Acclaim for David Cannadine's

MELLON

"A fascinating biography. . . . A compelling portrait of a dour and lonely financier who was wounded in love, disappointed in his children and, tragically, ill-rewarded by his government. . . . Mr. Cannadine paints a vivid picture of 19th-century Pittsburgh as a crucible of the Industrial Revolution. Among Mellon's customers or business partners were a Who's Who of American tycoons. . . . A sprawling work for a sprawling life."
—Roger Lowenstein, *The New York Times*

"Though scarcely known today, Andrew W. Mellon was a colossus in late 19th-century and early 20th-century America. He would come to play a major role in the management of the American economy, but first he built one of the country's great fortunes, one that would rank him today with Bill Gates and Warren Buffet. . . . David Cannadine, the distinguished British historian, [gives us] a well-written, richly detailed chronicle."
—Steve Forbes, *The Wall Street Journal*

"Magisterial. . . . David Cannadine's well-wrought account of Andrew Mellon's life, with its sometimes poignant echoes of a *Buddenbrooks* or indeed *The Great Gatsby*, is in its nuanced richness likely to remain another lasting memorial to a man who, for all his meticulous concern with day-to-day business, devoted surprisingly little attention to his posthumous reputation." —A. J. Sherman, *The Times Literary Supplement*

"David Cannadine has done readers on both sides of the Atlantic a great service in writing an erudite and compelling biography of a man immensely prominent in his day, virtually forgotten now, who believed, as his father did that the 'serious business of life was business.' . . . Cannadine shows exceptional skill in describing how, late in life, Mellon became a serious collector of art and the lasting contribution he made to American culture in creating the National Gallery in Washington D.C."
—Stephen Graubard, *Financial Times*

"David Cannadine, our foremost historian of the British aristocracy, has painted a rich, full-length portrait, warts and all, of one of the most important plutocrats America has ever produced. It turns out the taciturn old conservative and master collector Mellon had an inner life as well as an amazing career, which Cannadine re-creates with his usual thoroughness, humaneness, and wit."

—Sean Wilentz, Princeton University, author of
The Rise of American Democracy: Jefferson to Lincoln

"British historian David Cannadine brings this important and elusive figure to life in a book that is a model of the biographer's craft. . . . An extensive, careful, fascinating study that will satisfy the scholar and appeal to a general audience as well. . . . A welcome and much needed work."

—*The Christian Science Monitor*

"Of all of America's great men, Andrew Mellon is arguably the least-known and under-appreciated. Yet the life of this banking tycoon, politician and philanthropist was remarkable, and its impact on his country wider and far more beneficial than those who know of him generally believe. And it is a life that deserves to be studied more than ever, since so much of it raised issues that are relevant today. . . . [A] superb biography." —*The Economist*

"David Cannadine has spent the past 12 years on this brilliant and reclusive figure. . . . There is no easy way to sum up a figure so complex, influential, ruthless *and* benevolent, whose faults and virtues loom equally large. . . . Cannadine has accomplished the rare feat of describing in meticulous detail the personality of someone one can admire and even feel sympathy for, who is nevertheless not very likable."

—Meryle Secrest, *The Washington Post*

"Absorbing. . . . Cannadine . . . has the gifted writer's eye for a good story. He is a rarity among modern academics: a historian who writes well and has the storyteller's instinct for exploring personality and its effect on events. . . . [H]e dares to write history as if he wants his readers to enjoy reading it. . . . [T]he book often reads as compulsively as one of those immense fictional sagas that weigh down the bestseller lists. Sin and redemption are always close to the center of those family tales, and so they are in *Mellon*." —Russell Baker, *The New York Review of Books*

"Cannadine tells [Mellon's] story in copious detail with considerable skill and sensitivity. . . . One [can] appreciate the biographer's difficult but ultimately remarkable accomplishment of dispassionately reconstructing the history of the Mellon dynasty and the world it inhabited."
—Eric Arnesen, *Chicago Tribune*

"*Mellon* is an extraordinary life in the fullness of all its complexity and contradictions—of a man, a family, their associates, and of America from 1850 onward. An unvarnished portrait painted in the full light of day."
—Paul O'Neill, former Secretary of the Treasury

"Fine and very readable. . . . Indisputably the best written, most reliable and insightful biography of one of America's greatest capitalists and empire-builders."
—*The Plain Dealer*

"The rehabilitation . . . [of] the Alan Greenspan of his time. . . . Cannadine . . . a distinguished historian . . . enjoyed luxurious access to Mellon's records. . . . The outcome: a book that delivers on the dignity and the achievements of Mellon. . . . A complete biography, containing also—how could I forget to mention it?—details of Nora Mellon's adultery, Ailsa's self-absorption, and Paul Mellon's education in philanthropy. It introduces us to a man we need to know, and all there is to say is: Welcome, Andy."
—Amity Shlaes, *The New York Sun*

"Grand successes and epic failures, engrossingly recounted. . . . [A] lavish, multifaceted portrait of the early-20th-century American businessman, emphasizing the man rather than the money. . . . Cannadine's insightful account reveals Mellon as a man who took personal risks that seemingly defied his upbringing."
—*Kirkus Reviews*

"This biography . . . is incredibly useful as a guide to the pipelines of finance of the late 19th century. It is also a terribly sad story. . . . Ultimately, what saved Mellon from utter gloom—and utter unlikability as a biographical subject—was his love of art."
—*Louisville Courier-Journal*

"As Cannadine eloquently shows, Mellon was a true genius at the art of making money. . . . [His] recounting of Mellon's public career make[s] this a worthy contribution to our understanding of the man and his era."
—*Booklist* (starred)

DAVID CANNADINE

MELLON

David Cannadine was born in Birmingham, England, in 1950 and educated at Cambridge, Oxford, and Princeton universities. He is the editor and author of many acclaimed books, including *The Decline and Fall of the British Aristocracy*, which won the Lionel Trilling Prize and the Governors' Award. He has taught at Cambridge and Columbia universities, and is now the Queen Elizabeth the Queen Mother Professor of British History at the Institute of Historical Research, University of London. He is also Chairman of the Trustees of Britain's National Portrait Gallery, and is a regular broadcaster on radio and television. He lives in London, Norfolk, and Princeton.

MELLON

An American Life

DAVID CANNADINE

Vintage Books
A Division of Random House, Inc.
New York

FIRST VINTAGE BOOKS EDITION, FEBRUARY 2008

Copyright © 2006 by David Cannadine

All rights reserved. Published in the United States by Vintage Books,
a division of Random House, Inc., New York, and in Canada
by Random House of Canada Limited, Toronto. Originally published in hardcover
in the United States by Alfred A. Knopf, a division of Random House, Inc.,
New York, in 2006.

Vintage and colophon are registered trademarks of Random House, Inc.

The Library of Congress has cataloged the Knopf edition as follows:
Cannadine, David, [date]
Mellon : an American life / David Cannadine.
p. cm.
Includes bibliographical references and index.
1. Mellon, Andrew W. (Andrew William), 1855–1937. 2. Politicians—
United States—Biography. 3. Cabinet officers—United States—Biography.
4. United States Dept. of the Treasury—Officials and employees—Biography.
5. Diplomats—United States—Biography. 6. Bankers—United States—Biography.
7. Industrialists—United States—Biography. 8. Philanthropists—United States—
Biography. 9. United States—Politics and government—1901–1953. I. Title.
E748.M52C36 2006   336.73092—dc22   [B] 2006 045116

Vintage ISBN: 978-0-307-38679-3

Author photograph © Kristopher Dan Bergman
Book design by M. Kristen Bearse

www.vintagebooks.com

Printed in the United States of America
10 9 8 7 6 5 4 3 2

TO THE ANDREW W. MELLON FOUNDATION

How much more satisfactory [than a painting] would it not be if we could have a true representation of [a person's] course through life from first to last, as in a panorama: showing his thoughts and actions, his good and bad qualities, what were his feelings on trying occasions; how he bore prosperity or adversity; what were his views on the current affairs of his day; what his motives and methods, and what he accomplished or wherein he failed; how he performed his duties as a citizen and fulfilled his domestic relations.

Thomas Mellon and His Times, pp. 3–4

Contents

PART THREE

The Rise and Fall of a Public Man, 1921–33

PART FOUR

Old Man, New Deal, 1933–37

Preface

> He was one of a class of men rarely met with: modest and retiring of manner, shunning notoriety, and averse to anything having the appearance of ostentation.
>
> *Thomas Mellon and His Times,* p. 78

LATE ON THE AFTERNOON OF NEW YEAR'S EVE 1936, Franklin Delano Roosevelt, then at the zenith of his domestic renown as the architect of the New Deal, received at the White House a visitor who might have seemed almost the last person the president would have joined in sipping a cup of tea. The man in question was a millionaire, and though his once-great fortune was now much depleted, he had been in his financial prime one of the richest men in America. He had been extraordinarily successful as a banker and businessman, he believed in individualism and competition and (when it suited him) monopoly, and he had always hated organized labor. He was a lifelong Republican who had been a major donor to the party for many decades, and he had held high office throughout the administrations of Presidents Harding, Coolidge, and Hoover. He was, in short, the embodiment of the discredited political and economic order which Roosevelt detested, and which he had been elected in 1932 to overthrow and re-elected one month before to bury. The president's visitor knew this only too well. For more than three years, he had been unrelentingly harassed by the New Deal administration, and he had been charged with fraud and tax evasion on a massive scale. His so-called tax trial had only recently ended, and the outcome was not yet known. A paragon of the Republican twenties, he had become almost a pariah of the Democratic thirties. Yet here he was, at Roosevelt's invitation, taking tea at the White House. The president's visitor was Andrew W. Mellon.

As a symbolic confrontation between the Republican old guard and the

Democratic New Deal, this meeting between Mellon and Roosevelt is difficult to equal and impossible to better. But what made the encounter even more unusual was that, despite the gulf which separated the two men, both politically and personally, there was nothing confrontational about it: on the contrary, FDR had invited Mellon to tea in the hope that they might be able to come to an agreement about a remarkable plan. For at least a decade, Mellon had been America's greatest collector of art, and he now wanted to donate his pictures and his sculpture to the American people. He hoped his art might become the nucleus of a great national collection, and to further that aim, he was willing to build a great gallery in Washington, and to provide it with a handsome endowment. But he needed the president's consent, and also that of the Democratic-dominated Congress. And he needed it fast, for Mellon had been stricken with cancer and must have known that he did not have much time left. Roosevelt promptly gave his authorization, the necessary legislation was soon passed, and work on the gallery began in midsummer 1937. Soon after, Mellon died, with the outcome of the "tax trial" still pending and his own reputation at best problematic. But in his last months, he had brought to fruition an unprecedented gift to the American people—who, in recently re-electing Roosevelt, had repudiated virtually everything that Mellon himself was deemed to have stood for and believed in. It was a remarkable, and ironic, finale to a very remarkable life.

Andrew W. Mellon was born in 1855, six years before the American Civil War broke out, and he died in 1937, when Pearl Harbor was barely four years away. At his death, he was himself half the age of the United States, and for much of his life, he played a formative part and significant role in its history. Indeed, the years from 1865 to 1933 have rightly been described as "The Age of Gold," when the United States became the first "billion-dollar country," and the fact that they almost exactly encompass Mellon's life is not coincidence.[1] As a Pittsburgh banker, he financed and facilitated the massive industrial expansion of western Pennsylvania (and beyond) in the late nineteenth and early twentieth centuries, making himself a prodigious fortune. A lifelong Republican, he became the most highly acclaimed, longest-serving, and most controversial secretary of the treasury in modern times. Although he prided himself on wealth without ostentation, and a restrained style of life, he was the supreme and unrivaled collector of his generation, and the National Gallery of Art was a unique instance of self-effacing, patriotic generosity. Mellon was thus preeminent in four fields of endeavor—business, politics, art collecting, and philanthropy—and this was a distinction he shared with none of those near contemporaries (among them Rockefeller, Carnegie, Frick, Ford, Morgan, and Hearst) who were sometimes lumped together, with varying degrees of appropriateness and plausibility, as the "Robber Barons."

In its length, its range, its importance, its accomplishments, and its long-term significance, Andrew Mellon's was one of the biggest American lives of its times, and like the lives of many of his wealthy contemporaries, it was also tainted by controversy, almost continuously during the last two decades. As a banker and venture capitalist, Mellon was criticized for being intransigently anti-labor, for being indifferent to the wretched deterioration of the Pittsburgh environment, and for his unfair and monopolistic business practices; and as a result, the companies in which he was a major shareholder were regularly in court from the 1910s to the 1930s. Unlike those of his parents and his brothers, his marriage was brief and unhappy, ending in a sensational and acrimonious divorce trial lasting from 1910 until 1912. His low-tax, pro-business policies while he was secretary of the treasury were severely criticized by such prominent opponents as George Norris, James Couzens, Wright Patman, and John Nance Garner, culminating in demands that he be impeached for impropriety in continuing business activities while holding high office. In 1933, the muckraking journalist Harvey O'Connor published a savage indictment, *Mellon's Millions*, which charged him with corruption, monopoly, and ill-gotten gain and depicted him as a compulsively greedy monster. And all this was but the prelude to the infamous "tax trial" that followed.

Like many men with a Midas touch, Mellon's personality was both complex and flawed, and while he was outstandingly successful in business, he was a conspicuous failure in personal relationships. From an early age, he was by turns shy and sad, silent and secretive, self-sufficient and self-enclosed. Despite a large and loyal family, he was always a loner, cut off from close contact, and fenced in against the world. He made little small talk, was a poor public speaker, rarely smiled and hardly ever laughed. Perhaps in an effort to break out, he launched himself headlong into an ill-judged marriage, which brought him more humiliation than happiness, and which drove him even further in upon himself. After his divorce, he confined his attentions to beautiful women long since dead, but immortalized by such painters as Gainsborough and Reynolds: two-dimensional creatures, safely confined within their wooden frames, whom he owned and possessed completely, and who could neither touch him nor do him harm. Not surprisingly, he would become a distant and forbidding father, and both his children suffered in his dark and brooding shadow. His daughter, who became Ailsa Mellon Bruce, lived unhappy and insecure, and died lonely and unfulfilled. His son, Paul Mellon, would spend decades coming to terms with the double burdens of paternal disappointment and colossal inherited wealth.

Andrew Mellon has now been dead for almost seventy years, but no full-scale life has been published during that time, and its absence constitutes a major gap in American biography and in American history. Shy in life, secretive in business, self-effacing in philanthropy, Mellon has all but vanished in death, except for his reappearance in two family sagas, written in the 1970s, which were more concerned with unfolding a lively dynastic chronicle than with probing the complexities of any single life, however extraordinary and worthy of close attention.[2] This biographical blank was not what had originally been intended. Soon after Mellon's death, Paul Mellon and Ailsa Mellon Bruce commissioned the Pulitzer Prize–winning author Burton J. Hendrick to undertake their father's life, putting him on a full-time salary of $25,000, but reserving to themselves the ultimate decision whether to publish or not.[3] Hendrick's view, having already completed a biography of Pittsburgh's "other Andrew," was that "Mr. Mellon lacks the personal qualities that made Mr. Carnegie so attractive a subject, nor, in other ways, was he so great a man, but his career, both in public life and business, was an historic one."[4] Beginning in January 1940, he worked his way through Mellon's letterbooks and volumes of press cuttings (all of which have subsequently disappeared), he conducted interviews with many of Mellon's (long since dead) relatives and business associates (the transcripts of which have been invaluable in writing this biography), and the whole thing was finished on schedule by March 1943.[5] The thirty-three chapters comprise well over 200,000 words, and the still-extant typescript remains the essential starting point for any subsequent biographer.[6]

But Hendrick's book was never published. While the Second World War raged, and while FDR was president, the life of Andrew Mellon was, as Hendrick himself admitted, "a little remote from the interests that are now exciting the nation," and publication was postponed for the duration of the conflict.[7] Andrew Mellon's tax affairs with the U.S. government had been finally settled, and the National Gallery of Art had triumphantly opened in Washington; it seemed better to let him rest in peace. At a time when New Deal liberalism was still in the ascendant, and when American history was increasingly being written along what Samuel Eliot Morison called a "Jefferson–Jackson–F. D. Roosevelt line," there was nothing to be gained from reopening controversies about Andrew Mellon's business ethics, his conduct at the Treasury, or the tax trial.[8] There were also personal reasons. Ailsa Mellon Bruce and her husband, David Bruce, had divorced in 1945; both of them were eager to move on. And so was Paul Mellon: he had largely withdrawn from Pittsburgh, his first wife had recently died and he would soon remarry, he had no wish to play any part in American public life, and he, too, was anxious to avoid re-igniting controversy about his father.[9]

This was not the only reason for the biography's suppression. For meanwhile, Andrew Mellon's nephew William Larimer Mellon, whose memories stretched back to the 1880s, had decided to write what was in effect his own autobiography, which would deal not only with his business career at Gulf Oil, but also with his father and his uncles, and their relations with the family's patriarch, Thomas Mellon. W. L. Mellon enlisted the support of Boyden Sparkes, a well-known collaborator and ghost-writer, who clearly did most of the work.[10] Like Hendrick, he interviewed many people, and these transcripts have also been invaluable in writing this biography. *Judge Mellon's Sons* duly appeared in 1948: it provided a vivid and immediate account of the upbringing of Andrew Mellon and his brothers; and it shed some light on Mellon business activities from the late nineteenth century onward. W. L. Mellon's memory was not always accurate, though, and the book was further diminished by a reticence about private matters; it was also stridently (if understandably) anti-Roosevelt and pro-Republican in tone. Still, its appearance made it even harder to justify the belated publication of Hendrick's biography.

Paul Mellon did not abandon the project entirely, however, and during subsequent decades he regularly sought the advice of academics as to whether the Hendrick typescript might be revised and updated for publication.[11] But as scholars got to work on the times of Andrew Mellon's life—on the Civil War, on Reconstruction, on the American economy, on Pittsburgh as an industrial city, on the politics and finances of the 1920s, on FDR and the New Deal, and on the international art market—they produced an increasingly rich and complex account which made Hendrick's work seem narrow, superficial, and outdated. By the early 1990s, now in his late eighties, Paul Mellon had become increasingly concerned with ensuring there would be an adequate historical account of his particular branch of the Mellon dynasty. He completed his autobiography, *Reflections in a Silver Spoon*, in which he likened his father to Soames Forsyte, both for his remorseless desire to accumulate money and art and for his indifference to human relations, an indelible and unflattering portrait.[12] (He might equally have likened Andrew to Adam Verver in Henry James's novel *The Golden Bowl*.) Soon after, Paul arranged for a new edition of his grandfather's autobiography, *Thomas Mellon and His Times*, and he contributed a preface to this stern chronicle of self-denial and self-advancement.[13] But that left Andrew Mellon still without a published biography. Paul Mellon now concluded that the Hendrick version was beyond rehabilitation, that a wholly new life of his father should be written, and that I should undertake it.

Only a lifelong Anglophile would have made such a choice. "For an Englishman," Harold Nicolson wrote in the introduction to his study of Dwight Morrow (a man, incidentally, whom Mellon much admired, but whom Nicolson came greatly to dislike), "to write a biography of an American may seem a hazardous, and perhaps impertinent, enterprise."[14] It is a salutary warning. Moreover, if I had been an American during the 1920s and 1930s, I like to think I would have cast my vote against Harding, Coolidge, and Hoover, and subsequently in favor of Roosevelt. So I was not at the outset exactly well disposed toward Andrew Mellon: I found him a fascinating biographical subject but an unsympathetic person with unappealing politics. But in researching and writing this book, I have learned much more about him than his son or his daughter ever knew, and I have sought to reach as evenhanded a verdict about him as the evidence allows. Roosevelt's treatment of Mellon, for instance, was certainly not the president's finest hour—but it is also easy to see why the New Dealers had Mellon so squarely in their sights. That extraordinary episode is one of many controversies surrounding him that seem to belong to a world far removed from our own. Yet in other ways, as a rich Republican in politics, believing that business was a higher calling than government, there is much about Mellon's life that still resonates with our own times. I have also come to appreciate the importance of Andrew Mellon's father, Thomas Mellon, who was born on the other side of the Atlantic, and who was in some ways an even more extraordinary man than his most gifted, flawed, successful, complex, and controversial son. But Thomas Mellon was himself the offspring of the first recorded Andrew Mellon, and it is with him, rather than with his grandson and namesake, that this biography must properly begin.

MELLON

A FAMILY IN HISTORY

Is a knowledge of our ancestors of any use to us? Is there any benefit to be derived from knowing their character and habits, and what manner of men they were of? We may have inherited no worldly possessions from them, but never can ignore the legacies of good or bad qualities they are sure to have left us by heredity.

Thomas Mellon and His Times, p. 3

I. FROM ULSTER SCOTS TO SCOTCH-IRISH AMERICANS

On or about the first day of October 1818, a coasting vessel reached Baltimore, Maryland, en route from St. John in New Brunswick, and among its passengers were the first Andrew Mellon, his wife, Rebecca, and their only child, Thomas, who was five years old. They had left their Irish home at Camp Hill, in Lower Castletown, County Tyrone, and had endured a rough twelve-week voyage across the Atlantic from Londonderry to Canada, intent on beginning a new life in the New World. Their ultimate destination was not Canada but the United States, and it took them a further two weeks' sailing to get from the British colony to the American republic. Like many new arrivals, they were part of an extensive and extended "chain migration": seventeen Mellon relatives had already made the crossing in the previous twenty years.[1] One of them was Andrew's father, Archibald Mellon, who had done so in 1816, settling as a farmer in western Pennsylvania. Another was Thomas Mellon, Andrew's elder brother: the first in his family to turn his back on the land, he had established himself in business in New Orleans, later retiring to Philadelphia.[2] Encouraged by their example, the first Andrew Mellon packed up his wife and child to follow his relatives west. The day of their arrival in Baltimore was a hotter one than any their son could recall in Ireland, and along with his parents, he was quarantined for what seemed the interminable whole of it. Fortunately, his father managed to obtain some fine ripe peaches, and over half a century later, Thomas could still recall his amazement at encountering this strange new fruit.[3]

By the time young Thomas Mellon and his parents landed at Baltimore, Irish immigration to America had been under way for more than a century; approximately one million made the crossing between 1700 and 1840, seeking freedom and opportunity, and a better, more secure life. The majority of them came from the north rather than the south of the island; they were modestly circumstanced rather than bitterly impoverished; they were Presbyterian rather than Roman Catholic; and they were recent settlers in Ireland rather than part of the indigenous population.[4] Their forebears had originated in the Scottish lowlands and had headed west during the seventeenth century, as part of the concerted campaign of "plantation" designed to secure British rule in Ireland. Known as "Ulster Scots," they were intended to form a loyal, Protestant bulwark between the native Irish and their lordly superiors. But since many settled as tenant farmers on estates confiscated from the native Catholic population and given over to alien landowners from Britain, this meant the Ulster Scots occupied a position in Irish society both intermediate and beleaguered: they were economically and socially inferior to the Anglo-Irish Ascendancy, but they looked down on the Irish laboring class as idle, impoverished semi-savages; as Presbyterians they resented paying tithes to the established Protestant church, yet they were also staunchly anti-Catholic; and while lacking secure tenure from their landlords, they were loathed as alien interlopers by the majority of the population.[5]

In such uncertain and inhospitable circumstances, the communal ties of family and congregation remained very strong, but association with the land was brief and territorial roots were tenuous; many Ulster Scots Presbyterians decided that Ireland was no place to settle permanently. Many moved on again—across the Atlantic to the New World, where the British colonies on the eastern seaboard held out the better prospects of abundant land, free of tithes and rents and landlords and Catholics. Between 1717 and 1775, an estimated 250,000 Ulster Scots left Ireland for North America, and by the early 1770s they were doing so at the rate of 10,000 a year.[6] As the second Andrew Mellon would later observe, when he was secretary of the treasury, they brought with them "their sturdy qualities of independence, love of civil and religious liberty [and] a sense of thrift and order," which enabled them "to build up a civilization out of a wilderness." Like the Pilgrim Fathers before them, they initially headed for New England, but they felt rebuffed in the northern colonies by what seemed to them intolerant Puritanism, and so turned south to Pennsylvania which, thanks to the terms of its founding by William Penn in 1682, was the most religiously relaxed colony in British North America. Most of the Ulster Scots initially settled in Philadelphia and in the southeast of the colony, but they soon moved south and west, fanning out through the Cumberland Valley in their search for land, crossing the Allegheny Mountains, and eventually reaching the Ohio River.[7]

At this point, the Ulster Scots immigrants faced a choice: many would keep moving, heading farther south and west, to the backcountry of Virginia, the Carolinas, and Georgia; but others preferred to put down roots in western Pennsylvania, where, by the middle of the eighteenth century, they had emerged as a coherent, politically assertive, and well-defined ethnic group.[8] There, in close-knit communities on the British colonial frontier, they established villages and churches, and created farms on the Ulster model: dispersed homesteads with a mixture of tillage and pasture, mingling agriculture with the production of flax and yarn and linen, and sometimes the lucrative distilling of whiskey. Here was the fuller and richer existence that they had sought—but these seemingly sylvan settlements were not quite as idyllic as they seemed. For one thing, the Ulster Scots were constantly at odds with the other significant immigrant group in the region: Germans with very different mores and religion—Lutherans, Moravians, and Anabaptists fleeing the central European version of intolerant Catholicism. In addition, as if in ironic re-creation of their woes in Ulster, they again found themselves in beleaguered insecurity: caught between what seemed to them the condescending Anglican elite of the colony's east coast and the Native Americans to the west who bitterly resented their threatening and acquisitive presence.[9]

On this remote western frontier of the British Empire, relations between the Ulster Scots and the indigenous tribes were often vexed and bloody, a situation intensified by the neighboring French, who were moving aggressively south from Canada into the backcountry of New York, Pennsylvania, and Virginia, and who sought to extend their own North American empire by inciting the Indians against the British army and the British colonists. The climax of these intrigues and confrontations was the French and Indian War of 1757–63, known in Britain as the Seven Years War, when the French were effectively ejected for good from the North

American continent. Most of the fighting was done by British enlisted troops, but on the western boundaries of Pennsylvania, the local Ulster Scots formed a militia that helped drive the French out of the Ohio Valley.[10] Their most significant success was the capture in 1758 of Fort Duquesne, a recently established French stronghold strategically located where the Allegheny and Monongahela rivers merge to form the Ohio River, and which was simultaneously an outpost of the east and a gateway to the west. The British constructed their own defenses, which they named Fort Pitt, in honor of their great war leader William Pitt. Soon after, a small frontier settlement and trading post began to grow up nearby; with the same patriotic inspiration it was named Pittsburgh.[11] By the 1770s, the American colonists were increasingly unwilling to pay the taxes levied for the upkeep of this enlarged imperium, and in the ensuing War of Independence against Britain, most of the Pennsylvanian Ulster Scots sided against the mother country—although they did not share the generally espoused revolutionary enthusiasm for "self-evident" democratic equality, or for religious toleration that encompassed the Roman Catholics, or for the abolition of slavery.[12]

The independence of the American colonies from Britain and the birth of the United States did not lessen the New World's attraction to the middling prosperous of Ireland, especially those in Ulster.[13] For during the late eighteenth and early nineteenth centuries, life in Ireland became less congenial, while the new republic became more socially and economically appealing. Between 1780 and 1820, the Irish population increased by 75 percent, creating unprecedented pressure on land and other resources; during the Napoleonic wars, rents and taxes rose dramatically; and after 1815, the abrupt postwar slump brought Ireland's agrarian economy to the verge of crisis. The result was that 450,000 people left Ulster for the United States between 1800 and 1845, and by the late 1810s the Ulster Scots were migrating at the rate of 20,000 a year. Most of them were engaged in farming or trade, they had both the motive and the means to travel, and they generally reached the United States, as Andrew and Rebecca Mellon were to do, via Canada: for as Thomas Mellon would later explain, Britain "would clear no ships except to ports in her own dominions," making it both difficult and expensive to go direct to the United States. They tended to settle where their co-religionists were already established, and by end of the eighteenth century, there were 100,000 Ulster Scots in Pennsylvania. They made up 20 percent of the population of the state, a quarter of the Ulster Scots population of the whole country, and more were eager to come.[14]

From the late 1840s, in the aftermath of the great potato famine, the Ulster Scots in the United States were confronted by the massive influx of those very poor Catholic Irish they had so disliked and had fled from. And it was at just this time that they began to describe themselves as "Scotch-Irish," to distinguish themselves from the very different Irish now pouring into the country, whom they scorned, and perhaps feared, not only for their indigence and their Catholicism, but also for their desire to remain unassimilated and their potential to make trouble as the "serfs of Rome and Tammany Hall."[15] The Scotch-Irish, by contrast, were assimilating rapidly by midcentury. They retained their traditional loyalty to family and congregation, but their religious fervor gradually weakened, along with their belief in predestination, and they became increasingly attracted to the secular doctrine of individualism and self-reliance. It was no coincidence that cities like New York, Philadelphia, Baltimore, and New Orleans—and Pittsburgh—would count Scotch-Irishmen among their most substantial merchants, lawyers, and politicians throughout the antebellum period. Some were also drawn into public life at a high level: from John Adams to Bill Clinton, fifteen American presidents have claimed Scotch-Irish ancestors. Three were the sons of Ulster Presbyterian immigrants: Andrew Jackson, James Buchanan, and Chester Arthur. Indeed, the ship *Alexander* which conveyed Andrew, Rebecca, and Thomas Mellon across the Atlantic from Londonderry to St. John was owned by James Buchanan's uncle.[16]

The three Mellons who landed at Baltimore harbor in October 1818 were recognizably—indeed, quintessentially—Ulster Scots of their time and class. Their forebears had crossed over from lowland Scotland during the second half of the seventeenth century, when the Scots migration to Ulster was at its height.[17] They were Presbyterian, and shared their kind's prevailing dislike of lower-class Catholics. They were farmers by occupation, combining crop production and livestock husbandry with flax cultivation and weaving. And they settled in County Tyrone at Lower Castletown, by the River Strule, where they gradually accumulated from the Viscounts Mountjoy (subsequently the Earls of Blessington) family holdings of one hundred acres on leases so long that they amounted almost to freeholds. This meant the Mellons were neither poor laborers nor rich landowners, but middling prosperous by the standards of the time.[18] By the 1780s, eight separate Mellon households were located in the district, and it was in one of these that the first Andrew Mellon was born in 1785. Rebecca Wauchob, whose family lived close by at Kinkitt, was four years his junior, and the couple married in 1812 at the austere

Crossroads Meeting House, where Thomas would later remember listening to interminable sermons. At that time, twenty-three acres of the Mellon family holdings were made over to Andrew, who was "comfortably fixed or comparatively so as to his neighbors," and on them he built Camp Hill Cottage, a traditional three-room, thatch-roofed farmhouse, with walls of field stones mortared together and whitewashed.[19]

It was in Camp Hill Cottage that Thomas Mellon was born on February 13, 1813, and although he would live there only five years, he retained a "vivid and permanent impression" of the place, and remained sentimentally attached to it all his life. In 1875, his second son, James Ross Mellon, would visit the cottage and be astounded at the accuracy with which his father had described it. After a second visit in 1899, James constructed a full-size replica in the garden of his house in Pittsburgh, with a few stones brought back from the Irish original.[20] In 1882, by which time he was rich, successful, famous, and semi-retired, Thomas Mellon himself would be overcome with emotion when he paid a return visit to the cottage with his youngest son, George. There, more than sixty years before, he and his parents had dreamed of America, of "the richness and abundance of the lands, and the liberty and freedom of the people from taxation and rents." "It was all again before me," he recalled, "like a vision of the past." That dream had come true for him and his family, who had indeed found "a wider field and better opportunities to rise in the world," but not for those who had stayed behind. The lower-class Catholics were still mired in poverty and indigence, ignorance and superstition. There was "one old man of our name and connection," who was "poor and obscure," whose heart was "gladdened" with "a gold piece." And their once-proud landlords, the Earls of Blessington, had been destroyed by idleness, dissipation, and debt, and had subsequently vanished.[21]

The unprecedented influx of Ulster Scots to the United States during the late 1810s had included Thomas Mellon's parents, who like many of their kith and kin settled in western Pennsylvania, at Crabtree in Westmoreland County. Encouraged by "letters from America [which] were eagerly looked for," and by "gazetteers and books of geography descriptive of the country and its resources [which were] eagerly read," Andrew and Rebecca Mellon had resolved to put behind them the darkening Irish scene and to seek a more promising life for themselves and their infant son. They parted with the lease on the farm, and disposed of most of their belongings, eventually setting sail with two hundred guineas, which Rebecca Mellon sewed into a belt she wore—a prudent and portentous precaution, for this would constitute a significant part of the seed capital from which the gigantic Mellon fortune eventually grew.[22] They were the last Mellons to make the transatlantic crossing. On reaching Baltimore, and having procured his peaches, Andrew Mellon chartered a four-horse Conestoga wagon to carry his family the three hundred and fifty miles to Westmoreland County for the eagerly awaited reunion with his mother and father. The trip was long and tedious, for there was as yet no turnpike, but the child Thomas Mellon was enthralled: "to my young mind," he later recalled, "the luxuriant vegetation and luscious fruit gave the country the appearance of paradise." No one had ever said that about Camp Hill and its neighborhood in County Tyrone.[23]

The family reunion duly took place at Crabtree Farm, where Thomas Mellon and his parents stayed until the spring of 1819, reacquainting themselves with the extended Mellon clan already settled nearby, who were busy re-creating the same sort of family "patch" they had occupied on the banks of the River Strule. Andrew Mellon set about searching for a property of his own, eventually buying a farm twelve miles from Crabtree, in an area known as Duff's Hill or (less propitiously) Poverty Point, consisting of one hundred and sixty acres of meadows and woodland, with an orchard and a log cabin which "presented a cozy and home-like appearance, with its pleasant streams and meadow and the alternation of woodland and clear field."[24] The down payment came from what remained of the original two hundred guineas Rebecca had carried with her from Ireland, and there seemed every prospect that the balance would soon be paid off. Thomas Mellon never forgot his first sight of this new home, or his parents' sense of triumph. "The cares and apprehensions of the great journey were now at an end," he recalled, and "we had gained our object": his mother and father were now in possession of a farm "seven times larger" than the one they had left behind in Ulster, and when paid for it would be clear of those dreaded exactions, "rents and tithes," and be subject only to "nominal taxes."[25]

Once settled, Andrew and Rebecca Mellon were soon able to extend both their family and their farm. Between 1819 and 1828 were born Elinor, Elizabeth, Samuel, and Margaret. In accordance with his fierce family loyalty, Thomas, formerly the only child, would remain devoted to his siblings (he would, indeed, outlive them all), though not without disapproval of their shortcomings, especially Samuel's failings as a man of business. During the same period, Andrew took American citizenship and was commissioned in the Pennsylvania Militia. Meanwhile, the farm was gradually enlarged, the log cabin replaced by a more substantial dwelling, and a distillery built for converting surplus apple and peach crops into brandy. For fifteen years Thomas lived on the farm, where he came to find, as he later put it in a school essay, that "the cultivation of the earth is congenial to the nature of mankind."[26] "Here," he subsequently recalled, "were implanted in my nature those root principles of right and duty, tenacity of purpose, patient industry and perseverance in well doing which have accompanied me through life." His parents were strict but affectionate, and he retained many "bright and happy memories" from this time. But there were also "occasions of anxiety and alarm." The most challenging of these occurred within months of their arrival, and it nearly ruined the Mellons' incipient farming venture. Although he was then only six, it would prove the formative experience in Thomas Mellon's life.[27]

The abrupt economic downturn which had begun after the end of the Anglo-American War of 1812 and the final defeat of Napoleon three years later reached its low point in 1819. It was global in scope and deep in impact: industry and agriculture in western Pennsylvania were hard hit, and so was Pittsburgh, the nearest big town, which since American independence had evolved from a frontier post into a thriving place with a population of more than 10,000. Settlers swarmed through in the thousands en route to the wide open hinterland. It was the center of an elaborate trading network by land and river that extended north to the Great Lakes, south via the Mississippi to New Orleans, and east to Philadelphia and Baltimore. And it was an expanding industrial center, where iron founding, metalworking, glass manufacturing, boatbuilding, and shoemaking were flourishing local industries.[28] But many of these enterprises were speculative ventures, which had been financed during the war years on the easy and uncertain credit of paper money, and they were devastated in 1819. "All the merchants, manufacturers and dealers of Pittsburgh," Thomas Mellon remembered, "with the exception of about a dozen, went under," as did most of the banks, "and it was nearly ten years before business and prices began to recuperate." Agriculture also suffered, and land values tumbled, thereby precipitating a potentially ruinous financial crisis for the first Andrew Mellon. The farm which he had so recently purchased with such pride and optimism was suddenly worth less than half of the deferred payments still owed against it, and with his agricultural income drastically reduced, "the prospect of making those payments was, to all appearances, hopeless."[29]

But not quite: for by sheer chance, the purchase deed had stipulated that the payments could be made "in money and bags and oats at market prices."[30] Throughout western Pennsylvania, money had all but disappeared and barter was back. Still, the Mellon farm produced oats, and bags could be made from spinning and weaving flax—something Ulster Scots immigrants knew well how to do. Determined to keep their land, Andrew and Rebecca Mellon worked with indomitable industry and perseverance during the next four years: farming by day, spinning and weaving by night, all the while assisted by their firstborn son, who was no "idle spectator" but was an active participant in these desperate endeavors. The payments were made on time, and the farm was saved. Between the age of six and ten, Thomas Mellon matured rapidly and learned many lessons. Some were financial: the dangers of indebtedness; the need to keep expenditure within income; the value of sound currency and prudent investment; the corrosive effects of easy credit, rampant inflation, and speculative mania; and the recognition that booms and slumps were intrinsic to the economy. Some were familial: the benefits of close collaboration across the generations; the importance of strong clan identity; and the galvanizing power of a shared urge to better the family condition. And some were individual: the vanity of recreation and leisure, ease and luxury; the virtues of "hardship and restraint," and "untiring energy, industry and perseverance"; and the value of a life of "energy, industry, determination, self-reliance and self-denial."[31]

II. A PITTSBURGH PATRIARCH IN THE MAKING

Following the financial panic of 1819, Thomas Mellon would ever after consider life to be a struggle that must be waged unremittingly and unrelentingly. During the 1820s, it took the form of what he would later describe as a period of "long and anxious mental conflict of deciding the question of a vocation, or what I should follow for a living when I grew up." In western Pennsylvania as in Ulster, most Mellons were farmers, and the first Andrew Mellon thought it "the best, safest, most worthy and independent of all the occupations of men," and that "anyone who forsook it for something else" had been "led astray by folly and nonsense." He clearly hoped that his son would succeed him, and the omens were good: at age six, in the aftermath of the crash, the young Thomas Mellon was already working beside his father in the fields, and at twelve, by which time he considered his boyhood ended, he was put to the plow. Here, surely, was another Mellon farmer in the making.

But Thomas Mellon's horizons and ambitions were already broadening. From 1821 to 1827, he attended local schools during the winter months when he could be spared from the farm, and he was a curious,

determined, hardworking, and able student who soon revealed remarkable powers of mind and application.[32] He rapidly mastered writing and
arithmetic, and acquired the habit of voracious general reading which
would continue throughout his life: Burns was already a great favorite,
followed by Pope and Goldsmith, and he leafed through Shakespeare
(whom he appreciated rather less) during the interludes in the fields while
the plow horses rested. But he was not drawn only to poetry and fiction. His uncle Thomas Mellon in Philadelphia encouraged him to read
widely, and sent him "books and papers of the most miscellaneous variety
on all imaginable subjects." Uncle Thomas also took a more general
interest in his nephew's welfare and, as befitted the first of his family to
break away from the land and go into business, he now inspired in his
namesake and protégé "the ambition to better my condition and rise to
something higher than farm life."[33]

By then, young Thomas had glimpsed what that "something higher"
might be, for in 1823, at the age of nine, he had paid his first visit to Pittsburgh. It was twenty-one miles west of his parents' homestead, and he
made the journey in both directions on foot. On the way there he was
accompanied by a farmer who told him he would see more in the town in
a day than he could at Poverty Point in a lifetime. At first, Thomas took
offense at the aspersion cast on his own locality, but Pittsburgh was
already recovering from the slump of 1819, and the boy would be much
impressed by the "numerous wonders" he saw. It was his first visit to a
large city since his family had left Baltimore for western Pennsylvania,
and he immediately sensed the exciting opportunities that might exist for
someone of spirit, determination, and ambition in a town that contemporaries were already predicting was "destined to become one of the greatest cities in the world."[34] He took in the "neat and trim" suburban houses,
and the greater dwellings of the leading citizens. He saw steamboats and
cotton factories, ironworks and glassworks. But he was most captivated by
the 1,500-acre estate of Jacob Negley, which encompassed a steam mill, a
village with a school, a store, a tavern, and a church, and a great mansion
on the outskirts of Pittsburgh, an area that was then known as Neg-
leystown, before it became East Liberty and finally the East End.[35]

The Negleys were one of the original founding families of Pittsburgh,
and Jacob's father, Alexander Negley, had lived there since the time of the
American Revolution.[36] But antiquity and appearance were alike deceptive, for Jacob Negley had been all but ruined in the panic of 1819.
Although rich in land, he was poor in money, and he would soon die a
broken and beaten man. But at that time, Thomas Mellon knew nothing

of this, and he saw in the Negley house and its ample estate only the embodiment of the security, position, success, and reputation to which he himself was already beginning to aspire. "The whole scene," he later recalled,

> was new to me, and impressed me with an idea of wealth and magnificence I had before no conception of. I remember wondering how it could be possible to accumulate such wealth, and how magnificent must be the style of living, and what pleasures they must enjoy who possessed it. I remember also of the thought occurring whether I might not one day attain in some degree such wealth, and an equality with such great people.[37]

No doubt Thomas Mellon exaggerated the importance of this epiphany in the light of subsequent events. But he did now know what a better life looked like, and he was determined to have it for himself.

These gradually stirring ambitions were powerfully reinforced when, in 1827, he read Benjamin Franklin's *Autobiography*. This experience became a "turning point" of his life, for in Franklin's account of his journey "from the poverty of obscurity in which I was born and bred to a state of affluence and some degree of reputation in the world" was the proof that all Americans, however humbly born, had the potential to make what they wanted of their own lives, and to become "learned and wise, and elevated to wealth and fame."[38] All one had to do was to cultivate the qualities of temperance, silence, order, resolution, frugality, industry, sincerity, justice, moderation, cleanliness, tranquillity, chastity, and humility, and to apply them.[39] Thomas Mellon had already displayed many of these attributes, especially resolution, frugality, and industry, in helping his family weather the aftermath of 1819. But it was Franklin's *Autobiography* that first connected these virtues with such worldly success as he saw among the Negleys. "I read the book again and again," Thomas later recalled, "and wondered if I might not do something in the same line by similar means. . . . I had will and energy equal to the occasion," he went on, "and could exercise the same degree of industry and perseverance." He never forgot the *Autobiography*, which became his secular gospel, and whose tenets he would instill in all his sons. When he moved his fledgling Pittsburgh bank to custom-built premises in 1871, a statue of Franklin was given pride of place above the entrance, and when he wrote his own life story in the early 1880s, he took Franklin as his model and paid him copious tribute.[40]

Inspired by Franklin, encouraged by his uncle, and also clandestinely supported by his mother, Thomas Mellon resolved to reject what he had come to regard as his family's confining agrarian tradition. But toward this end, he needed a decent education. In 1828, he enrolled for four months at the County Academy at nearby Greensburg, where he studied geometry, history, grammar, and geography, boarding with a well-to-do family whose wealth and standing stirred the same passions as the Negley mansion near Pittsburgh. He returned home more determined than ever that "farm work" would not be his life. Two years later there was a dramatic encounter between father and son.[41] Convinced that Thomas would become a farmer, Andrew had decided to buy land for his son adjacent to his own property. "The die was cast," Thomas remembered, "or so nearly so as to be almost past recall." It seemed that all his "air castle and bright fancies of acquiring knowledge and wealth and distinction" were about to be "wrecked and ruined, and to be abandoned forever." On the day the purchase was to be completed, in nearby Greensburg, Thomas was so overwrought that he abandoned his work on the farm and ran the ten miles to the town in the hope of putting a stop to the transaction. His father seemed initially "bewildered at such determined self-assertion," but eventually he gave way with better grace than his son had expected. And so came another "turning point" in Thomas Mellon's life.[42]

He continued to work on the family farm for two more years, gaining firsthand knowledge of construction work by building houses and barns, and all the while brooding on how best he might set about acquiring that "knowledge and wealth and distinction" on which he was now so determinedly set. "Knowledge" would clearly come first, and in his limited spare time, he read yet more widely and acquired the rudiments of Latin. In 1832 he enrolled at the Rev. Jonathan Gill's Tranquil Retreat Academy near Monroeville in Allegheny County to prepare for college. During the next two years, he mastered Murray's Latin grammar, learning all seventy-six rules of syntax by heart; he read Caesar, Virgil, and Ovid; and he made a good start at Greek.[43] As he would later recall, with more pride than self-pity, he was "pursuing a course of classical study under difficulties." This was partly because Gill was more than a touch eccentric—he was confident that the world would end in 1837—and partly because Thomas was still working for his parents, who in 1833 moved from Poverty Point to a new and bigger farm at Monroeville. Once more, his character was tested, and again he triumphed. "In all my experience," he later recalled, "whether of study or business, I succeeded the best when hardest pushed to overcome difficulties." "The greater the obstacle," he concluded, "the stronger my desire grew to overcome it, and my power to succeed seemed to rise with the occasion for it."[44]

Thomas Mellon was now ready to begin that college education which he believed was the essential stepping-stone to the "wealth and distinction" he craved. He thought of Jefferson College in Canonsburg, but on observing the students at commencement, he concluded that they "did not present the earnestness of purpose for knowledge and mental improvement which I had expected." Instead, he enrolled in October 1834 at the Western University of Pennsylvania (which would later become the University of Pittsburgh), then located on Third Avenue between Smithfield and Grant streets. There he found, to his satisfaction, "a very different state of affairs."[45] Both faculty and students were eager and energetic; the university was well run by the Rev. Dr. Robert Bruce, another Scotch-Irish Presbyterian; the tuition was lower and the requirements for a degree could be met in less time than at Jefferson. This was Mellon's first experience of life in Pittsburgh, and although still required for work on his father's farm eleven miles away, he threw himself into undergraduate activities. He studied Latin and Greek, mathematics and philosophy, and read Bacon, Descartes, Berkeley, Locke, Hume, Thomas Reid, Dugald Stewart, and Thomas Brown. He joined a literary society, set up a dining syndicate, and generally avoided what he regarded as the distractions of female company.[46] In order to pay his way, he worked during summer vacations, teaching (successfully) for three months in a local school, and working (less successfully) as a book salesman in Ohio. "Money," he observed in an essay written at this time, "is to society what the element of fire is to matter, diffusing warmth and vigour through all its parts." Thomas Mellon graduated in October 1837, after only three years of study. Seventy years later, he was awarded an honorary degree as the oldest living alumnus, but it was the last year of his life, and he was too frail to attend the ceremony.[47]

By dint of determination and hard work, Thomas Mellon had obtained a far better education than any of his forebears, and for a few months in 1838, he returned to the university to teach Latin, filling in for a professor on sick leave. In later life, he played down the benefits of higher learning, thinking it better to be rich than to be educated, and he found no reason for his sons to be as well schooled as he had been. "In the professions and business management," he subsequently observed, "certificates of either ability or learning are valueless." Yet for him, the "prize" had been well worth "the cost of time, money and exertion required."[48] For his aim was to enter a profession, not so much for its own sake, but as a means to

wealth and position. Indeed, for someone of his relatively humble background, with no capital, it was the only route outward and upward. But
which profession should he enter? The church did not appeal: it was
scarcely a path to the renown and security he sought; he had no wish to be
subject to the "prejudices and whims" of those who dominated Presbyterian congregations; and like his hero, Benjamin Franklin, he was never a
wholehearted believer. He appreciated the church as a place of moral discipline and social instruction, but as a vehement anti-Catholic, he loathed
superstition and blind belief. Even more than his father, he "inclined to
rationalism."[49]

The alternative was the law, and although his father thought it a "tricky
and dishonest profession," Thomas Mellon considered it highly attractive. It was intrinsically much more lucrative than the church, of course,
and clients, he imagined, would be easier to deal with than congregants.
Moreover, the close connection between the law and property promised
access to the world of business that was already his ultimate ambition.[50]
And so, having resigned his temporary Latin professorship, he began to
study law in Pittsburgh under the direction of the Hon. Charles Shaler, a
former judge of the Court of Common Pleas of Allegheny County. He
threw himself into his work, but he still needed to support himself, and in
March 1838, he won appointment as assistant deputy in the office of the
prothonotary, or chief clerk of the Court of Common Pleas. One of his
friends from university days was William Liggett, the prothonotary's son:
here was an early example of Thomas Mellon's capacity to turn personal
connections into professional advantage. His salary was twenty dollars a
month, which later rose to twenty-five.[51]

This was more than enough for Mellon to get by on, and there were
other advantages in his position. His studies in Judge Shaler's office, combined with his work for the prothonotary, meant he gained experience in
both the theory and the practice of the law: a fortunate arrangement
which was "essential to proficiency in any profession or calling." He also
came into contact with many Pittsburghers who were lawyers or businessmen (and who were often Scotch-Irish Presbyterians), and he would later
exploit such connections with single-minded determination.[52] It was an
indication of Thomas's networking skills, as much as of his studiousness,
that he passed his bar examinations with relative ease. He had learned the
law, but he was also already acquainted with all the members of the board:
their questions were brief and perfunctory, and he received his license to
practice on December 15, 1838. He remained in the prothonotary's office
for a few months longer, investing his savings in a law library, and he

opened his own law office in June 1839 on Fifth Street at Market Alley, one block from the city courthouse.[53] It was twenty-one years to the month since he had reached Baltimore with his parents. In the intervening period, he had gained control of his life, and the prospects now seemed fair before him.

From the very outset, Thomas Mellon was a sure-footed and successful attorney whose fortune improved along with that of his adopted city. There had been another slump in 1837, but it was less deep and protracted than that of 1819, and by the early 1840s, Pittsburgh was once again prospering. Since the frontier of American settlement had moved on, it was no longer the gateway to the west. But the wagon trains kept passing through, its position as a national center of commerce and business was consolidated by the completion of the Pennsylvania Canal in 1834, and its manufacturing activities, especially in the iron and glass industries, continued to expand. There were rich coal seams beneath the surrounding hills and abundant timber in the nearby forests; iron ore was also readily available nearby. As steam-powered industrial output increased, there were already complaints that the city was among the most polluted in the country. But this did not deter immigrants who by now were pouring in, and by 1840, the place that Charles Dickens called the "Birmingham of America" and its immediate environs boasted a population of more than forty thousand.[54]

By now, Pittsburgh had moved well ahead of its former rivals in the region, Cincinnati and Louisville, and so it was a good location, as well as a good time, for the young and determined Thomas Mellon to set up his practice.[55] The city was booming, he had already made numerous connections, many litigants he had assisted in the prothonotary's office brought him their business, and by the end of his first year his profit amounted to $1,500. He worked hard, from seven in the morning until seven at night. He was knowledgeable in the law and experienced in court procedures; he preferred civil cases, specializing in estate litigation, and soon became renowned for his fierce loyalty to his clients. He also made a point of not charging excessive fees. He was efficient, dependable, and thorough; he despised the "display and notoriety" of such flashy and glib litigators as Samuel Black; and he much preferred to make money in the background and on the sidelines of the law. "Those growing rich in the professions," he soon learned, "were seldom seen in court"; and "success" was more important than "display."[56]

Thomas Mellon did not regard the law as an end in itself. It brought him a certain income and recognition, but even more, it brought him into direct contact with mortgages, foreclosures, real estate, and property development, all of which held out the prospect of far greater financial returns than legal advocacy as Pittsburgh prospered and expanded. Already, during his time at the prothonotary's office, he had ventured into "little speculations in the purchase of small judgments, mechanics' liens and like securities," which had yielded a nice and encouraging profit. Now he began to invest shrewdly in foreclosures and the buying and selling of mortgages (his 1840 business card included "debt collection" among his specialities), and to move into bricks and mortar.[57] As the central business district encroached on the area where his office was located, Thomas Mellon persuaded the landlord to grant him a five-year lease for the whole of the floor he occupied. He sublet it at good rates, and soon netted $1,000. He also began to purchase properties which he renovated and sold at a profit. He was determined to obey the injunction of his favorite poet, Robert Burns, "to gather gear by every wile that's justified by honour," and by so doing he calculated that he was worth $12,000 at the beginning of 1843—a substantial sum "for a young lawyer so short a time at the bar," and the equivalent of about $300,000 today. Thus established, he looked about him and resolved to "make a change in personal relations." He accordingly "set out in search of a wife."[58]

His earlier experience with what he termed the "fair sex" had not been quite as "limited" as he would subsequently claim: he had encountered girls at Tranquil Retreat Academy, and he already knew a few "good families" with daughters of marriageable age. Hitherto, he had been too preoccupied with his studies and his work to contemplate matrimony, but now he showed the same careful calculation and mighty resolve that had served him in other pursuits, and he was confident of a similarly successful outcome. He would not be "easily led astray in my selection by premature emotional excitement or falling in love," and he was determined to "consider and decide impartially regarding favourable and unfavourable qualities." He sought neither great beauty nor great accomplishments, but looked for "family, ancestry and health," and he wanted a "helpmate" who would support him in adversity and delight in his successes.[59] Ephemeral emotion and fleeting feeling were less important than lifelong companionship and constant support. The search for a wife was thus another test of willpower. Yet it could not have been all cold calculation, for he also admitted that "a happy home with loving wife and bright children" was "the ultimate consummation of my hope."

Thomas Mellon initially courted Sarah Liggett, the daughter of the prothonotary who had first employed him in Pittsburgh: she was a suitable prospect, being "of a good family and very wealthy"; but he feared the Liggetts were tainted by "hereditary consumption," and he accordingly turned his attentions elsewhere. Through Sarah Liggett, he had met Sarah Jane, the daughter of the very Jacob Negley whose house and estate had so fired his imagination on his first visit to Pittsburgh in 1823, and about whom he had also heard from one of his university friends, Dr. Richard Beatty.[60] Sarah Jane Negley was four years younger than Thomas Mellon, but by chance they shared the same birthday: February 3. After several months' courtship, Thomas proposed to Sarah Jane and was accepted. They were married on August 22, 1843—or, as he would later put it, "the transaction" was "consumated." It was the "most important" event of his life: a marriage born of "judgment and discretion" which subsequently ripened into lasting if understated love.[61] In marrying Sarah Jane Negley, Thomas Mellon moved a significant step closer to realizing his dreams: both financially, because of the resources she brought into the marriage, and socially, because of the Negleys' high standing and good connections, it was a good match for an ambitious man of relatively humble origins who for twenty years had striven to achieve "an equality with such great people."[62]

But as Mellon well knew by then, all was not exactly what it had seemed back in 1823. Jacob Negley had died in 1827, worn out by the futile struggle to save his magnificent but indebted estate. His property had been taken into receivership by the sheriff, then auctioned to pay his creditors. James Ross, a family friend and former U.S. senator from Pennsylvania, intervened to save a portion of the estate for Negley's children, purchasing some of the plots at auction, and holding them until Jacob's formidable widow, Barbara Anna, and her children could afford to buy them back.[63] Eventually, they recovered some five hundred acres, or about one-third of the original Negley property, and in 1837 it was divided up among the eight children, with the larger portions going to the men. But even the smallest plots were worth $50,000, which meant Sarah Jane was still a substantial heiress, at least four times richer than her suitor, so for Thomas Mellon, who aspired to deal extensively in real estate, the "transaction" was very well worth consummating. Indeed, in the foundation of the Mellon fortune, Sarah Jane's dowry must be accounted at least as important as the two hundred guineas Rebecca Mellon brought with her across the Atlantic in 1818, and some members of the Negley family still resented this one hundred years later. After honeymooning in Buffalo, Toronto, Albany, Boston, New York, and Philadelphia, Thomas Mellon and his bride returned to Pittsburgh via the Pennsylvania Canal, and with his resources thus augmented, he went back to work.[64]

Pittsburgh was then at the beginning of a long boom which would last until the middle of the next decade. To be sure, there was the "Great Fire" in 1845, which destroyed one-third of the city, including the university that Thomas Mellon had attended, followed by a general economic downturn two years later; but the rebuilding was rapid, and by 1850 the population of greater Pittsburgh was roughly 100,000, mostly as a result of immigration, including a young Scotsman named Andrew Carnegie, who had arrived almost penniless in 1848. It was now a nationally preeminent industrial center, famous for its mills, forges, foundries, factories, steamboats—and its sky-darkening smoke. Not to be outdone by Dickens, Anthony Trollope thought it "the blackest place which I ever saw," with its smoke and dirt and "floating soot." But it was also a great metropolis, positioned to unique advantage at the junction of three great rivers, and now simultaneously the most western of the East Coast cities and the most eastern of the midwestern ones. The Pennsylvania Railroad linked Pittsburgh to Philadelphia in 1852, thereby shortening the journey from two weeks to thirteen hours, and thereafter lines were built to New York, Baltimore, Washington, Chicago, and beyond.[65]

In these buoyant times, aided by his wife's contacts and connections, Thomas Mellon's law practice grew rapidly. He built himself a much grander office in the summer of 1844, at the intersection of Fifth Avenue and Wylie Street, which would survive the 1845 fire. This may also have been the time when he learned about how Senator James Ross had saved part of Negley estate. Born in 1762, in York County, Pennsylvania, Ross was of Scotch-Irish descent, like so many of the Pittsburgh elite. He became a lawyer, and briefly taught Latin at Jefferson College. He represented Pennsylvania in the United States Senate from 1794 to 1803, and made unsuccessful bids for governor in 1799, 1802, and 1808. He settled in Pittsburgh in 1795 and resumed his legal practice in 1803, specializing in real estate. During the 1820s and 1830s he had become a major investor, buying up agricultural land on the outskirts of Pittsburgh and selling it at a substantial profit for housing development as the city limits expanded. James Ross, then, had successfully followed the very route from law to land to riches that Thomas Mellon envisioned, and he became, along with Benjamin Franklin and the uncle for whom he had been named, a model and inspiration.[66]

Not that Thomas Mellon needed much inspiration in the aftermath of the Great Fire, which provided an ideal opportunity for real estate speculation. He continued to trade in mortgages, but now he entrusted this business to brokers. In 1846, he became a building contractor, constructing eighteen small dwellings, renting them out at 10 percent of the cost, and eventually selling them at a substantial profit. He acquired properties at "sheriff sales," like those where the Negley estate had been liquidated, obtaining court judgments invariably in his favor. He bought farm land on the edge of Pittsburgh, subdivided it into plots for development, and by judging his sales carefully realized as much as six or seven times his initial outlay.[67] And he acquired coal-bearing acres near the Pennsylvania Canal, where, anticipating the model of management and investment that his son Andrew would perfect, he entrusted the operations to the "energy and business" of Benjamin Patterson while he put up the capital. "Hence," Thomas Mellon would later write, "my means, aided by a good professional income, accumulated rapidly."[68] By placing his money "in the safest and most profitable investments," he became ever more prosperous. "Wealth rightly acquired," he later reflected, "and wisely managed, possesses a power and an advantage never to be despised or disregarded." Mellon may have rejected agriculture, but all his investments—in mortgages, real estate, and minerals—were rooted in property. As a farmer's son, he had no doubt that the only tangible and dependable form of wealth ultimately rested on (or under) broad (or narrow) acres.[69]

By such means, Thomas Mellon now settled down to live an increasingly comfortable married life as a prosperous Pittsburgher, though he always remained something of a loner and an outsider, not being himself a member of one of the city's original founding families.[70] He wanted to reside downtown, near his work, and in October 1845 moved into a house on Fifth Avenue and Wylie Street. But Sarah Jane did not like the ever more grimy and polluted atmosphere, and in April 1848 they withdrew from the center of the town to a cottage on the estate of his mother-in-law, Barbara Anna Negley, at East Liberty. Thereafter, Thomas rode to work on horseback, leaving home at six in the morning and returning twelve hours later. During the next few years, he also oversaw the construction of what he called his "country home," less than half a mile from the original Negley mansion. In 1851, Thomas and Sarah Jane moved into their new house, at what would eventually be known as 401 Negley Avenue, and there they would remain together for fifty-seven years. It stood on twenty-five acres, with a large garden and a fine orchard. As befitted a former farmer, Thomas grew fruit and vegetables on his small estate, and also raised cattle and sheep.[71]

In accordance with the conventions of the day, Sarah Jane Mellon yielded up the ownership and management of her property to her husband. She devoted herself to running the house, to doing good works, especially at the local East Liberty Presbyterian Church, for which her parents had donated the land, and to bearing and rearing the children her husband devoutly desired. She became pregnant soon after the wedding, and repeatedly thereafter. Their eldest, Thomas Alexander, born in 1844, was named for his father's uncle, who had been Thomas Mellon's first mentor and benefactor. James Ross appeared in 1846, named after the senator. Then came two daughters: Sarah Emma, born in 1847, named for her mother, and Annie Rebecca in 1851, so called for her paternal grandmother. Samuel Selwyn arrived in 1853 and was named for his Mellon uncle.[72] By now, it seemed that Thomas Mellon had everything he had ever dreamed of and worked for: "knowledge and wealth and distinction," together with a "happy home with loving wife and bright children." He was a Pittsburgh patriarch in the making. But what sort of a man was he?[73]

A portrait by John Glogger, painted in the 1860s but based on a photograph taken a decade earlier, depicts Mellon with flowing black hair, bushy eyebrows, and a full mouth; but also with a firm chin, a high forehead, and a determined look. This is recognizably the man who would assert in his autobiography that individuals should be rounded personalities, with "co-operation between the emotional and mental part of our nature": not for nothing was his favorite poet Robert Burns, who combined mawkish sentiment with practical wisdom.[74] By the standards of his time, Thomas Mellon was very well educated. He had been brought up on the Bible, he knew Greek and Latin and French, and he was fascinated by history, especially that of his native Ireland, economics, philosophy, and sociology. He was a keen observer of the natural world, and he could describe buildings with accuracy and expertise. He was also a person of powerful feeling. He may have rejected his father's calling, but he remained a devoted son. He may have regarded his marriage as a business transaction, but he undoubtedly came to love his wife. He thought himself a warm and sympathetic father, eager for close and affectionate relations with his children, and so when both his daughters died—Sarah of heart disease in 1850 (she was three) and Annie of dysentery two years later (she was barely one)—his grief was profound: "keen sorrow which time alone can comfort." He was a passionate and warmhearted man, moved by the tragedy of the human condition, and by the transience of human life. As such, he seemed a typical Ulster Scot: deeply affected by sentiment, but determined to keep it in check—certainly in public, and usually in private too.[75]

As a lawyer and a businessman, Thomas Mellon appeared hard, cold and forbidding, and scornful of the "tender emotions." He believed that life was a perpetual battle, in which victory depended on willpower, determination, perseverance, hard work, and self-discipline. He admired self-denial and self-control, and accordingly despised those who fell into debt or drank too much.[76] He hated extravagance, display, waste, and ostentation, feared the corrupting allure of ease and luxury, and disapproved of those possessed of "festive disposition." His voracious reading was his only recreation: he rarely went to the theater, never gambled or saw a horse race, and was indifferent to art and music. Frowning upon "spasmodic and indiscriminate gifts of money," he took little note of the long hours, meager wages, tense labor relations, degraded environment, and cholera epidemics which most inhabitants of Pittsburgh were obliged to endure.[77] He welcomed inequality, which he believed was based on the necessary division of labor, and he distrusted democracy, he disliked radical politics, and he despised Irish Catholics. He thought politicians, except for Senator James Ross, were self-seeking and dishonest, fiscally extravagant and financially irresponsible; they plunged cities and states into debt, resulting in inexorably and inexcusably rising taxes. For him, the government was best that taxed the least.[78]

These were not atypical opinions for a self-made professional-cum-businessman at midcentury in Protestant Europe and North America. On the contrary, thrift, self-reliance, hard work, and individual responsibility were essential to the bourgeois culture, experience, and worldview.[79] Whatever "tender emotions" decorum obliged him to conceal, Thomas Mellon espoused these austerities with unusually rigid resolve and in noticeably unforgiving form. His principles explained his achievements, justified his existence, and vindicated his triumphs. They were the key to self-mastery and to a success that was best summarized as "acquisition and accumulation." And they made him a formidable character with a siege mentality, conspicuously lacking in charm or empathy or compassion. He may have modeled himself on Benjamin Franklin, but unlike Franklin, he did not love his fellows, and he held no brief for public service. There was in Mellon a downright mean streak which some members of his family could not fail to notice.[80] As such, he was a quintessential Scotch-Irish, middle-class Pittsburgher: a calculating, conservative, and belligerent member of the mid-nineteenth-century bourgeoisie, rather than a benevolent, liberal, or cosmopolitan one.

Thomas Mellon's Pittsburgh was dominated by such men: all proud of "their shrewdness in money matters; their possession of a certain mental hardness or rigidity, and a lack of imagination; their contempt for many of the social amenities." For western Pennsylvania was very much a cultural extension of Protestant Ulster, and that was in turn an extension of Presbyterian Scotland. According to a local joke, when John Knox asked God to give him Scotland, the Lord not only granted his prayer but threw in Ulster and Pittsburgh for good measure.[81] In leaving Ulster for western Pennsylvania, the first Andrew Mellon had taken charge of his own future. In leaving the countryside for Pittsburgh, his son Thomas had done likewise, and thereafter the name of Mellon would be increasingly identified with the city. During the next generation, these links would become ever closer as the Mellons grew richer and Pittsburgh grew bigger. It was Thomas's fourth son, Andrew William Mellon, born on March 24, 1855, and named for his paternal grandfather, the immigrant and farmer (who died in the following year), who would be primarily responsible for the family's remarkable financial aggrandizement and success. He would be known as Andy or AW, and more than any of his elder or younger brothers, he was quintessentially Thomas Mellon's son. So much so, indeed, that in later life, when confronted by any challenging problem, his invariable reaction would be to ask: "What would Father do?"[82]

PART ONE

In the Shadow
of His Father, *1855–1900*

Every man who comes into the world has his own peculiar qualities, and must find his level before he can accomplish his mission satisfactorily. He must rise or fall, or flounder about till he finds his proper place. Faculties, aptitudes and abilities are infinitely various, but all are equally worthy and deserving when rightly applied.

Thomas Mellon and His Times, p. 424

1

THE PATRIARCH PRESIDES

Father and Sons, 1855–73

Make your child a partner in your joys and sorrows, your hopes and fears; impart your plans and purposes; stand not on your dignity, but let yourself down to his capacity, if need be, and show your trust in him. You will be surprised to find how much a five or ten year old boy can understand of the ways of men, and how readily he will enter into your views. . . . I experienced the benefit of such training myself, and applied it in raising my own family with the most satisfactory results.

Thomas Mellon and His Times, p. 29

I. A THRIVING CAREER

Andrew Mellon was the sixth child of Thomas and Sarah Jane Mellon, but he was only the fourth to survive infancy. His two sisters were already dead, and although he would not long remain the youngest son, he grew up among brothers only, in what Burton Hendrick called a "eugenic" family.[1] Only the fittest would survive. At the time of Andrew's birth, his eldest brother, Thomas Alexander, was eleven: the next, James Ross, was nine: and Samuel Selwyn was two. The two elder boys were close in age and interests: Andrew and Selwyn soon became a second pair, as would Richard Beatty ("Dick" or "RB"), who was born in 1858 and named for one of his father's oldest friends, and George Negley, who arrived two years later and was named for his mother's uncle. Even depleted by two early and wrenching deaths, this was a large bourgeois family by the standards of the time. But it was very much a Scotch-Irish

Presbyterian household, and while Andrew Mellon knew far more comfort and security than most Pittsburghers, the atmosphere was intense and serious, rather than joyful or easy. Although surrounded by a lush and bountiful garden, the house at 401 Negley was gloomy and forbidding inside. For Thomas Mellon disdained the vulgar ostentation which he feared was "common among those grown suddenly rich," whom he dismissed as the "shoddyocracy," and his house was devoid of the elaborate ornamentation, both inside and out, that would became popular among the local plutocracy in subsequent decades. The blinds were often drawn, and the interior was a drab amalgam of Brussels carpets, heavy draperies, and somberly papered walls, with no pictures of any artistic merit.[2]

This was the morose world of Andrew Mellon's boyhood, but unlike his surviving siblings, he would continue to inhabit it as an ever more solitary son until he was in his mid-forties. Sarah Jane Mellon was the presiding matriarch, and although Thomas Mellon wrote little about her in his autobiography, she was clearly a redoubtable woman for her time. She was not only rich but tough, having survived eight pregnancies between 1844 and 1860. More conventionally religious than her husband, she was responsible for getting the family to East Liberty Presbyterian Church on Sundays. She also oversaw the household, baking the bread and cooking many of the meals herself. There was a domestic staff of three, including an intimidating housekeeper, Mrs. Cox. On the day of Andrew Mellon's birth, the housekeeper instructed James Ross Mellon to convey the news to his grandmother, Barbara Anna Negley, who lived nearby, and she soon appeared bearing a willow basket full of yellow apples which perfumed the birth room.[3] Andrew Mellon's earliest recorded recollection was another scene of purposeful feminine domesticity—which he disrupted. When two years old, he crawled beneath a table at which his mother and her sister were sewing, and began cutting the edges of the tablecloth with a pair of scissors which had fallen to the floor. Given his father's "high opinion of the strict exercise of parental authority," it is difficult to believe this misdemeanor went unpunished.[4]

From the very beginning, Andrew Mellon was at the center of that large and growing family over which it had always been his father's ultimate ambition to preside. These were generally prosperous times in Pittsburgh, despite another slump in 1857, two years after Andrew's birth, which lasted to the end of the decade: thus he was also at the center of a large and growing industrial region.[5] Oil was discovered nearby in 1859, and the iron industry continued to expand. By 1860, there were twenty-six rolling mills, twenty-three glassworks—and fourteen banks, all of which had survived the recent depression. With a population that had reached 50,000, the city ranked sixteenth in the United States, and Allegheny County as a whole claimed 178,000 inhabitants. Pittsburgh was also the birthplace of the Republican Party, which held its first convention there in February 1856: the Mellon family would be among its faithful for the next hundred years and more.[6] In this buoyant, fertile environment, Thomas Mellon grew in wealth and stature. In 1857, the Allegheny County commissioners decided to double the real estate tax to pay the interest on bonds that they had imprudently floated to help finance railroad extension in the area. As befitted a lifelong opponent of tax increases and irresponsible speculation, an outraged Thomas Mellon helped organize public protests, and he spoke at many meetings. But his chief activities remained business and the law, at which he would work harder during Andrew Mellon's formative years than at any other time.[7]

Thomas Mellon continued to deal in debts, mortgages, real estate, and property developments, not just in Pittsburgh, but also more widely.[8] In 1856, he took control from a defaulting mortgagor of a furnace property of 1,700 acres in West Virginia; it was his first acquaintance with iron production, but he chose against continuing operation because of the prohibitive costs of obtaining ore from nearby mountainsides. Three years later, he ventured more deeply into the coal business, and went into partnership with his wife's cousin, Felix Casper Negley. He financed the purchase of coal works at Braddock and Sandy Creek, but despite kinship, Negley proved an unreliable partner, and Mellon was later obliged to resort to "vexatious litigation."[9] This was not his only business association that would go sour, and in his autobiography he would lament that his judgment of men and character was defective, and that he was too trusting and easily persuaded. Much more successful was a partnership with James B. Corey, David Shaw, and George M. Bowman, all of whom became trusted lifelong friends. The group invested in numerous collieries, among them the Waverly Coal and Coke Company, and they prospered mightily. "As to the coal business," Thomas wrote to his son James Ross, "I consider it one of the best, and it is highly respectable." "Coal," he would conclude, was "the most important article in productive manufacturers."[10]

At the same time, Thomas Mellon's legal practice was growing, and here, too, he sought partners, among them William B. Negley, his wife's nephew. But again collaboration created more problems than it solved: "I found it impossible," he later lamented, "to transfer clients who relied on me to my partners, without losing them altogether." By 1859, he was feeling "overwhelmed and oppressed" with his increasingly "taxing and monotonous" legal work, but fortunately an opportunity to lighten his load presented itself.[11] In April that year, he was approached by three powerful and politically connected friends—Thomas M. Marshall, A. M. Watson, and Stephen Geyer—who invited him to run for the new position of associate law judge in the Court of Common Pleas. With their help, he secured the Republican nomination. The recently established party was Mellon's natural political home: northern-based, pro-business, anti-immigration. But he "knew nothing about party maneuvering and electioneering," and his dislike of the political process was such that he refused to campaign personally: "I did not go out at all or appear in public," he later recalled, "leaving electioneering in that line to my friends." They worked hard for him, and he won easily in the November election. He promptly dissolved his practice, and was duly sworn in on the first Monday of December 1859. Thereafter, Thomas Mellon was always known in Pittsburgh as "the Judge," or "Judge Mellon," and for the rest of his life, even after leaving the bench, he would dress in his formal attire from that time: a long-tailed frock coat and white shirt with a high, starched wing collar.[12]

For the next ten years, he shared the duties with a senior colleague (initially William B. McClure, whom he had met in 1838 at the prothonotary's office, and subsequently James P. Sterrett, who would end his days on the state supreme court), and they sat together, or separately, as they saw fit or as the pressure of the docket dictated, except in capital cases, where two judges were required. Previously renowned as a ferociously committed and determinedly partisan advocate, the Judge now moved with unexpected ease to Olympian impartiality.[13] But in other ways, he remained characteristically forceful and unyielding. He had no qualms about sentencing criminals to death "if they clearly deserve it," and he was predictably unsparing in his criticism of those he deemed to be hopeless or idle or failed—or Catholic. He believed that there was "entirely too much sympathy and consideration for criminals" on "the part of the unthinking multitude," and he soon became equally skeptical of the collective wisdom of juries. His initial inclination was to let the jurors hear the evidence and make up their own minds, with no direction from the bench. But he soon concluded that they were rarely capable of reaching a sensible conclusion about complex issues, and came to favor firm-handed direction from the bench. "The judge . . . ," he later observed, "may even go so far as to tell the jury how on the whole the weight of evidence strikes him: indeed it is his duty in most cases to do so." In later life, Andrew Mellon would have cause to remember—and indeed to share—his father's skepticism of jury trials.[14]

Although the Judge applied himself with predictable efficiency and thoroughness, he had been correct in anticipating that the job would be less stressful and demanding than his practice. With time on his hands, he was able to return to his relentless regime of solitary self-improvement which he had grudgingly abandoned after college. But since then there had been a revolution in political, theological, economic, and philosophical thought, as Bacon, Descartes, Berkeley, Locke, Hume, Reid, Stewart, and Brown were now joined—and in some cases supplanted—by Darwin, Spencer, Wallace, Huxley, Tyndall, Buckle, and Argyle, the "deities now installed in the temples of philosophy." From among these new thinkers, Thomas Mellon particularly relished Charles Darwin and Herbert Spencer. He found it easy to reconcile the theory of evolution with the tenets of Christianity: the history of the world extended forward in a long chain of cause and effect, while the great First Cause of it all remained unknown and unknowable. And he found Spencer even more congenial: in his insistence that life was a struggle which only the fittest survive; in his belief in individualism and laissez-faire; in his hatred of socialism and militarism; in his abhorrence of state interference; and in his stress on the need for practical, problem-solving education.[15] Darwin's and Spencer's were transformative books for the Judge's middle-aged thinking in the way that Franklin's had been during his youth. The *Autobiography* had sketched out an individual course of self-help and self-advancement; Darwin and Spencer provided the broader natural and sociological vindication of such a trajectory. The Judge had experienced life as a struggle; they explained his experience. And so he determined to prepare his sons to fight and to win in their turn.

Judge Mellon's mature, solitary self-education proceeded amid searing and stirring national events. Indeed, the events initially facilitated his efforts, for the Civil War broke out scarcely a year after he was elected to the bench, and the resulting decline in litigation gave him more time to read and reflect. But while he appreciated the opportunity, he deplored the reason for it. Although abolitionist sentiment was overwhelming in western Pennsylvania, giving Lincoln a massive majority in Allegheny County, the Judge did not feel strongly either way about slavery.[16] He thought "the Rebellion" was another foolish armed conflict, characterized by "imbecility and petty tyranny" on the part of military officers and by "folly and wickedness" on the part of politicians. For war meant more government intervention, and more government spending, and this in turn meant more debt and more taxes. "The waste and extravagance," he would later recall, "indulged in by the state and local authorities in military affairs was amazing." He thought military service a great mistake, and approved of enlistment only among those who combined low class and low intellect, and who would not be missed if they failed to return. By contrast, he thought "men of better qualities" should stay at home, and "the parents and friends of young men of promise" should "use all their influence" to guard them from the mistaken temptations of "military excitement." War, by Mellon's lights, was not a matter of glory and heroism and righteousness, but of waste and folly and ruin, and he lamented the death in uniform of his former foe-cum-friend at the Pittsburgh bar, Samuel Black.[17]

Whatever his feelings about it, the Civil War inevitably impinged on the Judge's affairs and on his family, making him "gloomy and melancholy." His brother Samuel and his uncle Thomas both supported the Confederacy, but a cousin of Sarah Jane's, General James S. Negley, served in the Union forces. Cargoes of coal that the Judge shipped downriver to New Orleans were impounded by Confederate troops, and he could secure the $40,000 he was owed in the transaction only by calling on his connections with the war secretary, Edwin Stanton, who had been a fellow Pittsburgh lawyer before joining Lincoln's cabinet.[18] But these were not his only anxieties. A ballooning national debt and rising taxes led the Judge to fear that the entire Mellon fortune might be wiped out, and that the family would have to leave the state; nothing of the kind happened. A more creditable worry was that industrial Pittsburgh would be a target for the Confederate army, and in 1862 and 1863 the threat seemed clear and present: "our homes and property," the Judge remembered, "were at one time in actual danger of destruction by the rebels." Trenches were dug and defensive earthworks constructed; they passed close to the Mellon house, behind the orchards. Andrew Mellon was not yet ten, but he vividly recalled the workers digging and shoveling, and he stood guard over the Mellon cherry trees with an unloaded shotgun. He also remembered seeing Abraham Lincoln in February 1861, when his train stopped at Pittsburgh on the way to Washington for his inauguration. When the president-elect rose to speak, he amazed the boy as he "un-spiraled himself, like a snake," to a great height, and spoke in "gentle and well modulated" tones.[19]

On balance, the Civil War brought more prosperity than trouble to Pittsburgh, just as the War of 1812 had done earlier in the century and as the First World War would do decades later. For this was the first large-scale modern conflict, fought by mass armies equipped with heavy weaponry, and it was Pittsburgh that helped provide the sinews of war for the Union forces. The city fabricated locomotives, freight cars, steamboats, artillery, small arms, ammunition, armor plate, and clothing in unprecedented quantities, and 5.5 million tons of coal were mined in the vicinity to power the factories, foundries, and furnaces. By the mid-1860s, Pittsburgh was producing two-fifths of America's iron; there were 100,000 people living inside the city boundary, and 230,000 in the greater metropolitan region.[20] Among its five hundred factories were such great undertakings as the Fort Pitt Foundry, and Jones and Laughlin's American Iron Works. The influx of population, the industrial expansion, and the accompanying noise, smoke, fire, and pollution meant Pittsburgh was now described as "Hell with the lid taken off." But whatever the atmosphere, the Civil War had transformed the city from a river town into an emerging industrial colossus. As the Judge would later recall, in the resulting period of sustained prosperity general business became so active that "such opportunities for making money had never before existed in all my former experience."[21]

Thomas Mellon took full advantage of them, despite his disdain for the war, "investing all my loose means in coal lands, which turned out very profitably afterwards." "In all my experience," he would later write, "I never knew any trade so profitable as the coal business continued to be for several years afterwards." He was also expanding his interests in real estate and property development, and not only in Pittsburgh itself. For nearby, up and down the three rivers, satellite towns were springing up, at Braddock, McKeesport, Mansfield, Duquesne, Etna, Sharpsburg, Allegheny, South Pittsburgh, and Birmingham, and the Judge hastened to buy up land in these rising neighborhoods.[22] He was also beginning to invest farther afield: in Baltimore, perhaps combining a well-concealed sentiment and manifest shrewdness; and at Fort Leavenworth, Kansas, now a major gateway to the still-advancing western frontier. The Judge continued to believe that carefully chosen parcels of strategically located land were bound to increase in value. Accordingly, at Leavenworth, his aim was to acquire holdings "near a great city unimproved," and wait for the town to expand. To be sure, it was not easy to manage properties at such a distance: local agents were unreliable, and the judgment of his brother Samuel, who was also involved, was unsound. But what had worked, and was still working, on the creeping urban frontier of Pittsburgh would surely work elsewhere.[23]

By the late 1860s, the Judge's many ventures were prospering beyond his imagining. Growing in wealth and local standing, he was appointed a director of the Farmers' Deposit National Bank and the first president of the People's Savings Bank.[24] With his professional income dwarfed by his investment returns, he decided that time spent on the bench could be put to more profitable and self-interested use. For the profession which had originally been his route to recognition and riches had served its purpose, and had now become a constraint on further accumulation. "My salary," he candidly recalled, "afforded no adequate compensation for the loss sustained by declining passing opportunities for making money."[25] Accordingly, when his ten-year term as judge was up in late 1869, he did not seek re-election. "Attention to other people's business," he later insisted, "is a waste of time when we have profitable business of our own to attend to." But there was another reason. "All through those busy years of professional and judicial labors," he subsequently wrote, "my heart was in my home; it was there I was happy and there my feelings centered."[26] So it was, and so they did. And what warmed his heart most was the prospect that one day his sons might join him in business. By now, there was every hope that they might prove the happy, rewarding, and successful collaborators he felt he had so rarely found outside the family. How did this come about?

II. PATERNAL CONTROL

Judge Mellon did not mellow with middle age or parenthood: on the contrary, he drove himself ever harder to acquire and to accumulate. It wasn't easy getting on with his children when they were very small—indeed, he never found infancy very attractive—but as they grew, "the tendrils of the young vine take hold on the parent's heart," and he became deeply involved with them.[27] The involvement was much more on his terms than theirs, and as usual, his brain was at least as engaged as his feelings. He liked to think he enjoyed close and warm relations with all his boys, but the family environment he had created was predictably stern. There was little light or laughter at 401 Negley, and meals were generally taken in silence (unless business was being discussed), even on the four great family feast days: Thanksgiving, Christmas, New Year's Day, and the shared birthday of Thomas and Sarah Jane on February 3.[28] Displays of emotion were frowned upon: in public, Mellon men never kissed Mellon women; handshakes were as demonstrative as they ever got. Reinforced now by Darwin and Spencer, the Judge's Presbyterian ethos was mostly secular— a social network and a social imperative rather than a deeply held religious belief. It was in this austere and intimidating environment that he set about molding his sons to his inflexible will. "As a general rule," he later noted, "parents, especially such as are in easy circumstances or engaged in extensive enterprises, hold their children at too great a distance from them." He, by contrast, was determined, after his fashion, to keep them as close as he could.[29]

Though Judge Mellon had rebelled decisively against his own father, he had no intention of tolerating any such conduct in the next generation. Never doubting that he had his boys' best interests at heart, he ensured that their upbringing furthered his aims for them. There was the odd interlude of teasing and fun and games, but generally he was intolerant of frivolity. They might be the children of an increasingly rich man, but that only intensified the imperative that they not succumb to the insidious temptations of ease, idleness, irresponsibility, and self-indulgence. He made all his sons learn Burns's "Epistle to a Young Friend" by heart, a paean to canniness, practical wisdom, and self-advancement: essential qualities for winning the struggles of life, which only the fittest would survive.[30] Rigid though he was, he genuinely believed that he was listening to his children, and responding to their interests and ambitions: "I would explore and forecast from the views and sentiments expressed in their free and joyous utterances the manner of men they were to become." But he also seemed aware that he was practicing more cunning than empathy: "I secured free admission to their confidence from the first and participated in all their plans; *and in return secured their willing co-operation in my purposes for their benefit.*"[31]

There was a significant measure of self-delusion about all this. "What appeared to me at the time very remarkable," he later recalled, "was that we never seriously disagreed, but seemed to see everything pretty much alike." In more brutal terms, the Judge regarded his sons as essentially extensions of himself, and this in turn explains why he would not entrust their education to schools, either public or private. He thought the former were full of low-class and low-aptitude people, given to "vulgarity, disobedience and contempt for study"; the latter, he found, were selling a service rather than providing a serious and disciplined apprenticeship for life. Determined that his own sons not be thus contaminated or corrupted, he built his own schoolhouse on his land at 401 Negley and employed a full-time teacher named Taylor.[32] There, in a school that was an adjunct of home, were educated, according to their father's principles, Thomas, James, and Selwyn, along with "a few other pupils of proper character in order to lessen the expense"; when Andrew turned five, he joined the class. The curriculum was predictably strict, and it was also extremely practical: reading, writing, and arithmetic, but not poetry or fiction or the classics or science. "The studies," the Judge later explained, "were such as would be most necessary and useful in the subsequent business of life; and the method was to train the pupil in the way best calculated to produce thoroughness in whatever was studied."[33]

For Judge Mellon was convinced that all his boys were destined for business, and that they should therefore be taught alertness to money-making opportunities at the earliest possible age. Later, having thus controlled and confined and conditioned them, his relief and joy would know no bounds when "their inclination seemed to concur with mine spontaneously." "I soon discovered," he triumphantly concluded, with a surprised delight both endearing and absurd, that "they were out and out business men."[34] And he drew a further conclusion: that being endowed with "first class business talent," they need not train for any profession. He himself had been well educated and had acquired professional qualifications, but given a lack of capital that had been his only route to advancement. His sons, by contrast, could count on him to set them up, and the sooner they started, the better. Accordingly, neither Thomas nor James had much education after leaving their father's school. Thomas did not proceed beyond the grammar grades, and James spent a brief spell at Jefferson College in Canonsburg, which the Judge had thought insufficiently serious for his own purposes.[35] The eldest sons were thus significantly less well educated than their father. That was deliberate.

When barely in their teens, the two elder Mellon brothers had shown an early aptitude for business by expressing an interest in becoming blacksmiths. The Judge immediately constructed a smithy on his grounds, where the boys worked diligently after school. For a time, he later recalled, "the hammer and anvil afforded constant recreation, with no other inconvenience than blackened hands and faces." "Thus," he concluded characteristically, "the gratification of a whim was easily converted into the improvement of bone and muscle!" This enterprise did not last long, but it was a significant portent of subsequent endeavors by the Mellon boys: paternal finance, leadership and support, and brotherly collaboration.[36] Thus did the Judge convince himself that he was merely an enabler and facilitator, whereas in fact he continued to be the dominant and controlling influence. A letter to James and Thomas in the festive season of 1862 makes this abundantly and overbearingly plain:

There is a Christmas gift which I would prize more than all things, but I am afraid to ask you for it lest you should be unwilling to give it, or should promise and afterwards fail to perform. The gift I would desire is your confidence—to trust all your secrets to me; to keep nothing back; to confide in me all your troubles and desires and all your hopes, fears and plans; to consult freely with me about everything without fear or backwardness; making me your most intimate friend—never deceiving; always relying on me for sympathy and advice, for what you do wrong as well as for what you do right.[37]

At this time, the Judge became convinced that Thomas and James were "ready and eager for the earnest work of life," and despite his gloomy anxiety about the Civil War, he proceeded to launch them in their early careers. He advanced Thomas $3,000 so he could buy a local nursery from General James Negley, who was then away on active duty. The enterprise specialized in fruit and trees and flowers, quite a natural occupation for someone reared on the lush and verdant grounds of 401 Negley. Thomas made a success of it, and soon repaid his father with interest.[38] Meanwhile, the Judge had withdrawn James Ross Mellon from Jefferson College and sent him out west, primarily for reasons of health. James had intended to go to St. Paul, Minnesota, but he was unable to reach the city because of inclement weather, and eventually found work in Milwaukee, in the law office of Finches Lynde and Miller, where he obtained practical knowledge of property transactions and bookkeeping. "Your vocation," the Judge instructed him, "is to acquire general useful information and experience, and in that time we can decide for a permanent occupation." "Learn the modus operandi," he urged on another occasion, "of the coal business and merchandising and iron business or other important branches of manufacturing. It may be useful to us hereafter." "A man," the Judge further warned, "never ought to risk much. I have always speculated in real estate or something that I knew had intrinsic value in it equal to my investment."[39]

In addition to drawing his second son's attention to the perils of undue risk, the Judge subjected him to a relentless bombardment of exhortations and admonishments. Naturally, he is against drinking, smoking, and "female company keeping." "Being unemployed is a serious evil," and it is essential to "resist temptations of all kinds." Casual friendships are a great mistake: "Be extremely cautious of social young men. Make no intimate, confidential friends till you know the private moral character. Make no friends, that is companions of theatre-going, party-going, or young men who talk of the pleasures of company and the like."[40] Recreation is an equally serious matter: "Read no light or frivolous works like novel reading and light literature—it unhinges the mind entirely for manly employment." And correspondence should always be conducted with care: "I notice your handwriting and spelling has improved some, which is an important matter in business. Your mode of folding a letter is rather awkward. I put this one in an envelope in order to show you the usual way."[41]

As the Civil War continued, both elder Mellon sons briefly fell victim to those "temptations" of "military excitement" which the Judge so feared and distrusted, and they sought to enlist in the Union forces opposing their "rebel" Uncle Samuel. Thomas Alexander briefly joined a regiment of emergency men and served for a hundred days in 1862 guarding prisoners at the Maryland border, fortunately arriving at Antietam just after the bloody battle was over. And from Milwaukee two years later, James Ross sent his father what seemed like an ultimatum: "If I do not get an answer next week," he wrote, with unprecedented daring, "I will suppose you have consented and will enlist." The Judge's rage at this impertinence knew no bounds, though his reply could not have been more succinct: "Don't do it. I have written," read the return telegram.[42] In subsequent letters, he vented his wrath at length: "You say if you don't get an answer this week you will take it for granted. You have no right to take it for granted until I have had time to reply and you know I would not let such an important matter pass without advising you about it." And again: "I had hoped my boy was going to make a smart, intelligent businessman, and was not such a goose as to be seduced from his duty by the declamations of buncombed speeches." And again: "Your constitution is not fit for soldiering." James's "military excitement" was thus broken by the relentless barrage of paternalistic invective.[43]

Young Thomas Mellon went back to his nursery after serving his hundred days in Maryland, his father having expressly forbidden general enlistment in the Union forces. According to the Judge, Thomas Alexander ultimately learned a great deal on the job, and closed the enterprise out with "a net profit of several thousand dollars": "quite a promising beginning" for his first business venture. Meanwhile, a chastened James Ross Mellon had returned from Milwaukee, anxious to atone for his high crimes and misdemeanors and get down to business himself. "I want to have you with me," the Judge had written at the end of one diatribe against military service, "and get you into constant employment of some kind as I have Thomas."[44] While out west, James had originally expressed an interest in overseeing iron foundries, but on his return, he preferred to enter the coal business, and the Judge put him in charge of the Osceola Coal works, a recent purchase intended for resale—at a profit, of course. Although only in his late teens, James managed the company, oversaw more than one hundred miners, supervised sales, and dealt with the accounts. He paid his father rent on the property, and when he eventually sold the business to C. Shad and Co., he made a profit of $5,000. Like his elder brother, James Ross had done well in his first solo entrepreneurial foray. In both cases, the Judge was pleased.[45]

Selwyn and Andrew were clearly next in line for correction and guidance; but Selwyn was carried off by diphtheria in September 1862. He was nine years old. The usually stern and stoical Judge was heartbroken: "Vigorous and healthy, thus cut down in the early morning of life! Time has brought me consolation in all other deaths but this: for Selwyn I cannot be comforted. The recollection of every little unkindness I subjected him to affects me with remorse." Thereafter, the Judge would claim that he had come to regret the harsh treatment of both his elder boys, and resolved to be more lenient with Andrew, Richard, and George—which, up to a point, he would be.[46] For his part, Andrew was left bereft at the particularly tender age of seven; he and Selwyn had been inseparable as the middle pair of brothers. His sense of isolation may have been intensified when, on Selwyn's death, the Judge closed down his school: having spent two years there, Andrew was sent away, perhaps to escape the diphtheria epidemic. The boy stayed with his father's sister, Elinor Mellon Stotler, about five miles outside East Liberty at McKeesport, where he attended the local school, returning to 401 Negley at the age of nine. By this time, his father seems to have overcome his earlier aversion to public education, and Andrew was enrolled in a Pittsburgh school at the corner of Grant and Strawberry streets. Father and son commuted daily together on the horsecar line from East Liberty to downtown which had opened in 1859.[47]

This shared routine—to and from school for Andrew, and to and from the courthouse for his father—ensured that of all the boys, Andrew would become particularly close to the Judge. "There was daily communion between father and son," W. L. Mellon later recalled, but it was predictably undemonstrative. Like his older brothers, Andrew soon showed a good eye for an opportunity and, encouraged by his father, evinced an interest in moneymaking and accumulation at an early age.[48] As a child, he cut grass from the meadows at 401 Negley, and he sold it to passing farmers for horse feed at five cents a bundle. Later, equipped with a donkey and cart provided by his father, and enlisting the labors of his younger brothers, Dick and George, Andrew sold fruit and vegetables from the family garden—with such success that his mother sometimes had to visit the local shops to buy her own garden produce back.[49] Like his brothers before him, Andrew was obliged to learn Burns's "Epistle to a Young Friend" (dedicated, by agreeable coincidence, to another Andrew), and as a boy of ten he recited the lines in front of the Judge, who rose to his feet to join his son in declaiming the most stirring verse:

> To catch dame fortune's golden smile,
> Assiduous wait upon her;
> And gather gear by every wile
> That's justified by honour;
> Not for to hide it in a hedge,
> Nor for a train attendant;
> But for the glorious privilege
> Of being independent.

At 401 Negley, "the air was heavy with the imperative to acquire." "They had absolutely no fun," a Mellon in-law recalled. "It was work, work, all the time . . . The one thing they understood, the end of all their efforts, was money."[50]

Andrew Mellon happened to be in his father's courtroom when the news came of Lee's surrender, and thus of the end of the Civil War. There was an uproar in court, forcing the Judge to pound his gavel, and he adjourned the session. Father and son left together, the Judge pausing to wind the clock on the way out, as if to express his scorn for a popular rejoicing he did not share. By the end of the war, his family was growing up, and each of the brothers had responded differently to their stern upbringing. Thomas and James were beginning to make their way in business. Dick was lively, expansive, and outgoing, and very much his mother's favorite. And George was showing signs of a kindness of heart which would make him of all the brothers the most popular in the town. But Andrew, light-haired, blue-eyed, and slight of figure, already seemed the most distant and remote of the boys. Perhaps it was the death of Selwyn, or perhaps it was those daily journeys with his father that set him apart. For as W. L. Mellon recalled, the Judge talked to Andrew "not as a little boy but as to one with a mature intellect, and thereby challenged the youngster to think as a man." "Indeed," he concluded, "I sometimes think that this companionship shortened AW's boyhood"—more, perhaps, than any of his brothers.[51]

As the 1860s drew on, the Judge's eyesight began to fail, and although the candles became more numerous, and the magnifying glasses got bigger, he found reading ever more difficult. For someone so devoted to book learning, who had inherited a magnificent library from his late father-in-law, Jacob Negley, and who had augmented it greatly, this deprivation was severe. Anxious to reread old favorites and to keep up with new writing in politics, religion, economics, philosophy, and sociology, the Judge would summon his wife, his sons, and eventually his grandchildren to read to him, first the newspapers, and then more specialized matter. As always, he did not expect honest labor to go unremunerated, and paid a fee of fifty cents for two or three hours. It was a wearisome duty, and the Judge was a far from passive audience—exhorting and cajoling his readers, and arguing and disputing with the authors.[52] But given their own deliberately limited education, this would prove the only way for his children to gain access to their father's rich but otherwise solitary intellectual life. Andrew read extensively to the Judge, and may thereby have learned more than he did by formal education. He certainly encountered Herbert Spencer that way, and he later told John Bowman, chancellor of the University of Pittsburgh, that he honed his own analytical skills by repeated reading of Spencer's *First Principles* to his father in the evenings.[53]

By the late 1860s, the older generation of Mellons and Negleys was dying off, and a new one was coming into being. The first Thomas Mellon, the Judge's uncle and mentor, died in 1866; Barbara Anna Negley, the Judge's mother-in-law, passed on in the following year; and Rebecca Mellon, the Judge's mother, died in 1868.[54] Truly, he was now the Mellon patriarch. Meanwhile, the Judge's two eldest boys were on their way to the altar. Returning home from Milwaukee in July 1864, James Ross Mellon stopped off at Fort Leavenworth to check on his father's property holdings, and there he met and fell in love with Rachel Larimer.[55] She was of impeccable Scotch-Irish lineage and her father, Major General William Larimer, had been a significant business figure in Pittsburgh and one of the Judge's clients. But he had gone bankrupt in 1854, and had headed west to make a fresh start, leaving the Judge to settle his affairs back home. Eventually, he restored his finances, founded the city of Denver in 1858, and apparently resumed business contacts with the Judge.[56] James Ross returned to Pittsburgh eager to be married. The Judge initially withheld his consent because his son was only nineteen (he believed that men should enter into this "transaction" between the ages of twenty-five and thirty-five), but he eventually relented, and the couple were married in 1867.[57] Within a year, James and Rachel had produced the first grandchild, William Larimer Mellon, named for the general and subsequently known in the family as WL. The boy was close enough in age to the Judge's younger sons that he was almost their contemporary—and would eventually become their business colleague.

One of Rachel Larimer's closest friends was Mary Caldwell, whose brother Alexander, born in Pennsylvania, was now one of the leading businessmen in Fort Leavenworth and also a major railway promoter in the Kansas area.[58] In due time, Thomas Alexander Mellon was dispatched to inspect the Judge's properties, and Rachel took the occasion to introduce Mary Caldwell to him. The result was a second Pittsburgh-Leavenworth romance, with Thomas Alexander and Mary exchanging vows in 1870 (without fuss, since Thomas, at twenty-six, was well within the Judge's matrimonial parameters). Like those of their parents, both of these marriages would turn out to be lifelong: James and Rachel eventually produced six children, and Thomas and Mary five. Again following the parental example, there was a mingling of sentiment and calculation: not only had Rachel Larimer's father been an associate of the Judge's in Pittsburgh, but after Thomas married Mary Caldwell, the Mellons became closely involved in business in Kansas with her brother Alexander.[59] Both brothers eventually settled down in houses close to 401 Negley, on land which Sarah Jane gave them, thereby establishing a third "Mellon patch," following Lower Castletown in Ulster and Greensburg in western Pennsylvania. Such was Judge Mellon's family in the years between the end of the Civil War in 1865 and his retirement from the bench four years later, when his third surviving son, Andrew, was in his early teens.

III. SETTING HIS SONS TO WORK

Having heard his last case in 1869, the Judge was honored with a testimonial dinner in Pittsburgh at Monongahela House, the best hotel in town. His eyesight may have been deteriorating, but with the law behind him, he was eager to embark on what would turn out to be the most creative and influential phase of his business career. This was partly because, as he later recalled, "the period between 1863 and 1873 was one in which it was very easy to grow rich," and as a free man, he was determined to take full (and full-time) advantage of the postbellum boom.[60] But it was also that he could now see a new and better way of doing so. Although he had prospered during the 1850s and 1860s, he had not found association easy, either in business or the law. He had often tried to work with and through his wife's relatives, but this had always been unsatisfactory: joining with Felix Negley in the coal business had not turned out well; the law partnership with William B. Negley had not been an unalloyed success; and even the purchase of the nursery from General James S. Negley had resulted in a serious disagreement. But now his elder sons, already tried and trained and tested, were ready for bigger challenges and greater opportunities. They were "two bright boys, just out of school, the idols of my heart, merging on manhood, and with fine business capacities," and he was "eager to launch [them] on this flood tide of business prosperity, and to pilot them in the channel for some part of the way."[61]

There were various matters he considered. Thomas had disposed of the nursery, and James would soon withdraw from his coal-mining venture. The Judge's own dealings in coal, in land, and in real estate held considerable business potential. He also had some experience of finance, having served on the boards of two of Pittsburgh's banks. And the death of Barbara Anna Negley in 1867 had made available further plots of land that might be profitably developed. Accordingly, the Judge devised an elaborate new business scheme by which his sons would take advantage of this propitious confluence of circumstances. He decided that Thomas Alexander and James Ross should go into partnership together in East Liberty, dealing in coal, lumber, building supplies, and real estate development; and at the same time he founded the East Liberty Savings and Deposit Bank, a joint stock venture which was partly an investment in itself, but also a way to finance the brothers' business.[62] Here was an interconnected and mutually reinforcing group of enterprises, well described by David Koskoff: "The Mellon boys subdivided acreage into home sites sold at a profit; sold their buyers lumber with which to construct their humble dwellings at a profit; financed the transactions through the bank, profitably; and then sold the coal with which to heat the houses, again at a profit."[63]

The new Mellon business arrangement was both intrinsically satisfactory and historically portentous. "I had now," the Judge recalled with evident relief and pleasure, "hearty and reliable coadjutors to execute with judgment, prudence and alacrity whatever I should plan. This was a condition I had never enjoyed before." The Judge was thus establishing the prototype Mellon business which in future years Andrew and Richard would carry to much greater heights of scale, sophistication, and success. Meanwhile, "a thriving and profitable trade was soon established" under James Ross and Thomas Alexander.[64] Before either of the brothers was twenty-one, their combined net worth approached $100,000 (which should be multiplied by at least twenty for its contemporary equivalent). The Judge exulted:

The gratification to me from the uniform good judgments, good habits, industry and aptitude manifested, and the congeniality of feeling between themselves which produced such results at so early an age, can only be fully comprehended by a parent whose life and hope is centred on his children.[65]

After such a flying start, Thomas Alexander and James Ross stayed in business as Mellon Brothers until the 1890s, and their real estate holdings eventually surpassed those of their father.[66]

Within a month of his retirement from the bench, and still casting about "for a new vocation," the Judge took a step which in retrospect was much more significant than the establishment of Mellon Brothers: he set up a second small bank in Pittsburgh at 145 Smithfield Street, near Sixth Avenue, called T. Mellon & Sons. Although initially he was in charge, it seems clear that from the outset the Judge regarded the enterprise as an eventual prospect for his younger boys: "in view of the condition of the times, *and the position it might afford for some of my younger sons,* I concluded to open a banking house."[67] He rented a single room in a small two-story brick building, with a desk for himself, a counter, a safe, and an iron stove. There were two assistants: a cashier, Samuel McClurken; and a messenger, Walter S. Mitchell. As the Judge had already explained in his letters to James Ross, the work demanded no particular expertise: "There is nothing in banking but what you ought to be able to learn in a week or two," he had then written. "As to bank books, keeping [them] is the simplest of all kinds. I know very well I could commence and manage a bank." It was a good time to begin such a venture and his self-confidence seemed amply rewarded: "the banking business was more than usually active at that time," he recalled, and it "continued more and more so until the collapse of 1873."[68]

The Judge's second bank was one of more than twenty new such enterprises established across the city at the height of the boom. When he founded T. Mellon & Sons, his financial standing in Pittsburgh was high, and he took pride in never having defaulted on a monetary obligation. "My credit was good," he later wrote, "and attracted depositors to both our banks." T. Mellon & Sons opened its doors in December 1869 with $10,000 of initial deposits; by early 1873 the deposits in the two banks totaled $800,000, or about $11 million at today's values.[69] But although the Judge was the dominant figure in both enterprises, they were significantly different undertakings. The East Liberty Savings and Deposit Bank was a joint stock affair, in which other investors held interests. By contrast, T. Mellon & Sons was a wholly private undertaking, with no partners and no stockholders. At the end of each month, a balance was struck. If there was a profit, it was placed in the Judge's private account; if there was a loss, then it was charged to the same account and the Judge put down the cash needed to make the deficit good. As such, T. Mellon & Sons was as much the Judge's personal property as 401 Negley, or the coal companies and the real estate he owned.[70]

From the beginning, the bank's lending criteria were thus entirely up to the Judge. In line with his lifelong principles and practice, he sought to minimize risk and to invest in land or property or mortgages of sound intrinsic worth. For the many Pittsburghers eager to buy a plot of land or a house, the Judge was well placed as a mortgage provider, and also as a major property dealer himself. Within a year, his expanding affairs obliged him to move to larger premises nearby; he purchased 116 (subsequently 512–514) Smithfield for $30,000 where he constructed a new, four-story building for an additional $28,000.[71] It was iron-faced, in the fashion of the time, with marble steps, a shining brass railing, and a statue of Franklin placed conspicuously above the door—not so much an ornament as an icon. Initially, only half the ground floor was occupied by the bank; the rest was rented to an insurance company, and all the other floors were also let. One room housed the bank itself, the other the "Mellon interests," especially those of the Judge. There dutiful clerks ensured that rents and interest were collected, upkeep and repairs undertaken, mortgages negotiated, taxes paid, obligations met. Behind these two areas was another room, an inner sanctum where the Judge transacted his business undisturbed, read as much as his eyesight allowed, or talked to customers.

For the next half century, this building would be the headquarters of T. Mellon & Sons and also of other Mellon family enterprises, and as the bank and the other businesses expanded, they eventually came to occupy the entire premises. But for now, the Judge's business was confined to the ground floor, which he entered every morning, with scarcely a word to anyone, not even greeting his staff, and then made straight for his private sanctum. Soon he would not be entirely alone, for he was joined by Andrew, whose active presence legitimated the multigenerational name of the bank. Although only in his early teens, Andrew was already eager to learn about loans, mortgages, bookkeeping, and foreclosures. And from the very beginning, he enjoyed his father's trust: he was the only other person whom the Judge would allow to handle the padlock on the steel cable wrapped around the safe for additional security. In joining in his father's business so young, Andrew was repeating family history. But unlike the Judge, who had worked on the Mellon farm, Andrew would not reject the path his father had marked out for him. Having learned the rudiments of banking, he would make it his lifelong profession—and, in a way, his lifelong passion. But not for a while yet. For now Andrew worked at the bank only on Saturday mornings and during time off from his studies; perhaps as a response to Selwyn's death, he was receiving the higher education that the Judge had effectively denied his two elder sons.

Between 1869 and 1872, Andrew Mellon attended the Western University, as his father had before him. It had burned down in the Great Fire of 1845, and again four years later. At that point it had ceased to function, but it was re-established in 1855 on the corner of Ross Street and Diamond, on a site where the house of the late Senator James Ross had previously stood. Under the leadership of George Woods and supported by a handful of faculty, the university offered a three-year preparatory course, leading on to a four-year college degree. But it was not the institution it had been in the Judge's day: the trustees exercised little supervision, resources were very limited, control of the curriculum was lax, students came and went during the year, and the courses offered did not always match those in the catalogue.[72] Andrew Mellon first appears in the university's records in the fall of 1869, age fourteen, studying arithmetic, algebra, elementary physics, and German. In the fall semester of the following year, he took Latin, algebra, physics, and grammar. He also studied penmanship, bookkeeping, and rhetoric, but he skipped the fourth quarter. For the year 1871–72 he was enrolled in the collegiate "special course" and took mathematics, physics, mental and moral sciences, essays, rhetoric, and German. His grades were good but not outstanding, and unlike his father, he seems to have had no extracurricular undergraduate life—though he did make some connections that would be important to him in later life, among them a young, ambitious, would-be lawyer named James Reed.[73]

Some of Andrew's essays have survived, on subjects as varied as history, civilization, country graveyards, and veracity. Although too much should not be made of these adolescent effusions, several of his observations are of interest.[74] Among American poets, he preferred Longfellow and Edgar Allan Poe. He believed the supernatural was merely that which science could not yet explain, but one day would. He considered classical studies a "great mistake" for students preparing themselves "for practical business." He thought Queen Elizabeth "knew how to manage her own interests pretty well, and had a good share of her father's temper." He gave Oliver Cromwell low marks for untidiness of clothing, "but what he lacked in manners and personal appearance he made up for in energy and perseverance." He held that getting up early was "essential to health and stimulates and sharpens the faculties," and approvingly quoted Franklin's maxim about the virtues of being "early to bed and early to rise." And he liked the custom of calling on New Year's Day: "the businessman who at other times is so immersed in business that he cannot find time to visit his acquaintances, now goes from house to house fulfilling his social obligations." Here he is at his most patriotic: "we hope that the United States will continue to advance, and will some day stand forth as the most civilized nation of the world." And on the merits of locomotion: "nothing is more beneficial to a nation than a system of rail roads." And here he shows himself a confident geologist: "Pennsylvania itself has more workable coal than the whole of Europe."

These writings lack the brilliance, originality, and sheer rhetorical force of the Judge's at the same age. But they do suggest that Andrew Mellon had absorbed his father's abiding convictions, that he believed in hard work and self-reliance, that he was fascinated by the evolving industrial economy, and that he was readying himself for an active life in business. In the light of subsequent travails and triumphs, three essays merit closer attention. One addressed the question "should females be admitted to the university." Though his experience of girls his own age was very limited, he seems to have held rather advanced views on the subject. Their "position in society has been gradually advancing for many years," he believed, which meant "the time was fast approaching when women will take degrees at colleges, study professions and hold office the same as men." They were, he reasoned, "as well qualified to master the higher studies and practice professions as men, and in some positions excel them by their quickness and foresight." Would this have appealed to the Judge? It seems unlikely. Was Andrew a budding feminist? His later (and limited) relations with women suggest not. In an essay on art galleries, he defined them as "exhibitions of sculpture and painting for the purpose of gratifying and instructing the community," and portentously opined that they were "generally productive of good influences, as they help to refine the minds and characters of men and divert them from selfish and sordid enjoyments." Perhaps this was the germ of a notion that many years later would blossom into the National Gallery of Art in Washington.

In an essay on Daniel Webster, Andrew expresses his admiration for "truly a great orator and statesman," noting also that as a young man, Webster had been deficient in but one thing, and that was declamation. No doubt Andrew sympathized, but unlike Webster, he would never conquer his shy discomfort at public speaking. Indeed, Mellon mythology has it that he left the university a few months before graduation to ensure that he would be spared the ordeal of delivering a commencement address, required of all prospective graduates. This account was later reprinted in the university's official publications, but there is no evidence that Andrew enrolled in any courses for the academic year 1872–73, and thus nothing to support the claim that he had come close to graduating with the class of 1873. More likely he was an intermittent student, dipping in and out of both preparatory and college curricula; he probably took preparatory courses for his first two years before enrolling in the collegiate course during his third year, but he never registered for a four-year college degree. So, while Andrew was undoubtedly better educated than his elder brothers, he was less well schooled than his father, who had come to doubt the value and "circumstances of having a diploma." And years later, one Mellon in-law insisted that the Judge had actually "compelled" Andrew to leave so he could begin to earn his living.[75]

It is clear that by now the Judge was anxious that his younger boys get on with the serious business of life, namely business itself. "In 1872," he later wrote, "my sons Andrew and Dick were through school, and eager for active employment"—though Andrew was only seventeen, and Dick was three years younger. The Judge soon dispatched Andrew to Philadelphia, to collect overdue mortgage payments on the Chestnut Street Theater, and from there to Baltimore to buy eighty acres along the turnpike to Washington.[76] Andrew already seemed suited to such work, but in the aftermath of Selwyn's death, the Judge was now more cautious about his sons' health, and acceded to Dick's request for something out of doors.[77] Accordingly, he would continue managing T. Mellon & Sons by himself for the time being, while setting up Andy and Dick in a business similar to that of their elder brothers, though prudently somewhere they would not be competitors. In the spring of 1872, he settled on Mansfield (later Carnegie), eight miles west of Pittsburgh, where he laid out $40,000 on another integrated Mellon enterprise. It was the first partnership of the two brothers, and the only time Andrew undertook manual work. They built an office, sheds, and warehouses; they shipped in coal and lumber for sale; they did their own surveying, laying out building lots for development. The two of them also served as their own bookkeepers and salesmen. In a short time, this profitable business—and formative experience—"greatly exceeded" even the Judge's expectations.[78]

Andrew Mellon was now launched on the business career in which he would eventually outshine all his brothers as well as his father, and he was already revealing the solitary drivenness from which would emerge his complex and powerful character. Having resolved matters at the Chestnut Street Theater, he attended performances for a month to satisfy himself that all was well. But it became a family joke that he was so preoccupied in counting and assessing the audience that he couldn't remember the play.[79] Even in the Mellons' undemonstrative household, he was something of a loner: at dinner at 401 Negley he sat at the end of the table, consuming his meal while lost in thought, rarely speaking, much less smiling or laughing. From an early age, he seems to have learned to keep his own counsel. His classmates at Grant Street School remembered him as courteous but aloof. Indeed, his salient characteristic, even as he moved from late adolescence to early adulthood, was an almost contradictory amalgam of inhibiting shyness and confident self-sufficiency. One survivor from these early years recalled the young Andrew Mellon as "solitary but not melancholy; seclusive but not moody; achieving but never boasting; timid but not fearful; silent but never stupid; removed but not eccentric; rivaling but not envious." "Andy never had an intimate," agreed one of his later business associates. "Not even to his brothers did he open the soul within." Had he "got religion" he would not have "told it to God."[80]

IV. PROSPERITY AND PANIC

As the slumps of 1819, 1847, and 1857 had already demonstrated, the Judge was joining a very precarious profession when he set up his two banks. The nineteenth-century American financial system was ramshackle and haphazard, and inadequately regulated or protected by a federal government uneager to intrude itself far into the world of business and finance. There had been no central bank since Andrew Jackson destroyed the Second Bank of the United States thirty years before, and thus no official "lender in the last resort," as was the case with, for example, the Bank of England. To be sure, there were American finance houses called national banks, which had been made possible by the National Bank Act of 1863, amended in the following year. But this designation meant that they (rather than the federal government) could issue the nation's bank notes, not that they were allowed to spread their branches across the union. They were superintended by the Office of the Comptroller of the Currency, but only very superficially. There were also state banks, which were chartered and regulated at the local rather than the federal level, but again in a cursory manner. And there were private banks, like T. Mellon & Sons, many of them no more than "pawn shops," run by "little corner grocery men calling themselves bankers."[81]

National and state banks were subject to minimum capital requirements and lending limitations, the notes issued by national banks were secured by U.S. bonds, and the Treasury stood ready to redeem instantly the notes of all failed national banks. With these provisions, it was hoped future financial panics would be avoided. But they proved inadequate, not least because many private banks placed deposits with both state and national banks, and in times of crisis, their sudden withdrawal of funds to meet their depositors' demands could put the whole system at risk. Moreover, private banks were often intrinsically unsound. They were essentially solitary institutions, wholly unregulated and unsupervised, and frequently undercapitalized: lending was easy, and security often inadequate; they regularly failed when times were good, and when financial panics hit, they fell like dominoes. To survive and succeed in private banking in postbellum America, it was therefore essential to lend prudently, and to take advantage of the good times, but also to possess the resources and the determination to ride out the bad times, which came with dismaying regularity, as the economy lurched and rolled from boom to slump and back again.[82]

Andrew Mellon recalled these early and uncertain times in a characteristically low-key address he delivered to the Pittsburgh Chamber of Commerce more than half a century later, in 1928. Until the mid-1860s, he suggested, "the demands made upon our banking resources were relatively small," the nation's "greatest undertakings, such as railroads, were partly financed from abroad," and "industrial America, as we know it, hardly existed." "It was," he further noted, perhaps paying homage to the Jeffersonian and Spencerian convictions of his father, "a period of individual effort in which business and industry were carried on by a multitude of competing units, mostly controlled by individuals or co-partnerships," and when there were "no great corporations or vast industrial enterprises such as we know today." Such was indeed the world in which the Judge had established T. Mellon & Sons. It was also an era, Andrew Mellon went on, when there was no "sound or continuous national banking policy," when "loose banking methods . . . obtained throughout the country," when banks made money from issuing notes and from holding and investing deposits, but when neither these notes nor these deposits were adequately secured. As a result, the "average banker" lived in "constant fear that, from causes remote or unforeseen, a financial crisis might develop at any moment and threaten him with ruin."[83]

Nevertheless, and as the Judge later recalled, the period between 1863 and 1873 was one in which it was "easy to grow rich."[84] It was a time of broad-based prosperity, during which the nation's railway mileage doubled in ten years. As with many long booms, the economic growth was cumulative. The cause was simple: during the immediate aftermath of the Civil War, the United States began its belated industrial revolution, and Pittsburgh was poised to prosper mightily. By the early 1870s, the city was turning out half of the nation's glass and a similar proportion of its iron; it had also become a major center of oil refining, producing 36,000 barrels a day, which were mainly used for machine lubrication and (as kerosene) lighting. To finance all this, there were more than one hundred banks in the city, and everywhere signs and portents of an even more prosperous future. Henry John Heinz had recently started his food-processing business, George Westinghouse had just begun to manufacture air brakes, and Andrew Carnegie would soon introduce the Bessemer process, proclaiming, "The day of iron is past! Steel is king!" Between 1867 and 1872, Pittsburgh absorbed and annexed many of the adjacent suburbs and neighboring townships, so that the area under its control increased fifteenfold, and the total population of the greater metropolitan region was fast approaching 300,000. In 1872, the Duquesne Club was founded for the elite of the town, and in future years, Andrew Mellon and his business and political associates would regularly meet there for lunch.[85]

In such heady circumstances, the Judge and his family found themselves "on the floodtide of prosperity": the companies run by Thomas and James and by Andrew and Dick were doing well, and so were the two banks. During its first three years of operation, T. Mellon & Sons netted just under $20,000 in profits for the Judge. He continued as well to deal in coal, real estate, and construction, and he would eventually own four hundred houses. At the same time, he expanded his land holdings across the Midwest. "One only had to buy anything and wait," he later recalled, "to sell at a profit: sometimes, as in real estate, for instance, at a very large profit in a short time."[86] Experience bore out his optimism: Thomas and James bought sixteen acres at Homewood for $25,000, and sold them soon afterwards for $125,000. But the Judge did not take pleasure in profit for its own sake. He also delighted to have succeeded with his flesh and blood. The partnerships with his sons, which he both financed and directed, were succeeding brilliantly. "Hitherto," he recalled, "I had devised many well-planned enterprises which failed through the inefficiency of those entrusted to execute them." But now he enjoyed the collaboration of "hearty and reliable coadjutors to execute with judgment, prudence and alacrity whatever I should plan." And it was likewise gratifying that after their marriages, Thomas and James had "chosen" to settle close to 401 Negley, "occupying elegant homes beside me—the fruits of their industry and ability—and conducting profitable business wisely and well."[87]

This is not to say the Judge had lost his taste for solitary success. In January 1872, he acquired a controlling interest in the Pittsburgh, Oakland and East Liberty Passenger Railway, which had earlier been disposed of by sheriff's sale. It was the line on which he traveled to work, an obvious appeal, but it also represented a first foray into a world of public transportation in Pittsburgh which would become increasingly important to the Mellons as the late nineteenth century drew on.[88] He also undertook another venture which in hindsight was more significant than it could have appeared at the time. On the same ship from Ireland that had first brought him to the United States was his Omagh neighbor Robert Fulton Galey, who was seven years old. The friendship forged aboard ship was continued in western Pennsylvania, and when he was a university student, the Judge had briefly lodged with Galey, who was by then a blacksmith in Pittsburgh. Soon after, Galey's health deteriorated, and he left the town and set up as a farmer in Clarion County, forty miles away to the northeast. Following Edwin Drake's pioneering work in petroleum exploration in 1859, Clarion County became a mecca for oilmen, and two of Galey's sons, Sam and John, were among the prime prospectors. In the early 1870s, the Judge advanced "moderate sums" from the bank, and along the Clarion River little wooden derricks were soon to be found bearing the names "Mellon No. 1," "Mellon No. 2," and so on. They yielded only a few barrels a day and soon dried up, and the Judge quit the oil business for good. But these were important connections with the Galeys, which would persist and develop in the next generation.[89]

One more relationship was inaugurated in these boom years, which would eventually matter far more to Andrew Mellon than to his father. In 1871, the year that he moved T. Mellon & Sons to its custom-built premises in Pittsburgh, Judge Mellon made a loan of $10,000 to a young man named Henry Clay Frick. The money was used to buy land and build fifty "beehive" ovens to bake Pennsylvania soft coal into coke, which would soon be in high demand for steel manufacture by the revolutionary Bessemer process that Andrew Carnegie was about to introduce. Frick had little experience of the business, but he had connections and convictions to commend him at 116 Smithfield: the Judge had known Frick's mother, Elizabeth Overholt, as a girl, and he recognized in Frick a determined, persuasive, and audacious entrepreneur after his own heart.[90]

Soon after, when Frick requested a second loan of $10,000, the Judge sent his friend and business associate James B. Corey to investigate. Corey's advice was perceptive: "Lands good, ovens well built," he noted; "manager on job all day, keeps books evenings; may be a little too enthusiastic about pictures, but not enough to hurt; knows his business down to the ground; advise making the loan." Although the Judge would not have been impressed by Frick's predilection for paintings, he advanced him the additional loan, thereby establishing a relationship between Frick and the Mellons that would endure across the generations, and in which "pictures" would come to play a significant part.[91]

The early 1870s had thus witnessed the launch of what would eventually become four of Pittsburgh's greatest enterprises: Carnegie Steel, Heinz food, Frick coke—and the Mellon Bank. But then came the financial crash of late 1873, inaugurating the "great depression" of the late nineteenth century, which nearly ended these ventures before they were established. The Judge rightly described it as "the most disastrous and extensive panic and collapse since that of 1819," and he was well placed to make the comparison.[92] Like that earlier downturn, only more profound, it was a global slump, beginning with a panic in Vienna and Berlin in May, which rapidly spread across most of Europe. The crisis reached the United States in mid-September with the failure in New York of Jay Cooke's banking empire in the aftermath of the bankruptcy of the Northern Pacific Railroad. The bubble of the postbellum boom burst almost overnight: the administration of Ulysses S. Grant, mired in financial scandal, could do little to moderate the national downturn, Wall Street was forced to close for ten days, and because many local banks held their cash reserves in New York, the devastation soon spread across the whole country.[93] "That demon of credit had destroyed confidence," the Judge vividly recalled, "and suddenly called a halt in the mad career of speculation." "The vitals of trade," he went on, warming to his theme, "were destroyed by the canker worm of credit; bloated inflation spread and increased until the decayed carcasses dropped dead."[94]

The panic hit Pittsburgh on September 22, four days after Jay Cooke went under in New York, and soon after, the Security Trust Company, the Nation Trust Company, and the Lawrence Savings Bank closed their doors.[95] There were no bank failures in the city in October, but industrial activity plummeted: the demand for iron and glass collapsed, both locally and nationally; coal mining, dependent on the iron industry, was similarly depressed; railroads, foremost the Pennsylvania, laid off workers; the price of oil fell from $2.36 a barrel to 70 cents; those fortunate enough to keep their jobs were compelled to take substantial cuts in wages; and 20,000 men were thrown out of work, nearly one-third of the labor force. Many could no longer pay their rent or interest on their mortgages; foreclosures reached unprecedented numbers. And things had not yet hit bottom. A second wave of bank failures began in November, including McVay and Company, the Duquesne Savings Bank, and the Mechanics' Bank. Eventually, close to one-half of Pittsburgh's banks succumbed, and it would take the better part of a decade for the city—and, indeed, the nation—to recover. Although only five then, William Larimer Mellon would never forget the lines of the embittered jobless: "the soup kitchens," he recalled, "made a lasting impression on me."[96]

It was much worse for WL's grandfather. "Loss of property or business disasters do not strike in like the death of dear ones," the Judge had written about the death of Selwyn.[97] But the slump of 1873 struck very hard and very close all the same, and the two Mellon banks came within a hair's breadth of failure. As a survivor of the 1819 crash, the Judge prided himself on his prudence and risk-aversion; he had always abhorred speculation as mere greed, and in 1864 James Ross Mellon had warned him that "there will be a terrible financial crisis sooner or later." But as the Judge later recalled, "prolonged prosperity had thrown me off my guard" during the early 1870s, and he had invested too much of his banks' deposits in loans or mortgages that could not be easily recovered, as well as other unconvertible securities, most critically a substantial recent purchase of Pennsylvania Railroad bonds.[98] When the panic broke, only $60,000 was available in both Mellon banks to meet $600,000 worth of deposit obligations. To make matters worse, the Mellon balances in New York and Philadelphia were also lost because the banks there failed before the Judge was able to secure the funds. In urgent need of cash, he dispatched his sons to collect as much as they could from those who owed them money, for lumber, building materials, mortgage payments, or lot sales, and he also tried to liquidate some of his real estate holdings. But many of his debtors were "utterly unable to pay anything on the emergency," and no one was willing or able to buy property with values plunging and with no end to the crash in sight.[99]

To be sure, the two Mellon banks were, as always, backed by the Judge's still substantial personal fortune, but as the crisis intensified during October, panicked depositors in great numbers began to withdraw funds, and the man "always looked upon as impregnable" now found himself in grave difficulties. On November 11, 1873, when the combined deposits of both banks had plummeted to a mere $12,000, the Judge closed the doors of the East Liberty Savings and Deposit Bank. The next day, he stopped payment at T. Mellon & Sons to all but a few of the most needy clients.[100] As the Judge conceded, "it was a bitter pill" to admit defeat in this way, and it "caused a very great sensation, as we were supposed safe if there was safety in a bank anywhere." In the end, both institutions survived, but it had been close, and the Judge felt humiliated: "the contemplation of a suspension," he recalled, "and having actually to succumb at last to a condition which I had never anticipated as possible, gave me more vexation and mortification than all the other adverse circumstances of my business life put together."[101] He resolved to close the East Liberty Savings and Deposit Bank, despite its unimpaired capital and a 30 percent surplus after the final settlement, and he also gave serious thought to shutting T. Mellon & Sons as well.[102]

The trauma inflicted by the panic of 1873 was clearly as impressive for Andrew Mellon as 1819 had been for his father. For just as the Judge's business career was defined by the slumps of 1819 and 1873, so Andrew's life would be bounded by those of 1873 and 1929–33. The young man drew the same conclusions in 1873 that his father had drawn fifty-four years earlier, namely that the American economy was liable to spurts and spasms, to booms and busts, which could be neither moderated nor eliminated, but which must be endured. One reason he would seem to some so inflexible, unimaginative, and unaccommodating as secretary of the treasury in the years after 1929 was his confidence that he had seen it all before. But in 1873, Andrew also seems to have been more prescient than his father in anticipating what he would later describe as this "Waterloo to Pittsburgh."[103] At the beginning of the year, when he and Dick had been in business together less than twelve months, he had concluded that the bubble would soon burst, and he availed himself of an unexpected opportunity to get out while still ahead. Early in the autumn, the lumberyard of a neighbor and competitor was destroyed by fire. Fearful about the length of time it would take to settle the insurance claims, and anxious to preserve himself in what was then still a booming business, the distraught owner happily leased the flourishing Mellon yard from Andrew at a good price. The neighbor's deep gratitude lasted only until he found himself foundering in ballooning interest payments when the crash came.

"It was a masterly stroke," his father later wrote, with his conscience untroubled by such profiting from others' misfortunes, "and gave good promise of the future."[104] But for the time being, it also brought to an end Andrew Mellon's first business partnership with his younger brother. Dick was sent back to school, to the Western University. He would become, in 1876, the only one of the Judge's sons to obtain a university degree. (Perhaps in his more generous forbearance respecting the education of Andrew and Dick, as compared with that of Thomas and James, the Judge was indeed attesting to the lessons of Selwyn's early death.) Meanwhile, the Judge had decided to reinstall Andrew at T. Mellon & Sons soon after it reopened for business. He now worked full-time, and he would stay there for nearly half a century, becoming richer and more powerful with each passing decade. No one could have foreseen that this was the beginning of the great Mellon fortune that would far surpass any accumulated by the Judge or his two elder sons. At the time, Andrew Mellon was but one of five brothers, and T. Mellon & Sons merely one of many family enterprises. He was only nineteen years old, the bank was barely three, and his salary was $75 a month.[105]

Half a century later, at the zenith of his fame as secretary of the treasury, Andrew Mellon was occasionally asked to give advice to young men considering going into business, and in proffering it, he drew on these early, formative years. It was partly, he thought, a matter of background and family: the desire to work in "banking or other branches of trade and commerce" was sometimes the result of "an hereditary inclination in this direction," which might lead to "an inherent liking for business of a financial nature." But it was also a matter of schooling. "A certain amount of business experience," he advised, "is an invaluable part of a boy's education": because it gives him "that most necessary contact with a competitive world." But while "knowledge gained through a school or college course" provided "a substantial foundation," success could "only come through that knowledge and practice which is obtained from direct work in some business line." For "business in the world of finance must be learned from the ground up, so that a thorough and comprehensive knowledge of it shall be acquired." And, finally, it was a question of character: the habit of "thrift and accumulation" should be acquired early in life, and it would be "a large factor towards future success," because "carelessness in respect to personal expenses" would naturally influence "action in the administration of business affairs and constitute an obstruction in their successful development."[106]

The Judge would surely have approved. But the successful following of these joyless and demanding precepts with such single-minded determination had left Andrew Mellon a very un-rounded and un-warm personality as he embarked on his professional life. He was already visibly precocious in business, but he would always remain stunted and limited in other ways. Financial success came at a high personal price. Shy and self-sufficient, he hated to be made conspicuous. He would get on with business associates in the shared task of acquisition and accumulation. But while some thought he longed for close friends and for intimate personal relations, he had little idea where to find them or how to get them, beyond the confines of his family or his work. There may have been color and warmth in his life, sometime and somewhere, but if so, he suppressed them so much that no one later knew where to find them or how to draw them out. As Paul Mellon later observed, his father had "reached adulthood as a thin-voiced, thin-bodied, shy and uncommunicative man."[107]

2

THE FAMILY IN BUSINESS
Boys and Banks, 1873–87

> Success in life depends greatly on the occupation we perma-
> nently adopt at the outset; and that again depends so much on
> whether we are suited for the occupation selected, that the ques-
> tion should rather be the fitness of the individual for the occupa-
> tion than the merits of the occupation itself.
>
> *Thomas Mellon and His Times*, p. 65

I. RECESSION AND RECOVERY

The sudden crash of 1873 ushered in a global downturn so deep and protracted that it would be known as "the great depression" until superseded by the even greater cataclysm of 1929–33. For the next twenty-five years, times were generally hard across North America and Europe, and this quarter century encompassed half of Andrew Mellon's working life in private enterprise. It was not only 401 Negley that was a bleak formative environment: as a fledgling banker and businessman, AW matured in stern and competitive times. The American economy took the rest of the decade to stage even a mild recovery, but there was a further recession between 1882 and 1886, and prices, profits, and interest rates remained low almost to the end of the century.[1] The global glut of agricultural products hit farmers severely, even as the Midwest became one of the great granaries of the world, and as cattle and cowboys populated the prairies. (Sharing his father's disdain for farming, Andrew Mellon would never be much concerned about the state of the rural economy.) Across the country, with unemployment at previously unimagined levels, the conflict between labor and capital became more bitter, and a succession of Republican administrations, mired in a succession of financial scandals, and led by such mediocre presidents as Hayes, Garfield, Arthur, and Harrison, were disinclined to intervene by way of fiscal policy or labor mediation.[2]

For the most part, then, the American economy was left to itself: the very idea that the federal government should intervene seemed to many (including the Judge, and by now his sons) to be at best unrealistic, at worst socialistic. To be sure, they welcomed federal intervention in the form of a high protective tariff, to shelter and nurture the nation's burgeoning industries, or in other ways that might create a more favorable climate for business, but that was all they cared for it to do. And the wisdom of such laissez-faire attitudes seemed well borne out: left largely to itself, the American economy evolved and strengthened and developed during these years, despite (or because of) the great depression. Indeed, the late nineteenth century was also a period of unprecedented urban growth, and of exceptional innovation and entrepreneurial success, as great cities became for the first time "the controlling influence in American life," and as the economy industrialized intensively around railroads and steel, oil and electricity, and soon became the biggest and the strongest in the world. For the great depression, taking the form it did, was also a powerful spur to cost cutting, to innovation, and to technological progress, all of which eventually stimulated greater productivity, and this in turn proved a powerful incentive to find new markets. In Pittsburgh, as across the whole of rapidly growing urban-industrial America, this was a period of unregulated, free-market Darwinism, in which only the fittest, leanest (and often the meanest) businessmen survived.[3]

One of those resolved to survive was Judge Thomas Mellon, who was committed to ensuring "the safety and permanence of what we have" and determined to weather the "cyclone" that he reproached himself for not having anticipated.[4] By early 1874, T. Mellon & Sons had resumed payments to its depositors, but it was a challenging time for the seventeen-year-old Andrew to be beginning a career in banking; throughout Pittsburgh, things would get much worse before they began to improve, and recovery from the depression took several years. "Real and fictitious wealth had become so mixed up," the Judge recalled, "that the refining process of bankruptcy and sheriffs' sales became necessary to separate the dross from the true metal." Nearly half of the city's banks went under, and all its major industries—glass making, railroad construction, coal mining, ironworking, and oil refining—were hard hit, as demand collapsed across the whole country.[5] The situation was already bleak by the end of 1873, and for the next two years, the gloom and anxiety intensified. By January 1876 the whole economy was contracting, confidence was at rock bottom, and the depression was deeply settled in; it would remain so for the next three years. In 1874, forty-five million bushels of coal and coke were shipped on the Monongahela River; in 1879 the figure was only twenty-nine million. There was scarcely a sign of recovery until the end of that year. "Real estate was unsaleable at any price," the Judge remembered, "and business of all kinds was equally depressed, and employment by workingmen could hardly be obtained." It was a period of liquidation—"an awful time," as Henry Clay Frick put it more pithily. He was another of those who—just—survived.[6]

Those desperate to stay in business did everything they could to reduce their costs, not only through layoffs and pay cuts, but also by suppressing the strikes that invariably followed in the mines, the rolling mills, and the glassworks. In the most notorious episode, which took place in the coalfields of western Pennsylvania, associated with a group who called themselves the Molly Maguires, mining superintendents were killed and miners hanged. But the most violent local clash occurred in July 1877, after the Pennsylvania Railroad cut wages in Pittsburgh, doubled the length of its trains, and halved the size of their crews. There were widespread and well-supported protests, and the railroad was brought to a standstill. The company called in the Philadelphia militia, which tried in vain to arrest the leaders; shots were fired, killing at least twenty strikers and injuring many more. The workers retaliated by burning a thousand railcars and a hundred engines, as well as sixteen buildings, including Union Station, the Union Hotel, and a nearby grain elevator. For forty-eight hours, the rioters held the city, and order was not re-established until federal troops arrived, backed by a local defense committee. By then, the railroad strike had become the first industrial conflict to spread across the whole country, and it seemed to portend a new civil war, this one between capital and labor. Since the Allegheny County authorities had conspicuously failed in their duty to maintain order and protect property, they were compelled to compensate the Pennsylvania Railroad and other companies for their very substantial losses, and three million dollars had to be raised in a new bond issue.[7]

Judge Mellon was predictably outraged by these events, which reinforced both his fears and his siege mentality. He attributed the riots to the "vicious classes," whose members he denounced as socialists and anarchists who sought to overturn the established order and bring ruin and revolution. His political commentary was not that of a disinterested party: some of the railcars destroyed were full of lumber and coal, the very commodities whose trade helped sustain the Mellon fortune. The family's links with the Pennsylvania Railroad were even more direct: the Judge's favorite uncle, old Thomas Mellon, had been a director of the company from 1856 to 1864, T. Mellon & Sons traded in its stock, and Andrew Mellon (who still recalled the strike with a shudder half a century later) would become a friend of Robert Pitcairn, head of the company in Pittsburgh in the next decade.[8] The Judge's fierce partisanship was further engaged because the local vigilance committee that eventually helped restore order had among its leaders his in-law General James Negley. But it was the fiscal consequences of anarchy that ultimately pained him most: for months after, he complained of the burden to Allegheny County taxpayers caused by the huge bond issue following the confrontation.[9]

The 1873 crash thus left the Judge anxious both politically and financially. "Our losses by this panic," he recalled, "whilst in no wise remarkable under the circumstances, were nevertheless serious." Across Pittsburgh and in the townships beyond, property was abandoned or sold for a relative pittance, and many buildings and lots remained empty for the better part of the decade.[10] But this crisis was also the Judge's opportunity—to obtain at knocked-down prices yet more land and property, which would appreciate in value when times were better. He foreclosed on defaulting mortgagees, bought avidly at sheriff's sales, and evicted tenants who were behind in their rent. Not surprisingly, the Judge acquired a reputation as the scourge of debtors, dilatory tenants, and careless mortgagees, and for being obsessed with getting his legal due.[11] "By outsiders," he wrote revealingly during the late 1890s, "throughout the business period of my life, I was regarded as a hard, practical man, disposed to acquire wealth by every fair means." "This," he added, with a rather winning candor, "is true to a certain extent, and I have never discovered its wrong!"[12]

The Judge's code may have been "hard," but it was a code nonetheless. As a landlord, he expected payment on time, but his houses were substantial, well constructed and well maintained, and little resembled the squalid tenements in which most members of the Pittsburgh working class were obliged to live. And his correspondence shows that in certain circumstances, he could be a sympathetic creditor to those whose misfortunes were beyond their own control: cutting interest rates, sometimes shaving the principal, occasionally giving them more time to pay. He had not forgotten his parents' "struggles and deprivations to save themselves" after the crash of 1819, and was lenient after his fashion in 1873. "We foreclosed no mortgages," he later recalled, "and forfeited no contracts where the parties were doing the best they could to pay for and hold their property."[13] But it seems likely that these were the exceptions. Throughout the mid- and late 1870s, the Judge and his sons were exceptionally active in the Pittsburgh land market, and Dick Mellon was assisting his father virtually full-time. All they had to do was to sit tight and wait, until the "liquidation process" was over, confidence returned, and prices began to rise again—which, by 1880, they were doing.[14]

For the Judge as for many contemporary entrepreneurs, the recent crash was opportunity couched in misfortune: the rich eventually got richer, and he would amass more Pittsburgh property than ever before. In 1873, on the very eve of the panic, there had been signs of determined optimism among future tycoons. Andrew Carnegie established his Edgar Thompson Steel Works on the edge of Braddock's Field, named after the president of the Pennsylvania Railroad, who he hoped, rightly as things turned out, would become his biggest customer. The Judge did not altogether approve of steel or large factories, but he at once began building houses for prospective workmen, and as the great Carnegie enterprise prospered, even amid depression, so did Thomas Mellon. He was also buying up more land out west, in anticipation of the railroads and the prosperity and enhanced values they might bring.[15] During the 1860s, he had bought acreage in Missouri, Kansas, and possibly Colorado, and he was probably doing business with General Larimer as well as Alexander Caldwell. Now he turned his attention to the northwest, and began purchasing in Wisconsin, Dakota, and Idaho. The result of these activities, as Andrew once observed, was that the Mellon name was sprinkled all over the title records of many midwestern states.[16]

It was also during the later 1870s that the Judge ventured into the only business to involve all his sons: the construction and operation of a twelve-mile-long narrow-gauge railway from Ligonier through the Loyalhanna Gap to Latrobe, where a junction was formed with the Pennsylvania Railroad. The line had been authorized a quarter century before, and in 1877 a syndicate presented the Judge with a proposition: he was offered four-fifths of the capital stock of $100,000, a bonus of $10,000, to be raised by subscription among the people of the valley, and a mortgage on the railroad for whatever it might cost him to complete and equip it, with this mortgage to be paid off from the net earnings. The Judge was on principle "averse to outside enterprises of any kind," and he also saw immediately that unless the railway produced "net earnings," he would never get his money back.[17] But all his sons seem to have been convinced that the line would pay, especially Thomas and Dick, and the Judge was won over by the chance for business experience and brotherly collaboration it would furnish them. He agreed to finance the enterprise—but on his own terms: Thomas, assisted by Dick, would oversee construction and manage the laborers; James would furnish the rails, ties, and building materials (no doubt from Mellon Brothers); Andrew would look after the paperwork; and James's nine-year-old son, W. L. Mellon, would count the wagons and pedestrians that passed through the gap to gauge the potential business.[18]

The first train left Latrobe for Ligonier on December 1, 1877, with the Judge, Sarah Jane, and all their sons and grandsons aboard. Upon its arrival, the locals were delighted, and so was the Judge, as he explained to his uncle Archibald Mellon a few days later:

> My boys have got through with their little Rail Road project and are highly pleased with the prospects. It is . . . taking in a good deal more money than they expected, and it is a great convenience to the Ligonier people. My greatest happiness is in my family. My sons are of my own way of thinking and acting; willing to work and never above their business. Dick, although but eighteen, is conducting the train and works at loading and unloading freight like a labouring man. Thomas bosses the hands yet engaged in blasting and other work, James attends to outside contracts for cars etc., and we have it all paid for and no trouble with it so far.[19]

Eventually, Thomas was installed as the railroad's first president, and Dick managed the day-to-day business, selling tickets, dispatching freight, operating the telegraph, and serving as conductor. Indeed, it may well have been for him that the Judge promoted the line. The railroad not only carried passengers, but also conveyed lumber and granite into Pittsburgh, much of it, no doubt, destined for Mellon Brothers. Soon after, Dick persuaded his father to rent four hundred acres and built a picnic resort called Idlewild Park as a weekend destination for Pittsburghers. In 1882 the line was widened to standard gauge in the hope of further expansion. Ultimately, however, it was not an especially profitable enterprise, in part because the hoped-for link with the New York Central Railroad never materialized. Still, the train to Latrobe remained in family ownership throughout its seventy-five years of operation.[20]

Andrew was made treasurer of the Ligonier line. This may well have reflected his expertise with figures, but another consideration was his growing involvement with the business at T. Mellon & Sons, which left him little time for the railroad, beyond what could be done from his desk at the bank. By late in 1874, deposits were back to $600,000, where they had stood on the eve of the panic. It was an impressive recovery given the general, lingering loss of confidence, and it may have been in recognition of this accomplishment that the Judge made over to Andrew a one-fifth share in the business the following year. In 1876 he would be given power of attorney to direct daily operations at the bank.[21] But it was still a very small-scale enterprise, and for all the changes, the Judge remained emphatically in charge. The total profits between 1876 and 1880 were scarcely $14,000, of which $2,250 (slightly less than the one-fifth he was due) went to Andrew. And while Andrew was ever more knowledgeable about the business, the Judge felt (perhaps mistakenly) that he had a thing or two yet to learn. "It is of the greatest importance," he told his son in November 1881, "to have strictly correct and clear accounts in all departments." On one occasion, the Judge even betrayed hopes that a loan Andrew had approved would turn out badly, so as to teach him a lesson in caution. Instead, it proved a lesson for the Judge: the loan was fully repaid, with interest, on time.[22]

It was at T. Mellon & Sons, in 1876, that the Judge introduced Andrew to Henry Clay Frick. Thus began one of the younger Mellon's few truly close and revealing friendships, albeit one sustained thereafter by business as much as by pleasure. The Judge had just designated Frick a preferred customer by granting him a credit line at the bank of $100,000. Clay, as he was generally known, needed the money, for the post-1873 recession had severely taxed his resources. He was six years Andrew's senior, and both of them came from reasonably well-to-do backgrounds, although Andrew's father was richer than Frick's. Both were eager to make money and do well: "the demands of modern life," Frick once wrote, in words equally applicable to Andrew, "called for such works as ours."[23] But Frick was much better read than Andrew: on one of their earliest meetings, Mellon found his friend engrossed in Addison, Macaulay, and Lord Chesterfield's letters to his son. He was also interested in the fine arts, an accomplished amateur painter with a passion for pictures. Unlike Andrew, Frick was also poised and authoritative: he had a ready sense of humor, mixed easily with others, and combined aspiring gentility with adamantine resolve— especially when dealing with labor. By age thirty, he was already a millionaire.[24] Whether because of Frick's slight seniority or Andrew's shyness, Andrew called him "Mr. Frick," while he always spoke of "Andy."

By the end of the 1870s, deposits at T. Mellon & Sons stood at more than $1 million—an impressive amount for a private bank only a decade old, and perhaps the equivalent of $20 million in today's values. As property prices revived, the family's expanded real estate holdings reverted to their pre-panic values. Indeed, for the Mellons and others who had survived the "liquidation" of the depression, the late 1870s and early 1880s seemed an encouraging time. Pittsburgh's position as a premier industrial city had been consolidated, as the ironmasters enthusiastically and eagerly embraced the future that was steel: by 1880, it produced half of the nation's glass, one-twelfth of its pig iron, one-quarter of its rolled iron, and two-thirds of its crucible steel.[25] Demographically, too, the city continued to grow, despite the panic: between 1870 and 1880, the population shot from 86,000 to 156,000; for Allegheny County as a whole, the increase was from 262,000 to 355,000. For the majority, living conditions were not good: the rivers and the atmosphere were ever more polluted; workers in blast furnaces toiled twelve-hour shifts for two dollars a day; and the bicameral municipal corporation was both cumbersome in its structure and grudging in its provision of the most basic public amenities such as schooling and sanitation, police and fire services. As Pittsburgh resident and writer Elizabeth Moorehead recalled, "business was the chief concern of the majority, and it promoted a solid, orthodox, materialistic attitude to life."[26]

The Judge no doubt endorsed these sentiments wholeheartedly: for him, hard work was the key to survival and independence, and so the corporation owed nothing to those who refused responsibility for the consequences of their own idleness. He himself was now in his mid-sixties, and although his zest for life (and learning) remained keen, his eyesight continued to deteriorate, and there were three sharp intimations of mortality. General Larimer, his old friend, business associate, and in-law, died in 1875. Then brother Samuel passed on in 1879. Theirs had not been an easy relationship, primarily because Samuel was a much less gifted and responsible businessman, and the Judge remained convinced he had lost money at Leavenworth through Samuel's mismanagement. At his brother's death he reacted with characteristic sentiment and calculation. He lamented Samuel's passing—"how wild the emotions which that significant expression on your pale, silent features excites in my heart."[27] But he also insisted that his widowed sister-in-law pay him back $2,000 of an outstanding $3,000 loan, and he would later caution his sons not to invest as unwisely as their late uncle had done in the Midwest. In November the same year, the Judge lost his brother-in-law, friend, and partner George Bowman, who was married to his sister Eliza, and who was by turns a farmer, civil engineer, and coal-mine owner, and had been a co-investor in such enterprises as James B. Corey and Co. since the 1850s.[28]

As his own generation passed from the scene, and as his five surviving sons reached maturity, the Judge mellowed—a little. On Christmas Day 1878, he addressed his children in his customary seasonal letter: "I wish to give you all," he wrote, "some acknowledgement of the great pleasure and satisfaction it affords a father to see his children well doing and agreeable." "It is," he concluded, "my greatest happiness, and repays all the labor and care of my life." In November 1881, he told his second son, James, that his property and bonds and mortgages "will have to be managed without me before long, even if life is prolonged, as failing faculties already have practically unfitted me for active business." "It is," he went on, "a joy to me to see that you are all able to manage so well and that our numerous affairs do not suffer from my absences."[29] Early in 1882, the Judge gave practical expression to this view, turning over both the management and the income of T. Mellon & Sons entirely to Andrew in the following proposition:

> He to have the entire net profits of the Bank from January 1, 1881, including my salary, the books to be readjusted accordingly from 1st January instant. He to have entire net profits of bank and pay me an annual salary of two thousand dollars as its attorney and fifteen hundred dollars per annum rent for the banking room: and I to allow him forty five hundred per annum for attending to my private affairs and estate selling lots collecting rents etc. as done heretofore. This arrangement to last till superseded by another or annulled by either party.[30]

In practice, there was little to transfer—no capital stock or partners, only the good name and modest profits—which may explain why the Judge chose this rather strange (and scarcely legally binding) mode of handing things on.[31] But it did represent a significant surrender of power from father to son, and it seems clear that it was recognized as such in the family. Two years after the death of Samuel Mellon, his son William A. Mellon (who should not be confused with A. W. Mellon, or with W. L. Mellon) had taken up residence at 401 Negley. Like his father, he was something of a black sheep in the Mellon family, failing both in business and in journalism, and ending his days in semi-poverty in Pittsburgh, living on a Mellon pension.[32] His lengthy late-life memoirs are an unreliable amalgam of disappointment, resentment, exaggeration, and embellishment, and must be taken with a grain of salt. But they do give a vivid

picture of Andrew and his father at the brink of the handover. All the
family, W. A. Mellon recalled, were by now deferring to Andrew, not
because he sought authority or worked for it; he just exercised it naturally. While Andrew habitually asked "What would Father do?," the Judge
now saw things the other way round: " 'What would Andy think? What
would Andy wish? How would Andy have it?' ruled his every answer to
questions."[33]

II. THE JUDGE'S NEW LIFE

Although the Judge urged his other sons in the future to "consult with
Andy" on matters of business, his notion of retirement and withdrawal
would prove deceptive. He still came into the bank each day, occupying
the back room; he retained an active (and no doubt opinionated) interest
in its affairs; and he continued to receive a steady procession of visitors.
He attended to his other interests in coal, real estate development, and
the Pittsburgh, Oakland and East Liberty Passenger Railway, and through
the latter he became involved in a public controversy about whether
trains should run on Sunday (it was good for business, so he was in favor).
He also developed an interest in the construction of inclined planes,
which transported people and freight up and down Pittsburgh's steep
river valleys, and founded the St. Clair Incline Company. He continued to
invest in the Midwest along the routes of both the Union Pacific and the
Northern Pacific railroads.[34] For someone as energetic and determined as
the Judge, retirement meant not so much the cessation of activity as a
change of direction; he also became a more public figure about town and
set about writing the story of his life. He did not regard such activities as
important or as worthy as being in business full-time; but they did provide
him with the means to dominate and influence his children—and also
their issue—by reaffirming his stern and trenchant outlook in new settings and in new ways.

Having spent a decade on the bench, and then ten years as a banker, the
Judge decided his next venture would be to take a more active part in
Pittsburgh's municipal affairs. In 1879, he had been elected to the Common Council, and two years later to the Select Council, representing
the Nineteenth Ward, his own affluent neighborhood of East Liberty. It
might seem an odd choice, as he could not have expected to enjoy himself
in any democratic context, and his low expectations of the structure, functioning, personnel, and ethos of local government were amply borne out.

"No more unsatisfactory position," he later recalled, "could be held by one of my disposition. I have for over forty years been combating municipal abuses without any appreciable effect. The drift has been steadily towards folly and extravagance, and those who oppose it are usually in the minority."[35] During the six years that he held office, this "unsatisfactory position" was frequently the Judge's lot. He distrusted popular rule; he disliked local government even more than he disliked national politicians; and he was convinced that the city officials, in collusion with local businessmen, were profiting from the flotation of bonds, while property owners like him suffered higher taxes to service and repay them. Although a Republican by party, the Judge was fiercely and sometimes obstinately independent, often finding himself in a minority, along with William B. Negley, Sarah Jane's nephew and his former law partner, who represented the adjacent Twentieth Ward.[36]

In addition to a handful of like-minded independents, there was also a minority of Democrats in city government. But they tended to be both Irish and Catholic, and thus were doubly anathema to the Judge. And so, too, were most of the ruling Republicans. For the early 1880s witnessed the rise of city political machines and city bosses, and Pittsburgh was no exception, as Christopher Magee and William Flinn created a corrupt caucus which would dominate local politics to the end of the century and far beyond.[37] They were supported by grocers, butchers, and saloon keepers, the sort of small-scale and easily influenced businessmen whom the Judge despised, and they made their fortunes by awarding themselves and their cronies lucrative municipal contracts: Magee in transport and natural gas, and Flinn in construction. For a man like the Judge, proud of his integrity and acumen, it was better to be poor than to get rich by such heinous means. Yet in the tight-knit world of Pittsburgh politics and business, matters were too complicated for categorical imperatives. For T. Mellon & Sons held Magee's mortgages and underwrote his bonds, and the Ligonier Valley Railroad carried granite blocks from Flinn's quarry for the construction of Pittsburgh's streets and sidewalks. The Judge may have been their critic, demanding economy and retrenchment, the reduction of debt and the lowering of taxes, and despising their corruption; but Magee and Flinn were his clients, all the same.

In his newfound freedom, the Judge also applied his dyspeptic outrage to confronting and confounding organized labor, which, as he saw it, had posed such a threat to order and property and security in 1877. Three years later, in response to an attempt by management to lower prices by cutting wages, there was a strike at the Waverly Coal and Coke Company, led by David Jones, general secretary of the recently created Miners' Association. The Judge was part owner, along with James B. Corey, and he was determined not just to defeat Jones and his union, but also, if possible, to ruin them. Accordingly, Jones was arrested and charged with criminal conspiracy: for seeking to fix the price of coal and labor at an artificially high level, for hindering miners from accepting work, and for exhorting them to break their employment contracts. All these were illegal activities under state law, and the charges were brought by the Judge, who was also Waverly's counsel. The jury found Jones guilty according to the letter of the law, but he was sentenced to only one night in jail and fined a mere $100.[38] The Judge ascribed the leniency to what he regarded as the blatantly prejudiced coverage the trial had received in the *National Labor Tribune*, which inveighed against how "corporate capital" was using the law to attack workingmen, in a "way that portended a fast-approaching" crisis between capital and labor. Early in 1882, the Judge and his associates filed for damages of $70,000 against the paper and against Jones, on the grounds of libel and conspiracy, hoping to bankrupt them both. But the following year, the state supreme court dismissed the suit.[39]

Meanwhile, a major controversy had arisen within the Pittsburgh city government. In November 1881, Andrew Carnegie offered $250,000 for the construction of a municipal library, on the condition that the corporation commit $15,000 a year to its maintenance.[40] To meet this condition, state law would have to be changed, enabling the corporation to earmark public funds for this purpose. The Judge believed in reading, he was acquainted with Carnegie, and they shared Scottish ancestry, a devotion to Burns and Spencer, and a passion for free enterprise. But he was vehemently against this gift, fearing that any such statutory alteration would open still wider the floodgates of municipal profligacy, civic debt, and caucus corruption. He proposed an alternative scheme, whereby a library would be built and maintained by the public subscriptions of rich individuals, and for a time his plans carried the Select Council. But the Flinn-Magee machine was determined that the Carnegie scheme should prevail, and the ensuing battle would last five years. Eventually, in October 1886, the Select Council accepted Carnegie's terms, with the Judge casting the only dissenting vote. Meanwhile, Carnegie had increased his gift to one million dollars, to finance not only a library but also more extensive buildings devoted to the arts, science, and technology. As a result, the city's annual obligation for maintenance rose to $40,000 a year, confirming the Judge's worst fears about municipal profligacy and waste.[41]

While in office, he fought another much-publicized and equally futile battle for retrenchment and restraint. It was a county rather than a city matter, but it was also very much a local issue. In May 1882, the Allegheny County Courthouse in Pittsburgh burned down, and the county commissioners organized a competition for its replacement. The architect H. H. Richardson prevailed in January 1884, proposing a Romanesque revival design that in its imaginative use of space and suitably imposing silhouettes ranks as one of his very finest works.[42] But the projected cost of construction was more than two million dollars, and the Judge fulminated in the pages of the *Pittsburgh Commercial Gazette*, denouncing the fiscal recklessness (the county debt was bound to increase) and the architectural ostentation (he thought the building too big and too pompous). In October 1884 he filed a bill of complaint against the Allegheny County Commissioners in the Court of Common Pleas, and having secured no redress, he took another case to the state supreme court. It was dismissed in January 1886, but once again the Judge felt vindicated when Allegheny County floated a hefty $800,000 bond issue to finance the enterprise. By early 1887, the Judge had had enough of local politics. He cast his final vote on March 28, 1887, against a resolution that funeral processions should enjoy right-of-way.[43]

Notwithstanding these protracted and hard-fought battles, against what he saw as the selfish machinations of labor on the one hand and the "folly and extravagance" of "municipal abuses" on the other, the Judge did enjoy the "leisure and opportunity" of retirement, taking a journey to Ireland and Great Britain in August 1882, in the company of his youngest son, George. James Ross and Rachel Mellon had visited the family's ancestral haunts in 1875, and Judge Thomas Mellon had long nurtured the ambition of returning to the land and place of his birth.[44] Father and son set off on a White Star liner from New York, reaching Queenstown (later Cobh) nine days later, and moved on to Cork, where they encountered "wild Catholic natives" and "Irish hoodlums" in the pernicious sway of anti-British "priests and demagogues," who filled their heads with "ignorance and superstition," "malice and depravity," "bigotry and prejudice."[45] Thence to Dublin, where George left for London, leaving the Judge to travel alone on to Ulster, and his birthplace at Camp Hill in County Tyrone. More than sixty years had passed since he had left in pursuit of the freedom and opportunities of the New World, but all seemed exactly as he recollected it. "My heart was full," he later recalled. "There was no spot on the place or its surroundings which I did not remember and know where to find." Then he went on to Londonderry, his original point of embarkation, and walking the city walls again, he said farewell to "the places and people near and dear to me as old friends, around whom my early memories clustered."[46]

During his brief return to the Old World, the Judge was eager to make another pilgrimage. He crossed to Glasgow, on the overnight steamer from Belfast, and took the train down to Ayr, to visit the birthplace of his hero and exemplar, Robert Burns, the poet whom he believed "above all others has revealed the inward springs of the Scotch disposition." "None," the Judge felt, "but those imbued with the Scotch nature can fully appreciate the truth and beauty of his poetry," with its unique combination of "sunshine and wisdom." Having paid his respects to the bard, and given thanks for the blessings of the Reformation as "a rationalistic movement against ritualistic formality," the Judge went on to Edinburgh and took in Melrose, Abbotsford, and Dryburgh before he reached London, where he met up again with George.[47] England interested him much less than Scotland or Ireland: "when or where," he wondered, "has Scotch philosophy been excelled in the analysis of the intellectual and emotional faculties?" But father and son duly saw the sights of the great city, though the Judge was decidedly disappointed by the dome of St. Paul's. They took the train to Liverpool, and returned to Pittsburgh, after fourteen days in Ireland and Britain and nineteen days at sea. Thus ended the Judge's only journey abroad since he had reached America: "the most interesting and pleasurable trip I have ever experienced; one of those which we like to go over again in memory, affording some of that enjoyment which makes life worth living."[48]

In keeping with his advancing years, "memory," especially of the most distant past, was increasingly important for the Judge, and his retrospective inclinations were reinforced and punctured by the passing of his oldest acquaintances and kin. In 1883 Archibald Mellon died, the Judge's lifelong friend and last surviving uncle, and he was followed the next year by Elinor Mellon Stotler, the Judge's sister, who had looked after Andrew in the early 1860s, and also by George Negley, brother-in-law and one-time business partner.[49] By now, he was the last of those twenty-odd Mellons who had crossed over from Ireland in the late eighteenth and early nineteenth centuries, and so he resolved to set down his family's early history and experiences, as the surviving custodian thereof. In what he called "the evening of life, with a competence for all reasonable wants, and sons both able and willing to manage *my* affairs as well as I could myself," he began to write his autobiography. For a man with deteriorating eyesight, this was a formidable undertaking. But the Judge was typically indomitable: between mid-1883 and the summer of 1885, he produced a quarter of a million words in his "back parlour" at the bank. Initially written in pencil in a huge, sprawling hand, the text was subsequently dictated to a stenographer.[50]

By turns rambling and repetitive, self-aggrandizing and self-critical, candid and selective, *Thomas Mellon and His Times* is a remarkable book— one of the great American autobiographies of the nineteenth century, and an essential document for understanding the matrix from which his favorite son, Andrew, emerged. The professional peaks may have been behind him, but the Judge's enthusiasm for life informs every page. The prose is vivid and vigorous, with memorable evocations of people and places. The tone is that of a thoughtful, confident, practical man, one also formidably well-read across an astonishing range of subjects. And he broods with wisdom, compassion, anger, and occasional bewilder- ment on his life and times. The outsized personality manifest throughout is unapologetically prejudiced and imposing, often infuriating but just as often admirable—a self-fashioned character, a self-taught intellect, and a self-made millionaire. Three predictable exemplars inform the Judge's account. The first is Benjamin Franklin, whose own autobiogra- phy inspired the Judge's striving life of self-improvement, and which also provided the model for these recollections. The second is Robert Burns, through whose sentimental poetry the Judge came to see his life as a romantic adventure. And the third is Herbert Spencer, whose hard-nosed sociology of struggle reinforced the Judge's belief in the survival of the fittest.[51]

The Judge devotes much attention to describing his ancestors and those of his wife. This was partly out of family piety, but it was also because his notions of surviving and thriving were essentially eugenic: he firmly believed that "hereditary transmission of ancestral traits is of momentous consequence," and it was thus important to come from "a family of good healthy stock" with "good mental and moral qualities."[52] This the Mellons and the Negleys most certainly did: across the gen- erations, as his researches showed, they were honest, sober and thrifty, earnest, energetic and industrious, with no trace of "hereditary disease or insanity," much less criminality; they possessed "a horror of running in to debt lest they should not be able to discharge their obligations."[53] To these quintessential Mellon attributes, the Judge ascribes the successes of his own life and those of his sons. He devotes relatively little space to great events or public affairs, or to his business and banking activities, and after his account of the courtship and marriage, his wife is scarcely men- tioned. In all, he presents a stirring narrative of struggle and achievement, the objective being not so much wealth or fame as what he more than once terms "a competence" or "independence."[54]

Of course, there were dangers and impediments to what Burns had called that "glorious privilege of being independent": in a country where life expectancy at birth was scarcely forty years, the incidence of ill health was serious; and in a land where the economy was unregulated and the taxes were ever mounting, the specter of financial disaster was always present. A powerful sense of constant risk and impending ruin permeates the Judge's pages, feeding the Scotch-Irish Presbyterian siege mentality. He had managed to meet and overcome these perils thanks to sheer good fortune, as well as by coming from good stock. He had applied determined calculation to his choice of wife, no less than to management of his many and varied professional activities. And he had successfully fashioned his sons in his own image. Still, he had made his share of mistakes, especially before the panic of 1873, and had shown faulty judgment, often with potential partners and collaborators; and sadly, some of his children had not been fit or strong enough to survive. So while, indeed, "a happy home with a loving wife and bright children" had been "the ultimate consummation of my hopes," he had not been able to shake off deep, abiding anxiety, or to escape an inconsolable sorrow. As he had come to realize, not every risk could be minimized, let alone eliminated.[55]

Following his account of his ancestors and his accomplishments, the Judge reflects on the current state of the world. There was much he did not care for: the cost of living in 1885 was twice what it had been only sixty years before; unprecedented material abundance had encouraged extravagant spending in pursuit of "artificial wants"; and saving was no longer honored as prudent and important. He also lamented a now widespread aversion to hard work and honest effort; the unprecedented spread of "murder, robbery and violence of every degree"; the slothful and superficial impertinence of youth; and the general decline of politicians in the past half century into corrupt, self-interested men, keen to line their pockets.[56] To make matters worse, workingmen were being infected by the "virus" of socialism: "the desire of him who has nothing to share with him who has; the desire of the idler, the worthless, the good for nothing, to place himself on a footing of equality with the careful, industrious and thrifty." And the transit from socialism to anarchism was but a step: to those "organized bodies of men in the different cities boldly and openly advocating the destruction of the present social system."[57]

These jeremiads contain few surprises: they were long-held views that had merely intensified as the Judge got older. Less expected was his

lament for the passing of the independent producer: those "small proprietors who own their own tools and work on their own materials are better
contented and make better citizens."[58] Despite railing against organized
labor, he regretted that workingmen were now crowded in squalid slums
and herded into large factories. Gone were the independent individuals,
with broad social contacts, and in their place was a "separated distinctive
community," increasingly antagonistic to capital. Such workers had no
direct interest in the success of the firm employing them: their only ambition was "to exact the highest rate of wages from it," and "individual honesty and good character" were "no longer a means to that end." The
malaise had been vividly and terrifyingly demonstrated during the rail
strike of 1877. Demoralized and beaten, regarded as automatons, laboring men were "all subjected to the same routine, and treated alike: too
much like the soldiers of an army or the inmates of a prison"—two of the
Judge's least favorite social cohorts. In this way, Thomas Mellon reveals
himself as a "closet Jeffersonian" who now discerned a better moral atmosphere in "rural democracy" than in urban and industrial Pittsburgh.[59]

There are many ironies here, which were apparently lost on the author.
To begin with, he now idealized that world of small-town, agrarian
democracy from which he had determined to escape during his youth for
something bigger and better. Moreover, the Judge himself had contributed to, and benefited from, the expansion of the Pittsburgh mills and
mines whose social transformations he now lamented—though, to be fair,
he had always avoided the steel industry, and complained of Carnegie's
massive mills at Braddock, Homestead, and Duquesne. He may have
deplored corruption in politicians, but his in-law Alexander Caldwell had
been compelled to resign from the U.S. Senate on those very grounds in
1872.[60] And the employment practices which he described and abhorred
were those for which his client Henry Clay Frick was already notorious in
the region. But irony was never the Judge's forte. Worried by the growing
division between capital and labor, and concerned by the inexorable
expansion of the state and of socialism, he wondered how free enterprise
would ever survive. "The general drift of my own time . . . ," he concluded, "seems to be in the wrong direction." He was "unable to take so
rosy a view of the future as I should wish," and he feared that those who
came after him "will not have as good opportunities for well-doing and
bettering their worldly condition; and will not be blessed with such peace
and prosperity."[61]

Yet for all its elegiac pessimism as a book, the autobiography was primarily intended for his progeny: for his grandchildren (he may well have

had W. L. Mellon in mind) and for generations of Mellons yet unborn. Hoping for the posthumous reach of his "indomitable perseverance," he was determined to prolong his influence, not only on the sons he had molded but also on those who would come after, so that he might "continue in some degree as a mentor to them and their descendants" from beyond the grave.[62] As such, the book was sacred writ, and the Judge's final investment in his family and their future. "I cherish the hope," he wrote in his preface, with a characteristic mixture of sentiment and steeliness,

> that, should an old copy of the book happen to fall into the hands of some poor little boy among my descendants in the distant future who, inheriting a share of my spirit and energy, may be desirous of bettering his condition, it may tend to encourage and sustain his commendable ambition. It may show him that industry and perseverance will overcome what without them would be insuperable; and the more insurmountable the obstacles in his way, the greater will be his satisfaction in overcoming them. It may serve to impress on him the truth of that important rule of life which demands labour, conflict, perseverance and self-denial to produce a character and accomplish purposes worth striving for. And it may tend to assure him that such a course carries with it more real satisfaction than a life of ease and self-indulgence.[63]

The Judge completed *Thomas Mellon and His Times* on "the twenty-second of August 1885, the forty-second anniversary of my marriage—the luckiest event of my life," these remarks from the conclusion being all there was by way of a brief and belated tribute to his wife. A limited edition was privately published by Johnston of Pittsburgh, and in accordance with his wishes, the book was distributed only among his family and close friends. It was generally well received. "No biography I have ever read," Henry Phipps told Frick, "has interested me so much." Despite their disagreement over the Pittsburgh library and the Judge's distaste for his large steel mills, Andrew Carnegie also admired the book, thinking it must "continue to influence succeeding generations of his family to live life well," and confessing it later served as the model for his own autobiography.[64] But although it was intended for family, and contained "nothing which it concerns the public to know," a few copies did circulate beyond his immediate circle, exposing the Judge's trenchant, controversial, and uninhibited opinions on courtship (especially his own), religion, trial by jury, capital punishment, education, democracy, politicians, and the Irish to a wider audience than he intended. Thereafter, his sons were forever seeking to retrieve copies that had slipped into public circulation, and in 1929, David Finley was still helping Andrew "to buy up any copies that might be in hands outside the Mellon family." But Andrew was as proud of the book as he was of his father: he gave copies away, despite his reservations, and he shared most of the opinions expressed therein.[65]

III. A PIVOTAL DECADE

"My capacity for usefulness," the Judge observed on the last page of his autobiography, "as well as for physical enjoyment, is declining, and already I begin to feel desolate." Although he was convinced that "the dark shadows of the evening of life are extended towards me," he lived another twenty-two years.[66] So while Andrew Mellon had become, in 1882, the acknowledged leader of the next generation, the Judge remained a powerful force in his life for at least another decade. In Pittsburgh, as across the country, the recovery of 1878–82 was followed by another recession, and though this one was not ushered in by a panic such as that of 1873, it lasted from 1882 until 1886. The Judge was jittery at the economy's cycles of boom and slump, which were now recognized as a pattern but still could not be precisely predicted: roughly "five [years] up and five down."[67] But the city's long-term growth continued, as it became the unrivaled steel capital of the United States, and waves of new immigrants poured in, not now from the British Isles and northern Europe, but from Poland, Hungary, Russia, and Italy. They were brought in to work in Carnegie's mills and Frick's coke ovens; they were prepared (or compelled) to work for less than the indigenous working class; they were Catholic and eager to organize themselves into unions; and naturally the Judge reviled them as "the spendthrifts, the desperadoes, and other criminal classes of the old world."[68] It was against this background that Andrew Mellon, now in his late twenties, sought feminine company and financial success—with mixed results.

For a brief period, and with Frick's help and encouragement, he began a much more active social life. In June 1880, they visited Europe together, accompanied by Frank Cowan, a journalist, and A. A. Hutchinson, a coke maker, and Frick took evident delight in introducing Andrew to the sights—and charms—of the Old World. The party reached Queenstown in Ireland, and proceeded to Dublin and Belfast, and thence to the Scottish highlands, England's Lake District, and London. They crossed the

Channel and visited Paris, Belgium, Holland, and Venice. They saw many galleries, and in London they consorted with "the fair Emma"—perhaps Andrew's first encounter with the opposite sex, though it is impossible to know just how close it was.[69] Seven years later, Frick recalled the trip in a letter to Andrew: "Paris is not so gay and attractive as in '80 as you would notice it at once. The buildings do not look so clean and bright. After we rest for a day or two we must begin seeing sights which is a great bore. No more trips for me to Europe which involve sight-seeing." ("The fair Emma" by now was on the stage in Berlin.)[70] Mellon lore has it that on this trip Frick (who would shortly begin his own collection) initiated Andrew into an appreciation of great art. But as he would not begin buying for another twenty years, the instruction—if such it was—apparently took some time to sink in. In any case, the Judge, whose "taste for the aesthetic was not sufficiently developed," thought such interests merely "artificial wants."[71]

Andrew Mellon showed no sudden or burgeoning interest in art, but he was certainly venturing into female society, often in Frick's company. (He grew his mustache at about this time.)[72] A clutch of letters have survived from "Minnie," whom Andrew had met at Fort Leavenworth and who was probably the daughter of Alexander Caldwell, and the niece of Mary Caldwell Mellon, and thus a very suitable match. Minnie was unabashedly ardent: "I am sure," she wrote to Andrew in April 1880, "if you had received all the letters I have commenced you could build a respectable landfill." In another missive, she recalls an equestrian date: "You know riding is a weak point of mine. I am always ready. I never will forget our ride at Idaho Springs [in Colorado] nor our horses." She also described Frick as a "heart-smasher," mentioned finding Andrew's gloves in a dresser drawer, and wrote chattily and flirtatiously about clothes and travel and friends.[73] The liaison fizzled, however, and eventually Minnie married a local doctor. Meanwhile, Frick and Mellon were regularly invited to social gatherings in Pittsburgh as a pair of eligible young men, and in the spring of 1881 they attended a party at the home of Asa P. Childs, an importer and manufacturer of footwear. Mellon apparently facilitated the introduction of Frick to Adelaide Childs, whom he would soon marry, after a three-month courtship which Andrew and Adelaide's elder sister chaperoned. Nearly twenty years later, Frick would reciprocate by introducing Andrew to his future bride—but with much less happy or lasting results.[74]

A serious romance soon developed between Andrew and Fannie Larimer Jones, who was even better qualified than Minnie Caldwell to join the Mellon clan. Her father was Thomas Mifflin Jones, whose family were partners in Jones and Laughlin's massive American Iron Works, which employed 2,500 workers in Pittsburgh, and her mother was the former Annie Larimer, sister of Rachel Larimer, who had married James Ross Mellon in 1867.[75] Moreover, Andrew Mellon was now in his mid-twenties, the right age for matrimony by his father's lights. "She was," the Judge later wrote, "of good family, and every way worthy of him," the "attachment" seems to have prospered, and the wedding was planned for the summer of 1882.[76] But as the great day neared, Andrew (perhaps urged to due diligence by his lawyerly and eugenicist father) made inquiries of her doctor; it emerged that Fannie was suffering from consumption and probably had not long to live. The Judge had declined to marry Sarah Liggett because her family had been tainted by that affliction and Andrew now followed his example, informing Fannie's mother that he was breaking the engagement with her stricken daughter. She forbade Andrew from seeing Fannie, who thus learned only indirectly that she had been dumped because she was dying. Andrew thereupon wrote Fannie a letter attempting both to comfort her and to defend himself. "I have been very wrong in not having confided all to you," he began. "It was only to save your feelings in your delicate condition that I did not." "My love is and always has been true and sincere," he went on, and he finished by admitting that "this has been the saddest day of many to me."[77]

Indeed, Fannie did not live much longer, and the Judge was convinced that this "unhappy experience" explained Andrew's subsequent withdrawal into himself: he henceforth went "but little into ladies' society, and became more and more absorbed in business pursuits." Paul Mellon would find this account of his father's actions "singularly unconvincing"; but after these early attempts at courting women of the right sort, Andrew does seem to have abandoned the chase and given himself over to the ever growing demands of his professional life.[78] At the same time, his own health seems to have been a source of some anxiety, and throughout the 1880s, his father was constantly concerned that his favorite son was doing too much, eating poorly, and generally not looking after himself. "Your constitution," he warned, "is not a strong one."[79] "You appear so thin and worried looking sometimes," he wrote later from Atlantic City. "When I return, I would have you come here for a vacation." "Health," the Judge fervently believed, was "the greatest of all treasures to be watched and guarded, more especially in the young and middle aged." Andrew weathered this difficult time, and although his personal life did narrow, he was certainly making a financial success of things. On May 1, 1884, he calculated the family's total wealth to be in the region of $2.5 million (perhaps $50 million in today's dollars): "my sons in the lot and lumber business, and Andrew and I at the bank," the Judge noted, "were again doing nearly as well in all branches of our business as before the panic [of 1873]."[80]

Andrew Mellon was indeed beginning to operate much more aggressively and confidently, through shrewd and selective purchase of other local banks, so as to expand his own lending base. In partnership with Frick, he acquired control of the Pittsburgh National Bank of Commerce in 1881. This gave him access to the smaller deposits of workers, widows, and orphans, and because it was a national bank, it also enabled him to issue bank notes—something not permitted a private bank, like T. Mellon & Sons. Two years later, Mellon acquired the Union Insurance Company, and also helped to start the Braddock Bank; and in 1886 he purchased the City Deposit Bank, a savings institution primarily serving the affluent East End, the Mellons' own part of Pittsburgh. But family pride may have been as much the motive as financial calculation, for with this purchase, and the installation of James Ross Mellon as president, the Mellons redeemed their earlier failure, the retreat and closure of their savings bank in the aftermath of the panic of 1873.[81] Later in 1886, again in collaboration with Frick, Andrew Mellon became involved in the formation of the Fidelity Title and Trust Company, the second trust organization established in Pittsburgh, which administered estates for individuals and corporations. Small wonder that in the closing pages of his autobiography, the Judge noted with a characteristic mixture of pride and possessiveness that Andrew "manages *my* banking business with eminent ability and success."[82]

By expanding his banking interests in this way during the 1880s, Mellon was also positioning himself to invest these greater resources in the region's burgeoning industrial activities.[83] He deliberately stayed out of oil during this decade, telling Sam Galey, a son of the Judge's old friend Robert Fulton Galey, that he "did not feel sure enough of the situation" to take the risk. But in 1883, he became a director of the Pittsburgh Petroleum Exchange, which was established to facilitate the purchase and sale of that commodity by the barrel. In January 1886, reorganized as the Pittsburgh Petroleum, Stock & Metal Exchange, it became the local securities market for newly formed transportation and natural gas companies.[84] By this time, natural gas was booming in Pittsburgh, in part thanks to the efforts of another Galey family friend, Colonel James M. Guffey, who had discovered the Grapeville field in Westmoreland County, Pennsylvania. With Guffey's help, Andrew Mellon created and controlled two companies, the Westmoreland and Cambria Gas Company and the Southwest Pennsylvania Natural Gas Company. Together, the two enterprises held over 35,000 acres of gas lands, and were capitalized at $2.5 million by 1887. Nor was this the full extent of Andrew's involvement in these new utilities, for he was also a substantial investor in the Bridgewater Gas Company and the Shenango Valley Gas Company.[85]

These activities show Andrew Mellon taking emphatic charge of the family fortune and expanding its financial operations far beyond the confines of T. Mellon & Sons. To that private bank he had added a national bank, a savings bank, and an insurance company, and he had also established a trust company. Not to be confused with the use of the word "trust" as a shorthand term for great industrial agglomerations, trust companies were chartered by the state, and they could do many things that national and state banks were not allowed to do. They could lend on real estate, provide safety deposit facilities, deal in stocks and bonds, disburse interest and dividend payments, as well as receive deposits and operate checking accounts. As America became richer, trust companies would play an increasingly important part in financing the nation's industrial expansion, and Mellon would be one of the first to see and grasp those possibilities.[86] At the same time, he was also moving beyond the Judge's world of mortgages and coal and real estate—not into oil or steel, but into utilities and also, in 1883, into the Pittsburgh Plate Glass Company, which he helped establish, at the behest of John Pitcairn. Here was active Mellon involvement with other people's businesses of a kind the Judge had never undertaken. He was no longer just extending credit; he was beginning to finance enterprise.

While expanding his business activities in Pittsburgh, Andrew Mellon was playing an ever greater part in the family interests out west. He seems to have traveled a good deal during the early 1880s, and there are occasional glimpses of him in Kansas, in Colorado, and in Idaho—three states in which the Mellons' concerns had for some time been mixed up with those of their Larimer and Caldwell in-laws (in 1885, Alexander Caldwell owed T. Mellon & Sons $125,000). His visit to Leavenworth was not wholly taken up by flirting with Minnie Caldwell: he was also studying her family's wagon business, and would later sell horses for Alexander Caldwell in Idaho and elsewhere in the West (though it is difficult to imagine the taciturn Andrew as a voluble horse trader) and purchase his own mounts from the same supplier.[87] In addition, Andrew and his father were major investors in the Idaho and Oregon Land Company, which Alexander Caldwell founded in 1882. Its purpose was to buy up acreage and create towns and irrigating canals along the Oregon Short Line Rail-way, from Salt Lake City to Portland, a line eventually absorbed into the continually expanding Union Pacific. As with all Mellon ventures out west, the evidence is patchy, but Andrew certainly seems to have had a hand in founding the town of Caldwell, Idaho, and he held mortgages on the Alturas Hotel and the Merchants' Hotel, both at Hailey, in the same state.[88] With such a burden of work, and of travel, it is scarcely surprising that the Judge worried about the health of his favorite son, and it is equally understandable that at this time, business was the all-consuming activity of his life—with, perhaps, one exception.

During the 1880s, Andrew Mellon's friendship with Henry Clay Frick intensified, politically, socially, and financially. Like the Judge, they were champions of capital over labor, and stalwart Republicans. After Frick's marriage to Adelaide Childs, the couple settled at Clayton, one of the grandest houses in Pittsburgh, and Andrew was a regular visitor: for din-ner, for poker, and sometimes staying the night. When Frick established the South Fork Fishing and Hunting Club in the Allegheny Mountains forty miles northwest of Pittsburgh as an exclusive enclave for friends and associates, Andrew Mellon was naturally one of the first members.[89] The relationship between Frick and T. Mellon & Sons, which the Judge had inaugurated, also continued to thrive: Frick's personal loans stood at $71,000 in 1882, rising to $148,000 in 1885, but dwindling to $9,000 in 1887; similar credit was extended to the H. C. Frick Coke Company; these sums were roughly equivalent to Alexander Caldwell's indebted-ness to the bank. When Frick and his wife departed for a grand tour of Europe in July 1887, he left all his stocks in Andrew's hands, giving him "full authority" to sell at prices he thought proper; and the letters they exchanged during that trip were frequent, friendly, and full of details about the Fricks' holiday as well as about business and financial matters.[90]

Mellon's business relations with Frick were clearly very different from, and also much happier than, those which Frick maintained with Andrew Carnegie. Frick and Carnegie invested in each other's companies, which produced coke and steel, respectively; they merged their interests for a time, and later fell out spectacularly. Mellon, by contrast, was Frick's banker, but did not invest much in his companies or play any part in their management. Nevertheless, they did invest together during the 1880s: in banks and coal properties and natural gas companies in Pittsburgh, and in the Fort Smith and Western Railroad, a coal line in Oklahoma.[91] And there was one more novel venture: in 1887, Frick persuaded Andrew, along with his brother Dick, to purchase an interest in the Overholt Distillery, founded by his maternal grandfather, Abraham Overholt, in 1810. They owned the entire stock between them, and although it was sold at a great profit soon after the First World War, there would be reverberations throughout Mellon's tenure as secretary of the treasury, when he was responsible for enforcing Prohibition.[92] Their joint ownership of the distillery was a symbol of their close friendship, which involved work as much as recreation. When invoking Andrew's name at a business meeting during this period, Frick described him as "a gentleman on whom I can rely." And Andrew always believed Frick was "a strong character, with good impulses and broad and generous ideals"—opinions that were emphatically not shared by his labor force.[93]

IV. GO WEST YOUNG MELLONS

As the Judge drew *Thomas Mellon and His Times* to a conclusion in August 1885, he summarized the state of what he called his "family affairs." Of his surviving sons, Thomas was well settled in "his elegant and comfortable home adjoining mine," and was "happy in the possession of a most excellent wife and three interesting children." James occupied "a home equal to that of his brother, immediately across the road from me," and his elder son, William Larimer Mellon, gave cause for particular satisfaction. "Just out of school," the Judge noted, "he has taken the situation of shipping clerk in his father's and uncle's firm, and works industriously every day from seven o'clock in the morning till quitting time in the evening, giving promise of steady habits and attention to business highly commendable." Andrew was still at home, and "more and more absorbed in business pursuits," while Dick was "the successor in form and disposition to our lost Selwyn," and "a model with his brothers in the management of business affairs."[94] All this gave the Judge much pleasure and pride. But there was also George, the youngest brother. In 1880, when George was twenty, the Judge had thought he "gave high promise of energy, industry, and a first class business capacity." At a time when the market was recovering from the post-1873 recession, he was set to work in Pittsburgh, like his brothers before him, building houses and selling lots. He showed himself "ready and eager for the enterprise," and "soon had some fifteen to twenty buildings under way."[95] But then things started to go wrong.

Early in 1881, George Mellon was stricken with what was eventually diagnosed as the dreaded consumption, and the Judge feared that another of his sons would die. "Was the pain and sorrow of Selwyn's loss to be repeated?" he wondered in the later pages of his autobiography. "I could not bear to see so bright and valuable a life, so dear to me, and just merging into manhood, going down gradually but surely to the grave." Characteristically combining what he hoped would be successful recuperation with business activity, the Judge sent George to Kentucky to buy horses for the Pittsburgh, Oakland and East Liberty Passenger Railway, and then on to Missouri to check out some of his landholdings; and soon after, father and son journeyed to West Virginia, to look over a 27,000-acre property which they eventually decided not to buy.[96] But despite the fresh air and modest, salutary exercise which these travels had provided, George's condition worsened; a Philadelphia doctor confirmed the Judge's worst fears, and he "resolved at once on energetic action, and to leave nothing undone that money or skill might do" to save his son. In October 1881, the Judge, Sarah Jane, and George set off to Aiken in South Carolina, where George received specialist treatment from Dr. William Geddings. The Judge read all the medical manuals he could find and took out a subscription to *Scientific American*. His mood fluctuated with George's malady. "His condition is a very distressing one," the Judge concluded, in one bulletin to his children, but he also insisted that he was "full of hope" for a better outcome.[97]

There was also another concern. George was not just mortally ill: despite a promising beginning in the building business in the late 1870s, he thereafter demonstrated little of his brothers' interest in work and accumulation, and had revealed himself a spendthrift, unable to keep his expenses within his income—an unforgivable character defect in Mellon eyes. Accordingly, the Judge concluded that for reasons of health and probity alike, George should always be watched over by another member of the family. When he was obliged to leave Aiken and return to his affairs in Pittsburgh, he left Sarah Jane behind, and she was later joined by Dick and James. In August 1882, when he made his sentimental pilgrimage back to the Old World, the Judge took George with him, partly in the belief that the sea air would do his son good, and so that he could consult doctors in London, but also (no doubt) in the hopes of improving his character to some degree. Soon after their return, the Judge sent George to Dakota, again with the thought of combining business with therapy: the change of climate might prove beneficial, there were Mellon properties to be superintended and developed, and at the Judge's behest, he was accompanied by his elder brother Dick. "None of us," William Larimer Mellon later recalled, "Dick included, believed that George could ever return to Pittsburgh for a long stay; consequently, should George have to live in exile, some one of us would need to share that exile. Dick had been chosen—and Dick had accepted the situation. That's the kind of family we were."[98]

Once again, the Judge's will was done. His boys still went where he sent them, and (with the ominous exception of George's working and spending habits) they did as he told them. Now, with their father's backing, and following the example of Thomas and James in East Liberty, Dick and George opened a small bank in Bismarck, Dakota, and named it Mellon Brothers. They attracted substantial deposits and were able to lend money easily and profitably: they dealt in Northern Pacific Railroad stock and local bonds, and for a brief time there seemed to be a promise of more profit than at T. Mellon & Sons. They also acquired a 1,000-acre farm on the edge of the town, planted it with wheat, and bought cattle. Following family precedent, they began to deal in real estate.[99] It seemed a propitious time: the cattle business was booming; the Northern Pacific Railroad was completed in 1883; in the same year Bismarck was made the capital of what was then Dakota Territory; and as Dick explained to Andrew, the local real estate men were "going crazy" with excitement. Dick looked after the bank and the property, served as treasurer of the Bismarck Loan and Trust Company, and became involved in local politics. Meanwhile, George managed the farm as his health and disposition allowed, and in June 1883, young William Larimer Mellon visited his uncles, and worked for a time as a cowboy.[100]

While the brothers were in Bismarck, the Judge regularly corresponded with Dick, in a manner reminiscent of the letters he had exchanged with James Ross in Milwaukee twenty years before. Once again, the Judge made it plain his sons must act in conformity with his "ideas" and "plans." Once again, there was an unending stream of advice on business matters: "beware of too much investment in town lots"; "it is easier lending money than getting it back"; "mortgages on cattle can never be safe"; "straightforward manly conduct will always command respect, but some men buy their popularity at a very dear rate"; and so on.[101] But in at least two ways, these later letters differed from the earlier dispatches from Pittsburgh. The Judge had given up the hectoring and haranguing of two decades earlier. He still wanted "fuller details" of all their "views and opinions," and more frequent and speedy replies, but there were no longer the insistent and precise guidance and warnings about girls, friends, drinking, smoking, handwriting, and spelling. Even more important, the substantive correspondence about the conduct of the business ventures in Bismarck was not between Dick and his father, but between Dick and Andrew. They had, after all, been partners briefly before the panic of 1873, and now it was Andrew who authorized the funds, from T. Mellon & Sons, which financed the Bismarck ventures. It was a sign that practical power in the family was shifting, and a portent of things to come.[102]

But as this correspondence also made plain, George was not improving: he could not settle down, he was "loafing about," his heart was not in his work, cyclical bouts of illness sapped his energy, and he continued to overspend. His personal account at the Mellon Brothers Bank in Bismarck was closed without his consent, and while he was still permitted to draw modestly on his father's funds in Pittsburgh, any overdrafts were to be deducted from his eventual inheritance. He also fell out with his brother Thomas Alexander, over whether he should play any part in the affairs of the Ligonier Valley Railroad.[103] George thus became the only Mellon boy whom the Judge had failed to bend to his will, and the father's disappointment at his son's "extravagance and folly" was matched only by his anxiety for his bodily infirmity. By January 1885, he had come to accept defeat. Even if George did recover, the Judge wrote to Dick, he doubted "whether his long idleness won't take all the sand out of him for business." "I hope not," he went on. "A man has a poor excuse to this world who could spend all his life as a dude." It is not known whether George ever saw this letter, but he can scarcely have been unaware of his father's anxious and pained comments about him in *Thomas Mellon and His Times*: "I still hope," the Judge wrote in one passage, "that robust health and vigour will restore his desire and capacity for regular employment"; and that George's "good common sense" might "restrain him at all times within the bounds of his income."[104]

In September 1886, almost twelve months after the publication of the Judge's book, George joined his brothers on a two-month tour of the United States, in a private railcar named *Glen Eyre*. The party fluctuated in number, as family and friends joined and left along the way, though the Judge himself does not seem to have been present at any stage. It was presided over by Sarah Jane (who would later write a lengthy account of the trip), and she was accompanied by Thomas Alexander and his family, by James Ross and his family (including WL), by Andrew, Dick, and George, and by assorted Larimer and Caldwell in-laws.[105] Andrew, who was certainly there when they embarked, is scarcely mentioned thereafter. The trip seems to have had several aims: to search for better and more salubrious weather; to survey the extensive and dispersed Mellon holdings in the Midwest; and to see as much of America as possible on one journey, something the recent expansion of the railroads had made possible for the first time. And so the Mellon party went its agreeable, windy way: to Chicago and on to Bismarck, where they met up with George and Dick, and where Andrew left to return to Pittsburgh; on to Yellowstone, Portland, Salt Lake City, Reno, San Francisco, and Los Angeles; then south to El Paso and Mexico City; and eventually returning via Denver and Kansas City to Pittsburgh.

Sarah Jane Mellon's account of this unique family expedition also provides the only sustained opportunity to encounter her at first hand, and she emerges from her journal as highly intelligent, deeply interested in history, strongly opinionated, and of greater religious conviction than her husband. Her descriptions of mountains, coastlines, waterfalls, canyons, rivers, and deserts rival the Judge's for color and atmosphere, and she provides vivid portraits of the Mormon Tabernacle at Salt Lake City, the great railroad junction at El Paso, and the cable cars and Chinese restaurants in San Francisco. Her attentiveness to detail is compulsive: the frequency with which their private railcar was cleaned, the facilities of the hotels in which they stayed, the crops and cattle and fruit and buffalo glimpsed as they pass. She had a good eye for the material circumstances of life: the price of land, the significance of railways, the importance of natural resources, the need for an educated labor force, the virtues of "thrift and energy," and the opportunities created by new inventions. She also shared her husband's disapproval of the Catholic church, which she thought held back human progress and individual opportunity, and she was delighted to learn that in Mexico, the monasteries had recently been suppressed.[106] She must have made as formidable a parent as her husband.[107]

Meanwhile, the Dakota enterprises were looking more doubtful, and not only because of George Mellon's diseases and delinquencies. The land boom was the thinnest and most fragile of bubbles, and it was soon clear that Bismarck would not be another Chicago. Wheat prices had declined and farmland bought in the expectation of rising values was rapidly going down in price. The bank was also proving to be less profitable than originally hoped, and there were terrible winters in 1885–86 and 1886–87. The Judge decided it was time to call a halt: "it is the true policy always to make the best of a bad bargain."[108] Mellon Brothers was liquidated, thereby making it the second family bank to be closed, and the properties were put in a "safe condition." Decades later, Dick Mellon ruefully lamented that when Bismarck was chosen, the alternative place for Mellon investment had been Winnipeg, in Canada, by then a thriving city of 300,000 inhabitants. But he had been convinced Winnipeg would not prosper, whereas Bismarck must succeed. The result was one of the few Mellon ventures that failed almost utterly. But the family stubbornly (or optimistically?) retained its property holdings. A memorandum by David Finley in September 1936 records a recent trip to Bismarck, and the extensive Mellon holdings that still existed. "I saw," he recalled, "the site now occupied by a jewelry store on the corner of Fourth Street and Broadway, where Mr. R. B. Mellon had a bank in a one story building during the early 80s when he was there."[109]

At almost exactly the same time that the Judge decided the Dakota venture was a bust, George's life came to its sad and seemingly inevitable end. He had never been happy or fulfilled in Bismarck, where Dick's obvious competence and enthusiasm left little for him to do—except socialize and spend. The Judge had hoped that George might take over Alexander Caldwell's Idaho and Oregon Land Company, or the Sioux Falls Waterworks, but he showed no interest in that, or in his father's alternative proposal that he should go back to Pittsburgh to build and sell houses once more.[110] In late 1886, having journeyed home with his family in the *Glen Eyre*, George returned to Bismarck and set out for Denver with a team and a buck wagon, and nothing but a compass to guide him, journeying through the Badlands, the Wyoming wilderness, and the Colorado Rockies, in what would prove a vain and final quest for health and freedom. Before leaving, he had reassured his mother he would be back in Pittsburgh the following spring. And he was. For having reached Denver, he fell ill again, this time with spinal meningitis. His brother Dick was urgently sent for, and he arrived from Bismarck just before George succumbed on April 15, 1887.[111] He was the fourth of the Mellon children to predecease his parents.

Now that he had closed down the Bismarck businesses, and brought George's body back to Pittsburgh, what was Dick to do? He had spent the better part of five years living ruggedly out west, and he was the poorest of the surviving brothers. Moreover, both his partnerships, initially with Andrew, and now with George, had been dissolved. "You have had," the Judge wrote to him with a mixture of candor and concern, "a rather worse start than the rest [of the brothers] in money making. Two declines: one at each start you made, and I hope to see you overcome it all eventually."[112] Far from leaving Dick to his own devices, however, the Judge once again acted swiftly and decisively in ordaining what a son of his should do next. For in June 1887, Dick returned home and joined T. Mellon & Sons. The decision to bring him in has widely been regarded as Andrew's; but in matters of grand family strategy, the Judge was still in charge, and as this letter makes plain, he does not seem to have ventured to discover "what Andy thinks":

> After you do all that can be done to get things in a safe condition to leave, it seems to me the thing to do is to go into the Bank here with Andy. There ought to be two in it. His outside business keeps him too busy to give it sufficient attention. *I have not spoken to him, but know how he would be pleased.* He is nowise selfish and this would give you a regular business, and you could take advantage of any outside matter that should turn up.[113]

Dick Mellon duly joined T. Mellon & Sons early in 1887 as vice president, and Andrew, as his father had predicted (or decreed?) immediately assigned him one-half share in all profits (and losses): "It was an outright gift," he later recalled. "I just said to come in, and he came in, and then we were partners."[114] It was the fourth such arrangement that had been made between the Mellon brothers: first Thomas Alexander and James Ross in East Liberty, then Andrew and Dick in Mansfield, then Dick and George in Bismarck, and now Andrew and Dick again. The Judge had always preferred collaboration in business, initially with associates of his own choosing: when those had proved unreliable, he formed, in effect, partnerships with his sons. These had worked and promised better, and had ultimately inspired him in setting up such arrangements among the brothers. Such joint ventures, the Judge had earlier told Dick, were "more satisfactory to yourselves": two of them working together was "safer" than being "entirely alone," and their "different business capacities" were complementary. But this second partnership between Andrew and Dick would turn out to be incomparably more successful than any of the three that had gone before. On the basis of this informal arrangement, T. Mellon & Sons would operate for the next fifteen years, and the phrase "My brother and I," which both of them would use in their financial dealings with others, would soon become almost legendary in Pittsburgh business circles.[115]

3

THE "MELLON SYSTEM" INAUGURATED
"My Brother and I," 1887–98

The Scotch and Scotch-Irish—the latter but a Scotch colony—
monopolize business and wealth, and almost dominate politics
and religion wherever emigration carries them. They owe this
to their qualities of thrift, economy, intelligence and industry.

Thomas Mellon and His Times, p. 331

I. THE JUDGE "RETIRES"

Shortly before he brought Dick back to join Andrew at T. Mellon
& Sons, the Judge had sold his interest in the Pittsburgh, Oakland and East Liberty Passenger Railway. Together, these two decisions
bespeak a more serious determination to withdraw from business than he
had evinced hitherto. Moreover, his eyesight was getting worse, making it
hard to read at all, even with the help of the state-of-the-art electric light
that seventeen-year-old William Larimer Mellon had recently installed at
401 Negley.[1] As he affirmed both in his autobiography and after its completion, the Judge had never "desired wealth on its own account," still less
for ostentation and display, but for what Robert Burns had described as
"the glorious privilege of being independent." He had long since achieved
that coveted Burnsean state of a more than modest competence, but he
was also finding increasingly burdensome the "labors and special attention" attendant upon "acquisition and accumulation," "possession and
ownership." He wanted "freedom" from such "care and responsibility,"
and so he resolved to give his wealth away.[2] This might have seemed "a
most unusual and reckless act," but at almost exactly the same time,

Andrew Carnegie had been dispensing advice on how to dispose of one's accumulated assets, insisting in 1889 that "the man who dies thus rich dies disgraced." The Judge may have agreed with some of Carnegie's views, and Carnegie admired the Judge's "long career of honour and usefulness"; but the Judge did not follow Carnegie's prescription.[3]

According to Carnegie, "the problem of our age" was "the proper administration of wealth."[4] He believed that the accumulation of large fortunes was both commonplace and defensible: the challenge was not to amass money, much less to justify the act, but to give it away in an honorable and improving manner. Avoidance of inheritance taxes was not the issue—at the time they scarcely existed—but rather how to ensure that the money was put to the worthiest use. There were, as he saw it, three possibilities. The first was to leave the fortune to one's family: this was "most injudicious" and was based on "misguided affection," for the inheritance of vast sums could only corrupt one's descendants. The second was to bequeath the money for public purposes, but this would likely produce monuments to the benefactor's folly. The third option was to dispose of it oneself, by donating it before one's death to specific public causes such as universities, libraries, hospitals, parks, concert halls, public baths, and churches, but not to charities or for the support of idle and impoverished individuals. In his writings, Carnegie paid homage to such pioneering American benefactors as Astor, Vassar, Cornell, and Stanford; he himself had already begun to give away his money—to the Pittsburgh Public Library, for example. He would soon make over much more; and other rich men like John D. Rockefeller and J. P. Morgan would also begin to part with substantial sums.[5] As for the Judge, while he shared Carnegie's disapproval of indiscriminate giving to wastrels, he had no intention of handing over his fortune for the public good. "An equal distribution of the wealth of the nation," he had written nearly sixty years before, "must inevitably be followed by bad consequences"; he would go to the grave still believing in the necessity and virtue of inequality.[6]

Instead, he transferred some of his assets, along with those of his wife, to his four sons; since he had "full confidence in the[ir] sound judgment and other qualities," he sensed no risk, either to his fortune or to their happiness. The means whereby the Judge chose to accomplish this transaction were both audacious and revealing. On the occasion of his seventy-seventh birthday, February 3, 1890, instead of receiving gifts, he gave them. He transferred "all the lands, tenements and hereditaments, or real estate" which he and Sarah Jane owned in the United States to their son Andrew, who was to hold them on behalf of the four surviving brothers, disbursing the revenues equally among them. On the same day, Andrew signed "A Declaration of Trust," which set out the terms of his steward-ship of the family property.[7] Essentially it was a pledge of fraternal loyalty and good behavior. He would manage the real estate in consultation with his three brothers, and sell no part of it without their consent. The family home was not to be disposed of in the lifetime of his father or mother, and he accorded his parents the right to reclaim the income should they ever need to do so. Otherwise the four brothers would share the revenue equally, and whenever the cash balance exceeded $20,000, it would be so divided. Having created the sons in his own image, the Judge was happy to pass his wealth on to them; and the three brothers just as happily acqui-esced in an arrangement which was also proof of Andrew's growing authority and unrivaled leadership within the family.[8]

But the valedictory interlude that saw the publication of the autobiog-raphy and the passing on of some of the Judge's property did not last for long. Freed from his civic responsibility, as well as from active involve-ment in business, he seems to have experienced a last surge of vitality, to the point that for a time he stopped complaining about his eyesight. As one contemporary publication explained, he was proud of having "never failed of success in any enterprise he ever seriously undertook," and he was "as energetic and vigorous mentally and physically, and as sound of judgment as at any former period of his life."[9] As he passed from his late seventies to his early eighties, the Judge carved out a wholly new existence for himself in Kansas City, where he would spend most of his time until 1894, and where his determination and discernment would be tested yet again. It was a part of the Midwest he knew: he had owned property in the region, his late brother Samuel had lived at Fort Leavenworth, two of his sons had found their brides there, and his Larimer and Caldwell in-laws resided nearby. Moreover, Kansas City was now a boomtown, with an expanding population and a thriving building industry. It ranked next to Chicago among American cities in packinghouse and stockyard business, had more miles of operating cable road than any city in the world, and was a great railway hub from which thousands of settlers headed west across the plains.[10]

Here was another place of opportunity, as Pittsburgh had been for him a generation earlier, and the Judge had already been drawn there once before. Late in 1888, he was visited by Louis Irvine, a lawyer and pro-moter, with interests in transport companies. He lived in Kansas City, which was then being built up on uneven terrain, a town divided between a low-lying area known as "the Bottoms," of factories, freight yards, and warehouses, and the residential, business, and retail district on a nearby plateau. A logical way to connect these areas was by constructing incline planes, and Irvine hoped to draw upon the Judge's experience in building and operating such structures in Pittsburgh. He invited him to Kansas to assess both the challenges and the possibilities. The Judge duly visited in early 1889, and was sufficiently impressed to take up the mission himself. He founded and financed the Kansas City Incline Plane Company specifically "to construct, maintain and operate a system of incline railways in that city," and he appointed as its directors Irvine, Dick Mellon, Alexander Caldwell, W. H. Larimer (son of the general), and Walter S. Mitchell (of T. Mellon & Sons). In addition, he purchased $60,000 worth of land, brought engineers in from Pittsburgh, and only then applied to the city council for the franchise to build and operate the inclines. But there was serious opposition: from residents who considered the inclines to be ugly, dirty, noisy, and fatal to property values, and from corrupt councilmen, who resented "Banker Mellon" as a rich outsider. They expected him to pay handsomely for the council's consent, which the Judge naturally refused, retorting "not a cent for boodle."[11]

During the second half of 1889, with his application bogged down in the council's Committee for Public Improvements, he returned to Pittsburgh to oversee the transfer of his property to his sons. But once this was settled, he went back to Kansas City, determined to do battle with the corrupt council, to build his inclined planes, and to make a substantial profit. Sarah Jane did not accompany him, remaining at 401 Negley, but the Judge wrote regular letters to her, and also to his sons. They radiate zest and pleasure in new freedom and new opportunity: "I feel able to make a fresh start in the world," he told "all at home" in early February 1890, "with as good health as ever I had in my life."[12] Yet there were still traces of the incorrigibly domineering patriarch. He expected "Ma" to correspond frequently and Dick to "keep me posted on all business matters." "Ma" duly obliged, writing "every week, regularly enough," but the Judge lamented that "I hear nothing about business." When he did, he responded with typical directness, about the St. Clair Incline Company in Pittsburgh, about the Waverly Coal and Coke Company, and also about the bank: "I know that Andy must be very busy," he opined, "and I know also that Dick's department needs all the attention he can afford it."[13]

Still, the Judge's main concern was his Kansas City council campaign. "I am sure of success sooner or later," he told his sons, with, as it turned out, seriously misplaced optimism, "and it affords rather a pleasurable excitement than otherwise." No stranger to rough politics, he established a newspaper, the *Penny Press*, with Dick Mellon as publisher and William A. Mellon (son of the Judge's brother Samuel) and his wife, Lillian, as editors. On its pages, the Judge penned ferocious screeds against the council and praised the inclined planes.[14] In November 1890, he gave away 20,000 copies of a 17,000-word pamphlet, *The BOSS and BOODLE Fight Against Incline Planes and Non-Resident Investors*, which accused particular councilors of soliciting graft. This caused a local furor. There were official investigations into his accusations, leading councilmen were indicted, and the Judge was sued for libel. This was excellent publicity for his plans and his planes, but his counter-attack soon fizzled. The *Penny Press* was put out of business, and the Judge quarreled with William and Lillian Mellon as a result. He was obliged to withdraw his application for the franchise in February 1891, and the indictments against his adversaries were dismissed. The only consolation in this debacle was that in taking his stand, the Judge became something of a local hero, several of his enemies were subsequently voted off the council, and when the suit against him came to trial, the jury found for him. But these were pyrrhic victories: the chimerical structures were never built, the properties he had bought were sold off, and the Kansas City Incline Plane Company was eventually liquidated, no doubt at a substantial loss.[15]

Despite this unprecedented reversal, the Judge stayed on in Kansas for the better part of the next three years, perhaps to enjoy his political celebrity, perhaps to undertake other commercial ventures, the details of which have not survived. But he also returned to a subject which had interested him thirty years earlier and was now very fashionable on both sides of the Atlantic, namely spiritualism.[16] During the late 1850s, a young servant girl, Mary McClean, had worked in the Mellon household; her presence was accompanied for a time by mysterious rappings, and before she moved on she had attracted substantial attention in Pittsburgh as a "natural medium." This scarcely seems a phenomenon likely to commend itself to the hard and calculating Judge, but the heartrending deaths of his two sons (though apparently not those of his daughters) left him susceptible to the notion of re-establishing contact with their spirits. So after his incline planes scheme failed, he began attending séances in Kansas City (where he thought he re-encountered Selwyn) and Cincinnati (where he believed himself in contact with George). His surviving sons were deeply skeptical, but the Judge for once could not reach a definite opinion. Part of him believed that "so many repetitious meetings with George and others afterwards" removed "all doubt as to the possibility and reality of spiritual forms." But in other, more typically unbelieving moods, he concluded that "there's nothing to it," insisting that he was no more a spiritualist than a socialist.[17]

Sometime in 1894, the Judge left Kansas City and returned to Pittsburgh for good.[18] It was not a moment too soon. His years there were the least successful of his career, and now he was falling prey to charlatans. He was indeed an old man by this time, which may explain why he also abandoned the passing thought of setting up a newspaper in Pittsburgh. During Christmas 1894, he consigned the rest of his assets—mortgages, bills receivable, coal mines, and other wealth—on the same terms as the earlier transfer, which meant that by January 1895, Andrew Mellon was "the unquestioned autocrat of the family estate."[19] The size of the Judge's fortune at the time was measured exactly: official appraisals and inventories fixed the value of real estate at $861,986.77, and the remainder at $1,595,562.02, bringing the total assets turned over to Andrew to almost $2.5 million. The Judge would later observe that his boys possessed "wealth equal to my own," so that at a conservative estimate, the collective Mellon family wealth in the mid-1890s was in the region of $5 million (about $110 million in today's currency), and might have been substantially more: William Larimer Mellon put the market value of the Judge's assets at closer to $4 million. In any case, the New York Tribune had not been mistaken to include six Mellons—the Judge, his four sons, and grandson William Larimer—in the list of American millionaires that it had published in May 1892.[20]

Andrew Mellon's stewardship of the family legacy would last from 1890 until 1919.[21] During that time, the official value of the principal increased from nearly $2.5 million to almost $4.2 million, even after taking into account the Judge's substantial losses in Kansas real estate ($50,000) and also in the Idaho and Oregon Land Improvement Company ($42,000). In those twenty-nine years, it also generated a third of a million dollars in revenue, the apportionment of which is quite telling, given the original terms of transfer. Of that sum, close to $100,000 was distributed as dividends to the four brothers, an annual average of only $1,600 per brother; Sarah Jane Mellon received $13,000 for personal expenses; and the Judge received $44,000 for household costs. But the most substantial outlay was $186,000, also to the Judge, for his personal expenditure, which was no doubt especially high during the early 1890s when he was living in Kansas, tilting at his incline planes, maneuvering in city politics, and publishing. By a substantial margin, then, the Judge was the primary beneficiary of the fortune he had "given away" to Andrew to manage for the benefit of the four brothers. Such was Thomas Mellon's notion of divestment. It was a characteristically shrewd arrangement for the sunset years of his life.

Having parted with his capital fortune, the Judge saw no need to make a will, but later, in September 1895, he sent a letter to "my dear sons" containing some final wishes and reflections. It was a recognizable blend of grudging charity, well-meaning censure, and heartwarming family sentiment. He was anxious that Henrietta, a former playmate of the children who might also provide later companionship for Sarah Jane, should be given a pension of $200 a year. He also hoped to assist the two children of William and Lillian Mellon of Kansas City, though "without helping to support the good-for-nothing father and child-like conceited mother in comparative idleness." (The failure of the planes and the *Penny Press* clearly still rankled.) "I have no idea," he went on, "of helping anyone, young or old, to shirk the duties and labors of life belonging to their condition. Everyone should be self sustaining according to his or her ability and the conditions in which they are placed." And he paid this last tribute to his immediate family:

> I have now only to mention the great comfort and happiness which I enjoy and have always enjoyed from your good qualities and uniform course of life since your infancy. I have been favored remarkably in all my immediate family relations. I was blessed in a mate and can see her good qualities in our children and grandchildren. Even our daughters in law have filled the place of our little daughters who left us in childhood. In the character, ability and fidelity of those who come after me, I am surely overpaid for all their arduous care and labor of a long life.[22]

It was a more gracious valediction than the closing words of his autobiography, but he still had another thirteen years to live.

II. NEW INITIATIVES

From 1890 onward, Andrew Mellon had responsibility for his father's fortune in real estate, coal lands, mortgages, bonds, and the like; he also had real estate and shares of his own, including holdings in the banks and utility companies he had acquired during the 1880s. But progress was slow. From July 1, 1887, according to the Judge's wishes, the surplus (or losses) of T. Mellon & Sons were divided equally between Andrew and Dick. On January 1, 1889, a small but significant adjustment was made: the brothers would each take 48 percent, the remaining 4 percent to be shared with their two senior clerks, Walter S. Mitchell and A. M. Thorne. (Mitchell, who had worked for the Judge as a cashier when the bank first opened, would be a Mellon retainer for the rest of his life, eventually becoming a director of Mellon National Bank in 1903, and vice president in 1916, positions he held until his death in 1930.)[23] But for a decade after Andrew and Dick took over, the profits of T. Mellon & Sons were decidedly modest: from 1888 to 1890, the surplus disbursed to each of the brothers averaged just below $13,000, dipping to $4,719 in 1891 and recovering to $12,288 in the following year.[24] These were a considerable improvement on the returns of the 1870s, but scarcely substantial sums—proof that economic recovery from the recession of the mid-1880s was very slow indeed, and also that T. Mellon & Sons was still a small-scale operation. As late as 1895, it had only seven employees, its total resources, measured as deposits or liabilities, were roughly ten million dollars, and as a private bank, it still did not clear its own checks or issue notes. As one early Mellon employee told Burton Hendrick, it was at that time only "a minor financial institution" in Pittsburgh, and "not of great account."[25]

The same was also true of the Fidelity Title and Trust Company which Andrew Mellon had established with Frick in 1886. It was the second trust in Pittsburgh and the first to receive deposits, but as late as 1895, these barely amounted to one million dollars, and the company had paid no dividend before 1893. The main purpose of the trust had been to administer estates for individuals and corporations, but it was unable to represent both sides in probating a client's will. The solution was to create a second, subsidiary company, so all business could be dealt with in-house, and in October 1889, Mellon, Frick, and other partners from Fidelity founded the Union Transfer and Trust Company, with Andrew as president and capital of $250,000. The new trust was very much a subsidiary of Fidelity: initially located in the same building, its business was largely determined by Fidelity's transactional needs. In 1892 the word "Transfer" was dropped (many Pittsburghers seem to have been mistaking it for a furniture moving company), and in 1893 it purchased the old Pittsburgh Oil Exchange building, moving in the following year. But in these unbuoyant times, it, too, languished and underperformed, with no particular focus or purpose. Under an 1889 state law, such trusts enjoyed full banking powers. But there was no sign of such enjoyment here: between 1889 and 1894, Union Trust's total profits were a mere $2,000, and the directors several times considered liquidation.[26]

The deep slump of 1884 may have passed, then, but the gloom of the "great depression" would linger until 1897.[27] It was in this dispiriting context that Andrew and Dick took two important steps toward involving themselves more aggressively and innovatively with local industry. The first concerned the Pittsburgh Reduction Company, a new business that was inadequately funded and had only a potential market for its product. It had been established in August 1888 by Captain Alfred Hunt (a graduate of MIT, an internationally respected engineer and metallurgist, and proprietor of the Pittsburgh Testing Laboratory), George Clapp (a young chemist and Hunt's co-proprietor), and four colleagues. They had scrimped, saved, and borrowed $20,000 to set up a workshop on Smallman Street in the city's Northern Liberties district. Their pilot scheme aimed to exploit the inventiveness of Charles Martin Hall, a prim and precocious chemistry graduate from Oberlin College, who had recently developed and would soon patent the first practical method known in America of electrolytic reduction of aluminum from bauxite. Soon after, Hall was joined by Arthur Vining Davis, fresh from Amherst College, whose skills as manager and marketer would eventually match Hall's inventive brilliance.[28]

The scheme worked—after a fashion. Within six months, the company was producing fifty pounds of aluminum a day, which was kept in the office safe and sold at $5 per pound; by September 1889, the daily output had climbed to 475 and it was now offered at $2 a pound. Accordingly, in that month the directors pronounced the pilot a success and authorized an increase in the company's capital stock to one million dollars, to be held in 10,000 shares worth $100 at par. But it was not clear sailing yet: aluminum was still both difficult and expensive to produce, and the market for it at $2 a pound was not promising. Why should those industries and consumers who relied on iron, lead, copper, tin, and zinc buy this manmade metal instead? If the company was to survive, it must produce more and cheaper aluminum. In order to do so, it would have to expand, and in order to expand, it would need more money to increase its capacity. At the suggestion of Charles Orr, a lawyer, Hunt, Clapp, and Davis visited Andrew Mellon late in 1889, in the hope of securing a loan of $4,000 to discharge a note they owed another Pittsburgh bank. Mellon was impressed by these men, and went over their (not very promising) accounts in detail. He was also captivated by the idea of aluminum; he was optimistic about its future, and concluded that the Pittsburgh Reduction Company needed substantially more than $4,000.[29] He offered them a loan of $25,000, which would enable them to discharge their bankers' debt and also provide them with much-needed working capital.

This was the beginning of a long and lucrative relationship between the Mellons and Pittsburgh Reduction, one that very soon intensified. Andrew Mellon bought his first sixty shares for $6,000 in January 1890, he became a director twelve months later, and by early 1893 he had acquired nearly one thousand shares. He was soon joined by Dick, who bought his first hundred shares in 1895 and became a director in the same year. With most of the 10,000 shares held by Hall, Davis, and Hunt, this was scarcely a dominant stake.[30] But Andrew and Dick were both extremely attentive directors, and they wielded a disproportionate influence because of the additional support they were prepared to provide. They urged, and financed, the company's relocation from Pittsburgh to a larger fabricating plant nearby at New Kensington, where the land was furnished by a real estate company in which they had an interest, and where coal and gas were readily available. And in 1894 they proposed, and again financed, the opening of a new plant at Niagara Falls, where hydroelectric power was both cheap and abundant. Thanks to reduced costs and expanding output, the price of aluminum continued to fall: to 85 cents a pound in 1892, and to barely 50 cents a pound two years later. And the demand increased correspondingly: in 1895, the company sold over 600,000 pounds, exactly one hundred times the output of its first year. The markets were both industrial (sheets, rods, wire, tubes, cables, and castings) and domestic (cooking utensils and kitchenware). The company was also beginning to develop into an integrated enterprise, mining its own bauxite in Georgia and also taking steps to manufacture its own finished products.[31]

The Pittsburgh Reduction Company was the first significant beneficiary of what would prove to be Andrew Mellon's extraordinary gift for spotting and nurturing outstanding individuals with promising ideas—though in this case, as in others, it would be some time before the promise was abundantly redeemed, both for them and for him. But Mellon was prepared to wait, riding out losses if need be (especially in the early 1890s) and plowing back profits when they came (during the company's first decade dividends were paid out only twice). By 1893, it seemed as though the corner had been turned: the company posted a profit of $139,000, its products were displayed at the World's Columbian Exposition at Chicago, and the future looked bright.[32] It bears emphasizing that Pittsburgh Reduction was an enterprise which the Mellons could influence and finance—indeed, influence *through* finance—but they did not completely control it. Although Andrew sought to buy more shares at this time, the Mellon stake was still only 12.35 percent in May 1894. Between them,

Hall, Hunt, and (increasingly) Davis were the dominant owner-managers. Almost forty years after his initial involvement, Andrew recalled: "For a great many years, I have depended entirely on Mr. Davis . . . You might say that he was practically the whole business."[33]

In the same year he ventured into aluminum, Andrew Mellon entered another industry: petroleum. This was a significant change in direction, for while the Judge had briefly flirted with oil in the early 1870s, Andrew had adamantly refused to involve himself during the early 1880s, even though Pennsylvania was then the preeminent oil-producing state and Pittsburgh was a major oil metropolis.[34] (At this time oil was primarily used as a lubricant for machining and, as kerosene, for lighting.) Three reasons underlay this change in family policy. The first was the discovery in 1889 of new sources of oil in southwestern Pennsylvania, near Coraopolis, in what became known as the McDonald Field. The second was that among the local wildcatters and prospectors were the Galey brothers, Sam and John, friends of Andrew's, and also James Guffey, with whom he had collaborated in the natural gas business during the late 1880s. The third was that William Larimer Mellon decided that oil was where his own future lay. The Judge's eldest grandson had already logged experience as a cowboy in Dakota, as a clerk in the lumberyard of his father and his uncle, and as the first installer of electric light at 401 Negley. WL was tall, energetic, boisterous, high-spirited, and something of a rough diamond. He had no college education, he liked hunting and shooting, he was "a harder worker with his hands than his father ever was," and he took after both his Mellon and Larimer forebears: from the former he inherited a passion for money and an eye for an opportunity, from the latter a delight in roughing it in the great outdoors. The oil business gratified both of these impulses. Bored with his desk job at Mellon Brothers, he accepted John Galey's invitation to join him at the new Pennsylvania oilfield in the autumn of 1889.[35]

There, W. L. Mellon fell in with the adventurers, prospectors, and wildcatters who were transforming the McDonald Field with their derricks, shanty hotels, saloons, and gambling houses. Roaming the country on horseback, sleeping under the stars or in local farmhouses, and trying to stay ahead of his competitors, he soon secured many "oil leases," not only in southwestern Pennsylvania, but in the Sistersville region of West Virginia too—often in collaboration with Galey and Guffey.[36] He would dig his wells, give the owner of the property a percentage of the profit when oil was found, build "gathering lines" to bring his oil to the central point at Coraopolis, and sell the crude to John D. Rockefeller's Standard

Oil Company, which by then controlled virtually all the pipelines and refineries in Pennsylvania—and far beyond. WL was operating as a front-line businessman in a way that his uncles never did, but it was they who financed him, partly through a "W. L. Mellon Special" account at the bank, and also by personal loans, which had reached almost half a million dollars by September 1894.[37] As with the two brothers at the bank, so now with the uncles and their nephew: the family arrangement was initially informal and was not written down until 1894. The three would be partners, Andrew and Dick would each take 35 percent of the profits and WL 30 percent, on top of a salary of $200 a month beginning in July 1893.[38]

The Mellon wells and gathering lines were duly consolidated into the Crescent Oil Company, and the family also began making their own petroleum products at the Bear Creek refinery, twelve miles from Pittsburgh, in which they acquired a half share.[39] Both operations were overseen from a second-floor office of T. Mellon & Sons. In 1890, their business had been further expanded when another local petroleum company, owned by Elkins and Widener, the Philadelphia streetcar millionaires, was sold to Standard Oil. Three of their former customers, two of them French and one of them Spanish, did not wish to deal with Standard Oil, preferring to do business with the Mellons.[40] Here was both a challenge and an opportunity: to risk the wrath of Rockefeller by building up a new and lucrative business as a direct competitor. W. L. Mellon decided the risk was worth taking, and that a fortune might be made defying Standard Oil; he purchased two hundred railroad tank cars, to transport his own crude from Coraopolis to the East Coast for shipment to Europe. Standard Oil, of course, was not amused by this threat to its near monopoly on oil transport in the state, and applied pressure on the Pennsylvania Railroad—pressure which the railroad could scarcely ignore since the Standard was one of its biggest customers. And so the railroad raised its rates for transporting Mellon tank cars, especially when returning them empty from the eastern seaboard to western Pennsylvania. By squeezing the Mellons' profit in this way, Rockefeller determined he would force them out of business.[41]

But W. L. Mellon and his uncles were not of a mind to succumb, and they resolved to transport their oil by a different and cheaper way which they themselves would control. Late in 1891, they established the Crescent Pipeline Company and began constructing their own line from Griggs Station near Pittsburgh to Marcus Hook on the Delaware River, eighteen miles south of Philadelphia, where they would build a refinery and storage facilities. They were able to do this thanks to a general pipeline law passed in Pennsylvania in 1883, which had declared such lines to be common carriers and thus entitled to exercise the right of "eminent domain," acquiring private property as needed for the line. Once again, Rockefeller sought to thwart the Mellons: Standard Oil tried to buy up land in the path of the projected line, thereby inflating the price the Mellons would have to pay for it, and the Pennsylvania Railroad held up construction by filing for injunctions and instituting trespass proceedings at the many points where the Mellons' pipeline ran under the company's tracks. All this delayed construction, but in November 1892 the Crescent Pipeline was completed. It was 271 miles long, its capacity was 7,500 barrels a day, and it cost one million dollars—by far the Mellons' biggest outlay to date, and the only line in all Pennsylvania that Standard Oil did not dominate or control.[42]

As Andrew Mellon explained to a prospective customer the following month, with evident satisfaction and pride, the family petroleum companies were now the largest of the so-called independents in the state.[43] There were five altogether, for Pennsylvania law required oil producers and refiners to be separate firms, but the result, nevertheless, was a fully integrated business encompassing production, gathering, piping, refining, storing, and marketing. Concentrated in southwestern Pennsylvania, but with their operations extending into Virginia, the Mellons dealt in both crude and refined oil. Altogether, Andrew and his brother Dick had invested $2.5 million in these ventures, a very substantial outlay for them at the time, especially given the determined opposition of Rockefeller. "We have," Andrew added pointedly, "every facility possessed by the Standard Oil Company, [and] receive and deliver oil under as favourable conditions in every way." "You will," he went on, "always be served as reliably and favourably as by our competitors, both in regard to supply and as to prices in the future." "We are," he concluded, "in the business to stay." So, it seemed, they were. In early 1894, the Mellon companies were producing 10 percent of America's oil exports, they were beginning to look beyond Pennsylvania, and the two brothers and WL had recently formed the Troy Company to prospect in Kansas.[44]

Together, the Pittsburgh Reduction Company and these varied oil ventures were the first examples of what would later become famous (or infamous) as the "Mellon system." As this term implies, the approach that Andrew and his brother took to nurturing and developing these infant businesses was in some ways uniform and coherent. To begin with, and in the manner of such earlier Mellon undertakings as the East Liberty partnership between Thomas Alexander and James Ross, they were, or were becoming, vertically integrated enterprises, from the extraction and provision of raw materials, via refining and production, to sales and marketing. Moreover, in seeking out partners and collaborators, whom they were happy to finance but were willing to allow to get on with the daily business, the brothers were following the very mode of business organization that their father had pioneered. The Mellon "system" owed much to this paternal example, but it also surpassed the Judge's model. For Andrew and Dick were now venturing into regions far beyond those with which old Thomas Mellon had been comfortable: he had dealt in coal and iron, they preferred hydroelectric power and aluminum; he had dabbled in oil wells, they were concerned with pipelines and large-scale refining. Andrew may habitually have asked "What would Father do?," but it is not clear that his answers would always have convinced the Judge.

Yet even in this earliest phase, the Mellon system was never wholly monolithic or uniform; it was continually being adapted to different technologies, different markets, different modes of production, different structures of ownership. In the case of Pittsburgh Reduction, the Mellons were, and would always remain, minority shareholders. It was a "Mellon company" to the extent that their financial support was crucial at certain critical phases, but it was never a "Mellon company" in the sense of outright ownership. It was also a monopoly, protected in the United States although not in Europe, by both federal tariffs and Hall's patents. As for the Mellons' involvement in their oil companies: it was unique among all their industrial ventures, for not only were the two brothers the major suppliers of capital, but another member of their family was also actively and publicly in charge of the business. W. L. Mellon was not a banker; he was always a frontline businessman in ways that Andrew and Dick never were. And far from being monopolists, the Mellons were in direct competition with the ruthless leviathan of Standard Oil. So while similar in some ways, the two new Mellon enterprises represented distinct approaches in this aggressive new phase in the history of T. Mellon & Sons, and their trajectories would soon dramatically diverge.

The subsequent success of Pittsburgh Reduction contributed to Andrew Mellon's reputation for near infallibility when it came to spotting and supporting great inventive and business talent. In years to come, he would score many such successes, but like his father, he also made some mistakes. In 1890, for example, George Westinghouse had sought a $500,000 loan from the Mellons to provide himself with much-needed cash during a period of structural organization of his business, following his decision to expand the manufacture of air brakes for railroad cars.

Mellon was willing, but demanded in exchange a high percentage of equity in Westinghouse's companies, along with the power to fill key managerial positions. Westinghouse was not prepared to surrender control, and to Mellon's chagrin refused the offer and thereafter sought assistance from the New York capital market. Here was a whole sector of the Pittsburgh economy that Mellon could have assimilated if he had played his hand more carefully, and he regretted ever after that a major local industry had slipped into the hands of New York financiers.[45] Another story of Mellon dating from this time did the rounds in Pittsburgh for many years. One of the earliest visitors to T. Mellon & Sons was a young man who wanted to establish his business in the city, and had even picked out a site for his factory. He sought to borrow $30,000 to get started. But Mellon turned him down flat, telling him that there would never be any future for his product. The product was an early version of the "horseless carriage," and the man's name was Henry Ford.[46] It is a good story, but there is no evidence for it in either the Mellon or the Ford archives.

In later life, Andrew Mellon looked back on this phase of American business as a time of unprecedented industrial transformation, in iron and steel, and in petroleum, natural gas, and aluminum. It was also, he recalled, accompanied by a major revolution in organization, as "great, self-contained" enterprises were created which superseded the "thousands of competing units" and made possible large-scale and integrated production. (Standard Oil was, of course, the classic example.) Such a transformation, he believed, had required "business daring and organizing genius" on the part of an "extraordinary group" of entrepreneurs, but it had also necessitated a corresponding expansion in the scale and scope and substance of banking, as "industrial financing" had become "a recognized banking function." The Pittsburgh banks, he noted, had been among the first to "adapt their methods to the requirements of industry": they had helped to promote the development of local businesses, and in so doing they had grown dramatically themselves. In supplying the capital for such undertakings, bankers had been "drawn more and more into industry" as they became involved in the businesses they were helping to finance; meanwhile industrial leaders were putting their "knowledge and judgment" at the disposal of banks, on whose boards they were more and more often found. These were big changes. During "the early nineties," Mellon recalled, this "particular phase of banking development was looked upon as something new and not altogether conservative." It was an apt description of what he and his brother had just been beginning to do.[47]

III. URBAN TENSIONS,
POLITICAL AFFILIATIONS, BUSINESS ETHICS

Between the mid-1880s and the mid-1890s, the Pittsburgh economy lurched from panic to recovery to crisis again, all within that broader context of depressed prices, profits, and interest rates which had begun in 1873 and would not be ended for nearly twenty-five years. Yet Pittsburgh was also in the very forefront of America's dramatic and depression-induced economic advance: between 1880 and 1900 its population exploded from 235,000 to 451,000; and that of Allegheny County as a whole grew even more rapidly, from 356,000 to 775,000. It was the site and scene of a "frenzy of capital accumulation," in which local banks did, indeed, play a crucial part, as the City of Iron successfully transformed itself into the City of Steel, by the wholesale adoption of the Bessemer and, subsequently, open-hearth methods of production.[48] By 1894, Pittsburgh was producing almost one-half of the nation's steel output, and it had become the greatest center of steel production in the world. Four years later, the massive agglomeration of the Carnegie Brothers mills, which was chaired and managed by Mellon's friend Henry Clay Frick, declared profits of $11.5 million and produced more than two million tons of steel. This great enterprise was the proud symbol of the city's industrial triumph. By comparison, the Mellons' dealings in aluminum and oil were small-scale endeavors, and despite his friendship with Frick, Andrew Mellon showed no inclination to invest directly in steel.

Steel was not the only industry that was flourishing in Pittsburgh: in addition to manufacturing air brakes, George Westinghouse was pioneering the delivery of electricity from alternating current generators, and illuminated the World's Columbian Exposition in 1893, and H. J. Heinz was purveying his "57 varieties" of food to a wider mass market than ever before. As a result of this explosive growth in numbers, industry, and prosperity, the face of Pittsburgh was itself transformed (though the intensifying pollution often made this difficult to discern): in the central business district, skyscrapers such as the fifteen-story Carnegie building suddenly appeared; middle-class suburbs spread eastward, with the help of new electric streetcar lines; and steel mills and working-class housing proliferated along the Monongahela River at townships such as Braddock, Homestead, and Duquesne.[49] This was the world in which Andrew Mellon and his brother were now operating, albeit as still relatively humble participants: one of rampant and triumphant capitalism, presided over by a powerful and tightly knit business class. It was the newly established order of things, but it was becoming more established year by year, and Andrew and Dick accepted it unquestioningly.

The agents and beneficiaries of these economic and urban transformations were great industrialists (among them ironmasters, steel masters, and glass manufacturers), financial intermediaries (bankers, insurance agents, and stockbrokers), and professional associates (especially lawyers and railroad managers).[50] Like the Mellons, many of them were Scotch-Irish Presbyterians (or Scottish immigrants), and many lived in the East End, the most fashionable neighborhood in town, where the Shady Side Academy provided for the exclusive early education of their sons. Like the Judge, these men were devoted to making money, they accumulated wealth and advantage over the generations, they despised leisure and, even more, idleness, and they had little appreciation of culture or the arts. Increasingly, they formed a self-sufficient and exclusive coterie, with a strong sense of their own moral rectitude and superiority—at least in Pittsburgh. For they had little to do, either socially or financially, with the East Coast elites of Boston, New York, and Philadelphia, whose cosmopolitan condescension at their parochialism, their unremitting devotion to work, and their lack of refinement they much resented. As a result, they sent their sons to the Western University of Pennsylvania or to no university at all. Harvard and Yale and Princeton and Columbia were not (yet) for them.[51]

As in many western cities at the time, the upper class in Pittsburgh was elaborately connected and increasingly interrelated, as they tended to marry among themselves. (Despite the example of Carnegie, there were in fact very few rags-to-riches stories.)[52] In an earlier generation, this had been true of the Judge's marriage to Sarah Jane Negley, which resulted in a large (though not always amicable) Mellon-Negley clan. James Ross Mellon's marriage to Rachel Larimer Mellon was an example in the next generation. Both these marriages gave rise to business dealings, which were happier in the second case than in the first. But elite networking in Pittsburgh went far beyond the extended Mellon family: when Andrew set up the Union Trust Company, he put not only Henry Clay Frick and Dick Mellon on the board, but also, among others, J. M. Schoonmaker, president of the Pittsburgh and Lake Erie Railroad; George Whitney, partner in the stockbroking firm of Whitney & Stephenson; Henry Phipps, a partner in Carnegie Brothers; James B. Finley, another coke king; and Philander Knox. Of these, Knox was by far the most important. He was a partner in the law firm of Knox and Reed, which was established in 1877 and which specialized in corporate law. James H. Reed, who was Scottish and Presbyterian, had been a near contemporary of Andrew Mellon's at the Western University, and was a lifelong friend, and Knox was a consummate business lawyer. He helped Mellon and Frick buy the Pittsburgh National Bank of Commerce in 1881, and he was in a good position to do so, because he was one of its directors. By the end of that decade, Knox and Reed included the Mellons, Carnegie, and Frick among their clients, and were counsel to many of the biggest companies in the city, in railroads, steel, iron, traction, and utilities.[53]

Somewhere between family and business came ties of friendship and structured sociability. The most famous and enduring Pittsburgh friendship was that of Mellon and Frick. During the late 1880s and 1890s, T. Mellon & Sons continued to lend money to Frick and to his coke company, and he and Andrew did more business in coal properties together, including buying their way into the Connellsville Coke Company. Frick helped put up both brothers for the Union League Club, and they went on more joint trips to Europe.[54] They also played poker at Frick's house at Clayton on Thursday nights, often in the company of Philander Knox and George Westinghouse, where they enjoyed "old time jolly evenings." These four were also to be found, along with James Reed, Robert Pitcairn, and others, at the Duquesne Club, where they met in a private room for lunch, whisky, and cigars, forming a sort of club within a club, with their own rules and traditions and admission procedures.[55] For more spiritual (and inclusive) fellowship, there was the East Liberty Presbyterian Church, home away from home for the Scotch-Irish fraternity, to which the four Mellon brothers, following their parents, retained a lifelong attachment—although Andrew Mellon attended much less regularly than his younger brother. And for recreation, there was the countryside, where Carnegie, Frick, Mellon, Knox, and their friends established exclusive hunting, shooting, and fishing clubs, at which they gathered occasionally on weekends and for summer vacations. This was not an especially refined society, but in a city where work was the gospel and where the aim of life remained acquisition and accumulation, there was little time—or inclination—for anything else.[56]

Not all of Pittsburgh's late-nineteenth-century businessmen and bankers and lawyers were rich, of course; many operated on a more modest scale of prosperity. Beneath the second tier, in what was becoming an increasingly segregated and stratified city, were doctors, clergymen, schoolteachers, shopkeepers, and publicans (and, just occasionally, bright men with bright ideas, who would seek Andrew Mellon's support); and on the next rung down was the large labor force whose heroic exertions in the mines and the mills ultimately made possible Pittsburgh's astonishing industrial growth. As factories grew in size, and became ever more mechanized, the demand for labor—especially the unskilled kind—seemed to expand exponentially, and more workers, usually lumped together as "Hungarians," were brought in from central Europe, as well as from Poland and Russia.[57] They were prepared to accept lower wages than the indigenous working class, and they often made less than two dollars a day. Shifts in the mills were usually twelve hours long; the only holidays were the Fourth of July and Christmas; industrial accidents were frequent and ghastly; most workers were unable to continue beyond their forties; and unemployment was an ever present anxiety. Their experience of Pittsburgh was a world away from that of the affluent East Enders: housing was squalid, unsanitary, and overcrowded, especially near the mills; the atmosphere, the streets, and the rivers were polluted with industrial effluent; and disease, especially typhoid, was endemic. The city government felt little obligation to the poorer areas or people of Pittsburgh, and at the end of the nineteenth century there was still no water filtration system. And what use were the local libraries donated by Carnegie for those who worked all day, every day, from dawn until dusk?[58]

Late-nineteenth-century Pittsburgh was, then, a metropolitan Janus: one aspect a dynamic industrial region, the other lacking in many of the most elementary amenities; an economic miracle, but also "Hell with the lid taken off." Truly, it was a place of extremes. As one contemporary put it: "First prince, then pauper; overwork, then underwork; high wages, no wages; millionaires, immigrants; militant unions, masterful employers; marvellous business organization, amazing social disorganization." It inspired both awe and revulsion among inhabitants and visitors alike, and it witnessed the confrontation between unbridled capital and organized labor at its most raw and antagonistic. By the early 1890s, Pittsburgh ranked third after New York and Chicago in frequency of labor disturbances.[59] On the one side were the industrial working classes: some who had acquired skills in the heyday of iron resented the massive influx of unskilled labor in the new steel mills; others supported the Amalgamated Association of Iron and Steel Workers and were adamant in demanding better wages and conditions. On the other side were the bosses, who regarded labor as just another production input, who by the inexorable logic of market forces were determined to drive down all costs, labor included, still further, and who (like the Judge) reviled trade unions and were determined to crush them. This perception of Pittsburgh, as a city caught in a "system which makes one man a millionaire [and] makes tramps and paupers of thousands," was vividly and horrifyingly dramatized in two infamous episodes in which it was very clear where the Mellons stood.[60]

The first resulted in the tragic Johnstown Flood of 1889. Johnstown was an industrial community in the Conemaugh Valley in Cambria County, and ten miles northeast of there, in the Alleghenies, Frick had established in 1878 the South Fork Fishing and Hunting Club as one of the first of those exclusive local recreational societies which would later proliferate. Its members included Carnegie, Knox, and Andrew Mellon, and it was known with good reason as "the bosses' club." Its central feature was an artificial lake, five miles in circumference, with excellent boating and fishing facilities and, along its shore, a clubhouse and private cottages. It was maintained by an earthen dam. In order to preserve the fish stock, the club was fenced off, and poachers were dealt with severely. On the night following Memorial Day 1889, after an unprecedentedly heavy rainstorm, the lake overflowed, the dam broke, and twenty million tons of water crashed into the valley below. Johnstown was overwhelmed, 2,000 people perished, and 1,600 homes were destroyed. There was an immediate outcry against those privileged rich whose pleasure park had put so many lives in jeopardy, and the club was sued for negligence in its maintenance of the dam. A relief fund was set up: Carnegie gave $10,000, Frick $5,000, and Mellon $1,000. The legal defense was mounted by Philander Knox, who successfully argued that the flood was an act of God and that therefore the club was not to blame. He also donated, on behalf of Knox and Reed, $50 to the relief fund. Most of the club members, including Andrew Mellon, declined to make any public comment.[61]

Three years later, an even more controversial episode occurred at the Homestead steelworks, which was owned by Carnegie and managed by Frick.[62] The Amalgamated Association of Iron and Steel Workers was well entrenched there, and in 1889 they had wrung some concessions from the management, much to Frick's wrathful dismay. Both he and Carnegie were determined that come the next showdown, the union would be defeated and organized labor expelled from the mill. For three years, Frick laid his plans, and when negotiations with the union collapsed in the early summer of 1892, he made his move. (Carnegie had conveniently absented himself in Scotland, from which safe distance he urged Frick on in private.) Having fortified the steelworks, Frick discharged the labor force and brought in Pinkerton agents for protection, while he employed scab labor to break the strike and the union. But the Pinkerton men met with stout resistance, and after a fourteen-hour-long "Battle for Homestead," which resulted in deaths on both sides, they surrendered to the proletarian mob. Thereafter, eight thousand Pennsylvania National Guardsmen were sent in to restore order. They protected the works until November, by which time the strike was effectively over. Meanwhile, Frick survived an assassin's bullet, largely thanks to the timely intervention of John G. Leishman, and realized his ambition of breaking the union. He was advised throughout by Philander Knox, who ensured that Frick's actions remained legal, and later prosecuted the strike leaders for murder. Frick's outstanding virtues, Knox concluded, were "charity, generosity, justness and patriotism."[63]

The steelworkers would not have agreed, but the Mellons certainly did: their support of Frick against labor was no less staunch than it had been during the great rail strike of 1877. Soon after hearing of the attempt on Frick's life, which he claimed was the heaviest shock he had ever received, the Judge wrote Frick to urge upon him "the necessity of quiet and mental repose." "You need," he went on, "a complete rest." "The public," he concluded, "as well as your friends have a deep interest in your perfect recovery."[64] In January 1893, he welcomed home Andrew Carnegie with an even more stirring letter of support and encouragement, saluting his recent "noble utterances" on "the Homestead affair," in which Carnegie had praised Frick's "ability, fairness and pluck." The Judge went on to declare that Frick was "by no means the hard and arbitrary man who had been depicted by labour parasites." The stand taken by Carnegie Steel and "the firmness with which it has been maintained" had, he insisted, "met the general approbation of the best and wisest classes." The labor leaders, who were irresponsibly supported by the press, he continued, were "corrupters of public sentiment" and "promoters of socialism and anarchy." And he concluded by expressing the confident hope that time "will purify the public mind on the aspersions so unfairly cast upon your firm and its management."[65] These hopes would prove vain, and the bitter memory of Homestead would linger. But like his embattled Ulster Presbyterian forebears, the Judge, ever determined not to yield an inch, rejoiced in the union's defeat and demise.

Like father, like son: in any confrontation between capital and labor, Andrew Mellon was on the side of capital, and in any battle between Republicans and Democrats, he was on the side of the Republicans. Since the rise of the Flinn-Magee Republican machine, Pittsburgh was in effect a one-party city, and it soon became notoriously corrupt, as Lincoln Steffens would show in *The Shame of the Cities*, an eloquent muckraking tract published early in the new century, but drawing much of its evidence from the 1890s. It was, Steffens believed, virtually impossible to do business in Pittsburgh without coming to terms with the Flinn-Magee organization. How involved was Mellon? He was certainly a financial contributor to the party, and when the politicians wanted special outlays, they invariably went to him. Also, since Magee's fortune was in transport and natural gas and Flinn's in road construction and building contracts, it seems inconceivable that their paths did not cross Mellon's in the course of doing business—as they had with his father.[66] He may personally have kept his distance from the machine bosses (after all, he kept his distance from most people); but it was widely believed that W. L. Mellon did his uncle's "dirty work," especially during the late 1890s and early 1900s, when the family became deeply involved in streetcar lines in the city.[67]

Mellon clearly took the same detached, pragmatic view of politics at the state level, where the Republican Party machine was similarly dominant.[68] The Pennsylvania legislature, in which both Flinn and Magee sat, was one of the most corrupt in the country, not least because of the influence exerted on it by the Pennsylvania Railroad and Standard Oil, and also by Carnegie and Frick. Indeed, it was jocularly known as being the best that money could buy. And that was not all the Republican dominance that big business bought. So complete was the machine's control of the state that between the end of the Civil War and the beginning of the New Deal, only one Democratic governor was elected in Pennsylvania. During the same period, no Democratic senators were appointed or elected to represent the state in Washington. And between 1860 and 1928, Pittsburgh and Allegheny County never voted for a Democratic presidential candidate. To all intents and purposes, Pennsylvania was a one-party state, and for much of this time, the Republican organization was dominated by three men: by Simon Cameron from 1865 to 1877, by Matthew Quay from 1877 to 1904, and by Boies Penrose from 1904 until his death in 1921. All three of them were corrupt, even by the lax standards of the time.[69] For nearly half a century, no other state party was as well entrenched, and it was generally recognized that the Pennsylvania Republicans ran "the most unscrupulous machine in the country."

Andrew Mellon accepted this Republican dominance in Pittsburgh and Pennsylvania as part of the natural order of things—indeed, as the best of all possible worlds. Union Trust, Philander Knox, and Frick all dealt with Matthew Quay concerning jobs and money and spoils, and he was given whisky from the Overholt Distillery and a portrait that Frick had commissioned. According to Arthur Vining Davis, Mellon used his influence in Washington, via Quay, to ensure that adequate burdens were placed on imports of foreign aluminum in the McKinley Tariff of 1890, which effectively protected the domestic monopoly of Pittsburgh Reduction.[70] (He was probably rather less enamored of the Sherman Antitrust Act, passed in the same year, which declared monopolies and combinations "in restraint of trade" illegal.) Like his father, Mellon never doubted that politicians were a low and inferior form of life. But he also accepted that a close connection must exist between business and politics, and since "business was the supreme occupation of man," it was important that those in politics understood this. The Republican Party did.[71] As someone who was "primarily a businessman in my training and outlook," Andrew Mellon wished "to see policies adopted which will make for the prosperity of business," and he was perfectly willing to exert himself and to spend money to ensure the election of pro-business legislators and their continued espousal and promotion of such policies.[72]

Two relationships explicitly illustrate Mellon's complex combining of friendship, business, and politics. One was with Benjamin Franklin Jones, a friend and neighbor, whose niece was the ill-fated Fannie Larimer Jones whom Andrew had courted in the early 1880s. Jones was a founding partner in the American Ironworks, which later evolved into the Jones and Laughlin Steel Company, one of the greatest enterprises in the city after the Carnegie and Frick conglomerate; his son, B. F. Jones Jr., would later become a director of Union Trust and of the Mellon National Bank. During the 1880s, Jones Senior was chairman of the Republican National Committee, with responsibility for obtaining generous benefactions from fellow manufacturers, who naturally expected (and got) consideration when the party did well.[73] The second relationship which bears further scrutiny was with Philander Knox, whose lawyerly skills had been so important for the business elite after the Johnstown Flood and during the battle for Homestead. In the aftermath of Frick's bloody and brutal triumph, Knox was involved in some very shady property dealing with Frick, Carnegie, and Magee, in which fraud and perjury undoubtedly took place. Four years later, in December 1896, after McKinley's electoral victory (to which Knox and Reed had donated ten times the amount they had given for relief in the aftermath of the Johnstown Flood), both Frick and Carnegie urged the president-elect to appoint Knox as attorney general. The appointment was not made, but it was a portent.[74]

Andrew Mellon and his brother Dick were both fiercely partisan, and there was an obvious synergy between their commitment to capitalism and their support for the Republicans, which intensified as the free soil/free labor party of Lincoln became increasingly allied with rich men and big business. Yet despite their determined allegiances, they were inconspicuous in the battles of the time, whether against labor or the Democrats. Andrew loathed the limelight, and as bankers and financiers, he and Dick were always distanced from the production and manufacturing processes. Their names were rarely on public display, and like Carnegie, they were happy to see others, such as Frick, bear the burdens (and opprobrium) of prosecuting the battle against labor.[75] They were also very secretive about the details of their business dealings, preferring their companies to be closely held, with few shareholders, and without publicly traded issue. "Why list a good stock on the Exchange?" Andrew Mellon once asked. They published the briefest of annual reports and did all they could to keep out of the newspapers. "We have your recent request for a statement," T. Mellon & Sons informed R. G. Dun on January 18, 1898, "and beg to say in reply that it would not suit us to make you a statement of our affairs, especially in the form you desire, as we have always kept the particulars of our business . . . to ourselves."[76]

To Lincoln Steffens, such opacity was selfish, irresponsible, rapacious, dishonest, corrupt—and widespread. "The typical businessman," he opined in *The Shame of the Cities*, "is a bad citizen . . . He is a self-righteous fraud." "The commercial spirit," he went on, "is the spirit of profit not patriotism; of credit not honor; of individual gain not national prosperity; of trade and dickering, not principle."[77] Yet all his life, Andrew Mellon believed such criticisms to be ill-founded and malevolent. Like his father before him, he saw no shame in acquisitiveness, and he thought himself a businessman of probity, integrity, decency, and honor, who was motivated by the highest ideals of local allegiance and devotion to country. Indeed, the brothers were very loyal: to each other (Dick once threatened to strike Frick for a comment mildly disparaging of Andrew); to their clan ("try to keep the family together" was Dick's repeated exhortation); to their collaborators in business (there were exceptions later, but they were rare); to their subordinates (many of them, like Mitchell, would stay on for a lifetime); and to their depositors (whose requests for credit were treated sympathetically). And after their own fashion, they were abidingly loyal to their city. "We are here to do all we can for Pittsburgh" was another constant refrain of Richard Mellon's. "There is," Andrew agreed, "no reason why these large companies in which we are interested should be here in Pittsburgh except that we have always lived here and have a natural civic interest . . . That is why these companies are here, instead of New York or any other convenient city."[78]

Andrew and Dick believed that their style of banking was both creative and public-spirited, and its fruit was "enduring and abiding work." Like the Judge, they considered greed and dishonesty in business as sins to be despised, and more typical of Wall Street than Pittsburgh. "I have never made anything myself in speculation," Andrew told one correspondent who had asked advice on making money quickly. "My father taught me to shun it, and I must say that all my observation in business had corroborated the fact that money cannot with any degree of safety be made in that way. Investment for prospective increases in value is another thing, but that method would be too slow to accomplish what you desire."[79] It was, however, the method Mellon preferred and perfected. He rarely sought quick profits, nor did he demand especially high dividends; he was committed to nurturing companies to prosperity, and once the business was in the black, he would always plow the earnings back into it and build up a surplus. Only occasionally would he allow profits to be distributed among shareholders, and then usually in the form of "stock dividends." In eschewing financial fast breaks and in their devotion to "making something grow," Andrew and his brother believed themselves not just high-minded, but statesmanlike and patriotic, building up the nation's economic resources and productive capacity in ways that would ultimately be of widespread benefit. For the result of an expanding economy would be "the general prosperity of all," since "the condition of industry necessarily affects all the other elements in the community."[80] In this they were early trickle-down fundamentalists.

By common consent, Andrew was the cleverer and the more gifted brother. "If you want to borrow $5,000, you see Dick; if you want to borrow $25,000, you see Andy" was soon a popular saying in Pittsburgh. He was thought to possess exceptional powers of judgment, both of the character and capacity of the men who sought help and of the feasibility and potential of the schemes which they presented—and he was especially open to the commercial possibilities of emerging science and technology. Having read Herbert Spencer to his purblind father, he retained the lessons of thoughtful analysis of any problem, the value of breaking it down into its constituent parts, and then putting it back together.[81] "How can I help you?" or "What can I do for you?" was invariably his professional greeting, the inquiries expressing both his sense of himself as a creative enabler and his wish to ascertain the facts. He was widely regarded as the best listener in Pittsburgh; in fact, it was his trick to let the visitor do all the talking, and stop him but occasionally with a pointed question: "What makes you think so?," "Can this thing be owned?," "Whom have you done work for?" And his eye for the balance sheet was unerring, homing in as if by instinct on the pertinent (or most suspect) figure: "What does this mean?" he would ask of one item, having glanced over several columns of figures that would have left a lesser man dazed. Most applicants for loans were turned away, some summarily ("Here's the trouble with the whole scheme"), others with painfully elaborate explanations ("There are five good reasons, gentlemen, why your undertaking is bound to fail"). But there were also the fortunate few who heard: "I may be able to help, but I cannot, of course, guarantee that," "I must consult my brother," or "See Mr. Mitchell. He will fix you up."[82]

Part of Andrew Mellon's strength as a banker derived from those very traits that inhibited his sociability: his shyness, his aloofness, his self-sufficiency, his calculating reticence, his inscrutable silences, his determination to keep his innermost thoughts to himself. He was invariably courteous with customers, but his face gave nothing away (it is not surprising that he was good at poker), he rarely looked them in the eye, and he seldom spoke, and then only haltingly. On entering the bank each morning, he followed his father's habit of never speaking to the staff, which may only have magnified the awe they felt for him. Slight in build, with brown hair and mustache, and with blue eyes which to some seemed dreamy and distant (when he was withdrawn into himself) and to others like "sharp blue daggers" (when he was about to pounce in some transaction), he gave the impression of a pensive abstraction that somehow coexisted with decisive efficiency.[83] He dressed well, but not ostentatiously: he was someone who could "wear a two hundred dollar suit and no one be aware of it." In fact, he was beautifully turned out and manicured, and very proud of his hands (in later years, when his portrait was regularly painted, he always checked to see that they had been done full justice). He was thus the very antithesis of the popular, hostile stereotype of the overfed, loudly dressed, bulbous-nosed, coarse-voiced capitalist, and there was no hint about him of the robber baron, much less the shop floor, the steel mill, or the coal mine. His friends were few, his recreations limited and conventional, his way of life understated. He chain-smoked small cigars, "needles" to him, "rat tails" to his friends. Obsessively and compulsively hardworking, he seems to have had neither time nor inclination for emotional involvements after his brief liaisons with Minnie Caldwell and Fannie Jones.[84]

Dick Mellon was wholly different from his brother in appearance, temperament, tastes, and habits. He was large, well-fed, hearty, with a round, genial, smiling face, and full of life and fun. He had a ready tongue, a lively sense of humor, a pretty wit, and he was a good storyteller. On entering the bank, he greeted the staff with warmth and good humor. But he was also subject to moods that took him from gaiety to depression, and on occasions to ferocious outbursts of bad temper. Where Andrew was

cool and detached, Dick was warm and spontaneous, never so hardworking or focused on business as his elder brother. His daughter Sarah would
sum them up quite aptly: "Uncle Andy had great business ability. Father
had a little more of the human ability, and a great sense of humor which
Uncle Andy lacked."[85] When they jointly interviewed customers or loan
applicants, Andrew would ask his few pointed questions, while Dick
would reminisce or make small talk to fill the silences. He loved the
details of the banking business, rather than the big picture, and he followed Andrew rather than leading in those industrial ventures that eventually made them two of the richest men in America. But Andrew had
great respect for his younger brother's abilities, never making a major
decision without consulting him, and when Dick took over as head of the
bank in the 1920s, it thrived as never before.[86]

At T. Mellon & Sons, they famously worked in adjacent offices, regularly passing back and forth through the connecting doors, which swung
both ways, for communion and consultations, always "Dick" and "Andy"
to each other. In his younger brother's company, all Andrew's shyness and
reticence seemed to melt away. His frequent use of the phrase "My
brother and I" can only hint at the close personal bond, the mutual
esteem and regard, and their collaborative business methods. (It also
meant that responsibility was shared, and saved Andrew from having to
face anyone alone.)[87] To be sure, they occasionally invested separately,
and the management of their father's fortune had devolved exclusively on
Andrew. But in general, they aimed to put identical amounts into the
companies and concerns they supported, and to ensure that they were
equally involved in their affairs. The capital they provided came from various sources: from their personal wealth, from the Judge's fortune, from
T. Mellon & Sons, or from the other banks they owned, but its disposition
was always decided as if by one mind. Though based only on the informal
agreement imposed on them by the Judge in 1887, theirs was an airtight
partnership. Their talents and temperaments were complementary, and
their persons were inseparable, both at the bank and at 401 Negley.
"They were entirely different," Dick's son Richard King Mellon later
recalled of his father and his uncle. "But the pair, I might say as a son, was
almost unbeatable . . . I never saw a better team."[88]

IV. SETBACKS AND SUCCESSES

Like the 1870s and 1880s, the mid-1890s saw a financial panic ensnare
Pittsburgh: across the whole economy, the Judge's rule of "five [years] up

and five down" still obtained. But the crisis which began in April 1893 was much more serious than that of the mid-1880s, and W. L. Mellon would later judge it worse than those of 1873 or 1907.[89] Once again, there was a global recession, in part because of overproduction in agriculture, in part owing to a delayed international reaction to the Baring Crisis of 1890, when excessive involvement with dubious Argentinean securities brought one of London's most venerable merchant banks close to ruin. But there were also particularly American reasons. Many of the railway companies were financially unsound, with too many redundant lines. The Sherman Silver Purchase Act of 1890 had furnished the flexibility of backing the U.S. dollar with silver as well as gold, but this had had the unintended consequence of hurting domestic business confidence and weakening the currency on foreign exchange markets, which in turn made America's European investors jittery. And from the beginning of his presidency in early 1893 there were doubts about Democrat Grover Cleveland's competence as steward of the economy, especially in regard to the tariff question. At almost exactly the time that Cleveland's term began, the New York Stock Exchange collapsed, gold reserves fell, and businesses, banks, and railroads (among them both the Union and the Northern Pacific) failed across the land.[90]

"On every hand," the Pennsylvania Republicans asserted, "can be seen evidence of Democratic times, the deserted farm, the silent factory and workshop, and in large cities soup societies (the only industry created by the Democratic Party) abound." In Pittsburgh, Frick steered Carnegie Steel relatively unscathed through the dismal aftermath of Homestead, but the winter of 1893-94 was especially severe, with factories closing, workers laid off, and unprecedented amounts of relief disbursed by the city and by private individuals. In March 1894 a civic fund was established to put unemployed men back to work, and in the following month the vanguard of Jacob Coxey's "army" of unemployed passed through Pittsburgh en route to demonstrate in Washington, D.C.[91] Although the traumas of 1873 would not return, these were difficult times for Andrew and Dick Mellon. Real estate values went down again; T. Mellon & Sons generated no surplus for the brothers between 1892 and 1896, and they were obliged to carry over losses; they were only able to continue lending money to their clients and their companies by drawing on the Judge's fortune; and the profits of the Pittsburgh Reduction Company slumped from $139,000 in 1893 to barely half that in each year from 1894 to 1896. It was not easy to make money, and as his father had done in the aftermath of 1873, Andrew responded to these challenges with varied strategies and various degrees of success.[92]

One response, certainly aggressive but ultimately fruitless, was the attempt to take control of the Pittsburgh Petroleum, Stock & Metal Exchange. The aim was to consolidate the Mellon position in the city's economy by acquiring another potential source of industrial capital, which might effectively become a subsidiary of T. Mellon & Sons and Union Trust, and one that should generate a substantial income when trading in stocks picked up again.[93] Andrew Mellon had been a director of the exchange since 1883, but hardly an active one. In truth, it didn't merit much attention: its level of activity had always been low, and its part in the capitalization of Pittsburgh's growing businesses and expanding firms had been modest to date. Industrial securities were slow to catch on, oil was scarcely traded after the Standard Oil Trust took control of the local markets, and after the 1893 panic, trading virtually halted, and the exchange could barely justify its existence. Indeed, it was all but insolvent, when its property was sold for $150,000 in August—to the Union Trust Company, which soon after moved to its premises. Meanwhile, Andrew Mellon had coaxed many members of the exchange to give up or sell their seats to him, so that by the end of 1893, he controlled three-quarters of them, as well as owning the building through Union Trust.[94]

Mellon seemed on the brink of an audacious success, but he did not possess the rights to the exchange's charter, and this fact emboldened those brokers and directors who had opposed his heavy-handed intrusion to organize a new exchange for themselves early in 1894.[95] Initially it was located in the same building that now belonged to the Union Trust Company—not exactly a declaration of independence—but by 1897 the refurbished exchange was independently established in its own place. Mellon's bid for ownership and direct control had failed. Beaten but unbowed, he remained a force in its affairs, reverting now to his preferred means of exerting indirect influence via one of his many local business colleagues. Among the leading brokerage houses operating in the new exchange was Whitney & Stephenson: George I. Whitney not only invested with Andrew Mellon, but also advised him on securities transactions, and later helped him underwrite and syndicate many of his corporate takeovers. He had a wide range of business interests in coke and transport companies; he also sat on the boards of Mellon-backed companies, and was a director of the Union Trust and of the *Pittsburgh Chronicle-Telegraph*. Thereafter Union Trust was always represented on the exchange, and so was T. Mellon & Sons.[96]

At the same time that the Mellons failed in their bid for control of what had become the Pittsburgh stock exchange, they also gave up the struggle against Standard Oil—but only at what may have been a fair, or even a good, price.[97] To be sure, they were the largest of the "independent" producers in Pennsylvania, but their companies were still new, and the recent pipeline construction had been a drain on their time and resources. In addition, the depression was wreaking havoc on the oil business: domestic demand dropped, there was a serious slump in overseas trade, and there were growing (and justified) fears that the McDonald Field would soon run dry. Such dismal circumstances provided the ideal opportunity for Standard Oil to crush its remaining competitors with the brute force of its superior financing. When their burgeoning Lima Field in Ohio and Indiana came on full stream, already depressed oil prices went down still further. At the same time, within Pennsylvania itself, the Standard resorted to price-fixing chicanery, driving the price of crude oil up in the west and that of refined oil down in the east. For the Mellons, who needed crude to be cheap so as to profit by refining it, the squeeze was unbearable.[98]

The remaining independents formed an association to resist the Standard's strangulation tactics, and protest meetings were held in many towns in western Pennsylvania, Pittsburgh included. Despite their earlier insistence that they were in the business to stay, the Mellons decided it was the better part of valor to do no further battle with Goliath: at the end of 1895, they sold all their oil operations to the National Transit Company, a subsidiary of the Standard. The negotiations were complex and protracted, initially between Andrew Mellon and H. H. Rogers for Standard Oil. Subsequently, W. L. Mellon took over. Foolishly taunted by Rogers for his youth, he determined to drive a harder bargain, and the final selling price was variously reported as between $2.5 million and $4.5 million.[99] If the lower figure is correct, the Mellons barely recovered their initial outlay. But if the upper figure is nearer to the mark, they made a very substantial profit indeed. Either way, it was for them a much-needed infusion of capital, and for Standard Oil the coup de grâce in its monopoly of pipelines in Pennsylvania. As WL recalled, the Mellons "were out of oil, and meant to stay out." Indeed, the Rockefellers maintained the deal included a pledge never to go into oil again, a promise the Mellons would later vehemently deny.[100]

Andrew Mellon may have invested some of the proceeds in a new venture, the Carborundum Company, which had been founded in Monongahela City, thirty miles south of Pittsburgh, by Edward G. Acheson in 1891.[101] Unlike his college-educated counterparts at the Pittsburgh Reduction Company, Acheson was a self-taught inventor who had worked for Thomas Edison at his Menlo Park laboratory in New Jersey (they subsequently fell out), and also at Westinghouse's laboratories in Pittsburgh, where he had invented an anti-induction wire. He was a great enthusiast of thermally generated electricity, and it was with the aid of a crude electric furnace that he first fabricated the new abrasive substance he called carborundum (a misnomer, since the crystals making it up were not of carbon and corundum but of silicon carbide). The stuff was incredibly strong and diamond-hard: a thin sliver could slice a pane of glass with relative ease, a wheel edged with it could tear through rock and stone, and in powdered form it could also smooth and polish metal.[102] To produce this new substance, Acheson founded his company with $200,000, allocating a majority holding to himself in consideration of his patent rights.

Eventually, the industrial demand for this remarkably versatile material would prove almost unlimited. But early on, and as with the Pittsburgh Reduction Company, high production costs restrained demand and ate up the profit: the only real takers were dentists interested in his product for their drills. In addition, Acheson was a poor manager, his former mentor had shortsightedly decided the product had no future, and buyers for the patents in France and Germany could not be readily found. Then came the panic of 1893. In the following year, Acheson determined to move his plant to Niagara Falls, in search of cheaper power, and he also proposed to issue $75,000 worth of first mortgage bonds. His original backers now pulled out of the company, and Acheson had to find new ones in the depths of the depression. Sometime in 1895, he met Andrew and Dick, and demonstrated to them the properties of the material. The brothers were deeply impressed, especially when Acheson scored a paperweight on Andrew's desk with one of his crystals. As with aluminum, the Mellons instantly grasped the commercial potential. They bought $50,000 of the bonds, receiving in the deal one-sixteenth interest in the common stock of Acheson's company, amounting to $12,500, in consideration of the attendant risk.[103] Andrew became a director, and thereby enjoyed an option to purchase further blocks of stock on favorable terms.

Little did he know just how risky an enterprise Carborundum was—as long as Acheson continued in command. For despite the Mellon infusion, the company remained in the red, with bills left unpaid and salaries in arrears. An accountant dispatched by Andrew to Niagara Falls found the books chaotic and impossible to balance. Nevertheless, during the next two years, the Mellons poured in more money and were granted additional stock bonuses: they soon became very significant shareholders.[104] Still things got no better. "The whole concern," Dick Mellon wrote to Acheson in August 1897, "is sadly in need of push and energy," and, he added ominously, "unless an immediate improvement is shown, we shall have to put in some one to protect our interest." When no such improvement took place the following year, Andrew wrote, pulling no punches: "I am sorry to see the disposition on your part to treat the Carborundum Company as if it were an outside concern in the welfare of which you are not interested." The business, he went on, "was practically bankrupt": it would "have been wiped out of existence beyond any doubt had it not been for our support," and there was a real danger that "my brother and I will have lost an immense sum of money." "I still hope and believe our investment will come out right," he concluded—but while Acheson remained in charge, that seemed unlikely.[105]

During their early years with Pittsburgh Reduction, Andrew and Dick found the managers, who were also the principal owners, exceptionally able, and these men blossomed with Mellon support. In the case of Carborundum, however, the management was very bad, and the Mellon money seemed to make no difference. By mid-1898, the Mellons had secured a majority interest, and they now made good on Dick's threat.[106] Acheson remained president of the company, continuing to hold one-third of the stock (which would eventually become exceptionally valuable). But the Mellons, no longer prepared to tolerate him as chief executive officer, moved to put the day-to-day management of the company in the hands of Frank W. Haskell, long a protégé of theirs in Pittsburgh, as well as secretary and treasurer of the South West Connellsville Coke Company, in which Mellon and Frick had joint controlling interest. Haskell was no inventor and no scientist, but he was a good accountant and an efficient administrator. The results were immediately apparent. In the fiscal year ending June 1897, the company deficit was $53,000; by the following year, it had been reduced to $8,000. But while the future looked less bleak, Carborundum was, after four years of Mellon involvement, still a struggling uncertainty, a gamble that had yet to pay off. Was the Judge aware of the situation? If so, what did he think? "What would Father have done?" Probably not what Andrew was doing.[107]

Setbacks with the Pittsburgh stock exchange, in the oil business, and now with Carborundum made the depression of the mid-1890s a particularly anxious time for Andrew Mellon and his brother. But there were two bright spots on this otherwise dismal horizon. Pittsburgh Reduction was "growing" promisingly, and seemed well positioned to become a self-sustaining and highly profitable enterprise. Output in 1898 was up nearly fivefold from three years before, and the price of aluminum was down to 36 cents a pound. Earnings had dipped severely in the mid-1890s, with a net loss in '97, but profits in the next year were the best since '93, and thereafter they rose year after year until 1902. The company's vertical integration also went on apace: the acquisition of new mines in Alabama enlarged the secure supply of bauxite; all smelting operations were consolidated in the Niagara Falls plant; and the manufacture of aluminum products, especially kitchenware, continued to expand.[108] Indeed, by 1898 aluminum was a well-recognized commodity, for both industrial and domestic use, making Pittsburgh Reduction the first authentic triumph of the "Mellon system," and Andrew and Dick were eager to acquire more shares in the company.

But the brothers' greatest success during these years was in an industry rarely associated with them, since the evidence of their involvement in it is extremely sketchy. One of the reasons for the Pittsburgh Reduction Company's slow start with aluminum was the mounting production of competing minerals: not only copper, zinc, tin, and lead, but also (in part because of concerns about the dollar) gold and silver. Indeed, mineral prospecting was almost as intense as the quest for oil, and it was greatly assisted by the transformation of mining and milling technology, with the introduction of dynamite, electric power, and machine drilling. Mining had ceased to be an old-style, amateur, and individual enterprise; now it was big business: it was mechanized, it needed substantial capital, and the profit potential was enormous. Not surprisingly, moneyed men from the East Coast were attracted, among them Charles Schwab, the Harriman brothers, and the Rockefellers. H. H. Rogers, who had negotiated the purchase of the Mellons' oil business, oversaw the Rockefellers' mineral interests, and in 1899 he would put together another two mineral combinations, the Amalgamated Copper Company and the American Smelting and Refining Company, which was devoted to silver.[109]

Although bloodied in their previous battle with the Rockefellers, the Mellons, too, were drawn to mining during this costly, expansive, and profitable phase. Thanks to the Larimer and Caldwell families, they had by now long-established connections out west. They also acquired another interest in a utility at this time, the Colorado Light and Power Company, which further consolidated their business interests in that region, and the Pittsburgh Plate Glass Company would soon open a plant in Denver. Moreover, both John Galey and James Guffey were as excited about searching for minerals as for oil. It is possible, though unprovable, that the Mellons developed extensive mining interests across several mountain states, perhaps using spare proceeds after the sale of their oil companies to Rockefeller. If it was so, however, it was probably not with Galey. In a letter of March 1897, Andrew Mellon observed that he had, "in the last year, been scattering money here and there in the West in several mining operations, unwisely I think." Andrew went on to write that he had consistently declined to lend Galey money, "because it is so difficult to collect that I always feel we can keep better friends by refusing in the first place."[110]

Guffey, on the other hand, collaborated closely and profitably with Andrew Mellon at just this time. In July 1891, the Trade Dollar Consolidated Mining Company was incorporated in Kentucky; by 1895 its president was James Guffey, and by 1897 its vice president was Andrew Mellon. The financial records have not survived, but it is scarcely conceivable that Mellon was not a major investor. The headquarters were in Pittsburgh, but operations were near the aptly named Silver City, on the southern slopes of the Florida Mountains in Idaho, where the Mellons had previously dealt in land and property. It was an extensive undertaking, with five miles of tunnels and three miles of track, as well as a mill, shops, and offices. A local directory called it "a full and complete mining and milling outfit," and it was further claimed that "the officers at the eastern end have been liberal and progressive, and management at this end conservative and intelligent."[111] For the best part of a decade, the returns were very handsome indeed. In 1897, the mine's output was worth $735,000, of which $420,000 was profit. And on May 15 the following year, Thomas McKaig, the company secretary, wrote to James Hutchinson, the mine superintendent: "We have deposited in the bank here since April 1st $159,123.57, and if that is not turning out money fast, nothing is."[112]

He was right. It seems highly likely that a considerable portion of the revenue went Andrew Mellon's way, and that may in turn have helped him finance more ambitious ventures at the very end of the nineteenth century and on into the first decade of the twentieth. In 1899, Trade Dollar Consolidated merged with the Black Jack Mining Company and the Florida Mountain Mining and Milling Company, but the Trade Dollar's management remained dominant.[113] Throughout this time, Guffey continued as president, but Andrew Mellon kept tight control, regularly attending directors' meetings and occasionally going to Silver City on site visits. He would retain his interest as long as the mine remained profitable, which was until about 1910, when output declined rapidly and the business was subsequently sold. This may explain why Trade Dollar has never appeared in any accounts of the Mellons' financial empire.[114] But in the late 1890s, it was probably their most successful venture, its profits far outstripping those of the bank or of Pittsburgh Reduction. It was a bright spot on what was still, in many ways, a bleak financial and economic landscape.

4

THE GREAT LEAP FORWARD
Mergers and Matrimony, 1898–1900

We were now in the way of material progress. Industry and thrift, with reasonable judgment to guide, will always prosper.
Thomas Mellon and His Times, p. 33

I. ON THE THRESHOLD OF CHANGE

The years of the "great depression" had been interesting times for the Mellon brothers, but no one looking to the future in the mid-1890s would have predicted the major enlargement in their fortunes that Andrew would very soon bring about. Suddenly, and unexpectedly, the global economic climate changed, as did the national mood, and Mellon, like many in business, would be both an agent and a beneficiary of this transformation. The Spanish-American War heralded the arrival on the world stage of the United States as a great power, and Theodore Roosevelt, the most charismatic and assertive president since Lincoln, would welcome the opportunity to project his country's influence around the globe. This remarkable display of national confidence and assertiveness was underpinned by an equally exceptional economic boom. In the brief period from 1898 to 1900, before Roosevelt entered the White House, America extricated itself from the great depression and suddenly surged forward in ways that amazed and intimidated observers, assuming the position of the world's most powerful economy—a position which, a hundred years later, it still occupies. One indication of this new energy and expansiveness was a sudden mania for mergers and consolidations.[1] So many vast new enterprises were created, and so great was their power and reach, that some Americans began to worry that these trusts (as they were all called) and their owners were becoming so rich, powerful, and monopolistic as to be above, beyond, and outside the law.

On the eve of this great transformation, and as the nineteenth century waned, in some ways the Mellon family seemed unchanged. Now in his late eighties, the Judge still occasionally ventured downtown to visit T. Mellon & Sons, the bank he had founded nearly three decades before, clad in his formal, antebellum business attire and leaning on a knotted hickory cane, to withdraw a few dollars for his now-meager wants. He habitually lunched at the Henry Hotel on Fifth Avenue, but as he refused to spend more than the twenty-five cents he had paid for lunch his whole life, Andrew arranged for the bank to cover the tab as prices rose. Most days, however, the Judge was found at home, in his rocking chair, beside his wife, with his grandchildren and staff taking turns reading to him. "Time lies heavy on one's hands when we cease to need it," he lamented to his son James Ross in 1897. "After spending as long a life-time as I have done in its profitable use, then ceasing to make any valuable use of it at all is too radical a change to be agreeable." He was no more cheerful writing to his niece Lillian: "I need hardly inform you," he declared in the same year, with a typical lack of self-pity, "that I am dying. It may be years before I pass out, and happily I am suffering no pain, only the gradual decay of mental and vital faculties. My mind is breaking down, especially as to recent events, and physical faculties weakening, from which I had derived most pleasure in the past, and general weakness prevailing."[2]

He still sometimes engaged with the world. He gave interviews to the local newspapers about his early life, and he corresponded with James B. Corey, one of his earliest business partners and by now one of his very few surviving contemporaries. "In this life I have arrived at the outlet gate," the Judge observed, "and have no better friend than you to tell me where I am to go, when let out." "Mistakes or untruths in religion," he went on, in his familiar vein of scientific skepticism, "if they are found to exist, should be eradicated by all religious men." As he had always insisted, faith alone was not enough: reason was also essential. Still he believed and trusted in God, and had "hope for a future life."[3] He also remained in touch with Andrew Carnegie, who sent a comforting letter informing the Judge that "I think often of you. There is a freemasonry between characters that commonplace people cannot enter. You are always in that circle in my thoughts." How far the Judge reciprocated these feelings is uncertain. He had never liked Carnegie's monstrous industrial agglomerations, he disapproved of his philanthropic efforts (and, indeed, of philanthropy in general), had hardly disposed of his wealth in the way Carnegie had recommended, and (had he known of it) would have scorned Carnegie's weak and vacillating stance vis-à-vis Homestead. Carnegie's world in Pittsburgh was never really that of the Judge, who, like his sons, much preferred Frick.[4]

Although his days of striving for himself, and of painstakingly charting his family's course, were long since over, the Judge reigned still as the Mellon patriarch. Since the death in 1898 of his last remaining sister, Eliza, he had no siblings left. Meanwhile, Sarah Jane continued to preside over the house and carry out her charitable activities, clad in black funereal enough for Queen Victoria and wearing a wig that merely drew attention to her increasing baldness. She supported local organizations concerned with the welfare of the aged, and she worshipped at East Liberty Presbyterian Church, still eagerly mobilizing as many of the Mellon clan as possible to attend on Sundays. The service was followed by a long, silent lunch at one of the Mellon homes, where uncles and aunts, brothers and sisters, and assorted cousins consumed roast beef, watery peas, and lumpy mashed potatoes, all washed down with iced water. Wine was conspicuous by its absence, though the men allowed themselves a whisky and cigar afterwards. The Mellons did not go out in Pittsburgh society, for which the Judge had neither liking nor respect, preferring to keep to themselves, and the annual calendar of family occasions remained unchanged. The New Year was still rung in at 401 Negley, and the shared birthday of the Judge and Sarah Jane celebrated there as always on February 3. At Thanksgiving, the Judge and his wife, accompanied by Andrew and Dick, joined James Ross and Rachel, and for Christmas Day they went on to Thomas Alexander and Mary's.[5]

As these arrangements suggest, the extended yet exclusive family life of the Mellons was largely sustained by the two elder married brothers; the financial life of the clan was, of course, nurtured by Andrew and Dick. For Thomas Alexander and James Ross, home now came before business, and after their initial spurt of Mellon enterprise, they never again demonstrated the drive, energy, or originality that Andrew and Dick were beginning to display. But for Thomas Alexander this settled existence proved fleeting: in 1898, when still in his early fifties, he was diagnosed with cancer of the mouth and throat, no doubt brought on by the cigars that he had chain-smoked for decades. He lingered the best part of a year before dying a painful and gruesome death.[6] Though considered a millionaire earlier in the decade, his personal estate when he died was not large: scarcely in excess of two hundred thousand dollars. But it did not include property, and perhaps he had, following the example of his father, already passed some of his wealth on to the next generation. His investments included shares in the H. C. Frick Coke Company, the St. Clair Inclined Plane Railway, the Pennsylvania Railroad, and the Union Insurance Company. Thomas Alexander left his estate to be managed not by Andrew but by his brother James Ross Mellon, who had been his business partner for most of his life.[7] Of the eight children that Sarah Jane had borne, only three now survived. They were, indeed, the fittest of this "eugenic family": James Ross, Andrew, and Dick would all live into the 1930s.

For his part, James Ross, having turned forty in 1886, was happy to take things easy. He retained his presidency of the East End Savings and Deposit Bank, a largely titular office, and he soon withdrew from active involvement in the Mellon Brothers coal and lumber business. For many years, he had been only a part-time Pittsburgh businessman, preferring to winter with Rachel and the children at Palatka in Florida. In 1899, he made a second sentimental journey to Ireland, and on his return he set out to create a replica of the Mellon house at Camp Hill in his garden in Pittsburgh. Neither particularly driven nor particularly talented, James Ross had made enough money to live comfortably and happily, and while his other children were something of a disappointment in business, he took pride in his confident (and accurate) prediction that his son WL would one day be richer than he was.[8] Meanwhile, freed from the demands of the oil business, William Larimer Mellon had fallen in love with Mary Taylor, whose parents were neighbors of James Ross and Rachel's at Palatka. Mary's father, Matthew Taylor, had been born in Glasgow; a graduate of the university there, he had been a civil engineer, and had entered the asphalt business in Trinidad. So his daughter was appropriate Mellon bride material; she was regarded in the clan as "a fine girl." WL married Mary in Florida in March 1896, and while the Judge was too frail to attend the wedding, he was soon presented with his first great-grandchild.[9]

Soon after, in November 1897, Dick Mellon married Jennie King, who had been something of a childhood sweetheart, and whose father, Alexander King, was one of the great glass manufacturers in Pittsburgh. Like Mary Taylor, she was from appropriate stock. Born in Ireland, Alexander King had immigrated to America, carrying with him a passion for Burns to rival the Judge's, even naming one of his sons Robert. Jennie was as outgoing, sociable, and gregarious as her husband and brought money to the marriage; eventually they set themselves up in a massive Tudor-style house at 6500 Fifth Avenue, which boasted sixty-five rooms, eleven bathrooms, and extensive gardens.[10] It was one of the grandest dwellings in Pittsburgh, and soon became the center for lavish social occasions, where liveried footmen stood in waiting at elaborate dinners. The furnishings were heavy and fussy in the manner of the time, and the decorations were generally of dubious taste, including several buffalo heads, mementos of Dick's Dakota years, which he would increasingly romanticize as the happiest and freest of his life.[11] The marriage of Dick and Jennie left Andrew the only unwed brother, still at home with his parents at 401 Negley, and when their son Richard King Mellon was born in 1899 (he would be known as RK), his uncle Andrew was doubtless given to feel that life outside business was passing him by. If Andrew, rather than his eldest brother, had died in 1899, he would have been remembered as a Pitts-burgh bachelor businessman of only the second rank.

Judged by the high (and hedonistic) standards of the late-nineteenth-century American plutocracy, Andrew Mellon did not have much to show for himself or his labors. The 1890s had witnessed the spectacular growth of some colossal American fortunes, reaching not only tens of millions of dollars (among them those of Huntington, Havermeyer, and Morgan), but now for the first time hundreds of millions (notably those of Rocke-feller, Gould, and Stanford)—and all of these figures must be multiplied by at least twenty for their present-day equivalents.[12] Already in his early forties, having been in business for over two decades, Andrew was not in this league: T. Mellon & Sons was still a private country bank; his oil busi-ness, while prospering for a while, had come and gone; the Pittsburgh Reduction Company and the Carborundum Company had not yet taken off; and his silver-mining ventures out west, although undeniably success-ful, were dwarfed by the Rockefeller copper combine. To be sure, the Pittsburgh working class might regard Andrew Mellon as a prodigiously wealthy man, but in a nation that already boasted four thousand million-aires, their ranks growing year by year, his wealth was nothing special. Noting the recent and "rapid growth of riches" in the previous twenty years, the New York society leader Ward McAllister observed in the early 1890s that "millionaires are too common to receive much deference; a fortune of a million is only respectable poverty."[13]

Put another way: as the century neared its end, Andrew Mellon could not have afforded to emulate those East Coast "robber barons," with their palatial chateaux on New York's Fifth Avenue, their ornamented "cot-tages" in Newport, their extravagant parties, their oceangoing yachts, their retinues of servants, and their arranged marriages to impoverished but titled European aristocrats. Nor did he wish to do so. He liked traveling, but the vulgar, ostentatious world of the America's Cup, of East Coast high society and transatlantic cosmopolitanism, as depicted and dissected by Henry James and Edith Wharton, was decidedly not to his taste. He was amazed when his nephew WL bought himself an oceangoing yacht, the *Vagabondia*—though his surprise did not prevent him from availing himself of its comforts for vacations. For Mellon, New York was a place to do occasional business, and from which to board the ship to Europe; unlike Carnegie and Frick, he had no ambitions to own a house there, nor any wish to build himself a place in the country or a cottage on the coast.[14] He thought such living self-indulgent, wasteful, and unpatriotic; he did not like big houses, whether urban or rural; he was wholly uninterested in birds or flowers or trees or landscape; and although he could ride, he was not very good at it, and did not enjoy it. Nor did he have any fancy for the symphony or the opera or the ballet: indeed, years later Paul Mellon remained doubtful whether his father could have told Chopin from Cole Porter. The limits of his indulgence were cigars and whisky at the Duquesne Club, and low-stakes poker with Frick and other friends.[15]

By the end of the nineteenth century, both Philadelphia and Pittsburgh had their fair share of the ever more common breed called the millionaire: 206 and 86 respectively in 1890, which put Philadelphia ahead in absolute numbers, but Pittsburgh led in per capita terms, and many more would appear in the next decade as the steel industry continued to expand. Even in his hometown, Andrew Mellon by no means enjoyed financial preeminence. Carnegie and Frick, the steel and the coke kings respectively, outranked everyone else, their fortunes nationally rivaling all but the greatest East Coast accumulations, and Carnegie would soon surpass most of them, too. In August 1898, the combined value of Carnegie Steel and the H. C. Frick Coke Company was put at $300 million, and in that year, Carnegie's income from earnings, dividends, and interest was $10.52 million. But several others, mostly in the steel industry, were also significantly ahead of the Mellons, among them the Jones and Laughlin families, Henry Oliver, Henry Phipps Jr., and William Thaw.[16] Moreover, the style and mentality of these superrich Pittsburghers was beginning to change. Gradually, during the late 1890s, they acquired more cultured and more cosmopolitan airs, leaving behind their forebears' austere morality and philistine aesthetic, of which Judge Mellon had been such an intimidating upholder and exemplar, with his undying hostility to leisure and to any form of "artificial wants." Across Pittsburgh's affluent East End, what Elizabeth Moorhead recalled as the "worst mid-Victorian taste," along with "the whole Presbyterian repression," began to give way to a lighter and more leisured atmosphere.[17]

One sign of this change was the growth of cultural amenities in the East End itself: a theater, a dance academy, two preparatory schools, and a "society" journal appeared in the late 1890s. At the same time, there was the gradual establishment of what might be termed civic culture and civic philanthropy, exemplified by the creation of Schenley Park, the establishment of the Pittsburgh Symphony Orchestra, and the inauguration of a public conservatory and a zoo. But most significant was the opening of the Carnegie Institute in November 1895, an elaborate cultural complex containing a scientific wing, a library, a museum, a concert hall, and an art gallery, developed out of the original benefaction which the Judge had so vehemently opposed during the 1880s. The opening was marked with a great exhibition, displaying more than two hundred paintings by European and contemporary American painters.[18] No such thing had ever been witnessed in Pittsburgh before, and it stimulated a burgeoning interest in art among the industrial elite, so much that by the end of the century there were several major collections in the making: not only that of Frick, but also those of Alexander Byers, Charles Lockhart, Henry Porter, and David Watson, to name those only of the first rank. With this developing local market came the aim of serving it (and also of stimulating it), and so the New York dealer M. Knoedler & Company opened a Pittsburgh branch in 1897. Presided over by Charles Stewart Carstairs, this outpost would remain in the city for a decade.[19]

Pittsburgh was the only place outside New York where Knoedler maintained a gallery during this period, and Carstairs was probably the single most important dealer in helping to form the tastes of the city's industrial rich. He built up a good business, even though most clients considered paintings primarily as wall decorations and their tastes ran to the very conventional. No matter: Carstairs took care not to push, and was not in the business of inducing aesthetic epiphanies. Most buyers sought pleasing landscapes or family portraits by commission, and this explains Knoedler's vigorous local promotion of Robert W. Van Boskerck, a landscape artist born in New Jersey, and Théobald Chartran, a French portraitist.[20] Also popular were such now largely forgotten painters as Cazin, Harpignies, and Ziem, who specialized in rather predictable landscapes and historical scenes. The slowly emerging exception to this rather drab uniformity was Frick, although his interests and tastes evolved more slowly than is sometimes recognized. During the late 1880s and early 1890s, his purchases had been very conventional, and it was only at the very end of the nineteenth century, perhaps in some sort of delayed reaction to the Homestead debacle and the deaths of two of his children, that he became more adventurous, and began to move toward fine eighteenth-century English portraits and European old masters, buying his first Romney in 1898 and his first Rembrandt in the following year.[21] But in end-of-the-century Pittsburgh, he was rather an exception.

As late as the mid-1890s, the Mellons played no part in the local revolution in sensibility, nor did they participate in the more relaxed, convivial, and civically oriented phase of Pittsburgh society. Andrew did join the boards of the Carnegie Institute and his alma mater, but he was recruited more in recognition of his financial acumen rather than for his cultural interests or passions.[22] Despite his friendship with Frick, he was not interested in buying art, and his introduction to pictures, perhaps unsurprisingly, was born of an impulse more dynastic and commemorative than aesthetic or cultured. In January 1896, sponsored by both Frick and Knoedler & Company, Theobald Chartran arrived in Pittsburgh, seeking work from the town's most prominent citizens. Frick took the lead, commissioning portraits of Henry Phipps Jr., Andrew Carnegie— and Judge Mellon. This last proved an arresting work, depicting its subject as "a man of fine, strong intellectuality," but with glazed eyes that seem almost unseeing.[23] The painting, destined to be a gift to the Pittsburgh Bar Association, was such a good likeness that the Judge's sons, apparently led by Andrew, instructed Chartran to make a copy, and to complement it with a matching portrait of Sarah Jane. The two commissions, negotiated through Knoedler at $5,000 apiece, were completed in the spring of 1896; and at the same time, Dick Mellon paid Chartran another $2,000 to paint a portrait of his bride-to-be, Jennie King, which would hang at 6500 Fifth Avenue.[24]

Thus was Andrew Mellon indirectly introduced to fine art, with Frick as the catalyst, although rather later than is generally supposed. Indeed, it seems likely that it was only on their travels to Europe in the summers of 1896, 1897, and 1898 that Frick and Mellon began to talk seriously about art, and it was during precisely the same period that Mellon began— tentatively, conventionally, and cheaply—to buy.[25] There was nothing distinguished or discerning about his first purchases, certainly not in their cost, but not in their quality either: they were very much what any rich Pittsburgher of the time might have acquired, and not remotely in the league of Frick's recent acquisitions. But they were all undertaken through Knoedler, with whom Mellon established a close relationship that would endure, with occasional interruptions, for the rest of his life. Between August 1896 and October 1898, he bought six paintings for a total of $10,000, including a modest landscape by Henri-Joseph Harpignies (*Soleil Couchant sur l'Étang*), and a large historical genre portrait by the American Frank D. Millet (*Anthony van Corlear, the Trumpeter of New Amsterdam*). The latter had been shown at the Royal Academy in London, the National Academy of Design in New York, and the Carnegie Exhibition of 1895 in Pittsburgh, which is where Mellon must first have encountered it. Frick was a great supporter of Millet's, and the purchase met with his resounding approval.[26]

Of course, as a middle-aged bachelor still living at home with his parents, Andrew Mellon had no walls of his own on which to hang pictures: indeed, the Millet was soon on loan to the Duquesne Club, where it hung over the mantelpiece in the room where he and his friends gathered daily for lunch. His next purchases were also intended to adorn other people's walls. In December 1898, Mellon bought six landscapes by Van Boskerck for $3,500, and instructed Knoedler to distribute them one apiece to his parents, his three brothers, and WL as Christmas presents. Mellon legend has it that he commissioned the artist to travel to Ireland to paint the family homestead and the surrounding sights. But Knoedler records suggest that Andrew simply called at the gallery one day and, seeing some paintings he liked, bought them on the spot.[27] In any case, he was by now a regular client, and from August 1899 to July 1900, he would spend $25,000 on six more canvases, including Troyon's *Cows in a Meadow*, which at $17,000 was by far his most expensive purchase to date; Cazin's *Moonlight, Écluse sur le Loing;* and two more tableaux by Van Boskerck, *Sunset, Pulborough, Sussex* and *Mid-Summer, Brandon, Vermont*. By mid-1900, his total expenditure at Knoedler, including the portraits of his parents, which he seems to have paid for entirely from his own pocket, was just under $50,000 (or $1 million in today's value).

These early purchases hardly prefigured a great art collection, or even suggested a good eye. Many years later, John Walker, who eventually became director of the National Gallery of Art in Washington, D.C., would dismiss them as "mediocre" and expressed relief that they had "mercifully disappeared." Doubtless they were well within the provincial parameters established by Lockhart, Byers, Watson, and other Pittsburgh art collectors of the time. Mellon bought what they bought, his interests developing in line with theirs, and like them he was guided by Charles Carstairs, who would become his closest friend at Knoedler. Unlike Frick, who was already outstripping his peers in taste and ambition, Mellon showed no interest at this time in old masters or in outstanding specimens of eighteenth-century English portraiture. Many years later, he asked Roland Knoedler: "When I first started buying pictures, why didn't you offer me Gainsboroughs, Rembrandts, Frans Hals, etcetera?" To which the dealer replied: "Because you would not have bought them." He was probably right. Still, there was the odd glimmer of habits and ambitions to come: in September 1899, Mellon spent $750 on an untitled portrait of a woman by the English artist Henry Singleton. He was no great painter himself, but he had been a follower of Sir Joshua Reynolds.[28]

"He was all business," one associate would later recall of Mellon in these years; "he had no time for or interest in much else. Except pictures— his one hobby."[29] And even that recreation had scarcely begun. He was in his early forties and had a few male friends, but he was both shy and self-sufficient. He worked prodigiously hard, poring over figures and accounts and reports day and night, on weekdays and weekends. But after twenty-five years of such ceaseless, unrelenting endeavor, his name was hardly known outside Pittsburgh, partly because of his highly localized base of operations, partly because of his unostentatious wealth (much of it tied up in private companies), and partly because of his tendency toward secrecy and self-effacement. Much to his great contentment, he was hardly ever in the newspapers, and if nothing else, the relative modesty of his success happily allowed him to be overlooked by the burgeoning antitrust campaigns. By the end of the 1890s, those two titans of an earlier generation, Rockefeller and Carnegie, were about to retire from business and devote themselves full-time to giving away some of their vast fortunes. But for the younger Andrew Mellon, the great phase of accumulation was just about to begin, and in just the next two years, he would propel himself toward the very top tier of American wealth.

Notwithstanding his differences from the general style of the super-rich, Mellon's drive to acquire was an essential, perhaps preponderant, element of his nature, and had already become largely a substitute for, and an escape from, personal intimacies and commitments. Such single-minded pursuit of money is often associated with some form of stunting in emotional growth, which success at accumulation intensifies rather than relieves. Thus it was already with Mellon.[30] Not surprisingly, many among the superrich were dour and anxious and humorless men, especially those of Scotch-Irish background: "Millionaires who laugh are rare," Andrew Carnegie once observed, and Andrew Mellon was mirthless in proportion to his wealth. To be sure, he himself believed that there was "no typical case" of the extremely affluent. Perhaps he was right. But as Mellon's career moves into a more intense phase of activity, and as he simultaneously embarks disastrously upon matrimony, we should remember F. Scott Fitzgerald's dictum that "the rich are different from you and me."[31]

II. MELLON AND MERGER MANIA

Andrew Mellon was so retiring that it was easy to miss two of his even more defining traits: his ambition and his aggressiveness. He was as eager to acquire and to accumulate as his father had been, and despite the life-long filial deference embodied in his mantra "What would Father do?," he had already shown himself to be more skilled and more adventurous at acquiring and accumulating than the Judge had been. Indeed, as David Finley later recognized, Mellon could in some ways be startlingly asser-tive, especially when it came to closing a deal.[32] He was too reticent to be called personally overbearing or intimidating, but he was clearly excited by many aspects of business, especially the execution of his own plans. This was never more so than during the boom years on either side of 1900, the most successful period of his career, when for the first time he operated in a generally buoyant and expanding economy and his range of activities substantially broadened. To be sure, he still sought to develop businesses vertically, both backwards to their sources of supply and for-wards to their market operations. But he also now took part in some of the major consolidations of the time, involving the horizontal integration of companies with similar products; in various ventures (some successful, some not) in the steel industry; and also in public utilities in Pittsburgh. Such, indeed, was the scale of his endeavors that on two occasions he set aside his normal preference for "closely held" companies and sought pub-lic funding via the stock exchange.

During these boom years, established Mellon enterprises enjoyed un-precedented prosperity. After the lean mid-1890s, when the brothers had drawn no profits, T. Mellon & Sons now began to show a substantial sur-plus. From 1896 to 1898, Andrew and Dick each received an annual aver-age of $26,629; but in 1899 the figure was $40,707 each, and in 1900 it was $103,936, the largest individual disbursement yet recorded, and the equivalent of $2 million in today's currency.[33] At the same time, the Trade Dollar Consolidated Mining Company was at its most productive and prosperous, and the profits of Pittsburgh Reduction, which had returned a loss of $14,000 in 1897, rose year by year from $87,000 in 1898 to an all-time high of $322,000 in 1900, when dividends were once again paid. Sensing that the company was at last "increasing wonderfully," with the additional plant at Niagara Falls, Mellon resolved that Arthur Vining Davis and his friends should cease to "dominate the business." He accordingly set out to buy up more shares and thus obtain a "clear majority" holding. Despite his determined efforts, he did not succeed and was obliged to "make the best of the situation."[34] Yet another sign of the times (and of the Mellons' shrewd choice of manager) was Frank Haskell's remarkable success at turning Carborundum around. Acheson was still proving difficult, and Mellon had no regrets at casting him aside. It was one of those rare occasions when a collaboration failed, and when Mellon might be said—certainly by Acheson—to have been "disloyal."[35]

Then there was a near-miraculous transformation in the fortunes and functions of the Union Trust Company, which suddenly became a much more important agent of capitalization and source of wealth than T. Mellon & Sons, which remained a private bank. In 1894, when, following five years of desultory underperformance in the transfer and registration of stock, Union Trust had seemed on the brink of dissolution, Mellon undertook a timely and prescient intervention. He insisted it venture into commercial banking and extend its range of activities by accepting deposits and making collateral loans. He also installed James S. McKean, former postmaster of Pittsburgh (who no doubt had excellent municipal contacts), as the new president, even though there was scarcely enough to pay his salary. In 1899, the capital stock of the trust was increased from $250,000 to $500,000, and the company moved to a lavish neoclassical building on Fourth Avenue, "second to none for convenience, elegance and general security."[36] On McKean's death in May 1900, Mellon tapped Henry C. McEldowney, once a messenger boy for the Pittsburgh National Bank of Commerce (which he owned, along with Frick), who by the age of thirty-one had risen to assistant cashier. Frick thought McEldowney too young, but Mellon admired his initiative, energy, and judgment and was sure he would go far. He was right. McEldowney would remain a lifelong loyal Mellon man, heading the Union Trust Company until his death in 1935, when he left an estate worth more than five million dollars.[37] Not bad for someone who had started in the mail room.

When McEldowney took over, the trust was already thriving in ways that would have seemed impossible five years before. In 1898, deposits had stood at a mere $513,000, but a year later they reached $5.13 million, and this was only the beginning. Having produced scarcely any surplus before 1895, for which year the figure was only $31,000, the trust's profits now soared: to $116,856 in 1898, to $276,343 in 1899, and to $318,972 in 1900.[38] By 1900, there were three separate, but interconnected, areas of business: a banking department, which accepted both checking and savings deposits; a trust department holding trust funds and investments for corporations; and a bond department, which bought and sold high-grade investment securities, and underwrote issues of approved corporate stock and bonds. Thanks to the trust, Andrew Mellon was now able to mobilize unprecedented sums to support his other business ventures, and it underwrote more new corporate capitalizations than any other finance house in the region. In 1899 alone, these included Pittsburgh Coal for $25 million, Monongahela River Coal for $10 million, National Glass for $2 million, and the Pennsylvania Water Company for $1.5 million. With an impressively well connected board of directors, and handsome profits now flowing in, Union Trust suddenly became the most important and strategically placed institution through which Mellon could prosecute his more aggressive ambitions in these prosperous years.[39]

At the same time that Union Trust was thus prospering, Andrew Carnegie and Henry Clay Frick had a spectacular falling-out. Early in 1899, Frick and Henry Phipps were eager to promote a consolidation of Carnegie Brothers Steel and the H. C. Frick Coke Company, with Frick buying out Carnegie. The scale of the undertaking was such that a syndicate was put together, involving the Chicago financier Judge Moore. In keeping with his new boldness, Mellon was very eager to be in on the action, but Judge Moore blackballed him, much to Frick's embarrassment and regret. "I tried to get Mr. Moore to agree to sell you an interest in his promotion," Frick awkwardly wrote Mellon in May 1899, "but without success."[40] In any case, the deal fell through later that year, largely on account of Carnegie's opposition. Frick and Carnegie thereupon quarreled bitterly, and scarcely spoke to each other again. Frick was forced out as chairman, though he remained a shareholder (as did Mellon, by virtue of his earlier holdings in Frick's coke company, which was now absorbed into the new combination). Disenchanted with the whole business, Frick considered selling his shares, and asked Mellon to conduct negotiations with an English merchant banker, Arthur Hill, a partner in Gordon, Hill and Company. In the end, this deal also fell through, because it proved impossible at the time to sell American stock in England.[41] But Frick and Mellon were clearly moving closer together, and Mellon was beginning to show an interest in the steel industry that neither he nor his father had evinced before.

The first indication of this came in December 1899, when Mellon and Frick created the Union Steel Company, in collaboration with another noted steel manufacturer, William H. Donner, who had previously been in charge of the Cambria Iron Works. It was from Donner that the original initiative for this venture had come.[42] One of the most rapidly expanding and promising areas in steel by the end of the century was the production of wire: to make nails, but also to fabricate barbed wire, the demand for which was increasingly rapidly, especially from farmers in the West who were using it to make and mend fences. Mellon was impressed by the prospects, and with his brother he established a one-million-dollar capital account in the name of Union Steel at Union Trust, bringing in Frick as well. There was to be a fully integrated steel mill at a site on the Monongahela River just below Monessen, and three hundred acres were cleared along the northeastern bank to make way for a rod and wire mill and blast furnaces. In the light of the Frick-Carnegie rupture, some saw a deliberate and direct challenge by Frick (and Mellon) to the Carnegie company in the production of steel wire. But it was Mellon who had brought Frick in, and he took pains to consult Carnegie, visiting him at Skibo Castle in Scotland in late August 1900 (where he had been promised "a highland welcome") to explain his intentions and obtain his consent.[43] The result was another closely held Mellon company, with only four investors: Andrew, Dick, Frick, and Donner held equal shares.[44]

Frick and Mellon undertook one more joint enterprise at this time, again following the familiar pattern.[45] With rising American militarism in the Pacific and the Caribbean, the massive increase in American exports to Europe and beyond, and the growing importance of sea power as recognized by Admiral Alfred Thayer Mahan, shipbuilding suddenly became as attractive an investment as the manufacture of barbed wire. So thought Henry G. Morse, who after a career in railways and engineering, and as president of the Harlan and Hollingsworth shipyard in Wilmington, Delaware, now sought to establish a great naval construction company on the East Coast for mass-producing ships, to which he hoped to attach his own plate-manufacturing steelworks. Having split with Carnegie, Frick took an interest, and Mellon also joined the venture as an "organizer." By the summer of 1900, the New York Shipbuilding Company was in business, with Morse as president and Mellon and Frick as major shareholders.[46] As the name suggested, the intended location was New York, specifically Staten Island, but it proved impossible to acquire the desired site. Instead, Camden, New Jersey, on the east side of the Delaware River across from Philadelphia, became the base of operations. By September 1900 the company was already employing 1,350 men, and the keel of its first ship was laid two months later, a tanker named *J. M. Guffey*. (The Mellons may have been out of oil at this time, but their friend was not.) Orders for more tankers and cargo ships soon followed.[47]

But Mellon and Frick did not always collaborate during these two heady and hectic years.[48] Early in 1900, and thanks to the assistance and mediation of W. L. Mellon, two engineer-inventors, Howard H. W.

McClintic and Charles D. Marshall, approached Andrew Mellon about backing a new business which would produce structural steel for skyscrapers, bridges, and other major construction. They had risen as far as they could within their department in the Shiffler Bridge Works Company, and fearing that the business would be purchased by J. P. Morgan's American Bridge Company (as it subsequently was), they foresaw that their own prospects would be much diminished. They explained to Mellon that they needed $50,000 to get their own venture started. With due diligence Andrew and Dick checked out McClintic's and Marshall's backgrounds, informed themselves about the burgeoning boom in skyscraper building (in Pittsburgh and elsewhere), and concluded that there was, indeed, an expanding market for structural steel. But they also believed the company needed twice what was asked, and a quarter was put up by Andrew, a quarter by Dick, and the rest by McClintic and Marshall—with a Mellon loan, which they later paid off from the company profits.

Capitalized in March 1900 at $100,000, the McClintic-Marshall Construction Company thus had only four shareholders: Andrew and Dick (who took 60 percent of the stock), and their two partners (with 40 percent). Frick had once again been asked, but had refused to join. "Don't touch it," he warned Andrew. "There is no chance whatever for success." He could not have been more wrong, as McClintic and Marshall became the greatest steel-fabricating business in the world, and an outstanding example of a Mellon-developed company. No stock was ever sold, requests to put the company on the stock exchange were declined, and during the thirty years of its existence, it never paid a dividend: McClintic and Marshall took living expenses out of the profits, and plowed the rest back. As with Pittsburgh Reduction, the Mellons left the management to the managers: McClintic was responsible for design and construction, Marshall oversaw contracts and daily finance. But without fail, they consulted Andrew and Dick in major matters of policy, strategic finance, organization, and acquisitions. Charles Marshall regarded Mellon as "the greatest business man he had ever known," and toward the end of his life he offered a romanticized but essentially accurate account of the relations between management and capital: "All we ever had to do was to state and explain our problem to Andrew Mellon. Invariably, he replied with a double-barreled question: 'How much do you want? and when?' "[49]

A final Mellon venture into steel was different again: the creation, in 1900, of the Crucible Steel Company, which consolidated a loose association of thirteen of the region's leading specialty manufacturers, among them La Belle Steel works, owned by Philander Knox's father-in-law.[50]

The combined companies were purchased for $19 million, and subsequently capitalized at $50 million, half in common stock, half in preferred. In tightening this alliance, whose members specialized in producing very high quality steel by the crucible method, Mellon was moving away from growth and vertical integration to consolidation and horizontal integration. It was a novel move for him, and he sought a novel method of financing. Generally with new ventures, Andrew and Dick were the leading, often majority, shareholders in what were unlisted enterprises: Pittsburgh Reduction, Carborundum, Union Steel, and McClintic-Marshall. But with Crucible Steel, Mellon turned to the open market, because the many ventures being consolidated were heavily capitalized and their existing stock amounted to a substantial sum. Since new stock would be needed to replace it, Mellon decided that the easiest way to raise the necessary funds was to float the combine publicly. Once again, the company began well, soon enjoying a near monopoly in the production of high-quality steel. Indeed, for a time it was the world's largest producer using the crucible process.[51]

In scarcely twenty-four months, then, Andrew Mellon had amassed an unrivaled portfolio of interests across the Pittsburgh region and beyond. No longer just a small-scale, private banker, he was now a major financier and businessman, hungry for action and eager to intervene. During the same period, he was also involved in the creative reorganization of the local coal industry in a manner far beyond anything his father had achieved or envisaged. By orchestrating a bold consolidation of Pittsburgh's coal production, he believed he could increase profits. His plan was to combine hundreds of small companies (many previously owned by the Judge) into two large enterprises according to how they distributed their coal, which was either by rail or by river. This was easy to do, because most used one means or the other and had either railroad spurs or river coal tipples. But very few had access to both. Accordingly, Mellon resolved to create two new, consolidating companies, Monongahela River Coal (for those using the water) and Pittsburgh Coal (for those dependent on the railroad).[52] Ostensibly they were separately managed businesses. But Mellon closely coordinated the two firms, devising different funding streams for each, in the determined belief that this would result in increased efficiency, reduced transport costs, and bigger profits.

Pittsburgh Coal began with authorized capital stock of $2,000, divided into twenty shares, preferred and common in equal numbers, of which Mellon's Union Trust owned seventeen. In order to buy out the many small operators who depended on rail transport, Mellon increased the capital to $64 million, creating 640,000 shares at a par value of $100. To ensure that this amount of capital stock was subscribed, Mellon once again (as with Crucible Steel) veered from habit and went outside, seeking out Judge Moore of Chicago, the very broker who had recently vetoed his involvement in the abortive Carnegie buyout. But Mellon never allowed personal matters to interfere with good business, and Moore, too, was a pragmatist: he helped underwrite the stock and bond offering, along with Union Trust. The new company promised investors handsome dividends on both preferred and common stock, and this, along with the combined prestige of the Moore and Mellon names, meant that within the first year, nearly all of the $64 million had been subscribed, much of it by "widows and orphans." Thus launched, associates of Mellon and Moore fanned out across the region, attempting to bring every coal mine located on a rail spur into the new combine. The effort netted 80,000 acres of coal lands and 5,000 railcars, and Mellon believed that this new, streamlined monopoly would result in an additional profit of $6 million a year.

Meanwhile, in June 1899, the Monongahela River Coal Company began operation, with $1,000 capital. One of the directors was George I. Whitney, also on the board of Union Trust, with close ties to the Mellons, who held sixteen of the twenty shares. During the summer Whitney and Mellon obtained pledges and covenants from the many local companies that they wanted to merge. In September (no doubt at Mellon's behest, since the Union Trust Company was the underwriter), Monongahela River Consolidated Coal & Coke Company (as it was now known) raised its capital stock from $1,000 to $30 million, which enabled it to acquire "the lands, mines, coal, leaseholds, steam boats etceteras" of eighty-one coal and manufacturing properties. Monongahela also absorbed forty-four riverboat companies which owned 80 steamboats, 3,000 coal barges, dozens of tipples, and coal ports from Pittsburgh to Cincinnati, Memphis to New Orleans. The board was increased from four to nine, of whom three were Mellon nominees, including James B. Finley as chairman. Finley had been a founding director of the Union Trust Company, and was clearly installed to do his master's bidding. From the beginning, the company controlled more than 70 percent of all river coal traffic and nearly half of all river freight tonnage. Not for nothing was it known as the "queen of the waterways." By 1901, the Monongahela River Consolidated and Pittsburgh Coal combined were responsible for 11 percent of U.S. coal production.[53]

During these years, the Mellons also intervened assertively in Pittsburgh transport. As with oil, the family had some previous experience in the business, thanks to the Pittsburgh, Oakland and East Liberty Passenger Railway and to the Judge's later mixed legacy in incline planes. But here, too, Andrew adopted a much more aggressive approach, though again he personally stayed out of it and thrust WL forward as the public face of the enterprise, with help from Walter S. Mitchell and George S. Davison, both loyal family retainers.[54] After the sale of the family oil companies to Rockefeller and his marriage to Mary Taylor, WL urgently needed something to do, and Andrew and Dick took him back as their "outside man" at the bank: in part to sniff out new investment opportunities; in part (one suspects) to handle the unavoidable dealings with the Pittsburgh city government and the Flinn-Magee ring. Late in 1897, WL concluded that it would be a good idea to bridge the Monongahela River, linking Braddock on the north side with Homestead on the south, both mill towns with large Carnegie factories. There was substantial potential traffic, not only in people, but also in freight, and so it seemed an excellent opportunity. WL took over a bankrupt bridge-building company, and the West Braddock Bridge was duly constructed, strong enough in the end to carry a streetcar line. This led WL to imagine there might be more opportunities in building, operating, and consolidating streetcar lines in the city. With Andrew and Dick's blessing, he was back in business.[55]

By the late 1890s, Pittsburgh streetcar lines were dominated by two companies: the Philadelphia Company, which took over the United Traction Company in October 1899 (and which, despite its name, was a private company and not a municipal undertaking); and the Consolidated Traction Company, owned by Elkins and Widener of Philadelphia, who had already had dealings with the Mellons in the oil business. Unintimidated, the Mellons now entered the fray from their base at Homestead and Braddock. They bought lines, consolidated them, built new ones, and soon were expanding to the north and east of Pittsburgh, and south along the Monongahela Valley.[56] They also arranged with Consolidated Traction for essential access to downtown, Pittsburgh being the terminus of most of the lines. W. L. Mellon was the ideal agent for these activities: he had bought farmland for oil prospecting earlier in the decade, and now he was acquiring franchises for streetcars. In the distant suburbs, he purchased land and negotiated with the local authorities, buying up the votes as necessary to obtain the franchises. Such is the clear implication of Burton Hendrick's account: "No capitalistic group," he wrote, clearly knowing more than he let on, "in any American city obtained franchises for street railways and other like utilities except by making terms with the corrupt politicians who held such matters in their hands."[57] As a result, there were fifty-five miles of "Mellon lines" by the end of 1900. Along with T. Mellon & Sons, they carried the family name throughout their city.

More than ever, Pittsburgh was the focus of Mellon enterprises, but for at least two decades the family had been "mixed up in mining" in states well beyond Pennsylvania and in minerals other than coal. The recent success of the Trade Dollar Consolidated Mining Company may have led to, and probably helped finance, the acquisition of the Spring Valley Mining and Irrigation Company in 1900.[58] It was based at Cherokee in California, the mountainous area which had witnessed one of the earliest gold rushes half a century before, and had been established in 1862. The method of mining was hydraulic, meaning that water was used to wash gold out of gravel; hence the enterprise required an extensive network of reservoirs, ditches, siphons, and flumes. The Mellons bought the business via Union Trust, renamed it the Cherokee Company, and installed as manager L. J. Hohl, who immediately undertook an extensive program of repairs, and then began renewed operations, "washing down the mountain." The business paid its way but was never a spectacular success, and the power potential of the water rights would eventually prove more valuable than the gold deposits. "In the end," Mellon once told David Finley, "the greatest profit we made was from something we never thought of at first."[59] Compared to the other initiatives, the Cherokee Company was scarcely a moneymaker, but it is a reminder of the broad reach of Mellon interests, and one more indication of their astonishing level of business activity and intervention at this time.

For Andrew Mellon, groomed to be a private banker, this two-year foray into the industrial world represents a quantum leap of endeavor and imagination. He saw the moment, seized the opportunity, and took his chance, with an impressive combination of calculated aggression, right timing, and cool nerve. And the result, an elaborate structure of interlocking enterprises, transformed him almost overnight into a much more significant figure on the Pittsburgh business scene. The demands on his attention must have been unrelenting: he was required not only to devise and oversee so many complex and varied deals, but also to provide funding packages, management assistance, and even technological advice for numerous companies.[60] This unexampled feat of acquisition and accumulation had its sordid side: the determined monopoly of local coal companies and the dirty political dealing over streetcars. But as with the Republican Party in the city and the state, Mellon turned a blind eye, tacitly condoning corruption in politics while, with some exceptions, striving to be high-minded in business. In any case, and despite the pressing demands of work, he also had other things on his mind. "Are you married yet?" Carnegie asked in August 1900, as they were discussing the future of Union Steel. Mellon's answer would very soon—and, as it turned out, very unfortunately—be yes.[61]

III. AN ILL-JUDGED MARRIAGE

As the nineteenth century gave way to the twentieth, Andrew Mellon's life was transformed in another way: he fell suddenly, completely, and hopelessly in love. At the relatively advanced age of forty-three, he briefly threw off the silent, self-absorbed, and self-sufficient persona he had inhabited since his mid-twenties.[62] Since the late 1870s, he had risen early, taken the train to work, spent the day closeted at the bank, breaking only for lunch at the Duquesne Club, and retired in the evening to 401 Negley, usually bringing documents home with him for intensive study, after a silent supper with his parents and perhaps a little time spent reading to the Judge. But as for himself, "he read few books, spent little time in outdoor sport, saw few plays and heard almost no music; business, tireless and unremitting, formed the consuming passion of his life."[63] To be sure, there were his local duties with the Carnegie Institute and the Western University of Pennsylvania, but they scarcely amounted to much time or diversion. And despite being one of Pittsburgh's most eligible bachelors, he had become almost incorrigibly antisocial. "I would rather have a panic day at the bank," he once wrote to a friend, "than the burden of an evening function of that nature"—by which he meant a social event.[64]

Yet in the summer of 1898, as Mellon suddenly began to transform himself "from the status of country banker to that of industrial financier," he also turned no less deeply and abruptly and assertively to love.[65] In June, he had been traveling with Frick and his wife from New York to England, on one of their regular summer trips, aboard the White Star liner *Germanic.* In the course of the voyage, Frick introduced his friend to Mr. and Mrs. Alexander McMullen of Hertford, and also to their daughter Nora, who was nineteen. Thus did Frick present Andrew with his future wife, just as Andrew had assisted Frick in meeting his bride, Adelaide Childs, seventeen years before. The McMullens were returning to England after a round-the-world tour that had included India, China, and Japan (where, it was claimed, they had witnessed a public execution); their journey would later become the basis of "pleasant and instructive lectures" to local literary and debating societies. Nora was the youngest of nine children, and all her siblings were boys. According to Burton Hendrick, she "had all the qualities of the typical English out-of-doors girl":

she was an energetic and accomplished horsewoman; she sang and painted in an amateurish way; and "her fresh complexion, blond hair, graceful slender figure, quiet and friendly manner, and charming, buoyant youth made a strong impression on her new friend."[66]

Unlike almost anyone else upon first encountering Andrew Mellon, Nora McMullen found him easy to talk and to listen to, and they were soon conversing at length, with Andrew holding forth on a variety of subjects with a vivacity and a fluency that would have amazed Pittsburgh. "In her presence," Hendrick subsequently wrote, "the famous Mellon reserve vanished like a cloud before an April breeze. To establish talkative relations with Andrew was at best a difficult, long drawn out process, but this girl evidently possessed the gift, known to few, of immediately putting him at his ease."[67] When strolling on deck or taking tea, he talked about business, inventions, industry, finance, art, galleries, and travel. Nora, having met few men of the world and being utterly inexperienced, was much flattered by the attentions paid her by this older and wealthy man. Perhaps it was her very naïveté that freed him from his customary conversational inhibitions. After scarcely a week aboard ship, they were getting on so well that the McMullens invited Mellon to Hertford before he began his continental excursion.

There he found a county town that dated back to Saxon times, with a population of less than ten thousand. Though scarcely more than twenty miles north of London, it seemed little attracted to the metropolitan orbit. Hertfordshire was a traditional, almost Trollopian English county, with rolling countryside and woodlands "offering an extraordinary sense of rural peace," with a nearby cathedral city at St. Albans, and with grandly housed aristocratic families, such as the Salisburys at Hatfield and the Cowpers at Panshanger. There was no industry or significant population centers in the county, which was predominantly Tory, and Arthur Balfour, the nephew and successor of the prime minister, Lord Salisbury, had represented the local constituency from 1874 to 1885.[68] Hertford's main business consisted of servicing the surrounding agricultural region, and it was a center of banking, brewing, and printing. The town was dominated by a Norman castle which had been a royal residence for centuries, and where Queen Elizabeth had spent some of her childhood. Thereafter, much of the original medieval structure was demolished, and in 1628 Charles I ceded it to the Salisbury family as their residence. During the late eighteenth century, it had been occupied by Lord Downshire, an Irish peer and Salisbury relation, who enlarged the place, and beautified the grounds, to make it a fit private dwelling.[69]

Hertford Castle was Andrew Mellon's accommodation for this brief visit in the summer of 1898, for Alexander McMullen lived there with his large family as tenants of Lord Salisbury. (There is no truth in the later rumor that he had deliberately rented it so as to impress his prospective son-in-law.)[70] Like the Mellons, the McMullens were of Scotch-Irish descent. William McMullen, Alexander's grandfather, had migrated from Donaghadee, County Down, to Hertfordshire, where he worked as a gardener at Hatfield House and eventually became steward to Lord Downshire. His fourth son, Peter McMullen, lived all his life in or near Hertford, and sometime during the late 1820s he became a brewer, an especially good occupation in the county because of the exceptional water that benefited from the gypsum in the soil. On his retirement in 1860, two of his sons formed a partnership to run the brewery, and the elder of them was Alexander McMullen.[71] Beyond his large family and the castle walls, he was a notable figure in the area, having long served on both the county and the town councils, and as mayor of Hertford in 1887, 1888, and again in 1896. His view of municipal government was very different from that of Judge Mellon, and he was an active supporter of the water-works, the public library, the school of art, and many other local ventures. He was, then, a quintessential civic worthy and gentlemanly capitalist, whose only daughter had been born at Hertford Castle in 1878.[72]

It would be only the first of several brief visits to Hertford: Andrew was captivated by the quaintness of the town, the romance of the castle, and above all by Nora McMullen. Although he had only been in her company for a few days, and knew little about her or her family, it seems he made up his mind very fast that he was going to marry her. On his return to Pittsburgh, he sent Nora's father a copy of the Judge's autobiography. His motivation is far from clear. Ever since the book had appeared, Andrew had been anxious to prevent it from falling into the wrong hands, fearful that his father's trenchant words on the working classes, on Irish Catholics, and on politicians might cause embarrassment or anger. But here he was, sending this idiosyncratic and opinionated chronicle to those who he hoped would become his in-laws: perhaps it was a sign of esteem and regard; perhaps he wanted the McMullens to learn what sort of family the Mellons were, despite the Judge's warts. It was certainly a confident gesture, consistent with his assertiveness in all matters at that time. Reading it nowadays, with Thomas Mellon long since gone, one might be both impressed and infuriated by this stern and ardent account of striving and success. But over a hundred years ago, with the author alive and his world and values still very much a reality, it must have seemed a most intimidating and alarming disclosure.

The Judge's utilitarian views on matrimony must have given particular cause for grave concern. To be sure, his own marriage to Sarah Jane Negley had been long and happy (after their fashion), and he had concluded the autobiography by describing his wedding day as the luckiest of his life. Nor was he indifferent to the "tender passions," writing with great warmth about the joy and comfort his family and home life had brought him.[73] But he had also written of his own marriage in exceptionally cold and calculating terms: as an enterprise, a business, a transaction, in which determination was all, and where romantic love and effusive sentiment had played little part. Had his proposal been rejected, he would have been merely "annoyed at [the] loss of time." His advice that men should marry between the ages of twenty-five and thirty made Andrew too old, and that women should do likewise between the ages of twenty and thirty made Nora too young. And his brief account of the life and personality of his favorite son can scarcely have seemed a recommendation, with its allusions to the unhappy love affair with Fannie Jones, its suggestion that he had little subsequent experience of women, and its portrayal of him as being wholly absorbed in work. As a matrimonial prospectus, it would seem a disastrous miscalculation.[74]

Having read the book, and having no doubt pondered Andrew's motives in sending it, Alexander McMullen reached the not wholly unreasonable conclusion that the Mellons were "a strange family," and since Andrew was old enough to be Nora's father, he found the age gap between them a further formidable basis for objection to their marriage.[75] But Andrew was not to be deterred: he persisted in his suit with the same determination that his father had displayed in his courtship of Sarah Jane Negley. Throughout the winter of 1898–99 he continued to correspond with Nora—and she continued to reply. In late March 1899, she wrote to "Dear Mr. Mellon," enclosing a recent photograph of herself on her horse Knapp (she loved to ride, and was more at home in the saddle than Andrew) and informing him that she would soon be traveling in Italy with her parents. "With very kind regards," she concluded, "I am, yours sincerely."[76] Andrew wrote back immediately from Pittsburgh to "Dear Miss McMullen," duly thanking her for the picture, which he had been "delighted" to receive, expressing his wish to see her again in England later in the year, and "sending kindest regards to your father and mother," he signed off "Yours sincerely, A. W. Mellon."[77]

In the summer of 1899, with business more than ever crowding in upon him, Andrew returned to England and visited Hertford again. Despite his continued reservations, Alexander McMullen clearly made him welcome, and Andrew spent several days at the McMullen holiday home at Guisnes Court at Tollshunt d'Arcy in Essex. He was taken to a garden party at Hatfield, where he met the great Lord Salisbury, Queen Victoria's last prime minister, and he later glimpsed him "lumbering into the train at Hertford Station, where a special compartment was always reserved for him." And he also visited Panshanger, the magnificent house owned by Lord Cowper, where he glimpsed for the first time the magnificent Raphael Madonna which, to his great satisfaction, he himself would later own.[78] This was a world of established wealth, of aristocratic grandeur, and of venerable houses and splendid art collections wholly unlike anything he had encountered in Pittsburgh; by association, it may have increased his longing for Nora. In any event, one of the purposes of this visit was to obtain her consent, and when he returned to Hertford later in the summer, he formally asked her to marry him. She was completely taken aback, but politely declined, refusing even his request to postpone her decision, declaring it to be final.[79]

This was confirmed in a friendly but definite letter addressed again to "Mr. Mellon," which reached him at the Carlton Hotel in Pall Mall on his return to London.[80] "I have been thinking long and earnestly about what you have said to me," Nora began, "and it pains me, more than I can tell you, to say that I have come to the conclusion that I do not love you enough to marry you." "You know without my telling," she went on,

> how much I honour and respect you, and I thank you a hundred times for the honour you have done me in asking me to be your wife. But it would be utterly unfair to you to ask you to wait at all, because even if you asked me again in time to come, there might be no change in my feeling and then you would be just as unhappy as you are now, whereas if you take my final answer now, you will get over this sad mistake you have made. For it is a mistake I am sure—you only know the best side of my character. I feel certain that if you ever got to know me well, you would be terribly disappointed—I am simply telling you this because I sincerely think it—if I thought that we should be happy, it would be different, but it would be downright wicked of me to promise to marry you when I know that I do not love you as you do me—you must see that it would mean nothing but unhappiness for us both. So do not waste your life in waiting for me, for at present I do not see any probability of changing my mind.

As subsequent events were to show, Nora was astonishingly perceptive and prescient here, especially given her youth and lack of worldliness.

(Perhaps her worried parents had helped her write the letter.) "Please forgive me," she went on, "for all the trouble I have caused you, and do not think of me as being hard hearted. . . . I am sure you will see things as I do if you look at them in the right light. . . . I cannot tell you," she concluded, "how unhappy I have been; it seems cruel not to be able to give you what you ask." And then again: "Please forgive me." She also expressed the hope that he would write, and that he would come to see her family when he was next in England. This was all the encouragement Andrew Mellon required. Before leaving for America, he responded by sending her the gift of a riding whip. "It was most awfully good of you," Nora replied to "Dear Mr. Mellon," "and I fully appreciate your kind thought." "I do wish," she went on, "I could have made the voyage a happier one to you. Of course, I cannot prevent your still hoping that I shall someday change, but I am afraid I cannot give you any encouragement for at present I do not see any likelihood of my altering. . . . You see, I am rather young still, and have never thought much about leaving home."[81]

But Andrew refused to be discouraged and sent her a letter on reaching the United States. Nora replied, belatedly, to tell him how much she appreciated the whip: "I hope you will write again when you have time and I will not be so long in answering." Then she reverted to what was by now her leitmotif:

> I still think that if ever you got to know me better I should bore you terribly. You see you really do not know anything about me and I do not know you very well. But you must be tired of hearing me say all this as I'm sure I have said it before.[82]

Shrewd and prescient comments indeed. For if Andrew had troubled himself to investigate his would-be bride and her family, as he would have done anyone visiting T. Mellon & Sons in search of a loan, he would have found that all was not to his liking. Nora herself had confessed her callowness, her limited education and experience of life. True, she had been to finishing school in Germany, and had traveled round the world, but she had rarely visited London, and she knew next to nothing of the urban and industrial nation that lay, sprawling and ugly, just beyond the confines of traditional, Tory Hertfordshire. As the youngest child and only daughter, she had clearly been indulged by her parents and brothers, her judgment was not good, and she had little awareness of the importance or value of money. Her interests were almost entirely rural and recreational, in complete contrast to those of her urban, workaholic suitor.[83]

As to the complementarity of family backgrounds, true, both were of Scotch-Irish ancestry, but Nora's family was very unlike Andrew's: the Mellons were dour, silent, embattled, and unemotional immigrants, while the McMullens were warmhearted, friendly, spontaneous, and affectionate, with no grudge against the place from which they had come. But behind the façade of civic worthiness, they were not quite as prudent or as respectable as they appeared. Peter McMullen, founder of the brewery, had been "an unruly youth" who had been fined for poaching. Alexander McMullen, the family patriarch, was more interested in spending money than in making it. Moreover, the heavy financial burden of nine children was not lessened by his sons, most of whom were also variously irresponsible. Among them, the eldest, Howard, got into gambling trouble, and was banished to South Africa. Leonard, onetime head brewer at the family business, was fired for drunkenness on his watch, and his finances were always precarious. Murray was large and lazy. Kenrick was an engineer, but never profited a whit from his inventions. Alan set out to be a schoolmaster, but wound up working at the Guinness brewery in Dublin—a profession and a place which would scarcely have endeared the McMullens to the Judge. Finally, Percy, a minor civil servant, proved to be another incorrigible lifelong gambler.[84] Taken together, these résumés suggest a family seriously deficient in both prudence and judgment—qualities which the Mellons habitually regarded as being of the utmost significance.

If Andrew Mellon knew anything of this, he chose to disregard it. He continued his postal wooing, and by early 1900, Nora was showing signs of weakening, though her father remained very anxious and unenthused. "I was very glad to get your letter," she wrote to Andrew in mid-January. "I was beginning to think you had forgotten all about me"—as she had earlier and wisely urged him to do. But now she wanted to see more of him. "There certainly does seem to be a fate against your coming over again. I hope that nothing will turn up to prevent you this time." "With kindest regards," she concluded, "I am yours very sincerely."[85] So, indeed, she now was. Presently, "Dear Miss McMullen" gave way to "My dear Nora" and "Dear Mr. Mellon" to "Dear Andrew" and, eventually, to "Dear Andy." By the spring of 1900, her change of heart was clear. Andrew returned to England in April, and she accepted his renewed proposal—as he reported in a letter to Frick; perhaps ominously, business matters took up most of the space, with the news of the engagement added as if an afterthought.[86] Mission accomplished, Andrew left his prospective in-laws to arrange the wedding and returned to Pittsburgh, where the news that he was to marry a twenty-year-old English girl from Hertfordshire proved something of a bombshell. Without consulting his bride-to-be, he bought a house, at 5052 Forbes Street in East Liberty, filled it with furniture, and engaged a staff to run it, then eagerly awaited the great event set for September.[87]

During the intervening period, Nora and Andrew corresponded as regularly as transatlantic post allowed. Only Nora's side of it has survived, with her letters now signed "ever your loving," but even half the exchange reveals much about both of them on the eve of their marriage. There are continual expressions of longing and love: "come back again quickly as you can"; "am so looking forward to letter from you." And there are encouraging signs of goodwill toward her from people in Pittsburgh: "am so glad your mother is pleased, and I hope I shall never disappoint her"; "Mrs. Frick kindly wrote to Mother and Father."[88] But there are also some disquieting straws in the wind. Nora shows herself not much interested in being a domesticated wife: "You can't think how I dread housekeeping— what dreadful muddles [I] shall get in." There are hints of sickliness, both physical ailments and neurasthenia: "my rheumatism is so much better"; "am feeling dreadfully depressed today." And there is the first iteration of what would subsequently become a regular complaint: "I expect you are so busy you are only reminded of my existence by these letters—I do wish you need not be quite so busy."[89]

It was not a union of altogether good augury. Andrew and Nora had spent little time together, and as Nora had rightly and repeatedly insisted, they knew next to nothing about each other. Their backgrounds and temperaments were wholly dissimilar, Hertford was about as unlike Pittsburgh as an English town could be, and until the day of the wedding, Nora's mother remained convinced "her daughter wasn't ready for marriage."[90] As for Andrew, he doubtless knew he was marrying far outside the normal circle for a rich Pittsburgh male. His three brothers and his nephew William Larimer Mellon had all taken wives of the right sort—proper family background and appropriate social position—who understood what was expected of them in Pittsburgh, and who happily conformed. Even Minnie Caldwell and Fannie Jones, Andrew's first two liaisons, had been women of appropriate circumstances.[91] Nora McMullen, by contrast, was not bred for this singular and straitlaced society. Indeed, the fact that Andrew had strayed so far to find a wife would later cause much resentment in the city where he had long been an eligible bachelor. Of course, transatlantic marriages were very fashionable at about this time. But they were usually between impoverished British male aristocrats and well-endowed American heiresses—another matrimonial formula to which the impending Mellon-McMullen union did not remotely conform.[92]

For her part, Nora seems simply to have succumbed to Andrew's relentless determination and persistent blandishments, but perhaps she also came to appreciate his qualities: he was probably the richest man she would ever meet, and she well knew that as her father's ninth child, she would be little provided for. But how could Andrew Mellon, who prided himself on being careful and prudent, and whose judgment of men and business was already legendary, have erred so catastrophically, rushing in where men of less sense would have feared to tread? Of course, there is no necessary connection between business acumen and emotional intelligence, and if Andrew did feel any qualms, his growing sense of midlife loneliness and isolation clearly swamped them. For as W. L. Mellon would later recall, since his own marriage and that of Dick, "AW had been growing increasingly wistful . . . There had been plenty of opportunities to notice this on those frequent evenings when he would come to my house to watch my children romping before they were put to bed. If he did not come to see me, he would go to RB's house and share the felicity there."[93] Perhaps, then, this was his final, desperate effort to break out of his self-made emotional fortress, in the hope of finding that close, personal, intimate warmth which, somewhere in the recesses of his innermost being, he craved and desired.

He was also ignoring all the advice on matrimony from his father's autobiography—the very counsel that Alexander McMullen found so abhorrent.[94] Marriage, as the Judge saw it, was both "the most momentous event of our lives" and also "a frightful risk": Andrew seems to have considered the risks not at all. "Character, temper, disposition, taste, sentiment and inclination should all be ascertained with certainty and considered carefully": this, in the case of Nora, Andrew notably failed to do. "Family, ancestry, health and position should be allowed their due weight and considered carefully": these, too, Andrew neglected to investigate. The three women the Judge had most admired were his mother, his wife, and his mother-in-law, all of them strong characters with shrewd heads for business: Nora was nothing like any of them. "Beauty" was "an excellent but dangerous substitute for either money or other good qualities in a lady": Nora in a nutshell. Not surprisingly, the Judge was against the marriage: "Don't marry an English woman, Andy," he is reported to have said. "Their manner of life is different from ours."[95] Andrew may thus have been indulging not only in an act of middle-aged desperation, but also in his one open rebellion against his father and his family. Only in his persistence and determination did he show himself his father's son.

Thus did Andrew Mellon return to Britain in August 1900, accompanied by friends and relatives, to marry a woman who was less than half his age, about whom he knew virtually nothing, a woman who was green in the ways of the world, who was not in love with him, and who had warned him that their marriage might not work (he had clearly forgotten his university essay about women's predictive powers). There were stag parties in London, hosted by Dick and W. L. Mellon, attended by such Pittsburgh luminaries as H. J. Heinz and a contingent of Duquesne Club regulars, and there were also receptions arranged by art dealers who no doubt hoped that Mellon would become a serious client, having now a house and a wife. These junkets were, WL recalled, "a test of anyone's physique to survive them all."[96] The wedding itself took place on Wednesday, September 12. A special train conveyed the Pittsburgh contingent (including Mr. and Mrs. Robert Pitcairn, Charles Carstairs, and Roland Knoedler) and other guests from Kings Cross Station, and reached Hertford at 1:40. It was a bright, fine day, and the whole town was celebrating, in recognition of Alexander McMullen's high local standing, and of Andrew Mellon's wealth and transatlantic origins: the route from the railway station to the castle, and from the castle to St. Andrew's Church, was lined with spectators and well-wishers, festooned with streamers and bunting, the Stars and Stripes and the Union Jack much in evidence.[97]

The bride's dress was made of ivory satin and chiffon, and she carried a large bouquet of roses and jasmine from the castle garden. The groom sported lily of the valley in his buttonhole, there were six bridesmaids, and Dick Mellon was the best man. There were many telegrams, including one from the relatively effusive Fricks ("cordial congratulations and best wishes for much happiness"), and another from the Judge and his wife, who had paid as little as they could ("congratulations" was the only word they transmitted), and were clearly not enthused.[98] The gifts were appropriately lavish, including silver fruit dishes from Mr. and Mrs. Andrew Carnegie, a silver tea and coffee service from the Fricks, and a silver punch bowl and ladle from W. L. Mellon and his wife. A wedding photograph of the couple seems peculiarly stiff and artificial, even by the standards of the time. Nora looks at the camera, with a mixture of vagueness and indifference, while Andrew regards her with pride and possessiveness: not a hint of physical or emotional chemistry between them. The day after the wedding, the castle grounds were opened to the public, for feasting at the expense of the bride's parents. Toasts were proposed, speeches were made, and sports enjoyed, culminating in a tug-of-war in which five Hertford villagers were set against the five strongest brothers of the bride. The McMullens won.

By then, Mr. and Mrs. Andrew Mellon had already departed on a brief honeymoon, visiting the town of Schwerin in Germany, where Nora had attended finishing school. But as in the days before the wedding, Andrew was much preoccupied with business, especially relating to Union Steel, and the chief reason they visited Berlin was because he needed to discuss aluminum and Carborundum matters. On October 3 Nora's mother wrote to her in Paris, in part about troubles with Howard, who needed money in South Africa, in part to try to console her, having apparently got word of her disappointment: "I am awfully sorry for you for dear you must not keep Andy here if he is wanting to get back to his business."[99] The Mellons paid a brief, valedictory visit to Hertford, and took the boat back to America, reaching Pittsburgh in mid-October. Nora had no idea what to expect. The world of big cities, endless suburbia, thundering factories, and smoking chimneys was wholly unknown to her. When Andrew had shown her a picture of 401 Negley, she had assumed it was in the middle of a great estate. But now, nearing the "City of Steel," via the mill towns of Braddock, Homestead, and Duquesne, she suddenly realized what an alien environment she was entering: the hills seared with outcropping seams of coal, the rivers dark and polluted, the atmosphere thick with soot. As the train neared East Liberty Station, and Andrew made ready to alight, she could scarcely believe that this blighted and benighted place would now be her permanent home. "We don't get off here, do we?" she asked. "You don't live *here*?"[100]

From this rude first encounter, Nora was appalled and bewildered by Pittsburgh. The whole Mellon clan welcomed the bride and groom to a breakfast; but their prim and reserved manner toward Nora was never to warm. She loathed the silent formality of dinners at the Judge's house, so unlike the convivial gatherings at Hertford. She thought the Judge "far gone mentally," she could barely understand Sarah Jane's accent, she found Dick and his wife relatively friendly, but coarse and lacking in fine feelings, and Frick seemed no better. Feeling their resentment at her arrival, she thought Pittsburghers to be smug, parochial, and materialistic. She hated the Forbes Street house, with its drab red brick and its pitifully bleak garden, made even less congenial by the unrelenting noise of the streetcars outside. She was disgusted by the dirt and squalor of Pittsburgh's environment, and she repudiated the entire industrial system: the factories, the mills, the dependent workers.[101] Almost immediately, she was lonely, homesick, and disoriented. But her husband, embroiled in his most complex business dealings yet and eagerly hoping for a first child, did not seem to notice any of this. "We were," he would blandly recall, "devoted to each other, and it seemed to me to be a state of happiness seldom reached." How could two people, even when living together for the first time, be so unaware of each other's feelings?[102]

PART TWO

Wealth's Triumphs, Fortune's Travails, 1900–1921

I have for many years been rated a millionaire, and perhaps justly so. But gratification or happiness does not increase proportionately with wealth . . . Wealth adds nothing to enjoyment.

Thomas Mellon and His Times, p. 382

5

THE TRANSITION COMPLETED
Family Man and Venture Capitalist, 1901–1907

My business, which was good before marriage, continued to improve afterwards, not only in extent, but in quality and profit.
Thomas Mellon and His Times, pp. 122–23

I. MARRIAGE AND PICTURES

Mr. and Mrs. Mellon were in residence at 5052 Forbes Street by November 1900, and their daughter was born in Pittsburgh on June 28 in the following year.[1] She was christened Ailsa, certainly not a Mellon name, and in further disregard of family convention, Andrew did not bestow on her any additional moniker. The name, chosen by Nora, referred to a small island at the mouth of the Firth of Clyde called Ailsa Craig, so at least offered homage to the Caledonian part of the Mellons' Scotch-Irish ancestry. Andrew was forty-six when Ailsa arrived, and so roughly as old as the Judge had been at the birth of George Negley Mellon, his eighth and last child, in 1860. Nora was only twenty-two, and so, by contrast, younger than her mother-in-law, Sarah Jane, had been at the birth of Thomas Alexander, her first, in 1844. Andrew was, in his fashion, a delighted (if predictably distant) father: "I never took an interest in babies before," he told Frank Haskell, "but now find myself comparing every one I see." In accordance with the custom of the time, a nurse was immediately engaged for Ailsa, named Miss Abernethy. She was Scottish, and she would remain with the family for the better part of a decade, taking a larger and more controversial part in the Mellon ménage than such a position properly required. Eventually she would depart amid high drama, bitter unhappiness, and deep recrimination all round.[2]

All marriages are ultimately unfathomable to outsiders, especially when the couple have long since passed on, and when the surviving record is both spotty and not produced in equal parts by each of them. It is likely that in the light of subsequent traumas, both Andrew and Nora would exaggerate in their recollections of these early years, Andrew positively, Nora negatively. But it also seems that from virtually the very outset, each saw the marriage in a way the other would scarcely have recognized. The difference in roles and expectations of privileged married women on opposite sides of the Atlantic may have figured in this, but this was something neither Andrew nor Nora fully understood. In the United Kingdom, such a woman would have naturally played the "lady bountiful," doing good works among the less fortunate; this is how Nora had imagined her life in Pittsburgh, envisioning herself, rather fancifully, "in the role of the mistress of the manor who lightens the burden of the peasant." But wives of rich American men were not generally supposed to be so active; at the same time, they were expected to support and comfort their husbands, who were so tired after another long, hard day making yet more money that they had no energy or emotion left to spend before the hearth.[3]

This was certainly Nora's frustration: Andrew was so busy he offered her no time (or tenderness?), and yet there was nothing she could do to contribute to his labors. And his easy talking, which she had so effortlessly drawn out of him on their initial encounter on the boat, now gave way to stern and stony silence. That, according to Paul Mellon, was Nora's unhappy recollection of their early married life:

> There is no first hand account from Mother about this period, but she often told me how terribly uprooted and lonely she felt in those early days in Pittsburgh and how the drabness and dirt of the city appalled her . . . It is not difficult to imagine [Andrew] returning to the house after spending long hours at the Bank, kissing his wife, and scanning the financial pages of the newspapers before having dinner in the gloomy dining room. The meals probably went uninterrupted by any conversation because his mind would still be preoccupied with business matters, and Mother knew by then that he did not enjoy small talk. Any remarks she made were likely to be subjected to analysis and questions . . . Many of them must have been childish and frivolous, but . . . his attitude and his treatment must have hurt and discouraged her. It was always a case of "Oh, you don't really want that, do you?" or "What makes you think that is a good idea?"[4]

Nora did not know it, but these were the standard complaints of many wives of rich Americans early in the twentieth century. She was not, as she thought, uniquely unfortunate or deprived, though that knowledge would not likely have brought her comfort. Here, by contrast, is Andrew's recollection of his marriage, a picture of contentment if not ecstatic happiness:

> We immediately became much occupied socially. My mother, Mr. and Mrs. Frick and several others gave receptions for us and for her. Later in the winter we settled down. I had before our arrival engaged a housekeeper, but Mrs. Mellon after a few months expressed her preference to manage the household affairs herself, and the housekeeper was dispensed with. She did the marketing and managed everything beautifully. She had the English instincts of economy which appealed to my admiration but I made everything easy and smooth. She kept the accounts and paid the bills carefully. In the evening when not going out she would play or sing and sometimes read the papers to me.[5]

From the very beginning, then, Andrew and Nora each seem to have been living in a different marriage. Little wonder, for a couple who had spent only a few days in each other's company before their honeymoon, at which time he was still infatuated, and she had just overcome her doubts that the marriage would work. Andrew, middle-aged and set in his ways, with no recent romantic involvement with women, let alone sexual experience, readily thought Nora had accommodated easily and happily to his life and routine. Nora, still so young, headstrong, and high-spirited, knowing little about herself, must have been in awe of the powers of her charms to inspire such an ardent suitor, only to discover his unsuspected true self: a husband who treated his wife like a client at the bank, seeking a loan to finance an ill-conceived venture. Nor did they have any friends or interests in common: she cared not a whit for business or balance sheets; he rode horseback dutifully but without enthusiasm or skill. Clearly irreconcilable, too, were their ideas of the benefits of marriage: he sought friendship, loyalty, support, and companionship; she craved warmth, fondness, demonstrative love, and perhaps passion. Add to this divergence the difference of more than twenty years in age, and it is impossible not to be reminded of another union that in both prospect and retrospect seemed equally ill-starred and ill-fated: that of the Prince of Wales and Lady Diana Spencer.

To be sure, Andrew Mellon had determined to conduct himself in what he thought was an appropriately honorable, courteous, and considerate way. He gave Nora all the money she asked for, never stinting but lavishing clothes and jewels on her, not so much from Pittsburgh but New York and London and Paris. (Needless to say, such "artificial wants" were not the Mellon family style.) Despite her claims that he was obsessed with work, they took long holidays together in the United States, they would spend considerable time in England almost every summer of their marriage, and Andrew soon began to contemplate buying a house there that Nora might decorate and think of as her own.[6] He was also exceptionally generous to her relatives: Nora's mother was a regular visitor to Pittsburgh, and Andrew got on well with her from the beginning; several of her dodgy brothers also came to stay, and he invariably paid their way; and within a few years of their marriage, Andrew was already lending money to both Norman and Leonard McMullen.[7] He must have found Nora's family as "strange" as her father had found his, but he clearly resolved to do his duty—indeed more than his duty—by them. Yet none of this was enough for Nora, trapped as she was, and against her own better judgment, with one of the most famously cold, taciturn, and repressed men of his generation. Not surprisingly, she spent a great deal of time in bed, afflicted by vague illnesses such as the age allowed, which must often surely have been psychosomatic.

Andrew seems to have been oblivious to all of this, bounding ahead to establish himself as the prosperous married man about Pittsburgh, according to the conventions of the time. Now that he had a house to furnish, he began to buy pictures more seriously than in the days before he possessed walls of his own, and this brought him closer to Knoedler & Company, and especially to Charles Carstairs, who was still in charge of the Pittsburgh branch.[8] Considering it took place abroad, both Carstairs and Roland Knoedler had been conspicuous at Andrew and Nora's wedding. Thereafter, Mellon and Carstairs (perhaps scenting a better client in a married man) got on particularly well: "Don't work yourself to death, but come to New York and have a spree with me," the latter wrote to the former early in 1903. Carstairs also befriended Nora and Ailsa, providing inexpensive landscapes and decorative vases for the house, and he encouraged Mellon and Frick to discuss their purchasing plans with each other as well as with him. By 1904, he was beginning his letters "My dear Andy," something even Frick did not do.[9]

Almost as soon as Andrew and Nora reached Pittsburgh, he started buying again through Knoedler, following the pattern of most prosperous but aesthetically conservative Pittsburghers. In December 1900, he purchased Harpignies's *Grave Affair* (for $1,450), which he returned in 1904;

Thaulow's *La Rivière* (for $1,500), which Frick had previously owned and returned; and *Bords de la Meuse* by Daubigny (for $9,000), a painter whom Frick had urged Carstairs to show Mellon three years before.[10] By the end of 1901, he had acquired seven pictures through Knoedler, spending more than $50,000 for works by Dupré, Maris, Ziem, Israels, van Marke, Rico, and Mauve. "I want you to understand," Carstairs wrote to him at about this time, "that it is our desire to do anything in our power and [we] trust you are satisfied. You should be, the paintings you have purchased are of the finest quality and worth every cent of the above prices." He also assured Mellon that he could return any canvas at any time, and be credited with the full purchase price, a courtesy of which he would very soon after begin to avail himself.[11]

In praising these pictures as being of the "finest quality," Carstairs flattered both his company and his client. Whatever their merits, they represented no advance beyond the conventional French landscapes of the Barbizon School that Mellon had tentatively begun to buy during the late 1890s. With such acquisitions, he was not even a middling collector in an era dominated by such titanic figures as Frick, Collis P. Huntington, Benjamin Altman, P. A. B. Widener, and Isabella Stewart Gardner, who were gobbling up, often accompanied by great publicity, some of the very finest works of European art, especially old masters and eighteenth-century English portraits.[12] These were individuals creating and commanding the new transatlantic market in art, but Mellon, by contrast, played it safe and small. In 1902 he paid $6,000 for two works by Diaz; in 1903 he spent $16,000 on paintings by Mauve, Maris (which he returned two years later), and Russell; and in 1904 he laid out $1,600 on one minor work by Chennevières and two by Rossi. "You will always like the pictures you have just purchased," Charles Carstairs reassured Mellon.[13] This was not true: all would eventually be returned to Knoedler or sold.

Yet Mellon's taste was beginning to develop during this period: Carstairs's influence did have some effect, and his continuing friendship with Frick played its part, as did his marriage to Nora, which may have stimulated his interest in British art. As a result, he became slightly but significantly more adventurous, beginning to spend larger sums on works of higher quality.[14] In December 1900, he bought one portrait by Sir Henry Raeburn (*Mrs. Hill*) and another by Sir Joshua Reynolds (*Robinetta*): the two together cost $41,000. Perhaps these were housewarming presents for Nora, intended to make her feel more at home in alien Pittsburgh. Twelve months later, Mellon acquired his first Corot landscape for $12,000 (though he would sell it back to Knoedler in March 1904 at a profit of $1,000); in September 1902 he purchased another (*Le Lac de Garde*) for $70,000, and in March 1904 a third by the same artist (*Une Idylle, Rond des Enfants*) for $63,000, along with Troyon's *Le Passage du Lac* for $70,000. Later that year, Mellon spent $29,000 on a second Daubigny, *Printemps à Anvers*, and in April 1905 he bought Cuyp's *Herdsmen Tending Cattle* for $62,000. Then, in September 1906, he acquired his first work by Gainsborough, *Portrait of Mrs. John Taylor*, for $115,000, his most expensive purchase to date.[15]

Andrew Mellon spent more than $400,000 in the years up to and including 1905 "without buying a single picture which he ultimately considered worthy of the National Gallery of Art," according to John Walker, who would be its second director. "Thus," Walker notes, "his education as a collector was expensive and wasteful." Indeed, at his death, his Corots were valued at scarcely one-tenth of what he had paid for them.[16] But in buying them Mellon was signaling that, like others in Pittsburgh, notably Frick, he was beginning to venture beyond genre painting and the Barbizon school. Moreover, three of these early purchases *did* find their way into the National Gallery: the Raeburn, the Cuyp, and the Gainsborough. Above all, it is anachronistic to judge Mellon by the standards of the major contemporary purchasers or his own later and greater acquisitions. For he did not yet see himself as a "collector": he was buying for himself, to please his wife, and to adorn his far-from-grand house.[17] And insofar as he ventured beyond the tastes of the Pittsburgh haute bourgeoisie, it was toward landscapes and portraits of Englishwomen (revealing preferences for someone who disliked the countryside and was distant to his wife) rather than old masters. Titians, El Grecos, Rembrandts, and Vermeers were not out of place in the great plutocratic palaces on New York's Fifth Avenue, but they would have looked ridiculous on the walls of 5052 Forbes Street.[18]

II. BANKING RESTRUCTURED, BUSINESS ADVANCED

Like the United States as a whole, the Pittsburgh to which Andrew and Nora Mellon returned after their honeymoon was booming as never before. Banking and business were feeding off and stimulating each other, new industrial combines were being formed, and the loans and profits (and investments) of finance houses were increasing accordingly. Both in terms of the rate of capital accumulation and of the increase in industrial output, Pittsburgh had reached its apogee of significance and influence in

American economic life. Indeed, in 1901, the city ranked second only to New York in floating new corporations, far ahead of Chicago and Philadelphia, and the local stock exchange witnessed the transaction of an unprecedented volume of business.[19] The most famous deal of the time was the sale of Carnegie Steel to J. P. Morgan in January 1901 for $480 million; Morgan promptly reorganized it as the United States Steel Corporation and recapitalized it at $1.4 billion, to make it the largest company in the world. Carnegie cashed in, and became a full-time philanthropist. Frick, though he remained a shareholder, largely withdrew from management, and became increasingly close to Mellon in his business interests. And Philander Knox, who had helped broker the sale, thereupon departed for Washington to become attorney general, first under President McKinley, then, after McKinley's assassination, in Theodore Roosevelt's cabinet until 1904, when, on the death of Matthew Quay, he became a U.S. senator from Pennsylvania.[20]

One indication of the generally buoyant state of the American economy was the growing scale of operations of East Coast banks as they played an ever greater part in the financing of industry. In New York, the National City Bank had merged with the Third National in 1897, and the new company boasted combined assets of $100 million. Soon after, there were consolidations in Boston and Providence, where the National Shawmut Bank and the Industrial Trust Company emerged as the major local financial powers.[21] But in 1902, the comptroller of currency forbade national banks from acting as investment banks, which provided a great spur to the growth of trust companies, whose numbers increased from 276 in 1899 to 924 in 1904, and whose varied functions meant they were now described as the "department stores of finance."[22] This in turn led to a much closer relationship between many national banks and trust companies, which increasingly saw their businesses as complementary. The Philadelphia National Bank largely controlled the Philadelphia Trust Safe Deposit and Insurance Company, the First National Bank of Chicago set up the First Trust and Savings Bank, and the First National Bank of New York formed the First Securities Company.[23] Here was a wholly new phase and scale of banking organization, in which Mellon determined to participate so as to consolidate and enhance his own position in booming Pittsburgh. He did so in a manner reminiscent of his first major financial foray in the mid-1880s, but this time on a greater scale and with more marked success.

Back from his honeymoon, he remained preoccupied with "statistics and business statements," often spending Saturdays in his office, and even preferring the bank to church on the Sabbath.[24] Crucial to his designs was the now-established Union Trust Company, which under its new president, Henry C. McEldowney, became the major agent and beneficiary of the industrial expansion and consolidation of the time. The trust had grown very slowly until 1899; but in 1900 its assets had suddenly skyrocketed to $7 million; in the following year they nearly tripled to $20 million; and by 1903 they had virtually doubled again to $37 million. Meanwhile, its deposits increased threefold, from $5.13 million in 1899 to $17.2 million in 1901, and its dividends exploded from 6 percent in 1902 to 60 percent the following year.[25] By early 1902, Union Trust was overwhelmingly a Mellon-Frick affair, as Mellon's holdings of 2,413 shares and Frick's of 1,503 formed a majority of the total capitalization of 5,000 shares. From this prosperous and powerful platform Mellon now resolved to execute his most audacious financial maneuver yet, by radically transforming and modernizing T. Mellon & Sons, and by linking it much more closely and strategically to the Union Trust Company.

To be sure, the Judge's old-fashioned country bank was still paying Andrew and Dick substantial profits ($58,000 each in the first four months of 1902), but it could no longer hold its place as a serious financial institution in a Pittsburgh of giant corporations, steel trusts, and huge manufacturing concerns with a national reach. It also seemed increasingly outdated: indeed, by 1902, only two such private finance houses remained in Pittsburgh, and as Andrew Mellon recalled, "some of our best customers were being offered inducements to interest themselves in other banking organizations."[26] Accordingly, he determined to transform his privately owned establishment into a full-fledged and federally chartered national bank, in which he and Dick would be the only shareholders. On July 1, 1902, Mellon National Bank came into being, immediately superseding T. Mellon & Sons, as well as absorbing the Pittsburgh National Bank of Commerce and the City Deposit Bank, which had been owned by the Mellons, along with the Citizens National Bank, which had been owned by Frick. The new bank's resources soon amounted to more than $24 million, which meant that at a stroke it had become the second biggest in the city, after the Farmer's Deposit National Bank. And the directors Mellon appointed were among the most powerful men in Pittsburgh, many of whom were also directors of Union Trust: steel magnates like Frick, Phipps, and B. F. Jones, oil barons like the Lockharts, and lawyers like George Shaw, a partner of James Reed's. (Philander Knox, as attorney general, was now ineligible, but his son, A. C. Knox, was elected in his stead.)[27]

This overlap was deliberate, for the relationship between the new bank and Union Trust was crucial to Andrew Mellon's plans to assert himself financially in Pittsburgh as never before. He and Dick immediately exchanged their stock in the new Mellon National Bank for shares in Union Trust, thereby placing the bank under the control of the trust. Andrew was president of the new bank, and also a vice president of Union Trust, while Dick became vice president of the bank and a director of the trust. Five thousand new shares in the Union Trust Company were now issued, three thousand of them in payment for the Mellon National Bank stock, and when joined to Andrew's previous holdings, this gave the Mellon brothers indisputable control: 5,416 shares out of a new aggregate of 10,000. The two Mellons plus Frick owned almost exactly 7,000 of the 10,000 shares, and under a new private arrangement, drawn up by Frick, these shares were reallocated: 2,750 each to Andrew and Frick, and 1,500 to Dick.[28] Thus was formed an insuperable triumvirate, exerting undisputed control over the Union Trust, and by extension over the new Mellon National Bank. But something significant *had* changed, for with 4,250 shares between them, the two Mellon brothers were no longer the controlling shareholders in the trust, whereas Andrew and Frick, with 5,500 shares between them, did command a majority.

Strictly speaking, then, the new Mellon National Bank was not a Mellon enterprise in the way that T. Mellon & Sons had been, though by sharing control with Frick, they made him "virtually an adopted member of the Mellon family, so far as banking and financial influence were concerned." "I take great pride," Frick wrote to Andrew in May 1903, "in the several financial institutions with which we are connected, and especially the one that bears your name."[29] In practice, however, not much changed. Frick was now spending much more time in New York than in Pittsburgh; Andrew was still de facto head of the Mellon Bank; and he continued working closely with his younger brother.[30] At the same time, the Mellons and Frick created another new financial intermediary, the Union Savings Bank, which offered a high rate of return on deposits and accepted them by mail, allowing it soon to win customers across the nation, as well as in Canada and Europe. Like Mellon National, Union Savings was owned by Union Trust, which made the trust the most significant financial institution in western Pennsylvania, with combined resources in 1903 of more than $65 million. From this enhanced and consolidated position, Andrew Mellon grew more boldly acquisitive. He soon enfolded the Pittsburgh National Bank of Commerce into his Union Trust empire, and also intruded himself onto the boards of local banks in nearby Braddock,

Scottdale, Wilkinsburg, Charleroi, Duquesne, and Donora. There, even with a minority interest, Andrew Mellon enjoyed disproportionate influence, being who he now was and what he was now worth.[31]

As a wholly owned subsidiary of Union Trust, the newly chartered Mellon National Bank expanded rapidly during the buoyant early 1900s. The numbers tell the tale. Eleven months after opening, deposits had increased from $13.7 million to $20.9 million, and total resources from $15.8 million to $24.3 million. During the first six months of operation, the bank's clearances were ranked sixth in the region; a year later, it headed the Pittsburgh Clearing House list. For the first twelve months of its existence, up to June 1903, net earnings were $465,342; for the corresponding period to June 1906, they were $523,935. However, no dividend was paid during the first three years: the money was set aside to build up a surplus. Nor were these the only signs of growth. As soon as the new bank opened, a foreign department was established, and close links were forged with banking houses in London (Brown, Shipley & Co.), Paris (Hottinguer & Co.), and Berlin (Mendelssohn & Co.). The bank also began to issue its own traveler's checks in January 1905—appropriately enough to Nora Mellon, though there is no record of her journeying abroad at this time. Not surprisingly, the whole of the original building of T. Mellon & Sons had long since been taken over, and the bank was now expanding to fill up most of the Smithfield Street block from Fifth to Oliver avenues.[32]

The carefully contrived combination of Union Trust, Union Savings, and Mellon National Bank—two state-based, one national—gave the Mellon brothers exceptional flexibility and power in their business dealings. It was these changes and innovations in 1902 which almost overnight transformed Andrew Mellon into the most powerful financial force in Pittsburgh, albeit at the relatively advanced age of forty-seven. Leveraging Union Trust's rapidly expanding resources, to which both Union Savings and Mellon National Bank now contributed, he was freely underwriting securities or subscribing to the stock of corporations he intended to bring within the bounds of his industrial empire.[33] The name T. Mellon & Sons now officially disappeared from the public eye; but Andrew and Dick appropriated it for their joint private account, which held their personal investments in shares and bonds and real estate, usually in equal portions. This was partly a matter of sentiment: to perpetuate an old and honored name. But it was also a matter of Scotch-Irish frugality: there were unused stocks of stationery and ledgers bearing the name "T. Mellon & Sons," and it seemed wasteful to destroy them.[34] One final change took place in October 1905, when the arrangement whereby Andrew had managed his father's estate on behalf of Dick, James Ross, and the descendants of the late Thomas Alexander came to an end. A new trust was created which would last until June 1919, when it was dissolved and the assets distributed among the beneficiaries.[35]

The heady economic climate which witnessed the transformation of the Union Trust Company and the Mellon Bank was also a period of unexampled prosperity for those Mellon companies which had been nurtured in earlier times: all were now accumulating substantial surpluses, which were either plowed back in immediately or used, via Union Trust, to finance new business ventures and consolidations. Pittsburgh Reduction, distributing one million dollars in share certificates to stockholders in 1904, and reporting its first million-dollar profits in the following year, was on the march: both its bauxite mining operations in Arkansas and its smelting and manufacturing centers in New Kensington, Pennsylvania, and in Niagara Falls and Massena, New York, were expanding. At Carborundum, the company's performance improved markedly after Frank Haskell replaced Acheson as president in 1901, and phrases such as "satisfactory and gratifying" and "another record-breaking month" regularly appear in Andrew Mellon's appreciative letters to him.[36] In April 1905, Thomas McKaig, secretary of the Trade Dollar Consolidated Mining Company, was reporting dividends of $60,000 per share, and noted that profits were higher than in any previous month. Meanwhile, McClintic-Marshall was milling the steel for the Grand Central terminal in New York, and had won the contract to make the construction machinery for the locks on the Panama Canal.[37]

In these ways, Andrew Mellon was showing outstanding business command and aplomb in the years immediately after his marriage; and these expansive successes, with a broad financial and industrial reach, constantly sustained and reinforced one another. (He was also more closely involved with his alma mater, recently renamed the University of Pittsburgh, where a new president, Samuel McCormick, now sought to raise its standards and profile, and relocate from downtown to Schenley Fields at Oakland.)[38] But as his dealings with Rockefeller in 1895 had shown, his astute sense of timing could sometimes move him to shed businesses, as well as create them. In this heady period, two instances stand out, each in its different way a great success or (depending on one's point of view) an outrageous scandal, since the terms of disengagement were disproportionately beneficial to Mellon. The family's extended holdings in Pittsburgh streetcars had continued under the direction of W. L. Mellon ever since he had ceased to be an oilman. He had been involved in a variety of (unrecorded) political deals and (suspect) financial transactions, as he bought up franchises, consolidated existing lines, and oversaw the construction of new ones. By late 1900 the Mellon system extended over fifty miles, and there were plans for a further expansion, amounting to a doubling of the track. But during the following year, the streetcar scene in Pittsburgh changed in a variety of ways, and so, more than once, did the Mellons' policy.[39]

To begin with, the Philadelphia Company, one of the rival lines, became much more aggressively expansionist, establishing a new subsidiary to pull together the lines in the West End of Pittsburgh, and acquiring all the track of another local operator, Consolidated Traction.[40] This gave the Philadelphia control of the greater part of the city's transport system, with the "Mellon lines" as the only major competitors left. Having been prepared to fight Rockefeller for oil, W. L. Mellon was now prepared to fight the Philadelphia for track: he constructed a new line through the Monongahela Valley to Charleroi; he bought out the Pittsburgh and Birmingham Company to gain better access downtown; and he began acquiring streetcar franchises in Allegheny, north of the river, which was the Philadelphia's home base. But then the Mellons suddenly changed tack, and agreed to lease out all their lines for 999 years in January 1902—to none other than their former rivals, the Philadelphia Company. In fact, it was a good deal for them, furnishing an annual rental of $2.3 million. But it came at a price which Burton Hendrick described as "the general sacrifice of the public convenience to the financial necessities of the capitalists in control." Nevertheless, the Mellons continued to draw their income, and their interests were safeguarded at the Philadelphia Company by the presence on the board of the ubiquitous James Reed (president), and Henry C. McEldowney (director).[41]

The second enterprise from which Andrew Mellon withdrew—again to great financial advantage—was Union Steel, inaugurated just before his marriage but only established afterwards, on two hundred acres on the Monongahela River just below Monessen, at a new town called Donora, in honor of the company's founder, William H. Donner, and Andrew's new wife.[42] Once in operation, the Union Steel Company mounted an aggressive but brief challenge to J. P. Morgan's recently established United States Steel Corporation in the manufacture of wire products. In 1902, Union sharpened its competitive edge with a stock swap arrangement for ownership of the Sharon Steel Company in nearby Lawrence County. Rather than compete, the directors of United States Steel resolved to acquire and absorb their rival, and Andrew Mellon proved willing to acquiesce. It is easy to see why. One month after the Union-Sharon merger, United States Steel agreed to pay a sum variously put at $42 million or $75 million, depending on the source, for Mellon's original $1 million investment. As he laconically admitted, this was "a fair profit to all concerned."[43] Certainly a spectacular profit—but was it also fair?

The evidence suggests not. For Union Steel had scarcely been in existence for three years, hardly time enough for it to grow from its relatively modest beginning to the scale of enterprise reflected in the sale price, whichever sum was correct.[44] In the aftermath of the Union-Sharon merger, and knowing United States Steel was watching, Mellon and Frick (Donner had by this time left to form his own steel company in Buffalo) had hurriedly issued a $45 million debenture, and also increased the company's capital stock from $1 million to $20 million. All of these manipulations were purely paper transactions: there was no time to sell the bonds or pay in cash for shares of the new stock issue. By the end of 1903, when the sale was finally completed, Mellon and Frick were out of the steel nail and wire business, with many millions in their pockets which they no doubt put to good use elsewhere. In 1912, a House of Representatives subcommittee on trusts reviewed the Union-Sharon merger, and the later takeover by United States Steel. It concluded that Mellon had vastly inflated the values of the plant and equipment, citing, for example, a $150,000 parcel of coal land valued at $4 million in the sale. The Union Steel affair, therefore, was no case of a company successfully developed over the long term: it was a short-term speculation and a paper profit of just the kind Mellon had always professed to abhor.[45] There is no evidence his conscience was troubled.

Nor was it troubled by developments in the two coal companies which he had created on the basis of their means of distribution—the Pittsburgh Coal Company (rail) and the Monongahela River Consolidated Coal & Coke Company (water)—neither of which lived up to its promising beginnings.[46] Mellon had created two separate enterprises, bringing together a majority of local mines, and had financed them differently (the former publicly, the latter privately), confident that the result would be reduced production and transport costs, and thus increased profits. But the subsequent histories of the two companies belie Mellon's reputation for unerringly backing winners. During 1902 and 1903, the Pittsburgh Coal Company acquired 98,000 additional acres of land (much of it from company directors, including Mellon) that was suitable for either surface or underground mining; it also added nearly two thousand coal cars to its rail fleet during the same period; and in November 1903—at Andrew

Mellon's instruction—Pittsburgh Coal negotiated a majority sharehold-ing in Monongahela Consolidated.[47]

These ventures cost altogether some $40 million, almost the equiva-lent of the entire Pittsburgh Coal Company's capitalization, and since only $14 million of it came from revenue, the company was left $26 mil-lion in the red. It proved impossible to float the debt publicly, and in 1904 it was taken over by the Union Trust Company, which thereby became the effective owner of both Pittsburgh Coal and its subsidiary, Mononga-hela Consolidated. But Pittsburgh Coal struggled to make its interest payments, and in June 1904 it was obliged to borrow more money *from* Union Trust to meet its obligations *to* Union Trust. This unpromising situation indicated serious underlying difficulties. Although the com-panies' combined landholdings were 250,000 acres, production never approached the initial predictions on which Andrew Mellon's calculations had been made. Moreover, the merger had proceeded so slowly that it failed to deliver the much-needed economies of scale.[48] Above all, it proved impossible to create a satisfactory management structure, or to find an outstanding figure to put in charge—a rare Mellon failure of judg-ment and leadership.

III. ENTER A VILLAIN

The year 1902 would expose another failure of Mellon's judgment, which would have far more devastating consequences. Just seventeen months after Andrew and Nora had married, a momentous meeting took place that would soon put his domestic life in jeopardy. In February, Nora was summoned by telegram to England, where her father was dying of cancer. Andrew could not go (Mellon National Bank would soon be launched), and having seen Nora to the boat in New York, he left her to cross the Atlantic by herself, reaching Hertford just in time. Alexander McMullen died soon after, and following the funeral, Nora returned to America, bringing her mother with her.[49] Andrew was there to greet them at the New York dockside, where Nora introduced a fellow passenger, named Alfred George Curphey. He was young, tall, good-looking, well-dressed, possessed of abundant charm, and he claimed (falsely) to have served as an officer in the Boer War.[50] It is possible that Nora and Curphey had met in England, or they may have encountered each other aboard ship. In any case, Curphey was traveling with James P. Scott, an associate from Philadelphia, and by agreeable coincidence (if such it was), the two were bound for Pittsburgh on business. Nora urged Andrew to invite them to dinner at Forbes Street, where the four of them subsequently spent an evening together.[51]

Who was Alfred Curphey? In brief, he seems to have been a villain straight out of a nineteenth-century melodrama: a cad and a confidence man who seduced the wives of unsuspecting husbands; a predator of unhappy women of means, whom he cast ruthlessly aside after taking their money. He was devious, dishonest, and unscrupulous, but with considerable roguish charisma: as such, it seems incredible yet somehow almost inevitable that he would have insinuated himself into the Mellons' precarious married life. Formed a million miles away from the prim and correct world of Pittsburgh Scotch-Irish Presbyterianism, Curphey operated on a scale of ill repute far exceeding that of Nora's most wayward brothers, except perhaps Howard McMullen. His pose was that of a gentlemanly capitalist with military bearing, but his true pedigree was far less impressive. His father, Samuel Curphey, had died at the County Lunatic Asylum in Sutton, Lancashire, in 1878, at the age of thirty-five, from "disease of the brain with general paralysis." He had begun life as a joiner, later describing himself as a contractor and builder, but he was clearly a suspicious character. He spoke more like a dandy than a working-class boy from Lancashire, he claimed to have made and lost several fortunes, and he had a deserved reputation as a spendthrift—a characteristic he passed on to his equally wayward son.[52]

Alfred Curphey was born in Wallesey, near Birkenhead, in 1872, one of three children. He spent much of his early life in the poorhouse, but he was allowed home when his mother remarried, to a schoolmaster from whom he obtained his education. He learned how to talk and how to charm, how to dissemble and how to deceive, and in June 1893 he married Grace Dundas Hamilton Souter Robinson, the daughter of Stuart Souter Robinson, chaplain to the Duke of Hamilton. On the marriage certificate, Curphey imaginatively listed his father's occupation as "gentleman," and although only twenty-one, he gave his age as twenty-six, the same as his bride.[53] The couple lived in London, there were no children, and via Grace's family and connections, Curphey began to make his way in the world socially and professionally, eventually establishing himself as a surveyor and land agent. From shreds of their correspondence, Grace Curphey emerges as a woman of considerable dignity, fortitude, and forbearance. She was also possessed of some private means, and one of her complaints in his wake was that Curphey made off with her money. By the time Curphey met Nora, his marriage to Grace was a sham, and he was on the lookout for new opportunities—and for new conquests.[54]

Later in 1902, Andrew, Nora, and Ailsa sailed for England, where they spent a long summer, from June to September, mainly at Hertford, so Nora could be near her widowed mother, but also visiting Paris and London. No doubt sensing that this might be the opportunity of his life, Curphey reappeared (had Nora let him know of their visit?), and the three of them dined together occasionally, and went out to the theater in London. Andrew saw nothing untoward in Curphey's attentions: "I regarded him then," he later wrote, "as a casual acquaintance along with many others." He also visited Curphey's office on Victoria Street, and naïvely concluded that "he appeared to have a prosperous business as an estate agent, valuer and surveyor."[55] During their stay, Andrew bought from Curphey a pair of coach horses as a present for Nora, and had them shipped to America because she admired them so much. He paid £350 (approximately $1,700) for the animals, and Curphey arranged their insurance and transport— at Andrew's expense. "We named one Curphey and the other Cope," Andrew would later recall ruefully, "the name of a friend of Curphey's. Cope was all right, but Curphey turned out to be of little account." By Andrew's recollection, the Mellons returned from their summer sojourn, and Nora "spent the fall and winter at home, all being happy and uneventful."[56]

Early in 1903, at their invitation, Nora joined Dick and Jennie at Palm Beach, Florida, so she might recover from a cold. She left Andrew (and Ailsa) in Pittsburgh, their first time apart since marrying, and so the letters they exchanged were the first since the interlude between their engagement and their wedding.[57] Nora wrote virtually every day, addressing Andrew as "Fatty" and signing herself "Norchen." Her letters are generally affectionate, and for the most part consist of artless holiday palaver—the weather, the meals, the accommodations—written in flighty, breathless, and ungrammatical prose. There are brief descriptions of fellow guests, which are candid though superficial: "the Duke and Duchess of Manchester are here—also John Jacob Astor. What an awful looking creature he is." There are requests for funds: "I think I would probably telegraph to you for some money or I would not get it in time." And there are conventional blandishments: "Fatty dear I do miss you so, I wish you were here."[58] But Nora also vents her by now perennial frustration and disappointment at Andrew's enslavement to work. "Take care of your self Fatty dear, and baby too," she writes on February 24. "I'm afraid what with your horrid business and all, you will not miss one so very much, or I would apologize for leaving you all alone." "Heaps of love, dear Fatty," she ended. "Ever your loving Norchen."[59] She returned to Pittsburgh in the second week of March.

By this time, Curphey was back in New York, and he hastened to contact the Mellons, clearly judging this the moment to strike. He informed Andrew that while he had many business ventures—including coal lands in West Virginia, and a patent for electric railway signals—he was temporarily in urgent need of $20,000. Andrew duly provided a loan, which was to be repaid on April 4.[60] Meanwhile, Nora invited Curphey to stay with them in Pittsburgh, and once ensconced at Forbes Street, he showed no inclination to depart. Before long, word reached Andrew that Nora had been seen about town "accompanied by a good-looking Englishman." Andrew urged Nora to suggest Curphey should leave, which he promptly did, returning to New York. Later regretting his behavior, Andrew apologized when he next saw Curphey, but Curphey put things right after his own fashion. Once, when Andrew was away, he made another visit to Pittsburgh, ostensibly on business, and spent the night at Forbes Street.[61] And when Curphey was back in New York, Nora suddenly became very enthusiastic about accompanying her husband on his business trips to the city. Andrew and Nora met up with Curphey at their Manhattan hotel: the three of them dined together and went to the theater. But when April 4 came round, Curphey was unable to repay his loan, and Mellon was obliged to renew it before Curphey returned to England. He would never have continued extending such easy credit to a client at the bank or a business associate.[62]

In June 1903, Andrew, Nora, Ailsa, and Miss Abernethy were booked to cross the Atlantic to spend the by now customary summer in England, intending to find a house to rent there. But the sudden death of Henry G. Morse of the New York Shipbuilding Company—he collapsed from a fatal stroke during a meeting—forced Mellon, at the very last minute, to have his luggage removed from the ship, and so the others sailed without him. He promised to follow as soon as he could, but meanwhile Nora seethed over his absence and the reasons for it.[63] On reaching England she went straight to Curphey, and together they found an attractive house to rent by the Thames, called Sandlea, at Datchet, near Windsor. At this point, Nora seems to have considered taking up residence with Curphey in England and parting from Andrew in Pittsburgh, and she took Miss Abernethy into her confidence, threatening dismissal if the nanny betrayed her. What did Nora see in Curphey? She knew nothing of his background, least of all that he was already married (about which Andrew likewise had no clue at this time). He does, however, seem to have offered the demonstrative affection her husband could not give, and perhaps, as well, a sexual excitement and danger of which marriage to Andrew emitted not a trace. As for Curphey, Nora's attraction was obvious: a means to some of the Mellon millions.[64]

Soon after Nora had settled in England for the summer, her brother Leonard wrote to her. Having learned that she had been "seen" with Curphey, who was "unfavourably known to many," he urged her to break off the relationship. Instead, Nora told Curphey, who phoned Leonard, demanding an apology. There was a heated exchange: Leonard informed Curphey that he was no gentleman; Curphey threatened Leonard with a good thrashing (never administered). Finally Leonard warned Nora that he was minded to write to Andrew. He never did, so when Andrew finally reached England, he was "entirely ignorant of Curphey's character and of this incident," and anticipated a pleasant summer. As he later recalled:

> It was delightful at Datchet. We had many visitors including Mrs. Mellon's family, and friends and acquaintances of hers and mine. The time was employed with excursions on the river, riding, driving, etc . . . We went riding then almost daily in Windsor Park, mostly just Mrs. Mellon and myself, but frequently some of her brothers were with us, and several times Mr. Curphey.[65]

But this conviviality soon frayed. Curphey's extended loan came due a second time, and once again, he could not discharge his debt. There was an incident when he was so drunk that he fell off a punt into the Thames, and had to be taken home and put to bed. And when the three of them visited London for theater and supper, or took excursions, even Andrew now began to notice Curphey's excessive attentions to his wife.[66]

Mr. and Mrs. Mellon returned to Pittsburgh at the end of the summer, and Nora, with the connivance of Miss Abernethy, initiated an extensive secret correspondence with Curphey—who, unbeknownst to Nora (or Andrew), formally left his wife at about this time for another woman named Alice. At the end of the year, Curphey's debt to Andrew still remained outstanding, and early in 1904, Andrew and Nora went to Florida, where they were joined by two of her brothers, Murray and Norman.[67] In June, Andrew booked the tickets for their next transatlantic summer trip, but just before they were to leave, Nora blurted out that she wanted a divorce and wished to live with Curphey in England. Andrew was "horrified" by what he regarded as such "madness," but he tried to discuss the matter calmly with her, and thought he had dissuaded her from her plan. "On the way over on the steamer," he recalled, Nora was "especially demonstrative of her love for me and I believed the Curphey outbreak of no consequence." He could not have been more wrong. As they journeyed to London from the ship, Nora was "quite animated and excited," and when they went down to dinner in their hotel, Curphey was sitting at a nearby table. He would meet with Nora later that evening, and the two of them were together for much of the next day.

Andrew and Nora had again taken the house at Datchet, and soon after they arrived, Nora arranged a clandestine assignation with Curphey nearby at St. George's Chapel, Windsor. Andrew learned about their meeting, and promptly confronted Curphey in his London office on Victoria Street. The rogue's response was a consummate piece of theater (tears welled up in his eyes) before an audacious demand for more money:

> Mr. Mellon, I know that I was wrong, but I cannot help it, I haven't the power to keep away from her, although I know it is all wrong. It is terrible to have such love under the circumstances—I would have chucked up everything and gone away, but my affairs are so tangled and in such shape financially that I cannot do it. I would leave now and go to South Africa if I could get the means to go. I feel how wrong it all is to you and what a cad you must think me to be after all your kindness to me, etc.[68]

Andrew subsequently informed Nora that Curphey was a "fraud" and a "forger," and there was another confrontation in his office, where Andrew called him a "blackguard." Mrs. McMullen learned with dismay of her daughter's behavior, but Nora, renewing her plea for a divorce, retired to bed with an unspecified but lengthy illness.[69]

By now Andrew sensed what looked like a potential deal: if he provided him with further funds, Curphey might go away for good. Meanwhile, Nora's continuing bedridden distress derived at least in part, she said, from Curphey's precarious finances, for he claimed that his "ancestral home" at Ballamoar on the Isle of Man was about to be seized. (Curphey is a Manx name, and one of Ballamoar's previous owners had married a Suzannah Curphey of Ballakillingham, but Alfred Curphey had no connection with the place.) Andrew went along with this, making inquiries as to what it would take to redeem the estate, though not, apparently, discovering that Curphey did not own it. But he did learn that Curphey was already married—though that would not last much longer. Andrew decided that the sum Curphey asked for was worth paying, until he realized that the figure had been quoted in British pounds, not U.S. dollars.[70] He wavered, but Nora offered him her shares in the McMullen brewery, and he finally agreed; in July 1904 he transferred £20,000 to

Curphey's account with Barclays—the price, he believed, of renewed marital happiness and also of Curphey's permanent disappearance from their lives.[71]

Andrew and Nora thereupon went back to Pittsburgh after the most traumatic, and expensive, summer of their marriage. Andrew had been "almost distracted," though more by Nora's illness than by Curphey's importuning. Nora had taken a tearful but final farewell of Curphey, vowed she would never think of him again, and undertook to be "a true and loving wife" from then on. Andrew was prepared to believe her an innocent victim of a rascal who had unscrupulously "worked upon her feelings": "she was young," he believed, "and would gain strength of character as she got older."[72] (Shades of the Judge.) Sometime after their return, Andrew informed Nora that Curphey was married, and she admitted to him "how foolish she had been." She seemed genuinely remorseful and reiterated her pledge "to be a good and true wife." Early in 1905, Nora and Ailsa went to Pinehurst, North Carolina, and once again, her letters to Andrew were pleasantly, reassuringly inconsequential: "Baby is well and beginning to look better. The people in the hotel are most uninteresting. Old John D. Rockefeller sits at the next table. Baby will have none of him!" That summer, Nora seemed determined indeed to make amends, even giving up her annual British sojourn. Instead, the Mellons vacationed at Pride's Crossing in Massachusetts, where Andrew thought they had a "delightful" time, "riding, motoring and entertaining occasionally," and where Frick was then building his own summerhouse.[73]

During the same vacation, having planned a visit to India to see friends of Nora's family, they decided to make it a round-the-world trip. It would be Nora's second, but Andrew's first, and he was clearly making a greater effort than ever to spend more time with his wife and away from business. Andrew booked the tickets, and they planned to embark for the east from London in December 1905. But it was not to be: in the autumn, Alan McMullen's wife, Mary, fell dangerously ill in Dublin, and Nora crossed the Atlantic to be with them and her mother. When Mary McMullen died, Nora joined her mother on a trip to Monte Carlo, and then brought her back to the United States.[74] In February 1906, Nora was operated on in New York for an unspecified ailment, and Andrew, more uxorious than ever, stayed for two weeks in the hospital while she recovered. They returned to England in the summer, renting Sunninghill Park. Like Sandlea, it was a large place near Windsor, allowing for family house parties and outings, but blessedly without Curphey, who now seemed gone for good. Nora's health had recovered from the traumas of

LEFT: Thomas Mellon, ca. 1850. A self-made man in full, he was the most potent influence in his sons' lives, especially Andrew's. RIGHT: Sarah Jane Negley, mother of eight, of whom five predeceased her. Thomas Mellon, a man known to make his own luck, described their marriage as "the luckiest event of my life."

CAMP HILL COTTAGE.
My birthplace.

The birthplace of Thomas Mellon: Camp Hill Cottage near Omagh in County Tyrone.

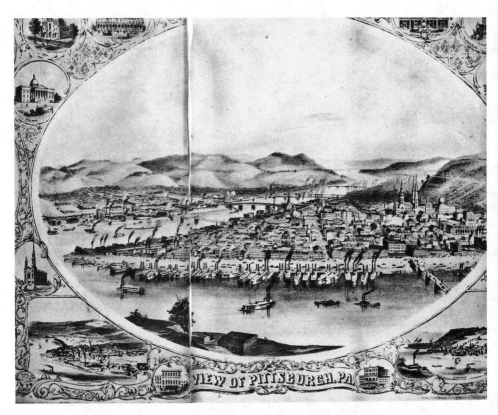

ABOVE: Pittsburgh in 1859 was already a thriving port and a major manufacturing center, but at exorbitant cost to the environment: the town would soon be described as "Hell with the lid taken off." BELOW: T. Mellon & Sons, just one of many private banks in the city when it opened at 145 Smithfield Street in December 1869.

Two years later the bank had moved to 116 Smithfield Street, occupying a cast-iron structure with a statue of Benjamin Franklin, the god of thrift, looming conspicuously over the entrance.

Mellon Brothers Bank, the Bismarck branch in the Dakota Territory in 1882. One of many family ventures outside Pennsylvania, it was managed by Dick Mellon but ultimately did not prosper.

The earliest extant photograph of Andrew W. Mellon,
whose hooded eyes and distant gaze already herald the shy, withdrawn,
and secretive man he would become.

The family home at 401 Negley. In summer the spacious grounds would have been
full of flowers and fruit trees, but inside the atmosphere was ever wintry,
heavy with the grim imperative to acquire.

LEFT: Andrew W. Mellon in his mid-twenties. Handsome and well set up, he was an attractive yet intimidating prospect for the marriageable daughters of Pittsburgh's elite. RIGHT: Andrew seated among three friends, as the four set off to tour Europe in June 1880. Henry Clay Frick, his comrade in accumulating wealth and collecting art, stands to the left.

The Mellon family, ca. 1895. Though a loyal and self-sufficient clan, there was little emotional connection among them. Behind Sarah Jane and Thomas are, left to right, James R., Andrew W., Richard B., and Thomas A. (seated right).

The McMullens of Hertfordshire, Christmas 1885. Nora sits at the center between her parents, among her many brothers, who later would become more or less dependent on Andrew's long-suffering generosity.

Nora McMullen (far left) and Andrew Mellon (center) crossing the Atlantic on the *Germanic* in the summer of 1898, when they were first introduced by Frick.

Andrew and Nora's official wedding photograph, at Hertford Castle on September 12, 1900. Even by the standards of the time, they appeared an awkward couple, and so they would remain until put asunder amid scandal.

Early-twentieth-century Pittsburgh, a nexus of soot, wealth, and Presbyterian primness. Shown the booming, polluted metropolis that was her new home, Nora Mellon exclaimed to her husband, "You don't live *here*?"

LEFT: Paul, Nora, Ailsa, and Andrew, soon after Paul's birth in 1907, when Andrew and Nora were briefly reconciled. Andrew's pose and dress are unusually jaunty, but his face betrays anxiety, perhaps financial as well as personal.

BELOW: 5052 Forbes Street, where Andrew Mellon installed his young bride. With grimy air that precluded opening the windows, hardly any garden, and nearby streetcars clanging past all day and all night, it was hardly a setting an English country girl would find congenial.

The gloomy interior furnished by the groom without consulting the bride. It would become the scene of great unhappiness, first Nora's, and when she left him, Andrew's.

ABOVE LEFT: Alfred Curphey,
the melodramatic villain, who lived off
what he could extract from the wives of
rich, unsuspecting men. The number II
suggests that this photograph may have
been intended for use as an evidentiary
exhibit in the divorce proceedings.

ABOVE RIGHT: Nora Mellon's portrait, by
James Jebusa Shannon, which Andrew had
commissioned in 1908. By the time it was
completed, two years later, Nora had
effectively ceased to be his wife.

RIGHT: A family shattered. At the time
of the divorce, Andrew's family shows the
toll of Nora's scandalous departure.
Ailsa regards her tired and drawn father
with pent-up fury, while a disconsolate
Paul already seems vulnerable,
defensive, and unloved.

<small>CLOCKWISE FROM TOP LEFT:</small> Loyal, and well-rewarded, colleagues and retainers: Charles Martin Hall, inventor of aluminum; Arthur Vining Davis, who built up Alcoa; Colonel James M. Guffey, involved in Gulf Oil until the Mellons "throwed me out"; and James Reed, Andrew Mellon's attorney.

Thick as bankers: Andrew W. Mellon, Henry C. McEldowney, and Richard B. Mellon at a dinner in the early 1930s.

CLOCKWISE FROM TOP LEFT: Not so strange bedfellows: Christopher Magee and William Flinn, who ran the Republican Party machine in Pittsburgh; Senators Boies Penrose and Philander Knox, who helped obtain the Treasury secretaryship for Mellon; and David A. Reed, who represented and defended Mellon's interests in the U.S. Senate. All were stalwarts of the Republican status quo.

Family collaborators: in addition to his brother Dick, these included Andrew's two nephews, E. P. Mellon, left, in architecture, and W. L. Mellon, right, in (among other things) Gulf Oil.

ABOVE: The house on Woodland Road, in Pittsburgh, which Andrew Mellon purchased in 1917. From here he would launch Ailsa into society with much champagne on the very eve of Prohibition. Grander and less gloomy than Forbes Street, it was still surprisingly unimpressive as the sole residence of one of America's richest men. BELOW: Ailsa's wedding, May 29, 1926. For Washington, it was the social event of the decade, although Ailsa's marriage to David Bruce would eventually fall victim to her fragile health and self-absorption.

ABOVE: Andrew and Paul in Cambridge in June 1931.
As Paul graduated, Andrew received his fifteenth
honorary degree, though doubtless distracted by portents
of collapse in the European economy and the international
financial system. RIGHT: Ailsa's husband, David K. E. Bruce.
Some said that the Mellon Bruce truly loved was not Ailsa
but Andrew. For his part, Andrew's relations with his
clear-headed, ambitious son-in-law were far easier than
with his dreamy, bookish son, Paul.

Syosset, the grand mansion on Long Island that Andrew bought for
Ailsa and David Bruce soon after they married.

Henry Clay Frick was not only Mellon's friend and business associate; he was also influential in Mellon's development as an art collector. But his influence, though significant, came later than is generally supposed.

Andrew Mellon bought his first pictures from Knoedler & Company. After the retirement of Roland Knoedler in 1928, the business was run by four partners: from left, Carman Messmore, Charles R. Henschel, Charles Carstairs, and Carrol C. Carstairs.

Joseph Duveen, the greatest art dealer of his generation, who would eventually nudge Mellon toward establishing the National Gallery of Art in Washington, D.C. Mellon delighted in almost invariably paying less for pictures than Duveen asked, and to Duveen's dismay he often exercised his option to return purchases for a full refund.

Edward Sorel's fanciful depiction of the first encounter between Duveen and Andrew Mellon in an elevator in Claridge's Hotel, London, in the early 1920s. In fact, Duveen had previously met the collector who would become his prey and his best client.

The secretary of the treasury in his Washington apartment.
View on the High Road, by Hobbema, is over the mantel,
and Cuyp's *Herdsmen Tending Cattle* is in the background.

the previous year sufficiently that she became pregnant again—a further sign of reconciliation. In December, with his wife in a "delicate condition," Andrew borrowed his nephew's yacht, the *Vagabondia*, for a river party in Florida, and they were joined by James Ross Mellon, by the owner, William Larimer Mellon, and also, once again, by Norman McMullen and his brother Murray, as well as a nurse.[75]

And so matters stood between Andrew and Nora by the end of 1906. What of Curphey in the aftermath of the tearful farewell to Nora? In August 1904, with money extorted from Mellon and recently transferred to his account, he duly purchased the Ballamoar estate on the Isle of Man that he had previously but erroneously claimed had been his—or, at least, his ancestors'. Located near the town of Ramsey, it amounted to just over five hundred acres, plus a rather dilapidated mansion, and it cost him £13,600. Now a country gentleman, he brought over a motorcar and a motor launch, and he set about constructing a new "palatial mansion" in Tudor style, complete with servants' quarters, stables, and extensive out-buildings. It cost at least as much again as the original estate purchase, and it "astonished" the locals by its "magnificence," and perhaps, too, by its incorporation of the "ancestral" arms of Curphey of Ballakillingham.[76] (It was during this construction, in December 1904, that Grace Dundas Hamilton Curphey filed for divorce. The final decree, on the grounds of desertion and adultery, was granted in May of the following year, and Curphey was ordered to pay his former wife maintenance of £6 a week.) In September 1906, Curphey took up residence at Ballamoar, and welcomed a large house party, who toured the island in his new ten-seat motorcar, which was fitted with electric light. To the locals, it all seemed very grand and glamorous.[77]

Having long since spent all his ill-gotten money from Mellon, Curphey urgently needed to find new sources of income, and as a country gentleman, he was better placed to do so. He became associated with the Antwerp-based Société Générale pour l'Agriculture et le Commerce, and also with the Belgian-based bank of Rom & Venderlinden. Through them, he obtained directorships of the Egyptian Mail Steamship Company and the Cairo Electric Railways and Heliopolis Oasis Society. The first of these enterprises aimed to provide a regular service between Marseilles and Alexandria, and the other was intended to develop a high-class residential suburb on the outskirts of Cairo, complete with palaces, villas, a church, and an amusement park.[78] The British armaments manufacturer Lord Armstrong was a member of both boards, but otherwise the directors were at best obscure. Curphey seems to have invested substantially in these two ventures, and while the work was taking place at Ballamoar, he was much involved with the launching of steamships and with developments in Cairo. By November 1906, with everything to his liking on the Isle of Man, he left for Egypt—partly on business, but also to look for his next female victim.[79]

IV. RIDING THE BOOM

As Andrew Mellon's businesses flourished in Pittsburgh during the early 1900s, the political climate in Washington began to change, primarily on account of the energetic and charismatic Theodore Roosevelt.[80] Although a Republican, he was never a party zealot, and he was not wholly to the taste of the Pennsylvania machine: he had a patrician disdain for big business and parvenu wealth, and he believed government had a duty to intervene on the side of the people to regulate what he regarded as irresponsible corporations (the "trusts") and those mega-rich individuals whom he loathed both for their vulgarity and for their irresponsibility. Ironically, it was Philander Knox, that consummate corporation lawyer, who was responsible for initiating the first major antitrust suit early in 1902, invoking the Sherman Act against J. P. Morgan, James J. Hill, and E. H. Harriman for consolidating their railroads into a single holding company, Northern Securities, which was second in size only to United States Steel. But as a lawyer, Knox was always willing to argue his client's case, whether it was that of a great capitalist or the people of the United States, and the Supreme Court ruled in his favor in 1904. This was scarcely what Mellon and Frick thought the government should be doing, and it was certainly not what they paid the Republican Party to do for them. As Frick put it: Roosevelt "got down on his knees to us. We bought the son of a bitch and then he did not stay bought." But for now, this new anti-business ethos passed Mellon by, and he continued with his work unmolested.[81]

For the restructuring of his banking interests, the continued expansion of "his" companies, the disposal of Pittsburgh streetcars and Union Steel, and the challenges of coal, did not consume all of his energy. There were also two new investments in growing companies, as Mellon again passed positive judgment on the promise of innovation.[82] The first was the creation of the Standard Steel Car Company. Like Union Steel and McClintic-Marshall, this was essentially a product of the unraveling of the Frick-Carnegie partnership.[83] One secondary effect of that falling-out were convulsions at the local Pressed Steel Car Company, previously owned by Carnegie Steel and now in the possession of United States Steel. Three executives—Charles T. Schoen, John M. Hansen, and "Diamond Jim" Brady—fearing for their future there, now sought to establish a new business for the construction of passenger and freight railcars. Along with Henry Oliver and Frick, the Mellon brothers made a substantial investment in the new $3 million corporation in 1902, which was floated on the Pittsburgh and New York stock exchanges. Hansen became president, and with Mellon support began production on a site in Butler, Pennsylvania, near the major railroads that served Pittsburgh: the Pennsylvania, the Baltimore and Ohio, and the Baltimore and Lake Erie. It was a brilliant ploy. Even before the plant was finished, Standard Steel was receiving orders from both the Pennsylvania and the Baltimore and Ohio, and within two years they had produced more than sixty thousand cars.[84]

Thanks to its superior technology, its founders' previous experience in steel car manufacturing, its committed financial support from the very beginning (Dick was even more enthusiastic than Andrew), and its unparalleled access to markets, the Standard Steel Car Company was an instant success, and although it had been launched as a public company, Andrew and Dick soon acquired a majority of the stock.[85] Along with Crucible Steel, Union Steel, and McClintic-Marshall, it represented another astute venture into an industry in which the Mellons had scarcely been a presence before 1900. And as a Mellon company, it benefited from the brothers' strong commitment to backward integration: they not only funded the Standard plant, but also the suppliers of many of its critical components, including the Butler Forged Steel Wheel Company and the Butler Bolt and Rivet Company. Colonel Frank Drake, a later Standard president, contended that "one of AWM's outstanding traits was that he gave his executive terrific authority, never interfered with details." But he knew the terms of his free rein: "until you did something that he himself judged to be wrong or showing poor judgment, he would back you against anyone and under all conditions."[86]

The most momentous new Mellon brothers move of these years was their return to the oil business, not in Pennsylvania, but in Texas and subsequently in Oklahoma.[87] Late in 1900, hoping for a gusher near Beaumont on the Texas plain, James Guffey and John Galey, those two incorrigible wildcatters and prospectors, had joined with Anthony Lucas to form the James M. Guffey Petroleum Company, with initial capital of $300,000. One-quarter of the shares went to Galey, one-eighth to Lucas, and five-eighths to Guffey. Somewhere behind the scenes were Andrew and Dick Mellon, who lent large sums to Galey and Guffey at the time.[88] Extensive drilling took place in the Beaumont district, and in January 1901, the greatest oil well then known was discovered near Spindletop, which was soon pouring black gold onto the prairie at the rate of 100,000 barrels a day. During the next five months, six additional wells were discovered, all very productive; a million acres in Texas and Louisiana were leased; a pipeline was built from Spindletop to the coast; and a hundred tank cars were acquired. But Guffey would need far greater sums to make the new field profitable, and although he had connections with Standard Oil, Rockefeller had resolved to stay out of Texas, where he had recently been indicted in a local court.[89]

Accordingly, Guffey sought out his old friend Andrew Mellon to finance this new enterprise much more lavishly than he had been willing to do up to now. Andrew was not eager to backtrack more deeply into oil, and a brief visit Dick made to Spindletop left him distinctly unimpressed: he told his elder brother "there's nothing in it for us."[90] Eventually, however, and in part because of John Galey's personal plea, they reconsidered the enterprise, and in May 1901 the Mellons refinanced the Guffey Petroleum Company through a Pittsburgh syndicate that included such associates as James Reed and William Flinn. (Frick again declined, believing the venture would never amount to much.) The company came into existence with a capital stock of $15 million, represented by 150,000 shares. But the initial subscription was $1.5 million, of which the Mellons put up $600,000, in payment for Guffey's wells, leases, and pipeline, and also for the storage tanks and tank cars he had assembled during the previous six months and now turned over to the new corporation. From these transactions, Lucas and Galey made a considerable profit and eventually retired from the business altogether, but Guffey stayed as president, collecting a large cash payment, and also becoming for a time the largest stockholder.[91]

With this massive infusion, Guffey Petroleum began to make essential improvements and to scale up. A modern refinery was built at Port Arthur; distributing nodes were established in several large cities; and a fleet of tankers (many of them constructed by the New York Shipbuilding Company) began conveying the oil from Texas to select markets. In November 1901 the Gulf Refining Corporation, a wholly owned subsidiary of Guffey Petroleum, was established to manage the Port Arthur refinery, and the following June Andrew and Dick subscribed $2.5 million of a $4 million bond issue.[92] But these early years were not easy. Just before they made these additional commitments, and at almost exactly the time that he was getting out of Union Steel and Pittsburgh streetcars, Andrew had once again thought of selling out these new oil interests to Rockefeller. Accompanied by WL, he went to New York to discuss such a proposal with H. H. Rogers and John D. Archbold. But having paid once to buy the Mellons out in Pennsylvania, Standard Oil proved unwilling to do so again, least of all over Texas, and the Mellons were left to make the best of what then seemed a rather chancy proposition. Years later, when Gulf Oil was producing annual profits of twenty million dollars, Andrew Mellon remarked of Standard Oil's decision: "They weren't so smart, were they?" But for now, as he admitted to Charles Schwab, there was "no possibility of returns to shareholders for a long time to come."[93]

Why was this? Guffey Petroleum faced many difficulties and uncertainties. For one, massive capital was needed for the drilling and refining and piping necessary to establish another fully integrated operation, but so much oil was being produced in Texas that the selling prices were too low to allow for much profit. Moreover, oil from the Beaumont field was so poor (it was low-grade high-sulfur oil) that there was scarcely any market for it, and in the middle of 1902, the Spindletop yield also began to fall off alarmingly. There was in addition the problem of Guffey himself. Although an old friend and a genius at locating oil, he was no businessman: he did not understand numbers and was a poor manager, preferring to spend his time prospecting (it didn't help matters that he was also a lifelong Democrat).[94] Hence Andrew and Dick decided to send down George Davison, who was now free of his earlier involvement with Pittsburgh streetcars, to report on the business, and also to install William Larimer Mellon, who was likewise in need of a new job, as vice president of Guffey Petroleum, charged with implementing Davison's recommendations.[95]

W. L. Mellon and Davison began to turn the business around by recruiting a new management team, appointing Frank A. Leovy to supervise production, George H. Taber to oversee refining, and Gale R. Nutty to head sales.[96] At the same time, a new field was discovered twenty miles south of Tulsa, Oklahoma, yielding crude of much higher quality than that in Texas. Standard Oil was there too, but Theodore Roosevelt took a dim view of the company: indeed, his administration was then preparing to file its antitrust suit of November 1906 against Rockefeller. Unmolested, the Mellons were allowed to construct a four-hundred-mile pipeline from Tulsa to Port Arthur (WL may also have bribed some officials from the Department of the Interior), for which project they formed the Gypsy Oil Company.[97] The final problem was Guffey's leadership, but in his very incompetence lay the possibility of a solution. For by 1905, he owed the Mellons some one million dollars in loans and back interest, and he had pledged, among other things, his 24,000 shares in Guffey Petroleum as security. The Mellons now foreclosed, took his shares, and got rid of him. "They throwed me out" was Guffey's typically colorful rendering of his enforced retirement in 1906.[98]

As at the Carborundum Company, the Mellons were unsentimental and determined when it came to ousting successful pioneers who turned out to be inadequate managers. But their relations with Guffey were by no means fully severed. He remained president of the Trade Dollar Consolidated Mining Company, in which the Mellons had substantial interests, and they subsequently advanced more money to him for coal-mining ventures in West Virginia. These turned out badly: from 1910 to 1920, Guffey's affairs were in the hands of the receivers, and between 1925 and 1927 he unavailingly sued the Mellons, claiming partial credit for the late success of Gulf Oil Company—Guffey Petroleum's successor—and therefore a share of the subsequent (and substantial) profits. But that was not the end of the story. For, since 1920 he had been receiving a Mellon pension of $12,000 a year—paid, not to him, on the grounds that he would squander it, but to one of his daughters. Perhaps the Mellons felt a twinge of regret? Perhaps they sentimentalized Guffey's association with their father? Whatever their motives, the pension mollified Guffey somewhat. He lived till 1930 and was ninety-one when he died.[99]

Such was Andrew Mellon's consuming and expanding business life as the turn-of-the-century boom reached its peak, and as industrial Pittsburgh prospered as never before. Two sets of figures give some indication of what this meant in terms of his accumulating personal wealth. When the Mellon National Bank was established in 1902, he declared himself worth "more than fifteen million dollars over and above his debts and liabilities," in real estate, stocks, bonds, and other assets.[100] This is a "book value," not a "market value," and is only an estimate, but in 1902 Andrew Mellon may well have been worth twenty million dollars (about four hundred million dollars in today's money): a significant advance, reflecting the recent frenzy of activity and accumulation, yet still not a stupendous figure compared to the titanic fortunes of the time. By January 1906, Mellon declared himself to be worth almost thirty-one million dollars (nearly six hundred million dollars now)—again at book, and not market value.[101] If, for example, his substantial holdings in Pittsburgh Reduction, or Carborundum, or McClintic-Marshall, or Union Trust had been offered publicly for sale, they would have fetched many times their book value. To put the real extent of his fortune at fifty million dollars might seem an exaggeration (it would make him close to a billionaire in our time), but probably not a great one. By this time, Andrew Mellon was so rich that it was virtually impossible for anyone to know the true magnitude of his wealth.

From "his perch atop the Union Trust Company," in alliance with his brother Dick and with Henry Clay Frick, and through his widely distributed and strategically placed investments, Andrew Mellon had established himself by the mid-1900s as the single most significant individual in the economic life and progress of western Pennsylvania. It had happened very suddenly in the few years since 1898, and his newly established status was reflected in his directorships of forty-one companies (more than anyone else in Pittsburgh; Dick was next with thirty-one). Through these and through his co-directors at Union Trust, who also sat on many additional boards, Mellon's reach extended that much further. His was an extraordinarily diversified portfolio: of banks and financial institutions; of property and real estate; of utilities and transportation; of nineteenth-century industries such as coal and steel; and of their twentieth-century successors, such as oil and aluminum.[102] Having made some notable strategic decisions during the great depression following 1893 that would accrue great long-term advantage, Mellon had ridden the boom years that followed with exceptional skill and flair. Indeed, in many ways, this was his most successful time as a creative capitalist and (as he would see it) as a patriotic statesman of American business.

But this was not the whole truth of things. Although a believer in free enterprise and the free market, Mellon, like many businessmen of the time, also rather liked monopolies. Alcoa was one, based on its patents, and Pittsburgh Coal functioned like one, because of its local dominance. Mellon gobbled up rival banks in the region, and he had happily leased his streetcar interests to the Philadelphia Company, which thereafter controlled all the local lines. They had been built by corrupt methods, and as in many American cities, the consolidated utility was much criticized by Pittsburghers for the poor quality of its service.[103] But Mellon did not care. A quarter of a century later, when he was secretary of the treasury, the Philadelphia Company opened a grand new building in the city. At the last minute, Mellon was unable to attend the ceremony but he sent a letter of congratulation in which he made his views plain: "The opening of this great house of service," he noted, was "a striking example of the earnest and intelligent effort" which utilities were making "to give the public adequate and efficient service." For forty years, he went on, the company had been "doing work of remarkable value," proving itself "an asset to the community" and enjoying "the confidence of the people."[104] Like the Judge, Andrew Mellon was wholly opposed to any form of municipal enterprise: he preferred his monopolies to be private rather than public.

This was more financial self-interest than financial statesmanship. Nor, in these heady and frenzied years of opportunity and temptation, was Mellon as hostile to making fast money as he and his admirers would later claim. "I have never made anything myself in speculation," he would later write to a Miss Stephens.[105] But the sale of Union Steel at grossly inflated prices showed that Mellon was capable of the very greed he deplored in others, and the consolidations of the Pittsburgh coal mines and streetcar lines were solely motivated by profit. Indeed, when Burton Hendrick showed a copy of this speculation-denying letter to John Nelson, Mellon's financial secretary from 1902 to 1908, Nelson threw up his hands and laughed. Mellon, he insisted, not only speculated, but he had three separate accounts through which he did so. He would "buy on the margin, lose and make" and "in the end came out about whole."[106] Nelson had no reason to lie, but the evidence for such activities has not survived. It may never have been a major activity for Mellon. But in the boom years of the 1900s, when he needed all the money he could lay his hands on to pour into new enterprises, he may have found the allure of quick profit irresistible.

V. A (BRIEF) TIME OF HOPE

From the late autumn of 1906 to the summer of 1907, Andrew Mellon's private affairs and business matters converged and intermingled in ways that gave him cause for optimism on all fronts. The refreshed domestic happiness that he believed he enjoyed with Nora was accompanied by signs of his maturing confidence and growing ambition as a collector. To be sure, M. Knoedler & Company had recently closed its Pittsburgh gallery and sent Charles Carstairs to head its branch in London.[107] But his correspondence and friendship with Mellon continued uninterrupted and moved to a higher level of art and acquisition. Just after Christmas 1906, Carstairs offered Mellon George Romney's painting *Miss Willoughby*, which he described as "one of the most beautiful Romneys you ever laid eyes on." "A charming little girl," he went on. "I thought of you the moment I bought it." "It was painted," he concluded, making the connection he knew would ring bells, "just two years later than Mr. Frick's *Lady Hamilton*, and is of Romney's finest period." Miss Willoughby was, moreover, just about the same age as Ailsa Mellon, a further incentive for Andrew to acquire such a beguiling image of youthful ardor, innocence, and hope. Purchased soon after for $50,000, it was the fourth and last of his acquisitions from this early period to find its eventual way into the National Gallery of Art in Washington.[108]

At the same time, Mellon (and Knoedler) sought to establish a closer link between his family and his pictures. In late January 1907, Carstairs was in correspondence with John Singer Sargent, wondering "when you would be likely to paint the portraits of Mr. & Mrs. Mellon?" "The time they will visit London," Carstairs explained, "is somewhat dependent upon your decision."[109] Sargent, the most famous and fashionable portraitist of the day, had painted P. A. B. Widener (twice); Alexander Cassatt, president of the Pennsylvania Railroad; Joseph Pulitzer, the newspaper tycoon; and Mrs. J. P. Morgan, though not her husband. Clearly, the negotiations, though now stalled, had already gone forward some way. Sargent had twenty-odd portraits on the easel that year, and he would not paint in autumn or winter. "He is," Carstairs wrote in anxious exasperation to Mellon, "such a slippery bird," and "so overworked it is always agreeable for him to postpone an order." In the end, nothing came of the proposal, perhaps because in that very year Sargent resolved to limit his future commissions. (In the early 1920s, Mellon would toy with the idea of commissioning Sargent to paint his own portrait, but again nothing ever came of it.)[110] Meanwhile, Knoedler's finances were "pretty low," and Mellon discounted several notes for them which were due in the late spring, and continued to do so into the winter (Frick had already been supporting the gallery for some years).[111]

At just the time when he was closing the deal on *Miss Willoughby* the first pipes were being laid in the trunk oil line from Tulsa to Port Arthur. The Guffey Company was precarious enough that Andrew and Dick had to give their personal guarantee of payment, but in eight months the pipeline was finished, and the oil soon began to flow. Mellon's risks had been rewarded, Standard Oil had been vanquished, and in this newly buoyant environment, the Mellons moved quickly to reorganize their interests.[112] On January 30, 1907, they established the Gulf Oil Corporation, which absorbed Guffey Petroleum, the Gulf Refining Company, and the Gulf Pipeline Company, and was headquartered in Pittsburgh. The capitalization was not increased, and the stock of the new company was the same $15 million as that of the old Guffey Petroleum. The usual elaborate swap of stocks and bonds took place, at the end of which Andrew and Dick were left with a comfortable majority control in what was, again, a close and privately held company. William Larimer Mellon became president of Gulf and would remain so for twenty-two years, during which time it would become the Mellons' most profitable and most famous enterprise. In the same year, another new name appeared in the Mellon portfolio, as Pittsburgh Reduction, citing the market necessity of matching its name to its product, rebranded itself as the Aluminum Company of America, or Alcoa.[113]

With the launching of Gulf and the renaming of Pittsburgh Reduction, most of the great Mellon enterprises were now in being, and as they continued to expand and to prosper, they would soon become more widely known. Only Koppers, Mellbank, and, to a lesser extent, Pan American Airways lay some distance in the future. Many of these businesses, such as Alcoa and Carborundum and Gulf, were fully integrated concerns, extending all the way from the extraction of raw materials, to processing and refining, to production and sales. This was a crucial, and ever more permanent, characteristic of Andrew Mellon's concerns. But integration was not only promoted *within* each Mellon company: the more extensively the portfolio diversified, and the more completely the directorships interlocked, the more the goal of coordination was promoted *across and between* Mellon companies. As David Koskoff puts it:

> Not only were most of [Mellon's] enterprises wholly integrated operations, but his interests as a whole were integrated. New York Shipbuilding built Gulf tankers out of Union Steel, all financed and insured through Mellon companies. Alcoa's laborers lived in houses financed by Union Trust, built on Mellon lots out of Mellon lumber, heated by Mellon coal, lit by Mellon utilities, and they rode to work on Mellon streetcars. If they had any money left at the end of the week, it went into a Mellon bank.[114]

Some of the details here are incorrect: Union Steel had been sold before Gulf Oil came into being, and most Alcoa workers didn't live in Pittsburgh. But the general picture is wholly accurate.

In the midst of these signal developments, Paul Mellon was born on June 11, 1907—the most tangible result of the recent reconciliation between Andrew and Nora. As he had done with Ailsa, Andrew gave him only one Christian name, departing from Mellon custom, so while there was AW, RB, WL, and RK, Paul would not be known by his initials.[115]

(Later in life, though, perhaps finding the pull of family tradition irresistible, Paul's senior staff and associates would refer to him as "PM.") At the end of July, Andrew, Nora, Ailsa, the infant Paul, and Miss Abernethy departed to England, where they again settled at Sunninghill Park. As Andrew would recollect, they "enjoyed a happy summer." In early October, he took Nora, her widowed brother Alan McMullen, and her sister-in-law Maude McMullen over to Paris, intending to stay a week or so before returning to Sunninghill, where he left the two children with Miss Abernethy and a housekeeper. But in Paris, Mellon received word of a sudden and severe panic in Pittsburgh, and judging "the bad state of financial affairs at home" to be critical, he immediately took passage for New York, leaving Nora, her brother, and her sister-in-law to make their own way back to England. Arriving at Sunninghill in late October, they remained until the end of the year, and Paul was baptized in St. George's Chapel, Windsor—a telling choice, considering Nora's earlier assignation there with Curphey, but also a presentiment of the lifelong Anglophile Paul would become.[116]

6

THE FIRST SCANDAL

Separation and Divorce, 1907–12

The faculties, abilities and proclivities of every human being are in some respect more or less different from all others; and if . . . the suitability of each to the other for such a union might with greater clarity be ascertained beforehand, . . . much misery, dissatisfaction and necessity for divorces [would be] avoided.

Thomas Mellon and His Times, p. 105

I. THE DARKENING SCENE

After Paul Mellon was born in the summer of 1907, relations between Andrew and Nora went rapidly downhill, though Andrew remained sublimely—or naïvely—oblivious to this. The immediate catalyst was the major financial crisis in October 1907, which necessitated Andrew's hurried return from Paris to Pittsburgh. He had good reason to go, but Nora was furious at his once again putting business before marriage. Her subsequent letters were full of rage and resentment, but also of a desperate sense of abandonment and loneliness back at Sunninghill: "It was such a shock and a disappointment your going off like that"; "Do tell me you like to get my letters, for it is so disheartening to write when I imagine you do not read them"; "Do you love Ailsa's mother, darling? Do you love Paul's mother, too, Fatty? Do you really love me?"[1] It was unbearable to her that, owing to what seemed an obsession with work, she had "so little" of him, while he had "all" of her. "I have been feeling so horrid for more than a week," she wrote in mid-November, "feeling that you had forgotten me after you got back to your horrid old business." "Oh Fatty," she went on, "if you only knew how jealous I am of it all the time. That is really why I have not written for so long, for I thought, what does he care?" Or, as she put it with pithy naïveté in another letter: "Will business always have to come before me?" "It is so easy for you to make me love you," she would write more poignantly later, "and yet you never seem to think that it is worth the trouble."[2]

Nora had also come to hate the regular summer ritual of living in England in rented accommodations: "I am so weary of knocking about and living in hired beds that I could cry"; "I hate to think of parting with these servants." Just before the Mellons departed for Paris, they had looked over a house called Park Close near Windsor Park. Nora wanted Andrew to buy it then and there, and it seems that his sudden departure to America dashed this very specific hope as well: "Just when the one wish of my heart, after all these years, seemed coming true, to have to give it all up *again*."[3] Before Andrew left, she renewed her plea that he buy the house, "and let me stay over and furnish it for you ready for next summer." "You could," she entreated, "come over and stay with me for a couple of months soon, for surely things are better now." "I implore you," she wrote, "if you have any love for me, let me stay here with the children and mother and you come back as soon as you can."[4] But it was not to be. Andrew could not come to Nora; she and the children were obliged to return to him. And she made her feelings plain, in a letter pouring out all her accumulated wrath and disillusion:

> I never can understand how you can possibly miss me or want me when I am away from you, for you never seem to want me when we are together. I am feeling altogether broken up at the thought of leaving the country. Everything is so ideal and the children so well and healthy, and now I have to give it all up and come back to housekeeping and other joys! I would not care a bit of it if I had *you* to look forward to, but the thought of those long dreary lonesome days and those silent preoccupied evenings almost kills me. Why must that loathsome *business* take all the strength and vitality which you ought to give to me? Why should you only give me your tired evenings? Why should I give you all my strength and health and youth and be content with nothing in return? For I am not content and never shall be as long as I have to be second—always second. I am feeling so desperately lonely tonight I could almost kill myself, but I would rather be lonely here than in Pittsburgh.[5]

Nora and the children returned to Pittsburgh in late December. Early in 1908, Judge Mellon died, his life having overlapped by six months that of his most recent grandson, Paul. And he manifested his patriarchal prerogative to the last, quitting life the morning of February 3, with perfect timing, on his ninety-fifth birthday, and Sarah Jane's ninety-first, when the entire Mellon clan was due to assemble at 401 Negley. The Judge had often seen death, and had thought about it a good deal; and he had had plenty of time to contemplate his own, to come to terms with it, and to make his plans. "A long life," he had observed philosophically toward the close of his autobiography, "is like an ear of corn with the grains shriveled at both ends." "The few years at the end of an old man's life," he went on, "are of as little account to him or others as the few years at its beginning." He hoped "to depart in peace, with as little pain and suffering as possible," and he wished "to be laid quietly, without display of public funeral, between my parents and only brother, with room for my loving wife beside me." There he would "rest as I have lived, quietly and unostentatiously, with merely a modest stone to mark the spot."[6] In 1895, he had further elaborated on these instructions, asking that his grave should be covered with "a rough granite block, such as those at the entrance of our home, though not so high, perhaps, with no more lettering than the name, age and date of death to be chiseled on the lower or outside face of the stone."[7]

The Judge's funeral took place two days later and, as he wanted, it was a private affair, appropriately quiet and unostentatious, conducted at 401 Negley by the pastor of East Liberty Presbyterian Church. He spoke a few words, a string quartet played "Nearer, My God, to Thee," and the impossible yet indomitable old man was later laid to rest in Allegheny Cemetery, on a cold, stormy winter's day, with heavy sleet falling. Andrew Carnegie wrote a letter of condolence, to which the other Pittsburgh Andrew replied: "Your beautiful and appreciative words are appreciated by all of us—especially my mother." "He was," William A. Mellon later observed, "one of those strong souls that loved life for the chance to think and do, and such souls abhor death."[8] On February 10, the Allegheny County Bar Association met especially in the Judge's honor. "He held," his colleagues noted, "to the old-fashioned doctrine that honesty and common sense were as essential in the administration of public as of private trusts. Stealing was stealing, whether done by the professional pickpocket, the respectable politician, or the dishonest contractor."[9] Almost a year later, on January 19, 1909, Sarah Jane Mellon followed her husband, and as befitted the daughter of Jacob Negley, she was mourned in the local press as the "last of the old East Liberty pioneers." Her funeral took the same form as the Judge's. "Nearer, My God, to Thee" was played for her as well, and she was buried in Allegheny Cemetery beside him.[10]

One reason why the Judge had "not the slightest fear or concern about the time or manner of going" was his confidence to the end that his sons would, without fail, do as he told them. After all, except for George's debts and Andrew's marriage, they had always done just that. And so he left no detailed will, partly because his substantial property had already been passed on, but also because he felt no need for any legally binding request, certain as he was that his sons would "cheerfully satisfy my wishes without it." He was right. Moreover, although he was gone, he did not intend to be far away: "I have very strong hope and assurance," he had written in 1895, with equal tenacity and faith in the hereafter, "that I shall be with you all as much afterwards as before until we all meet again face to face." Indeed, the unforgettable imprint of his personality and philosophy would ensure his continued presence in the lives of those who had known him; while for Mellons yet unborn the inspiring and intimidating pages of his autobiography, with its exhortations to effort and warnings against ease and self-indulgence, would serve well enough. In death, as in life, his unsettled contradictions would remain. He eventually expected "to enjoy happy communion with all my children and other loved ones" in that next world in which, despite his rational Darwinian skepticism, he had some-how never ceased to believe.

With the passing of his father, Andrew Mellon's place as head of the family was assured; he wasn't the eldest surviving brother, but he clearly was the most talented, the most able, the wealthiest, and the most com-manding. His ascent to dominance was partly a consequence of the Judge's decision, more than thirty years before, to put him, rather than one of his two elder brothers, in charge of T. Mellon & Sons. At that time the Judge already had the greatest of respect for his abilities, and Andrew had proved the esteem to be amply and abundantly justified. Indeed, in his audaciousness and multifaceted expertise, Andrew far surpassed his father, though it must always be remembered that he began his profes-sional life with all the advantages of wealth and connection that the Judge had had to create for himself. But where Andrew failed to equal, let alone surpass, his father was in the range and richness of his humanity. Behind the Judge's implacably stern façade was a warmhearted and emotional spirit, moved by the tragedy and transience of life. Yet behind Andrew's no less steely exterior, it often seemed to many people, and especially by now to Nora, that there was either something vaguely unpleasant— or nothing at all. He was a hollow man, with no interior life. He could judge men and business, but not women and love. In warning Andrew against marrying Nora, his father had been wholly correct.

The period immediately after Judge Mellon's passing cannot have been easy for Andrew; nor was it easy for Nora. Although she had returned from England only in late December 1907, she was on the move again the following March, this time to Aiken, South Carolina, and once more with Dick and Jennie Mellon. She seems to have suffered another bout of sustained illness, perhaps nervous exhaustion, and her equivocal, high-strung letters show the strain. "Do try to come down for a few days," she urged Andrew, on the one hand. Then: "Your letter did not seem to miss one very much! Do you darling?" "Terribly disappointed that you are so *un-anxious* to come down," she wrote again. "It is *wicked* to be so tied!"[11] Eventually Andrew did join her, and they returned together to Pittsburgh in early April 1908. In mid-May, they departed for their usual summer in England, staying at Park Close: Andrew, eager to obtain for Nora the English residence she ardently desired, had now acquired an option to purchase it for £20,000. If Nora still liked the place at the end of their stay, he decided, he would buy it. Sometime in June, the actress Maxine Elliott, a guest at Park Close, asked Nora to accompany her to Paris. Andrew initially refused to let her go, "disliking to have her seen about Paris alone with Maxine," who was getting divorced that year. Faced with Nora's hurt and disappointment, however, Andrew relented. The plan was for him to join them after a few days, so they might all return together. But soon after her arrival in Paris, Nora wrote to Andrew asking him to send money, and saying that, as the remaining time was so short, it scarcely seemed worth his while to come. She signed the letter "always your loving Norchen"—a distinct hypocrisy this, for her need for money, and her suggestion that Andrew not bother coming, had a less-than-loving reason: Curphey was in town.[12]

He had made his way from Egypt to Paris via a new conquest, Lady Vivian, his grandest to date. She was born Barbara Fanning, with money of her own, and she had married into an ancient Cornish family, with eight thousand acres and a fine mansion at Glynn near Bodmin. The third Lord Vivian had been a career diplomat whose final posting was as British ambassador to Rome; his son, born in 1878, had succeeded him as the fourth baron in 1893, and (unlike Curphey's) his service in the Boer War was authentic, and left him severely wounded. In 1903, the maimed Lord Vivian had married Barbara, and she bore two children, in July 1904 and March 1906.[13] Toward the end of that year, Lord and Lady Vivian went to Cairo, where they met Curphey, recently arrived from Ballamoar. Lord Vivian took an instant dislike to him ("he was not a desirable person"), and urged his wife to eschew him.[14] His lordship thereupon departed for a month's shooting in the interior, while Lady Vivian remained in Cairo and, in defiance of her husband, became well acquainted with Curphey and agreed to join him in a motoring party from Marseilles to Paris on her way back to England. On returning to Cairo, Lord Vivian informed Curphey that her ladyship would not be joining the party, and the trip was abandoned.

But Lady Vivian continued to consort with Curphey back in England, and in April 1907 she left her husband, informing him that she would not return. Lord Vivian made repeated efforts to dissuade her, but they were to no avail, and from October 1907 Curphey and Lady Vivian lived together at Ballamoar.[15] Lord Vivian thereupon filed for divorce, alleging both desertion and adultery, and citing Curphey as the co-respondent. A provisioned decree was granted on December 17, 1907, the suit being undefended. Meanwhile, Curphey was fully occupied as a notable in the Isle of Man: he presented various trophies at the local livestock show, he donated an x-ray machine to the Ramsay Cottage Hospital, he received the local schoolchildren for tea, and it was rumored he might run for a seat for the local parliament, the House of Keys.[16] Early in 1908, Curphey presided at the annual dog and poultry show, where Lady Vivian's canines won the first two places; in the same month, he announced an ambitious agricultural venture costing some quarter of a million pounds, which he and unnamed banker friends were to finance (could he have had Andrew in mind again?). The plan was to purchase and drain the nearby wastelands, and to lay out smallholdings for fruit and vegetable farms whose produce would find a ready market across the Irish Sea in Liverpool and Manchester.[17]

When *The Times* reported the Vivian divorce, it obligingly described Curphey as "a man of considerable means, who lives in the Isle of Man and spends a good deal of time in Cairo." But within days of this announcement, Curphey had left the island, accompanied by Lady Vivian, never to return. According to the local newspaper, he would be "absent for some time, but the closing of Ballamoar is only temporary."[18] In fact, the self-made man-about-Man had been ruined when investments in Egypt, including £40,000 in the Egyptian Steamship Company, had been wiped out in the same crash of fall 1907 that had necessitated Andrew Mellon's return to Pittsburgh. In February 1908, Curphey parted with all his personal effects—furniture, pictures, linen, glass, horses, carriages, and motorcars—for £4,000, and in the following month, he sold the whole Ballamoar estate to his associate Francis Rom for a sum rumored to be near £60,000. He had set out for Paris with Lady Vivian, but when her final divorce decree came through in the summer, he dumped her, and she remarried soon after.[19] And so Curphey found himself in Paris once again in need of a big cash infusion. The arrival of the lonely Mrs. Mellon could not have been more propitious.

Andrew Mellon, meanwhile, still apparently basking in his fool's paradise of domestic felicity, continued to purchase paintings, and even sought to commission a permanent pictorial record of what still seemed to him his happy family. In August 1908, he acquired, through Knoedler, J. M.W. Turner's painting of the Thames, *Mortlake Terrace: Early Summer Morning*. It had previously been offered to Frick, who initially turned it down, and Mellon bought it for $70,000. Both in price and in quality, it was well up to the standard of his recent acquisitions of Cuyp, Gainsborough, and Romney, and as only the second Turner bought by a Pittsburgher (the first had been *The Wreckers*, acquired by Alexander Byers in 1899 for $50,000), it was a further indication of his evolving taste and growing confidence as a collector.[20] It may also have been a sign of his budding Anglophilia, and of his desire to please Nora: it could be intended as a memento of their summers spent in England in houses near or on the Thames. Yet little more than a year later, Mellon sold the painting to Frick, who'd evidently reconsidered it, for $82,875, a substantially higher price than he had paid Knoedler for it. It remains in the Frick Collection in New York to this day.[21] It is not clear why Mellon parted with the painting so quickly. But it may be no coincidence that he began to realize the disintegration of his marriage at just this time. Indeed, as his domestic life imploded, he suddenly ceased to acquire, buying no paintings between late 1908 and early 1918, retiring as a collector before he had ever made a significant mark.[22]

But until then, Mellon was seriously set on the family portraits. Charles Carstairs had failed to lure John Singer Sargent, but there were other possibilities, among them the artist Harrington Mann. He had started as a member of the Glasgow School, painting Yorkshire fishermen and historical scenes, but his attention had recently turned to high society subjects, his works combining Whistler's tonal approach with bravura brushwork reminiscent of Sargent. Upon his first visit to the United States in 1907, he was quickly taken up by Knoedler (he would later paint Charles Carstairs's wife, and also his colleague Carman Messmore's). Thereafter, Mann made regular Atlantic crossings, maintaining both a home and a studio in New York. In part because of his tact and charm, he came to specialize in depicting children, and by the end of his career he had produced more than three hundred such portraits.[23] One of his earliest was of Ailsa and Paul, in the front hall of the Forbes Street house, which he completed in the early summer of 1908: Ailsa in a silken dress, her hand resting on a side table; Paul nearby on the ground, holding a big orange. It was an attractive tableau of a youthful sibling innocence that would soon be lost forever. The picture itself eventually suffered the same fate: having passed from Ailsa to Paul, it unaccountably disappeared during the 1930s.[24]

Having arranged a painting of his children, Andrew Mellon contemplated a portrait of Nora—though he found it neither appropriate nor necessary to commission a picture of himself at this time. James Jebusa Shannon, an American-born but British-trained artist, specialized in high society portraits, and had spent much of the mid-1900s in the United States.[25] Like Harrington Mann, Shannon had been taken up by Knoedler, and they mounted several exhibitions of his work. But he was based in Britain for most of his career, and in the summer of 1908, he was able to begin a full-length portrait of Nora, who visited his studio in London once or twice a week. Reminiscent of a Sargent, this Nora is a commanding presence in a flowing gown, a rose in her right hand, and a fountain playing behind her. The commission cost almost $8,000, twice the sum Andrew had paid Harrington Mann, and the account was not finally settled until 1911. But by the time it was completed, Andrew and Nora were separated and well on the way to divorce. Which of them should enjoy the custody of the painting, Andrew as the patron or Nora as the subject? In November 1912, Andrew had the portrait put in storage, "uncertain yet about its disposition." But the following year he instructed Knoedler to deliver it to Nora, and it remained in her possession until her death, when it passed to Paul.[26]

II. THE MARRIAGE DISINTEGRATES

By the summer of 1908, as Andrew Mellon obliviously thought of art, Nora and Curphey in Paris thought of being together. She had had her fill of married life, including the recent attempt at reconciliation; he, after his recent financial reversals, was running on empty. Whether she suspected any venial motive or no, Nora was willing to try to get Curphey some additional cash from the most obvious and plentiful source. Sometime after her return from Paris to Park Close, she asked Andrew for a regular allowance. Hitherto, he had always given her as much as she asked, as and when she requested it, but he now agreed to a more regular arrangement.

He initially suggested ten thousand dollars annually, but Nora rejected this as inadequate. Eventually they settled on a yearly sum of twenty-five thousand dollars—perhaps the equivalent of half a million dollars today.[27] Much of it seems to have been earmarked for Curphey, who had crossed over from Paris, and whom Nora was seeing at every opportunity: on days she went to London to sit for her portrait, on an overnight trip to Arundel, and also when driving or riding in the parks at Windsor. With Nora's money, the flat-broke Curphey was able to buy expensive clothes, eat in the best restaurants, travel widely, and live as the gentleman he pretended to be.[28]

Emboldened by Nora's renewed attention and the money that flowed with it, Curphey appointed one Charles Ernest Long as "steward" of his "estates." By this time, of course, he owned no land: Long's job was as a go-between for Curphey and Nora in England, the same task Miss Abernethy was discharging in Pittsburgh. According to Long's later testimony, it was at about this time that Curphey and Nora were each tattooed: her name on his left breast, his pet name, "Pig," over her heart (although Paul Mellon thought this untrue).[29] Meanwhile, Andrew had come upon a new property called Stoke Park, "a beautiful estate with large meadows not far from Windsor," which "had been the ancestral home of the Penns." It was on the market, and he made an offer. But as the summer dragged on, Nora, desperate not to return to America, constantly nagged Andrew about expediting the negotiations over the place. By now he was belatedly beginning to notice her growing indifference toward him, and so he withdrew the offer on Stoke Park. Eventually, it was settled that Nora, Andrew, and the children would return to America on September 17, accompanied once again by Nora's mother, who traveled as usual at Andrew's expense. But as the date neared, Nora left Andrew to oversee the closing of the house, then to go to Wimbledon, where her mother now lived, and to the Savoy Hotel in London, where she could be with Curphey in a suite for which she was likely paying.[30]

Nora rejoined her husband for the return voyage in mid-September, and to his unconcealed delight, he found her warm and agreeable. He immediately renewed his offer for Stoke Park, without telling her, planning a surprise. His offer was accepted, but the deal ultimately foundered on litigation concerning the title.[31] Mrs. McMullen stayed chez Mellon for the whole of the autumn, and in mid-December, Nora escorted her back to Britain on the *Lusitania*, leaving the children with Andrew to spend Christmas in Pittsburgh without her. (Nora's devotion to her widowed mother would prove a reliable alibi for her trysts.) In London, she stayed at the Berkeley Hotel; Curphey was by now living nearby in rented "gentleman's chambers" on Bury Street, St. James's. In mid-January 1909, Nora reluctantly returned to America, without her mother, but in the company of two of her sisters-in-law, Maud (Percy McMullen's wife) and Gee (married to Leonard), who were due to holiday in the United States at Andrew's expense. Also on board were Curphey and Long, registered on the passenger list under the names of E. Long and C. Long.[32]

Nora had told both Maud and Gee of her unhappiness with her husband, and of her great love for Curphey, and both of them accepted her account and agreed to keep her secret. Nora and Curphey were openly a couple onboard ship, and the party of five had a very enjoyable crossing—all, effectively, courtesy of Andrew Mellon. He was at the dockside in New York to meet them, having attended his mother's funeral in Pittsburgh the day before. He had telegraphed this sad news to Nora on the high seas, but instead of greeting him with the gentle sympathy he might have expected, she seemed anxious and jumpy, and only when prompted did she utter some perfunctory words of condolence.[33] It had been agreed that she and Andrew would show Maud and Gee the sights of New York, but Nora now insisted on going to Pittsburgh immediately to see her children, from whom she had, indeed, been separated for more than a month, and she left Maud and Gee (and also Curphey and Long) in New York. The McMullen wives stayed at the Plaza (where Andrew paid), Curphey and Long in less magnificent accommodations, initially at the Majestic Hotel, subsequently in rooms on Sixty-eighth Street (where, no doubt, Nora paid).[34]

Nora stayed at the Forbes Street house only very briefly, returning to New York the next night with the children and Miss Abernethy, and Andrew followed the day after. He was busy for the next few days keeping office hours downtown, which created the ideal opportunity for Nora and Curphey to see each other.[35] After the Mellon party returned to Pittsburgh, Nora arranged to take Maud and Gee to Niagara Falls, and she went to great lengths to persuade Andrew not to accompany them. He reluctantly agreed. The three women stayed at the Iroquois Hotel in Buffalo, where Curphey and Long were also guests, and once again Nora and Curphey were together.[36] But soon after, when Nora and her sisters-in-law went to California in a private railcar, Andrew came along as well. Nora, now without easy or certain access to Curphey, was cross and restless throughout. Back in Pittsburgh, she met up again with Curphey, who was staying at the Hotel Schenley. One evening, as she and Andrew were being driven to dinner, Nora indulged in a final act of defiant and amorous bravado: she saw Curphey standing on a street corner, and removing a large rose she was wearing, she dropped it through the car window at Curphey's feet. Andrew, still apparently suspecting nothing, did not notice.[37]

In early April 1909, Curphey and Long returned to England from New York on the *Mauretania*, this time registered as Messrs. Murphy and Song. By this time, and despite Nora's assistance, Curphey's finances had deteriorated still further: his total liabilities were more than £18,000 and his assets were only £60, and when he stepped ashore an action was brought against him by Barclays Bank, to which he owed £13,000. Describing himself as a "financial agent," Curphey confessed to having been ruined by the crash of 1907, and to having been since then "without occupation and dependent on friends." It was one of the few truthful declarations of his life, and he was duly adjudged bankrupt.[38] But neither his divorce nor his precarious finances diminished Curphey's attractions in Nora's eyes; on the contrary, she had by this time resolved to leave Andrew for him. Just as Curphey and Long were leaving New York, Andrew and Nora were also there to meet Leonard McMullen, who had sailed over to meet up with Gee, see the sights, and accompany her back to Britain. (Maud had already gone home.) It was while they were still in New York that Nora brought Andrew's domestic happiness to a sudden and brutal end.

On Easter Sunday morning, she went to church with Grace Chadbourne. On her way out, Nora told Andrew, almost as an afterthought, that Grace's husband, Thomas, his friend and a New York corporation lawyer, would be paying him a call. Chadbourne indeed appeared, and after much prevarication and circumlocution, and with evident embarrassment and concern, he finally informed Andrew that his wife had made an irrevocable decision to leave him and to obtain a divorce.[39] She had, Chadbourne reported, been unhappy for the last two years, and could not continue as she had been doing. No mention was made of another man, only of Nora's wish to go back to live in England. For unsuspecting Andrew, "it was a bolt out of a clear sky." As he later recalled: "I had been going happily along without the slightest misgiving or knowledge of any trouble, nor had I the least intimation of unhappiness on her part." He was comforted to learn he had no rival, but on hearing the news, Dick Mellon immediately guessed what had been going on: "You will find it is Curphey," he told Andrew, who initially refused to believe it. Eventually he accepted the ugly truth.[40]

This was an unprecedented crisis for Andrew Mellon, not only pri-

vately, but also, potentially, publicly. In prim, prudish, Presbyterian Pittsburgh, where decency and dignity were an essential element of elite living
(at least in public), divorce was frowned upon: even for the innocent party,
it could spell social disgrace—or worse.[41] In 1907, William E. Corey, the
second president of United States Steel, had been forced to resign for
just such a reason. And American divorce rates had increased dramatically during the 1890s and 1900s, leading to a growing public discussion
which climaxed between 1909 and 1912. Some religious leaders, especially Catholics and Presbyterians, thought the solution was to reaffirm
that divorce was contrary to the laws of God and the teachings of Christ.
Other commentators advocated the rationalization of the varied state laws
into a unified national legal code. And a new generation of feminist writers urged that more women were seeking to end marriages they regarded
as intolerable.[42] The issue was much debated in Pennsylvania itself. The
governor, Samuel W. Pennybacker, had convened a national conference
in 1906 to draft model uniform legislation on divorce; soon after, Professor James P. Lichtenberger of the University of Pennsylvania wrote a
treatise linking the emancipation of women with the rising divorce rate,
and applauding divorce as the means whereby victimized women freed
themselves from the shackles of marital bondage and male tyranny.[43]

In such generally unpropitious and personally worrisome circumstances, Andrew Mellon naturally turned to his lawyer, James Reed, who
counseled that a divorce might be averted by dealing with Nora "in a
fatherly way."[44] But this heavy-handed condescension was to no avail. She
wanted three things, and she wanted them fast: a clean divorce (she could
not endure Andrew as her husband one moment longer), sole custody of
the children (Andrew, she claimed, did not care for them and scarcely
knew them), and a settlement that would enable her to live in England
supporting them (and, implicitly, Curphey) in the accustomed comfortable manner. Soon after, Andrew discovered Miss Abernethy's complicity
in Nora's deceptions, and promptly dismissed her. (On leaving, she took a
suitcase full of Nora's letters from Curphey.) But this drove Ailsa to the
verge of hysterics; she called her father a "wicked man," whereupon he
promised to bring her nurse back. Meanwhile, Leonard and Gee had
reached Pittsburgh from New York, to find the Mellon household in
utter disarray and acrimony. Nora, Gee, the restored Miss Abernethy,
and the two children took their meals in the nursery upstairs, while
Andrew and Leonard ate together downstairs. Not surprisingly, Leonard
and Gee left as soon as they decently could, taking a boat for England in
early May.[45]

By now, Nora had engaged her own lawyer, Paul Ache of Ache and Wassel in Philadelphia, and she threatened to make Pittsburgh "ring with scandal" unless Andrew met her demands. She would accuse him of being infected with venereal disease, of having procured an abortion for a young girl, and of keeping a woman in New York. (None of it was true.) When Andrew asked whether she had no regard for the well-being of Ailsa and Paul, or for the distress they would suffer from such (unfounded) allegations, Nora replied, with true or calculated sangfroid: "If the children suffered, they would have to suffer."[46] Andrew dreaded not just the prospect of scandal, but also that during any time with Nora, Ailsa and Paul would be exposed to Curphey's poisonous influence, and it enraged him to imagine that any money he paid to Nora might end up in that rogue's feckless and incontinent pockets. He made a last effort at reconciliation, telling Nora that "if she couldn't be happy in Pittsburgh, I would arrange my affairs so that I could live elsewhere, live abroad with her." For such a devotee of his native city, the home of his clan and the focus of all his business interests, this offer represented an enormous sacrifice. But Nora told him it was too late: she could never be happy living with him, wherever it might be.[47]

His back against the wall, Andrew at once hired a detective, dispatching him to Europe with letters of introduction from the chief of detectives in Allegheny County to the head of Scotland Yard, and also from the acting U.S. secretary of state to U.S. diplomatic and consular officials. His mission was to find out the truth of Nora's activities, in Paris, in London, and on the high seas.[48] But as Nora had calculated, it was too late: while these investigations were proceeding, Andrew would have to come to terms, if scandal was to be avoided. A legal separation was agreed in the summer of 1909, preliminary to the dissolution of their marriage, on grounds of desertion, after two further years. A first trust fund of $150,000 was established for the maintenance of Paul and Ailsa, a second of $600,000 to provide Nora an income, and a third of $400,000, whose proceeds she would also enjoy, as long as she did not remarry. She also received a direct cash payment of $250,000 (approximately $5 million in today's currency). It was further agreed that Andrew and Nora would have joint custody of the children on an equal and alternating basis, several months at a time with either parent, and that Nora would promptly leave for Europe to commence the two-year period required for divorce on the basis of desertion. She also gave an oral undertaking to Andrew (who failed to get it in writing) that when Paul and Ailsa were with her in Europe, she would not bring them into contact with Curphey. Indeed, she claimed that "her family were so opposed to him that she had decided to give him up entirely."[49]

With these matters apparently settled, Nora departed in early August, taking with her most of the silver and linen from Forbes Street, including all of the wedding presents. (She later denied this.) She was not bound for England, where she (rightly) anticipated trouble with some of her brothers, who disapproved of her conduct, but for Paris, where she planned to stay with Alan McMullen, who still took her side. In the end, he was not able to be there, and so she set herself up in an apartment at 41, avenue du Bois de Boulogne.[50] In accordance with the separation agreement, Andrew crossed the Atlantic at the end of the month, bringing Ailsa and Paul, accompanied by Miss Abernethy, for their first period in Nora's custody, returning to Pittsburgh solitary, baffled, and bereft. Thereafter, Nora wrote to Andrew regularly about the children, their health, and their schooling, and Ailsa sent occasional, affectionate, homesick letters, thanking her father for his presents: "I love you so dearly for being so good to me"; "only a few weeks now and I can be with you in my playhouse." On the way back to Pittsburgh, passing through London, Andrew had learned that Curphey was leaving for South Africa. He promptly hired another detective, this one to travel on the same boat and ensure that the scoundrel reached his destination. But by December, Curphey was back in Paris with Nora, and thus with Ailsa and Paul. Their mother was already reneging on her promise to their father.[51]

Andrew was dismayed at being thus separated from his children. He sought to be as attentive, and as vigilant, a father as circumstances and his own distant temperament allowed. One of Andrew's nephews, Edward P. Mellon, son of his late brother Thomas Alexander, happened to be in Paris at the time, studying to be an architect. At Andrew's behest, he kept his uncle informed as to how Ailsa and Paul were getting on; he also, on their father's behalf, provided the children with, respectively, a dollhouse and a train for Christmas 1909. The following month, Paris was flooded: the children, EP informed AW, were fine, but Nora was away. Truly, as Edward admitted to his uncle, with more candor than comfort, it was "a wretched condition of things."[52] Meanwhile, Andrew wrote regular letters to Ailsa, reporting on the playhouse he had bought her and lamenting the disappearance of her dog ("I have been doing everything I could to trace him"). He was an eager correspondent, and regretted that his daughter seemed less than enthusiastic in reciprocating (this would be a lifelong trait of hers). "I am looking for a letter from you," he concluded one of his own epistles, rather sadly, "and I hope you and Paul are keeping happy. I shall be glad to hear from you." And he signed off "with lots of love and kisses from your loving father."[53]

This was a deeply anxious time for Andrew, but since his children would be back with him in eight weeks, he decided the best course was to wait. He did, however, hire more men to shadow Nora and Curphey, including George F. Taber, then in charge of refining at Gulf Oil, who was now dispatched to Paris to make "confidential inquiries" about them. In March 1910, Mellon crossed to France and brought Ailsa, Paul, and their nurse back to Pittsburgh, where they remained until June, the children's condition reported in regular letters he sent to Nora. They were generally well, but Andrew feared that Miss Abernethy was a bad influence: "It is a shame to have the child taught deceitfulness, and Ailsa is just at an age when such influence is harmful."[54] Nora's replies were taunts: "Although you are probably paying first-class prices to these detectives, the work is being done in a very crude and third-rate manner." Andrew denied having any "such work done." Then family illness obliged Miss Abernethy to go home, and Andrew took the occasion to dismiss her finally and employ a new nurse, Miss Jordan, in her stead. (Miss Abernethy wrote a tearful farewell letter to Nora, pledging her undying devotion, which also extended to Ailsa, Paul, and Curphey, but emphatically not to Andrew.)[55] In April, Nora crossed the Channel to be with Curphey in London and they arranged to summer at Vale Farm, near Windsor, taken on a six-month lease. The children would be there with them, a further breach of her earlier assurances to Andrew. By this time, Curphey had fallen out with Charles Ernest Long, to whom he owed money, but he obtained a new associate, one Captain Kirkbride, and it was he who accompanied Nora on her return visit to America.[56]

Nora reached Pittsburgh on June 11, 1910, which by coincidence or design was Paul's third birthday. After what must have been a tense and somber celebratory lunch, Andrew informed Nora that he knew she had not honored her promise to keep the children away from Curphey. Eventually, her lawyer, Paul Ache, provided assurances that Ailsa and Paul would hereafter have no contact with Curphey, though it was not disclosed to Andrew where in England his wife and children would be. Reluctantly accepting this, Andrew set out on June 14 to take the children and Miss Jordan from Pittsburgh to New York on the night train to meet Nora. But just as he was leaving the house, he received a cable from one of his detectives, informing him that Curphey was in residence at Vale Farm, that Nora intended to bring Ailsa and Paul there, and that if he let them go, he might never get his children back.[57] Andrew continued the journey, but when he reached New York the next morning, he refused to take them and their nurse to the ship. Instead, leaving all three at a hotel, he went to confront Nora about not disclosing her destination in England, which he now knew all too well.[58]

Following Andrew back to his hotel, Nora demanded to see her children, enraged that her plans had now been thwarted—she could scarcely remove them by force and make a run for the ship. Andrew took Ailsa and Paul back to Pittsburgh with him, and though willing to let Nora have them for her next period of custody, he was adamant that she not take them out of Pennsylvania. Eventually it was agreed that she could spend July and August with the children at Forbes Street, which Andrew would vacate for the duration, taking up residence at the University Club.[59] It was a crucial precaution, but he mightily resented abandoning his own house to his estranged wife, who would now enjoy his food and wine, his servants and his cars. Encouraged and emboldened by letters and telegrams from Curphey extravagantly proclaiming his love for her, Nora began a concerted campaign to turn her children against their father. On his daily visits to them in the morning and evening, on his way to and from work, Ailsa seemed much colder, Paul once hit him with a stick, and Nora would always remain in the room, offering caustic and belittling remarks about him. Though hurt and mortified, Andrew refused to respond in kind, and he never spoke ill of his wife in his children's presence, then or thereafter.[60]

On September 1, when Andrew appeared at Forbes Street to collect the children for his next period of custody, Nora would not let him see Ailsa. Once again fearing that the children would be spirited away to England to sojourn with Curphey, never to see their father again, Andrew prohibited Nora from taking them off the premises without his permission. "Watchmen" were posted in the house to enforce Mellon's edict, and primitive listening devices were installed so that he would know of Nora's movements, conversations, and even her telephone calls.[61] In addition, Andrew now abandoned the previous strategy of a legal separation, which after two years would lead to divorce based on desertion. It now seemed too long for him to wait and for his children to suffer. And so he filed for divorce on the grounds of adultery, which he alleged had taken place on two continents as well as on the high seas. In addition to James Reed and his colleague, James H. Beal, Mellon retained Rody P. Marshall, Pittsburgh's leading criminal lawyer; William A. Blakeley, Marshall's great courtroom rival; William A. Stone, a former governor of the state; and the firm of Watson & Freeman. He did not need so many lawyers, but buying up the competition was part of the way he did business, and he was eager to ensure that none of the city's best attorneys worked for Nora, who would thus have to rely on out-of-town counsel. This, he reasoned, would be a disadvantage in a place like Pittsburgh. It proved a major miscalculation.[62]

By now, Andrew Mellon enjoyed the support of most of Nora's relatives, excepting Alan McMullen, who still remained loyal to his sister. Leonard McMullen, who seems to have been the best informed of the brothers, strongly encouraged Andrew from the time of the separation in the summer of 1909. "It is preposterous," he wrote, "to think, as she seems to, that she can have your money and your children and a lover." Nora was "absolutely hopeless," while Curphey was "a brute" and "a blackguard"; Leonard was further ashamed that for a time his wife, Gee, had been party to Nora's deceptions, and had taken her side. With his financial affairs more precarious than ever, and constant requests to Andrew for money (to whom he now owed more than £5,000), Leonard may have felt constrained in his views.[63] But other brothers who were not beholden to Andrew were of the same opinion. "I cannot see," Norman McMullen wrote, "how you could do anything else but divorce her. She has lost all sense of honour, and I cannot see any hope of her changing now. It is the most dreadful case I have ever heard of, and I cannot say how sorry both Helen and I are for you." Another brother, John McMullen, agreed: "You were a good and generous husband to her in every way that she could expect or had a right to expect." Nora, by contrast, "never seems to have had the slightest consideration for anybody but herself," and he deplored "her vanity, selfishness and lack of common intelligence." But it was Mrs. McMullen who was hurt "most of all," and she, too, took Andrew's side against her own daughter.[64]

Despite this unequivocal support from Nora's flesh and blood, the strategy that Mellon and his advisers had decided upon was fraught with risk. Divorce on the grounds of adultery was relatively rare in the United States at the time, for it not only carried for the proven adulterer social ostracism and personal disgrace, but also the threat of a criminal indictment and potentially a jail sentence. Did Andrew really want to send Nora to prison? What impact would *that* have on the welfare of the children? Moreover, because of the criminal dimension, the commonwealth of Pennsylvania allowed such cases to be tried before a jury, should either party wish it, and juries were unwilling to convict unless the evidence for adultery was absolutely conclusive. Had Andrew forgotten his father's warnings of how wayward juries might be without strong direction from a judge?[65] And what, for someone who hated to be conspicuous, was the risk of his own public humiliation? Unfortunately, in seeking to end his marriage, Mellon showed no better judgment than he had in initiating it. As he and his lawyers should have realized, by forcing the issue in this way, they were not so much resolving it as playing into Nora's hands.

III. THE MARRIAGE ENDED

By the autumn of 1910, Andrew Mellon was determined to move against Nora with the full force of the law, and with every other means at his disposal. But it did not prove to be easy. She soon discovered the listening devices he had installed in their home, and she retaliated by playing up before the microphones, knowing her words would be written down, get back to Andrew, and might even reach a wider audience. He was, she declaimed, suffering from "a horrible disease," he was "in such a state that it is impossible for him to live very long," and he also went "with some woman nearly every evening, for I am having him watched."[66] It was true that Nora had hired "watchmen" of her own, and with warring snoopers, spying on the family and on each other, life at Forbes Street became intolerably tense and insecure. Now, when Andrew visited to see his children, he was obliged to endure not only Nora's usual caustic ridicule, but also the offensive hostility of her hired retainers. Thus the Mellons' marital breakdown became the talk of Pittsburgh, an utter embarrassment for Andrew, and even more upsetting for Ailsa, age ten, who was repeatedly asked cruel questions at school about what was going on in her home. In truth, she had no idea.[67]

In November 1910 Andrew filed an application to the Orphan's Court to have his children made wards of court under a guardian. Fräulein Bertha Meyer was legally appointed to look after them, living with them (and with Nora) at Forbes Street. But it was not enough for Andrew, who was now determined to curtail what he regarded as Nora's abrasive and hostile influence: early in 1911 he entered a second court application to remove Ailsa and Paul from Forbes Street, along with their guardian, to a rented house.[68] Later that year, Fräulein Meyer and the children took up residence in a dwelling on Sewickley Heights, and in October they were on the move again to another house on Morewood Avenue in East Liberty. Under this latest ruling, Andrew and Nora were allowed access to Ailsa and Paul on alternate weeks. These were terrible times for the Mellon children: by turns lonely and fearful and bored, they were uprooted, hauled off to unfamiliar and impermanent surroundings, and looked after by a strange German lady, "a little grotesque and ugly" in Paul's recollection. Ailsa, who already possessed a high-strung temperament, must have been at her wit's end, not knowing what was going on, nor whom to believe; and Paul, though too young to be as affected as his sister, was continuously ill, with days of nausea and weakness and headaches.[69]

To Andrew, these were but temporary solutions to the impossible situation that, he believed, Nora had deliberately and irresponsibly created—by her return to Forbes Street, by the campaign of vilification, and by her cruel and heartless action in manipulating the children's feelings. For Nora it was but further indication that her husband was a malevolent and calculating monster who had never cared for her, and who would stop at nothing to gain possession of her children, whom he sought to own but did not love. Meanwhile, the action for adultery which Andrew had brought the previous year was under way. The onus was on him to prove his case, and this meant he had to achieve at least one of two objectives: first, to provide conclusive and convincing evidence of Nora's adultery; or, second, to circumvent somehow the jury trial on which she had understandably insisted. It proved exceptionally difficult to do either, let alone both. And it eventually resulted in revelations about Andrew's marriage and private life that to his clannish and secretive family were at best intolerable, at worst humiliating: "the first time the Mellons have ever been 'in print.' "[70]

Reviewing Nora's movements during the years since she had first met Curphey, Andrew and his lawyers thought it self-evident that she must have committed adultery with him on countless occasions, on both sides of the Atlantic and in between. Since the middle of 1909, Andrew's agents and detectives had been scouring Europe and North America, interviewing stewards and chambermaids and servants, offering them financial inducements to testify to this effect. But while much circumstantial evidence was accumulated, no witnesses could be produced who were willing to say that they had ever seen Nora and Curphey in bed together, let alone in flagrante.[71] They had always been careful to register in separate rooms, even in Paris, and many of the underlings whom the Mellon agents interviewed, loyal to Nora and Curphey, were affronted by the presumption that they would testify for a price. (It was relatively easy for W. L. Mellon to buy up streetcar franchises in Pittsburgh and oil leases in Pennsylvania, but family money could not sway the actors in this drama, which was personal rather than political.) Even Charles Ernest Long could aver only that, on many occasions when the couple had been

together, Curphey's bed was not slept in. In the end, Andrew's best hope
was that Curphey himself would break down under cross-examination;
but getting him to the stand would prove impossible.[72]

The second difficulty facing Andrew was Nora's insistence on her right
to a jury trial, and all the damage she would inflict on him and his children
when she had her day in court. As some of her letters had shown, she was
not without histrionic gifts, and the opportunity to make Pittsburgh "ring
with scandal," and to humiliate her husband, was one she was unlikely to
pass up. And since convincing evidence of her adultery could not be
obtained, all she had to do was to deny it outright, thereby further damaging her husband. It bears repeating that in seeking divorce on these
grounds, Andrew and his lawyers had freely chosen to open up this terrible prospect; now they were obliged to try to find a solution to the problem they themselves had created. "Had I been on hand," John G.
Leishman (who had earlier saved Frick from assassination, and later
became president of Carnegie Steel) wrote Mellon, "my inclination
would have been to influence you as far as possible to reach an amicable
settlement even at considerable cost." This was wise advice. But, he went
on, rather less prudently, "now that the battle has begun, there should be
no surrender, as you have everything to gain and nothing to lose."
"Don't," Leishman concluded, more loyally than presciently, "allow the
damned newspapers to hurt your feelings, as abuse is the only weapon on
the other side."[73] It would prove a powerful one.

In seeking a way forward, Mellon and his advisers now showed themselves at their most manipulative, audacious, and overbearing. For they
resolved to overturn the state law providing for a jury trial, so that the case
would instead be heard privately before a judge. (There were precedents
for such high-handed action: in 1901, Henry M. Flagler, the Rockefeller
partner and Florida railroad and real estate developer, had successfully
divorced his wife, having persuaded the state legislature to add insanity to
adultery as reasonable grounds.)[74] Assisted by Dick Mellon and Henry
Clay Frick, the Mellon team set about lobbying their highly placed political friends, especially Senator Boies Penrose in Washington, to support
the necessary local legislation. Many such meetings are recorded in the
diary that Andrew Mellon had begun to keep in 1910, particularly with
Cyrus Woods, a lawyer and leader of western Pennsylvania's Republican
Party machine, and with John R. K. Scott, a member of the state House of
Representatives, who was charged with seeing the bill through the Pennsylvania legislature.[75] This calculating resolve to subvert the democratic
and legal processes to one's own ends might strike us as shocking: "the

intercession of the legislature," Burton Hendrick wrote, "in the private interest of an influential citizen is something that can hardly be viewed with equanimity"; "the present biographer," he concluded, "is the last one who would apologize for such an abuse of power or seek in any way to extenuate it."[76]

But to Andrew and his associates, there was nothing extraordinary or malevolent about proceeding in this way: in their day, by their lights, politicians existed to create a climate favorable to businessmen, so they might enhance the wealth of nations, and here, albeit in slightly odd circumstances, was another opportunity (indeed, necessity) for them to do just that. Chambermaids and stewards and servants might be impervious to bribes, but politicians could always be relied upon. And Mellon's men reasoned that the end justified the means: Nora was clearly guilty, Andrew's reputation needed protecting, the divorce ought to go through, and the children should be spared the worst. There was every call for secrecy, and every need for haste. In April 1911, the Pennsylvania legislature duly amended the state divorce law without any opposition: the need for a jury was now left to the discretion of the divorce court. But there was no discretion, and jury trial was strictly forbidden, when it "could not be held without prejudice to public morals." In such circumstances, the court was empowered to appoint a special master to depose witnesses in Pennsylvania, in other states in the union, and in foreign countries, and to render, with his report of the proceedings, an opinion of the case. Moreover, the new law applied not only to future cases, but to those already pending. It was, in short, specifically tailored to Andrew Mellon's requirements, namely his wish to deny his wife a public platform, on the artfully contrived grounds that the lurid details would indeed be prejudicial to public morals.[77] So speedily and surreptitiously had the measure passed the state legislature that some representatives were later amazed to learn that they had voted for it.[78]

Having bought up Pittsburgh's best lawyers, launched inquiries into his wife's relationship with Curphey, put her under surveillance in Paris and Pittsburgh, and changed the state law to his advantage, Mellon and his advisers were clearly, and chillingly, determined to prevail. They enjoyed another advantage: the Pittsburgh press, generally Republican and pro-business, would be unlikely to give attention to the court proceedings now under way.[79] There were also more specific reasons: natural deference and discretion to a family that remained loyal to the city, direct appeals by Mellon's lawyers that "nothing must be printed," their use of a press agent who daily censored what would be published, an extensive advertising campaign in some papers on behalf of Mellon National Bank, influence exerted by the local Republican leadership and city bosses, and reminders that mortgages could always be foreclosed on. By such means, ranging from persuasion to coercion, Andrew and his lawyers succeeded in keeping the matter mostly out of the local papers—a vivid example of "the great power the Mellon family exercised in the community and their disposition to use this power in their personal interest."[80] Of the major dailies, the *Press* (which had been acquired by Oliver S. Herschman with a Mellon loan) scarcely mentioned it; the *Sun*, the *Chronicle-Telegraph*, and the *Post* contained only brief and occasional court reports; and the *Dispatch* and the *Gazette-Times*, although following the case closely, buried it in their general litigation section. Only the *Leader*, generally the most sensationalist, covered the trial in detail.

But that was in Pittsburgh. Denied her jury trial and local coverage, Nora now appealed to the wider Pennsylvania public, especially in Philadelphia, which Paul Ache knew well, and sympathetic newspapers were successfully enlisted, eager to mock the upstart city and tainted plutocrat in the western part of the state. On May 7, 1911, Nora gave an electrifying interview to the *North American*. The article was framed with a feminist denunciation of the new law, which "robbed" women of their "constitutional right to trial by jury," and thus "makes it easier for rich husbands to get rid of their wives." There was also plenty of ad hominem criticism of Andrew Mellon for letting spies and bugs and snoopers loose on his wife. But the heart of it was Nora, who portrayed herself as the woman deeply wronged, and she made her case with shameless venom and considerable rhetorical and histrionic force. Artfully appealing to "the mothers of this state," she begged them not to turn away from her own battle "against the combined money-making and law-making powers of the state for possession of my children." She was, she continued, "all alone in this country with my two children, my two babies." "Were my sins," she went on,

> as enormous and self-evident as my accusing husband claims, would the laws as they have been here for a hundred years not have been sufficient for my case? Is it fair, is it honourable, six months after suit has been instituted against me, to adjust the laws to fit my particular case? Is that justice? Is it honourable to go to such extremes against one lone mother?[81]

There was more in the same vein. Nora's only sin, she went on, was having "failed to realize the dream of a foolish young girl." She had come to Pittsburgh, a healthy country maid from England, hoping to play the part of lady bountiful on her "wealthy and powerful husband's vast estate." She saw herself "in the role of the mistress of the manor who lightens the burden of the peasant," thereby forming "a link between the old and the new world." At the beginning she had loved and admired her husband, and even "looked up to him as a great man, a master mind." But all this, she subsequently discovered, was no more than "idle dreams." She soon came to loathe the "gray-smoke and dust-filled air" of her husband's "gold and grim estate," with its "unreasoning hoarde [*sic*] of wage slaves"; and she despised Andrew, "locked in his study," accumulating his "dollars, millions of dollars, maddening dollars, nursed larger and bigger at the cost of priceless sleep." Moreover, he was now seeking divorce, "not on the grounds he had agreed to, but on the absurd grounds of infidelity," and he had tried "every means and artifice to get my babies away from me," including the recent change in the state law, which had "abrogated my right to a jury trial." Having thus made her case, Nora moved to her peroration, challenging the very scruples of the country and state she was loath to have adopted and longed to flee:

> Gold fighting against one lone woman is unscrupulous in its methods. Gold may crush me. Gold and politics may take my babies from me. But if they do, it will be because the manhood of Pennsylvania has sunk so low that it is willing to surrender the motherhood of the state to the pillage of gold and politics. I don't believe it. That's not American, and I don't believe it is Pennsylvanian.[82]

Hers was, to say the least, a very tendentious account: Nora's so-called babies were ten and four years old, and she made no allusion to her irresponsible relationship with Curphey; did not acknowledge her initial aspirations to the "manor" of life in Pittsburgh were embarrassingly naïve; and omitted to mention Andrew's generosity to her and to her many relatives. But in essence her case was both plausible and powerful and, as she and Paul Ache intended, it evoked widespread public sympathy across the state, and they ensured that two thousand copies of the paper were distributed in Pittsburgh—to good effect. The Episcopal bishop of Pittsburgh issued a statement deploring the provisions of the new divorce act, especially its curtailment of the right to jury trial; the president of the National Congress of Mothers blasted the amendments as "outrageous," while the president of the Federation of Women's Clubs labeled them "iniquitous"; the *Pittsburgh Leader* attacked the state legislature for what it had done, and on whose behalf; some lawyers expressed doubts as to the constitutionality of the legislation; and the story was taken up by newspapers on the East Coast and also in the British press, prompting a question to be asked in the House of Commons of the foreign secretary about this reported ill-treatment of an Englishwoman abroad.[83]

In the resulting public relations triumph for Nora and Ache, their version of events and personalities dominated the media. The Mellons were indeed "in print." Andrew's associates did all they could to prevent copies of the *North American* and other East Coast papers from reaching Pittsburgh, and to hold up, lose, or garble the copy journalists tried to file via Western Union.[84] But their efforts were unavailing, and each new episode in the continuing court battles was presented in the *North American* as the latest encounter between a virtuous and wronged woman and a vile and vengeful man. By the time Fräulein Meyer and the children left Forbes Street for Sewickley Heights, in accordance with the court order, the melodrama of the "innocent" mother watching her "sobbing and heartbroken children" forcibly "torn" from her by "strong-arm men" was only more grist for the mill. Reporters harassed Andrew unrelentingly, and his replies ranged from the untruthful to the unconvincing. He denied any part in the change to the law—an outright lie. And when pressed, the best he could say in bad-tempered reply was "What right have you to come here and ask me such questions about my private affairs? What business is it of yours, tell me that?"[85]

In June 1911, Alfred Curphey and Captain Kirkbride appeared in Pittsburgh, ostensibly to help Nora with her defense, and perhaps in the hope that they might negotiate another financial advantage with Andrew. Curphey was at his most shameless, insisting that he was an English gentleman, that Nora was an English lady, and that there was no foundation to any of Mellon's malicious accusations about the relationship between them. He had the cheek to demand an apology from Andrew, and threatened to thrash him within an inch of his life; the *North American* printed silhouettes of the two of them, making plain who would win such a contest, and whom the paper was rooting for. Curphey paid a much-publicized visit to the Mellon Bank, expressly to confront Andrew in his office, but he was not there.[86] Instead, both Curphey and Kirkbride were served summonses to appear as witnesses. They immediately fled to New York, where they were arrested and promptly released on bail, as reported in the British press.[87] The governor of Pennsylvania requested extradition, and the governor of New York agreed, but before any further action could be taken, both fugitives jumped bail and boarded a ship bound for South Africa, thereby denying Andrew's lawyers their best chance to prove adultery if and when the case came to trial. Soon after, Charles Ernest Long appeared in Pittsburgh, his travel expenses covered by Mellon lawyers, and in his extensive deposition, he gave a full account of the relations between Curphey and Nora during the period that he had known them.[88]

During the next six months, both sides won and lost important battles in the courts, and these encounters were vividly reported in the *North American*, which remained strongly committed to Nora's cause.[89] When challenged by Ache, Andrew's lawyers failed to provide proof of Nora's adultery with Curphey (Long's testimony, though graphic, gave no conclusive evidence), but they did win their request that a special master be appointed to adjudicate the case, and an examiner empowered to gather evidence abroad. At the same time, Nora's lawyers failed in their general challenge to the retroactive application of the new divorce statute, but they did, nevertheless, win their right to the jury trial that Andrew so dreaded.[90] Nora's victory was hailed in the *North American*: "I win back everything," she was reported as saying, "everything that money and politics conspired to take from me—my children, my fair name and my right to a full and public vindication before a jury of my peers."[91] This was not good news for Andrew: his lawyers had failed to secure a hearing in camera, Curphey was not available for cross-examination, Nora was determined to protest her innocence, and it would be virtually impossible to prove her adultery before a judge, let alone a jury.

Despite these undeniable legal victories, Nora's morale had been undermined in one significant way: Curphey had deserted her when she most needed him, and when he fled the country, their relationship seems to have come to a decisive end. Perhaps on the rebound, she now took up with Charles Mustin, organist at a Pittsburgh church, who also played the piano in silent movie houses.[92] Stripped of her illusion of Curphey's love, burdened with the substantial debts she had incurred through supporting him, and knowing that her case against Andrew was far from watertight, her resolve weakened, and in late May 1912, she authorized Paul Ache to visit her husband, to report her "a changed woman, remorseful, penitent." She realized, Ache told Andrew, how much she had wronged him and the children (though still denying she had ever committed adultery), could not understand why she had behaved as she did, and feared she must have been "dominated" or "hypnotized" by Curphey. She offered no excuses for what she had done, throwing herself on Andrew's mercy. Her whole desire was to put matters right for him and the children, "as far as she was able." Eager that they should be reconciled, she would "devote herself toward redeeming the past." She knew that they had been happy once, she both hoped and believed they could be so again, and she now wished to live for nothing but Andrew and their children.[93]

Not surprisingly, Mellon was unmoved by this appeal. He did not wish "to say anything that would make her position harder," but he insisted that she understand why "reconciliation was impossible." He could not "again trust her": it was in her nature to change her opinions radically and unpredictably, as when she protested her love for him in her letters of June 1908, when she was already back with Curphey in Paris. She had also treated her mother and brothers badly, and she had no shame. "In my mind," Andrew concluded, "the future is hopeless as to living together." All that remained, he insisted, was to reach agreement as to the divorce.[94] By this stage, the outlines of a compromise were beginning to emerge, in part because the two-year period needed to establish divorce on the grounds of desertion would soon be over, making moot any advantage of speed in pursuing dissolution on the grounds of adultery. And both parties were by now glad to settle. Accordingly, Andrew abandoned the adultery charge and reinstated his original claim of desertion; Nora ceased talking to the newspapers and dropped her demand for a jury trial. Andrew further agreed to lend Nora $120,000 to deal with her (clearly substantial) debts.[95]

The divorce hearing was held privately in Pittsburgh in the office of the special master, John Hunter, on May 20 and 21, 1912. The witnesses were James Reed, Andrew Mellon, and three of his servants. Also in evidence were the parts of Charles Ernest Long's deposition that related only to Nora's desertion. There was no cross-examination, and the decree was granted on July 3, on the grounds that Nora McMullen Mellon was "guilty of willful and malicious desertion."[96] The *North American* hailed the verdict as "a victory for wife of Pittsburgh banker who tried to besmirch her name."[97] But in legal and financial terms, at least, Andrew had eventually emerged the winner. Nora's wrongdoing was now a matter of record, and Andrew was established as the injured party. In the future, Ailsa and Paul would spend eight months of every year with their father, and only four with their mother. The domicile of the children was to be "at all times" within the commonwealth of Pennsylvania, and they could not be taken out of Allegheny County without Andrew's written consent or that of the court. And if the parents could not agree on the educational and religious training of their children, then Andrew could "decide and direct" as he saw fit. By consent of counsel for both parties, all the papers in the case were withdrawn from the records, so that nothing remains on file except the decree of divorce itself—proof that to the very end,

Andrew was determined to keep the matter out of the public eye as much as he could. In more senses than one, it was a costly victory. Mellon's bill from Reed Smith was more than $100,000, which would be close to $2 million in today's money.[98]

IV. PERSPECTIVES AND CONSEQUENCES

Even allowing for the later scandal of the so-called tax trial, his divorce must be rated the most extraordinary episode in Andrew Mellon's life. Its impact was lasting, but some of the threads may be easily tied up. John R. K. Scott continued his lawyerly and legislative career, but he was defeated in his bid to be elected lieutenant governor of Pennsylvania in 1918. Cyrus Woods fared better, insisting that Mellon lobby Philander Knox, who was by now secretary of state, for a senior diplomatic posting overseas in recompense for his labors. He duly became minister to Portugal in 1912, and after a period as secretary to the Commonwealth of Pennsylvania, he was subsequently ambassador to Spain and then Japan.[99] Charles Ernest Long worked briefly for a firm of locksmiths after leaving Curphey's employment, and Mellon eventually paid him £2,000 in appreciation of his testimony. Thereafter, he took to drink and lost his job, and despite additional entreaties from his wife, Mellon declined to help further.[100] As for Curphey—he married again in 1921 and, as if in ironic homage to Andrew Mellon, his bride, Celia White, was twenty-seven years younger than he was, and her father was described as a financier. Thereafter, Curphey disappears from view until late 1937, when he went to live with the widow of George Bedlam, a cricketer, inventor, and photographer, who had recently died. Curphey settled down with Mrs. Bedlam at Farnham in Surrey, and he stayed with her until his death from cancer on October 4, 1938. Twenty years later, Mrs. Bedlam scattered his ashes in Dorset at a point near Wimborne known as Three Legged Cross. Apparently she had loved him.[101]

So much for the minor characters in this astonishing melodrama: but what of the central figures? Had he lived to see the marriage of his favorite son unravel, Judge Mellon would have taken no pleasure in having rightly counseled against it, and against the woman who had "broken up this man's life, and ruined the fortune of his children, and all that through a *whim*."[102] To be sure, this was not the first divorce in the Mellon family: as the Judge recounted in his autobiography, he himself had urged his sister Margaret to part from her debauched and dissolute hus-

band, Robert Shields. But it was the first Mellon divorce to be sensation-
ally newsworthy in a manner appropriate to the era of Henry James and
Edith Wharton. For it was indeed a story of power, money, and sex; of
love and lies, calculation and deceit, pain and anguish; of transatlantic
emotional entanglements; of a drama played out both above stairs and
below, with servants taking sides and collaborating in deception;[103] of
great ocean liners, private railcars, country houses, and grand hotels; of a
flawed millionaire, an unhappy wife, and a predatory villain. Yet neither
James nor Wharton could have credibly published as fiction anything so
pyrotechnical, with so many dizzying plot turns, or such outrageous over-
reaching—what the *North American* described as a battle between "millions of dollars and powerful political pull on one side, and publicity on
the other."[104]

Taking sides in a bitter divorce is rarely wise, especially when it
occurred nearly a century ago. For her part, Nora had been against the
marriage to Andrew from the beginning, insisting that it would not work.
From the very outset she had hated Pittsburgh, and although she enjoyed
the comforts which his wealth provided, she soon came to hate her
husband as a moneymaking automaton, lacking sympathy and human
emotion, with little evident feeling or concern for her or the children.
Whatever his true nature or motives, Alfred Curphey was (at least for a
time) demonstratively loving and affectionate, and he was also a fellow
Briton. She had understandably sought her freedom, only to be confronted by her hostile husband at his most malevolent and manipulative.
How could he not have known that she was so unhappy? He had turned
her own family against her, prevented her from taking her children to
Europe, had her stalked by spies and detectives, gagged the local press,
and even contrived to change the state law on divorce in his favor by
coercing and corrupting the Pennsylvania legislature. By going public,
she had defended herself in the only way available, and by forcing him to
abandon the adultery charge, she had been vindicated.

But Andrew did not see things that way. After his own fashion and
according to the conventions of his family, he had been a loyal and loving
husband, generous both to his wife and to her many relatives. True, he
worked long hours, but he had also taken extended breaks to be with her
in England, and he even volunteered to move there permanently. She had
repaid him by falling in love with a scoundrel and a gigolo. That Nora
wished to expose their children to the moral contagion of this reprobate
was emphatic proof of her unfitness as a mother; and in her determination
to blacken Andrew's name and to set Ailsa and Paul against him, she had

shown a wanton disregard for truth, loyalty, decency, or consideration. In never speaking ill of Nora in public or in private, Andrew had displayed exceptional high-mindedness and forbearance, as well as his personal concern for the well-being of Ailsa and Paul. It was scarcely surprising that, once it was clearly over, he sought to use his financial, political, and legal influence to bring this disastrous marriage to an end in the most rapid and least public manner possible. And what stronger vindication could there be than the almost unanimous support of Nora's family? Andrew had been deeply abused, ill-used, and sorely tried, and yet he had behaved with dignity and consideration in exceptionally difficult circumstances—as thereafter, by his lights, he always continued to do.

As so often in divorce cases, these positions are impossible to reconcile. All that can be concluded is that Andrew and Nora were clearly unsuited to each other, that the marriage was ill-fated from the beginning, and that had there been no Curphey there would sooner or later probably have been someone else. Nora's behavior was by turns understandable and impossible; Andrew, however justifiable his sense of being betrayed, had let his lawyers make a hash of the divorce strategy. It is equally clear that all four of those most closely involved sustained lasting emotional and psychological damage. The two children were terribly scarred, notwithstanding Leonard McMullen's breezy prediction that "they and others will hardly remember it when they grow up": Ailsa, who had already demonstrated an early tendency toward the neurasthenia that characterized her mother, was ever after high-strung, easily upset, and inclined to illness, whether physical or psychosomatic; while Paul turned in on himself, becoming shy and lonely, self-conscious and insecure. Both children were ever after left uncertain and distrustful of their father and their mother and, indeed, of all close human relationships.[105] For her part, Nora had obtained her freedom, but at a very high price, for her dream of returning to England in triumph with her children was never realized, and she was never forgiven in Pittsburgh for what was regarded as her selfish, disloyal, and errant behavior. And Andrew's one attempt to establish a close human relationship had been an abject and humiliating failure. As one of Mellon's associates would later observe, for all those involved, the divorce "was a source of great mental distress and bitterness," and thereafter, in deep, lasting, and unassuageable ways, Andrew, Nora, Ailsa, and Paul would all be wounded people as well as wealthy people.[106]

7

LIFE GOES ON

Business (Almost) as Usual, 1907–14

> There is a great deal of humbug and nonsense afloat about people breaking themselves down with hard work. I have never known hard work to hurt anyone in good health and strength, if the work and will went together.
>
> *Thomas Mellon and His Times*, p. 413

I. PANICS AND PROGRESSIVES IN PITTSBURGH AND BEYOND

While the devastating drama of Andrew Mellon's divorce was unfolding, his daily business life in the city went on. His office at the bank was a refuge, and since he rarely spoke to his staff, there was no danger that any of them would mention the matter to him (except, perhaps, to warn him when Curphey threatened to show up). But in Pittsburgh, as across America, both the economic climate and the political mood were changing. To be sure, at the beginning of 1907, Andrew Carnegie had predicted, in the pages of the *Pittsburgh Post*, that "never has the future dawned upon the American republic more brightly."[1] After almost ten years of unprecedented prosperity, this seemed a portent that the good times would continue. So, in some ways, they did. That very year, Pittsburgh and Allegheny City were merged into a new supermetropolis. Their combined populations increased from 450,000 in 1900 to 534,000 ten years later, while the head count in Allegheny County as a whole grew from 775,000 to slightly more than one million. Immigrants still poured in from southern, central, and eastern Europe (a quarter of the city's population was foreign-born in 1910), and Pittsburgh's coal, steel, and glass industries continued to expand.[2] Between 1900 and 1913, the annual output of the city's rolling mills doubled from twelve million to twenty-five million tons, and production of steel ingots and castings increased from ten to thirty-one million tons.

All this seemed to suggest that business was continuing to boom. Yet in other ways, the economic reality was less than reassuring, not only in terms of short-term fluctuations and long-term trends, but also because of sagging local morale and hostile national perceptions of the city. Early in 1907, Pittsburgh suffered a flood which was the greatest local disaster since the devastating fire of 1845.[3] Situated at the junction of the Allegheny, the Ohio, and the Monongahela rivers, and low-lying at the Point, Pittsburgh was always vulnerable to rising water levels, and on March 13 the three rivers burst their banks. For a time, sixteen hundred acres of the city were submerged, rendering one hundred office buildings inaccessible and thirty-three miles of streets impassible, and putting seventeen miles of railroad out of action. Commerce and manufacturing in the central business district came to a halt, and so, too, did the steel mills and blast furnaces along the riverbanks. The loss to the city was in excess of ten million dollars, a costlier catastrophe than the rail strike of 1877 or the Homestead battle of 1892. A commission, chaired by H. J. Heinz, was appointed in February 1908 to investigate and recommend future precautionary measures. The eminently sensible proposals it put forward in 1911 came to nothing because of a lack of state and federal support.[4]

The city had scarcely begun to recover from the flood when, in October 1907, a sudden economic downturn ripped through the Northeast, starting in New York and spreading rapidly to Boston and Philadelphia, and west to Chicago—and Pittsburgh. There were many reasons for it. On the basis of Judge Mellon's principle of "five [years] up and five down," the turn-of-the-century boom was due to go bust.[5] Almost a decade of muckraking journalism and lurid stories of dishonest speculators and avaricious entrepreneurs had fed widespread distrust of the stock exchange and big business. And on Wall Street itself, weeks of jitters and rumors eventually brought the roof down on October 21, when the Knickerbocker Trust Company, the Mercantile National Bank, and the brokerage firm of Otto C. Heinze and Co. all collapsed. The resulting panic on the Street spawned a national currency crisis, mushrooming bankruptcies, an abrupt halt to railroad building, a reduction in industrial output across the nation, and widespread unemployment. Only the intervention of J. P. Morgan, who, with the assistance of Andrew Carnegie and J. D. Rockefeller, put together a syndicate mobilizing fifty million dollars to prop up ailing trusts, banks, and brokerage houses, prevented complete financial devastation in New York. The nation's banking system held—barely.[6]

As the American economy came close to collapse, western Pennsylvania was especially hard hit. On October 23, shares quoted on the Pittsburgh Stock Exchange lost 40 percent of their value, and its doors were closed until January 26, 1908.[7] But this was only the beginning. Two national banks would subsequently go into receivership: the Fort Pitt and the Allegheny. So did the Iron City Trust Company. Likewise three brokerage houses: Whitney and Stephenson, James Carothers, and George MacMullen. Such major (indeed, iconic) businesses as the Westinghouse Electric and Manufacturing Company, the Westinghouse Machine Company, the Hostetter-Connellsville Coal and Coke Company, and the National Glass Company also went under.[8] As Thomas McKaig of Trade Dollar Consolidated Mining wrote from the firm's Pittsburgh headquarters in November 1907: "The general opinion prevails that hard times will be felt here for some time." "General opinion" was quite correct, and financial activity in Pittsburgh remained crippled for much of the following year. "I have not noticed a summer for a long time," James Ross Mellon wrote to Andrew in August 1908, "that business was at such a standstill in the bank and everywhere else." And it was the same in industry: coal and coke production was down by 50 percent, steel output down by one-third, river and rail traffic down by 30 percent, and a quarter of local firms ceased operations.[9]

These were trying times. "Pittsburgh," as one contemporary observed, "looms up as the mighty storm mountain of Capital and Labor. Here our modern world achieves its grandest triumphs and faces its gravest problems."[10] It was against this somber background that the political picture in the city briefly changed. The death of Christopher Magee in 1901, combined with the publication of the muckraking exposé by Lincoln Steffens, *The Shame of the Cities*, meant that for a short time the local Republican machine lost its grip, and that even in Pittsburgh there was an interlude of more progressive government. From 1906 to 1909, George W. Guthrie held office as a reforming mayor, and in a radical departure from precedent, he and his successor both sought to get things done and make things work. They remedied some of the city's worst abuses: a filtered water supply was provided, dramatically reducing the incidence of typhoid, and there were successful prosecutions of corrupt city officials in the departments of Public Works, Public Health, and Public Safety. And they reorganized local government. First, Pittsburgh and Allegheny City were merged. Then, in 1911, Pittsburgh's large and unwieldy two-chamber council, where one hundred and forty members were elected ward by ward, was replaced with a body of nine members, each elected citywide, in an attempt to ensure more efficient (and less salable) civic leadership.[11]

In this more liberal political climate, Pittsburgh now became the focus of a social survey, overseen by Paul U. Kellogg, sponsored by the Russell Sage Foundation of New York, and initially supported by the Civic Club of Allegheny County. When undertaken, it was an investigation unique in American history, and matched only by Charles Booth's monumental investigation of *Life and Labour of the People of London* thirty years before. The results were published in six volumes between 1909 and 1914, an encyclopedic and utterly devastating indictment of the city, especially of its degraded and polluted environment, its squalid and inadequate housing, its terrible working conditions, and its deplorable standards of public hygiene.[12] Part muckraking polemic, part objective sociological investigation, the published results of the survey depicted Pittsburgh as being obsessed with wealth and work to the exclusion of virtually everything else. The report of twelve-hour shifts in the steel mills was but one notorious manifestation. The city's fabled success had been bought at too high a price, paid by the many for the benefit of the few. For while business was concentrated, dynamic, and rational, and filled the pockets of the leading industrialists, local government was wholly inadequate and private charities unequal to answering the widespread poverty and deprivation. There was thus virtually no sense of Pittsburgh as a unified or coherent civic, as distinct from economic, community.[13]

The detailed exposé of Andrew Mellon's hometown made national news. But not surprisingly, it found no favor with the targets of its criticism, so its recommendations were virtually ignored. The Civic Club withdrew its support, and the local press launched a vigorous counter-offensive, denouncing the survey's authors as ignorant outsiders and malevolent mischief-makers, and their report as an exaggerated, inaccurate, and selective defamation of a fine city.[14] But Mayor Guthrie and his reformist successor recognized that the issues raised could not be brushed off, and they promoted a series of initiatives and investigations, including a civic commission, an economic survey of the region, a report on its transportation, a city planning commission, and a municipal art commission, which exposed in further detail the dark and squalid side of life in Pittsburgh. But the city was now back in Republican control, and these efforts were ultimately ineffectual. A 1911 attempt to enlarge its boundaries into a greater Pittsburgh—so as to create a bigger unit in which contemporary problems might be more comprehensively addressed—also met with failure. In western Pennsylvania, the brief progressive era was nearing its end.[15]

Such renewed municipal infirmity lent credence to the survey's contrast between a vigorous, innovative economy and inadequate local government. Yet ironically, at the very time the survey results appeared, even Midas-touch Pittsburgh was slowing down: the aftershocks of 1907 were still being felt, and despite its sluggish recovery, the city's heyday was beginning to draw to a close. The age of heavy industry was ending: after 1907, demand for rails and railcars would begin to decline, and no new steelworks would be constructed in the Pittsburgh region after 1911. Even in realms of traditional dominance, there were ominous signs of faltering: in 1901 the area had produced 80 percent of the nation's coke; by 1910 the figure was down to 50 percent.[16] As this suggests, Pittsburgh was now dangerously overconcentrated and overspecialized in a limited range of heavy industries which were no longer at the leading edge of the American economy. By 1910, that era of rapid industrial and population expansion was virtually over, and growth in output began to taper off markedly. Nor was there any sign that "new" industries were settling in town: such Mellon companies as Alcoa, Carborundum, and Gulf Oil kept their corporate headquarters in Pittsburgh, but by now most production, manufacturing, and sales were carried on elsewhere. Relatively, though not yet absolutely, the city and the region were beginning to stagnate after 1907.[17]

One indication was that the Pittsburgh Stock Exchange never recovered from its protracted closure. A vital provider of capital from 1898 to 1907, it thereafter languished at the margins of industrial securities activity, trading only in oil and mining stocks.[18] A second sign was that the Pittsburgh Chamber of Commerce later published a report showing that between 1909 and 1914 the aggregate value of the city's businesses had declined. At best, these were years of limited recovery, tentative expansion, and widespread pessimism and uncertainty. A third pointer was that in July 1913, Andrew Mellon was in Europe, but so concerned about the prospect of another panic that he wondered whether he should return home, as he had done in 1907.[19] Brother Dick counseled against it, but in the following month, he warned Andrew of a coming period of tight money. There had been another bank failure, the First-Second National, and Dick had notified all Mellon companies that for the time being they would have to manage "without any assistance from us." New building work at Carborundum was halted, drilling by Gulf was cut back, McClintic-Marshall "got along without money," Standard Steel Car borrowed in New York and Philadelphia. "I find," Dick concluded, with characteristic, tight-lipped Mellon pragmatism, "they all get along with less money if we are more strict with them."[20]

Such were Pittsburgh's economic, environmental, and political conditions as Andrew Mellon suffered the public humiliation and private desolation of his divorce. Across the nation, the progressive movement was even stronger, especially in Washington, and Mellon did not like it.[21] As Theodore Roosevelt's ostensibly Republican presidency galloped toward its close in 1908, he became more determinedly radical, calling for the increased regulation of big business, initiating more antitrust suits, and urging the introduction of an inheritance tax and an income tax. Indeed, there were some who claimed that it was TR's anti-business rhetoric and his energetic interference in the economy that had helped to precipitate the crash of 1907. In its aftermath, Roosevelt went on the rampage against the selfish rich, the "huge monied men to whom money is the be-all and end-all of existence," the "malefactors of great wealth," who are responsible for "wrongdoing in many forms."[22] (He also called for the establishment of a national gallery of art in Washington at about this time.) Roosevelt's successor in the White House, William Howard Taft, though lacking TR's charisma, was in some ways yet more of a progressive: he initiated twice as many antitrust suits in the four years of his administration than Roosevelt had in eight. As far as Mellon was concerned, this was not what a Republican president was supposed to do.

In these progressive years, Mellon was appalled by the muckrakers' "revelations" about the supposed misdemeanors of big companies and rich businessmen, and he was dismayed by the government's antitrust suits. In particular, he was much aghast at the prosecution of John D. Rockefeller and Standard Oil, which had been initiated in 1906 under Roosevelt. "The evil effects," he noted in a letter to Frank Haskell of Carborundum early in 1911, "accomplished by these muck-raking magazines, and their followers, a large portion of the daily press, is an actual menace to the welfare of people generally."[23] He had read, he explained, some of the articles by Ida Tarbell denouncing Rockefeller, but "became so disgusted" at their contents that he "couldn't continue reading." Many purported facts he knew personally to be "utterly unfounded," the whole sordid activity "jarred upon my sense of truth and justice," and he was sure that "the crusade by the Government and a great many states against the Standard Oil Company would not have arisen but for these false and exaggerated statements." To be sure, he went on, there were "a great many things done which should not have been done" by businessmen in "times past"; but from his own personal knowledge, Mellon was convinced that "there is no foundation for ninety-one one-hundredths of the slanderous charges which have been published against the company."

Having read the briefs and arguments presented by both sides, Mellon was confident that the Supreme Court would find for Rockefeller and Standard Oil. "No fair-minded man," he went on, "can read the proofs without being convinced that irrelevant and unfounded charges generally are the basis of the contention upon the part of the government." And as the proprietor of Gulf Oil, he had reached this benevolent conclusion "from the standpoint of a competitor in the business." His sense of sportsmanship was clear: "We meet with their competition everywhere, but it is fair and open competition. We have not had to complain about any underhand or unfair methods."[24] Such was the freemasonry of big business—but it was underpinned by faulty recollection. For in the early 1890s, Standard Oil's methods in Pennsylvania had scarcely been aboveboard, and the Mellons' dealings with the company had been far from happy. But now, forgetting the past, and out of touch with the mood of the time, Mellon breezily predicted that the Court would find for the Standard. Instead, it ordered the complete dissolution of Rockefeller's giant corporation, a trust that had defied twenty-seven years of legal assault, into thirty-four independent entities.[25]

Later that year, no longer a shocked observer of antitrust action, Mellon himself became a target when the federal government turned its attention to Alcoa. From 1889 to 1909, the company had enjoyed a legal monopoly to produce aluminum in the United States, based on Charles Martin Hall's original patent. But the right applied only in America, and in any case its term was finite. The management had therefore taken steps to secure Alcoa's position at home and abroad, anticipating the expiration of its legal domestic monopoly. Their efforts were undoubtedly "in restraint of trade," and thus in breach of the Sherman Antitrust Act of 1890. But they were only behaving in a manner consistent with American big business practice of the time. No great American capitalist had expected the act to be rigorously enforced by future federal administrations. Between 1896 and 1908, Alcoa entered into agreements with the major European producers of aluminum, handing over the continent to them but keeping America for itself, thereby establishing a cartel which helped keep world prices buoyant until the slump of 1907. In addition, Alcoa had struck various domestic deals, with the General Chemical Company, the Norton Company, and the Pennsylvania Salt Company, restricting their rights to make aluminum or sell bauxite. It had also made another pact with an independent aluminum utensils manufacturer that limited the competitor's markets geographically, to Alcoa's advantage.[26]

It is not clear how or when the federal government became interested in Alcoa. But with its elevated profitability, and the continued antitrust vigilance of the Taft administration, it was likely to come under scrutiny sooner or later. In May 1911 the Department of Justice filed a complaint, charging illegal participation in foreign cartels, restrictive covenants in the purchase of bauxite, and the undertaking of other unfair competitive practices.[27] Officials soon found ample evidence in support of the department's complaint concerning domestic restrictions on trade; it also emerged that new international agreements had recently been struck, reviving arrangements that had lapsed in 1908, although Arthur Vining Davis initially denied this. Mellon seems to have distanced himself from these proceedings: he made only one laconic entry in his diary, dated May 16, noting the formal filing of the federal suit. However, these were also the months when the fat was in the fire during his divorce proceedings.[28] Faced with such overwhelming evidence of wrongdoing, Alcoa's directors capitulated, and after yearlong negotiations a "consent decree" was signed in June 1912, obliging the company to admit its position was indefensible, in return for which the federal government agreed to drop its suit, provided Alcoa pledged to play fair in the future.

While the company was not judged to have built its "substantial monopoly" illegally, it was forbidden in the future to enter into any cartel. In addition, its collusive agreements with other American companies were struck down, and it was enjoined from combining in any way with other manufacturers to control output.[29] The relative speed of the settlement and the absence of any penalties has been taken to imply that the government had merely intended to fire a warning shot across Alcoa's bow, and it is undeniable that for a time thereafter, management did all it could to conduct its business carefully, even consulting the Justice Department in 1915 before acquiring the Southern Aluminum Company of North Carolina. In fact, the federal government was not yet done with Alcoa. Since 1890, the company had benefited from the strong protectionist policy sustained by every administration since the Civil War. Federal tariffs, initially levied at $0.15 per pound on aluminum ingot, had subsequently been reduced to $0.08 per pound in 1897, but protection was extended to semifinished and fabricated products. Woodrow Wilson then decisively overturned this policy with the Underwood Tariff of 1913, when Congress slashed the duty on aluminum ingot to $0.02 per pound, despite Arthur Vining Davis's (distinctly implausible) claim that this would spell ruin for Alcoa.[30]

Clearly, Andrew Mellon found progressivism emanating from Washington as bilious as progressivism in Pittsburgh. And there was more of it to come, for in the aftermath of the 1907 crash, public opinion turned against finance in particular: against small-town banks, which were often mismanaged, and against the great banking houses that had recently become more prominent than ever on the East Coast. According to the comptroller of the currency, 69 percent of bank failures between 1865 and 1911 could be attributed to fraudulent management, the granting of loans in excess of the legal limit, or other injudicious acts. And according to Woodrow Wilson, the banker was "the most jealously regarded and the least liked instrument of business," and "the people" considered bankers as "belonging to some power hostile to them."[31] Those who shared this view found ample corroboration in 1912 and 1913 in the hearings of the subcommittee of the House Banking and Currency Committee, chaired by Representative Arsène Pujo of Louisiana, which was charged with investigating "the money trust," by which was meant the elaborate inter-locking connections between East Coast business and bankers, personi-fied by J. P. Morgan. The committee's findings were inconclusive, but the hearings, and the great publicity they were given, increased demand for some sort of banking regulation and reform.[32]

While the Pujo Committee was sitting, the political climate swung further against big business as a result of the presidential election of November 1912. It was a three-way contest between Taft, the Republican incumbent; Roosevelt, who had bolted and founded his own Progressive Party; and the Democrat, Woodrow Wilson. To Mellon's dismay, Wilson won. He disapproved of the new president as an intellectual and a do-gooder, as someone who would sponsor "adverse legislation in Washing-ton," by which Mellon meant laws designed (by his lights) to constrain and cripple private enterprise.[33] As Frank Haskell wrote to Mellon early the following year, no doubt echoing his master's own thoughts, "with the existing uncertainty as to what Washington will do with business, we should not consider heavy investments in new plants."[34] Like Roosevelt, Wilson was "against the trusts," and against "a government by the opinion and duress of small groups of dominant men." One of Wilson's advisers was Louis D. Brandeis, who in 1914 published a book drawing on the hear-ings of the Pujo Committee, entitled *Other People's Money—and How the Bankers Use It*, which painted a graphic picture of financial oligarchy, greed, and overweening power.[35] The new president, Mellon noted in his diary in June 1914, "proposes to pass Anti-Trust and Trade Commission Bills." They would, he added, be "bad for [the] country," but pass they did.[36]

In September, and spurred on by Wilson, Congress established the

Federal Trade Commission to police business practices; it was authorized to investigate the activities of all corporations engaged in interstate commerce, and to move against those using unfair methods of competition. The following month, the Clayton Act was passed to strengthen the original Sherman Antitrust Act, under which previous prosecutions had been brought. Its aim was to outlaw certain specific business practices: price discrimination that lessened competition or promoted monopoly, discounts given on condition that purchasers refrain from buying from other suppliers, and (something that must have been particularly worrisome to Mellon) interlocking directorates in industrial firms with capital of more than one million dollars. The Clayton Act also declared trade unions to be legal, and not to be combinations in restraint of trade; peaceful strikes, picketing, and the payment of strike benefits were found lawful; and court injunctions were not to be used in labor disputes "unless necessary to prevent irreparable damage to property."[37] By then, Wilson had also signed into law a federal income tax, to compensate for the reduced revenue as a consequence of lowering tariffs, and he supported a constitutional amendment whereby U.S. senators would henceforth be directly elected, instead of being nominated by the state legislature.

Wilson's aim was to try to undermine Republican Party machines. Unsurprisingly, he scored no success in Pennsylvania, where things went on as before, with Penrose and Knox (now back in the Senate) still emphatically in charge. But in this hostile political climate, Mellon suddenly seemed vulnerable. For there was not only the investigation into Alcoa, but also the inquiry into his dealings over the Union Steel merger and sale. He kept his distance from both investigations, but the findings were seriously critical. And, had anyone chosen to make the comparison, the picture of the Morgan Bank, at the center of a vast, interlocking empire—of finance houses, insurance companies, transport, and utilities—was merely a larger-scale, East Coast version of what Mellon and his brother had created (and controlled) in Pittsburgh. For now, most of the public ire against bankers in the aftermath of the panic of 1907 was directed against those in New York and on Wall Street: Mellon was still relatively inconspicuous. But next time around, a quarter of a century later, with a more devastating economic crisis, another Roosevelt presidency, and popular clamor against bankers at record levels, it would be very different.

Meanwhile, Woodrow Wilson passed one more major piece of legislation: the Federal Reserve Act in December 1913, which reformed the monetary and banking system in response to the panic of six years before. Twelve Federal Reserve banks were established across the nation, owned by local banks, and with directors recruited from local banks, which could support individual finance houses in their region by holding their surplus funds, or by lending to them in the event of difficulty. These banks, in turn, were to be generally supervised by a new agency, the Federal Reserve Board, which consisted of the secretary of the treasury, the comptroller of the currency, and five other presidential appointees. The board was empowered to set the rediscount rate at which Federal Reserve banks would lend, and it was also able to buy or sell U.S. government securities in "open market" operations. By these means, it was hoped that the board would be able to control the total volume of money and supply of credit, thereby eliminating the booms and slumps of earlier times. Bank notes issued by national banks were no longer secured by U.S. government bonds. Instead, Federal Reserve notes were created, which were issued by the twelve regional banks on the basis of a 40 percent gold reserve. Woodrow Wilson believed the act would usher in a new era of prosperity and happiness. "We will," Charles Hamlin predicted in 1915, "never have any more panics."[38] Mellon's response to the Federal Reserve Act is unrecorded. But it seems unlikely that he would have approved of any legislation initiated by the Wilson White House, and inconceivable that he would have shared Hamlin's naïvely optimistic opinion.

II. MAKING MONEY, MANAGING MEN

A week before the Pittsburgh Stock Exchange was forced to close in panic in October 1907, Henry Clay Frick had written Andrew Mellon from New York, urging prudence. "I trust you are keeping the bank in good strong shape," Frick wrote, "as you cannot tell these times what may happen." "We occupy," he went on, "a very important position in [the] Pittsburgh financial world, and we must see to it that we are in a good strong position, ready at all times to give our depositors the money when they want it."[39] He was not speaking hypothetically. On Mellon's abrupt return to Pittsburgh later that month, the news was grim: shares in two of his (very few) publicly traded quoted companies, Crucible Steel and Pittsburgh Coal, were especially hard hit, their earnings in sudden decline; currency was scarce, while both the Allegheny Bank and the Oakland Saving and Trust Company were near collapse. It was rumored that even such Mellon associates as James Reed were for a time in dire straits. Indeed, Thomas Galey, son of Sam Galey, would claim that the Mellons "almost went broke" in 1907, and were saved only by Andrew journeying to New

York to borrow twenty million dollars from J. P. Morgan—but there is no evidence of this.[40]

Since Union Trust Company reported a surplus of twenty-four million dollars on the first day of January 1908, it seems highly unlikely that the Mellon brothers were in serious trouble.[41] But there were also rumors that Mellon and Frick had fallen out over the relative importance of safeguarding bank reserves in Pittsburgh (which was Mellon's view) or in New York (as Frick allegedly preferred). The local situation presented two other causes for worry. The lesser was the bankruptcy of both the Westinghouse Electric and Manufacturing Company and the Westinghouse Machine Company. Although Westinghouse had long been an iconic local entrepreneur, in air brakes and in electrical products, he was a much abler inventor than businessman, and after brushing off Mellon, had sought financing from New York rather than Pittsburgh.[42] In March, 1907, the Westinghouse Electric and Manufacturing Company authorized an increase of twenty-five million dollars in capital stock, to enlarge its capacity and meet growing overseas demand. But the new issue was ominously undersubscribed, and thus began a downward spiral: by the time of the October crisis, share prices had collapsed, and two of the Westinghouse companies faced bankruptcy. A rescue package was put together, which incidentally presented Mellon with an ideal opportunity to move in on a local enterprise he had long coveted. However, apart from installing W. H. Donner on the board of the refurbished Westinghouse Machine Company and distributing three other colleagues over the other salvaged Westinghouse enterprises, he stayed out.[43]

The reason for this may well have been the general strain of that terrible year, but there was also the more serious and time-consuming bankruptcy of the brokerage house of Whitney and Stephenson. George I. Whitney was a member of the stock exchange in Pittsburgh, as well as those in New York and Philadelphia. He was a director of Union Trust, and he had helped Mellon consolidate his two coal companies in 1899. He was also a manager of various local firms, including the Hostetter-Connellsville Coal and Coke Company. He was, then, almost as much a Mellon man as Mitchell or Reed or McEldowney. In the recent boom years, he had overextended himself, making dubious investments in mining stocks and fraudulent pledges of security on collateral loans, and leveraging his firm's resources far beyond prudence. When the panic hit in October 1907, his brokerage was highly exposed. The immediate response of Mellon and Frick was to try to shore up Whitney's firm: in mid-November, Whitney sold his shares in Hostetter-Connellsville to

Frick, and in return received a million-dollar infusion from Union Trust. But it was too little too late: Whitney's company folded, with liabilities of nearly twenty million dollars and assets of only seven million.

Once it was clear that a million dollars would not rescue Whitney, Mellon and Frick refused to offer any more, and stood by watching their friend's business collapse. Though major creditors, they made no attempt to recover Union Trust's loan, preferring to distance themselves from the whole affair. But they did not fully succeed. For in the aftermath of the bankruptcy, a suit was brought against Frick and Mellon and Union Trust by the other creditors. Among the charges, it was alleged that Whitney had had no right to sell his shares in Hostetter-Connellsville without permission of its secured creditors; that with the Pittsburgh Stock Exchange closed, and the value of the shares thus depressed, Frick had bought below market price; and that Frick had colluded with Union Trust to make available the abortive rescue package of one million dollars (that much was incontrovertibly true). Frick, Mellon, and Union Trust were artfully defended by James Reed, who simply denied many of the charges, and the case against them petered out. In truth, Mellon and Frick were lucky to get off scot-free.[44]

In general, Mellon's consolidations in traditional Pittsburgh industries were not faring as well as the newer companies that he had developed in the city and, increasingly, elsewhere. One of the older companies, Crucible Steel had been an overcapitalized amalgamation from the beginning, and its shares had fluctuated wildly. They plummeted in 1907, and in March 1908 the company reported losses of $500,000 for the preceding half of the fiscal year. Mellon's solution was to increase his investment, and in 1910–11 a new integrated steel mill was constructed at Midland, Pennsylvania, on the Ohio River—the last to be built in the greater Pittsburgh region.[45] He was much less inclined to put money into Pittsburgh Coal and Monongahela River Consolidated Coal & Coke. The merger of 1903 had not really worked, 1907 was a severe setback, and neither of the Mellons' chiefs—first James B. Finley, then Francis L. Robbins—proved up to the job. Consolidation was resumed in 1910, and completed during the next five years, but profits were sluggish and market share declined. At the same time, more than 40,000 acres of coal-bearing land were sold off, along with subsidiaries such as the Pittsburgh Coal Car Company. All these were bad omens—signs of a business poorly led, and one that failed to achieve the hoped-for economies of scale. Mellon's original optimistic expectations had not been met.[46]

But across most of the Mellon empire, there was generally rapid recovery from 1907, and Dick Mellon's anxieties about tight money six years later were also short-lived. McClintic-Marshall expanded its production facilities, bought up rival companies, and in December 1911 won the contract to build the Hell Gate Bridge, which brought the Pennsylvania Railroad as well as the New Haven and Hartford lines into Manhattan from New England. By June 1913, Standard Steel Car's six freight plants were producing 250 cars a day, its three passenger car plants were turning out 115 cars a month, and there were orders on hand worth $37 million.[47] In addition to other contracts, the New York Shipbuilding Company constructed seven battleships for the U.S. Navy—including its first dreadnought, the *Michigan*—and six tankers for Gulf Oil. Two additional double slipways had to be installed between 1912 and 1915. They were the largest in any American shipyard. (The company had lobbied hard in Washington, via Philander Knox, when he was secretary of state, for government contracts, and its direct line to Gulf must also have helped.)[48]

While these businesses based on coal and steel boomed, the Mellon petroleum and aluminum companies did even better. The recently restructured Gulf Oil, now directly led by W. L. Mellon and his associates, soon paid off its Guffey-era debts, and by 1910 it was a thriving company, with assets including 20,000 acres of land, more than 1,000 producing wells, and over 100 gas stations across the country. In 1913, Gulf reported a net profit of $8.2 million and paid a 100 percent stock dividend; capitalization was later increased from the original $15 million to $60 million. Alcoa was also flourishing. Thanks to extensive vertical integration and expanding markets, both domestic and industrial, pretax earnings leapt from $1.2 million in 1908 to nearly $6 million in 1909, prompting the distribution of a 500 percent stock dividend (which may, in part, have triggered the 1911 federal inquiry), which increased the company's capitalization from $5.6 million to $24 million. Even though its legal domestic monopoly lapsed in 1909, the company was now too large and secure for any other enterprise to challenge it.[49]

Part enablers, part beneficiaries of these developments were the two flagship financial enterprises, the Mellon National Bank and the Union Trust Company, which both prospered mightily during these years. The bank's initial capital of $2 million had been doubled to $4 million in 1904, and even after Mellon National disbursed a 50 percent stock dividend in March 1911, it again increased, to $6 million. In the following eighteen months, another $500,000 was added to its surplus, and a sum close to that was also paid out in ordinary dividends. Put another way, from 1902 to 1912, the assets of Mellon National Bank grew fivefold—a complete vindication of Andrew's decision to restructure the business.[50] At the same time, Union Trust was even more successful: from July 1903 to January 1910, it was paying a 60 percent dividend annually; from 1905 on there was an additional 6 percent Christmas dividend; and from 1911 to 1916, it was paying a 100 percent dividend each year, not counting the Christmas bonus. These were astonishing figures. In 1908, Union Trust topped the "Financial Roll of Honor of the United States" as the most prosperous trust in the country. Through its connections with Mellon National and Union Savings, it controlled one-third of the banking resources of the city. And its accumulated surplus, which then stood at $24 million, grew to over $30 million in the next six years.[51]

A further indication of Mellon financial might: of eighty-five banks in Pittsburgh in 1912, Mellon National was preeminent in terms of deposits ($40 million), investment securities ($11 million), and loans ($21 million). And it was first by several lengths: next came the Farmer's Deposit National Bank ($25 million, $5 million, and $15 million, respectively), and then the Bank of Pittsburgh ($19 million, $4 million, and $13 million). This Mellon primacy was further buttressed in another round of aggressive acquisitions and assimilations, launched soon after the midsummer 1913 jitters that had unnerved Dick. In October, Union Trust bought out Farmer's Deposit, in the largest consolidation of financial institutions ever carried out in the city. The Judge had been one of the original directors from 1858 to 1865 and again from 1869 to 1871, and Andrew had been a member of the board since at least 1900.[52] At the same time, the McKeesport National Bank and the Bank of Pittsburgh were also brought under Mellon influence through overlapping directorships, a substantial Mellon equity holding, and "moral and financial support." The result was that over 40 percent of the region's banking deposits and half of the investment securities owned by its national banks were now controlled by Andrew and Dick Mellon, via Union Trust, the Mellon National Bank, subsidiary ownerships, and interlocking directorates. According to Mark Samber, the Mellons "had a lock on virtually half of the region's banking resources," and controlled de facto most of the major financial decisions made in Pittsburgh.[53]

In these tumultuous years of the new century, then, most of Andrew Mellon's enterprises were more buoyant than the Pittsburgh economy generally, which meant that whatever his personal distractions and marital misfortunes, his private wealth continued to grow significantly—indeed, inexorably. In 1906, Mellon had declared himself to be worth $31 million at "book value," which probably meant $50 million at "market value." By 1908, the "book value" of his fortune had increased to $36 million, of which nearly $18 million was his own personal holdings of stocks and bonds and $15.5 million was his half of the holdings he kept jointly with his brother in the account under the name of T. Mellon & Sons. (By contrast, Mellon's art collection at this time amounted to a little over $600,000, barely one-sixth of what Frick's was worth.)[54] Thereafter, the book value of his wealth increased to $42 million in 1910, to $50 million in 1911, to $53 million in 1912, and to $55 million in 1913.[55] In six years, his fortune was well on the way to doubling, and so at market value, Andrew Mellon may have been worth approximately $100 million by 1914–15, which means that in present-day currency, he was certainly a billionaire.

This accumulation, far beyond anything the Judge could have imagined or achieved, was significantly more than the $80 million estate that J. P. Morgan left at about this time, but it was barely half of what William Vanderbilt had been worth back in the 1880s, and not remotely in the league of J. D. Rockefeller, who in 1913 was a billionaire in the value of his time and who did not consider Morgan a seriously wealthy man.[56] In terms of stocks and bonds, the Mellon fortune was primarily distributed across the largest and most famous companies that Andrew and Dick had helped develop: some shares were individually held (Union Trust, Carborundum, Alcoa, McClintic-Marshall), while others were in the brothers' joint T. Mellon & Sons account (Gulf Oil, Union Steel, New York Shipbuilding, Standard Steel Car). As befitted the brothers' constant avowals of civic loyalty, most of these Mellon enterprises were headquartered in Pittsburgh, and some operated within the region: the two coal companies, Crucible Steel, McClintic-Marshall, the Philadelphia Company, and Standard Steel Car. But just as the Judge had bought land far from Pittsburgh, so too did the next generation's businesses operate within a much wider geographical radius: New York Shipbuilding was based in Camden, New Jersey; Alcoa had expanded far beyond Niagara Falls, New York, to Quebec, North Carolina, Tennessee, Arkansas, and Georgia; Standard Steel Car also had plants in Indiana, Maryland, and Massachusetts; Gulf Oil was in Texas, Oklahoma, Kansas, and Louisiana; and there were the mining interests in Idaho and California.[57]

But it was not only geographically that the Mellon fortune transcended the bounds of Pittsburgh. It had never been based primarily on the city's great staple industries of the nineteenth century. To be sure, the Mellons were shareholders in the Pittsburgh Plate Glass Company and the two great local coal businesses, and they were deeply involved as well in the fabrication, though not the production, of steel. But they had also been interested in utilities: in natural gas companies since the 1880s, in streetcar lines since the 1890s, and (farther afield) in the Colorado Light and Power Company. Most important of all, in helping to develop Carborundum, Alcoa, and Gulf, they had connected themselves to what would prove among the most profitable industries of the first half of the twentieth century. This was especially so with Gulf, whose prodigious expansion, thanks to the demand that would soon be generated via the automobile and the airplane, could be only dimly discerned, even as late as 1914. (If Mellon had indeed turned Henry Ford down, he was not alone in being skeptical of the internal combustion engine.) As these companies prospered, along with the Mellon Bank and the Union Trust Company, Andrew's private fortune increased commensurately. At the same time, he also lived relatively cheaply, spending barely a quarter of his annual income of approximately one million dollars. The suspension of art collecting, plus his incorrigible determination to live unostentatiously, allowed him to accumulate money faster than some of his significantly richer contemporaries who were spending lavishly on houses, yachts, old masters, and other conspicuous consumables.

With the exception of the years of his divorce, Mellon was neither conspicuous nor a consumer, and thus he was an atypical plutocrat. Nor was he a pioneer in the new methods of business management and control that were becoming widespread during the first decades of the twentieth century, as inventors and owners were superseded by salaried managers and corporate hierarchies.[58] Although he was dealing with enterprises and technologies far beyond his father's experience and imagination, Andrew adhered all his working life to the Judge's managerial formula, applying it at altogether higher levels of success and profit: "If he [an inventor and/or entrepreneur] would furnish the energy and industry to operate the business and carry it on in his own name, I would become the silent partner with him and furnish the money necessary."[59] "Silent partner" was certainly an apt description of Mellon, befitting his legendary taciturnity, and also his wish to avoid publicity. He always distanced himself from the front line of business—the coal face, the oil refinery, the shipyard, the assembly plant—and especially from potential labor unrest. But such distance was not so much an abdication of control as a discreet means whereby control was exercised more effectively. As Andrew once put it in a letter to his nephew WL, he and Dick "had always been in the position of entirely dominating our own operations."[60] That may have been an exaggeration, but not by much.

As in the Judge's day, the essence of the Mellon management system was the "intensely personal and informal" reliance on loyal associates and subordinates, who came in various guises and operated on a variety of different levels (though they all ranked below those attorneys and politicians who helped create a legal and legislative climate favorable to business, in which cohort Philander Knox and James Reed were preeminent).[61] There were the inventors-cum-entrepreneurs: Hall of Alcoa, Acheson of Carborundum, McClintic and Marshall of their eponymous company. There were the lifelong managers, such as Walter S. Mitchell at Mellon Bank, Henry C. McEldowney at Union Trust, and Frank H. Haskell at Carborundum. There were those who moved around from one place to another, mixing business, politics, and personal matters: George S. Davison, who was involved with the "Mellon lines" in Pittsburgh, and subsequently with Gulf Oil;[62] William H. Donner at Union Steel, and later at Westinghouse, who claimed that he had "done a lot of work for A. W. Mellon personally that nobody knows anything about, in investigating";[63] and George F. Taber, who was sent off from Gulf Oil to Paris in January 1910 to shadow Nora and Curphey, and who was eventually paid an extra $15,000 for his pains.[64] And there were the lower-level functionaries: Howard M. Johnson, who went to work for the Mellon Bank as a clerk in 1907, and from 1913 on was responsible for completing Andrew's federal income tax returns; Arthur E. Sixsmith, Andrew's private secretary from 1908 to 1931; and Henry A. Phillips, who looked after the dockets and wallets containing the two brothers' individual and joint investments.[65]

Frick once recommended one such individual to Mellon as being "a valuable man to look after your interests," and this is precisely what they were and what they did.[66] They were competent, tough, discreet, and loyal. Managerially, entrepreneurially, technologically, financially, and (where necessary) politically, the whole "Mellon system" depended on this mobile cadre of reliable associates, expected to do whatever was asked and to go wherever was needed: "When I send for a man, I want him to come" was Andrew Mellon's initial summons to Howard M. Johnson.[67] Likewise, in 1910, George S. Davison renewed a contract with Andrew and Dick, undertaking to devote "so much of his regular working time and services as may be necessary as advisory to and manager of such companies, corporations, partnerships, associations or other organizations, owned in whole or in part" by the brothers.[68] These retainers were disproportionately Scotch-Irish Presbyterians; never Catholics or Jews (who played no serious part in Pittsburgh industry or banking), or Slavs or blacks. Cut from such cloth as the Mellons themselves, they contributed to that dour, philistine, insular male culture so typical of the place.[69] In return, Andrew and Dick were "immensely loyal and treated you well if you followed what they said." Many of their associates became rich men

(Hall of Alcoa was worth $30 million when he died in 1914, and McClintic, Marshall, and McEldowney all left substantial estates). "Real success," Mellon would later observe, "comes from making others successful." Nor was ceremony neglected: Andrew and Dick were assiduous mourners at the funerals of their lieutenants.[70]

Of course, there were those exempt from grace: to Acheson at Carborundum and Guffey at Gulf were now added Finley and Robbins and Whitney in Pittsburgh who, having simply failed to meet up to the Mellons' exacting standards, were unsentimentally cast aside ("cut their throats" was one description of such dismissals).[71] Which brings us back to Nora Mellon; for she, too, proved incapable of nurturing Andrew's "interests" in the manner that he hoped for and expected. Knowing no other way, Andrew treated Nora essentially as one more business collaborator: he was faithful, considerate, dutiful, loyal; he made available to her ample means and abundant resources, hoping that with such support her wifely and maternal enterprises might prosper. But to Andrew's utter bafflement, she was unwilling to settle for a marriage that was more a business partnership than a human one. And her infractions of this code were many and blatant: she did not give a fig for loyalty or discretion or secrecy, virtues the Mellon clan and their associates prized as essential for their survival and success. Hence Andrew's rage, anxiety, and—eventually—ruthless determination to move against her with every instrument he could command: not as a flawed and fallible wife, but as a wayward and inadequate associate who must be silenced and neutralized. As one interviewee told Burton Hendrick, in a passage which—unsurprisingly—did not make its way into his unpublished biography: Mellon "was just as ruthless to her when she fell from grace and no longer held his confidence, as he was to business associates and the like against whom he turned."[72]

Indeed, all the distasteful publicity of the divorce, combined with the simultaneous federal investigation into Alcoa, must have reinforced the Mellons' lifelong belief in confidentiality and secrecy as cardinal virtues, no less for the "private" individual than the "public" conduct of business or politics. Not surprisingly, then, many of the most important discussions of their affairs were never written down, the decisions made during telephone calls or over lunch at the Duquesne Club, or at Dick's house or at WL's mansion. The Mellons' surviving business correspondence is almost invariably about day-to-day matters, scarcely recording higher levels of strategy such as they must have discussed, for instance, in response to the crash of 1907 or the Alcoa investigation four years later. Likewise, their companies provided as little documentation and reporting as the law allowed. Nor did they ever give information to the press, for as

Burton Hendrick noted, "to publish detailed reports, and spread all the facts of a growing business before their competitors, or prospective competitors, seemed to them sheer folly." "Referring to your inquiry about the standing of the Standard Steel Car Company, and your request for a statement," Andrew Mellon replied to one such question, "I have to say that the company does not give out any statements as to its condition." As Howard M. Johnson recalled, Mellon, like Vanderbilt, maintained a "the-public-be-damned attitude. It was none of their business."[73]

Nevertheless, the Mellon brothers and their associates continued to believe and to proclaim, among themselves and to the general public, a devotion to the highest good of the nation and its people. Just before Christmas 1910, Frank W. Haskell sent a letter to Andrew Mellon to reassure him that, though his marriage and personal life were in disarray, his work and professional life were both admirable and of the greatest significance. "There is in this place," Haskell observed, writing from the Carborundum plant at Niagara Falls,

> a business institution that is not only serving its purpose of earning good returns for its owners, but is, to my mind, doing a greater and nobler work in training scores of young men to look upon integrity and dignity as being unavoidably associated with business success. . . . The active, enthusiastic, energetic department heads of that concern today were the office boys of a few years ago. . . . They are not only good workers, but good citizens, and they are this because they were secure in the knowledge that good and faithful service would not fail of recognition, and their undivided attention was thus left for the work in hand, instead of being diverted by worries over business politics.

Moreover, the success and expansion of Carborundum had "made thousands of people comfortable, it has made hundreds of people happy, and it has made Niagara Falls a better community." "For the part I have taken in the work," Haskell concluded, "I am proud and happy." "But," he insisted, "an agent can only do what his principal permits. You are the man who is responsible for the good that is beyond expression."[74]

Haskell would soon have even greater cause to thank the Mellons, who stood by him during a nervous breakdown he suffered in January 1913, and his subsequent several months' sick leave.[75] Pride and happiness, goodness and greatness, integrity, dignity, and nobility: these are very powerful words, and they must have swelled Mellon's heart, even as they may now seem to us at best only selectively true, at worst monumentally hypocritical. For how can they be reconciled with the darker realities that contradicted Mellon's professed business ethics: his excessive profits from the sale of Union Steel, or his abandonment of George I. Whitney in 1907, or Alcoa's blatantly illegal actions "in restraint of trade"? And how do they relate to the suspect purchase of streetcar franchises, or of witnesses for the divorce case, or of legislators in Pittsburgh, Harrisburg, and Washington, D.C.? For Mellon and his generation of businessmen, these were minor aberrations and necessary activities in pursuit of a greater goal which they genuinely believed to be admirable, patriotic, and for the general welfare. Their self-image was that of industrial statesmen, who bore greater burdens than mere politicians, and who also did incomparably more good. Occasional lapses were unavoidable, but what was most important was that the nation's business must be carried on. It was a different time from ours. Or was it?[76]

III. SHORT BREATH AND SECOND WIND[77]

By the late 1900s and early 1910s, Andrew Mellon's varied business activities had settled into a recognizable pattern that had been developing since the early 1870s: a slump, weathered with difficulty but determination, then a recovery; burgeoning profits for the banks, the Union Trust Company, and many of his companies; one or two undertakings performing below par but with long-term prospects of growth and profit; and one or two just performing below par. To that extent, the years 1907–14 were business as usual, consistent with this latest phase of the economic cycle. But with neither the financial nor the political climate as propitious as it had once been, both Andrew and Dick were also beginning to feel their age. Dick, who had been seriously ill for several months early in 1914, was looking forward to creating at Ligonier a country estate which would come to be named Rolling Rock, where he could live out his last years hunting, shooting, and fishing with his male relatives and friends in a rural version of the Duquesne Club.[78] As for Andrew, for all his awesome (or loathsome) obsessiveness, he had in fact been a part-timer for a long while: he had taken regular, extended trips to Europe with Frick from the 1880s onward; he had spent two or three months away with Nora most years of their marriage; he had been prepared to buy her a summer home in England; and he had even been willing to take up full-time residence across the Atlantic to save his marriage.

With his sixtieth birthday in 1915, there were more definitive indications that Mellon was withdrawing from work, and wishing to withdraw even more. Like Dick, he was by now showing up in his Mellon Bank office at Smithfield Street for only a few hours in the middle of every day. Humiliated by the very public collapse of his marriage, discouraged by the anti-business ethos of progressivism, and with his spirits further weakened by a bad attack of pneumonia in March 1911, Mellon seriously considered quitting altogether the banking and business which had hitherto been the mainstay of his life.[79] He was also giving thought to selling off particular enterprises. Public utilities no longer seemed financially or politically attractive, and he parted with the Colorado Light and Power Company in the autumn of 1911.[80] "There seems," he observed, in explaining his unwillingness to invest in a similar enterprise in Nashville, Tennessee, "to have developed in legislative bodies and municipalities such an attitude unfavorable to individual ownership and property rights that such investments do not appeal to me."[81] And despite massive profits between 1912 and 1917, Andrew, Dick, and WL also made several serious attempts to sell Gulf Oil, via the investment banking house of Kuhn, Loeb & Co. in New York (perhaps an unexpected choice, given the bank's strong Jewish identity).[82]

These are not the actions of a man who necessarily saw his future in business—or even in Pittsburgh, despite his lifelong protestations of loyalty to the place. It was, after all, the done thing for many of the city's wealthiest and most famous to withdraw once their fortunes had been made, leaving the smoke and the smog for the less polluted and more sophisticated and cosmopolitan East Coast. Carnegie had long since left, building himself a sixty-four-room Manhattan palace in 1898. Soon after, Charles Schwab constructed a New York town house modeled on a Loire Valley château, and Frick moved to the city in 1902, initially living in a hotel, then renting a Vanderbilt residence, and finally putting up a grand mansion of his own on the corner of Fifth Avenue and Seventieth Street, where his best pictures still hang. Late in March 1914, Frick urged Mellon to follow him, and establish himself in a house nearby.[83] Yet apart from the sale of Colorado Light and Power, none of these exit strategies ever came to anything, which suggests that they may never have been wholly serious. For however he spent his time, business had always been the very essence of Andrew Mellon's life, existence, purpose, and identity, and what would he have done without accounts to pore over, or directors' meetings to attend, or old and new schemes to brood on even when he was not, ostensibly, at work?

Moreover, Mellon was also aware of new challenges and new opportunities now presenting themselves in the business world, and to varying degrees he was stimulated by and attracted to them. He may not have appreciated the censorious tone and lurid reporting of the social survey published between 1909 and 1914, but he was concerned by the problems of Pittsburgh's traditional industries, he recognized that the city's environment and infrastructure were not all they might be, and he understood the need to bring new businesses to the region. He also remained well aware that the "new" industries of the early twentieth century were beginning to depend on technology and applied science: Alcoa, Carborundum, and Gulf Oil were all becoming increasingly reliant on what in a later era would be called "research and development," and although American industry was thought to lag behind Germany in these matters, it was an aspect of business that fascinated Mellon.[84] He also knew that philanthropy was becoming a serious pursuit of the rich, in a way that the Judge would never have endorsed, as businessmen like Carnegie and Rockefeller, perhaps feeling guilty about their prodigious wealth, and certainly anxious to neutralize progressive hostility toward it, became ever more active in the financing and promotion of good causes.[85] Here were new problems, new prospects, and new possibilities, and during those very years when Mellon toyed with the notion of withdrawing from business, he also involved himself, to varying degrees, in three novel endeavors, emerging from, and as responses to, the change and challenge of unprecedented circumstances.

The first was his tacit support for the Pittsburgh Industrial Development Corporation (PIDC), established by the city's Chamber of Commerce in 1911. It was one of the many local initiatives launched following the publication of the controversial survey, with the aims of projecting a more positive image of the city across the nation and attracting new industries which might reinvigorate the flagging and overspecialized economy. It seems unlikely that Mellon looked with favor on most of the committees and commissions of this time, but he was certainly sympathetic to the objectives of the PIDC, and although not personally involved, he gave it an emphatic nod of approval. Its offices were located in the Farmer's Deposit National Bank, which the Mellons would absorb in 1913, and two of its initial twelve directors were Mellon men: William H. Donner, of Union Steel and Westinghouse, and John M. Schoonmaker, a director of both the Union Trust Company and the Mellon National Bank. It is inconceivable that they would have signed on without Mellon's knowledge and support.[86] During the next three years, the

PIDC helped bring thirty new businesses to Pittsburgh, creating eight thousand new jobs. There is no evidence of Mellon's direct involvement in any of them. But he was busy developing two new enterprises of his own which also addressed Pittsburgh's current problems.[87]

One of these ventures was Mellon's second new endeavor. Though research-oriented, it was as much a project of philanthropy as of business, and it developed into an essentially unpremeditated departure for Mellon. The Judge had famously given his fortune away, but to his own family; Andrew likewise had shown no interest in charity beyond home before he married. Only in the early 1900s had he begun to make some limited donations, but he gave less than he was then spending on paintings or on Nora. Most of his benefactions were local good causes: the Western Pennsylvania Hospital, the YMCA and YWCA, the Pittsburgh Association for the Improvement of the Poor, the Industrial Home for Crippled Children, the Pittsburgh Orchestra Association, the East Liberty Presbyterian Church, and so on.[88] But these were regular annual contributions rather than substantial one-time gifts, and they do not seem, all told, to have amounted to more than twenty-five thousand dollars a year. Indeed, it was a disappointment to Samuel B. McCormick, the new chancellor of the recently renamed University of Pittsburgh, that Andrew Mellon, by now a trustee for the better part of a decade, was not a conspicuous benefactor to his (and his father's) alma mater. He assiduously attended board meetings, and chaired the finance committee, but he was not prepared to give money to an institution he thought poorly run and lacking in business principles.[89]

But that mind-set was about to change, thanks to the energetic intervention of Professor Robert Kennedy Duncan, who visited Andrew Mellon in March 1911. Duncan was a Canadian, born in 1868, educated at the University of Toronto, who had been a professor of industrial chemistry at the University of Kansas since 1906. He had spent much of his earlier career traveling in Europe, where he had been greatly impressed at the sophistication of German science, at its close links with industry, and at the benefits that accrued to business as a result. He was himself no great researcher, but he was a passionate believer in and propagandist for the natural complementarity of science and industry. He was also concerned to describe and establish the sort of jobs and institutions that would be mutually beneficial to both domains of human endeavor. In particular, he advocated what he termed industrial fellowships, to be sponsored by business but conducted in universities, positions for promising scholars working in areas likely to yield findings of interest to both the funder and academia. His views and proposals appeared in a succession of articles, which were soon consolidated and expanded in his most important book, *The Chemistry of Commerce*, published in 1907.[90]

Three years later, when Mellon was trying to learn French (perhaps so he could follow Nora's misdeeds in Paris in greater detail), a teacher from the local Berlitz School arrived at Andrew's home bringing with him a letter from his father in France, in which the father claimed to have made a major scientific discovery. Mellon passed it on to George F. Taber, chief chemist at Gulf Oil, who concluded that the discovery was of no practical value, but along with his report he sent Mellon a copy of Duncan's book.[91] Although he had many other things on his mind at that time, Mellon was engrossed by Duncan's arguments and his recommendations. He already believed, as Duncan argued, that inventors and scientists of a practical bent were essential for continued wealth creation, and that the key to general human advance was not "governmental or political action," but the application of "new discoveries and inventions" which "increased production, lowered costs, raised wages, elevated the standard of living, and so brought about a greater participation of the human race in these benefits." Mellon immediately grasped that Duncan's fellowship scheme would enable industry "to utilize the services of qualified scientists to solve its problems," especially if they were brought together in a new institute with a university affiliation. Dick Mellon was equally enthusiastic, and so the brothers invited Duncan to Pittsburgh.[92]

It was a more timely invitation than they could ever have known, for Duncan's tenure as a professor at Kansas had not been wholly happy. To be sure, eight fellowships had been provided by business, which resulted in some interesting and commercially valuable work on subjects ranging from finding new uses for waste buttermilk to keeping fabric from wearing out during laundering.[93] But he had received very little support or encouragement, his laboratory quarters were cramped, the pure scientists at the university resented this "applied" interloper with his industrial connections, he was accused of being a propagandist rather than a scholar, and there was midwestern resentment that local taxes were being used to fund schemes designed to benefit eastern capitalists. So, by 1910, Duncan was eager to find another home, preferably nearer to a great industrial region. He first tried the Northeast, but Harvard turned him down, as did MIT and Clark University. Then came the summons to Pittsburgh. Duncan duly explained, with considerable eloquence and persuasiveness, the work he had been doing in Kansas, the benefits already reaped by industry, the limitations of working in a predominantly agricultural region, and the great possibilities presented by western Pennsylvania, with its coal, steel, gas, glass, electrical, and oil industries. Both Mellon brothers were so impressed that they were now willing to contribute to the University of Pittsburgh in support of a cause in which they believed.[94]

Duncan hoped the result would be an elaborate building, full of laboratories and workrooms, libraries and lecture halls, with fellows and funding to match. But Mellon would not commit himself to so grandiose a scheme while the basic idea was still germinating. He was willing to finance a small, inexpensive wooden building on the university grounds, and to pay for a two-year trial period. If this bore fruit, he would consider a more substantial contribution. This was hardly the answer to Duncan's dreams, but there was no alternative, and so over the period from 1911 to 1913, Andrew and Dick each contributed $52,000. Duncan moved from Kansas to become professor of industrial chemistry at the University of Pittsburgh, and a two-story structure was put up.[95] He brought several colleagues with him, and succeeded in persuading Pittsburgh companies (including Alcoa and Gulf Oil) to fund fellowships. The enterprise was a success from the outset. One problem that the institute addressed, at the behest of Gulf, was how to convert petroleum into gasoline. A second was smoke pollution—which suggests that Mellon or Duncan or McCormick, or perhaps a combination, was genuinely worried about Pittsburgh's undeniable environmental problems. Indeed, the institute concluded that the economic cost was ten million dollars a year in terms of wasted resources, and that the damage it did to individuals, their homes, and their businesses should "not be tolerated by the public."[96]

By 1913, with the enterprise a success, it was clear the initial accommodation, now overcrowded, was no longer adequate. Accordingly, Andrew and Dick funded a permanent structure, in brick and granite, which closely resembled the building Duncan had originally sketched out after his first interview at Smithfield Street. The Mellons together allotted $325,000 for this purpose, including the costs of equipment and a library, and also pledged $40,000 a year in maintenance. Here, in response to Duncan's urgings and examples and (more important) results, was Andrew Mellon's first large-scale philanthropic endeavor, and his diaries record many meetings on the subject during this time.[97] It would be named in memory of the Judge, a recognition of his lifelong interest in scientific philosophy. The full title was somewhat unwieldy: the Mellon Institute of Industrial Research and School of Specific Industries of the University of Pittsburgh.[98] Accommodation was provided for sixty industrial fellows, with the institute now set up to serve as a nucleus for the development of graduate study and research at the university. As such, "their" institute followed the model Andrew and Dick had perfected in starting and developing their many companies. With this, their first large-scale gift, Chancellor McCormick had finally extracted something substantial from hitherto reluctant benefactors.[99]

Apart from their shared interest in applied or useful science, Andrew Mellon and Robert Duncan had little in common. The former was shy, taciturn, aloof, retiring; the latter was enthusiastic, fluent, outgoing, charismatic, ingratiating, and a brilliant propagandist. Mellon hated the limelight, but Duncan was a supersalesman for his subject.[100] While Mellon's domestic life was in collapse, Duncan's marriage was almost famously close. Yet in the three years of their acquaintance, a warm friendship seems to have developed between them. "Duncan," Mellon once inquired of him, "are you happy at home?" "Yes, Mr. Mellon," he replied, "most happy." "Then you are a far richer man than I am," Andrew allegedly answered. In March 1911, Duncan sent the two brothers a letter of appreciation which vividly captures his eloquence and charm. "It is impossible to convey to you," he wrote,

> through written or spoken words my feelings of the treatment that you have accorded me during the two and a half years of our acquaintance. You have treated me invariably with utter kindness; have given me, I am embarrassed to think, of how much of your time in conference; have given me large sums for the support of any work and of me—and always cordially; have defended me against I know not what attacks; and have trusted my honor and my discretion.[101]

But Duncan was also nervous, high-strung, and a chain-smoker, and as the new institute building was taking shape, he was stricken with a mortal illness. He entered the hospital early in 1914, and Mellon's diaries record many visits to see him there until his death on February 18. In his last weeks, Duncan's chief anxiety had been for the future well-being of his wife and small daughter. Mellon reassured him, and a diary entry for April 3 shows that he honored his deathbed promise: "arranged trust for Mrs. Duncan and daughter."[102] Duncan was followed as director by Raymond F. Bacon, and the new Mellon Institute building was dedicated jointly, not only to the Judge but to Duncan as well. The inscription beneath a memorial plaque described him as an "interpreter of scientific knowledge" and "founder of the system of practical co-operation between science and industry" who "dedicated his life to the ideal that the laboratory shall be the servant of the nation for the material needs of men."[103] It was an expression both of Duncan's virtues and of Andrew Mellon's views. "I cannot think of anything," W. P. Potter, a justice of the Supreme Court of Pennsylvania, wrote soon after, in words that must have cheered the Mellons mightily, "which would be of more lasting value, and the research work which you make possible is of particular and especial worth to a community like Pittsburgh."[104]

As the Mellon Institute was being ushered into full being, Andrew had other reasons to think about applied science, and about Germany, then its mecca. For he was also being approached about another scheme, one likewise meant to address America's lag behind its prime European competitor in the harnessing of science for industrial production, and which would become the third of his new initiatives during these years. Once again, Mellon eventually decided to invest in response to a personal appeal, yet this time, the beneficiary was not an institute but an industry— and an industry which had begun from a familiar local endeavor, namely coking, but then headed off in an innovative new direction.[105] Most of the coke produced in western Pennsylvania that fed Pittsburgh's voracious blast furnaces and steel mills was made in dome-shaped beehive ovens by heating the region's rich bituminous coal to high temperature. The resulting coke was 85–90 percent carbon, and by the 1900s there were, largely thanks to Frick, more than fifty thousand such beehive ovens. This was a cheap and easy way of making coke, but it required coal of the highest quality, and it failed to utilize the volatile gases burned off, which were vented into the air through an aperture on top of the ovens, with devastating environmental impact, as the Pittsburgh survey (and the Mellon Institute) had recently recorded and lamented.[106]

But in Europe, high-grade coking coal was in much shorter supply, and from the mid–nineteenth century onwards, the by-product method was used. This new process involved the construction of much more complex coking ovens, which made possible the retention of the waste gases, from which were derived such by-products as tar, benzene, toluene, naphtha, and xylene. Rather than becoming ambient toxins, they could be used for such purposes as the paving of highways, the manufacture of insecticides— and the production of explosives. By the end of the nineteenth century, Europe, and especially Germany, had adopted the by-product method as both economically and environmentally superior. But as late as the 1900s, the beehive ovens remained overwhelmingly popular in western Pennsylvania (and across the United States), partly because of the extensive investment already undertaken, and out of deference to Henry Clay Frick; partly because the by-product ovens were more sophisticated and thus more expensive initially to finance and install; and partly because, in Pittsburgh as elsewhere in America, the local demand for the chemical by-products was largely met by Europe, notably Germany.[107] Indeed, in 1910, the United States scarcely possessed a recognizable chemical industry at all: here its lag behind Germany in bringing together science and industry was most manifest.

One of the foremost European exponents of the by-product method was Heinrich Koppers, a German. Born on the lower Rhine in 1872, and poorly educated, he soon became connected with his country's steel industry, building his first battery of ovens in 1889, and by the early twentieth century he had established himself in Essen. He earned an international reputation for his improvements and refinements to the by-product process, and in 1906, he was invited to construct what would eventually become nearly three hundred by-product ovens in Joliet, Illinois, for the United States Steel Corporation's new plant. This revolutionary undertaking was an immediate success. Thereafter Koppers would establish his own American company, bearing his name and based in Chicago, to manufacture his by-product ovens, demand for which soon exceeded all expectations.[108] But such expansion required a large capital outlay, not easy to secure in the United States for a technology so unconventional. Koppers rarely visited America, but sometime in 1913, he approached two Pittsburgh men, Harry W. Croft and Hamilton Stewart, executives at Harbison-Walker Refractories, a local company, offering to sell a substantial interest in his business in order to obtain much-needed capital.[109]

Koppers had close ties with both men because Harbison-Walker manufactured the refractory bricks he used in his by-product ovens. Croft and Stewart concluded that he would need roughly $1.5 million. They were willing to put up perhaps one-third, and for the rest they approached Henry B. Rust, a Virginian now living in Pittsburgh, who was renowned for his energy, drive, and resourcefulness and had extensive interests in the iron and steel business. He was also known to be sympathetic to this new mode of production, and it was thought he would find like-minded men to join him.[110] There was an obvious potential synergy between Koppers and Pittsburgh, with its high output of coking coal and steel products. But even more obvious was the potential fit between Koppers and Andrew Mellon, with his matchless resources, massive investments in coal and steel, and avowed interest in industrial research and development. Approached early in 1914 by Rust, who said that one million dollars was needed, Mellon promptly discussed the matter with Thomas Lynch of the Frick Coke Company, and during the summer, while vacationing in Massachusetts, he was often in conversation with Frick, whose holiday home at Prides Crossing was nearby. Although the new process rendered obsolete the ovens with which Frick was so closely identified, both men recognized where coke's future lay.[111]

Meanwhile, Koppers himself departed for Europe, and after war broke out, he remained there, not to return to America for eight years. Mellon got back to Pittsburgh in October 1914, and the negotiations were resumed with Koppers, now in absentia, via Sweden.[112] It was eventually agreed that Mellon would put in one million dollars, and he and his brother took a 37.5 percent equity interest in the firm. In addition to Andrew and Dick Mellon, the other stockholders were Harry Croft and Hamilton Stewart, as well as Koppers himself, who kept a 20 percent investment. As had been agreed, Henry Rust was put in charge, and his expertise, ambition, and connections, combined with Mellon funding, enabled the company to expand its production, not least because it immediately benefited from extensive interlocks with other giant Mellon enterprises such as McClintic-Marshall and Crucible Steel. With so much Pittsburgh money and management, it was scarcely surprising that the decision was soon made to relocate H. Koppers Company to the city. The first employees, numbering no more than eighty-five, moved from Chicago to Pittsburgh in May 1915, where a few rooms in the First National Bank Building were immediately set aside. Following the lead of Alcoa, Carborundum, and Gulf Oil, the company immediately set up a fellowship at the Mellon Institute.[113]

The timing could not have been better, for the battle by then raging between Britain, Russia, and France on one side and Germany and Austria-Hungary on the other was already turning out to be as much a clash of chemicals as it was of coal and steel. Andrew Mellon might have had a bad marriage, but there was every prospect that he and Pittsburgh would have a good and profitable war. Although the summer of 1914 witnessed renewed financial jitters, and the New York Stock Exchange was closed from August to November, wartime demand was soon manifest in 1915, bringing to an end the years of recession and sluggish recovery that had dogged much of western Pennsylvania since the 1907 panic.[114] Because of the nature of many of its products, war had always been good for Pittsburgh, and the First World War resulted in unprecedented demand and unprecedented local prosperity. Under these flush circumstances, the anxieties of the preceding years abated; attempts to pursue diversification, economic restructuring, and civic reform were abandoned; and the Pittsburgh Industrial Development Commission disintegrated.[115] For this was not business as usual, it was business better than ever, and what was good for Pittsburgh business was invariably good for Andrew Mellon. Despite his marital misfortunes, his advancing years, and his occasional hesitations, he was still creatively enthralled by acquisition and accumulation.

NEW CAREERS FOR OLD

Single Parent, Aging Plutocrat, Emerging Politician,
1914–21

The advance of our nation in power and material prosperity in
the last half century has been unprecedented.

Thomas Mellon and His Times, p. 368

I. FATHER AND CHILDREN—AND NORA

In divorcing Nora, Andrew Mellon had been legally vindicated as
the responsible and wronged husband, while branding her as the
disloyal and irresponsible wife. He had finally got his way. But it left him
with an abiding sense of personal failure and public humiliation, and it
was in this depressed and dispirited state that he was obliged to start over.
He continued to reside at 5052 Forbes Street, always a drab and unwelcoming house, now further darkened by painful memories and associations. He was often home from work soon after lunch, usually spending
the rest of the day alone in his den, before going out for the evening,
"RBM's for dinner" being his most frequent destination. He rarely read
books; his only recreation—a characteristically solitary and uncommunicative activity—was lengthy walks in the city, and like his parents, he did
not seek out Pittsburgh society. "Home 4 pm. Got mush and milk for dinner. Out to walk and then to bed" is a typically dismal diary entry from
this time. Mellon may have been a rich man, but this was a deprived mode
of existence; according to Burton Hendrick, "probably the loneliest part
of his life were the five years from 1912 to 1917."[1]

Or were they? Paul Mellon believed that—apart from those in the portraits on his walls, who could neither touch nor hurt him—there were no

other women in his father's life after the trauma of divorcing Nora. But a regular entry in his diaries of these years suggests there may have been another liaison at a time when Paul was too young to have been aware. On August 20, 1912, scarcely one month after the final divorce decree, the entry "M——" is recorded for the first time, and it reappears on sixty-two occasions until the last on October 22, 1917.[2] Apart from the summer months when Mellon was away with the children, the entries, which are at the beginning or the end of the day, appear about once every two weeks. This could indicate a regular activity or a professional meeting rather than a personal encounter: medicine? mesmerist? something to do with the children? Or was he perhaps seeing another woman? In April 1910, he had met his old flame Minnie Caldwell, along with her parents, at dinner with his nephew Thomas A. Mellon, Jr.[3] But although she had just been widowed for the second time, Minnie Robertson (as she now was) remained resident in Kansas.

One other possibility is that Mellon was regularly visiting a whore. Prostitution and corrupt city politics went together in early-twentieth-century America, Pittsburgh was amply supplied with brothels in its tenderloin districts, and some of them catered to men from the higher echelons of local society.[4] And for Mellon, an amalgam of riches and repression, a commercial arrangement for sexual favors may have seemed more appealing and secure than returning to the treacherous reefs of emotional entanglements. Yet it is impossible to imagine him as an habitué of any Pittsburgh brothel, however exclusive and discreet. There is no evidence, either before or during his marriage, that his sexual needs were great. There would be terrible risks—of venereal disease, of blackmail, of exposure—and it is hard to imagine him running them after the public drubbing of his divorce. And it was in these very years, too, that prostitution and "white slavery" were widely cited as the leading "social evil" of Progressive America, and prim Pittsburgh was, in 1913, the first American city to establish a Public Bureau of Morals—first in this reform, if no other.[5]

It seems highly unlikely that Mellon would have ventured into the demimonde, when prostitution, like divorce, was being discussed as one of the great evils of contemporary American society. Perhaps he was visiting a courtesan (or mistress) in her own home.[6] She might have offered him not only comfort and companionship but loyalty and discretion. Mellon's long, solitary walks in the city (a comparison with the British prime minister William Gladstone springs immediately to mind, although he had rescued prostitutes rather than availed himself of them) would have provided the perfect cover for such visitations. Coincidentally, one of the few books that Mellon makes note of reading is *David Copperfield*, which is partly concerned with the redemption of Martha, a prostitute.[7] The average career of such women was about five years, just the length of time during which "M——" entries appear in Mellon's diary. And the only occasion when postdivorce melancholy moved him to acknowledge feeling "lonesome" was in April 1919, almost a year and a half after that last entry.[8] The evidence, of course, is no more than circumstantial, yet something regular, personal, and important was happening at this time in Mellon's life in Pittsburgh, which he wanted to record, and in a way others would not readily decipher.

In any event, with custody of his children for two-thirds of each year, and responsibility for all the major decisions concerning their welfare, Andrew had his hands full—lady friend or no. In the early twentieth century, male millionaires (indeed, males in general) were not closely involved with child rearing, but Mellon's diary from 1912 to 1915 shows that he devoted much effort and thought to the task, spending a great deal of time with Ailsa and Paul and genuinely delighting in their company. "Glorious day with children" is one typical entry.[9] He rode and drove with them in the summer, he went sledding with them in the winter, he bought them dogs and ponies and birds, and he played hide-and-seek in the evenings. On Sundays, he took them to East Liberty Presbyterian Church, on other days to the zoo and the circus, and there were trips to New York and to Atlantic City, which was a rather more wholesome and exclusive seaside resort then than it is now. On birthdays and at Christmas, he lavished them with presents—a ring, a watch, a camera, and perfume for Ailsa; a train set, a bicycle, a toy gun, and a typewriter for Paul—and he was unfailingly attentive to such Yuletide rituals as trimming the tree and filling their stockings. As W. L. Mellon recalled, Andrew "entered wholeheartedly and with touching delight into every compartment of their lives." They were, at this time, the "bedrock" of his existence.[10]

Mellon also went to considerable trouble arranging their long summer holidays, taking several months off from the bank (and also forgoing M——) though still keeping in touch with business in Pittsburgh. In the summer of 1913, he journeyed with Ailsa and Paul back to England, where they stayed at Down Place, an eighteenth-century country house on the Thames near Windsor. It was a vacation very much like those Andrew and Nora had taken together during their marriage ("ride in morning, find Vale Farm" is one laconic diary entry recalling that unhappy past), with boating trips on the Thames, visits to Windsor, London, Bath, and Salisbury, and a trip over to Paris. He took the children to Hertford, to see the castle, and to Wimbledon to see their widowed McMullen grandmother, when she was also receiving Nora and several of her brothers.[11] But this was the last such transatlantic vacation for some years, and in 1914, Mellon took the children to Sewickley, the country area west of Pittsburgh where they had spent the summers in 1911 and 1912, and then on to the North Shore, outside Boston, where the family stayed near Frick, and Andrew talked to him about Koppers. Despite the outbreak of war in Europe, Paul Mellon recalled this as a particularly happy summer, when he felt closer to his father than at any other time.[12]

Both in Pittsburgh and on vacation, this comfortable existence was made possible by gardeners and servants, a chauffeur and groomsman, all presided over by the housekeeper, Mrs. Richards. The day-to-day work of bringing up the Mellon children was undertaken by governesses and nurses, who attended to their early education, got up for them at night, and taught them their manners. Fräulein Meyer departed soon after the divorce, and was followed by Miss Askey, who was succeeded by Miss Sylvester, in whom Andrew confided his doubts about the influence of Nora on the children. With his strong support for her efforts to bring them up correctly, she remained with the family until Ailsa married in 1926.[13] Realizing that these women were essentially surrogate mothers, and no doubt remembering the earlier trouble with Miss Abernethy, Mellon took pains with their appointments, going "into the matter even more searchingly than when he was selecting a McEldowney for Union Trust or a Haskell for Carborundum." Ailsa had also been settled at the Winchester School, which she had been attending since 1906, and Paul joined her there briefly in the autumn of 1912. Three years later, he was moved to Shady Side Academy, the school of choice for the sons of the Pittsburgh plutocracy. There he was bullied but also befriended, and began to acquire a taste for poetry and literature. Andrew recorded evidence of his children's progress with interest, and its lack with concern, and he doggedly attended school events.[14]

Yet the doting and dutiful parent who emerges from the pages of his own diary, and whose devotion would be noted by W. L. Mellon, was not as he appeared to Ailsa and to Paul during these years. In part this was a matter of age: in 1915, Ailsa was fourteen, Paul was eight, and Andrew was sixty, which meant he was old enough to be their grandfather. This was a big gap, but as with Nora, bridging distances in emotional terms was for him even more mystifying a problem than the chronological divide. His long, cold silences do not seem to have melted before the children's laughter and high spirits, and like the Judge before him, Andrew appeared a stern and stiff and distancing father. He may have adored Ailsa and Paul, but only in a characteristically "shrinking and embarrassed way," and as he could not express the love he felt for them, it was difficult for them to return it.[15] Ailsa had been at a particularly vulnerable age when the marriage exploded, and being closer to her mother, whose version of events she was inclined to believe, she wept regularly and fruitlessly for her, and begged her father to take Nora back. And she naturally resented the governesses for usurping her mother's place in the household. Paul was too young to have been so traumatized, but he was always intimidated and overawed by his father, whom he found "dry and censorious and negative," and he got on much better with the servants, the chauffeur, and the groom.[16]

There was also the continuing presence—and for Andrew the continuing problem—of Nora, of whom he was now rid, but not fully free: she remained in the Pittsburgh she despised, setting herself up in a place on Howe Street. There were constant phone calls and disagreements over the rights and wrongs and logistics of ferrying the children back and forth between the two houses, not only respecting changes in custody, but also shorter visits. For a time, Nora telephoned Ailsa every day, and never missed an opportunity to disparage Andrew in front of her. He responded to this calumny with threats to "cut off communication entirely unless she desists."[17] Much to Andrew's dismay, Nora also introduced both Ailsa and Paul to Charles Mustin, to whom she had turned after Curphey deserted her, and dropped hints that she was thinking of marrying him (which she may have hoped would get back to their father). But Nora also hankered for England, where she vacationed in the summers of 1913 and 1914, and in January 1916 she considered moving there permanently, ceding complete custody of the children to Andrew, provided he pay off her debt of $45,000 and buy her a house.[18]

Believing that he had made more than adequate provision for Nora, and failing to understand how she needed more than $30,000 a year—he was on principle unwilling to "pay her money she had wasted on Curphey"—Andrew was not inclined to enter into an arrangement which might be publicized as a cynical scheme to pay for her banishment and obtain full-time custody of the children.[19] In any case, Nora changed her mind again, and decided to stay in Pittsburgh. Despite her new liaison with Mustin, she still longed for Andrew to accept her offer to reconcile, which he had roundly rebuffed (and she may in part have taken up with

Mustin in the hope of making him jealous). She regularly put this proposition to Ailsa, who tearfully begged her father to accept. Preying on his
dread of gossip, Nora planted stories in the local press that a reconciliation was pending, and at one emotional meeting with Andrew, she wept
bitterly, telling him "how sorry she was that she had wronged me and
given me so much trouble." But her ex-husband was unyielding: he did
not trust her, he resented her manipulation of their daughter, and
he still entertained fears that she might spirit the children off to England.
There would be no deal.[20]

Nora also attributed her need for more money to her claim that she
was supporting her brothers in England, but Andrew thought it false
considering the bad blood that had come between them. He himself
remained friendly toward the McMullens, every year sending Christmas
letters and cards. He felt especially close to the widow McMullen, with
whom he regularly corresponded, and after her death in September 1914,
Nora gave Andrew her mother's gold pen and holder.[21] By then, the
McMullen brothers had been drawn into the Great War: Norman served
in the Royal Navy, hunting submarines in a motorboat for which Andrew
provided the purchase price of £3,000; Percy was also at sea on HMS
Agincourt, and received cigarettes and tobacco from Andrew (as did Norman); Kenrick and Murray worked at the War Office, forwarding engineering matériel to various fronts; Leonard (still a debtor) enlisted in the
Hertfordshire Regiment, later becoming a musketry instructor; John
eventually became a second lieutenant, looking after the electrical appara-
tus of a flying squadron and lecturing the young pilots in navigation;
John's son Don was at Gallipoli, and earned the Distinguished Service
Order for his work in the advance on Palestine. Remarkably, all of the
brothers survived—along with their debts, which Andrew once again
began to make good.[22]

In a personal way, the war impinged much less on the Mellons than on
the McMullens. There was a brief scare at the outset of hostilities when it
seemed that W. L. Mellon, on vacation in Italy with his family, might be
stranded. But for Andrew, the most significant engagement during the
war years was with his daughter's adolescence. "Is Ailsa too much pam-
pered?" he wondered in February 1914. Taking her to see *Poor Little Rich
Girl* soon after may have provided a sort of answer. "Ailsa looks very
pretty in party dress," he proudly recorded in the summer, one of many
appreciative and admiring entries, but soon he was rebuking her for visiting friends "in my absence and without permission."[23] Yet he willed himself to be sociable for her benefit: "Ailsa's first real party," he recorded

with genuine satisfaction, early in 1916, "about sixteen couples at Forbes Street. Everything fine. Ailsa looking very pretty." But there were anxieties, too. "I realize Ailsa has developed," her father noted after she had clashed with Mrs. Richards and expressed her wish to live in New York, "and is not a little girl." So, indeed, she had: "Mrs. Richards consulted me about Ailsa's period sickness," he recorded in August 1916, to which he responded by urging his housekeeper to consult the family doctor. But he did offer his daughter advice on less intimate matters, urging her to be truthful and to improve her manners.[24]

This final homily was occasioned by Ailsa's departure to the Low and Heywood School, in Stamford, Connecticut, in the autumn of 1916— a harbinger of the shift in family orientation from western Pennsylvania to the East Coast.[25] Twelve months later, she moved on to Miss Porter's School in Farmington, Connecticut—the famous finishing academy for daughters of money old and new—and there she stayed until the summer of 1919. Andrew wrote her regularly, bought her expensive clothes, jewelry, and, eventually, a car, and arranged through Knoedler for Alphonse Jongers to paint her portrait at a cost of $3,000.[26] She went to proms at Yale and at Princeton, and increasingly gravitated toward social life in New York. Try as Andrew might to please her, Ailsa still inclined to her "darling" mother's side, rather than that of her father, who seemed a perpetual scold: finding fault with her care of her clothes, her casual attitude toward money, seeing too much of one boy, and for deceiving him about her rooming arrangements at Miss Porter's. There were arguments concerning where she should go and how long she should stay out: "I object and then give in" is a frequent paternal refrain during these years.[27] Above all, Ailsa disliked Miss Porter's, where she was prostrated by a succession of mostly vague ailments, to do with her "nerves," her "glands," and her eyes. By March 1919 she determined to leave school and to "come out," as "all her friends" were planning to do.[28]

By now, Paul, too, was growing up, though he made significantly fewer appearances than Ailsa in his father's diary. Although less nervous and high-strung, Paul had grown up shy and diffident, not unlike his father, and he was sent away to summer camp in New Hampshire in 1915, 1916, and 1917 for "toughening up." It seems to have worked, for when not at Shady Side Academy, he spent time on horseback at Rolling Rock, the three-hundred-acre estate to the west of the city which Dick Mellon was now developing in earnest as an exclusive club for the family and their close friends and business associates.[29] It was at Rolling Rock that Paul initiated himself into business, purchasing large supplies of soft drinks and selling them at a profit to the workmen building the clubhouse. One is reminded of his father's sale of cut grass from 401 Negley, but whereas in Andrew's case, early entrepreneurship was a portent, in Paul's it would be an aberration. Soon after, in July 1918, Andrew had a talk with him concerning "what a boy should know. Warn him against sexual bad practices and about bad boys' influences."[30] It seems unlikely it was an easy conversation.

II. TRIUMPHANT CAPITALIST

"War," Harvey O'Connor would later opine in *Mellon's Millions*, "is Pittsburgh's fairy godmother. The darker the pall that shrouds the battlefield, the blacker the cloud over the City of Iron and Steel."[31] He was right. To be sure, the stock markets were unsettled during the summer of 1914, and Andrew Mellon was much concerned at the guns of August and September, when money was tight and bank reserves low.[32] To the dismay of many Republicans, Mellon included, Woodrow Wilson did everything he could to keep the United States out of the war: despite the sinking of the *Lusitania* in April 1915, America did not officially join the fray for two more years. But long before then, Pittsburgh's furnaces and steel mills were busier than ever, with munitions orders from overseas, which would in time be augmented by those from Washington. Demand pulled the city out of the prolonged post-1907 slump, for a time dispelling the doubts and anxieties that had beset Pittsburgh and its economy. As early as February 1915, the United States Steel Corporation took on an extra eight thousand workers to meet the increased demand for its products, and by November 1918, government war contracts executed in the city totaled more than $200 million.[33]

As in all conflicts, finance was a crucial element in the First World War, and the Mellon banks were heavily involved in the transatlantic lending to the Allies before the United States became a belligerent. These loans were famously orchestrated by J. P. Morgan and Company, which mounted an intense effort to involve as many American banks and finance houses as possible, and Andrew Mellon was willing and able to join in. Of the $500 million Anglo-French loan that was raised in 1915, the Union Trust Company contributed $15 million: it held $10.8 million for its own account and sold $4.2 million to its customers. This was a substantial sum, and few East Coast institutions took bigger shares. The Mellon banks also subscribed $2.5 million to the $100 million lent to France in April 1917, and $9.5 million to three large loans made to the United Kingdom between August 1916 and January 1917.[34] As soon as the United States entered the conflict, in the spring of 1917, Mellon personally subscribed to $1 million worth of Liberty War Bonds in May 1917, and in October both Union Trust and the Mellon Bank upped their subscriptions to the bonds from $5 million to $25 million.[35] By this time, Mellon was also chairing the Red Cross War Council appeal in western Pennsylvania, launched with a dinner at which former president Taft spoke. A million dollars was immediately raised, including $50,000 from Andrew himself, as much again from Dick, and the same from Alcoa, Gulf, and Carborundum, and within a month, nearly $4 million had been subscribed.[36]

Even before the United States joined them, Mellon very much wanted the Allies to win, and his businesses helped them to do so—especially (and ironically) Koppers, the fledgling company created by a German in which Mellon had become a major investor just before European hostilities broke out in 1914.[37] From Mellon's standpoint, the timing was extraordinarily lucky, for among the substances which the by-product method yielded were benzene and toluene, two of the essential ingredients for making the high explosive TNT. At the outbreak of the war, Germany manufactured twenty-three million gallons of benzene and four million gallons of toluene annually, whereas the figures for the United States were three million and less than one million respectively; Britain and France scarcely produced either substance. This gave Germany an immense initial advantage, but thanks to Koppers, by-product ovens were soon being produced in massive numbers in the United States (including a $7 million contract from United States Steel). Even before it joined the war, America became the major supplier of benzene and toluene to the Allies, significantly surpassing Germany's output by war's end.[38] To the extent that the First World War was a war of chemicals and especially of explosives, Koppers made a major contribution to the Allied victory.

Its eponymous founder was not so fortunate. As organized in November 1915, Koppers was held by five stockholders: Andrew and Dick (37.5 percent); Heinrich Koppers himself, with much diminished holdings (20 percent); and Hamilton Stewart and H. W. Croft (who owned the rest, 42.5 percent). Having left for Europe in the summer of 1915, Koppers was unable to return to America, and in April 1917, his shares in the company became subject to recent federal legislation authorizing the confiscation of all property held in the United States by enemy aliens. "Meeting Koppers Company," Mellon noted in his diary for October 15, 1917. "Voting out Koppers as Alien Enemy."[39] A year later, Koppers's stock was auctioned off in Washington in accordance with the rules laid down by the Federal Bureau of Sales, which, as it happened, was run by Joseph F. Guffey, the nephew of James M. Guffey, Mellon's former colleague in the oil business. The shares were appraised at their 1914 value of $100 each plus interest, and although the auction was publicly advertised, there was only one bidder: a syndicate consisting of the Mellons, Stewart, and Croft. They acquired the shares for $302,250, and this sum was eventually transmitted to Koppers after the war ended. The business was now entirely American-owned, and in recognition of this, its name was changed slightly from H. Koppers Company to the Koppers Company.[40]

Thus did Mellon win control of the business, and his fortune was further and substantially enriched as a result. With wartime success, Koppers had greatly increased in size and value, and so the market worth of the additional shares he had just acquired was probably ten times what he had paid for them.[41] In the following year, Croft and Stewart pulled out and sold their shares, and the Mellon brothers brought in their colleagues McClintic and Marshall to be the co-owners. After the war, orders dwindled, and Henry Rust later led the company in different (and not always successful) directions, as it morphed into a mining and utilities conglomerate. But Mellon was determined that the enterprise should remain "closely held," even to the extent of keeping out its founder. After the armistice, Heinrich Koppers sought to re-enter the company he had created, and in 1921 he visited Pittsburgh for that purpose. But Mellon refused, believing he had treated his former associate fairly: "I could see no reason," he wrote at the time, "for giving the proposition favorable consideration." Like his father, he believed unsentimentally in "acquisition and accumulation," and having acquired and accumulated Koppers, he was not of a mind to part with any of it.[42]

Koppers was not the only Mellon company to thrive, as wartime demand soared for coal, steel, aluminum, and oil, among other things. Alcoa's pretax earnings jumped from $8.9 million in 1915 to $25 million the following year, and by 1919 the company ranked as forty-third largest in the United States. Gulf Oil's assets grew from $142 million in 1917 to $254 million by 1920, making it thirty-first among the nation's biggest corporations. Even the now fully merged Pittsburgh Coal Company showed a respectable improvement, with profits increasing from $104 million in 1914 to $160 million in 1919.[43] And what was good for Mellon's businesses was also good for his banks. In July 1916, Union Trust increased its dividend from 25 percent quarterly (excluding a 6 percent Christmas bonus) to 35 percent quarterly (though the bonus remained the same). In that year its assets equaled those of all the other trusts in Pittsburgh combined, and in 1918 it acquired the City Deposit Bank and Trust Company. As business continued to expand, Andrew, urged on even more enthusiastically by Dick, recognized that both Union Trust and Mellon National Bank needed bigger and modernized headquarters, and he turned to his architect nephew, E. P. Mellon, for ideas and advice.[44]

As his companies prospered, Mellon's personal fortune continued to grow, and from 1916 onward, there is systematic, annual data about its extent. In that year, his capital account showed him worth $72.5 million, and by 1921 that figure had grown to $80 million.[45] Considering that he had been worth "only" $55 million in 1913, this was a very significant surge. Once again, these were book values, not market values. For example, Mellon's 252,185 shares in Gulf Oil were valued at $17.4 million, but on the basis of the few shares actually traded at that date, a more realistic figure might have been in excess of $100 million. The same was true of his 26,555 shares in Standard Steel Car: They were deemed to be worth $3.5 million, but quoted prices would have raised their market value to nearly $14 million. However, these calculations can themselves mislead, for in the unlikely event that Mellon had sold all of his Gulf or Standard Steel Car stock at one go, the effect on the market worth would have been problematic, and more than likely a downward one. The true extent of his fortune was then, and is now, a matter of guesswork, but Burton Hendrick's 1921 estimate of $135 million may not have been far wide of the mark. Even allowing for wartime inflation, Andrew Mellon was, in our currency, a substantial billionaire.[46]

Yet the Great War also brought him his share of concerns and anxieties. The belligerent European powers went off the gold standard, which effectively brought to an end the relatively stable world of early-twentieth-century international finance. The Bolsheviks seized power in Russia, pledging to overturn capitalism and to confiscate all private property. In Washington, the federal government expanded, as new departments were established to superintend the war effort, and on the very eve of hostilities, it commandeered all the Gulf Oil tankers "for supplying the war fleet." The national debt increased ninefold, and federal spending by twice that amount. Mellon's companies were hit by the new excess profits tax, but even so, and on into the early 1930s, he would be criticized for having been a wartime profiteer. There were also drastic increases in income tax (and inheritance tax) and a new surtax of 40 percent was imposed on incomes of over $1 million. The result was that Mellon's federal taxes went up more than tenfold, from $168,000 in 1916, to $305,000 in 1917, to $1.2 million in 1918, and to $1.9 million in 1919, which helps explain why his net income fell from more than $4 million to $1.3 million during the same period.[47] And in July 1917, Mellon noted that there was a "whisky in Senate bill," portending Prohibition, and leading him to wonder what the future of his Overholt Distillery might be.[48]

Mellon viewed these wartime developments with dismay, and once the fighting was over, the abrupt collapse of demand for matériel led to a global recession, intensified in the United States when the Federal Reserve raised interest rates to 7 percent in June 1920.[49] Pittsburgh was especially hard hit: thousands were laid off, and relations between capital and those who were still employed deteriorated. Fearful for their jobs, and believing themselves protected by the Clayton Act, workers organized into trade unions. The result was an unprecedented outbreak of strikes. During the summer of 1919, the streetcar system was in disarray as motormen and conductors walked off the job, and there were riots across the city when the Philadelphia Company tried to break the strike, which in the end it did manage to do. In September, Pittsburgh steelworkers were in the vanguard of a national strike seeking to secure recognition for a trade union, a reduction of the twelve-hour day, and to avenge labor's defeat at Homestead in 1892. This action, too, was brutally suppressed after four months. And in November 1919, forty-two thousand coal miners in the Pittsburgh district walked out, as part of a nationwide strike which lasted more than a month.[50] Mellon was especially concerned about the labor troubles on the trolley lines in which he still had an interest; urging the management "not to be afraid of strikes," he joined a local political committee "to organize safety."[51]

In Pittsburgh, both rich and poor alike had much to be concerned about as the Great War ended, but as usual, their anxieties were different. For those suddenly thrown out of work, or returning from military service, or afflicted by the influenza epidemic that would carry off more lives in the city than had been lost during the war, the anxieties were about keeping body and soul together. But for those with money, property, stocks, and works of art, the scale and intensity of the unrest seemed to portend socialism, bolshevism, or even anarchy: "Fifth Avenue swept by machine gun fire . . . Pittsburgh, Detroit, and Cleveland in the hands of revolutionary committees of workmen after wild scenes of pillage and mob passion . . . The rich daughters of millionaires stripped of their pearls and of their furs," according to one fanciful English observer.[52] To be sure, Pittsburgh avoided revolution, and Ailsa's by now substantial accumulation of pearls and furs remained intact, but times were bad for many people, and Mellon's own companies shared in the general down-turn. After the annus mirabilis of 1915, Alcoa's profits had declined to $15.4 million by 1918 and to $6.6 million in 1920, and it reported losses in 1921 and again in 1922. With his taxes higher than ever, Mellon began "selling securities to establish losses" for tax purposes, and by January 1921, despite being richer than he had ever been, he was complaining of a "scarcity of funds."[53]

Mellon had now turned sixty-five, and his business priorities were beginning to change. He sold the New York Shipbuilding Company for $13 million in 1916, he declined William H. Donner's invitation to take a one-third interest in the Pennsylvania Steel Company, and after bringing in McClintic and Marshall, he rather lost interest in Koppers, whose organization he found increasingly "unsatisfactory."[54] The family trust which had been set up in 1905 to hold the Judge's estate for the benefit of his descendants was also dissolved in 1919, and the assets distributed among the beneficiaries. And he was increasingly drawn away from Pitts-burgh toward the East Coast, where he now attended meetings as a director of the American Locomotive Company, the National Bank of Commerce, and the Pennsylvania Railroad.[55] Not even counting holidays, he was absent from western Pennsylvania more than he had ever been, regularly taking the night trains to and from New York, Philadelphia, and Washington. Perhaps, too, he had come to realize that while his own for-tune seemed set on a course of inexorable expansion, Pittsburgh's greatest days were past: the postwar slump merely intensified the problems of eco-nomic stagnation, environmental degradation, and civic disarray which had been diagnosed before 1914, but which had been temporarily masked while the Great War raged and the steel mills hummed.[56]

By 1919, Andrew Mellon was the last survivor of the great innovators and entrepreneurs of Pittsburgh's heroic age. Westinghouse had died in 1913, and Heinz and Carnegie both passed on in 1919, as did Haskell of Carborundum. But for Mellon, the greatest loss would be the death of Henry Clay Frick at the end of the same year. Like Carnegie, Frick had long ceased to be a Pittsburgh resident, but he and Mellon had remained in close touch about matters of business and, increasingly, art, and Mellon had become a regular visitor to Frick's New York palace. At the funeral in Pittsburgh, he was one of the honorary pallbearers, along with Dick Mel-lon, Philander Knox, and Henry McEldowney.[57] Eight years later, Mellon recalled the occasion in a letter to George Harvey, Frick's authorized biographer. It was "with a strange feeling," he wrote, after his friend's "sudden death," that he attended the funeral on that "wintry day" and "witnessed the performance of the last rites over his body." "Was this," Mellon had wondered, "the end of that eager, masterful character? It was hard to realize that he could even then be confined within those narrow bounds." It was certainly not the end for Andrew: he was the executor of Frick's will, and he would later help oversee the transformation of Frick's Manhattan mansion into a collection open to the public.[58]

Lifelong friends, close business associates, and (at least recently) united in their love of pictures, Frick and Mellon were nonetheless in many ways very different sorts of entrepreneur. Like Astor in real estate, Vanderbilt in railroads, Rockefeller in oil, Carnegie in steel, and Morgan in finance, Frick was associated in the popular mind with one particular business endeavour—in his case, coke making—and his very public stance as champion of capital and enemy of labor brought him both admiration and opprobrium. By contrast, Mellon was not associated with any single industry, and apart from the years of the divorce scandal, his name scarcely registered in the public mind at all. His fortune had been made in an astonishing range of activities, from the old industries of coal and steel to the newer ones of oil and chemicals. None of the great undertakings he had nurtured and supported bore his name, and few were quoted on the stock exchange. Only the Mellon Bank and the Mellon Institute drew attention to the family; the former, now owned by Union Trust, had been founded by his father, and the latter, a memorial to the Judge, was part of the University of Pittsburgh. Compared to most of the great contemporary fortunes, Mellon's was most remarkable for being mostly invisible. That was no accident.

How would Andrew Mellon have been remembered had he died in the same year as his two great Pittsburgh peers, Carnegie and Frick, when halfway through his seventh decade? As a man who had been briefly and unhappily married, but who had fathered two children who were destined to be among the richest Americans of their generation. As a highly successful banker and industrialist, who had helped transform western Pennsylvania and thus the late-nineteenth- and early-twentieth-century American economy. As the bearer of a name well-known in Pittsburgh, though scarcely mentioned in the *New York Times* since the divorce scandal had died down, and who had only recently been admitted to *Who's Who in America*.[59] As a relatively minor art collector and philanthropist, whose benefactions were wholly confined to his native city. He would, in short, have been remembered, in select circles, as someone who had lived an important and influential local life, but not (with the exception of a shameful mistake) a public or a national life.

III. HOUSES, PICTURES, AND PARTIES

As Ailsa grew up, her father's desire to create the appropriate life and setting for her obliged him to expand the narrow confines of his own existence. Suddenly and (to others) unexpectedly, Andrew Mellon started
going out in local society, attending dinners and dances (he was a very
bad dancer), and he recorded in his diary events heretofore inconceivable: "Go in Pierott costume 9 pm to masked ball. Home 3:30 am." He
took an interest in Rolling Rock, where he (rather inexpertly) rode and
played golf, but drew the line at fox-hunting, which Dick (and later Paul)
adored.[60] Here, too, Mellon was now looking beyond Pittsburgh. After
1915, he stopped vacationing at Sewickley and instead rented a house
every summer on Long Island, initially in Easthampton, subsequently in
Southampton, where Ailsa and Paul could ride and swim and play tennis
with other children of the rich, and bring their school friends for extended
stays. He began visiting the theater in New York when on business trips,
often taking Ailsa with him to see popular dramas and light musicals, and
he even purchased a Rolls-Royce—already the ultimate symbol of riches
and status, and the very sort of "artificial want" the Judge abominated.[61]

   Such doings would not bear comparison with Mellon's extravagant plutocratic contemporaries, but they did signal a major shift in the style,
scale, and tempo of his life. One sign of this was his decision to part with
the "house of sad memories" at 5052 Forbes Street and buy a home more
befitting Pittsburgh's richest resident.[62] It was on Woodland Road, and it
had belonged to Alexander Laughlin, a partner in Jones and Laughlin's
American Steel Works, who had built it in 1897. A forty-room mansion in
the Tudor revival style, with gables, chimneys, half-timbering, stained-
glass windows, wood paneling, and carved fireplaces, it was hidden a long
way from the road, on twenty-seven acres landscaped with trees, lakes,
and formal gardens.[63] In March 1916, Mellon's bid was accepted, and on
December 23, 1917, exactly two months after the last mention of M——
in his diary, the family moved in. "We go to the new place," Mellon
recorded. "Everything pleasing. Ailsa seems much pleased. Send for
Paul." Here was a new beginning in a new home. But the past was not to
be effaced that easily. On Christmas Day, Dick and Jennie Mellon came to
visit with their two children, and while Andrew was taking them on a tour,
"Mrs. M. comes. I show Mrs. M. through the house." He then added one
word in his diary, which he underlined: "cruel."[64]

In an effort to expunge his previous life, Mellon gave the house on Forbes Street to the Carnegie Institute of Technology, which converted it into a girls' dormitory. Meanwhile, with the advice of his architect nephew, E. P. Mellon, and at the urging of Ailsa, he lavished much attention (and money) on the extension and refurbishment of the new place, which would continue long after the family had moved in: it was not completed until the summer of 1919. A porte cochere and ballroom were added, the dining room was remodeled, an organ was installed, and a radio system was wired up. Fittingly, though peculiarly, Mellon's dressing room was made of aluminum (he would later have a car made from the same material), and a swimming pool and bowling alley were added to the basement.[65] Mellon intended his new house, unlike Forbes Street, to be a place where he could entertain, and where Paul and Ailsa could bring their friends. To this end, he also revived the Judge and Sarah Jane's custom of inviting the whole clan on New Year's Day. Here is his diary entry for January 1, 1918: "Have all family connections at lunch in new house, twenty-four in all with the children. In afternoon, swimming in the new pool and bowling. Successful day."[66]

Mellon took comparable pains adorning his grand new residence. The Forbes Street house had been drably decorated, its furnishings were philistine, its paintings were mostly commonplace, and Mellon had stopped buying once his marriage began to disintegrate (which may explain why Carstairs had come to describe him as a "cold proposition"). But he had continued a desultory sort of correspondence with Knoedler, and after the divorce his interest in art began slowly to revive. In 1913 both Benjamin Altman and J. P. Morgan died, and when their collections were exhibited in the Metropolitan Museum of Art, Mellon and Frick went together to have a look.[67] Soon after, Frick began to hang his best paintings in his New York mansion, where Mellon was a frequent visitor, sometimes with Ailsa and Paul. By now, Frick was also purchasing porcelain, furniture, and carpets to match his pictures, and he was beginning to think about leaving it all to the public, provided the inheritance taxes could be arranged to his advantage, as Altman and Morgan had managed to do. Mellon looked on, and in March 1920, when visiting California with Ailsa, he took time out to call on Henry Huntington in San Marino, and admired his array of eighteenth-century English portraits.[68]

This new interest in collectors and collecting reawakened Mellon's own acquisitive impulse. After a ten-year lapse, he suddenly began to spend as he never had during the years of his marriage. In decorating and furnishing the house at Woodland Road, he was again guided by E. P.

Mellon. He also turned to Knoedler and to French and Company, a New York firm which specialized in supplying interior decorations and furnishings for rich people. Between 1918 and 1920, he spent over half a million dollars on Chinese porcelain vases, sixteenth- and seventeenth-century Dutch and Flemish tapestries, and eighteenth-century French furniture.[69] Ailsa was much involved in the discussions on interior decoration, and letters went back and forth from Pittsburgh to Farmington about fabrics, color schemes, and furnishings. "Father," she wrote, after reading some suggestions made by E. P. Mellon, "don't you think Cousin Ed is a little bit wrong about the upstairs guest room? In a big Tudor house in the country in England it would be all right to have an old pine dressing table and odd pieces of furniture. But this house is in Pittsburgh, and although it needs to be as homelike and English as possible, yet I still think it will be a great mistake if too many old and antique things are put into it."[70]

For the public rooms at least, "old and antique things" were very much in evidence, as they helped show off the pictures that had now become Mellon's major concern, in terms of both outlay and quality. In January 1918, scarcely a month after moving to Woodland Road, he acquired through Knoedler three paintings for $160,000: Cariani's *Portrait of a Man*, Gainsborough's *George IV When Prince of Wales*, and Goya's *Pepito Costa y Borrello*. This was only the beginning, for by December 1920, he had purchased a further eighteen canvases through Knoedler, at a total cost of nearly one million dollars, including two Rembrandts, Constable's *View of Salisbury Cathedral* (a favorite family visiting place), Romney's portrait of Sir William Hamilton, a Gainsborough seascape, Frans Hals's portrait of Nicholas Berghem, George Washington painted by Gilbert Stuart, and Raeburn's portrait of Miss Eleanor Urquhart. Mellon's last purchase for the Pittsburgh house was Turner's *Thames at Mortlake Terrace: Summer Evening*, a companion piece to the picture he had bought in 1908 but then sold to Frick. In worth and quality, these acquisitions were far beyond the earlier acquisitions at Forbes Street. In a mere two years, Mellon had become a serious collector.[71]

Although he remained loyal to Knoedler, and regularly visited their showrooms in New York, Mellon now became acquainted with a dealer who would eventually become no less significant in his collecting life: Joseph Duveen. The exact date of their first encounter is uncertain, but they were probably introduced in New York in 1913, appropriately enough by Frick. By this time, Duveen was the major force in the firm founded by his father, having built a magnificent new showroom in New York the year before, and he was as much the agent as the beneficiary of the transatlantic boom in art sales which characterized these prewar years. Morgan and Altman had been his customers, and so were Huntington, Frick, Morgan, P. A. B. Widener, and Isabella Stewart Gardner. He studied their moods, he bribed their butlers and their servants, and he delighted in playing them off against one another, thereby driving his prices (and his profits) up. Duveen was by turns pushy, determined, overwhelming, duplicitous, intimidating, unscrupulous, ingratiating, manipulative, loquacious, and addicted to his own hyperbole. And he paid Bernard Berenson to authenticate his (sometimes dubious) Renaissance pictures. In short, he was a brilliant but shameless salesman, and as Mellon himself would observe, paintings never looked so good as when Duveen was standing in front of them.[72]

It is difficult to imagine two people less alike than Joseph Duveen and Andrew Mellon, but when Frick introduced them, he told Duveen that one day his friend would be "the greatest collector of us all." Duveen determined that this should happen, and that he should make a fortune as he made Mellon's reputation. With the deaths of Altman and Morgan, he was on the lookout for new clients of such means, and he now laid siege to Mellon with all his might, as anxious to court the retiring titan as Mellon seemed to evade him.[73] By 1915, Mellon was indeed visiting Duveen's New York showroom, and before long Duveen was assisting with the refurbishments at Woodland Road, helping remodel the drawing room. Now he began urging his pictures on Mellon, in the extravagant language for which he was notorious. In 1920, Sir Joseph Duveen (as he had by now become) facilitated the meeting between Mellon and Huntington in California, and in the same year he made his first sale: a Frans Hals, *Portrait of an Elderly Lady*. Duveen described it as a work "of the very highest quality and very celebrated." At $220,000 it ought to have been; it was certainly Mellon's most expensive purchase to date. For Duveen, this was the shape of things to come. Mellon was, perhaps, less farsighted.[74]

As a married man, Mellon had bought his (generally indifferent) canvases from Knoedler's sale room in Pittsburgh. Now he bought much better art through Knoedler and Duveen in New York. Between 1918 and 1920, he "traded back" many of his earlier Barbizon School paintings to Knoedler, finding them distinctly inferior to his more recent acquisitions.[75] He was also very particular about the new pictures he was buying: of the eighteen that he acquired from Knoedler during these years, he would return seven, among them the Goya portrait, El Greco's *San Ildefonso of Toledo*, Rembrandt's portraits of King David and King Saul, and Moro's portraits of Mary Tudor and Lord Essex. There was no penalty for changing his mind: by this time, Knoedler had agreed that Mellon could keep any picture in his house, with complete freedom to return it for up to two years, thereby giving him "every possible opportunity for mature reflection and consideration in their acquisition." However, with the downturn of the economy following the end of the First World War, and Knoedler being short of funds, Mellon was urged to make up his mind more promptly. "We cannot afford," Roland Knoedler pleaded, "to be without our finest pictures indefinitely."[76] But knowing it was now a buyers' market, Mellon did not budge.

Nor was he any more yielding with Duveen, whose flamboyant salesmanship he delighted in countering with poker-faced silence. Along with the Frans Hals, Duveen had sought to press upon Mellon two Tintoretto portraits of Venetian senators, and *The Suitor's Visit* by Gerard ter Borch. "It is difficult, if not impossible, to exaggerate their importance," Duveen grandly declared. "It is my conviction," he went on, "that their rarity and beauty, and their high artistic standard, place them on the same plane as those creations of rare art which form the nucleus of the finest collections." Having "made a commencement" with Mellon by selling him the Hals, Duveen was willing to offer him a 10 percent discount on the Tintorettos and the ter Borch, asking $513,000 for the three works. Mellon hung them on his walls, to ponder in his own good time.[77] Soon after, Duveen was pressing on him portraits by Titian and by Rembrandt. He had acquired them in Paris, but he could not bring them to New York immediately as he had "an engagement to re-arrange the King's picture gallery," and he had "an appointment to see His Majesty in London" in October 1920. When the pictures finally arrived early the following year, Mellon was no more impressed by the royal name-dropping than by the delay. With the onset of the postwar depression, and with income taxes still high, it was to Duveen that Mellon now complained of "scarcity of funds." "I have to say," he told him, "that however much they may appeal to me, I shall be unable to contemplate making any substantial purchases under present circumstances."[78]

This new splendor was never meant to encompass Nora. But shortly before Christmas 1918, she again told Andrew "how much she felt of how wrong she had been." Insisting that she had always loved him, she said it was her wish—and also Ailsa's—that they should remarry. But Andrew's response was no more yielding than before: "I answer," he confided to his diary, "that she is mistaken, that after what has happened, it could not be. It would never be what she thinks." "I was sorry," he concluded, that "I could not say to her what she would like to have me say."[79] Nora had many reasons to feel sorry. Since the divorce, she had been ostracized by Pittsburgh society and only invited to two receptions. In March 1919,

Paul Ache reported that she was "very unsettled, sometimes in good spirits, other times depressed and despondent." By now, she had realized that when she married Andrew, she had "had everything she could ever want," but then "threw it all away over Curphey." Andrew remained unmoved. But the scars lingered. A month later, on the anniversary of learning in New York that his marriage was over, he noted in his diary: "Bright Easter morning. Just ten years since Chadbourne broke news to me."[80]

Despite the generous terms of the settlement, Nora's finances remained precarious. Old ways died hard: she had given money to Charles Mustin to buy a farm at Brookwood in the Hudson Valley, where, in certain moods, she hoped they might settle down together. Indeed, she inquired of Andrew through Ache whether he might waive the provision of the settlement whereby she would forfeit one of her trust funds if she remarried. Andrew refused that request, too, unconvinced that her fondness for Mustin was any less a "whim" than her mad love for Curphey had been.[81] By then, Mustin had been badly injured in a car accident and needed constant medical supervision: one more strain on Nora's resources. Andrew helped with her income tax bills and Mustin's medical expenses, but by the summer of 1919, Nora had reluctantly accepted he would not take her back. With Ailsa now more in New York than in Pittsburgh, she concluded it was time for her to move on as well. She put the Howe Street house up for sale, and rented a Manhattan apartment at 340 Park Avenue. Andrew's relief at her departure was not unalloyed: "Nora leaves Pittsburgh," he recorded with notable if laconic regret. "Feel sorry." He told her she was "to call on me if help wanted." Soon after, he would loan Leonard McMullen another $600.[82]

Wistful jottings notwithstanding, Nora's continued presence in Pittsburgh would have been a serious embarrassment with Ailsa about to come out. Nora could scarcely be absent from her own daughter's presentation to society and entry into adulthood, but since many in Pittsburgh no longer recognized her, there would inevitably have been awkwardnesses. It was both a personal sacrifice and a tactful solution to remove herself from the scene, and such uncharacteristic selflessness was not lost on Andrew, who was genuinely touched.[83] In deciding how and when Ailsa should come out, he was guided by Miss Sylvester and Jennie Mellon, Dick's wife. He took endless trouble inviting the right people to the event, ordering the dance cards, and bringing in cases of Italian "champagne" and Scotch (Prohibition was due to come into force in 1920, which made 1919 a bumper year for comings-out). He also bought Ailsa additional expensive dresses and furs, and, most impressive, a $50,000 pearl necklace from Tiffany's in New York. After last-minute arrangements of the furniture and carpets and pictures, she duly emerged at a reception held at Woodland Road, on December 16, 1919. Her father was never prouder: "Stood with Ailsa from four to seven receiving," he recorded in his diary. "Rooms full of flowers sent to Ailsa . . . House beautiful and full of people." A week later, Andrew put on a ball for her at the Pittsburgh Club: "Dance lasts to 3:30," he noted. "Great success. I go home about four."[84]

At the beginning of that year, Ailsa had tearfully begged her father to remarry Nora. "Herself was largely the motive, it seemed to me," Andrew noted caustically, and now explaining his refusal, he told Ailsa something of Nora and Curphey. It did not make relations between them any easier. Like many daughters of wealth, Ailsa was both overindulged and underschooled, but such had been her dislike of Miss Porter's that she had no intention of staying on for a third year—despite the advice of the headmistress and of Miss Sylvester, and the rare agreement of Andrew and Nora, that she needed "further education."[85] Starting in the autumn of 1919, Ailsa divided her time between Pittsburgh and New York, preferring the much brighter social scene of Manhattan, and her mother's company to her father's. She danced and stayed up late, often not rising before midday. Andrew worried that she had taken up smoking (unacceptable for ladies of quality) and that she was seeing too much of a wild drinking man called Tom Jones (from the same family as the ill-starred Fannie). There was a bitter row in June 1920, as Andrew was leaving for the Republican National Convention in Chicago: "she argued and contended that I was unkind," he recorded, "and that she was not a child." Later that month he declined to give her a birthday present because she had recently lost an expensive bracelet. But by the autumn, Andrew was providing Ailsa with an allowance of $500 a month, and they were planning a spring trip together to Egypt.[86]

In the autumn of Ailsa's coming-out and her effective flight from the Pittsburgh nest, Paul was sent away to Choate, the fashionable boarding school in Wallingford, Connecticut. Although established only twenty years before, it had found favor with the Pittsburgh rich. There Paul did poorly at mathematics but he was increasingly drawn to English and literature. These were scarcely subjects in which his father was interested, let alone knowledgeable: like his sister, Paul was growing up in a world very different socially and culturally from the one Andrew had known as a boy.[87] But he remained a watchful and attentive parent: writing regular letters, scrutinizing his son's reports, visiting him when possible, donating $10,000 to the Choate Memorial Building, making arrangements for him to have his teeth straightened by a dentist in New Haven, and commissioning a portrait by Weber, which was completed in the summer of 1920. Like Ailsa, Paul was now often in New York, sometimes seeing his father, sometimes staying with his mother.[88] Andrew may have belatedly made his family a home of warmth and opulence in Pittsburgh, but his single parenting was largely done. More than ever, Ailsa and Paul were drawn toward the East. And their father, increasingly, was drawn after them.

IV. MR. MELLON GOES TO WASHINGTON

In 1919, while negotiations were taking place overseas which would culminate in the Versailles Treaty, Andrew Mellon was making his peace with momentous changes in his own life: the deaths of Heinz, Carnegie, and Frick, Nora's departure to New York, Paul's enrollment at Choate, Ailsa's coming-out, and the impending prospect of Prohibition. But it was also a sea-change year in American politics: amid persistent widespread unemployment and popular unrest, along with high taxes, high-interest rates, and high levels of government debt, the progressive impulse which had informed the Roosevelt, Taft, and Wilson administrations was now clearly spent. Moreover, and as if to prove politics no less cyclical than economics, it was superseded by a new conservative era much more to Mellon's taste. Wilson had been criticized for keeping America out of war, then for taking her in, and then again for his increasingly intrusive government. The Republicans, on the other hand, had done very well in the midterm elections of 1918, and with the death of Theodore Roosevelt early the following year the GOP's reformist wing was marginalized. There now seemed every prospect they would win the White House back in 1920 on a conservative platform harking back to McKinley—whose monument in Miles, Ohio, Mellon and Frick had visited in October 1919 on what may have been their last meeting.[89]

However disenchanted with its lurch toward progressivism, Mellon had always supported the Republican Party, at city, state, and national levels. His first recorded donation was $1,000 to the Harrison presidential campaign of 1888, and since then he had never had any qualm about using the influence his gifts had bought—in obtaining his Pittsburgh streetcar franchises, in changing the state divorce law, in securing high federal tariffs to protect Alcoa, and in lobbying for battleship orders for the New York Shipbuilding Company (where even the devoted and normally imperturbable Philander Knox thought Mellon rather overdid things).[90]

By the time of Roosevelt and Taft, Mellon was established, along with Frick, as a major party benefactor, his diary abounding with figures and supportive sentiment: "RBM gives $3,000 for campaign"; "contribution $10,000"; "E. V. Babcock soliciting for Republican Committee. We pledge $25,000"; "draw $40,000 T. Mellon & Sons for Senator Penrose to pay debts state organization"; "agree to contribute $12,500."[91] Early in 1919, Frick and Mellon each agreed to pledge $10,000 in support of the Irreconcilables, a group led by Henry Cabot Lodge and Philander Knox, that was determined to prevent the ratification of the Treaty of Versailles, which would have obliged the United States to join the League of Nations. In this endeavor they succeeded, thereby effectively bringing the Wilson presidency to an end.[92]

By the time the Republicans had to choose their own nominee for 1920, the GOP was re-established, to Mellon's pleasure, as the party that was hostile to activist government, strongly pro-business and finance, and viscerally opposed to organized labor and anything the least redolent of socialism. Mellon, having quarreled with Ailsa immediately prior to his departure, attended the convention in Chicago in June as part of the Pennsylvania delegation. With the nomination wide open, he hoped to secure it for Philander Knox, although he initially joined his fellows from the Keystone State in support of its governor, William C. Sproul.[93] Neither bid came to anything, for it was Senator Warren G. Harding of neighboring Ohio who won the nomination after the Pennsylvania delegation finally decided to back him. Mellon did not get his candidate, but he was delighted with the platform all the same: it urged a return to pre-war "normalcy," favored "honest money and sound finance," and was committed to "free business from arbitrary and unnecessary control." And Harding's running mate, Calvin Coolidge, was well-known for his hostility to labor, having memorably observed during the Boston police strike of 1919: "There is no right to strike against the public safety by anybody, anywhere, anytime."[94]

Politics had not looked so good to him in ages, and Mellon threw himself into the 1920 election with unexampled vigor. He advanced a loan of $150,000 to the party (subsequently repaid), and he personally donated $56,000 to the campaign. He also served on the Republican Committee on Ways and Means, with responsibility for fund-raising in Allegheny County. The target had been set high, at $400,000, but by mobilizing his friends and contacts across Pittsburgh, and by using his own staff and employees, Mellon met it.[95] For the first time he became a familiar sight at the Republican campaign headquarters in New York, and he earned the appreciation of the party's high command, as Allegheny County gave twice as much as the rest of Pennsylvania: it was the only district to meet its goal, with every prominent Republican located and tapped.[96] Mellon had read the tea leaves correctly: Harding not only defeated James M. Cox for the White House by an overwhelming command of the popular vote, but the Republicans also piled up majorities in the House and the Senate. Another victim of the rout was the assistant secretary of the navy, Franklin Delano Roosevelt, the Democrats' vice presidential candidate. In the heady aftermath of the Republican triumph, he was soon stricken by polio, and it seemed unlikely that he would ever be heard from again.

With victory in hand, Pennsylvania's senators, Boies Penrose and Philander Knox, joined Henry Cabot Lodge in lobbying hard to win Mellon an appointment in Washington.[97] Knox had been in close touch with Harding since the convention, and in late November 1920, he entertained hopes of his own reappointment as secretary of state, the office he had held under Taft. If that materialized, Knox would urge the president-elect to appoint Mellon to his vacant seat in the Senate or, alternatively, to make "the ablest financier in America" secretary of the treasury.[98] Equally influential was Boies Penrose: he was the party boss in Pennsylvania, and he had broken the deadlock at the Chicago convention by persuading the GOP leaders to nominate the senator from Ohio. This gave him Harding's ear, and he, too, lobbied hard in November and December, insisting Mellon was "the best appointment he could make." Dick Mellon also welcomed such a new career path for his brother, while Ailsa was "delighted with the idea of living in Washington." With many associates in Pittsburgh also on his side, Mellon's claims were soon being "boosted" in the local and national press.[99]

But he was a reluctant nominee. In the middle of December, Mellon told Cyrus Woods he "could not contemplate taking the job" and urged him to advise Penrose of this. On New Year's Day 1921, he wrote to Knox "thanking him for his offices in my behalf at Marion [Harding's home town in Ohio] and telling him why I am not prepared to accept Secretaryship of Treasury if offered me."[100] There was nothing coy about this demurral: indeed, Mellon had many reasons for it, some of which he unsystematically confided to his diary during the ensuing days. Having seen his banks and his businesses through the Great War, he had reached an age when retirement beckoned. He had always preferred to exercise power and influence from the background, and he hated the glare high public office would inevitably bring. He was apprehensive about doing what would be a difficult job during the period of postwar adjustment, and he feared his industrial and financial connections would prove a liability, creating perceived conflicts of interest. If he left Pittsburgh, the whole burden of banking and business would fall on Dick, who was yearning for the open spaces of his Rolling Rock estate. Andrew also worried that if Ailsa accompanied him to Washington and was obliged to act as his hostess, she would fall easy prey to every "fortune hunter" in town.[101]

But the day after Mellon had written his letter to Knox, he received one from Harding, inviting him "to run out to Marion for a short interview."[102] The president-elect was now courting him directly. He needed someone acceptable to Wall Street, but wanted someone who was not of it. His first choice had been another non–New York banker, Charles G. Dawes of Chicago, head of the Central Union Trust Company of Illinois, but Dawes bowed out at an early stage. Harding was initially loath to accede to the lobbying of Knox, Penrose, and Lodge. This was not because he had never heard of Mellon: Harding was well aware of him as a party backer and as a figure in his own right. Nor did he consider Mellon's riches any sort of political liability: like many Americans, Harding believed that a few great figures controlled the economic destiny of the world, and he was eager to put one of them in the service of the nation's prosperity and his own political success.[103] But together with their support for Mellon, Penrose and Lodge also expressed opposition to Herbert Hoover (whose loyalty to the GOP they doubted), whom Harding was eager to appoint secretary of commerce. Harding insisted it must be "Mellon and Hoover or no Mellon," and it was only when he had secured their acceptance of Hoover that he agreed "to have a look" at their candidate.

Mellon duly journeyed to Marion, where he was obliged to walk the mile from the railway station to Harding's house, and over lunch the two agreed that the country needed a prompt and thorough revision of the tax code, emergency tariffs, and the creation of a federal budget system. It remains less clear exactly what Mellon told Harding, for he would leave behind two accounts of the meeting which are not wholly consistent.[104] According to a memorandum he dictated some time later, Mellon had gone to Marion "determined not to take the appointment under any circumstances." He insisted that his business and industrial connections would be a "handicap" to the incoming administration, and that his ownership of stock in the Overholt Distillery would be an embarrassment in the era of Prohibition. Harding brushed aside these arguments, pointing out that he himself owned shares in a brewery. But as Mellon left, he urged the president-elect, as a "personal favour," to "find someone else for the Treasury and relieve me from going to Washington." However, Mellon's diary records a rather different version of the conversation. He was, he told Harding, "not seeking the place" and would feel "much relieved" if he "would pass me by," but he had nevertheless decided that "should I have to face the offer, I would not shrink from accepting." It was on this basis that he informed Knox and Penrose that his visit had been "satisfactory."[105]

By now, Philander Knox had abandoned his own claims to office—not least because Harding made it clear he thought him too old—and this made him all the more determined to propel Mellon forward. On January 23, 1921, he wrote to the editor of the *Boston Evening Transcript*, outlining and extolling his old friend's "character, aptitude and attainments." He did so "not with a view of serving Mr. Mellon, but to help Senator Harding make good his promise to the American people that he would surround himself with the most capable advisors available." "Mr. Mellon's entire life," Knox insisted,

> has been given to constructive work—to translating great capacity into great accomplishment. He is one of the few cases where his wealth is an accurate measure of his ability. He has never financially debauched any enterprise with which he has been concerned. He has never multiplied his fortune over and over again by resolutions to increase capital stock. He has never floated issues of stock upon the market in connection with any of his great work of industrial development. With marvellous vision and imagination he has spent his entire life in developing new fields for American energy and opportunity, and in my deliberate judgment he is the greatest constructive economist of his generation.[106]

Much of this endorsement was duly incorporated, with barely any revision, into an editorial appearing in the next day's edition of the *Transcript*.[107]

This scarcely reflects what Knox truly knew about his friend's business career and ethics: it was a selective account by an accomplished advocate making the best case he could. What about the inflated capital stock of Union Steel just prior to its sale, which Mellon and Frick had orchestrated, and the infringements by Alcoa of the Sherman Antitrust Act? Knox must have known that Crucible Steel and the Pittsburgh Coal Company were both floated and quoted on the stock exchange. In April 1920 the senator had himself secured the passage of a bill which authorized the payment of over $700,000 to McClintic-Marshall for additional expenses incurred in their work in connection with the lock gates of the Panama Canal. And he knew full well that Mellon's "vision and imagination" did not encompass organized labor.[108] But Knox did catch the essence of Mellon's creative achievements, and insisted he was "only expressing the opinion of those who know Mr. Mellon best, who admire him for his great ability and love him for his modest and unassuming personality, his patriotism, his un-flaunted charities and loyalty to the men and principles to which he is attached." That much was defensibly true.

Meanwhile, Mellon had turned back to business and personal matters: he attended meetings of Alcoa, Standard Steel Car, and Crucible Steel; he was obliged to resign as a director of the Pennsylvania Railroad because of the Clayton Act; he overheard his cook talking on the telephone and "inferred" that Duveen had bribed the servant; he learned that Ailsa had lost the bracelet he had given her for Christmas; and he sent Paul ten dollars to cheer him up after he had been hit in the mouth with a hockey stick.[109] Ailsa was still eager for her father to accept the post, "as she wants to live in Washington," but her father's worry had not abated that his "corporation connections" would be a "cause of criticism in case of acceptance," and in the middle of January, James Reed discovered a statute of 1789 which prohibited anyone engaged in trade or commerce from becoming secretary of the treasury. Mellon was relieved, and took the night train to Washington to confirm his ineligibility to Knox. But the senator argued that in the light of several subsequent court decisions, the statute was no obstacle. All his friend would have to do was to resign his many directorships, since the mere possession of stocks and shares had long since been distinguished from active engagement in business. Reluctantly, Mellon now concluded that there would be "no really serious objections" to his appointment.[110]

Late on the evening of February 1, Knox telephoned Mellon to inform him that the treasury secretaryship had indeed been "settled in my favor." Lukewarm to the last, Mellon recorded his response: "Tell him I am not sure that the news is pleasing to me." The next day, Penrose telephoned his congratulations, the papers began reporting the appointment as a settled matter, and letters of congratulation started to pour in. "I have a talk with Ailsa about Washington," Mellon recorded in his diary. "Tell her I am accepting the office on her account, and depend on her to use good judgment in Society when we go. Talk to her about the men she associates with, and that I think she should be more discriminating and particular."[111] Can his decision have been wholly selfless? With Paul in Connecticut, Ailsa spending more time in New York, and Nora permanently there, he was once again facing loneliness in Pittsburgh. He was himself increasingly being drawn to the East Coast, and if he went to Washington, a whole new life would open up before him, allowing him also to keep a much closer eye on Ailsa. In taking the Treasury post "on her account," he was also tacitly acknowledging that his own life was changing: beyond banking, beyond business, beyond Pittsburgh.

Andrew accordingly wrote to Paul with the news he would "likely accept office and go to Washington," and by special delivery he received a "letter from Nora congratulating me on appointment and with best wishes."[112] But the matter was still not yet definitely decided, as two more obstacles had to be circumvented. One concerned Mellon's ownership of shares in the Overholt Distillery, a point Harding had dismissed on the visit to Marion. The press had got wind of the story, and with gleeful exaggeration the *New York World*, which numbered among its opponents injustice, corruption, public plunderers, and the privileged classes, depicted Mellon as "the largest distiller of whisky in America," who had made a large part of his fortune in a trade recently declared illegal; though as secretary of the treasury, he would be responsible for enforcing Prohibition.[113] The other obstacle, discovered by James Reed, was a provision in the Federal Reserve Act of 1913 that prohibited any member of the Federal Reserve Board from owning bank stock. The secretary of the treasury was ex officio chairman of that board, and Mellon's shareholdings in banks were both extensive and of great sentimental value, being the very essence of his dynastic pride and individual identity.[114]

In the case of the Overholt Distillery, Mellon's original investment of $25,000 in 1887 had given him one-third ownership (Frick and Dick owned the other two-thirds). The business had prospered, and his holdings had been assigned a book value of $1.1 million in December 1918. But output had declined during the war years, in part because of the government's requisition of grain, but also because of looming Prohibition. (By way of preparing for the worst, from October 1918 to January 1919, Frick had been hastily sending Overholt whisky to many of his friends, including twenty cases to Philander Knox.)[115] Accordingly, in 1916, Overholt had suspended manufacture, but Mellon recognized that this did not solve his problem. In late January 1921, he and Dick, as the two surviving partners, entered into an agreement for the Union Trust Company to acquire Overholt's property and remaining stocks of liquor, which would be sold in 1925 to the Schulte Drug Stores for medicinal purposes. This enabled Mellon to state that "the distilling company absolutely ceased from doing any manufacturing business over three years before the Prohibition Amendment went into effect and the entire business was subsequently wound up." But his copious denials could not kill a good if spurious story. During the next ten years, rumors continued to circulate that he had made his money as a distiller, and that he continued to do so as a bootlegger.[116]

At the same time, James Reed was addressing the requirements of the Federal Reserve Act by arranging for Mellon to divest himself of his bank stock holdings. But this cut to the dynastic quick only renewed Mellon's uncertainties: he wrote to Paul that "Washington matter not settled yet," and Ailsa worried that he was going to withdraw. Knox and Penrose kept insisting that the problem could be solved, and urged Mellon "not to back out." Reed duly came up with a solution, and Mellon informed Knox that it would "enable me to qualify in case of appointment." But, in "sincere" pleading he urged Knox to communicate to Harding that "I will consider it a favor if he will find another for the post. . . . I dislike to refuse and will [accept] if he persists, but hope he may select someone else."[117] His hope was in vain. "I have not found anybody as yet," Harding wrote to Knox on February 20, "who speaks in hostility concerning him. I note that the *New York World* has been hammering him, and trying to discredit him, but that has helped to confirm me in my impression that he is a very suitable candidate." Four days later, Mellon learned from Knox that Harding had "asked him to see me and say he hopes I would accept the Treasury Portfolio." Mellon now felt obliged to do so. So the matter was settled, and that evening Andrew discussed Washington apartments with Ailsa.[118]

Although rich businessmen such as Bernard Baruch and Charles Schwab had held temporary appointments in Washington during the war, it was unusual for a successful financier to hold public office in peacetime, and the only precedent most commentators could find was the first and greatest treasury secretary, Alexander Hamilton. For Mellon's supporters, his indubitable abilities justified the innovation, particularly as many of the problems facing the new administration were economic: industrial depression, high taxes, mounting debt. But those who disliked the prospect of a Republican administration took Mellon's appointment as a sign that Harding intended "to reseat the power of special privileged interests, the powers of avarice and greed, the powers that seek self-aggrandizement at the expense of the general public, and to reseat the powers of capital on the throne where they can un-molestedly antagonize labor at will."[119] And while Mellon could render himself technically eligible by selling his banking shares and by resigning his directorships, he still possessed a great (though invariably overstated) fortune, and any policy he implemented to the benefit of business could be legitimately criticized as promoting his self-interest. Harding and Knox were unconcerned, but James Reed's worry that Mellon's large portfolio might render him vulnerable to "possible investigation by some hostile members of Congress" would prove well founded.[120]

But all this lay in the future on February 28, 1921, when Mellon made a final visit to Washington as a private citizen. Accompanied by Philander Knox, he visited the Treasury building, where he met with the assistant secretary, S. Parker Gilbert; from there, he went on to the Capitol, and then saw the apartment that he was thinking of renting, one block east of Dupont Circle, on Massachusetts Avenue. In the evening, Knox gave a dinner for Mellon to which twelve Republican senators were invited.[121] Then it was back to Pittsburgh, in time for the official announcement on March 2, and the inevitable rituals of transition. There were letters to reply to, and photographs, biographical details, and statements to provide for the press. "We are rejoicing," Frick's daughter had written, "seeing Mr. Harding's wonderful selection, and feel that the whole country is to be congratulated in having you for Secretary of Treasury." Mellon duly made over all his bank stock, nominally worth slightly more than ten million dollars (of which nine million was in the Union Trust Company), to his brother Dick, who gave him his notes in payment at 5 percent interest. At the same time, he resigned the directorships of more than sixty companies. In a formal and a legal sense, this was the end of his banking and his business life, and it marked the official dissolution of the remarkable partnership both spoke of as "my brother and I."[122]

On March 3, with a party of twelve supporters that included Henry McEldowney, James Reed and his son David, and the mayor of Pittsburgh, Andrew Mellon boarded the night train for the nation's capital. ("I wish I could be in Washington on Friday," Paul wrote rather plaintively from Choate, but the school would not let him go.)[123] It was a journey he had taken many times, especially in recent years, but never so portentously as on this occasion. The following morning, Warren Harding was inaugurated in the first such presidential ceremony to be broadcast on radio, and the entire cabinet was rapidly confirmed by the Senate. That afternoon, Mellon was the first to be sworn in by the Chief Justice, appropriately enough in the office of Senator Knox. (He had to be resworn the next day, after it was learned that the Chief Justice was not a notary public and thus could not lawfully administer the oath.) On the morning of March 5, 1921, not quite three weeks short of his sixty-sixth birthday, Andrew Mellon began his new life as secretary of the United States Treasury. He arrived at eight o'clock, an hour before most of his staff turned up for work. Such a thing had never happened in the memory of any of the Treasury's night watchmen.[124]

PART THREE

The Rise and Fall
of a Public Man, *1921–33*

All the past history of the world goes to show that continued peace and prosperity produce luxury and idleness,
which in turn corrupt the morals and deteriorate the character of the people.

Thomas Mellon and His Times, p. 357

9

HARD TIMES WITH HARDING

Political Realities, Getting Started, Settling In, 1921–23

Ignorance of economic principles blinds our governing class to the evils of extravagance and undue public burdens, increasing the cost of living to rich and poor alike.

Thomas Mellon and His Times, p. 340

I. CONTEXTS, CHALLENGES, AND CONSTRAINTS

Not since the laissez-faire heyday of McKinley at the turn of the century had Washington seen an administration so unequivocally in favor of private enterprise and individual self-advancement as that which Andrew Mellon now joined. "The business of America," President Harding observed, in words anticipating Calvin Coolidge's later and more memorable formulation, "is the business of everybody in America. . . . This is essentially a business country. . . . We must get back to methods of business."[1] One emphatic sign of this change was the abrupt smothering of those progressive, prewar, pro-labor impulses. The antitrust laws were still on the books, but they were no longer enforced with anything like the zeal shown under Roosevelt, Taft, and Wilson, and although Harding was by nature more conciliatory than confrontational, his administration aggressively supported employers in industrial disputes. In 1921–22, nationwide strikes of coal miners and railroad workers were successfully put down with troops and court injunctions. For its part, the Supreme Court dealt the trade unions a succession of hammer blows, including a ruling that the Clayton Act of 1914 had not conferred immunity on them after all. Here was a government whose ideology, at least, was completely after Mellon's own heart.[2]

The pro-business and anti-labor stance was integral to what Harding described as a return to "normalcy," by which he meant restoring the pre-war climate of low taxes, balanced budgets, manageable national debt, limited government, and a functioning international economy backed by the gold standard. It now fell to Mellon to do what he could to bring back these good old days.[3] Both domestically and internationally, it was a serious task. The financing and fighting of the First World War had increased annual government spending from $1 billion in 1916 to $18.5 billion in 1919, and it was still above $6 billion in 1920; the national debt had exploded from less than $2 billion in 1916 to $26 billion in 1919. Of these obligations, $7.5 billion consisted of short-term loans, due for payment by May 1923.[4] Interest rates were at 7 percent, and the tax structure was in chaos: many rich people were evading the recently imposed income tax, and new taxes had been added haphazardly in a frantic scramble to raise revenue. And the armistice, the collapse of wartime demand, and the return of two million demobilized troops had plunged the nation into recession, with factory closures, business liquidations, bank failures, and widespread unemployment and social unrest. Mellon had witnessed all this firsthand in Pittsburgh, and he would conclude that "the crisis of 1921 was one of the most severe this country has ever experienced."[5]

The domestic economic scene might have been dark, but the international scene that Mellon now contemplated was, by comparison, dire. For the financial problems by which the United States was beset were as nothing compared to those that afflicted the exhausted and impoverished European powers, both vanquished and victors alike. The Allies had only been able to continue fighting because of American financial support, and more than $10 billion of the U.S. national debt was owed by them. But they were in no position to repay the loans: their economies were in deep recession, many had suffered serious damage to their industries, and their currencies, no longer backed by the gold standard, were prone to violent fluctuations. At the same time, Russia had abandoned itself to Communist revolution and civil war, Austria-Hungary had been broken up, and Germany was faced with a reparations bill it claimed it could not afford—but the Allies depended (and insisted) on German compliance if ever they were to repay their loans to the United States.[6] This was a stricken world—and a stricken world economy. As Mellon later noted, Europe was "in a state of political turmoil and disagreements which prevented any solution of the reparations problem and hindered her economic recovery. Her currencies went from bad to worse, industry dragged along at a slow pace, and in many countries, all incentive to save and accumulate capital virtually disappeared."[7]

Of course, there were many aspects of both the domestic and the international economy of the early 1920s that no one expected Mellon to deal with. Few Americans thought it was the responsibility of the secretary of the treasury to try to iron out booms and slumps, to redistribute wealth, to provide pensions to retired workers, to eradicate unemployment, or to regulate the entire banking system. Nor would Mellon be expected to solve the myriad difficulties that now beset the European economies. Officially, the United States had nothing to do with the issue of German reparations, which were primarily owed to Britain and France. From now on, loans to the continent, to help rebuild its devastated industries and infrastructures, would be privately arranged by American finance houses, and it would be the State Department, rather than the Treasury, that would exercise oversight of this so-called dollar diplomacy. And to the extent that they concerned the United States, future negotiations over the return of European currencies to the gold standard would be carried on between continental central bankers and Benjamin F. Strong, the formidable governor of the New York Federal Reserve Bank. In none of these matters would Mellon be extensively involved, and his participation would be largely confined to making encouraging noises about restoring the international economy to its prewar stability.[8]

In conformity with this limited role, the department over which the new treasury secretary presided was a relatively small organization, employing only 70,000 people even after wartime expansion. Its chief traditional responsibilities were the currency, customs and excise, public buildings, and the Coast Guard. Recently added to its portfolio were collecting taxes, settling foreign debts, and enforcing Prohibition. Like the federal government as a whole, which spent less than 3 percent of gross national product, the Department of the Treasury scarcely intruded into the lives of many Americans, and official data on such matters as employment, and unemployment, hardly existed.[9] Mellon was wholly comfortable with this minimalist fiscal regime. His concern was to ensure that the nation's finances were prudently managed, which, as for any responsible individual, meant living within income, firmly controlling expenditure, paying off accumulated debts, borrowing only on the soundest terms, and providing carefully for the future by building up a surplus. In short, Mellon aimed to run the Treasury, and to oversee the national finances, just as he had run the family bank, with few notions beyond such stewardship as to what he should be doing.[10] And insofar as he was concerned with international economic affairs, his efforts would be focused on the matter of settling the debts which European nations owed the United States, which took precedence over all other continental considerations.

So Mellon was generally comfortable with a narrow definition of his job and jurisdiction, but there were externally imposed constraints on his freedom of action with which he was less happy. To begin with, President Harding and Secretary Mellon remained strange bedfellows. Once they were together in Washington, Mellon occasionally received the Hardings for dinner in his apartment, and sometimes played poker at the White House, but he was never part of the president's inner circle. Relations were always correct rather than warm, and Mellon was the only member of the cabinet not to campaign during the midterm elections of 1922.[11] Someone who had begun life as a small-town newspaper proprietor and then became a professional politician (two occupations Mellon vehemently disliked) was hardly likely to win his heart. Mellon thought Harding an inefficient man of business and would never (according to his nephew) have dreamed of giving him a senior job in one of his companies. Also dismaying was the president's enthrallment to the "Ohio gang," and his wish to give important and responsible Treasury posts to party hacks and Republican loyalists. For his part, Harding thought Mellon ignorant and naïve about politics, he did not always support him in his battles with Congress, and he failed to understand the technical complexities of many of the issues with which the secretary had to deal.[12]

Within the Harding cabinet, Mellon was similarly detached and aloof. Most of his colleagues were in their forties or fifties, at least half a generation younger than he. It did not help that Mellon was substantially richer than all of them put together (the secretary of commerce, the self-made Herbert Hoover, by comparison, had been worth a mere $4 million in 1915). And he rarely spoke except on matters within his own jurisdiction. "I think there is a good deal to be said on both sides" was his best answer when once asked to comment on a nonfinancial matter.[13] Mellon seems to have got on well enough (if very formally) with Vice President Calvin Coolidge and Secretary of State Charles E. Hughes, but with others, especially those whose portfolios overlapped his own, relations were less satisfactory. He regularly clashed with the attorney general, Harry Daugherty, who, following the president's lead, sought to fill the Treasury through patronage appointments, regardless of qualifications. He disapproved of Henry C. Wallace, secretary of agriculture, for stridently championing the claims of farmers over what he regarded as the more compelling interests of industry and business. And Mellon was enchanted least by Herbert Hoover, the secretary of commerce, whom he regarded as rigid, narrow, and "too much of an engineer," with a distasteful flair for self-promotion. In addition, Hoover continually interfered in other departments, as when he took over the Bureau of Customs Statistics from the Treasury.[14]

Nor, despite the Republican majority in both houses, were Mellon's relations with the Congress easy. From the outset, Harding failed to provide decisive leadership, and Mellon himself scarcely dazzled before House or Senate committees.[15] Late in 1921, both Philander Knox and Boies Penrose died, thereby robbing Mellon of his two most effective advocates in the upper chamber (Penrose had been chairman of the Senate Finance Committee). The Republican Party, though ascendant, would remain riddled with divisions, especially between those representing the eastern industrial areas, and those representing the agrarian South and Midwest. The self-styled "agrarians," the "farm bloc," were (rightly) convinced that the administration was more concerned with the business of industry than with the business of agriculture. Supported by the progressive, populist Senator Robert "Fighting Bob" La Follette of Wisconsin (a visceral opponent of Mellon's) and allied with the Democrats, the farm bloc was sufficient to threaten any proposals the new secretary might make. This situation worsened after the midterm elections of November 1922, when the Republican margin in both Houses was so diminished as to leave no effective working majority.[16]

These constraints were already clear during the opening months of Mellon's secretaryship, as he suffered a succession of political defeats, lost turf battles, and other challenges to his authority. A Bureau of the Budget was belatedly established, to produce for the first time comprehensive calculations of federal income and expenditure. The measure had originated in the later Wilson years, in response to the contingencies of wartime, but it had been vetoed by the president, and by the time the Harding administration took office, there were two alternatives before Congress: one which placed the bureau under the control of the Treasury, and another which put it under direct control of the president. Mellon predictably preferred the first, Harding vacillated, and to Mellon's dismay, the second version was adopted.[17] To make matters worse, the first director of the bureau was Charles G. Dawes, Harding's first choice for treasury secretary, who would now have primary responsibility for overseeing and cutting government expenditure. In fact, Mellon and Dawes worked well together for the twelve months the latter held his post, but it was a serious diminution of Mellon's authority and prestige for the bureau to have been established outside the Treasury, and his department was now obliged to defend figures for government income and expenditure that were not of its own construction.[18]

There was also the problem of the Federal Reserve Board, which had been established in 1913, with the intention of avoiding a repetition of the panic of six years before.[19] Its members were appointed by the president, and their task was to oversee the local Federal Reserve banks, and also to set discount (and thus interest) rates. But the board's functions and responsibilities had not been fully or precisely defined, and the new and uncertain economic conditions precipitated by the war left its relations with the Reserve banks, and with the Treasury, even more uncertain. There were also serious disagreements among the board's members, many of whom knew little about banking, as to what interest rates should be.[20] Although the secretary of the treasury was nominally chairman of the board, he was unable to prevent the president from using it for patronage and political advantage. Harding appointed one of his Marion cronies, Daniel Crissinger, comptroller of the currency, thus making him an ex officio member; and he later yielded to pressure from the farm bloc in adding Milo D. Campbell, president of the National Milk Producers' Association, to represent the agricultural interest. Mellon disapproved of both men, but he was powerless to stop them.[21]

Nor did the secretary have much control of tariff policy, since Congress held the initiative, and in this area Harding again was weak. Mellon thought tax reform should come first, because European exports to America had declined significantly during and since the war, and so tariffs raised a lower proportion of federal revenue than they had previously done. But the Republicans were pledged to restore the high protective barriers that the Democratic administration had abolished in 1913, and an emergency tariff was passed in May 1921, soon after the new administration took office, in the vain hope of protecting American agriculture.[22] But thereafter, little got done until September 1922, when Congress passed the Fordney-McCumber Tariff. There had been serious disagreements between the agricultural and the business interests, and the result was little more than a hodgepodge compromise of political expediency and vested greed. Mellon was interested in the measure insofar as it related to his own companies, but lamented the inordinately long and ill-tempered time the Congress had spent on it, while the more urgent matter of tax reform had been left languishing.[23]

Mellon's hands were also tied when it came to trying to resolve the complex issues of European indebtedness to the United States. On taking up his post, he believed he should have full freedom to deal with this matter, and in the summer of 1921, a bill was introduced in Congress proposing "the grant of broad powers to the Secretary of the Treasury to handle the problem."[24] But despite Harding's initial support, Congress balked, in part because his critics believed, quite erroneously, that Mellon favored canceling the debts, and so they resolved to impose on him such terms and conditions as to make this impossible. Led by La Follette, the Senate set out to constrain the secretary by establishing a Debt Commission to carry out the negotiations. To be sure, Mellon was chairman, but he was obliged to share authority with two other cabinet members, as well as one senator and one member of the House. And stern parameters were set to the terms of any settlement that might be negotiated: all debts were to be paid within twenty-five years, by 1947, at a fixed rate of interest of 4.25 percent. Once again, Harding gave way. But as Mellon would discover, no negotiations would succeed on terms so stringent: they were, as Stanley Baldwin later noted, "a stone given by Congress to Mr. Mellon when he had asked for bread."[25]

Even within the Treasury itself, Mellon's position was far from secure. During the war, the department's staff had expanded considerably, especially in the Bureau of Internal Revenue, and after eight years of Democratic rule, Republican officials, senators, congressmen, and state bosses were eager to get their noses back in the patronage trough and to discharge accumulated obligations. Harry M. Daugherty, leader of the "Ohio gang," whom Harding had unwisely appointed attorney general, yielded to no one in this sentiment, and his view was well summarized in the slogan "Throwing the Democrats out and putting Republicans in." Though he had kept his distance from the Pittsburgh and Pennsylvania political machines, Mellon was not ignorant of the claims of political obligation. But he was also committed to running an efficient and responsible bureaucracy, and he sent out an early signal to this effect when he appointed David Blair, a North Carolina lawyer, to the important post of Commissioner of Internal Revenue. Meanwhile, Daugherty (and Harding) had other priorities.[26]

There was a preliminary skirmish in November 1921, when the president was lobbied by the attorney general to name one of his political protégés, James F. McConnochie, to be an assistant secretary at the Treasury. But he was so bereft of claims and qualifications that even Harding blenched at this.[27] Instead the president urged Mellon to take McConnochie on as supervising internal revenue agent in charge of the District of New York, leaving to the secretary the task of determining whether the man was "entirely capable and wholly worthy of such an assignment." Mellon concluded that McConnochie was neither, explaining himself in a long and unyielding letter to the president. For what he termed the most important field position in the Bureau of Internal Revenue—the agent oversaw a staff of more than five hundred—Mellon insisted McConnochie had no appropriate experience; indeed, at the Customs Service he had been criticized for "negligence of duty." Rumors of Mellon's impending resignation were rife, but Harding gave way, and the secretary appointed J. C. Wilmer, long-time Treasury staffer. "He has real capacity," Mellon bluntly informed Harding, "tact, and a fine personality, is an excellent executive, and knows how to handle men."[28]

But the battle of the trough was not yet won. In December 1921, without Mellon's knowledge or approval, Elmer Dover was appointed assistant secretary in charge of customs and internal revenue.[29] He came from Tacoma, Washington, but had spent much of his life in Ohio, as another member of the "gang." Active in Republican politics, he was a friend of Daugherty's and of Harding's, and notwithstanding his job description, his real task was to "Hardingize" the Treasury staff. In January 1922, his first month, he dismissed thirty long-serving employees of the Treasury's Bureau of Engraving "for the good of the service," replacing them with political hacks. Mellon learned of this shake-up, and also that Harding had authorized it, from the newspapers. Dover had charged these devoted public servants with improper conduct, but a subsequent inquiry ordered by Mellon exonerated them all. Still Dover was set to make further "reorganizational" purges, and it was rumored that staff in the Bureau of Internal Revenue would be next to go.

Early in April, Mellon responded to the stories in the press. "These reports," he wrote, "do not emanate from any official source, and are absolutely without foundation." "No such reorganization," he concluded, "is now or has been at any time contemplated." But in June, a list was leaked naming one hundred and fifty senior staffers in the bureau, all alleged to be Democrats, who would be the likely targets of the next partisan blast. There were many inaccuracies, and although the author was never identified, Dover was naturally suspected, and it was (rightly) assumed he was doing Harding's bidding.[30] Mellon dismissed the list as "so false and for the most part so ridiculous that in ordinary circumstances I should hesitate to take notice of it." "The affairs of the Treasury," he said, "are of too great importance to allow of interference to its proper conduct through the introduction of petty politics." "This department," he went on, "particularly the collection of revenue and the handling of the public debt, must be conducted on business principles and kept free at all times from detrimental influences." The administration might be in Republican hands, and Republican policies would be followed, but, he concluded, "those Democrats who hold positions in the Treasury have been retained because of their qualifications for the offices they hold, and I have no evidence of partisan activity on their part."[31]

Writing to Representative J. W. Dunbar, Mellon acknowledged the "great deal of gossip and misinformation" concerning the affairs of the Treasury, both "political and otherwise." But he insisted it "should not receive serious attention," and once again, amid rumors that Mellon might quit, Harding gave way. On July 18, 1922, he announced the resignation of assistant secretary Elmer Dover, who promptly returned to Tacoma.[32] In seeking his successor, Mellon declared himself guided by qualifications above all other considerations. Confidential inquiries Mellon initiated about one candidate sought to uncover "his general character, his business ability, whether he possesses administrative capacity for such an important and administrative position, and also the aptitude for handling a large volume of correspondence."[33] To be sure, the man in question would be a banker and a Republican, although the secretary's prime concern was ability, not affiliation. It was not a view designed to win favor with his boss, but Andrew Mellon had never had a superior before.

II. MAKING POLICY, MIXED RESULTS

When he entered the unknown, unfamiliar, and perilous territory of official Washington, the new secretary of the treasury had prudently brought with him two reliable Pittsburgh hands from that cadre of male Mellon minions who went where they were sent, did what they were told, and never talked about it. One was Arthur E. Sixsmith, who until 1931 served in Washington as Mellon's personal secretary, dealing with family, business, and salesroom correspondence.[34] The other was Colonel Frank Drake, previously at Gulf Oil as assistant to W. L. Mellon, and who remained on the company's payroll while he was seconded to Washington. At Gulf, Drake had handled the negotiations with the Treasury concerning taxes the business owed on wartime profits, which dealings he had successfully concluded before Mellon's appointment. He therefore knew his way around the corridors of power, and for two years would serve Mellon in a "private and confidential capacity." At breakfast time and in the evenings, Drake was a friendly face and a trusted confidant, but his chief task was to make discreet inquiries about Treasury staff, both existing and prospective. He would thus prove an essential adjutant in Mellon's battles with the president and the attorney general.[35]

Mellon could create his own private entourage by the familiar expedient of shifting around some loyal retainers, but his appointment had been so long delayed that he'd never had the chance to recruit his own official staff, as was customary at the time; thus he was obliged to retain the senior figures of the Wilson administration.[36] It turned out to be a great piece of luck, for among them, and by far the most important, was S. Parker Gilbert, who had resolved to leave before Mellon persuaded him to stay. A graduate of Harvard Law School and later a partner in J. P. Morgan and Company, Parker Gilbert was so able that in June 1921 Mellon convinced Congress to create the special post of undersecretary of the treasury for him. In this capacity, he served as a bridge between the previous and present administrations, as well as being the most potent influence on Mellon's policymaking. He drafted much of his new master's official correspondence and memoranda, from the very beginning urging upon Mellon those very policies which had been advocated but not implemented during the last, directionless months of the Wilson administration: a lowering of interest rates and domestic debt, tax reform in preference to tariff adjustment, a tight rein on government spending, and the rationalization of foreign debt.[37]

When Mellon was appointed, interest rates were running at 7 percent, the Federal Reserve Board having raised them in the immediate aftermath of the war. Some board governors believed that high rates were essential to prevent stock market speculation, but Mellon was worried that recent increases had helped bring about what he regarded as "the present unfavorable conditions." He argued that lower rates would be more beneficial as an economic stimulant, and during his first months in office, he persuaded the board to reduce rates to 5 percent, signaling a significant change in policy.[38] As he explained to Joseph Fordney, chairman of the House Ways and Means Committee, "the tendency now is toward somewhat of a relaxation or reduction of interest rates generally over the country, but the movement will be slow." "There is," he went on, "nothing which I know of that can be done toward accelerating the return to lower rates, other than the extent to which they may be influenced by changes in the discount rates of the Federal Reserve Banks." These, he said, were being lowered, and it would "be the policy of the Federal Reserve Banks to make further reductions from time to time."[39]

But this was not the only reason for Mellon's concern about interest rates. The biggest and most immediate difficulty confronting him was the $7.5 billion of short-term government debt, accumulated at rates varying from 3.75 percent to 6 percent, some of which would come due for repayment in only two years.[40] There was no possibility of paying these debts in that time: the economy was depressed, government revenue was declining, and there were widespread demands for tax reduction. Here was a banker's problem, and Mellon devised a banker's solution to make the short-term debt "more manageable": he refinanced the loans at lower rates, thereby saving the Treasury (and the taxpayer) $200 million a year, and he extended the term of repayment, by staggering the dates of maturity on the new loans from 1923 to 1928.[41] Between 1921 and 1923, Mellon offered the American public $7.5 billion of his new securities, all redeemable by 1928, and bearing the average rate of interest of 4.75 percent. The First Lady inaugurated the new scheme, all the issues were oversubscribed, and this enabled Mellon to pay off the miscellaneous tax certificates, notes, war savings warrants, and other forms of floating debt that had been clogging federal finances since the armistice.[42]

Mellon was also turning his attention to the longer-term matter of reforming the federal tax code. His aims were clear, and at the time were widely shared by Republicans and Democrats alike. He sought a system that would be more rational and coherent. He believed that reducing taxation on business earnings would enable more of the profits to be plowed back in for expansion and growth, thereby creating new jobs and promoting economic recovery. And he wanted to reduce rates of personal income tax on the very wealthy—not to let them pay *less* tax but, on the contrary, to encourage them to pay *more*. For it was clear to Mellon that with the prevailing high rates on individual incomes, most of the rich were avoiding federal income tax by investing in "tax-exempt" securities: state and municipal bonds whose interest the federal government could not legally tax.[43] (Mellon had not availed himself of this strategy, as his own large tax bills clearly attest.) If federal taxes were significantly reduced, Mellon reasoned, it would then become rational for the rich to move their investments out of tax-exempt securities, which produced low yields, and into taxable industrial stocks, on which the return was generally higher. With the top federal tax rate reduced to an optimal 25 percent, Mellon calculated that the net income rich individuals would draw from industrial investments would be higher, even after paying federal taxes at the lower rate, than the gross income that could be enjoyed from the tax-exempt bonds.[44]

Here were the lineaments of what in a later guise would be called the American supply-side revolution. Advised by Parker Gilbert, Mellon had fully worked out his reform plans by the end of the summer.[45] He wanted to reduce the top surtax rate from 65 percent to 32 percent for 1921 and to 25 percent thereafter, and he was eager to repeal some of the minor wartime "nuisance" taxes. He also wished to abolish the excess profits tax, effective January 1, 1921, provided he could increase the corporation tax from 10 percent to 12.5 percent, which he calculated would still leave business on balance better off.[46] But in the House of Representatives, the farm bloc objected to the immediate repeal of the excess profits tax, which it insisted should be retained another year, and personal exemptions were increased from $1,000 to $1,500 for single men, and from $2,000 to $2,500 for married men, which would be much more attractive to lower-income taxpayers than Mellon's original scheme. In the Senate, where the farm bloc was better organized, Mellon's proposals were further modified. Eventually passed just before Thanksgiving, the Revenue Act of 1921 postponed the repeal of the excess profits tax, accepted the increase in the corporation tax, reduced the maximum surtax rate to 50 percent, and kept the increased exemptions for those with lower incomes. President Harding took comfort in having fulfilled his campaign pledge to cut taxes, but Mellon's proposed reductions for those with high incomes had been emasculated, and he was unhappy with the final outcome.[47]

As Mellon's tax reform proposals were variously implemented and rebuffed, additional pressure was being exerted on the federal budget as a result of demands that the government pay what was called "the bonus." From the day the Harding administration took office, the American Legion and its political sympathizers began their first campaign for "adjusted compensation" (as "the bonus" was properly called), namely cash gratuities for all able-bodied Americans who had served in the First World War. At that time, the Treasury was already spending $500 million a year for the care of disabled veterans; it was estimated that payment of "the bonus" would cost as much as $5 billion more. Mellon approved of payments to disabled ex-servicemen, but he drew the line at a measure that would oblige him to raise money for men who had returned healthy and uninjured.[48] The levies and loans necessary to generate sufficient revenues would jeopardize his hopes for tax reform and debt reduction. (He also shared his father's dislike of ordinary military men.) "It would be the greatest relief to the Treasury and the country as a whole," he wrote to Charles Hamlin at the Federal Reserve Board, "if the bonus question could be disposed of, once and for all."[49]

But the issue stubbornly refused to go away. In the spring of 1921, a bonus bill was introduced into the House, which it carried by a solid majority. Although Mellon voiced strong objections, the bill reached the Senate, where it was killed only after President Harding, in a rare display of public support for his secretary of the treasury, visited the floor in the summer of 1921 to speak against it.[50] But early the following year, with midterm elections coming up that autumn, Congress was more determined than ever to give the voters what they wanted. Mellon made it plain that the bonus would require additional taxation, but with the support of Democrats and the farm bloc, the measure had passed both the House and the Senate by Election Day.[51] Once again, Harding exerted himself: he vetoed the bill. In a statement co-authored with Mellon, he deplored the attempt to establish a "precedent of distributing public funds whenever the proposal and the numbers affected make it seem politically appealing to do so." While the House managed the two-thirds majority needed to override the veto, the Senate did not. Thus was thwarted a demand Mellon would always deplore, and which he dismissed as a financially irresponsible piece of "class legislation" in favor of a minority group.[52]

At the same time, the secretary was confronting the problem of American loans to foreign countries, which had exceeded $10 billion between 1917 and 1920.[53] They had been temporary expedients organized on an ad hoc basis, a jumble of notes and IOUs payable on demand at 5 percent, and they had been negotiated on the presumption that more permanent and thorough arrangements would be made when hostilities were over. Most of the money borrowed by the Allies, especially Britain and France, had been spent on the purchase of war matériel in the United States, so this was not a dead loss for the economy. But there were in all more than twenty debtor nations, who owed an additional $1.5 billion in unpaid interest due. With Europe mired as deeply in depression as America, and with its economies devastated after the war, there was a real fear that no solution acceptable to all could be reached. Across the Atlantic, the predominant sentiment was that all debts between nations should be canceled, and that America, whose casualties did not come close to those of its European allies, should write off the whole amount in the interests of goodwill and the global economy. The British especially, owing almost half the total amount, were of such a mind, and the governing Lloyd George coalition was vigorously calling for cancellation.[54]

Despite certain fears in Congress to the contrary, Mellon was strongly against any policy of debt cancellation. "We ended the war," he noted, "with everyone owing us and our owing no one," and as a banker no less than a patriot, he was appalled that Britain might renege on what he described as "the greatest credit operation in the history of the world."[55] But while the American in him was determined to collect the debts, the practical banker knew that a debt could be repaid only on terms which were acceptable and realistic for both parties. It was not possible for the

European nations to pay in gold, because after spending so much on the war, their reserves were insufficient. Nor could they, with a global recession and high new American tariff barriers, be realistically expected to pay in goods. What was needed was a brokered settlement: here was a bankers' problem which Mellon had looked forward to solving—until the establishment of the Debt Commission eroded his autonomy. In setting parameters of term and rate, the commission had codified provisions which Mellon believed unrealistic, and which threatened to tie his hands. But encouraged by his success in addressing the problem of domestic debt, he now turned his attention overseas.

The obvious place to begin was Britain, America's closest ally and greatest debtor, where the political situation became more favorable to a settlement with the fall of the Lloyd George coalition in November 1922. In the new Conservative government headed by Andrew Bonar Law, the chancellor of the exchequer was the then relatively unknown Stanley Baldwin. Unlike their predecessors, both the prime minister and the chancellor shared Mellon's view that Britain was honor-bound to meet its obligations. Early in 1923, Baldwin sailed to the United States, accompanied by Montagu Norman, governor of the Bank of England, and Auckland Geddes, the British ambassador. In addition to Mellon, and as required by Congress, the American commission consisted of Charles Hughes and Herbert Hoover (from the cabinet), Reed Smoot (chairman of the Senate Finance Committee), and Theodore Burton (from the House). Between them, these men sought to settle what Baldwin, knowingly echoing Mellon, described as "the largest single financial transaction in the history of the world." Not surprisingly, in reaching an eventual settlement, Mellon and Baldwin were the central figures.[56]

Mellon got on well with both Baldwin, who was a businessman by profession, and Norman, a fellow banker. Encouragingly, Britain had recently resumed interest payments on the debt. But the country was in no better shape than the other impoverished European powers. Its gold reserves were too depleted and its goods too expensive to repay America in treasure or wares, and the congressionally mandated rate of 4.25 percent was fantasy, as was full repayment within twenty-five years. Mellon realized this and, taking command of the proceedings in a way that no one had expected, urged that negotiations proceed informally, on the understanding that it was better to reach a settlement based on Britain's ability to pay than not to reach one at all.[57] He presided at the meetings, which all took place in secret (the final gathering was in his apartment), and there eventually emerged a proposal to present to the U.S. Congress and the British

Parliament. By making an immediate cash payment, Britain would reduce the outstanding loan from $5 billion to $4.6 billion, and the balance would be paid off within sixty-two years, at 3 percent for the first ten years and at 3.5 percent from 1933 until 1984.

These terms were far more generous than any Mellon and his committee had been legally empowered to authorize, and the rates of interest were particularly lenient. Even so, and as Murray McMullen explained to Mellon, many in Britain regarded the terms as "unduly onerous." But the secretary believed "the arrangement made was the best that could be accomplished under the circumstances." "There was," he went on, "a great element of public opinion, and particularly of sentiment in Congress, that the terms finally arrived at were too favorable to Great Britain, their contention being that the rate of interest should be equivalent to that which is being paid by our government on its war debt." "The rate arranged," he concluded, "was from 1.25 to 1.75% below that which is being paid upon our government obligations."[58] Eventually, Mellon prevailed, and the deal, ratified by both Congress and Parliament, set the precedent for subsequent negotiations with the remaining debtor countries: all loans would be repaid in full over sixty-two years, at interest calculated on the basis of each country's ability to pay.[59] It was also a precedent in another way: this settlement of international obligations opened the way for the debtor nation to return to the gold standard.

Against this early undoubted success must be set Mellon's less happy experience with Prohibition. Despite the president's nagging, his heart was never in it, not so much because of the Overholt Distillery, but because he was no teetotaler himself, and thought the measure extreme and unproductive.[60] He also regretted the Treasury's responsibility for enforcing a law he knew to be unenforceable, which needlessly burdened a government department whose prime concern was raising revenue, not the alien duties of detection and policing. Indeed, before Mellon took office, there had been talk of transferring enforcement to the Justice Department, and he would vainly press for this change during most of his time as secretary.[61] Moreover, the funding was inadequate, the Treasury staff assigned to the task were generally unenthusiastic and of low caliber, and they were scarcely inspired by Roy A. Haynes, the chief of the Prohibition Unit, formerly the editor of a small-town Ohio newspaper and a crony of the president's.[62] Moreover, speakeasies, bootlegging, and smuggling were already rampant. In his report for 1921, Mellon passed over Prohibition in two vague paragraphs, and he incurred the wrath of zealous "drys" by urging the medicinal uses of alcohol.[63]

As befitted someone who had been a banker, the signal achievements of Mellon's first two years as secretary of the treasury concerned interest rates, debt, and income. He had persuaded the Federal Reserve Board to lower rates from the record postwar level, although thereafter he generally kept his distance. "At no time," Benjamin Strong wrote to Parker Gilbert early in 1923, "has the Reserve System been so free from anything approaching control by the Treasury as it has since Mr. Mellon took office."[64] The national debt had been reduced from $24 billion to $22.3 billion, and at that rate it would be paid off in full by 1952. With the president's support, Mellon had fended off congressional demands for "the bonus," and government spending had fallen by almost 50 percent, helped by the belated transition from war to peace. The fiscal years of 1922 and 1923 had both ended with a surplus of some $300 million.[65] But there was plenty undone and still to be done. The Revenue Act of 1921 was unsatisfactory, and he was determined to try to lower surtax rates still further. In the following year, he failed to push through Congress a constitutional amendment prohibiting tax-exempt bonds. As high priest of Prohibition, he was a "dismal flop," something Mellon did not mind but others emphatically (and increasingly) did. And the European economic scene was still dark, with few faint glimmers of recovery.[66]

III. KEEPING BUSY, STAYING IN BUSINESS

With so much to do, Andrew Mellon found himself putting in longer hours at the Treasury than had for some time been his custom at the Mellon National Bank.[67] "The work of the Department," he explained when refusing an invitation to an evening event, "in these early days of my administration is so heavy that I am compelled to start early and work late each day, and even then it is very difficult to accomplish all that is necessary." "After remaining in the office from nine until six," he went on, "it is physically undesirable, and I might say almost impossible, to continue on through the evening. I must save myself for the next day." Nor was this merely a matter of long days and full weeks, for even when Congress was not in session, the work of the department went on. Neither in 1921 nor in 1922 was Mellon able to take his cherished long summer vacation in Europe with the children. Instead, he rented Barton Lodge, at Hot Springs in Virginia, from July to September 1921, and Avalon at Prides Crossing, Massachusetts, from July to October of the following year. But such were the demands of his job that Mellon was only able to get away from Washington for long weekends to join Ailsa and Paul.[68]

Why was Mellon so much busier in Washington than in Pittsburgh? To be sure, the Treasury, the cabinet, and the Congress absorbed much of his time, but he was also doing other things. One such activity was talking to the press. Given Mellon's famous dislike for newspapers and his dread of publicity, it was scarcely surprising that in the beginning, journalists did not know what to make of "the most widely unknown plutocrat in the firmament." Some reporters found "an aesthetic, almost a spiritual aspect to his countenance," while to others it seemed that "gray is the color that most effectively expresses his personality." He was variously described as resembling "a tired double-entry book keeper who was afraid of losing his job" and as looking like "a dried-up dollar bill that any wind might whisk away."[69] The biographical information he provided for the *Congressional Directory* of 1921 amounted to scarcely six lines, and when pressed by newspapermen for more personal details, Mellon initially dismissed such questions as "unduly digging into a man's private life." "Just why should the Secretary be expected to talk to the reporters?" he responded to one who wanted to know more.[70]

But he was now a public man, heading one of the most vital departments of government, and since he needed popular and congressional support for his proposals, he was obliged to spend time explaining and justifying them by talking with reporters and by giving regular press conferences. A notoriously poor public speaker, Mellon found the former activity easier than the latter. He regularly gave long interviews to individual journalists, which easily blended personal detail, information about the nation's finances, and general reflections on government policy. But although he was unfailingly courteous, he did not enjoy facing forty-odd importunate newsmen, and he found it difficult to look reporters straight in the eye. Many of his responses were a compound of hesitation, discomfort, and evasion: "I don't know"; "No man can answer that"; "There is a great deal I have to learn." He never gave the impression that he knew all the answers. "You know," he observed after three years in office, "the press conferences have been an education to me. The newspaper men come in here and ask me a lot of questions about things I know nothing about, and when they leave I send for somebody who knows, and find out all about them. And the next time they come I know."[71] Given his dislike of journalists, Mellon's relations with the press would prove generally better than expected, mainly because he put his mind to it.

The secretary also worked on the bestowal of patronage, at both federal and state level, with greater zeal and enthusiasm than his opposition to Elmer Dover's appointment might have suggested—a blatant contradiction that was somehow lost on him. In politics as in business, Mellon regarded patronage as indispensable, provided the right people were appointed, and that those dispensing favors did not interfere in his purview, although—another contradiction—he might interfere in theirs. He lobbied the secretary of state and the president on behalf of Cyrus E. Woods, who had been so useful at the time of the divorce, obtaining for him the embassy in Tokyo after he had served as ambassador to Spain. He made inquiries for his nephew E. P. Mellon, in the hope (vain, as it happened) of obtaining for him federal commissions to design hospitals and embassies.[72] He corresponded, too, with Pennsylvania senators and local leaders about such positions as the mayoralty of Pittsburgh, the (quaintly named) appraiser of the port, and vacant judgeships. "I am in entire accord with your suggestions," he wrote to Senator Boies Penrose early in his tenure at the Treasury, concerning various matters of patronage, "and in my consideration of these matters shall be guided accordingly." Mellon would regularly claim that while in Washington he had not "kept touch with affairs at home or with [the] politics of the state," but he was more involved than his denials implied.[73]

Indeed, he had little choice in the matter, for the deaths of Senators Knox and Penrose within a few weeks of each other at the end of 1921 compelled him, suddenly and unexpectedly, to assume a more prominent position in Pennsylvania politics than he had ever expected or desired. One reason he had agreed to accept the Treasury in the first place was the assurance that Knox and Penrose would champion his policies, defend his interests in the upper house, and try to get Prohibition enforcement moved from the Treasury to the Justice Department. Moreover, as the boss of Pennsylvania politics, Penrose was determined to keep the state machine well oiled and working for the Republican administration. But within months of Mellon's taking office, his two main props were suddenly knocked out from under him. He would mourn Knox as "an affectionate friend from boyhood days" whose death left "an aching void." Knox's Senate seat was Mellon's for the asking, but he had too much to do at the Treasury and so declined.[74] Knox's term was served out by William A. Crow, the Republican state chairman, but he was old and ailing, and in office only briefly. In November 1922, with Mellon's support, David A. Reed, son of James Reed and also a lawyer, was elected for a full six-year term, on the clear understanding that he would take on the task of supporting and defending the secretary and his policies on the floor of the Senate. As a loyal Mellon man, he effectively did so for the remainder of the decade. By convention, the other Senate seat was held by someone from the eastern part of the state, and so, again with Mellon's support, it was effectively offered to the Philadelphia lawyer George Wharton Pep-per, who in 1922 was elected to serve out Penrose's term, which would expire in 1926.[75]

So far, so good for Mellon: the successors to Penrose and Knox had been deftly arranged to his satisfaction. But this ease was deceptive, for the death of Penrose left no acknowledged head of what had been "the most unscrupulous machine in the country."[76] Even under Penrose, the Republicans in Pennsylvania had been incorrigibly fractious and they were often at war with themselves. Mellon had neither the enthusiasm nor the skills to deal with them in the way that Penrose had habitually managed. He hoped that his nephew W. L. Mellon might handle day-to-day matters for him at the local level. Mellon clearly believed that WL's wheeler-dealer skills at obtaining oil concessions and streetcar franchises could be adapted to state politics. But WL had no political judgment, and having no serious interest in politics, he was unwilling to put in the daily work required, preferring to spend more time away from Pennsylvania on his yacht.[77] In consequence, Mellon's position in state politics soon began to deteriorate, and neither in Pennsylvania nor in Congress was he able to provide the sort of leadership that Penrose and his predecessors had.

Even as Reed and Pepper were being pushed forward into their senato-rial seats, the Mellons suffered their first significant reverse.[78] In the spring of 1922, W. L. Mellon had accepted on behalf of his uncle a "har-mony" agreement with the Vare brothers, who had taken over as bosses in Philadelphia and now had designs on the Republican machine statewide. The Vares were willing to let David Reed run unopposed in the forth-coming Senate primary, provided the Mellons supported the Vares' can-didate for governor, George C. Alter, the state attorney general. It was an indication of the limits to Mellon power, and it was soon followed by another. For within weeks, Alter was unexpectedly challenged by Gifford Pinchot, an old Bull Moose Republican and a onetime Roosevelt sup-porter. Although the Mellons and the Vares backed Alter, Pinchot won the Republican primary by a narrow margin, and he was duly elected gov-ernor in the autumn, when Reed and Pepper won their Senate seats.[79] The Mellons and the Vares had reluctantly decided not to oppose him, but Pinchot was a maverick, vehemently in favor of Prohibition, and he held no brief for those who, like the Mellons, had preferred Taft to Roo-sevelt in 1912. "Pinchot's administration seems so far to be satisfactory and in harmony with most of the party leaders," Mellon informed Cyrus Woods early in 1923. He could not have been more wrong: the governor was no Mellon supporter, and his election represented a repudiation of the Harding administration, of which he would soon become an outspoken critic. Instead of spending less time (and money) on Pennsylvania politics, Mellon would soon be spending more.[80]

Dealing with the press, dispensing patronage, and trying to herd cats in his home state's GOP: altogether these constituted a great drain on Mellon's working hours. But there was another and more dubious explanation: his continuing involvement with his brother in business. To be sure, Andrew rarely visited Dick in Pittsburgh, and Dick went to Washington infrequently, but as soon as Andrew arrived in the capital, he had installed a private telephone line in his office linking him directly to his brother at the bank. There are no records of their conversations, but they certainly did discuss business, as Colonel Drake made plain when he recalled W. L. Mellon's explanation of why he himself would eventually be summoned back to Pittsburgh from Washington: "AW and RB have been talking about Standard Steel Car. There are some things there they do not like, and so on, and they want you to go over and run it."[81] The brothers also corresponded about their companies. In November 1921, for example, Andrew sent Dick a letter urging that surveyors from Koppers should look into some coal property which had reverted to the brothers from James Guffey. "We should have this drilling and investigation carried out," Andrew insisted, "in order to have some more definite knowledge of the property, and I would advise authorizing them to go ahead on the matter."[82] Though no longer legally bound as partners, "my brother and I" were still a collaborative entity, and it seems unlikely that Dick made any major decisions without consulting Andrew first. He had always been the subordinate figure, and although he was now ostensibly (and somewhat reluctantly) in charge of affairs, that continued to be essentially the case.[83]

Mellon also remained in regular contact with those senior company executives whom he had personally picked and promoted: their surviving letters make plain that substantial matters were discussed and decided in this period. He corresponded at length with Charles D. Marshall about the "current business earnings and prospects" of McClintic-Marshall, and when Marshall went on a visit to investigate the operations of another Mellon company, Andrew told him he "would be very much interested in hearing a report resulting from your inspection trip."[84] He alerted H. B. Rust of Koppers to "some operations in the vicinity of Washington that have been developing a process of extracting the by-products from coal and eliminating the ash." "I only mention the matter for your information," he added coyly. In March 1922, Mellon received an advance proof of the annual report of the Pittsburgh Coal Company. "I have just looked over," he replied to the chairman, "the comparative balance sheet of January 1, 1916, and January 1, 1922." "These indicate," he went on, revealing an undiminished zeal for columns of figures, "a very gratifying financial and operating condition, and I congratulate you on the showing you have been able to make, notwithstanding so many unfavorable conditions of the industry."[85]

It was not all discreet oversight. Mellon spent much time in Washington lobbying openly and persistently on behalf of "his" companies. When McClintic-Marshall put in a bid for the construction of the Yellow River bridge in China, he took the matter up with Charles E. Hughes. "The State Department," Mellon informed Marshall, "cannot recommend a particular tender or form, but all will be done that can be done." When the House Committee on Rivers and Harbors refused to sanction the expenditure of $250,000 on a project in which Gulf Oil was "specially interested," Mellon approached Congressman Morris, "who promised to assist us," and the committee duly agreed "to re-open the matter."[86] And when the provisions of the Fordney-McCumber Tariff were being discussed, Mellon did all he could to ensure they were favorable to his companies. Alcoa benefited from a substantial rise in the duty on aluminum, from two to five cents per pound on ingot, and from five to nine cents per pound on sheet, which effectively perpetuated its monopoly. And in the case of Carborundum, Mellon made no secret of his eagerness to see supplies of aloxite from Canada remain "on the free list." "I wish," he wrote to the company president, F. J. Tone, "you would send me a memorandum of your argument on the subject for use of one of the Senators to whom I have spoken."[87]

With so many irons in the fire, it was scarcely surprising that Mellon was working longer and harder than before. But the extent of his exertions was obscured because he would not own up to everything he was doing. From the very beginning, he had been adamant that he had "not kept in touch with any outside business," and he would later claim that in 1921 he terminated all active connection with his companies "as completely as if I had died at the time." "I have not," he flatly insisted, "concerned myself with their affairs, and I have not endeavoured to control or dictate their operations in any way."[88] W. L. Mellon corroborated the claim that when his uncle "got on the train to go to Washington, on March 3, 1921, he had divorced himself from business . . . He was really getting out of business. There is no doubt about that." Instead, he had "imposed on himself strict devotion to public service."[89] But uncle and nephew protested too much. From the very beginning of his time at the

Treasury, Mellon was contravening the spirit, and perhaps also the letter, of the 1789 statute that prohibited the secretary of the treasury from participating in trade or commerce, either directly or indirectly.

Almost from the outset, there were critics and enemies who suspected as much, though they had no details of Mellon's secret exchanges with family and retainers over business. During the debates about his role in the settlement of foreign loans, Senator Thomas E. Watson, a Democrat from Georgia, who had been William Jennings Bryan's running mate on the People's Party ticket in 1896, was first to openly challenge Mellon's eligibility to hold office. The secretary, Watson insisted, was in clear breach of the 1789 statute, and as a result "could on any day we see fit be impeached." But at this early stage, Mellon was given the benefit of the doubt: Watson's criticisms were easily dismissed, and he died soon after. "There have," Mellon wrote disingenuously, "been many such vicious and unfounded attacks since I have been in office, and I have constantly ignored them. Without any foundations of truth, they cannot have any serious effect." But they *did* have substantial foundations of truth, as he must have known. At the beginning of his tenure, as the economy first recovered and then boomed, the charges gained little political traction or momentum. But as Mellon's term of office lengthened, and as his reputation collapsed in the aftermath of the depression of 1929–32, such charges would become more frequent, and the chickens would come home to roost.[90]

The secretary's day of reckoning was also delayed because opposition to him, even as it mounted, came from divergent quarters: from veterans disgruntled over being denied their bonus; from farmers resentful of his relative indifference to the plight of agriculture; from those in Congress, both Democrats and Republicans, who disliked him personally or disapproved of his policies; from members of the public who (erroneously) thought his tax reforms were primarily designed to make the rich richer; and from committed Prohibitionists who (rightly) believed that Mellon was derelict in his enforcement duty and (wrongly) thought he still maintained an interest in the Overholt Distillery.[91] When opponents wrote in, as they often did, Mellon replied at length: insisting (not always honestly) on the legality of his conduct, and defending (not always plausibly) the vigor and energy of his department in "doing everything possible" to enforce the Eighteenth Amendment.[92] But facts are facts: Mellon knowingly continued to participate in business, repeatedly blurred the lines between enterprise and government, and enjoyed taking and serving a drink. When criticized, he responded with disdain, and insisted that he always acted with the strictest propriety and for the most patriotic and honorable ends. He may genuinely have believed this. It was not the whole truth, but for the time being, that did not seem to matter.

IV. THE PRIVATE LIFE OF A PUBLIC MAN

Among the many letters of congratulation that Mellon received on his appointment to the Treasury were one from Carman Messmore of M. Knoedler & Company and another from Sir Joseph Duveen. "Although I realized," Messmore wrote, "it is going to be a tremendous amount of work, I am truly thankful that our country has a man of your caliber at the helm in these troubled times." Duveen, by contrast, "permitted himself the pleasure" of sending his good wishes, and soon after he, the most importunate of salesmen, informed Mellon that the Washington home of Mr. and Mrs. Belmont would be available, either for purchase or for rent.[93] Both realized that Mellon would need a residence appropriate to his high office—and pictures for its walls. At a time when the international art market was as depressed as the rest of the economy, and when the sale of paintings in America was still burdened by a wartime "luxury" tax of 10 percent, Mellon's new need presented a lucrative prospect. But he was not to be rushed: although he had already got his eye on an apartment, he told Duveen he had decided "for the present to defer consideration of any permanent location until later," and he insisted that "with the pressure of matters here in the beginning, interest in the way of art has to be dropped." He added, teasingly, that he was "hoping soon to have the business in control, so that I may have some time for other than Department matters," but he would buy few paintings in 1921.[94]

Naturally, during his first months in Washington, Mellon's prime domestic concern was to establish a residence. Initially, he lodged in the New Willard Hotel, where he took his breakfast at the coffee shop in the basement before walking the short distance to the Treasury building.[95] But this was only a temporary accommodation. He had discussed the matter with Ailsa before the job had been formally offered him, and quickly settled on an apartment on the fifth floor of the recently constructed McCormick Building, one block east of Dupont Circle, at 1785 Massachusetts Avenue. Designed by Jules H. de Sibour, in the Beaux-Arts style, it was the finest place of its kind in the capital, the individual apartments being the largest and loftiest in the city. Mellon took the whole top floor. There were six bedrooms, extensive quarters for the butler and the maids, an oval reception hall, a salon, a living room measuring forty-five feet by twenty-four, and a dining room that was only ten feet shorter.[96] This opulent abode would be Mellon's home throughout his Washington years, and the annual rent of twenty-five thousand dollars was more than twice his official salary. "Remember Andy," his brother James Ross warned (or teased?), "father always said we should live within our income." Mellon had no difficulty in so doing, but for most Washington-based politicians, such a place, at such a price, was inconceivable.[97]

With Mellon thus established in the capital as a major public figure, Duveen redoubled his efforts to ingratiate himself with him. He offered to arrange a meeting with his "friend and client Henry Goldman, of Goldman Sachs," who had recently returned from Europe, and would welcome the chance to talk to the new treasury secretary about financial conditions across the Atlantic. There is no evidence that Mellon took him up on this offer. But Duveen and Mellon certainly met several times in Washington during the first half of 1922, as the dealer insisted he had "many matters of some importance" to discuss.[98] By the summer, Duveen was determined to win the contract for furnishing and decorating the Mellon apartment, and he brashly sent him extensive (and expensive) estimates. But Mellon eluded him again, turning once more to French and Company, whom he had recently employed at Woodland Road. Duveen was "very grieved" at the news: "cannot understand what has happened," he cabled in dismay from London.[99] French and Company duly provided the eighteenth-century French furniture, a specially designed Steinway baby grand, and Oriental rugs costing $125,000. The Flemish tapestries were moved from Pittsburgh to Washington, as were some of the pictures, including Gainsborough's portrait of George IV as Prince of Wales, Gilbert Stuart's portrait of George Washington, and Turner's evening view of the Thames at Mortlake Terrace.[100]

But Duveen was determined to capture Mellon as a major client, and in the aftermath of his decoration defeat, he opened up other lines of approach and attack. Mellon had been quite correct in surmising earlier that Duveen had bribed members of his household: Duveen continued to do so throughout the Washington years. It was also rumored that an underling at the Treasury was in his pay, and that the contents of Mellon's wastebasket were forwarded to the Duveen salesrooms in New York on a regular basis.[101] Armed with such intelligence, Duveen was able to plan and time his approaches carefully. Early in 1923, he urged Mellon to have his portrait painted by Oswald Birley, in whom Duveen reposed "great confidence." "I am well aware," he pompously informed Mellon, "that I assume a great moral responsibility in recommending any artist, but in this instance I do so with perfect frankness, feeling confident that the result would be to your entire satisfaction." Almost as an aside, Duveen added that Birley would also be painting Mr. and Mrs. Henry E. Huntington, who had recently bought Gainsborough's *Blue Boy* at a record price: surely Mellon deserved no less? Soon after, Duveen shipped a canvas and easel to Mellon's apartment, and the artist began work. "I understand from Birley," Duveen wrote to Mellon in April 1923, "that he is making wonderful progress with your portrait, and that he considers the head to be one of the finest that he has ever executed."[102]

Later that year, Mellon and Duveen encountered each other in the elevator at Claridge's Hotel in London, a meeting that was later immortalized in a cartoon by Edward Sorel, who depicted Duveen as a huge pussycat, in top hat, spats, and striped trousers, stepping into the lift, where Mellon, his prey, cowered as an aged, tiny, shriveled bird. "Mr. Mellon, I presume?" Duveen's likeness purrs—disingenuously, for the "spontaneous" encounter had been carefully planned. "What a delightful surprise." According to Duveen, Mellon was now as "ready" for him as he was for Mellon.[103] But this account cannot be literally true. It was not their first meeting, as is often alleged; and it seems more likely to have taken place in 1923 than two years earlier, the date normally given, for Mellon did not visit Europe in 1921. Nor is there any evidence that Duveen had arranged things so he might "accidentally" encounter Mellon in the hotel elevator. But Duveen did go to great trouble to establish where Mellon would be staying during his visit, as coded telegrams flew back and forth between his offices in London and New York; and he definitely met Mellon in London in July 1923, when he urged upon him a Van Dyck and a Cuyp, quoted at "$220,000 and $130,000 respectively." "So," Duveen grandly instructed an underling in New York, "kindly make a note of these in your prices asked book."[104]

But Mellon was not as easily cornered by Duveen as Sorel suggests. At the time of his move to Washington, he had on his walls in Pittsburgh the two Tintorettos of Venetian senators and ter Borch's *The Suitor's Visit*. For the three pictures, Duveen wanted $513,000, which included a 10 percent discount. The Tintorettos were subsequently returned, and in June 1922, Mellon offered $175,000 for the ter Borch. With the discount, Duveen wanted $220,000 for it. Mellon expressed a willingness to go up to $200,000, if Duveen could produce proof that the painting was worth it. As Duveen could only insist that it was "the finest and most important ter Borch that exists in any private collection in the world," Mellon got it for $175,000.[105] Nor, despite Duveen's hopes, did Mellon show any interest in the Cuyp or the Van Dyck: his only other major purchase from Duveen was Sir Thomas Lawrence's portrait *Lady Templeton and Child*, for which he paid $250,000. It was his most expensive acquisition yet, but Mellon again had the last word. "I have not received from you," he wrote Duveen, "the usual description and date regarding this picture, which please send, together with your understanding of the arrangements as to your repurchase of it on my moving from Washington to Pittsburgh, in [the] event that I do not find it appropriate or desirable in size for my house there."[106]

In dealing with Duveen, Mellon was now displaying the sort of cunning and strong-nerved bluffing of an accomplished poker player, or of a businessman who had preferred to make his money in the shadows rather than in the glare of publicity. His determination to get the best terms more than matched Duveen's mastery of the hard sell. And Mellon was equally unyielding with Knoedler. As they moved his pictures from Pittsburgh to Washington, they urged upon him the need to repeal the wartime "luxury tax," and Roland Knoedler assured his "dear Andy" that he was "a friend of the house, besides being a valuable client whose interests will always be ours."[107] But Mellon was not wholly of the same opinion. His relations with Carman Messmore and Charles Henschel, who were now carrying on most of the business, were not as warm as those with Charles Carstairs or with Knoedler himself, and both of them addressed him as "Mr. Mellon." They pressed many pictures on him once he reached Washington, but they failed to interest him in Vermeer's *The Flute Player* (which for a time hung in his apartment), or in a *Nocturne* by Whistler. "I think it is a shame you did not buy the picture," a mournful Messmore wrote to him about the Vermeer, "as it is a wonderful opportunity and is one of the rarest things of its type which will ever come up in the entire world."[108]

By now, Mellon was much more confident in his own judgment of a painting's excellence and worth, and his commerce with Knoedler was more on his terms than on theirs. In February 1922, he bought back El Greco's *San Ildefonso of Toledo*, which he had originally purchased from them in October 1918, only to return it three months later for a full refund. Having paid $65,000 for the painting earlier, he now reacquired it for $35,000.[109] Soon after, he offered $40,000 for Raeburn's portrait of Colonel Francis James Scott, on condition that he might return it at any time during the next two years for a full refund. Knoedler did not want to make this term "an absolute obligation," but in the end they had no

choice but to agree.[110] At about the same time, Mellon acquired two portraits by Gainsborough, of Georgiana, Duchess of Devonshire, and of
Miss Elizabeth Lindley, for $75,600 the pair; but after they had been
hanging on his walls for well over a year, he refused to pay the final $735
that Knoedler believed to be due.[111] Finally, in December 1922, Mellon
paid $52,000 for the *Portrait of a Cavalier*, by Frans Hals. Messmore
assured Mellon that it was "as fine in quality in every respect" as the
Laughing Cavalier, but Mellon paid for it in part by returning two Rembrandt panels of King Saul and King David which he had acquired in
April 1918, and thereafter he purchased no more paintings through
Knoedler for the better part of a year.[112]

Mellon's collecting in the capital thus got off to a relatively slow start.
Between the spring of 1921 and the summer of 1923, he spent less in total
with Knoedler and Duveen on pictures in Washington than he had
between January 1918 and December 1920 in Pittsburgh. And as his letter to Duveen concerning the Lawrence portrait made plain, he was not
expecting to stay all that long in the capital, or to take back to Pittsburgh
all of the new pictures. Among those he would certainly have planned to
keep were those associated with his family and those of himself. Mellon
had previously commissioned portraits of his wife and his children; now,
in addition to the likeness by Birley, he was himself a willing sitter for the
British artist William Orpen, and again Knoedler nursed the vain hope
that Sargent might also paint him.[113] Late in 1920, Mellon had commissioned a bust of the Judge from the sculptor F. Lynn Jenkins, and once he
reached Washington, he asked Jenkins for two busts of himself. He soon
added two more busts by the French sculptor Soudbinière. Finally, in
September 1922, he acquired a painting, allegedly by Lawrence, of Harriet Mellon, later Duchess of St. Albans, whom the Judge believed to be a
relation. Mellon paid $30,000 through Lewis and Simmons, which made
the duchess's portrait one of the few major works he would buy from a
dealer other than Knoedler or Duveen.[114]

By these purchases Mellon was creating an opulent setting for political
entertaining and for accommodating visiting family and friends. Ailsa,
though still chaperoned by Miss Sylvester, was also living at a faster
tempo, acting as her father's hostess. "Does Ailsa seem to like Washington?" Paul had asked his father soon after Andrew and his daughter
moved there. The answer was an emphatic yes. Her life at this time was
almost entirely social, to judge by a telegram Andrew dispatched to her on
April 26, 1922: "You are invited to dinner Saturday evening by Miss
Beack; to tea Sunday afternoon by Mrs. McKormick to meet Lord and

Lady Astor; to dinner Sunday evening by Olive Graef; to dinner Thursday fourth by Mrs. Larz Anderson.[115] As one of the richest heiresses of her generation, Ailsa was soon appearing regularly in the society pages of the Washington papers, but she was also criticized in some quarters for being aloof and standoffish (like her father), and she continued to suffer from nervous exhaustion or other unspecified ailments (like her mother). "Ailsa is much better," Nora wrote to Paul Ache, after one of her convalescent visits to the Hudson Valley farm, "but has become terribly dipped about herself, and it has been very difficult. I don't wonder that Andy turns her over to me at such times, but it really is no laughing matter, she has become so self-centered."[116]

There were no such difficulties with Paul, who was much happier at Choate than Ailsa had been at Miss Porter's. Although still lacking in confidence, he showed "industry and perseverance" and corresponded regularly with his father (as well as with his sister), whether about meeting up in Pittsburgh or New York or Washington, or about the fruit and food he had recently received; and he usually reported his grades, the latest school sports news, the friends he was making, and the movies he had seen.[117] "Paul's work is good from start to finish," his report card recorded in May 1921. "And he is in fine physical shape, too!" "It is a delight to see Paul's average make such a good gain," the headmaster noted a year later. "You will be glad to know that in Latin and French Paul now leads his divisions—no mean accomplishment."[118] But what would Paul's future be? "I do not wish," Andrew wrote to the headmaster, "to have his preparatory course prolonged, nor would I think it desirable for him to spend more time than may be necessary in college." "He is not," Andrew concluded, evoking his own father's cynicism and desire to be succeeded in the family business by a son, "likely at all to follow any professional occupation, so that a limited course in college, I believe, is all that will be required."[119] Like the Judge, he wanted no superfluous tuition.

Both Ailsa and Paul (when he was on vacation from Choate) divided their time between their father's apartment in Washington and their mother's farm on the Hudson. Now that all four of them were away from the tainted Pittsburgh environment, relations between Andrew and Nora became much easier. He helped her with the financing of the farm, and they exchanged news about the children in a friendly manner, dropping the acrimonious edge of the years immediately after their divorce. "Paul is having a good time," Andrew told Nora, after father and son had spent a weekend at Rolling Rock. "He drives about in the pony cart, goes fishing, and enjoys himself generally." And he signed himself "yours sincerely,

Andy."[120] "Paul looked very well, I thought, but rather thin," Nora informed Andrew after a visit, then added, "but of course he has grown up so quickly that that is natural." And she ended the letter, "With kindest regards. Always most sincerely. Nora." "Ailsa and I are thinking of going over to Philadelphia for a few days . . . to do some shopping," she wrote on another occasion. "Ailsa's cold has been quite bad," Nora continued, "but is much better today and she is quite cheerful. She sends her love."[121] Nora also seems to have been devoid of jealousy, indeed genuinely proud of Andrew's grand new public position. "I read all your utterances in the papers with great interest," she told him. "Paul seems to think he is getting a lot of exercise! Are you quite well?" She signed off, "Always affectionately, Nora."[122]

Their letters also touched on the continuing financial problems of her brothers, who were not finding life easy in postwar Britain. Leonard, having tried and failed to get "a settled job," had in desperation become a bookmaker, convinced that he would do well at it "in the long run." Andrew was predictably opposed to such a dubious and unseemly employ, but since, as he told Nora, it afforded her brother "his only opportunity to make a living," he reluctantly accepted the idea, and eventually "furnished the capital." "It is absolutely *final*," Leonard replied, for the umpteenth time. "I will never worry you again as long as I live." Three months later, he would again be pleading with Andrew for more cash.[123] Norman McMullen was also hard up, and in March 1923 he asked Andrew for a loan of £3,000: "I have not been able to live within my income for the last three years," he went on, offering a feeble explanation that was scarcely consistent with Mellon morality. It was not until the end of the year, and after further entreaties from Norman, that Andrew agreed to help him out.[124] In the case of Percy, Andrew was more immediately accommodating, advancing him loans totaling £1,400 in April and May 1923. Percy was appropriately grateful for this "opportunity to retrieve [his] position," though regretful that he could "never wholly regain [his] self-respect."[125]

To someone brought up on the Judge's stern injunctions about debt, the McMullen brothers must have seemed an incorrigible lot, and Andrew must by now have realized that he might never be free of their importuning. Even Nora, who had already shown herself inept at managing money, was "worried to death" about Leonard, to whom she was sending five thousand dollars a year, and she told Andrew of her brother's "wretched gambling" with dismay. But she remained grateful for his generosity toward her siblings, and now there were also some lighter moments between the former husband and wife.[126] "I have had an offer to buy a case of genuine Scotch Whisky in Newport!" Nora informed Andrew, fully aware of his responsibility to enforce Prohibition, which forbade the transport of alcohol across state lines. "Can you tell me how it would be possible to get it from there to here?" Andrew's reply has not survived, but the need was clearly urgent: "instead of expecting *less*," she told him on another occasion, "I find that people expect *more* at a dinner party than *before* Prohibition."[127] Such playfulness was something new, and it signaled the thawing in relations long wished by Nora and Ailsa. How had such a new tone—and, in Andrew's case, such a change of heart—come about?

Paradoxically, it was Nora's recent second marriage that had precipitated the very reconciliation with Andrew she had always wanted, but which he had continually refused following the bitter disillusionment of the divorce. It came about in the following way. In 1922, having ended her relationship with Charles Mustin, Nora began a new liaison, with Harry Lee, an Englishman who had recently established himself as an antiques dealer in New York.[128] Remembering what had happened the last time Nora had taken up with an itinerant Englishman, Andrew made inquiries about her latest beau, as to his matrimonial status and career and so forth. Nora was enraged when she found out about this latest investigation. "Do you not think," she told Andrew, "it would be more dignified and satisfactory to find out by direct methods whatever you feel you may wish to know about Mr. Lee?" "I am at a loss," she went on, "to know why you should take it for granted that I know nothing about him. I assure you it is quite the contrary." In response, Andrew sent her such information as he had been able to glean about Lee. "I was not disturbed by the report you sent me," Nora responded, "as I knew he had never been married. I happen to know everything else about him there is to know."[129]

In the autumn of 1922, Nora and Lee became engaged, and with the wedding date set for the spring of the following year, her main concern was once again her own precarious finances. Under the terms of the divorce settlement, one of the trust funds that Andrew had originally set up for her would cease payment when she remarried. The prospect of her income being halved was far from appealing, not least because following Mustin's long illness, the farm in the Hudson Valley had fallen into terrible neglect.[130] There was, Nora reported to Andrew, "not even a pig or chicken"; most of the implements had been "stolen or broken"; and the house needed repairs and alterations just "to make it possible to live there during the winters, as we expect to do." In the face of these anxieties, Andrew's formerly immovable and punitive resolve turned to sympathy: he agreed to waive the terms of the divorce settlement so that Nora could continue to enjoy the income from all her trust funds; and, following the precedent he had set with her Pittsburgh house, he bought the Hudson Valley farm and then returned it to her as a gift.[131]

By late February 1923, Nora and Lee had obtained their marriage license, though they did not intend to wed for some days. But the newspapers got hold of the story, and the very public announcement of Nora's plans, about which he had already known in private, came as a revelation to Andrew. His hostility to reconciliation suddenly dissolved, and he determined to try to get Nora back for himself before it was too late. His letter to her has not survived, but Nora's reply of March 7, the very day of her wedding to Lee, leaves no doubt as to what he must have written and proposed:

Andy, dear Andy, nearly all night I have thought and thought and prayed to do what was right. I cannot do what you ask me, dear, I simply cannot break my word. Even if I had a misgiving (which I have not) that it would not turn out well, it is better I should do what is honourable now. I realize only too keenly the other side, and it tears my heart to pieces. The children. Yourself. But Andy, I am not taking myself away any more now than I have been all these years. As far as my own personal happiness (which I think you do realize is not my first thought) I know I have nothing to fear. I am going to live the life I have always longed for, and for which I have waited so long. I do implore you Andy not to ask me again. I can do nothing but refuse, and it breaks me to pieces. Forgive me again for hurting you, but it is too late dear. Always the same, Nora.[132]

She clearly intended this to be final. Yet in two days, which though the first of her new married life seem to have been spent thinking more about her previous than her present husband, Nora wrote to Andrew again, in a state of high emotion. "Please destroy this, won't you?" she put in the top right corner. It is clear why she asked him to do so; it is equally clear why he instead kept the letter. "Dear, dear Andy," she began:

I miscalculated my strength when I thought that the fact of my doing what I still hope and pray was the right thing, would uphold me and give me comfort. The comfort has not come, and the awful pain in my heart does not lessen . . . I do so earnestly long to have you understand why I felt it was impossible to go back on my word at the last moment. Oh why, dear, did you not say something when I first told you of my engagement last fall?

If only you could have given me the faintest hope during all these years I would have waited till I died. But the hope I had had gradually died, and it was then that I felt I could bear no longer that dreadful loneliness. This is not a reproach, dear Andy, I have not even the shadow of one in my heart for you . . . I have known for many years that if you still cared for me I could have made you happier than you ever dreamed of being before, because all that horrible part of me that, in looking back seems to have been "devil-possessed," was dead and buried even before we were divorced . . .

Dear, dear Andy, even though I feel I have a mortal, inward, bleeding wound, still, I am so grateful not to have died without telling you how much I have loved and missed you all these years. As long as I live, it will always be the same . . . Think kindly of me sometimes, and if you can, write me. I should love if it will not bore you to write you from time to time of my life . . . This is the only letter I shall ever write you like this, dear, for it would be disloyal; but this time I cannot help it. Always, your devoted, Norchen.[133]

To this wrenching, heartfelt (perhaps theatrical?) missive, Andrew responded with unprecedented sensitivity and magnanimity, in words addressed, for the first time in ages, to his "Dear Norchen":

I have read your letter, and it has grieved me deeply, while at the same time bringing solace and abiding comfort. I have been sadly wrong, but must tell you how it was that I did not speak sooner. In the years of contention, there was on your part a seeming animosity and bitterness which I did not believe could disappear. When suggestions were made of conciliation, I believed you unfeeling, and did not think you could really care for me. However wrongly, I attributed to you motives of expediency and convenience . . .

I did not believe that any love existed for me, and so when I heard of your engagement to Mr. Lee it only gave me a heavy heart. When I learned that the day was so close at hand, I had a twinge of pain, and felt that I must see you. It was then [that] revelation and understanding came to me. It proved too late—your letter was so final. The old love was in my heart even while I was so obtuse and blind, and it makes me heartsick to think of you in all this time suffering so sadly alone. The past cannot be brought back, and we must look to the future. You have had more than your share of unhappiness, and are entitled to brighter days.

I want to be helpful to you now and always. You must look forward

and not allow anything of the past to distress you. Interest in farm and
garden will do much, and your married life can become a happy and contented one. For myself, aside from all else, the truth of our understanding
remains, and is an abiding comfort in my heart. I shall be interested
in your life, and pray for your happiness . . . God bless you, dearest
Norchen. Your ever loving Andy.[134]

Nora had come as close as she ever did to apologizing for the pain and
suffering she had caused him and to regretting her mishandling and
manipulation of Ailsa, which "hurt my little girl so much"; she owned up
to being "an unskilled mariner on life's seas, always doomed to dash my
ships on the rocks." (There would be more choppy waters ahead.) As for
Andrew: the disillusionment and embarrassment of the divorce years had
fallen away like scales from his eyes. He could now see himself and Nora
in a new light, revealing if but fleetingly the empathy and imagination,
tenderness and insight, tolerance and warmheartedness which many, not
least Nora herself, had long believed him to lack. There is no extant
response to Nora's firm yet loving rebuff. But it seems likely that he
shared her bittersweet sense of what was "just a dreadful tragedy" that
"our understanding of each other has come too late." Whether such an
understanding would have survived had they actually remarried must
remain an open question, but it is evidence of unsuspected depths in both
of them.[135] For his part, Paul didn't "care much" for his stepfather, and
regretted his mother had changed her name from Mellon to Lee.[136]

V. THE DEATH OF A PRESIDENT

In March 1923, which witnessed both this mournful reconciliation with
Nora and the end of the congressional session, Andrew Mellon had been
secretary of the treasury for exactly two years. Despite the constraints
under which he labored, the limits of his accomplishments, and the enemies he had made among the politicians and the public, there prevailed a
general impression that the nation's prosperity was being rapidly restored.
In his report for 1923, Mellon would note that "labor has been in strong
demand, and in most localities fully employed"; that in the principal manufacturing industries, "the volume of production has been the greatest in
our history"; and that "the traffic handled by the railroads has surpassed
all records." The "Roaring Twenties" were in sight: in 1923, many economic indexes reached levels that would not be surpassed until the spring

of 1929.[137] To be sure, there was much of this for which Mellon could take (and claimed) no credit: the impact of the motor car and electricity, the building boom, the construction of highways, and the like. And there were still large parts of the country, especially in the South and the Midwest, that would never be reached by this prosperity. But for unprecedented numbers of Americans, the good times were indeed beginning to roll, and Mellon was seen as the man who had turned things around through a mastery of complex fiscal issues seldom seen in public life before—or since.[138]

As a result, and much to his own surprise, Mellon was increasingly regarded as the administration's star figure; soon he was being acclaimed as "the greatest Secretary of the Treasury since Alexander Hamilton," praise first bestowed by Representative Simeon D. Fess from Ohio in a speech in the House on December 7, 1922. (It was a premature encomium, Mellon himself was never comfortable with the comparison, and it would later come back to haunt him.)[139] Even the censorious *New York World* abandoned its earlier "misgivings": "Andrew W. Mellon," it noted in an editorial on February 24, 1923, "is today the outstanding figure in the Harding cabinet." "In all his conduct of the country's finances," it went on, "he showed possession of breadth and clarity of mind as well as a technical mastery of the problems involved."[140] Honorary degrees now began to flood in: from Rutgers, New York University, Dartmouth, and Princeton. Mellon was happy to accept, and even liked dressing up (hat size 7¼, height 5 feet 10½ inches, weight 145 pounds), but he refused to make speeches. He also declined to deliver the commencement address at Choate in the summer of 1923: "on the few occasions," he explained to the headmaster, "that I have ventured even a very short address, it has been a painful ordeal."[141]

After two stressful years, Mellon clearly felt the need to pause and take stock, not least because Parker Gilbert was determined to resign that autumn, to take up the career in banking on which he had long sought to embark. While Mellon wholly understood his decision, it remained for him an "occasion of extreme regret."[142] But with Gilbert still there to look after things and Congress no longer in session, Mellon resolved to take Ailsa and Paul back to Europe during the summer of 1923, from late June until mid-September. He had long "promised" them this trip, and refused almost all official invitations from local dignitaries, because he had made his plans "more particularly on their account."[143] On the eve of their departure, Andrew received an affectionate note from Nora: "I do hope I shall see you if only to wish you 'bon voyage,' " she wrote. "I am so very glad you are going to get a rest, though I shall feel terribly lonely when you are all gone." She sent him some books for the boat. "The voyage brings me many happy memories of others in the past," he wrote in thanks, "and also tinges of regret." On this visit Mellon would meet Duveen (though not in the elevator) and, violating his own ordinance, attend an official dinner hosted by the lord mayor of London. By now, and to Mellon's delight, Stanley Baldwin was prime minister, and he took this occasion to express his satisfaction at the outcome of the Anglo-American debt negotiations, convinced that they had succeeded on account of having been conducted by two businessmen rather than lawyers or politicians or statesmen.[144]

Mellon also took the opportunity to visit Nora's brothers, who were unaware of the recent reconciliation between him and their sister, unhappy at her remarriage, and skeptical about its prospects. "It was a great pleasure to see you again," John McMullen would write soon after Andrew had returned to the United States, going on to express delight that someone "now such a prominent man of politics" should still have time for his former in-laws. But, John continued, that was not the only reason Andrew might by now have turned away from them. For

> there is always in the background the shadow of past tragedy. It can be called nothing less than a tragedy, the mess that foolish sister of ours has made of her life. The pity of it is lamentable from many points of view other than our own . . . It is good of you to take any interest in us at all, and not to class us all as rotters. We may, as a family, be a poor lot from a business point of view. We were unfortunately brought up that way, but some of us are not such bad sorts from other points of view.[145]

Norman was likewise ignorant of the recent rapprochement: "She has made a bad mistake," he had earlier informed Andrew. "We can only hope for the best." Likewise Leonard: "So Nora married," he wrote, even more brutally, to his former brother-in-law. "Well, I have found a bigger fool than myself at last. But unfortunately it is in the same family."[146]

One London journalist described Mellon as being "modest almost to shyness, tranquil almost to quietude, the feeling I got from his face is one of a very winning if thoroughly subdued sweetness of temper." No such sweetness would be manifest, however, when he received word of President Harding's sudden death. Exhausted by the cares of office and overwhelmed by the looming scandals about to break, Harding expired in San Francisco on August 2, succumbing to an apoplectic stroke. There followed a display of national mourning such as had not been seen since Lincoln's assassination, with industrial workers weeping as the president's funeral train passed through Pittsburgh. Mellon's tribute to his former chief would be, in comparison, perfunctory at best: "there was evident a growing confidence in his judgment and his sincerity."[147] Perhaps, indeed, he had got wind of the abuses and irregularities that would soon come to light, culminating in Teapot Dome (Senator David A. Reed seems to have had an ear to the ground), and he may have set off for Europe as much in flight from this taint as toward a happy interval with his children. Nevertheless, he would subsequently consent to become treasurer of the Harding Memorial Fund, himself donating $12,500. Upon informing the secretary of the president's death, Parker Gilbert urged that there was no need for Mellon to return: he would attend the funeral on his master's behalf. Harding would be buried in Marion, on August 10; Mellon left for the United States later in the month on the *Aquitania*.[148]

10

BETTER YEARS WITH COOLIDGE
Mellonizing America, Aggrandizing Himself, 1923–26

It has been a memorable period of material progress, the
most so, perhaps, in the world's history; and the changes of
public sentiment and condition of society have not been
less remarkable.

Thomas Mellon and His Times, p. 338

I. IMPLEMENTING THE "MELLON PLAN"

Of the three Republican presidents with whom Andrew Mellon
served, Calvin Coolidge represented much the closest and the
happiest relationship. Having been reassured by Parker Gilbert that
the new president was "well informed and absolutely sound" on taxes,
the bonus, and agriculture, and also generally enthusiastic about Mellon's
handling of the Treasury Department, the secretary understood that
Harding's death would "make no difference to his staying in office."
Unlike Mellon, Coolidge came from New England Yankee farm stock
and had no firsthand experience of business; but their personal styles and
worldviews were very similar. Both were inscrutable men of few words:
indeed, it was suggested that they often "conversed almost entirely in
pauses."[1] Both abhorred ostentation and trade unionism, and neither had
been comfortable with the moral and financial laxity of the Harding
regime. Coolidge's administration would be a strong supporter of private
enterprise: "the business of America," he famously observed, "is business." (He added that "the idealism of America is ideals," but that resonated rather less.) There were those who inferred from this that the

president was merely the treasury secretary's creature and mouthpiece; among them was, predictably, Senator La Follette, who declared at Pittsburgh in November 1924 that "Andrew W. Mellon is the real President of the United States. Calvin Coolidge is merely the man who occupies the White House." But this was untrue and unfair: Mellon needed Coolidge's political support as much as Coolidge needed Mellon's financial expertise; Coolidge's backing was more determined and effective than Harding's had ever been; and Mellon placed great "confidence in the President's courage and political sense."[2]

By the autumn of 1923, both Colonel Drake and Parker Gilbert had departed the Treasury; the former returned to Pittsburgh (where he would eventually become president of Standard Steel Car), and the latter went to Wall Street (though only briefly). Drake had no successor as Mellon's private and confidential fixer, but Parker Gilbert was followed as undersecretary by Garrard B. Winston, a Chicago lawyer and an able administrator, who would never become as close to his master as Parker Gilbert had been.[3] More important was the arrival of a young man named David Finley. Born in 1890 to a prominent South Carolina family of Scotch-Irish descent and Presbyterian beliefs, he had trained as a lawyer and worked on the War Finance Corporation before moving to the Treasury Department in early 1923. Although Finley was a fervent Wilsonian Democrat, Mellon took a great liking to him and soon promoted him to be his personal assistant. Finley would later claim that he was merely a junior functionary, acting at the behest of the secretary, but the records tell a very different story. No one saw Mellon without first going through his office; it was Finley who passed all the secretary's directives on to underlings, and it was he who followed up on the execution of all decisions. Virtually every letter or paper or statement or press release that emanated from Mellon's desk was initiated, drafted, or composed by Finley, and he wrote the newspaper articles about tax reform that appeared in the newspapers under Mellon's name. During Finley's frequent travels with Mellon, the secretary reminisced about his early years and business career, and expounded his views on the contemporary world. And so he soon became Mellon's most important professional associate, staying close to him until his death and becoming in time something of a surrogate son.[4]

From the outset of the Coolidge administration, Mellon needed all the help he could get from the president and officialdom. Congressional hostility had increased with revelations of scandal during the Harding presidency, and as inquiries were launched into the malfeasance at the

Veterans' Bureau, the no-bid oil contracts and corporate venality soon to be known as Teapot Dome, and the Justice Department's involvement in corruption at the highest level. But Mellon was determined to press ahead with his own program, both domestic and international, and shortly before Armistice Day 1923, he wrote to William R. Green, acting chairman of the House Ways and Means Committee, outlining a "scientific tax plan," whose details had been completed by Parker Gilbert before he departed.[5] Once more, Mellon aimed to reduce the surtax rate from 50 percent to 25 percent as an incentive to the wealthy to shift their investments out of tax-exempt bonds and into industrial stocks. He further sought a reduction of 25 percent in the tax on earned income (as distinct from investment income), and the repeal of several nuisance taxes that fell disproportionately on those same low earners.[6] He also proposed to limit the deduction a business could take for capital losses to 12.5 percent, equal to the tax on capital gains, rather than the 100 percent then allowable. And he sought to create a Board of Tax Appeals independent of the Treasury which, in the event of a dispute, would serve as "an informal court before which the Government and the taxpayers could present their respective cases, and have a prompt determination of tax liability."[7] (He could scarcely have imagined that he himself would appear before that body in a decade's time, and that the determination of his liability would be anything but prompt.)

These proposals became known as the "Mellon Plan," and though they came with the "unqualified approval" of President Coolidge, many of them died in Congress.[8] The Democrats and the farm bloc were in effective control of both houses; William R. Green was an independent Republican opposed to drastic tax cuts; and Reed Smoot, chairman of the Senate Finance Committee, supported the bonus and proposed a sales tax to pay for it. The resulting Revenue Act, reluctantly signed by the president in June 1924, thus bore little relation to Mellon's original program. Instead of a 25 percent maximum surtax on incomes in excess of $100,000, Congress voted a 40 percent levy on those over $500,000. The estate tax was raised from 25 percent to 40 percent on accumulations of more than $10 million, and a gift tax was also introduced to close off that potential method of avoidance. In a further rebuff to the secretary, the details of individual tax returns were made open to public inspection. Most damagingly, Congress rejected another proposal for a constitutional amendment prohibiting the issuance of tax-exempt securities, and it authorized the veterans' bonus, overriding the president's veto. Fortunately, the economy was performing so well that paying this extraordinary entitlement did not lead to the dire consequences Mellon had predicted. The secretary did win one victory with the establishment of the Board of Tax Appeals. Even so, the Revenue Act of 1924 was a major blow.[9]

Although defeated in Congress, Mellon had already taken his arguments and proposals to the American public. Copies of his original letter to Chairman Green had been sent by the Treasury Department to prominent businessmen and Republicans across the country. A National Citizens' Committee in Support of the Mellon Tax Reduction Proposals was formed, led by Major John F. O'Ryan, and supported by such esteemed economists as Frank W. Taussig, Charles W. Bullock, Thomas S. Adams, and E. R. A. Seligman. The ostensibly "non-partisan" American Bankers' League also pressed for the implementation of the original Mellon proposals, and these groups gathered for an intensive public relations campaign during their self-proclaimed National Tax Reduction Week, April 6-13.[10] Meanwhile, Mellon gave interviews and contributed articles to a variety of newspapers and periodicals, in writings that were drawn together by David Finley in *Taxation: The People's Business*. The book was published in April 1924, and its proposals were essentially those the secretary had sent to Congress the previous autumn.[11] Mellon insisted the Treasury should be run "on business principles," and that federal taxation should be "the least burden to the people" while yielding "the most revenue to the government." Such a system required that wealth must carry its share, yet it should be freed from federal estate and gift taxes, which were counter-productive to the "accumulation of capital" upon which civilization was based. In the world according to Mellon, those who could not afford to pay taxes should be exempt from doing so, and "tax revision should never be made the football either of partisan or class politics, but should be worked out by those who have made a careful study of the subject in its larger aspects."[12]

In the short run, this publicity campaign availed Mellon nothing. House minority leader John Nance Garner shrugged it off as "an organized conspiracy [which] attempts to coerce Senators and Representatives to support the Mellon tax bill before they have had an opportunity to study or understand its provisions." And when the Revenue Act was finally passed, Mellon warned the president that as a "permanent expression of government fiscal policy," the provisions inserted by Congress were "not only unsatisfactory" but also "harmful for the future of the country."[13] Yet this disappointing period soon came to an end. At the Republican national convention, held in Cleveland in the summer of 1924, Mellon was chairman of the Pennsylvania delegation, and when

Aelbert Cuyp, *Herdsmen Tending Cattle*, 1655/1660.
Oil on canvas. Acquired from Knoedler & Company in 1905.

George Romney,
Miss Juliana Willoughby,
1781–83. Oil on canvas.
Acquired from Knoedler &
Company in 1907 as
Portrait of Miss Willoughby.

J. M. W. Turner, *Mortlake Terrace: Early Summer Morning.*
Acquired from Knoedler & Company in 1908, but soon sold by Mellon to Frick.

John Constable, *Salisbury Cathedral from Lower Marsh Close*, 1820. Oil on canvas.
Acquired from Knoedler & Company in 1918 as *A View of Salisbury Cathedral*.

Sir Henry Raeburn, *Miss Eleanor Urquhart*, ca. 1793. Oil on canvas.
Acquired from Knoedler & Company in 1920.

Johannes Vermeer, *Girl with the Red Hat*, ca. 1665/1666.
Oil on panel. Acquired from Knoedler & Company
in 1925 as *Girl with a Red Hat*.

Thomas Gainsborough, *Georgiana, Duchess of Devonshire*, 1783.
Oil on canvas. Acquired from Duveen in 1925.

Raphael, *The Niccolini-Cowper Madonna*, 1508.
Oil on panel. Acquired from Duveen in 1928.

Francisco de Goya, *The Marquesa de Pontejos*, ca. 1786.
Oil on canvas. Acquired privately via Knoedler & Company in 1931.

Rembrandt van Rijn,
A Polish Nobleman, 1637.
Oil on panel. Acquired from the
Hermitage via Knoedler & Company
in 1930.

Sandro Botticelli, *The Adoration of the Magi*, ca. 1478/1482.
Tempera and oil on panel. Acquired from the Hermitage via Knoedler & Company in 1931.

Raphael, *The Alba Madonna*, ca. 1510.
Oil on panel transferred to canvas. Acquired from the Hermitage via
Knoedler & Company in 1931 as *Madonna of the House of Alba*.

Veronese, *The Finding of Moses*, probably 1570/1575. Oil on canvas.
Acquired from the Hermitage via Knoedler & Company in 1931.

Jan van Eyck, *The Annunciation*, ca. 1434/1436.
Oil on canvas transferred from panel.
Acquired from the Hermitage via Knoedler & Company in 1930.

Raphael, *Saint George and the Dragon*, ca. 1506. Oil on panel.
Acquired from the Hermitage via Knoedler & Company in 1931.

Petrus Christus, *The Nativity*, ca. 1450.
Oil on panel. Acquired from Duveen in 1936.

Sandro Botticelli, *Madonna and Child*, ca. 1470.
Tempera on panel. Acquired from Duveen in 1936.

RIGHT: Desiderio da Settignano, *A Little Boy*, 1455/1460. Marble. Acquired from Duveen in 1936 as *Life-Size Marble Bust of Boy*.

BELOW: Andrea della Robbia, *Madonna and Child with Cherubim*, ca. 1485. Glazed terra-cotta. Acquired from Duveen in 1936 as *The Madonna and Child—Tondo*.

Thomas Gainsborough, *Mountain Landscape with Bridge*, ca. 1783/1784.
Oil on canvas. Acquired from Duveen in 1937 as *Landscape with a Bridge*.

called to the podium to propose a routine motion, he received an ovation. It may have been staged, and he was certainly embarrassed, but it was the greatest expression of public approbation Mellon would ever receive.[14] The convention nominated Coolidge by acclamation, with Charles G. Dawes as his running mate. The Democrats put up the lackluster John W. Davis, and the opposition was divided because Mellon's bête noire, Senator La Follette, ran on the Progressive Party ticket. Coolidge and Dawes managed to distance themselves from the scandals of the Harding years, and with the economy booming, the result was both a triumph for the president and a new Congress in which the Republican majority was such that the Democrats and the farm bloc together could no longer obstruct legislation.[15]

Of course, there was still the matter of Prohibition, and in the aftermath of Coolidge's victory, Mellon tried to reapply himself. Although he remained personally opposed to this "new law," recognizing that "the temptations for its violation are extraordinary," he had been stung by the unrelenting criticisms from the "drys" that enforcement was lethargic. Reluctantly, he decided to redouble his efforts, since it now seemed there was no likelihood the work would be transferred from the Treasury to the Justice Department any time soon.[16] The secretary had become convinced of the top-to-bottom weakness of the Prohibition Unit, from the poor leadership of Roy Haynes, a Harding crony, down to its foot soldiers, who had been drawn from the dregs of the Treasury's workforce. Accordingly, in June 1925, he announced a reorganization of the unit by a career army officer, Brigadier General Lincoln C. Andrews. Instead of the old state-by-state operation, there would be twenty-two administrative districts. Each district would have a director, and the directors would report to Andrews, thereby sidelining Haynes. In this more decentralized system, the Treasury would be less concerned with direct enforcement and more focused on general oversight and coordination. It took Andrews six months to effect his plan, and late in 1925, confident of success, he pledged to resign if it failed.[17]

At just this time, with the administration riding high, Mellon proposed a new revenue bill. This was passed with remarkable speed, and scarcely any modifications, by February 1926, and finally brought into law his long-fought-for tax reforms. The clear, orthodox Republican majority had little to fear from party insurgents, who were now leaderless, following the death of Senator La Follette soon after his failed presidential bid. There were even defections among Democrats who, discouraged by their recent drubbing at the polls, opted to support the reform and reduction of taxation.[18] At the same time, assorted tax clubs, together with the American Taxpayers' League, continued to lobby in support of the Mellon Plan. The result was dramatic, and for the secretary hugely gratifying. Most of what he regarded as the objectionable features of the 1924 Revenue Act were abandoned: the gift tax was repealed, the public disclosure of federal income tax returns was abrogated, and although the estate tax survived, the rate was halved. And all of the measures that Mellon had wanted were now implemented: the top rate of surtax was reduced to 25 percent, the remaining nuisance taxes were repealed, and with an effective exemption from taxes of every householder's first $4,000 of income, most Americans paid no federal income tax whatsoever. As Mellon proudly noted, a married man with an income of $3,000 a year had paid $40 in federal tax in 1920, $20 in 1921, $7.50 in 1924, "and under the 1926 [Revenue] Act he pays nothing." "The income tax in this country," he concluded, "has become a class rather than a national tax."[19]

As Mellon had promised all along, the restructuring of federal revenue via taxation, combined with the postwar reduction in federal spending, meant that by 1926 the surplus was running at almost $400 million. This, in turn, made it possible for the secretary to make substantial progress in the progressive reduction of the domestic debt. When he took office, the total national debt stood at $24 billion, but by the end of the fiscal year 1926 it was reduced to $19.6 billion, creating an annual savings of $40 million in interest payments. Mellon was convinced that the domestic encumbrances should be reduced as rapidly as possible, even if it meant keeping taxes higher than some wished. To let debts linger, or to allow them to mount, violated his most basic convictions: for a country, as for an individual, it was "a sign of debility and denoted an absence of the essential vigor and foresight which insure future success." "It was," he concluded, in words that might have issued from the mouth of the Judge, also "the policy of the thriftless, the ne'er do-well."[20] Reducing debt sooner rather than later not only lessened the cost of interest payments, it also took advantage of economic prosperity which would not last indefinitely. As of 1926, his policy was to apply one year of the government's surplus revenue to tax relief, and the next year's to the debt. Despite subsequent criticism of his judgment, Mellon genuinely believed that by 1942 all the domestic debt would be gone, leaving only the overseas debt to be whittled down, according to an agreed-upon framework and schedule.[21]

After a discouraging start under Coolidge, these were substantial achievements on the home front, and Mellon would also make significant advances internationally—though here, too, the initial prospects were scarcely rosy. The only foreign loan that had been settled was Britain's, which meant more than $7 billion of overseas debt was still outstanding; economic and political conditions in Europe remained uncertain; and Germany, with its currency in free fall and much of its economy in ruins, had recently defaulted on its reparation payments. Thus provoked, the French and the Belgians had occupied the Ruhr in January 1923, piling a political crisis on top of an economic one, and the prospects of continental peace, let alone prosperity, plummeted. But within little more than a year, the picture suddenly brightened. France and Belgium withdrew their troops, and a reparations settlement was brokered by Charles G. Dawes (formerly director of the budget and soon to be Coolidge's vice president) by the late summer of 1924. As a result, America (via the J. P. Morgan Bank) effectively agreed to finance an (independent) German central bank, a (newly minted) German currency, and (substantially reduced) German reparations. This, in turn, meant Germany's economy was stabilized, and that it could now pay an agreed-upon, and reduced, sum in reparations to the victorious European powers.[22] The agent-general appointed to oversee this operation was none other than Mellon's former underling, S. Parker Gilbert, plucked from a banking career that had scarcely begun. Although German reparations to the Allies and the Allies' indebtedness to the United States were ostensibly separate issues, the adoption of the Dawes Plan also made possible the settlement of most of the outstanding obligations of European nations to America.[23]

Mellon had been unofficially present for some of the negotiations concerning the Dawes Plan during the summer of 1924, and within a year he sensed that circumstances in Europe were indeed beginning to improve.[24] He thereupon returned to the issue of foreign debts and began receiving a succession of foreign finance ministers. The first delegation was from Belgium, and a settlement was reached relatively fast, on terms more generous than those that had been extended to Britain: sixty-two years to pay, but virtually no interest charges before 1935. "I think we were exceedingly fortunate," Mellon observed, "in having to deal with businessmen who had come over to settle this difficult problem with us." "Our next task," he concluded, presciently as events would turn out, "may prove a harder one."[25] Later that year, the French Republic dispatched its finance minister, Joseph Caillaux, to Washington, with the mission of obtaining a deal for his country that was even more favorable than Belgium's. After Britain, France was the largest debtor nation, with $4.2 billion outstanding. Caillaux insisted that his country owed the United States only

$3.3 billion, and he was so intemperate and inflexible that negotiations soon broke down, as Mellon had evidently foreseen. But Latvia, Yugoslavia, Finland, Lithuania, Poland, Czechoslovakia, Estonia, Romania, and Italy all subsequently settled, as did the Austrians and Hungarians, former enemies to whom America had lent money once the peace treaties were negotiated. Like Belgium, all obtained more favorable terms than those to which Britain had earlier agreed.[26]

Throughout these negotiations, Mellon's aim was "orderly funding and gradual liquidation." Every deal that he and the Debt Commission negotiated had to be ratified by Congress, and since they were all on terms more generous than those Congress had originally laid down, there was always a degree of political jeopardy: some lawmakers denounced the secretary's formula for collection, based on "capacity to pay," as cancellation by another name. Mellon was never a cancellationist, but after Italy's debt was "adjusted" to barely one-fifth of what had been owed, a major congressional rebellion loomed. The crucial vote came in February 1926, but with Coolidge's strong advocacy, the Italian deal won easier ratification than Mellon had expected.[27] Thus encouraged, he returned to the vexed and lingering matter of the French debt, finally securing a settlement in April that year with the new French ambassador, Henri Béranger, who, unlike Caillaux, conducted the discussions with "dignity and fairness." They agreed that France owed $4 billion, and a repayment schedule and interest rates were also fixed. Although it would take three years for the French National Assembly to ratify the settlement, Mellon could now confidently predict that virtually all overseas debts to the United States would be discharged by 1988 (with the exception of Soviet Russia, which repudiated all government obligations that had been incurred by the Romanovs).[28]

The settlement of these overseas debts was Mellon's highest international priority at the Treasury. But although, as both a banker and the secretary, he regarded such agreements as essential, they were not just an end in themselves: they were also the essential starting point for the financial stabilization and reconstruction of Europe, and thus of the world economy that had been shattered by the war. As soon as European nations had settled their debts, Mellon encouraged American bankers to invest in their industries and their infrastructures, and on occasion to lend money to help them balance their budgets. With their economies thus gradually rehabilitated and their currencies strengthening, the nations of Europe could contemplate returning to the prewar gold standard. Britain was the first major nation to do so in April 1925, and it was followed by most other European countries, once they had settled their debts to America.[29] Thus, it seemed, was the pre-1914 world regained in the mid- to late 1920s: the return to gold was the international analogue of the domestic restoration of "normalcy." In the attendant negotiations, Mellon played little part. They were largely conducted among the governors of the central banks of Europe. The prime American participant was Benjamin Strong, who negotiated a two-year standby loan for Britain of $300 million if needed to ease its return to the gold standard.[30] But Mellon was a strong advocate of such policies; he was eager to see the gold standard restored, and he helped persuade the Federal Reserve Board to lower its interest rates still further, from 4.5 to 3.5 percent, in May 1924. This was domestically sensible, for cheap money encouraged the economic boom. But it was also internationally worthwhile: keeping rates low in America would encourage the movement of gold to Europe, where interest rates were higher and where gold was now needed to back the recently stabilized currencies.[31]

In an almost miraculous way, it seemed as though the needs of both the American and the international economy were served by the same interest rates set by the Federal Reserve Board, and it was a policy Mellon was eager to endorse during the mid-1920s. To be sure, the question loomed as to what would happen if the needs of the United States and Europe diverged, but for now the financial sky seemed clear and promising. For private profit and public esteem, this was a golden time to be a banker. In an earlier era, J. P. Morgan and his contemporaries had seen themselves as patriotic statesmen, rescuing the American economy in 1907 from slump and ruin. Now, a new generation of financiers saw themselves as international statesmen, rescuing a stricken continent and gradually restoring a world order that had crashed between 1914 and 1918. That was the self-image and the ambition of both Benjamin Strong and his close friend Montagu Norman of the Bank of England.[32] And there were others who moved back and forth from banking to government in pursuit of the same objectives, among them Parker Gilbert and Charles Dawes. As America prospered, and as Europe recovered, these international bankers were the heroes of the hour: national icons, global saviors, altruistic leaders. And behind them, urging them on, was the most distinguished financier-statesman of them all, Andrew W. Mellon.

In a succession of letters, articles, interviews, and speeches, the treasury secretary set out the domestic and international prosperity his policies and his colleagues were helping to create. "No one," he observed in a letter to the Pittsburgh Clearing House Association, "is in a better position than the banker to know the pulse of the nation's business and, what is of more importance, to regulate in some degree that pulse." "As the distributor of the credit resources of the country," he went on, "the banker possesses a powerful instrument for good or ill. The great desideratum in business today is stability, and bankers through credit control can probably do more to maintain business on an even keel than any other group." And having settled the broader, international framework of financial relations between states, it was now up to businessmen to get on with business. "With the excellent credit machinery and strong position of our Federal Reserve System," he continued, "with most nations again on the gold standard, with the reparations plan in successful operation, with the debt settlements completed or in near prospect, and with Europe every day making progress toward normality, business in America should fear few obstacles."[33] And with a prosperous United States and a Europe at peace, there seemed every possibility that the continent might emulate the United States still further, by embracing the model of minimal state intervention in the economy in which Mellon so passionately believed: "To get the government out of business," he wrote to a congressional colleague, "whether it be in banks, utilities or monopolies, has become one of the most essential steps to a permanent fiscal restoration of Europe."[34]

During these triumphant years, Mellon received many indications that his work had made him the most admired member of the Coolidge cabinet. The honorary degrees continued to flow in—from Columbia in June 1924, and from Kenyon College, Amherst, Yale, and Harvard in the summer of 1926—perhaps encouraged by all the economists who supported his tax cuts. The Chamber of Commerce of the State of New York commissioned a portrait of him by Philip de Laszlo, and a dormitory in what would eventually become Harvard Business School was named after him.[35] There can be no doubt that Mellon warmed to this celebrity, noticeably loosening up as a result: indeed, the man who had been famously silent in Pittsburgh became on occasion almost garrulous in Washington. But he took the acclaim in his stride. "I cannot think," he replied to the managing editor of the *New York Herald Tribune*, "of any period or occasion in my life that would have the outstanding importance or character to render it of enough interest for the purpose of your abridged biography." And he was too experienced in business, too much his father's son, to doubt that booms in the economy—like the one fueling his popularity—always ended. "We cannot expect," he wrote to William Howard Taft, former Republican president, now Chief Justice of the Supreme Court, in words all too prescient, "that in the course of years the country will not again suffer severe industrial depressions, and while we are prosperous we should put our house in order to meet subsequent difficulties."[36]

As during the Harding administration, Mellon was also up to some other things—rightly suspected by his critics, but known in detail to only a few close associates—which would, if widely exposed, have won him rather less acclaim. He kept a finger on the pulse of Pennsylvania politics, consulting with Senators Pepper and Reed about the next speaker of the state's House of Representatives, the outlook for the 1924 elections, and so on.[37] And, despite his repeated denials, he remained involved in his businesses—not, to be sure, on a day-to-day managerial level, but certainly in regard to major strategic issues. In March 1924, Undersecretary Winston sent Mellon the following memorandum: "No new developments today. Think it advisable we have conference on Gulf nine o'clock Monday morning." Such a discussion at the Treasury was hardly proper, and Mellon wrote many letters during these years concerning Gulf, especially to the secretary of state, as the company expanded its operations into Mexico and sought official diplomatic assistance. A year later, when Marshall and McClintic sent Mellon a congratulatory telegram on the day of President Coolidge's inauguration, Mellon addressed his reply to his "dear partners"—hardly consistent with his claim that in 1921 he had withdrawn from business as if he had died. At the same time, Mellon was actively assisting Alcoa in its negotiations with James B. Duke concerning the latter's hydroelectric interests on the Saguenay River in Canada. The company was anxious to acquire a major share in this plentiful power source in order to establish a new aluminum works nearby, which it duly did in July 1925.[38] And there were also those long phone calls to Dick in Pittsburgh. Clearly, Mellon was still doing more than one job. Little wonder his time was rarely his own.

II. PICTURES, FAMILY, AND FORMER IN-LAWS

As such a popular and powerful figure in the capital, Andrew Mellon entertained extensively, and invitations to his apartment were highly prized. The talk was rarely scintillating, but his canvases constituted the finest single art collection in the notoriously culture-starved capital. "Pictures," Arthur Sixsmith recalled, for his employer "took the place of friends." "I am," Mellon once observed, alluding to the eighteenth-century "English beauties" adorning his walls, "surrounded here by some very nice people."[39] During the three-year period starting in the middle of 1923, Mellon spent more money on art than he had in the whole of his previous collecting career, primarily because the shamelessly importunate Duveen had superseded Knoedler as his principal dealer and artistic adviser. Duveen had already established personal contact, made two successful sales, and arranged for Oswald Birley to paint Mellon's portrait. His intelligence network of wastebasket pickers and spying servants kept him well informed about the moods and movements of the man he eyed as his biggest fish. Now Duveen set out to overwhelm Mellon with pictures of such surpassing quality and in such numbers that he would find it impossible to refuse to make a significant number of purchases. Every summer, Duveen would cross the Atlantic, returning to New York with what he insisted (not always correctly) were the choicest English portraits and European old masters, acquired at auction or by private treaty from the continent's impoverished aristocrats and deceased businessmen. Tasting long-schemed-for success at last, he now offered the best of them to Mellon.

"I hesitated about writing to you at the present time," Duveen informed him on returning in late October 1924, "because of the election." But by the end of the year, Mellon had agreed to buy four paintings: Rembrandt's *An Old Lady with a Bible*, Pieter de Hooch's *A Dutch Courtyard*, Meindert Hobbema's *A View on a High Road*, and Sebastiano Mainardi's half-length *Portrait of a Lady*. Mellon paid $650,000 for this quartet early in 1925, his most significant foray yet into continental European art.[40] Duveen kept up the pressure, urging other pictures on his client: in particular, "one of the finest Botticellis existing, also a Vermeer portrait, and a Titian." But Mellon's next purchase from him would be British: Gainsborough's second portrait of *Georgiana, Duchess of Devonshire*, which at $410,000 was his most costly acquisition to date. During the summer of 1925, Duveen acquired the plums from the sale of Sir George Holford's collection at Dorchester House in London, and in the autumn descended on Mellon in Washington with six "great pictures." "I expect to sell most of them," Duveen confidently predicted. In the end, Mellon settled for three portraits: Van Dyck's *Marchesa Balbi*, Raphael's *Giuliano de Medici, Duke of Nemours*, and Reynolds's *Lady Caroline Howard*. He paid Duveen $1.2 million, including $450,000 apiece for the Van Dyck and the Raphael, which made them the two most expensive paintings he had yet bought. And he took them on the condition he could return any or all of them within the first year for a full refund, or in the second year for the purchase price less 5 percent.[41]

"Of course," Duveen wrote to Mellon in his grandest manner, "I have purchased many other fine things," but these were "the gems, and I am losing no time in telling you about them." Duveen's eagerness was understandable: in a market of uncertain supply and demand, in which prices rose and fell with bewildering speed and to unpredictable extremes, sales to Mellon represented relatively reliable and certain profit. He had, for example, valued the Van Dyck *Marchesa Balbi* at only £35,000 and had taken his chances buying it for twice that amount (roughly equivalent to $350,000); fortunately he managed to sell it to Mellon for $450,000, netting some $100,000.[42] But although Mellon was now spending more than ever before, he continued to drive hard bargains, still refusing more paintings than he accepted and almost invariably forcing down the prices. For the Raphael, the Reynolds, and the Van Dyck, Duveen had asked $1,450,000; but was obliged to settle for $250,000 less. Behind the bluster, he was in a weak position: Mellon's fortune was massive and secure, but Duveen's finances were precarious, and his acquisitions obliged him to lay out large sums that might take years to recoup. "It is very rarely," Duveen wrote to him early in 1926, "that I am hard-up," but "unfortunately, pay days, like income tax days, will come around, and I find I have to make a very large payment at the end of this month. My purpose in writing to you is to inquire whether you can conveniently assist me." Mellon apparently did so, thereby demonstrating that Duveen needed him more than he needed Duveen.[43]

Likewise, when a disagreement arose between them concerning the terms of any potential repurchase of *Georgiana, Duchess of Devonshire*, Duveen had no choice but to give way. He agreed that he would buy back the picture if Mellon, returning from Washington to Pittsburgh, did "not find it appropriate or desirable in size" for his house there. The arrangement would stand for five years or until the death of Duveen, whichever came sooner, and Mellon would be refunded 90 percent of the original net purchase price. But while Mellon agreed to the time frame and the percentages, he insisted his right of return was "not contingent upon my moving to Pittsburgh, or of not finding it appropriate in size for my Pittsburgh house." Duveen again capitulated immediately: "I turned the matter over to my secretary for his attention." "My mind," he explained, rather splendidly, "must have been upon other things when I signed the letter."[44] Mellon kept the Gainsborough, but soon sent the Raphael back: "It seemed to me a strong work," he explained to Frick's daughter, "but not particularly attractive for a private living room." He preferred his "English beauties" to men of power. Within a year, Mellon had returned it at full price (a wiser move than he could have known, for it was later deemed to be a copy). One evening at a dinner party, the wife of the Belgian ambassador noticed that the portrait had disappeared, and inquired after it. "Mr. Mellon sent it away," she was told by David Finley, "because he did not like it." The ambassador's wife exclaimed: "How wonderful! To be able to say, 'Take away that Raphael. I don't like it.' Who but Mr. Mellon could do *that*?"[45] Who indeed?

Mellon may have been dealing less with Knoedler, but he had not abandoned them: in November 1923 he bought Romney's *Countess of Derby*, Hoppner's *The Frankland Sisters*, and two Turners (*Van Tromp's Shallop Entering the Scheldt* and *Approach to Venice*) from the Glenconner collection. The total price was $495,000, making it his largest purchase from them to date.[46] Once again "English beauties" and sylvan scenes dominated. Thereafter, however, the pace and scale of his Knoedler purchases noticeably slackened, as he turned increasingly to Duveen. In late 1924, he acquired Sir Henry Raeburn's *Miss Davidson Reid* for $30,000, and another Hobbema, *La Ferme au Soleil*, for $108,000; but despite Carman Messmore's hope that it had been "improving very much upon further acquaintance," he sent back Reynolds's *Miss Ridge*, for which he had been asked to pay $50,000.[47] During 1925, Mellon again purchased only two major pictures. In July, he acquired Holbein's *Portrait of Prince Edward, Afterwards Edward VI* for $437,400, by far his most expensive acquisition from Knoedler. "This painting," Charles Henschel wrote, with bombast to rival Duveen's, "is one of the great outstanding works that have come in the market in many years. The fact of it being one of the kings of England adds tremendously to its interest, and we know of no picture that has a finer history than this one." Five months later, Mellon bought Vermeer's *Girl with a Red Hat* for $140,000. "We congratulate you," Messmore noted, in similarly effusive language, "on the acquisition of this wonderful little gem." "We know of none," he went on, "that is finer in quality, and certainly none that is more brilliant in colour."[48]

Thereafter, Mellon bought nothing from Knoedler for more than a year, except for a painting by Manet for $8,500—one of his very rare forays into modern art. To be sure, there was other business being carried on between them at this time, concerning the lending of pictures to exhibitions, the possible reduction of tax on the sales of works of art, the completion of the painting by Orpen (which Mellon did not much like), and the commissioning of another portrait by John da Costa at the behest of Dick Mellon. And Duveen was furious to learn that Knoedler had beaten him to the Holbein, which he thought had been in his grasp: it was, he lamented, "a great loss of prestige."[49] But he took comfort from the definite cooling in relations between Mellon and Knoedler and did not hesitate to exploit it. His intelligence network was critical to the effort, providing detailed reports on his rivals as well as his client: about the frequency of Messmore's visits to Washington, about the items and issues he discussed with Mellon, about the hanging of the Holbein (for which Duveen, swallowing his pride, eventually provided the frame), about the other pictures Messmore brought down, and even about his state of health (Messmore had his tonsils removed in the early summer of 1925 and was "laid up in hospital for two and a half weeks"). For his part, Mellon seems to have enjoyed playing the rivals off against each other, asking Duveen's opinion of the pictures he had acquired from Knoedler, and Henschel's and Messmore's assessment of works he had bought through Duveen. Henschel's verdict was a model of truthful tact: "I think your pictures look splendidly," he wrote to Mellon after one visit, "and that you have an unusually fine assemblage of great works."[50]

Beautiful pictures, Washington society, high political office: all this was a world away from Pittsburgh. Meanwhile, life was very different for Nora McMullen, then Mellon, now Lee. She was often indisposed, and effectively confined to her farm on the Hudson with her new husband. "I have not been awfully well and have been in bed a good deal since Christmas," she wrote to Andrew at the end of January 1924. Soon after, she underwent a major operation, requiring extensive convalescence, in the course of which she caught pleurisy and, later, bronchitis, interspersed with an endless succession of coughs and colds. The farm was too big for her and her husband to manage; staff and servants were difficult to obtain and never stayed for long, which meant Nora, as she wrote, frequently had "to do everything for myself." No wonder she took to her bed so often. She also lost the beauty that had captivated Andrew and began to put on weight. All she had "to look forward to" were the visits of Paul and Ailsa, though she was mournfully aware of being unable to accommodate and entertain them in the style to which they were accustomed.[51] The combination of divorce and remarriage made Nora, in social terms, more of a nonperson than ever. Choate had stopped sending her copies of Paul's school reports when she became Mrs. Lee, "a slight," she told Andrew, "which has hurt very much and has made Paul feel badly." As for visiting Pittsburgh to see her dentist: "I have given up the idea . . . I cannot face being there alone in a hotel." It was a friendless, forlorn, and generally circumscribed existence: "I have no news," she once wrote Andrew. "Everything is much the same." That just about summed things up.[52]

Correspondence with Andrew and occasional meetings in New York or

Washington had never been more precious. "I am very distressed that you did not get my letter," she wrote in August 1923, on learning that it had not reached him at Claridge's. "Not that there was anything of importance in it," she went on, "but still I would not like it to fall into any hands but yours." She was as concerned about his health as about her own: "I hope your trip refreshed you and that you are very well," she concluded. "Shall look forward to seeing you later. As always, your Nora." "I was sorry to hear from Paul that you had a bad cold," she wrote on another occasion, "and could not go to New York. Are you better? I hope so." She asked for Andrew's help and advice: "Could you spare me one bottle of Overholt [whisky]?"; "Will you please tell me what to do about a passport?"[53] She took pleasure in contemplating a "charming picture" of her ex-husband, "standing on the terrace at Southampton," and she was delighted to receive a copy of *Taxation: The People's Business*—"although it taxes my intelligence," she rather artlessly replied, "I am enjoying reading it." And she commiserated with him over politics. "I am, of course, intensely interested in your [Revenue] *Bill*," she wrote in February 1924, "and before I am through I shall make myself quite ill over Congress." "It must be exasperating," she went on, "when you have really put your life blood into evolving a measure which you *know* to be right and essential, to have those ignorant, unscrupulous politicians hold things up." "Yours is indeed a most thankless task," she wrote on another occasion, "and I marvel at your patience."[54]

The deeds (and misdeeds) of their children also figured prominently in Nora's letters. Since Ailsa was "quite nervous of taxis," she urged Andrew to provide her with a car. (He did.) She was concerned about her daughter's continuing hypochondria: "I am sorry to see she is still worrying over herself, although I think she is really *very* well."[55] Nora feared that in her self-involvement, Ailsa was becoming increasingly casual, forgetful, unreliable, and indecisive. In the spring of 1925, mother and daughter went on a trip to England and France (Andrew paid: "you should have everything comfortable and of the best," he insisted), but the reports Nora sent back were not encouraging. Ailsa was endlessly fussy and particular about hotel accommodations, she forgot to tip waiters and chauffeurs, and she was "very naughty" about returning hospitality. And planning their itinerary was a nightmare, for getting Ailsa to make up her mind was "the most difficult thing in the world for her." Paul caused his mother rather different anxieties, more easily remedied. "I was so dreadfully distressed," Nora wrote to Andrew in April 1924, "to hear of poor Paul having measles, but I do hope he will escape all complications." (He did.) As for college:

Should he go to Princeton? "I do hope there is really no doubt about it," she mused, with a characteristic display of impassioned and opinionated ignorance, "for I do feel so strongly that almost *any* other is preferable to Yale. I have a real horror of it."[56]

Meanwhile, Nora's brothers remained indebted and accident-prone, writing and appealing separately to their sister and her ex-husband, in the hope of getting money out of each. Unknown to them, Nora would share all the details with Andrew—though not with her new husband. Leonard McMullen, still working as a bookmaker, was losing money on the wagers he was accepting and wanted to sell his house, which both Nora and Andrew had lent him money to improve. "How he can really feel that the place is his to sell," Nora exploded, "in the face of what he owes you, is something more than I can understand."[57] Then Norman (who was also in debt) gave notice that he would visit; Nora was "terribly worried" that she could not get to the dock to greet him, and wondered whether Andrew might send someone instead. Then Percy was diagnosed with "concussion of the brain" and needed help with his hospital bills. "I am almost distracted," Nora wrote, "for you know how devoted I am to him." Then, as if in turn, Murray fell ill, and Nora invited him to stay with her to convalesce. "Could you tell me," she asked Andrew, "how I can get a permit to go on the dock to meet him, for I feel I ought to, as he is not well?" Then Kenrick suffered a succession of heart attacks "which seem to be getting more severe each time." "I am afraid he cannot last much longer," Nora concluded. Even she was by turns appalled and dismayed at her brothers' behavior, ranging from the "despicable" (Leonard) to the "pathetic" (Percy).[58] Andrew continued to treat his former in-laws with remarkable forbearance and generosity, especially Leonard, who was by turns self-loathing and self-pitying, fearful of insolvency, and threatening to take his own life (which he never did).[59]

Reproachful of her brothers' profligacy though she was, Nora remained financially irresponsible herself. Her income was in the region of $4,000 a month, a substantial sum, which should be multiplied by ten for a present-day equivalent, but she could never live within it. Time and again, she wrote to Andrew and to Bruce McCrory, who had succeeded Paul Ache as her lawyer and trustee, lamenting her continuing and irremediable financial woes: "completely broke"; "I have just $3.65 in the bank"; "I seem to have got out of my depth again"; "I seem to have managed extra poorly this month."[60] The Hudson Valley farm was a money sink, her medical bills were high, it was expensive to try to entertain Ailsa and Paul and their friends in the expected manner, and there were also her brothers' visits and debts. "It seems incredible how the money goes," she told McCrory, "for I have really had no clothes for a year, because I have been wearing some of Ailsa's 'hand-me-downs,' I never take a taxi unless I absolutely have to, and I don't entertain one quarter as much as I should like to." She sought loans from Andrew, and advances against the monthly payments from her trust-fund income. Like her brothers, she always insisted that "it will never happen again"; but while she declared herself "mortified" at such "disgraceful behaviour," happen again it would. "This is a busy place," she told Bruce McCrory, "and I don't have much time to puzzle over what life means—which is a very good thing!" But she was forced to admit that it was too demanding and expensive, and in the autumn of 1925, she decided to sell the farm and take a "tiny apartment" in New York.[61]

Ailsa, by contrast, continued her extensive socializing in Washington, interspersed with visits to New York or overseas, when she was accompanied by Andrew or Nora or Miss Sylvester. Whenever father and daughter were separated, Andrew was a diligent and (after his reticent fashion) devoted correspondent—much more so than Ailsa ever was in return. His letters were an amalgam of family news ("I have just returned from Bermuda with Paul and three of his schoolmates"), political intelligence ("everything is bright and promising for Coolidge and the Party"), social gossip ("it is very quiet in Washington"), musing over art acquisitions ("I might buy the Gainsborough"), offering paternalistic advice ("don't fail to declare your purchases for the customs on your return"), and fatherly affection ("with very much love").[62] But aside from traveling and shopping and being social, Ailsa's main business now was to make her best choice among the many grandees who eagerly sought her hand, among them Prince Bismarck (grandson of Germany's Iron Chancellor), Sir Robert Horne (chancellor of the exchequer at the end of the Lloyd George coalition), and Prince Gelasio Caetani (Italian ambassador to Washington). This was never going to be easy for Ailsa: she had a deserved reputation for being distant and standoffish, she had never mastered the art of small talk let alone of sparkling conversation, she was understandably suspicious of fortune hunters, and she was not good at making up her mind.[63] But in May 1926, she consented to marry David Kirkpatrick Este Bruce, a multiple-named fellow for a girl who lacked even a middle initial.

Like the Mellons, the Bruces were of Scottish origin, but their trajectory had been very different, establishing them by the mid–nineteenth century at the apex of Virginia plantation gentry, with a great estate, three hundred slaves, and a Gothic mansion at Staunton Hill, built by David's grandfather, Charles Bruce.[64] By American standards, they could boast heritage and lineage aplenty; the intermarried elite to which they belonged was the closest thing to an aristocracy that the republic would ever produce. In the aftermath of Emancipation and Reconstruction, the Bruces suffered the economic decline that befell their class generally, and the next two generations remained in thrall to the faded antebellum values of pride, honor, chivalry, Anglophilia, ancestral piety, and noblesse oblige. Staunton Hill would always be David Bruce's spiritual home, the place where he felt territorially rooted and socially defined. When Charles Bruce died in 1896, he left behind eight children, of whom the sixth was William Cabell Bruce. With the family fortune evaporated, William had no choice but to make his own way in the world, and he qualified as a lawyer. He joined a flourishing practice in Baltimore, took up progressive politics, and won a seat in the state Senate. In 1887, he married Louise Este Fisher. It was a union of which Judge Mellon would have approved, for the bride's father was the senior partner in William's law firm, and a very rich and well-connected man besides. David Bruce, the fourth and youngest child of William and Louise, was born on February 12, 1898.

David's upbringing combined the material urban comforts of Baltimore with the declining but resonant gentility of Staunton Hill, and from an early age he liked to read widely and to go shooting. His elder brother died when he was twelve, a greater trauma than many would later appreciate, though perhaps not one to rival what Ailsa had suffered on account of her parents' divorce. In 1915, David Bruce enrolled at Princeton, where Scott Fitzgerald befriended him and later modeled the character of Amory Blaine in *This Side of Paradise* on him. David left Princeton after two years (never to return) and volunteered for the U.S. Army, but he reached France too late to see action on the Western Front. Instead, he soaked up French culture and history at the University of Bordeaux and the Sorbonne and soon found himself a courier of American government documents between the Paris peace conference and various embassies and legations across the continent. But his father, who was now at the point of selling Staunton Hill, and would soon be elected to the U.S. Senate as a Democrat from Maryland, wanted his son to follow him into the law, and he summoned David home to study—initially at the University of Virginia, subsequently at the University of Maryland. Practicing for a brief time in Baltimore, David regarded the law as little better than Dickensian drudgery, and he would be no more enamored of politics after serving one term in the Maryland state legislature. Whenever he could, he escaped back to Europe, and was increasingly drawn to a diplomatic career. But his father had taken up residence in Washington, and for now David also gravitated to the capital, where his good looks, his swank attire, and his effortless patrician charm made him welcome.[65]

Sometime in 1925, David Bruce met Ailsa Mellon, perhaps at a Washington dinner dance or a diplomatic reception. Although strikingly eligible, he was not regarded as a front-runner in the Mellon marriage stakes by the gossip columnists: he was not seriously rich, he was neither a prince nor a peer nor a knight, and he had little in common with Ailsa. He was brilliant, well-read, outgoing, impeccably mannered, and professionally ambitious; she was self-centered and aloof, intellectually lazy, inadequately educated, and easily bored, as well as inclined to hypochondria. But Andrew Mellon and William Cabell Bruce had recently become acquainted as relative newcomers to Washington (Bruce *père* had by now evolved into a very conservative Democrat), and David pursued Ailsa with a resourceful persistence that eventually prevailed.[66] Despite their temperamental differences, their union was a classic wedding of old status and new money: David would bring to the marriage a position based on lineage; and Ailsa would eventually bring to it an ample share of her father's fortune, though in the beginning, and despite the recent repeal of the gift tax, it was far less than the $10 million it was rumored Andrew had given her. Initially, he transferred to his daughter "only" 10,000 shares in Alcoa, which had a book value of $1 million, and provided her an income of $60,000 a year; he also gave her a wedding present of $150,000 in cash. But despite gossip to the contrary, there was nothing yet for David.[67]

The Mellon-Bruce wedding was the greatest society event that the nation's capital had witnessed since Presidents Roosevelt and Wilson married off their daughters in the years before the First World War. Andrew himself had long ceased to be a practicing Presbyterian (indeed, he attended no church regularly during his Washington years), but the ceremony, which took place at the National Cathedral, was a quintessentially establishment affair, as a scion of old lineage married a daughter of new wealth, in the presence of a veritable *Who's Who* of American church and state.[68] The Bishop of Washington performed the service on May 29, 1926, in the Bethlehem Chapel, the only part of the great edifice that was then complete. Space was limited, but in addition to the Mellon and Bruce clans, the guests included the President and Mrs. Coolidge, Chief Justice William Howard Taft, General Pershing, most of the cabinet, and many ambassadors (David Finley made the seating arrangements). The bride wore a gown of lace over satin, with a court train and a tulle veil, held in place by a coronet of pearls—an ensemble which she had helped to design. The groom's best man was his brother James, and he was supported by twenty ushers, one of whom was Paul Mellon. The reception was held at the Pan American Union building, and two thousand additional guests were invited; each received a slice of wedding cake in a box on which the monograms of Ailsa and David were embossed in silver.[69] So many and valuable were the wedding presents received by the golden couple that they were displayed in an apartment Mellon had rented for the purpose just below his penthouse.

For Nora, the wedding was a predictably bittersweet occasion. On one hand, she was greatly relieved that Ailsa had finally made up her mind. "I think we ought to be very happy about it," she wrote to Andrew on learning of the engagement. "I did not realize quite what an anxiety it had been all these years, as to whom she would choose, until I experienced the relief in hearing it was David." At the same time, however, Nora was "terribly exercised" that she would have to buy her daughter a present, and eventually spent $2,400 on "the only thing I could find that she wanted." Ailsa little understood that her mother was in no position to afford such a sum, though as Nora admitted, "Of course I ought to be able to if I managed right."[70] She was also "dreading" the ceremony itself: "it is not easy," she told Bruce McCrory, "to be a guest at one's own daughter's wedding." In the end, it "went off very nicely," proving "less of an ordeal" than she had expected: "I was allowed to sit in the front pew," she reported with evident pleasure and satisfaction. But two things rankled. She had to take her chance with "the rest of the crowd" at the reception, and "waited in line for more than an hour for the honour of shaking hands with the wedding party." "It seemed," she thought, "an unnecessary humiliation after all I have had these years." And she remained a nonperson to the newspapers, which "never mentioned" her name. "These things, unfortunately, still have power to hurt," she told McCrory, "not for myself, but because I see they hurt Paul." "They," she went on, with a fine and familiar combination of theatricality and imprecision, "swore they would break my heart, and I doubt not that they will accomplish it sooner or later. There is a limit to even my endurance."[71]

While Nora's feelings were understandably mixed, Sir Joseph Duveen's response was unequivocal: he spied a new potential client. In March 1925, when Nora and Ailsa visited Europe together, Duveen had sensed an opportunity to get Miss Mellon "interested in art," in the hope that she might "develop into a future buyer," and to this end, he offered to arrange visits to all the great museums and principal collections on the continent, and sent her flowers to decorate her cabin. (There is no evidence that Knoedler & Company was similarly imaginative or aggressive in targeting Ailsa.) Later that year, he arranged for Oswald Birley to paint Ailsa's portrait, and on learning of her engagement, Duveen drafted (but apparently did not send) an effusive letter, offering his "sincere congratulations." "I do so," he wrote, "because of the interest I have always felt since you were a little girl, and realized that you bore the same name as my wife."[72] (This was not strictly true, for Lady Duveen was named Elsie, which may explain why he thought better of sending the letter.) Sir Joseph and Lady Duveen were naturally invited to the wedding, and the day before the ceremony, a gold and enameled box was dispatched from New York to Washington. Four days after the ceremony, Mr. and Mrs. David Bruce boarded the SS *President Harding* en route for Europe, where David would take up the position of junior vice consul in Rome. The couple were not expected to live on his diplomatic salary of $2,500 a year. It was rumored that the Bruces would soon return to Washington, and that they would settle down with Andrew in a grand house. Such a residence, of course, would need more furnishings and more pictures than those Mellon had already purchased for his apartment.[73]

Ailsa Mellon had been brought up with little other purpose than to marry well; now that she had done so, her only work in life was to support (as well as to finance) her husband's diplomatic career, to produce the children which others seem to have anticipated more eagerly than she, and (if Duveen had his way) to spend money on pictures. But what of Paul Mellon, now that his education at Choate was almost complete? Because it was in the East and because it was founded by Presbyterians, Princeton drew a disproportionate number of the sons of the Scotch-Irish Pittsburgh elite during the late nineteenth century. Two of Paul's cousins, Matthew (son of WL) and Richard King (son of Dick), had already attended, as had David Bruce, and Paul was duly admitted in his turn, and was all set to head to Old Nassau in the autumn of 1925, much to Nora's satisfaction.[74] But on the very threshold of the academic year, he abruptly changed his mind, partly because the Princeton freshman handbook had given him the impression of a prim and stuffy place, and partly because he came to think his burgeoning interest in history and English would be better nurtured at Yale, with its outstanding departments in both subjects. Paul summoned up the courage to tell his father, who was concerned at this late change of mind, but he "put up no objections when told the reason." Nor, in the end, despite her irrational anti-Yale sentiment, did his mother. "I was terribly disappointed myself," Nora told Andrew, on learning the news, "but when I realized it was not for any frivolous motive and that it meant so much to him, I felt more satisfied." "I feel sure," she concluded, "he will do his best wherever he is."[75]

Paul did, indeed, do his best at Yale. Although still shy, he was gradually building his confidence, and would make some lifelong friends, among them George Wyckoff, who would later represent his financial interests in Pittsburgh, and Chauncey Hubbard, who went to work in the Mellon Bank. Paul was tutored by a coterie of brilliant teachers in Yale's English department, among them Chauncey B. Tinker and William Lyon Phelps, who reinforced and refined his love of literature, and his grades were generally good—except in chemistry. He took up student journalism, writing for the *Yale Daily News* and joining the editorial board of the *Yale Literary Magazine*, to which he began to contribute poetry and essays. Thanks to his father's influence, he obtained an interview with President Coolidge and an article from the new secretary of state, Frank Kellogg. But his attainments were also his own: in May 1926, he was awarded the first McLaughlin Prize for his essay "Donn Byrne—His Place in Literature."[76] In addition to studying hard, Paul was also playing hard, thereby anticipating the well-struck balance between work and leisure that would characterize his later life. He rowed on the "filthy" Quinnipiac River, and he spent weekends in New York, making new friends, meeting his first girls, and imbibing bootleg liquor. As he later recalled, his generation of undergraduates drank a great deal, despite (or because of) Prohibition. Though well aware that his father was responsible for its enforcement, there he was, "the Secretary's son, lapping it up in speakeasies." The speakeasy owners paid protection money to the police, and there was little chance of his being caught, but had he been, the political embarrassment to his father would have been considerable.[77]

For this and other reasons, Paul's relationship with his father had settled into an uneasy distant reticence, blending wary affection and mutual misunderstanding. So it would remain while Andrew lived, and for Paul a long time after that.[78] At Yale as at Choate, Paul saw little of his father, except during university recesses, when they took vacations together. But as he came to appreciate how rich, powerful, and successful Andrew Mellon was, Paul became more intimidated by him, and preferred to correspond with David Finley, both about his work and his living and traveling arrangements. Yet in some ways, the father was more sympathetic than the son ever realized. In selecting Yale over Princeton, Paul had imagined himself rebelling against paternal authority; but Andrew had not objected. In taking up poetry and literature, Paul embraced subjects that his father was widely believed to disdain; yet Andrew carried with him copies of his son's published poems and essays, proudly showing them to anyone in Washington who expressed interest.[79] Much more difficult and potentially divisive was the question of what Paul would do with his life. With a famous name and superabundant riches, he would never want for anything, or need to work. His father's existence had been built around banking, business, public service, and art collecting. His mother preferred country pursuits, spending money, and romantic adventure. Andrew and Nora had signally failed to reconcile their needs and priorities in their marriage, and for many years, Paul would find it hard to reconcile them in his own life.

III. PITTSBURGH, PENNSYLVANIA, AND POLITICS

Andrew Mellon's public activities and his private affairs were by now almost wholly focused on Washington, and apart from Christmas holidays, when he habitually returned to Pittsburgh, he spent most of his limited leisure time in Bermuda, on Long Island, or in Europe. He turned down many invitations to public functions in Pittsburgh, yet with his unrivaled wealth, his high office, and his national fame he remained a favorite son in his hometown.[80] There was an unmistakable element of nostalgia about this continued adulation, for despite the general prosperity that Mellon's policies had helped to promote across much of America during the 1920s, Pittsburgh was becoming a town whose great days of innovation and advance were past. No comparable generation of entrepreneurs had arisen to replace the Heinz-Carnegie-Frick-Westinghouse-Mellon cohort, of whom Andrew was now the sole great survivor. And while he was still involved in the businesses he had helped to create and which sustained his wealth, he was more interested in buying old pictures than in promoting new companies. Under Dick's leadership, no new Mellon enterprises of any significance were being established. The 1920s were, then, a stagnant decade for Pittsburgh: coal output declined, no more steel mills were built, and problems with housing, labor, and the environment, laid bare before the First World War, remained largely unaddressed. Pittsburgh had been the quintessential industrial metropolis at the turn of the century, but now it had been overtaken by Henry Ford's Detroit. In the ten years beginning in 1919, the population of Allegheny County grew a scant 200,000, from 1.2 million to 1.4 million, and expansion came to a virtual halt compared with the head-spinning decades before the First World War. In early 1929, with the American economy booming as never before, unemployment in Pittsburgh was running at somewhere between 5 and 10 percent.[81]

More and more, Pittsburghers were doughtily proclaiming a faith in their city's continuing industrial greatness which they no longer truly felt, and one indication of this was a perceptible shift in Mellon attitudes and priorities.[82] To be sure, the basic financial infrastructure that Andrew and Dick (and Frick) had created at the turn of the century remained in place. Henry C. McEldowney continued to run the Union Trust Company, and it unfailingly recorded massive profits, boasting the largest surplus of any trust company in the world. For ten years from July 1916, it was paying dividends of 35 percent quarterly with a 6 percent Christmas bonus; in January 1927 that increased to 50 percent quarterly plus the 6 percent bonus. As for Mellon National Bank, by March 1924 its deposits were nearly $112 million, up from $94 million just four years earlier, and its total resources were close to $137 million; three years later the figures would be, respectively, $155 million and $187 million.[83] But while this was recognizably business as usual in terms of dollars, there were also signs of a generational shift in the Mellon dynasty. When Andrew left for Washington, and sold his shares, Dick had taken over as president of the Mellon National Bank, and at almost the same time, his son, Richard King Mellon, had begun work there as a messenger. After gaining experience in several departments, RK was appointed assistant cashier in 1924; he became a director of the bank the following year and was appointed vice president in 1928. Clearly, Dick was grooming his son to succeed him at the helm of the Mellon National Bank, and Andrew was already hoping Paul would occupy a similar position at Union Trust, thereby ensuring that the second-generation collaboration between the two brothers would be perpetuated into a third generation of collaboration between the two cousins.[84]

More visible were the changes in the Mellon physical presence in Pittsburgh. Hating ostentation and coveting a low profile, Andrew had never wanted the "Mellon interests" to be conspicuously headquartered in great buildings. But now that policy was dramatically abrogated, in part out of necessity, as continued expansion of the banking business demanded larger and more rational accommodation, in part because Dick was now wielding greater authority, and he had always been a keener builder than his elder brother, as he had already shown in his own home and in the creation of Rolling Rock.[85] In November 1923, the Union Trust Company moved into the Union Arcade, an ornate Gothic building originally built by Frick between 1915 and 1917 in the Flemish style, modeled on the city hall of Brussels. It was originally a speculative venture of mixed office and retail use, situated at the intersection of Fifth Avenue and Grant Street between Frick's two other great real estate initiatives in downtown Pittsburgh, the William Penn Hotel and the Frick Building. The architect was Frederick J. Osterling, who had designed Frick's house at Clayton, and his flamboyant, arcaded, pinnacled, stained-glassed, high-roofed fantasy had been a dramatic reproach to prim, sooty, utilitarian, philistine Pittsburgh.[86] With limited modifications, the building now became the headquarters of the Union Trust Company; thousands of people visited on the first day it was open to the public, and both Andrew and Dick attended the inaugural dinner, along with many East Coast bankers brought in on a special train from New York.[87]

At the same time, new accommodations were being constructed nearby for the Mellon National Bank, which was awkwardly housed in an agglomeration of buildings, acquired around the "Iron Front" structure that Judge Mellon had put up in 1871, and which now filled the entire block on the east side of Smithfield Street between Fifth and Oliver avenues. The architects were Trowbridge and Livingston of New York, whose clients included the Bankers Trust and J. P. Morgan; for this commission they were assisted by E. P. Mellon. They produced a building which combined classical simplicity with the latest electronic and aluminum technology.[88] Measuring 232 feet by 117, it was on completion the largest structure in the country devoted solely to banking. The gray granite exterior was dignified and restrained, the massive banking hall was 62 feet high and supported on Ionic columns, and the Judge's statue of Benjamin Franklin was placed in a prominent position. On the floors above, the offices were arranged around a courtyard with a central skylight, and included adjacent accommodation for RB and (in anticipation of his return) AW. The new building was dedicated in March 1924, with the secretary of the treasury as guest of honor. Mellon's speech described the origin and growth of the family bank, and acclaimed "a success beyond our most ambitious dreams of those early days." No one who had been involved with the bank from the beginning, he concluded, "could have imagined that we should ever require a building of such dimensions, nor that this or any other bank in Pittsburgh would ever have a hundred million [dollars] of deposits."[89]

As the Mellon presence in Pittsburgh ceased to be so entrepreneurially innovative, it became more immediately manifest in these two grand buildings, respectively a cathedral and a temple to finance. At the same time, Andrew Mellon was becoming increasingly interested in philanthropy. Previously, his benefactions had largely been confined to local good causes, such as hospitals and colleges, and his only two serious gifts had been to the Mellon Institute, in memory of his father (and in pursuit of a closer relationship between science and industry), and to Paul's preparatory school, Shady Side Academy, to which he gave nearly $180,000 between 1915 and 1927. During the early 1920s, his annual donations were nearer $50,000 than $100,000; they were in no way systematic, and he funded them out of his current income. As such, they were a small part of his personal expenditure rather than a self-conscious act of creative or engaged giving from what he had accumulated. But now he became a major donor to two institutions. Between 1923 and 1928, he gave $250,000 to finance the library at Choate. (There is no evidence, incidentally, of an equivalent donation to Miss Porter's School, whose results may have impressed him rather less.) He took the same businesslike care with this project as he did when purchasing pictures. He reviewed the designs with his architect nephew, E. P. Mellon, insisting that the scheme be realistically budgeted and asking if his gift could be tax-exempt. Having satisfied himself, he duly laid the cornerstone of the new library at a ceremony coinciding with Paul's graduation.[90]

Mellon's second, and much more substantial, act of largesse concerned his own alma mater, the University of Pittsburgh. Its new chancellor, John G. Bowman (whom Mellon, as a trustee, had helped to appoint just before his departure to Washington), was determined to reinvigorate the university by building an entirely new campus on a neighboring site known as Frick Acres. The eventual result was the construction of the forty-two-story Cathedral of Learning, at a cost of $15 million.[91] From the very beginning, Bowman had sought to interest Mellon in the project, hoping he would finance the purchase of the land. Andrew (and Dick) duly obliged, not least because the university had recently agreed to take over the management of the Mellon Institute, and also because this new venture might yield another major commission for E. P. Mellon, whose work on the new bank building was now done. (EP did indeed produce a design, but it was not accepted.) "It seems to me appropriate," Mellon observed, "that the University of Pittsburgh should be the first to adapt science and architecture to the need of modern conditions in the educational world, for Pittsburgh is associated in the public mind not only with inexhaustible sources of iron and steel, but with the energy and initiative of new undertakings." As when assessing a new business proposition at the bank, Mellon was initially cool and skeptical, and as when buying a picture, he took his time to decide. But Bowman eventually won him over, the land was acquired, and the ground was broken for the Cathedral of Learning. By the time it was topped out in October 1929, Mellon's gift to the university was $1.6 million. Though this represented barely one-tenth of the whole cost, it was nevertheless his most substantial benefaction to date, and his first major foray into the realm of capital giving.[92]

These buildings and donations signaled distinct and portentous changes in Mellon's preoccupations and priorities. But in accepting the economic and social and political order of Pittsburgh, with its harsh inequalities and its fierce partisanship, he remained as unquestioning and as unthinking as ever. One indication of this was in the copious tributes he paid to the prominent Pittsburghers who were one by one passing on. In February 1924, William Flinn died. He had been one of the most notorious of America's big-city bosses, an unrivaled master of graft and corruption, and to his many ethical failings Mellon had always turned a blind eye. "The community," he wrote to Flinn's widow, "will long mourn the loss of a great man of sterling character and wide influence." Flinn was neither a great man nor one of sterling character, but his influence had undoubtedly been extensive.[93] Three years later, James Reed died. Mellon had known him since they had been together at what would become the University of Pittsburgh, and Reed was thus his oldest (and some said closest) friend, as well as his lifelong legal adviser, business associate, and a director of many Mellon companies. In a statement to the press, Mellon eulogized a man of "great ability" and "unquestioned integrity," who possessed both a wide circle of friends and one of the best legal minds of his day; a man who had played a major part in many great undertakings "which have had so much to do with Pittsburgh's growth and prosperity." Reed's work, Mellon concluded, "has been constructive and enduring, for he used his great talents in bringing together and harmonizing men and interests that were in conflict."[94]

But the antagonisms Reed sought to harmonize, in the furtherance of industrial growth and expansion, were those of such warring capitalists as Frick and Carnegie; he had no interest in reconciling managers and trade unions, and remained to the end of his life a vehement opponent of organized labor. So, of course, were both Andrew and Dick, as their father had been before them. To be sure, they publicly endorsed the idea of industrial harmony and amity. In October 1924, Andrew wrote to Howard Heinz, regretting that he could not attend a dinner in Pittsburgh to celebrate fifty-five years of peace in the Heinz family's food-processing plant. Such an occasion, Mellon observed, "is an inspiration to all of us who believe that, when men seriously attempt to understand each other and realize that their primary interests are the same, industrial conflicts will become impossible"; and the example of the Heinz Company held out the hope that "men can yet reach an era of better understanding, which will end industrial strife."[95] But there was not the remotest prospect of such a "better understanding" between the managers and the miners of the Pittsburgh Coal Company, in which both Mellon brothers were major investors, and of which Dick Mellon had become chairman in 1924.[96]

Soon after, Pittsburgh Coal, along with most of the major producers, signed with the United Mine Workers union the so-called Jacksonville agreement, establishing a $7.50 daily wage. Indeed, Mellon himself had brought pressure from Washington to bear on the company to participate and settle. But by 1925, as production and profits declined across the northern United States, and as the mines faced increasing competition from the lower-cost bituminous operations in the South, most of the coal companies would repudiate this accord, even though the Coolidge administration—of which Mellon was a member—was anxious to maintain it. Among the renegers was Pittsburgh Coal, which closed its operations, with the immediate aim of forcing the workers to accept lower pay, and with the broader goal of breaking the UMW and replacing it with an open shop. By these means, the company hoped to bring down its costs and thus return to prewar profitability. Four months later, the defeated miners straggled back to work, having accepted the open shop and a pay cut to $6 a day. But they did so with a great sense of grievance, and in the strikes that followed, many would suffer at the hands of the so-called company police, armed guards employed by the steel and coal firms of western Pennsylvania to protect their property and browbeat malcontents. By then, Dick had long since resigned as chairman, resorting to the familiar Mellon stratagem of distancing himself from events he found distasteful—and potentially embarrassing. But as late as 1927, the Mellon brothers were still aggressively buying more shares in the company.[97]

It was not as easy for the Mellons to stand aloof from Pennsylvania state politics, especially during the months leading up to the senatorial and gubernatorial elections of 1926, by which time W. L. Mellon was state chairman of the GOP.[98] Despite Andrew's initial optimism, Gifford Pinchot had turned out to be a wholly unsatisfactory governor: he soon became a fierce critic of Mellon's money, power, and failure to enforce Prohibition, and of the Coolidge administration generally. For Pinchot was a Republican populist, hostile to machine politics, who frequently inveighed against the fact that for years the state had been run "as part of the business of certain moneyed interests," by which he meant the Mel-

lons among others.[99] Barred by law from running for a second consecu-
tive four-year term, Pinchot now announced that he would oppose the
incumbent senator, George W. Pepper, in the Republican primary. Unlike
Pinchot, Pepper supported the Coolidge administration, and Mellon was
determined to see him re-elected. To make matters even more uncertain,
William A. Vare, the boss of Philadelphia, announced that he, too, would
challenge Pepper, in what was threatening to become a three-way Republican brawl.[100] Mellon now saw no choice but to intervene, and he summoned Vare, his nephew, and other prominent politicians to Washington
for the purpose of agreeing on another "harmony ticket" and stopping
Pinchot. But the negotiations broke down, with Vare determined to run
and convinced he would win.

Thus rebuffed, Mellon turned to Joseph Grundy, president of the
Pennsylvania Manufacturers Association and a prominent Republican
fund-raiser in the state. Though he disliked Pepper, Grundy agreed to
support him as Mellon's candidate, in return for Mellon's support of his
gubernatorial candidate, John S. Fisher. Neither in these negotiations,
nor in those that had taken place earlier, was George Pepper himself consulted; when this later "harmony ticket" was settled, he was merely presented with a fait accompli.[101] The ensuing Republican primary in May
1926 was as acrimonious as it was—for the Mellons—expensive and disappointing. It would later be alleged that the Mellon-Grundy faction had
spent nearly $2 million on their candidates, and that 35,000 so-called poll
watchers had been hired (i.e., bribed) in western Pennsylvania, at a cost of
$10 each. Between them, AW, RB, and WL may have contributed a quar-
ter of a million dollars; and Andrew made a rare political speech, in a joint
appearance with Senator David Reed and Secretary of Labor James
Davis, at a rally in Pittsburgh. He expected "a good margin of favorable
votes," but the result was a divided outcome, which revealed the Pennsylvania Republican Party's disarray and lack of leadership.[102] Supported by
Mellon and Grundy, John Fisher narrowly beat Vare's candidate in the
gubernatorial primary, but in the Senate primary, Vare bested both Pepper and Pinchot. In November 1926, Fisher easily beat his Democratic
rival for governor (Mellon spoke in his support), and Vare won as easily a
seat in the U.S. Senate. But after lengthy hearings, held intermittently
over more than two years, the Senate eventually refused to allow Vare
to take his seat, and Governor Fisher duly appointed Grundy to serve
out the term.[103] It was a triumph for Grundy, at best a partial success for
Mellon, and a humiliating rebuff to Vare.

Vare was denied his seat because the Republican primary in Pennsylvania had become a cause célèbre even before the November election took place. A congressional investigation, chaired by Democratic Senator James Reed of Missouri (not to be confused with Republican Senator David Reed from Pennsylvania), was launched in mid-June 1926 in response to widespread allegations of corruption. Called upon to justify his campaign financing, W. L. Mellon blamed the primary system for causing expensive intraparty factionalism and making the high costs of advertising, letter campaigns, and "poll watchers" unavoidable.[104] He vigorously denied any illegal disbursements, maintaining (for example) that poll watchers were essential in a state that generally lacked voting machines, and he affirmed that, given time, he could account for every dollar they had spent. His uncle artfully avoided testifying by departing to Europe in July 1926 for his annual three-month vacation. As a parting shot, Andrew Mellon noted that giving money to a political party was no different from making a donation to a church—a remark that prompted even the normally pro-Mellon *New York Times* to observe that "the real Pennsylvania scandal is the fact that Pennsylvania did not seem to know that it was doing anything scandalous."[105] The investigations would still be going on when Mellon returned from the continent, as a result of which Vare was duly unseated; but by February 1927, Senator David Reed of Pennsylvania successfully filibustered them to death.

These congressional criticisms of the Mellons' electoral shenanigans in Pennsylvania were but part of a growing chorus of dissatisfaction with the treasury secretary. The tax reductions of the "Mellon Plan" had repeatedly been denounced as the self-serving maneuvers of a rich man who wanted to make all millionaires, including himself, even richer. "It is clear," observed Representative John Nance Garner, one of the secretary's foremost critics, "that Mr. Mellon's design is to reduce his own and the taxes of other wealthy people."[106] But Mellon's reforms were supported by the best American economists of the time, and also by his Democratic predecessors at the Treasury, Carter Glass and David Houston. Hence there was some plausibility to Mellon's claim that taxation was "just like any other business" and that his proposals were both "scientific" and "non-partisan."[107] Like them, Mellon genuinely believed that the rich should pay their just share of taxes, and that they should pay more than they did under Woodrow Wilson. Hence tax *cuts* as a means to discourage tax avoidance; hence his deep hostility to tax-exempt bonds; and hence his limitations on business deductions for capital losses. Like the "supply side" economists decades later, Mellon also believed that the rich could be motivated by tax incentives to invest their savings in productive enterprises, while lower-income earners would benefit by higher employment and rising wages: here was "trickle down" economics three generations before the term was coined.[108]

Despite the considerable cogency of these arguments, the spectacle of a rich man urging rate reductions for the highest income brackets was a political gift Mellon's opponents could not refuse. They also charged that while he treated the rich so generously, he "at the same time decline[s] to give the small taxpayer the same consideration he gives himself." Mellon's "sole purpose," his critics alleged, was "the reduction of the larger taxpayers at the expense of the small taxpayer."[109] In fact, there is no evidence to suggest that Mellon was seeking to shift the burden of tax in this way: he merely wanted to maximize revenue. Indeed, he accepted that the rich should be seen to pay their full share, in order to fill the Treasury's coffers but also to diffuse radical attacks on capital. And in insisting on "the fairness of taxing more lightly incomes from wages, salaries and professional services than the incomes from business or from investments," Mellon actually favored the worker over the plutocrat. This was not sympathy for labor, but calculated pragmatism. For by its nature, earned income was "uncertain and limited in duration; sickness or death destroys it and old age diminishes it," whereas unearned income "may be disposed of during a man's life and it descends to his heirs." Moreover, Mellon preferred direct taxes of a mildly progressive kind to indirect taxes, which tend to be inherently regressive. In absolute dollar terms, his tax reductions were greater at the higher levels, but he sought to reduce taxes at all levels, and in particular to "lessen, so far as possible, the burden of taxation on those least able to bear it." The result speaks for itself: by 1927, the overwhelming majority of Americans did not pay federal income tax.[110]

Criticism of Mellon's tax reforms invariably turned ad hominem, particularly during the immediate post-Harding period, when the Congress was awash with what has been called "investigation hysteria."[111] He was peripherally (and tellingly) involved in the Teapot Dome affair, named after a piece of federally owned oil-bearing acreage that had been illicitly leased out. One of the disreputable figures who in April 1922 had obtained a no-bid lease was Harry F. Sinclair. The transaction was effected by the interior secretary, Albert Fall, at the suggestion of Attorney General Harry Daugherty. Sinclair was also a major benefactor to the Republican Party's 1920 campaign, after which Mellon was approached to "lend" the party $50,000 in exchange for the equivalent in U.S. bonds that had been donated by Sinclair. Mellon refused, returning the bonds after ten days and writing a check of his own for $50,000 which he sent directly to the

Republican Party as an outright gift. As the Senate committee investigating Teapot Dome delved doggedly into Sinclair's misconduct, Mellon remained quiet about his own brief encounter with the man. Eventually, when his nondeal with Sinclair came to light, he was obliged to testify and defend his silence. He insisted that he had known nothing sinister about Sinclair or his bonds, which in any case he had not taken. To Senator La Follette and other critics, this was clear evidence that Mellon's character and connections were irredeemably tainted, and they called for his resignation. But pro-Mellon newspapers, such as the *New York Times*, accepted his testimony as a "complete explanation" and the matter went no further.[112]

Mellon could not escape another critic so easily. In the autumn of 1923, Senator James Couzens, Republican of Michigan, initiated what would become an increasingly acrimonious correspondence, by questioning the secretary's arguments and figures concerning tax-exempt bonds and surtaxes. It was a subject in which Couzens was much interested, for he was reputedly the richest man in Congress: in 1919, he had sold out his stake in the Ford Motor Company, of which he had been general manager, for a reputed $30 million, much of which he had placed in tax-exempts.[113] He had then embarked upon a political career, establishing himself in the Senate as a supporter of La Follette and thus a persistent critic of Mellon's. Couzens took exception to the secretary's reasoning that a higher surtax led to increased investment in tax-exempts, and he also argued that the municipal expenditure financed by tax-exempts was as much to the public benefit as the business spending that stocks financed. "Do you contend," he asked Mellon, "that it is less productive to invest money in thousands of schoolhouses, to invest money in waterworks [and] lighting plants . . . than it is [in] theaters, [and] office buildings?"[114] Mellon responded by pointing out that most of Couzens's fortune was held in the very bonds he was praising for their benefit to the common good, but which also significantly reduced his own tax liability. To which Couzens retorted that his investments at least precluded conflict of interest, whereas Mellon, by contrast, was bound to benefit from his own policies after taxes were reduced.[115]

Early in 1924, Couzens moved his attack to the Senate floor, calling for an investigation into the workings of the Internal Revenue Service, on the grounds of many perceived irregularities in its handling of taxation. Mellon replied that such an investigation was unnecessary and would be disruptive, but he would not object because the Treasury had nothing to hide. A committee was duly established; it was chaired by Senator

James E. Watson, a staunch administration supporter, but Couzens was a member, and if he voted with the Democrats, he could command a majority. With such a broad mandate, the committee could investigate the tax rebates given during the war to Mellon companies, especially Gulf Oil, which had received for the years 1917–19 refunds totaling $4.6 million.[116] Mellon denied any wrongdoing, pointing out that the rebates had been settled under the Wilson administration, and that the negotiations, conducted on the company's behalf by Colonel Drake, had all been completed before the Harding administration took office. True, the Treasury had actually paid the refund to Gulf during Mellon's tenure, but that was merely because of the bureaucratic backlog from wartime. In any case, his supporters insisted, the whole episode had been taken out of context and blown up out of all proportion. Between 1917 and 1923, only 1 percent of federal taxes collected had been refunded by the government, whereas new assessments were running at eight times that amount.[117]

But as Mellon might by now have suspected, Couzens would prove a tenacious antagonist in what was dubbed "the battle of the millionaires." In April 1924, he persuaded the committee to hire a special investigator, Francis J. Heney of San Francisco, whose salary would be paid by Couzens personally. Mellon appealed to the president, insisting that the inquiry was based on "personal grievance," that the investigation had disclosed that "no company in which I have been interested has received any different or better treatment than any other taxpayer," and that it was impossible to carry on work while the Treasury Department was being pried into by a privately hired and politically motivated agent: in short that "government by investigation is not government."[118] Coolidge thereupon denounced the arrangement in a letter to the Senate, which the *New York Times* called "one of the most sensational utterances that have come from a President of the United States in years." The Senate condemned Coolidge's interference with legislative prerogatives, and promptly voted funds to hire an investigator other than Heney. Soon after, the chief economist for the committee, T. S. Adams, resigned, and Senator Watson vacated the chair. Both men had concluded that no good would come of the hearings, and they were eager to avoid responsibility for the outcome: Watson as a loyal Republican, Adams as a longtime Treasury adviser. Consequently, Couzens now became chairman, and the hearings were resumed in the autumn. They dragged on well into 1925, and the transcripts ran to more than four thousand pages, but they were generally inconclusive: no misconduct was proved, no civil or criminal proceedings were initiated, and no corrective legislation was recommended or enacted.

Some questionable practices were revealed, but they were insufficient for Couzens to initiate any viable prosecution.[119]

As the Couzens hearings resumed in the autumn of 1924, Mellon found himself under attack from another quarter. During the summer recess, the Senate released a report, compiled by the Federal Trade Commission, charging Alcoa with unfair trade practices.[120] These were the interim findings of an investigation that had begun in 1922 and would last eight years. The report contained testimony by Alcoa's chief executive, Arthur Vining Davis, to the effect that the company "really consist[ed] of A. W. Mellon and R. B. Mellon"—an assertion scarcely consistent with the secretary's oft-repeated claim that he had withdrawn from business. The report also found that the company had "a practically complete monopoly of the aluminum in the United States," that it enjoyed a "high protective tariff," and that as a result, it was able to "control the price of aluminum." The FTC concluded that Alcoa was engaging "in various practices forbidden by judicial decree under the Sherman Act." Mellon hastened to rebut these charges, repeatedly avowing there was "no basis whatsoever" to substantiate them; President Coolidge would later restaff the FTC with men more sympathetic to the "needs" of business.[121] But by coupling the commission's report with the findings of the Couzens committee, the Democrats sought to depict Mellon as being at least as corrupt as his former cabinet colleagues, Daugherty, Fall, and Denby, in the hope that he, too, might be compelled to resign. Their attacks enlivened the last weeks of the election campaign of November 1924, but Coolidge's overwhelming victory meant that they were again forgotten, and the charges were eventually dismissed by the FTC in 1930.[122]

Still, the Couzens committee hearings continued past Election Day, and although inconclusive, they were taxing to Mellon's patience. By the spring of 1925, he was determined to retaliate. Early in March, the Treasury informed Couzens that it was reopening his 1919 tax return, and soon after, he was reassessed to the tune of $11 million in back taxes, based on a recalculation of the imputed profit on the sale of his Ford stock that year. Mellon seemed vindicated by the disclosure.[123] But the secretary's rejoicing was premature, for this tactic would prove to be as ill-judged and ham-fisted as his scheme to alter divorce law in Pennsylvania fifteen years earlier. On further investigation, the independent-minded Board of Tax Appeals (which Mellon himself had created) concluded in May that Couzens had actually *overpaid* his 1919 federal taxes by $900,000 and was entitled to a refund.[124] This decision was the greatest humiliation Mellon had yet suffered at the Treasury, and there were two disadvantageous consequences, one immediate, the other delayed. The first was that Couzens's hatred of Mellon was now incandescent: he was more determined than ever to bring the secretary down. The second was that Mellon himself had shown how the technical issue of income tax compliance could be used to pursue a politically motivated vendetta. In this case, the quarry escaped unscathed, but a decade hence, the Roosevelt administration would use the same weapon to mount a devastating attack on Mellon himself.[125]

The years from 1923 to 1926 witnessed Mellon's greatest successes at the Treasury, but they also unleashed opposition elements whose claims would thereafter increasingly dog him. There was, at the least, more evidence that Mellon was still involved with his family companies than those who pursued such investigations could know. Indeed, in the spring of 1924, at the very time the Couzens committee was beginning its work, Senator Kenneth McKellar again raised the matter of whether Mellon could serve as treasury secretary in the light of widespread suspicions concerning those continued connections and activities. Once again, Senators David A. Reed and Henry Cabot Lodge answered the allegations, in what seemed a comprehensive and convincing way. Moreover, as Mellon approached the peak of his political success and national popularity, he seemed virtually invulnerable to attacks he dismissed as so many expressions of envy, malice, and partisan spite. Impervious as ever to nuance or differing opinion, he saw himself as a man of integrity who had satisfied all the legal requirements for holding office, who was doing his public duty in the interests of the nation as a whole. He saw no peril, much less legitimacy, in the backbiting of opportunistic rascals who sought to denigrate and belittle him. To his admirers, and he had many, "Mr. Mellon" was simply "the sincerest man in public life today."[126]

IV. POSSESSIONS AND POSSIBILITIES

The passing of the Revenue Act in February 1926 and Ailsa's wedding three months later were significant milestones in Andrew Mellon's professional and personal life. (The Pennsylvania Republican primary was another sort of milestone, but Mellon distanced himself from that.) His major goals were accomplished at the Treasury, his daughter was suitably and (it seemed) happily married, and he himself was approaching the zenith of his public fame as well as of his private fortune. He had effected the tax reforms he had advocated since joining the government, he had reduced the national debt by nearly a billion dollars a year, federal spending had been cut from $6.5 billion in 1921–22 to $3.5 billion five years later, and he would have funded almost all of America's overseas loans by the time the Foreign Debt Commission ended its business in 1927.[127] Europe was heading toward stability and prosperity, and America was being transformed into an urbanized, mass consumer society. This was the age of skyscrapers and airplanes, of motorcars and film, of radios and refrigerators, of jazz and the Charleston; and it was the age whose jagged, strident rebellion and dislocation would be evoked and proclaimed by Scott Fitzgerald and George Gershwin. Ironically, it was shy, silent Andrew Mellon who was widely credited with having ushered in these buoyant, booming modern times (though the credit was due at least as much to the extraordinary inventiveness of Thomas Alva Edison, to whom Mellon would personally present the Congressional Gold Medal in October 1928).[128]

"We are now," the secretary observed in November 1926, "at a very high tide of prosperity," of which he was not only the architect but also, as his critics alleged, a conspicuous beneficiary. The resources and liabilities of the Mellon National Bank grew from $176 million in 1926 to $204 million two years later; the Union Trust Company continued to pay prodigious dividends; Alcoa, Gulf, and Standard Steel Car were expanding beyond the United States to become multinationals; McClintic-Marshall and Standard Steel Car had their order books full. (Only Koppers and the Pittsburgh Coal Company seemed to be losing their way, the former for want of a coherent business plan, the latter as prey to the general economic stagnation of the region and the industry.)[129] In all, Mellon's net income increased from $2.4 million in 1923 to $6.5 million in 1925, but fell back to $5.2 million in 1926—and this was after paying federal income tax that was $950,000 in 1923, $880,000 in 1924, and averaged $1.5 million for 1925 and 1926. As the third greatest taxpayer after John D. Rockefeller Sr. and Henry Ford, Mellon could not be accused of shirking his fair obligation, or of failing to practice what he preached. But the greatest taxpayers necessarily benefited most from across-the-board cuts, even those proportionately favoring the less advantaged. While Mellon's income more than doubled during these years, the tax he paid on it went up rather more slowly, and he was not paying as much as the $1.9 million and the $1.7 million that he had paid on a smaller income at higher rates in 1919 and 1920.[130] And as Mellon's income increased, so did his principal: in 1923, the book value of his fortune was $81.7 million, and by 1926 it had just passed $100 million—a figure which, in real terms, must have been closer to $150 million, and may even have exceeded that. In our time and currency, he would have been a very substantial billionaire, and his wealth was growing at a rate that only serious art collecting and philanthropy could dampen.

There were other ways in which Mellon did well thanks to his own policies and those of the rest of the Coolidge administration.[131] The repeal of the gift tax, a provision of the Revenue Act of 1926, was to him of national importance, a way to safeguard the sanctity and mobility of accumulated wealth, which he regarded as the essential reservoir for the industrial investment that was vital for economic growth. But the repeal also made it possible for Mellon himself to begin transferring his immense holdings to his children, and toward the end of the decade, he would begin to make such untaxed gifts in increasing amounts. (That repeal of the gift tax would also help furnish the wherewithal for irresponsible stock speculation, and thus help bring about the catastrophe of 1929–33, is no small irony of Mellon's life.) The passing of the McFadden-Pepper banking act in February 1927 was also to his personal advantage. Its prime aim was to provide for the indefinite extension of reserve bank charters; but another provision allowed national banks to set up subsidiary branches in their localities, something that had previously been forbidden in many states, including Pennsylvania, for fear it would lead to vast, irresponsible financial conglomerates. If the Mellon National Bank was to maintain its dominance in Pittsburgh, and extend its reach out into the steel towns along the three rivers, it would need to complement its grand new Smithfield Street building by considering some form of branch extension. Not surprisingly, Mellon was strongly in favor of the measure, which he described as "the most important piece of banking legislation enacted since the Federal Reserve Act." Two months later, however, the Pennsylvania legislature effectively rendered the law inapplicable in the state. For Andrew and Dick, the challenge of extending the territorial reach of Mellon Bank remained unresolved.[132]

Here was an ethical quagmire. To be sure, Mellon had never sought to avoid federal taxes by investing in tax-exempt bonds, and he had been paying substantial sums since 1913. Moreover, his primary objective in promoting national prosperity was certainly not to enrich his own companies, nor did he reduce surtaxes principally to enrich himself. Had these been his priorities, he would have done better to stay out of Washington and continue in banking and in business. But even though the consequences were unintended, Mellon and his companies *were* doing very well thanks to his own policies, and he undoubtedly benefited from other legislation enacted while he was a cabinet secretary. If Mellon saw the slightest ethical or moral complication in this state of affairs, he never breathed a word of it to anyone. More likely, he was blinkered by his absolute faith that a buoyant economy, based on a genuine growth in productive resources and in employment, was good for everyone. In his view, his self-interest, the interest of industry and finance, the interests of workers and their families, and the broader national interest were identical and inseparable. "Business prosperity," he wrote to the president in June 1926, "is the barometer of the individual prosperity of our citizens."[133] And, he might have added, the measure of his own national standing. But while this was fine as the twenties roared, would it continue to be so when the boom ended, as all booms eventually did (something Mellon knew as well as anyone), and when the good times he personified, and for which he was widely praised, suddenly ceased to roll?

Through the second half of 1926, the criticism of Mellon's policies and personal affairs continued as background noise. The delay in completing the belated French debt settlement (Congress would not ratify it until the French National Assembly did) led to revived attacks on his unauthorized negotiations of foreign loans—from the cancellationists like Frederick Peabody, who thought the sum total should be written off; from revisionists, including many academic economists who had supported the secretary's tax plans, who now wanted the debt scaled down faster; and from the hardliners in Congress who had consistently deplored his "ability to pay" formula because it meant the United States would not get back the full amount of capital and interest it was legitimately owed.[134] Mellon replied at length to these various objections, while at the same time speaking out against the McNary-Haugen Farm Relief Bill, which sought to establish a new federal agency aimed at helping to drive up domestic prices for farmers' produce. Mellon was deeply opposed: he had never shown much sympathy for agriculture, he did not believe that the federal government should intervene to assist ailing sectors of the economy, and he insisted it was wrong to try to modify the "fundamental economic law" of supply and demand. For these opinions Mellon was criticized in turn: How could a man who supported tariffs on behalf of industry be opposed to intervention on behalf of the farmer?[135] There was strong support for the measure in the rural South and the West, and only Coolidge's veto prevented it from becoming law.

As the complaints of Congress continued, the secretary increasingly turned his attention to his paintings. In September 1926, Mellon and Duveen met in London, and soon after, Duveen visited him in Washington, where more pictures had been hung in his apartment. "Business prospects marvellous," Duveen exulted. "I expect to sell all of them." In fact, Mellon turned down paintings by Velázquez, Rubens, and Giorgione, but agreed to take Rembrandt's *A Young Man Seated at a Table*, Rogier van der Weyden's *Portrait of a Lady*, and Vermeer's *The Smiling Girl*. The three cost him $975,000; but having returned Raphael's *Giuliano de Medici*, he only had to pay $525,000.[136] Later that year, Duveen bought two outstanding paintings from the sale of Lord Michelham's estate: *Miss Catherine Tatton*, by Gainsborough, and *Pinkie*, a portrait of Sarah Goodin Barrett Moulton, by Lawrence. "The *Pinkie*," Duveen advised Mellon with familiar hyperbole, "is one of the greatest and most beautiful of all English pictures in the world, while as regards the Gainsborough, *Miss Tatton*, there is nothing finer painted by the master." Despite the fact that *Pinkie* reminded Andrew of Ailsa, the painting eventually went to Huntington, to whom Duveen had in any case promised it first, but Mellon finally took the Gainsborough for $224,000—a sale on which, at the current rate of exchange, Duveen made no profit. "We have done [the] right thing by Mellon," Duveen wrote, perhaps feeling guilty about *Pinkie*, "which is all I care about."[137]

At this stage, Mellon still saw himself as essentially a private collector. "I have," he told the Duchess of Rutland in 1926, "only those paintings and a few tapestries which I have acquired from time to time when I had suitable places of residence." "I have not had," he added, "occasion to consider the acquisition of such for public purposes."[138] But Duveen saw his self-appointed task as being to educate and encourage Mellon to make his collection the equal of any rivals, and to see it as an evolving enterprise with an ultimate purpose at which he may already have been hinting. Accordingly, he suggested that Mellon should welcome visits from people of "great artistic taste and appreciation": fellow collectors and directors of galleries. He urged him to buy "seven or eight great Rembrandts," because "he could not hope to form a great collection to beat Widener's unless he had some." He advised there was nothing worth his attention in the sale of the Leverhulme and Castiglione pictures: "both these gentlemen spent much money in their time, but in my opinion were merely accumulators, not collectors."[139] He talked at length with Mellon when they were in London in September 1926: "have been with him daily this week," Duveen reported with satisfaction to his New York office, "and have had marvellous interviews. Am very enthusiastic for the future. Closer to him than ever." And they spent many hours visiting the National Gallery in London: perhaps Duveen was even then suggesting that the ultimate purpose of Mellon's collection was to be the nucleus of a similar institution in Washington.[140]

Meanwhile, after a leisurely honeymoon spent motoring across Europe, Mr. and Mrs. Bruce had reached Rome, where they settled into a palatial apartment, and David began work for the State Department as American vice consul in July 1926. But on the very first day that her husband appeared at the office, Ailsa was suddenly afflicted by a mysterious illness that left her constantly listless and prone to low-grade and intermittent fever; she did not eat and was losing weight. Soon after, Andrew arrived with Paul on summer holiday, and he took Ailsa to Évian-les-Bains on the shore of Lake Geneva, in the hope that the fashionable French spa might revive her—which, for a time, as long as he was there, it did.[141] Supported by a personal appeal from his eminent father-in-law to the secretary of state, David Bruce applied for a leave of absence so he could take Ailsa to a more salubrious climate. Once David had joined his wife in France, Andrew left for home. But Ailsa's condition promptly worsened, and it was thus a solitary return to Washington for her father. After fifteen years in service, Miss Sylvester had retired to Boston, with six hundred shares of preferred stock in Alcoa; Paul "saw very little" of his father at this time, and Ailsa was ill and an ocean distant. "You are so far away," Andrew wrote to her, "that the top of 1785 Mass Ave seems a very lonesome place this Sunday." "I do miss you!" he concluded, and signed himself "Your ever loving father."[142]

Ailsa's health showed no sign of sustained improvement, but Andrew now resolved to secure her financial well-being, and by the end of the year, he had completed the transfer to her of 6,000 shares in the Pennsylvania, the Illinois Central, and the Baltimore and Ohio Railroad companies, along with 2,000 shares in the Pennsylvania Water Company and 1,000 in the Oil Well Supply Company. They were together worth $800,000, and with the million dollars of shares in Alcoa he had already given her, they provided Mr. and Mrs. Bruce with an assured income of $110,000 a year. In his accompanying letter, addressed to Ailsa at the Bellevue Palace Hotel in Bern, Switzerland, Andrew sought to explain "everything definitively." The securities were all now in her name, a deposit box would be provided at the Mellon National Bank, and the dividends would be credited to her account. "I have learned," he went on, "to have confidence in your ability to intelligently manage your own affairs, and am pleased and gratified that I can feel so." (Wishful thinking, this, for if Ailsa had given him cause, the proof has not survived.) "On your part," Andrew continued, "I want you to feel settled and independent." "I have complete confidence," he told her, "in David's judgment also. You are fortunate in having a husband of such sterling character and dependability." (So, indeed, she was: Andrew got on very well with David—much better, in fact, than with Paul—and the admiration seems to have been mutual.) "This is a long letter," he concluded, "but all about your business affairs. I will bring it to an end and write you of other things again today or tomorrow."[143]

As Christmas 1926 approached, Andrew would write Ailsa another letter, revealing much about his life, both private and public, in the wake of the passage of the Revenue Act, and of her wedding.[144] She was then in a hospital in Switzerland, and he had heard nothing from her for two weeks. "I know," he gently scolded, "it is irksome sometimes to write letters, but if only a word or two, or a cable now and then, it would be a great satisfaction." "I hope," he went on, "you received my letter telling you about your investments, and that you understood it all." Being "kept so busy, every day," he was turning down numerous invitations to dinners and social events, but still felt obliged to accept "a great deal" of them, and many people he met asked after her. "I tell them all 'You are getting on very well.'" Hoping to join Ailsa and David for Christmas, he had looked at the sailing schedules, contemplating a brief trip, "just to go over and back with Paul and have even a day with you." But there was simply too much to do, and the dates would not work. "You both seem so terribly far away," he again lamented. But he would "be with you in love and spirit." (However "independent" Andrew may have wanted Ailsa to be in financial terms, her departure from the nest obviously pained him.) Meanwhile, Paul was finishing midterm exams at Yale, "getting through them very well," and Andrew would be spending Christmas with him in Pittsburgh. He had recently talked to Nora on the telephone: she was also well, but "Mr. Lee has been very seriously ill with some kind of intestinal attacks." As for the weather in Washington: "today we are having our first snow."

Such, as the year neared its end, was the domestic humdrum of the financial guardian of the richest nation on the planet, himself one of the wealthiest men in the world, surrounded by one of the greatest (and growing) private art collections in existence. Meanwhile, at the United States Treasury, there were significant and portentous changes in the offing. "I am trying," Andrew told Ailsa in the same lengthy letter, "to organize my office so that some of the things I am having to do may be taken over by assistants." Garrard Winston was leaving as undersecretary; he was replaced by Ogden Mills, as able a man as his two predecessors, and one who passionately believed in low taxes, orthodox financing, and a balanced budget. But in other ways, Mills was cast from a rather different professional mold than Winston and Parker Gilbert. For he was every inch a Republican politician: he had been a member of the House for much of the decade, serving on the Ways and Means Committee; he had staunchly supported the administration, especially over the passing of the 1926 Revenue Act; he ran unsuccessfully for governor in New York later that year; and—though Mellon may not have noticed it—he clearly had set his sight on higher office.[145] From March 1927, Mills would take most of the routine Treasury work from Mellon's shoulders, much to the secretary's contented acquiescence. This was partly because he believed his main work was done, and at seventy-three, he wanted to take things more gently. But it was also, paradoxically, that he was finding something new to do.

As Andrew explained to Ailsa in the same pre-Christmas letter, he was looking for "a new assistant (not yet selected) particularly to have charge of some new activities that I have been made responsible for." One matter of direct interest would be the design of a new dollar bill, which would be smaller than those that had been in circulation since 1861. His motive was economy rather than aesthetics: a smaller bill would not be folded as much or so often as a larger bill, and would therefore last longer, thereby saving the government an estimated $2 million a year. The change would be completed by 1929, and Mellon would describe it as "one of the most important steps ever undertaken in connection with our currency."[146] But the most important of his "new activities" was "public building to be constructed in Washington and elsewhere." In the very month of Ailsa's wedding, Congress had appropriated $165 million for this purpose, "and put the responsibility on me for final approval of locations and selection of the architects and designs." "It is," he told his daughter, "interesting and important work, as there may be opportunity to make a large part of Washington equal to or superior in beautiful planning and architecture to Paris or any city in the world." "That work," he concluded, "is taking more of my attention now than any other." Here was a new task, of constructive statesmanship and of statesmanly construction, which would increasingly take up Mellon's attention during the remainder of his time at the Treasury, and which, in ways he could not yet foresee, would eventually occupy him for the rest of his life.

11

CARRYING ON WITH HOOVER
Great Ideas to Great Crash, 1927–29

I had never failed in anything on which I had set my mind so far,
and why might I not succeed in this also?

Thomas Mellon and His Times, p. 154

I. TREASURY, CONGRESS, AND PRESIDENCY

By the beginning of 1927, Andrew Mellon's work at the Treasury
was largely done. Taxes had been cut, government spending had
been halved, and the debt had been reduced by $6 billion. The surplus for
fiscal year 1927, at first estimated at $180 million, had been revised to
$300 million; but it eventually attained the record level of $636 million,
which speaks better of the government's capacity to generate revenue
than its ability to make projections.[1] Fewer poor people were paying
taxes; more rich people were doing so; the national economy was full
speed ahead. "I see nothing to indicate that business will not be good
throughout the country," Mellon observed in late March 1927, before
embarking on a brief trip to Europe:

> The stock market seems to be going on in very orderly fashion, and I see
> no evidence of over-speculation. There is an abundant supply of easy
> money throughout the country which should take care of any emergen-
> cies which should arise. I do not look for any change in the Federal
> Reserve Rate for some time to come, because I can see no reason for
> changing it ... Our government will have about $500,000,000 surplus
> on hand as of June 30 ... All signs and indications at the moment point
> to the country enjoying a successful business year.[2]

Until the time of the presidential election early in November 1928, Mellon remained generally pleased with the economy, and thus relatively relaxed about it.[3] But while the boom continued, its nature was changing. Previously, it had been largely based on productive investment in the growth of resources and output. But with unprecedented deposits and accumulating surpluses, banks and businesses now began to lend to brokers and speculators, who promised high returns based on buying and selling shares, encouraged by Wall Street's and Main Street's belief that prices could only go up. One select group of stocks, averaging 186 on March 23, 1927, reached 196 on April 5, 200 on April 12, and 217 on June 2, a gain of 31 points in ten weeks.[4] Mellon did not generally approve of stock speculation, and scarcely understood the greedy, gambling mentality behind it. But he did not wish to take any corrective fiscal action that might cause the economy to stumble before an election, and the Federal Reserve Board likewise showed no inclination to raise interest rates, which fluctuated between 3.5 percent and 4 percent from the beginning of 1925 until the end of 1927. Yet for the board, for Mellon, and for Benjamin Strong, the reason for holding rates down was increasingly international rather than domestic: the need to encourage gold to flow to Europe to support the newly stabilized currencies there. (Herbert Hoover would later denounce Strong as "a mental annex to Europe.")[5]

Much of Mellon's business at the Treasury during 1927 and early 1928 thus seemed predictable and routine. Having only recently succeeded in having his tax reforms included in the Revenue Act of 1926, he wanted to wait to see how they worked out. Arguing that the massive federal surplus of 1927 would not reappear the following year, and with his best estimates putting it at only $252 million, he proposed only minor tax reductions, to the extent of $225 million, in the next revenue bill he sent to the House.[6] He sought a reduction in corporate income tax from 13.5 percent to 12 percent, the first notable relief for business since the repeal of the excess profits tax in 1922. He proposed that surtaxes on those earning between $10,000 and $70,000 be adjusted downward, and he urged that the federal estate tax be repealed altogether, leaving it to states to tax inheritance if they wished. In the autumn of 1927, these proposals were discussed by the House Ways and Means Committee, but Mellon preferred to let his undersecretary do most of the talking: Ogden Mills had been a member of the committee earlier in his career, and would increasingly become the Treasury Department's front man.

But once again, Mellon (and Mills) met with resistance, for with elections pending in 1928, the Democrats now took up the very cause of tax reduction they had previously so derided. The House minority leader,

John Nance Garner, wanted the corporation tax rate lowered to 11 percent and the automobile tax repealed, along with all wartime excise taxes. Meanwhile, the Ways and Means Committee came up with its own proposals: there should be no repeal of the estate tax or adjustment of surtaxes, but a reduction in corporation tax greater than Mellon wanted but less than Garner proposed. The resulting bill got bogged down in the House, and Mellon became increasingly worried that, with the surplus dwindling and additional tax cuts likely, the balanced budget was in jeopardy. It was, he maintained, in a public letter to President Coolidge, "an essential element of any sound fiscal system, and as long as I am Secretary, the Treasury Department will resist the undermining of the principle." He also took issue with the Chamber of Commerce's advocacy of $400 million in tax cuts.[7] That a Republican organization should be supporting the Democrats seemed to Mellon both reckless and opportunistic, and in letters and speeches he made it plain the business community could expect no special favors from him.

By spring of 1928, the revenue bill had finally reached the Senate, where it was batted back and forth between the Finance Committee and the floor. Eventually, the corporate income tax rate was set at 12 percent, the surtaxes remained unchanged, the estate tax was preserved at current levels, and an attempt to make tax returns public again was successfully beaten off. Meanwhile, Democrats in both chambers complained that the Treasury estimates of the surplus were being constantly manipulated in order to make the case against further tax cuts. The eventual legislation was a tepid compromise. The Democrats had failed to make political hay by reducing taxes as sharply as they wanted, while the Republicans could claim that they had reduced taxes for the fourth time since they had taken power, although this cut was relatively small. Assisted by Senator David A. Reed on the Finance Committee, Mellon had successfully fended off calls for greater cuts which would have depressed federal revenue by as much as $500 million, thereby making it impossible to balance the budget. The secretary who had wielded the tax ax with increasing determination in 1921, 1924, and 1926 was now more concerned with trying to hold the line.

During the same period, the enforcement of Prohibition remained an intractable problem. Since mid-1925, the reorganization of the Prohibition Unit had been in the hands of Brigadier General Andrews, who was by now an assistant secretary of the Treasury.[8] He was eager to dismiss all Haynes-era political appointees, and Mellon generally approved; but he was not eager to wrangle with Congress over political appointments, or to reactivate his (temporarily quiescent) "dry" critics. In March 1927, Congress finally passed the Mellon-Andrews Reorganization Act, establishing a new Prohibition Bureau within the Treasury but putting it under the authority of Haynes, the very figure Mellon and Andrews had tried to sideline. Relations between Haynes and Andrews were predictably uneasy, and so amid continuing criticism of the Treasury's lack of zeal, Mellon eventually had to sack both men. In their places, he promoted chief chemist James Doran to commissioner and brought in Seymour Lowman, former lieutenant governor of New York, as assistant secretary. Both were capable, but given such pervasive flouting of the law, real enforcement of Prohibition remained a fantasy. And the secretary was still branded the owner of a distillery by the drys, no matter how often he denied it.[9]

By early 1928, the stock market "began to rise, not by slow, steady steps, but by great vaulting leaps," and the volume of shares traded broke one record after another. With Mellon's approval, the Federal Reserve Board—recently unburdened of Harding crony Daniel Crissinger, who had been replaced by Roy A. Young, for eight years governor of the Minneapolis Federal Reserve Bank—now reversed its low-interest policy and sanctioned three separate increases of 0.5 percent in the first half of the year, bringing the rate to 5 percent by the summer of 1928, the highest since 1921.[10] These measures proved ineffectual: stock speculation intensified, and gold began returning to the United States for the first time in three years, not only feeding the domestic speculative frenzy but also threatening to destabilize the recently restored international economy. But Mellon saw no cause for great worry. In February 1928, he wrote an article in praise of American capitalism and its work ethic, which might have been penned by his father. There had, he insisted, been "built up in this country an economic and industrial organization under which we have achieved not only a vast amount of wealth, but a distribution of it that is unprecedented, and a standard of living that is the best justification, if any is needed, of the American system." So long as Americans believed that "work is the only honorable occupation, and that life has more to offer than merely the spending of money on selfish enjoyment," then there was nothing to fear.[11]

As Calvin Coolidge's term of office drew to a close, there was widespread political speculation about whether he would run for re-election. Mellon had no doubt that he would, or that he would win. But on August 2, 1927, with Mellon away in Europe on his summer holiday, the president stunned Washington by announcing "I do not choose to run."[12]

What did this characteristically cryptic statement mean? Had he decided that he would not seek re-election under any circumstances? Or was he testing his popularity, and perhaps angling to be drafted at the Republican convention? In fact, Coolidge had made a firm decision not to run again under any circumstances; he meant what he said when he urged the Republican National Committee to "vigorously continue the serious task of selecting another candidate." Mellon, fervently hoping that Coolidge would reconsider, expended a great deal of time, effort, and political capital trying to persuade him to do so. It was a mistake, both in retrospect and at the time: in the first place, Coolidge "was serious and firm in his conviction not to be a candidate"; in the second, promoting Coolidge would likely disadvantage Mellon with whoever eventually became the Republican nominee.[13]

In the wake of Coolidge's announcement, there was a brief bubble of support for Mellon himself, which lasted until the spring of 1928. The Hearst press and the Pittsburgh Republican machine both boosted his presidential prospects, and so did such independent journals as the *Denver Post*, the *New York American*, and the *Los Angeles Examiner*. News of this possibility even reached England. "Should your ambition include the presidency of the USA," Percy McMullen wrote to him, "no one prays for your attainment of it more fervently than your humble servant."[14] Early in 1928, Henry A. Rose of the National News Service produced a widely distributed pamphlet citing Mellon's achievements, and one bankers' journal issued an editorial explaining "why the times call for a president of Mellon's type." Henry Ford expressed his enthusiasm for the idea, and one of Mellon's foremost congressional critics, John Nance Garner, who would later be FDR's first vice president, insisted that he was the logical Republican nominee. "Mr. Mellon," he told the House of Representatives, "has dominated the financial, economic and fiscal relations of the United States for the past four years." "Every Republican in the administration," he observed with considerable exaggeration, "has done his bidding." As such, Mellon was the most powerful man in the world, and Garner doubted "whether the Democrats could beat him."[15]

But there were also serious difficulties attending a Mellon presidential bid—which may, indeed, have been why Garner had made a point of so strongly favoring it. The secretary was in his mid-seventies, and so if elected would be by far the oldest president yet; the prospect of Mellon stumping vigorously and effectively across the length and breadth of the country was less than zero; and much would be made of his controversial activities in business and in Pennsylvania politics. Indeed, at just this time, Mellon received a sharp reminder of how embarrassing were his connections as a coal owner. Following the recent, brutal defeat of the miners' unions, the Senate had set up a committee to investigate the industry (on which sat both William Cabell Bruce—Ailsa's father-in-law—and James Couzens), and some of its members traveled to Pittsburgh to see the mines at first hand. They found the conditions of work and life appalling, and it was clear that the company police had harassed and frequently assaulted unionized workers when the owners had brought in scabs to break the strikes. The Senate inquiry was a devastating indictment of a declining, inefficient, unprofitable, badly managed, and inhumanely run industry. Dick Mellon was summoned to appear before the committee in Washington on March 23, 1928, both as a former chairman of the Pittsburgh Coal Company and also as a major shareholder.[16]

He gave a lamentable performance, and it was an embarrassing blow to the secretary. In reply to sharp questioning from anti-Mellon senators, Dick admitted that his company had violated the Jacksonville agreement; that he had not visited his Pittsburgh mines recently; that he had no idea under what conditions his employees and their families were living; that he had never done anything to "alleviate this suffering or destitution"; and that he had "perfect confidence in the men who are operating the business."[17] But most damaging was Dick's exchange, toward the end of his testimony, with Oliver Eaton, attorney for the United Mine Workers union, concerning Pittsburgh Coal's private police force, and its so-called equipment:

MR. EATON: You never heard of the question of machine guns being bought [for the company police]?

MR. MELLON: I never heard of that. They may have.

MR. EATON: Would you approve of them having machine guns—

MR. MELLON: Such as the police here have them?

MR. EATON: I beg your pardon.

MR. MELLON: The same as the police have here.

MR. EATON: Well, would you approve of that?

MR. MELLON: It is necessary. You could not run without them.

MR. EATON: You could not run a coal company without machine guns?

MR. MELLON: No, I didn't say without machine guns.

MR. EATON: Well, I am asking you about machine guns.

MR. MELLON: Well, I don't know anything about machine guns. I don't know whether the police have them there.[18]

To be sure, Dick Mellon never quite said, as some critics alleged, "you can't run a coal mine without machine guns." But he came very close, and his whole shifty testimony left a deplorable impression of managerial ignorance and human indifference. It exposed the dark realities of life in the mines of the Allegheny region, and would certainly have been used to very damaging effect had Andrew Mellon decided to seek the presidency. But there was never any real likelihood of that. As the normally pro-Mellon *New York Times* observed, there were many reasons why his "nomination for the Presidency would be absurd to the point of impossibility." Mellon would decline all invitations, citing his age as an insurmountable barrier, and in January 1928 he issued a public statement that he would not consider the use of his name in connection with the Republican nomination "now or at any time." But even this formal disclaimer could not quell the draft-Mellon movement completely. "Pressure on me," he recorded in his diary in May 1928, after a meeting with the Pennsylvania Republicans, "to allow my name as a candidate, but I refuse . . . I feel sure it would be a mistake." Two days later, he recorded that Frank Kellogg, secretary of state, "thinks I should have assented to be Presidential Candidate." And almost on the eve of the Republican convention, there were still some senators whose "almost universal regard for myself" allowed them to believe that Mellon would really be their man.[19]

Who, then, did Mellon want as the next Republican president, if neither he nor Coolidge was available? On his return from Europe in September 1927, it was briefly rumored that he might support Charles Evans Hughes, Harding's secretary of state, who had previously been a presidential candidate in 1916. But Hughes was not interested. Mellon would not back the vice president, Charles Dawes, because of his support for the McNary-Haugen Farm Relief Bill. And he did not want Herbert Hoover, the long-serving secretary of commerce. Their unlikely inclusion in successive Republican administrations had been the by-product of an internal party squabble, and they had been in constant competition for dominance in both the Harding and the Coolidge cabinets. Mellon, moreover, thought Hoover "too much inclined to have his own solution of problems, frequently unsound"; and he also doubted his rival's conservative credentials.[20] For Hoover had once allowed his name to be entered in the *Democratic* primary in Michigan, and in 1922 he had supported a government-sponsored public works program which Mellon had thought a threat to a balanced budget. Hoover, Mellon believed, was a closet interventionist, and not truly wedded to the sanctity and independence of the markets, and as secretary of commerce he had asserted himself across a whole range of government departments, in a self-aggrandizing and intrusive way.[21]

By early 1928, however, the Hoover bandwagon had definitely begun to roll, and among Mellon's subordinates at the Treasury, both assistant secretary Ogden Mills and David H. Blair, commissioner of internal revenue, became strong supporters of their boss's bête noire. At least Mellon's former deputy, Parker Gilbert, shared his hostility to Hoover and was convinced he would not do well at foreign policy. When questioned about his preferences in January, Mellon equivocated: "I am not indicating any position on the matter, and I have not done so to anyone . . . At this time I am not for or against anybody." "In leisure there is luck," he concluded, somewhat enigmatically.[22] A month later, it was rumored that Mellon, along with Charles Hilles of New York and the national party chairman, William Butler, might try to block Hoover's nomination at the Kansas City convention, forcing the delegates to call for Coolidge. But there was no encouragement from the White House, and in the spring of 1928 Hoover, having won a succession of Republican primaries, gained the support of enough state conventions to emerge as the front-runner. In May, the Pennsylvania delegation met in Philadelphia, on Vare territory, and the delegates resolved to go to the convention uncommitted. Mellon observed that Hoover "seems to come closest to the standard we have for the presidency," which seemed an endorsement to Hoover's followers but was actually a dispirited yearning for an alternative.[23]

He failed to find one. At the outset of the convention, the *New York Times* claimed that "Mellon Holds Key to Nomination," but it was not true. For with the Pennsylvania delegation moving closer to Hoover, Mellon's position as the state's senior Republican began to weaken. One indication was that he failed to install either W. L. Mellon or Senator David A. Reed as national committeeman; the position went instead to W. W. Atterbury, a Vare supporter. When the GOP gathered in Kansas City in June 1928, Mellon seemed less the kingmaker than the reluctant courtier; in the words of the *New York Times* Washington correspondent Richard V. Oulahan, he was "all dressed up but he has no place to go but the Hoover party."[24] This turned out to be exactly correct. Having released a terse statement that he would abide by the dictates of his state's caucus, Mellon stood by as Vare and his crew pledged their support for Hoover, thereby guaranteeing him the nomination. Vare had been denied his Senate seat, but he was still in local terms a very powerful man. In one fell swoop, he had decided the Republican presidential nominee and seized control of the party in Pennsylvania. As one observer put it, "Mellon had the money, but Vare had the votes," and the votes beat the money decisively.[25]

Once Hoover won the nomination, Mellon faded even more into the background. Reed Smoot and Ogden Mills praised his record at the Treasury as "unrivaled and unsurpassed," but the secretary whose appearance had been a highlight of the 1924 convention was now moving into the political shadows. On his return to Washington, Mellon sought to regain some lost stature by proclaiming that "the outcome at Kansas City was very satisfactory," but no one was taken in. In July 1928, he departed for his customary European summer holiday.[26] On his return, he participated briefly in the campaign, to which he and Dick jointly donated $50,000. Mellon insisted, despite the ever more frenzied stock market, that there was "no cause for worry. The high tide of prosperity will continue." "In no other nation," he went on, "and at no other time in the history of the world, have so many people enjoyed such a high degree of prosperity or maintained a standard of living comparable to that which prevails throughout this country today."[27] Hoover duly won in another Republican landslide in November, and David Reed was easily re-elected senator from Pennsylvania. But Hoover carried what had long been the impregnably Republican Allegheny County by only 4,000 votes, and lost to the Democrat, Al Smith, in Pittsburgh, the first time the city had gone to a Democrat since 1856. Earlier that year, W. L. Mellon had resigned as chairman of the Republican Party in Pennsylvania. He had not done well. An era was ending.[28]

II. FORTUNE AND FAMILY

Throughout the boom of the second half of Coolidge's presidency, and despite repeated protestations to the contrary, Mellon continued to be closely involved in his business concerns. He was constantly on the phone to his brother, and he attended meetings in New York, Washington, and Pittsburgh where matters concerning Gulf, Alcoa, Carborundum, Koppers, and other Mellon companies were discussed. Many entries in his diary make this plain: "I spent Saturday at the Bank on affairs"; "business meeting, McClintic Marshall, at RBM's"; "H. B. Rust about coal properties, etc."; "Colonel Drake at office about [Standard Steel] Car business"; "Arthur V. Davis at house about forming new Canadian Company for foreign holdings and business"; "RB telephones about coal strike"; "give [Secretary of State] Kellogg Gulf Oil correspondence with Ambassador Morris relating to present status of oil situation in Mexico"; "talk with Rust about Pittsburgh Coal, also about Koppers utility interests"; "C. D.

Marshall about re-organization McClintic-Marshall stock"; "meeting on subject of Carborundum Co. getting power in Canada from Aluminum Co."; and so on.[29] This is scarcely consistent with Mellon's later claim that in 1921 he had withdrawn from business "as if I had died." That was a bald-faced, brazen lie.[30]

Helped by his continued involvement in major strategic decisions, Mellon's companies duly prospered in this, the most prosperous decade of his life. Alcoa's operating profit, for instance, increased from $20.2 million in 1927 to $27.8 million in 1928, and to $32.9 million in 1929—a figure that would not be surpassed until 1937. In the thirty years since 1908, Gulf's assets had grown nineteenfold and its gross income thirty-three-fold; the company was well entrenched in Mexico and Venezuela and was beginning to cast covetous glances toward the Middle East. Koppers had also been expanding, acquiring coke plants nationwide and expanding into gas and lighting utilities in New York, Connecticut, and Massachusetts. The construction of the giant Koppers Building in Pittsburgh, at the intersection of Grant Street and Seventh Avenue, between 1927 and 1929, offered even more eloquent and public testimony to this unprecedented Mellon prosperity. It was a thirty-four-story art deco skyscraper, faced in Indiana limestone and topped with a green copper cap; locally it was known as "the house that coke built."[31]

As the companies prospered, Mellon's personal wealth grew more rapidly than ever, the book value of his fortune increasing from $100 million in 1926 to $105 million or thereabouts by 1928. Of this, $12 million was in bonds, $10 million in coal lands, $3.2 million in real estate, $8 million in works of art, $12 million in proprietary accounts, and $11 million in receivables (probably the notes given by Dick when Andrew sold his bank interests). The rest was stock, most of it held in the great Mellon enterprises. It is difficult to be clear what this portfolio was actually worth, because so many Mellon companies were closely held and were not publicly traded, and thus had no market value. In the case of Gulf, Mellon owned 70 percent of the company, along with Dick and WL, and his personal holding amounted to $1.5 million. In 1928, Gulf's net assets were valued at $650 million, meaning his holdings were worth between $150 million and $200 million, yet this was not included in the estimate for that year of his total fortune. In the case of Alcoa, Mellon listed his ordinary and preferred shares as being worth $17 million. But according to Hendrick, who asked people who should have known, the real value of his holdings was between $75 million and $90 million, four times the sum included in his 1928 balance sheet. As for McClintic-Marshall, the book value assigned to Mellon's holdings in 1928 was barely $1 million, but the real value was in the region of $21 million.

There are many other examples of such undervaluations, which simply signifies that Mellon was so rich that he had no idea precisely how wealthy he was. Some of those to whom Hendrick talked believed that at peak of his fortune, in 1929–30, Mellon was worth $600 million. But Hendrick concluded that a figure of between $300 million and $400 million was more likely.[32] Unlike Rockefeller, he was never a billionaire in his own day (though he would have been worth several billion at today's values); but for each of the three years from 1926 to 1928, his after-tax income was well above $5 million. Sooner or later, Mellon would have to give thought to the disposition of his riches, as his father had done a generation before. But his more pressing concern at the moment was his immediate family. In different ways, Nora, Ailsa, and Paul all had their problems, both temperamental and circumstantial, and then there was the continuing tragicomedy of the McMullen brothers. Although a busy public figure, and with far greater involvement in business than was legal, Mellon remained, after his fashion, a devoted family man.

Following her daughter's wedding, Nora had crossed the Atlantic, visiting those McMullen relatives with whom she was on speaking terms, and staying with Paul, who was also in England for the summer. On her return, she sold her farm on the Hudson and bought a smaller house in the country, at Farnborough Hill, near Litchfield, Connecticut. "The only trouble," Nora informed Andrew, "is that I feel if I went up there I should see practically nothing of you." And her own loneliness made her more sympathetic to his: "I expect you are very busy now with social events," she said. "I wish the conventions were other than they are, so that I could come and help you, Ailsa being away." The deal went through in February 1927, and Nora and Harry Lee took up residence in mid-April 1927.[33] But the house was seven miles from the railroad station and two miles from the nearest village, and it did not have even a mailbox. Once again, Nora turned to Andrew for help. "It seems they have been trying for years to get an R.F.D. on this road," she explained, "but it can only be acquired by someone asking the Post Master General in Washington, and nobody has ever had anyone they could ask to do it. Do you think you could possibly do this for me?" Andrew duly obliged, and a mailbox soon appeared. "Ever so many thanks for your kindness," Nora wrote back.[34]

Her new married life was a combination of familiar troubles and new ones. She gave up her Manhattan apartment, but it was both difficult and expensive to get the new house in order—there were plumbers' and carpenters' bills (it was Nora, not Lee, who paid, and she got further in debt). Her letters to her lawyer were on the usual subjects: a lack of money in her account ("I have $20.47 in the bank"), inability to pay her taxes ("I suddenly had an awful panic about my state income tax"), and requests for advances against her next month's income ("I am afraid, after all, I shall have to borrow $3,000"). Enjoying nearly $40,000 a year from her trusts, Nora was scarcely hard up, but it was never enough.[35] In September 1927, she borrowed $10,000 from Andrew to buy a small place in Essex, near her brother Percy. She planned to repay it in monthly installments, but at Christmas, no doubt bowing to the inevitable, Andrew converted the loan to an outright gift. "I shall be glad if you will allow me to do this," he wrote. "I simply don't know how to thank you," she replied. "It is so good and generous of you."[36] She was also frequently ill, and her letters were becoming a chorus of complaints about being bedridden or crippled with arthritis, with her circumstances made worse because the servants (perhaps understandably) never stayed.[37]

But the crowning disaster and indignity for Nora was the collapse of her marriage to Harry Lee early in 1928. The precipitants are unknown, but, as Andrew may have surmised at the outset, Lee seems to have been another of those disreputable, itinerant Englishmen (though mercifully not in Curphey's class) for whom Nora had a fatal weakness. "She tells me she wants to divorce Lee," Mellon recorded in his diary. "I give her advice." (What could it have been?) "It has been such a strain these last few weeks," she wrote to Andrew. "I feel as if a steam roller had gone over me!" The divorce came through (from Reno) in May, Nora spent part of July and August in England with Paul, and Norman McMullen hoped his sister would "be happy now."[38] It seems as though Nora bought Lee off for $25,000, and Andrew thereupon wrote off another $38,000 of her debts. Her opinion of her second ex-husband was characteristically equivocal—she would "probably be seeing Harry from time to time," but she was "too heartily disgusted with him and his character to ever entertain" the "impossible idea" of going back to him.[39] By the 1930s, Lee would be established in the cigar business in China and Manila; during the Second World War, he would be interned in Shanghai by the Japanese, and he would return to the United States at the end of 1945.[40]

Nora's second divorce naturally led to rumors that she might finally go back to her first husband. During the early months of 1929, Paul Ache, Percy McMullen, and Nora herself all urged Andrew to take her back. Mellon told Ache he had "no answer now," and that he would have to think about it; he informed Percy that he had not "considered on [the] situation fully."[41] In May, he met Nora in New York and "explained to her the difficulties" of any such remarriage. These he specified as "my absorption in work" (nothing had changed there), and also that it would not be satisfactory to her to be the "wife of one in my position." Nora was "hurt" at these "reasons against re-marriage," but she seems to have accepted Andrew's decision.[42] "We are quite friendly and see each other often," she later wrote to Roland Knoedler, "and there is absolutely no straining about the children or anything, but I know he has absolutely no desire or *intention* of altering our personal relationship." It is not clear why Andrew had changed his mind since his second proposal in 1923. Rumors of an impending reunion continued to resurface, but they were always denied by both parties. Nora and Andrew settled into being friends, and so they would remain until Andrew's death. "With love, yours always, Nora" was how she ended one letter to him. She meant it.[43]

One constant theme of their affectionate correspondence was a shared concern—and, increasingly, anger—at the financial incompetence and incontinence of the McMullen brothers, and at their continued, shameless importuning of their former brother-in-law. Norman hoped Andrew might get him a job in France, with a subsidiary of Standard Steel Car, but nothing came of it.[44] Percy fared rather better, with Andrew making him a substantial gift toward the end of 1927: "you have relieved my mind of an ever present anxiety," he replied, "and from the bottom of my heart I thank you for your generosity and still more for your magnanimity."[45] But Leonard was pushing his luck, not least by begging in by far the most irritating and peevish manner. His foray into bookmaking had merely increased his debts; he constantly teetered on the brink of bankruptcy, and his letters to Andrew became increasingly frenzied: "I am at the end of my tether"; "I want £2,000"; "Am I to go to the workhouse or worse?"; "I wish I had been young enough for the trenches"; and so on. Andrew refused to respond, but eventually relented again, although he did not send Leonard as much money as he had asked: "I received . . . the cheque for £300," Leonard wrote. "Many thanks indeed. But I cannot understand and never shall understand why you reduced it [by] £100." Then, in the summer of 1927, having fractured the base of his skull, he lost hearing in one ear "for ever" and suffered "slight paralysis." "It was nearly the end," he told Andrew, "and a pity it was not." By late 1928, Andrew's patience with the McMullen brothers was wearing thin.[46]

This seamy life of genteel poverty, constant insecurity, and the ever-looming threat of bankruptcy and social disgrace was a world away from Andrew Mellon's native values of stern self-reliance and prudent financial rectitude, and in some ways it was Nora's most lasting, ironic, and tainted gift to him. It was equally remote from the assured opulence and social confidence of the privileged, Gatsby-esque world to which David and Ailsa Bruce now belonged, that heady swirl of old status and new money, gossip-column celebrity and international travel, cocktail parties, transatlantic liners, and polo ponies. But though the Bruces were a glittering couple, their marriage had got off to a shaky start, from which it seems (at least in retrospect) to have never fully recovered. Ailsa's personal inclinations, as well as her bodily and mental infirmities, clashed with David's professional preferences and devastating charm—and for the time being Ailsa's disposition won. When Bruce returned to work in Rome at the end of 1926, Ailsa's doctors forbade her to join him, and her health continued poor. David took indefinite leave without pay and accompanied his wife across Europe in search of a cure. Swiss clinics were unavailing, as no convincing diagnosis was adduced. They journeyed on to Paris, where Ailsa's appendix was removed (Andrew rushed across the Atlantic to be with her, and Duveen sent her a "beautiful lot of my favourite deep orchids"), but there was no improvement.[47]

Although Ailsa was forever in and out of hospitals for more bodily afflictions, her illness was also psychosomatic, and it would be lifelong. It derived from the inexpungible emotional trauma of her parents' divorce and also from having long since transferred her emotional allegiance from her mother to her father: she was now appalled at the prospect of being separated from him, as she would perforce be as a diplomatic wife on the other side of the world. David Bruce remained loyal to Ailsa throughout this difficult time, but some friends began to whisper that his wife's name should really be "What Ails Her?" There was also speculation as to why she was not yet pregnant (had she miscarried?), and it was an open secret in Washington that her father wanted her back by his side. In the summer of 1927, Andrew and Paul joined Ailsa and David in Europe, and for two months they cruised the Mediterranean on a rented yacht. By then it was clear to David that his wife was unwilling and unable to remain abroad with him, and so he could not continue in the Foreign Service. Putting Ailsa and his marriage (and his father-in-law) before his own career, he decided to resign, and the couple returned for good to the United States, where Ailsa underwent another operation, at the Johns Hopkins Medical Center in Baltimore.[48]

On their return to America, Andrew lavished more money on his daughter to help them settle on the East Coast in the very grandest style. In November 1927, Andrew gave Ailsa $25,000 in cash, 10,000 shares of common stock in Gulf Oil, and 30,000 shares of common stock in rail-road, mining, and steel companies, worth altogether $3.8 million. Soon after, he bought her a country house at Syosset on Long Island, an Italianate villa of thirty-six rooms, surrounded by sunken gardens, set in a hundred acres, and costing $1.5 million.[49] "Personally," Paul wrote to his sister soon after, in a splendid piece of satire (those Yale English classes were clearly bearing fruit), "I am all for laying the foundation of a new feudal regime on Long Island—with the Bloody Bruces of Syosset as overlords"; when he visited, he expected "to be able to shoot deer from my bedroom window, and to hunt wild boar, civets, and aard-varks in the neighboring cappets."[50] In April the following year, Andrew gave Ailsa another 15,000 shares of common stock in various steel and railroad companies, and a further $75,000 in cash, and in September he bought the couple an apartment on one of New York's most fashionable streets, Sutton Place. Toward the end of the year, he wrote off $135,000 of Ailsa's debts, incurred in the "additional outlays" made necessary by the refurbishment and redecoration of her two grand new residences.[51]

Although, or perhaps because, Ailsa was by now deeply dependent on her father, both psychologically and financially, relations between them were never easy. For in addition to being shy, aloof, distant, and generally difficult, she was also greedy and unwell—"Ailsa asks me for money" is one entry in Mellon's diary for this time. "She says it is 'so little to me and so much to her.'" "She seems," he noted, "obsessed with Craving for Money," and she also wanted some of his pictures for herself.[52] Perhaps it was understandable insofar as she was constantly "depressed about her health": she had her adenoids removed in Baltimore in December 1927; there was "recurrent fever and pain in her side" in August 1928; two teeth were taken out following fears of tuberculosis in September; and her kidneys were examined in May 1929, shortly before a recurrence of her bad throat. As Andrew recorded, after a conversation with Ailsa's mother-in-law, one doctor had told her that "the best thing for her general health condition would be to have children."[53] But she showed no inclination to do so. Andrew also seems to have discussed Ailsa's financial and medical condition openly with her husband: "Have talk with David," his diary records, "about Ailsa's health and also about her money affairs." Within his own means and limitations, Mellon was a generous and attentive father, but it is difficult to avoid the conclusion that the more he lavished on Ailsa and the more operations she underwent, the unhappier she became.[54]

With her father's substantial assistance, Ailsa had become an East Coast grande dame, with a New York palace and an estate in the country:

both, incidentally, places and types of residence that Andrew had always disdained for himself. David Bruce possessed a sufficiently strong sense of identity and station in life not to be overawed by this opulence, but he cannot have found it easy: his first, privileged foray into government service had ended in virtual humiliation, and he must by now have realized that Ailsa was—body and mind—seriously damaged, and that she could scarcely bear any separation from her father. All of which left David no choice for now but to accept these constraints as the price of being a Mellon in-law—and beneficiary. One sign of his acquiescence in the "Mellon embrace" was his venture into banking, where it naturally helped to be the son-in-law of perhaps the greatest financier of his generation, who was also secretary of the treasury. He began working at Bankers Trust, but in early 1929 moved to W. A. Harriman & Co., an investment firm at 38 Broadway. (Mellon lent him $100,000 to buy himself into the Harriman Investment Trust.) "I am sure I shall prefer banking to a diplomatic career," David tactfully told a skeptical reporter, and in the fat days that were fast approaching an end, he made a substantial sum for his personal account, also acquiring lucrative directorships in Mellon or Mellon-associated companies.[55]

The two grand Bruce residences provided Paul with new places to stay during weekend breaks from Yale, and now he also visited his mother's house in Litchfield and saw his father mainly on vacations. At the beginning of his junior year, in the autumn of 1927, he became vice chairman of the *Yale Daily News*, devoting much effort to recruiting eminent speakers for its next annual banquet in March 1928.[56] "I have been unable," Andrew informed him, "to obtain Vice President Dawes' agreement to attend," and "Hoover also failed me, but with some good reason on his part." Eventually, Mellon produced Ogden Mills, and pledged to appear himself. But at the last moment he withdrew: "considering Mills will complete the program," he explained to Paul, "I may as well be left out." Even so, Paul "enjoyed the whole evening thoroughly, and believe[d] it was really a great success."[57] By this time, he was finding his allowance of $300 a month insufficient. It covered his regular expenses and was "theoretically correct," but it was "a little inadequate" for such extra items as travel. Paul asked for an increase, and his father immediately deposited $200 in his son's account. Soon after, with Paul's twenty-first birthday approaching, Andrew made over to him his first major gift: one thousand shares of preferred stock in Alcoa, which was followed in November 1928 by two thousand shares of common stock in the Monongahela Street Railway Company.[58]

Throughout his time at Yale, Paul continued his journalism and creative writing, assiduously attending classes. But he also drank hard, suffered from occasional bouts of mild depression and, increasingly, stomach pains, and he felt a general lack of direction in his life. Although he was in both body and spirit more robust than Ailsa, he was still painfully shy, and in September 1928 he had a lucky escape when the car he was driving, en route to Ailsa's house at Syosset, skidded off the road and overturned, leaving him uninjured but shocked and shaken for several months after.[59] But his greatest anxiety was the "hidden worry" about what he was going to do with the remainder of his life. He knew his father longed for him to work at the bank, where Dick's son, RK, had recently been appointed a vice president, but Paul had no aptitude for business and feared being bored. For his part, Andrew was determined that his own son should eschew the unhappy example of the elder son of his friend Henry Clay Frick. Like Paul Mellon, Childs Frick had endured a disturbed youth: his sister and his younger brother both died young. And like Paul again, Childs wrote poetry, traveled a great deal, and showed no interest in his father's business. He preferred wildlife and natural history, eventually donating many of the animal specimens he had stuffed to the Carnegie Institute in Pittsburgh. He was a great disappointment to his father, and Andrew invariably ended discussing Paul's future by citing (and scorning) Childs Frick as a cautionary tale. "And you know," Paul remembered his father saying, "what he finished up doing—taxidermy."[60]

III. GRAND DESIGNS AND GRANDER PAINTINGS

As his letter to Ailsa at the very end of 1926 had rightly predicted, Andrew Mellon had acquired a new and absorbing interest in the building and beautification of Washington. Although he liked life and work in the capital, he had no illusions about its shortcomings as a world city. Apart from the Capitol, the White House, Union Station, the Library of Congress, and the Treasury itself, Washington boasted few official buildings of real grandeur or architectural merit, and the National Cathedral, of which Mellon had been treasurer since 1923, was far from completion. The original plan of L'Enfant had long been given up, and despite the urgings of the McMillan Commission of 1900–1902 that it be revived, much of the Mall was cluttered by railway lines and temporary buildings put up during the First World War, and Pennsylvania Avenue, which linked the Capitol and the White House, was disfigured by what Mellon would later describe as "gasoline stations, lodging houses and Chinese laundries."[61] Moreover, hundreds of thousands of dollars were being wasted by the federal government on rented office space, and efficiency was greatly impaired with many departments spread across town, in more than forty buildings. Both aesthetics and economy dictated the city should be replanned, and that there should be a major construction program to house government departments in buildings of appropriate location, dignity, and design.[62]

As secretary of the treasury, Mellon was in charge of federal public buildings, through the Office of the Supervising Architect. But Congress held the purse strings, and for nearly two decades, it had refused to sanction spending, which partly explains the scant progress following the McMillan Report. Since he took office, Mellon had been prodding Congress to find money, and in early summer 1926 he had finally obtained the necessary initial appropriations under the Public Buildings Act, which also included an amendment, sponsored by Senator William Cabell Bruce (who had just become Ailsa's father-in-law), calling for the highest quality of construction and design.[63] But although Congress had authorized the building program, and confirmed that it should be overseen by the Treasury Department, it resolved to vote appropriations on an annual basis. Nor was this Mellon's only problem, for there were three different statutory bodies which also had jurisdiction in these matters. In 1910, President Taft had set up the Commission of Fine Arts (CFA), with responsibility for approving the design of buildings in Washington; in 1916 Congress created the Public Buildings Commission (PBC), to recommend solutions to the problems of housing the federal government; and in 1924 the National Capital Park and Planning Commission (NCPPC) was established, to prepare plans for the improvement of Washington, with discretion over land use, as well as the construction (or closing) of streets. The chairmen of these three bodies—respectively Charles Moore, Senator Reed Smoot, and Frederic A. Delano—were powerful men, and Mellon would need to win over each of them.[64]

The broader issues—of the layout of the Mall, and of the great open spaces in the center of the city and by the Potomac—were not Mellon's main concern. From 1926, his chief responsibility was with the construction of new government buildings in what became known as the Federal Triangle, a large area bounded by Pennsylvania Avenue to the northwest, Fifteenth Street to the west, and a proposed grand new thoroughfare to the south on the Mall, which would be called Constitution Avenue.[65] For most of 1926, Mellon does not seem to have paid the matter much attention, and for much of that time, there was no assistant secretary of the treasury in charge of buildings. Nor did the federal government yet own all the land within the triangle. The result was chaotic and inconclusive wrangling among various departments, each of which wished to stake a claim to a site, and the three statutory bodies, with the Department of the Treasury providing little by way of leadership. Meanwhile, Congress did set funds aside for the construction of the Department of Commerce building and the Internal Revenue Service building.[66] But it was only at the very end of the year that Mellon, about to become the "architectural czar of Washington," began to take serious interest in the matter: he appointed Charles S. Dewey as assistant secretary for buildings, and on Dewey's advice, he brought in the architect and urban planner Edward H. Bennett to sketch out a coherent plan for the triangle, to determine the location of buildings within it, and to begin work on designing them.[67]

Here, for once, Mellon's instinct for collaborators failed him, for while Bennett was a good urban planner, he was a mediocre architect, and though it might have been acceptable at the bank, it was also an extraordinary step to make such a federal appointment without soliciting advice or holding a competition. Bennett duly produced a plan at the very end of 1926, but Charles Moore, the chairman of the CFA, strenuously criticized it.[68] It was at this point that Mellon realized he was going to have to involve himself much more in the matter. In the spring of the following year, Moore sent him a letter, urging the need for "considerable change in the grouping of the buildings for the Triangle from the plan prepared by Bennett," and proposed giving the triangle "a treatment similar to the Louvre in Paris, with colonnades, open courts and arched driveways, and an extended façade for units of a very large building rather than many individual buildings."[69] Under pressure from the CFA, the NCPPC, and also the American Institute of Architects, Mellon accepted this advice, and in May 1927 he appointed a board of architectural consultants to oversee the whole project, with Edward Bennett as chairman. The triangle would be designed by committee, thus adding yet another string to an already exceptionally knotty skein of jurisdictions.[70]

Nevertheless, many of America's most distinguished architects in private practice were included on the board, with the understanding that, despite federal regulations insisting that government structures must be designed by government employees, they might each be expected to produce detailed designs for one of the buildings, as most eventually did. At Mellon's insistence, the board was instructed to produce a grand array of dignified edifices, in the prevailing neoclassical style, in harmony with the White House and the Capitol, with interior courts and plazas modeled on those of the Louvre.[71] The board duly set about apportioning plots and sketching out preliminary designs, and work began on the IRS building and the Department of Commerce building (Hoover having insisted on a massive bloc abutting Fifteenth Street). As the pace of activity quickened, Congress authorized the purchase of the remaining privately owned land by eminent domain, and in October 1928, Mellon spoke of the scheme in the Founders' Day Address at the Carnegie Institute of Technology in Pittsburgh, in the presence of President Coolidge. For the first time, the secretary publicly revealed the details of the Federal Triangle scheme, in a lyrical speech, promising "beautiful harmonious buildings" expressing "the soul of America"; but as they so often were, his words were almost completely inaudible.[72]

From 1927 onward, the Federal Triangle scheme became a very high Mellon priority. But it also seems to have stimulated another interest. Ever since his arrival in Washington, Mellon had been aware of talk of creating a national gallery of art in the city, a dream dating back to the 1880s.[73] Theodore Roosevelt had thrown his weight behind such a proposal in 1907, and soon after a National Gallery of Art was actually established, with a limited number of indifferent paintings that had been bequeathed to it; from 1910 they were exhibited in rooms in the National Museum Building (subsequently the Natural History Museum) on the Mall. In 1920, this National Gallery of Art was designated a separate bureau of the Smithsonian Institution, with its own commission to oversee it, and W. A. Holmes was appointed director.[74] Soon after, the Smithsonian raised $10,000, of which Joseph Duveen contributed $1,000, and commissioned the architect Charles A. Platt to produce a design. He did so in 1924, proposing a neoclassical building 60 feet high, measuring 560 feet by 300 feet.[75] At the same time, the project was also taken up by Senator Henry Cabot Lodge, who persuaded Congress to set aside space on the Mall for a national gallery, to be located near the National Museum Building. However, he failed to secure the $2.5 million appropriation as an initial, federal contribution toward the estimated $7 million cost of construction.

Nevertheless, this gallery scheme was being widely talked about, both officially and unofficially, during Mellon's early years in Washington, and he was certainly in the loop. He was "very much interested" in the Lodge proposal, he discussed the Platt designs with Charles Moore, and he was sent a full set of architectural drawings.[76] By the middle of the decade, the project was being actively promoted in the press, a better site had been suggested on Fourth and Sixth streets at Pennsylvania Avenue, and there was talk of a public appeal and of another approach to Congress. The matter was definitely considered by the CFA, and there are some draw-

ings of the Federal Triangle scheme which show the south side of Constitution Avenue filled with grand public buildings, of which a national
gallery was undoubtedly one.[77] Such was the buzz that in the winter
of 1926–27, Senator Reed Smoot, chairman of the Public Buildings
Commission, "sent rumors abroad that a rich American would give his
collection, and perhaps a building, to the nation." This was wholly
counter-productive: it effectively killed any further effort to persuade
Congress to fund the enterprise; and since no rich benefactor actually
stepped forward, the whole scheme came to a halt. But the man who was
rumored to be that rich benefactor was Andrew Mellon.[78]

Until 1926, Mellon had rightly considered himself to be no more than
a private buyer of art, and not a purchaser in the front rank. To be sure, his
collection had expanded in recent years, but it was still relatively small in
numbers and restricted in range: to northern Europe, to beautiful En-
glishwomen, and to restful landscapes. There were few Italian paintings,
no religious scenes, and not many portraits of men of power. It was a personal accumulation rather than a comprehensive display. But though he
denied the rumors that were circulating in Washington, it is clear that
sometime during the mid-1920s Mellon did decide that he wanted to create his own national gallery.[79] Duveen later claimed that he had first
broached the issue with Mellon in 1923, shortly before he gave his
donation toward the cost of commissioning architectural drawings, and
Mellon certainly discussed the matter with Edward Bennett, Henry
Huntington, and David Finley late in 1926 and in early 1927.[80] Paul Mellon was also convinced that 1927 was the year his father made up his
mind, and there are two powerful pieces of corroborating evidence. At the
beginning of that year, David Finley decided against taking a well-paid
job in a New York bank, because Mellon had "some work" for him to do.
Accordingly, he created a new position for Finley as his special assistant,
and thereafter he was as much involved in his master's art collecting as in
his work at the Treasury. And in October 1927, Mellon plucked another
promising young official from the Treasury, Donald D. Shepard, employing him as his personal lawyer on special tasks in Washington.[81]

This, then, was the time when Mellon's interest as a collector and his
concerns as secretary of the treasury connected and converged. He had
more money than ever, and he could afford to buy the best pictures in the
world to extend and embellish his collection. And as the authority presiding over the Federal Triangle scheme, he was perfectly placed to locate a
gallery on a site of his choosing, in which his best canvases might reside as
the nucleus of a great national display. By early 1928 at the latest, these

matters had crystallized and come together in his mind, as two diary entries make plain. On February 26, 1928, he wrote: "Ailsa telephones in morning . . . Asks if I have given art gallery to the government." And on September 3, 1928: "Go over 'Triangle.' View work on location of Commerce and Internal Revenue Buildings. Also view site for National Gallery."[82] And at the same time, the pattern and ambition of Mellon's art purchasing changed and intensified. Now that he was no longer acquiring according to fancy to cover his own walls, he began to buy on a greater scale than ever before. And his collection grew more comprehensive, with purchases of those Italian and religious paintings to which he had previously been indifferent, despite Duveen's tireless prodding.

In the spring of 1927, Duveen offered Mellon a portrait of the Earl of Newport and Lord Goring by Van Dyck, and *The Intruder* by Gabriel Metsu, both from the estate sale of Lord Northbrook. Even by his own standards, Duveen was ecstatic about them. The first was "one of the finest English Van Dycks that I know of"; the only one comparable to it was in Windsor Castle. As for the Metsu, "there does not exist one so fine, not even in the Rijksmuseum at Amsterdam, the home of the great Dutch pictures." "Will you pardon me," Duveen went on, "for advising you not to let these pictures go? I am sure you will never regret their acquisition, and would like to feel that you are guided a little by my judgment as to quality, because my feeling of responsibility to you makes me always extremely careful in my statements to you." The paintings were duly hung in Mellon's apartment, and the below-stairs spies informed Duveen how Mellon and Ailsa were reacting to them. But the vendor's hyperbole did not prevail over the purchaser's hardheadedness. Duveen had wanted $700,000 for the pair; Mellon got them for $450,000 and later returned the Van Dyck.[83] At the end of the year, Mellon went back to Duveen and bought Vermeer's *The Lace Maker*, Hans Memling's *Madonna and Child with Angels*, and Titian's *Virgin and Child* for a total of $1,050,000 (Duveen had originally asked $1,280,000). Mellon would return the Titian, which, like his first Raphael, eventually proved to be of doubtful provenance. (The Vermeer, like the predecessor bought through Duveen, was one of several forgeries floated on the market during the 1920s, but this would not be known until after Mellon and Duveen were dead.)[84]

By comparison, as the spies informed a gleeful Duveen, Knoedler was now trailing, and Mellon bought no paintings from them for the better part of 1926.[85] In December, he had shown no interest in Rembrandt's portrait of his son, Titus, or in paintings by Titian or Renoir; and although he bought Raeburn's portrait of Mrs. Robertson Williamson, for $131,000, he would return it two years later. There was a slight improvement in 1927. In March, Mellon bought a Velázquez, *Woman Sewing*, for $275,000, and there seems to have been no disagreement about the price. But in May, he purchased two Fragonards, for $100,000 the pair, despite Messmore's insistence that they were worth at least $110,000 and that they were "two of the most important examples by the master and are known all over the world."[86] Later that year, Messmore offered Mellon Dürer's *Portrait of a Man*, on which Knoedler had an option, in conjunction with Colnaghi & Co. of London and the Berlin dealer Francis Zatzenstein. The asking price of $250,000 was, he explained, "very little for a rare work of art of this character. There are very few pictures in the world by the artist, and they are practically all in museums, and this is a very great opportunity." Mellon got it for $200,000. At about this time, he also lent Messmore $50,000. "I have always considered it," Messmore wrote in abject appreciation, "the greatest honour that I have ever had in my life to have had the pleasure of serving you in the small capacity that I have, and I can only add a sincere hope that my future will prove to you that your confidence has not been misplaced."[87]

All this was but the prelude to the year 1928, when Mellon, now increasingly set on his gallery scheme, at least in outline, spent more money on more paintings than he had done in any previous twelve-month period. "Mellon wonderful humour and very interested," Duveen cabled from New York to Paris. "Anticipate enormous business greater than you realize therefore urge dispatch all fine things." There were "splendid prospects" of "marvellous sales." For once, Duveen had not exaggerated. Within six months, he would sell to Mellon *Mrs. Davenport* by Romney, *Portrait of a Lady* by Bernardino Luini, *Youth with a Black Cap* by Rembrandt, *The Dancer, La Camargo* by Nicholas Lancret, *Madonna and Child* by Titian, and *Dirk Berck of Cologne* by Holbein. In all, Mellon spent almost $2 million on these paintings: it was for him, as for Duveen, an "enormous deal."[88] But increased expansiveness did not mean the end of financial prudence: Mellon had again paid less than Duveen asked, and he would later return the Rembrandt and the Holbein. During the second half of the year, he would show no interest in the "greatest" Rubens to come Duveen's way, or in a "world famous" Watteau, or in Gainsborough's *George IV*, or in "a very important Sir Joshua Reynolds." Once again, Mellon became elusive: with both men in Europe during the summer of 1928, Duveen insisted he had "many interesting matters to speak to Mellon about," but the object of his attention kept his distance.[89]

At the same time, relations with Knoedler & Co. were being rekindled.

With them, too, Mellon was still driving hard bargains, and he may have had particular cause since 690 shares of preferred stock and 3,450 shares of common stock in the company had been assigned to him as security until Carman Messmore paid off his loan. In January 1928, Mellon acquired Titian's *Portrait of Andrea dei Franceschi* for $135,000 but, growing more circumspect, he insisted that it must be sent to Europe for authentication by "the leading authorities there on the Italian school"; should their findings not prove satisfactory "in every way," Knoedler would be obliged to take the picture back. (In the end he kept it.)[90] In June he purchased for $18,000 Rembrandt's tiny *Têtes du Viellarde "Grisaelles,"* which, as Messmore explained, was "a unique little picture of the very highest possible quality"—"the smallest painting by the artist to exist" and also "one of his greatest gems." Mellon took it on condition that he could return it "at any time within five years," but he held on to it.[91] Toward the end of the year, when he was dodging Duveen, he bought Van Dyck's *St. Martin Dividing His Cloak*, Jan van de Cappelle's *View on the River Excaut*, and Goya's portraits of King Carlos IV of Spain and of Queen Maria Luisa, at $100,000 for the quartet; and also Sir Joshua Reynold's *Portrait of Lady Elizabeth Compton*, for $500,000. It was, Messmore explained, "a more beautiful composition" than anything else Reynolds had ever painted, "and there is nothing finer in quality or period in existence."[92]

IV. A FATEFUL DECISION

The landslide election of Herbert Hoover in November 1928 should have been a major turning point in the life of Andrew Mellon, but unfortunately he failed to recognize any of the signs. By now, at seventy-three, Mellon had achieved everything he could at the Treasury. Although popular in many quarters, and admired by the outgoing president for his "patriotic devotion and wise financial leadership," he had not silenced the growing chorus of criticism his business and political activities provoked.[93] There was also the disagreeable prospect of serving under a president whom he did not much like and who had been a rival in the cabinet. Mellon could and should have retired, spending his time and his money on the new and remarkable project which had captured his imagination late in life. Had he done so, the public acclaim attending his departure would have only been enhanced by the announcement that he would devote the remainder of his life, and a substantial part of his fortune, to the creation of a national gallery for the benefit of all Americans. Why, then, did he not take Hoover's victory as the occasion to retreat gracefully from the public stage, at the peak of his reputation, as Coolidge had so shrewdly chosen to do?[94]

There can be no doubt that Mellon was widely expected to retire. Analyzing the likely course of the impending presidency, William C. Murphy opined that it was "inconceivable" that Mellon "would want to stay another four years," as he was becoming the "representative of a fast vanishing race." But Mellon had no intention of vanishing. For all the battles, criticism, and turf squabbles, he enjoyed being secretary of the treasury, had grown accustomed to working and living in Washington, and had no wish to give up public life. "At my age," he told one reporter during the presidential campaign, "I might as well work here as anywhere else. I have made no plans about retiring."[95] In addition, Mellon doubted whether Hoover would be as zealous in support of his policies as Coolidge had been. Hoover might find it expedient to retard domestic debt reduction or to renege on the Federal Triangle scheme, and his affection for the "noble" experiment of Prohibition was but one token of his more interventionist sense of government. Mellon was determined to ensure his fiscal policies were continued and to drive the Federal Triangle scheme through to completion, while continuing to accumulate pictures for the National Gallery that would form an integral part of it.[96]

There was another reason for Mellon to stay in Washington and in government. By now he had surrounded himself with a group of younger men with whom he very much liked working (and, on occasions, socializing). In Pittsburgh, such collaborators as Walter Mitchell, Henry McEldowney, Arthur Vining Davis, and McClintic and Marshall had been near contemporaries, they were often self-made, and they and Mellon (and their businesses) grew and aged together. But in Washington, his associates belonged to a younger generation, they came from a different social and geographical milieu, and they tended to be university-educated: Parker Gilbert, Garrard Winston, David Finley, David A. Reed, Donald Shepard—and David Bruce.[97] Mellon relished their company, and they came to form an extended Washington family. Indeed, with Ailsa often in New York or on Long Island, and with Paul away at Yale, they often provided the only family that was available. Perhaps these bright young men became surrogate sons: for they showed a commitment to work and business that Paul conspicuously lacked. Indeed, Paul's relationship with Andrew may have been so distant and difficult in part because he knew his father was more at ease with these young men than with him.[98]

Mellon was also determined, with his native stubbornness, to face down the critics who had dared doubt his integrity. Shortly before Christmas 1928, the House minority leader, John Nance Garner, accused him of granting secret tax refunds to his corporations; in demanding an official investigation, he denounced Mellon as "the greatest Santa Claus in history." It was a repeat performance of the tax-refund drama that Senator James Couzens had first staged after the Internal Revenue Service investigation of 1924–25. Couzens himself also returned to the fray, insisting that his earlier quashed investigation had turned up tax files bearing the notation "this is a Mellon company." Garner and Couzens were soon joined by Senator Kenneth McKellar, the Tennessee Democrat who had first called for Mellon's impeachment back in 1924. McKellar now proposed that all refunds in excess of $10,000 be reviewed by the Board of Tax Appeals in open, public hearings. Once more, Mellon denied the charges, pointing out that it was not the treasury secretary but the commissioner of internal revenue who adjudicated all such refunds, and that those in excess of $75,000 were, in any case, subject to examination by the Joint Congressional Committee on Taxation. Proof was never presented of the "this is a Mellon company" accusation (even Couzens's biographer would conclude that the refunds were legal), and McKellar's proposals failed to gain enough congressional support.[99]

By the early months of 1929, others were circling the secretary. Senator Pat Harrison, Democrat from Mississippi, stirred up the zealots perturbed by the Treasury Department's still unconscionably lax enforcement of Prohibition. While the Prohibition Bureau was being reorganized, Mellon's "dry" critics had generally held their fire, but after the election, the chief of the bureau, James Doran, argued that effective enforcement would require $300 million each year, an absurd and deliberately inflated sum which brought the issue back to the political fore. With his tongue very much in cheek, and anticipating overwhelming rejection, Senator William Cabell Bruce proposed that Doran's request be granted; such was the support for Prohibition that his motion failed by only two votes. Thereupon, Senator Harrison proposed an appropriation of $25 million, which seemed likely to gain approval. But Mellon was deeply opposed to any such expenditure: he did not believe that more money would make enforcement easier, and he considered the proposal a reckless use of appropriations power, nothing more than political grandstanding. But as with tax refunds, criticism was now starting to take hold, and by early 1929, there was a growing demand in Congress for a thorough investigation into Prohibition enforcement.[100]

Mellon also found himself attacked on a third front when Senator Gerald P. Nye of South Dakota informed Hoover that his fellow insurgent Republicans would oppose the secretary's reconfirmation.[101] Mellon had always had his critics among these Republican dissidents, and by joining with the Democrats, they could muster enough votes to unseat him. It was a serious problem for the recently inaugurated Hoover: he had no wish to begin his term with a congressional defeat that would cast a pall over his legislative program; yet, and although he knew how Mellon felt about him, Hoover had no wish to sacrifice the secretary, who was still widely supported by Republican voters and the business community. Indeed, immediately after his victory, he had invited Mellon to stay on, and even asked his advice about cabinet appointments.[102] And even if Mellon had entertained any notions of retiring, the threat to his reappointment after eight successful years would have been enough to make him stay and fight. For his part, Hoover was still "deeply anxious" to keep Mellon, and in the spring of 1929 he came to his rescue.[103]

The new president cleverly blunted all three lines of attack.[104] First, by executive order Hoover declared that all future tax refunds, abatements, and credits in excess of $20,000 be made public, thus appeasing McKellar and his gang, while preventing the full disclosure of tax returns or the assignment of refunds to the Board of Tax Appeals, which Mellon opposed. Second, Hoover would appoint a bipartisan panel (which came to be known as the Wickersham Commission) to examine the problems of enforcing Prohibition, and he later let it be known that he favored shifting the bureau from the Treasury to the Justice Department, as had been proposed at the beginning of Mellon's tenure. As a result, both the Harrison appropriation bill and the demand for a congressional investigation disappeared.[105] Finally, Hoover determined to keep Mellon as secretary without submitting his name for congressional confirmation. Senator McKellar demanded an investigation, raising again the issue of Mellon's compliance with the 1789 statute preventing the treasury secretary's involvement in "trade or commerce." But Senator David Reed persuaded the Senate Judiciary Committee, by eight votes to five, not only that the secretary was compliant, but that by law and tradition Mellon could continue without confirmation as a holdover from the previous administration. A minority report by the chairman, George Norris, averred that Mellon was in violation of the statute, but the general sentiment was that it was too vague for a definitive finding, and the whole matter was dropped by May 1929. In any case, as the pro-Mellon *Pittsburgh Press* noted, Mellon's three Democratic predecessors at the Treasury had all owned stock.[106]

Mellon had survived these congressional attacks with the president's help ("my estimate of him rises," the secretary noted in his diary), but Hoover was not wholly on his side.[107] Early in the term, David H. Blair, commissioner of internal revenue, decided to retire. Mellon had fought and won a battle with Harding over appointing Blair; now he fought and lost a battle with Hoover concerning the successor. For Hoover insisted on picking the new man, with an eye to party political considerations. He was determined to reward Robert H. Lucas, who had transformed previously Democratic Kentucky into a Republican stronghold. Mellon, however, wanted to promote Blair's assistant, Charles R. Nash. The president got his way, at least in the short run, with a messy compromise. He appointed Lucas but stipulated that if he did not prove himself to Mellon within six months, he would resign. Six months later, Lucas duly did so.[108] It was a minor skirmish, but it proved that Mellon was damaged and no longer invulnerable. It seemed likely his critics would soon regroup, and the newspapers were full of stories predicting he would step down, with Ogden Mills and the Los Angeles banker Henry Robinson mentioned as possible successors. Mellon stood fast, but the ground was shifting beneath his feet: Hoover was relying more and more on Mills, and from March until October 1929, Mellon avoided the public eye, devoting himself to other things.[109]

"No sincerer greetings or happier wishes will you receive on your birthday than these," Percy McMullen wrote to Mellon on March 23, when he turned seventy-four. "May you emulate your father, and look forward to many years of peace and contentment, and see the fulfillment of your project to make Washington the most magnificent city in the world."[110] The second of these wishes would come closer to fulfillment than the first, and Mellon was much preoccupied with the Federal Triangle scheme during these months. The Board of Architectural Consultants had completed its overall design, which was officially unveiled in Washington on April 1929, at a glittering occasion presided over by Mellon.[111] It featured a scale model, twenty-two feet long and nine feet wide, and a film (suggested by David Finley) tracing the development of Washington and showing the present blight along Pennsylvania Avenue; there were speeches (written by Finley) by the secretary, the president, and Senator Reed Smoot, all urging that Washington be made dignified and beautiful in an inspiring and timeless classical style.[112] But the Commission of Fine Arts was still unconvinced, either by the merit of many of the detailed designs, or by the way the buildings related to one another: as the work of a committee, the plan lacked unity or coherence. Accordingly, they urged the appointment of "one very able designer." John Russell Pope, one of the most outstanding architects working in the neoclassical idiom, had not responded to an invitation to join the original board in 1927. Now, in September 1929, he accepted Mellon's invitation.[113]

At the same time, Mellon determined to expand his art purchasing to include those Italian and religious paintings that Duveen had insisted were essential to any collection comprehensive enough to form the nucleus of a national gallery. In late 1928, he scored his greatest, and most expensive, coup yet, when he bought through Duveen what was known as the *Niccolini-Cowper Madonna*, by Raphael, for $836,670. The painting, so-called for its former owners, the Earls Cowper, had hung in their great palace at Panshanger in Hertfordshire, where Mellon had first glimpsed it on a visit with his McMullen in-laws at the turn of the century.[114] Now it was his, and he had paid the highest price yet for any old master, far surpassing what Huntington had spent on *The Blue Boy*, so much so that when the newspapers reported that Mellon had paid £200,000 (approximately $970,000), he took pains to deny it. It was his first recorded denial of a purchase price, but it would not be his last, and the news that he was spending so lavishly and, it seemed, so selfishly further angered his congressional critics. But Mellon had now successfully acquired a painting by the Italian artist who had been most prized and sought after by American collectors since the turn of the century. It was his first permanent Raphael—a trophy picture obviously better suited to the walls of a great gallery than even the grandest plutocrats' sitting rooms.[115]

Of course, Mellon had already sent back one spurious Raphael, and he would eventually acquire two more real ones. But for now, this acquisition inaugurated a spending spurt that extended into the following year. In January 1929, Mellon went back to Knoedler, acquiring Frans Hals's *Portrait of a Young Man in a Large Hat* for $50,000 and Rembrandt's *Self-Portrait* for $475,000. The latter couldn't hold a candle to his Raphael invoice, but it was a major purchase all the same. "We congratulate you," Carman Messmore wrote, "on the acquisition of this great portrait by Rembrandt, which is considered to be the finest portrait of the artist by himself in existence." "We have never," he concluded, "had a greater picture pass through our hands in all the years that this firm has been in business."[116] But Mellon turned again to Duveen and bought Titian's *Portrait of a Lady* for $550,000 (he would later send it back), and Frans Hals's *Balthasar Coymans* for $350,000 (this he would keep). Even apart from the Raphael, this was audacious purchasing. As Duveen informed his Paris office, following a "marvelous interview" with Mellon in New York, the secretary was now a "big buyer" who wanted only "great topazes." "Greatly encouraged," he signed off, "and have further business which hope conclude before sailing."[117]

By now, Mellon had clearly raised his sights as a collector, and David Finley was playing the increasingly important part that his master had sketched out for him. Between August 1928 and February 1929, Finley attempted, on Mellon's behalf, to acquire Vermeer's *The Artist in His Studio* from Count Czernin in Vienna. At just the time that negotiations fell through, Finley took Leonello Venturi to see Mellon's collection.[118] Venturi, professor of the history of art at the University of Turin, was an expert on the Italian Renaissance, the very period that was so far underrepresented in Mellon's holdings. Together they spent two hours looking at his pictures, Venturi communicating to Finley thoughts the latter found "very valuable." He liked the Dürer, the Vermeers, and the Rembrandts, and was especially impressed by the small Filippino Lippi ("very fine"), the Hobbema ("a masterpiece"), and the Van Dyck *Marchesa Balbi* ("very fine also"). Of the pictures hanging in the apartment that Mellon was considering for purchase, Venturi rejected the Filippino Lippi *Virgin and Child* (as being only the "school of") and Titian's *Old Man in a Red Coat* (as a fake). But he was strongly in favor of Piero della Francesca's *Crucifixion*, a small picture by Domenico Veneziano, a *Portrait of a Woman* by Luini, and a Lawrence likeness of Prince Metternich. But despite this expert opinion that these would be most desirable additions, Mellon never acquired any of them.[119]

Nevertheless, his collection was now beginning to evolve from a personal accumulation into a potential national benefaction. Meanwhile, Andrew's son was evolving from a student—into what? Paul would be graduating from Yale in the summer of 1929, and he had already made public his interests, priorities, and ambitions—very different from those of his father—in a thinly veiled short story that appeared in the *Yale Literary Magazine* in March 1929, titled "To Sail Beyond the Sunset." The central character, a young man named Robin Bennett, seeks to devote his life to writing, painting, and travel, in defiance of his father's plans for what he regards as his wayward son. In a scene of dramatic confrontation, Robin explains that such activities "mean more to me than a hundred of your factories or fifty thousand of your bloody whistles blowing" (a fairly unambiguous allusion to Pittsburgh). Robin's father responds: "This is your life—here, with us, doing as we have always been doing. You've gone off at a tangent and you've got to come back." At the end of the scene, he allows his son twelve months of travel to do what he likes, but decrees that "one year from today I shall expect you." Robin's income will continue in the meantime, but if he then fails to return home and begin work, it will be cut off.[120]

The lineaments of Paul's distant and difficult relationship with his own father could hardly be more evident. Andrew was generally proud of his son's literary endeavors, but this story cannot have given him any pleasure, especially when it was picked up in the American press, fueling speculation that Paul might "follow a literary career" after his graduation.[121] Such a possibility was emphatically denied, but it was no secret that Paul had been happy at Yale, with his books and his poetry and his history, and had never expressed any wish for a life in business, or in Pittsburgh. As his mother's son, he increasingly felt himself drawn to England and to country pursuits, and Nora, while careful not to take his side against his father, was naturally gratified and supportive. Eventually, Andrew agreed that Paul might go abroad and study for a year at Cambridge University, beginning in the autumn of 1929. A friend of Percy McMullen's, Henry Thirkill, was a fellow of Clare College, and it was at his suggestion that Paul enrolled there. Nothing as vulgar as disinheritance was ever broached between father and son, but Andrew made it plain that after this final year of idle learning, he expected Paul to return to Pittsburgh to accept his dynastic obligations and his financial destiny, buckle down to work, and "learn actual contact with affairs." For his part, Paul saw Cambridge as a reprieve, and as a deferral of an inevitable decision and real-life confrontation he dreaded.[122]

As Paul's thoughts were turning toward the homeland of his maternal relations, Andrew resolved to put an end to the brothers' interminable importuning, by providing each of them with a regular income. In July 1929, he set up six trust funds for them, and endowed them with shares in Alcoa, Koppers, and the Monongahela Street Railway Company, worth approximately $50,000 each, and giving a net annual income to each beneficiary of $3,165.[123] "You will get tired of hearing me say 'thank you,' " Nora wrote to Andrew, "but I must repeat how grateful I am—you have no conception of what happiness it has given me!" Likewise, Norman McMullen was "simply overwhelmed by this extraordinary gift," which had come at a "crucial time" and freed him from worry about his wife's future. Percy, too, thanked him for generosity which could "only be described by the three M's—munificent, magnanimous, and magnificent." ("Your junior by twenty years," he had earlier written to Andrew, "regrets he will not live to read the biography of, in many ways, a wonderful man.") And John McMullen thought it was a better tonic for his wife than all the medicine she was taking. "They are too grateful for words," Nora told Andrew.[124] Except Leonard: for in his case, uniquely, the trust beneficiary was his wife, since "if he had the handling of it, he would find one excuse or another for putting it into some worthless business like he always has." A shrewd move, perhaps, but it left Leonard angry, disappointed—and still in debt.[125]

By this time, Mellon's art purchases had abruptly halted: he bought no paintings between June 1929 and January 1930. In the case of Knoedler, he may have held back while the Titian was being authenticated, which would also have given Carman Messmore time to begin repaying his loan.[126] In Duveen's case, Mellon may also have decided that it was time to set his face against irrepressible importuning. Late in July, Duveen reported to Mellon that Ramsay MacDonald would again be leading a Labour government in Britain, following the recent general election. "I understand," he went on, in his grandest manner, "that he intends to visit America to see you early in October, and I expect that I shall accompany him upon his steamer." In the same letter, Duveen informed Mellon that "due to hard work, persuasive powers, and a long purse," he had "been quite successful in securing a few great pictures," among them two Van Dycks, "one of the greatest Botticellis you have ever laid your eyes upon," and "also a portrait by Bellini and a Holbein." Mellon was unmoved, and in the ensuing chill Duveen became distinctly anxious. By August, Mellon still owed him half a million dollars from purchases made earlier in the year, and in the following month he would refuse Duveen's invitation to dinner in New York "to meet Mr. Ramsay MacDonald and daughter."[127]

V. THE BUBBLE BURSTS

Mellon may have had his personal reasons for eluding both Knoedler and Duveen during the second half of 1929, but the picture on the economic horizon was more distracting than any a dealer could have shown him. With Hoover's election, the stock market had taken off once again. On November 10, 1928, shares soared as never before, and on November 21, Wall Street recorded for the first time a volume of 6.5 million trades, an astonishing number in the days before digital computation.[128] Mellon would later describe the unprecedented frenzy as "partly due to the activities of powerful groups of speculators, and partly due to the fact that the public in general believed and acted as if the price of securities would indefinitely advance."[129] It was a shrewd assessment. Encouraged by Hoover, he delivered one public statement in March 1929 which, if carefully read, made his concern clear. "For prudent investors," he told a reporter asking about the state of the market, "I would say, if making a suggestion, that now is the time to buy good bonds. This does not mean that many stocks are not sound investments. Some are, however, too high a price to be good buys."[130] In our era of twenty-four-hour financial reporting, this sounds like the sort of pronouncement that would send shares tumbling. But Mellon's warning was so carefully and coyly worded—for fear of precipitating the very collapse he was anxious to avoid—that few investors paid any heed or even noticed.

As the stock exchange boom continued, there were demands that the Federal Reserve Board raise interest rates again, beyond the 5 percent set in the summer of 1928. But there were also fears that going much beyond this level might well paralyze legitimate business activity (as had happened in 1920–21), while failing to stem the tidal wave of speculation. Accordingly, in early 1929, the board decided on a policy of "direct pressure" or "moral suasion," whereby it urged member banks to refuse discount privileges when the funds in question would be used for speculative purposes. Mellon objected to the policy as overextending the powers of the board, and he did not attend the meeting at which it was adopted. The result was that word leaked to the press that the secretary was at odds with the body of which he was the chairman. Adding to confusion, the New York Federal Reserve Bank refused to implement the "moral suasion" policy, concluding that raising the discount rate would be more effective. By early March 1929, Mellon felt obliged to issue a statement denying that the Treasury and the Federal Reserve Board disagreed over how to deal with the overheated economy; in fact, that was precisely the situation. He wanted interest rates to rise, but the majority of the board (and, for now, Ogden Mills) did not.[131]

At the second meeting of the Hoover cabinet, held on March 12, 1929, Mellon recorded the president's concern about the stock market. Hoover, he noted, "thinks something should be done to curb speculation." "Give my views," he went on. "Everything possible has been done."[132] Indeed it had, for by then Mellon was prescribing measures deemed not "possible." In concert with Ray Young and Edmund Platt, both members of the Federal Reserve Board, the secretary was urging an increase in the discount rate. Between February and early August 1929, the Federal Reserve Bank of New York, now led by George L. Harrison following the death of Benjamin Strong, petitioned the board ten times to raise the rate to 6 percent.[133] Mellon and his allies supported such an increase, but they were outvoted by a majority who refused to give in to what they regarded as improper pressure from the Hoover administration. His diary records disappointment and frustration. On March 26, 1929, he wrote: "Meeting Federal Reserve Board. I vote with Board, but state I think increase in the discount rate to be inevitable." April 25: "Long session Federal Reserve Board. Subject New York rate. New York Bank raise to 6 percent voted down. I vote for raise." May 16: "Federal Reserve Board meeting discuss New York Bank rate raise. I vote for raise. Majority carried disapproving raise." May 23: "Conference with President on reserve rates and financial conditions. I criticize the Board on not raising rate."[134]

By now, Mellon was clearly concerned about the speculative mania and he was vigorously if vainly prescribing the only obvious remedy. But as treasury secretary he was limited in what he could do, and in any case, there was no way of predicting whether his proposed monetary answer would solve the speculative problem or exaggerate it. A sudden full point hike in rates might, as in 1921, lead to the very panic and crash he feared; on the other hand, a slow, incremental increase might be shrugged off, not calming the markets at all but harming legitimate commerce and industry by making credit more expensive.[135] Higher rates might also seriously destabilize the already wobbly transatlantic economy, militating against the supposedly still paramount imperative: to get gold flowing out of America and toward Europe (especially Britain), and not the reverse. Raising interest rates might dampen Wall Street's mania, but this was a far less certain outcome than the flight of money toward higher rates in America. Such a capital flight might shatter Europe's recent, rickety reconstruction effort, and along with it the recently negotiated foreign debt deals and reparation payments. As Mellon had written back in 1925, "the Federal Reserve System is not a panacea for all economic and financial ills, and cannot entirely prevent business crises and depressions." Hoover was more brutal: the Federal Reserve Board, he later opined, had been "a weak reed for a nation to lean on in time of trouble." But in 1929, no other reed was available.[136]

Despite these uncertainties, Mellon persisted, and on August 8, 1929, he got his way when the Federal Reserve Board finally approved the New York bank's request to increase the discount rate to 6 percent.[137] The stock market promptly crashed but instantly reversed itself, and soon it was soaring upward again. By the end of August, the Dow Jones Industrial Average was at a record high of 380.33, up nearly 30 points for the month, and the volume of summer trading had shattered all records. With bullish speculators imagining an equally unprecedented autumn market, the first trading day after the Labor Day weekend, September 3, 1929, saw the Dow climbing even further, to 386.10. Three days later, a "storm of selling" broke out on the New York Stock Exchange, but it, too, proved a passing squall: the market soon recovered, and the second week of September saw variable weather, sharp sell-offs alternating with modest gains. In all this, though, something had changed: the mood in New York had grown edgy, the drunkenness looking more and more like a hangover. Surely contributing to the shift was a recent speech by Roger Babson to the National Business Council, in which he had predicted that "sooner or later a crash is coming." After a sharp rally on September 16, the market turned sour, with heavy selling a week later; for the rest of the month, the Dow would register only three up days. By the end of September, half of what had been made in August had been wiped out.[138]

As these first "rumbles of distress" were heard, rumors were again circulating that Mellon would resign from the Treasury. In reply to one such speculation, he quoted Benjamin Franklin: "I am deficient, I am afraid, in the Christian virtue of resignation." And in response to another, he quipped: "I have become resigned to rumors that I have resigned."[139] These words were reproduced in Philip Love's just-completed biography of Mellon, an admiring portrait that would be published in October. It rehearsed the main episodes in his life ("crammed with accomplishment"), informing Mellon's cold and aloof personality with a certain pale warmth ("quiet, patient, dignified, industrious, sincere and loyal") and insisting that his life had been "replete with romance—the romance of achievement." Most of Love's pages were devoted to a vindication of Mellon's debt-reducing and tax-cutting policies at the Treasury, and to denouncing his critics and enemies as selfish, partisan, and narrow-minded. "No finer man than he," Love concluded, "has ever served the American people." "And," lest there was any doubt, he declared Mellon "a great Secretary of the Treasury."[140]

Mellon had not welcomed this biography—it represented unwelcome intrusion and publicity—but there would soon be other reasons to regret it. Its heroic view of the secretary, which had seemed so plausible to so many for most of the 1920s, would soon be overturned by national (and subsequently global) events that were fast outrunning both control and comprehension.[141] During the first week of October, the stock market gyrated wildly, and in an effort at instilling confidence, the White House issued the following statement: "The President has asked Mr. Andrew Mellon to remain in his cabinet for the next three and a half years, or for the balance of the administration." Hoover had indeed made the request, but Mellon had not acceded to it unequivocally. "I had made no promise," he confided to his diary. "I tell the President that he has made his statement too strong. But he understands I shall be free to resign if that may become desirable on my part."[142] Morale on Wall Street was briefly boosted by the announcement, and Mellon remained "optimistic" about the "business outlook"; but by the middle of the month, after several days of unexpectedly violent sell-offs, the Dow was down to 323.87, more than 60 points below its high in early September. On Monday, October 21, there was evidence of heavy distress, which one analyst described as "overwhelming and aggressive" selling—though Mellon made no mention of it in his diary.[143]

Two days later, on Wednesday, October 23, the New York Stock Exchange was hit by what has been described as a "hurricane of liquidation": more than six million shares changed hands, wiping out over $4 billion in paper values. Bad as that was, what followed was twice as bad. For on the morrow, immediately christened "Black Thursday," nearly thirteen million shares were traded, and by noon, losses had reached $9 billion. A rally later in the afternoon gave little cause for optimism. Mellon's diary is laconic: "Stock market crash in New York. Dinner Belgian Embassy, and go to Belgian exhibit at Corcoran Gallery later." Black Thursday would look merely gray by the following Tuesday, October 29, as sixteen million shares were sold and bought—a Wall Street record that would stand for thirty-nine years. "Stock market panic," noted Mellon. "RBM telephones from Pittsburgh asking [about] conditions as to money. Duveen comes to lunch." He offered "two Van Dycks [from the] Anhalt Collection: $750,000 for the two."[144] Mellon did not buy them. For three more weeks, shares continued to plummet: "stock market still slumping, New York very disturbed," Mellon noted on November 13. By then, some $26 billion, roughly one-third of the value of stocks at their early September peaks, had evaporated, in belated reaction to what had been an "orgy of speculation."[145]

Yet the crash itself left the American economy, and the American people, mostly unaffected. As Herbert Hoover observed in late October 1929, "the fundamental business of the country, that is production and distribution of commodities, is on a sound and prosperous basis," a pronouncement he made after consulting Mellon. Contrary to much retrospective popular opinion, that assessment was in essence correct. At least 97.5 percent of the American population owned no shares in 1929, and so the crash had little direct or immediate effect on them.[146] As for Mellon himself: although he held some shares in companies such as the Bethlehem Steel Corporation, the majority of his holdings were in the great family enterprises—Gulf, Alcoa, Carborundum—which were not publicly traded. His own finances, therefore, like those of ordinary Americans whom in other ways he did not resemble, were largely unaffected, and he continued to prosper. In 1929, his net income after federal taxes was $7.8 million, compared to $5.2 million for the previous year, and even the book value of his fortune rose from $105 million to $112 million. Such steady accumulation vindicated Mellon's faith in nurturing companies, and reinforced his general disdain for those reckless sorts who chased mere paper profits and were now reaping the whirlwind.

Still, there was a crisis in the economy, and at the end of October 1929, Mellon tried in vain to discourage Hoover from making any more public statements on the subject, for fear they would only make things worse. Meanwhile, he was willing to act, within the limits of his own authority. At his urging, in late October, the Federal Reserve Board announced a cut in the discount rate by 1 percent to its pre-August level of 5 percent.[147] Thereafter, the Fed would ease and expand credit incrementally, until the rate was down to 2 percent by mid-1930 (by which time there was criticism that such cheap credit might rekindle speculation, with even more disastrous consequences).[148] In mid-November, Mellon also recommended an across-the-board one-year cut of 1 percent in personal and corporate income taxes. He insisted he had been planning this for some time, in anticipation of a further federal surplus (which he predicted would be $225 million in fiscal 1930, and $122 million in fiscal 1931), and he denied claims that he was reducing taxes to encourage spending. These proposals met with bipartisan support, and a revenue bill was pushed through Congress in less than a month, with John Nance Garner, the House minority leader and normally a strong critic of Mellon's, collaborating with Willis Hawley, chairman of Ways and Means, to get it passed. Only the insurgent Republicans voted no.[149]

It was as much as Mellon was prepared to do in the immediate aftermath of the crash: adjust interest rates and taxes downward. Otherwise, he did little and stayed quiet, still governed by his faith in the self-regulation of markets. Hoover itched to do more, and began to formulate his own interventionist economic policy. He summoned American business and financial leaders for open-ended discussions, urging them to keep on their employees in active and productive work, while reassuring the public about the underlying soundness of the economy. In private, Mellon thought such meetings "premature," and likelier to worry the public than reassure them; having staged such a conference, the administration "[had] 'shot its wad,' " leaving no card left to play.[150] In public, however, the secretary reluctantly supported the president, but despite his unrivaled banking and business connections, he did little to help. Hoover, fearing there might be worse to come, sought to increase government spending on public works, so as to stimulate what he feared might become a more generally flagging economy. Mellon was more enthusiastic about this, but for his own good reasons: it would mean more funding for, and thus progress on, his Federal Triangle project. Accordingly, in mid-November 1929, the Treasury proposed and secured from Congress an additional $175 million for public construction over the next decade.

During the last months of 1929, and not yet seriously affected by or implicated in the Wall Street crash, Mellon could concern himself at least as much with personal and social matters, and with his own businesses, as with the nation's economy. He spent a great deal of time at the dentist. He visited New York, calling—though just looking—at Knoedler & Company and Duveen Brothers, and also seeing Helen Frick. He congratulated Henry C. McEldowney on the fortieth anniversary of the establishment of the Union Trust Company, and was delighted to learn that David Bruce had weathered the crash unscathed.[151] He seems to have had a disagreement with Ailsa about paintings for Syosset ("she asks for pictures") and she underwent another operation in Baltimore. He received his first letters from Paul at Cambridge, looked forward to seeing him over the Christmas vacation, and planned a yachting trip from Miami to Puerto Rico.[152] He was, as always, in regular touch with Dick, and paid a lengthy visit to Pittsburgh to catch up on business and local politics. He attended meetings or made phone calls concerning Alcoa, Koppers, Pittsburgh Coal, and the Union Trust. He discussed the Connellsville Bank with Dick: it seemed "about to fail," but they decided "not to try to save it." They also gave further thought to "acquiring banks" in the greater Pittsburgh region, but Andrew firmly advised Dick against "forming [a] holding company yet."[153]

The secretary of the treasury was, then, still much involved with his banks and businesses at a strategic level, and the most important decision he made at this time was to sell the Standard Steel Car Company. Established by Andrew and Dick early in the 1900s, it had been one of their most successful enterprises. But by the late 1920s, Jim Brady was dead, John M. Hansen was ill and would not live to see the next decade, and of Mellon men, only Colonel Drake was left as president. Accordingly, Andrew and Dick decided that the time was ripe for the first sale of a major Mellon business since the New York Shipbuilding Company in

1916. The one potential buyer was the only other large-scale producer of railcars, J. P. Morgan's Pullman Company. Negotiations, begun shortly before the stock market fall, were completed by the end of the year. Although the consolidation would not take effect until March 1930, the valuations remained those agreed on before the crash.[154] For each share in Standard, the Mellons received two shares in Pullman, plus $21.71 in cash, which meant they came out of the deal with $4.3 million and 400,000 Pullman shares. Colonel Drake became the chief executive of the consolidated company, and Dick's son, Richard King Mellon, joined the board of directors. The disengagement could not have been more deftly handled or better timed.[155]

At the beginning of December 1929, Andrew sent Nora a letter, apologizing for not having written for so long. He confessed to having been "rather driven with work," and he proceeded to explain, thereby revealing much about his own outlook and limitations:

> Mr. Hoover is a most active and tireless President, prolific of new ideas and movements from day to day, which adds to our responsibilities. It is all interesting, but sometimes over much in quantity. The stock market crash upset business greatly, and the President is endeavoring to mitigate the effects of it in order to prevent as far as possible a threatened widespread unemployment situation, so we have been busy starting new government building and other work, at the same time having conferences with leaders of large businesses in order to encourage the starting of new work. The stock market collapse has entailed a terrible lot of distress among people who have lost their savings and incomes. The gambling instinct in England runs to betting on horses which is bad enough, but stock speculation has disastrous consequences.[156]

For now, these "disastrous consequences" were the hardships of the less than 3 percent of Americans who owned stock. Scarcely anyone, in business or government, anticipated the great unraveling that was to come, least of all Andrew Mellon.

12

TRIUMPHS AMID TROUBLES

Fortune's Zenith, Russian Pictures, Pittsburgh Woes, 1929–31

> Such inflation of the currency gave further impetus to new proj-
> ects, and only added fuel to the flame which was consuming the
> vitality of legitimate business pursuits. The end came at last, the
> bubble burst, and all went down with a crash.
>
> *Thomas Mellon and His Times*, p. 24

I. ECONOMIC VICISSITUDES

By the end of 1929, Andrew Mellon had concluded that the federal government had done quite enough—and Herbert Hoover more than enough—to allay anxieties engendered by the recent Wall Street collapse. It was the nature of the market: shares went up, shares went down; speculators made money, speculators lost money. "They deserved it," Mellon once brutally told the president.[1] But meanwhile, the growth of companies, the support of innovation, the increase of output, and the general enrichment of America went on, and as 1930 began there was scarcely any reason to think that the productive American economy, as distinct from the speculation-addled securities market, was in trouble. Sketchy reports about rising unemployment were worrisome, but not unduly alarming. As Mellon put it at the beginning of the new year, echoing the general view: "I see nothing . . . in the present situation that is either menacing or warrants pessimism . . . I have every confidence that there will be a revival of activity in the spring, and that during the year the country will make steady progress." Most evidence soon seemed to bear this out. By mid-1930, the stock market had recovered one-fifth of its value before the black days of October, and the banking system had shown great resilience under stress. Many, now believing that the worst was over, expected that recovery would soon be under way.[2]

Across the Atlantic, the picture was more equivocal. Between February and August 1929, a new reparations deal for Germany, with further reduced payments on an again extended schedule, had been brokered by Owen D. Young (another American emissary with a business background whose status was no more than quasi-official), and the "Young Plan" was ratified by all the interested European powers by May 1930. As a result, the Reparations Commission was wound down, Parker Gilbert came home, and the Bank for International Settlements was established to oversee the new arrangements. The postwar international order that Mellon and his fellow banker-statesmen had labored throughout the 1920s to put in place still seemed to be holding.[3] But only just. Although of limited domestic significance, the Wall Street crash had had international repercussions. American loans across the Atlantic collapsed, as did American demand for European goods. Industrial and agricultural prices fell, manufacturing output declined, and by mid-1930 unemployment had begun to rise across the continent. The currencies (and thus the banks) of Germany and Austria came under particular pressure, and the Weimar Republic under Chancellor Heinrich Brüning began to look distinctly shaky. Nevertheless, from November 1929 to June 1930, there was still hope that this was only a temporary lull, and that conditions would soon improve.[4]

For much of 1930, Mellon shared the general view that the American economy was basically sound and that business would soon pick up in Europe. To be sure, the crash had occurred on his watch, denting the reputation of "the greatest secretary of the treasury since Alexander Hamilton" and shaking the expectation that under his stewardship, things could only get better and better and better. He sought to avoid the shadow of incipient doubt by increasingly leaving the details of administration to Ogden Mills and initiating an unprecedented public relations campaign, breaking his long-standing rule of privacy and granting interviews that touched on his personal life and habits.[5] But this was mere window dressing. More important, when the fiscal year ended on June 30, 1930, with a federal surplus of $184 million, it looked as though Mellon's analysis had been vindicated: the downturn was temporary and recovery just around the corner. That the Democrats didn't seek to exploit the crash and its aftermath, accepting the Republican view that this was a minor economic setback, indicates the extent of the faulty consensus. As Jouett Shouse, chairman of the Democratic National Executive Committee, noted: "Of course, Secretary Mellon is honest in his assertion that the panic is the result of natural conditions."[6]

Early in 1930 Mellon did his reputation another favor by finally managing, with Hoover's support, to rid the Treasury of the loathsome responsibility of enforcing Prohibition. Appearing before the House Committee on Expenditure by Executive Departments to speak in support of a bill transferring the Prohibition Bureau to the Justice Department, he reiterated his view that it was "illogical" for the Treasury to be responsible for law enforcement, a task wholly at variance with his department's other duties of raising and disbursing revenue. He declined to answer questions concerning the effectiveness of current policies; he insisted they were not germane to the bill under consideration and said only that the Treasury had "made every effort to enforce the prohibition law."[7] With the blessing of the attorney general, the bill passed both houses within four months, and the transfer duly took place in June 1930, almost nine years after Senator Boies Penrose had assured Mellon it could be accomplished within six months of his confirmation as secretary. Some critics took advantage of this last opportunity to lampoon Mellon's failings as the commander of the dry brigade, but from now on, that buck no longer stopped with him.

During the first half of 1930, Mellon was also much concerned with international trade. Although exports from western Europe to America were declining, the Soviet Union had recently begun dumping large quantities of grain, lumber, and oil on the American market, in a desperate drive for foreign currency to finance the new five-year plan, which aimed to bring the chronically backward Soviet economy into the modern world. Mellon was concerned, both as treasury secretary and as a major shareholder in certain American businesses that were by now getting involved with the Russians (Koppers was building a processing plant in the country). Accordingly, he issued embargos on the import of Soviet lumber, safety matches, and asbestos—but not on manganese, which was needed by Mellon-controlled steel companies.[8] More generally, as he explained to Nora, he was "continually occupied from morning to night" in discussions concerning the tariff. This was more a congressional than an executive-branch initiative, and the resulting Smoot-Hawley Tariff of June 1930 raised protective duties to the highest level ever. Hoover disliked the measure, rightly fearing it would reduce international trade still further. But he failed to prevent its passing; Mellon, by contrast, was generally content with the outcome.[9]

Nevertheless, by this time, Mellon had come to believe that Hoover was demonstrating "a firm grasp of the economic and business problems of the country" along with "a very remarkable and intimate knowledge of essential details and facts, together with fine business judgment." And it was the president's judgment that, having persuaded industrialists to maintain wage rates and state governments to join the federal government in increasing spending on public works, the prospects looked encouraging. "I am convinced," he told the U.S. Chamber of Commerce in May 1930, "we have passed the worst, and with continued effort we shall rapidly recover." The following month, he told a delegation from the National Catholic Welfare Conference that their pleas for the further expansion of federal public works were "sixty days too late. The Depression is over."[10] Hoover would, Bernard Baruch predicted, be "fortunate enough, before the next election, to have a rising tide and then he will be pictured as the great master mind who led his country out of its economic misery."[11]

Freed from the weight of Prohibition enforcement and guardedly optimistic about the future, Mellon concentrated on driving forward his Federal Triangle project, which moved ahead in early 1930 with a confidence that reflected the mood of the time in the Republican administration.[12] The arrival of John Russell Pope had brought energy and coherence to the planning for the first time, and very soon, he had reconfigured the buildings, especially these fronting on Constitution Avenue, where he persuaded the Commission on Fine Arts to switch the positions of the Justice Department and the National Archives. An amendment to the Public Buildings Act of 1926 enabled Mellon to award design contracts to architects in private practice, as well as to federal employees, which meant he could share out commissions among members of the Board of Architectural Consultants, as he had always wanted to do. And in 1930, Congress authorized the construction of four additional buildings: the Post Office Department was designed by Delano and Aldrich; the Department of Justice went to Zantzinger, Borie, and Medary; the Department of Labor and the Interstate Commerce Commission (which formed one building, together with the Departmental Auditorium) was assigned to Arthur Brown Jr.; and the National Archives, which would be the most elaborate and ornate of the lot, with its plethora of Corinthian columns, was given over to Pope himself.[13]

The result was what has rightly been described as "the most active phase of the Triangle development." The Internal Revenue Service and the Department of Commerce buildings were nearing completion; during the first six months of 1931, all the land was cleared for the next phase of construction; the foundation stones of these four additional buildings would be laid during Hoover's administration; and they would all be completed by 1935.[14] But there remained one vacant plot, and also one seriously dissatisfied architect: Edward H. Bennett, who had been associated with the project from the beginning (albeit not in an especially distinguished way), had not yet been commissioned to design a building, and he was eager to obtain the commission for the last site, at the eastern apex of the triangle, where Constitution Avenue and Pennsylvania Avenue intersected. By the autumn of 1930, Bennett was lobbying Mellon hard for the job. In March 1931, Congress authorized the expenditure of $3 million on the building (which was originally intended to house the United States Coast Guard), and in April, the Treasury signed a contract with Bennett's firm to prepare preliminary sketches for it.[15]

Such progress meant that by the spring of 1931, Mellon could look forward, with justifiable confidence and in reasonable time, to the realization of the greatest single piece of neoclassical construction that the world had ever seen. It was, of course, rather ironic that the self-proclaimed champion of small government and fiscal restraint was presiding with such zeal and interest over this unprecedented monument to administrative bureaucracy. Nor was this the only irony: for by agreeable coincidence, this federally funded scheme reached its high point at exactly the time when Hoover was advocating public building programs as the best way to keep the economy moving in the aftermath of the crash. Already, criticisms were being leveled at the Federal Triangle from a younger generation of architects who preferred the modern style and who averred that the buildings were elitist, pretentious, and anachronistic; and later they would seem to have unacceptable affinities with Communist and Fascist architecture of the same decade. But as the 200th anniversary of the birth of George Washington approached in February 1932, Mellon believed they would form "a succession of beautiful and harmonious buildings." No secretary of the treasury before or since has left his imprint so impressively and enduringly on the nation's capital.[16]

But long before then, the optimism of early 1930 had begun to fade, as the American economy suddenly took a downward slide which defied explanation. By the end of the year, business failures had reached a record 26,355, and the gross national product had slumped 12.6 percent from its 1929 level. Production of durable goods was down sharply—as much as 38 percent in some steel mills, and about the same throughout the automobile industry. In the face of softening demand, employers could no longer keep up wages or keep on their workers as they had promised Hoover in the immediate aftermath of the crash. By December 1930, an estimated four million were out of work, and Mellon joined a presidential committee to coordinate the government's "activities in unemployment."[17] By various criteria, 1930 had not been as bad a year for the American economy as 1921, but Mellon admitted that things did not look good. "We thought the stock market was at the bottom after the stock market crash last fall," he wrote to Paul in Cambridge in October, "but it has gone much worse." "The depression in business," he went on, "and fall in values has gone further than anyone believed possible, and the prospects indicate a long period of readjustment. There will be much hardship from unemployment this winter."[18]

Not surprisingly, the popular mood was beginning to turn against the government, and in the midterm elections of November 1930, the GOP lost its majorities in both houses. "We have not yet learned how to avoid industrial depression," Mellon mournfully observed in an election eve broadcast. The country must go through "a painful process of readjustment."[19] In fact, many races for the House and the Senate had turned on Prohibition as much as on the economy, and as midterm losses went, they were not unusual. But Hoover's prestige was considerably weakened as a result. Then, at the very end of the year, an epidemic of failures spread through America's financial system. In 1929, there had been 659 banking suspensions, a figure easily within the normal range for the decade, and through October 1930, there were a similar number of collapses. But in the last sixty days of the year, 600 banks closed their doors, beginning with Louisville's National Bank of Kentucky and culminating in New York, where the Bank of the United States closed its doors on December 11. This was the largest commercial bank failure in American history up to that time: it had held the savings of some 400,000 people, totaling nearly $300 million. The Federal Reserve System failed to persuade Wall Street to organize a rescue operation, and business morale and depositor confidence were both hard hit.[20]

As Mellon had feared, the winter of 1930–31 was indeed bitter: unemployment continued to rise, and his own position now began an inexorable decline. With tax revenues down and a deficit soaring to $300 million during the first five months of fiscal 1931, the secretary's reputation for prudence and competence took a battering. In selecting a new member of the Federal Reserve Board, Hoover ignored Mellon's preference for Parker Gilbert and appointed Eugene Meyer without even consulting the secretary. When the Treasury position was presented to Congress or the press, it was Ogden Mills who now did most of the talking, while Mellon looked on, mute and detached. The recent biography of him by Philip Love had sold poorly, leaving the publishers with 2,500 copies "still on hand," which they duly pulped.[21] Most damaging was Mellon's opposition to another bonus bill, which aimed to make immediately available to impoverished ex-servicemen their adjusted compensation certificates, which were not due to mature until 1945. Supported by Hoover, who would eventually veto the measure, Mellon argued against it: it would cost $3.4 billion, it would damage public credit, and it would thus retard economic recovery.[22] As a result, Mellon earned the "hatred" of "ex-servicemen all over the country." "It is to your own interest," one of them wrote to him in February 1931, "to prolong unemployment, and to keep the poor of the country from getting a fair chance. . . . If I had one wish granted before I die, I would wish you and others like you could suffer hunger and poverty."[23] It was but one of many such letters.

Although admitting to Paul that "conditions as to unemployment" were "distressing," Andrew was unmoved by such missives. The government, he insisted, was "doing what it can to improve the situation." (At just this time, he received with Dick an award from the American Institute of Chemists "for service to the science of chemistry.")[24] Moreover, no one quite yet knew whether the banking panic of December 1930 was the last spasm of events that had begun in October 1929 or the portent of something worse. On the whole, it seemed to be no more than the delayed consequence of the stock market crash. During the first quarter of 1931, when Mellon's reputation was beginning to go down, the rate of bank failures slowed dramatically and indexes of economic activity turned upward. Industrial production rose, and so did payrolls and income. Many Americans permitted themselves the guarded hope that the financial convulsions of late 1930 might have marked the beginning of the end of the bad times. As Hoover himself would later write, by the spring of 1931 "we had begun to entertain well founded hopes that we were on our way out of the depression." Some later observers agreed. "All in all," two monetary historians would conclude, "the figures for the first four or five months of 1931, if examined without reference to what actually followed, have many of the earmarks of the bottom of a cycle and the beginning of a revival."[25] There was, then, something to be said for the view that sitting it out was the right thing to do, and that recovery really might be around the corner. That, unsurprisingly, was the opinion of Andrew Mellon.

On May 5, 1931, the secretary of the treasury spelled out his unchanged economic philosophy in a speech at a meeting of the American Bankers Association.[26] It was inevitable, he again insisted, that from time to time the economy had to undergo painful but necessary periods of readjustment, and this latest period, coming so soon after a great war, was no worse than those which had gone before. "Conditions today," he said, "are neither so critical nor so unprecedented as to justify a lack of faith in our capacity to deal with them in our accustomed way." This in turn meant that now was "no time to undertake drastic experiments which may conceivably result in breaking down the standard of living to which we have become accustomed." As before, solutions would come from individual initiative, and not "by surrendering the management of business and industry to government or to any board or group of men." "I have no means of knowing," he concluded, "when or how we shall emerge from the valley in which we are now traveling. But I do know that, as in the past, the day will come when we shall find ourselves on a more solid economic foundation and the onward march of progress will be resumed." But that day, that foundation, and that progress would not come in what remained of Mellon's lifetime.

II. MONEY, McMULLENS, AND MELLONS

In 1930 and in early 1931, Andrew Mellon's fortune reached its zenith, and he reached the age of seventy-five. It had been a long lifetime of "acquisition and accumulation." In capital terms, his wealth peaked at a book value of $127 million, and his income was also the highest he ever recorded: $8.8 million after paying federal taxes, and doubtless helped by the recent cash payment from Pullman on his Standard Steel Car stock.[27] What did all this money mean to Mellon personally? He rarely spoke about his fortune, but two comments are worth recording. Like many rich men, he had no idea how just rich he was: "How can I tell what I am worth?" H. M. Johnson remembered him once asking. "It changes from day to day."[28] And on his arrival in Washington as treasury secretary, he offered the following observation, which was true as far as it went:

> I suppose I am what they call a rich man. They tell me so. I'm not particularly conscious of it. I don't use money for myself. I don't spend much on myself. I have always just worked, done what needed to be done in business. I didn't try to make money especially. I'm not interested in money.[29]

One indication of the increased riches, sustained confidence, and continued commitment to their city of both Andrew and Dick was that they had recently been aggressively buying up more shares in the Pittsburgh Coal Company. Another was that in February 1930, work was begun on a new Gulf building, directly across Seventh Avenue from the recently completed Koppers headquarters. At forty-four stories and 582 feet high, it would be the tallest skyscraper in the city, and at the very top, in a stepped-back pyramid that recalled the Mausoleum at Halicarnassus, it would be lit by neon tubes in the company colors of orange and blue, which displayed the local weather forecast: steady blue meant precipitation and rising temperatures; flashing blue, precipitation and falling temperatures; steady orange, clear and rising temperatures; flashing orange, clear and falling temperatures. The building was designed by Trowbridge and Livingston, who had been responsible for the Mellon National Bank; E. P. Mellon was again involved; and the structural engineering was undertaken by McClintic-Marshall.[30] It was in a very different stylistic idiom from the Federal Triangle in Washington, and along with the Union Trust, the Mellon Bank, and the Koppers buildings, it would proclaim the continued dominance of the "Mellon Raj" in the city. It is not difficult to imagine what the Judge would have made of such ostentatious display, and Andrew was less comfortable with it than Dick.[31]

This was not the only sign of the buoyancy and expansiveness which the Mellon brothers felt: they also began spending on two more personal enterprises, both the results of family piety, in one case joint and dynastic, in the other case single and religious. By the late 1920s, the Mellon Institute building had long since become too small, and in 1930, Andrew and Dick resolved that they would finance a grander new home: between 1931 and 1937, Andrew would give four million dollars for new construction, and Dick (and subsequently his estate) the same.[32] During this time, Dick also decided that he would pay for the complete reconstruction of the East Liberty Presbyterian Church, where the Mellon boys and their parents had worshipped, and which Dick and Jennie still attended regularly. During the remainder of his life, Dick lavished another four million dollars on this building project, rightly described by its architect, Ralph Adams Cram, as "a church of cathedral size."[33] (It would be popularly known as "the Mellon fire escape.") But this time, there was a difference: apart from Rolling Rock, this was the only undertaking embraced by Dick in which Andrew did not join, and it was later alleged that the one time he entered the church was for his funeral. Insofar as religion still mattered to Andrew, he was an Episcopalian, and insofar as he was interested in an ecclesiastical building, it was the National Cathedral in Washington.

Despite Andrew's continued protestations that he was no longer active in business, he was now concerning himself, along with Dick, in two additional ventures, one familiar and local, the other novel and distant.[34] The local venture was the creation, at the very end of 1929, of the Mellbank Corporation as the vehicle for expanding and consolidating Mellon involvement in small-town banks in the greater Pittsburgh area. This could be seen as the altruistic extension of Mellon protection to local, neighborhood banks with limited resources and reserves. But it also enabled Andrew and Dick to become yet more influential in Pittsburgh, as they offered financial and management support to more than twenty banks in places like Donora, New Kensington, Latrobe, and Ligonier. Thus did altruism and self-interest converge: the more stable the financial structure of greater Pittsburgh, the more powerful the Mellons became. To run this new corporation, Andrew and Dick appointed a young man named Frank Denton, who had previously been employed in the Treasury as assistant chief national bank examiner. Only thirty, he was exceptionally able, and Mellon had no qualms about plucking a promising young employee from government service (as he had already done with Donald Shepard) and putting him in charge of this new realm in the family's financial empire.[35]

At the same time, Andrew and Dick also involved themselves in one final new business enterprise: air transport. As they were getting out of Standard Steel Car, they took an interest in a local firm, the Pittsburgh Aviation Company, and through it they also became shareholders in Pittsburgh's recently opened Butler Airport. Crucial to the viability of any American airline at this time was the securing of federal contracts to carry airmail, and Mellon naturally used his influence with the postmaster general, Walter F. Brown, to obtain such contracts for his company. This had the further advantage of driving out potential competitors, who complained (justifiably yet ineffectually) of the pressure the Mellons had brought to bear via the federal government. One such defeated rival was Clifford Ball, who had been operating an air route between Cleveland and Pittsburgh, and who had obtained the mail contract for it. But under pressure from the Mellons, and also from the postmaster general, his federal contract was not renewed—until he agreed to sell out to the Pittsburgh Aviation Company, to which the government then promptly awarded the Pittsburgh-Cleveland contract until May 1936.[36]

By this time, the Mellons were extending their interests in this new form of transport in an easterly direction, to the Aviation Company of Delaware (AVCO). Formed in March 1929, it boasted close links with the administration (a former postmaster general was a director), the Harrimans and the Lehman Brothers were involved in it, and both David Bruce and R. K. Mellon were put on the board. Once again, the company obtained preferential treatment from the federal government in the form of lucrative airmail contracts. AVCO, in turn, was one of the four major domestic airlines that supported Pan American, the country's only international airline at the time, of which both Bruce and RK became directors.[37] In seizing this new opportunity, the Mellons characteristically sought to overwhelm competitors, and used privileged contacts in Washington to achieve their ends. This venture was also an indication that, in business as in politics and social life, they were moving into closer contact with the East Coast establishment. David had recently become involved with the Harrimans in New York, and Andrew Mellon may have hoped that while Paul took over the family interests in Pittsburgh, David would become a major financial figure on the eastern seaboard. (If so, he would be disappointed in both expectations.)

Mellbank and AVCO were Andrew Mellon's last business initiatives. By now he was giving more thought to selling off some of the family companies. Standard Steel Car had recently gone, and next it was the turn of McClintic-Marshall. The reasons were essentially the same: Andrew and Dick were both getting on in years, and so were the eponymous founder-managers whom the brothers had financed and supported since the early 1900s. Like the Mellon brothers, McClintic and Marshall were eager to be relieved of further managerial responsibilities, and were happy to convert their interests into an investment. So, in 1930, they began negotiations for the sale of virtually all the company's assets to the Bethlehem Steel Corporation in exchange for Bethlehem stock and bonds, and they also conveyed some of its property to Koppers. The cash value of the stock distribution to Andrew and Dick was nearly $20 million apiece, and McClintic and Marshall each received some $13 million. Both acknowledged that it was thanks to Mellon funding that they had made their fortunes. Of the iconic Mellon companies, this left Alcoa, Carborundum, Koppers, and Gulf. This would not be the last, however, that Andrew Mellon heard of McClintic-Marshall.[38]

Selling companies lessened responsibility, but it increased Mellon's fortune, rather than diminished it. To be sure, he had recently set up a trust fund for the McMullens, he was always giving money to Nora, and he had established Ailsa and David at Sutton Place and Syosset. But despite rumor to the contrary, Mellon had not yet settled many multiple millions on Ailsa, and Paul was living on an allowance from his father. Andrew had also given some money for philanthropic purposes, most noticeably to the University of Pittsburgh, and he had recently committed significant funds to the new Mellon Institute building. But he had taken no steps toward establishing the legal and financial structure that would be necessary if he was to realize his scheme of creating and endowing a national art gallery and of donating his picture collection to it. Yet Mellon was reaching the age at which his father had divested himself of his wealth, and he now began to consider how he might do the same. A diary entry notes that he was thinking about "personal corporation matter" and also about "question of making charitable or other trust."[39] Here was the germ of an idea which Mellon, assisted by Donald Shepard, would now bring to fruition. He would give away his fortune in approximately equal proportions: for new philanthropic purposes (which would mean the National Gallery of Art) and for familial purposes (which meant Ailsa and Paul and, eventually, their descendants), thereby ensuring that at his death, he would be far less wealthy than he had been in his prime.

To realize the first of these aims, he established the A. W. Mellon Educational & Charitable Trust in December 1930, the purpose of which was to give "considerable funds and properties" exclusively "in aid of such religious, charitable, scientific, literary and/or educational purposes as, in the judgment of the trustees, shall be in the furtherance of the public welfare, and tend to promote the well-doing or well-being of mankind."[40] As such, the trust would receive the Mellon money that would eventually provide the endowment and pay for the cost of building the gallery, and also hold the Mellon pictures that would later hang on its walls. As an indication of his intentions, Mellon immediately handed over to the trust a cash gift of $10,000 and also Raphael's *Niccolini-Cowper Madonna*, which he had bought through Duveen in November 1928. Like the Carnegie Corporation and the Rockefeller Foundation, the trust was named after its creator, and it was set up as a family affair, with the first trustees being Andrew himself, Paul, and Donald Shepard. (David Bruce was subsequently added.) But unlike Carnegie and Rockefeller, Mellon had no intention of setting up a permanent foundation. Once the trust's aims had been achieved, the remaining money was to be spent, the trust wound up, and Andrew Mellon's name would disappear from any list of American philanthropic endeavors.

During the next few years, Mellon would make over stock and art to the trust in increasing amounts. At the same time, he also resolved to begin giving more substantial sums to his children. In May 1931, he transferred 75,000 shares of common stock in Alcoa, with a book value of half a million dollars, to Ailsa, and he also handed over the same amount to Paul—an indication that in future he intended to turn over roughly equal sums to each of his children as a "permanent provision" for them.[41] Soon after, he set up two new private companies, Coalesced and Ascalot, to which he would transfer some of the shares he intended to pass on to Ailsa and Paul. (Within a year, Dick Mellon had followed suit, establishing the Aloxite and Riscar Companies, through which he would pass on his wealth to his wife, son, and daughter.)[42] In December 1931, Andrew Mellon made over to Paul and Ailsa 100,000 shares each in Coalesced common stock, with a combined book value of $20 million, retaining the preferred stock in his own name. This was the first major transfer of wealth to his children, and it was a portent of what was to come. It also in large part explains why, by the end of that year, the book value of Mellon's fortune had declined from $127 million to $101 million—making 1931 the first year in the twentieth century that it had diminished.[43]

These strategic decisions, which inaugurated the long-term disposal of Mellon's wealth, were made against a background of continuing day-to-day uncertainty and unhappiness in his family. It might have seemed that by the autumn of 1929, various issues and relationships had been settled, but that soon turned out not to be the case. The establishment of trust funds for the McMullen brothers had been met with acclaim and appreciation—but would it be sufficient for the troubled times they were headed into? Nora had obtained her divorce from Harry Lee—but what sort of new life would she make for herself this time around? Paul had begun his studies at Cambridge—but would this be an interlude before he got down to work and business in Pittsburgh, or would it lure him further in his love of the English countryside? And Mr. and Mrs. David Bruce were grandly ensconced in Sutton Place and Syosset—but where were the grandchildren that Andrew looked forward to, as the next generation and as a solace to his old age?

In providing for the six surviving McMullen brothers scarcely two months before the Wall Street crash of October 1929, Mellon had acted just in time. "Things are pretty bad here," Kenrick McMullen later wrote from Britain, when the depths of the slump were reached, but he had not forgotten "that it is your generosity which enables us to keep our noses above water."[44] This was the general view among the brothers, most of whom ceased to harangue their former brother-in-law—all except Leonard, whose share of the trust fund had been made over to his wife, Gee, who wisely kept him on a minor allowance. Leonard, therefore, teetering constantly on the brink of bankruptcy, continued to deluge Andrew with begging letters by turns enraged, disappointed, self-pitying, and pathetic: "I do think you might put aside past failures and lend me this

£300"; "I have not a single real friend"; "Gee cannot pawn her trust fund without your permission"; "all I wanted you to do was give me £500 in cash"; "this is not life, it is just hell"; "I could think of nothing more unkind or inhuman"; and so on. Andrew declined to give Leonard any further assistance, and Nora also refused to help him, though she did give money to Gee. In the spring of 1931, Leonard's daughter Phyllis was to marry, but he could barely afford a present, and he feared he might be unable to attend the service: "I cannot go to the church to give her away as bankrupt," he wailed. Nora was furious, and Leonard responded in kind. "I don't want Nora to help," he complained to Andrew. "She hates me."[45]

Continued concern for her brothers was one reason why, in the aftermath of her divorce from Harry Lee, Nora remained unhappy and uneasy.[46] In the autumn of 1929, she went to England, where she set herself up in a "small service apartment" in London for six months and saw a great deal of those McMullens with whom she remained on good terms. "I wish I could settle down here," she wrote to Andrew, and "it is wonderful to be wanted, but I know I could not." "I do not seem to fit in anywhere, anymore," she reflected, "and get rather discouraged." At the end of the year, Andrew settled another substantial sum on Nora, guaranteeing her an additional income of $25,000 a year; this was not in the form of a trust fund, but an outright gift to her, to do with as she wished. "I seem always to be thanking you for something," she wrote back, "and now you have done this wonderful thing for me . . . I do thank you from my heart—but words are poor things!"[47] Soon after her return to America, in June 1930, she decided to change her name back from Nora Lee to Nora McMullen Mellon, for (as she explained to Bruce McCrory) "Paul and Ailsa both wish it, and Mr. M. is agreeable to it." Indeed Andrew was, and Nora delighted in seeing the name Mellon once again on letters addressed to her from family and friends. She was, however, very discomfited when a reporter from the *New York Times* tracked her down in Litchfield and asked whether the reversion implied that she and Andrew would be getting back together again.[48]

Later that year, Nora suffered a bad attack of shingles, which led to a complete nervous collapse, and she decided to sell the Litchfield house—partly because, as she admitted to Andrew, "Ailsa hates Connecticut and calls it the 'wilds,'" and partly because she wanted somewhere in the country where she could ride again before she got too old.[49] Virginia beckoned as an inviting possibility: it was good hunting country, near the nation's capital, and the home state of David Bruce's family. But there were disadvantages, too. "If I were nearer Washington," Nora lamented to Andrew, "I should always be hoping to see you," but her recent encounter with newspaper reporters made her realize that she could "only hope ever to see you in a more or less secret way, and I simply cannot do it." Nor would undue proximity to Ailsa be a good idea: "I always feel in some way I am more or less of an embarrassment . . . I know not one of Ailsa's friends . . . It has always been a great grief." "I think," Nora concluded—in a letter which she thought "very selfish," but from which Andrew, evidently moved, copied out sections in his own hand—that "if Paul shows he does not want me, that will finish life for me."[50]

In fact, Nora's relations with her son were much easier than with her increasingly distant and self-absorbed daughter, and the main reason she had gone to England for a long visit in the autumn of 1929 was to be near Paul, as he took up his place at Clare College, Cambridge. She had a "dreadful time" persuading the authorities to make his traditionally spartan rooms "fairly comfortable." But, with Andrew's agreement, she took care to ensure that everything was "made comfortable but not better than the others have."[51] Paul would have to walk across the college court to find a bath, his diet would consist of such staples as "boiled potatoes, cabbage, marrow, veal and ham pies," and it would be some time before he accustomed himself to such Cambridge idiosyncrasies as gyps and gowns, bicycles and lectures and supervisions. But he was enthralled by the beauty of the buildings, rowed with relish in the college boats, and having got over his debilitating stomach pains, began to enjoy the "general education" which the history tripos provided. "I don't see," he wrote to David Finley, "how any intelligent criticism or appreciation of any form of art, literature, science or philosophy can be attempted without a fairly sound background of historical knowledge; and I don't know anything better for mental discipline than the training in historical analysis and synthesis." Nora had this much cause for contentment, at least. "Paul is extremely happy at Cambridge," she wrote to Bruce McCrory, "which of course has made me very happy. He has done awfully well rowing, and hopes to have a little time to study during the vacation!"[52]

Early in 1930, Paul predictably decided he wanted to spend a second academic year in Cambridge, and wrote to his father, anxiously seeking approval. Nora rightly sensed that Andrew would be opposed, and while insisting she had never encouraged Paul to resist his father's wishes, she strongly supported her son's request. "Don't you think," she reminded Andrew, not unwisely, "one has to remember how steady and faithful he was all through years at school and Yale, when he might so easily have been different in his position." Paul was indeed thriving at Cambridge:

the rowing had "made a different man of him, and he fairly radiates health and strength now and seems so very happy," but he had "hardly got settled into work yet." Nora was sure that, if Andrew insisted, Paul would capitulate, for he "would never want to cause you any distress"; but she also knew it would be "a very bitter disappointment" to him. "It is not," she continued, "as if he were trying to shirk his initiation into business. He is, I believe, looking forward with interest to it, but I can't help feeling he will do infinitely better when he does start, if he has gratitude in his heart rather than a feeling of disappointment and frustration." "If," she concluded, "you have any feeling that the extra time there might give him a taste for English life, I think you should dispel it at once. It is the last thing I would wish for him, but I am convinced that it would have the opposite effect, and he would be more than satisfied to return home and take up whatever work seems best."[53]

In these predictions, Nora would be proved entirely wrong: Paul would soon fall in undying love with English life, and he never harbored a wish to work in the Mellon Bank. But Andrew was "greatly impressed" by her "fine letter," and admitted to feeling "at heart just as you have expressed yourself in favor of conforming to Paul's desires," even though his "best judgment has supported the other side of the problem."[54] Accordingly, he sent his son what he acknowledged was "an unusually long letter for me," recognizing that it was "a difficult decision to make," setting out the arguments for and against Paul's staying on, but conceding in the end that it was for him to decide, "for I want you to be satisfied with whatever you do, so that there will be no regrets later." "The line of least resistance," he began, "or rather I may say my inclination (which is always prompted by desire for your happiness and enjoyment) is to follow your wishes in the matter." "I sympathize with you," he went on, "in your desire to finish whatever you have begun, and can understand your reluctance to stop a course when you are half way to a degree." And he certainly recognized the value of what Paul was learning, especially "the importance of an understanding of history as a preparation for life and for enabling you to see things in their proper perspective." Clearly, his year at Cambridge had been "of real value," and if Paul thought that another year would be "vitally important" to him, his father would not prevent it. "I am willing to abide by whatever conclusion you come to, for I know it will be an honest decision and made for reasons which seem to you justifiable."[55]

Andrew may have thus resigned himself to Paul's decision, but he was far from pleased with it. "The degree can add nothing to your equipment," he argued, for "you never intend to teach or to use the degree in after life," and his stay in Cambridge was merely to provide him with "cultural background." But too much time spent in such academic pursuits "would make it difficult for you to become really interested in and adept at the practical, concrete matters with which you will be obliged to deal in business." It was, Andrew felt, essential that Paul should accustom himself in his "early, formative years to dealing with business matters so that you will acquire a facility which in time will become second nature and give you that experience and judgment which will enable you to protect yourself and to meet the great responsibilities which will some day be yours." "A year or two of business training," he went on, "such as you would get now at your present age in the Bank, is as necessary for your later business life as your preparatory school was for your college education." "It is this experience," he continued, "that I want you to get before your habits of thought have become fixed, as they surely will be before you are very much older." "I do," he insisted, "want very much to see you established along lines that I feel will ultimately bring you the greatest satisfaction," which could only be achieved by returning to Pittsburgh "for the work which you will come home to do."

It was a powerful letter, in its earnest effort to be evenhanded and in its insistence that "my inclination is always to let you do what will make you happiest." But there was a proviso—that Paul's "choice" was "also for your own good." Like the Judge a generation earlier, Andrew was sure he knew where his son's best interest lay. He feared that Paul was being excessively influenced by his "present surroundings, whereas if you were at work at home instead, you might feel very differently about things." With his cousin Dick and others "at the Bank, I think you would have congenial occupation. I feel sure of your aptitude, and I see great opportunities for you which I am confident will arouse and hold your interest, without it being necessary for you to become in any sense a slave to business." A business career, Andrew was at pains to point out, was not incompatible with "opportunities for abundant cultural enjoyment." There was another consideration. "I am getting old," he wrote, "and before a great while, our positions will be reversed. I will be more or less dependent on you for advice and guidance, rather than the one to lead." But in the meantime, he was anxious to help Paul "to make no mistake now." Still, he seems to have recognized that the plan would succeed only if Paul was willing. In a letter to Nora at this time, he describes Paul's proposal to go into the bank for the summer: encouraging news on the face of it, but, Andrew allows, "unless he feels perfectly strong and well when the time comes, I think that may not be good for him."[56]

When Paul returned to the United States for the summer vacation in early July 1930, rumors were circulating that he would turn his back on the "Mellon Interests" as he contemplated a career in publishing. "I do not think," he was quoted in the *New York Herald-Tribune*, "I would be a great success as a banker or industrialist. Commerce and banking hold no particular interest for me and I think it is wiser to enter a field which is more attractive. There are other members of my family who are far better fitted than I am to look after the family interests." Nevertheless, within twenty-four hours, Paul reported for his first day at the Mellon National Bank, escorted by his father, who had journeyed to Pittsburgh especially for the occasion. But before long, Paul was again quoted as saying that "the idea of becoming a banker is not attractive to me, and that I'd much rather be in the publishing business."[57] Both quotations, Paul told Ailsa, were "fictitious," and he spent the summer working at Mellbank Corporation, auditing small banks in western Pennsylvania under the tutelage of Frank Denton. "It is," he wrote to his sister, evidently attempting to convince himself as much as her, "fairly interesting and a good way to get a bird's eye view of what a bank is for, besides being in at the beginning of something that may be pretty important later." In subsequent years, he would confess to being "bored to tears" by the work; he couldn't wait for the evenings, "for music and dancing with some of the very attractive girls we knew around town."[58]

In the autumn of 1930, Paul returned with obvious relief to Cambridge, "this fool's paradise of sloth and procrastination," as he described it to Ailsa. He knew that his father had been "rather disappointed" at his decision, which he defended to David Finley as "the best thing and not a waste of time." In any case, Andrew soon relented. "I feel glad that you are there now," he wrote, no doubt biting his tongue, soon after Paul's return, "and that you are finding it so pleasant and beneficial. It would have been a cause of regret had you not gone back."[59] As in the previous year, Paul went home for the Christmas vacation, but he was now far more settled in Cambridge, he had been elected to the Pitt Club, and his father had agreed to raise his allowance. The increase would support not generally higher living but one passion in particular, for in his second year, Paul took up hunting with great gusto, often going out two days a week, and maintaining a pair of horses and a groom. In this, he was manifestly Nora's son. He rode with the Harriers, the Fitzwilliam, the Quorn, the Pytchley, the Cottesloe ("more than worth the extra distance"), and even the Belvoir ("especially swank"). The Easter vacation of 1931 would be spent mostly in the saddle. "This winter," he told Ailsa, "has given me a love of England and of hunting that I can never lose. I feel so well now that I could burst." "England must be delightful at this season," Andrew wrote soon after, not yet realizing—or perhaps accepting—what an ardent Anglophile his son had become.[60]

Throughout his time at Cambridge, Paul corresponded regularly with his father, with Nora, with Ailsa, and with David Finley. "No doubt you will find very little out of the ordinary to write about," Andrew opined in October 1930, eager to coax a correspondence, "but I am interested to hear from you as may happen, whether what you have to say is of consequence or otherwise." His own letters to Paul were full of important items: the depression in Pittsburgh, politics in Washington, and the purchase of pictures.[61] But there was also news of Ailsa and David and Nora, as well as more personal matters. "I regard boat racing as injurious," Andrew wrote on one occasion, taking issue with his son's increasing relish for sport. "Reasonable athletic activity is beneficial, but too much is positively harmful." "I notice you use the word 'gotten' instead of got," he mentioned in another letter, "which is all right, but I remember that one time while in England, I was questioned as to the use of that word, it being stated that gotten was not a proper form, and that got was the appropriate word and was usable wherever gotten might be used. I am not mentioning this in the way of criticism, but only from recollection of the incident I speak of." And there were also hints about the great scheme for Washington, and the part his son might play in it. "I hope," Andrew wrote to Paul, "you are having some time to spend at the National Gallery, as it will be useful to you to have some knowledge of the important pictures in the Gallery in view of the contact you will have with work of a similar character in the future here."[62]

There was one other important issue between father and son during Paul's second year at Cambridge, and that was the purchase of the four-hundred-acre Rokeby farm in Virginia's horse country, near Upperville. Andrew bought it in March 1931 for $125,000, and it was registered in Paul's name; but it was Nora who, having finally sold her house in Litchfield and overcome her doubts about Virginia, would be living there full-time.[63] After her divorce and her illnesses, Paul was adamant that "she simply must be made to take life more easily and to live in the country as much as possible," where she could live the life of an English country lady such as she had naïvely expected to do when she married Andrew. With the dismal prospect of returning to work in the bank at Pittsburgh, Paul was also eager to have a country place of his own, a reminder of the England for which he constantly yearned from across the Atlantic, and to which he could repair at weekends for fox-hunting and other rural diversions. As Rokeby was an easy distance from Washington, the press naturally got wind of the purchase, fanning renewed rumors that Nora and Andrew might be reconciled. "I sometimes think," Paul had earlier written to Ailsa, "that it might almost be the best solution for father to marry her again," for "he must certainly at times have a great loneliness, and I am sure she would be happy as long as she would be able to see us occasionally." But, he went on, "I suppose things will always drift on haphazardly and uncertainly, as they always have in this more than strange family."[64]

III. THE SALE OF THE CENTURY

The establishment of the A. W. Mellon Educational & Charitable Trust was one clear indication that, despite the crash, Andrew Mellon was determined to move forward with his plan to establish a great gallery in Washington. His treatment of W. A. Holmes, who had been appointed director of the unbuilt National Gallery of Art back in 1920, was another. Early in 1930, it transpired that, according to government regulations, Holmes would have to retire in August that year. Mellon was not eager that he should be replaced, because there would then be a director already in the post, and one not of his own choosing, when he got around to announcing his own plans. Accordingly, Mellon resolved that he would keep Holmes on, paying him an annual salary of $4,000 from his own pocket, thereby ensuring that he could get him to resign at any time.[65] But Holmes only stayed in office for little more than a year; he died in 1933. Accordingly, Mellon requested the secretary of the Smithsonian Institution not to appoint a successor, but to keep the job in abeyance. For as he explained, with uncharacteristic candor, he had "definitely in mind a very large gift, concerning not only the erection of a building, but its sufficient endowment to enlarge it fifty years hence," with the aim of ensuring that the United States would possess "the leading National Gallery in the whole world."[66]

In further pursuit of this ambition, Mellon continued throughout 1930 to purchase fine pictures from both Knoedler and Duveen. He had more money to spend than ever, and he could also enjoy an unprecedented buyers' market: the international art trade came close to collapse in the aftermath of the crash, as many rich people, cut off from the dividends on which they depended, suddenly stopped spending on such luxuries. Dealers were in tight straits indeed, with both credit lines and demand evaporating simultaneously. Stuck with pictures they had bought at inflated prices during the twenties boom, they now faced selling at a loss—if they could sell at all.[67] Early in January 1930, Charles Henschel noted that Duveen had "done very little business lately," and Mellon later informed Duveen that the prices of pictures would have to fall, in line with the value of "other commodities." Markets being markets, they duly did. It was no better at Knoedler: the second half of 1929 was a time of "bad business" for them, of excessive inventory that did not move. By the end of 1930, Henschel was lamenting that "business is almost at a standstill, and it is very difficult to get in any money."[68]

Bad times for the vulnerable and overleveraged, depressions are also golden opportunities for those who can ride them out. Following the crash of 1873, Judge Mellon had bought Pittsburgh property at bargain-basement prices. Now, having briefly cut back on his picture purchases during the second half of 1929, Andrew Mellon re-entered the art market, eager to make deals. Having cold-shouldered Duveen for the better part of six months, he moved to re-establish contact, paying off his outstanding balance and inviting Sir Joseph and Lady Duveen to their first dinner in the secretary's Washington residence, to meet the vice president. "May I also say," Duveen wrote in his thank-you letter, "that your apartment looked simply wonderful. I had never had an opportunity of seeing it at night, and my wife and I were charmed with the delightful atmosphere."[69] Such sociability would be a prelude to doing business again. For in February 1930, Mellon bought five paintings through Duveen: *Señora Sabasa Garcia* by Goya, *Portrait of a Youth* by Bellini, *Portrait of the Artist* by Antonis More, *The Madonna and Child with Infant St. John in a Landscape* by Titian, and *Cardinal Borja y Velasco* by Velázquez. Altogether, they cost him $1.6 million, which made this one of his largest purchases, though he could not have bought the five at that price the year before. He paid up promptly.[70] Even though he would later return the Velázquez, at $500,000 the most expensive of these pictures, this was a substantial outlay, and for Duveen a desperately needed infusion of funds.

Mellon also thawed his account with Knoedler, having done no major business with his original dealer for more than a year. In March 1930, Carman Messmore offered him two major works: *Saint Martin and the Beggars* by El Greco and *Portrait of a Donor: A Knight of the Order of Calatrava* by Master Michael. As Messmore explained, the retail prices of these paintings would be $150,000 and $100,000 respectively, but he offered them to Mellon for "a special cash price" of $120,000 and $80,000. "I cannot urge too strongly," he went on, "the acquisition of these two extremely fine works." The El Greco was "equal in importance" to Mellon's Rembrandt *Self-Portrait*, which he had bought the previous year (David Bruce also admired it as a "really exceptional picture"), while the Master Michael was an "extremely rare and outstanding work" by a painter "of which there are only five known examples." But Mellon pressed for a further reduction, and in the end, acquired the Master Michael for $60,000, the pair for $180,000. It was substantially less than even Knoedler's "special cash price."[71] Soon after, he purchased Holbein's portrait of Sir Bryan Tuke for $440,000 through Knoedler, but once again, he made them pay for his custom. For he also expressed a liking for a small portrait of William Pitt by Thomas Gainsborough and a little Degas pastel of L'Opéra, which meant, as Henschel would admit, that "we really had to throw these pictures in" as well, for the relatively trivial sums of $3,000 and $12,000 respectively.[72] For Mellon, such hard bargaining signified a return to business as usual: to say the least, he liked to keep his dealers on their toes, and to get the best terms; to say the worst, he took advantage of their depression-induced hardship.

But by this time, he was also undertaking through Knoedler what would turn out to be his most daring buy, his *coup de maître* as an art collector: a covert acquisition of twenty-one of the very finest paintings from the Hermitage—that remarkable constellation of buildings, part shrine, part palace, part art gallery, adorning the city formerly known as St. Petersburg and now called Leningrad, which had been founded by Peter the Great in 1703.[73] The Hermitage collection had originally been assembled by Empress Catherine the Great, who had acquired pictures from Britain, France, Prussia, and the Netherlands during the second half of the eighteenth century. Thereafter, her successors made their own great additions, so that by the early twentieth century the Hermitage merited comparison with any of the great accumulations of European royalty, including those at the Hofburg in Vienna, the Prado in Madrid, and Windsor Castle. Few western Europeans had visited the place, but accounts of its treasures gradually emerged in guidebooks, catalogues, and newspaper articles.[74] Estimates varied, but in all, the Hermitage collection amounted to more than two thousand items, including classical antiquities, coins and medals, and (especially) works of fine art from medieval times to the eighteenth century; approximately fifty of its paintings, representing Leonardo, Raphael, Rembrandt, Velázquez, and Titian, among others, were outstanding old masters.[75]

Having survived the Bolshevik Revolution intact, the Hermitage and its collections were subsequently nationalized in the name of the Russian people, and the keepers, curators, and directors were compelled to accept Marxist ideology. Throughout the 1920s, there were whispers that the Soviet government was considering selling off some of its greatest works of art to the West. For the first half of the decade, these rumors were largely without foundation, as only a few works of art were sold, most of inferior quality, and the sales were badly managed by the Soviets. But in 1925, the People's Commissariat for Foreign Trade set up a new organization, the Central Office for State Trading of the USSR for the Purchase and Sale of Antique Objects, to organize and oversee future transactions. Called the Antiquariat for short, it was headed by Nicholas Ilyn, who "had been locked up in Siberia for ten years by the Czar." The Antiquariat began compiling lists of the most valuable art in the Soviet Union, including many of the European old masters in the Hermitage.[76] During the winter of 1929–30, following the announcement of Stalin's five-year plan, the politburo authorized the Antiquariat to begin making sales abroad, to help obtain the foreign capital Stalin needed to transform the Soviet economy. But two conditions were imposed on its transactions: with the aim of generating substantial revenue, only items of the highest quality and value could be selected for sale; and the negotiations must be conducted in complete secrecy, since the Soviets did not want it generally known that they were selling off their greatest national treasures to the capitalist enemies of the revolution.[77]

The challenge for Ilyn was to find potential western purchasers who possessed sufficient wealth, enthusiasm, and discretion. There was an initial approach to Armand Hammer and his brother Victor (who were already trading with the Soviet regime), in which Duveen may also have been involved, and one of the paintings offered was Leonardo's *Benois Madonna*. But it proved impossible to agree on prices, and the deal collapsed. Next in line of the Antiquariat's suitors was Calouste Gulbenkian, an immensely rich Armenian, who was building up an impressive collection in Lisbon, and whose Iraq Petroleum Company was then prospecting for oil in the Ukraine. Between late 1929 and mid-1930, Gulbenkian made four separate purchases through the Antiquariat, mainly of antique silver and sculpture, but also including a Rubens and three Rembrandts, at a price in excess of $1.5 million.[78] But then negotiations stalled: the buyer believed he was paying too much, the sellers thought they were getting too little. Before pulling out, Gulbenkian offered several bits of unsolicited advice to the Soviet authorities: it was a mistake to sell off the national heritage piecemeal, Soviet prestige would plummet if the news got out, and the revenue generated would be insufficient "to help the finance of the state." Understanding the effects of the Wall Street crash of October 1929, he added a further admonition: "all sales have ceased in America, and there is a drop in prices and no buyers."[79]

Sometime in late 1929, Charles Henschel of Knoedler heard about these sales to Gulbenkian, and he also gathered that the Soviets might consider selling more art if another suitable buyer could be found.[80] The intelligence source was a well-connected dealer in Berlin, Francis Zatzenstein, proprietor of the Matthiesen Gallery. (Also known as Catzenstein or Matthiesen, he would leave Berlin in 1935, foreseeing the fate of German Jews under Hitler, to re-establish the Matthiesen Gallery in London.)[81] Involved with the Gulbenkian purchases, Zatzenstein was represented in Moscow by his agent, Heinz Mansfeld, who was in direct touch with Ilyn of the Antiquariat.[82] It was Mansfeld who had informed Zatzenstein that more sales might be in the offing; Zatzenstein hastened to pass this news on to Otto Gutekunst and Gus Mayer, who were partners in the Colnaghi Gallery in London; and they in turn alerted Knoedler in New York (Charles Henschel was Gus Mayer's uncle). Thus was established a chain of dealership extending from Moscow to Manhattan, by agreeable coincidence exactly the same combination that had sold Dürer's *Portrait of a Man* to Mellon late in 1927. "There has," Henschel wrote in mid-January 1930, "been a lot of talk for the last year of some of the Hermitage pictures being sold; this now seems to have come to a definite head."[83] At a time when Knoedler, like all dealers, was short of cash, however, the only hope of getting in on the action was to persuade a rich client to put up the money in advance, and when it came to rich clients, Andrew Mellon was at the very top of the list.

Yet despite his enormous wealth, Mellon must have seemed in some ways a less than ideal party to such an extraordinary transaction. He was an extremely cautious collector, anxious about provenance and authenticity, always insisting on inspecting a picture before he bought it, preferably over several months with it hanging in his own home. Would he be "willing to spend vast sums on the purchase of paintings he had never seen"?[84] And would he be prepared to hand over what would likely amount to millions of dollars to the Communists? No less than any member of the Republican administrations in which he had served, Mellon was viscerally hostile to the Soviet Union as a nation based on the contradiction of almost everything he held dear and true in economic values. It had reneged outright on its international debts, it had nationalized and confiscated private property (including the Hermitage collections), it was pledged to the overthrow of global capitalism in favor of workers' rights, and it exalted the role of the state vis-à-vis the individual. Not surprisingly, Mellon enthusiastically supported Harding, Coolidge, and Hoover in their determined refusal to grant official recognition to the USSR; and it bears repeating that as secretary of the treasury, he was much concerned during 1930 and 1931 with what was deemed to be "unfair" Soviet competition, when cheap Russian goods were "dumped" on the American market, as Stalin sought other ways to obtain western currency.[85]

But Knoedler was not going to let global ideology stand in the way of what might be its biggest deal in years in a decidedly flat market. They rightly sensed not just a unique opportunity to bolster their precarious finances, but also that the prospect of acquiring some of the greatest pictures from one of the world's most fabled collections would be a challenge Mellon could not resist. As David Finley once remarked, his master had "a very keen sense of the possibilities of a situation," and here was a situation of potentially limitless possibilities: the ultimate business deal, carried out in complete secrecy, which would be a triumph of capitalism over communism. And with its completion, Mellon's collection would be transformed from what was still an essentially private accumulation, no matter how magnificent, into a glittering cynosure befitting the great national display he wanted to create.[86] (Moreover, and despite his hostility to the regime, some of Mellon's companies had recently begun trading with the USSR.) In January 1930, Henschel dispatched one of his agents, George Davey, to Leningrad, with instructions to obtain photographs and particulars of the finest paintings. His departure was delayed, but in mid-April, Davey reported back, not altogether enthusiastically (for he doubted the Soviets' seriousness about selling), but with a lengthy list of prospects, including Raphael's *St. George and the Dragon* ("in a word, irreproachable"), Van Dyck's *Susanna Fourment and Her Daughter* ("the most wonderful picture"), and several works by Hals ("I would buy any of them without hesitation").[87]

Meanwhile, Knoedler had succeeded in obtaining their first Russian picture, Van Dyck's *Philip, Lord Wharton*. As soon as they had it in their possession, Henschel and Carman Messmore hastened to Washington to show it to Mellon. The painting was not in good condition, and it had been by no means the greatest in the Hermitage, but it indicated that the Soviets were serious and it whetted Mellon's appetite. He duly instructed Knoedler to "go ahead."[88] "You realize," Messmore told him, during the course of the negotiations over the El Greco, the Master Michael, and the Holbein, "that for the present, nothing must be said about the Russian situation, as it might hurt us in the acquisition of other pictures if any-thing was disclosed about them."[89] By April 1930, Mellon formally autho-rized Knoedler to purchase for him what were laconically described as "certain paintings from the Hermitage Collection in Petrograd." The deal would not be entirely on the Kremlin's terms (or on Knoedler's), however: although Mellon would be buying pictures for the first time sight unseen, he was determined to get them at the lowest possible prices, and he also kept his options open as far as he could. "If you decide to retain them," Messmore wrote to Mellon when confirming the terms of acquisition,

> you will pay us a commission of twenty-five per cent of the cost price. In the event you do not wish to keep any of them, it is understood that we will sell them for your account, and pay twenty-five per cent of the profit on the price we receive for them. We have shown you reproductions of the paintings which we decided to purchase from the above collection, and it is understood that we will acquire them at a price at which we con-sider they can be disposed of, should you not care to retain them, of approximately fifty per cent profit.[90]

During the next twelve months, Mellon would acquire through Knoedler, on just these terms, an additional twenty paintings from the Hermitage. As the Russians gradually released more pictures, this transat-lantic dealing assumed a recognizable pattern, albeit with occasional vari-ations. Ilyn at the Antiquariat would reveal that he might have more art to sell, whereupon the news was passed to Knoedler, via Mansfeld and Zatzenstein and Colnaghi. Knoedler then consulted Mellon as to whether he would be prepared to buy, providing him with photographs and details of provenance. Once his assent was secured and an upper price limit had been agreed on, Knoedler instructed Zatzenstein as to how much he could offer the Russians. When a deal was eventually struck, Mellon's money was wired, in pounds sterling, by Knoedler to Zatzenstein in Berlin, who lodged it in a blocked account, after 10 percent was paid to the Russians as a deposit.[91] At the other end of the chain, in Moscow, instructions were sent to the Hermitage to remove the pictures from the walls and to hand them over to an agent who would arrive at an appointed time. Meanwhile, the adjacent paintings would be rearranged to make it look as though nothing had been removed. The pictures were then trans-ported by train to Berlin and handed over to Zatzenstein, who then released the balance of payment. They were subsequently shipped to

Knoedler's gallery in New York, and eventually, after cleaning, restoration, and (often) reframing, they made their way to Mellon in Washington.

The first transaction following these arrangements was completed very rapidly, in April and May 1930. As a result, Mellon acquired Frans Hals's *Portrait of a Young Man*, two Rembrandts (*A Girl with a Broom* and *A Polish Nobleman*), and Van Dyck's *Susanna Fourment and Her Daughter*, all for a quarter of a million dollars.[92] Thus encouraged, Charles Henschel set out for Europe, in the hope that he might bypass Mansfeld and Zatzenstein and negotiate more sales directly with the Russians. He traveled across the Atlantic on the *Olympic*, which by chance was one of the first ocean liners to be equipped with a radio telephone, and while on board he learned from Mansfeld, Zatzenstein's agent in Moscow, that the Russians were prepared to sell Jan Van Eyck's *Annunciation* for half a million dollars. Henschel contacted Messmore in New York, who immediately left for Washington to secure Mellon's approval. Mellon agreed to buy ("as cheaply as you can"), and within a few days Nicholas Ilyn himself turned the painting over to Henschel in Berlin.[93] (The downcast Hermitage staff, desperate to prevent the removal of one of their most prized treasures, willfully misrepresented the telegrams from Moscow, instructing them to remove the picture from their walls, as referring to a nonexistent *Annunciation* by Van Dyck, but these efforts were to no avail.)[94] On its arrival in Knoedler's London office, the picture was cleaned, varnished, and framed. "It looks magnificent," Messmore was informed, "and I am sure Andy will be delighted with it." He was.[95]

In August 1930, Henschel visited Moscow and Leningrad with Gus Mayer. Subsisting on a diet of vodka, sturgeon, and caviar, he made notes on the pictures in the Hermitage, twitted the staff about the whereabouts of *Lord Philip Wharton* and the *Annunciation* (they claimed the missing canvases had been sent away to be cleaned), and successfully negotiated the sale of Rubens's portrait of Isabella Brant, Van Dyck's *Portrait of a Flemish Lady*, Velázquez's *Pope Innocent X*, and Rembrandt's *The Turk*.[96] (At the same time, Mellon also acquired, through Knoedler, Botticelli's *Portrait of a Young Man* from the Lichtenstein collection: "bought three fifty, sold Andy four.")[97] In 1930, Mellon had disbursed over two million dollars on Hermitage paintings, and this, combined with his other purchases from both Knoedler and Duveen, meant he had spent in that year even more on art than in 1928. Of course, in accordance with their original agreement, he might instruct Knoedler to sell any of the pictures. But, as he explained to Paul in Cambridge, he had not "made up my mind whether I shall allow any of them to be sold. The trouble is that they all seem to be of high quality and quite low in cost. While I can make good profit on any that I may let go to be sold, I am reluctant to do so, notwithstanding the large cash investment which the purchases are requiring during these hard times." In any case, he was still, rightly as it turned out, "expecting more of them to come as for some reason they only decide to sell one or two at a time with long intervals between when nothing is doing."[98]

While these transactions via Knoedler were proceeding, Mellon did scarcely any business with Duveen in 1930, after his purchases from him in February of that year. At that time, Duveen lunched with Mellon, who told him "he had been offered some of the pictures in the Hermitage Museum, and asked me whether there was anything to it." "I told him," Duveen reported to his firm's Paris office, "it was not serious, as everybody had been offering them for the last three years."[99] He rightly guessed that the dealer was Knoedler, but wrongly thought the matter trivial. For the next few months, Duveen, wholly ignorant of Mellon's Russian purchases, pressed upon him the so-called Brunswick Vermeer and Sir Thomas Lawrence's *The Pink Boy*. Mellon's partiality for Vermeer was well known, and it was also believed that he regretted not having acquired Gainsborough's *The Blue Boy*, which had gone to Henry E. Huntington after hanging briefly in Mellon's Washington apartment in the course of its journey from Britain to California. But Duveen's offerings were very expensive: the Vermeer had cost him $650,000, and the owner of *The Pink Boy*, the Earl of Durham, wanted at least £135,000 for it. By early September, Mellon decided, much to Duveen's surprise and chagrin, that he would purchase neither of them: unbeknownst to almost everyone, he was getting better value for his money buying from the Hermitage.[100]

Fast upon this rebuff, Duveen belatedly learned that Mellon was indeed acquiring pictures from the Russians through Knoedler. He was enraged to learn that his great rivals for Mellon's purse had stolen a march on him, and mortified not to be involved in such a spectacular sale. At the same time, from sour grapes he pressed a wine of some hypocrisy: Mellon, he opined, was taking a big risk, for if it should become known in the United States that he "was having business dealings with the Soviet Government of Russia, he would be forced out of political life." (No doubt his concern and scruples would have been different had the spectacular deal been his.) Duveen duly dispatched his moles to Washington, to confirm that Russian pictures were now hanging on Mellon's walls, while Mellon admitted that he was after "great pictures" from the Hermitage, but that he did not want Duveen to compete with him for them.[101] Meanwhile, Duveen pressed upon Mellon another clutch from his inventory, by Cimabue, Domenico Veneziano, Rembrandt, Gainsborough, and Filippino Lippi, asking more than $2.8 million for the lot.[102] In the end, Mellon settled for a *Madonna and Child* by Veneziano and *Aristotle Contemplating a Bust of Homer* by Rembrandt, paying $1.3 million for the pair. But Mellon returned both pictures in April of the following year, and would buy nothing more through Duveen until the very end of 1936.

Meanwhile, Duveen, heedless of Mellon's wishes, went to Berlin in the autumn of 1930, in the hope of making personal contact with the Russians. But he would be frustrated in this venture, perhaps because the Soviets knew of the flamboyant Duveen's taste for publicity; perhaps because, as Henschel told Zatzenstein, Duveen was not "anxious to spend any large sums, as he has been not only disappointed in making sales, but in recovering monies that were due." It was, as John Walker later observed, the outstanding failure of Duveen's career.[103] But it was just as well that Duveen presented no challenge, for the transatlantic syndicate was in some disarray by the end of 1930. There were disagreements about sharing the commission; Zatzenstein was cross with Henschel for intruding himself into direct negotiations with the Russians; Henschel (no doubt influenced by Mellon) complained the prices the Russians were asking were too high; and Mellon decided that Knoedler should try to sell Rembrandt's *The Turk*.[104] Trying to calm the waters, Henschel informed Zatzenstein that "you can tell the eastern representatives that we are perfectly willing to buy and pay fair prices, but not exorbitant ones." Among his client's specific fancies, he mentioned the Raphael *St. George and the Dragon*, Titian's *Venus with a Mirror*, and Botticelli's *Adoration of the Magi*, as well as three works by Hals and two by Chardin. "You must realize," Henschel concluded, "that we are in a very unique position of being able to buy these pictures at this time, and I think it is equally important for the eastern people to realize that they ought to take advantage of the opportunity they have in being able to sell to us." In six months' time, Henschel pointed out, he might not be able to offer such high prices "on account of the business depression which is spreading rapidly in America."[105]

"Personally," Zatzenstein responded, "I never can understand why the eastern people do sell"; they could, he rightly observed, by exporting raw materials "get amounts of money so much more important than these comparatively poor sums." He also expressed regret at Knoedler's apparently scant confidence in his negotiating abilities. But with the air cleared and the syndicate reinvigorated, Zatzenstein now returned to the task, and early in 1931 he obtained Botticelli's *Adoration of the Magi* and Rembrandt's *Joseph Accused by Potiphar's Wife,* for one million dollars the pair.[106] He was simultaneously negotiating for two more Rembrandts, *The Holy Family* and *Woman Holding a Pink:* "need directions," he telegraphed to Knoedler, "as every day pressed." Knoedler duly obliged. "Angels in Holy Family rather disturbing to composition," Henschel cabled back. "Do not negotiate further for this picture. Try Raphael and Titian." Soon after, Zatzenstein managed to obtain *Woman Holding a Pink,* along with Van Dyck's *William II of Nassau* (later reattributed to Adriaen Hanneman, and deemed to be of Henry, Duke of Gloucester), Veronese's *The Finding of Moses,* and the much-coveted Raphael *St. George and the Dragon,* which alone cost $745,000.[107] While these negotiations were in process, Andrew wrote to Paul at Cambridge, revealing that he had lately acquired "more of the Russian paintings. They are among the most important, if not *the* most important of the Gallery. They will not arrive for several weeks, but I am not bringing them to Washington as for the present I do not want it to be known that I have them." He was still cautious: "If they do not come up to expectations when I see them I will have Knoedler dispose of them."[108]

At this point, the action suddenly shifted to New York, where Nicholas Ilyn and Boris Kraevsky from the People's Commissariat of Foreign Trade decided to negotiate with Knoedler in person. As befitted their status as comrades, they traveled across the Atlantic in steerage, and put up in "some obscure little [Manhattan] hotel in West 23rd St.," lodging there for six weeks. It was soon agreed that they would sell Frans Hals's *Portrait of an Officer* and Chardin's *The House of Cards,* and these were followed by Perugino's *Crucifixion*—the first and only depiction Mellon would buy of this most painful Christian image, but agreeable perhaps for being more tranquil than agonizing in tone, unlike most great renderings. All were subsequently consigned by the Antiquariat to the Matthiesen Gallery in Berlin on the usual terms.[109] Soon after, Henschel informed Zatzenstein that he had "made large deal. Keep absolutely quiet." For he had obtained Titian's *Venus with a Mirror* (the closest the prudish Mellon ever came to buying a nude), and Raphael's *Madonna of the House of Alba,* for $1.7 million the pair.[110] With this transaction, Mellon became the only American to have purchased *three* Raphaels, and his second Madonna became his most expensive picture to date, supplanting the *Niccolini-Cowper Madonna* he had acquired via Duveen three years before.[111] "I have," he explained to Paul, "gone deeper into the Russian purchases—perhaps further than I should in view of the hard times and shrinkage in values, but as such an

opportunity is not likely to again occur, and I feel so interested in the ultimate purpose, I have made quite [a] large investment." "However," he
concluded, "I have confined myself entirely to examples of ultra quality.
The whole affair is being conducted privately, and it is important that this
be kept confidential."[112]

Though there was no sense of finality at the time, this would be the end
of Andrew Mellon's Russian purchases. He had acquired nearly half of the
Hermitage's fifty greatest paintings, for a sum very close to $7 million: to
be sure a colossal figure then, in the midst of a global depression, but also
one to which it is virtually impossible to assign a contemporary value.
Today's monetary equivalent is in the region of $90 million; but thirty
years later, one Velázquez alone fetched more than Mellon had paid for all
twenty-one of his Russian paintings, and when the National Gallery in
Washington finally acquired a Leonardo in the late 1950s, with generous
financial help from Ailsa, it was rumored to have cost in the vicinity of
$10 million.[113] The clandestine negotiations, the transatlantic telephone
calls, and the coded telegrams were the means by which the representatives of two societies—opposed in every assumption of economics, politics, and ideology—sat down to do business. But they only did so because
of a brief, extraordinary conjunction of supply and demand: a Russian
government eager to sell, and one rich American eager to buy. Mellon's
greatest purchasing triumph would prove the most remarkable coup of
any twentieth-century art collector: acquiring the crown jewels of one
great gallery, eventually to make them the founding treasures of another.
As for the Russians: Kraevsky and Ilyn were so pleased at their sale that
they promptly laid ideology aside and moved to the Biltmore Hotel, ultimately returning to Russia as first-class passengers on the *Bremen*. Nor
did they perceive any ideological defeat in what they regarded as only the
temporary surrender of their great masterpieces to their capitalist antagonist par excellence. Shortly before their departure, Charles Henschel
asked them about this. In reply, they expressed certainty that within ten
years, the American system would collapse, and "come the Revolution,"
the pictures would be on their way back to the Hermitage.[114]

Although there were no further Mellon purchases, the transatlantic
negotiations continued throughout the spring of 1931. Indeed, they took
a turn upmarket, with Giorgione's *Judith* and the two Madonnas allegedly
by Leonardo da Vinci now offered for two million dollars, considerably
less than the Russians had asked of the Hammer brothers for one Leonardo
only three years before. "If we can conclude this deal advantageously,"
Messmore wrote triumphantly to Mellon, "we will have secured all of the

greatest pictures in the entire collection." But what appears a steal in ret-rospect seemed much too expensive at the time, and the negotiations stalled. The Russians threatened to sell the Giorgione to Duveen instead, and in anticipation of the publicity they feared he would generate, Knoedler went so far as to draft their own version of the Hermitage pur-chases, being very careful to keep Mellon's name out of it. But the Soviets were almost certainly bluffing (they stopped selling art altogether within little more than a year), and Duveen never got a look.[115] Meanwhile, Mel-lon bought one painting directly from a private owner: Goya's portrait of the Marquesa de Pontejos, whose descendants were willing to sell the ancestral likeness as the political situation in Spain deteriorated in the run-up to the civil war. David Finley handled the negotiations, and a price was agreed upon; but the Spanish government threatened to withhold an export license, obliging Knoedler to send an agent who "had to bribe sev-eral persons" to obtain it. In the end, the picture made it to Washington, with Mellon paying $193,140 directly to the vendor and $19,560 in com-mission to Knoedler. He bought no more major pictures from Henschel and Messmore until early in 1935.[116]

What, meanwhile, was Mellon to do with the Russian pictures that were making their way across the Atlantic, via Berlin, London, and New York, and eventually reaching him in Washington? The essence of the deal with the Soviets had been secrecy on both sides, which meant that Mellon could scarcely display the pictures in his apartment, where even his least knowledgeable and discerning dinner guests could not fail to be entranced by them. Initially, two or three of the canvases were hung there, but then Knoedler realized the danger: "If anyone knows for sure that the pictures are out of Russia, we may never be able to get any more."[117] Nor would it have been politic to admit to such lavish spending while so many millions of Americans were struggling to keep body and soul together. They were duly taken down and hidden in a cupboard. Then, in March 1931, Mellon was lent a room in the Corcoran Gallery in Washington, where he would store them until the National Gallery of Art was con-structed. Of course, rumors were already circulating that many great Hermitage pictures had been sold, and that Mellon was the buyer. (It could scarcely have been otherwise, given the even peripheral knowledge of Duveen.) But Mellon and Knoedler simply denied everything: appro-priately enough, he had effected his triumph by honoring the code of secrecy which it was always his preference to observe.[118] In June 1931, Mellon transferred four of his recent Hermitage purchases to his educa-tional and charitable trust: the Raphael *Alba Madonna*, the Titian *Venus with a Mirror*, the Perugino *Crucifixion*, the Van Eyck *Annunciation*, and the Botticelli *Adoration of the Magi*. They were collectively valued at $3,246,796. Together with his substantial gifts to Paul and Ailsa, this meant he had given away $25 million in 1931—more than ten times that amount in today's currency.[119]

Although Mellon had succeeded in concealing the Hermitage transactions from the public—even the Russians "never knew who was buying them"—the deals had absorbed so much of his attention and money between early 1930 and mid-1931 that they nevertheless had public consequences, which were not to his benefit.[120] In his excitement and preoccupation, Mellon was not altogether engaged in his duties as secretary of the treasury, with the exception of his diligent oversight of the building of the Federal Triangle. Buying pictures covertly from the Soviets captured his imagination in a way that presiding over an uncertain economy did not, and he may have been more enthralled in making deals than at any time since the days when he had been running the Mellon Bank, inventing new companies and sponsoring new technologies that helped transform American industry. One story from the time certainly reflects his priorities. In September 1930, Mellon kept a group of bankers waiting in his Washington apartment for the better part of two hours while he discussed pictures and fended off inquiries about the Hermitage sale, with one of Duveen's representatives.[121] Such was his outlook: ride out the downturn, and concentrate on the pictures. Thus was the treasury secretary ever more detached from the economic whirlwind blowing around him, and it is scarcely surprising that he so willingly ceded responsibility for his government's economic policy to Hoover and Ogden Mills.

IV. RECESSION IN PITTSBURGH, RETREAT
IN PENNSYLVANIA

On March 24, 1930, shortly before the Hermitage purchases began in earnest, a dinner was held at the Pittsburgh Golf Club to celebrate Andrew Mellon's seventy-fifth birthday. Before more than two hundred guests, the organizing committee, which included Arthur V. Davis of Alcoa and Henry C. McEldowney of the Union Trust Company, presented Mellon with a large gold cup, engraved with images of the T. Mellon & Sons façade and that of the United States Treasury.[122] Thus did Pittsburgh's social, economic, and political elite—many of them still Scotch-Irish Presbyterian—gather to honor the man who, since the deaths of Frick and Carnegie, had been their most illustrious citizen. In his acceptance speech—written, as usual, by David Finley—Mellon declared that he would "not exchange the period in which I have lived (and the circle of friends among whom my lot has been cast) for any other in the world's history." He went on to reaffirm his faith in America and in Pittsburgh, after almost a decade of Republican rule. "The average person in this country," he noted, "now commands the means of comfortable subsistence to a greater extent and with less effort than ever before in the history of the world." The recent past had been one of unprecedented progress, and the future beckoned with bright and clear promise: "if I were given the opportunity to exchange my own period of time for any other, I would choose, without hesitation, the next three quarters of a century and, needless to add, I would live it in America and preferably in Pittsburgh." "Life has been," he concluded, "and still is, both full and interesting; and I shall go, when the time comes, 'as a satisfied guest from life's banquet.' "[123]

While none of the guests could have known it, this occasion was something of a last hurrah, not only of a man still very much alive, but also for an urban patriciate that would very soon be overwhelmed and undermined by the greatest crisis to hit America since the Civil War. For the dominance the tightly knit Scotch-Irish elite had enjoyed over Pittsburgh throughout Mellon's lifetime depended on a set of conditions, all of which would soon be severely threatened. The first was that the city's economy, built on coal and iron and steel, would continue to prosper—but the 1920s had been a slow decade, and much worse was in store. The second condition was unchallenged Republican dominance, of Pittsburgh, of Allegheny County, of the state house, of the governor's mansion, and of Pennsylvania's congressional delegation—but Hoover's narrow victory in 1928 was but one portent that the party's hegemony would not go unchallenged much longer. The third condition was the deference, sometimes genuine, often coerced, that those in charge of the city's economy and politics had traditionally received from most of the community—but this, too, would not last much into the 1930s. No less than the rest of urbanindustrial America, Pittsburgh was about to undergo an economic and political sea change, as a result of which Andrew Mellon and his friends, hitherto confident in their power and entitlement, would be reviled and cast aside.

The recent commitment of the Mellons and their companies to the Gulf building, the Mellon Institute, and the East Liberty Presbyterian Church reflected their ample riches, and also their abiding confidence in and loyalty to Pittsburgh itself. It was not altogether unfounded. In January 1930, United States Steel reported record profits of nearly $200 million, and soon after Jones and Laughlin announced a $20 million plan to expand its steel plants in Pittsburgh and Aliquippa.[124] But by the end of the year, the forecast was abruptly less optimistic, as Pittsburgh was drawn into the general downturn, and unemployment began to rise and businesses began to fail. In October, the city council passed an emergency proposal to set up a fund of $300,000 to aid needy local families. But the measure provided merely temporary employment for only 2,600 men and soon proved both its woeful inadequacy and city hall's misjudgment of the magnitude of the crisis. Of course, whatever the hardship for others, Mellon could not help seeing opportunity in depression. "We have," he wrote to Paul at Cambridge, referring to the recently established Mellbank scheme, "stopped the program of acquiring more banks for the present," because with a recession in prospect, "we believe we can acquire others in the future to better advantage than at present"—a strikingly candid comment on the self-interested nature of their newest financial enterprise.[125]

Mellon's predictions were well borne out, as the winter of 1930–31 was one of the worst in Pittsburgh's history. Though at the beginning, he had briefly hoped that "there will be improvement and everything more cheerful later on," by mid-January 1931, more than 28 percent of workers were jobless; local relief agencies had run out of money and were warning that nearly 50,000 residents faced the immediate prospect of starvation. As new relief funds were organized during 1931, Mellon gave $50,000 to the Allegheny County Emergency Association, $20,000 to the American Red Cross, $20,000 to the Presbyterian Ministers' Fund, and $26,250 to the Welfare Fund of Pittsburgh, and Dick and W. L. Mellon apparently each gave corresponding amounts.[126] (The continuing construction of the Gulf building, the Mellon Institute, and the East Liberty Presbyterian Church, conceived in times of plenty, was now a significant source of employment.) "We organized in Pittsburgh," Andrew told Paul, "endeavoring to take care of the situation there by creating new sources of work, to which I subscribed quite substantially." For someone of Mellon's robustly individualistic views to pledge more than $100,000 to the aid of the poor and unemployed was unprecedented, and a clear indication of just how serious he feared things were becoming. "It will not be so bad through the summer," he told Paul, "while there is garden and farm work, but if business conditions do not improve the problem will be a serious one to cope with next winter."[127]

It was an astute prediction. For now, however, the slump had no impact on the politics of western Pennsylvania, allowing Mellon to remain unrepentant about the corruption of Republican power there, and unapologetic about his failure to provide adequate party leadership. "You remark," he wrote to James Witherow, shortly before his seventy-fifth birthday,

> that it is always a regret when you find my name associated with many of the political excesses which are carried out in my native state, but you are convinced that individually I have not been connected with such dishonorable means as seem to have been used. . . . I may say that most of these alleged political excesses are not what they have been represented, and personally I feel no regret or apology for any act or connection of mine in the political affairs of the State. . . . It would take too long to explain the present political situation which has been the object of so much criticism, often from persons unfamiliar with the actual state of affairs or from those having adverse political motives. . . . I will only say, however, that we have in Pennsylvania the best state administration that has existed there for many years, [and] in Governor Fisher we have an executive of high principles and great administrative capacity. . . . We have an effective budget system, a State treasury in fine condition, and there are more public improvements already accomplished or under way than has ever been the case.[128]

Neither Mellon's utopian fantasy of Pennsylvania politics nor his panegyric to Governor Fisher enjoyed much credence now.[129] Here is one example. In February 1929, a miner of immigrant stock had been beaten to death by two of the armed police privately employed by Pittsburgh Coal Company. They were both drunk, they dragged the miner from his home, and they set upon him with an iron poker, pistol butts, brass knuckles, and heavy boots. A public outcry followed, and two bills were immediately sponsored in the state legislature: one was intended to disarm the company police and convert them into night watchmen, the other essentially kept the present arrangements intact. Determined not to antagonize the corporate interests on whom he depended, Fisher made it plain he would sign the weaker bill, which he duly did in April 1929. There then erupted another protest in the press and in the pulpits, with Fisher denounced as the tool of "money interests" and a "Mellon stooge." His action, it was claimed, had again shown the Republican Party in Pennsylvania to be "the servant of coal and iron barons who cared little for humanity and justice." The Mellons quickly distanced themselves from Fisher, with W. L. Mellon even announcing he could "stew in his own juice." Any ambitions the governor may have entertained of being elected to the U.S. Senate promptly faded away.

With one senate seat and the governorship both up for election in

1930, the fall of Fisher's star may have simplified things somewhat, but not much.[130] In the Senate race, Mellon was committed to the incumbent Republican, Joseph Grundy, whom the governor had appointed to fill the place of William S. Vare after the Senate declared the Pennsylvania seat vacant in the aftermath of the notorious 1926 primary.[131] Since, conveniently, Fisher could not run again, Grundy chose as the ticket's gubernatorial candidate the former state treasurer, Samuel Lewis. Not surprisingly, in the light of his past quarrels with Mellon, William S. Vare had other ideas. His support of Hoover at the Kansas City Republican convention had yielded no dividends for him in Washington; indeed, he was still outraged at his expulsion from the Senate. He now determined to reassert himself across the state, backing another Republican candidate for the Senate seat he himself had unceremoniously been compelled to vacate: James J. Davis, Hoover's secretary of labor and a former Pittsburgh resident. As Vare intended, this put Mellon in a difficult position. By convention, one senator represented the west of the state, deferring to Pittsburgh, the other the east, deferring to Philadelphia. The western senator was David Reed, who would be up for re-election in 1934. If Mellon swung his allegiance to Davis, he would outrage Grundy and the eastern wing of the party would be galvanized to knock out Reed in 1934; but if he continued to support Grundy, he would oppose and antagonize a cabinet colleague.

In late March 1930, while in Pittsburgh for his seventy-fifth birthday celebrations, Mellon sought once again to broker a harmony ticket for the Republicans that would placate the Vare faction. His proposal was that Lewis withdraw and yield the Republican candidacy for governor to Francis Brown, a former state attorney general, who was believed to be acceptable to Vare and his eastern wing. Lewis obliged, but that was as far as Mellon got at negotiating a harmony ticket, something he had failed at before. For Grundy refused to accept Brown—who thereupon joined the slate headed by Davis, and thus became beholden to Vare. To complicate matters still further, the Republican maverick Gifford Pinchot, an old friend of Grundy's and enemy of Mellon's, reappeared on the scene, jumping into the gubernatorial fray. Meanwhile, Mellon's unsuccessful candidate for senator in 1926, George Pepper, also defected and now supported the Davis-Brown ticket. The result was "one of the most complex Republican tangles that a state has ever experienced": the Mellon forces were once again pitched against Vare; many people who liked Grundy also liked Pinchot; but Mellon disliked Pinchot deeply, and had no intention of countenancing a Grundy-Pinchot ticket, even though Hoover and Stimson would have preferred it.[132]

In the end, both Grundy and Brown lost: Davis won the senatorial primary, and Pinchot the gubernatorial. Since the GOP was still dominant in the state, Davis and Pinchot prevailed in the general elections of November 1930. This was well enough for Pennsylvania Republicans, but for the Mellons it was a twofold "smashing defeat": for not only had both their candidates been drubbed in the primary, but the election of Davis, another westerner, boded ill for David Reed's prospects in 1934. Nor was this the full extent of the rout. The Mellons had planned to ease out the incumbent mayor of Pittsburgh, Charles H. Kline, but unlike his predecessors, Kline had refused to step aside at their behest and was re-elected with huge popular support, in what was described as "the greatest shakeup in the history of Pittsburgh."[133] Once again, Andrew Mellon had failed to provide effective political leadership in his hometown, let alone statewide. For all the Mellons' vaunted financial resources, there was no effective "Mellon machine," despite the contrary claims of their opposition. In the Pennsylvania primaries of 1930, as at the Republican convention in Kansas City two years earlier, Mellon had the money, but Vare had the votes, and it was Vare who won.

To be sure, Pittsburgh was still effectively a one-party town, and Pennsylvania a one-party state: in 1930, there were only 675,584 registered Democrats, compared to 2,659,850 registered Republicans.[134] But while the Republicans had remained in power almost without interruption since the Civil War, it was no longer the same party that had been beholden (and subservient) to Frick, Penrose, Knox—and Mellon. The party elders who had helped send Mellon to Washington had long since gone, and he could not dominate state politics from the nation's capital. But this was not the only or, ultimately, the most troubling issue Mellon faced in Pennsylvania: for despite his large national mandate, Hoover had not done well in Pittsburgh in the election of 1928. It might be that those who toiled down the mines and in the mills, many of them first-generation immigrants, were beginning to experience a political awakening. If so, the recession of late 1930 and 1931, which had put so many of them out of work, might he expected to drive them into the arms of Democrats as fresh recruits. Such a development hardly seemed inevitable or even foreseeable in the fall of 1930. But in hindsight it is not surprising.

With politics in Pittsburgh on the brink of turning anti-Mellon, the journalist R. L. Duffus wrote a caustic essay on the city, and on the Scotch-Irish elite who had created and controlled it. The tone may be well gathered from the title: "Is Pittsburgh Civilized?"[135] The question was purely rhetorical, for the author described a philistine city which was a lurid example of that supreme paradox of the industrial age: "our civilization rests upon coal and iron," but "in almost every spot where coal and iron are brought together, civilization is blighted and begrimed." Where the Monongahela and the Allegheny joined, "quiet valleys have been inundated with slag, defaced with refuse, marred with hideous buildings. Streams have been polluted with sewage and the waste from the mills." Life for the general population had been rendered "unspeakably pinched and dingy," with people serving machines, rather than the reverse. Far from enjoying what Mellon had recently characterized as "the means of comfortable subsistence," the workers in Pittsburgh lived "amid ugliness and dirt, in congested quarters, next door to vice and crime." Labor was just another raw material, to be bought as cheaply as possible, and the facilities for recreation were utterly inadequate. Indeed, the city was almost wholly without culture. It had "the wealth to buy a high degree of civilization," but it remained, "on the whole, barbaric."

Similar indictments had been penned in virtually every decade from the 1880s onwards. But what was new about Duffus's essay was its sustained attack on the Scotch-Irish, Presbyterian elite who, he insisted, bore full responsibility for this deplorable state of affairs, and whose very epitome was Andrew Mellon himself. "If any large American city," Duffus observed, "is so narrowly, so religiously, I might even say so conscientiously dominated by so small a group, I have yet to hear of it." These leading families had decreed that Pittsburgh would be the laboratory wherein "the theory of laissez-faire has been allowed to work itself out almost without let or hindrance." They had fashioned an economy based on "gigantic material production with as much profit-taking as the traffic could bear." They were a self-perpetuating, self-selecting elite, hostile to Catholics and Jews, dull, narrow, arrogant, and anti-democratic, committed to a "code of proper behavior" with "relentless severity," enforcing it and all else they willed with "absolute power." But they possessed no "corresponding sense of responsibility," no generosity or enthusiasm, no "broader conception of what the pleasures of a civilized life are." Duffus predicted (presciently, as it turned out) that the "Presbyterian bloc" would not "always have the power and dominion that they now possess." In time, a "truly civilized Pittsburgh" might emerge, created by those now thought only fit to work in the mills and the mines. Meanwhile, he suggested, the city was in urgent need of less Calvinism, and of "a few first class funerals."

To be sure, as Duffus admitted, Pittsburgh was not unique in its miseries and deprivations, and there were "general causes" which explained how many cities had become so blighted in industrial America: "the machine age itself, and the excessive individualism which characterizes

that age." But there was something especially virulent about the manifestation of individualism and mechanization in the place Mellon and his ilk
had created: small wonder he averted his gaze from this face of the city,
just as he had always kept his distance from the seamier side of Republican
politics and civic corruption. There might be cultured citizens in Pittsburgh, especially those art collectors who had gone before Andrew Mellon, but their accumulations were either still in private hands or had long
since gone under the auctioneer's gavel. In the case of Frick, the best pictures he had bought off the sweat of Pittsburgh's workers had been hauled
off to Manhattan, eventually to be enjoyed by far less deprived New York-
ers. And although Mellon's decision, when it was eventually made public,
would be presented as an act of broader-minded patriotism, it might be
said that in deciding to create a national gallery in Washington, he had
resolved to do something similar: despite his protestations of abiding loyalty to Pittsburgh, his native city would not be adorned and enriched by
the paintings he had acquired thanks to the wealth he made there.

Among those few who could claim to be genuinely cultured in Mellon's
hometown, and who picked up the rumors about his gestating benefaction, the news was received with ambivalence. Early in 1932, Samuel
Harden Church, the president of the Carnegie Institute, after learning
from Duveen that Mellon's pictures were destined for Washington,
applauded this "worthy patriotic act of a great citizen," but he wanted "to
say one more word for Pittsburgh." "Your family," he urged Mellon,
"stands in its relation to Pittsburgh just where the great Medici family
stood in relation to Florence." Lorenzo the Magnificent disregarded the
pope's wish that he send all his pictures and sculptures to Rome, because
he believed that "the city in which he had won both fame and fortune
should enjoy the prestige and honor of his collection." There had been a
"universal feeling of regret" when Frick "bestowed his pictures upon the
city of New York," and "there would be an even greater feeling of desolation if this marvelously beautiful and comprehensive collection of yours
should be given to any other city than Pittsburgh." If the Mellon collection came to the banks of the Allegheny, it "would make this city as
famous and as distinguished as an art center as Florence, Dresden and
Munich now are." "Washington," he concluded, "has many friends, while
Pittsburgh has only a few, and my heart is so full of a desire for the fame
and glory of this city that I ventured upon this expression of my views."[136]
It was a vain appeal. When the National Gallery of Art was finally opened
in the nation's capital, Church wrote a magnanimous letter to a Pittsburgh paper: "the glory of the nation exceeds the pride and longing of
the city."[137]

13

"THE MAN WHO STAYED TOO LONG"

Depression, Departure, London and Back, 1931–33

> After the panic commenced, money matters grew worse daily,
> until a condition of affairs was reached which no one who has
> not gone through the like could conceive of.
>
> *Thomas Mellon and His Times*, p. 263

I. ECONOMIC MELTDOWN, POLITICAL COLLAPSE

Within days of his speech to the American Bankers Association in early May 1931, when Andrew Mellon reiterated his long-held philosophy that economic storms were to be weathered and that no politician (least of all himself) could reasonably be held responsible for recent events, the United States plunged into another financial crisis. Both different and deeper than anything that had come before, it would usher in almost a decade of woe, ruin, hardship, and distress for unprecedented numbers of Americans. From October 1929 until April 1931, the causes of economic concern had been essentially domestic and, in the long view, they were scarcely unusual: the collapse of the New York Stock Exchange, a crisis in the national banking system, and an increasingly sluggish industrial output. But although these troubles may have seemed local, familiar, and bearable, they were this time the harbingers and portents of an unprecedented disruption of the worldwide economic order. Soon after Mellon's speech, the crash of 1929, which in 1930 was already heading toward a depression, plunged headlong into a great depression that was far deeper and more devastating than the late-nineteenth-century downturn that had hitherto been known by that dismal accolade. Nothing like this had ever before been experienced in American history.

It would transform the economic, political, and social landscape of the country, and Andrew Mellon himself would be one of its most prominent victims.

This international economic meltdown began in Europe on May 11, 1931, with the failure of Louis Rothschild's Creditanstalt, the largest bank in Austria, and also one of the major financial houses in middle Europe. Rumors had been circulating for some time about the possible creation of a German-Austrian customs union, something explicitly prohibited in the Versailles treaty, and to which the French government and people were viscerally opposed. Dismayed at such a prospect, many French depositors had withdrawn their funds from Vienna, and the panic thus engendered in Austria spread northward, where a sudden "flight" from German capital and the German mark caused many banks to close in Berlin and elsewhere.[1] Neighboring nations such as Hungary and Romania were also engulfed in the crisis, and thus began what Herbert Hoover would later describe as "a gigantic explosion, which shook the foundations of the world's economic, political and social structure." For with their banking and financial systems now in chaos, the Germans could no longer make their scheduled war reparations to the Allies, and this made it increasingly difficult for Britain and France to continue repaying their debts to the United States. Here, then, was a breakdown in the international monetary system, which Mellon and his fellow banker-statesmen had labored so hard to create in the aftermath of the First World War; and the unraveling of this delicate web of European and transatlantic obligation would soon bring further troubles and traumas to the already battered American economy.[2]

Under these circumstances, Mellon's decision to discontinue negotiations with the Soviets for further Hermitage treasures in the spring of 1931 was well timed (he may have genuinely thought the Leonardos too expensive, but there were broader considerations), yet notwithstanding these international disruptions, it was family matters that now claimed his immediate attention. On June 6, before the full dimensions of the global economic crisis had become apparent, the secretary left Washington to attend Paul's graduation at Cambridge, where Ailsa and David Bruce joined him. At the same event Andrew also received his fifteenth honorary degree, acknowledging a reputation that was now very soon to fade.[3] Paul had obtained only a third-class degree in the history tripos, scarcely an outstanding performance, but his McMullen uncles were especially proud. "My best congratulations on his good degree," Norman wrote. "Probably not at all bad," Alan opined, "considering that he only had two years when most of the others probably have had three." "Paul has pulled his weight, and you must feel proud of him," Percy added. "Every letter from Clare has attested what an asset he has been to the College."[4] (He would be an even greater asset in later years, becoming an exceptionally generous benefactor to Clare as well as to Yale.) According to his tutor, Henry Thirkill, "Paul Mellon has been a very acceptable member of the College, and has taken an active and most useful part in College life while he has been in residence. I have been very glad indeed to have him here."[5]

President Hoover took advantage of Andrew Mellon's absence to work with Ogden Mills and the secretary of state, Henry L. Stimson, and on June 20 he proposed a brave but controversial plan for a yearlong moratorium on all international debt payments and German reparations. By these measures, Hoover hoped to provide a breathing space during which the beleaguered international economy might regain stability.[6] But the moratorium was deeply unpopular in America, where it confirmed the worst fears of those who had always suspected that the country's foreign loans would never be repaid, and the French government also opposed the suspension of German reparations. The day before he left for England, Mellon had expressed his "unqualified disapproval" of such a policy, but he now reversed his views. He was given the task of commending the moratorium to the British cabinet and to Montagu Norman, governor of the Bank of England, and also of trying to persuade the French to agree to the plan. In this, he was little more than an emissary for the administration to which he belonged: he was given strict instructions on the transatlantic telephone by Hoover, Stimson, and Mills, and as he told reporters, he could say nothing unless Washington said it or approved it first.[7]

Although hailed in Britain as the "great financier" who it was hoped would solve the current crisis, Mellon was now implementing the economic policy of the Hoover administration rather than making it, being "instructed" and "authorized" by Washington, rather than consulted.[8] After discussing matters with Montagu Norman, he shuttled back and forth between London and Paris during late June 1931, but the French prime minister, Pierre Laval, took great exception to not having been consulted about the original moratorium announcement, and he now balked at the terms, insisting that Germany must continue its (already much-reduced) reparation payments.[9] Disturbed by being shunted around from one European capital to another (in those days, shuttle diplomacy was a sign of diplomatic weakness rather than of strength), and realizing that reporters were beginning to sense his impotence, Mellon reacted in a hos-

tile, bad-tempered, tight-lipped way to their questions. "I grant no interviews," he told them, "outside the United States, and as few as possible
there."[10] The discussions dragged on more than two weeks, and eventually agreement was reached: as the French had insisted, Germany would
continue making certain payments during the moratorium year, but they
would be deposited in the recently established Bank for International Settlements, and then be promptly lent back to Berlin. The principle of reparation repayment was thereby preserved, but the reality was effectively
over.

With the business concluded in Paris on July 7, 1931, Pierre Laval
observed, perhaps ironically, "Now, Monsieur Mellon, you can take up
again your interrupted vacation." So he did. Accompanied by David, Ailsa,
and Paul, he spent what remained of the summer on the French Riviera at
Cape Ferrat. But he had little peace. The lengthy negotiations with the
French had robbed Hoover's audacious initiative of its desired psychological impact, and the moratorium did nothing to arrest the economic
cyclone in Germany, where all private banks closed on July 13, following
the collapse of the Darmstädter- und Nationalbank.[11] Mellon was summoned back to London later in the month, to take part in another round
of meetings, this time accompanied by Stimson, whom Hoover had dispatched to Europe to take charge of negotiations—a further indication of
Mellon's declining prestige. As a result, a so-called standstill agreement
was reached, whereby it was reaffirmed that foreign credits would be
maintained to Germany until early the following year.[12] But by then, the
contagion had spread to Britain itself, which held a high proportion of
Germany's long-term debt. There was a run on sterling, the Labour government collapsed, a national coalition was formed in its stead, and in
September 1931, Britain abandoned the gold standard, to which it had
returned only six years before. This was the greatest shock the global
financial system had yet received: within four weeks, eighteen other countries would also go off gold, and another twenty would follow before the
end of 1932.[13]

This was no time to be on vacation, and Mellon now drew his interrupted holiday to a close: "everything," he told Nora during the third
week of August, "at home, politically and in the business world, is so
unsettled that I feel now I should be in Washington."[14] Even by his own
laconic standards, this was a major understatement, for Germany's panic
and Britain's abandonment of gold portended not only the unraveling of
the international financial system he and his fellow financiers had struggled to reconstruct during the 1920s, it also meant there would be further

punishment for the already crippled American banks, which were still shuddering from the rash of failures during the closing weeks of 1930. Foreign investors, worried that the United States was holding so much European debt, now began massive withdrawals from the American banking system, and in the week after Britain went off the gold standard, the United States lost $180 million worth of gold. At the same time, jittery domestic depositors forcefully renewed their own demands for cash, thereby precipitating a liquidity crisis that would dwarf the earlier panic. In the one month following Britain's abandonment of gold, 522 American banks failed, and by the end of the year, 2,294 had suspended operations, nearly twice as many as in 1930 and an all-time national record. The banks were now bleeding profusely from two open wounds, one inflicted by domestic runs on deposits, and the other by foreign withdrawals of gold and capital.[15]

Mellon's return to the United States, in late August 1931, was thus a tense one, and on leaving the ship, he snapped at reporters (not wholly accurately) that he had been "able to get along quite well in Europe without any interviews" and that he intended to maintain that policy now he was back stateside.[16] But while he was an ocean away on a protracted vacation, the nation's finances, for which he was ostensibly responsible, and the American economy as a whole, had been falling headlong toward disaster, and he was now forced to recognize the grim prospect that confronted him. "Business has been going from bad to worse," he wrote to Paul (who had remained in Europe, saying he wanted to improve his French) in early September, "and conditions are deplorable." Banks were still failing, factories were running at a loss if they were running at all, next year's unemployment promised to be even more serious, and "besides our troubles in this country, the British and European situation is still disquieting" (another understatement). In October, the Federal Reserve Board raised interest rates to 3.5 percent, in the (vain) hope of stemming the flow of American capital abroad. This merely made matters worse domestically, as credit became more expensive. And as taxable income fell, government revenue "slumped badly," nullifying all Mellon's previous efforts to keep the federal budget in surplus and pay off the national debt.[17] In December 1930 the budget deficit for fiscal year 1931—the first of his tenure as treasury secretary—was projected at $180 million; the actual figure came in at $903 million.[18]

Within barely a month of the secretary's return to the United States from Europe, a financial crisis in Pittsburgh not only provided a vivid local illustration of the by-now parlous state of the American economy, but also greatly damaged the public standing of Mellon and his family in their native city. Among the victims of the panic of September 1931 was the Bank of Pittsburgh, the city's "most venerable institution," which had been founded in 1810, before the Judge was born.[19] Despite the Mellons' efforts to establish a controlling connection before the First World War, it was the city's only major bank effectively outside their financial reach, and its continued independence was both a reproach and a provocation. Hard hit in the stampede triggered by Britain's abandonment of the gold standard, the bank had closed its doors on September 21. "Its condition," Andrew explained to Paul, "was found to be pretty bad," for it had been in "a weak condition for many years." And although he and Dick were "doing all we can to assist where we can do so safely," the Bank of Pittsburgh had not qualified for such help. "Fortunately," Andrew went on, "our own institutions—the Mellon and the Union Trust as well as the others in which we are interested—are all in sound and fine condition. Many of those withdrawing from other banks are coming to the Mellon and the Union Trust."[20]

This typically bland report belied what had been a most traumatic event in Mellon's hometown and a most damaging episode for him personally. For while the Bank of Pittsburgh had indeed been mismanaged, a new team installed in early 1931 had been gradually but impressively turning things around, so that by July the bank listed deposits just short of $47 million and total assets in excess of $53 million, a much more healthy position than Andrew's account to Paul suggested. To be sure, as the financial crisis deepened toward the end of the summer, the bank had voluntarily closed its doors, but this was not so much an admission of insolvency as a preemptive act to buy time to make its improved position completely secure. Hoover took a personal interest in the matter, and a local syndicate was put together with the aim of creating a rescue package, to which both Dick and W. L. Mellon were willing to contribute, and Andrew journeyed from Washington to Pittsburgh for a meeting held at his house late in the evening of September 19. Only $1 million were needed to complete the rescue package, but Mellon would provide the money only on condition that his family be given a controlling majority of the bank's stock.[21] Not unreasonably, the directors refused, and so the Bank of Pittsburgh went to the wall.

More closures followed in the city in the fall of 1931. Two affiliated institutions, the Highland Bank and the Franklin Savings and Trust Company, shut their doors; and two more unaffiliated institutions went under in the aftermath: the Pittsburgh-American Bank and Trust, and the Merchant Savings and Trust Company. Here, in cameo, was the sort of chain reaction afflicting the whole national financial system at this time, and Hoover was furious at Mellon's demurral in the bailout effort.[22] But Mellon knew exactly—and coldly—what he was doing. For by imposing such conditions, he would either obtain the Bank of Pittsburgh for nothing or terminate it for nothing. Either way, the result would be to increase Mellon financial dominance in the city, even at the price of impoverishing many of its citizens, which is duly what happened. For Andrew, as for his father, recession was an opportunity for the strong to overwhelm the weak, and such opportunities did not come around very often. But in acting as he did, he was clearly putting his own personal and financial interests as a banker (even though he technically owned no stock in either the Mellon National Bank or the Union Trust Company) ahead of his duty as treasury secretary to the banking system as a whole and to the national economic good, both of which would have been better served had the Bank of Pittsburgh been saved.

Mellon's inaction generated bitter local criticism at the time, from which his reputation would never recover, despite the money he was spending on building and the substantial donations he would soon be giving to help the unemployed. "An extraordinary thing has happened in Pittsburgh," the journalist Frank R. Kent wrote in a local newspaper scarcely two months after the bank failed. "The Mellon family is in disrepute. The shine is off them individually and as a group—not only politically but personally, in the matter of business prestige and other ways." In the old days, Andrew and his relatives could do no wrong; but now "the awe is gone, the worship has ended, the glamour has utterly disappeared." Instead of being venerated, the Mellons were now "terribly unpopular," it was unsafe for members of the family to appear in public, and things were thrown at Mellon houses and the Mellon National Bank. A reply was immediately penned by James Francis Burke ("always a good Mellon friend"), but the damage was done.[23] And the political repercussions would be considerable, both locally and nationally. "I was a depositor in four banks," one Republican-turned-Democrat Pittsburgher recalled, "and all went under. I was in bad shape. I felt we couldn't let the Republicans get away with it." The same view would hold in New Deal Washington, and during the "tax trial," Mellon's failure to rescue the Bank of Pittsburgh would receive extensive attention.[24]

Meanwhile, Hoover would not let the matter rest. On October 4, 1931, a meeting was held at Mellon's Washington apartment with nineteen senior bankers, whom the treasury secretary had summoned at the president's behest. During this long and anxious encounter, Hoover urged that the stronger private banks create a $500 million credit pool to assist weaker institutions, in the hope of avoiding such calamities as the Bank of Pittsburgh's failure. The result was the National Credit Association, which attests to Hoover's continuing preference for private and voluntary initiatives, though he had virtually commanded it into being.[25] But as a private bankers' pool, it would prove a great disappointment to the president, for after only a few weeks of activity, in which it dispensed a mere $10 million in loans and support, the NCA (as Hoover later recalled) "became ultra conservative, then fearful, and finally died." Like Mellon, strong and sound bankers had no interest in helping those who were poor and weak, and they did not believe it was their patriotic responsibility to prevent a national financial crisis, as J. P. Morgan and his associates had done in 1907. In January 1932, Hoover responded by setting up the Reconstruction Finance Corporation, which made tax dollars directly available to support private financial institutions. Funded by Congress to $500 million, and authorized to borrow up to $1.5 billion more, this was the most intrusive foray yet by the federal government into the private sector. Mellon did not like it, preferring "further study" of the problems to what he regarded as ill-advised and "hasty action."[26]

The collapse of Mellon's reputation in Pittsburgh during the second half of 1931 was soon replicated across the country, where both the treasury secretary and the president suffered a massive loss of public confidence. Hoover was genuinely pained by his inability to deal with unemployment, and he became increasingly isolated, both personally and politically: the man who had once been acclaimed as the "Great Engineer," who could fix anything, was now derided as the "Great Scrooge," who would eagerly mobilize federal relief for banks, but not for ordinary men and women. Second now only to Hoover in the nation's list of loathed leaders was Andrew Mellon. A story making the rounds at the time recounted a conversation between the president and the secretary, wherein one asked the other for a nickel to make a phone call to a friend. "Here's a dime," came the reply. "Call both your friends." Their interchangeability in the telling is an indication of how the reputations of both had collapsed. And it was also from just this time that Paul Mellon painfully recollected some words that he found scrawled on a urinal in the men's room at a gas station where he had stopped when driving from Washington to Pittsburgh:

> Mellon pulled the whistle,
> Hoover rang the bell,
> Wall Street gave the signal,
> And the country went to hell.[27]

As Howard M. Johnson later recalled, Mellon now "found himself as much abused by the populace as he had previously been praised. The one-time idol became something to throw vegetables at. All his great work in reducing the debt and taxation was forgotten." So it was, even among his supporters. At the very end of 1931, the Republican James M. Witherow reported to Mellon the results of investigations made by his "political scouts" over a "large portion of the western half of the United States."[28] Their findings were not encouraging. "Outside of the office-holding and professional Republican politicians," Witherow reported, "it is very hard indeed to find anybody who is unbiased, who is not only lacking in confidence, but in a great many cases resentful toward the administration." But Mellon just did not get it. "I am sorry," he replied to a similar letter,

> that you feel as you do about the President. He works long hours, and is trying to improve present conditions. I think, on reflection, you will agree with me that it is not fair to hold him responsible for things beyond his or any man's control. I am sure that if you could see him at close range as we do here, you would feel only a desire to help the administration, and not cherish any feeling of resentment.[29]

But resentment there undoubtedly was, and it would only increase. One figure who saw the way the wind was blowing was Senator David A. Reed, whose relationship with his increasingly beleaguered master now began to unravel. After the deaths of Knox and Penrose, Mellon had effectively anointed the son of James Reed in 1922, with the idea that he would now carry the secretary's standard in the Senate as Knox and Penrose had briefly done before. And Reed's re-election to the Senate six years later had been Mellon's only success in Pennsylvania politics during a decade of dismal defeats. Throughout these years, Reed had defended Mellon from every line of attack, and as a member of the Finance Committee he had loyally supported his patron's revenue bills. Early in 1928, the writer Silas Bent had pronounced the relationship between the two men "as near Cabinet representation on the legislative floor as anything we have seen in this country."[30] So much for the separation of powers. But in late 1931 came the first conspicuous rupture: as Mellon sought congressional approval of the foreign debt moratorium, indicating that further negotiations of the settlement might be necessary, Reed voiced strong opposition to any concession beyond the temporary suspension of payments. The elected officeholder was clearly distancing himself from his mentor: it would, he surely reckoned, be his only chance of keeping his seat in the upcoming elections of 1934.[31]

By the end of 1931, Mellon was no more popular within the administration than he was outside it. Henry L. Stimson thought the secretary's analysis of current events "childlike," and Hoover regretted the fact that in government (though not, he might have noted, in business) Mellon was invariably reactive rather than proactive. Although now beleaguered to the point of utter ineffectuality, the president preferred to take what actions he did attempt in tandem with Ogden Mills, who was now widely recognized as the de facto secretary.[32] Mellon made no fuss over this preference for Mills. But others took note, including the *New York Times:* "A chief more jealous of his authority than Mr. Mellon might resent Mr. Mills's position as a direct advisor to the White House." And, it went on, "a subordinate less sure of himself than Mr. Mills would have been in difficulty long ago." By now, all the indications were that the secretary of the treasury had overstayed his welcome in Washington: as Robert Allen and Drew Pearson put it, he would "go down in history as the man who did not know when to quit."[33] Yet even with his friends and colleagues wishing to see the back of him, Mellon determined to stay. It was partly calculation, partly emotion: by March 1933, when Hoover's term would end, the economy (and his own reputation) might, Mellon reasoned, be in better shape. More viscerally, he wanted to see the Federal Triangle development through, and to promote his plan for the National Gallery of Art. His legislative and executive legacy was fast becoming but a memory; now, more than ever, he needed to leave a permanent impression on the city to which he had devoted his later life.

II. SUDDEN EXIT

By January 1932, Andrew Mellon had been secretary of the treasury for more than ten years, and the United States was in its third winter of an unprecedented economic downturn which was now both domestic and global, and which seemed to some so devastating as to portend the end of capitalist civilization as they knew it. In the words of Arnold Toynbee, 1931 had been "distinguished from previous years by one outstanding feature," and that was that "men and women all over the world were seriously contemplating, and frankly discussing, the possibility that the Western system of society might break down and cease to work."[34] By early 1932, well over ten million Americans were unemployed, nearly 20 percent of the labor force; in big industrial cities like Chicago and Detroit (and, of course, Pittsburgh), the rate was much higher, sometimes approaching

50 percent; and one-third of those who were lucky enough to remain working were on short hours. Tens of thousands took to the roads and the railroads in search of jobs; many more, having lost their houses in mortgage foreclosures, huddled in squalid shantytowns known as Hoovervilles. Never before in American history had there been joblessness at this level. It would remain persistently high throughout the whole decade, and there were many who wondered whether the nation's economic or social fabric would survive.[35]

Yet in the face of such wrenching and pervasive human suffering, Mellon constantly lectured the president on the importance of letting things be. The secretary belonged (as Hoover would recall) to the "leave it alone, liquidationist school," and his formula was "liquidate labor, liquidate stocks, liquidate the farmers, liquidate real estate." For the economy to recover, it had to find its true level, which meant for the time being that many individuals would be out of work. This, Mellon believed, was in the nature of capitalism, which necessarily had no human face: as in 1873 and 1907, so in 1930, the depression must run its course until the system had been purged of its excesses and rottenness, which would ultimately be to the good because "people will work harder, lead a more moral life."[36] And since the depression was caused by "uncontrollable forces" as much international as domestic, the voters should not "blame any group of men or party for something that could not have been prevented . . . by any action that might have been taken." This was, indeed, Mellon's sincere belief, but to his critics, it seemed a convenient and unconvincing way of avoiding responsibility for what had happened. Such devotees of laissez-faire were now denounced as unreflective and uncompassionate "lazy fairies." "The great advantage of allowing nature to take her course," observed the liberal journalist Stuart Chase, "is that it obviates thought . . . Just sit and watch with folded hands."[37]

As Mellon sat and watched with folded hands, he experienced his own version of the Great Depression, as his personal income was "very much reduced." As he explained to Paul, "None of our companies are earning anything (except the Bank and the Union Trust) and I am having to resort to borrowing." He did not exaggerate. In 1930, Mellon's income after taxes had peaked at $8.8 million; in 1931 it plummeted to $712,511, and in 1932 he reported a loss of $1.9 million.[38] There would later be serious disagreement as to how real this reduction was, but there can be no doubt that, within barely twelve months of resolving to begin giving away his unprecedentedly vast fortune, Mellon had entered a much bleaker financial world, in which he would never again know an income running into several millions. Despite its continued profits, the resources of Mellon National Bank would decline from nearly $300 million in March 1931 to barely $200 million two years later, and the other Mellon companies were hard hit like the rest of the economy. Alcoa's net income of $24.9 million in 1929 became a loss of $2.3 million in 1932; Pittsburgh Coal stock collapsed from 78.5 to 4; Gulf Oil lost $23.6 million in 1931, but clawed its way to a $2.7 million profit in 1932. No wonder W. L. Mellon found the new Gulf building "a little luxurious for these times." There was a further difficulty. The precise details are obscure, but it seems that Andrew and Dick were obliged to underwrite a $60 million loan to Gulf Oil, which the company would not pay off before 1934. They committed both their personal fortunes and those of their banks. "It very nearly ruined the Mellons," Colonel Frank Drake would recall. "Who ever got me into this awful scrape?" Mellon himself would ask at about this time.[39]

Small wonder that, in late December 1931, Charles Henschel reported to Heinz Mansfeld that "Mr. Mellon is feeling rather depressed," as a result of which "we have done no business with him and see very little prospect of doing any." Since the early summer, when he acquired the *Alba Madonna, Venus with a Mirror,* and the portrait of the Marquesa de Pontejos, he had withdrawn from the art market completely, especially where Russian pictures were concerned. If anything, he was now more interested in selling than in buying. In addition to Rembrandt's *The Turk,* he had instructed Knoedler to try to dispose of the same master's *Joseph Accused by Potiphar's Wife* and also Van Dyck's *Portrait of a Flemish Lady.* His view of microeconomics was perhaps no less blinkered than his view of the larger realities: he wanted, reported Henschel, "his original cost in dollars, and feels he ought to get a profit"; but with business "absolutely at a standstill," the chances were slight, and the pictures did not find a buyer.[40] There was still a possibility of getting Giorgione's *Judith* (indeed, it was rumored the Russians were now very eager to sell), but Ilyn asked $750,000 for it, and Mellon did not see that as a bargain. As Henschel told Mansfeld, "I don't think your eastern friends realize the crisis the world is going through. You can tell them that we cannot sell any pictures, irrespective of price. For them to quote prices such as you cabled us is ridiculous." "Mr. Mellon," he informed Mansfeld early in March 1932, "has not bought anything this winter, and there is no prospect whatever of getting any money out of him."[41]

Andrew had not drawn much comfort from his son's belated return to Pittsburgh either. After Cambridge, Paul had stayed on in Europe, ostensibly to improve his French. But after an unrewarding month of conversational immersion in Saumur, relieved by riding with an officer cadet from the nearby cavalry school, Paul reluctantly returned to Pittsburgh, to begin work in the Mellon National Bank.[42] He would stick with it for eighteen months, not out of any enthusiasm for the work, but because his father insisted it was his duty and his destiny. Andrew's aim seems to have been for Paul to acquire a comprehensive knowledge of the bank's operations by being assigned in turn to various different departments. But it proved neither as instructive nor as agreeable as his father might have hoped. Paul hated his working days and looked forward to parties at night and weekends at Rolling Rock, which was only an hour away from Pittsburgh. There he rode and hunted foxes in the company of his cousin R. K. Mellon (master of fox hounds as well as vice president of the bank), and his friends George Wyckoff and Adolph Schmidt (who both worked for the Union Trust) and Chauncey Hubbard. They were loyal friends and good company, but there seemed a real danger Paul would succumb, as the Judge had feared his descendants might, to the life of "idleness and ease" which often blighted the third generation of rich and successful families.[43]

Very little was going right for Andrew Mellon by now, even with the construction of the Federal Triangle. To be sure, the four new buildings that had been commissioned in 1930 were definitely going ahead, but there were now serious difficulties with the structure that Edward Bennett and his associates had begun to work on, which was destined for the intersection of Constitution Avenue and Pennsylvania Avenue, at the eastern corner. The architects' preliminary sketches had been for a building with curves and colonnades and cupolas, which would have been an appropriately dignified neighbor to Pope's ornate design for the National Archives. These were approved by both the Treasury and the Commission for Fine Arts in early February 1932. Almost immediately, Bennett and his colleagues began on the working drawings, and test borings at the site were commenced soon after. But then, as the economy continued to worsen, Congress barred the use of the three million dollars it had authorized twelve months earlier for the building's construction, and the project was indefinitely postponed.[44] With a presidential election looming in the autumn, the prospects that the Federal Triangle would be completed according to the agreed-upon plan had suddenly dwindled.

But it was the state of the nation's finances that caused Mellon most concern at this time. His tax-reduction and debt-reduction policies now lay in tatters. The deficit for the fiscal year 1931 had been five times what was originally anticipated. The first sixty days alone of fiscal 1932 saw an imbalance of $400 million, and the federal budget would end up $2.7 billion in the red for the year—by far the largest peacetime shortfall in American history to that date. "Deficits are certainly not so pleasant as surpluses, especially, as you say, to a Scotch-Irish temperament," Mellon had earlier written to James M. Witherow.[45] Indeed, both Mellon and Hoover insisted that for the government of the United States they were both unacceptable and unsustainable. With a depression that was now global as well as national, they believed that the surest way of re-establishing domestic and international stability was to make an aggressive effort to balance the federal budget. Honoring the government's commitment to the principles of sound finance would, they reasoned, restore confidence at home (especially in the banking system) and overseas, thereby curtailing the flight of gold. But, as Mellon admitted to his son, the only way to do this was to "impose additional taxes upon industry and commerce that are in no condition to bear additional burdens," as well as on the American people.[46]

Some of the details of what would become the Revenue Act of 1932 were spelled out by Mellon in a statement before the House Ways and Means Committee in January that year, though, as had been the case for many months, it was Ogden Mills who did most of the talking.[47] "We are," Mellon began, "in the midst of a grave emergency," and the paramount need was to "maintain unimpaired the credit of the United States government." The deficit for fiscal 1932 was estimated at $2.1 billion, and for fiscal 1933 was predicted to be $1.4 billion. It was imperative that the government stop borrowing to bridge this gap by the end of June, but even then, the national debt was going to increase by $1.5 billion. The only way to avoid further encumbrance was by increasing revenue, which meant broadening what was still a very narrow federal tax base. "The necessary relief to the Treasury," Mellon urged, "can be accomplished by giving up for the time the reductions in tax effected by the Revenue Acts of 1928 and 1926, and returning to the general plan of the Revenue Act of 1924." Mellon claimed that this would increase the number of federal taxpayers by 1.7 million; but even then, there would be barely 4 million of them in a nation with a population of 200 million.[48]

In addition to proposing increases in income tax, Mellon and Mills sought to maximize federal revenue by raising corporation and estate taxes, and by increasing (or in some cases, levying) taxes on items of "wide use but not of first necessity," among them tobacco, radios, phonographs, long-distance phone calls, telegrams, and bank checks. They also proposed taxes on cars and gasoline, which was unexpected from a major shareholder of Gulf Oil and an indication of how seriously Mellon viewed the current situation.[49] This scheme to restore taxes to 1924 levels marked the end of Andrew Mellon's decade-long attempt to bring them down and keep them low. As the Speaker of the House noted during the debates on the bill, "the country at this time is in a condition where the worst taxes you could possibly levy would be better than no taxes at all."[50] But these proposals, along with the recent increases in interest rates, would be profoundly deflationary in their impact: they *might* lead to a balanced budget, but they would do nothing beyond that to revive the economy. Yet despite all the modifications made as it passed through Congress, the 1932 Revenue Act did succeed in widening the tax base, and thus it set the essential features of the federal tax structure for the remainder of the decade. But even before the measure was passed, Mellon had ceased to be even nominally responsible for it.

By the early months of 1932, both local and national politics and public opinion were moving with irresistible momentum against the secretary: in Pittsburgh, in the rest of Pennsylvania, in Congress, and in the cabinet, he was increasingly regarded as out of touch and out of date. One further episode illustrates this vividly. In February of that year, hundreds of thousands of angry veterans, outraged at Hoover's veto of the bonus bill in 1931, descended on Washington. They had three particular enemies, for each of whom they dug symbolic graves at their encampment. The headstones were labeled Herbert Hoover, Andrew W. Mellon, and Senator David A. Reed. (It was prescient symbolism, for all three would soon find themselves metaphorically buried.) So seriously was the implicit threat taken that the three men were offered police protection. Hoover and Reed took it; Mellon refused.[51] (Hoover would eventually disperse the protesters by setting the troops on them, an act of chilling heartlessness to which Mellon's reaction is unrecorded.) But such a display of courage could not redeem the secretary's by now untenable political position. After Hoover himself, who was determined to stay and seek re-election, Mellon was the administration's greatest liability. Even his friends wanted him gone; his enemies wanted his scalp, and they would soon come close to getting it.

Among the sternest of Mellon's new critics was a freshman Democratic congressman from Texas, Wright Patman, who barnstormed the country during 1931, addressing veterans' organizations, fulminating against "Mellonism," and scorning the treasury secretary as little better than Al Capone.[52] At the same time, he was accumulating mounds of incriminating material concerning Mellon companies and Mellon's conduct in office. He went to great lengths to investigate the secretary's financial arrangements and business interests, writing to the Treasury, the War Department, the U.S. Shipping Board, the Library of Congress, and all manner of public officials and private individuals.[53] Patman also received a mass of letters from ordinary people, who were enraged and resentful at what Mellon had done and not done, and who denounced him as (among other things) a rascal, a scoundrel, a dictator, an autocrat, a bootlegger, a monopolist, a money-grabber, a traitor, a hypocrite, a strikebreaker, and America's Mussolini. One letter must do proxy for many hundreds: "He is the most hated man in Pittsburgh, and when his picture appeared on a moving picture theater screen recently in one of our local theatres, the boys in the gallery yelled ROBBER, ROBBER!" Here were the unheard multitudes, angry and far-flung voices of protest, not so much of the very poor, but of the middle class, the bedrock of American democracy, whose lives now seemed ruined.[54] Riding his campaign of fact-finding and rabble-rousing for all it was worth, Patman declared that he would move to impeach Mellon when Congress reconvened.

He was as good as his word. On January 6, 1932, Representative Patman stood up in a packed House to raise what he described as a matter of "constitutional privilege." "On my own responsibility as a Member of the House," he declared, "I impeach Andrew William Mellon, Secretary of the Treasury of the United States, for high crimes and misdemeanors."[55] Patman's indictment was an amalgam of all the charges previously leveled against Mellon in successive Senate investigations, but some new accusations were added: he had actively engaged in trade and commerce, in deliberate breach of the 1789 statute; he had granted illegal tax refunds and rebates to companies in which he had a substantial interest; he continued to own bank stock when as a member of the Federal Reserve Board he was explicitly prohibited from doing so; he was still a manufacturer of liquor in defiance of the Prohibition laws; he had insisted that aluminum be used in public buildings while he was a major stockholder in Alcoa, virtually the only source of aluminum; and he had interests in companies trading with the Soviet Union, in violation of the law preventing the importation of goods manufactured by convict labor. As before, Mellon was determined to fight: having quashed successive Senate inquiries, he was not to be intimidated by a first-term congressman from Texas, and he promptly retained Alexander W. Gregg, the former general counsel of the Internal Revenue, to defend him.[56]

But the world had changed. When he was attacked during the 1920s, Mellon had been widely hailed as the symbol, if not the author, of national prosperity. Senate grievances gained little political traction either inside Congress or beyond, and were dismissed as little more than political back-biting. Now, however, his star had fallen, and the nation's banker was commonly reviled as a false prophet, a plutocrat who fiddled while the world burned around him. Charges of corruption and malfeasance now found much more sympathetic ears among the American people and their elected representatives. Nor, despite his junior status, was Patman alone in the House in his anti-Mellon campaign: Representative Fiorello La Guardia, Republican of New York, was also compiling evidence for impeachment proceedings.[57] Procedurally and politically, this constituted a new threat to Mellon's position. For while previous attempts to oust him had originated (and also died) in the Senate, that body was constitutionally unable to act without prior action in the House of Representatives. The House had previously shown no inclination to act, but now the calls for impeachment were originating there, and if Patman succeeded, the Senate would be obliged to proceed. To be sure, conviction required a two-thirds majority in the upper house. While that seemed unlikely, the proceedings were bound to be lengthy and damaging, and given the public temper there was no knowing what the final outcome might be.

The House hearings began in mid-January 1932, and almost at once, Mellon was forced to admit that when parting with his bank stock, in order to make himself eligible to be treasury secretary, he had in fact sold it to none other than his brother.[58] This was potentially extremely damaging. President Hoover, himself on the ropes, hardly needed this additional problem. Rightly, if ruthlessly, he now resolved to rid himself at last of this laconic priest of laissez-faire, for whom he had already put himself out enough, and who was now a conspicuous political liability to his own embattled administration. Moreover, Ogden Mills, already de facto head of the Treasury, was an obvious and immediately available replacement. And so it remained for Hoover only to determine how Mellon could be eased out with the measure of dignity he deserved, and while conceding nothing to Patman, for the administration's sake no less than the secretary's. By agreeable coincidence, Charles Dawes, Coolidge's vice president, architect of the reparations settlement of 1924, and Harding's first director of the Budget Bureau, had recently resigned as United States ambassador to Britain, in order to become the administrator of the Reconstruction Finance Corporation—Hoover's latest idea for pulling the American economy out of the doldrums, toward which Mellon had been decidedly lukewarm. On February 1, Hoover offered Mellon the London embassy; two days later he informally accepted it, pending a consultation with his doctor that turned out satisfactorily, and on February 5 he was confirmed by the Senate.[59]

The post was a perfect political gold watch: Mellon had been a prime participant in the recent inter-governmental debt negotiations, and now that they were unraveling, serious issues loomed between the United States and the United Kingdom. Mellon would be well placed to undertake discussions on the international economy with the many European finance ministers and bankers he already knew. And with affairs in the Far East looking increasingly worrisome—Japan had recently attacked Shanghai—Hoover and Stimson wanted an ambassador to London of genuine weight and cabinet experience, as Charles Dawes had been.[60] But for all that, there was about Mellon's appointment an inescapable sense of demotion and exile. Caught between Patman (who wished to impeach him), Mills (who wished to succeed him), and Hoover (who held no brief for him), Mellon's position had become as untenable in Washington as it was in Pennsylvania. And so he accepted the posting to Britain, but without enthusiasm. It was a divorce, he told reporters; given his personal experience, this did not suggest a pleasant parting.

In addition to the Finance Bill, there was one major item of government business which it must have pained Mellon to leave unfinished, and that was the Federal Triangle. For his departure left "a vacuum into which no one with the same guiding force, determination and vision could feasibly step to continue the fight for the total realization of the master plan"; and with the subsequent defeat of Hoover and the Republicans, who had been so closely associated with the enterprise, momentum waned further. Congress still refused to release the money for Edward Bennett's "apex building," nor would it authorize the tearing down of the Old Post Office Department and the District of Columbia buildings, to make way for the final extension of the Internal Revenue Building complex and the north arm of the Grand Plaza. Architectural landscaping that would have brought cohesion and context to the overall plan now seemed an unjustifiable extravagance. And the Roosevelt administration would be far less sympathetic to the grandiose neoclassical style that Mellon and his friends so admired.[61] Governments, committees, and Congress were not the best instruments for the realization of any grand building plan: when Mellon eventually returned to his own gallery scheme, it was a lesson he took to heart.

As Hoover had hoped, Mellon's resignation rendered Patman's impeachment charges moot, and the House Judiciary Committee investigation was discontinued on February 13, 1932. In a minority report, Patman, La Guardia, and two other members of the committee assented to the ter-mination, but declared that this should not be construed as exoneration.[62] Mellon, Patman insisted, in comments reported in the Pittsburgh newspapers, "had violated more laws, caused more human suffering, and illegally acquired more property to satisfy his personal greed than any other person on earth, without fear of punishment and with the sanction and approval of three chief executives of a civilized nation."[63] Indeed, he would always believe that Mellon was guilty of the charges he had leveled at him. A year later, he was still receiving letters from the public denouncing the former secretary. In 1934 Patman would publish a book, *Bankerteering, Bonuseering, Melloneering*, that set out the evidence of Mellon's lifelong wrongdoings, and thirty years later, in October 1965, when he was chairman of the House Banking and Currency Committee, Patman addressed a Veterans' Day celebration at the Texas State Fair, reiterating his firm conviction that Mellon had fled the country for London to avoid prosecution.[64]

But not everyone saw Mellon's record in such a hostile way. The Chapter of the National Cathedral recorded its "deep appreciation" of Mellon's "great services to the nation as a member of the cabinet of three presidents and to the cathedral as Treasurer of its Executive Committee." "The wisdom and courage and devotion," Parker Gilbert wrote to his former boss, "with which you have administered the Treasury through these eleven trying years have had no parallel, I think, in the history of the country, and you leave behind you in Washington a record of public service and of sound finance which should be a constant inspiration for the future."[65] In formally resigning as secretary of the treasury, on February 8, 1932, Mellon described his term of office as "a period of absorbing interest," and counted it the "highest privilege to have had this opportunity for public service." And he took with him the "greatest respect" for the staff of the Treasury, and the "highest regard" for Hoover and his administration "of which I have had the honor of being part." The president's reply was tactful to the point of disingenuousness: he noted the "magnificent tribute" embodied in the "universal expressions of the press and the public toward you during the past few days" (a decided exaggeration), and he recorded "the feeling of personal loss I have after these years of association in the Cabinet" (of which the same could be said).[66]

Two private responses to the announcement of his new appointment were wholly characteristic. Thus Nora:

> I am heartsick at what you have just told me. Not only for my own selfish sake, but I hate the idea of your going to that climate. You do not realize how dreadful it is in winter. The thought of not seeing you again for a

year and perhaps not then just paralyzes me and there seems no point in this place. I know, however, if you feel you must go, you will, but I do hope and pray it won't be necessary.[67]

And thus Sir Joseph Duveen:

My first reaction was that it will of necessity mean a temporary break in the enjoyable luncheons I have had with you, and which form so pleasant a recollection to me, but this is completely overshadowed in the thought that the country is indeed fortunate in having at its disposal, in these unprecedented times, the service of one who has such wide and long experience of public affairs.

Ten days later, and with his incorrigible eye ever to business, Duveen was trying to persuade Mellon to take Allington Castle for the summer as his English country residence—but to no avail.[68]

Mellon had less than a month to clear his desk at the Treasury, and there were also urgent financial matters demanding his attention. Howard M. Johnson visited from Pittsburgh, bringing his master's as yet incomplete federal tax return for 1931, which Mellon hurriedly signed, without having a chance to scrutinize the details.[69] And just before his departure, Mellon made his second substantial gift of pictures to his educational and charitable trust, handing over nineteen of his choicest works, valued at $5.9 million, including three Vermeers, two Rembrandts, two Rubenses, two Van Dycks, and two Holbeins. Some of these he had owned for several years, among them Holbein's *Portrait of Edward VI as a Boy* and Vermeer's *Girl with a Red Hat*; others were from his recent Hermitage purchases, including Rembrandt's *A Polish Nobleman* and Raphael's *St. George and the Dragon*. At the same time, he also made over $3.3 million worth of stock to Ailsa (in Alcoa, common and preferred, and in the Pittsburgh Coal Company), $4 million worth to Paul (from the same issues, plus Carborundum), and $238,000 worth of Alcoa shares (5,000 preferred, 5,000 common stock) to David Bruce—his only recorded benefaction to his son-in-law. He also reclaimed his shares in Mellon National Bank and the Union Trust Company from Dick, still valued at $10 million, which were now divided between Paul and Ailsa.[70]

All that remained were some staffing arrangements to complete and some formal farewells to make. As Donald Shepard and Frank Denton had done before, David Finley now resigned from the U.S. Treasury and government service, and became a full-time Mellon employee. He and his wife would accompany the ambassador to London, and Finley would continue to work for Mellon thereafter. The president and the members of his administration donated Mellon his cabinet chair as a farewell gift, and as a memento of his long public service.[71] On March 15, Hoover gave Mellon a farewell dinner at the White House, and the following evening the cabinet and congressional colleagues put on a banquet for him at the New Willard Hotel, where Mellon had lodged for a time at the very beginning of his official Washington sojourn, almost exactly eleven years before. Calvin Coolidge was also present. "While the Treasury is passing through an extremely difficult period," the former secretary observed, "its policies are well-established and its direction is in capable hands." Soon after, and with the ever loyal Finleys by his side, Andrew Mellon left Washington, via New York, for the Court of St. James's in London, on a liner appropriately named the *Majestic*.[72]

III. MR. AMBASSADOR

When Ambassador Mellon reached Southampton on April 8, 1932, the journalists assembled at the dockside expressed slightly mocking concern as to whether the official representative of the American republic would wear the knee breeches and silk stockings customary when presenting one's credentials to the sovereign. (Franklin D. Roosevelt would be much exercised by the same question when he appointed the uncourtly Joseph P. Kennedy to the same post six years later.)[73] Breeches aside, Mellon's appointment had been widely welcomed by the British. He had served three American presidents, including the incumbent; he was by far the richest man yet to be assigned to the London embassy; and he was known to possess a fabulous art collection. Moreover, Mellon knew the country as a regular visitor for more than thirty years; he was the former husband of an Englishwoman and the father of an already ardent Anglophile son. He was on friendly terms with members of the royal family as well as the cabinet, and with various important bankers and captains of industry.[74] On the British side of the Atlantic, it was Mellon's renown as both a businessman and a statesman that had accompanied him, rather than news of his recent political difficulties. Thus he now found himself in a generally more friendly and sympathetic environment than official Washington or American public opinion had lately afforded him. Indeed, as the Prince of Wales put it, there was an eager sense of expectancy concerning "the advice which the great financier can give Europe."[75]

Ailsa and David Bruce joined Andrew soon after (though Ailsa was promptly ill, and David would make regular business trips to the States and back). The three duly installed themselves in the ambassador's official residence at 14 Prince's Gate, where J. P. Morgan had lived before he donated it to the American government for this purpose.[76] Morgan's pictures had been removed after his death, and apart from official portraits of some of Mellon's predecessors, the walls were almost completely bare. Accordingly, the new ambassador brought forty-seven canvases with him (which would be expertly mounted on the walls by Knoedler's London staff), though he left the works painted on wood panel behind in Washington, for fear they would be damaged by the change of climate.[77] Thus his Raphaels and his Vermeers did not make the journey, but Van Dyck's *Marchesa Balbi* hung on the stair landing; into the library, which Ailsa had paneled in oak for the purpose, went the Rembrandts, the Frans Halses, and the remaining Van Dycks; and the drawing room, redecorated in pale gray, was adorned with the English pictures by Gainsborough, Romney, Hoppner, and Reynolds.[78] As a result, some of Mellon's aristocratic guests became briefly reacquainted with formerly family-owned portraits of ancestors. But not every visitor was so keenly aware of the ironies of the display. "What wonderful pictures you have, Mr. Mellon!" one appreciative but ill-informed caller exclaimed. "Do all American embassies have paintings like these?" Mellon's answer is unrecorded.[79]

As the reporters at the Southampton dockside had warned and jested, the new ambassador's first diplomatic conundrum would be what to wear at the royal court. The matter did not arise when he presented his credentials, because he did so informally to King George V and Queen Mary, the first Windsors, who invited him to lunch at their eponymous castle, where the sovereign showed himself particularly knowledgeable about Mellon's pictures.[80] But there was much speculation about how Mellon would be outfitted for his first evening appearance at Buckingham Palace. His two immediate predecessors had both disdained the customary knee breeches as anachronistic tokens of pre-revolutionary Europe, and had preferred the more contemporary formality of white tie, tailcoat, and trousers, such as were worn at formal presidential receptions in the White House. Mellon's diary for May 11, 1932 reveals he followed their example: "First Court in evening. I do not wear knee britches." For the duration of his stay this would remain his costume at court, though at gatherings in private houses which royalty attended, he thought it more tactful to don his "britches."[81]

A second immediate challenge that Mellon faced in Britain was less expected and more personal. His arrival coincided with the publication of

Lloyd George's book *The Truth About Reparations and War Debts*, a vitriolic attack on Stanley Baldwin's alleged mishandling of the settlement with the United States in 1923. As Lloyd George described it, the terms America had imposed had been punitive, and the British delegation in accepting them had gone like lambs to the slaughter. Baldwin, Lloyd George insisted, had been "casual, soft, easy-going and then woefully 'raw,' " whereas Mellon had been "keen, experienced, hard and ruthless"; the latter had completely outmaneuvered the former. Their "business transaction," Lloyd George concluded, "was in the nature of a negotiation between a weasel and its quarry"—scarcely a flattering description of the new American ambassador.[82] But it made little impact, at least initially, partly because Lloyd George was now widely regarded as an embittered, marginal figure and partly because Mellon's aura of soft-spoken distinction gave the lie to these imputations of hardness and ruthlessness, though he undoubtedly possessed both. "Tall, thin, elegant, composed, detached," observed the *London Graphic*, as if struggling to describe a whole equal to the sum of these parts, "he has even the fragile face of a dreamer and a poet."[83]

Following a long-established custom, Mellon's first public address was at a dinner given in his honor by the Pilgrims, the foremost Anglo-American organization in Britain; it took place on April 14, only six days after his arrival, and was presided over by the seventeenth Earl of Derby.[84] His speech articulated all the right sentiments. "Nowhere," Mellon began, "outside my own country, could I feel so much at home as here," and he went on to extol the common language and literature and liberty that the United Kingdom and the United States possessed. But his main concern was to comment on "the present crisis," which, though serious, was not unprecedented. As in 1873, too rapid expansion after a war had led to the recent crash; yet, Mellon argued, the economic life of nations went in cycles, and even at the darkest times "quick or spectacular remedies" should be avoided. This might be a "difficult transition period," but "no one should be discouraged about the ultimate outcome." "In the light of past history," he concluded, "it is not unreasonable to expect that opportunities greater than any we have yet known will come as the result of forces now at work and constantly being discovered." His remarks were greeted with cheers. "My speech seems to go well," Mellon noted in his diary. "He really delivered the speech very well indeed," David Finley informed Ogden Mills. Or, as one gossip columnist put it, less enthralled: "in an almost inaudible voice he carefully read platitudes to the assembled company."[85]

Mellon's days in Britain fast settled into a conventional ambassadorial

routine, an unrelenting schedule of "receptions and dinners and presenta-
tions."[86] Assisted by David Bruce and Ailsa, he entertained with characteristically understated style, his reputation and (even more) his pictures
making invitations to his lunches and dinners as sought after by London-
ers as they had been by Washingtonians. Mellon was also a regular in the
high life of the capital, where the cream of society mingled with diplomats
and holders of high office ("dining with princes and lunching with kings,"
as David Bruce put it). He also spent many weekends in great country
houses, the guest of such grand personages as Lord and Lady Desborough, the Duke and Duchess of Sutherland, Mrs. Ronald Greville, and
Mr. and Mrs. Ronald Tree.[87] He attended more formal banquets in his
honor given by the English-Speaking Union and the lord mayor of London, delivering speeches, invariably written by David Finley, in his inim-
itably inaudible style of declamation. He was asked to join the Prince of
Wales in opening the new Shakespeare Memorial Theatre at Stratford-
on-Avon, in recognition of the substantial American contribution to the
building costs. He received his sixteenth and last honorary degree at the
University of Edinburgh. He put on the customary Fourth of July party
for the benefit of American citizens resident in London, and he endured
the swarm of transatlantic debutantes, daughters of the nation conceived
in defiance of the British monarchy, who nevertheless wished to be presented at the royal court—as did (and was) Ailsa herself.[88]

Shortly before the Mellon entourage left for Britain, David Finley told
Paul that "the only real flaw in what will be a perfect time in London is
that you will not be there this year."[89] Throughout his father's ambassadorship, Paul continued working in the Mellon National Bank in Pittsburgh, although his heart was scarcely more in it now than on the day he
had begun. As he confessed to Andrew in November 1932, in a letter
delayed by "plain procrastination," he had been at Rolling Rock virtually
every weekend, where the hunting had been "exceptionally good" and
where David Bruce had joined him for the shooting. He was "fairly busy"
at the bank, buying and selling bonds for the Mellbank Corporation. He
reported finding the duties "much more interesting and not subject to the
dullness" of other departments he had worked in, which suffered from
general "lack of activity," though this may well have been a sop to please
his father. Paul then provided a description of life at Woodland Road
("things here at the house are going on as usual"), an account of a visit to
his mother in Virginia ("quite well and the place in very good condition"),
and a suggestion concerning a renewal of their subscription to the Pittsburgh Symphony Orchestra ("I feel we ought to help them again").

Would the election result, Paul asked, mean that Andrew would return to America in December or in March? "Much love," he signed off.[90]

It was not a busy or fulfilled life. Paul avoided Pittsburgh as much as he decently could. Indeed, although ostensibly working at the bank, he was often in England during his father's ambassadorship. He went about with some of his Cambridge friends, attended weddings and garden parties, spent weekends at country houses, got in some fox-hunting and point-to-point riding, and was painted on his favorite horse, in full hunting regalia, by A. J. Munnings.[91] In London, he went to the theater, and to nightclubs, and soon became engaged to a "pretty girl" named Delphina Burt, whom he met at "an informal and somewhat disorganized party at a minor embassy in London." Knowing no one, he had sought refuge in the kitchen, and as fortune had it, he found Delphina there for the same reason. She was five years older than he was, a strict Roman Catholic, and, like his own mother, English. Paul took her out dancing at the Café de Paris, and introduced her to his uncle Percy McMullen, and also to his mother, who was then visiting her brother. Naturally, they were delighted at the prospect of his marrying an Englishwoman.[92] (Might Delphina also have suggested an honorable ticket out of Pittsburgh?) As Paul later recalled, this seemed a golden time, of dancing, songs, and laughter, all the more brilliant for being set against the gloom and hardship of the Great Depression, and of his far-off hometown.[93]

In truth, the whole of Andrew Mellon's ambassadorship was conducted in the shadow of a still-darkening economic landscape that stretched across Europe and the United States, its valleys showing no signs of renewed life—if anything they were growing yet more desolate. The whole capitalist system now seemed to be heading for a terminal crisis. This was not lost on Mellon, who became "very depressed" for much of the time, despite the occasional relief afforded by his breeches.[94] In every major western European nation, unemployment was higher in 1932 than it had been in 1931, and in the United States, the ranks of the jobless swelled from ten million to twelve million. National currencies collapsed and so did international credit. Early in 1931, forty-seven countries had been on the gold standard, but by the end of 1932, following Britain's departure, only seven remained.[95] At the Lausanne Conference in the summer of 1932, Germany's reparations were effectively voided, making it virtually inevitable that Britain, France, and other European nations would soon default on their debt repayments to the United States. (Britain and France, the two greatest debtors, would both do so within a year.)[96] All this was doubly dismaying for Mellon. Most immediately, as U.S. ambassador, he was obliged to endure increasingly strident attacks by British ministers on a U.S. government still intent on being repaid (perhaps Lloyd George had had a point after all). Much more demoralizing was the comprehensive collapse of the whole postwar settlement of debt accords, stabilized currencies, and the revived gold standard, on which Mellon and his fellow statesmen-financiers had labored so long and successfully during the 1920s: this was the end of the new world order they had tried to create.[97]

The political consequences of such economic cataclysms were also on a global scale, though the particulars differed from country to country, continent to continent. In the United States, Hoover's reputation was at rock bottom in the months following Mellon's departure from Washington. Throwing the treasury secretary overboard had brought the beleaguered president no relief from unrelenting public criticism, and he seemed ever more overwhelmed by the scale and momentum of events. All the same, in June 1932, a listless and lackluster Republican convention could think of no alternative but to renominate him. The November election turned on only one issue, though the Democratic challenger, Franklin Delano Roosevelt, governor of New York, offered no more concrete solutions to the depression than Hoover. Unlike the incumbent, however, Roosevelt did manage to convey confidence and hope in the form of a "New Deal for the American people," and he blasted the recent policies of Hoover (and Mellon)—higher taxes and tariffs, reduced government spending, and shrinking money supply—as the worst that could be devised. He also promised an "enlightened administration" that would govern in the interests of the American people as a whole, and would no longer be in thrall to that unholy trinity of "the speculator, the manipulator, even the financier."[98]

Across the Atlantic, and still in some ways in denial about the depression, Mellon believed that there was "not much doubt" that Hoover would be re-elected, because his "constructive measures are working very effectively," and he looked forward to staying on in the London embassy for another four years. "I am confident," Ogden Mills wrote in similar vein to David Finley, "that our case is so strong that if we make a vigorous campaign . . . the American people will not be foolish enough to take a chance on a man who, in my judgment, has no qualifications whatsoever for the office he seeks."[99] But the American people were both angrier and wiser than Mills allowed, and the result was a landslide victory for Roosevelt in November 1932: he carried forty-two of the forty-eight states (though Pennsylvania was not among them), which meant he garnered 472 votes in the Electoral College to Hoover's 59, and the Democrats also won massive majorities in the Senate and the House. This was a triumph for democracy as a transformative principle. But elsewhere in the world, under the impact of widespread economic disaster, democracy was more often at risk than triumphant. In the Far East, Japan, having already attacked Shanghai, advanced across China from Manchuria to Jehol in January 1933, and left the League of Nations soon after.[100] And that very same month, with the Weimar Republic on the brink of collapse, Adolf Hitler became chancellor of Germany.

Mellon had donated $22,500 to the Republican National Committee in 1932; it had proved an uncommonly poor investment.[101] Beyond keeping up appropriate state at the embassy, he did not spend substantially while he was in London. Given the constriction of his own assets, the anxieties over Gulf Oil, and the sums he had spent on the Hermitage paintings, it is not surprising that he showed little enthusiasm for acquiring pictures. Within weeks of his arrival, Duveen tried to tempt him with the late Count Czernin's "great Vermeer in Vienna," which Mellon had earlier but vainly sought to acquire. "If you and I co-operate," Duveen advised, "we shall, I am sure, be able to secure it eventually at the right price." But Mellon was "not interested" in "hearing about any pictures" until the economic situation had "clarified." Convinced there would be "many opportunities" to buy fine paintings in a few years' time, he prepared to wait.[102] Even *The Red Boy*, by Sir Thomas Lawrence, which Lord Durham had recently put up for sale and which Duveen had always coveted, could not arouse his interest. Mellon was now so "pestered" by people offering to sell him their pictures that David Finley prepared a "stereotyped letter" of refusal. As Duveen's spies would verify, when Mellon visited the von Auspitz collection, on display in Agnew's gallery, he was "very cold," and dealers "could not get close to him."[103]

Knoedler fared no better. Their business was now "at an absolute standstill," and as it was proving impossible to sell Mellon's three Hermitage rejects, salaries at the firm had to be cut by 20 percent to 50 percent. Soon after reaching the London embassy, Mellon learned that the Guaranty Trust had refused to renew Knoedler's credit line of $500,000. The situation was a "terrible strain," and Charles Henschel felt "reluctantly compelled" to ask his "old friend and client" to "help us out." The ambassador duly did so, arranging a new credit line for Knoedler at the Mellon Bank of $120,000.[104] But that was as much as he was willing to do. Henschel and Messmore still cherished the hope of another deal between Mellon and the Russians: perhaps the Giorgione in exchange for the Rembrandt *Turk* and the Van Dyck *Portrait of a Flemish Lady*, and an additional $300,000. The Giorgione was, as Messmore pointed out in January 1933, the "only one left" that Mellon wanted, and there "may not be another opportunity." But Mellon had had his fill of Russian treasures, and he was even less interested in the French impressionists that Knoedler tried to press on him later that year. As he had told their London staff when they were hanging the paintings he already owned at Prince's Gate: "at present" he was "not buying anything."[105]

Even with the assistance of Zatzenstein in Berlin, Knoedler failed to devise a tempting enough scheme to rekindle Mellon's interest in the Hermitage. The great collector from 1928 to 1931 had become the great abstainer. He had "too many things on his mind" (was this an allusion to his anxieties about Gulf Oil?), and he thought it "not a propitious moment to try and undertake any purchases," even if "something very fine turned up." He was also convinced that pictures were now worth "about a third of the price they were two years ago, and they will sell even cheaper in a year from now."[106] To be sure, he had not lost interest in art generally, or in his great scheme for Washington, and he spent a great deal of time in the National Gallery in London, getting a sense of how the place worked, how the spaces were organized, and how the pictures were hung. But as Knoedler's London office reported to New York in June 1932, their former star client was now seriously concerned about the protracted economic downturn: he was "worried about the unemployment situation next winter," and he did not think that "anything very constructive" was "being done to get us out of the rut we are in"—though there is no sign that Mellon had any "constructive" ideas of his own at this time.[107]

This unwillingness to acquire art was not the only indication that Mellon was downcast, cautious, beleaguered, and perhaps more damaged by the criticisms he had recently endured than he was willing to let on.[108] To be sure, in May 1932 he handed over another $3 million worth of shares to Ailsa (Gulf, Koppers, and Standard Steel Car), and an additional $4.75 million to Paul (the same). This meant that during the first five months of that year, he had given away in all more than $5 million worth of pictures to the educational and charitable trust, $10 million worth of bank shares to Ailsa and Paul, and $16 million worth of shares in Mellon companies. Not surprisingly, the book value of his capital account declined from $100 million in 1932 to $70 million in the following year: his disposal of his fortune seemed to be gaining serious momentum.[109] But then disbursement stopped almost as suddenly as it had started: during the remainder of 1932, Mellon made no further gifts of paintings to the trust or of stock to his children, and this moratorium would last through the whole of 1933—another indication that he was feeling under serious financial pressure, and that everything was on hold for the time being.[110]

IV. OPPORTUNITIES AMID DISASTER

Yet even in these bleak times, Mellon may have been nurturing another project for the cultural enrichment of his nation's capital. Washington not only lacked an art gallery, it had no building displaying images of the great men who had made the history of their nation. A national portrait gallery had existed in London since the late 1850s, and by coincidence, Duveen (who was a trustee of the gallery, and in 1933 would be ennobled as Lord Duveen of Millbank) had recently paid for an extension to it, adjacent to the National Gallery on the north side of Trafalgar Square.[111] Mellon had previously shown little interest in American art, although since his arrival in Washington, he had hung Gilbert Stuart's portrait of George Washington in his bedroom at 1785 Massachusetts Avenue. But now he learned from David Bruce that an oil portrait of Pocahontas, after an engraving dating from 1616, was on sale in London. He had resolved not to purchase any pictures during his ambassadorship, but with his new interest, this was too good an opportunity to miss. Accordingly, he authorized David Finley to acquire the painting, transferred $22,500 to his bank account, and Pocahontas was secured.[112]

Mellon's sharp eye for the possibilities of a situation was even more in evidence in business, for during his spell in London he was actively engaged in furthering the fortunes of Gulf Oil.[113] Given its recent collapse in profits and his own substantial financial commitment to it, he had strong incentives to do all he could to restore the enterprise to prosperity, and he eagerly availed himself of an opportunity which now presented itself. By the late 1920s, the Persian Gulf had become an attractive field of operation for multinational oil companies, though the British jealously insisted on their rights, enshrined in treaties with the local rulers; concessions could be granted only with their consent, and so, in practice, not to foreign-owned businesses.[114] In late 1929, when still secretary of the treasury, Mellon had exerted himself on behalf of Gulf, urging the State Department to press the company's claims for a concession in Kuwait with the Foreign Office in London, despite the British government's known opposition to such attempts at intrusion into a region it claimed wholly to control, and he continued to press during the remainder of his time in Washington. Despite the continued opposition of the Admiralty, the India Office, and the government of India, the Foreign Office eventually signaled a change of policy, urging the British government to adopt a more permissive attitude to foreign companies seeking concessions in Kuwait, which essentially meant American companies. At a time of increasing uncertainty in Europe and the Far East, and with Britain soon to renege on its war debt repayments to the United States, Whitehall saw this as a modest way to stay on good terms with the Americans.[115]

This was the view Mellon would sponsor as U.S. ambassador, and while lodged at Prince's Gate, he did everything he could to plead the cause of Gulf Oil in Kuwait to the Foreign Office. To be sure, he did so as the American representative of the State Department, which was by now officially supporting Gulf. But it was lost on no one in Whitehall that he was also Gulf's creator and (with RB and WL) majority shareholder. His zeal as the company's champion moved the State Department to urge caution upon him on more than one occasion; it suggested he leave negotiations in the hands of Ray Atherton, the senior American Foreign Service official in the London embassy.[116] Undeterred and unashamed, Mellon held several meetings during the autumn of 1932 with Sir Robert Vansittart, the pro-American permanent secretary at the Foreign Office; and by the time his appointment expired the following spring, he had negotiated the basis of an extremely good deal for Gulf.[117] To take the new Kuwait concession, a new company would be set up, owned in equal shares by the (British) Anglo-Iranian Oil Company, and by the (American) Gulf Oil Company. Advantageously for America and for Gulf, the British would continue to bear the whole cost of overseeing the administration and defense of Kuwait, thereby at least preserving its sphere of influence. The agreements between the two companies and between their consortium and the sheikh of Kuwait would not actually be signed until early 1934. But by the time Mellon's ambassadorship came to an end, the deal was effectively done, and he had played a major part in it.[118]

Mellon had always believed that the ultimate purpose of diplomacy, no less than that of government, was to secure a world in which American business could thrive, especially (if not exclusively) the businesses he owned. Here, once again, he had seen the possibilities of a situation, and this may well have strengthened his determination to stay on in London after Roosevelt's crushing victory, when, as Paul put it to him, there was an argument for returning home at once.[119] To be sure, Mellon understood that "Washington and the world seems to be marking time and waiting, but looking forward" to the new president, but the incoming administration was less likely to be a friend of American oil companies than Hoover's had been, and so there was every reason for Mellon to remain for as long as he legitimately could, moving negotiations with the Foreign Office as far and as fast as possible.[120] As during his time at the Treasury, the ambassador felt no tension between the demands of office and the imperatives of industry. The interests of America and the interests of Gulf Oil were identical, and so no reasonable, patriotic person could see abuse of power in his helping the producer of a commodity vital to the national well-being. The British war debt settlement with Washington might be unraveling, but where there was a promising opportunity for Gulf, there was also one for the United States.[121]

Beyond that, and as Hoover and Stimson had foreseen, Mellon's only substantial foray into the realm of international diplomacy while in London concerned the rapidly deteriorating situation in the Far East, in the aftermath of the Japanese attack on Shanghai in January 1932. As the secretary of state had explained to the new ambassador just before the latter's departure from Washington, he had been working "to secure a solid alignment with Britain," and it would be Mellon's mission to further that policy. In reality, when the situation was at its most tense, during the first five months of 1932, most of the diplomatic business at the London end was handled by Ray Atherton.[122] Thereafter, Mellon himself was directly involved, and he held regular meetings with the British foreign secretary, Sir John Simon, between late May 1932 and early February 1933. (He also informally visited the Japanese ambassador in London.) Mellon duly expressed American support for Britain (which doubtless strengthened his hand when making the case that Gulf should be given a share in the Kuwait oil concession). There was talk of a possible international conference—conciliation via the League of Nations was tried and failed—and by the end of Mellon's ambassadorship, it was agreed that the lead in the formulation of future policy should be taken by Britain, with U.S. support.[123]

At the farewell dinner given for him by the Pilgrims, on February 21, 1933, Mellon delivered a valedictory speech (drafted, as usual, by David Finley), in which he said all the things that were appropriate to the occasion: he spoke of his lifelong love of this "enchanted country," of his great belief in Anglo-American friendship and cooperation, and of his determination to revisit Britain frequently in the future. But the ambassador also surveyed the current scene and, despite everything that had happened since the crash of October 1929, he still insisted that the American economy remained fundamentally strong. "Our economic system," he contended, "is not in any danger of breaking down." Despite unemployment and reduced purchasing power, there was "no lack of production, and the processes of distribution continue to operate as usual." And although there were defects in "our over-individualized banking system," the nation's financial structure had "stood the strain remarkably well." This was at best an over-optimistic account of the continuing economic cataclysm, at worst an indication that Mellon still failed to grasp the magnitude of the challenges which his country faced. In the last twelve months, he concluded, the "inexorable march of events" meant that "much history has been made"; "what the next twelve months hold for us I do not know."[124] Perhaps, for him personally, it was just as well.

The reality was that during the lame-duck period from November 1932 to March 1933, when Hoover had been defeated but was still in office, and while Roosevelt was triumphant although not yet president, the American economy—and the global economy—had continued to go downhill. In a memorandum to Senator David A. Reed of Pennsylvania, Hoover maintained that recovery was already under way, and it was only Roosevelt's determined refusal to continue his program (which he did not seem to notice that FDR had been elected to terminate) that had effectively sabotaged it. In truth, all the indicators made plain that the American economy was still in free fall. There had been five thousand bank failures in three years, wiping out seven billion dollars in deposits; 45 percent of homes had suffered or were in danger of mortgage foreclosure; and national production had declined by approximately one-half. Between the peak of 1929 and early 1933, the volume of check transactions and stock market deals had contracted by 60 percent, the amount of new capital financing was down by 95 percent, the volume of new building contracts had fallen by 75 percent, and the Dow Jones Industrial Average had plummeted by 90 percent.[125]

On the eve of the new president's inauguration, then, the country's financial institutions seemed on the brink of complete collapse. Most states (including Pennsylvania) and municipalities (including Pittsburgh) had reached the legal limits of debt; banks continued to fold and fail across the nation, as anxious depositors sought to retrieve their life savings. Confidence declined still further, as the hearings before the Senate Committee on Banking and Currency and before the Senate Finance Committee revealed not only widespread mismanagement, impropriety, and recklessness, but also an almost complete dearth of ideas on the part of business leaders about the causes of the depression or any likely remedy. The Federal Reserve Board raised interest rates yet again, but things just got worse.[126] By March 2, more than half the states in the union had been compelled to shut their banks, and the New York Stock Exchange and the Chicago Board of Trade had both closed down, along with many local bourses. "I am fully confident," Mellon observed in one of his last speeches before leaving, "that this is a temporary crisis." But by the evening of Friday, March 3, thirty-two states had shut their banks indefinitely, six were in virtually the same position, while in the remaining ten states and the District of Columbia, withdrawals were limited to 5 percent of deposits. "Conditions are not improving," W. L. Mellon informed his uncle; "in fact, I have never seen them worse." "It is a most amazing state of affairs," Nora wrote to Andrew. "None of us has any cash." Hoover was going out, and Roosevelt coming in, "to the sound of crashing banks."[127]

This nightmare world of panic and poverty, crisis and collapse, fear and hunger seemed a long way from Andrew Mellon's opulent London bower at 14 Prince's Gate, where dukes and duchesses dined and danced, enthralled by his pictures and doubtless a little envious. But as he well knew, thanks to the transatlantic telephone, the situation was nowhere worse than in Pittsburgh. In early March 1933, the Mellon National Bank and the Union Trust Company both faced major crises, with the now all-too-familiar sight of anxious depositors queued up at the door. On Friday, March 3, both banks were open, despite Governor Pinchot's declaration of a statewide bank holiday, and more than 10,000 people flooded the Mellon Bank to obtain cash. Dick Mellon was conspicuously present (as was Henry McEldowney at Union Trust), and turned in a bravura public performance, of which his cleverer elder brother would have been utterly incapable. Though stricken (as Andrew knew by this time) with the angina and the bladder infection that would shorten his life, Dick climbed a stepladder at 1:30 that afternoon, and announced to the anxious and assembled multitude below, "Please don't be apprehensive. We have just obtained all the cash you could possibly need or use, so withdraw any amount you want." "There's one good thing about a bank run like this," he added. "It enables me to get acquainted with all of my customers."[128]

As a display of cool nerve, jaunty confidence, and determined resolution, this was an act that was hard to beat, and since both Mellon National Bank and Union Trust were highly liquid, all deposits were duly honored in full. Indeed, many Pittsburghers who withdrew their money from one bank merely crossed the street and promptly deposited it in the other. In its way, this was the greatest financial triumph that Andrew (in absentia) and Dick (very much present) ever achieved, and both the bank and the trust company came through the panic of 1933 much better than had T. Mellon & Sons in the lesser disaster of sixty years before. And all the nearby banks which were part of the Mellbank Corporation, to which Andrew and Dick had recently pledged $6 million in support, also survived. Yet in the disenchanted and resentful mood of the times, this triumph of Mellon solidity and survival merely added to their unpopularity in their hometown: "they were so strong, when everyone else was so weak." The Mellons might claim that they were "saving banks" in Pittsburgh, but the reality was that they saved none but their own, which meant they became more dominant in Pittsburgh than they were before.[129] Once again, the Mellons had made the best of hard times. As in the Judge's day, some would see in their perseverance a continuous and generous public-spiritedness; others would take it for a sign of coldhearted willingness to benefit from the misfortunes of others.

Early in March 1933, Franklin Roosevelt finally took office, and Andrew Mellon's ambassadorship to Britain thus came to an end after only eleven months. In that interval, he had twice returned to the United States (during these visits he was on leave from the State Department without pay), and for more than half of his tenure, he was the lame-duck representative of a discredited Republican regime which the American voters had scornfully and vengefully rejected.[130] Mellon had enjoyed living in Britain, and had looked forward to continuing in the post had the Republicans been returned to power for a fourth time. Despite witnessing the further collapse of the global economy, and the undoing of so much he had sought to accomplish during the 1920s, both domestically and internationally, he had found the ambassadorship an adroit and dignified way to evade the specter of impeachment in Washington (although his enemies had not given up, but were merely biding their time). He had furthered the interests of Gulf Oil, about which he entertained no more qualms than he had on any occasion he might have been said to abuse his power. And the Bruces and the Finleys had been comfortably close at hand. But now his embassy and his official career were both over, and as he approached his seventy-eighth birthday, retirement finally beckoned.

Though spurned and rejected by the American people, Herbert Hoover wrote Mellon a letter, in the dying days of his defeated and derided presidency, which was more magnanimous than that which he had penned a year before, on the eve of his departure for London:

> Before I leave this position, I should like to express to you, as far as words can express it, the appreciation which I have for the most distinguished service which you have given to the American people over these many years. That service needs no recounting from me, but it is due that

I should express my gratitude which I have for your many years of friendship.[131]

Mellon's gracious reply matched the president's high tone:

I deeply appreciate all that you say about my work in the years that we have been associated together. I value your friendship and want to thank you now, on the eve of my departure from London and public life, for the courtesy and consideration you have always shown towards me. No president has ever had a more difficult term of office than yours, nor has any president ever brought to the office greater devotion or higher endeavor than you have shown in the service of the American people.[132]

Although Roosevelt had swept all before him, Hoover and Mellon, each in his own ways, were still unrepentant and uncomprehending, drawn more closely together in defeat than ever they had been in power. Hoover finally and formally accepted Mellon's resignation early in March 1933. Looking back on his own official life, Judge Thomas Mellon had concluded that "its experiences were altogether pleasing and satisfactory to myself, and their retrospect leaves nothing to regret."[133] Despite the recent collapse in his reputation, and the adverse comment and hostile publicity he had endured, Andrew Mellon probably felt the same way. But as he set sail for the United States aboard the liner *Leviathan* on March 17, 1933, focused not on retirement but on getting back and getting on with his great gallery plans, he could not have foreseen that, although his public service had just ended, his public life most emphatically had not.[134]

PART FOUR

Old Man, New Deal,
1933–37

To the general public which surrounds me now, I am as a stranger in a strange land.

Thomas Mellon and His Times, p. 386

14

HIS WORLD TURNED UPSIDE DOWN
An Unhappy Homecoming, 1933–34

The spirit of the age tends rather towards socialism, or the performance by the state of duties which ought to be left to individual enterprise.

Thomas Mellon and His Times, p. 351

I. THE ROOSEVELT REVOLUTION

Andrew Mellon arrived in New York on the *Leviathan* on March 24, 1933, accompanied by Ailsa and, as on his first voyage over as ambassador, by David Finley. It was, by agreeable coincidence, his seventy-eighth birthday. He was followed across the Atlantic by five van-loads of pictures and furniture, which had been taken down and packed by Knoedler's staff in London, and which for caution's sake traveled on five different ships.[1] It would be several months before the crates were unpacked and their contents rehung, because it would take Mellon that long to rearrange his life in two places of residence—a life which he fully expected to be one of retirement and freedom, his only remaining work the realization of his dream for the National Gallery of Art. "We'll start on it right away," he had told Finley on the ship.[2] By now, Franklin Delano Roosevelt had been president for twenty days. While Mellon was busy reorganizing his life, Roosevelt was even more urgently reorganizing the battered country. At this stage, there was no reason to believe that the patrician president's efforts would set a collision course with the aging Pittsburgh plutocrat, much less that the confrontation would result in the most public and ad hominem clash between old guard, business-loving Republicans and New Deal, business-loathing Democrats.

On the eve of the inauguration, David Bruce predicted to Ailsa that "Washington is going to be the most interesting place in the world in the next few months."[3] It is a great irony that his prophecy would be fulfilled in such varied ways (not all of them welcome to him and his in-laws) and that those few months would prove epochal indeed. For when FDR took office on March 4, 1933, there was scant hint that his presidency was to become, both in duration and in achievement, by far the greatest in the twentieth century. Like George Washington and Abraham Lincoln, Roosevelt would be deified in circumstances of unique national crisis and trauma, and would prove himself—as had been said of Washington, albeit in different order— "first in peace, first in war, and first in the hearts of his countrymen." But FDR would never be first in the hearts of *all* men, certainly not among those people and professions with whom Andrew Mellon had spent and made his life: the rich bankers, leading businessmen, captains of industry, and high-living plutocrats who had heard themselves damned in the heyday of trust-busting progressivism by Franklin Roosevelt's predecessor and distant cousin Theodore as the "malefactors of great wealth."[4]

Educated at Groton and Harvard, a Hudson Valley squire of ancient lineage (at least by American standards), the younger Roosevelt shared his kinsman's patrician disdain for what he regarded as the selfish and irresponsible excesses of the parvenu super-rich. But this hostility was not merely a matter of social disapproval or economic envy; it was also, as FDR had explained in a speech to the San Francisco Commonwealth Club in September 1932, a matter of historical examination. The last half century, he insisted, had been "in large measure a history of a group of financial Titans" (of whom, though he named no names, Andrew Mellon was undoubtedly one). Society had chosen to give these ambitious men "free play and unlimited reward," on the supposition that "the business of government was not to interfere but to assist in the development of industry." In an era of unprecedented depression and hardship, however, there was need for "a re-appraisal of values." Under these very different circumstances, Roosevelt insisted, "a mere builder of more industrial plants, a creator of more railroad systems, an organizer of more corporations" was "as likely to be a danger as a help." "The day," he concluded, "of the great promoter or the financial Titan, to whom we granted everything if only he would build or develop, is over."[5] Here was a vision, and a history, of the United States as a capitalist society that was wholly at variance with the heroic narrative of Andrew Mellon and his fellow bankers, businessmen, and industrialists. Needless to say, they did not share FDR's view that their day as "great promoters" and "financial Titans" was past.

Roosevelt, it must be said, was never hostile to capitalism per se. On the contrary, he saw his prime task in 1933 as saving the American nation, which essentially meant saving the American economy. To that extent, there was no disagreement between FDR and those titans he had rhetorically (for now) brushed aside. But while they might have agreed on ends, they differed quite profoundly on means. This was partly a matter of divergent attitudes toward the business cycle and its ups and downs. For Roosevelt, the Great Depression had a human face: it was above all a terrible, wrenching human catastrophe for millions and millions of ordinary Americans, and one wholly unacceptable in a modern, urban, industrial democracy; like any scourge, it must be battled and beaten, routed and remedied, by all the urgent, determined and vigorous action government could muster. Yet for Mellon and his ilk, this latest downturn, however unprecedented in its deep and widespread severity, was but a part of the natural economic order of things. It was a symptom of a disease whose only cure was a harsh purgative of previous excesses, and the inevitable suffering must be stoically endured by every patriot until the poison had drained out of the system and good times returned—as, by immutable law, they naturally would. The last thing that was needed was "hasty and unwise legislation that might lead to new evils."[6]

This disagreement was fundamental, but it was only part of a much broader divergence of views, about the nature of the American economy and the sort of society to which it had given rise; and also about the role of government and the legitimate reach of the American state. For FDR wanted not merely to mobilize latent, as yet unused executive power to tame the excesses of economic fluctuations; he also wanted to deploy it to remedy what he regarded as capitalism's more deep-rooted problems and systemic abuses. On the one hand, the greedy, selfish indulgences of the rich, the heedless unaccountability of their great corporations, and the inadequate regulation of business and finance; on the other, the lack of trade union rights, of provision for health care, of unemployment benefits, and of old-age pensions for ordinary people—in other words the total lack, in this state of nature known as the American economy, of what we today call a social safety net. These imbalances, Roosevelt believed, urgently needed to be righted, because without such reforms American capitalism might not survive. Mellon et al. disagreed point for point: they took for granted the blessings and inequities alike of the free market; they believed in individual liberty, self-help, and self-advancement; and they accorded labor no rights but a day's (meager) pay for a day's work. And they viscerally opposed, indeed dreaded, government intervention, which would perforce be malevolently intrusive and financially irresponsible, no matter how apparently benevolent its motives.

Fundamental philosophical and ideological differences between right and left suddenly came into sharp focus in America, as FDR advanced a new and radical national agenda into the nation's politics, mobilizing popular opinion against what he graphically depicted as the old, tired, unsympathetic, discredited Republican order of politicians and businessmen: Andrew Mellon and his brethren. But there were also differences of style as much as of substance. Despite the ravages of polio, Roosevelt was a man of exceptional charm, charisma, and physical presence. He radiated confidence, buoyancy, purpose, and hope; he was articulate, eloquent, and a maker of memorable phrases. He also possessed remarkable insight, imagination, and intuition, including a rare instinctive feel for American public opinion. It was an odd facility for one to the manor born—and one largely absent in his self-made predecessors, Harding, Coolidge, and Hoover, and completely absent in the case of Andrew Mellon. They would never have said, in the words of Roosevelt's first inaugural, that "the only thing we have to fear is fear itself," nor would they have dreamed of calling for a period of "continuous experimentation" so that "bold executive power" might be wielded to wage war against "the emergency" with which America was now faced.[7]

The inaugural address made an electrifying impact, as FDR denounced the incompetent and finance-enthralled administrations of the past twelve years, which he himself had been elected to overturn and supersede.[8] He painted a harrowing picture of the economic and social devastation over which Hoover and his cabinet colleagues had so impotently and ineptly presided:

> Values have shrunken to fantastic levels; taxes have risen; our ability to pay has fallen; government of all kinds is faced by serious curtailment of income; the means of exchange are frozen in the currents of trade; the withered leaves of industrial enterprise lie on every side; farmers find no market for their produce; the savings of many years in thousands of families are gone . . . ; a host of unemployed citizens faced the grim problem of existence.[9]

Roosevelt laid the blame for this dismal and deplorable state of affairs squarely on the "false leadership" of three successive Republican presidencies: a "generation of self-seekers" and "unscrupulous money changers" who had sought to seduce the American people with the "lure of profit," but who now stood "indicted in the court of public opinion" and who had been summarily "rejected by the hearts and minds of men."[10] It was a favorite rhetorical and political device of FDR's, one that he had frequently deployed during the campaign and would continue to employ throughout his presidency: the diatribe against vaguely but resonantly defined social groups, which he described only in broad moralistic caricatures. And there could be no doubt that this was the group to which Andrew Mellon belonged.

The rest of the speech dealt in similarly broad generalities, some distinctly more conciliatory than these flights of scapegoating rhetoric. "Happiness," the president insisted, "lies not in the mere possession of money; it lies in the joy of achievement, in the thrill of creative effort." Mellon would certainly have agreed with that sentiment: indeed, he might have regarded those words as both a summary and a justification of his own life in banking, business, and government. He might also have taken some comfort in learning that Roosevelt was determined to restore "an adequate but sound currency," and also to make "income balance outgo." But alongside such reassuring expressions of fiscal conservatism, the new president was also proposing an unprecedentedly radical executive interventionism, of "action and action now" that included putting the people back to work, raising agricultural prices, providing aid to rural and urban homeowners, bringing "an end to speculation with other people's money," launching some "greatly needed projects to stimulate and reorganize the use of our natural resources," and introducing comprehensive regulation of utilities and of the financial securities industries.[11] This was a sweeping agenda of government interference in the economic and social life of the nation, the like of which had never before been outlined in any president's inauguration speech, and to some the more unsettling for being so heavy on rhetoric but light on detail.

During the first hundred days of Roosevelt's presidency, from early March to mid-June 1933, his deeds matched his words: Congress was inundated with bills, all of which were passed with remarkable (and often bipartisan) alacrity.[12] The first matter to be addressed was the deepening financial crisis, and almost immediately after he took office Roosevelt issued a proclamation closing all the banks in the country until Friday, March 10. Meanwhile, the Emergency Banking Act was rushed through Congress, authorizing the issuance of special currency backed by bank assets, which was immediately distributed around the banking system to deal with further heavy withdrawals, should these continue once the banks reopened, as they began to do on Monday, March 13. At the same time, the banks were encouraged to improve their own positions by recapitalization or by merger, facilitated by the heavy investment of the Reconstruction Finance Corporation. As they were certified sound by the Treasury, banks gradually reopened across the country. The Mellon banks in Pittsburgh were among the first to do so.[13]

Recovery was also encouraged by FDR's expressions of confidence (not wholly consistent with statements made in his inauguration speech) in the banking system and in the great majority of bankers, as proclaimed in his first presidential press conference and his first "fireside chat."[14] Later in the year, Congress would pass what became known as the second Glass-Steagall Act, which guaranteed all bank deposits up to $2,500 and divorced commercial from investment banking; both provisions were aimed at strengthening depositors' security. In the future, Americans of modest means with bank accounts could rest assured that they were backed by the federal government, and it would no longer be so easy for bankers to speculate "using other people's money." This was a major piece of interventionist legislation, more a congressional than a presidential initiative, and bank failures in the United States became extremely rare thereafter.[15] It was informed by the revelations of the recent and still-continuing congressional inquiries into the banking system, which provided abundant evidence of the irresponsible investments that had been made by many bankers, who had misused the deposits entrusted to them. As such, it was a serious blow to the Mellons, for it meant that in future the Union Trust Company, like all such organizations, could no longer both accept deposits as a bank and also be involved in underwriting and issuing corporate securities.[16]

Two further measures showed that Roosevelt was determined to deliver on his promise—which the Republicans never took seriously—to put people back to work, by bold experimentation and executive order. One was the creation of the Civilian Conservation Corps. Charged with tidying up the countryside, it was empowered to recruit across the nation from among the young unemployed. By June 1933, three-quarters of a million Americans had been enrolled to clean up forests and national parks, and to make trails and build camping grounds; the program was so successful that it lasted until 1942. Even more important was the establishment soon after of the Tennessee Valley Authority, a vast program of rural development encompassing some of the poorest parts of the country, ranging far beyond Tennessee itself, over Virginia, North Carolina, Kentucky, Georgia, Alabama, and Mississippi. Here deep rural poverty was exacerbated by regular flooding and widespread malaria, and only 3 percent of farms were supplied with electricity. No region was more desperately in need of a "new deal." Dams were constructed, the floods were controlled, and irrigation schemes were created. The dams generated electricity which was transmitted across the region, stimulating new industries, better education, and improved health. There were some initial teething troubles, but no one could deny the success of this major transformation of a hitherto-forgotten region.[17]

The TVA was one sign of FDR's concern for the rural sector, which distinguished him from his Republican predecessors, especially Mellon; he constantly insisted he was a farmer himself. The Agricultural Adjustment Act was another. Designed to rationalize agricultural markets, where surpluses had driven down prices and thus farmers' incomes, the bill made it possible to pay farmers *not* to grow the staple products of wheat, cotton, hogs, and tobacco—an utter heresy to free marketeers. It was, in short, a much strengthened version of the McNary-Haugen bills, which Mellon had so vehemently opposed, and it aimed to mitigate the squalor and near despair to which many American farmers had been reduced since the early 1920s. At the same time, Roosevelt also signed the National Industrial Recovery Act, showing himself equally concerned with the other side of the economy. Its most conspicuous result was the establishment of the Public Works Administration, which would fund building projects across the nation. But there was also an initially little-noticed provision, in section 7a, which mandated federal regulation of maximum hours and minimum wages in various industries, and which stipulated the right of industrial labor "to organize and bargain collectively through representatives of their own choosing." With the authority of the federal government behind the right of workers to organize themselves, there was soon a sudden upsurge in trade union membership, and for the remainder of FDR's presidency, American labor was overwhelmingly Democratic.[18]

Roosevelt addressed one more matter during these early months, again in a decisive and mold-breaking way. On April 19, 1933, he voluntarily suspended dollar convertibility. Unlike Britain and many other European countries, America was not forced off the gold standard; rather, the dollar was strategically floated in the belief that this would help raise domestic prices, which it duly did. But FDR had another purpose. Within days, the World Economic Conference, which Andrew Mellon had helped to plan and organize during his final months as ambassador, met in London. It was the last major gathering of those bankers and financiers who had tried (with some success) to restore national currencies and international credit in the aftermath of the First World War, arrangements that had unraveled in the aftermath of the events of 1929–32. By the end of the proceedings, the British, French, and American delegates reached an agreement limiting exchange-rate fluctuations among their respective currencies, and they issued a cautious commitment to return to the gold standard under "proper" but unspecified conditions. When he learned of the agreement, the president decisively rejected it: the dollar would stay off gold, and the national economy was far more important than any temporary agreement to calm international nerves. And he dismissed the stabilization pact as no more than an amalgam of the "old fetishes of so-called international bankers."[19]

Virtually all of the actions of FDR's first hundred days were anathema to Andrew Mellon (only the repeal of Prohibition, which Roosevelt also undertook during the summer of 1933, commanded his approval). Anathema and utterly counter-intuitive: if, for instance, bankers did not behave prudently and responsibly, it would be better for them to go out of business than to be bailed out by Washington.[20] The separation between commercial and investment banking, apart from being bad news for Union Trust, seemed wrongheaded and retrograde. Government expenditure on job creation, whether in national parks or in the Tennessee Valley, must have smacked to him of socialism. As for schools and courthouses and hospitals, these were no more qualified to receive federal funds during the 1930s (out of tax revenues) than they had been to receive the state funds that had been lavished on them during the 1920s (from the sale of tax-exempt bonds). Never having harbored a shred of agrarian romance, he must have thought the notion of paying farmers *not* to produce was better suited to a satire of statism than to thoughtful policy. Like his father, like Frick and like everyone in his circle, Mellon had always opposed organized labor, and the last thing any government should have been doing was coming to its support. The market should be left alone—except, of course, on the international scene, where it was the duty and obligation of bankers to try to restore and maintain a stable monetary system built on the gold standard. Perversely, Roosevelt now viewed this essential interventionism with scorn, and rejoiced at its demise.

As the summer of 1933 proceeded, Andrew Mellon was hardly alone in his growing disenchantment with the new president and his policies, for these months witnessed a marked deterioration in relations between Roosevelt and bankers and big businessmen. At the outset, and with the whole financial system (and thus, potentially, their own fortunes) at risk, they had been willing to give him the benefit of the doubt, despite the hostile tone of his inaugural. That had certainly been Mellon's own view. But as confidence in the banks returned, as industrial production picked up, and as unemployment began to fall, their relief at what he had done turned to hostility at what he was now doing and threatening to do, and they began to denounce FDR in extravagant terms as a communist, a fascist, a socialist, a dictator, a tyrant, and a traitor to his class. "Our institutions," Ogden Mills would soon write to Mellon, showing the paranoia by which many of his views were afflicted, "are today in greater danger than at any time since the founding of the Republic." David Finley wholeheartedly agreed, and so did Mellon himself.[21]

For his part, the new president returned the bankers' disdain. During the 1920s, financiers had been held in high public regard throughout the western world, as the altruistic and seemingly infallible architects of domestic economic recovery and of international economic stabilization. Now they were scorned as the proud, selfish, irresponsible incompetents who had presided over a false boom before 1929, and had brought the world close to ruin thereafter: "usurious money-lenders from the temple of international finance," who must be curbed, regulated, and controlled.[22] In the new world of the New Deal, public esteem for bankers was decidedly out of fashion—a change in mood well symbolized at just this time by the appearance of J. P. Morgan Jr. before the Senate Committee on Banking and Currency. When asked why he had paid no income tax for nearly three years, he replied that he did not know and that it was a matter for his accountant. It was a feeble, humbling spectacle compared to the bravura confidence and patriotic conviction that his father had displayed before the House's Pujo Committee investigating the "money trust" just twenty years earlier.[23]

Before Roosevelt, it had hardly occurred to most Americans to blame the current depression on the banking plutocracy in general rather than on Andrew Mellon in particular. The shift in public regard, away from financiers as the guardians and geniuses of the economy, in favor of the federal government assuming a much-enlarged mandate of management and regulation, indicated the radicalism of what FDR had wrought within a few months of assuming office. Every sacred truth, spoken and unspoken, of Andrew Mellon and his colleagues—about the trade cycle, about individual self-reliance, about laissez-faire, about bankers and bosses, about workers and unions, about minimally intrusive government—and above all the overarching belief that the late nineteenth century was the best of all possible worlds, were simply washed away. And this was a political revolution that the ideologues and intellectuals soon hastened to join and to proclaim. During the 1930s, the political affiliation of most American professors turned markedly leftward, where it generally remains today. Figures like Nicholas Murray Butler, president of Columbia University and a major force in Republican politics for decades, became utter anachronisms. Likewise, a whole new generation of writers emerged, among them John Steinbeck and John Dos Passos, whose work conveyed with indelible vividness those terrible aspects of American life for which the Republicans were now blamed, ranging from the pollution and poverty of Pittsburgh to the dirt and devastation of the Dust Bowl.

Thus was Andrew Mellon's political world turned upside down by the first "hundred days" of FDR's New Deal, and it would continue thus inverted during the remaining years of his life—and beyond. Indeed, the America to which Mellon returned in April 1933 was becoming a starkly different country from the one he had left in March 1932. In the midterm elections of 1934, continued and intensified popular support for FDR was translated into Democratic gains in Congress: their seats in the House increased from 313 to 322, and in the Senate from 60 to 69. This was wholly contrary to the conventional midterm pattern, whereby the ruling party usually got taken down a peg or two, and it was an ominous indication that Roosevelt's revolution was by no means over. For Mellon, the consequences were very serious, portending reversals for himself, for his companies, and for his political fortunes in Pennsylvania. Having lived most of his life in the mainstream of American business, politics, and history, it would come as a most unpleasant shock to find himself, in his declining years, very much at odds with the new and irrepressible spirit of the times. These were wrenching upheavals and disorienting circumstances for any man in his late seventies to confront, especially one so closely identified with the now-derided Republican old guard. As the ocean liner carried him westward across the Atlantic, at the end of his year t Prince's Gate, to what he hoped would be a peaceful and creative retirenent, Mellon could not have imagined that the most challenging and controversial years of his life still lay ahead.

II. PENNSYLVANIA POLITICS TRANSFORMED

The political revolution that Roosevelt was creating in Washington also undermined Mellon's position in Pennsylvania and in Pittsburgh.[24] As it had been since the death of Boies Penrose, the state Republican Party as it headed into the elections of 1932 remained disputatious and divided over personalities, priorities of the eastern versus the western parts of the state, and the issue of Prohibition. As the Pennsylvania economy tumbled still deeper into recession, the state-wide standing of the GOP suffered further. The Republican senatorial primary, held that spring, shortly after Mellon's departure for London, showed Governor Pinchot still at war with the Vare machine in Philadelphia, whose man, the incumbent Senator James J. Davis, would be carried to decisive victory. Governor Pinchot, although a Republican, had never been an admirer of Hoover's, and now came out strongly against his renomination. For their part, the Mellons still disliked both the Vare faction (the Philadelphia antagonists to Pittsburgh interests) and Pinchot (a friend of Prohibition and an enemy of big business, as well as a long-standing family enemy whose wife was a strong supporter of organized labor). But with Mellon away, and WL ineffectual and out of touch, the family was in little evidence in state politics during 1932.

Meanwhile, the Democrats' hopes rose with each new dip in the local economy. Since the Civil War, Pennsylvania had elected only one governor and two senators who were Democrats: despite the Republicans' internal quarrels, it was still a single-party state. Andrew Mellon had always accepted this dominance as a matter of course and promoted it accordingly as but another facet of the natural order of things. But all this now gave way to a most unnatural change, as jobless rolls swelled, local relief efforts were overwhelmed, and the state became dotted with Hoovervilles. The pastor of Old St. Patrick's Roman Catholic Church, Father James R. Cox, led the Pittsburgh jobless on a march to Harrisburg (where Governor Pinchot fed them) and to Washington (where President Hoover mostly averted his gaze) early in 1932. At the same time, Joseph Guffey, a nephew of Andrew Mellon's partner-turned-adversary and like his uncle a lifelong Democrat, began to revive the state's largely dormant party machinery. He fielded promising young local candidates, such as David Lawrence, Warren Van Dyke, and Lawrence Rupp; and he established close, cordial contacts with Roosevelt, who was by then the Democratic front-runner, to whom Guffey would deliver a majority of the state's delegates at the party's national convention in July 1932.[25]

Part cause, part consequence of these developments was a significant abandonment of the state GOP by hitherto loyal constituencies. Blacks had supported the party since the days of Lincoln, but during the early 1930s, their allegiance began to shift. As mostly unskilled workers, their suffering was especially severe during the Depression, and the Democrats exploited their disenchantment and misery with great effectiveness. Sensing a voting bloc of potentially major significance for his party, Guffey cultivated close relations with their leaders, including Robert Vann of Pittsburgh, whose newspaper, the *Pittsburgh Courier,* with a national black readership, now came out strongly for FDR. At the same time, large numbers of Italian immigrants, reliable Republican voters in the past, began to swing over, in part because Senators Reed and Davis were backing immigration policies unfavorable to their fellow countrymen. Union leaders, much closer to the bosses when there was nothing to be gained by confrontation, had also been traditional Republicans; but as the Depression deepened, such powerful voices as John L. Lewis of the United Mine Workers and John Phillips of the Pennsylvania Labor Federation now declared their allegiance to Roosevelt. Even some businessmen crossed the party line: the proprietors of the local Benedum-Trees oil company gave money to the Democrats instead of the Republicans, as did the owners of the *Pittsburgh Press.*

Despite these developments, Roosevelt failed to win Pennsylvania in November 1932: it was indeed the only major industrial state he did not carry. He won 1,269,000 votes to Hoover's 1,454,000. The incumbent Senator Davis also got himself re-elected by 1,375,000 votes to 1,200,000. Thanks to the Vare machine, the Republicans easily took Philadelphia again, and they held large parts of the rural regions, where, notwithstanding severe hardship, the "dry" farmers tended to prefer Hoover on Prohibition over Roosevelt and his call for repeal. Nevertheless, this was the poorest showing by the Republicans since they had gained control of the state during the Civil War. Most humiliating for the local oligarchs, Roosevelt carried Pittsburgh (by 27,000 votes), taking twenty-six of the city's thirty-two wards, and Allegheny County went Democratic (by 37,000 votes) for the first time since 1856. Guffey's rival machine was now up and running, collecting workingmen and -women and the unemployed, the immigrants and the blacks, as each group moved inexorably leftward.[26] It was not enough to overturn all at once more than half a century of entrenched Republican rule, but in Pennsylvania, as elsewhere in the country, the political tide in 1932 was running very strongly the Democrats' way, and transformation would be a matter of months rather than decades.

The Democrats' conquest of Washington only further strengthened their position in the state. With his direct line to the White House, Joseph Guffey was in effective control of all local federal patronage: Homer S. Cummings, FDR's new attorney general, made no appointments in Pennsylvania without the endorsement of the first of the "liberal bosses."[27] As a result, David Lawrence became collector of internal revenue for Pittsburgh, Warren Van Dyke was offered the same post in Philadelphia, and immigrants and blacks took a significant share of the blue-collar spoils. By mid-1933, the recently revived Democratic State Committee was as well organized as the venerable Republican Party machine. And with the help of the maverick Republican Governor Pinchot, who made common cause with FDR, Democrats in the state legislature passed a succession of reforms concerning child and female labor and old-age pensions. The New Deal had come to Pennsylvania, and the voters liked what they saw: the Republicans were now cast as "mean people," or "the rich man's party," whereas the Democrats championed "the little people." One prominent black leader maintained that two-thirds of his community was now openly Democratic, while a Vare lieutenant lamented that voters were "going toward the Democratic Party like an ocean tide."[28]

The metaphor was apt, for here was the beginning of a sea change in Pennsylvania politics: within two years, the electoral landscape, so permanent and so familiar to Andrew Mellon, would become utterly unrecognizable. Following the trend, and exacerbating his chagrin, was the publication, in August 1933, of Harvey O'Connor's sensational exposé, *Mellon's Millions*. The author, a muckraker in the tradition of Lincoln Steffens, was an acknowledged anti-capitalist who had produced the book with extraordinary speed. He had begun it in February 1932, just as Mellon was leaving the Treasury for London. It would, O'Connor informed his subject, in words that could be interpreted in different ways, be "an absorbing biographical study, illustrative of the rise of a great American fortune." Mellon refused to talk to O'Connor, claiming (via David Finley) pressure of work, nor did any of his associates have any dealings with the author.[29] Not surprisingly, then, there were some serious errors in the book, as in his account of the Carnegie Steel buyout (he completely misunderstood and overestimated Mellon's role), and in his wildly exaggerated calculations of the combined Mellon family wealth, which he put at $2.5 billion, yielding an annual income of $60 million.[30]

Nevertheless, O'Connor did undertake extensive researches, a surprising number of people were willing to talk to him, Wright Patman had gladly cooperated with him, and he made devastating use of the Judge's autobiography (especially the account of his marriage), as well as of Dick Mellon's embarrassing testimony on the Pittsburgh Coal Company to the Senate committee, which he reprinted in full as an appendix.[31] O'Connor depicted Mellon's upbringing as brutal and cold, the story of the divorce was retold with melodramatic effect, and he more than hinted at Mellon's temperamental failings. In describing the formation of Mellon companies, O'Connor alleged stock watering in the case of Pittsburgh Coal, and devoted much space to Alcoa's monopoly on aluminum and the congressional investigations which had been fended off during the 1920s. He described the blatant favoritism that the State Department had shown Gulf in the oil company's pursuit of licenses and concessions overseas. He also detailed the entrenched anti-labor attitudes which he insisted existed in all Mellon companies. Finally, he insisted that through his extensive investments and his multifarious family trusts and connections, Andrew Mellon had become a manipulative malefactor, unaccountable to anyone.

The Pittsburgh newspapers refused to publish reviews of O'Connor's work, and local booksellers declined to stock it; still, the timing of the publication could not have been more damaging for Mellon, and in the radical euphoria of Roosevelt's first months the book received a great deal of public notice.[32] To those who shared the president's dislike of bankers and big business, it offered support for FDR's denunciations, and although not sold or reviewed in Pittsburgh, it clearly benefited from, and added impetus to, a growing hostility to the Mellons that was developing in their hometown. To top it all, it had laid bare many details of Mellon's personal life and business career which he had always fought hard to keep secret. This was not the sort of treatment he had expected five months after ending what he looked back on as a lifetime of patriotic endeavor, financial success, creative entrepreneurship, and public service. And even some reviews which were more sympathetic to Mellon than to the book could not fail to note how rapidly and how completely his reputation had recently plummeted. "Few stars," *Time* magazine observed, "have receded into space more swiftly than, in a few months' time, the 'greatest-Secretary-of-the-Treasury-since-Alexander-Hamilton' has receded into history."[33]

Mellon was both enraged and wounded by the book. Instead of ignoring it, he went to extraordinary lengths in a vain attempt to combat it. He hired a lawyer, J. M. Daiger, on a retainer of $600 a month, but it proved impossible "to suggest any form of legal relief."[34] He issued a press statement, denouncing the "so-called biography" as a "travesty of truth." The figures for the Mellon family fortune were "so fantastic and imaginary as to be senseless." The book alleged "huge ownership in many companies with which I do not have, and never had had, any connection or interest whatever." There were "many false statements in respect to private affairs" and "malevolent innuendos in respect to personality." "To call it," Mellon concluded, "as it is advertised, 'a balanced and impartial story,' is to confuse scurrility with biography."[35] David Finley, himself aghast, assured Mellon the book was "so patently vindictive" as to "defeat its own end," but a great deal of the mud did stick. In its tone, its texture, its intent, and its impact, the book showed just how far the political pendulum had swung against Mellon since Philip H. Love's admiring biography of only four years ago.[36]

For national offices, 1933 was an "off" year, but in Pittsburgh and Allegheny County, the mayoralty, several seats on the city council, and even the county sheriff were all up for re-election. The Republicans put up John S. Herron, who had been acting mayor since his predecessor, Charles Kline, had been sent to prison, convicted on charges of abuse of office. But Kline's disgrace had shaken the local GOP, Herron proved uninspiring, and in both the city and the county, the Republican organization was in deep disarray. The Democrats nominated William N. McNair, who had long served the party in the district, and he was supported by Michael Benedum, Joseph Guffey, and David Lawrence, and a reinvigorated organization. McNair campaigned now negatively, now positively—but always effectively. Taking a page from O'Connor's book, he made an issue of the avarice of "Mellonism," and all the evils he insisted the family had inflicted on the city, including the present depressed economy. Contrasting Republican failure to end the Depression with the successes of the Democrats and their public works programs, he handily defeated Herron by 28,000 votes.[37]

McNair's victory was part of an unprecedented Democratic sweep in Pittsburgh and Allegheny County: the party won control of the city council, and they took all the other offices that were up for election, including the post of county sheriff. This "Democratic conquest" of Pittsburgh, rightly described as a "political revolution," mimicked at the local level, and drew momentum from, the one that FDR was effecting nationwide.[38] It irrevocably revised traditional patterns of voting and power in the city. In terms of registration, the Democrats remained the minority party in 1933, but a majority of registered *Republicans* had also voted Democratic. Where Roosevelt had failed to carry a majority of black and Italian votes, McNair had no such difficulty. And while only the *Pittsburgh Press* had thrown its allegiance to FDR, now the *Post-Gazette* and the *Sun-Telegraph* abandoned tradition and followed suit. Even more striking, such staunch Republican machine politicians as former mayor William A. Magee, son of Christopher Magee, refused to support Herron, and instead endorsed McNair and worked to elect Democrats. They could see the way the electoral wind was blowing: indeed, it was a veritable tornado, sweeping away the Republicans in the city and across Allegheny County.[39]

Elsewhere in the state, it was much the same for the once-invincible GOP organization. In Philadelphia, the Vare machine was jammed by a coalition consisting of a revived Democratic Party and disaffected Republicans who produced a "fusion ticket." It was supported by both Joseph

Guffey and Governor Pinchot, and most of its candidates were former Vare lieutenants who, like their fellow Republicans in Pittsburgh, had defected from the party they knew could not win. As in the western part of the state, there was a clamor for more radical leadership, a strong endorsement of FDR's more vigorous policies, and many immigrant and black voters abandoned the Republicans. And so, again, for the first time since the days of Lincoln, the voters of Philadelphia turned against the GOP: the fusion ticket overwhelmed the Vare machine and took the elected offices as well as the spoils of patronage. In Scranton, meanwhile, a Democrat was elected mayor; Erie City voted in a Democratic council; even some of the farming regions were beginning to sow a Democratic crop. The *New York Times* did not exaggerate in describing the statewide results as "a political revolution without parallel."[40]

The final reckoning in Pennsylvania came in 1934, when the Democrats swept almost everything before them.[41] It was a crucial midterm year: the governorship was up for grabs because Pinchot could not run again, but Senator David A. Reed was eagerly and anxiously seeking reelection. Pennsylvania had not sent a Democrat to the U.S. Senate since 1874 and to the governor's mansion since 1890. But the GOP was not only besieged from without, it was also seriously divided within. A bitter contest for the Senate nomination arose when the pro-Roosevelt Pinchot challenged Reed in the primary, depicting him as a Mellon puppet and a reactionary who would never support (as Pinchot himself had done) the legislation that was urgently needed to restore prosperity to the state.[42] After managing to win the nomination, Reed was joined on the ticket by William A. Schadner, the state attorney general, who was running for governor with the strong support of what remained of the Vare machine. Against them, the Democrats ran Joseph Guffey for senator, and George H. Earle for governor. Guffey, a lifelong Democrat and supporter of FDR's, was the key architect of the party's revival in the state; Earle, scion of an old Philadelphia family, had renounced inherited loyalties in 1932 to support Roosevelt, but he also had an impressive record of military and public service.

The ensuing campaign amounted to a referendum on the New Deal as it had so far been enacted. Reed's only hope was to distance himself from Mellon, but he took the conventional Republican line: he denounced Roosevelt's recent legislative torrent as nothing but a series of "broken promises," dismissed Democratic policies as "futile and fantastic," and warned that the country was headed for "complete chaos" unless the Republicans were returned to power. He insisted that FDR was leading the nation down the road to socialism, ruining the spirit of American individualism while amassing despotic power himself. For their part, Guffey and Earle campaigned along no less predictable but much more appealing lines.[43] They made it personal, retorting that there was no longer enough Mellon money to buy state elections, scorning Reed as a Mellon client, and denouncing the former treasury secretary for letting the Bank of Pittsburgh collapse. They indicted the Republicans for mishandling the nation's affairs, for their constant and determined oppression of ordinary people, and for being the party of big business. And they insisted that federal intervention in the economy was not socialism, but necessary action to protect people from the ravages of unrestrained "corporate interests." Echoing Roosevelt, they also promised to support old-age pensions and unemployment insurance.

The outcome of the election was never in doubt. Harold Ickes came down from Washington to speak in support of the Democratic candidates.[44] Most of the state's newspapers supported the Guffey-Earle ticket. Immigrant voters continued their march toward the Democrats, in part provoked by the charge that Reed had described the Italians as "an inferior race." Blacks also voted Democratic in unprecedented numbers, encouraged by David Lawrence's endorsement of Negro leaders like Homer Brown and Paul Jones for prominent public offices in Pittsburgh. Andrew Mellon was convinced that "the tide is now settling in against the Democrats and Rooseveltism," and that the Republican ticket would win "by a very large and satisfactory majority."[45] In fact, the GOP lost almost everywhere. Guffey defeated Reed, and Earle defeated Schnader, becoming the first Democratic governor since 1890 and only the second since 1860. A Democrat was also elected lieutenant governor (a former official of the United Mine Workers, who helped deliver the union vote), and the party gained a majority in Pennsylvania's delegation to the House, as well as dominating both houses of the state assembly. Carrying Pittsburgh and Allegheny County, and most other counties across the state, they even came within a whisker of taking complete control of that bastion of East Coast Republicanism, Philadelphia itself.

The devastation of Pennsylvania's GOP was the most extraordinary result of the 1934 midterm elections. In 1930, the Democrats had been able to control only 26 percent of the popular vote; two years later, 47 percent went to Roosevelt; now they had captured 52 percent of the vote.[46] Put another way, in a mere four years, the Democratic Party had advanced from being a hopeless and seemingly perennial minority to a formidable majority. For the first time in sixty years, a Democrat from Pennsylvania would now represent the state in the Senate, and for the first time in forty-four, a Democratic governor would sit in Harrisburg. And this was no mere ephemeral victory, for it marked the end of Pennsylvania as a Republican fiefdom. In 1936, FDR would carry the state, and he would do so again in 1940 and in 1944. In 1940, Senator Guffey would also be re-elected, and Pittsburgh itself would become a well-nigh impregnable Democratic fortress. To be sure, the Republicans were beaten but not dead: they would make significant gains in 1938, when they won back the governorship and held the second Senate seat, and they would stage a serious revival throughout the 1950s. But never again would Pennsylvania be the one-party GOP stronghold that it had been for most of Andrew Mellon's life, and never again would Pittsburgh be a one-party Republican town. To that extent, Arthur Krock of the *New York Times* was quite right in describing 1934 as the Pennsylvania Republicans' Austerlitz.[47]

In Pittsburgh as in Washington, then, a political revolution was under way, and few on either side failed to recognize it as such (though Sarah Mellon Grange, James Ross Mellon's daughter, who had assured her "Uncle Andy" late in 1933 that "President Roosevelt is losing public confidence" and that the "tide was turning" in favor of the Republicans, was not one of them).[48] The revolution's aim may in part have been the conservative one of preserving capitalism, but Andrew Mellon and his peers saw in it no such virtuous purpose. They resented Roosevelt's attacks on their patriotism, they disapproved of his dictatorial meddling in violation of every business precept, and they deplored the proliferation of federal agencies, with their competing jurisdictions, baffling acronyms, and bloated payrolls. The Mellon clan had another motive for loathing Roosevelt and all he stood for. Although Roosevelt's rage against Republican bankers and businessmen had been expressed in very broad terms at the national level, it had been much more tightly focused in Pennsylvania, and most particularly in Pittsburgh: on the Mellons, and above all on Andrew Mellon himself. The elections of 1933 and 1934 had been fought in terms of such explicitly ad hominem renunciation as never had been heard in Pittsburgh or the rest of the state. The political allegiance, public respect, and social deference previously accorded Mellon, his clan and cohort, and to which they still felt themselves entitled, had simply evaporated.

III. GLOOM AND STRIFE IN PITTSBURGH

Out of office and a private citizen once again, Andrew Mellon no longer felt obliged to be in Washington so much; with the capital now dominated by Roosevelt and the Democrats, and with the Federal Triangle project in abeyance, he was far removed from its social and political heart. But for Pittsburgh's most famous (or, by some lights, most infamous) son, the town he had helped create had also become hostile and unwelcoming. Mellon was no longer a political force in the city, the county, or the state, and he was widely blamed for the depression. "Why do they turn against me?" he once plaintively asked Chancellor Bowman of the University of Pittsburgh. "I am the same man now I was before."[49] That, for many Pittsburghers, was precisely the problem. Choosing the lesser evil, Mellon resolved to spend most of his time in Washington, where Donald Shepard, now joined by David Finley, was in charge of his legal affairs. For the remainder of Mellon's life, Shepard (along with Finley and David Bruce) would be closest to him. "He is," Duveen was informed by his New York office, "the man that we will have to keep in touch with in future when making any arrangements."[50]

Pittsburgh would catch sight of Mellon only "as business demands." It was a clear sign of his alienation—and of his resolution—that his paramount objective would be to realize his plan for a national gallery, rather than to re-insert himself in the banking and industrial life of his native city, or into the political turmoil of western Pennsylvania and Allegheny County. Nevertheless, Mellon spent much of the summer of 1933 in Pittsburgh, and he cannot have been encouraged by what he saw and heard. To be sure, the Mellon National Bank, the Union Trust Company, and the Mellbank Corporation had triumphantly weathered the storms of March 1933.[51] But the once-dominant Republican Party lay in ruins, and the idle, benighted industrial landscape presented a stark and sorry contrast to the official grandeur of Washington or London. On the radio, the New Deal evangelist Father Coughlin denounced Mellon by name in his broadcasts, as the embodiment of greedy capitalism in an increasingly impoverished land.[52] As his niece Sarah Mellon Grange informed him, the once-mighty City of Steel was a "discouraging place to live in just now," blighted as it was by "Old Man Depression."[53]

As the economy bottomed out in 1933, Pennsylvania was revealed to be one of the worst-hit states in the Union, and Pittsburgh one of the most beleaguered cities. The coal industry was exceptionally pummeled, and as Governor Pinchot observed, "in the whole range of depression, there is nothing worse than the condition of the soft coal miners" who, if they were lucky enough to have work, were on reduced wages and subject to the strong-arm tactics of their employers. It was not much different in the steel mills, where production was 40 percent off the level attained before the 1929 crash. As a result, by the winter of 1932–33, only two-fifths of the workforce statewide was employed full-time. Pittsburgh's particular hardship was that its core industries had already been languishing, underutilized, during the 1920s. The only justification for a place so blighted and polluted had been that in its prime, things were made there, and people had work. These benefits may not have excused the smoke and soot, the substandard living conditions, or the rampant inequality, yet at least Pittsburgh had functioned and thrived in its fashion. But now, as Lorena Hickok reported back to Harry Hopkins, one of FDR's top men in Washington, the local economy had collapsed, the mines were idle, the steel mills were silent, and the whole place was an environmental nightmare, an economic catastrophe, and a social disaster: "the human wreckage of a century of pell-mell, buccaneering, no holds barred, free market industrial capitalism."[54]

The extent of the local economic turmoil is also vividly indicated by the sudden and serious reduction in Mellon's income. The Mellon National Bank and the Union Trust Company still paid good and steady dividends, but the rest of his companies fared less well; Alcoa's $2.3 million loss in 1932 became a modest net profit of $1.7 million in 1933; but Pittsburgh Coal paid nothing to stockholders.[55] And his income was further reduced as a result of the large blocks of stock he had transferred to Ailsa and Paul. Accordingly, in 1933 and 1934, Mellon's after-tax income averaged one million dollars: a substantial improvement on the loss of 1932, but still a major reduction from the good years of the late 1920s. As a result, and for the first time in his life, he had incurred the "bad habit" of "running in debt."[56] From September to December 1932, he had taken a loan of $875,000 from the Mellon National Bank, returning for another $300,000 in April 1933; he also borrowed $1.6 million from the Union Trust Company in June 1934. Nor was that the end of it: between 1935 and 1937, Mellon would receive on credit another $1,125,000 from the Mellon National Bank, and an additional $5.1 million from the Union Trust Company. All in the form of notes payable at 2 percent, these loans, totaling some $9 million, were secured with stock in Mellon companies, and they would all be outstanding at the time of his death in 1937. Little wonder he bought no major pictures between August 1931 and November 1934.

At the same time, Mellon faced the demands of charity, which perforce began at home.[57] (Even the Judge had not called for a completely blind eye to abject misery: as ever, the question was one of the relative responsibilities of society and individual.) The construction of the new Mellon

Institute and the rebuilding of the East Liberty Presbyterian Church created employment opportunities that Andrew and Dick would have criticized if they had resulted from federal spending. And like Rockefeller Center, under construction in New York at just this time, these building projects expressed the continued confidence of the leading family in the future of their city. Nor did Andrew Mellon neglect charity in its purest form: he gave directly and generously to the Welfare Fund of Pittsburgh. In 1932, following his benefactions of the previous year, he had donated $325,000, and in 1933 he gave another $75,000—combined, these sums exactly equaled the amount he had paid Knoedler in November 1930 for Botticelli's *Portrait of a Young Man.*[58]

But Mellon's unprecedented gestures of private charity were mere palliatives; they could not come close to propping up the old economic, social, and political order. Under the combined impact of the Great Depression and the New Deal legislative response, industrial relations across western Pennsylvania were transformed from the old-style amalgam of "paternal" management, hostility to organized labor, and worker insecurity to a relationship of greater equality engendered by legal provision, collective bargaining, and trade unions. Section 7a of the National Industrial Recovery Act provided an explicit stimulus to union activity in the major mass-production industries. While direct ownership or management of steel companies had never been a major Mellon objective, Andrew and Dick had received substantial holdings in Bethlehem Steel following the sale of McClintic-Marshall, and developments in this quintessential Pittsburgh sector would lead to change in industries with which they had a much closer connection. Soon after he took office, Roosevelt dispatched Frances Perkins, secretary of labor, to the steelmaking communities of western Pennsylvania; she was appalled by what she saw. FDR prevailed upon the chairman of the leading companies, who had refused to recognize any unions, to allow the Department of Labor to negotiate on behalf of the workers. In the end, management reluctantly agreed to a forty-hour week and a minimum hourly wage of forty cents. Workers had been seeking both since the First World War.

Mellon's interests were much greater in other businesses, among them the troubled and unprofitable Pittsburgh Coal Company, where labor was notoriously discontented and where the union had been crushed in the mid-1920s. Here, too, were latent stirrings of redress in what had previously been the hopelessly unequal contest between the owners and the miners. The head of the United Mine Workers of America, John L. Lewis, had responded to Roosevelt's legislation by proclaiming in the summer of 1933 that "the president wants you to join the union." The campaign succeeded in reversing the sharp decline in enrollment over the previous decade, and strikes soon broke out across the coalfields of western Pennsylvania. When one miner was killed and many were injured, Governor Pinchot called out the National Guard. Roosevelt responded by setting up a tribunal chaired by Senator Robert Wagner, to arbitrate the dispute, and he also summoned the industry's leaders to the White House. By October 1933, the first-ever coal industry code had been agreed to: many union demands concerning wages and hours were met, and the feudal monopoly of company stores and lodging was broken. It was the beginning of a revolution in labor-capital relations in the coal-fields which must have turned Mellon's stomach and set Frick spinning in his grave.

Such developments might have been expected at the outset of the New Deal in distressed traditional heavy industries. But the pattern would also be followed in some of the more modern Mellon companies. Alcoa provides an instructive example. During the same summer, 1933, workers there began to organize for higher pay, job security, and better working conditions.[59] The management expressed willingness to recognize an in-house union, which they would effectively control, but in September, workers at New Kensington overwhelmingly rejected the company's feint. Soon after, Hugh Johnson, head of the National Recovery Administration Policy Board, declared his intention to "impose" rigorous labor regulation on the aluminum industry. Thus encouraged, Alcoa workers now sought to form unions independent of the company, and a local chartered at New Kensington demanded a labor contract. Determined to resist, management flatly rejected this demand. Inveighing against "the predatory wealth of the Mellons," the workers responded by going on strike in October 1933. They did not prevail, but this was just the beginning.

Within a few months, trade unions had formed in Alcoa's plants and factories across the whole country, and workers staged a ten-day wildcat strike at the company's Pennsylvania works in March 1934. This first major walk-out in Alcoa's history, involving five thousand employees in all, forced management to agree to a hefty 11 percent increase in wages, but the company still refused to concede legitimacy to the union, or to acknowledge its claim to negotiate on behalf of the workforce. Beginning in mid-August, therefore, a second strike was called. The management took no aggressive action to break it, and after five weeks, the workers eventually capitulated. The company made only those concessions it had been prepared to make before the action: it accepted the principle of

The president's men. Andrew Mellon, seated and second from the left, was the star of the Harding cabinet.

With Calvin Coolidge on the left and Herbert Hoover on the right. Mellon got on better with Coolidge, a kindred taciturn, than with the sharp-elbowed Hoover, formerly his cabinet colleague at the Commerce Department.

The secretary's men in Washington: S. Parker Gilbert (left),
David Finley (right), and Ogden Mills (below).
All a generation younger than Mellon, they, like
David Bruce, were devoted surrogate sons.

Laying a wreath at the feet of Alexander Hamilton, in front of the U.S. Treasury,
to mark the 174th anniversary in 1931 of the department's greatest secretary, to whom,
at the height of pre-Depression prosperity, Mellon was often compared.

ABOVE: Atlantic crossing sometime during the 1920s: one of the world's richest and most powerful men looking frail, lonely, wounded, and forlorn.

LEFT: Ailsa accompanies her father, ambassador to the Court of St. James's, to a reception at Buckingham Palace. Andrew eschewed the traditional knee breeches.

Returning to New York, August 24, 1932, on one of two long stateside visits as ambassador. Mellon would have gladly retained the post had the Republicans retained the White House.

The drawing room in the American Embassy in London during Andrew Mellon's posting. His own pictures adorn the walls, from left: John Hoppner, *The Frankland Sisters*; George Romney, *Portrait of Miss Willoughby*; Sir Thomas Lawrence, *Lady Templeton and Child*; Francisco de Goya, *Marquesa de Pontejos*.

Mellon's architectural stamp on Pittsburgh:
the Mellon National Bank, dedicated by him in May 1924;
the Mellon Institute, also dedicated by him, visibly failing, in May 1937,
during his last visit to his native city. Both exemplify his preference,
labeled reactionary by some, for neoclassical idiom over the art deco style
used in the Koppers and Gulf skyscrapers between 1929 and 1932.

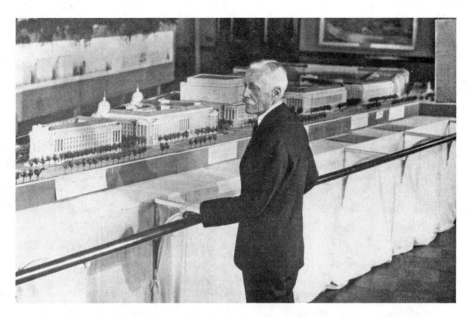

ABOVE: Contemplating the model of the proposed Federal Triangle in April 1929. It would be Mellon's largest building venture, his most enduring mark on the capital. BELOW: The Federal Triangle, ca. 1935. John Russell Pope's National Archive building stands nearest the Capitol. The missing corner of the triangle would eventually be occupied by the Federal Trade Commission, its construction for now delayed by the Great Depression.

FROM LEFT TO RIGHT: Political nemeses: Senator James Couzens,
who bettered Mellon in the "battle of the millionaires" (left);
Rep. Wright Patman, who moved unsuccessfully to have Mellon impeached
in January 1932 (middle); and John Nance Garner, a longtime foe,
who became FDR's first vice president (right).

The old guard and the new:
President Hoover riding glumly with the president-elect,
Franklin Delano Roosevelt, the short way from the White House to the
Capitol for FDR's inauguration, March 4, 1933.

Robert H. Jackson, who represented the U.S. Treasury during
Andrew Mellon's trial for tax evasion, would later be
appointed to the Supreme Court by FDR.

The tax trial: witness for the defense.
Lord Duveen's bravura testimony was a high point in the proceedings.

At the tax trial: impeccably dressed, self-possessed, at once fascinated
and dismayed by the proceedings. Despite his complete exoneration,
which he always expected, Mellon's reputation would not recover in his lifetime.

Fitzpatrick in The St. Louis Post-Dispatch

It seems there are two Uncle Sams and two Andy Mellons.

A cartoon from the time of the tax trial points up
Mellon's oddly paradoxical status
as national benefactor and accused tax cheat.

The National Gallery in London, Mellon's inspiration
and model for the National Gallery of Art in Washington.

The State Hermitage Museum in Leningrad at about the time of Andrew Mellon's art purchases, which transformed his personal collection into the nucleus of a great American benefaction.

The National Gallery dream made reality: (from left to right)
John Russell Pope, America's preeminent neoclassical architect;
Charles Moore, chairman of the Commission of Fine Arts;
and Frederic A. Delano, chairman of the National Capital Park
and Planning Commission (and FDR's uncle).

BELOW: An architectural drawing of the completed National Gallery of Art.
No expense was spared for materials to achieve a cool dignity that banished
any hint of ostentation. (Anticipating future benefactors, Mellon also ensured the
reservation of the adjoining lot for an eventual expansion.)

The most tender and touching image of the famously
austere Andrew Mellon, his granddaughter Audrey on his lap,
her pet hamster perched on his right hand.

LEFT: With Ailsa on Long Island toward
the end of his life. RIGHT: In extremis.

The site of the National Gallery of Art, shortly after groundbreaking in the summer of 1937, by which time the Federal Trade Commission building had been belatedly completed. This was as much of his dream as Andrew Mellon would live to see realized.

Tradition and progress: a semi-abstract neoclassical façade conceals steel construction and other state-of-the art technologies used in building the National Gallery of Art. Despite modern amenities, architectural critics would revile it as retrograde.

The reception to mark the opening of the National Gallery of Art in Washington, March 17, 1941, when FDR formally accepted Mellon's gift on behalf of the American people. The president is at the microphone, and Paul Mellon on the immediate left.

The three-cent commemorative stamp issued in 1955 to mark the centenary of Andrew Mellon's birth. The occasion happened to fall in the middle of the Eisenhower years, a propitious time for Republican friends to promote Mellon's official rehabilitation, though the effort achieved mixed results.

collective bargaining without recognizing the union as labor's exclusive agent, it promised to hold wages constant but not raise them, to refrain from discriminating against union members, and to establish a grievance procedure but one which management would effectively control. Union officials declared that this amounted to "unqualified recognition by the company of the fundamental principles and methods of collective bargaining," but having had a taste of what solidarity could accomplish, the workers believed the union had settled for too little. It would be only a matter of time before a more militant faction would pose a far more aggressive challenge.

There was also trouble for Mellon at his alma mater, the University of Pittsburgh, though it was not of his own making. In June 1934 Chancellor Bowman refused to renew the contract of Professor Ralph E. Turner, a young radical professor who was an ardent supporter of FDR and the New Deal. Various explanations were given for his dismissal, but one of them was that earlier in the year, Turner had delivered a speech at the Historical Society of Western Pennsylvania which, while never mentioning them by name, had been a scathing attack on the Mellon family. The president of the society was John S. Fisher, the former Republican governor, and he complained about Turner to Bowman. But when the news of Turner's dismissal was made public, there was an outcry, and Governor Pinchot demanded an investigation into the state of academic freedom at the university. "If the Mellons want a school to teach their ideas," he observed, assuming Bowman had been acting on instructions, "then let them support it. The Commonwealth cannot." In fact, Mellon had had no part in the affair, and he subsequently sent a letter of rebuke to Bowman, declaring that "if it were Doctor Turner's political beliefs or statements which caused his dismissal, I should be heartily in favor of his immediate re-instatement." But Turner was not re-instated and Mellon's letter was not made public.[60] In addition to his other failings, Mellon was now depicted by his enemies in the city as the opponent of academic freedom, and his battered reputation in Pittsburgh was dealt another blow.

IV. A FAILING AND FALLIBLE FAMILY

Andrew Mellon's family had always offered him at best an imperfect refuge, and at worst it had been a source of consuming agony and anxiety. These years of unremittingly harsh political and economic weather would prove no exception. But now the sadness would come most frequently. In the months immediately after his return from Britain, there was a glut of those "first class funerals" for which R. L. Duffus had called only a few years before, the first of them in some ways the most momentous. Soon after Dick Mellon triumphantly saw the bank through the financial panic of March 1933, his health began to fail. Around Thanksgiving, he went on an inspection tour of a water project related to one of the family businesses, he caught a cold that led to pneumonia, and he died on December 1.[61] Andrew rushed from Washington to Pittsburgh, and he was with Dick at the end. Flags were flown at half-mast across the city, there were fulsome newspaper tributes from Republicans and business leaders, and Dick's casket was placed in a temporary vault in Allegheny Cemetery until his final resting place in East Liberty Presbyterian Church was ready. But not all of Pittsburgh was in mourning, and not everyone shared the view that Richard Mellon had been an agent of "benevolent capitalism." As the funeral cortege wended its way from his house at 6500 Fifth Avenue to the cemetery, many ordinary people looked on—and they glowered. It was a sight one Mellon woman never forgot: for the first time in her life, she saw public hostility and knew real social fear.[62]

"There is a large amount of work to be done," Andrew told Nora, in settling Dick's affairs, so he would "have to help at that for a time. The newspaper articles concerning the extent of his estate are wildly exaggerated." (Dick was rumored to be worth $200 million, but his total stock holdings were subsequently valued at scarcely one-tenth of that figure.)[63] "I felt very sorry about Dick's death," Nora wrote back, "as I know you must feel it very much." It was clear to those close to Andrew that he was "visibly shaken." Dick was the brother with whom birth order had paired him, and with whom he conducted a lifelong and life-defining family partnership. With his death, Andrew had lost a piece of himself. For nearly half a century it had been "my brother and I." No longer. Dick's estate was split between his widow, Jennie; his son, Richard King; and his daughter, Sarah. R. K. Mellon now took over as president of the Mellon National Bank, a promotion that had long been inevitable, and that must also have reminded Andrew that Paul was still dragging his feet about his future career.[64]

Less than a year later, in October 1934, James Ross Mellon passed on. At eighty-eight he was the longest-lived of all the brothers. He had given up business many years before and spent long stretches of the year away from Pittsburgh in Florida; his funeral was a relatively low-key affair. But Andrew once again led the mourners. Of the eight children of the Judge and Sarah Jane, he was now the sole survivor.[65] Yet another sign of the passing of generations would come in March 1935 with the death of Henry C. McEldowney, who had headed the Union Trust Company ever since Andrew Mellon had appointed him more than a third of a century ago. He had been a pillar of the Mellon system, his life was a genuine rags-to-riches story, and his salary was alleged to be more than $150,000.[66] The Scotch-Irish Pittsburgh elite turned out in force for all these somber farewells, and the tribal loyalty in a time more noted for its betrayals must have held some comfort. But each funeral must have reminded Andrew Mellon of his own mortality. And while he still cherished the hope that Paul would take over at Union Trust, as his cousin RK had at the bank, he must have known in his heart of hearts that this was never going to happen.[67] "My brother and I" would not be succeeded by "my cousin and I."

Soon after Dick's death, Andrew was faced with a serious dynastic challenge which had been brewing since the late 1920s but which now asserted itself with formidable force.[68] During 1934, two of the children of his eldest brother (Thomas Alexander Mellon, who had died in 1899) sought to contest the generally accepted view that the Judge had consigned the family bank, T. Mellon & Sons, exclusively to Andrew and Dick, between the years 1875 (when Andrew began to receive one-fifth of the profits) and 1887 (when Andrew and Dick were established as equal partners and sole proprietors). Now Andrew's niece and nephew alleged that their grandfather had assigned ownership of the bank to all four surviving sons equally, as he had undoubtedly done with his real and personal property, which Andrew had managed in trust, on behalf of himself, his three brothers, and their descendants, until the trust was dissolved and its assets distributed in 1919. This claim was brought by Thomas Alexander Mellon Jr. and Mary Mellon McClung, with whom Andrew's previous relations had been friendly and cordial.[69] But now Thomas and Mary (who was married to the lawyer Sam McClung) threatened to bring a lawsuit against their uncle Andrew and against their uncle Dick's estate to secure what they deemed was rightfully theirs, even at the expense, as their attorney put it, of a "public scandal."[70]

At a time when he was already embattled, and with the experience of his divorce never far from his mind, Mellon took the threat very seriously, and his lawyers assembled a mountain of evidence proving his version of the Judge's bequest—which, as they also substantiated, had never previously been challenged, even when T. Mellon & Sons had been transformed into the Mellon National Bank in 1902 and sold to the Union Trust Company. After a bitter confrontation, at which Mellon refused to yield an inch, Mary and Thomas dropped their claims before the end of

1934 and never brought a suit to court.[71] (Their brother, E. P. Mellon, who had always got on well with Andrew, and who had helped design both the Mellon National Bank and the Gulf buildings in Pittsburgh, kept out of the affair altogether.) But it remains a strange episode, wholly inconsistent with the Mellons' usual sense of clannishness and solidarity under fire. Perhaps, in the aftermath of the publication of *Mellon's Millions*, some of Andrew's many enemies in Pittsburgh put Thomas and Mary up to it. Perhaps his relatives believed the exaggerations of his fortune and felt themselves comparatively needy. In the end, the family was reconciled, and in December 1936, Andrew made ten gifts of $5,000 cash to some of his relatives. Five of them went to Mary McClung, her husband, and their three children.[72]

As times grew harder, the desperate letters poured in from distant and increasingly impoverished cousins, on both the Mellon and the Negley sides: for $1,000 here and $500 there, to help with taxes, the mortgage, medical expenses, and dozens of other financial emergencies. Andrew seems to have given all these requests sympathetic consideration, for in 1932, he and Dick had set up a fund for "rendering financial assistance to their needy and worthy relatives, friends or associates," from which was disbursed $22,000 in 1933 and $29,000 the following year.[73] Across the Atlantic, Percy McMullen, who had promised never to appeal to Andrew again, was in new trouble, and doing just what he had sworn not to do. By contrast, Leonard McMullen, always the hardest case, had finally left London (and bookmaking) for Essex, where, according to Nora, he had become "quite the country gentleman, with his sports and bridge parties." But one of his grandchildren was severely crippled with a defective spine, and he continued to importune both Andrew and Nora for money, no longer to pay his gambling debts, but for his granddaughter's medical expenses.[74] As for Nora, Rokeby farm had not proved the home of her fondest wishes. "I felt," she told Andrew, with more wishfulness than realism, "that it was going to be a place for family re-unions and put my whole strength into making it attractive." But then, with Andrew's posting to London, "the whole family went off to England and left me alone with it," and as she had been warned by her neighbors, living in the country under such solitary circumstances was "a fearful risk." Two years later, she left Rokeby for Greenwich in "wild" Connecticut, and there she lived for the rest of her life.[75]

Amidst an abundance of family gloom there was a spot of true light: after seven years of marriage, chronic illness, and periods of depression, Ailsa had finally given Andrew his first grandchild in November 1933, a girl named Audrey Bruce. The general relief that a baby had at last arrived mingled with hope that the infant might improve her mother's mental and physical health, which all adults and medical ministrations had so far failed to accomplish. "I feel greatly gratified over the grandchild, and was so very pleased to see it looking so bright and well," Andrew wrote to Nora, gushing after his fashion, but with his usual clear-eyed view of his own daughter. "It is a blessing for Ailsa. Her interest in the child should take the place of much self-occupation." "Ailsa seems very well, and the baby grows so fast," Nora replied. "I am sure it will be a wonderful thing for Ailsa."[76] "Apart from the happiness it will bring David and Ailsa," David's mother wrote to Andrew, "I think it will be a wonderful thing for her health." But given Ailsa's clinical history, this was an optimistic assessment: within a few months, she would be prostrated once again, this time with chicken pox. Moreover, Ailsa turned out to be as aloof a parent as her father had been, and David Bruce had no particular paternal instinct either. Audrey's rearing would be largely left to governesses, and she would do nothing to cure Ailsa's woes or bring her parents closer together, as they continued on what seemed their glamorous and perpetually itinerant life.[77]

In fact, David and Ailsa were leading ever more separate existences. Within a year of Mellon's gift of Alcoa stock to his son-in-law, David had repurchased Staunton Hill in Virginia, the seat of his idyllic youth, which his father had sold in 1919. He now set about restoring the place to its former antebellum splendor, with the help of the architect William Delano, adding modern bathrooms in the style of the Ritz Hotel in Paris.[78] Eventually he expanded the estate to ten thousand acres, and having thus reestablished himself as the country gentleman he always was at heart, David Bruce resigned from most of his corporate boards early in 1934. He had, he announced, "moved my residence to Virginia," having no taste for "continuing as an idle director," and he was eager to "get out of New York business entirely." He now devoted himself to hunting and shooting and to acts of local charity and noblesse oblige, cherishing no greater ambition than to be elected to the Virginia state legislature. This artificially restored life of old landed money was a long way removed from Ailsa's Manhattan and Long Island life of plutocratic, rootless new wealth. "In the heat of Virginia," David wrote to her, in mild rebuke, "parties seem not only distant but rather undesirable compared with the really important things of life such as planting tobacco and beating rugs."[79]

David Bruce's withdrawal from business may have disappointed Andrew Mellon, but relations between the two remained good. Relations between

Andrew and Paul, however, continued uneasy, in both personal and professional matters.[80] Andrew (and Ailsa, too) had disapproved of Paul's engagement to Delphina Burt, and once father and son were both back in Pittsburgh in the summer of 1933, Andrew composed a chilling memorandum setting out the reasons why it should be broken off. First, he believed, "women grow old faster than men, and differences of age which seem immaterial at thirty are accentuated after forty." ("Differences of age" had, of course, been part of the problem between Andrew and Nora from the very beginning, though for different reasons than he was now implying.) Second, he pronounced "difference of religion" to be "especially troublesome," the more so "in the event of there being children," which would incite "tremendous pressure by the priesthood" to bring up the children in the Catholic faith, "especially in view of the Mellon reputation for wealth." (Paul found this objection "odd," since his father "was not particularly religious.") And third, he feared that "a woman of thirty, whose habits are more or less formed," would not "be happy if transplanted from England and set down in Pittsburgh where she has no friends and acquaintances." (The case of Nora was proof enough of this, though Paul may have intended himself to be the "transplant," as part of a plan to escape Pittsburgh.) "Differences of nationality," Andrew concluded, "are naturally unsettling for both parties."[81]

There were additional considerations, which reveal much about Mellon's still-calculating view of the world, and about the high and determined ambitions that he continued to entertain for his only son. Among his concerns, he deemed what he termed the "difference of social position" between Paul and Delphina to be particularly notable. "Paul's social standing," he recorded, "is of the highest, and anything he does is subject to publicity." By contrast, "the girl's family is apparently not well known," which meant Paul "would find himself on the defensive not only in America but in England." Ailsa, whatever her flaws of character and temperament, had at least married well. Now, amidst every sort of global reversal and social upheaval, Andrew sought to save his son from the error of having "lowered his position." As one of the most eligible bachelors of his generation, with friends on both sides of the Atlantic, Paul could "marry almost anybody in America or Europe whom he wished": why settle for Delphina, who also brought with her an "invalid mother and divorced sister"? Moreover, Andrew still believed that "Paul's future is in Pittsburgh," where his "business and civic position" were an asset "unique in this country." This asset was not likely to appreciate if he married an Englishwoman of relatively obscure background. "My hopes will be dashed and my visions unfulfilled," he concluded, with uncharacteristic theatricality, another indication of his anxiety amidst what he had described, in a reply to Herbert Hoover's letter of condolence about Dick's death, as the "kaleidoscopic changes in the country which seem to be taking place under our eyes."[82]

As before, when Paul wanted to pursue a second year of study at Cambridge, Nora took her son's part. She had met the girl, and made plain to Andrew that she thought her "a splendid lovely character," who was "sweet and cultivated and well-educated" and possessed of "a deep, unselfish love for Paul." And although Delphina was older than Paul, she "does not look a day over twenty." "I know," Nora went on, heading off one more likely objection, "she would want to marry Paul if he had not one cent." To be sure, she admitted, Delphina's Catholicism was a difficulty, but ever the romantic even after two marriages, Nora declared there was nothing "that cannot be overcome by a selfless love." Moreover, with Paul seeming "very much in love with her," his mother thought it would be "dishonourable" for him to withdraw now. It was unconscionable, Nora fulminated, that Andrew and Ailsa had not even written to Delphina: "You must realize," Nora said, "the humiliation to a well-bred gentle girl that she receives no acknowledgement from Paul's family," and she repeatedly urged that the couple be allowed to marry without delay.[83] But Andrew would not relent, and in the end, Paul bowed to the heavy pressure exerted by his father and sister. He sailed to Britain to break the news to Delphina in person, and she accompanied him back to Southampton to say a final goodbye. On the crossing back, feeling confused and unhappy with his life, Paul was drawn into a card game with some seagoing confidence men, who "won" $25,000 from him, which he was obliged to make good with a check. Fortunately, he caught on in time to prevent their cashing it, saving himself at least from that hardship and humiliation.[84]

There were other reasons why Paul would remember this as a "trying period of uncertainty in my own life." After a year of apprenticeship in the Mellon National Bank, he had gone to work temporarily at the Bankers Trust Company in New York. The routine was as dreary as in Pittsburgh, but the social life was a great deal more diverting. When Andrew returned from London in the spring of 1933, he realized that Paul's interest in banking had not developed, even though he had recently made over to him (and to Ailsa) all his stock in the Mellon National Bank and the Union Trust Company. Having consulted with Dick, he thereupon made Paul a director of the (very troubled and unprofitable) Pittsburgh Coal Company; both Andrew and Dick assured Paul that he would find it a rewarding and instructive experience.[85] Reluctantly, Paul accepted their proposal and soon found himself "floating down the river on coal barges, donning a helmet to go down the mines, and attending the meetings of the directors." He hated it all, especially the meetings, where he understood little about what was going on, and cared less. But this was only the beginning: Paul soon found himself a director of the Mellon Bank, of several associated companies, and of Gulf Oil. Contrary to the assurances of his father and uncle, he found none of these enterprises any more congenial or instructive than the coal mines. He had no real interest in business, however hard his father tried to stimulate it.[86]

Paul still wished to marry, however, and in December 1933, after returning to New York from Pittsburgh, where he had gone for his uncle Dick's funeral, he met the woman who would become his wife. She was Mary Elizabeth Conover; she had been born in 1904 in Kansas City, where her father was a doctor, and where, a generation before, Judge Mellon had spent so much time. Paul found her striking in appearance, easy to talk to, vivacious and enthusiastic, and with a wide range of interests, among which music ranked first. She had majored in French at Vassar, studied for a year at the Sorbonne and then at Columbia, and in 1929 had married Karl Stanley Brown, who was then working in advertising; he later moved to Wall Street. Within two years, the marriage was in difficulties: Mary left for Europe in 1932, and she and Karl divorced in the summer of the following year. Paul was instantly smitten, and within six months of their first meeting, they were engaged.[87] Mary had none of the most objectionable liabilities Andrew had found in Delphina, and she was well educated, but she was scarcely of high social position or of East Coast ancestry. In his intended marriage, as in his lack of an established career, Paul was widely regarded in Pittsburgh as "a great disappointment to everybody," and no one felt that more keenly than his father.[88]

In fact, Paul was only too well aware of his life's lack of focus and professional purpose. In August 1934, in a lengthy letter to Ailsa, who was staying with the Duke and Duchess of Sutherland at Dunkeld in Perthshire, he contrasted his own unhappy indifference and lethargy to his father's continued application and energy. Once again, he was back in Pittsburgh and the bank, a routine "dull as ditchwater" and "absolutely devoid of movement, to say nothing of action." His only friend in the office was a Yale classmate, George Wyckoff, and they spent "many hours pitching coins and discussing the incredible weather outside" for want of "something to do." Paul's abiding interests remained essentially extra-curricular: the building of a steeplechase course at Rolling Rock, and weekend visits to Rokeby. Their father would soon be returning from a short trip across the Atlantic. "Everyone was glad to see him go away," Paul told Ailsa, "because they all had their tongues hanging out from exhaustion. I sometimes think he will trail off into a mere comet of complete energy."[89] America, he later reported, was "lousy with strikes and general marauding," and Hoover had written an article decrying the Roosevelt administration. "However," Paul concluded, "the Mellon interests are still under control, although I am not sure it wouldn't be wiser to move them to Dunkeld. Ourselves too."[90]

Though he knew little of business, Paul clearly had some anxieties, and Andrew was even more concerned. On his return to America, he had initially been bullish about the economy and its prospects. "Very confident about existing conditions," according to Duveen's spies, he felt that "the worst was over," that there would be a "gradual upturn," and that there would be "good times here before most people realized it." He also noted with pleasure that "*his* bank" was "seventy percent liquid."[91] But Mellon was clearly chastened by what he'd seen in Pittsburgh, and not a little concerned about his own declining income: he would "wait until conditions in this country are more stable, until the railroads and great industrial plants are making money, and until he can see how the new government policies work out," before committing himself to purchasing any more pictures. Soon after he got back, Carman Messmore was again trying to interest Mellon in the Hermitage Giorgione, along with some "modern French pictures" they had "bought from the Russian government." The Soviets had previously wanted $900,000 for the Giorgione, but would now accept $300,000 plus unspecified pictures in partial exchange. Despite this reduction, and although Mellon wanted *Judith* very much, he would "not part with even that sum at this time." Messmore concluded that no "business can be done with Mellon until the fall." But the autumn came and went, with no revival of interest, and in February 1934, Duveen came to the same conclusion, lamenting to Mellon that "it seems a very long time since I had the pleasure of seeing or hearing from you."[92]

Except for a picture of Abraham Lincoln by G. P. A. Healey, acquired from Knoedler for $13,800 (another indication of his growing interest in American portraiture), Mellon bought no works of art in 1934. Nor did he make over any further stock to his children or pictures to the educational and charitable trust. But in December, by which time his anxieties over Gulf Oil seem to have been alleviated, he resolved to hand on another substantial piece of his fortune. He conveyed to the trust forty-five of his paintings, valued at almost $9 million, and including virtually all of the pre-Hermitage purchases that he intended for the National Gallery. Among them were the only three of his earliest acquisitions to which he remained attached—Cuyp's *Herdsmen Tending Cattle* (purchased in 1905), Gainsborough's *Mrs. John Taylor* (the same), and Romney's *Miss Willoughby* (1907)—as well as four Gainsboroughs, three Rembrandts, three Goyas, two Turners, two Romneys, and two Titians. In the same month, having recently celebrated Audrey's first birthday, and with Paul's marriage to Mary Conover set for early the following year, Andrew also decided to make serious provision for his grandchildren, setting up new trusts for Paul, Ailsa, and their heirs, into which he deposited shares in Alcoa, Gulf, Mellbank, Pullman, and the Bethlehem Steel Corporation, all told some $10 million worth. As a result, the book value of Mellon's capital was down to $55 million by the end of 1934: he was now less than half as rich as he had been only four years earlier.[93]

Donald Shepard explained all this to Ailsa as a strategy "designed to help Audrey in the event of confiscatory taxes and inflation of our currency in future years"—unwelcome possibilities which might have seemed remote under Mellon's stewardship of the Treasury, but which now seemed all too likely with the Republicans in retreat and the Democrats rampant.[94] By the end of 1934, there were clear indications that the Mellon clan was seriously set against FDR. Closing one of his letters to Ailsa, Paul wrote: "Best love to David and to Audrey, although she doesn't know me from President Roosevelt yet. I hope she will, and prefer me." A more forceful antipathy appears in a letter from Mrs. William Cabell Bruce. "I have just been called up," she wrote Ailsa, "by one of the Colonial Dames officers asking me to appear, in costume, at a Tercentenary celebration next week at which Mrs. Roosevelt is to be present!" But Mrs. Bruce had "declined with delight!"[95] Many rich families shared this distaste for FDR, but the Mellons were not only reacting as another disgruntled clan of wealthy Republicans who hated Roosevelt as a socialist, a dictator, and a class traitor. For in recent months, they had come to feel this animus in deep, bitter, and personal terms.

15

THE SECOND SCANDAL

The "Tax Trial" and the National Gallery of Art, 1933–36

Litigation affects the lawyer, the judge and the party involved in it quite differently. The lawyer is animated by the spirit of mastery natural to combatants; the judge regards it with cool indifference, only desirous to discover the truth; but the party involved in it is steeped in anxiety. He has more at stake than either of the others. Ambition to win, pecuniary loss, and pride of character are all involved: but, whether much or little is involved, he cannot avoid anxiety. And the intensity of feeling is greatly augmented if the litigation happens to be vexatious, unjust or unfounded, and is persisted in by a designing adversary who thinks he has or can obtain advantage by it.

Thomas Mellon and His Times, p. 182

I. THE BATTLE WITH ROOSEVELT BEGUN

Andrew Mellon visited the White House during the summer of 1933, at the very end of Roosevelt's "hundred days" of whirlwind legislative activity, to report on his stewardship of the American embassy in London. Throughout the 1920s, his access to the executive mansion had been regular and easy; now he was a stranger in hostile territory, an outsider and already a targeted enemy. Mellon had listened in London to FDR's inaugural address, of which he generally approved, as he had the president's initial steps to soothe the national financial panic by declaring a ten-day "banking holiday." Now they met, perhaps for the first time and, among other things, they discussed the Glass-Steagall Act recently passed by Congress, which would separate investment and commercial banking and establish federal insurance of bank deposits.[1] Mellon conveyed his doubts to Roosevelt, insisting that once bankers knew the federal government would bail them out, they would become careless lenders and be inadequately vigilant about the credit-worthiness of their customers. It seemed to Mellon that FDR agreed wholeheartedly, and promised to veto the measure. "What a charming man Mr. Roosevelt is," he concluded. The next day, the president signed the bill, welcoming it as a major piece of necessary and progressive legislation.[2]

When Roosevelt had excoriated Mellon in 1926 as "the master mind among the malefactors of great wealth," and from this recent—and wholly typical—encounter, Mellon might have learned that FDR's charm masked a complex character that was, among other things, duplicitous, ruthless, devious, and opportunistic. But for now, Mellon preferred to give him the benefit of the doubt and, according to Duveen's spies, was "inclined to believe that Roosevelt's policies will work out."[3] There was another reason why Mellon might have wished to think well of FDR: David Bruce had campaigned for him, and was eager to return to public service by obtaining a position in the new administration. The Treasury was out of the question, because an appointment there might be construed as an attempt by Mellon to reassert his influence via his son-in-law. But to be an assistant secretary of state seemed perfectly plausible, and very attractive. Like his father a Democrat in politics, Bruce had already undertaken diplomatic work in Europe, and relocation to Washington might please Ailsa. Accordingly, Senator Bruce mobilized his Democratic Party allies to lobby the new secretary of state, Cordell Hull, and even the president himself. In the end, nothing came of the effort, and David Bruce went off to cultivate his estate in Virginia.[4] If it had succeeded, the rest of Andrew Mellon's life might have turned out very differently.

Within one week of Roosevelt's inauguration, before he had even returned from London, Mellon had learned that the Bureau of Internal Revenue was auditing his 1930 federal income tax return.[5] Of particular interest was the fact that at the very end of that year, he had conveyed the Raphael *Niccolini-Cowper Madonna*, bought in 1928 from Lady Desborough, via Duveen, to his recently established educational and charitable trust, and that he had claimed its purchase price, in excess of $800,000, as a charitable deduction. The bureau wanted to establish whether this sum did indeed represent the "fair market value" of the painting. Mellon immediately cabled Duveen, then in New York. "My personal representative will call," Mellon informed him, "and explain to you [my] requirement, and I shall appreciate it if you will furnish him with affidavit necessary."[6] Duveen duly obliged, signing a document drafted for him by Donald Shepard, Mellon's Washington lawyer, attesting to his familiarity with the picture and confirming both its value and its sale price. The declaration apparently satisfied the authorities, for no more was heard of Mellon's 1930 tax return.[7]

By then, however, rumors were already circulating in Washington that Mellon's return for the following year would also be under official scrutiny.[8] On May 5, 1933, Louis McFadden, a Republican congressman from Pennsylvania who belonged to one of the state party's anti-Mellon factions, delivered a speech under privilege in the House, introducing into the record a letter written by one David A. Olson to David Burnett, the commissioner of internal revenue. The letter charged that during the latter part of 1931, Mellon had sold 10,000 shares in Western Public Service, showing a loss of $1 million, which he had then deducted from his taxable income for that year. The document further alleged a similar deduction of $5.7 million representing a loss realized on the sale of 123,000 shares in the troubled Pittsburgh Coal Company. Both these blocks of stock, the letter continued, had been sold to the Union Trust Company of Pittsburgh, a corporation "under the control of Mr. Mellon and his associates," and both had been repurchased by Mellon or Mellon interests after thirty-one days. It was Olson's view that these transactions were illegitimate under the federal tax code, making the $6.7 million loss deduction wholly improper. And this was neither an accounting error nor a misinterpretation of the code: "these transactions," Olson concluded, had "accomplished the fraudulent withdrawal of income taxes from the government."[9]

It was a sensational charge, accusing someone who had been secretary of the treasury for eleven years, and who was still one of the richest men in the world, of deliberately cheating on his federal income tax return. Since the publication of personal filings was prohibited by a law Mellon had helped to pass in 1926, Olson can only have obtained this information via direct access to Mellon's tax return, or from someone who worked at the Bureau of Internal Revenue. (By now, the Democrats had got their hands on many senior jobs in the bureau, and David Lawrence was collector of internal revenue for Pittsburgh, where Mellon's returns were filed.) To be sure, Olson was a well-known investigator and troublemaker, who specialized in bringing so-called informer proceedings against Treasury officials. And McFadden had been at odds with the Hoover wing of his party throughout the preceding Republican administration, castigating the Federal Reserve Board as a "den of thieves" and urging impeachment when the president proposed a moratorium on war debts. Yet although they were both fairly disreputable characters, Olson and McFadden put forth a case that had the virtue of a certain superficial plausibility. It was not illegal to sell securities at a substantial loss, nor to deduct such a loss from taxable income; and it was not illegal to buy them back after twenty-one days. But it *was* against the law to do so under a prearranged understanding between buyer and seller to that effect. Under such circumstances, the loss did not constitute a valid deduction; the money had in effect been laundered, and the transaction amounted to fraud.

McFadden duly forwarded the relevant correspondence concerning Mellon's tax affairs to Homer Cummings, Roosevelt's attorney general. In a recent speech, Cummings had declared that "financial crimes which have been committed in high places growing out of banking irregularities and income tax evasions will require unexampled activity upon the part of the Department of Justice," and he now informed reporters that he would thoroughly investigate the allegation against Mellon of a "specific tax evasion of $6,700,000."[10] Mellon responded to Cummings by demanding just such an inquiry, and offering him and the Justice Department "my fullest co-operation in connection with any investigation which you may wish to make in my tax affairs." No reply was forthcoming, but the matter was much discussed in the press, where Mellon's guilt was widely presumed. But in September 1933, two agents from the Bureau of Internal Revenue went over Mellon's 1931 return, and recommended that he be given a *refund* of $7,507.74. Late in October, three agents of the Justice Department were dispatched to Mellon's office in Pittsburgh, to undertake a more lengthy examination of his accounts. It lasted three weeks. Mellon turned over all his records, placed his entire staff at their disposal, and practically suspended all other activity while the investigation proceeded. But after an even more thorough scrutiny of his financial affairs for 1931, these investigators also concluded that there had been nothing irregular about Mellon's tax return.[11]

To Mellon, this was a wholly satisfactory outcome, but it was the outcome of a very unusual and offensive process. For in the first place, the responsibility for investigating tax returns lay with the Bureau of Internal Revenue in the Treasury, and not with the attorney general. Moreover, there was a well-established and legally sanctioned procedure at the bureau for dealing with income tax returns that called for further elucidation and investigation. In such circumstances, the bureau dispatched a printed form listing the items under suspicion. The taxpayer was then granted a hearing, on an appointed date, to which he was entitled to bring all relevant documentation and to answer questions from officials. In the majority of cases, negotiations between the taxpayer and the government usually ended with a mutually satisfactory determination, as had often happened with Mellon's own returns during the 1920s.[12] Only when an impasse was reached, and when no satisfactory "adjustment" was agreed upon, did the law and the courts become involved in the matter.

So it was highly irregular—indeed, wholly without precedent—that this procedure, enshrined specifically in federal law, was not followed in Mellon's case, and that the attorney general took up the matter from the very beginning, preempting due process. The deviation was even more extraordinary considering that the preceding routine examination of Mellon's tax return by the Bureau of Internal Revenue had discovered nothing of interest or suspicion. But what Mellon could not have yet known was that from the president on down, there were those in the new administration determined to pursue Mellon, regardless of any conclusions that the bureau, and thus the Treasury, might have reached. A short note written in FDR's own hand, undated but clearly from this time, refers explicitly to Mellon's 1930 income tax return: "why not have Cummings read it [and] make it public?"[13] That, of course, is precisely what the attorney general—in violation of federal law—had effectively done for the subsequent year's return, thereby lending credence to the charges leveled by McFadden and Olson. For his part, Henry Morgenthau Jr., who would become Roosevelt's secretary of the treasury at the beginning of 1934, thought it immoral for wealthy taxpayers like Mellon to exploit what he regarded as "loopholes" in the tax code, and he was eager to make examples of some of them.[14]

Now a total outsider to Washington politics, Mellon was oblivious to these goings-on as the Treasury and the Justice Department agents went through his books in Pittsburgh during late 1933. The Justice investigations terminated on November 9, but the department declined to comment, let alone acknowledge the findings. After waiting two months for public exoneration, Mellon sent Homer Cummings a lengthy letter in mid-January 1934.[15] It was a cogent and dignified plea. Ever since last summer, Mellon declared, the impression being given in the press was that "I have evaded payment of taxes due to the Government which your Department is now taking steps to collect." "For several months," he went on, "a campaign of character-wrecking and abuse against me and other large taxpayers has been carried on in the press and over the radio."

But "the time has now come when, so far as I am concerned, I am determined to put an end to it if facts and truth can do so." "I am not," Mellon insisted, "conscious of any wrong doing with respect to my taxes, and the Government has not made any such charge." He expressed confidence, naïve as it happens, that neither Cummings nor his department would "wish to appear to countenance a scheme for political sniping nor be a party to the machinations of any unscrupulous person."

Press reports, Mellon continued, were now circulating that he owed the United States Treasury twelve million dollars: "I know of no such tax that could be assessed against me or collected by the Government." "As the records will show," he went on, "all income taxes which have ever been assessed against me have been paid." "I have never," he stated, "sought to evade payment of any taxes legally claimed, and have always paid a very substantial income tax every year." "I have always," he further affirmed, "been scrupulous to stay well on what the Supreme Court calls 'the safe side' of the line of what is permitted not only by the letter but by the policy of the law."[16] Not surprisingly, Mellon noted, the tax investigators who had recently combed his books and records had "found no irregularities of any kind," yet he had heard no official response from Cummings's department. Moreover, the procedures for questioning a citizen's tax obligations, which "necessarily may be subject to dispute," had been ignored. He had not been "accorded the opportunity to meet such charges in the customary way," and there seemed a real likelihood that "the campaign of vilification mounted in the press" would continue "unchecked." "Only by prompt and final action by the Government in disposing of any questions that may have arisen in my tax affairs," Mellon concluded, could these unjustified and unsubstantiated charges be laid to rest. On that, at least, he and Cummings may have agreed.

The attorney general declined to reply, but soon after receiving the letter, he gave an interview, disclosing that the investigation into Mellon's tax returns was continuing, and that the Justice Department was working in perfect concord with the Treasury.[17] He also took the occasion to inveigh against the "one hundred percent aluminum monopoly" of Alcoa. Yet Cummings did admit that "any income tax case against Mr. Mellon would be a borderline case," a bit of forthrightness that must have pained him. For officials in the two departments most closely involved with the matter were not reaching the desired conclusions: a Justice Department memorandum of early 1934 insisted that the charges against Mellon were either invalid or could not be proved; and Elmer Irey, head of the Treasury's Intelligence Unit, who had helped to send Al Capone to prison on the grounds of tax evasion, was of the same opinion.[18] Nevertheless, Cummings announced in March 1934 that a grand jury would be empaneled in the Federal District Court of Pittsburgh, to consider the sufficiency of evidence to indict Mellon on the criminal charge of filing a fraudulent tax return. To plead the government's case, Secretary Morgenthau recruited Robert Jackson, a New York state "country lawyer," a Democratic activist, and a friend of FDR's, to become general counsel of the Bureau of Internal Revenue, and he told him: "You can't be too tough in this trial to suit me." "Thank God I have that kind of boss," Jackson happily replied. "I consider," Morgenthau went on, "that Mr. Mellon is not on trial, but Democracy and the privileged rich, and I want to see who will win."[19]

The first intimation of this impending proceeding came early in March 1934, when Cummings issued a press release naming several people whose tax violations would be brought before grand juries. Mellon was one of them, and he immediately issued a lengthy statement, describing this latest move as "politics of the crudest sort." "In all my years of experience in the administration of the tax laws," he went on, "I have never known of a single instance in which such unfair and arbitrary action has been taken.... All income taxes which have ever been assessed against me have been paid, and in no single year have I failed to pay a very substantial income tax. The total has amounted in the last twenty years to over twenty million dollars." He gave his own account of events since the previous May, deploring once more the irregularity of the Justice Department's preemptive investigation, and insisting that charges against him emanating from Congress had never been corroborated by any investigation. He also dismissed Cummings's remarks about Alcoa as irrelevant. "For many months now," he concluded, borrowing from his carefully crafted and ignored letter of January to the attorney general,

> a campaign of character-wrecking and abuse has been conducted against me in the press and over the radio. I know there has been no evasion of taxes on my part. I have, on the contrary, always been scrupulous to give the Government the benefit of every doubt in making up my tax return. I am glad the issue is joined at last, and am quite content to leave the outcome to the Courts and to the good sense and fairness of the American people when all the facts are known.[20]

The grand jury was duly seated in Pittsburgh on May 7, 1934, to consider whether there was enough evidence to indict Andrew Mellon for seeking to defraud the federal government by "willfully, feloniously, fraudulently and knowingly" filing a false income tax return for 1931.[21] The panel was composed overwhelmingly of laborers, mechanics, farmers, and craftsmen—men much more likely to be supporters of Roosevelt than of Mellon. The attorney for western Pennsylvania made the case on behalf of Robert Jackson, and five witnesses gave evidence. (Mellon was not present, nor was any evidence allowed controverting the charge.) After five hours of deliberation, the grand jury found by eleven votes to ten that the evidence was insufficient to warrant an indictment.[22] Mellon, who had declared the charges to be "impertinent, scandalous and improper," was naturally most gratified at this vindication: "the fact that the grand jury reached a sound conclusion, notwithstanding the unusual methods pursued in my case, is proof of the good sense and fairness of the American people." Or, as one newspaper put it more graphically: "the large outstanding fact is that a grand jury of such men as have little reason to love the rich tossed the Government's complaint into the discard."[23] And so, in what would only be round one of the battle between the combatants Henry Morgenthau had described as "democracy" and "the privileged rich," it was "the privileged rich" who had won.

Mellon's friends were delighted at his vindication. "The Federal Grand Jury," W. S. Morris informed W. L. Mellon, "sitting in Allegheny County this week exploded a nitroglycerine factory into Attorney General Cummings's office in Washington." "Congratulations on the recent Grand Jury decision," the architect Edward H. Bennett wrote personally to Andrew. "I am frankly delighted." So were former cabinet colleagues. "You have been subjected," Henry L. Stimson told Mellon, "to a prosecution which in my opinion has violated all basic principles of American justice as well as the well-recognized ethics of criminal procedure. I am greatly gratified that the Grand Jury in your district has vindicated your action and rejected the prosecution."[24] The most encouraging letter came from Herbert Hoover, who expressed "tremendous satisfaction" at the outcome. "The entire proceedings," Mellon replied, "was absolutely unprecedented and without justification, either in law or fact, so that I never felt seriously disturbed as to the final outcome if the case came to trial in the courts." "For more than a year," he went on, "and even before the Attorney General started his investigation of my tax affairs, I had warning that a concerted movement was being planned to attack me personally, either in connection with my tax affairs or with my administration of the Treasury. I have an abundance of very direct evidence to this effect."[25]

It was not only Mellon's family, friends, and former colleagues who took this view. Walter Lippmann, a former Wilson adviser and no son of privilege himself, also applauded the outcome, and declared the Department of Justice guilty of "a most discreditable performance," of a "low and inept political maneuver," which had compounded injustice with poor judgment.[26] The injustice was the protracted interval during which Mellon had stood accused of criminality before the matter was taken to the grand jury. By making and repeating such accusations against Mellon long before the grand jury had "even seen the evidence," Lippmann concluded, the attorney general had committed "an act of profound injustice." Cummings had also been exceedingly stupid, for as Lippmann reckoned, the chances of Mellon's having cheated on his tax returns "were not one in a million." "Is it conceivable," Lippmann asked, "that a man in his position, with an income of nearly $7,000,000 that year, would deliberately have cheated the government out of $700,000?" "To believe," Lippmann went on, with palpable outrage, "that Mr. Mellon would have the audacity and the downright imbecility to falsify his income tax is to believe the utterly incredible." The whole affair, he concluded, was "one of those stunts that politicians stoop to every now and then, thinking that they can gain some advantage by it for their party."

Lippmann, who had once famously dismissed Roosevelt as being no more than "an amiable boy scout," far underestimated the amount (varying from six to twelve million dollars) that Mellon's accusers claimed he owed, and also overestimated Mellon's income for 1931 by a factor of ten.[27] But his basic argument was well put (though naturally Homer Cummings did not accept it).[28] One of the main objectives of Mellon's policy at the Treasury had always been to get the rich to pay *more* taxes, not less. He had railed against tax-exempt bonds, refraining from investing in them himself (to his financial disadvantage), and he took conspicuous pride in having always paid his federal taxes. Not that his filings had gone entirely unquestioned before. It bears repeating that during the 1920s, they had been regularly revised, sometimes upward, sometimes downward, and he often paid additional amounts, or received refunds, several years after the return in question had been filed.[29] True, as secretary of the treasury, he had clearly transgressed both the letter and the spirit of the statute prohibiting the holder of that office from involvement in trade, but as a matter both of financial prudence and of personal honor, he was far more scrupulous about trying to stay within the letter of the law when it came to his financial affairs.

Throughout his tenure at the Treasury, Mellon had dutifully observed both the rules and the conventions for filing tax returns. His misfortune was that after 1932, the Roosevelt administration was determined to change those rules and conventions and, if possible, to apply those revisions retroactively, making public examples of particular rich men, thereby exposing and discrediting their whole rapacious cohort. Among the more extraordinary pieces of evidence unearthed by the Senate Committee on Banking and Currency had been that no partner in J. P. Morgan had paid a single cent in federal income tax in 1931 or in 1932, their huge salaries having been wiped out by claiming losses on securities. It might be legal, but at a time when so many Americans were suffering such hardship, it seemed unconscionable that these rich men should pay no federal tax whatsoever.[30] Mellon *did* pay his taxes; but that did not make him immune to attack. As *Fortune* magazine put it: "the plain fact of the matter was that Mr. Mellon had made out his tax return in one economic era, and was being prosecuted for it in another."[31] If to "economic" is added "political," then that observation becomes even more telling.

For Roosevelt fully reciprocated the enmity increasingly felt toward him by bankers, businessmen, and plutocrats. Like his kinsman Theodore, he looked on new money with a mixture of snobbery and disdain. As a man whose own business ventures had not prospered during the 1920s, he was also envious and disapproving of those who had done so much better. Even FDR's admirers conceded that beneath the charming, patrician façade there lurked a vindictive streak which was intensified by his disability.[32] Accordingly, Roosevelt relished using both the Bureau of Internal Revenue and the Department of Justice to pursue vendettas against some of his rich antagonists, encouraging them to unleash tax inspectors and prosecutors like crusaders against the "malefactors of great wealth." Their tactics were invariable: tax returns filed in good faith, with the customary expectation they might be questioned during subsequent discussion and renegotiation, were now recharacterized as something akin to sworn statements, every erring calculation adduced as proof positive of deliberate intention to defraud the federal government. (Ironically, indeed, hypocritically, FDR himself used every legal means to reduce his own federal tax liability, paying only $31.31 on his private income of $19,000 in 1932.)[33]

The 1930s would see a succession of high-profile prosecutions of rich men for tax evasion, initially including Thomas S. Lamont (a partner in J. P. Morgan), James J. Walker (the mayor of New York), and Thomas L. Sidle (a Cleveland businessman), and subsequently Moses Annenberg (the Philadelphia publisher). In such a vengeful political climate, Andrew Mellon was another marked man.[34] He was extremely rich, and he was a lifelong Republican. He had presided over the meretricious boom of the 1920s, and he had failed to avert the disastrous crash at the end of the decade. As such, he embodied everything about the "old order" that FDR so detested. But in addition, it was widely—and rightly—believed that throughout his time in office, Mellon had been in breach of the law by remaining actively involved in business. From 1921 to 1932, he had always managed to evade censure and impeachment. But now, with his political mantle in tatters, the long-frustrated Democrats at last spied an opportunity to get even. As the earlier conviction of Al Capone had shown (ironically during Mellon's own time at the Treasury), prosecution for tax evasion was a successful way of sending men to prison when other, and greater, charges against them could not be proven. So it was for the Democrats in the case of Mellon. As such, it was, indeed, "politics of the crudest sort." Or, as Mellon put it on another occasion, against him was launched "a campaign of terrorism, with the tax law as a weapon."[35]

Did the president know? The Washington bureau chief of the *New York Times*, Arthur Krock, wrote in early March, just before the grand jury hearing in Pittsburgh, that Roosevelt did not know what Cummings was planning.[36] This seems unlikely: FDR had already interested himself in Mellon's 1930 tax return, and would any attorney general begin criminal proceedings against a former secretary of the treasury, ambassador to Britain, and major figure in the Republican Party without consulting the president first? In any case, and as his diary makes plain, Homer Cummings *did* consult Roosevelt. Here is the relevant entry, dated March 10, 1934, recording a meeting at the White House with FDR, nearly two months before the grand jury convened in Pittsburgh:

> I discussed tax matters with him, and obtained his approval of a proposed release which I expect to give out to the newspapers that afternoon. This release in substance states that Attorney General Cummings had authorized the United States Attorneys in New York, Cleveland and Pittsburgh to present to Federal Grand Juries for tax violations the cases of Thomas S. Lamont, James J. Walker, Thomas L. Sidle, and Andrew W. Mellon. I talked to the president quite a while about these matters, and he concurred with me that unless we made an attempt to secure indictments in these cases we might as well give up the whole tax program.

This is unequivocal. "Let the cases go to the grand jury," Harold Ickes later recorded FDR as saying. Robert Jackson agreed: "as a matter of fair history, he [Roosevelt] did know about it."[37]

II. THE NEW DEAL CLOSES IN

From the spring of 1933 until May 1934, Andrew Mellon was thus much preoccupied with what would turn out to be only the first battle in an all-out war with the Roosevelt administration. But the attack on him extended beyond these imputations of tax fraud; he was also coming under renewed assault as the major owner of companies whose business practices and ethics were no longer deemed acceptable—or legal. This was especially so with Alcoa, in which Andrew and Dick were massive, if not quite majority, shareholders. In the changing atmosphere of the early 1930s, management had already been forced to give some ground in recognizing unions and collective bargaining; now Alcoa found itself increasingly on the defensive concerning its market monopoly. During the 1920s, successive Federal Trade Commission investigations had been easily (and suspiciously) fended off, but under the New Deal, Alcoa's monopoly was more widely exposed and attacked. To begin with, several small firms, claiming they had been driven out of business by the aluminum giant, began to file private antitrust suits.[38]

The most important of these actions was brought by the Bausch Machine Tool Company, whose own aluminum plant had closed down in 1931. The company's president, George Haskell, thereupon filed a suit in Connecticut District Court seeking $3 million in damages. He had already brought several unsuccessful actions against Alcoa, claiming, among other things, that he had been unfairly excluded during the mid-1920s from participation in the Saguenay water power projects. Now he alleged that Alcoa had systematically set out to undercut his prices for forgings and sheet of duralumin (an alloy of aluminum, copper, and magnesium) in illicit restraint of trade. Haskell further alleged that Alcoa had conspired with and coerced foreign producers to keep out of the American market. This was a most serious allegation, for if it was proved, the law required that triple damages be paid, which for Alcoa would amount to some nine million dollars—equivalent to 80 percent of the firm's operating profit, and more than five times its net income, in 1933. The case did not reach trial until the autumn of that year, and Bausch was represented by the law firm in which Homer Cummings had previously been a partner. The attorney general took care, formally at least, to distance himself from the matter. But to Mellon and Alcoa, it seemed just another sinister sign that the New Dealers were regrouping for revenge.

Following ten weeks of testimony, Alcoa was cleared by a Connecticut jury. But a federal appeals court ordered a new trial after finding that the judge's instructions to the jury had been too narrowly framed and that relevant evidence improperly excluded. In the second trial in 1935, the jury, operating on more liberal instructions, found for Bausch, awarding him $2,868,900, which by law would be tripled, and the company's attorney's fees added to it. Naturally, Alcoa appealed again, and again it won. Yet while the devastating damages were saved, in other ways it was a pyrrhic victory. For the court ruled in the company's favor largely on technical grounds, and when more rumbles were heard from Bausch, threatening further litigation, Alcoa agreed to settle out of court, even placing Haskell on retainer to neutralize him. But buying him off proved no guarantee of peace and immunity. To be sure, the final agreement was conditional upon a letter from the attorney general, promising that the settlement would not be used as a basis for any future action against Alcoa. But the business was widely regarded as a monopoly, and it was well-known to be a "Mellon company." Homer Cummings had clearly taken an interest in the recent proceedings; thus, although Bausch's private interest was settled, it would be only a matter of time before the Department of Justice moved in to investigate on behalf of the U.S. public.[39]

One reason for the initial rush of his "hundred days" legislation was that Roosevelt had been primarily concerned with preserving the capitalist system and the American economy, which was why he had sought to save the banks rather than nationalize them. But as these suits against Alcoa were proceeding, the president began to turn more explicitly against the "money changers" whom he had already denounced in his inaugural speech. One indicator was that, in the spring of 1934, Congress passed the Securities Exchange Act.[40] Among other things, the new measure required timely and detailed reporting on the financial performance of major companies, as well as a full disclosure of the compensation of company officers; it also mandated that such accounts be verified by independent auditors. In general, the measure was designed to make companies more publicly accountable, but its specific targets were clearly the overmighty bankers whose exclusive knowledge of big business and high finance had allowed them to wield, often irresponsibly, such vast power. To administer the new regulations, the law established the Securities and Exchange Commission, consisting of five members appointed by the president. For chairman FDR picked Joseph P. Kennedy, the reputed bootlegger whose dubious business and banking practices were widely known. But the president breezily dismissed objections with the response

"Set a thief to catch a thief." Indeed, knowing all the tricks that the new act was designed to prevent, Kennedy proceeded to run the SEC honestly and effectively.

Soon after, Congress passed the 1934 Revenue Act. It was partly in response to Roosevelt's call for "stringent preventive or regulatory measures" against "individuals who have evaded the spirit and purpose of our tax laws." But it was given more bite as it passed through the upper house, where Mellon's longtime enemy, Senator Couzens, sensed another opportunity to attack him and his financial dealings.[41] Eventually passed in what was described as a "savage, soak-the-rich atmosphere," the measure increased estate taxes, revived the excess profits tax and the gift tax, limited capital losses that could be claimed against income, imposed a special penalty tax on personal holding companies, and disallowed the claiming of losses in intrafamily sales of property or shares. In the future, it would be more difficult to reduce tax liability in the way the Morgan partners had done, and more costly to pass on wealth from one generation to the next in the way that Mellon had done. The act also revived a provision of the Revenue Act of 1924 which Mellon had succeeded in overriding two years later, mandating the release of every federal taxpayer's name, address, gross income, total deductions and credits, and tax payment. In addition it strengthened certain provisions of the Securities and Exchange Act by reaffirming the publication of the salaries of directors and executives of banks, public utilities, and large corporations.[42]

But this was only the beginning of a nascent New Deal radicalism which would soon become stridently hostile to the rich. In a September 1934 radio address, Roosevelt vented his growing impatience with businessmen, whom he now depicted as self-seeking, unimaginative, and increasingly critical. Soon after, he made the same point in a major speech to American bankers. He reminded them that in March 1933, he had asked the people to renew their faith in the banks of the country. "They took me at my word. Tonight I ask the bankers of this country to renew their confidence in the people of this country. I hope you will take me at my word." The implication was clear: FDR had come to the aid of frightened financiers when they had been in urgent need of help; if they now responded with enmity, then the popular opinion that he commanded would be directed more virulently against them, there would be further legislation to curb their freedom, and there would be renewed resort to the courts. The *New York Times* reported that Roosevelt had received an "ovation," but a member of the president's entourage described the atmosphere as "frigid."[43]

In the aftermath of his sweeping midterm victories in November 1934,

FDR embarked upon the implementation of what is sometimes called the Second New Deal, a campaign to "weed out the over-privileged" and "lift up the under-privileged" that was carried through during the congressional session of 1935. The Emergency Relief Appropriation Act created new work opportunities for the unemployed by financing the construction of schools, roads, bridges, and courthouses across the nation, as well as such large-scale projects as the Oakland Bay Bridge in California and the Triborough Bridge in New York. The Social Security Act was passed to provide workers with unemployment benefits in times of recession and pensions in their old age, and a new federal tax was levied on employers to help pay for it. The worthily compassionate goal was to lessen the sufferings of the majority of Americans, who did not earn enough to save for a rainy day, never mind retirement. Equally important was the Wagner Act, which strengthened Section 7a of the National Industrial Recovery Act by empowering the National Labor Relations Board to supervise elections of union representatives, and by prohibiting such unfair employment practices as discrimination against union members, refusal to bargain, and sponsorship of company unions—all practices that had historically characterized relations between workers and owners in Pittsburgh and other industrial cities.[44]

Two more precisely focused pieces of legislation were directed at the managers and owners of public utilities and coal mines. The Public Utilities Holding Company Act was passed to begin the breakup of large, extensively leveraged, elaborately interlocked, and often completely monopolistic entities providing heat, light, and transport, often to the great inconvenience of the consumer. Such undertakings had been long been regarded by progressives as being over-powerful and under-regulated, and this measure began to discipline and restructure them. In the same session, the Guffey-Snider Bituminous Coal Conservation Act also became law. Co-sponsored by the recently elected Democratic senator from Pennsylvania, the measure effectively embodied the soft-coal code which had been established by the National Recovery Administration Policy Board. The result was the unprecedented regulation of businesses like Mellon's Pittsburgh Coal Company, which in effect compelled them to recognize the unions they had so ruthlessly set out to destroy during the mid-1920s. Practicality as much as politics figured in the bill's passing: the United Mine Workers leader, John L. Lewis, had convincingly threatened a nationwide coal strike if the measure was not passed, and the president shrewdly threw his full weight behind it.

During 1935, Roosevelt also set out to reform the Federal Reserve System, which under Mellon had proved itself incapable of dealing with the events of 1929–33, and which FDR had only been able to tinker with during his first hundred days. Now additional legislation made the board more responsive to the public interest and more directly answerable to the president. The newly empowered board had discretion to adjust by up to 100 percent the reserves-to-deposits requirement; it had greater leverage over the money supply, through control of the Open Market Committee, which traded in government-issued securities; and it held sway over all state banks in exchange for eligibility for federal deposit insurance. The resulting system gave FDR unprecedented power over currency and credit, and the Federal Reserve Board now wielded more of the authority of a true central bank than any American institution since the demise of the Bank of the United States in Andrew Jackson's day. The panics and crashes of 1870, 1907 and 1929–31, which had been a recurrent and accepted feature of Andrew Mellon's whole business life, thus became things of the past, and the banking and currency systems of the United States could now enjoy security, albeit at the sacrifice of autonomy.[45]

In the same session of Congress, Roosevelt proposed a new revenue bill, designed unabashedly to "soak the rich."[46] "It may," FDR observed, raking the coals of class warfare once again, "be necessary to throw to the wolves the forty-six men who are reported to have incomes in excess of one million dollars a year [a category to which Mellon belonged in 1933 and 1934, but not immediately before or after]. This can be accomplished through taxation." He proposed a federal inheritance tax, to increase maximum corporate income taxes, and to levy a surtax on large personal incomes. "Americans," FDR insisted, "must forswear that conception of wealth which, through excessive profits, creates undue private power over private affairs and, to our misfortune, over public affairs as well." "The transmission from generation to generation of vast fortunes" was "as inconsistent with the ideals of this generation as inherited political power was inconsistent with the ideals of the generation which established our government."[47] But the measure was whittled down on its way through Congress, and some of the more radical provisions of the 1934 Revenue Act were also repealed. The result was that the 1935 Revenue Act generated little new income for the government and made no significant contribution to the redistribution of income. In practice, few people were affected by it: only John D. Rockefeller Sr. was subject to the highest rate of surtax (75 percent) on an income of more than five million dollars. This was gesture politics, aiming at "revenge rather than revenue—revenge on business."[48]

There was more to come. Early in 1936, Roosevelt took the occasion of his State of the Union address to deliver a fiercely partisan message that effectively began and set the tone of his campaign for re-election.[49] "We have earned the hatred of entrenched greed," he declared before an astonished but generally appreciative Congress, in what even his most sympathetic recent biographer describes as a "vituperative outburst." "They seek the restoration of their selfish power. They steal the livery of great national constitutional ideals to serve discredited special interests." If they succeeded in regaining power, FDR warned, these men would display in government the same deplorable traits they had shown in their own affairs: "autocracy towards labor, towards stockholders, towards consumers, towards public sentiment." "Give them their way," he concluded, and they would behave like every despotism in the past, seeking "power for themselves, enslavement for the public."[50] As he did so often, FDR refused to name names, and the rhetoric was all the more effective for its generalizing. Still, there was little doubting whom he had in mind, and it is easy to see why bankers and businessmen, like the Mellons, were so angered and, increasingly, worried to find themselves in the sights of a president they deplored as a self-righteous opportunist and irresponsible demagogue.

During the ensuing congressional session, Roosevelt resolved to tax the undistributed profits that had accumulated in corporate treasuries during the boom years of the 1920s. Billions of dollars, he insisted, were being selfishly withheld from stockholders by those in control of giant corporations, and his proposed legislation would liberate these funds. Here was a populist, anti-business proposal, entirely consistent with his State of the Union message. FDR put it forth without acknowledging that companies retained profits not necessarily for selfish purposes, but to provide resources for re-investment and as a hedge against difficult times; neither did he admit that the profits in question had already been taxed, which meant that what he proposed amounted to double taxation. And if, as a consequence of this proposed legislation, companies *did* distribute *all* their surpluses to avoid this new tax, the same earnings would be still taxed again as shareholders' dividends. In the course of the bill's journey through Congress, modifications were made and small businesses were largely exempted from its provisions. But for good or ill, the act did establish the principle that retained earnings could be taxed.[51]

Together, these measures constituted an extraordinary package of legislation to have passed in a single session, surpassing even Roosevelt's first hundred days in their force and significance. Walter Lippmann, who had come to repent of his earlier underestimation of the president, described it as "the most comprehensive program of reform ever achieved in this country in any administration." To be sure, as far as "soaking the rich" was concerned, much of the second New Deal was symbol rather than sub-stance, as FDR sought to outflank Huey Long and Father Coughlin and regain the radical initiative. But to Mellon and his friends, the program threatened to undermine the very free-market system that had allowed them to bring America to global economic supremacy—and to make their own fortunes along the way. Whatever value some may have grudgingly allowed in the measures of the president's first hundred days, they regarded this phase as a vindictive attempt to throttle industry and bank-ing, to impose controls and regulations inimical to free enterprise, to levy taxes for revenge rather than income, to privilege labor over capital, and to demoralize the private sector by constantly scapegoating it and by threatening yet more punitive legislation—all for political advantage. As Arthur Schlesinger Jr. put it, the first New Deal "told business what it must do," but the second New Deal "told business what it must not do"; and as a result, "in corporate boardrooms from Wall Street to the Golden Gate, fear and loathing of Roosevelt deepened."[52]

Andrew Mellon and his beleaguered breed could not have been more dismayed, for they disapproved of everything that FDR and his colleagues were now doing. The introduction of unemployment insurance and of old-age pensions ran counter to the ideal of sturdy independence, which Mellon regarded as essential for building not only business but also indi-vidual character. The measures in support of job creation and the rights of unions, and against coal companies, seemed an utter betrayal of the free market and of the creators of American wealth. While most Americans welcomed security for bank deposits, the reform of the Federal Reserve Board was opposed by financiers (and also by Ogden Mills) as an encroach-ment on the liberty of the private banking system. The gift tax made it harder to keep wealth intact from generation to generation, yet for Mel-lon and his colleagues, such long-lasting fortunes were an essential source of industrial investment. Finally, the taxing of retained surpluses struck at the heart of the Mellon way of business: the deliberate, long-term accu-mulation of capital whereby a company might grow and strengthen and, if necessary, wait out competitors and lean times. Of course, from the per-spective of the Democrats, and of many ordinary American working-people, these reforms were necessary and long overdue, but Mellon saw only antagonism and hostility.

Nor was this just a general change in the political climate and popular mood against big business and corporate finance: Roosevelt's policies impinged directly on Mellon's banking and industrial empire in many specifically targeted ways. Legislation regulating banks, companies, and public utilities, and requiring the annual provision of "comprehensive reports," portended the end of the Mellons' way of doing business, which had always been as secretive as possible, and obliged them to divulge (for example) the salary of Henry C. McEldowney as president of the Union Trust Company.[53] The separation of investment and deposit banking necessitated the establishment of the Mellon Securities Corporation, which took over the underwriting of stocks and bonds from Union Trust, thereby spelling the effective end of the interlocking financial structures Mellon had put in place in the early 1900s, and which had been central to his subsequent financial and industrial success.[54] Nor was this all: in February 1934, the Roosevelt administration canceled all pre-existing federal air mail contracts, on the (undoubtedly correct) grounds that many of them had been fraudulently granted and collusively gained. Among them were those held by the Pittsburgh Aviation Company, the last new venture undertaken by Andrew and Dick, which had depended for its success on their inside contacts with the Hoover administration.[55]

There was another, more visible sign that FDR wished to make a complete break with the Republican administrations that had gone before, and especially with the policies and practices of Andrew Mellon. The major buildings that the secretary had authorized during his time at the Treasury were completed by 1935, and he was "very pleased indeed with their appearance," but the remainder of the Federal Triangle scheme was languishing.[56] Work on the repeatedly postponed "apex" building at the easternmost corner of the triangle, which would house the Federal Trade Commission, finally began in January 1937. But although Edward H. Bennett was the architect, it was more a departure than a continuation. In line with new, radical, progressive thinking, both political and architectural, the final design was much less ornate than had originally been intended. Turning away from columns and cupolas, the Roosevelt administration inclined toward plainer, stripped-down, modernist architecture, as exemplified by the buildings it would later commission, among them the Department of the Interior, the Library of Congress Annex, the Social Security Building, and the War Department.[57] Just as the New Deal had changed the culture of politics, so it was also changing the politics of culture, and in both cases, Mellon would continue to be a prime target.

III. THE BATTLE WITH ROOSEVELT RESUMED

With the Pittsburgh grand jury's decision in May 1934 Andrew Mellon had decisively defeated the Roosevelt administration: the Treasury's auditors had found his returns to be in good order; three agents from the

attorney general's office, having spent several weeks in Pittsburgh exam-
ining his books and accounts, had found nothing amiss; and now a federal
grand jury in Allegheny County, composed primarily of the kind of
workingmen who were flocking to Roosevelt's banner, had refused to
indict him on the criminal charge of tax fraud. But as Mellon savored his
victory, his opponents were already planning their next move, which was
to bring a new, *civil* action against him, undertaken by an admittedly
reluctant Treasury, this time at the urging of the Justice Department and
the president, in accordance with the standard procedures which had
previously been disregarded. Even before the grand jury met, Mellon
had received, late in March 1934, a communication from the Bureau of
Internal Revenue, technically known as a "deficiency letter." It claimed
that, on the basis of further investigation into his 1931 tax return, he owed
$1,319,080.90 in addition to the $600,000 he had already paid. With the
penalty of 50 percent, this brought the total amount he was now being
asked to pay the federal government to almost $2 million.[58]

Not surprisingly, when Joseph Duveen inquired in May 1934 whether
he should congratulate Mellon on the Pittsburgh grand jury's verdict, he
was advised that it would be premature.[59] Still convinced of his innocence,
and outraged that the matter had not been settled, Mellon responded to
the deficiency letter by counter-suing, insisting now that he had actually
overpaid his 1931 obligations by omitting to claim as a valid deduction the
value of the five paintings he had conveyed to the educational and charitable trust in June that year: they were worth more than $3 million. Choos-
ing now to do so, he claimed a refund of $139,034 for 1931.[60] Four
months later, the bureau sent Mellon a second deficiency letter, reporting
another recalculation of his liabilities—again upwards. Upon additional
investigation, Mellon was informed, his federal income tax arrears had
ballooned from $1.3 million to $2,050,068.82 and, correspondingly, the
50 percent penalty had gone up to $1,025,034.41. By this latest reckon-
ing, Mellon still owed the government more than $3 million in unpaid
taxes for 1931. To be sure, this was significantly less than the figures of
$6 million and $12 million that were being bandied about in the media.
But even for a man of his prodigious resources, it was hardly a minor sum,
and it was raised slightly higher again in February 1935.[61]

This was no longer a matter of differing interpretations and calculations about which, as Mellon had repeatedly accepted, "the proper
amount of tax to be paid by a citizen necessarily may be subject to dispute." For one of the charges contained in the deficiency letters was that
he had deliberately sought to defraud the federal government of rightful
revenue, by establishing the A. W. Mellon Educational & Charitable

Trust, which was now alleged to be a bogus philanthropy, created for no purpose but to receive gifts that would enable him to reduce his taxable income. It was an accusation Mellon rejected root and branch: "I will spend the rest of my life in jail," he declared, rather than admit to having *knowingly* falsified his tax return.[62] Accordingly, he refused to countenance negotiations, he flatly denied any fraudulent intent, and he determined to take his case to the Board of Tax Appeals, which he himself had set up in 1924 during his tenure at the Treasury to evaluate taxpayers' claims of unjust assessments. He also retained Frank Hogan as his attorney. Hogan, Washington's leading trial lawyer, had defended many high-profile cases brought by the government, both civil and criminal, with spectacular success; he once observed that his ideal client was "a rich man who is scared."[63] Andrew Mellon was certainly rich, but it is impossible to know if he was scared. He was certainly angry.

Once again, Robert Jackson was in charge of the government's case. Despite his effusive words to Henry Morgenthau, he had not been altogether happy about the earlier failed criminal suit, and he was also worried about the civil action that was now being proposed. In a sense, he agreed with Mellon: there was a legitimate case for discussion and renegotiation concerning his 1931 tax return. Jackson had also recommended that "fraud not be charged and no fraud penalties be assessed," on the grounds that the burden of proof lay with the federal government, and that, whatever the truth of the matter, this would be very difficult to demonstrate.[64] But the Department of Justice was opposed to this view from the Treasury, and it is clear from an entry in Homer Cummings's diary for late May 1934 that he again took the matter to Roosevelt. Despite being warned by Henry L. Stimson—who insisted that Mellon had been very shabbily treated[65]—that the failure of the criminal suit did not bode well for its civil successor, the president personally authorized the attorney general to instruct the Treasury to press ahead with the fraud charges:

> After the cabinet meeting the President has his usual press conference. Mr. Morgenthau and I remained over and after the conclusion of the press conference we went into a discussion of the Mellon situation . . . The President, with an expressive gesture, held his nose . . . After considerable discussion, the President upheld my position at every point.[66]

Thus was the scene set for the infamous "tax trial" involving Andrew Mellon and the federal government. It took place before the Board of Tax Appeals, and would last from February 1935 until May 1936—a period

almost exactly coinciding with the climax of Roosevelt's public and legislative campaign against banking and big business. The mood of the
country was deeply hostile to men like Mellon, but the contest was not as
uneven as this might imply: the full board comprised twelve members,
and most of them had been Mellon appointees.[67] Even so, the three members who would actually hear the case could not be counted upon to be
collectively sympathetic: for they were E. H. Van Fossen (a Republican,
appointed by Mellon), Bolon B. Turner (a Roosevelt Democrat), and
Charles M. Trammell (a Democrat, appointed by Mellon). The proceedings began in Pittsburgh, but in May 1935 they moved to Washington,
and they absorbed most of Mellon's time and effort during that period—
along with a substantial sum of money, since his lawyers' fees eventually
amounted to $360,000.[68] In all, 47 witnesses appeared, 847 exhibits were
accepted in evidence, and the trial transcript amounted to 10,000 typewritten pages. The proceedings would vary from high drama or comedy
(as when Mellon was rebuked for smoking in the courtroom during a
recess) to lengthy discussion of technical and arcane financial questions.
Media interest was high throughout, and Roosevelt was kept fully informed by Jackson and Morgenthau.[69]

Mellon was closely involved with his own defense, attending the hearings virtually every day; and when he took the stand himself on April 1,
1935—his testimony would go on for a week—he revealed a mastery of
the details of his financial career which surprised no one, but also a sustained fluency that surprised many: it was as if sheer indignation had sil-
vered his tongue.[70] (He also celebrated his eightieth birthday during the
course of the proceedings, though hardly in a joyous mood.) He told of
his father and his own early days, of the growth of T. Mellon & Sons, of
relations with his brother Dick, of the companies they had helped to
establish, and of his hopes for his two children, especially Paul. To his
admirers, Mellon's testimony, which would fill six hundred pages of the
typewritten record, was a tour de force: here was one of the preeminent
bankers, businessmen, and public servants of his time, obliged to explain
himself by making what amounted to an *apologia pro vita sua*, and during
which he betrayed not a shred of rancor or resentment toward the federal
forces so vindictively arrayed against him. "We do feel," one of his admirers wrote, "it has been a perfect outrage to subject you to such an unjust
ordeal after what you have given of your time, experience and money to
the government."[71]

But in such extensive testimony, Mellon was bound to make some damaging admissions. Indeed, to his political opponents, one of the major jus-

tifications for these further proceedings was not so much to recover lost federal revenues, but to get such embarrassing details on the record, so they might provide the Roosevelt administration with additional ammunition in its continuing battle against selfish and irresponsible plutocracy.[72] Like J. P. Morgan Jr. testifying a few years earlier to the Senate Committee on Banking and Currency, Mellon admitted to delegating the preparation of his own tax returns to his staff (not such a commonplace in those days), and also to having signed his 1931 return without scrutinizing it carefully, in the rush before departing to London.[73] Like many rich men, he also failed to understand just how damaging it was to admit that he did not know how rich he was, when so many Americans knew precisely how poor they were. "I've never kept track," he explained, "for the simple reason that I never thought it was important to know. What's really important is that the money is at work, creating work." This had always been Mellon's belief and self-justification, but in the 1930s, when the responsibility of "creating work" seemed increasingly to fall to government rather than business, the claim seemed unpersuasive and self-serving.

In other ways, too, Mellon's testimony failed to convince those who were determined not to be convinced. He continued to insist that when he became treasury secretary, he had given up involvement in banking and business, "as if I had died." Yet again, this was a bald lie, as it had always been when Mellon's qualification for office had been challenged under federal statutes. But it was less credible after his damaging admission to the Patman inquiry that he had conveyed his banking shares to his brother, in what had been in essence a sham transaction. His "death," Jackson wryly noted, "certainly did not result in 'sleep perchance to dream no more.' "[74] The Treasury counsel also brought up the collapse of the Bank of Pittsburgh, pointing up the contrast between the Mellons' successful resolve to protect their own empire and their selfish indifference to the fate of other finance houses in the city.[75] And they depicted Mellon's elaborate financial machinations, involving the educational and charitable trust and the Coalesced and Ascalot companies, as a massive, elaborate, premeditated conspiracy to evade taxes. In responding, Mellon was obliged to divulge to the American public, and for the official record, many of the details of his banking and business life which, for more than half a century, he had so determinedly kept to himself and a few favored associates. It was at best an unsettling ordeal for an old man; at worst it was a sustained and bitter public humiliation. "He felt the wound," Herbert Hoover later wrote, "to a lifetime of integrity."[76]

Technically, as distinct from rhetorically, the tax trial centered on certain specific issues, several of them legitimately "subject to dispute" and which, had fraud not been charged, Mellon would have been willing to settle by quiet negotiation. The first concerned the sale, in January 1931, of about $8 million worth of the bonds Mellon held in the Bethlehem Steel Company, which he had received for the sale of McClintic-Marshall. That transaction had realized a capital gain on which Mellon had duly paid his taxes. But there was serious disagreement as to whether the gain had been calculated correctly. The law required a valuation of the McClintic-Marshall stock in 1913 (the year the federal income tax took effect), and the difference between that estimate and the price at the sale in 1931 was the capital gain on which tax had been levied. The higher the 1913 valuation, the lower the subsequent capital gain—and thus the tax on it. A simple matter in principle, but not in practice: the worth of the McClintic-Marshall stock in 1913 was problematic, because there were only four stockholders (Andrew Mellon, his brother Dick, and Messrs. McClintic and Marshall), and the stock had no market value because it had never been publicly traded or quoted.

In his 1931 tax return, Mellon had estimated that in 1913, the hypothetical market value of the McClintic-Marshall stock had been $350 a share: he made plain that the figure was "tentative," and thus subject to examination and review by the Bureau of Internal Revenue. Following the pre-Roosevelt rules and conventions, he had made what was in effect an opening offer, fully expecting that his representatives and those of the bureau could agree on a definitive value, perhaps resulting in a refund, though more likely in an additional payment for Mellon. But the deficiency letters had peremptorily fixed the value of McClintic-Marshall in 1913 at $158.54 a share, less than half Mellon's estimate, thereby claiming a very substantial additional liability. Accordingly, a succession of expert witnesses were summoned, both for Mellon's side and for the federal government's—but even experts could venture no more than opinions. As the minutiae and arcana on this matter accumulated day by day, the large crowds that had shown up since the opening arguments, expecting more star witnesses, bombshells, and pyrotechnics, thinned dramatically; and even Frank Hogan handed the matter over to associates who for months had made the issue one of "unsleeping study."[77]

A second area of contention, previously broached by McFadden and Olson back in early 1933, concerned Mellon's sale of 27,000 shares in the Western Public Service Corporation to the Union Trust Company for $108,000 on December 2, 1931. (McFadden and Olson had claimed it was only 10,000 shares.) Thirty-seven days later, on January 8, 1932, the stock, repurchased from the Union Trust Company, was again in Mellon's account. On the surface, this seemed a perfectly legal transaction: the law permitted the reacquisition of stock thirty days after the initial sale. But a finer point was in question. For during that thirty-day period, the purchaser was enjoined by law not only from repurchasing the stock, but also from "enter[ing] into any contract or option" to do so. In this instance, the burden of proof lay with Mellon to show that no such "contract or option" had existed between himself and Union Trust. But proving this negative was not easy. Mellon himself knew nothing about the transaction until the tax case brought it to light, and the two men who had executed it on his behalf, Dick Mellon and Henry C. McEldowney, were both dead and had left no records.

A third matter, also initially raised in 1933, concerned the sale of stock in the Pittsburgh Coal Company, a perennial runt among Mellon enterprises, which was also unusual for being quoted on the stock exchange rather than "closely held," and of which Paul Mellon had recently become an understandably unenthusiastic director. Following severe labor disputes during the mid-1920s, Andrew and Dick had both increased their shareholdings significantly, and at their peak Andrew's investment in the company was valued at $6,170,000. But by December 1931, the worth of that investment had shrunk to $500,000, and at the end of that month, Mellon sold this depressed stock to the Union Trust Company, thereby realizing a deductible loss of approximately $5,500,000. Three months later, Mellon sailed for London to assume his ambassadorial duties, and while he was away, in late April 1932, the same block of Pittsburgh Coal stock was bought from the Union Trust Company by the Coalesced Company for $500,000 plus interest and incidental charges. All the preferred stock in the Coalesced Company was held by Andrew Mellon himself, and he had made all the common stock over to his two children in December 1931.

The sale of stock in this way, to a private, family-owned company, or even direct to close relatives, for the sake of establishing a tax-deductible loss, had been recognized as being perfectly legitimate at the time Mellon disposed of his coal shares. As such, it was a fair means of tax avoidance (which was a wholly legal objective), but it did not constitute tax evasion (which was a felony). To be sure, Congress had taken some steps in the Revenue Act of 1934 to close up the loophole, but such legislation could not be applied retroactively; moreover, to make something illegal rather confirmed that it had been legal before. Nevertheless, there was one aspect of the transaction about which the federal government was suspicious, and that was Mellon's intentions at the time of the first sale. For if these had all along included the repurchase of the Pittsburgh Coal stock four months afterward by Coalesced, the deal amounted to a conspiracy, to which all companies and persons concerned were party. In the event of such collusion, the initial loss would be nondeductible, and Mellon would be guilty of tax evasion. Accordingly, Robert Jackson concentrated his efforts on proving just such a conspiracy, insisting that the sequenced exchange of securities between Mellon, Union Trust, and Coalesced was but a "shadow sale," and therefore fraudulent.

Only two men had been party to the first transaction: Henry C. McEldowney and Andrew Mellon. McEldowney had recently died, but not before making a detailed declaration that his purchase of the coal stock from Mellon on behalf of the Union Trust Company had been in good faith, with no understanding, either explicit or implied, that he would later be relieved of those securities by Coalesced at the price he had paid for them. And so it came down to Mellon's word. He testified that he had indeed sold the stocks in Pittsburgh Coal to establish a loss so as to reduce his taxes—as the law of the time had allowed him to do. He also pointed out that he had owned several more blocks of stocks showing substantial losses, and that had he sold them all and legally deducted these additional losses, he would have paid no federal income tax for 1931. Such complete avoidance would have been entirely legal, but it seemed to Mellon, as a point of honor, that because he had a "substantial income," he "ought to pay substantial tax," as he had done every year since 1913.[78] Accordingly, he had singled out the Pittsburgh Coal stock, because its value was so depressed. Once it was assigned to Union Trust and the price was paid, that was the end of the transaction.

Such was Mellon's account, which contradicted Robert Jackson's claim of a conspiratorial arrangement. Mellon emphatically denied this charge, pointing out, quite correctly, that if his real aim had been to sell the Pittsburgh Coal stock to Coalesced, he could have done that directly, without breaking the law.[79] There was no need for an intermediate sale to Union Trust, and it had never entered his mind to use that company as a "conduit" (Jackson's word) for a later transaction. Mellon further insisted that he had learned of the second sale, from Union Trust to Coalesced, only three months after it had been completed. He had had no part in that deal, which had been negotiated between McEldowney and the managers of the Coalesced Company, entirely at their own initiative, perhaps because they believed that the stock ought to be restored directly to the family portfolio. In reply, Jackson put on the stand a varied group of witnesses who insisted that there had been some kind of agreement or understanding or collusion. None of them, however, had been party to the transactions, and their evidence was never more than circumstantial.

The final, and most significant, issue concerned the legitimacy of the educational and charitable trust that Mellon had established in December 1930 to hold the pictures and the money that were destined for the National Gallery of Art. The federal government charged that it was not a bona fide trust but another sham created for the purposes of tax evasion.[80] In support of that claim, Jackson submitted that the trustees were Mellon himself, his son, his son-in-law, and his lawyer, Donald Shepard: a cozy coterie more concerned with the benefit of the Mellon family than that of the American public. Consigning them to such an entity, Mellon had not relinquished personal control of his paintings, which had yet to go on public display in the furtherance of any of the trust's ostensible objectives. On the contrary, they were housed in the basement of the Corcoran Gallery in Washington, where the only people who could see them were, again, Andrew Mellon himself and, at his invitation, close relatives and friends. As for the National Gallery: with no material sign of its existence, Jackson dismissed it as at best a delusion, at worst an outsize deceit. By assigning his art to a sham trust, established in bogus support of a chimerical gallery, and claiming charitable deductions, Mellon had knowingly, deliberately, and willfully sought to defraud the U.S. government.

Of necessity, a large part of the defense's case was devoted to justifying the aims and activities of the educational and charitable trust, which also meant itemizing the scope and describing the motivation of Mellon's picture purchases, and outlining the gallery plan as it had thus far evolved. Hogan rightly insisted that this was a vital part of the case for the defense, but Mellon himself was unconvinced. He still sought to keep the plan a secret, partly out of his usual preference for reticence, and also for fear that making the scheme public would drive up the price of any pictures he might wish to acquire in the future. During the course of his own testimony, he had done nothing to help his cause. "The report," he averred, "that I have arranged to build a gallery in Washington, is entirely unfounded. I have engaged no architects, have caused no plans to be drawn, and have made no commitment to build or endow a gallery at Washington, Pittsburgh, or elsewhere."[81] This was all true so far as it went; but it was not the whole truth, and Hogan successfully insisted that the trust had been legitimately created to be the vehicle by which Mellon would establish a national gallery in the nation's capital as a gift to the American people.

Of course, there had been rumors floating about Washington concerning Mellon and such a scheme since 1927. But it was only during the trial that his great plan was first publicly disclosed.[82] The news that Mellon had been actively working toward such a benefaction caused a sensation, and received extensive press coverage, especially as the details emerged concerning the scale of his collection, the intrigue of the Hermitage picture purchases, and the magnitude of his intended gift, which was conservatively valued at fifty million dollars.[83] Charles Henschel and Carman Messmore both testified on behalf of Knoedler & Company, outlining their firm's long business relations with Mellon, giving some account of the Russian acquisitions, and stating that his art collection was "unique and unlike any other collection ever known or even heard of . . . All his pictures are of great quality and marvelously collected with great patience."[84] And Frank Hogan made telling use of these revelations of his client's long-nurtured and carefully planned scheme of national philanthropy. "God did not place in the hearts and minds of men such diverse and opposite traits as these," he insisted. "It is impossible to conceive of a man planning such benefactions and at the same time plotting and scheming to defraud his government." It was a successful ploy. "Every time we bring out a bad point," Jackson ruefully observed, "Hogan brings out a picture."[85]

In making the argument that the A. W. Mellon Educational & Charitable Trust was a wholly bona fide trust, intended to hold Mellon's great assemblage of paintings which would plausibly form the nucleus of a great national collection, Hogan's star witness was, predictably, Joseph Duveen. On June 9, 1935, he turned in a bravura performance of histrionics and hyperbole that managed to aggrandize himself no less than the defendant.[86] Stating his name for the record as Lord Duveen of Millbank, he accepted the defense's flattering characterization of him as the greatest art dealer in the world, and confirmed his positions as trustee of Britain's National Gallery, National Portrait Gallery, and the Wallace Collection. He also claimed the credit for persuading Mellon to establish a great gallery in Washington, sometime back in the 1920s, and also for the unrivaled merit of the paintings he had acquired. "I consider the Mellon collection of pictures," he declared, "the greatest collection ever assembled by any individual collector"; it was "the finest private collection in the universe." By comparison, the Hermitage was "no more the greatest collection in the world, it has gone to pieces." And Duveen also insisted that he had agreed with Mellon as to the proposed gallery's ideal site, which he described as being "by the obelisk, near the pond." The court erupted with laughter when it was clarified that his lordship was referring to the Washington Monument and the Reflecting Pool.[87]

During his testimony, Duveen was wholly unfazed to be reminded that he had paid a penalty of one million dollars for having sought to evade tax on works of art imported to the United States in 1911; and he was sublimely indifferent to the profit or loss his company had made in 1931 and 1932, or whether he himself had paid any income tax in those years. He also lavished on Robert Jackson, a future justice of the Supreme Court, a truly impressive condescension. "Really, my dear fellow," Duveen scolded him, "art works do not rise and fall in value like pig iron. . . . They have a value, and that's all there is to it." Describing the Van Eyck in Mellon's collection, he observed, with sublime hauteur: "Perhaps you don't realize that there are only three small Van Eycks in America, and they can't compare with Mr. Mellon's." Duveen even admitted to having netted $85,000 from the sale to Mellon of his first Raphael Madonna for $836,000, which he had thought "a very low price. But Mr. Mellon thought it was a very high price. One day after lunch, I gave way." Here, according to *Newsweek*, "Duveen beamed at Mellon," and "the banker stopped chewing gum long enough to wink at Duveen." Once Duveen's testimony was concluded, Donald Shepard sent him "warmest congratulations upon deserved effective defense of Mr. Mellon and wise artistic utterances. Triumphant for him and for yourself."[88]

Throughout the trial, Mellon maintained his absolute innocence, convinced that the evidence supported him rather than the prosecution. In the case of the sale of his McClintic-Marshall shares to the Bethlehem Steel Company, the issue was one where Mellon had always admitted there was room for difference of opinion, and there was no question of fraudulent intent. In the case of the double sale of the shares in Pittsburgh Coal, it was up to the government to provide proof of deliberate fraud; moreover, there was no conceivable reason why Mellon should have entered into collusion, and there was no hard evidence that he had. As for the educational and charitable trust: the evidence was overwhelming as to its history, legitimacy, and purpose, and the unintended consequence of trying to show otherwise only revealed to the public that the man whom the government had tried to tar as a tax shirker had in fact made significant progress toward his plan to donate an unprecedented gift to the American people. Only in the case of the sale of the stock from the Western Public Service Corporation was Mellon on weaker ground, for in this matter, the burden of proof lay with him, and with his brother and Henry C. McEldowney both dead, it was proof he could not provide.

In terms of the specific legal and financial issues, the federal government's case against Mellon was thus decidedly weak. This had been the assessment that the Treasury officials had offered the Justice Department back in the spring of 1933, and they continued to maintain this view thereafter, until they were overruled by the attorney general, acting on Roosevelt's instructions. "We are expected to make bricks without much straw," Jackson lamented in the summer of 1934. Later he feared that the case would seem to be one of "political persecution." This was corroborated when a carbon of one of the Bureau of Internal Revenue's deficiency letters to Mellon was introduced in evidence at the trial, bearing the stamp "this case was not considered on its merits."[89] Nor did Jackson find the witnesses easy: he could not be seen to bully Mellon, and found him "the most difficult man I ever cross-examined," while David Bruce, Paul Mellon, and Donald Shepard simply refused to testify and could not be compelled to do so (though a halfhearted attempt would be made in the case of Paul). At one point in the proceedings, Jackson caught shingles; at another, he was so discouraged by Van Fossen's persistently pro-Mellon stance that he offered to resign.[90] He hoped to "give the newspaper boys a sensation a day," but in May 1935, the *New York Times* reporter covering the trial, who had been on the side of the government, was transferred by the editor to cover agriculture in Arkansas. And toward the very end of the trial, Charles M. Trammell, a Democrat, "mysteriously resigned" to represent the du Pont family in a tax claim he would argue before the Board of Tax Appeals of which he had recently been a member.[91]

Hogan certainly fought hard for his client. But the record generally bears out the views of Mellon's relatives and friends that the tax trial was politically motivated by an administration which, according to Ogden Mills, was "entirely lacking in an elementary sense of decency."[92] True, FDR usually denounced businessmen, bankers, "economic royalists," and "malefactors of great wealth" in very general terms between 1933 and 1936, but he was also prepared to name particular individuals, and to subject them to the sustained pressure and adverse publicity of scrutiny by the Bureau of Internal Revenue and the Department of Justice. Andrew Mellon was at the top of Roosevelt's list of those to be singled out. The president clearly disliked him, not entirely without cause: for his business success no less than for his business ethics, for his policies at the Treasury, for his willful flouting of the law while he held public office, and for being the embodiment of everything in the pro-business Republican world before 1932 that Roosevelt loathed and was determined to destroy. The precise details of Mellon's tax returns were probably of no concern to FDR, and he may not even have cared about the ultimate outcome of the tax trial. But he wanted to put Mellon on trial for being Mellon, to launch "an attack upon his character" and to "discredit" him.[93] In these endeavors, Roosevelt undoubtedly succeeded, and Mellon's standing in American history has never recovered. Was this rough, fair, and belated justice? Or was it low, mean-spirited political revenge?

IV. THE GALLERY AND THE FAMILY

The so-called tax trial ended in the summer of 1936 with the preparation of final briefs by both sides, after which the Board of Tax Appeals, now minus Charles M. Trammell, retired to deliberate. Although Mellon remained confident of eventual vindication, he was, as FDR had intended, exhausted and downcast by the degrading public exposure. "Mr. Mellon," Duveen's spies reported, "seemed a little bit tired and depressed," and this meant he was still not "in the mood for buying pictures." It was Carman Messmore's opinion that Mellon would not acquire art again "until the trial and other complications were over."[94] For that distraction was not Mellon's only concern. In May 1935, the Bureau of Internal Revenue attempted to impose a property tax not only on the pictures in his apartment but also on those stored in the Corcoran Gallery. Mellon was outraged at this further attack, and informed the revenue commissioners that in the event of enforcement, he would "take all his pictures and instantly move from Washington, as the price he is asked to pay is absolutely prohibitive." He seems to have fended off this attempt to tax him further, but compounding as it did the wounds of the tax trial and the Alcoa suit, Mellon must have felt himself under all-out siege by the Democrats: small wonder he had no enthusiasm for buying art.

This is not to say that he simply turned morose, for even as the tax trial was under way, Mellon was thinking about the future. It was not only the hearings that had virtually suspended his art purchases and delayed the planning of the gallery by almost three years; the depressed and uncertain state of the economy, and that of his own finances, were also responsible. But now, across America, it seemed that business was definitely picking up—not, as Mellon saw it, thanks to anything Roosevelt had done, but owing to the natural course of the economic cycle. (He would always bemoan FDR's reliance on "theorists" and professors over entrepreneurs as advisers, for they had "no experience whatever in running successfully the businesses they are now trying to dictate to.") The proof was close at hand. Between 1933 and 1936, the reserves and liabilities of the Mellon

National Bank increased from $207 million to $343 million.[95] In 1936, Alcoa's profit neared $32 million, almost the equal of 1929 (a record year), and more than the combined surpluses for the period 1930 to 1934. "Business is maintaining its improvement," Andrew wrote to Paul early in the year. Gulf stock was now 86; Alcoa common stock was at 100, and preferred at 114. "The trend is upward," he concluded, "but to what extent it will continue is presenting a problem."[96]

To be sure, this improvement in his companies did not translate into an upsurge in Mellon's personal resources. In 1934, after paying federal income tax just shy of half a million dollars, his net income was very close to one million. But in 1935, after taxes of $520,000, he made a net loss of $268,000, which only slightly improved in 1936 when, with taxes of $365,000, his net income was a mere $161,737. Nevertheless, after giving away no money during 1934, Mellon had resumed disposing of his fortune. In 1935, he passed on $12.7 million to the trusts he had set up for his grandchildren, and also $10.5 million to the educational and charitable trust, his first major donation to it of stock as distinct from pictures. Thanks to Roosevelt's recent legislation, he was also obliged to pay substantial federal gift taxes: $2.2 million in 1935, and $5.7 million in 1936.[97] And in March 1936 he gave a further half million dollars to the University of Pittsburgh, for the completion of the common room in the Cathedral of Learning—a benefaction which was, as usual, conditional on there being no publicity.[98] As a result of these gifts and payments, Mellon's personal fortune continued to dwindle inexorably: at book value, he had been worth $55 million at the end of 1934, but by the beginning of 1936, he was worth only $35 million.

During the same period, Mellon did return to buying art, after a lapse of more than three years, albeit on a reduced scale. In February 1935, when the tax trial was just beginning, he had purchased Duccio's *Madonna and Child* (subsequently declared to be in the style of Duccio) and Castagno's *Portrait of a Young Man* from Knoedler for $400,000; and in December that year, he acquired Hobbema's *The Holford Landscape* and Gerard David's *Rest During Flight to Egypt* for $250,000, again through Knoedler.[99] Two of these were religious works, further signaling Mellon's determination to broaden his collection to meet a public gallery requirement of comprehensiveness; his personal preferences had never tended toward sacred subjects. Moreover, the Duccio was not a portrait but a late-fifteenth-century marble bas-relief: it represented Mellon's first foray from paintings into sculpture, yet another sign that he was extending his purchasing beyond his own interests. David Finley was an advocate of sculpture, and now urged his master to acquire such works; he hoped that this initial acquisition was "a happy augury of more to follow."[100]

This was not the only way in which Mellon was looking to the future. The same impulse was evident in a more substantial purchase he made in February 1936, after lengthy negotiations, which Mellon financed via his educational and charitable trust rather than from his own pocket.[101] It was the first and only time he bought art in bulk: 175 pictures from the collection of Thomas Clark, through Knoedler, for $580,000 ("half its value," Andrew triumphantly reported to Paul). Most of these paintings were portraits of major American historical figures, among them John Quincy Adams, Stephen Foster, Benjamin Harrison, Nathaniel Hawthorne, and Andrew Jackson, and their purchase was a further indication, following the earlier acquisition of the painting of Pocahontas, that Mellon was seriously considering founding a national portrait gallery in Washington. (On learning of this deal, Duveen sniffed that he "was not interested in Americana.")[102] Later in the year, Mellon bought more American portraits through Knoedler, including John Calhoun, Dewitt Clinton, Daniel Webster, Henry Clay, and James Buchanan; he also acquired one major work by Hans Memling, *Portrait of a Man with an Arrow*, for $100,000 in June 1936. Like the Clark collection, these purchases were paid for by the trust rather than by Mellon personally.

In returning to buying pictures while the tax trial was still proceeding, Mellon not only confounded both Knoedler and Duveen; he also showed that his determination to see the National Gallery of Art created (and perhaps a portrait gallery too) was more powerful than the most adverse and dispiriting circumstances FDR and his minions could contrive. At the same time, he also decided that he should now appoint an architect, and that it should be John Russell Pope. The two men had been acquainted for some years: in 1929, Mellon had (belatedly) appointed him to the Board of Architectural Consultants overseeing the construction of the Federal Triangle, and Pope had subsequently designed the building that would house the National Archives. But there were also private connections: early in his career, Pope had built a house on Long Island for Ogden Mills; he had created the mausoleum for Arabella and Henry Huntington at San Marino; and in 1931, on the death of Henry Clay Frick's widow, he had been appointed by the trustees (of whom Mellon was one) to transform the Frick mansion in New York into a public museum by adding extra galleries, an auditorium, and a garden court. This commission he executed with such skill that on its opening to the public in December 1935, these extensions seemed organic parts of the original house.[103]

Pope was also strongly supported by two powerful, well-connected, and familiar figures. One of them was Charles Moore, an old friend of both Pope and Mellon, who was still the chairman of the Commission of Fine Arts. On learning from Mellon's tax trial testimony about his proposed Washington gallery, Moore immediately initiated a correspondence with him, the purpose of which was to champion Pope. The second was Lord Duveen who, on commending Pope to Huntington, had described him, with his customary certitude, as "the greatest architect of modern times and the only man for you."[104] For Pope specialized in those grand, neoclassical, Beaux-Arts buildings, in the Roman rather than the Greek style, which Duveen deemed the only setting equal to the display of great European art. Moreover, Duveen had insisted that Pope be engaged to design the modern foreign sculpture wing at the Tate Gallery in London, and also the wing for the Elgin marbles at the British Museum (both of which extensions his lordship funded).[105] And Duveen also employed Pope for the construction of galleries in his New York apartment and commissioned him to design a grand London house for him on the western edge of Hyde Park near Kensington Palace. During the second half of 1935, Duveen and Moore set out to persuade Mellon to appoint Pope to be the architect of his gallery.[106]

Since Pope was the undisputed American master of a conservative style of European architecture, there could not have been a better match for Mellon's essentially conservative taste in European art. And given his prior acquaintance with Pope and his work, the patron may have needed little persuading. Mellon interviewed him in December 1935, and they agreed upon the commission soon thereafter. Apart from the Jefferson memorial, Pope had no major projects under way at that time, and so he was able to split his staff, assigning equal manpower to both enterprises. Before all else, Mellon and Pope had to settle the location of the gallery, and they finally agreed on the area extending from Third to Seventh streets, bounded by the Mall and Constitution Avenue, not far from sites which had previously been considered for the same purpose during the 1920s. Within scarcely a month, Pope had also developed five designs for the gallery, drawing on his earlier work, both constructed and unrealized, for the Baltimore Museum of Art and the Art Institute of Chicago. The first envisaged a building 765 feet long, with projecting wings, interior courts, and four colonnaded and pedimented entrances. It was this design on which Pope came to focus, when Pope and Mellon met in mid-February 1936 to discuss it. The completed gallery would vary little in its general scheme from the one that they agreed on at that time.[107]

The proposed building was long, a double-H in shape, with a low dome set on a high drum, and with the principal entrance on the Mall. The east and west ends were given colonnaded porticoes, and the north and south façades were also treated with extended colonnades. There would also be large niches for sculpture, and the frieze was to be inscribed with the names of great artists. Inside, beneath the dome, there would be a central rotunda connected by corridors to two great enclosed courts toward each end of the building; they resembled the garden court that Pope had recently added on to Frick's house in New York. These large interior spaces were conceived to make visiting the museum an agreeable experience, by turns both stimulating and restful, and to that same end, all the galleries would be located on a single level. Initially, Mellon's pictures would be installed in the central area, surrounding the rotunda, with the more distant galleries to be brought into use only later. According to this vision, the building would be 829 feet long, 340 feet deep, and 140 feet tall at the top of the dome, which made it larger than Charles A. Platt's abortive design of 1924. On the south side, a massive flight of steps would lead up to the main entrance and the principal floor of the gallery; whereas on the Constitution Avenue side, the visitor would enter at ground level, where the offices as well as the power, heating, and cooling equipment would be located. From there, members of the public would ride up in elevators to the main gallery floor.

By the spring of 1936, as the tax trial was nearing its end, these outline drawings were ready. But while settling the design of the gallery, Mellon was also concerned to devise a governing structure for it that would best suit his purposes. He wanted to make his gift to the nation on terms the federal government would accept, but which would be matched by a commitment to federal assistance in maintaining the institution. At the same time, he also wanted the gallery to be guaranteed a substantial degree of independence from administrations which might be as malevolent and misguided as Roosevelt's.[108] Since Mellon's model had always been the building and collection of the National Gallery in London, it was scarcely surprising that he also looked to that example for ideas about governance. Accordingly, in January 1936, Duveen's London operation transmitted to its director, Kenneth Clark, a request for information as to "organization, maintenance, operation, etc.," and also inquiring "in whom is title of building vested." Clark confessed that it was "most difficult" to give "precise information" as the "whole system" had been "continually changed and complicated," but he replied at some length. "The constitution of the National Gallery," he began, "is like the British constitution: it has grown up gradually as the result of various traditions and adjustments, and on many important points it is impossible to find out how or where our constitution is defined."[109]

Nevertheless, Clark went on, it was clear that the Treasury was responsible for the upkeep, and that the building was (probably) vested in the Office of Works or, perhaps, the Treasury. Through Parliament, the British Exchequer provided the annual maintenance grant, and also a modest acquisitions budget, which had recently varied from £3,500 to £7,000 a year. Most gallery staff were civil servants, but the director was appointed by the prime minister, as were the gallery's ten trustees, in whom the ownership of the pictures was vested on behalf of the nation. On the whole, Clark concluded that "the constitution is a good one." Ten trustees seemed the right number, none of them was ex officio, and their function was largely "confined to purchasing," which left the director an agreeably wide area in which to exercise "a free hand." He was responsible to the trustees and to the Treasury "for the whole running, and to a large extent for the policy, of the Gallery," and in practice he was always given his head in such matters as "framing, cleaning and decoration." "The dual responsibility," Clark candidly allowed, "of the Director to the Trustees and Treasury gives him a valuable independence, by allowing him, in a critical situation, to play off one against the other." "It would be a great mistake," he concluded, "if the Director was appointed solely by the Trustees and was nothing more than their servant."[110]

Mellon rightly believed that if his gallery was to operate according to his wishes, the terms of its constitution were as important as the design of the building, and he was clearly influenced by this letter, in electing both what to emulate and what to avoid. He accepted that the eventual ownership of the gallery itself must be vested in a department of government on behalf of the people. He further approved of the arrangement whereby the annual cost of upkeep would be paid for by the Treasury, out of public funds. He also saw the sense of a small number of trustees and of an appointed director with career staff. All these elements of the British model would eventually find their way in some form into the constitution of the National Gallery of Art in Washington. But there would also be significant and telling differences. Mellon had no wish to charter his gallery on terms that might be modified over time, subject to political winds, which in his own later experience blew only ill. Nor did he want the trustees and the director being appointed by and beholden to the government of the day. He preferred a director who would serve at the pleasure of the trustees, and not one at liberty to play them off against the

Treasury. But he did want his gallery to be provided with a realistic acquisitions budget, so that the collection might grow and develop around the enabling nucleus of his own intended gift.

Mellon was determined to eradicate (Democratic) politics from the gallery's charter, but he could not do likewise concerning the allocation of the site and the acceptance of the proposal, which were still in many ways problematic.[111] The site that he had agreed upon with Pope had already been earmarked for the long-delayed George Washington Memorial Auditorium, and a design for it by Egerton Swartwout had recently been selected. A further difficulty might be expected in the form of opposition to the proposed closure of Sixth Street, from the National Capital Park and Planning Commission, whose approval was essential, as well as from concerned citizens' groups. Even if both of these matters could be resolved, it would still be necessary to gain the consent of the members of the Commission of Fine Arts for the design of the building, and this was also something that could not be taken for granted at a time of growing reaction against neoclassical architecture in favor of the modernist style. Finally, and most uncertainly: would Roosevelt advise the overwhelmingly Democratic Congress, on behalf of the American people, to accept such a gift from a man his administration had demonized and harassed for the better part of three years? There was always the chance that FDR might lose the 1936 presidential election, but he was riding high in the polls, and he was more likely to win by an even bigger margin than he had before.

None of these questions had been resolved as the tax trial drew toward its close in the summer of 1936. Nor had Andrew's relations with his son, which the glare and anxiety of the tax trial exacerbated rather than soothed. For Paul remained wholly uninterested in the Mellon bank and in Mellon businesses. It must have come as both an irritation and a disappointment to Andrew that it was R. K. Mellon who had successfully claimed leadership over the next generation in Pittsburgh, and it was already clear that Paul and RK did not get on with each other or even like each other very much. Moreover, Andrew had been obliged to discuss his relationship with Paul in his testimony at the tax trial. As the government attorneys had pointed out, the Mellon National Bank had always been a family affair: Did not Andrew intend it to continue in that way in the next generation? The father duly testified that it was up to his son to choose his own career, insisting that he and Paul were "congenial" and "comrades."[112] But this was obfuscation, to keep family disagreements private, and to avoid embroiling his son in a discussion of financial affairs which would be quite beyond him. In any case, Andrew's private comments at the time of Paul's aborted engagement to Delphina Burt doubtless still reflected his real feelings and intentions.

It did not help relations between father and son that Paul was abroad for most of the tax trial. No defiance or disloyalty was intended, but it must have been painful to Andrew to endure the bitterest public ordeal of his life without the visible support of his son and heir. And he could take no comfort in the reason for Paul's absence: he feared testifying about financial matters of which he knew very little because, as he later put it, "father had never really taken me into his confidence about his business life."[113] But the federal prosecutors were convinced that he might know things that would be embarrassing, if not incriminating, to his father. At the end of January 1935, just before the tax trial began, a court officer attempted to serve a subpoena on Paul in his office at the Mellon National Bank in Pittsburgh. Having been forewarned by an assistant, Paul escaped by climbing out of his office window onto the inner courtyard roof; he reentered the building through another window, took the elevator down, and went home. He had, in fact, a second good reason for wanting to flee: he was due to marry Mary Conover at Ailsa's house in New York in two days' time. The wedding duly took place, a low-key affair compared to Ailsa's high-society extravaganza of almost a decade before, and Mr. and Mrs. Paul Mellon set out for a lengthy honeymoon, beginning in Egypt, where they voyaged up the Nile to Abu Simbel before continuing to Paris, the Netherlands, and England and Scotland.[114]

As the tax trial dragged on, Paul grew ever more anxious about the outcome, yet he remained convinced that he must stay away from America until it was over.[115] While in England with Mary, he hunted in Wiltshire, and the couple witnessed the "magnificent" silver jubilee celebrations of King George V. But with future developments (and responsibilities?) in mind, Paul also set out to make a "thorough study" of "galleries here, especially the National," and to inform himself not only about the collections but also about "administrative problems and personnel."[116] Mr. and Mrs. Paul Mellon eventually returned to the United States in the autumn of 1935, by which time the tax trial testimonies had been completed, settling down at the family house on Woodland Road, where Andrew was often to be found when not in Washington. Indeed, it may have been to mark their return that he bought four pictures through Knoedler for $22,000, of subjects nearer to his son's heart than his own: Thomas Malton's paintings of High Street Oxford, and of the Senate House, the University Library, and King's College Chapel, Cambridge; and J. N.

Sartorius's studies of the Belvoir Hunt. The couple gave regular house parties in Pittsburgh for their smart New York friends, although Paul escaped to Rolling Rock or Rokeby as often as he could. For her part, Mary got on surprisingly well with her father-in-law, though in her letters she addressed him as "Dear Mr. Mellon" and signed herself "affectionately Mary."[117]

From the autumn of 1929, when he began his studies at Cambridge, to the middle of 1936, when the tax trial ended, Paul Mellon was as often in England as in America, the geographical distance from his father reinforcing the emotional gulf between them. By contrast, Ailsa and David Bruce were constantly at Mellon's side during the trial, keeping up the appearance of a happy marriage, and even living for a time in Pittsburgh, which Ailsa could never bear. During this period Andrew Mellon and his son-in-law became very close. Bruce was trained as a lawyer, he was good at dealing with people, and he knew about art, and although a lifelong Democrat, he had soon become convinced that the tax case was a political vendetta. He even wrote a satire, *Frankie in Wonderland*, which was privately printed for the family's enjoyment, and which included this courtroom scene, in which the King (FDR) is both judge and jury:

> "Order in court," said the king. "Who is the first prisoner?"
> "A banker from Pittsburgh who is in the aluminum business," answered the prosecutor, who was well known for his short cummings.
> "Guilty," shouted the King. "What crime is he accused of?"
> "He says he doesn't know, Judge," replied Short Cummings.
> "Never mind," said the King. "He's guilty anyhow, all Bankers are guilty! Especially Republican Bankers! Off with his head!"[118]

Bruce never forgave Roosevelt; he would vote Republican in 1936. As often occurs with flawed parents, Andrew found it easier to get on with David than with either of his own children. David, in turn, found Andrew more companionable than Ailsa. Indeed, some of David's friends mockingly suggested that the Mellon he was really in love with was not *his* wife but *her* father.[119]

There is a vivid picture of Andrew at this time painted by David in a letter to Ailsa of August 2, 1935, which gives some indication of the toll the tax trial was exacting. David was on the *Berengaria*, accompanying his father-in-law to England, while Ailsa remained at Syosset with little Audrey. It was during a break in the proceedings, and they had taken the opportunity to make brief visits to London and Paris. Paul and Mary had gone to the Manhattan dockside to see the two of them off, and David noted to Ailsa that Mary Mellon was "very attractive and sweet to your father. He is very pleased with her." The journey had been smooth and completely uneventful, largely because of Mellon's fatigue—he had clearly been "shockingly weak" before the crossing. "He told me the other day," David reported, "that walking from his office to the Duquesne Club" had been "enough completely to exhaust him." But the trip was "really doing him a great deal of good, and he says that he feels better than he has for months." Each day, Andrew arose at ten o'clock or later, lunched with David, watched a movie in the afternoon, dined early in his private sitting room with his son-in-law, then retired to bed. "Tonight," Bruce reported, "is the first time we expect to put on dinner coats and go to the dining room. It sounds very dull, but it is really most pleasant." And he concluded: "he is a sweet old gentleman, and it would have been ghastly for him if he had come by himself."[120]

With the trial still in progress, Paul and Mary Mellon went abroad again at the beginning of 1936. Despite the deep differences between father and son, Andrew clearly missed them, and he eagerly looked forward to "the pleasure of your return." They first visited Ireland, and then stayed for some time at Bibury Court in Gloucestershire, where Paul enjoyed a great deal of hunting with Mary occasionally following in the car. They invited Andrew and David Shepard to come over in April for a rest from their legal labors, but as there was "so much of importance" requiring Andrew's "personal attention," concerning especially the trial and the gallery plans, they were unable to accept. Paul now bought his first picture, a Stubbs of the Earl of Portland's horse Pumpkin (hardly after his father's taste), and he also visited the National Gallery again, armed with a letter of introduction from Duveen to Kenneth Clark.[121] While Paul and Mary were away, R. K. Mellon became engaged to the daughter of Seward Prosser, a senior figure in the Bankers Trust Company of New York. Like Mary Mellon, RK's fiancée had been married before, and Andrew thought her "attractive and of a thoughtful character," though when conveying the news in a letter to his son and daughter-in-law, he could not recall her name. The wedding was set for April 23, but Paul and Mary did not return for it, which Andrew thought "too bad." That they would soon nevertheless be back suggests serious coolness between Andrew's and Dick's sons.[122]

In May 1936, as both sides were preparing their final briefs for the Board of Tax Appeals, David Finley wrote to Lord Duveen on his master's behalf, warning him that "the Government's brief takes the position that you are interested only in what they choose to term 'the commercialization of art.' " Would Duveen accordingly provide information concerning his "great contribution to art in this country and England, and the fact that you are so highly regarded in both countries"? Duveen replied, noting "the uniqueness and impressiveness" of his London museum and gallery trusteeships, and adding that it would be "very useful for [the] judges to realize they in England have great faith in me."[123] At the time, Finley was keeping Mellon company in Pittsburgh, and the mood was somber. Otherwise, he told Duveen, his master was "entirely alone," as both his children and their spouses were away, and being unwell "Mr. Mellon is unable to leave the house, so time passes heavily for him just now." Soon after, Duveen spoke to Mellon on the phone and reached a quite different conclusion about his client's morale. "I must say," he told Finley, "that he sounded marvellous. You know how I dislike Pittsburgh, but I do think that he is most fortunate in having seven acres of park to loaf about in."[124]

16

BEGINNINGS AND ENDINGS
The Gallery Established, a Life in Its Fullness, 1936–37

It is a beautiful provision of nature to make life rosy at the beginning. It develops young hope and incites to action— renders work a pleasure and lures us on. As age approaches, and strength declines, the enchantment is removed and we see things differently . . . It is thus . . . we are brought to the point of departure. "Our little life," as Shakespeare has it, "is rounded with a sleep." And we are made to see, or at least feel, with the wise man, that all is vanity. And so we are prepared to step out without regret!

Thomas Mellon and His Times, p. 74

I. POLITICS, PICTURES, AND PAUL

Soon after Andrew Mellon's tax trial ended in Washington, the Democratic Party's national convention took place in Philadelphia in late June 1936. The setting was indicative of the party's determination to capture Pennsylvania this time. In his acceptance speech, Roosevelt turned in another bravura performance, depicting himself as the champion of the people's freedom against the "despotism" of those he denounced as "economic royalists." They were, he insisted, the owners and controllers of "corporations, banks and securities," who "impressed" the "whole structure of modern life" into their "royal service." There was no place under this "royalty," he went on, for anyone but greedy oligarchs "thirsting for power." And it was the "privileged princes of these new economic dynasties" (was he not a privileged dynastic prince himself?) who had during the 1920s "reached out for control of government" by creating "a new despotism," which they "wrapped in the robes of legal sanction" and which deprived "the average man," with whom FDR insistently identified himself, of his ostensibly inalienable rights to life, liberty, and the pursuit of happiness. "Against economic tyranny such as this," he went on, "the American citizen could appeal only to the organized power of Government. The collapse of 1929 showed up the despotism for what it was. The election of 1932 was the people's mandate to end it. Under that mandate it is being ended."[1]

This fiercely partisan account of the 1920s resonated powerfully with his rapt and delighted audience, and although Roosevelt once again named no names, it is inconceivable that he did not have Mellon in mind among the "economic royalists." To be sure, FDR admitted later in the campaign that "the overwhelming majority of businessmen in this country are good citizens," and that he was eager to do all he could to save the system of private property and free enterprise. But, he added, the greatest threat to the survival of that system was the existence, side by side, of "widespread poverty" and "concentrated wealth," and while he made more visible efforts to eradicate the former, he was equally determined on breaking up the latter. He took to the barricades once more in another coruscating speech at Madison Square Garden in New York, toward the very end of his campaign. Once again, he damned the previous Republican administrations, for "nine mocking years of the golden calf" followed by "three long years of the scourge." Once again, he denounced "business and financial monopoly, speculation, reckless banking, class antagonism, sectionalism, war profiteering": "never before in all our history have these forces been so united as they are today." "They are," he went on, "unanimous in their hate for me—and I welcome their hatred." "I should like to have it said of my first Administration," he concluded, "that in it the forces of selfishness and of lust for power met their match. I should like to have it said of my second Administration that in it these forces met their master."[2]

This was brilliant, barnstorming, unforgettable, infuriating raillery: "never in American history would the wealthy be scapegoated as they were in the 1936 presidential campaign."[3] With unemployment down to 60 percent of the figure that had greeted him at his inauguration, and with the *New York Times* index of business activity having risen to 100 for the first year since 1930, Roosevelt scented a massive electoral victory from the very beginning. A *Fortune* magazine opinion poll found that 53 percent of Americans thought the Depression was over, and all polls showed

60 percent or more to be well satisfied with the president's performance. The Republicans had put up a thoroughly moderate candidate in the person of Alfred M. Landon, governor of Kansas, but FDR simply annihilated him. Securing 60 percent of the popular vote, he carried every state in the union except Maine and Vermont, garnering 523 votes in the electoral college to Landon's 8. This was more than a landslide: it conformed and consolidated the recasting of American politics that had been taking place since 1932. The Republican majority that had existed since Lincoln's time was gone, and in its place Roosevelt had forged a mighty new, national Democratic base, encompassing the big-city working class, farmers and rural laborers, the liberal East Coast, and the white South, as well as Jews and Catholics and African Americans virtually everywhere.[4]

These were constituencies in American society toward which Andrew Mellon had been at best indifferent, at worst hostile. Among the pillars of his world that fell under the Democratic steamroller was that of Republican dominance at every level in Pennsylvania, a dominance Mellon and his associates had cherished throughout their lives as part of the natural, indissoluble order of things. Hoover had barely won western Pennsylvania in 1928; FDR had prevailed there in 1932, though he failed to carry the state. Now the Democrats had made off with Pennsylvania for the first time in fifty years. "I believe I'd vote for Roosevelt," declared one resident of a steel town, "because every banker is against him . . . I'm no red—just a common ordinary American." At the same time, Pittsburgh became a Democratic bastion and would continue as such throughout the twentieth century. For now, the downtrodden, disillusioned, and unemployed, whatever their national or ethnic origins, swarmed in protest and also in hope to Roosevelt's standard. FDR carried every ward in the city and garnered 70.6 percent of the vote.[5] This was a political earthquake to the Scotch-Irish Republican and Presbyterian elite who, as the town's employers, had previously commanded its voters, and for Mellon, it was another body blow to the understanding and practices of a lifetime.

Nor was this the only indication that the tectonic plates were shifting under his feet. In July 1936, in a powerful demonstration of labor's mounting confidence, two thousand steelworkers and coal miners had gathered at the Homestead battleground to pay homage to the "martyrs" of 1892, when Frick had turned the troops on the workers. The lieutenant governor of Pennsylvania, himself a vice president of the United Mine Workers union, made a speech before the crowd, declaring that the steel towns encircling Pittsburgh were now open to union organizers. And on behalf of Governor Earle, he promised public relief payments to workers and their families in the event of a strike. John L. Lewis now began a great drive to unionize steelworkers, and in an audacious gesture, he set up his local in Pittsburgh's Grant Building, headquarters of several steel corporations, where union leaders and steel executives routinely rode the elevators together in paralyzing, venomous silence. Thus was turned upside down the world which Andrew Mellon had always believed would endure for his lifetime and beyond.[6]

Neither Pittsburgh nor Washington offered him comfort or consolation, but at least he was now free of obligatory exertions for the first time in his life. He had withdrawn more fully from business, he had exited the public stage, and he no longer needed to show up daily in court. During the second half of 1936, he could, in a real sense, finally retire. He was now eighty-one, and it had for many years been a joke in the family that "Andy expected to live forever." He certainly had good reason, on the grounds of heredity, to expect a significantly longer life than most. True, some of his siblings had died young, but his father had lived to ninety-five and his mother to ninety-two (Paul in his turn would almost match his grandmother's years), and his older brother James Ross had made it to eighty-eight.[7] "You will get around to this matter at about the year 2000" had been a favorite quip of Dick's to his brother, pleasantly echoing Andrew's own supposed conviction (or failure of imagination) respecting his own mortality. Unlike Nora's and Ailsa's, his health had always been excellent, he had no use for doctors, and he scarcely ever had personal recourse to one; his examination before the London posting had been an exception. Until his early eighties, his appetite continued good, and there was no decline in the number of rat-tailed cigars he enjoyed, or in the vigor of his regular walks in Washington and Pittsburgh.[8]

It is impossible to know the effect of the tax trial on Mellon's hitherto robust constitution, and the opinion of family and friends was divided. There were those like David Finley who maintained the impact was negligible; that Mellon, steel-nerved and never doubting his innocence, was certain of vindication; the trial in this view represented little more than an irritating interruption of his planning for the gallery.[9] His performance on the witness stand had certainly shown him in full command of himself, of his affairs, and of the issues. Indeed, he had often seemed to regard the proceedings as a fascinating legal-cum-financial puzzle in which he was dispassionately engaged, rather than as a life-and-death struggle to save his reputation.[10] But Paul, Ailsa, and David Bruce claimed that the wearying days in court, the humiliating publicity, the constant exposure, and the uncertainty of outcome in such hostile times took years off Mellon's life, with Roosevelt and his cronies thus responsible for "hounding" Mellon to a relatively early grave.[11] More generally, there were those who felt that Mellon's later years were darkened by an overwhelming sense of futility and of a life ill-lived, with his proudest and heretofore most certain achievements reviled and likely to be forgotten. Indeed, Chancellor John Bowman claimed that Mellon would telephone him late at night, seeking reassurance that his life had not been lived in vain.[12]

Whatever the impact of the tax trial may have been, Mellon headed for Europe as soon as it was over, accompanied by Donald Shepard; they joined David Finley and his wife in London. His purpose was business as much as relaxation, the future rather than the past. While in the capital, he "visited all the larger galleries, had conferences with their officers, particularly as regards the organization and operation of the galleries, and the construction of gallery buildings."[13] In July, Mellon called on Duveen at his London salesroom, an encounter almost as celebrated as the (probably apocryphal) meeting between the two in the elevator at Claridge's a decade and a half before. Duveen and Finley were now corresponding regularly about Mellon's art collection, and his lordship had known for some time that a post-trial visit was planned, on which occasion he hoped to "open [Mellon's] eyes to the beauty of the eighteenth century," by which he presumably meant European rather than English paintings. "From that," Duveen told one correspondent, to whom he said he was "advising and helping Mr. Mellon form a collection for a museum in Washington," he hoped that "something might develop."[14] But when Mellon finally appeared, he was in a far more expansive and acquisitive mood than even Duveen had dared dream. "Expect make much larger deal with Mellon," he informed his New York office, "than one originally contemplated. He wants to buy all our great Italian pictures. Greatly encouraged after three hours with him yesterday."[15]

Sensing the opportunity of a lifetime, Duveen reacted with predictable speed and imagination, putting to Mellon a much augmented proposition which, if realized, would be not only the greatest sale of his career, but also Mellon's greatest purchase, surpassing even his acquisitions from the Hermitage. "I am going to retire from business," Finley recalled Duveen saying to his best customer, "and you are getting ready to give your collection for a national gallery. This is a combination of circumstances which could never happen again. I have quite a number of pictures of the first quality which are needed to build up your collection."[16] So, indeed, he had: for since 1929, he had been the owner of the great nineteenth-century Dreyfus collection, which he had purchased in Paris before the crash and urgently needed to sell. As it happened, the assemblage was strong in ways that Mellon's holdings were still weak: in Italian Renaissance paintings and in European sculpture, both categories which (Duveen repeatedly insisted) must be well represented in the Washington gallery. "They will," he told Mellon, "help you round out your collection before you give it to the country." Mellon agreed to meet Duveen in New York, to inspect the paintings and sculpture at his leisure when they would be on display in Duveen's showroom at 720 Fifth Avenue.[17]

Mellon returned to the United States in September, in time to receive an award from the Pittsburgh chapter of the American Chemical Society, in recognition of his contribution, and also that of his late brother, to the field of chemistry. But then he caught a severe cold, which forced him to send Finley to New York to see Duveen in his stead, with instructions to take to Washington for his own inspection "everything I thought good enough for the National Gallery." It was a remarkable, if unavoidable, show of Mellon's confidence in his adviser's judgment and loyalty. Finley duly departed to New York by the overnight train, and spent three days in a "velvet-hung room" at Duveen's gallery, as the staff came and went bearing objects for consideration. Later, he would confess to Duveen that he had been "overcome" by "the quality (and also the quantity of quality!)" of what he saw. He selected thirty paintings and twenty-one pieces of sculpture, all from the Dreyfus collection, which would soon be dispatched to Washington for Mellon's assessment.[18] It was intended that they would be stored in the basement of the Corcoran Gallery, along with Mellon's Hermitage acquisitions, so he might judge the two collections side by side, making his own selections at leisure from what Finley had chosen at Duveen's.

But the Corcoran Gallery was a dozen blocks from Mellon's apartment, and its basement, while fine for storage, was scarcely suited to contemplating art. Quite by chance, David Finley learned that an apartment directly beneath Mellon's, at 1785 Massachusetts Avenue, had become available for a sublet of two or three months. He passed the information on to Duveen, who immediately recognized the opportunity.[19] He took the apartment, decorated it with carpets and tapestries and porcelain, as well as with his choicest Louis XV and Louis XVI furnishings. He hung the paintings and installed the sculptures, creating a private gallery that would show the works to best advantage. Having engaged a caretaker and guards, he then handed the key over to Mellon. Naturally, the caretaker was in Duveen's pay, and that autumn he kept his employer well informed about Mellon's frequent visits downstairs. Apparently Mellon thought the

pictures and sculpture looked "*very, very* nice," and he often descended to
the apartment late at night, alone in his dressing gown and slippers. He
also took Charles Carstairs and Donald Shepard to this art-filled bower,
even entertaining some dinner guests there. On occasion, Duveen himself
appeared, to offer his customary voluble encouragement as Mellon looked
and pondered.[20]

Duveen had correctly surmised that this was an opportunity Mellon
could not resist, and in November 1936, scarcely two months after the
pictures and sculpture had been unpacked in Washington, negotiations
were under way. David Finley, the only witness to their discussions,
remembered that "both enjoyed the contest immensely": Duveen asked
what seemed "astronomical prices," wanting eight million dollars for the
pictures, and at least half that for the sculptures.[21] Mellon countered by
offering much less, though how much Finley declined to specify. At one
point, Mellon, resorting to his familiar poker tactics, observed: "Well,
Lord Duveen, I think you will have to take these things back to New
York." To which Duveen replied in kind: "Mr. Mellon, I would give you
these things for the National Gallery rather than take them away."[22]
When the brinkmanship was done, Mellon settled for twenty-four of the
thirty paintings, and for eighteen of the twenty-one sculptures. It was
rumored then, and the figure has continually been repeated since, that he
paid Duveen $21 million for them, which would have made it the largest
single art transaction to date. In fact, the sum was just short of $8 million,
which was greater than his outlay on the Hermitage pictures, though this
time the money had come from the educational and charitable trust rather
than from his own purse. The actual amount notwithstanding, the results
were just as Duveen had intended: Mellon secured for the National
Gallery the gems of the Dreyfus collection, and Duveen's finances were
restored by the liquidation of his most costly inventory. Now even this
most indefatigable of salesmen might begin to contemplate retirement.[23]

Beyond any doubt, Mellon's collection was substantially enhanced by
these purchases, which were finalized with unusual speed in December
1936. Most of the paintings were Italian old masters, such as Duveen had
always maintained would be necessary to correct the deficiencies of Mellon's collection—their selection suggests Mellon may have regretted his
failure to obtain the two Leonardos from the Hermitage. They ranged
from the Byzantine school of the thirteenth century to the High Renaissance, including works by Cimabue, Giotto, Filippino Lippi, Matteo di
Giovanni, Petrus Christus, and Botticelli. There was also, more typically
Mellonesque, a Joshua Reynolds (*Lady Elizabeth Delme and Her Children*)

and a Velázquez (*Portrait of a Young Man*). Equally noteworthy was the sculpture: Desiderio da Settignano's charming, life-sized bust of a little boy; Andrea della Robbia's glazed terra-cotta *Madonna and Child—Tondo*; Verrocchio's fabulously armored Giuliano de Medici; the two exquisite marble reliefs of Faith and Charity by Mino da Fiesole; Giovanni Bologna's *Mercury* (subsequently placed above the fountain in the rotunda of the National Gallery of Art); and many others. In the same month, and again through the educational and charitable trust, Mellon bought two pictures from Knoedler for a combined sum of $275,000: J. B. S. Chardin's *La Maîtresse d'École*, and Fra Angelico's *Madonna and Child*.

This sudden upsurge in acquisitions betokened Mellon's renewed confidence after the trial, but also his determination, now keener than ever, to assemble the best and most comprehensive collection for his intended gallery. Meanwhile, he was still in discussion with John Russell Pope about the design, and there remained the problem of settling the site in Washington with the appropriate authorities—a matter now taken up by Charles Moore of the Commission of Fine Arts.[24] In the autumn of 1936, Moore raised the issue with Egerton Swartwout, architect of the proposed George Washington Memorial Auditorium, which had already been granted the site. Moore now told him that the location must be used for another purpose and it would take him some effort to smooth Swartwout's ruffled feathers. He also initiated discussions with the National Capital Park and Planning Commission, chaired by Frederic A. Delano, which would have to approve the closure of Sixth Street; and he lobbied the district engineer and local citizens' associations. At the same time, Mellon himself made it plain that unless Sixth Street was closed, there would be no national gallery in Washington, and he would take his art elsewhere. With this powerful threat at their disposal, Moore and Delano set about obtaining the necessary permissions, and getting the interested parties and authorities aligned on their side.[25]

Although a trustee of the educational and charitable trust, Paul Mellon knew virtually nothing about the very significant purchase from Duveen, or about the site negotiations in Washington. His exclusion could hardly have made relations with his father any easier, and it may even have helped precipitate a major confrontation at just this time. But this was not the only cause. For the great issue between them remained unresolved, namely: What was Paul going to do with his life? In the autumn of 1936, he showed an interest in settling full-time at Rokeby in Virginia, and raised the subject with his father one day as they were being driven together into downtown Pittsburgh. Paul intended to begin by saying that he preferred country living to the urban existence of a banker, but feeling nervous and uneasy, as he always did when broaching any important topic with Andrew, he merely blurted out his wish to settle on the farm and add more acres to it. "Father replied," Paul recalled, "in his quiet voice that he considered that sort of real estate purchase a rather poor investment in the current economic climate." This discouragement reminded Paul of the time when he had asked his father for a pet, and Andrew had replied, "Oh, you don't want a dog." "There was," Paul remembered, "a forbidding quality in Father's cold attitude that always unnerved me, and made it very difficult for me to pursue a personal conversation with him."[26]

Paul, now twenty-nine, was becoming increasingly "discouraged over a growing feeling of stagnation" in his life. Urged on by Mary, he now set down his thoughts and feelings in a lengthy memorandum, which he would later use as a basis for discussion with his father, and which vividly conveys the difficulties, the resentments, the frustrations, and ultimately the sheer incomprehension that characterized Paul's relationship with him.[27] He began by conceding that he had never in his life asked his father a direct personal question, "never really tried to discover what the feeling is behind his strange exterior," and "never tried to have him put his philosophy or religion or hopes or emotions into words." Moreover, Paul allowed that "years of habit" had left him "encased in a lump of ice," with the result that whenever he approached personal conversation with his father, he became "congealed and afraid to speak." The ice age had endured so long "that it will be frightfully hard to thaw myself out and actually be able to feel my real emotions, and actually say them to him." But now he determined to express himself by whatever means he could, to talk about business, about values, about Nora, about hunting and love of country, about horse racing, and about paintings and the National Gallery.

As for business: What did his father "really expect me to do or to be?" Did he want his son to be "a great financier, to enter into the real spirit of business, to accumulate more wealth in addition to protecting this great mass of interests that have already fallen to me?" He was "appalled" at such a prospect, preferring his interests to be taken care of by "trusts or competent persons" so that he might be free to do the things he wanted with his life, though for now he was not sure what they were. As for values: Paul had no idea what his father thought life was for. "Why is business and the accumulation or protection of wealth more important than the acceptance and digestion of ideas?" "Why is he so afraid of the country and of country life?" "There is," Paul noted, "no use beating about the bush by trying to identify my sense of values with his." As for his mother: in his "instinctive nature" and in his "feeling for beauty and natural things," Paul felt himself to be much more like Nora than like Andrew. To be sure, he had inherited from his father "good judgment and sound natural sense and the sense of the importance of the outside world, and a respect for logic and order and money," all of which he recognized as "very important." But his father's "denial" (as he saw it) of his mother "and his complete reaction to anything to do with feelings or the personal side of nature," had "always had a dampening effect" on his own energy and emotions.

Turning to his own passions, Paul put "hunting and love of the country" very high, along with an "addiction" to English life, literature, and history, all of which he felt were owed entirely to his mother, and which only further set him at odds with his father. For Andrew had never owned a house in the country, or any land he valued for its own sake, in "a personal way," as distinct from properties he had bought for investment, whether in Pittsburgh or further afield. "What," Paul wondered, "is his aversion to owning land?" "Why haven't we, Ailsa and I, as children, ever had a permanent base, a real home with roots, in the country?" In the same way, he questioned his father's dislike of fox-hunting as a dangerous activity for his son to pursue: to Paul, it was an exhilarating endeavor, demanding skill and strength and nerve, and expressive of his dislike of "business, the city [and] modern industrial drabness." Andrew likewise had no use for Paul's love of horse racing, and this, too, had "always been a source of disagreement" between them. "Why," Paul pondered, "does he misunderstand the subject so? Is it because he thinks the whole thing is connected with gambling, drinking, fast horses, fast women? Is he influenced by Uncle Percy's lamentable addiction to betting and losing?" The answer to the second and third questions was almost certainly yes. But Paul loved to see his horses run more for the aesthetic experience than anything else: "the color, the movement, the speed, the excitement, the competition, the skill of riding, the cleverness of the horses, the primitive element of luck."

There was, Paul felt, simply no meeting of minds or feelings between himself and his father, and his collection and his scheme for the National Gallery of Art were prime examples. For he was convinced that to Andrew these enterprises were "just one more investment, one more tremendous Mellon Interest, one more prop for the scaffolding which holds up his gigantic, intensive, mysterious ego." It rankled that his father had donated all his best paintings to the educational and charitable trust without asking whether Paul or Ailsa would like to have any of them. The disappointment was compounded by his "terribly surprised" reaction when they told him that they would each "have liked just one picture, one favorite picture," partly as a token of childhood, and partly as a remembrance of "the only artistic or aesthetic thing" that Andrew had "ever permitted him-self"—some "tangible evidence" that there really was "a feeling side" to him. It also annoyed Paul that while his father had made him and David Bruce trustees of the trust, he had "never really consulted us about any important matter to do with it, and has never encouraged me to take any interest in it whatever." He had not discussed with Paul the great pur-chase of pictures and sculpture from Duveen, and he never even asked whether Paul had seen John Russell Pope's plans for the gallery. "It is just the same as it has always been in business," Paul concluded, bitterly: "he puts me into them and then ignores me, ignores my judgment or interest or actions. He has never encouraged me to do anything, never given me a word of advice or encouragement about business or my life."

There is no denying the genuine anguish of a son who had never man-aged to get close to his father. Paul's memorandum was both accurate and self-aware in its depiction of what had always been a cold and seemingly unbridgeable distance between the two of them. But it was not wholly fair. For one thing, Paul knew very little of Nora's relationship with Cur-phey, and knew nothing of the pain it had caused his father, and which his father had always sought to spare him. Nor does he acknowledge Andrew's efforts to meet him halfway at least, as when he encouraged and supported him, despite his own preferences to the contrary, in his two years of study at Cambridge. If Andrew dismissed fox-hunting as "need-less risk," this might reasonably be regarded as the legitimate, even lov-ing, concern of an elderly father for his only son and heir. As to Paul's description of the National Gallery as a megalomaniacal extravagance: this was as flatly false as it was ungenerous. Paul may have been correct that his father made an inadequate attempt to understand him, but he also made little serious effort to understand his father.

In late November 1936, Paul finally plucked up courage to talk the matter out. He found his father unexpectedly "understanding and appre-ciative" that he had "broached these issues with him." Andrew had no wish for Paul to take an "active part" in Mellon companies, much less that he be "tied down" by business. If he wanted to spend several months each year in England, as he had recently been doing, that was wholly accept-able. To his surprise and relief, Paul found his father more receptive than he had known him before. "There was," he recalled, "a reasonableness and a softness and understanding in him that took me back a little because I had always thought of him as being so different." Thus encouraged, Paul responded with a letter of unprecedented candor, setting out his own "ideas and feelings," "partly to clarify my own mind, and partly to be sure that you understand me thoroughly":

I have always been afraid to talk about these things with you because I felt for some strange reason that you might think the less of me or feel that I was being unreasonable or disloyal. I now realize that it would always have been much better to have you know what I was thinking or feeling, and that this is the only basis of a real understanding between us. I have always had the feeling that you would judge me and think about me in terms of business and of your own active, fruitful, and energetic life: but I now realize that even if that had been so it would not be worth the price to compromise with the feelings in me and to keep on in silence and mental compromise. In other words, I found that I would much rather have you disappointed in my attitude towards business and our material interests than in myself as a person, and that I would much rather have you respect me for my honesty and frankness than accept me as an inadequate replica of myself, a counterfeit. And there is no doubt about it, from your attitude, your chance questions, you have wondered what my position is, and what I have been thinking about for a long time. I want you to have confidence in me and an understanding of me as I am, just as my feeling and respect for you is for you as a man and my father, and not the same sort of respect and love and deference as the rest of the world has for you. It is much closer and more real.[28]

This overdue rapprochement between father and son bears comparison with another détente, thirteen years earlier, between the former husband and wife, on the eve of Nora's second marriage. Both new understandings were tellingly arrived at by correspondence rather than face-to-face contact. And while each must have gladdened Mellon to a degree, neither came in time fully to put to rights personal matters that had been so long awry. It is the great irony of Mellon's life that the hard carapace of his inscrutability and reserve—the very nature that had helped make him so rich, so powerful, so famous, and in the end so generous—was only pierced too late to redeem these vexed personal relationships, which may well have been more precious to him than he could ever show or say.

II. THE CULMINATING ENDEAVOR

Although he was retired, and finally free of the drama and distraction of the tax trial, the last weeks of 1936 were an eventful time for Andrew Mellon, both in terms of public events and private matters. He had to resign himself to the fact that his bête noire, Roosevelt, and the detested New Deal regime would continue to rule in Washington for the foreseeable future. With a major purchase of pictures and sculptures from Duveen, a veritable orgy of acquisition after the recent lean years, he had greatly enhanced and extended his collection at a single stroke. The negotiations with interested parties and local authorities in the capital concerning the site and design of the National Gallery of Art were gradually moving forward. Quite unexpectedly, Mellon had also reached a sort of understanding with his son, a satisfaction which had always previously eluded him, and which was likely intensified by the birth of Paul and Mary's first child, Catherine Conover Mellon, at the very end of the year. It may have seemed as if the verdict in the tax trial would never come. But at least Mellon saw the way now clear to carry his gallery project forward into its next phase. It was a progress too long frustrated by his political enemies, and he renewed his endeavors with redoubled urgency.

But he had also by now been compelled to recognize a more practical and pressing necessity for haste. In November 1936, the prominent physician Worth B. Daniels diagnosed Mellon with cancer. It is not clear whether the patient was told of the seriousness of his condition: Burton Hendrick insisted he was not, and Mellon certainly refused to admit anything was wrong, even to Ailsa or David or Paul. But he was subsequently given radium and X-ray treatment, the rigors of which can scarcely have left him in any doubt as to the seriousness of his condition. And since Duveen was well aware that Mellon's "health was causing concern," many other people on both sides of the Atlantic must have known about it, too. Indeed, Dr. Daniels would maintain that it was only on account of the treatment he prescribed that Mellon was able to survive the winter months of 1936-37, which he devoted to "completing his plans for the Gallery."[29] This may well explain why Mellon had concluded the deal with Duveen with what was, for him, uncommon haste, and why he now pushed so hard to get his gallery scheme accepted: he did not have much time left to bring his last great enterprise to fruition.

Despite the unremitting distractions of the tax trial, Mellon had worked out the details of the National Gallery of Art to his own satisfaction by the close of 1936: his pictures were now held by the educational and charitable trust or would soon be deposited there; he had settled the architect, the building in outline, and the structure of governance; and the remaining issues concerning the site seemed on the way to resolution. And so, with the boldness of one who knows his days are numbered, he decided to broach the subject with the president, whose support would be essential if the scheme was to be realized. Understandably, given their recent confrontation, Mellon preferred not to approach the White House directly. Instead, he elected to make his offer through Frederic A. Delano, an ideal intermediary. Delano was Roosevelt's uncle on his mother's side, Mellon knew him well as chairman of the National Capital Park and Planning Commission, and he was actively working to ensure the closure of Sixth Street. Delano was due to eat Christmas dinner with his illustrious nephew, and during the course of that meal he handed FDR a personal letter from Mellon. It was written in a lofty tone appropriate to the significance of its subject, it made no allusion to the tax trial, and it addressed Roosevelt as the nation's head of state, rather than as the man who had been his vengeful enemy ever since he had assumed the presidency. It was also very carefully drafted, for Mellon was not prepared to make good on his offer unless certain conditions were met by FDR and Congress. He would be a national benefactor only on his own terms.[30]

"Over a period of many years," Mellon's letter to Roosevelt began, "I have been acquiring important and rare paintings and sculpture with the idea that ultimately they would become the property of the people of the United States." They would be housed in a national art gallery to be maintained in the city of Washington, and form the "nucleus" of what Mellon envisioned as an expanding national collection. He had, he explained, given his own paintings and sculpture to the A. W. Mellon Educational & Charitable Trust, whose trustees were empowered to deed them to "a national gallery if and when such an institution shall assume and be prepared to carry out the proposals intended." He had also given the trust "securities ample to erect a gallery building of sufficient size to house these works of art, and to permit the indefinite growth of the collection under a conservative policy regulating acquisitions." The gallery, Mellon insisted, would be for the benefit of the general public, and he expressed the hope that, following his own example, other citizens might "contribute works of art of the highest quality to form a great national collection." To this end, Mellon stipulated that the intended gallery "shall not bear my name." Instead, and provided all his conditions were met, it "shall be known as 'The National Gallery,' or by such other name as may appropriately identify it as a gallery of art of the National Government."

In order to carry out this purpose, and with the approval of the other trustees, Mellon proposed to give his collection to the Smithsonian Institution or to the federal government, whereupon the trustees would "cause to be erected on public land a suitable building" at their expense, for which John Russell Pope "will furnish designs." The gallery would be placed on the Mall, on the site he had chosen, in part so that it would be "readily accessible," and also to ensure that there would be "sufficient surrounding property under [the] control of public authorities to protect it from undesirable encroachments." Mellon would additionally provide an endowment, which would pay the salaries of the senior administrative officers (who would thus be exempt from civil service regulations—and political manipulation), and also an acquisition fund for future purchases (which would be "limited to objects of the highest standards of quality"). In return, the building's upkeep, staff salaries, and "other administrative expenses and costs of operation" would be funded in perpetuity by Congress, though the governance of the gallery would be vested in "a competent and separate board of trustees," beholden neither to Congress nor to the president nor to his administration. "If this plan meets with your approval," Mellon concluded, "I will submit a formal offer of gift stating specifically the terms thereof, and the erection of the building may proceed immediately upon the acceptance of such offer and the passage of necessary legislation by Congress. Appropriate instruments of conveyance and gift will then be executed."

Thus did Andrew Mellon formally initiate the culminating endeavor of his life: a philanthropic gesture which in both its scale and the willful self-effacement of its benefactor had no precedent or parallel in the nation's history. Wholly unembarrassed by his harsh treatment of Mellon, or by his tireless denunciations of the class to which the former treasury secretary belonged, Roosevelt was clearly eager to accept the offer and move the matter forward. (Did he, perhaps, recall the remarks of his cousin Theodore of almost thirty years ago, calling for the establishment of a national gallery in Washington?) But there were important legal and political ramifications to consider, and before replying to Mellon's letter, FDR summoned Homer Cummings to the White House on the day after Christmas. The attorney general was expecting to discuss the looming problem of dealing with a Supreme Court intractably opposing some recent provisions of the New Deal, perhaps by appointing more justices than the usual nine. But the president began by reading out Mellon's letter, without revealing who had written it. Cummings soon guessed that the author of this "long, well-constructed and modestly-phrased document" must be Andrew Mellon. They agreed that the proposal needed careful thought as to the details, and that Congress would have to pass the appropriate legislation. "It is," Cummings confided to his diary, taking a more appreciative view of Mellon than had recently been his wont, "the sort of a gift that could not be rejected. Indeed, it is a magnificent conception and would supply a need which has been felt for a long time by those who have thought about the subject at all."[31]

Roosevelt and Cummings had met in the late afternoon, and that very evening, the president replied to Mellon's missive in a reciprocally gracious tone.[32] He was, he claimed, "completely taken by surprise" by the proposal, which can scarcely have been true, since Mellon's scheme for a gallery had been common knowledge in Washington ever since his testimony at the tax trial. Nevertheless, he was "delighted" at this "very wonderful offer to the people of the United States," and he acknowledged that it would meet a long-felt need for a great gallery in the nation's capital, and that Mellon's own pictures would provide an initial collection "of the first importance," which would "place the nation well up in the first rank." Naturally, Roosevelt noted, the gift would be subject to congressional review and "the necessary legislation" would have to be passed. "The formal announcement and the terms of it" would also need discussing. "May I suggest," Roosevelt concluded, "that you, or whoever you may care to designate, should come to see me some afternoon this week?" A meeting was duly scheduled for New Year's Eve, and on December 29, Roosevelt outlined Mellon's proposition to his colleagues at a cabinet meeting.

In the late afternoon of December 31, 1936, Andrew Mellon and Franklin Roosevelt met for what was probably the second and certainly the last time, in the White House library, a room Mellon had often frequented during the days of Harding, Coolidge, and Hoover. Both David Finley (who had come at Mellon's request) and Homer Cummings (who was there at FDR's) left accounts of an essentially informal, almost familial occasion at which tea was served, while assorted presidential grandchildren came and went.[33] After initial pleasantries, Mellon pulled a paper out of his pocket, which elaborated on his earlier letter: "Here, Mr. President, is my offer. I hope it can be carried out."[34] Roosevelt and Cummings read the document, and the attorney general immediately advised there should be no impediment to the government's doing everything Mellon had requested. "Then put it through," said FDR. After further general conversation, Mellon thanked the president for his assistance and, accompanied by David Finley, returned to his apartment on Massachusetts Avenue. Once again, Roosevelt had exerted the charm that was already legend, for on the way back, according to Finley, an implausibly dazzled Mellon allowed: "What a wonderfully attractive man the President is." He then added, in words crossed out but still legible in Burton Hendrick's typescript: "I came through it much better than I expected to."[35]

Mellon's gift was announced in the newspapers on January 3, 1937, and it caused as much of a sensation in London as in New York and Washington.[36] Now his private pictures became a matter of general public knowledge in a way that had never been true before. One indication was that the art critic Royal Cortissoz, who more than a decade before had written about the earlier, abortive national gallery scheme, wrote a series of articles in the *New York Herald Tribune*, which were published later that year as *An Introduction to the Mellon Collection*, paying particular attention to the Italian paintings and sculptures, many of which had been among the most recent acquisitions.[37] The building would be called the National Gallery of Art, it would cost between $8 million and $9 million to construct, and with Mellon's "priceless art collection" (estimated at $19 million) housed in it, there was every hope that Washington would become "one of the principal art capitals of the world." "Gratefully delighted," Dr. C. G. Abbot, the director of the Smithsonian, telegraphed Mellon, "at your princely gift, greatest in history."[38] (Nor was this the full extent of the benefaction, for there would also be a brief allusion in Mellon's scheme to the possibility of establishing a national portrait gallery, of which his own pictures of Americans, most of them recently acquired, would become the nucleus.)

Behind the scenes, the detailed negotiations FDR had authorized were conducted by Donald Shepard, on behalf of Mellon, and Judge Newman A. Townsend, the assistant solicitor general, for the government. In practice, and as Homer Cummings unhappily admitted to Roosevelt, "there was but little give and take," for in this matter, as in every transaction of business or art, Mellon drove a hard bargain. By calling the building the National Gallery of Art, he was appropriating a name already attached to a bureau of the Smithsonian. He insisted that the funds and pictures come from the A. W. Mellon Educational & Charitable Trust, where he had already deposited them, rather than from his personal fortune, even though the Roosevelt administration was still contesting the bona fides of the trust. And in seeking to establish a board of nine trustees, five of whom would be private citizens and "general trustees," all initially to be appointed by Mellon, he ensured that overall operation of the gallery would be independent of the federal government, although it was technically part of the Smithsonian and dependent on Congress for its upkeep. On all these points, Mellon would eventually get his way, largely because, as Cummings informed FDR, his lawyers "assumed, and adhered to the position, that as Mr. Mellon was making the gift, he was entitled to dictate the terms thereof."[39]

But in early January 1937, there was serious unease in the administration about both the terms and the possible consequences of this proposed benefaction. Robert H. Jackson feared that "the gift of the Art Gallery means the end of the tax case," because it might influence the Board of Tax Appeals to reach a lenient verdict, and help rehabilitate the donor "in public esteem." Roosevelt was adamant: "no change whatsoever," he wrote to Henry Morgenthau, "in the government's position in the A. W. Mellon tax trial has ever been agreed upon or considered, and no inference prejudicial to the government can properly be drawn from the acceptance of Mr. Mellon's gift." Indeed, Treasury officials soon busied themselves scrutinizing Mellon's tax returns for 1932 and 1933, believing them to reveal the same "transactions and circumstances" as the "fraudulent" return of 1931.[40] More worrying, as Homer Cummings explained to FDR, was Mellon's determination that the management of the gallery should not "pass out of private hands into government control," thereby perpetuating the anomaly of a "government property being managed by a private group." Various modifications were suggested: four ex officio and four general trustees, with a ninth trustee selected by the president; term limits for all trustees; a national advisory committee. All were rejected by Mellon's representatives. FDR hoped the gallery would not "be tied up in perpetuity," but his vice president, John Nance Garner, a lifelong critic of Mellon's, took a more realistic and calculated view: "while Mellon was Secretary of the Treasury, he made several millions of dollars which no Secretary of the Treasury could properly have made"; "the government would be getting back something at any rate if we took this art collection."[41]

Accordingly, in mid-January, Cummings sent Roosevelt a formal letter, accompanied by a draft joint resolution of Congress, setting out "the conditions which Mr. Mellon and his associates insist must be included in the legislation." "It is my opinion," the attorney general concluded, more dutiful than enthusiastic, "that the Congress, if it desires to do so, has full power to enact into law the provisions contained in the proposed draft." The president did not hesitate to send the draft to the Congress by the beginning of February, commending Mellon's "generous purpose" and "magnificent gift."[42] Thus did a Democratic administration urge upon a Democratic-controlled legislature a measure accepting a major benefaction from a much-hated Republican, who might yet be found guilty of fraud and tax evasion on a massive scale. For some longtime Mellonhaters, this was just too much. "The precedent is a very bad one," Congressman Wright Patman complained to FDR. "If we allow Mellon this privilege, Hearst and Morgan will come in next with an offer just as attractive." "Mellon's citizenship," Patman went on, "is nothing to be proud of. A lasting memorial in his honor should not be constructed in the nation's capital, even at his own expense." And Senator Robert M. La

Follette Jr., the son of another of the secretary's leading critics, raised the matter of Mellon's unresolved tax case and also took issue with the proposed composition of the board of trustees.[43]

Many others would look the gift horse in the mouth before all was said, done, and settled. The closure of Sixth Street was finally agreed to, and with it the earlier plans for a George Washington Memorial Auditorium were abandoned. But, despite Charles Moore's best efforts, the Commission of Fine Arts proved most obstinate, as politics extended into the aesthetic realm. Several of its members were young architects and admirers of Le Corbusier, Mies van de Rohe, and Frank Lloyd Wright; to them Pope's neoclassicism bespoke a tainted, dishonest, conservative, and Republican sensibility. Although the commission's members were willing to approve the site and welcome the gift at their January meeting, there was some uncertainty as to whether they had actually accepted the specific design.[44] And they were soon joined in their protests by the League for Progressive Architecture in America, which attacked not only Pope's designs for the gallery but also his proposed Jefferson Memorial, on the grounds that such imperial pomposity had no place in the capital of a democratic republic conceived in opposition to an empire.[45] For several months, there was no sign of resolution at the commission, though things were moving in Congress. Pope provided large perspective drawings, Finley and Shepard testified before the appropriate House committee, Tom Connolly of Texas guided the bill through the Senate, and the legislation was passed on March 24, 1937, barely three months after Mellon's initial approach to the president. By agreeable coincidence, this was his eighty-second birthday. It would also be his last.[46]

The gift was accepted exactly according to Mellon's wishes. It would be known as the National Gallery of Art; the Smithsonian bureau that had previously born the name was redesignated the National Collection of Fine Arts. It would be located on the Mall, the plot bounded by Seventh Street, Constitution Avenue, Fourth Street, and North Mall Drive. The intervening thoroughfares would be closed off, and the area directly eastward across Fourth Street reserved "for future additions," and the A. W. Mellon Educational & Charitable Trust would finance the building and furnish the collection of art to be exhibited there. In return, "the faith of the United States" was "pledged" to maintain, protect, curate, administer, and operate the gallery, and "for these purposes" Congress would appropriate "such sums as may be necessary." Though established as a bureau within the Smithsonian, the gallery would have its own trustees: four of them ex officio (the chief justice of the Supreme Court, the secretaries of state and of the treasury, and the director of the Smithsonian); five of them "general trustees" from outside government, who would be named initially by Mellon (with the formal approval of the Smithsonian's Board of Regents) and would thereafter elect their own successors. The board's decisions would be subject to no review by any federal officer or agency other than a court of law, and the gallery would display no works of art unless "of similar high standard of quality" to those already in the Mellon collection.

In insisting on calling the building the "National Gallery of Art" rather than naming it for himself, Mellon had shown his customary reticence, giving the lie to the false modesty of which some accused him. He had also demonstrated a characteristically shrewd appreciation of such anxieties and ambitions as preyed upon the egos of his fellow art collectors. All his life, he had used his family name but sparingly in public: the Mellon National Bank and the Mellon Institute in Pittsburgh, which were both in any case memorials to his father rather than to himself, were quite enough exposure. Moreover, and as with his businesses, Mellon wanted his gallery to *grow*, and he rightly reasoned that other collectors would be more likely to give their paintings to an institution whose aggrandizement would honor the nation as a whole, not the memory of an individual. Such "donor memorials" as the Huntington Gallery, the Carnegie Institute, and the Frick Collection had lost momentum after their founders died, because other major collectors did not want to give their art to be displayed in a building, however splendid, that was named for someone else.[47] Mellon, by contrast, had always intended his pictures to be the "nucleus" of something much greater. He would sooner his generosity be effaced and enabling rather than explicit and enervating. He never had his father's command of literature or history, but he knew enough to avoid the fate of an American Ozymandias.

But this was not the only reason Mellon did not want his name associated with the gallery. As with most of the enterprises with which he was engaged, he was more concerned with perpetuating Mellon power than he was in flaunting the Mellon presence, and here, too, he emphatically achieved his objective, by creating a structure of governance very different from that of the National Gallery in London as described by Kenneth Clark. Mellon would himself be the first "general trustee" of his gallery, and he would also nominate the other four people in this category: his son-in-law, David Bruce; his lawyer, Donald Shepard; his former subordinate at the Treasury, Parker Gilbert; and the collector Duncan Phillips, another scion of Pittsburgh wealth, who had recently founded the Phillips

Collection, which Mellon much admired.[48] (Significantly, Mellon preferred to appoint his son-in-law rather than his son as the second family member.) Together, these five trustees formed the majority of the board, and they were all close associates on whom he could confidently rely to oversee the construction and operation of the gallery, and to choose like-minded successors.

In establishing the National Gallery of Art along these lines, Mellon may have been giving belated effect to his ideas on such institutions expressed in his school essay on the subject of seventy years before. It is probably unwise to look too closely at juvenile musings, which in Mellon's case covered a wide range of topics. Suffice it to say Mellon was realizing an ambition nurtured for the better part of a decade, and this despite the enormous political, financial, and legal buffeting to which he had been subjected for so much of that time. Yet in so doing, he also gave life to his vision in conformity with the business precepts he had perfected almost half a century before: once again, the initial focus was on "acquisition and accumulation"; once again, he picked good and loyal men to oversee the operational details; and as so often before, he provided the seeding resources in the hope and belief that the undertaking might grow and prosper, eventually acquiring its own momentum. Perhaps Paul Mellon had had that familiar pattern in mind when he wrote his memorandum, wherein he had identified his father's gallery as being of a piece with his many businesses, another recognizable extension of himself: "one more investment, one more tremendous Mellon Interest."

These were, indeed, Mellon's methods, as they had always been—but what were his motives? According to J. P. Morgan, "a man always has two reasons for the things he does—a good one and the real one." It is still widely believed in certain quarters that Mellon gave his art and built his gallery in tacit exchange for his acquittal at the tax trial, and to escape from the onslaught of the Roosevelt administration.[49] But as should by now be clear, there is not a shred of evidence for that contention. Mellon had conceived the gallery many years before he was charged with tax evasion, and at a time when the rise of Roosevelt and the New Deal could not have been foreseen. Indeed, his creation of his educational and charitable trust as the instrument for endowing and realizing the gallery was one of the major acts upon which the tax charge was hung: to that extent, it was the gallery that led to the tax trial, rather than the tax trial that led to the gallery. In addition, the magnitude of Mellon's benefaction—which, including the art, the building and the endowment, was eventually reckoned in the region of sixty million dollars—was at least ten times the largest sum the government was claiming in back taxes. Moreover, throughout the negotiations during the winter of 1936–37, Mellon's tone was anything but that of a suppliant bargaining for his life and eager to pay for his acquittal: he dealt as one who held all the cards, leaving the federal government to take or leave his offer. It is also clear that Roosevelt and Cummings, when they agreed to accept Mellon's gift, had resolved that the gallery and the tax trial were separate issues.

In any case, Mellon was certain that, when the actors in the tax trial were all long dead and gone, the gallery would endure, growing and evolving year by year, as a treasure-house of beautiful things which all Americans might enjoy. "I am not going to be deterred," he replied to a colleague who questioned his perseverance in the face of such shabby treatment by the Roosevelt administration. "Eventually the people now in power in Washington will be dead, and I will be dead, but the National Gallery, I hope, will be there, and that is something the country needs."[50] In this reckoning, politics, and especially politics of the Roosevelt sort, was one thing, patriotism another. The edification of the American people outweighed the vindictiveness of any American president. In giving his art to the nation, Mellon was transmitting not only many paintings and sculptures of astronomical monetary value, but also the pleasure he had come to understand that they could give. For somewhere, somehow, deep in the inner recesses of his cold, shy, inscrutable, and inarticulate nature, Mellon *was* moved by art, and the gallery was the means whereby he hoped others might be moved by it, too. As he was once alleged to have told his friend John G. Bowman, chancellor of the University of Pittsburgh: "Every man wants to connect his life with something that he thinks of as eternal."[51]

III. LAST THINGS

We only have Bowman's authority for this remark, and as with his report of Mellon's concern that he had lived his life in vain, the uncharacteristically self-indulgent theatricality of these words should give us cause to question their strict veracity. While certainly aware that great art outlived great men, Mellon was in general far too interested in the here and now to have much time or thought for eternity. Metaphysical musing was hardly his style. In any case, and despite (or because of) his failing health, Mellon was determined to see the gallery to fruition, and his dealings with Roosevelt and his officials reveal that though his body might be failing him, his command of detail and his iron will remained in good order. He needed every ounce of the latter, for in the midst of these negotiations FDR had been sworn in for a second term on January 20, 1937. Although he was less adversarial than he had been during his re-election campaign, he continued to inveigh in his second inaugural against the "dulled conscience, irresponsibility, and ruthless self-interest" which he believed people like Mellon personified. "Private autocratic powers," FDR noted, had been "challenged and beaten," and brought "into their proper subordination to the public's government." But millions in America were still on the brink of disaster and destitution, and one-third of the nation was "ill-housed, ill-clad, ill-nourished." "The test of progress," he insisted, "is not whether we add more to the abundance of those who have much; it is whether we provide enough for those who have too little."[52]

In such a hostile and polarized political climate, it was scarcely surprising that Mellon was so adamant that the National Gallery of Art be as independent of the federal government as possible. Following the inauguration and the passage of the legislation that provided for the building, Mellon returned to the business of buying more art. Even after his great purchase from Duveen, there was still ample scope for consolidating and extending the collection, and as Mellon's health began to fail, David Finley came to play an even more prominent part. In January 1937, Mellon bought five American portraits from Knoedler, through the educational and charitable trust, for a little less than $90,000, including *Colonel Guy Johnson* by Benjamin West and *John Randolph* by Gilbert Stuart. Three months later, again through the trust, he purchased seven more works from Duveen, for $2.6 million. Four of them were religious subjects, in which area his collection was still weak: Andrea Mantegna's *St. Jerome in the Wilderness*, Giovanni Bellini's *The Flight into Egypt*, Duccio di Buoninsegna's *The Nativity with the Prophets Isaiah and Ezekiel*, and Masolino da Panicale's *The Annunciation*. There were also two outstanding Gainsboroughs, which Mellon could not resist: *A Landscape with a Bridge* and a full-length portrait of Mrs. Richard Brinsley Sheridan.[53] Finally, there was a painted and gilded terra-cotta statuette, *The Madonna and Child*, then thought to be by Donatello.

Although (or perhaps because) he knew that time was against him, Mellon continued to drive hard bargains. He was increasingly using Finley as an intermediary, but early in April 1937, Mellon and Duveen met in Washington for lunch, doubtless to discuss the latest artwork that he was considering.[54] Duveen had offered *The Annunciation* for $650,000, but he let Mellon have it for $500,000; he had wanted $600,000 for the Donatello, but settled for $460,000. *Mrs. Sheridan* went for $450,000, not the $580,000 of his longings; he sought the same sum for the Duccio before being obliged to accept the same reduction. "I am anxious," Duveen had written to Finley when naming his price for the Duccio,

> to do everything I can to please Mr. Mellon and to assist his purpose, but I hope you will delicately mention to him that I cannot reduce the price this time as I did on the last occasion. You see there were special reasons, as you know, last time that made it possible for me completely to meet Mr. Mellon's wishes; but I have invested a very considerable sum of new money in the things you now have under offer and so I cannot do what I did last time. I mention this because I am very anxious to co-operate with Mr. Mellon, and I would not want him to feel disappointed over the matter of price.

In the end, however, and as usual, the disappointment was Duveen's: he was forced to accept substantially less than he had asked for every work that Mellon bought. Mellon also sent back another six paintings and sculptures which did not interest him.[55]

These were the last works Mellon would buy from Duveen, and soon after he returned the Mantegna, which was sold to Joseph Widener, who eventually gave it to the National Gallery of Art. Despite Duveen's predictable urging to the contrary, Mellon was eager that there should be no publicity about these sales, "as it merely lets him in for more trouble."[56] But from April to June 1937, Duveen, Finley, and Mellon would discuss many other prospects. When John D. Rockefeller Sr. died, his son gave Mellon first refusal of Lawrence's portrait of Lady Dysart for $290,000. But Mellon, now more interested in following a "definite program" of "building up collection in schools other than English," proved unavailing, and so the matter was dropped.[57] Soon after, Duveen offered him a work by Giotto, probably his *Virgin and Child*, but as David Finley explained, "Mr. Mellon has seen the Giotto, and regrets that it would not be suitable for his purpose, as a gallery picture." (It was subsequently sold to Samuel H. Kress, who later donated it to the National Gallery of Art.) As the New York office reported to Duveen in London, Mellon and Finley wanted him to "concentrate [on] pictures they [are] short of," by such artists as Brueghel, Hogarth, and Simone Martini.[58]

Mellon's continued commitment to acquisition even after the establishment of the gallery was assured can be glimpsed in the further steps he now took to bolster the educational and charitable trust. Indeed, this was now his highest priority. Between January and August 1937, he gave no more money to his children or to the trusts for his grandchildren, but he did make over another $9.5 million worth of stock to the trust, bringing his total monetary contribution to nearly $22 million. The sum would suffice to pay for building construction, and also to furnish the endowment, which would be the source of future funding for salaries of the senior staff and also provide the acquisitions budget. In May and June 1937, Mellon conveyed ten more pictures and one bas-relief to the trust, including such Hermitage purchases as Rembrandt's *Joseph Accused by Potiphar's Wife*, and Frans Hals's *Portrait of a Young Man in a Large Hat*. Valued at $1.8 million, these brought the total worth of the art he had conveyed to the trust since 1930 to $20.7 million.[59] As a result, the book value of Mellon's fortune continued to go down: by the beginning of 1937, it had dwindled to $28 million, and it continued to fall thereafter. This was less than one-third of what he had been worth at the peak of his wealth a mere six years before and would be scarcely $300 million at today's values.

Once a public announcement of the gallery had been made, Mellon also engaged Duveen's and Finley's help in beginning to scout for other potential donors. One prospect was Joseph E. Widener, whose father, P. A. B. Widener, had made a fortune in Philadelphia streetcars, and who had almost certainly had dealings with Mellon concerning Pittsburgh streetcar lines at the turn of the century. Housed at Lynnewood Hall, near Philadelphia, the Widener collection was second only to Mellon's in both number and quality of paintings (which included fourteen Rembrandts, seven Van Dycks, three Titians, two El Grecos, and another Madonna by Raphael); it also included much decorative art, especially furniture and porcelain.[60] Joseph Widener, another client of Duveen's, had devoted himself to refining and consolidating his father's collection. In January 1937, Duveen arranged for the trustees of Mellon's educational and charitable trust to visit Lynnewood. It is not clear whether Mellon attended, but Duveen reported to Widener that the visitors were "most enthusiastic and greatly impressed"; he further expressed his hope that the "intimate contact" with the collection thus established might prove "enormously useful." In late April, Duveen arranged for Mellon and Widener to meet over lunch, in order to discuss the possible bequest of the Widener collection to the National Gallery.[61]

Such cordial ceremony would be the exception during the last months of Mellon's life, for even with the tax trial behind him, he knew no peace, as the New Deal continued to intrude. Overwhelmingly triumphant in Pennsylvania in November 1936, the Democrats had increased their majority in the commonwealth's House of Representatives and also captured its Senate, thus taking full control of the legislature. They proceeded to enact a "Little New Deal" in Pennsylvania, providing for unemployment insurance, restrictions on the use of court injunctions to halt strikes, and the abolition of some of the most detested aspects of "industrial despotism": company stores in company mining and industrial towns, and the company police. The right of Pennsylvania workers to unionize and bargain collectively with their employers was also guaranteed, and a workmen's compensation act was passed with provisions more radical than anything proposed in Washington. Of 371 bills introduced by Governor Earle during the first five months of the 1937 session, only 6 were voted down. Here was a new world for labor, reinforced in its battle with capital by the full force of the state. Neither economically nor politically was this the Pennsylvania in which Andrew Mellon had previously lived his life.[62]

One indication of these changed times was that in March 1937, United States Steel, one of Pittsburgh's most iconic corporations, announced recognition of unions, wage increases, an eight-hour day, and a forty-hour week. This time, there had been no strike: the company, having sized up the enemy, had surrendered to labor without a fight. In the following month, the U.S. Supreme Court handed down a ruling delivered in a case that had an even more immediate resonance for Mellon. It stemmed from a complaint to the National Labor Relations Board that ten men had been dismissed from the Jones and Laughlin Company steelworks in Aliquippa, Pennsylvania, for being union members. Known as "Little Siberia," the Aliquippa mills were among the state's most notorious. Moreover, the Jones and Laughlin families were two of the traditional Republican dynasties of Pittsburgh, and Andrew Mellon had courted— and then rejected—Fannie Jones more than half a century before. Dismissal of workers for belonging to a union was a clear violation of the Wagner Act's prohibition on unfair labor practices, but the company contended that the Wagner Act was unconstitutional and that the NLRB thus had no authority to receive or act upon the workers' grievance. Much to the chagrin of Jones and Laughlin (and also of Andrew Mellon), the Supreme Court upheld the constitutionality of the Wagner Act. It was another milestone for organized labor in western Pennsylvania. As one steelworker in Little Siberia put it: "I say good, now Aliquippa become part of the United States."[63]

For Mellon, Roosevelt's determination to restructure relations between capital and labor would soon strike even closer to home in the case of Alcoa. Worker discontent at New Kensington had been increasing since the unsatisfactory settlement at the end of 1934, and in the spring of 1937, the local shifted its allegiance from the American Federation of Labor to the more radical Congress of Industrial Organizations. Once the new union was certified by the National Labor Relations Board as the sole bargaining agent for the plant's workers under the terms of the Wagner Act, the writing was on the wall for Alcoa.[64] Collective bargaining was now established, along with a grievance procedure, which provided for (albeit limited) independent arbitration. In other company plants elsewhere in the United States, there were disputes as to which union would be certified, but the overall effect was clear: "unionism had triumphed at Alcoa." And with collective bargaining instituted by law, the company would soon be obliged to increase wages.

But the New Deal's business with Alcoa was not yet finished. In April 1937, just as union rights were being significantly advanced within the company, the Department of Justice filed suit under sections 1 and 2 of the Sherman Anti-Trust Act against Alcoa and sixty-one related corporate entities and individuals.[65] The general charge was that the company was illegally acting in restraint of interstate and foreign trade, to promote and maintain its monopoly in aluminum. But the details of the suit covered almost every aspect of Alcoa's business, and the proposed remedy was both radical and seriously threatening to the company: first, "to create substantial competition in the industry by rearranging the plants and properties of the Aluminum Company and its subsidiaries under several separate and independent corporations"; and second, to bring about "a divorcement" of Alcoa and its Canadian subsidiary, Aluminum Limited, "through which it is alleged that the Aluminum Company has conspired with other world producers to restrain imports and preserve the Aluminum Company's monopoly in the United States."[66]

If successful, this suit promised far more damage to the "Mellon Interests" than even the yet-undecided tax case. There was no attempt to dictate just how the parts and properties of Alcoa should be divided or the industry restructured. But if the government prevailed, Alcoa might be left, in the words of its official historian, "if not dead, [then] severely wounded and amputated, [and] no longer anything like the self-sufficient and powerful corporation it had become in a half century of business." This, of course, was precisely what Roosevelt, Cummings, and the New Dealers wanted. If the tax trial had represented their ad hominem attack on Mellon, the Alcoa suit was an assault on the very foundations of his industrial wealth and economic power. And in a political climate so hostile to business, the company's prospects did not look good. In the words of its historian, George Smith: "in public relations terms, Alcoa was a sitting duck for the New Deal attorneys who marched into Federal Court with their sweeping indictment in April 1937."[67] Leading the charge was Robert H. Jackson, who was briefly head of the Justice Department's Antitrust Division, fresh from his previous assignment as lead prosecutor at Mellon's tax trial. But the Alcoa case would be tied up for months in pre-trial maneuverings; it would not be heard till June 1938.

By the spring of 1937, it was becoming increasingly obvious to those closest to him that Andrew Mellon was seriously unwell. Soon after Congress passed the legislation accepting his gift of the National Gallery of Art, he began to appear tired and weak, on occasions apparently losing his train of thought, and sometimes blacking out temporarily.[68] This physical decline was made disquietingly manifest when he visited Pittsburgh in early May to dedicate the new facility for the Mellon Institute of Science and Technology. (Earlier in the year, he had refused a testimonial dinner from the Pittsburgh Chamber of Commerce on the grounds of ill health.)[69] Financed jointly by Andrew and Dick, and occupying a plot the size of a city block, it had taken seven years to complete, and was the Mellon brothers' largest benefaction to their hometown. Inside, the building contained state-of-the-art laboratories, classrooms, and lecture halls. Its exterior was girded by sixty-two Ionic limestone columns each forty feet high, and it was richly ornamented throughout with bas-reliefs, medallions, and panels. "This," one critic observed, echoing recent modernist condemnation of the Federal Triangle, "is what happens when rich men decide to bring Greece to Pittsburgh."[70]

Sensing his frailty, family and friends looked after Mellon attentively on dedication day, but it was an anxious and distressing occasion; even by his own standards, Mellon's speech was more than usually inaudible, rambling, and incoherent. He spoke about the first days of the institute and about his early dealings with Robert Kennedy Duncan, declaring that "it is science and not government or wars of conquest that open up to us new horizons"; he also reaffirmed his belief that "the new processes which science will discover will in the future give man the chance to live more abundantly."[71] If Americans lived with intolerable inequities of means, it was for science, with the benevolent sponsorship of industry rather than government, to assuage the circumstances. But few could hear Mellon's words: he seemed "badly rattled," left his glasses on the rostrum, and forgot his hat. It was his last public appearance, and he would never see Pittsburgh again.[72] Even the great celebrations to be held in connection with his alma mater, of which he was the most distinguished alumnus and to which he had been a princely benefactor, due to take place in June that year, could not draw him back to his native city. The University of Pittsburgh was one hundred and fifty years old; the Cathedral of Learning was finally completed, after being delayed by the Depression; and the cornerstone of the common room, Mellon's latest gift, was to be laid. But he stayed away.[73]

During this last visit to Pittsburgh, there was another falling-out between Andrew and Paul, notwithstanding what had seemed to be their reconciliation at the end of the previous year. The new disagreement concerned pictures, in particular two Corots which Andrew had recently decided not to make over to the educational and charitable trust because he considered them unworthy of a place in the National Gallery of Art. Whatever their aesthetic merits, however, they were among the earliest paintings he had bought, back in the early 1900s, when he and Nora were living at Forbes Street. As a result, they had always been part of Paul's life, and for this reason, he had clearly hoped that his father would either give them to him before he died or leave them to him in his will. Instead, Andrew now proposed to *sell* the two pictures to Paul, for $25,000 each, thus saving himself gift tax. There may have been a bit of elderly perversity in this, a foolish, Lear-like jibe at a well-meaning son. Or perhaps the thought of paying additional gift tax to FDR's Treasury stuck in his craw. But Andrew was perfectly willing to ask his son for $50,000 from money he himself had given him. Whatever his reasoning, Paul was outraged at such calculation, cold even by his father's standards: "I don't want to buy them," he insisted. "I should have thought you would have loved to have given me something that you knew I loved, not only for their own sakes and because of childhood memories, but also because of *you.*"[74]

Paul wrote his father yet another anguished letter, trying to make his feelings clear. It was not only "the present situation about the pictures," which might "in itself appear trivial," that pained him, but "the other problems that I have written you about before: my part in the businesses, my problems about not liking Pittsburgh, my seeming lack of interest in the things that have been your life, and which you would like to have me interested in." The main issue, he said, was that his father did not "seem to care about how I really feel about anything," that he never allowed "the emotional or sentimental aspect of anything" to enter his head, and thus failed to understand that "the matter of the Corots was a sentimental, not a business question." "Don't you see," Paul went on, "how difficult it is for me to understand your attitude in these things, when you find it difficult on the one hand to pay a gift tax of a few thousand dollars to give something to your children, and pay millions of dollars at the same moment on the other for the Gallery, a completely impersonal thing?" "The whole idea," he continued, "of keeping the Corots is spoiled for me now. I can't understand why you couldn't feel that tonight when I talked about it." "I didn't set out to write this letter to hurt your feelings," he concluded. "I did it purely to explain myself to you, in an attempt to be honest. If it makes you sad, if it makes you angry, or if you choose to ignore it altogether, I can't help it. But I felt you ought to know." "With much love," he signed off.

This was the last letter between father and son, a final and futile attempt to resolve misunderstanding in prose when speech had failed them utterly. If Andrew gave Paul's missive great thought, there is no evidence of it. In any case, on his return to Washington, he was once again fully absorbed in gallery business. The National Capital Park and Planning Commission insisted that the building be set back from the Mall, to align with extant or expected structures on adjacent sites. To this Mellon and Pope reluctantly agreed, consequently reducing the size of the gallery to 785 feet in length and 303 feet in width. Mellon now instructed Pope to begin working drawings, but there were further objections from the Commission of Fine Arts: some members insisted that they had not yet approved the design in detail; that the garden courts should not be covered; that the porticoes at the east and west ends should be removed; that there should be no central dome; and that the whole neoclassical style was inappropriate. Pope and Mellon gave way on the porticoes, but dug in their heels over the covered courtyards and the dome. There, in May 1937, the matter lay unresolved.

Despite these discouraging delays, Mellon was convinced he would prevail, and meanwhile was determined to press ahead with the gallery as he intended it to be. He believed it must be comfortable on the inside and simple on the outside. "Most galleries," he once observed, "are exhausting." His, by contrast, would be welcoming and easy on both the feet and the eye. Instead of the large, intimidating spaces, full of drafts and echoes, such as characterized so many museums built in the prevailing Beaux-Arts style, Mellon insisted on an inviting succession of intimate, restful, almost domestic little chambers, arranged around the central rotunda and the two garden courts, each to be adapted in size and decoration to the particular school of art displayed in it. He also discouraged Pope's inclination toward ornament and ostentation, which had reached its apogee in the nearby National Archives building, insisting he make his external elevations less cluttered and more chaste, and vetoing his proposals for windows and sculpture niches as contrary to his ideal of tasteful and understated simplicity.

By now Mellon was also much concerned with the choice of building materials. He wanted the best, and was willing to pay for it, but he feared that limestone or white marble, widely used in buildings that occupied the Federal Triangle, were too harshly reflective in the generally sunny Washington weather. Duveen seems to have been involved in this discussion, for in February 1937 he sent David Finley the following telegram: "Just returned from Morgan Library. Colour of marble divine. It has lovely rose tint which [is] so attractive. Sincerely hope Pope can get same."[75] Duveen was referring to the Tennessee marble of which the Morgan library in New York had been constructed, and which varied in color from pale rose to pure white. Pope duly obtained samples, and Mellon was pleased to authorize the use of the marble on condition that the darkest pink be employed closest to the ground, with the shades lightening as the structure soared upward, culminating in pure white at the dome. This feature would add greatly to the gallery's cost, but it would also enhance its dignity, and Mellon was willing to spend extensively in the cause of un-ostentation. As he observed to David Finley when considering other materials: "I don't care if they are expensive, if they don't look expensive."[76]

There still remained the obstacle of the Commission of Fine Arts, to which Pope now submitted two new sets of drawings, one with a dome, envisaging a building 135 feet high, the other without. He made plain his vehement opposition to any domeless version, but the commission still demurred and disagreed, some members insisting on the superior merits of a less majestic top. In June 1937, Mellon intervened, sending Charles Moore a determined letter, defending Pope's design and for the last time leveraging his mighty beneficence for the sake of having his way. As some commission members still balked, Moore now determined to force their assent. At a commission meeting held on June 21, 1937, also attended by David Finley and Donald Shepard, Moore pointed out that Congress had accepted Mellon's gift, including the gallery as designed by Pope; that it seemed to many observers that the commission had already consented last January; and that the commission was only an advisory body, with no powers to enforce its judgments. Thus exhorted and berated, Moore's colleagues formally agreed to the Mellon-Pope plans, and the final obstacle to the establishment of the National Gallery of Art was removed.[77] Soon after, the ground was broken, and Mellon expressed to David Finley "the greatest satisfaction in knowing that everything was to be as he had planned."[78]

IV. AN EVENING DEATH

The summer of 1937 was unbearably hot, even by Washington standards, and Mellon was now in visible discomfort—so much so that David Finley commandeered some of the contractors who had just begun working on the gallery to install a primitive form of air-conditioning in his apartment.[79] It was some temporary relief, but Andrew Mellon was clearly failing. He no longer had the energy to play with his granddaughter, Audrey Bruce; he gave up his walks; he lost his appetite and with it considerable weight; he even abandoned the "rattails" he had smoked all his life. A photograph taken by Paul at about this time depicts his father's gaunt face, lined and drawn, a cold pallor already heavy upon him. Yet Mellon did not seem overly concerned with his condition; he still refused to acknowledge his illness publicly, except to say that he "did not feel quite right." He was even planning another visit to Britain for the summer, but as Duveen's spies reported in late May, "sufficient pressure" from family and friends was "used to stop him."[80] Instead, now that work on the gallery had visibly begun, Mellon finally yielded to Ailsa and David's entreaties, agreeing to leave Washington for Long Island, where he would stay not with them at Syosset, but at a rented house on Southampton's Gin Lane, called, with fitting ancestral echoes, Bonnie Dune.

On the drive from his Washington apartment to Union Station, Mellon passed the Federal Triangle, most of its buildings now as complete as they would be, and also the site of the National Gallery of Art he had conceived and forced into being with his last strength, but which he would not see finished. Excavation was advancing, but there was no hint of the cool and majestic edifice that would eventually arise there. Yet while the gallery building had barely begun, Roosevelt's New Deal was nearing completion. In addition to upholding the Wagner Act, the Supreme Court had also recently found constitutional the provisions of the Social Security Act concerning unemployment insurance and social security. This decision embodied a view of labor and of life that had always been anathema to Mellon, the sanctity of personal independence, celebrated in the Burns poem he had learned at his father's knee, being sacrificed for what he regarded as the demoralizing security of state relief. It was a triumph for FDR, despite his recent failure to "pack" the Supreme Court to his liking. But the New Deal's reforming impetus was virtually spent by mid-1937. A coincidental downturn in the summer economy, known as the "Roosevelt recession," would lead to another ferocious anti-business outburst by the administration later that year: America's richest families were again denounced by FDR and Morgenthau as cheats and tax evaders, whom they blamed for organizing a conspiratorial "capital strike," restraining essential investment in industry, and thus holding back the recovery of the American economy.[81]

Roosevelt's New Deal had changed America indelibly, sounding the death knell for the unbridled capitalism and unregulated individualism of which Mellon had been a child, an instrument, a beneficiary, an icon, and, as some of his friends insisted, a scapegoat. His world was dying, and he was dying with it. Indeed, Mellon was now so frail that for his comfort and convenience a special car had been attached to the northbound train. "I have never before hired a private car for my own use," he observed, recalling a lifetime of abstinence and restraint, as he stepped aboard to begin a final journey from the nation's capital, which had been his home for the better part of fifteen years.[82] His last words to David Finley were that he looked forward to seeing him again soon. Once settled in on Long Island, Mellon remained in close touch with Duveen, via Finley, and he continued to be "most anxious" for news concerning possible acquisitions for the gallery. Among the works Finley discussed with Duveen on Mellon's behalf during July and August were the Allendale Giorgione, Count Czernin's Viennese Vermeer (whose saga seemed to know no end), the Morgan library marbles, a Sassetta, a Constable, a Piero della Francesca, and some unspecified "Elizabethan pictures." The "most important thing," one of Duveen's staff observed, was that Finley was showing "great interest" in "great names," and this promised well, since "we know his taste."[83]

The bulletins that reached Duveen in July and early August were encouraging: "all reports Mellon quite well"; "Mellon resting [and] getting on very well"; and so on.[84] But their optimism was exaggerated. By the time he reached Long Island, Mellon needed constant medical supervision, yet he remained predictably resistant to it. Accordingly, David Bruce invited a friend of his, who also happened to be a doctor, to come for a visit, installing him as a permanent house guest at Bonnie Dune without revealing to his father-in-law the visitor's profession. Mellon didn't mind his beloved son-in-law's friend, and the doctor became much attached to his patient as they spent more and more time together. As Mellon continued to weaken, taking to his bed in mid-August, his mind remained as alert and active as ever, and the matter which engaged his interest almost to the last was the progress of the gallery.[85] Eventually he succumbed to bronchial pneumonia and uremia: he died shortly before eight-thirty on the evening of August 26, 1937, scarcely five months after Congress had accepted his gift on behalf of the nation, and less than two months after the construction work on the building had been authorized. To the end, Mellon's nerves had remained as steady as his will was strong, and on the very threshold of death, he had brought to fruition his last, greatest, and most enduring enterprise, with a tenacity of which the Judge would have been proud. But it had been very close.[86]

Ailsa and Paul were at their father's side when he died, and David Bruce issued a brief statement that "the end was perfectly peaceful." For the next few days, they were inundated with telegrams and letters of sympathy. Again and again, friends and associates hailed Mellon's decency, integrity, patriotism, kindness, and generosity.[87] Thus his tax trial lawyer, Frank J. Hogan: "The nation loses one of its greatest men, and the people a modest, wise and exceedingly generous benefactor." Thus W. B. Pryon of Gulf Oil: "I consider him one of the outstanding American citizens, and industrially, socially and politically he has probably done more for this country as a whole than any other citizen." Thus Lauder Greenway of the Metropolitan Museum of Art: "In a way all the citizens of the country have suffered the loss of one of the few real public servants, and time will show how great a one."[88] Thus Helen Clay Frick: "He always had my devoted admiration. The world does not make such men any more as these fathers of ours." And thus Lord Duveen: "I have met in my time very many men of great eminence in many walks of life and in many countries, but never one whose greatness made so deep an impression on me as Mr. Mellon, and certainly no one who had more unselfishly and more effectively devoted his life to his country." "His loss to America," Duveen went on, "is irreparable, but it gives me great joy to know that his national work is to be perpetuated, as well as our memories, by the imperishable monument to be erected in Washington."[89]

Perhaps the most "splendid" tribute was never even intended for Ailsa or for Paul. It was from David H. Blair, commissioner of internal revenue for much of Mellon's tenure at the Treasury, delivered to Colonel Frank Drake, who had been responsible for bringing him to Washington.[90] Blair did not know Mellon's children, but Drake eventually passed the letter on to Ailsa, and it is easy to see why. "I wish," Blair began,

> it were possible for me to express in words my feelings in regard to Mr. Mellon. You and I know how he hated sham, pretense and fraud, in what contempt he held those tricks of the demagogue who used his name to kindle class hatred and set afire the passions of the ignorant and shiftless

against the thrifty and successful, and yet how tolerant he was towards those who for their own base and selfish purposes abused and slandered him. Without any noisy profession of high morals or religion he practiced the teachings of Christ in a far greater degree than any of his traducers, many of whom, in public, made great professions of morality . . . In spite of unwarranted abuse by high officials of the government, and in spite of their persistent attempts to discredit and to "despitefully use and persecute" him, without the slightest resentment he carried out a plan, conceived long ago, and gave to the Nation the most munificent gift it ever received from any source. I know of no other man who was big enough to do what Andrew Mellon did.[91]

While these private tributes were pouring in, Mellon's death also made the front pages across America, where opinion was much more divided.[92] In some cases, the man recently reviled for standing by while the Great Depression crushed the country, and accused of tax evasion and fraudulent conduct, was now acclaimed as an outstanding banker, an exemplary business leader, an indefatigable public servant, and a national benefactor who, sadly, would not live to see the dedication of the great institution that his imagination, generosity, and perseverance had made possible.[93] There were words of praise as well from Herbert Hoover ("his public service will be told by historians . . . his lifelong benefactions were studiously withheld from the public"), from Parker Gilbert ("he had a tranquility of spirit and a nobility of character which prevailed over all things"), from Governor John S. Fisher ("the name of Mellon is indelibly written in honor on the pages of American history"), and even from a cousin of FDR's, Theodore Roosevelt Jr. ("I have always found him a sincere and honest patriot"). And the *Washington Star* saluted Mellon as a creative and constructive figure, whose achievements in banking and business had strengthened the national economy and thus benefited the American people as a whole: "he sought to make his country strong and dignified, happy and content . . . by providing opportunity for self-improvement [and] self-advancement for all who were willing to try."[94]

But among the encomiums, note was also frequently made in the press of the two major government suits still pending against Mellon and his "industrial interests." At the Treasury, Henry Morgenthau put the legacy in a much cooler New Deal perspective when he opined that Mellon's life spanned "an epoch in the economic history of the nation, and his passing takes one of the most important industrial and financial figures of our time."[95] Indeed, pervading all the less sympathetic portrayals was a sense that Mellon was a figure from an age and a generation that were over, and that its passing was more cause for relief than for regret. "Like Rocke-feller, Gould, Carnegie, and the rest of the pioneering capitalists," opined the *Washington Daily News*, "Andrew Mellon belonged to a vanishing race." America had needed "their directive energies to mine its minerals, harness its waterfalls, and span its distances with ships and railroads, and it rewarded them with unprecedented wealth." But now the nation was "turning from the mere exploitation of wealth to its fairer distribution," and so in future it would be needing and rewarding "the energies of social engineers, economists and statesmen." In recent years, agreed the *Phila-delphia Record*, "America left the day when it needed great capital accumu-lations to produce goods, and entered the day when it needed a great spread of purchasing power to consume goods. To Mellon, this new era was as unfamiliar as if he had suddenly been transported to China."[96]

But the only journey remaining for Andrew Mellon was much shorter. On the day after his death, his body was taken by special train from Long Island to New York City, the casket conveyed, by ironic coincidence, in the same private railcar that had brought FDR home to Hyde Park from Washington the previous day. At Pennsylvania Station, the car was attached to the overnight train that Mellon had so often taken home in his days of wealth and power and fame, and it reached Pittsburgh on the morning of August 28, 1937. Flags were at half-mast across the city, and the funeral took place at two-thirty that afternoon—not, as was custom-ary with the Mellons, at the home of the deceased, but at the East Liberty Presbyterian Church where Mellon had worshipped with his family as a boy, and on which, to his great disapproval, his late brother Dick had lav-ished such charity in his final years.[97] "The casket was not opened," one local paper reported. "In death, Mr. Mellon remained as retiring as he had been in life." But there was nothing understated about the four hundred floral tributes which overflowed the church onto the grounds outside, and which had obliged the Pittsburgh florists to send to Chicago for more roses and chrysanthemums. Not everyone was so conventional in their choice: Duveen ordered a "large wreath" of the "finest deep orchids," while President and Mrs. Roosevelt sent a spray of gladiolus.[98] By con-trast, the service could scarcely have been simpler. There was no eulogy. The Twenty-third Psalm was read by the same minister who had con-ducted the funerals of Dick Mellon and James Ross Mellon only a few years before. And there were two hymns: "Abide with Me" and "Lead Kindly Light."

Three thousand people filled the church to pay their tributes to "Pitts-burgh's first citizen," as the local papers now described him, and there was also a large crowd outside. The Mellon clan occupied the first five rows, with Ailsa and David, Paul and Mary, and Dick's widow, Jennie, in the first pew. Only R. K. Mellon was absent, on a vacation in Alaska, from which he could not return in time. Braving the cold wrath of the Pittsburgh establishment who had never forgiven her for the pain and humiliation she had inflicted on their favorite son, Nora McMullen Mellon appeared to mourn the man whose life had diverted and dominated her own for nearly forty years. Did she recall the letter she had sent to "dear Andy" six years before: "I realize as I have always done that life would be a dreary affair if you were to go before me. I don't suppose this interests you, but I want you to know it is the truth"?[99] Most of the great Pittsburgh figures of Mellon's youth and middle years had long since passed: Carnegie, Frick, Heinz, Westinghouse, Magee, Knox, Reed, and McEldowney. But his surviving business associates, whose fortunes he had helped to make, turned out in force, among them Arthur Vining Davis and Roy A. Hunt (son of Alfred) of Alcoa, Colonel Frank Drake and George S. Davison of Gulf Oil, and C. D. Marshall and H. H. McClintic. They were joined by John G. Bowman, by Parker Gilbert, and by David Finley, and the now-vanquished Republican ascendancy, represented by David Reed, Ogden Mills, and John S. Fisher. In mourning the end of a life, they were marking the passing of an age.

After the service, Mellon's casket was taken to Allegheny Cemetery, where it was placed next to that of his brother Dick in an ivy-covered vault with two Gothic spires. "His death," the *Pittsburgh Post-Gazette* observed, in words which well caught the prevailing sense of epochal transition, "took from the American scene one of the last of its statesmen-financiers, and from Pittsburgh it took a modern Midas, whose gifted financial touch had helped to transform the city into one of the industrial wonders of modern civilization."[100] So, indeed, he had; but in depressed and Democratic Pittsburgh, all that now seemed a long time ago. Yet for those most closely associated with Mellon during his last years, the loss was much more immediate, especially for David Finley, who had never seen his master again after Mellon had left for Long Island in early July. "I did not have the opportunity," Finley wrote to Ailsa a few days after the funeral, "to tell you in Pittsburgh how beautiful I thought the funeral service was. The music could not have been more appropriate or more beautifully sung, and the whole service, it seemed to me, was just as Mr. Mellon would have wished it to be."[101]

A FORTUNE IN HISTORY

In the short voyage of a lifetime, we can see the eddies and rip-
ples upon the surface, but not the under-currents changing the
main channel of the stream. History alone can determine the
deep seated causes which have been at work to bring them
about.

Thomas Mellon and His Times, p. 338

I. UNFINISHED BUSINESS

Andrew Mellon's life was over, and naturally he had left his affairs
in good order. He had made a new will in July 1936, when he
appointed David Bruce, Paul Mellon, and Donald Shepard as his executors, and when he named the educational and charitable trust as his
residuary legatee. Nevertheless, the executors could do little until the
outstanding tax dispute had been resolved with the federal government.
"When will the Board publish its findings?" Mellon had inquired, almost
plaintively, during his last months, in a rare display of anxiety and concern
at the seemingly interminable delay.[1] The Board of Tax Appeals finally
delivered its judgment on December 7, 1937, a little more than three
months after Mellon's death, causing his many friends, relatives, and
admirers deep regret that he had not lived to learn the outcome. For its
main conclusion was an unequivocal exoneration, namely that the "petitioner did not file a false and fraudulent return for the purpose of evading
taxes." It then proceeded to elaborate:

Just as the law cloaks every man with the presumption of innocence, it likewise clothes him with a presumption of good faith in his business dealings. Fraud is never presumed. It must be proven by clear and convincing evidence. Having carefully considered all the evidence and all of the inference properly to be drawn therefrom, we find in our minds no doubt as to the correct determination. The record before us does not sustain the charge of fraud.[2]

Accordingly, the board struck down the government's claim against Mellon for three million dollars in unpaid taxes and fines, just as he had had almost unfailing faith that it would. Several of the more detailed findings were equally gratifying to Mellon's supporters. The prosecution's contention that the educational and charitable trust was fraudulent was dismissed outright: "The A. W. Mellon Educational & Charitable Trust was, in 1931, a valid and existing trust, organized and operating exclusively for Educational and Charitable purposes," which meant that "the transfer by petitioner to the Trust of certain paintings in 1931 was a complete and valid gift." And Mellon's transfer of stock in the Pittsburgh Coal Company to Union Trust was likewise held to be "a complete and valid sale, giving rise to a legal deduction."[3]

Only in two instances did the board direct revisions to Mellon's 1931 tax return, and these concerned technical complexities and had no bearing on Mellon's intentions or integrity. The first was his sale of stock in the Bethlehem Steel Company in January 1931, wherein the board ruled that Mellon had overstated the value of the original McClintic-Marshall shares for 1913, thereby underreporting his profit and thus his tax liability. Mellon had always assumed this would be a matter for revision and negotiation in accordance with standard practice; the final value of $300 assigned to each share in 1913 was much closer to Mellon's figure of $350 than the Treasury's of $158.54. There was also the sale of stock in the Western Public Service Corporation to the Union Trust Company in December 1931, wherein Mellon could demonstrate that he had not repurchased the stock within the thirty-day moratorium, but could not prove that he had not entered "into any contract or option" with the Union Trust Company to repurchase the stock at a later date. As a result, Mellon was deemed to owe $485,809.49 in unpaid taxes for 1931, and $158,778.94 in accrued interest on that amount. Altogether, then, his arrears came to $644,588.23: scarcely one-fifth of the sum the government had initially sought.[4]

The jubilation among Mellon's supporters at this vindication was inevitably bittersweet, and was well expressed in letters Lord Duveen wrote to Paul, David Bruce, and the Mellon legal team:

> None of his friends, among whom I am proud to count myself, ever doubted that the unworthy attack would be defeated, and that he would be entirely vindicated. At last this has come, and I share the happiness and pride that must be yours at so satisfactory an outcome. I shall always deeply regret that he was not spared long enough to know that the attack upon his good name had been so decisively defeated.[5]

"The decision," Frank Hogan wrote back, "is most gratifying, but not in the least surprising." Indeed, it was "unthinkable" that the federal government "could have countenanced the futile attack upon Mr. Mellon's honour." "I believe the attack on Mr. Mellon hurt me as deeply as it did him," Donald Shepard replied, "and it is a deep satisfaction to me to feel that I was of some help in resisting this unjustifiable action."[6] FDR's response was rather different. Asked at his first press conference after the verdict about the vindication of Andrew Mellon, he breezily replied that he had not read the board's decision, and he merely asked Homer Cummings for "a brief memorandum relative to the outcome."[7]

The conclusion of the tax trial, and a final agreement reached between Mellon's lawyers and the Treasury in June 1938, made it possible for the executors to settle what remained of Mellon's personal estate.[8] At the time of his death, there were often, thanks to Harvey O'Connor, wildly exaggerated notions as to just how many millions Mellon really commanded and personally possessed. The *New York Times* put Mellon's wealth at between $100 million and $500 million, while the *Washington Times* estimated between $200 million and $2 billion. On the basis of such stratospheric guesses, the *New York Post* calculated that the commonwealth of Pennsylvania would collect somewhere between $32 million and $80 million in taxes.[9] But these figures bear very little relation to reality, partly because Mellon had never been as rich as was popularly imagined, and partly because few knew how much money he had given away during his lifetime to his family and to the educational and charitable trust. The final reckoning was thus relatively modest for the man once ranked as one of the four richest in America, and it came as a shock to many. Mellon's remaining assets at the time of his death were valued at $31.5 million (which was higher than their assigned book value of $21.9 million), of which nearly $8 million was in bonds, $16 million in stocks, $1.8 million in works of art, $1.6 million in real estate, and $2.3 million in coal lands.

That figure was subsequently revised by the state appraisers to $36.6 million—perhaps $400 million in today's currency.[10]

From this sum, there were extensive deductions. The largest single item was the $9 million which Mellon had borrowed between 1932 and 1937 from the Union Trust Company and the Mellon National Bank, to compensate for his much-depleted income, when stock from various Mellon companies had been pledged as collateral. There were also unsecured debts of nearly $4 million, largest among these being the $2.8 million that was owed in back taxes. (The sum included not only the additional income tax for 1931, but also similar assessments for 1932 to 1934, as well as income tax for 1936 and the months of 1937 preceding Mellon's death, additional assessments for federal gift taxes in 1934 and 1935, plus accrued interest. The other major items of this unsecured debt were $360,000 in legal fees for the 1931 tax case and Mellon's medical expenses since December 1936, which amounted to $75,000.) Beyond these secured and unsecured debts, the executors took $1 million as commission, and the attorneys' fees amounted to the same amount. After other, miscellaneous deductions, the net worth of Mellon's estate was calculated to be $19 million, from which $3.3 million was then paid in federal estate tax and other death taxes.[11]

Andrew Mellon's financial affairs were finally settled in early 1939, when his residuary estate was determined to be worth just short of $16 million. After bequests to his former employees totaling $180,000, the remainder was duly disbursed to the educational and charitable trust. It is a modest sum when set against his years of peak wealth during the mid- and late 1920s, and it was far, far less than was popularly expected. But it bespeaks the speed and efficiency which he had set about disgorging his fortune in the years since Ailsa's marriage and the creation of the educational and charitable trust. Since then, it bears repeating, Mellon had settled $20 million on Ailsa, approximately the same sum on Paul, handed on $10 million in bank shares to the two of them, and established over $22 million in trusts for their children. During the same period, he had given another $22 million to the educational and charitable trust in the form of stocks and bonds, as well as conveying to the trust most of his art, which was valued at $20 million. When the residuary estate was factored in, it turned out that Mellon had divided his fortune fairly equally, between the $72 million that had gone to his descendants and the $58 million that went to the trust. Indeed, if his income had been greater during the 1930s and he had borrowed less from the Mellon National Bank and the Union Trust Company, the trust would have been the almost exactly equal beneficiary. (There had also been substantial bene-factions to Pittsburgh, especially during the 1920s and 1930s, including the university and the Mellon Institute, amounting to another $10 million.)[12]

Such was the division and disposal of the fortune that Mellon had methodically and shrewdly accumulated during the course of his long life. The final total of $140 million was no doubt a substantial underestimate: even in these depression years, its real worth, as distinct from its book value, may have been well above double that.[13] But however reckoned, the Mellon millions had never approached the wealth of a Carnegie or a Rockefeller (though his final estate was larger than that of John D. Rock-efeller Sr., who left only $26.4 million);[14] and assuming Mellon's art pur-chases made up one-sixth of his fortune, he had spent a significantly smaller portion of his total worth on art than had, say, Morgan or Frick. But in dividing his fortune as he did, Mellon knew exactly what he was doing to ensure the afterlife of his success and to compound its effect. To ensure the precise fulfillment of his wishes, he vested control of his affairs in the hands of three men of the next generation whom he knew he could trust. For David Bruce, Paul Mellon, and Donald Shepard were both his executors and trustees of the A. W. Mellon Educational & Charitable Trust, while Bruce and Shepard were two of the first general trustees of the National Gallery of Art, and Paul Mellon joined them on the board within a year.

While the gallery was being constructed, the trustees refused to con-sider purchasing any more art, much to Duveen's disappointment.[15] In any case, they bore heavier burdens than they might reasonably have expected, because the very day after Andrew Mellon's death, John Russell Pope, having been taken ill at his summer home earlier in the month, had also passed away at sixty-three. "That, on top of the other loss," a down-cast Duveen wrote to David Finley, mourning the architect whose career he had done so much to promote, "was too distressing and bewildering. It was indeed a cruel stroke of fate which took him away practically in his prime, when he was rapidly mounting to higher honours and achieve-ments in his brilliant career."[16] "I have felt dazed," Finley replied two weeks later, "as I know you have been, at the loss of two such friends as we have both sustained." "I find it hard," he went on, "to adjust myself to a world without Mr. Mellon. He has been such a vital factor for so many years, and my affection for him was such that I find myself missing him more and more each day." "Then," he continued, "the death of Mr. Pope less than twenty-four hours later was a great blow for me . . . The design had been approved, in toto—dome and all—and the matter of the Tennessee marble was settled." "It is," he concluded, "all the more incumbent on us to see that the Gallery is built and arranged as he and Mr. Mellon wished—and that we shall do, as of course you know. But much of the joy we would have had in working with Mr. Mellon and Mr. Pope has gone, and that can never come back."[17]

Along with Mellon and Pope, Lord Duveen was the third of the gallery's authentic creators. He may have (typically) exaggerated his contribution, but he had probably planted the original idea in Mellon's head during one of their many visits to the National Gallery in London, and he had constantly encouraged him to be more ambitious and comprehensive in his own collecting for this greater purpose. When it became a settled plan, Duveen was closely involved in the discussions of design and construction, and he sought to persuade other clients to donate their collections to the gallery. And after Mellon's death, Duveen's staff had moved his paintings out of the Washington apartment to join his other pictures at the Corcoran Gallery.[18] Like Mellon and Pope, however, Duveen would not live to see the building completed, for he died in London on May 25, 1939. David Finley paid tribute to the long relationship between client and dealer. "Knowing him as you did," one of Duveen's staff replied, "you are in a position to appreciate what a privilege it was to us to have that association, and how we treasure the memory of it."[19] Soon after, Duveen's executors offered to the gallery the oak paneling from a room in his New York house, which had been designed by John Russell Pope. They thought it fit to adorn the Founder's Room, which would be situated to the right of the entrance from the Mall, serving as a meeting place for the trustees and a commemoration of the prime movers in the establishment of the gallery. Alas, it proved impossible to adapt either the paneling to the room or the room to the paneling, and the offer was rejected.[20]

Despite the losses of Mellon, Pope, and Duveen, work on the gallery went ahead, and now with a growing urgency as the prospect loomed of American involvement in another world war. David Bruce and Donald Shepard superintended the effort (Paul Mellon served only briefly as a trustee, from 1938 to 1939: his close association with the gallery did not begin in earnest until 1945), together with Pope's assistants, Otto R. Eggers and Daniel Higgins of New York, and David Finley, who was formally appointed director by the trustees in March 1938.[21] There were many details to settle that Mellon and Pope had left undecided, especially concerning the further uncluttering of the exterior walls and also the size and configuration of the galleries themselves. As a feat of construction, the job was enormous: the building rested on 6,800 concrete piles, and more than 800 railcar-loads of pink Tennessee marble were eventually drawn from seven different quarries. The gallery was completed in December 1940, at a cost of $15 million, and soon after, David Finley moved in, along with the staff he had been busy recruiting in the meantime. Mellon's paintings and sculptures were installed early in 1941, and some pictures on loan from Samuel H. Kress and from Chester Dale began arriving soon after. The great Widener collection was also promised, and Finley now began in great earnest to cultivate other potential donors, and also to charm and woo President and Mrs. Roosevelt.[22]

On the evening of March 17, 1941, the National Gallery of Art in Washington was finally opened, with a glittering reception, entirely orchestrated by David Finley, for more than six thousand guests, who marveled at the size and style of the building, no less than at the pictures on display.[23] According to the *New York Times*, "all ranks of official, diplomatic and resident society" were present, along with "a cross-section of the *Who's Who* and social register of every large city in the United States" and many "outstanding artists and sculptors, directors of art museums, presidents of universities, connoisseurs and collectors." The ceremonies began promptly at 10 p.m. and were broadcast live on radio across the nation. In presenting the gallery "to be dedicated forever to the use and enjoyment of the people of the United States" on behalf of its founder, Paul Mellon noted that while secretary of the treasury, his father had

> felt the need of a national gallery in Washington, with a collection of art which might serve as the nucleus of a great collection. He saw in his imagination a building adequate to contain that future great collection. He hoped that the gallery would become a joint enterprise on the part of the government on the one hand, and of magnanimous citizens on the other.

Above all, it had been Andrew Mellon's wish that "the National Gallery would become not a static but a living institution, growing in usefulness and importance to artists, scholars and the general public."

While the gallery was being completed, FDR had been elected to an unprecedented third term in November 1940 (W. L. Mellon had predicted that Wendell Wilkie would win "by a landslide"), which meant it was Mellon's great adversary who now publicly accepted the gallery on behalf of the American people.[24] But as he had during his New Year's Eve meeting with Mellon in 1936, Roosevelt relished, rather than regretted, the ironies of the occasion. "The giver of the building," he observed, "has matched the richness of his gift with the modesty of his spirit, stipulating that the Gallery shall be known not by his name, but by the nation's." (Perhaps, Paul later speculated, the president "had come to realize that Father really had been a public-spirited man.")[25] It fell to Chief Justice Charles E. Hughes, secretary of state under President Harding and recently the New Deal's obstructionist in chief on the Supreme Court, to thank his former cabinet colleague more copiously.[26] "This treasure house," he noted,

> now formally presented to the nation, is at once a memorial, a symbol and an opportunity. It is a memorial to an eminent benefactor, whose patriotic ardor and love of art prompted the conception of this plan for public enrichment, now happily brought to fruition. This building, so admirably suited to its purpose in beauty of design and perfection of practical adaptation, does not bear the name of Andrew W. Mellon, as he requested it should not, but it will none the less always be a memorial to his public spirit, as it is a fitting crown of his public services.

Not everyone saw the building in such benevolent light. When John Russell Pope died, the *New York Times* opined that he had created "temples that sit serene in the moil and toil of commerce," and this was one reason why his work was so congenial to Andrew Mellon. But as the dissent on the Commission of Fine Arts had already made plain, a younger, more radical generation of architects had no more sympathy for Pope's classicism than for Mellon's politics.[27] Within a month of the gallery's opening, Joseph Hudnut, dean of Harvard's Graduate School of Design, mounted a ferocious assault in his article "The Last of the Romans," which insisted that classicism was inappropriate to a democratic republic with a Democratic administration. It was, Hudnut thought, a tired architectural deceit to clothe a steel structure in marble, and to conceal all the machinery by which it was heated and lit and cooled. The triumph of the modern international style, he concluded, could not be long delayed, at which point architects like Pope, and buildings like the gallery, would become anachronistic irrelevancies. Pope's reputation would not recover for half a century; it is not coincidence that the denunciation of his aesthetics as elitist, reactionary, and dishonest so clearly echoes many of the political attacks mounted on Mellon during the 1920s and 1930s.[28]

In June 1938, meanwhile, the suit against Alcoa, initiated by the Department of Justice, had finally come to trial. It was a significant part of the last major assault FDR would launch against bankers and businessmen in the aftermath of the "Roosevelt recession," leading even some of the president's friends to counsel restraint: it was a mistake, they averred, to be at perpetual war with the nation's foremost capitalists, who were now utterly demoralized after five years of continuous criticism and unrelenting investigation, and in a most uncertain and anxious state over what further provocations and penalties might yet be in store for them.[29] Nevertheless, the Alcoa trial was a significant investigation into the workings and ethics of big business, and as such it was also a major confrontation between what remained of the Democrats' New Deal and what had survived of the Republican old guard. From filing to verdict, the proceedings lasted longer than the American Civil War: the record of the trial amounted to some 58,000 pages, and before it was over, Alcoa would spend two million dollars defending itself: the U.S. government's costs amounted to one quarter of that sum. Almost all of the extensive publicity was unfavorable to the company, owing partly to the Justice Department's skill at news management and partly to Alcoa's being, as Mellon himself had so often been, ill-advisedly reticent.[30]

Nevertheless, the initial verdict delivered in March 1942 was a complete vindication of Alcoa, with the defendant found not guilty on more than 130 counts. In a decision that ran to 311 pages in fine print, Judge Francis G. Caffey of the United States District Court for the Southern District of New York observed that the Justice Department had failed to show proof of the company's *intent* to monopolize in the accumulation and concentration of resources, or proof that the company had committed unlawful acts.[31] His conclusion was therefore that Alcoa's success had been mainly the result of sound business practice and acceptable competitive tactics, and in most respects there was no demonstrable monopoly. A succession of independent aluminum manufacturers had also been enlisted to attest to Alcoa's helpfulness in developing their lines of production, and even George Haskell now maintained under oath that he had never previously believed the company had sought to drive him out of business. Caffey expressed himself full of admiration for the firm and for Arthur Vining Davis, who through thirty days on the stand had shown a mastery of detail that was widely recognized as extraordinary. His final observation was that "it would be greatly contrary to the public interest either to dissolve or to enjoin Alcoa."[32]

In essence, the judge had accepted Alcoa's argument that there was insufficient evidence in support of the government's contention of specific acts of wrongdoing; and he had declined to share the prosecution's broader view that monopoly, however attained, was an inherent social evil in any system of free enterprise. The Sherman act did not forbid de facto monopoly arrived at fairly, and on this rested Alcoa's innocence. The Department of Justice naturally appealed, ultimately to the Supreme Court. But as an unsettling number of Justices were found to have connections with Alcoa or other Mellon interests, the appeal wound up before the U.S. Court of Appeals for the Second Circuit and the most celebrated American jurist never to sit on the Supreme Court, Learned Hand. In March 1945, just a few weeks before President Roosevelt's death, Judge Hand delivered a decision, a landmark in case law and a boon to the Department of Justice. More sympathetic to the arguments against monopoly in principle, and less attentive to specific instances of wrongdoing, Hand concluded that Alcoa had begun as a legal monopoly, but its subsequent efforts to expand its business amounted to a goal of perpetuating its monopoly. It made no difference that the company had deterred competitors by no other means than its high efficiency and managerial excellence. Having run the company this well was in effect proof enough of illegal intent to perpetuate monopolistic power.

This was a controversial decision that would cause many to question the economic coherency of antitrust law. Applauded by some for aligning the courts with the powerful and prevailing anti-monopoly sentiments of the time, it was denounced by others for ignoring the practical realities within which Alcoa had operated with such remarkable efficiency. In the trial of worldviews we might call Roosevelt vs. Mellon, Hand had found decisively for Roosevelt. But perhaps out of consideration for market realities, and in particular for the extraordinary circumstances of wartime, the court opted for restraint in its recommendations, refusing to accept the Justice Department's request for the dissolution of Alcoa and for the severance of ties between the company and its Canadian counterpart.[33]

Ultimately, it was not court action so much as the unprecedented demand for aluminum during the Second World War that had already broken Alcoa's domestic monopoly. The company had been unable to expand output sufficiently to meet all the needs of the American armed forces: aluminum was essential for aircraft construction, among other things. So great was the demand that not only did serious private competitors now appear for the first time, but the U.S. government itself also entered the aluminum fabrication business. Thus was competition established in an industry that had been impervious to free market forces and the federal court rulings alike. At the end of the war, the government sold its own plants to the two companies that had now become Alcoa's chief competitors: Reynolds Metals and Kaiser Aluminum & Chemical Corporation. In 1950, the market share of each of the three major American producers was adjudged as follows: Alcoa with 50.86 percent, Reynolds with 30.94 percent, and Kaiser with 18.20 percent. For many, however, Alcoa still remained *the* Aluminum Company of America, though now operating in a wholly different economic and political environment from the one in which Andrew Mellon had helped transmute Pittsburgh Reduction into one of the nation's most successful corporate entities.[34]

Two years after the circuit court's decision against Alcoa, the political climate was changing significantly. A year and a half had passed since VJ Day, the galvanizing effects of war and Roosevelt's populist charisma were dissolving, and pent-up resentment at his heavy hand began to express itself. His successor, Harry Truman, was deeply unpopular and both houses of Congress were again under Republican control. Some of Mellon's remaining friends and admirers now spied an opportunity to obtain for him a long-overdue honor: a monument in Washington. In April 1947, two Pennsylvania Republicans, Senator Howard Martin and Representative James G. Fulton, introduced legislation authorizing the construction of a commemorative fountain, in the vicinity of the National Gallery of Art, for which private money had been raised. Their joint resolution was passed in July, and a site was selected that was bounded by Sixth Street and by Constitution and Pennsylvania avenues, opposite the north entrance to the gallery, and at the eastern corner of the Federal Triangle. Otto Eggers and Daniel Higgins, who had been John Russell Pope's associates, were chosen to design the structure in keeping with their mentor's adjacent building.[35] The Mellon Memorial Fountain was dedicated on May 9, 1952. It had cost more than $300,000; it was simple in design, with no statue or sculpture of Mellon, and the inscription recorded the briefest details of his life and nearby gift. The outward flow of water was deemed to represent Mellon's generosity: "the calm and steady giving away of itself." But on most passersby, the symbolism would be lost. On that same day, the first bay of the south outer aisle of the National Cathedral was also dedicated to Mellon.[36]

Mellon's political rehabilitation was further advanced during the Eisenhower years. The centenary of his birth in 1955 was marked by the issue of a three-cent commemorative postage stamp bearing his name and likeness. (It was unsuccessfully opposed by Congressman Wright Patman, whose hostility to Mellon lived on long after its object had died.)[37] Just before Christmas that year, at a ceremony held in the National Gallery of Art, Senator Martin of Pennsylvania paid tribute to a man of "outstanding achievement" whose life was devoted (in part) to expanding industrial enterprise, so as "to create new products for the benefit of mankind, to broaden employment opportunities for our working men and women, and to make a richer, fuller life for the community and the nation." Martin also paid tribute to Mellon's "splendid achievements" as secretary of the treasury, and to his imagination and generosity as a philanthropist—in sum, to his "practical patriotism." "His memory," Martin concluded, "should be honored by all Americans in recognition of his brilliant record of achievement, his unselfish devotion to the public good, his unfailing adherence to sound principles of government, and to his outstanding place as a benefactor of mankind."[38] This was scarcely sufficient to wash away or cover the blots left on Mellon's memory by the New Deal and the tax trial; and although a serious attempt to set the official record straight, it by no means garnered universal support.

Meanwhile, having seen the National Gallery of Art successfully completed and triumphantly opened, David Finley had been working to bring to fruition his late employer's last initiative, the creation of a National Portrait Gallery. When Mellon's paintings were given to the National Gallery of Art, it was with a proviso that those works primarily of historical interest, which he had begun to purchase during the last years of his life, should go to a national portrait gallery, provided such an institution became a reality within twenty-five years. Once the Second World War was over, Finley lobbied hard in Washington to get such a gallery established, and the necessary legislation was finally passed in 1958, transferring the Old Patent Office Building, which the government was about to vacate, to the Smithsonian Institution to be used for such a purpose. Four years later, and just within the time limit Mellon had set, President John F. Kennedy signed into law an act to provide for a National Portrait Gallery as another bureau of the Smithsonian, and it finally opened to the public in 1968. The first thirty-four portraits the gallery received came from the Mellon collection at the National Gallery of Art. David Finley was a member of the National Portrait Gallery Commission from the beginning (he had retired from the directorship of the National Gallery of Art in 1956), and he remained active in its affairs, and loyal to Mellon's memory, until his death in 1977.[39]

Not surprisingly, the "do-nothing" Eisenhower years were the best for Mellon's reputation since the 1920s. Thereafter, big spending government reached its zenith in Washington, not only under the Kennedy-Johnson Democrats (who saw themselves as completing FDR's New Deal and extending it into Lyndon Johnson's "Great Society"), but also under the Nixon-Ford Republicans (who carried federal spending and intervention to even greater heights, both at home and abroad).[40] In such a political environment, Andrew Mellon's spirit was preserved, if only marginally, among Goldwater Republicans; his name had disappeared from public discourse almost entirely, remaining in history's shadow-land until the "Reagan revolution" of the 1980s. In fact, Ronald Reagan had begun as a Roosevelt Democrat and New Deal supporter, but he ended a self-confessed free marketer and enemy of big government, and his administration was a deliberate repudiation of the political status quo as galvanizing as any since FDR's.[41] During his presidency, "new Republicans" and "supply-siders" rediscovered and hailed Mellon as the dishonored prophet of small government and fiscal responsibility, of committed and systematic tax cuts (especially for the rich), and of the universal benefits of "trickle down" economics.

Liberal commentators and politicians predictably denounced "Reaganomics" as a selfish and misguided return to the corrupt and ultimately disastrous Republican consensus of Harding, Coolidge, Hoover—and Mellon. But a kind of synthesis was perhaps inaugurated when Bill Clinton, a socially progressive Democrat, declared during his presidency that "the era of big government is over." However much the American political reality has strayed from that dictum, it has yet to be explicitly overturned as orthodoxy. These paradigmatic changes, looking backward as much as forward, were not confined to the realm of politics. As in the 1930s, cultural attitudes also shifted. Beginning in the 1980s, there was a growing reaction against the long reign of modern architecture, as exemplified by some of the newer museums recently constructed on the Mall, and in 1991 this backlash overlapped the fiftieth anniversary of the opening of the National Gallery of Art. Its cool, semi-abstract neoclassicism was now reappraised more positively, in the light of broader changes in architectural fashion, as was the whole of John Russell Pope's oeuvre. In this changed political and aesthetic climate, the Grand Plaza in the Federal Triangle was finally finished, after a fashion, in 1996.[42]

The administration of George W. Bush, who took office in 2000, stressed from its inception the importance of bringing people with business experience into government, of encouraging close links between the private and the public sectors, and of cutting taxes for those who invest and employ. These neoconservative nostrums certainly have a Mellon-like ring to them. But since the Bush administration has also accumulated an unprecedented federal debt and run unparalleled budgets, whatever they may espouse, it is difficult to believe Andrew Mellon would have looked with any favor upon their results. He might have sympathized with Vice President Dick Cheney, who has been repeatedly criticized for his continued links with the Halliburton Corporation, and for the large government contracts that company was awarded during his term of office. Whatever their merits, such attacks recall those mounted on Mellon eighty years before, when he claimed to have severed his business and banking connections "as if I had died." More likely, however, Andrew Mellon would identify with his fellow treasury secretary, Paul O'Neill, who was forced to resign halfway into the first term. O'Neill, who by compelling coincidence had been CEO of Alcoa, became the administration's Cassandra, making blunt pronouncements after Mellon's fashion. To be sure, Mellon remains something of a hero to those Republicans on the radical right who wish to dismantle the New Deal, but this objective does not seem likely to be achieved any time soon.

II. THE BALANCE SHEET

Since his death in 1937, Andrew Mellon has been by turns vindicated, ignored, rehabilitated, disregarded, acclaimed, and dismissed—though until now his remarkable story has never been laid out in full for public consideration. In death as in life, he remains a contentious figure, still a standard to which some partisans rally, and therefore also something of a contemporary political lightning rod. This would have greatly disappointed David Finley, who had looked forward to a day when "all the controversies" about his employer would have "died down," when "his record could receive the attention it deserved," and when his "career could be better assessed at its true value."[43] To be sure, nearly seventy years after Mellon's death, the particular disagreements surrounding his life and legacy have died down; the New Deal, in name if not effect, has been filed away as history, together with the less fondly remembered Republican administrations of the 1920s. To that extent, Finley's hopes have been fulfilled: from the vantage point of the early twenty-first century, Mellon's life, its triumphs and tribulations both, can be seen as belonging to a bygone world very different from ours. And when viewed with this distancing historical perspective, perhaps what the Judge would have called its "deeper undercurrents" may reveal themselves. But for all that has come to pass since Andrew Mellon lived, no easy agreement or obvious consensus as to his "true value" seems to have emerged, and in this account of his life, his admirers and his detractors will both have found timber to bolster their views.

Here is one version of Mellon's life for which these pages provide ample justification. He was a decent, loyal, honorable man, generous to his friends and family, but deceived and betrayed by his disloyal and dishonorable wife. He was a brilliant banker, with a rare, creative genius for business and an eye for opportunity, who became a transformative figure in America's economic growth during the late nineteenth and early twentieth centuries. As a result of his efforts, many thousands were gainfully employed who might otherwise have found no work, and America's economic might was greatly strengthened. He was also an outstanding secretary of the treasury, who rightly understood that what was good for business was ultimately good for America, who presided over the greatest boom in the nation's history, and who helped restore the stricken post–First World War world to something resembling financial stability. He could not be blamed for the collapse of this settlement between 1929 and 1933, and as Roosevelt's record shows, in terms of most economic indicators, Mellon was essentially correct in believing the Great Depression was an ill that had to be endured, rather than one responsive to a government cure. Mellon was also a preeminent collector and philanthropist, assembling the greatest accumulation of art of his day, which he generously donated to the nation. By this view, the extent of the vindictive attacks against him during the 1920s, and of the Roosevelt administration's calculated campaign of vilification during the New Deal, is merely a measure of how great Mellon loomed in the contemporary consciousness. Truly, as this image would have it, he represented the banker as heroic financier, the businessman as exemplary creator of wealth and livelihood—in short, he was a great American.

A motivated detractor could, however, equally well draw from these pages quite a different impression of the man: a sad and shriveled human being, lacking dimensionality of emotion, of intellect, of humanity. Relations with his wife and children tell the tale: he left them permanently scarred and damaged. He was cold, distant, and calculating: devoid of insight, warmth, or empathy. And as his attitudes to organized labor, and to the less fortunate in American society—hostile and unforgiving, even by the standards of the time—demonstrate, Mellon accepted the brutal inequities of capitalism at its harshest with nary a thought, much less a qualm. For all his vaunted commitment to principle and honor, there were episodes in his business life that were far from admirable. Also blameworthy was his unthinking acceptance of Republican dominance, the party's prostration before business interests, and the corruption that followed from it. Throughout his time at the Treasury, he cut taxes to the disproportionate benefit of the rich, and he was in continuous violation of statutes forbidding his involvement in business, about which he knowingly lied. During the Great Depression, he gathered Russian pictures while workingmen starved. Mellon, then, was the epitome of a discredited phase in America's history, which Roosevelt, more caring about ordinary people, was determined to end. For he sought to cleanse the Augean stables of entrenched greed and indifference, and to reform the United States into a more fair, decent, and secure society, and to this end it was fitting to make an example of Mellon. "Better the occasional faults of a government living in the spirit of charity," FDR observed in 1936, "than the consistent omissions of a government frozen on the ice of its own indifference."[44]

Such were the opposing views of the world, and therefore of Andrew Mellon, for much of his life, and they are views with which any assessment of him must reckon. On the one hand are the old guard Republicans, who believe that any individual who can harness market forces to create wealth is deserving of society's praise and thanks. On the other hand are progressives and, later, New Deal Democrats, to whom men such as Mellon were incarnations of the excess from whose predations it was the duty of the state to protect the many, and above all the underprivileged. In some form these opposing views of men and state have persisted in American political discourse ever since, and not coincidentally, the two views have been replicated in two very different modes and styles of American historiography, one generally pro-enterprise and practiced in business schools, and one generally pro-labor and flourishing in history departments.[45] They also inform, if sometimes inexplicitly, our popular debates about the role and reach of government, and about its proper relationship with business: the traditional conservatives and neoconservatives on one side, the liberal progressives and environmentalists on the other.

Those who do not think it is possible or wise to try to transcend such polarities would be well advised to skip the next few paragraphs. But historians and biographers do have a moral and professional obligation to regard their subjects as doctors regard their patients, with a mixture of sympathy and detachment. In Mellon's case, it may seem a great deal easier to maintain the detachment than to summon up the sympathy, but it is intrinsic to this biographical enterprise to attempt a summation that goes beyond the mere iteration of established views and contradictory interpretations. And the commitment to do so arises not only from a wish to discard reductive dualisms—although that purpose is creditable enough— but also from a conviction that individual and collective human experience are not simple matters. But for any summation of Andrew Mellon's life, an appropriate starting point is Karl Marx's famous dictum that while men (and we would now add women, without changing the spirit of the sentiment) make their own history, they do so under circumstances not of their own choosing.[46]

Individual actors do matter, but (and in this insight the typical historian is advantaged over the typical biographer) as individuals they cannot be assessed without appropriate perspective and a realistic sense of proportion relative to a specific temporal setting. Beyond any doubt, Andrew Mellon, along with Frick, Carnegie, Heinz, and Westinghouse, was one of the most significant figures in the economic development of Pittsburgh and of western Pennsylvania during the last quarter of the nineteenth century and the first decades of the twentieth. That is one very good reason to write about him. But this astonishing regional transformation was part of a broader national development, namely the emergence of the United States as the world's foremost industrial power—a position that it has sustained and consolidated during the hundred-odd years since. It is no belittlement of Andrew Mellon's life or achievement to note that this transformation would certainly have occurred whether he had lived or not. Contemporaries' encomiums notwithstanding, bankers and businessmen, like most other professionals, however exceptional, are almost never truly indispensable. "The demands of modern life," Frick once wrote, "called for such works as ours; if we had not met the demands, others would have done so."[47] Mellon, whose fortune was but a fraction of Carnegie's or Rockefeller's, agreed. "We are not really important, any of us," he once told David Finley, and this was not just self-deprecation, for he was certainly never as powerful as his many contemporary nemeses presumed.[48] Industrializing economies, especially those stretching across entire continents, are always much greater than the few individuals, however mighty, who in the popular imagination control them.

Mellon was, then, very much a figure of his times. There is also much about him, both his limitations and his achievements, that may best be explained with reference to his powerful yet inhibiting Scotch-Irish background and to the heavy hand of his parents: his taciturnity and secrecy, his coldness and distance, his sense of perpetual embattlement, his single-mindedness in pursuit of profit, his obsessive, pedantic concern for the technicalities of the law, which often served his determination to yield never an inch on anything or to anyone. Culturally conditioned, too, were his lack of humor or warmth, his incapacity to feel or express emotion, his indifference to and indeed contempt for public opinion, and his visceral abhorrence of ostentation and conspicuous consumption. Even Mellon's most salient trait was paternally ordained: his preference for narrow and intense self-application at the expense of well-roundedness, flexibility, nuance, and above all self-knowledge.

He was in some ways precocious at banking and at business, and nothing if not tenacious, but it is difficult not to implicate his single-minded drive when considering his emotional stuntedness. In this sense, he was never quite a three-dimensional figure. If he seemed uncommonly well equipped to be a financier and an industrialist, he was woefully ill equipped to be a husband or a father, a politician or any public figure, much less to defend himself with any dexterity against what he saw reductively as Roosevelt's simple vindictiveness. Had Mellon married Fannie Jones in the 1880s, and had she lived, his life might have turned out differently under her influence. But there was never the remotest likelihood that this would happen. As to his pyrrhic victory in winning Nora's hand, it was a testament to his persistence, however misguided. But persistence was more of a virtue in business than in wooing, and the odds must always have been against the marriage working or lasting: if Curphey had not come along, someone else almost certainly would have done so. By his own lights, Andrew Mellon was a loyal husband and a devoted father, but those lights were very dim: the loyalty was not reciprocated, and the devotion inadequately expressed, however hard he thought he was trying.

This temperamental and imaginative narrowness owes less to some general Scotch-Irish ethos as to the Judge's draconian version of it. The father was determined to spare the sons the useless trouble of such broad cultivation as he had profited from. Thus did Thomas, something of a fox, sire in Andrew an absolute hedgehog. This is not, however, to deny that Andrew was in many ways very much his father's son. Of all Thomas's boys, Andrew was the one most amenable to his will, and the one most abundantly possessed of the talent and determination to make a great career along the path that his father intended. He imbibed the Judge's approval of acquisition and accumulation, his admiration for independence, his intuition of the ups and downs of the economy, and his loathing of trade unions and organized labor. Whenever confronted by any major problem, his authentic reflexive response was to wonder what his father would have done—though many of the problems Andrew confronted, and many of the solutions he devised, would have been beyond his father's range. With but a half-formed nature of his own, he could, nevertheless, channel the Judge's wisdom and conjure his spirit.

This emotional incompleteness was most painfully manifest in Mellon's personal life—or, rather, the lack of it. He had all of the Judge's coldness of calculation, but none of his warmth of heart. And so in his signal act of independence, his marriage to Nora McMullen—whereby he rebelled not just against his father's views but against all the conventions of Pittsburgh's Scotch-Irish elite—the results were uniformly and all too predictably disastrous. Only in endeavors not taxing to his humanity did he exceed his father—at least initially. In business, he was far more audacious, ambitious, and successful than the Judge. He carried his successes beyond the old economy of his father's fortune—riches of railroads, real estate, and coal—into the new economy of chemicals and electricity, oil and airplanes. In collecting art, Andrew lavished money on what the Judge would have dismissed as "artificial wants." But what began as a way to decorate his drab marital home evolved into a personal interest and a delight in driving hard bargains, in which the aesthetic component, though probably present, remains largely inscrutable. In establishing himself as a local philanthropist and national benefactor, Andrew also repudiated his father's distaste for charity. But his conversion took time, and his sensibilities were not fully formed until relatively late in life.

As the Judge had anticipated, Andrew Mellon became an extraordinarily successful and innovative banker. At the time of his death, the joint resources of the Mellon National Bank and the Union Trust Company made them one of the ten biggest banks in the country. Indeed, because he was a banker before he was a businessman, Mellon would see every enterprise, even the foundation of the National Gallery of Art, from the creative perspective of a financier or an enabler. Was the idea a good one? What resources would it take to make it self-sustaining and self-sufficient? This outlook and activity inspired the accumulation of an unusually diverse and widely distributed fortune: Mellon was in this sense a forerunner in the now commonplace practice of portfolio diversification. It also distinguished him from such monolithic tycoons as Gould or Morgan or Rockefeller or Ford, and it is no coincidence that while the popular imagination associates each of these men with a specific industry, it holds no clear understanding of the sources of Mellon's wealth. But while he was unlike his fellow Midases in some respects, he also shared some characteristics with them.

Like many individuals gifted at making money, Andrew Mellon did not start out poor: on the contrary, he began life with many advantages his father lacked, and he was ideally placed and conditioned to make a fortune when and how he did. In an age when the business of America was held by many to be business itself, Mellon subscribed to the view that there was no higher calling to which a man could aspire. He took pride in his business ethics (which he regarded as being good by the standards of the time, as they generally were), and also in his unusual commitment to building up companies (which was a more selfless and patriotic act than speculating on the stock exchange). The self-image of the tycoon as patriot was common enough among his fellows. There is some justification for this pride, but Mellon's record was not as unblemished as he liked to think. His career does afford examples of sharp practices, and even of speculative gains; there must always remain the suspicion that unsavory things went on but weren't written down; and his loathing of organized labor was Frick-like in its intensity. In truth, none of the men in this cohort was a saint, and to some degree moral self-delusions coincided with emotional ones. Perhaps this was why Mellon was not unusual in falling out with his progeny: it happened in the richest of families, from Rockefellers to Gettys, and beyond.

In spending his business life in the Midwest rather than on the East Coast, Mellon followed what was increasingly the norm among his contemporaries. The generation of Vanderbilt, Gould, and Morgan were decidedly rooted in—indeed were creatures of—the East. But Rockefeller, Carnegie, Frick, Ford, and Westinghouse had all made their reputations (and their fortunes) well to the west of New York, coming east only latterly, in search of legitimacy and influence. In Mellon's case, it was only after his divorce that he was gradually drawn toward New York and Washington—and even then, the immediate motivations were more social and political than economic. Like his peers, Mellon passionately believed in individualism, self-help, and competition, yet his instincts were also (and increasingly) toward the monopolistic, as evidenced by his acquisitive attitude toward the Pittsburgh Stock Exchange, Alcoa, Pittsburgh streetcars, Pittsburgh coal, Pittsburgh banking, and the aviation industry. As a result, Mellon and his relatives obtained a degree of control over the increasingly diversified economy of southwestern Pennsylvania which was greater than that wielded by any other single family in any other single industrialized region. To be sure, the Mellons largely stayed out of United States Steel, Westinghouse, and Heinz, but through their bank and their businesses, they exercised exceptional and growing hegemony over the remaining industries. Small wonder that Andrew did not support the idea of a single building in Pittsburgh to house the "Mellon Interests": it would have drawn attention to a reality he was eager to obscure.

Mellon went to Washington an orthodox believer in the plutocratic creed that government existed to serve business interests—not in opposition to the public good but as the only sure way of furthering it. Likewise, his tax policies encouraging the accumulation of wealth were not born of any conscious greed or even some form of social Darwinism such as the Judge might have espoused. As Mellon understood it, the wealth of great capitalists *was* the wealth of nations. Without it, a national economy had no prospect of growing and providing the opportunities by which other citizens might sustain themselves. Although a contrary impulse in American public discourse had existed for most of his adult life (reaching its very apotheosis in the New Deal), Mellon, like others of his kind, never seriously considered it anything but pernicious to America. Whatever ethically dubious business or political dealings he may have undertaken, he was never shaken in his faith that the Mellon interests and the national interest went hand in glove. This was the political morality that Mellon carried with him to Washington. Hence his belief that, having satisfied the letter of the law by selling his banking shares and resigning his directorships, he could take on the Treasury, even though he continued to involve himself with Mellon businesses. Hence his genuine surprise when his political opponents attacked him on these grounds. And hence the brazen lies he told throughout his term of office, as he repeatedly denied these accusations. He simply never understood or accepted the notion of conflict of interest.

Yet in other ways, Mellon's tenure at the Treasury—at least up to 1929, and in some ways even beyond—does deserve a more sympathetic appraisal than it has generally received. After more than seventy years of big-spending federal government, it is difficult now to grasp just how little it was believed the United States Treasury could or should attempt to do to influence the economy during the 1920s. At most Mellon could have been realistically expected, according to conventional economic wisdom, to balance the books and reduce the debt, and this he undoubtedly did. And, in collaboration with men like Charles G. Dawes and Charles E. Hughes, he also went some way toward restoring the international financial system which the First World War had fairly ruined. These were substantial, constructive achievements, and two more should also be recorded to Mellon's credit. First, it is clear that in reducing counter-productively high tax rates, he arranged that the rich should not pay less, but more, while most Americans paid nothing. This was not an easy policy to sell politically, but Mellon never wavered in the principle that federal taxes should be in proportion to individual means. Second, it is equally clear that Mellon practiced what he preached: throughout the 1920s, he paid far more in federal taxes than he need have done—partly because he believed it was his duty, and partly because he thought it prudent to try to err on the side of caution. Mellon undoubtedly broke the law in denying his continued involvement in business, but when it came to paying taxes, he observed the rules as scrupulously as their vagueness and complexity allowed.

Between 1929 and 1932, the financial world that Mellon had helped administer and reconstruct crashed and burned, although it was hardly clear at the beginning that this would be the eventual outcome. Could he have prevented the initial spasm that was the great crash of October 1929? It seems highly unlikely, partly because of the very limited role and power then vested in the Treasury; partly because the admittedly belated raise in interest rates by the Federal Reserve Board was an inadequate mechanism for calming Wall Street speculation. Could Mellon have prevented the subsequent financial meltdown? Again, probably not: for the nation's banking system was so decentralized and so vulnerable that once the shock waves reached the United States from Europe, and once the confidence of depositors was lost, there was no way to arrest the domino effect. Perhaps the secretary could have done more to save individual banks, particularly the Bank of Pittsburgh. Steeped in the potential of the business cycle his whole life, and spying a prospect to gobble up a long-standing rival, he may well have neglected his public duty to do his utmost to support a major bank in difficulties. But in general terms, most of what happened in America between 1929 and 1932 would probably have happened regardless of who had been running the Treasury. The knife of politics cut both ways: having been overcredited for creating the great boom of the 1920s, Mellon was overcensured for being the man on whose watch the Great Depression began.

The more compelling criticism of Mellon attaches to his apparent lack of feeling or empathy when faced with the catastrophic human consequences of the collapse. As a financier notable for his creativity and imagination, he showed notably little of either in trying to mitigate its effects. To be sure, he knew how bad things were in Pittsburgh, and he and his brother and their companies gave substantial sums for the relief of the unemployed—though far less than he was spending on Russian pictures at the same time. But human sympathy was never Mellon's strong suit. The hardscrabble existence in Ireland, which his father had fled but never let his sons forget, may have inured Andrew Mellon to the notion that human history is full of convulsions that affect multitudes of people. His Presbyterianism, too, was more cultural than spiritual, and had long since been abandoned by this time. Unlike Rockefeller, a devout Baptist who gave away a tithe of his income from an early age, Mellon (like the Judge) was never disposed to charity, Christian or otherwise.

Even had he been capable of grasping the scale of what had befallen millions of average Americans, he was, in his mid-seventies, far too set in his nineteenth-century individualist, laissez-faire mentality to contemplate the sort of bold experimentation that Franklin Roosevelt would soon undertake. Mellon may have been correct in his view that the Depression would ultimately have to right itself: as late as 1940, after all, unemployment in America still stood at nearly 20 percent. Where Mellon went wrong—politically and perhaps ethically as well—was in his belief that in an industrial, urbanized, mass democracy, Washington could and should stay out of the mess. *Something* had to be done; the government could not afford to stand idly by, and FDR was rightly concerned with trying not only to provide security and hope for the millions of dispossessed Americans, but also to shore up the capitalist system itself. And this was as much a matter of politics as of humanity. In the era of communism and, increasingly, fascism, it was myopically complacent to believe that the American commitment to free enterprise could indefinitely weather such hardship and ruin. Though entirely predictable, and wholly characteristic of his background and generation, Mellon's hostility to the New Deal was imprudent, unimaginative, chilling.

There are many ironies attending Andrew Mellon's late-life conflict (and collaboration) with Franklin Roosevelt. One is that for all their disagreements, they were both equally committed to the survival of American capitalism—though this was scarcely apparent either from Mellon's vehement contempt for FDR's efforts to save it or from the president's conviction that men like Mellon were a serious threat to it. A second irony is that whatever his reasons for wanting to make an example of Mellon, Roosevelt's advisers erred when they chose to attack Mellon for dishonesty: in paying his federal taxes, it bears repeating, Mellon had always been scrupulous to stay within the boundaries of the law. No wonder he was determined to fight, and no wonder he eventually won. But as a result, Mellon and FDR were thereafter locked in a strange relationship: enemies over the tax trial, they cooperated in order to create the National Gallery of Art. It also bears repeating that Mellon did not donate his money and his art to help secure his acquittal. Instead, it was Mellon who set the conditions for his gift. He essentially said to Roosevelt: take it or leave it. And FDR sagely took it.

Perhaps the greatest irony in their strange unique relationship is the one that FDR relished least: that owing to the tax trial, as much as to his gift and its acceptance, Mellon achieved a certain kind of belated nobility and redemption. For all but the last five years of his life, he had lived unquestioningly with the grain of America's capitalist history. But by the time of Roosevelt's victory in November 1932, the feverish spirit of accumulation had cooled, and Mellon's economic, political, and social assumptions—and those of his class and his party—were overturned. No longer was the government best that governed least; now the order of the day was active (and expensive) intervention to secure and improve the lives of the many. Business would never again be as free or unaccountable as it had been during most of Mellon's life. Bankers were no longer seen as patriotic heroes, restoring international prosperity, but as selfish villains who had brought about national calamity. Western Pennsylvania ceased to be a Republican fiefdom and became a redoubt of the New Deal, and it remains predominantly Democratic to this day. Workers no longer faced intimidation (and worse) by armed company police: they now had the right to organize and bargain through unions. In Pittsburgh, the Mellons were no longer accorded the deference they had once enjoyed. And so on. In short, by the early 1930s, the whole nineteenth-century worldview which Andrew Mellon had learned at his father's knee had become an anachronism. Yet despite the end of so much he took for granted and cherished, and notwithstanding the attacks that the New Deal unleashed upon him, Mellon determined to bring his gallery scheme to fruition. Under such circumstances, it was, in its way, a noble gesture.

Although precociously good at making money, Mellon was a late bloomer in most other matters of his life. He came late to marriage, late to fatherhood, late to great wealth, late to public service, and late to art collecting. Not until the 1920s did he reach the sort of emotional accommodation with Nora that he should have striven for from the beginning of their relationship. Given her temperament, things might not have worked under any circumstances, but while they were married it never seems to have occurred to Andrew even to try to bridge the gap between them. He did not even know it was there. He made more of an effort with his children, a greater one than they would ever realize, but his age and his reserve meant he was never emotionally close to Ailsa, and his relations with Paul were always more distant than either would have liked. As for politics: Mellon came to high office at the age of sixty-five, and he never understood the compromises and conflicts that are at the heart of public life. Yet it was during the 1920s, when living in Washington in relative solitude, that he turned to art collecting with greater zeal. It is difficult to avoid the conclusion that the pictures he called his "friends and companions" were indeed a belated substitute for the genuine intimacies which he sadly never enjoyed.[49] Despite his many admirers and professional associates, he could never really give or receive love, whatever he may have felt.

Philanthropy, at least on a large scale, was also something to which Mellon came belatedly, and he had no family precedent to guide him as he concocted and pursued his great gallery scheme. In his secrecy, his relentless focus, and his determined wish to launch something that would subsequently grow and develop, his approach was very much that of the banker and the facilitator he had always been. And this last endeavor, combined with the unpleasant demands of the tax trial, meant Mellon's final years were among the most innovative, busy, and controversial of his life, and that he would need all eighty-two of them to accomplish all he wanted to achieve. Why, in the face of what surely seemed a popular repudiation of his service to the state, should he have been so determined to make a great gift to the nation? There is no evidence that he felt guilt, or a need to atone for anything. He did not want his name perpetuated, he was not much concerned with how future generations would judge him, and he left worries about the details of his posthumous affairs to loyal retainers like Donald Shepard and David Finley. But what was he to do with his money, and what was he to do with the pictures his money was buying?

By Mellon's own principles, accumulation across generations was justified by its beneficial effect upon the wealth of nations, and the Scotch-Irish sense of family identity was with him his whole life. But Ailsa had turned out frivolous, sad, and self-involved (and she clearly coveted the pictures); and Paul had decisively declared his unwillingness to carry on the dynasty, at least the business part of it. It was one of Andrew Mellon's great disappointments, though one to which he ultimately seems to have reconciled himself. He would provide generously for them, but he wanted to do more with his fortune (and his pictures). It seemed unlikely that Paul would ever enrich the nation with his business skills, which for his father was always the ultimate justification of business. But Andrew himself could enrich the nation by donating his pictures and creating a gallery. That he should have committed himself so doggedly, and under siege, to this purpose; that he should have arranged the gift with no thought of perpetuating his name; that he ensured that it would be accepted by his nemesis FDR: all this suggests that Mellon did come to appreciate a patriotic imperative and obligation attendant on his good fortune.

Whatever his motives may have been, Andrew Mellon's great benefaction, like so much else in his life that had gone before, becomes in some ways the more extraordinary as it recedes into history. Western Pennsylvania is no longer at the center of the industrial world, and petrochemicals have long since yielded to information technology at the cutting edge of the international economy. New Deal welfare and regulated capitalism, both anathema to Mellon, have been part of the American economic, social, and political order for two-thirds of a century, and no Republican administration has yet successfully overturned them. And it is impossible today to imagine anyone assembling an art collection to rival Mellon's, or pulling off such an astonishing personal coup with his gallery on the Mall. Truly, Mellon was a child of Mark Twain's Gilded Age, though he disliked gilt. He was a fin de siècle plutocrat, but he was no member of Thorstein Veblen's leisure class, with their lust for conspicuous consumption. He was much closer to the Anglo-American world depicted by Edith Wharton and Henry James, but he was not personally the happier for it. Had he read Scott Fitzgerald, he might have feared that his own son was becoming another idle, party-loving Jay Gatsby; and had he read John Dos Passos, he would probably have been enraged by its bitter, pervasive tone of anti-capitalist hostility.

Yet although the issues that Mellon's life raised and touched may have taken forms unique to their time, which were mirrored and distorted by contemporary fictional forms no less particular, they also in other ways transcend their temporal limitations. The means and morality of accumulating vast fortunes, the relationship between business and government, the scope and reach and obligations of the state, the sources and purposes of philanthropy: all these issues remain very much current and with us today. Whatever one thinks of it, Mellon's life, and the issues with which he grappled, at varying levels of success and comprehension, imagination and morality, continue to resonate—and they will continue to do so for as long as the United States remains, thanks to Mellon, his ilk, and his successors, the most successful wealth-producing nation the world has ever known. For some, it will seem an exemplary life, for others a cautionary tale; neither verdict does full justice to its complexity and contradictions. For good or ill, though more likely for good *and* ill, it could only have happened as it did and when it did in America.

III. THE LEGACY

Andrew Mellon left behind money, art, shares in companies, a charitable trust, the National Gallery of Art under construction, and a reputation that would see ups and downs across the ensuing decades. He also left two children, whose later lives were as much a comment on his own as any appraisal of his conduct as a banker, businessman, politician, collector, or philanthropist. Both Paul and Ailsa bore heavy paternal burdens—

financial, social, and psychological—and their difficult and unresolved relations with their father did not end with his death but only with their own. Indeed, both Ailsa and Paul found it difficult to shape their lives after losing the dominating force of their father's taciturn yet titanic personality; to some degree their subsequent lives oscillated between disapproval of him and sympathy for him, and between rejection and emulation. Paul had previously been unaware of the extent of his mother's involvement with Alfred Curphey, and he had tended to accept her highly selective version of the facts, which put Andrew in a bad light and thereby made relations between father and son more difficult than they might otherwise have been.[50] But soon after Andrew's death, Paul discovered the full details of the divorce for the first time, and came belatedly to realize that his father was at least as much sinned against as sinning. He confronted Nora with his discovery, there was a painful scene between them, and then something of a reconciliation. Thereafter, Paul later wrote, "we were friends, with a certain amount of affection between us, although I would not have called it love."[51]

Yet while Paul may have come to think better of his father respecting the divorce, both he and his sister turned their backs on his memory by turning their backs on Pittsburgh. Indeed, Ailsa had already long since departed, first to Connecticut and New York, then to Long Island and Washington. After she appeared during the tax trial and for her father's funeral, she rarely returned to the city of her birth. As for Paul, Andrew's death freed him to live the country life that he had always wanted. Accordingly, he left Pittsburgh for Virginia, donating the house on Woodland Road to the Pennsylvania College for Women, and soon after, he resigned his many directorships in the Mellon banks and businesses, installing George Wyckoff to look after his remaining interests in Pittsburgh and in the family companies.[52] Nor, for the time being, did either of Andrew's children show any serious interest in art or in collecting. During the 1930s, Ailsa made a few perfunctory acquisitions, and Paul had bought Stubbs's *Pumpkin* and commissioned portraits of himself out hunting, but for more than a decade after their father's death, that was it. Both of them had been upset that Andrew had not left them particular paintings—in Paul's case the Corots, in Ailsa's the portrait of Lady Caroline Howard by Reynolds that had always hung in her bedroom—and this may have put them off collecting for themselves. In addition, Paul had always disliked Duveen's bumptious manner, and this, too, may have discouraged him from visiting dealers or going to the salesrooms.[53]

There was, however, one of Andrew's pursuits that his two children soon took up, when they were both still relatively young, as compared with their father, who had come to it, like much else, late in life. That was philanthropy. Advised by Donald Shepard, Ailsa and Paul both concluded that they had been given more money than they needed, and each established foundations which they vested with a substantial portion of their inherited wealth. In 1940, Ailsa set up the Avalon Foundation, which she named after the house her family had rented at Prides Crossing in Massachusetts, near Frick's place, during the 1900s. A year later Paul established the Old Dominion Foundation, named after the Commonwealth of Virginia, where he was now happily settled as the fox-hunting, horse-breeding country gentleman he had so long wished to be. ("Any damn fool knows that one horse can run faster than another," his father had once rebuked him.)[54] Ailsa was characteristically detached from her foundation's gifts, but for Paul, philanthropy soon became very personally rewarding, and he derived far more pleasure and satisfaction from giving money away than he would ever have done from earning it. Between 1941 and 1969, the Old Dominion Foundation disbursed over $86 million, most of it to the arts and to higher education.[55] At the same time, the A. W. Mellon Educational & Charitable Trust still retained substantial funds after the completion of the National Gallery of Art, and these were now mainly used in support of ventures and organizations in Pittsburgh.

As American involvement in the Second World War approached, both Ailsa and Paul had arranged their finances satisfactorily, but they were soon faced with major personal challenges. By the time of Andrew's death, Ailsa's marriage to David Bruce was effectively over, there would be no more children, and after their appearances together at the tax trial, the two lived essentially separate existences—she primarily in New York and at Syosset, he in Washington and Virginia. More than ever, Ailsa was plagued by fears of ill health and was constantly in and out of hospitals; she could never settle down, she became increasingly reclusive and unstable, and when she and David were separated she showed little interest in replying (as had previously been the case with her father) to his still attentive, but increasingly dutiful letters. In this way, she not only continued to impede her husband's pursuit of the diplomatic career he still craved, but she also became more and more estranged from him, without seeming to realize it. In 1942, having helped see the National Gallery of Art to completion, David joined the U.S. Army once again, and was soon posted to London, where he became head of the European division of the Office of Strategic Services, which involved him in military and intelligence work at a high level. He also met Evangeline Bell. She was beautiful, intelligent, well-educated, self-possessed, and utterly captivating; within a few months, David Bruce was duly and utterly captivated.[56]

By October 1943, he had decided that his marriage to Ailsa was finished, and at the end of the year he wrote declaring that he had no intention of returning to her and asking for a divorce. In February 1944 he wrote again, announcing that he was "definitely in love with a woman whom I definitely want to marry." In April, while on leave, he visited Ailsa briefly in Washington, putting the hard facts to her directly. On his return to Europe the following month, he sent his wife another letter setting out the same arguments, now at greater length:

> There is no aspect of it which I have not considered with the greatest care, and the conclusion I reach invariably is that feeling as I do a divorce is the only possible solution. I love E[vangeline] very deeply and I want beyond everything to marry her. I know it is something that will not change under any circumstances, and with my conviction that my happiness depends on such a marriage, life on other terms would be completely unsatisfactory. I say this with a full awareness of how drastic and fundamental divorce is, and everything that it means in our particular case.

At the end of August 1944, David wrote to Ailsa again, insisting that it was "unfair and unreasonable that there be any further postponement of what from my point of view is inevitable, namely a divorce." He was deeply in love with Evangeline Bell, whom he wanted "above everything" to marry, and there was "no possibility whatever" that his sentiments would undergo any change.[57]

Ailsa was devastated by David's letters and news. She was now so self-absorbed that, like her father before her, she seemed hardly to have noticed the disintegration of her marriage. Faced with this unexpected crisis, she felt by turns shocked, upset, miserable, and humiliated, and both her physical and mental health suffered. She was depressed, she lost weight, she stopped eating almost completely, she could not sleep, and she did not go out. In October 1944, she finally resigned herself to the inevitable and headed for Florida, purchasing a house at Palm Beach, with the intention of beginning a new life for herself, with Audrey, in a healthier climate. But she was immediately taken ill with pneumonia, and could not establish herself at her new domicile until early in 1945. In March that year, she and David negotiated a separation agreement, in which neither made any financial claims on the other's estate, and David agreed to

give over full custody of Audrey to Ailsa, with the sole right to make decisions about her education and place of residence. Soon after, and by
prearrangement (no-fault divorce did not exist then), Ailsa brought an
action for divorce against David, charging him with "extreme cruelty, and
likewise with willful, obstinate and continued desertion for more than a
year." David did not appear or otherwise contest the suit, although he
(unsuccessfully) denied the charges of mental cruelty.[58] Ailsa had no difficulty in establishing that she was a bona fide resident of Florida, much less
that she had ample means to look after her daughter. Since all property
matters and custody issues had already been settled, the divorce was easily
granted.

The breakup of David and Ailsa Bruce was much less acrimonious and
much less public than that of Andrew and Nora Mellon: indeed, a greater
contrast could scarcely be imagined. For David, the divorce was the
beginning of a new and better life. Later in 1945, he married Evangeline,
and having freed himself from the stultifying "Mellon embrace," he found
both personal and professional fulfillment, as Mr. and Mrs. Bruce became
one of the great diplomatic couples of their generation, taking up a succession of demanding and high-profile ambassadorial postings to Paris,
Bonn, London, Peking, and NATO. At the time of the divorce, David had
resigned from the boards of the National Gallery of Art and the educational and charitable trust, but he remained on close and friendly terms
with his former brother-in-law, and he continued to write to Ailsa and
occasionally to visit her.[59] But her life, once ruined by her parents' divorce,
was now twice ruined by her own. She became ever more reclusive and
restless, moving from one great house to another, and from one Manhattan apartment to the next, nursing her real and imagined illnesses. She
could not sleep, and she could not make up her mind about anything. She
occasionally contemplated life with another husband, and nearly married
her friend Lauder Greenway. But on the morning of the wedding, unable
to find the right shoes to wear, she canceled the ceremony.[60]

Despite the birth of their daughter, Catherine, late in 1936, Paul's marriage to Mary Conover had also not been easy. Mary was intelligent,
warmhearted, and high-spirited, but she was also afflicted with asthma,
which worsened with proximity to horses, which inevitably attended life
with Paul. This soon put a strain on their marriage, as did Paul's continuing uncertainty about what to do with his life beyond avoiding Pittsburgh,
and riding and fox-hunting in Virginia and in England. He felt burdened
by family constraints as well as by the possession of too much money.[61]
Between 1938 and 1940, as war spread in Europe, Paul and Mary spent a

great deal of time in neutral Switzerland, where they were both in analysis with Carl Jung. (The sessions were not wholly successful, and Mary got more out of them than Paul did, but the two were so impressed with Jung that in 1945, they established the Bollingen Foundation, the chief purpose of which was to support the publication of his writings in English.) On their return to the United States, Paul enrolled as a mature student at St. John's College in Annapolis, where he hoped the exacting study of Greek language and literature and of Euclidean geometry (the school had a very specialized curriculum) would help him order his life. But he soon realized that the scholarly avocation was not for him, and after only one year, he joined the U.S. Army, soon finding himself at Cavalry School at Fort Riley.[62]

There Paul Mellon remained until March 1943, rising to the rank of instructor, bringing some of his horses out from Virginia, seeing Mary intermittently, and welcoming the birth of their son, Timothy. By this time, he had realized that "this was not, after all, a war in which the horse would be of prime importance," and soon after, he was posted to England, where he met up with his (not quite yet former) brother-in-law, David Bruce.[63] He, too, was recruited into the OSS, and three weeks after D-day he landed on Omaha Beach in Normandy, where he was promptly incapacitated by pneumonia. He later saw active service in France. On his return to the United States, he found himself "restless and irritated" as he rejoined Mary. "We had," he later recalled, "been leading separate lives for the last four years, so it was hardly surprising that we had developed separately, and had inevitably grown somewhat apart." In October 1946, after a day together fox-hunting, Mary suffered a severe attack of asthma, and she died soon after. Paul was almost forty; his daughter, Cathy, was nearly ten, and his son, Tim, just four. Burdened with an enormous fortune, and with responsibility for his mother, his sister, and his two young children, these were very difficult times for him. The trauma of Mary's death overshadowed all else, and he found himself unable to settle or to concentrate.[64]

Neither Ailsa nor Paul was thus in good shape or good spirits in the immediate aftermath of the Second World War: one divorced, the other widowed, and with the dark shadow of their father's memory still hanging over them both. If there was now any dominant figure in the increasingly dispersed Mellon family, it was Paul's cousin, R. K. Mellon. (W. L. Mellon would die in 1949, aged eighty-one.) Apart from a shared taste for military life, the two had little in common. While Paul had cut his ties to the city and fled, RK, through his presidency of Mellon National Bank and his many directorships in family companies, became the one Mellon of his generation willing to provide business and civic leadership in Pittsburgh. He merged the Mellon National Bank and the Union Trust Company in 1946, along with the Mellbank Corporation, into the Mellon National Bank and Trust Company. RK became chairman, and Frank Denton was appointed CEO.[65] In the same year, RK also established a family holding company called T. Mellon & Sons. It was an act of homage to his grandfather, invoking the original name of the Mellon Bank; and the aim was to bring together the four children of AW and RB (namely Ailsa, Paul, RK himself, and his sister, Sarah) in the hope of maintaining some family unity and financial coherence. From the beginning, RK was the chairman, but Paul disliked the arrangement, and he was a reluctant participant.[66]

Soon after, in May 1948, Paul Mellon married Rachel Lloyd, who was always known as Bunny, and who had previously been married to Stacey Lloyd, a mutual friend and Virginia neighbor. The couple had no children, but the marriage gave Paul a new stability and social confidence, and his life became more expansive as well as more focused. Possessed of a fine aesthetic sense, and also a talented amateur gardener, Bunny Mellon designed and decorated their new homes on the estate in Virginia (which eventually grew to more than four thousand acres), in Washington, New York, and also Antigua and Cape Cod. The Mellons began to entertain with characteristically understated lavishness.[67] Paul continued to hunt in Virginia, to visit England regularly and to breed racehorses, which now became a passion, and which were soon competing in America, Britain, and France. In 1971, one of them, Mill Reef, achieved the remarkable double victory in both the Epsom Derby and the Prix de l'Arc de Triomphe at Longchamp in the same season. Paul had no wish to take part in public life (though he could have followed his father to the American embassy in London at virtually any time, had he asked for it), but, encouraged by Bunny Mellon and Chester Dale, he now began to collect pictures: initially French impressionists, subsequently British artists, especially Gainsborough, Constable, Turner, and Stubbs. Though more plainly an aesthete, Paul Mellon was, like his father, a late developer in matters artistic; and as with his father again, his appreciation of pictures was informed more by instinct than by any critical scholarship or knowledge of the life of the painter or the period.[68]

By the early 1950s, Ailsa Mellon Bruce had also begun to acquire paintings. She was not as serious or systematic a collector as her brother: she bought art primarily to decorate her houses. This gave her plenty to do, for if Ailsa was a true collector of anything, it was of residences. Eventually, in addition to Syosset and her house at Palm Beach, she acquired two places in Greenwich and three in New York, as well as several estates in New Jersey. These houses provided settings both splendid and poignant for a life that was ever more restless and reclusive. Ailsa now visited Syosset only three weeks in every year, but she maintained a staff there of twelve domestics and twenty-two gardeners, and the cut flowers in each of the thirty-two rooms were changed daily, whether she was present or not.[69] She was deeply interested in interior decoration, but in a characteristically unsettled way, and her houses were always chaotic—full of unopened boxes of china, of furniture half unpacked, and with pictures stacked against the walls, or (since she especially liked small paintings) piled on tables. She began to collect seriously in 1951, with the purchase of the Molyneux collection of impressionist and post-impressionist paintings, and these would remain her preferences. She was advised by John Walker, who had succeeded David Finley as director of the National Gallery of Art, and they often visited the New York salesrooms together. But her indecisiveness drove dealers to distraction, and it would even have tested the mettle of a Duveen.[70]

Yet in their respective ways, both Ailsa and Paul had eventually become collectors, and although their interests differed from their father's, there was an element of honoring and emulating Andrew in taking up his enthusiasm. But it was in their devotion to the National Gallery of Art in Washington that their dynastic sense would manifest itself most strongly. Ailsa was a substantial benefactor, and gave large sums to assist with such acquisitions as Fragonard's *La Liseuse* and the Leonardo portrait of Ginevra di Benci.[71] Paul's association was even closer. He had resigned his trusteeship of the gallery in 1939, but upon his return from the war he was re-elected; he stayed on and became president in 1963, then served as chairman from 1979 until 1983. Throughout this time, he was not only intimately involved in the gallery's affairs, but once he became a serious collector, he also began to donate his pictures. In 1966, the National Gallery of Art marked its twenty-fifth anniversary with an exhibition of impressionist and post-impressionist paintings from Paul's and Ailsa's collections.[72] By this time, and just as Andrew Mellon had hoped, many other private donors had expanded the gallery's holdings, and they were beginning to outgrow John Russell Pope's original building. Fortunately, Andrew Mellon had anticipated that the gallery would eventually need more space, and when settling the site he had also ensured the reservation of the adjacent plot on the east side. There, a new building now arose,

funded by Ailsa, Paul, and their respective foundations. It was designed by
I. M. Pei in the modern style Andrew had so disliked, but it was faced with
the same Tennessee marble as the original building. It cost $93 million,
and was opened in 1978.[73]

Ailsa did not live to see the completion of this long-gestated project,
for her life had ended nine years earlier. Her lonely, rootless existence had
been rendered additionally bleak by the marriage of her daughter, Audrey,
to Stephen Currier, the greatest blow she had suffered since David had
divorced her.[74] The Mellon family deeply disapproved of the match, not
least because Currier used some of his wife's money to promote what they
regarded as distastefully radical political causes. The Curriers had three
children, but Ailsa saw little of them. In 1967, Audrey and her husband
were lost when the plane they had chartered disappeared in the West
Indies. Their bodies were never found, and their children were brought
up by John Simon, a professor at Yale Law School. From this terrible loss,
Ailsa never recovered.[75] She complained more than ever about her health,
but her few friends dismissed this as more hypochondria. She also resolved to settle herself in one home, in Manhattan, and determined to
create the most sumptuous and exquisite apartment in New York. But in
the summer of 1969, on the very eve of moving in, she was diagnosed with
cancer that was already so advanced that it could not be successfully
treated. Only on the day of the funeral did the mourners see her glorious
new residence, after which it was immediately dismantled: her two hundred pictures were left to the National Gallery of Art, while the furniture,
porcelain, and silver went to the Carnegie Institute in Pittsburgh (much
of it was subsequently sold off). She also left David Bruce a "handsome
legacy." It was a sad end to a sad life.[76]

Ailsa's bequest to Pittsburgh was a belated attempt to atone for her
father's decision to give his art to Washington, rather than to his native
city. Paul had also forged one close involvement with Pittsburgh: as chairman of the Mellon Institute, he came to feel that it was no longer a viable
enterprise, and in 1966, three years before Ailsa's death, he had successfully negotiated a merger with the Carnegie Technical Institute, thereby
creating Carnegie-Mellon University. Paul's involvement was rather resented by his cousin R. K. Mellon, who regarded himself as the leader of
the family in Pittsburgh throughout the 1950s and 1960s.[77] Despite their
deep political differences (RK was a strong Eisenhower supporter), RK
collaborated with David Lawrence, the Democratic mayor and long-
standing Mellon enemy, to bring about the "Pittsburgh Renaissance," as
the town began to diversify its economy, moving away from the declining

steel industry, and to clean up its polluted environment.[78] In 1969, the Mellon Bank celebrated its centenary, but both Frank Denton and RK had retired two years earlier, and by then, most of the iconic Mellon companies, so long "closely held"—Alcoa, Gulf, Koppers, Carborundum—had gone public. Increasingly, they abandoned the old style of interlocking family directorships, and the Mellons ceased to be the dominant stockholders. There were still occasional reports of the Mellons wielding irresponsible economic power in finance capital and heavy industry, but such a picture was more and more anachronistic. They were no longer able to do so, and with the possible exception of R. K. Mellon, they did not wish to do so.[79]

In addition to his horses, his houses, his pictures, and the National Gallery of Art, Paul Mellon's chief interests during the 1950s and 1960s centered on philanthropy. He created a fulfilling role for himself, via the Bollingen and the Old Dominion foundations, and also with many large personal benefactions, which eventually would amount to substantially more than half a billion dollars. Besides the National Gallery of Art, he was an exceptionally generous benefactor of Yale University, where his gifts culminated in the establishment of the Center for British Art, which he funded, endowed, and filled with his own paintings; and he also gave generously to (among others) the Choate School, St. John's College in Annapolis, Clare College and the Fitzwilliam Museum in Cambridge, and the Virginia Museum of Fine Art.[80] As a country gentleman, Anglophile, and horse lover, he took after his mother, but in organizing his busy life, Paul Mellon followed the pattern perfected by his father—putting loyal and able subordinates in charge, and then largely (but not entirely) giving them their head. Aided by a lifetime in analysis (Jungian, subsequently superseded by Freudian), he gradually became a much happier person than his parents or his sister. But for all his charm and cheerfulness and good humor, he was also recognizably his father's son, always keeping his distance, and with a great need for privacy. "He attracts people," John Walker observed, "but he is fundamentally a 'loner.' "[81]

The National Gallery of Art was not the only way in which Paul Mellon demonstrated his abiding filial regard. In 1980, the A. W. Mellon Educational & Charitable Trust was liquidated, in conformity with its founder's wishes, after exactly half a century in existence. One of its last and largest grants had been of $5 million toward the cost of linking the new East Wing of the National Gallery of Art with the original building. But well before then, and with Ailsa's blessing, Paul had seen through another merger: between her Avalon and his Old Dominion foundations.

The result was a new, much larger entity, which Paul decided to name the Andrew W. Mellon Foundation, a permanent philanthropy of which Paul served as a trustee from its inception in 1969 until 1985.[82] By so doing, he was at once honoring his father yet defying his wishes: the new foundation would perpetuate Mellon benefactions in a way that Andrew had not intended, and the Mellon name—indeed, *his* name—in a way that he would not have wished. The initial assets were $250 million, of which the larger share had come from Avalon. But within a year of its creation, it received a massive benefaction of almost $400 million from Ailsa's residuary estate, which transformed the Andrew W. Mellon Foundation into one of the largest and greatest grant-giving bodies in the country.

Since its inception, and following the precedents set by Ailsa at Avalon and Paul at Old Dominion, the Andrew W. Mellon Foundation has given substantial sums, especially (but not exclusively) in support of the arts, the humanities, and higher education (its heads have invariably been former presidents of colleges and universities). By December 1994, the market value of its assets had quadrupled to nearly $2.2 billion, making it the ninth richest foundation in the United States, and in the following year, it made grants of over $100 million. By the end of 2004, the foundation's assets had doubled again, to $4.5 billion, and in that year it gave grants totaling $186 million. It is not as large as the Hewlett or the Gates foundations, but it is about the same size as the MacArthur Foundation, and it is substantially bigger than the Rockefeller Foundation or the Carnegie Corporation.[83] With its relatively small staff and unpretentious offices, the organization exemplifies that dislike of ostentation so characteristic of Paul Mellon and his father. Yet in the areas where it gives most of its grants, the foundation is extremely well-known, and to many Americans today, the name Andrew W. Mellon is more likely to conjure up this great beneficent body, rather than the distant, shadowy historical figure after whom it is named, and whose prodigious fortune essentially created it, albeit in the next generation.

Just as Ailsa had outlived Audrey, so Nora outlived Ailsa. She lived the rest of her life in Greenwich, Connecticut, where she had moved after leaving Rokeby. Her finances remained precarious, and both Paul and Ailsa regularly supplemented them, as their father had done. Nora was eccentric and willful to the end, keeping a rifle for protecting the birds from the squirrels (she had always been a good shot). She died in 1973, just short of her ninety-fifth birthday. By then, Richard King Mellon had been dead for three years, and with his passing went the last embodiment of Mellon dominance in Pittsburgh business and public life. His was the grandest Mellon funeral seen in the city since his uncle Andrew's, with 1,600 attending the service in East Liberty Presbyterian Church. There would never be anything like it again. By then, the visible signs of the earlier Mellon generations had also mostly disappeared from the city, with the exception of the house at Woodland Road, which still stood, but which Paul had long since given away. In 1940, Dick Mellon's mansion had been demolished, the marble hauled off to build a new church in the Alcoa town of New Kensington. W. L. Mellon's house, with forty-five rooms and thirteen bathrooms, was the next to go in 1951. Four years later, the darkened sanctum from which all else issued, the Judge's residence at 401 Negley Avenue, was demolished; the grounds were divided into twenty-three modest lots for single-family houses. It had been just this sort of real estate development that had helped the first Thomas Mellon to make his fortune a century before; now someone else was profiting from the breakup of his home.[84]

With the passing of Ailsa Mellon Bruce, R. K. Mellon, and Nora McMullen Mellon, Paul was left the only close living link with his father's era. But immediately after RK's death, he insisted that T. Mellon & Sons should be wound up. There followed a difficult period at Mellon Bank which lasted from the mid-1970s until the late 1980s: the business lost its way, it became excessively involved in lending to South American countries, and in 1987 it reported losses of $844 million. As a result, professional managers were brought in to turn the enterprise around, and family control effectively came to an end. Today, the Mellon Bank does most of its business in Europe, far beyond Pittsburgh and western Pennsylvania, and the combined family interest is less than 2 percent of the stock.[85] Family shareholdings remained substantial in other core Mellon companies, but by the mid-1970s less than 20 percent of Gulf stock, and approximately the same portions of Alcoa and Carborundum, were Mellon-owned. The companies themselves have also changed, with successful takeovers, with ownership increasingly in the hands of institutional portfolio managers, and with professional, bureaucratized structures of corporate governance.[86] The Kennecott Copper Corporation bought Carborundum in 1977, Gulf Oil merged with Chevron in 1984, and Koppers was acquired by the British firm Beazer PLC in 1988. The Gulf and Koppers buildings no longer dominate Pittsburgh's skyline, and they no longer house the Mellon enterprises for which they were originally constructed. The bank and Alcoa remain, but the other iconic Mellon companies have disappeared. The Mellon family itself has also dispersed. Its "great days," one member acknowledged in 1977, were "over."[87]

The whole Pittsburgh region has changed almost beyond recognition since Andrew Mellon's day, both within the city limits and in the smaller towns along the riverbanks. As the later chapters in the story of the Mellon companies suggest, "corporations once integral to the history of Pittsburgh have departed, been absorbed, gone bankrupt," and those that remain are much less rooted in the local community. During the severe recession of the 1980s, most of the surviving steelworks were closed down, among them such notorious places as United States Steel at Homestead and Jones and Laughlin at Aliquippa, and even the once-mighty Westinghouse works became but a shadow of its former self.[88] The steel mills and factories, which with their smoke and flames had been the very totems of the world Frick and Carnegie and Mellon built, disappeared seemingly overnight. In their wake came a second civic renaissance, again combining public and private initiatives, but this time with a much-diminished Mellon presence. The new Pittsburgh would stress professional services, advanced technology, and applied research enterprises (headquartered in an array of new skyscrapers that have transformed and beautified the city's skyline). There is today cultural vitality and diversity as never before, exemplified by a proliferation of historic preservation societies, by the Pittsburgh Symphony, and by the Andy Warhol Museum, honoring the Andrew who is much better known in the city and beyond than either of the earlier pair, Mellon and Carnegie.[89]

During his last years, Paul Mellon's thoughts turned increasingly to the vanished world of his youth, and to his forebears. He arranged for his grandfather's autobiography to be republished, and in the preface, he explained that he identified with the Judge as someone who had likewise rejected the career his father had planned for him.[90] At the same time, and with the help of his friend John Baskett, Paul wrote an account of his own life, aptly entitled *Reflections in a Silver Spoon*. The tone was characteristically civilized and urbane, charming and self-deprecating, but Paul was candid all the same about his difficult relationships with both his parents, and the book made plainer than he may have intended just how long and hard he had struggled to create a good and worthwhile life for himself, when lesser men bearing similar burdens of wealth and expectation might have given up and gone to ruin. But in the end, Paul had achieved an existence that was balanced as his father's had never been, which was happy, fulfilled, and generous, achieving an integration of self that had eluded his line since the Judge first launched it on its great American adventure. He also commissioned this biography, for which he gave a series of interviews in which he spoke more warmly about his father than he had written about him in his book.[91] In January 1999, Paul Mellon died in his ninety-second year, and he was buried in a plot at Upperville churchyard in Virginia, next to his first wife, Mary Mellon. Nearby are the remains of Andrew Mellon, which Paul had brought from Pittsburgh for reburial, and also of Ailsa Mellon Bruce and of Nora McMullen Mellon. In death, the five of them are closer together than they ever had been in life.[92]

APPENDIX: THE MELLON FAMILY

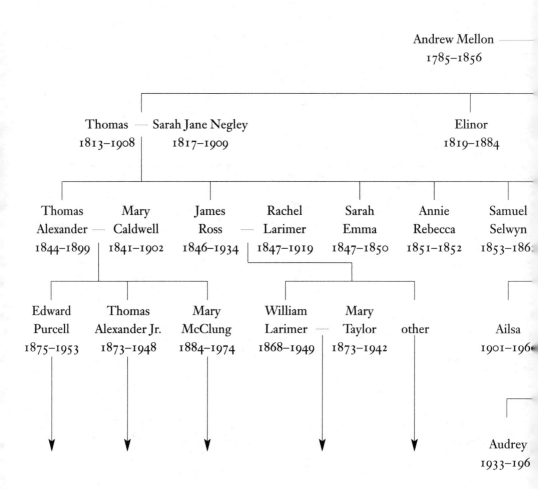

Andrew Mellon
1785–1856

Thomas — Sarah Jane Negley
1813–1908   1817–1909

Elinor
1819–1884

Thomas
Alexander — Mary
Caldwell
1844–1899   1841–1902

James
Ross — Rachel
Larimer
1846–1934   1847–1919

Sarah
Emma
1847–1850

Annie
Rebecca
1851–1852

Samuel
Selwyn
1853–186:

Edward
Purcell
1875–1953

Thomas
Alexander Jr.
1873–1948

Mary
McClung
1884–1974

William
Larimer — Mary
Taylor
1868–1949   1873–1942

other

Ailsa
1901–196·

Audrey
1933–196·

NOTE: This family tree is much simplified and includes
only those names mentioned in the text.

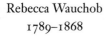 Rebecca Wauchob
1789–1868

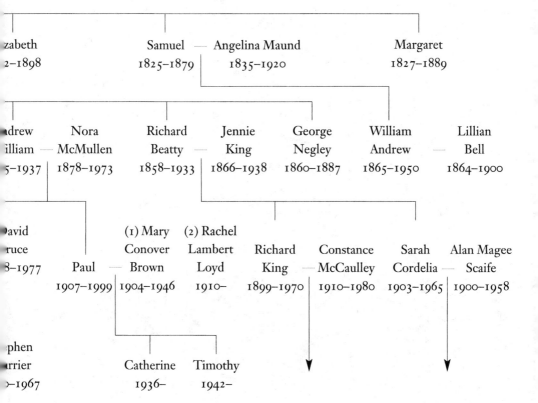

zabeth 2–1898		Samuel 1825–1879	—	Angelina Maund 1835–1920			Margaret 1827–1889	

ndrew illiam 5–1937	Nora — McMullen 1878–1973	Richard Beatty 1858–1933	—	Jennie King 1866–1938	George Negley 1860–1887	William Andrew 1865–1950	—	Lillian Bell 1864–1900

avid ruce 3–1977	Paul 1907–1999	(1) Mary Conover — Brown 1904–1946	(2) Rachel Lambert Loyd 1910–	Richard King — 1899–1970	Constance McCaulley 1910–1980	Sarah Cordelia — 1903–1965	Alan Magee Scaife 1900–1958

phen rrier)–1967		Catherine 1936–	Timothy 1942–				

A Note on Sources

IN THE COURSE OF PREPARING THIS BOOK, the following archival collections have been consulted:

Edward G. Acheson Papers (Library of Congress, Washington, D.C.)
Alcoa Papers (Alcoa Law Library, Pittsburgh)
Bank of England Archives (Bank of England, London)
Edward H. Bennett Papers (Ryerson and Burnham Library, Art Institute of Chicago)
Board of Architectural Consultants Records (National Archives II, College Park, Maryland)
John G. Bowman Papers (University Archives, University of Pittsburgh)
Ailsa Mellon Bruce Papers (National Gallery of Art, Washington, D.C.)
Daniel H. Burnham Papers (Ryerson and Burnham Library, Art Institute of Chicago)
Andrew Carnegie Papers (Library of Congress, Washington, D.C.)
Edward T. Clark Papers (Library of Congress, Washington, D.C.)
Commission of Fine Arts Collection (National Archives I, Washington, D.C.)
Calvin Coolidge Papers (Library of Congress, Washington, D.C.)
Court for Divorce and Matrimonial Causes Files (National Archives, Public Record Office, Kew, U.K.)
James Couzens Papers (Library of Congress, Washington, D.C.)
Homer Cummings Papers (Alderman Library, Special Collections, University of Virginia, Charlottesville)
Huntland Downs Papers (in private hands)
Duveen Brothers Papers (Getty Center, Los Angeles)
David E. Finley Papers (Library of Congress, Washington, D.C.)
David E. Finley Papers (National Gallery of Art, Washington, D.C.)
Ford Motor Company Archives (Henry Ford Museum, Dearborn, Michigan)
Foreign Office Papers (National Archives, Public Record Office, Kew, U.K.)
Henry Clay Frick Papers (Frick Art and Historical Center, Clayton, Pittsburgh)
Carter Glass Papers (Alderman Library, Special Collections, University of Virginia, Charlottesville)
Charles S. Hamlin Papers (Library of Congress, Washington, D.C.)

Warren G. Harding Papers (Library of Congress, Washington, D.C.)

George Harrison Papers (Federal Reserve Bank of New York Archives, New York)

Burton J. Hendrick Papers (in private hands)

Archive of the State Hermitage (State Museum of the Hermitage, St. Petersburg, Russia)

Herbert Hoover Papers (Herbert Hoover Library, West Branch, Iowa)

Henry L. Huntington Papers (Huntington Library, San Marino, California)

Harold Ickes Diaries (Franklin D. Roosevelt Library, Hyde Park, New York)

Idaho and Oregon Land Improvement Company Papers (Colorado State Archives, Denver)

Robert H. Jackson Papers (Library of Congress, Washington, D.C.)

Knoedler & Co. Papers (M. Knoedler & Co., New York)

Philander C. Knox Papers (Library of Congress, Washington, D.C.)

David Koskoff Papers (Historical Society of Western Pennsylvania, Pittsburgh)

Larimer Family Papers (Colorado Historical Society, Denver)

Samuel B. McCormick Papers (University Archives, University of Pittsburgh)

Robert McKnight Papers (Darlington Memorial Library, University of Pittsburgh)

Mellon Bank Papers (Historical Society of Western Pennsylvania, Pittsburgh)

Andrew W. Mellon Papers (National Gallery of Art, Washington, D.C.)

James Ross Mellon Papers (Historical Society of Western Pennsylvania, Pittsburgh)

Nora McMullen Mellon Papers (National Gallery of Art, Washington, D.C.)

Paul Mellon Papers (National Gallery of Art, Washington, D.C.)

Thomas Mellon Papers (National Gallery of Art, Washington, D.C.)

Mellon-Negley Papers (Darlington Memorial Library, University of Pittsburgh)

Ogden Mills Papers (Library of Congress, Washington, D.C.)

Charles Moore Papers (Library of Congress, Washington, D.C.)

Henry Morgenthau Papers (Franklin D. Roosevelt Library, Hyde Park, New York)

Montagu Norman Papers (Bank of England Archives, Bank of England, London)

Harvey O'Connor Papers (Labor History Archive, Walter Reuther Library, Wayne State University, Detroit)

Thomas Walker Page Papers (Alderman Library, University of Virginia, Charlottesville)

Wright Patman Papers (Lyndon Baines Johnson Library, University of Texas, Austin)

Pennsylvania Railroad Company Papers (Hagley Library and Museum, Wilmington, Delaware)

George Wharton Pepper Papers (Archives and Records Center, University of Pennsylvania, Philadelphia)

Pittsburgh Coal Company Papers (Hagley Library and Museum, Wilmington, Delaware)

Pittsburgh Railway Companies Papers (Archives of Industrial Society, University of Pittsburgh)

Pittsburgh Recorder of Deeds Indexes (Pittsburgh)

Pittsburgh Stock Exchange Papers (Historical Society of Western Pennsylvania, Pittsburgh)

Matthew Quay Papers (Library of Congress, Washington, D.C.)

Rainhill Lunatic Asylum Papers (Central Library, Liverpool, U.K.)

Rockefeller Family Archives (Rockefeller Archive Center, Sleepy Hollow, New York)

Franklin D. Roosevelt Papers (Franklin D. Roosevelt Library, Hyde Park, New York)

Russian State Archive of the Economy (Moscow, Russia)

Smithsonian Institution Archives (Smithsonian Institution, Washington, D.C.)

Boyden Sparkes Papers (in private hands)

Spring Valley Mining and Irrigating Company Papers (California State University, Chico)

State Department Records (National Archives II, College Park, Maryland)

Henry L. Stimson Papers (Manuscripts and Archives, Yale University Library, New Haven, Connecticut)

Benjamin Strong Papers (Federal Reserve Bank of New York Archives, New York)

Trade Dollar Mining and Milling Company Papers (Idaho State Historical Society, Boise)

Treasury Department Records (National Archives II, College Park, Maryland)

Bolon B. Turner Papers (National Archives, Washington, D.C.)

Union Trust Papers (Historical Society of Western Pennsylvania, Pittsburgh)

John Walker Papers (National Gallery of Art, Washington, D.C.)

Paul M. Warburg Papers (Manuscripts and Archives, Yale University Library, New Haven, Connecticut)

Western University of Pennsylvania Papers (Archives Center, University of Pittsburgh)

Waddy Wood Papers (Library of Congress, Washington, D.C.)

Abbreviations for Notes

Books and Printed Matter

Docket 76499	*Official Report of Proceedings Before the US Board of Tax Appeals,* A. W. Mellon, Petitioner v. Commissioner of Internal Revenue, Respondent. Docket no. 76499.
F&S	M. Friedman and A. J. Schwartz, *A Monetary History of the United States, 1867–1960* (Princeton, N.J., 1963).
Hendrick	B. J. Hendrick, "Andrew W. Mellon: A Biography" (unpublished typescript, 1943).
Hersh	B. Hersh, *The Mellon Family* (New York, 1978).
JMS	W. L. Mellon, *Judge Mellon's Sons* (privately printed, 1948).
Judge	James R. Mellon II, "The Judge: A Life of Thomas Mellon" (unpublished typescript, 2003).
Kennedy	D. M. Kennedy, *Freedom from Fear: The American People in Depression and War, 1929–1945* (Oxford, U.K., 1999).
Kopper	P. Kopper, *America's National Gallery of Art: A Gift to the Nation* (New York, 1991).
Koskoff	D. E. Koskoff, *The Mellons: The Chronicle of America's Richest Family* (New York, 1978).
Lankford	N. D. Lankford, *The Last American Aristocrat: The Biography of David K. E. Bruce, 1898–1977* (Boston, 1996)
Letters	J. R. Mellon, *Letters, 1862–1895* (privately printed, Pittsburgh, 1928).
Lorant	S. Lorant et al., *Pittsburgh: The Story of an American City* (New York, 1964).
Lubove	R. Lubove (ed.), *Pittsburgh* (New York, 1976).
Meltzer	A. H. Meltzer, *A History of the Federal Reserve*, vol. 1, *1913–1951* (Chicago, 2003).
MNBTC	[C. H. McCullough Jr.], *One Hundred Years of Banking: The History of the Mellon National Bank and Trust Company* (Pittsburgh, 1969).
Murray	L. L. Murray III, "Andrew W. Mellon, Secretary of the Treasury, 1921–1932: A Study in Policy" (Ph.D. diss., Michigan State University, 1970).

O'Connor	H. O'Connor, *Mellon's Millions: The Biography of a Fortune* (New York, 1933).
PPAFDR	*The Public Papers and Addresses of Franklin D. Roosevelt*, vols. 2–6 (New York, 1938–41).
RSS	Paul Mellon with John Baskett, *Reflections in a Silver Spoon: A Memoir* (New York, 1992).
Samber	M. D. Samber, "Networks of Capital: Creating and Maintaining a Regional Economy in Pittsburgh, 1865–1919" (Ph.D. diss., University of Pittsburgh, 1995).
Smith	G. D. Smith, *From Monopoly to Competition: The Transformations of Alcoa, 1886–1986* (New York, 1988).
Steiner	Z. Steiner, *The Lights That Failed: European International History, 1919–1933* (Oxford, U.K., 2005).
TMT	Thomas Mellon, *Thomas Mellon and His Times* (Pittsburgh, 1994 ed.).
White	E. White, *A Century of Banking in Pittsburgh* (Pittsburgh, 1903).

Names

EHB	Edward H. Bennett
AMB	Ailsa Mellon Bruce
CSC	Charles S. Carstairs
JD	Joseph Duveen, subsequently Sir Joseph Duveen, eventually Lord Duveen of Millbank
DEF	David E. Finley
HCF	Henry Clay Frick
BJH	Burton J. Hendrick
CRH	Charles R. Henschel
AWM	Andrew William Mellon ("AW" or "Andy")
NMM	Nora McMullen, subsequently Nora Mellon, then Nora Lee, and eventually Nora McMullen Mellon
PM	Paul Mellon
RBM	Richard Beatty Mellon ("RB" or "Dick")
RKM	Richard King Mellon ("RK")
TM	Thomas Mellon ("the Judge")
WAM	William Andrew Mellon
WLM	William Larimer Mellon ("WL")
CHM	Carman H. Messmore
FDR	Franklin Delano Roosevelt

Institutions and Collections

BAC	Board of Architectural Consultants
CFA	Commission of Fine Arts
CFOST	Central Files of the Office of the Secretary of the Treasury, 1917–1932

CFOST, 1933–56	Central Files of the Office of the Secretary of the Treasury, 1933–1956
FO	Foreign Office (United Kingdom)
HSWP	Historical Society of Western Pennsylvania
LOC	Library of Congress, Washington, D.C.
NA	National Archives, Washington, D.C.
NA: PRO	National Archives, Public Record Office, Kew, U.K.
NCPPC	National Capital Park and Planning Commission
NGA	National Gallery of Art, Washington, D.C.
OF	Official File
PPF	President's Personal File
SD	State Department (United States)

Notes

Preface

1. H. Brogan, *The Penguin History of the United States of America*, 2nd ed. (London, 1999), pp. 375–77.
2. Koskoff; Hersh.
3. BJH papers: D. E. Shepard to BJH, December 9, 1939; R. J. Rusnack, " 'To Cast Them in the Heroic Mold': Court Biographers—The Case of Burton Jesse Hendrick" (undated and unpublished paper), passim.
4. Rusnack, "Burton Jesse Hendrick," p. 15.
5. BJH papers: BJH to WAM, December 2, 1940.
6. Hendrick, "Sources," pp. 1–4; BJH papers: H. M. Johnson to BJH, April 11, 1940; BJH to WAM, January 20, 1943; D. K. E. Bruce to BJH, January 16, 1943; BJH to Mary Mellon, March 26, 1943.
7. BJH papers: BJH to D. K. E. Bruce [undated, February 1942]; Mary Mellon to BJH, March 13, 1943; Rusnack, "Burton Jesse Hendrick," p. 19.
8. S. E. Morison, "Faith of an Historian," *American Historical Review* 56 (1951), pp. 272–73.
9. Lankford, pp. 163–67, 173–77; *RSS*, p. 187.
10. Sparkes's collaborative works include the following: F. A. Vanderlip and B. Sparkes, *From Farm Boy to Financier* (New York, 1935); E. W. McLean with B. Sparkes, *Father Struck It Rich* (London, 1936); L. J. Horowitz and B. Sparkes, *The Towers of New York: The Memoirs of a Master Builder* (New York, 1937); W. P. Chrysler and B. Sparkes, *Life of an American Workman* (New York, 1938); A. P. Sloan Jr. and B. Sparkes, *Adventures of a White-Collar Man* (New York, 1941).
11. *RSS*, p. 415.
12. *RSS*, pp. 147–55.
13. *TMT*, pp. xiii–xv. The book was cut by removing many of TM's more hostile references to Irish Catholics (though there are still plenty left), and rearranged by putting the chapters in more appropriate chronological order and by relegating the early chapters on Mellon and Negley ancestry to appendixes: see Judge, pp. 239–40.
14. H. Nicolson, *Dwight Morrow* (New York, 1935), p. v.

Prologue: A Family in History

1. Judge, pp. 8–11, 338–40.
2. TM papers: "Transcript on the Death of [uncle] Thomas Mellon," January 15, 1866.
3. *TMT*, pp. 16, 419–24.
4. D. N. Doyle, *Ireland, Irishness and Revolutionary America, 1760–1820* (Dublin, 1981), p. 51.
5. K. Kenny, *The American Irish: A History* (Harlow, 2000), pp. 8–14.
6. Kenny, *American Irish*, pp. 14–23.
7. Huntington papers: AWM, Speech at Charlotte Chamber of Commerce, January 19, 1928.
8. D. MacCulloch, *Reformation: Europe's House Divided, 1490–1700* (London, 2003), pp. 542–43; W. F. Dunaway, *The Scotch-Irish of Colonial Pennsylvania* (Chapel Hill, N.C., 1944), pp. 56–64.
9. T. M. Devine, *Scotland's Empire, 1600–1815* (London, 2003), ch. 7; Dunaway, *Colonial Pennsylvania*, pp. 119–29; E. E. Evans, "The Scotch-Irish: Their Cultural Adaptation and Heritage in the American Old West," in E. R. R. Green (ed.), *Essays in Scotch-Irish History* (London, 1969), pp. 80–84.
10. M. A. Jones, "The Scotch-Irish in British America," in B. Bailyn and P. D. Morgan (eds.), *Strangers Within the Realm: Cultural Margins of the First British Empire* (Chapel Hill, N.C., 1991), pp. 296–97.
11. Lorant, pp. 19–34, 42–46; L. D. Baldwin, *Pittsburgh: The Story of a City* (Pittsburgh, 1995 ed.), pp. 19–26, 48–54; R. C. Wade, *The Urban Frontier: The Growth of Western Cities, 1790–1830* (Cambridge, Mass., 1959), pp. 7–11.
12. Kenny, *American Irish*, pp. 39–40; Jones, "Scotch-Irish," p. 310.
13. M. A. Jones, "Ulster Emigration, 1783–1815," in Green, *Scotch-Irish History*, pp. 46–68.
14. *TMT*, p. 16; Kenny, *American Irish*, pp. 45–46, 56.
15. Jones, "Scotch-Irish," p. 285; A. McKee, " 'A Peculiar and Royal Race': Creating a Scotch-Irish Identity, 1889–1901," in P. Fitzgerald and S. Ickringill (eds.), *Atlantic Crossroads: Historical Connections Between Scotland, Ulster and North America* (Newtonards, N. Ireland, 2001), pp. 37–41.
16. Kenny, *American Irish*, pp. 37–41, 57; Judge, p. 12; E. R. R. Green, "The Irish American Business and Professions," in D. N. Doyle and O. D. Edwards (eds.), *America and Ireland, 1776–1976: The American Identity and the Irish Connection* (Westport, Conn., 1980), pp. 195–203; PM papers: E. Montgomery to PM, July 8, 1996.
17. Judge, pp. 308–11.
18. Kenny, *American Irish*, pp. 48–49; P. D. Mowat, *Mellon Country: A Survey of Nineteenth-Century Mellon Farms in Castletown, County Tyrone* (Omagh, N. Ireland, 1991); Judge, pp. 317–22.
19. *TMT*, p. 12; PM, "The Irish Cottage Where an American Dream Was Born," *Architectural Digest*, August 1993, pp. 23–38; *RSS*, pp. 17–19.
20. *Pittsburgh Chronicle Telegraph*, November 28, 1902; *TMT*, p. 9; Judge, pp. 185, 192; Hendrick, ch. 1, p. 6.

21. Judge, pp. 329–31; *TMT*, pp. 9, 291–93, 302–306.

22. *TMT*, pp. 13–14.

23. *TMT*, p. 18; Baldwin, *Pittsburgh*, pp. 137–38; Carnegie Library of Pittsburgh, *Pittsburgh in 1816* (Pittsburgh, 1916), pp. 26–27; J. F. S. Collins Jr., *Stringtown on the Pike* (HSWP, n.d.), pp. 39–40.

24. Judge, pp. 13–14; *TMT*, p. 21; Hendrick, ch. 1, p. 15.

25. Judge, p. 14; *TMT*, pp. 21–22.

26. Huntland Downs papers: Andrew Mellon, naturalization certificate, October 7, 1825; Andrew Mellon, commission as first lieutenant in the Pennsylvania Militia, May 1, 1826; *TMT*, pp. 31, 437–43; TM papers: TM school essay, n.d.

27. *TMT*, p. 22.

28. Baldwin, *Pittsburgh*, pp. 129–53; *Pittsburgh in 1816*, passim; Lorant, pp. 47–80; Lubove, pp. 1–8.

29. Wade, *Urban Frontier*, pp. 11–13, 161–69, 174–82, 274; *TMT*, pp. 24–25.

30. *TMT*, pp. 26–27.

31. *TMT*, pp. 26–28.

32. *TMT*, pp. 22, 30, 32, 34; Judge, p. 17.

33. Judge, pp. 29–30, quoting [uncle] T. Mellon to TM, January 8, 1829; TM papers: TM to [uncle] T. Mellon, December 25, 1831 [typed copy]; *TMT*, pp. 34, 419.

34. Wade, *Urban Frontier*, p. 319.

35. Collins, *Stringtown on the Pike*, pp. 41–48; R. J. Jucha, "The Anatomy of a Streetcar Suburb: A Development and Architectural History of Pittsburgh's Shadyside District, 1860–1920" (Ph.D. diss., George Washington University, 1980), pp. 39–41.

36. J. F. Rishel, "The Founding Families of Allegheny County: An Examination of Nineteenth-Century Elite Continuity" (Ph.D. diss., University of Pittsburgh, 1975), pp. 40–41.

37. BJH papers: interview, Mr. Gettys, April 4, 1940, p. 1; *TMT*, p. 48.

38. J. A. Leo Lemay and P. M. Zall, *Benjamin Franklin's Autobiography: An Authoritative Text, Background, Criticism* (New York, 1985), pp. 249–79; G. T. Couser, *American Autobiography: The Prophetic Mode* (Amherst, Mass., 1879); E. Wright, *Franklin of Philadelphia* (Cambridge, Mass., 1986), p. 6; *TMT*, p. 3.

39. E. Morgan, *Benjamin Franklin* (New Haven, Conn., 2002), pp. 22–25; Wright, *Franklin*, pp. 44–47.

40. *TMT*, pp. xviii, 33, 62; *JMS*, pp. 21–24.

41. TM papers, TM to [uncle] T. Mellon, December 25, 1831 [typed copy]; *TMT*, p. 60; Judge, pp. 29–30.

42. *TMT*, pp. 64–65; Hendrick, ch. 1, pp. 17–18.

43. Judge, pp. 32–34; TM papers: TM to J. Coon, April 29, 1834, August 13 and 16, 1834 [all typed copies].

44. *TMT*, p. 73; TM papers: TM to [uncle] T. Mellon, March 23, 1833, May 17, 1834 [both typed copies]; TM to "Cousin," May 17, 1834.

45. *TMT*, pp. 75–76.

46. TM papers: TM to R. C. Beatty, April 19, 1834 [typed copy]; TM to J. Duff, March 4, 1836 [typed copy].

47. McCormick papers: S. B. McCormick to TM, April 12, 1907; TM papers: TM,

"Essay on Money," January 1835; TM to S. B. McCormick, April 26, 1907; *TMT,* p. 392; R. C. Alberts, *Pitt: The Story of the University of Pittsburgh, 1787–1987* (Pittsburgh, 1986), pp. 13–16.

48. *TMT,* p. 82. See also TM papers: TM essay "Is an Education Preferable to Wealth?," for Mr. Gill, 1832.

49. *TMT,* pp. 34, 84, 435; Judge, p. 27; Morgan, *Franklin,* pp. 15–22; TM papers: J. Coon to TM, May 19, 1835.

50. *TMT,* p. 321; Judge, p. 28.

51. *TMT,* p. 91; Judge, p. 40; M. Murphy, *Prothonotaries of Allegheny County, 1788–1993* (Pittsburgh, 1993), unpaginated entry on Thomas Liggett.

52. Rishel, "Founding Families," pp. 66–80, 188–89.

53. *TMT,* p. 85; Judge, p. 42.

54. Lorant, pp. 92–101; Baldwin, *Pittsburgh,* pp. 184–95, 218–30; C. E. Macartney, *Right Here in Pittsburgh* (Pittsburgh, 1937), pp. 74–78.

55. J. C. Holmberg, "The Industrializing Community: Pittsburgh, 1850–1880" (Ph.D. diss., University of Pittsburgh, 1981), pp. 58, 236.

56. *TMT,* pp. 93–94, 126, 130–33; Judge, pp. 40, 80–82; Hendrick, ch. 1, p. 25. Mellon-Negley papers: Day Book, 1853–60, lists TM's fees for the slightly later period, ranging from 50¢ to $5.00. See also McKnight papers: diaries, 1842–47, which give a vivid early picture of TM at the bar.

57. *TMT,* p. 91; Judge, pp. 134, 222.

58. *TMT,* pp. 96–97, 100.

59. *TMT,* pp. 100–101.

60. Collins, *Stringtown on the Pike,* p. 55.

61. *TMT,* pp. 97, 113.

62. F. C. Negley, *Traditional History and Family Record of the Negley Family* (Pittsburgh, 1898); A. C. Miller, *Chronicles of Families, Houses and Estates of Pittsburgh and Its Environs* (Pittsburgh, 1927), pp. 92–95.

63. *TMT,* pp. 444–45; Collins, *Stringtown on the Pike,* pp. 56–57; Miller, *Chronicles of Families,* pp. 27–29.

64. BJH papers: interviews, Miss Georgina Negley, April 6, 1940, p. 1; Mr. Gettys, April 4, 1940, p. 1; *TMT,* pp. 446–48; H. McCullough, "Negley Avenue and Jacob Negley," *Making History: The Bimonthly Newsletter of the Historic Society of Western Pennsylvania,* November 1994, unpaginated.

65. Baldwin, *Pittsburgh,* pp. 195–200, 202, 221–22, 228–30; Lorant, pp. 46, 89, 123, 464.

66. Baldwin, *Pittsburgh,* pp. 232, 243–44; Collins, *Stringtown on the Pike,* pp. 56–57; H. McCullough, "Ross Street and James Ross," *Making History: The Bimonthly Newsletter of the Historic Society of Western Pennsylvania,* January 1995, unpaginated.

67. TM's property dealings are itemized in the indexes held in Pittsburgh by the recorder of deeds: Deed Absecum [purchases], vol. 1, pp. 86–87; Deed Direct [sales], vol. 1, pp. 136–37.

68. *TMT,* pp. 146–49; O'Connor, pp. 27, 34; W. S. Hoffman, *Paul Mellon: Portrait of an Oil Baron* (Chicago, 1974), pp. 22, 26.

69. *TMT,* p. 96; Judge, pp. 63–64.

70. Holmberg, "Industrializing Community," pp. 286–87.

71. *JMS*, pp. 4–9.

72. Judge, pp. 303–304.

73. *TMT*, p. 9.

74. *TMT*, pp. 57, 319–23; Hendrick, ch. 1, p. 19.

75. *TMT*, pp. 12, 226–27, 241, 434–37.

76. *TMT*, pp. 104, 107, 126, 286; TM papers: TM, "School Essay on Drunkenness" [n.d.].

77. TM papers: "Memorial Meeting of the Allegheny County Bar Association," February 10, 1908; *TMT*, pp. 90, 98, 227, 343, 381, 391–92; Baldwin, *Pittsburgh*, pp. 201–17, 222–28, 275; Lorant, pp. 104, 107, 111.

78. TM papers: TM, "Essay on Money," January 1835; *TMT*, pp. 239–40, 340–43, 355–60, 420–21.

79. C. A. Jones, *International Business in the Nineteenth Century: The Rise and Fall of a Cosmopolitan Bourgeoisie* (New York, 1987).

80. Morgan, *Franklin*, pp. 23–24; *RSS*, p. 22; *JMS*, p. 15.

81. Baldwin, *Pittsburgh*, p. 72; Lorant, p. 47; L. K. Pritchard, "The Soul of the City: A Social History of Religion in Pittsburgh," in S. P. Hayes (ed.), *City at the Point: Essays on the Social History of Pittsburgh* (Pittsburgh, 1989), pp. 328–33. An instructive comparison is between the Scotch-Irish in the United States and the Scotch-Canadians, who crossed the Atlantic directly and did not stop off in Ulster on the way. They, too, were often Presbyterian and concerned about money. But they were less embattled, not so much driven in their professional lives, and more inclined to be liberal in politics. See J. K. Galbraith, *The Scotch*, 2nd ed. (Boston, 1985).

82. AWM papers: H. McCullough interview, July 8, 1996, pp. 2–3.

1. The Patriarch Presides: Father and Sons, 1855–73

1. Hendrick, ch. 2, p. 2.

2. *TMT*, p. 227; Hendrick, ch. 2, p. 27; Lorant, pp. 167–68; BJH papers: WAM, Notes for BJH biography, pp. 6, 11.

3. DEF papers (NGA): AWM, personal, 1928–32.

4. *TMT*, pp. 232, 241; AWM papers: J. R. Mellon to AWM, March 23, 1930; AWM to J. R. Mellon, March 28, 1930.

5. AWM papers: TM to J. F. Harry, January 2, 1860.

6. L. D. Baldwin, *Pittsburgh: The Story of a City* (Pittsburgh, 1995 ed.), pp. 221–22, 309–10; Lorant, p. 129; White, p. 20; C. E. Macartney, *Right Here in Pittsburgh* (Pittsburgh, 1937), pp. 31–52.

7. J. C. Holmberg, "The Industrializing Community: Pittsburgh, 1850–1880" (Ph.D. diss., University of Pittsburgh, 1981), pp. 231–34; M. F. Holt, *Forging a Majority: The Formation of the Republican Party in Pittsburgh, 1848–1860* (London, 1969), pp. 176–77, 200–63.

8. TM's property dealings from 1855 to 1869 are itemized in the indexes held in Pittsburgh by the recorder of deeds: Deed Absecum [purchases], vol. 1, pp. 87–89; Deed Direct [sales], vol. 1, pp. 137–47.

9.   AWM papers: TM to J. F. Harry, October 26, 1858, November 24, 1858, December 29, 1858, January 12 and 22, 1859, March 5, 1859, April 18 and 25, 1859, July 16, 1859, January 2, 1860; *TMT*, pp. 182–223.

10. BJH papers: WAM, Notes for BJH biography, p. 136; *TMT*, pp. 151–52; *Letters*, pp. 22, 35, 41, 80.

11. *TMT*, pp. 121–22, 152–53.

12. *TMT*, pp. 154–55; *RSS*, p. 23.

13. *TMT*, p. 165. For some of the Judge's decisions, see B. Crumrine (ed.), *Pittsburgh Reports: Containing Cases Decided by the Federal and State Courts of Pennsylvania Chiefly at the City of Pittsburgh*, vol. 2 (Philadelphia, 1872), pp. 82–85, 130–37, 172–76, 185–88, 211–16.

14. *TMT*, pp. 161–69, 171.

15. *TMT*, pp. 84, 174–77; R. Hofstadter, *Social Darwinism in American Thought* (New York, 1959), pp. 3–12, 31–50. See also, especially, H. Spencer, *Education: Intellectual, Moral and Physical* (London, 1860), *First Principles* (New York, 1864), and *The Study of Sociology* (New York, 1874).

16. *TMT*, p. 173; Lorant, p. 133.

17. *TMT*, pp. 177, 239–40.

18. TM papers: [uncle] T. Mellon to TM, February 26, 1864, March 20, 1864, June 24, 1864; J. S. Negley to TM, April 19, 1863; S. Mellon to TM [n.d. c. 1865]; S. Mellon to A. Ridell, December 8, 1862; Lorant, p. 138.

19. *TMT*, p. 177; *Letters*, pp. 62–63; *JMS*, pp. 9–10; *RSS*, pp. 65–66; Baldwin, *Pittsburgh*, pp. 318–20; Lorant, pp. 130, 141, 144; Macartney, *Right Here in Pittsburgh*, pp. 147–50; AWM, interviewed in *Washington Star*, March 22, 1931.

20. Baldwin, *Pittsburgh*, pp. 317–18; Lubove, pp. 9–13.

21. Lorant, pp. 137, 145–46, 168; *TMT*, p. 180.

22. *TMT*, pp. 158, 177–80, 185. For one example of the Judge's property development schemes, see: R. J. Jucha, "The Anatomy of a Streetcar Suburb: A Development and Architectural History of Pittsburgh's Shadyside District, 1860–1920" (Ph.D. diss., George Washington University, 1980), pp. 80–83.

23. *Letters*, pp. 147, 154–63; TM papers: Stinson and Havens to TM, October 17, 1863; S. Stoner to TM, December 29, 1863; TM to RBM, December 9, 1886.

24. Mellon Bank papers: f06-02-00-007-0008, records TM as a director of the Farmers' Deposit Bank for 1857–65 and for 1869–71.

25. *MNBTC*, p. 9; White, pp. 17, 62; *TMT*, p. 180.

26. *TMT*, pp. 146, 225.

27. *TMT*, p. 224.

28. BJH papers: interview, Mrs. J. B. Sellers, April 7, 1940, pp. 1–2; interview, Mrs. E. Frazier, April 10, 1940, p. 1; WAM, Notes for BJH biography, p. 73.

29. *TMT*, pp. 28–29.

30. *TMT*, pp. 99, 320–22; *Letters*, p. 19.

31. *TMT*, p. 228 (emphasis added).

32. *JMS*, p. 26.

33. *TMT*, pp. 228–31.

34. *TMT*, p. 229.

35. *TMT*, pp. 68, 146, 231–33; *Letters*, pp. 77–78.

36. *TMT*, pp. 229–30.

37. *TMT*, pp. 236–37; *Letters*, pp. 12–13.

38. *TMT*, pp. 234–35; TM papers: pamphlet, "East Liberty Select Nursery . . . Thomas A. Mellon, Box 415, Pittsburgh PA" [n.d. c. 1862].

39. *TMT*, pp. 235–36; *Letters*, pp. 30, 44, 50, 55, 75, 78, 133, 148.

40. *Letters*, pp. 19, 35, 49, 53.

41. *Letters*, pp. 42, 53.

42. *Letters*, pp. 95–97.

43. *Letters*, pp. 98–110.

44. *TMT*, pp. 111, 237; *Letters*, p. 104.

45. *TMT*, pp. 236–37; *Letters*, pp. 80–93.

46. *TMT*, pp. 234, 241–43.

47. Baldwin, p. 234; *Pittsburgh City Directory* (Pittsburgh, 1864), p. 377; Jucha, "Anatomy of a Streetcar Suburb," pp. 63–65; J. A. Tarr, *Transportation Innovation and Spatial Patterns in Pittsburgh, 1850–1934* (Chicago, 1978), pp. 6–7.

48. BJH papers: interview, C. D. Marshall, April 3, 1940, p. 1; *JMS*, p. 26.

49. *JMS*, p. 18.

50. *TMT*, pp. 321–22; Judge, p. 158; Hendrick, ch. 2, p. 36; BJH papers: interview, Mrs J. B. Sellers, April 7, 1940, pp. 1–2.

51. *JMS*, p. 28.

52. *JMS*, p. 16.

53. Sparkes papers: interview, J. G. Bowman, August 3, 1944, pp. 3–4.

54. *TMT*, pp. 426, 436, 455.

55. *Letters*, pp. 103–107, 121–22, 130, 134; J. Ostrom Beasley, "Unrealized Dreams: General William Larimer, Jr.," *Colorado Heritage*, summer 1996, pp. 2–20.

56. R. H. L. Mellon, *The Larimer, McMasters and Allied Families* (Philadelphia, 1903), pp. 20–22, 29–34; H. S. Davis (ed.), *Reminiscences of General William Larimer and of His Son William H. H. Larimer* (Pittsburgh, 1918), pp. 19–26, 123–25, 210–20, 222; J. W. Jordan (ed.), *Colonial and Revolutionary Families of Pennsylvania: Genealogical and Personal Memoirs*, vol. 3 (New York, 1911), pp. 1509–12; Larimer family papers: f179, TM to General Larimer, July 5, 1858; f180, TM to J. M. M. Larimer, November 3, 1858; f182, TM to J. M. M. Larimer, February 19, 1859.

57. *TMT*, p. 101.

58. W. S. Burke and J. L. Rock, *The History of Leavenworth, the Metropolis of Kansas* (Leavenworth, 1880), pp. 37–38; *Portrait and Biographical Record of Leavenworth, Douglas and Franklin Counties, Kansas* (Chicago, 1899), pp. 155–56; *Kansas City Star*, May 20, 1917.

59. *TMT*, pp. 241–43.

60. *TMT*, p. 238.

61. TM papers: [TM] to Gnl. J. S. Negley, March 6, 1865; BJH papers: WAM to BJH, March 18, 1940; *TMT*, pp. 181, 243.

62. *TMT*, p. 237.

63. Koskoff, p. 29.

64. *TMT*, pp. 237, 243.

65. *TMT*, p. 238.

66. The property dealings of Thomas Alexander Mellon and James Ross Mellon for 1869–73 are itemized in the indexes held in Pittsburgh by the recorder of deeds: Deed Absecum [purchases], vol. 1, pp. 89–90; Deed Direct [sales], vol. 1, pp. 140–53.

67. *TMT*, p. 244 (emphasis added); Mellon Bank papers: Box 1306, f06-03-00-001-0001, early advertisement for T. Mellon & Sons [c. 1870].

68. *TMT*, p. 245; *Letters*, p. 46; White, pp. 22–24.

69. *TMT*, pp. 244, 260; E. Wilson (ed.), *Standard History of Pittsburgh, Pennsylvania* (Chicago, 1898), p. 484.

70. AWM papers: Notes for an Address Delivered by AWM at Banquet in Connection with Opening of New Building of Mellon National Bank, March 20, 1924; docket no. 76499, p. 4611.

71. *TMT*, p. 256.

72. R. C. Alberts, *Pitt: The Story of the University of Pittsburgh, 1787–1987* (Pittsburgh, 1986), pp. 18–32.

73. Western University of Pennsylvania papers: RG 0/3/2, Register of Students Entering, 1865–1881, pp. 220, 344; Register of Students Entering, 1871–1873, p. 13; M. Brignano and J. Tomlinson Fort, *Reed Smith: A Law Firm Celebrates 125 Years* (Pittsburgh, 2002), pp. 15, 23.

74. For this and the next two paragraphs see AWM papers: AWM, School Compositions.

75. BJH papers: interview, Mrs. E. Frazier, April 10, 1940, p. 2; *TMT*, pp. xxii, 82; *JMS*, pp. 28–30.

76. *JMS*, p. 29.

77. *TMT*, p. 259; *Letters*, pp. 9–10, 22–23, 40–41, 58, 67, 83.

78. *TMT*, pp. 259–60.

79. Judge, p. 159.

80. BJH papers: WAM, Notes for BJH biography, pp. 7, 16; WAM to BJH, June 11, 1942, Review of Sheets, p. 14; Hendrick, ch. 2, pp. 31–32.

81. C. Bird, *The Invisible Scar* (New York, 1966), pp. 97–98; J. A. Schwartz, *The Interregnum of Despair: Hoover, Congress and the Depression* (Urbana, Ill., 1970), p. 218. For private banks more broadly, see: R. Sylla, "Forgotten Men of Money: Private Bankers in Early U.S. History," *Journal of Economic History* 36 (1976), pp. 173–88; L. Schweikart, "Private Bankers in the Antebellum South," *Southern Studies* 25 (1986), pp. 125–34; F. Redlich, *The Molding of American Banking: Men and Ideas* (New York, 1968), pt. 2, pp. 60–79.

82. F&S, pp. 8–9, 18–19; B. J. Klebaner, *American Commercial Banking: A History* (Boston, 1990), pp. 45–68, 92–101.

83. AWM, "Banking and Finance in Pittsburgh," in *Pittsburgh and the Pittsburgh Spirit* (Pittsburgh, 1928), pp. 257, 263.

84. *TMT*, p. 238.

85. *MNBTC*, p. 12; Lorant, pp. 145–61; Holmberg, "Industrializing Community," p. 2.

86. *TMT*, pp. 238, 260; AWM papers: T. A. Mellon and Mary Mellon McClung v. AWM and the Estate of RBM," Exhibit L: T. Mellon & Sons, Bank Earnings and Distribution, 1869–1902. For an example of TM's successful property dealings, see AWM papers: TM to RBM, December 14, 1884.

87. *TMT*, pp. 230, 243.

88. *TMT*, p. 465, n. 3; Pittsburgh Railway Companies papers 74:29: Book 22, p. 232.

89. Holmberg, "Industrializing Community," p. 100; Hendrick, ch. 11, pp. 3–6; BJH papers: interview, J. Galey, March 10, 1941, p. 1.

90. K. Warren, *Triumphant Capitalism: Henry Clay Frick and the Industrial Transformation of America* (Pittsburgh, 1996), p. 12; *MNBTC*, p. 11.

91. Warren, *Triumphant Capitalism*, p. 13; G. Harvey, *Henry Clay Frick: The Man* (New York, 1928), p. 62; H. O. Evans, *Iron Pioneer: Henry W. Oliver, 1840–1904* (New York, 1942), pp. 122–23.

92. *TMT*, p. 262.

93. G. H. Hull, *Industrial Depressions* (New York, 1926), pp. 149–52; R. Sobel, *Panic on Wall Street: A History of America's Financial Disasters* (New York, 1968), pp. 154–96.

94. *TMT*, p. 25.

95. F&S, p. 42. This paragraph draws extensively on D. Fisher, "The Economic Impact of the Market Crisis of 1873 and the Depression of 1873 to 1879 on the Pittsburgh Area" (M.A. thesis, University of Pittsburgh, 1957).

96. White, pp. 25–26; *JMS*, p. 42.

97. *TMT*, p. 241.

98. *Letters*, p. 141; *TMT*, p. 261.

99. *TMT*, pp. 191–92, 245, 265.

100. Fisher, "Economic Impact of the Market Crisis of 1873," pp. 32–33; *Pittsburgh Commercial Gazette*, November 12, 1873. TM gives the date when he ordered payments to be stopped to all except the most needy depositors as October 15; but his memory must have failed him: *TMT*, p. 266.

101. *TMT*, pp. 265–66.

102. *TMT*, p. 269; Mellon Bank papers: f07-02-00-001-0018, AWM, "A Hundred Years of Banking in Pittsburgh" [undated typescript, c. 1903], pp. 34–35.

103. AWM, "A Hundred Years of Banking in Pittsburgh," p. 33½.

104. *TMT*, p. 260.

105. Docket no. 76499, p. 4419.

106. BJH papers: AWM Letterbooks, AWM to L. Baer, March 10, 1922; AWM to C. H. K. Curtis, September 25, 1925.

107. BJH papers: interview, A. E. Sixsmith, March 5, 1941, p. 2; interview, F. Denton, March 14, 1941, p. 2; interview, E. R. Weidlein, April 14, 1940, p. 5; Sparkes papers: interview, H. M. Johnson, June 5, 1945, p. 10; *RSS*, p. 65.

2. The Family in Business: Boys and Banks, 1873–87

1. F&S, pp. 42–43, 97, 99; R. Sobel, *Panic on Wall Street* (New York, 1968), pp. 197–229.

2. E. Foner, *A Short History of Reconstruction, 1863–1877* (New York, 1990), pp. 217–22; L. Gould, *Grand Old Party: A History of the Republicans* (New York, 2003), pp. 65–75. For the general inferiority of American politicians at this time, see J. Bryce, *The American Commonwealth*, 3 vols. (London, 1888), vol. 2, pp. 403–11, 606–16.

3. M. A. Jones, *The Limits of Liberty: American History, 1607–1992*, 2nd ed. (New

York, 1995), p. 320; J. Livingston, "The Social Analysis of Economic History and Theory: Conjectures on Late Nineteenth-Century American Development," *American Historical Review* 92 (1987), pp. 69–95.

4. AWM papers: TM to RBM and G. Mellon, November 24, 1885.

5. Samber, p. 134; *TMT,* pp. xxii, 264.

6. *TMT,* p. 270; D. A. Fisher, "The Economic Impact of the Market Crisis of 1873 and the Depression of 1873 to 1879 on the Pittsburgh Area" (M.A. thesis, University of Pittsburgh, 1958), pp. 1–3, 8–9, 30–49; K. Warren, *Triumphant Capitalism: Henry Clay Frick and the Industrial Transformation of America* (Pittsburgh, 1996), p. 14.

7. R. V. Bruce, *1877: Year of Violence* (New York, 1977); Lorant, pp. 170–76; P. S. Foner, *The Great Labor Uprising of 1877* (New York, 1977), pp. 55–77; J. A. Henderson, "The Railroad Riots in Pittsburgh," *Western Pennsylvania Historical Magazine* 11 (1924), pp. 195–57; "Reminiscences of George B. Logan," *Western Pennsylvania Historical Magazine* 51 (1968), pp. 251–53; D. L. Mahrer, "Historical Society Notes and Documents: The Diary of Wilson Howell Carpenter: An Account of the 1877 Railroad Riots," *Western Pennsylvania Historical Magazine* 60 (1977), pp. 306–13.

8. *TMT,* pp. 264, 426; Pennsylvania Railroad Company papers: Board of Managers Minute Books, March 5, 1856, June 24, 1856, March 3, 1857, March 9, 1859, March 4, 1863, March 9, 1864; AWM papers: R. Pitcairn to AWM, June 19, 24, and 26, 1888; Mellon Bank papers: 07-02-00-001-0018, AWM, "A Hundred Years of Banking in Pittsburgh" [undated typescript, c. 1903], p. 34; BJH papers: interview, DEF, March 27, 1940, p. 1.

9. O'Connor, p. 33; *TMT,* p. 349.

10. R. J. Jucha, "The Anatomy of a Streetcar Suburb: A Development and Architectural History of Pittsburgh's Shadyside District, 1860–1920" (Ph.D. diss., George Washington University, 1980), pp. 88, 110.

11. O'Connor, p. 27; *TMT,* pp. 270–71.

12. Hendrick, ch. 3, p. 9.

13. BJH papers: interview, Mr. Gettys, April 4, 1940, p. 2; Hendrick, ch. 3. p. 10; *TMT,* p. 270.

14. *TMT,* p. 271.

15. Hendrick, ch. 3, p. 9; BJH papers: interview, Mr. Gettys, April 4, 1940, pp. 1–2.

16. Hendrick, ch. 3, p. 11.

17. Hendrick, ch. 3, p. 26; AWM papers: "An Act to Incorporate the Ligonier and Latrobe Rail Road Company," April 15, 1853; *TMT,* pp. 271–74.

18. Judge, pp. 166–67; *JMS,* pp. 67–78.

19. Hendrick, ch. 3, p. 27.

20. Judge, p. 170; Samber, pp. 139–40; AWM papers: TM to RBM, November 13, 1882, January 9, 1883; "In the Matter of Revenue Agent's Report Concerning the Income and Profits, Tax Returns for the Years 1922, 1923, 1924 and 1925, Filed by the Ligonier Valley Rail Road Co, Ligonier, Pa.," filed by RKM, treasurer, March 14, 1927.

21. Judge, pp. 161, 166.

22. AWM papers: TM to AWM, November 22, 1881; T. A. Mellon and Mary

McClung v. AWM and Estate of RBM Statement as to Claim, Exhibit L: T. Mellon & Sons, Bank Earnings and Distribution, 1869–1902; *MNBTC*, p. 14.

23. M. F. S. Sanger, *Henry Clay Frick: An Intimate Biography* (New York, 1998), pp. 25–26, 45–56, 77; Warren, *Triumphant Capitalism*, pp. 6, 14.

24. Judge, pp. 161–62; G. Harvey, *Henry Clay Frick: The Man* (New York, 1928), p. 66.

25. Samber, p. 138; Lorant, p. 145.

26. Lorant, pp. 161–62, 202; Lubove, pp. 22–29.

27. *TMT*, pp. 439–41.

28. *TMT*, pp. 151, 437; AWM papers: TM to RBM, 1882–86, TM to RBM, December 9, 1886.

29. AWM papers: TM to his sons, December 25, 1878; *Letters*, p. 181, November 6, 1881; *TMT*, pp. xxv–xxvi.

30. AWM papers: Proposition, January 5, 1882; *JMS*, p. 124.

31. Docket no. 76499, p. 4419.

32. BJH papers: interview, WAM, January 9, 1940, p. 1; WAM to BJH, July 3, 1942; PM papers: interview no. 5, pp. 13–14.

33. BJH papers: WAM, notes for BJH biography, pp. 22, 44; WAM to BJH, July 8, 1940; Judge, p. 172.

34. *Letters*, pp. 182–85, 192–94; *TMT*, pp. 382, 389; Judge, pp. 255–56; Hendrick, ch. 4, p. 13; M. P. Bothwell, "Incline Planes and People—Some Past and Present Ones," *Western Pennsylvania Historical Magazine* 46 (October 1963), pp. 311–46; W. H. Vincent, *Sunday Trains Demoralizing and Contrary to the Laws of God and Man: Review of the Reply of the Hon. Thomas Mellon* (Ligonier, 1880); TM papers: TM to ?, June 1883.

35. *TMT*, p. 382.

36. Judge, pp. 202–203.

37. Lorant, pp. 193–95, 201.

38. Judge, pp. 176–84; P. Krause, *The Battle for Homestead, 1880–1892: Politics, Culture and Steel* (Pittsburgh, 1992), pp. 88, 156, 194, 156–59; *National Labor Tribune*, 27 November 1880, February 19, 1881, October 29, 1881.

39. *National Labor Tribune*, January 7, 1882, February 4, 11, 18, 25, 1882, April 15, 1882.

40. Judge, pp. 206–208.

41. J. F. Wall, *Andrew Carnegie*, 2nd ed. (Pittsburgh, 1989), pp. 816–17; P. Krass, *Carnegie* (Hoboken, N.J., 2002), pp. 249–51.

42. J. K. Ochsner, *H. H. Richardson: Complete Architectural Works* (Cambridge, Mass., 1982), pp. 325–27; M. G. Van Rensselaer, *H. Hobson Richardson and His Works* (New York, 1968), pp. 89–93; F. K. B. Toker, "Richardson 'en concours': The Pittsburgh Courthouse," *Carnegie Magazine* 51, no. 9 (November 1977), pp. 13–29.

43. *Pittsburgh Commercial Gazette*, August 27, 1884; Judge, pp. 209–13.

44. Judge, pp. 185–99. In *TMT*, p. 286, TM gave the date of his son's visit as 1874, but he was in error.

45. Judge, p. 187; *TMT*, pp. 291–93.

46. *TMT*, pp. 304–306, 314. Almost half a century later, when he was secretary of the

treasury, AWM would urge his son, then an undergraduate at Clare College, Cambridge, to visit the Mellon ancestral home during his Easter vacation: AWM papers: AWM to PM, February 11, 1930.

47. *TMT,* pp. 319, 323.
48. *TMT,* pp. 331, 337.
49. Judge, pp. 229–31; *TMT,* p. 419.
50. *TMT,* p. 4 (emphasis added).
51. G. T. Couser, *American Autobiography: The Prophetic Mode* (Amherst, Mass., 1979); C. McGuirk, "Haunted by Authority: Nineteenth-Century American Construction of Robert Burns and Scotland," in R. Crawford (ed.), *Robert Burns and Cultural Authority* (Edinburgh, 1977), pp. 136–58; R. Hofstadter, *Social Darwinism in American Thought* (New York, 1959), pp. 3–13, 31–50.
52. *TMT,* pp. 402–404.
53. *TMT,* pp. 425, 431–33, 443.
54. *TMT,* pp. 64, 128, 238, 240, 382.
55. *TMT,* pp. 99, 220–22.
56. *TMT,* pp. 340–43, 347–55, 357–58.
57. *TMT,* pp. 349, 361–65.
58. *TMT,* p. 341–46.
59. *TMT,* pp. x, 347.
60. *TMT,* p. xi; Samber, p. 140; F. Bancroft (ed.), *Speeches, Correspondence and Political Papers of Carl Schurtz,* vol. 2, *December 13, 1870–February 27, 1874* (New York, 1913), pp. 450–72.
61. *TMT,* p. 339.
62. *TMT,* pp. 27, 386.
63. *TMT,* p. 5.
64. *TMT,* p. 386; Judge, p. 246; AWM papers: H. Phipps Jr., to HCF, November 28, 1887; TM papers: A. Carnegie to TM, January 11, 1897.
65. Mellon Bank papers: Folder TM, TM to I. Craig, May 26, 1890; DEF papers (NGA): DEF to J. P. Davies, December 2, 1929; DEF to AWM, December 2, 1929; *TMT,* pp. xix, 4; BJH papers: AWM Letterbooks, AWM to W. H. Gardner, December 28, 1927; interview, Mrs. E. Frazier, April 10, 1940, p. 3.
66. *TMT,* p. 386.
67. AWM papers: TM to RBM and G. Mellon, October 14, 1882; TM to RBM, December 14, 1884, January 5, 1885.
68. *TMT,* p. 349; Lorant, pp. 174–78, 187–88.
69. Sanger, *Frick,* pp. 78–80.
70. Sanger, *Frick,* pp. 92–93; AWM papers: HCF to AWM, August 25, 1887.
71. *TMT,* pp. 325, 341; *JMS,* pp. 514–15.
72. BJH papers: WAM, notes on BJH biography, p. 79.
73. AWM papers: Minnie —— to AWM, February 26, 1879, February 3, 29, 1880, April 25, 1880, April 25, 1880.
74. Sanger, *Frick,* pp. 82–83.
75. Lorant, p. 147; Lubove, p. 27.
76. AWM papers: F. Jones to AWM, April 7, 1881; E. H. Walker to AWM, June 30, 1881; *TMT,* p. 384.

77. *TMT*, p. 102; *RSS*, p. 64.

78. *TMT*, p. 384; *RSS*, p. 64; Hendrick, ch. 2, pp. 31a, 32; BJH papers: WAM, notes on BJH biography, pp. 83–85; interview, WAM, January 9, 1940, p. 2; WAM to BJH, October 9, 1940.

79. AWM papers: TM to AWM, November 3, 1881.

80. Hendrick, ch. 3, p. 17; *Letters*, pp. 182, 187; *TMT*, p. 271; AWM papers: TM to AWM, June 20, 1884.

81. White, pp. 28, 56, 70–71.

82. Samber, pp. 141–42; *TMT*, p. 384 (emphasis added).

83. For the growing interconnectedness of banking, insurance, and industrial investment, see Holmberg, "Industrializing Community," pp. 183, 194–98.

84. Samber, pp. 138, 154–55; Lorant, pp. 150, 154; AWM papers: T. Mellon & Sons Letterbooks, AWM to S. Galey, February 10, 1881, September 26, 1882, October 4, 1882. Alexander Caldwell also knew about (and may have invested in) natural gas in Pittsburgh: see his speech reported in "Proceedings of the Kansas Quarter-Centennial Celebrations," *Transactions of the Kansas State Historical Society*, 1883–85, vol. 3 (Topeka, 1886), p. 457.

85. Samber, pp. 201, 231–32; J. H. Reid, "Pittsburgh and the Natural Gas Industry," in *Pittsburgh and the Pittsburgh Spirit* (Pittsburgh, 1928), pp. 127–30; AWM papers: J. J. Vandergrift to AWM, March 26, 1885; Memorandum of Agreement, October 25, 1884; *JMS*, p. 153.

86. B. J. Klebaner, *American Commercial Banking: A History* (Boston, 1990), pp. 72–77; D. North, "Life Insurance and Investment Banking at the Time of the Armstrong Investigation of 1905–06," *Journal of Economic History* 14 (1954), pp. 209–28.

87. *JMS*, p. 135; AWM papers: P. A. Caldwell to AWM, June 2, 1888, April 13, 1889; A. Caldwell to AWM, July 17, 1888; TM to RBM, January 5, 1885; Sparkes papers: interview, DEF, March 1, 1945, pp. 17–18.

88. Idaho and Oregon Land Improvement Company papers: Articles of Incorporation, 1882; J. A. Lukas, *Big Trouble* (New York, 1997), pp. 19–22; C. A. Strahorn, *Fifteen Thousand Miles by Stage*, 2 vols. (Lincoln, Neb., 1998), vol. 2, *1880–1898*, pp. 41–42, 49–50, 68; R. E. Strahorn, "Ninety Years of Boyhood" (unpublished typescript, 1942, held at Idaho Historical Society), pp. 320–25.

89. Sanger, *Frick*, pp. 77–78, 92; BJH papers: J. W. Chalfant to T. Mellon & Sons, October 4, 1888.

90. AWM papers: Loans made by T. Mellon & Sons, 1882–October 1, 1892; HCF papers: Agreement Between HCF and AWM, July 12, 1887; AWM papers: HCF to AWM, June 29, 1887, August 15, 16, 25, 1887, September 15, 21, 1887.

91. HCF papers: HCF Letterbook, AWM to HCF, May 30, 1887; BJH papers: interview, H. A. Phillips, April 11, 1940, pp. 1–2.

92. *TMT*, pp. 31–32. For two versions of the sale price, see Samber, p. 138, note 43, and BJH papers: interview, Mr. Hick, March 14, 1941, p. 2.

93. Warren, *Triumphant Capitalism*, p. 40; HCF papers: AWM to Col. Harvey, June 25, 1927.

94. *TMT*, pp. 383–85.

95. *TMT*, p. 275.

96. *TMT*, pp. 275–78, 282–85; AWM papers: TM to AWM, November 3, 1881.

97. *Letters*, pp. 194–95; *JMS*, pp. 96–97.

98. AWM papers: T. Mellon & Sons Letterbooks, AWM to S. Galey, September 26, 1882; TM to RBM and G. Mellon, October 14, 1882; TM to RBM, October 28, 1882, January 9, 1883; *JMS*, p. 97.

99. *JMS*, pp. 94, 100–107; AWM papers: RBM to AWM, December 27, 1882, March 4, 1883, June 18, 30, 1883, July 13, 1883, September 27, 1883, November 8, 1883; Sparkes papers: interview, H. M. Johnson, June 5, 1945, p. 7.

100. *JMS*, pp. 93, 101; AWM papers: RBM to AWM, December 5, 1882, April 14, 23, 1884, June 18, 1884, April 20, 1885.

101. AWM papers: TM to RBM, October 14, 1882, January 9, 21, 1883, January 5, 1885, November 24, 1885.

102. AWM papers: TM to RBM, October 14, 1882, July 19, 1883; RBM to AWM, December 8, 11, 30, 1882.

103. *TMT*, p. 388; TM papers: G. Mellon to TM, August 6, 1884; AWM papers: G. Mellon to AWM, June 29, 1884, May 30, 1885; TM to RBM, January 9, 1883.

104. *TMT*, p. 385; AWM papers: TM to RBM, January 16, 1885.

105. Larimer Family papers: f365, RBM to W. H. H. Larimer, October 17, 24, 1886.

106. Huntland Downs papers: S. J. Mellon, "Glen Eyre," passim, esp. pp. 22–25, 31–32, 36–46.

107. *TMT*, p. 455.

108. AWM papers: TM to RBM, December 9, 1886.

109. *JMS*, p. 97; DEF papers (NGA): Box 1: Anecdotes of AWM.

110. AWM papers: TM to RBM, January 16, 1885, May 20, 1885, December 9, 1886.

111. *JMS*, p. 127; AWM papers: TM to RBM, December 17, 1886.

112. *JMS*, pp. 128–29; AWM papers: TM to RBM, January 16, 1885.

113. AWM papers: TM to RBM, December 9, 1886 (emphasis added).

114. Docket no. 76499, pp. 4420–22, 4605, 4610–12.

115. Hendrick, ch. 3, pp. 29–30; *TMT*, p. 389; AWM papers: TM to RBM, May 20, 1885.

3. The "Mellon System" Inaugurated: "My Brother and I," 1887–98

1. *JMS*, pp. 132–33, 183; Pittsburgh Railway Companies papers: 74:29: Book 22, p. 237.

2. Hendrick, ch. 4, pp. 7–8.

3. A. Carnegie, "Wealth," *North American Review* 148 (1889), pp. 653–64; A. Carnegie, "The Best Fields for Philanthropy," *North American Review* 149 (1889), pp. 682–98; AWM papers: A. Carnegie to TM, January 7, 1895. See also: W. E. Gladstone, "Mr. Carnegie's 'Gospel of Wealth': A Review and a Recommendation," *Nineteenth Century* 28 (1890), pp. 677–93; H. Edward et al., "Irresponsible Wealth," *Nineteenth Century* 28 (1890), pp. 876–700; A. Carnegie, "The Advantages of Poverty," *Nineteenth Century* 29 (1891), pp. 367–85.

4. J. F. Wall, *Andrew Carnegie*, 2nd ed. (Pittsburgh, 1989), pp. 804–16; P. Krass, *Carnegie* (Hoboken, N.J., 2002), pp. 338–51.

5. B. D. Karl and S. N. Katz, "Foundations and Ruling Class Elites," *Daedalus* 116 (1987), pp. 1–40; D. J. Kevles, "Foundations, Universities and Trends in Support of the Physical and Biological Sciences," *Daedalus* 121 (1992), pp. 194–96.

6. TM papers: "Essay on Money," January 1835.

7. Judge, pp. 262–64; TM papers: Deed of Transfer from TM *et ux.* to AWM, February 3, 1890; AWM, A Declaration of Trust, February 3, 1890.

8. Docket no. 76499, pp. 4417–18.

9. *History of Allegheny County* (Chicago, 1889), p. 220.

10. *TMT*, p. 390.

11. Judge, pp. 254–59; *Penny Press*, February 15, 1890.

12. AWM papers: TM to "all at home," February 7, 17, 1890; TM to "Ma," February 28, 1890.

13. AWM papers: TM to "all at home," February 7, 17, 1890; TM to AWM, February 25, 1890, March 29, 1890; TM to "my sons," March 3, 1890.

14. AWM papers: TM to AWM, February 25, 1890, March 12, 29, 1890; TM to Thomas Mellon, AWM, and RBM, February 28, 1890; *Penny Press*, February 15, 1890, March 7, 13, 15, 31, 1890, May 9, 1890, June 3, 1890.

15. Judge, pp. 267–80; *JMS*, pp. 191–92. WLM is mistaken in his claim that TM's newspaper was called the *Leader.*

16. *TMT*, p. 391; Judge, pp. 280–85.

17. *JMS*, p. 191; Sparkes papers: interview, DEF, March 1, 1945, p. 2; TM papers: TM ms., August 25, 1898 [typed copy], pp. 1–2, 4–7.

18. J. N. Boucher, *History of Westmoreland County, Pennsylvania*, vol. 2 (New York, 1908), p. 408.

19. Hendrick, ch. 4, p. 4; TM papers: Assignment by TM of certain bonds and mortgages to AWM, December 26–29, 1894.

20. *JMS*, pp. 185–86; J. N. Ingham, "Reaching for Respectability: The Pittsburgh Industrial Elite at the Turn of the Century," in G. P. Weisberg, D. E. McIntosh, and A. McQueen (eds.), *Collecting in the Gilded Age: Art Patronage in Pittsburgh, 1890–1910* (Pittsburgh, 1997), pp. 12–13, 345–46, n. 12; *New York Tribune*, May 1, 1892, pp. 45, 50, 51.

21. AWM papers: Miscellaneous Financial Records, 1892–1917.

22. TM papers: TM to "My dear Sons," September 24, 1895; Judge, pp. 290–91; *Letters*, pp. 205–11.

23. Hendrick, ch. 6, p. 30; Sparkes papers: interview, H. M. Johnson, June 5, 1945, p. 7.

24. AWM papers: T. A. Mellon and Mary McClung v. AWM and Estate of RBM: Statement as to Claim, Exhibit L: Miscellaneous Financial Records, 1892–1917.

25. Hendrick, ch. 6, pp. 1–2; BJH papers: interview, Mr. Kerrigan, April 9, 1940, pp. 2, 4.

26. Mellon Bank papers: f07-02-00-001-0018, AWM, "A Hundred Years of Banking in Pittsburgh" [undated typescript, c. 1903], p. 36; Samber, p. 143; *MNBTC*, pp. 24–25; White, pp. 48, 79; H. O. Evans, *Iron Pioneer: Henry W. Oliver, 1840–1904* (New York, 1942), pp. 127–28.

27. F&S, pp. 104–13.

28. Hendrick, ch. 7, pp. 1–30; ch. 8, pp. 1–21; R. A. Hunt, *The Aluminum Pioneers*

(New York, 1951), pp. 7–15; C. C. Carr, *Alcoa: An American Enterprise* (New York, 1952), pp. 5–50, 85–122; Smith, pp. 8–42.

29. BJH papers: interview, G. H. Clapp, November 3, 1940, p. 4; Sparkes papers: interview, A. V. Davis, 1945, p. 4.

30. Alcoa papers: Drawer 7, Envelope 185, J. R. D. Huston to R. A. Hunt, May 17, 1935, November 25, 1940.

31. Smith, pp. 81–82; Sparkes papers: interview, A. V. Davis, 1945, pp. 6, 17.

32. Smith, pp. 81–82.

33. Carr, *Alcoa*, p. 44; Hendrick, ch. 7, p. 21; Alcoa papers: Drawer 7, Envelope 185, AWM to M. Hunsiker, September 5, 6, 1894; T. Mellon & Sons to Messrs. Rolston & Bass, February 21, 1895.

34. Hendrick, ch. 11, pp. 7–27; *JMS*, pp. 139–78; Samber, pp. 56–60.

35. Larimer Family Papers: f 364, A. L. Jones to W. H. H. Larimer, December [c. 1884]; BJH papers: interviews, WLM, November 14, 1940, p. 1, March 17, 1941, pp. 1–2; WAM, March 7, 1941, pp. 1–2; Mr. Kerrigan, April 9, 1940, p. 1.

36. WLM insisted that he did not do business with Guffey (*JMS*, pp. 152–53), but this is contradicted by the evidence. See BJH papers: *Oil City Derrick*, September 12, 1893, January 25, 26, 1894, February 27, 1894, December 27, 1894; AWM papers: T. Mellon & Sons Letterbooks, AWM to C. M. Dow, June 21, 1888; AWM to J. Clark, July 7, 1888; AWM to J. McCrea, September 29, 1889; AWM to C. Smith & Sons, March 13, 1891.

37. AWM papers: Miscellaneous Financial Records, 1892–1917.

38. AWM papers: AWM, RBM, and WLM, Memorandum of Agreement, June 20, 1894; also reprinted in *JMS*, p. 185.

39. BJH papers: *Oil City Derrick*, February 2, 1894.

40. R. W. Hidy and M. E. Hidy, *History of Standard Oil Company* (New Jersey), vol. 1, *Pioneering in Big Business, 1882–1911* (New York, 1955), pp. 238–40.

41. BJH papers: interviews, WLM, March 17, 1941, p. 2; Mr. Hartman, March 13, 1941, p. 1.

42. AWM papers: T. Mellon & Sons Letterbooks, AWM to E. E. Robbins, March 3, 1892; AWM to J. C. Head, April 4, 1892; BJH papers: interview, Mr. Kerrigan, March 6, 1941, pp. 2–3.

43. AWM papers: T. Mellon & Sons Letterbooks, AWM to P. Stackhouse, December 27, 1892; Samber, pp. 202–203.

44. AWM papers: T. Mellon & Sons Letterbooks, AWM to D. M. Kennedy, March 31, 1894; AWM to W. D. Card, March 26, 1894; AWM to J. G. Strean, March 29, 1894.

45. Samber, pp. 344–45.

46. BJH papers: interview, Dr. M. A. Rosanoff, April 13, 1940, pp. 6–7.

47. AWM, "Banking and Finance in Pittsburgh," in *Pittsburgh and the Pittsburgh Spirit* (Pittsburgh, 1928), pp. 263–69; Samber, pp. 264–69; D. B. Houston, "A Brief History of the Process of Capital Accumulation in Pittsburgh: A Marxist Interpretation," in J. A. Tarr (ed.), *Pittsburgh—Sheffield: Sister Cities* (Pittsburgh, 1986), pp. 29–46. For the broader picture see J. A. James, *Money and Capital Markets in Postbellum America* (Princeton, N.J., 1978); V. P. Carosso, *Investment Banking in America: A History* (Cambridge, Mass., 1970).

48. F. G. Couvares, *The Remaking of Pittsburgh: Class and Culture in an Industrializing City, 1877–1919* (Albany, N.Y., 1984), pp. 81–82; Houston, "Capital Accumulation in Pittsburgh," pp. 29, 35, 38.

49. Lorant, pp. 178, 198, 232–35, 249–54; J. A. Tarr, *Transportation, Innovation and Changing Spatial Patterns in Pittsburgh, 1850–1934* (Chicago, 1978), pp. 17–18; J. A. Tarr and D. di Pasquale, "The Mill Town in the Industrial City: Pittsburgh's Hazelwood," *Urbanism Past and Present* 7 (1982), 1–7; S. P. Hays, "The Changing Political Structure of the City in Industrial America," *Journal of Urban History* 1 (1974), pp. 6–25.

50. J. N. Ingham, "Steel City Aristocrats," in S. P. Hayes (ed.), *City at the Point: Essays on the Social History of Pittsburgh* (Pittsburgh, 1989), pp. 265–94.

51. J. N. Ingham, *The Iron Barons: A Social Analysis of an American Urban Elite, 1874–1965* (Westport, Conn., 1978), esp. pp. 6–7, 228–29; J. N. Ingham, *Making Iron and Steel: Independent Mills in Pittsburgh, 1820–1920* (Columbus, Ohio, 1991), pp. 169–71; Couvares, *Remaking of Pittsburgh*, pp. 31–35; J. F. Rishel, "The Founding Families of Allegheny County: An Examination of Nineteenth-Century Elite Continuity" (Ph.D. diss., University of Pittsburgh, 1975), pp. 199–200.

52. F. C. Jaher, *The Urban Establishment: Upper Strata in Boston, New York, Charleston, Chicago, and Los Angeles* (Urbana, Ill., 1982), esp. pp. 1–14, 711–30; Rishel, "Founding Families," pp. 164–76.

53. Samber, pp. 182–83; R. H. Demmler, *The First Century of an Institution: Reed Smith Shaw & McClay* (Pittsburgh, 1977), pp. 3–9, 14–24; M. Brignano and J. Tomlinson Fort, *Reed Smith: A Law Firm Celebrates 125 Years* (Pittsburgh, 2002), pp. 23–25.

54. HCF papers: Memorandum of Agreement between HCF and AWM, February 9, 1889; Passenger lists: *Lucania*, Liverpool to New York, August 15, 1896; *St. Louis*, New York to Southampton, July 14, 1897, Southampton to New York, August 21, 1897, all record Mr. and Mrs. Frick and AWM.

55. Hendrick, ch. 5, p. 18; Sparkes papers: interview, W. H. Donner, June 25, 1945, p. 27; HCF papers: AWM to Col. Harvey, June 25, 1927; Judge, p. 163. WLM, although he had attended many lunches earlier by invitation, was only elected to the group after Frick's death in 1919: *JMS*, pp. 367–68.

56. Couvares, *Remaking of Pittsburgh*, p. 36.

57. AWM papers: HCF to AWM, July 14, 1894.

58. Couvares, *Remaking of Pittsburgh*, pp. 128–29; Ingham, *Making Iron and Steel*, pp. 166, 177; S. J. Kleinberg, *In the Shadow of the Mills: Working-Class Families in Pittsburgh, 1870–1907* (Pittsburgh, 1989), pp. 27–40, 65–78, 96–99, 303; Lorant, p. 189; J. A. Tarr, "Searching for a 'Sink' for an Industrial Waste: Iron-Making Fuels and the Environment," *Environmental History Review* 28 (1994), pp. 9–35.

59. Lorant, p. 207; Lubove, p. 17; Couvares, *Remaking of Pittsburgh*, pp. 83–86.

60. Lubove, p. 32; D. Montgomery, *The Fall of the House of Labor: The Workplace, the State and American Liberal Activism, 1865–1925* (New York, 1987), pp. 11–24.

61. Demmler, *First Century*, pp. 14–19; M. F. S. Sanger, *Henry Clay Frick: An Intimate Portrait* (New York, 1998), pp. 77–78, 102–21; N. D. Shappe, "Spoliation and Encroachment in the Conemaugh Valley Before the Johnstown Flood of

1889," *Western Pennsylvania Historical Magazine* 23 (1940), pp. 23–48; N. D. Shappe, "The Johnstown Flood and Pittsburgh's Relief," *Western Pennsylvania Historical Magazine* 23 (1940), pp. 79–98; D. G. McCullough, *The Johnstown Flood* (New York, 1968), passim.

62. Montgomery, *Fall of the House of Labor,* pp. 36–40; Sanger, *Henry Clay Frick,* pp. 178–98, 207–10; K. Warren, *Triumphant Capitalism: Henry Clay Frick and the Industrial Transformation of America* (Pittsburgh, 1996), pp. 63–112. For the two fullest accounts, see L. Wolff, *Lockout: The Story of the Homestead Strike of 1892— A Study of Violence, Unionism and the Carnegie Steel Empire* (New York, 1965); and P. Krause, *The Battle for Homestead, 1880–1892: Politics, Culture and Steel* (Pittsburgh, 1992).

63. Demmler, *First Century,* pp. 20, 31; Warren, *Triumphant Capitalism,* p. 373; Krass, *Carnegie,* 275–302; Wall, *Andrew Carnegie,* pp. 537–82; Krause, *Battle for Homestead,* pp. 348–50.

64. Judge, p. 249; Warren, *Triumphant Capitalism,* p. 97; Frick papers: TM to HCF, July 25, 1892.

65. Carnegie papers: Box 18, TM to A. Carnegie, January 30, 1893.

66. Couvares, *Remaking of Pittsburgh,* pp. 63–65; Ingham, *Making Iron and Steel,* p. 165; Lorant, p. 193; H. Zink, *City Bosses in the United States: A Study of Twenty Municipal Bosses* (Durham, N.C., 1930), pp. 230–56; L. Steffens, *The Shame of the Cities* (New York, 1957), pp. 101–33. The book was first published in 1904. For an earlier denunciation of the corruption of politics in American cities see J. Bryce, *The American Commonwealth,* 3 vols. (London, 1888), vol. 2, pp. 278–357, 450–91.

67. Hendrick, ch. 6, pp. 40–41; BJH papers: interviews, G. S. Davison, December 19, 1941, p. 5; J. F. Grundy, March 4, 1941, p. 3.

68. S. J. Astorino, "The Decline of the Republican Party in Pennsylvania, 1929–1934" (Ph.D. diss., University of Pittsburgh, 1962), pp. 1–7; B. M. Stave, *The New Deal and the Last Hurrah: Pittsburgh Machine Politics* (Pittsburgh, 1970), pp. 24–32.

69. Lorant, p. 186; H. Brogan, *The Penguin History of the United States of America,* 2nd ed. (London, 1999), pp. 410–11; R. G. Crist (ed.), *Pennsylvania Kingmakers* (Philadelphia, 1985), pp. 25–37; R. D. Marcus, *Grand Old Party: Political Structure in the Gilded Age, 1880–1896* (New York, 1971), pp. 129–34.

70. Quay papers: 7/7, J. S. McKean to M. S. Quay, February 25, 1896; 6/6, HCF to M. S. Quay, January 29, 1896; 6/8, HCF to M. S. Quay, February 5, 7, 1896; 7/6, HCF to M. S. Quay, October 2, 1896; 9/11, HCF to Mrs. Quay, May 8, 1902; 7/7, P. Knox to Governor McKinley, August 17, 1897; HCF papers: Letterbook, November 17, 1894–October 18, 1895, HCF to RBM, November 22, 23, 1894; Sparkes papers: interview, A. V. Davis, 1945, pp. 9–10.

71. Hendrick, ch. 5, pp. 27, 33; Bryce, *American Commonwealth,* vol. 3, pp. 73–74.

72. Hendrick, ch. 5, pp. 34–36; Judge, p. 225.

73. Hendrick, ch. 5, p. 34; Samber, p. 121.

74. Demmler, *First Century,* pp. 28–29; Brignano and Tomlinson Fort, *Reed Smith,* p. 37; Krause, *Battle for Homestead,* pp. 270–83.

75. *Letters,* p. 176; Houston, "Capital Accumulation in Pittsburgh," p. 39.

76. Hendrick, ch. 6, pp. 34–35; BJH papers: interview, G. H. Clapp, November 3, 1940, p. 1; Sparkes papers: interview, H. M. Johnson, June 5, 1945, p. 9.

77. Steffens, *Shame of the Cities*, pp. 3–4.

78. Hendrick, ch. 6, p. 25; Evans, *Iron Pioneer*, p. 130; BJH papers: interview, Mr. Kerrigan, April 9, 1940, p. 4.

79. Hendrick, ch. 5, pp. 31–32; Brignano and Tomlinson Fort, *Reed Smith*, p. 53; BJH papers: interview, G. H. Clapp, November 3, 1940, p. 5.

80. BJH papers: AWM Letterbooks, AWM to J. M. Witherow, April 24, 1930; Hendrick, ch. 6, pp. 38–40; *JMS*, p. 182; Sparkes papers: interview, W. Donner, June 25, 1945, p. 27.

81. Hendrick, ch. 6, pp. 18–20; BJH papers: interview, H. A. Phillips, April 11, 1940, p. 3; Sparkes papers: interview, W. Donner, June 25, 1945, p. 8; J. G. Bowman, August 3, 1944, p. 5; DEF, March 1, 1945, p. 16; PM papers: interviews, no. 1, p. 11; no. 3, p. 2.

82. Evans, *Iron Pioneer*, p. 121; BJH papers: interviews, Mr. Kerrigan, April 9, 1940, p. 3; G. H. Clapp, November 3, 1940, p. 3.

83. Judge, pp. 165, 216; BJH papers: interview, Mr. Kerrigan, April 9, 1940, p. 3; Sparkes papers: interview, DEF, pp. 7–10.

84. Hendrick, ch. 6, pp. 16–18; BJH papers: interview, Mrs. Bothwell, March 11, 1941, p. 1.

85. Sparkes papers: interview, S. Mellon Scaife, November 18, 1944, p. 1.

86. Hendrick, ch. 6, pp. 21–27; BJH papers: interview, Col. F. Drake, June 9, 1942, p. 9; Sparkes papers: interview, J. G. Bowman, August 3, 1944, p. 4.

87. AWM papers: interview, C. H. McCullough, July 8, 1996, p. 3; BJH papers: interview, H. A. Phillips, April 11, 1940, p. 5.

88. Sparkes papers: interview, RKM, October 18, 1944, pp. 15–16.

89. *JMS*, p. 180.

90. R. Sobel, *Panic on Wall Street* (London, 1968), pp. 230–72; C. P. Kindleberger, "International Propagation of Financial Crises: The Experience of 1888–93," in C. P. Kindleberger, *Keynesianism vs. Monetarism and Other Essays in Financial History* (London, 1985), pp. 226–39.

91. L. L. Gould, *Grand Old Party: A History of the Republicans* (New York, 2003), p. 116; Lorant, p. 196; Warren, *Triumphant Capitalism*, p. 125.

92. Smith, p. 445; AWM papers: T. A. Mellon and Mary McClung v. AWM and Estate of RBM: G. D. Wick to J. J. Frazer, May 31, 1934; Statement as to Claim, Exhibit L.

93. Samber, pp. 154–56; F. Spreng, "The Birth of the Pittsburgh Stock Exchange," *Western Pennsylvania Historical Magazine* 58 (1974), pp. 68–80.

94. Pittsburgh Stock Exchange papers: Minute Books of Meetings of Board of Directors, 1894–July 3, 1907, page pasted in opposite p. 1; *Pittsburgh Commercial Gazette*, August 18, 1893.

95. Pittsburgh Stock Exchange papers: Minute Books of Meetings of Board of Directors, 1894–July 3, 1907, March 26, 28, 29, 1894; *Pittsburgh Commercial Gazette*, March 27, 1894.

96. L. M. Williamson et al. (eds.), *Prominent and Progressive Pennsylvanians of the Nineteenth Century* (Philadelphia, 1898), vol. 1, pp. 493–95. HSWP: HG5133

P692, *The Pittsburgh Stock Exchange, 1894–1924* (Pittsburgh, 1924), pp. 12–13, lists H. C. McEldowney (Union Trust Company), W. S. Mitchell (Mellon National Bank), and Eugene Murray (Fidelity Title and Trust Company) as members.

97. Hendrick, ch. 11, pp. 27–37; *JMS*, pp. 1279–82.

98. BJH papers: interview, Mr. Kerrigan, March 6, 1941, p. 3.

99. Larimer Family Papers: f311 A. L. Jones to W. H. H. Larimer, December 8, 1895; BJH papers: *Oil City Derrick*, November 18, 19, 1895; AWM papers: T. Mellon & Sons Letterbooks, AWM to H. H. Rogers, March 9, 1895, May 23, 1895, October 12, 1895; AWM to J. Bushnell, May 16, 31, 1895, June 6, 1895; AWM to T. R. Cornick, December 24, 1895; BJH papers: interview, J. Galey, March 10, 1941, p. 2; Hidy and Hidy, *Pioneering in Big Business*, pp. 241, 274, 281.

100. *JMS*, p. 264; BJH papers: interviews, WLM, March 17, 1941, p. 3; Mr. Kerrigan, March 6, 1941, p. 3; Mr. Hartman, March 13, 1941, p. 1.

101. Hendrick, ch. 9, pp. 1–39; W. H. Wendel, *The Scratch Heard 'Round the World* (New York, 1965), pp. 8–11.

102. AWM papers: E. G. Acheson, "Carborundum: Its History, Manufacture and Uses" (n.p., n.d.).

103. Acheson papers: Box 17, Agreement Between E. G. Acheson, AWM, and RBM, July 6, 1895.

104. BJH papers: interviews, F. H. Manley, February 4, 1941, p. 1; Acheson papers: Box 17, Agreements Between E. G. Acheson, AWM and RBM, March 31, 1896, July 16, 1896, November 14, 1896; Box 18, Agreement Between E. G. Acheson, AWM, and RBM, April 13, 1897.

105. Hendrick, ch. 9, pp. 30–31, quoting RBM to E. G. Acheson, August 2, 1897; Acheson papers: Box 18, AWM to E. G. Acheson, August 20, 1898; BJH papers: Acheson Letterbooks, E. G. Acheson to AWM, August 22, 1898.

106. Acheson papers: Box 18, Agreement Between E. G. Acheson and AWM, June 17, 1898.

107. BJH papers: interview, F. H. Manley, February 4, 1941, p. 3; Acheson Letterbooks, E. G. Acheson to W. W. Acheson, October 21, 1898; Warren, *Triumphant Capitalism*, p. 266; E. G. Acheson, *A Pathfinder* (Port Huron, Mich., 1965), pp. 41–43.

108. Smith, pp. 34, 84, 88, 95, 445.

109. P. N. Limerick, *The Legacy of Conquest: The Unbroken Past of the American West* (New York, 1987), pp. 105–106; A. Derikson, *Workers' Health, Workers' Democracy: The Western Miners' Struggle, 1891–1925* (Ithaca, N.Y., 1988), pp. 2–9; R. H. Peterson, *The Bonanza Kings: The Social Origins and Business Behavior of Western Mining Entrepreneurs, 1870–1900* (Lincoln, Neb., 1977), pp. 93–94; J. A. Lukas, *Big Trouble: A Murder in a Small Western Town Sets Off a Struggle for the Soul of America* (New York, 1997), p. 100; M. P. Malone, *The Battle for Butte: Mining and Politics on the Western Frontier, 1864–1906* (Helena, Mont., 1981), pp. 132–41.

110. *JMS*, pp. 156–57, 159–60.

111. AWM papers: T. Mellon & Sons Letterbooks, 1871–1902, AWM to J. Guffey,

September 23, 1895; *A Historical, Descriptive and Commercial Directory of Owyhee County, Idaho, January 1898* (Silver City, Idaho, 1898), pp. 28–32.

112. *Annual Reports of the Department of the Interior for the Fiscal Year Ended June 30, 1899, Twentieth Annual Report of the U.S. Geological Survey*, pt. 3, *Precious-Metal Mining Districts* (Washington, D.C., 1900), p. 140; Derickson, *Workers' Health, Workers' Democracy*, p. 10; Trade Dollar Consolidated Mining Company papers: Box 3, T. B. McKaig to J. Hutchinson, May 15, 20, 1898.

113. Trade Dollar Consolidated Mining Company papers: Box 1, T. B. McKaig to F. Irwin, April 6, 25, 1905.

114. Trade Dollar Consolidated Mining Company papers: Box 2, T. B. McKaig to F. Irwin, November 6, 1909, May 26, 1910, June 6, 1910; M. W. Wells, *Gold Camps and Silver Cities: Nineteenth-Century Mining in Central and Southern Idaho*, 2nd ed. Idaho Dept. of Lands, Bureau of Mines & Geology, Bulletin 22 (1983), p. 49.

4. The Great Leap Forward: Mergers and Matrimony, 1898–1900

1. F&S, p. 138; A. D. Chandler Jr., *The Visible Hand: The Managerial Revolution in American Business* (Cambridge, Mass., 1977), esp. pp. 315–39; N. R. Lamoreaux, *The Great Merger Movement in American Business, 1895–1904* (Cambridge, 1985); M. J. Sklar, *The Corporate Reconstruction of American Capitalism, 1890–1916: The Market, the Law and Politics* (Cambridge, 1988); A. P. O'Brien, "Factory Size, Economics of Scale and the Great Merger Wave of 1898–1902," *Journal of Economic History* 48 (1988), pp. 639–49.

2. *Letters*, pp. 203–204; Judge, pp. 285, 288, 293.

3. TM to J. B. Corey, December 31, 1900, quoted in Judge, p. 292.

4. TM papers: A. Carnegie to TM, January 11, 1897.

5. Judge, p. 286; BJH papers: interview, Mrs. E. Frazier, April 10, 1940, p. 3.

6. Judge, p. 288; *JMS*, pp. 310–11.

7. O'Connor, p. 56; TM papers: Last Will and Testament of Thomas A. Mellon, January 23, 1899.

8. BJH papers: interviews, WLM, March 17, 1941, p. 5; WAM, March 7, 1941, p. 3; PM papers: interview no. 2, p. 16.

9. *JMS*, pp. 193–207; Larimer Family Papers: f 311, A. L. Jones to W. H. H. Larimer, December 8, 1895.

10. J. N. Ingham, "Reaching for Respectability: The Pittsburgh Industrial Elite at the Turn of the Century," in G. P. Weisberg, D. E. McIntosh, and A. McQueen (eds.), *Collecting in the Gilded Age: Art Patronage in Pittsburgh, 1890–1910* (Pittsburgh, 1997), pp. 18–20; Lorant, p. 233; Samber, p. 120.

11. Judge, p. 221; *JMS*, pp. 311–12; Sparkes papers: interview, RKM, October 18, 1944, pp. 2–7, 10; S. M. Scaife, November 18, 1944, pp. 2, 12; PM papers: interview no. 3, pp. 1–3. RBM paid a sentimental visit to Bismarck near the very end of his life: *Bismarck Tribune*, October 17, 1932.

12. P. Krass, *Carnegie* (Hoboken, N.J., 2002), p. 248; J. Strouse, *Morgan: American Financier* (New York, 1999), p. 216; R. Chernow, *Titan: The Life of John D. Rockefeller Sr.* (New York, 1998), pp. 343–44.

13. Quoted in F. C. Jaher, "The Gilded Elite: American Multimillionaires, 1865 to

the Present," in W. D. Rubinstein (ed.), *Wealth and the Wealthy in the Modern World* (London, 1980), pp. 195–97.

14. Ingham, "Reaching for Respectability," pp. 34–35; PM papers: interview no. 1, pp. 4, 25.

15. PM papers: interview no. 1, pp. 25–27.

16. Ingham, "Reaching for Respectability," pp. 12–13, 38–39; K. Warren, *Triumphant Capitalism: Henry Clay Frick and the Industrial Transformation of America* (Pittsburgh, 1996), pp. 226, 229.

17. F. G. Couvares, *The Remaking of Pittsburgh: Class and Culture in an Industrializing City, 1877–1919* (Albany, N.Y., 1984), pp. 96–97; E. Moorehead, *Whirling Spindle: The Story of a Pittsburgh Family* (Pittsburgh, 1942), pp. 233, 256.

18. Krass, *Carnegie*, pp. 322–27; Couvares, *Remaking of Pittsburgh*, pp. 97–99, 105–107.

19. W. J. Hyett, "Some Collections of Paintings in Pittsburgh," *Art and Archaeology* 14 (1922), pp. 323–29; Department of Fine Arts, Carnegie Institute, Pittsburgh, *An Exhibition of the Alexander M. Byers Collection of Paintings* (Pittsburgh, 1932); A. McQueen, "Private Art Collections in Pittsburgh: Displays of Culture, Wealth and Connoisseurship," in Weisberg et al., *Collecting in the Gilded Age*, pp. 53–105; D. E. McIntosh, "Demand and Supply: The Pittsburgh Art Trade and M. Knoedler & Co.," in Weisberg et al., *Collecting in the Gilded Age*, pp. 112–14, 165.

20. McIntosh, "Demand and Supply," p. 166.

21. M. F. S. Sanger, *Henry Clay Frick: An Intimate Biography* (New York, 1998), pp. 287, 541–43. The Rembrandt attribution has subsequently been shown to have been mistaken.

22. BJH papers: interview, Mr. Richards, March 15, 1941, p. 1; R. C. Alberts, *Pitt: The Story of the University of Pittsburgh, 1787–1987* (Pittsburgh, 1986), pp. 47–48.

23. McQueen, "Private Art Collections in Pittsburgh," pp. 62–63.

24. Ingham, "Reaching for Respectability," p. 19.

25. McQueen, "Private Art Collections in Pittsburgh," p. 95.

26. McIntosh, "Demand and Supply," p. 153.

27. AWM papers: Knoedler & Co. to AWM, January 18, 1899.

28. McIntosh, "Demand and Supply," p. 155; J. Walker, *Self-Portrait with Donors* (Boston, 1974), p. 104.

29. BJH papers: interview, C. D. Marshall, April 8, 1940, p. 4.

30. Jaher, "The Gilded Elite," pp. 189–90, drawing on O. Fenichel, "The Drive to Amass Wealth," *Psychoanalytic Quarterly* 7 (1938), pp. 69–95.

31. A. W. Attwood, *The Mind of the Millionaire* (New York, 1926), p. 10; A. Carnegie, *Problems of Today* (New York, 1908), p. 35; H. Brogan, *The Penguin History of the USA*, 2nd ed. (London, 1999), pp. 388–89.

32. Sparkes papers: interview, DEF, March 1, 1945, pp. 7, 18.

33. AWM papers: T. Mellon and Mary McClung v. AWM and Estate of RBM, Statement as to Claim, Exhibit L.

34. Hendrick, ch. 7, pp. 27–29; ch. 8, pp. 13–14; Smith, p. 445; Alcoa papers: Drawer 7, Envelope 185: B. Hendrick to R. A. Hunt, January 20, 1941; AWM to F. W. Matthiessen, February 1, 1899; AWM to J. G. A. Leishman, February 10, 1899; W. S. Mitchell to J. W. Seaver, February 28, 1899.

35. AWM papers: RBM to F. Haskell, April 18, 1900, October 12, 1900; BJH papers: interview, F. H. Manley, February 4, 1941, p. 2.

36. White, pp. 48–50.

37. Hendrick, ch. 6, pp. 5–6; *Pittsburgh First*, May 30, 1925, p. 3; *Pittsburgh Press*, August 22, 1935.

38. Samber, pp. 175–89; *MNBTC*, pp. 24–29; Union Trust papers: 06-01-00-011-0009, Capital Surplus and Profit and Loss Account, 1898 to 1908.

39. For the general picture, see L. Neal, "Trust Companies and Financial Innovation, 1897–1914," *Business History Review* 45 (1971), pp. 35–51.

40. *JMS*, pp. 297–98; Hendrick, ch. 5, p. 19; HCF papers: Miscellaneous Letters, HCF to AWM, May 10, 1899.

41. M. Brignano and J. Tomlinson Fort, *Reed Smith: A Law Firm Celebrates 125 Years* (Pittsburgh, 2002), pp. 31–32; Warren, *Triumphant Capitalism*, pp. 204–68; Krass, *Carnegie*, pp. 360–95; Frick papers: Miscellaneous Letters, HCF to AWM, April 13, 19, 1900; AWM to HCF, April 20, 1900.

42. Samber, pp. 193–95; *JMS*, pp. 299–300; Hendrick, ch. 5, pp. 20–21.

43. Warren, *Triumphant Capitalism*, pp. 279–86; Frick papers: Miscellaneous Letters, AWM to HCF, August 25, 1900, AWM to Col. Harvey, June 25, 1927; Letterbook, December 2, 1899, to December 7, 1900, HCF to AWM, August 23, 1900.

44. AWM papers: A. Carnegie to AWM, August 28, 1900; AWM to HCF, September 7, 1900; BJH papers: interview, W. H. Donner, May 23, 1940, pp. 1–3.

45. Warren, *Triumphant Capitalism*, pp. 288–94.

46. HCF papers: Letterbook, April 30, 1898, to February 16, 1899, HCF to AWM, February 13, 1899.

47. *50 Years: New York Shipbuilding Corporation* (Camden, N.J., 1949), pp. 11–19.

48. Samber, pp. 195–97; *JMS*, pp. 300–304.

49. *JMS*, p. 309; BJH papers: D. E. Shepard to AWM, February 14, 1935, enclosing Memorandum in re: McClintic-Marshall Corporation, pp. 1–2.

50. Brignano and Tomlinson Fort, *Reed Smith*, p. 23; Samber, pp. 199–200; BJH papers: interview, C. D. Marshall, April 8, 1940, pp. 1–6.

51. W. H. Colvin Jr., *"Crucible Steel of America": 50 Years of Specialty Steelmaking in the U.S.A.* (New York, 1950), pp. 11–12.

52. This and the next two paragraphs draw heavily on Samber, pp. 207–16.

53. G. H. Love, *An Exciting Century in Coal (1864–1964)* (New York, 1955), pp. 11–12.

54. *JMS*, pp. 239–52; J. W. Jordan, *A Century and a Half of Pittsburgh and Her People*, vol. 4 (Pittsburgh, 1908), pp. 362–63; R. J. Spence (ed.), *Yearbook of the Pennsylvania Society, 1931* (New York, 1931), pp. 94–95; L. C. Walkinshaw, *Annals of Southwestern Pennsylvania*, vol. 4 (New York, 1939), pp. 402–403.

55. Pittsburgh Railway Companies papers: 74:29, Book 20, pp. 60–61.

56. For examples, see Pittsburgh Railway Companies papers: 74:29, Book 9, pp. 1118, 1125; Book 27, p. 805; Book 28, pp. 975–76; Book 29, pp. 1090–91.

57. Hendrick, ch. 6, p. 40.

58. Spring Valley Mining and Irrigating Company papers: Box 5, f6, AWM to L. J. Hohl, April 24, 1900; f24, AWM to L. J. Hohl, June 15, 1900; f34, AWM to L. J. Hohl, July 27, 1900.

59. DEF, notes of a conversation with AWM, July 28, 30, 1929. I am most grateful to David A. Doheny for this reference.

60. Samber, pp. 220–24.

61. Warren, *Triumphant Capitalism*, p. 285.

62. *JMS*, p. 312; Hendrick, ch. 10, p. 4; PM papers: interview no. 1, pp. 4–5.

63. Hendrick, ch. 10, p. 2.

64. Hendrick, ch. 10, p. 3.

65. Hendrick, ch. 5, p. 26.

66. Hendrick, ch. 10, p. 5.

67. Hendrick, ch. 10, p. 5; BJH papers: interview, NMM, November 25, 1940, p. 3.

68. H. J. Hanham, *Elections and Party Management: Politics in the Time of Gladstone and Disraeli* (Hassocks, U.K., 1978), pp. 42, 44–45, 397, 410; H. Pelling, *Social Geography of British Elections, 1885–1910* (London, 1967), pp. 68–74; L. Stone and J. C. F. Stone, *An Open Elite? England, 1540–1880* (Oxford, 1984), pp. 45–47.

69. F. M. Page, *History of Hertford*, 2nd ed. (Hertford, U.K., 1993), pp. 73, 162–63, 170, 180–82; N. Pevsner and B. Cherry, *Hertfordshire*, 2nd ed. (Harmondsworth, U.K., 1953), pp. 185–87.

70. BJH papers: interview, NMM, November 25, 1940, p. 1.

71. M. Cornell, "The McMullen Story," *The Labologists Society Newsletter*, no. 4, September 1980, pp. 1–3; J. Burgess, "Hertfordshire's Only Brewers Have Been 150 Years in Business," *Hertfordshire Countryside*, vol. 32, June 1977, pp. 32–33; M. Small, "Peter the Poacher," *Hertfordshire Countryside*, vol. 46, December 1991, p. 22.

72. *Hertfordshire Guardian*, March 6, 1902; *Hertfordshire Mercury*, March 8, 1902; P. Kingsford, "Interest and Policy in the Hertfordshire County Council, 1889–1908," in D. Jones-Baker (ed.), *Hertfordshire in History: Papers Presented to Lionel Munby* (Hertford, U.K., 1991), p. 267.

73. *TMT*, pp. 99, 228, 386.

74. *TMT*, pp. 100–14, 384.

75. Hendrick, ch. 10, p. 12; BJH papers: interview, NMM, November 25, 1940, p. 4; *TMT*, p. xix; *RSS*, p. 28.

76. AWM papers: NMM to AWM, March 20, 1899.

77. AWM papers: AWM to NMM, April 9, 1899.

78. DEF papers (NGA): Box 37, DEF Memorandum, June 8, 1935.

79. BJH papers: interview, NMM, November 25, 1940, p. 4.

80. AWM papers: NMM to AWM, August 28, 1899.

81. AWM papers: NMM to AWM, August 31, 1899.

82. AWM papers: NMM to AWM, October 6, 1899.

83. *RSS*, pp. 26–27; BJH papers: interview, NMM, November 25, 1940, p. 2; PM papers: interview no. 1, pp. 5, 15.

84. PM papers: interview no. 2, pp. 6–7; notes on the McMullen family by Launcelot McMullen, undated and in the author's possession.

85. AWM papers: NMM to AWM, December 15, 1899, January 14, 1900; BJH papers: interview, NMM, November 25, 1940, p. 4.

86. HCF papers: Miscellaneous Letters, AWM to HCF, May 4, 1900.

87. *RSS*, p. 30.

88. BJH papers: NMM to AWM, May 11, 25, 1900, June 5, 1900.

89. BJH papers: NMM to AWM, May 18, 1900, June 5, 6, 16, 1900, July 26, 1900.

90. *JMS*, p. 314.

91. J. N. Ingham, *The Iron Barons: A Social Analysis of an American Urban Elite, 1874–1965* (Westport, Conn., 1978), p. 224.

92. BJH papers: interview, NMM, November 25, 1940, p. 8; M. E. Montgomery, *Gilded Prostitution: Status, Money and Transatlantic Marriages, 1870–1914* (London, 1989), esp. pp. 29–65.

93. *JMS*, p. 313.

94. *TMT*, pp. 103, 228, 411, 455.

95. BJH papers: interview, C. D. Marshall, April 8, 1940, p. 6.

96. BJH papers: interview, NMM, November 25, 1940, p. 1; *JMS*, p. 315.

97. Huntland Downs papers: RBM diary, September 12, 1900; AWM papers: RBM to F. Haskell, October 12, 1900.

98. AWM papers: Wedding of AWM and NMM, congratulatory cables, September 12, 1900.

99. Warren, *Triumphant Capitalism*, p. 285; BJH papers: NMM, November 25, 1940, p. 5; Frick papers: HCF Letterbook, December 2, 1899, to December 7, 1900, HCF to AWM, August 23, 1900, September 7, 1900; AWM papers: Mrs. McMullen to NMM, October 3, 1900.

100. Hendrick, ch. 10, pp. 18–20; BJH papers: interview, NMM, November 25, 1940, pp. 5–6 (emphasis added).

101. BJH papers: interview, NMM, November 25, 1940, pp. 6–8; PM papers: interview no. 1, pp. 24–25; interview no. 5, p. 19.

102. *RSS*, p. 31; AWM papers: AWM divorce deposition, p. 3.

5. The Transition Completed:
Family Man and Venture Capitalist, 1901–1907

1. AWM papers: AWM divorce deposition, p. 2.

2. *RSS*, pp. 34–35; AWM papers: AWM to F. Haskell, November 25, 1901.

3. Koskoff, p. 128; M. E. Montgomery, *Gilded Prostitution: Status, Money and Transatlantic Marriages, 1870–1914* (London, 1989), pp. 59–62; J. Gerard, "Lady Bountiful: Women of the Landed Classes and Rural Philanthropy," *Victorian Studies* 30 (1987), pp. 183–210; P. Gordon, "Introduction," in P. Gordon (ed.), *Politics and Society: The Journals of Lady Knightley of Fawsley, 1885 to 1913* (Northampton, U.K., 1999), pp. 1–43.

4. *RSS*, pp. 32–33.

5. AWM papers: AWM divorce deposition, p. 3.

6. AWM papers: N. McMullen to AWM, February 2, 1904; AWM Letterbooks, 1903–1925, AWM to T. Jefferson Coolidge Jr., June 2, 1906.

7. AWM papers: L. McMullen to AWM, September 8, 1905, December 3, 1907, February 4, 1908, March 16, 25, 1908; N. McMullen to AWM, February 2, 1904, June 2, 1908.

8. BJH papers: interview with CRH and CHM, November 10, 1941, pp. 1–2.

9. Knoedler papers: Domestic Letterbook, February 15, 1901–April 24, 1901, CSC

to AWM, February 23, 1901; Domestic Letterbook, January 9, 1903–March 24, 1903, CSC to AWM, February 20, 1903, March 14, 17, 21, 1903; Domestic Letterbook, December 28, 1903–April 11, 1904, CSC to AWM, February 2, 1904; Domestic Letterbook, April 11, 1904–October 19, 1904, CSC to AWM, October 20, 1904; D. E. McIntosh, "Demand and Supply: The Pittsburgh Art Trade and M. Knoedler & Co.," in G. P. Weisberg, D. E. McIntosh, and A. McQueen (eds.), *Collecting in the Gilded Age: Art Patronage in Pittsburgh, 1890–1910* (Pittsburgh, 1997), p. 159.

10. McIntosh, "Demand and Supply," pp. 156, 159.

11. Kopper, pp. 53–54; Knoedler papers: Domestic Letterbook, October 22, 1901–January 2, 1902, CSC to AWM, November 11, 14, 27, 1901.

12. W. G. Constable, *Art Collecting in the United States of America: An Outline of a History* (London, 1964), pp. 91–120; F. G. Santori, *The Melancholy of Masterpieces: Old Master Paintings in America, 1900–1914* (Milan, 2003), pp. 11–70.

13. Knoedler papers: Domestic Letterbook, October 22, 1901–February 2, 1902, CSC to AWM, December 27, 1901; Domestic Letterbook, January 4, 1902–March 24, 1902, CSC to AWM, February 6, 1902; Domestic Letterbook, September 2, 1902–January 9, 1903, Knoedler & Co. to AWM, October 30, 1902; Domestic Letterbook, January 9, 1903–March 24, 1903, CSC to AWM, February 20, 1903, March 12, 14, 1903; Domestic Letterbook, April 11, 1904–October 19, 1904, CSC to AWM, October 27, 1904.

14. Kopper, p. 55; McIntosh, "Demand and Supply," p. 159.

15. Knoedler papers: Domestic Letterbook, December 28, 1903–April 11, 1904, CSC to AWM, March 9, 1904; Domestic Letterbook, April 11, 1904–October 19, 1904, Knoedler & Co. to AWM, October 17, 1904.

16. J. Walker, *Self-Portrait with Donors: Confessions of an Art Collector* (Boston, 1974), p. 104; AWM papers: Estate of AWM, Paintings at Woodland Road, Affidavit of CHM, February 10, 1938.

17. McIntosh, "Demand and Supply," pp. 166–69.

18. BJH papers: interviews, Dr. E. R. Weidlen, April 14, 1940, p. 2; S. and A. Scaife, November 4, 1940, p. 3.

19. F&S, pp. 152–53; Samber, pp. 143–47, 151–52, 158–62, 375–83.

20. K. Warren, *Triumphant Capitalism: Henry Clay Frick and the Industrial Transformation of America* (Pittsburgh, 1996), pp. 295–99; J. Strouse, *Morgan: American Financier* (New York, 1999), pp. 403–405; J. F. Wall, *Andrew Carnegie*, 2nd ed. (Pittsburgh, 1989), pp. 780–93; P. Krass, *Carnegie* (Hoboken, N.J., 2002), pp. 409–13; R. H. Demmler, *The First Century of an Institution: Reed Smith Shaw & McClay* (Pittsburgh, 1977), pp. 22–27, 28–32; M. Brignano and J. Tomlinson Fort, *Reed Smith: A Law Firm Celebrates 125 Years* (Pittsburgh, 2002), pp. 31–38.

21. T. R. Navin and M. V. Sears, "The Rise of a Market for Industrial Securities, 1887–1902," *Business History Review* 29 (1955), pp. 105–38; M. V. Sears, "The National Shawmut Bank Consolidation of 1898," *Business History Review* 39 (1965), pp. 368–90; N. Lamoreaux, "Bank Mergers in Late Nineteenth-Century New England: The Contingent Nature of Structural Change," *Journal of Economic History* 51 (1991), pp. 537–57.

22. F. Redlich, *The Molding of American Banking: Men and Ideas* (New York, 1968), pt. 2, pp. 175–81, 186–93.

23. J. J. Binder and D. T. Brown, "Bank Rates of Return and Entry Restrictions, 1869–1914," *Journal of Economic History* 51 (1991), p. 52; P. B. Trescott, *Financing American Enterprise: The Story of Commercial Banking* (New York, 1963), pp. 69–70; B. J. Klebaner, *American Commercial Banking: A History* (Boston, 1990), pp. 70–77, 90–91.

24. BJH papers: interviews, DEF, March 27, 1940, p. 3; S. and A. Scaife, November 4, 1940, pp. 2–3.

25. Samber, pp. 179–80, 183–84.

26. Hendrick, ch. 6, p. 4; Samber, p. 185; AWM papers: T. A. Mellon and Mary McClung v. AWM and Estate of RBM, Statement as to Claim, Exhibit L.

27. Samber, pp. 145–46; White, pp. 19, 51–53; AWM papers: W. S. Mitchell to Messrs. R. G. Dun & Co., June 7, 1902; List of Board of Directors of Mellon National Bank, January 12, 1904.

28. AWM papers: Agreement Between AWM, RBM, and HCF [undated, 1902]; T. A. Mellon and Mary McClung v. AWM and Estate of RBM, [copy] meeting of Board of Directors, Mellon National Bank, July 3, 1902; transcript of article in *Pittsburgh Dispatch*, May 29, 1902; Docket no. 76499, pp. 4615–20.

29. Hendrick, ch. 6, p. 6; AWM papers: HCF to AWM, April 17, 1902, May 2, 1902; HCF papers: Letterbook, March 20, 1903–March 26, 1903, HCF to AWM, May 11, 1903.

30. Warren, *Triumphant Capitalism*, p. 334.

31. Hendrick, ch. 6, p. 8; White, pp. 21, 50; Mellon Bank papers: Box 1310, Union Savings Bank of Pittsburgh, f06-05-00-002-0001, Report for July 14, 1902; f06-05-002-0002, *The Union Savings Bank of Pittsburgh* [Pittsburgh, n.d.].

32. *MNBTC*, pp. 23–24, 33; Mellon Bank papers: Box 604, f04-01-02-002-0001, *The Story of Mellon Bank* (Pittsburgh, 1911), tables; f04-01-02-002-0003, memorandum [undated].

33. Samber, p. 177.

34. Hendrick, ch. 6, pp. 9–10.

35. AWM papers: T. A. Mellon and Mary McClung v. AWM and Estate of RBM, memorandum [undated], pp. 5–6; trust agreement, October 16, 1905; trust dissolution document, June 19, 1919.

36. Smith, pp. 82–87, 96–97, 445; AWM papers: AWM to F. Haskell, July 6, 9, 20, 1901, November 12, 1901; AWM Letterbooks, AWM to F. Haskell, November 3, 1906; Acheson papers: Container 20: Agreement between E. G. Acheson and Carborundum Co., July 5, 1901; E. G. Acheson, *A Pathfinder: Inventor, Scientist, Industrialist* (Port Huron, Mich., 1965), pp. 43–47.

37. Hendrick, ch. 8, p. 6; Samber, pp. 190, 193, 197. For the New York Shipbuilding Company, see Warren, *Triumphant Capitalism*, p. 294; AWM papers: AWM Letterbooks, 1903–1925, AWM to T. Jefferson Coolidge Jr., June 2, 1906.

38. McCormick papers: AWM to S. B. McCormick, June 2, 1906; S. B. McCormick to AWM, January 2, 1907, December 10, 1907; R. C. Albers, *Pitt: The Story of the University of Pittsburgh, 1787–1987* (Pittsburgh, 1986), pp. 56–62.

39. *JMS*, pp. 252–54.

40. *Pittsburgh Commercial Gazette*, October 1, 1901.

41. AWM papers: Letterbooks, vol. 6, pp. 370–75 (undated [June 1911]); Hendrick, ch. 6, p. 42; *Pittsburgh Commercial Gazette*, October 8, 1901; *Day and Night for*

Forty Years: Philadelphia Company and Affiliated Corporations (Pittsburgh, 1925), list of officers and directors.

42. HCF papers: Letterbook, December 2, 1899–December 7, 1900, HCF to AWM, September 7, 1900.

43. Hendrick, ch. 5, p. 21; HCF papers: AWM to HCF, September 20, 1903; AWM papers: AWM to Col. Harvey, June 25, 1927.

44. Hendrick papers: interview, W. H. Donner, May 28, 1940, p. 4.

45. Samber, pp. 193–95.

46. Samber, pp. 207–21.

47. Pittsburgh Coal Company papers: Minutes of the Board of Directors, November 10, 1903.

48. Pittsburgh Coal Company papers: Minutes of the Board of Directors, February 19, 1904; Minutes of Executive Committee, May 29, 1906.

49. *Hertfordshire Guardian*, March 6, 13, 1902; *Hertfordshire Mercury*, March 8, 1902.

50. Koskoff papers: K. G. Raffield to D. Koskoff, March 18, 1977, October 7, 15, 31, 1977, November 7, 1977.

51. AWM papers: AWM divorce deposition, p. 4.

52. Rainhill Lunatic Asylum papers: Sutton County Lunatic Asylum, Record Book, entry under Samuel Curphey; *St. Helens Newspaper and Advertiser*, December 17, 1878.

53. *The Times*, June 20, 1893; marriage certificate of Alfred Curphey and Grace Robertson, June 15, 1893.

54. TNA: PRO: Court for Divorce and Matrimonial Causes papers: J77/833/5342: G. D. H. Curphey v. A. G. Curphey, Document no. 1, G. Curphey to A. Curphey, November 16, 1904.

55. AWM papers: AWM divorce deposition, pp. 4, 7.

56. AWM papers: AWM divorce deposition, p. 5.

57. AWM papers: AWM divorce deposition, p. 8.

58. AWM papers: NMM to AWM, February 26, 28, 1903.

59. AWM papers: NMM to AWM, February 24, 1903.

60. AWM papers: A. Curphey to AWM, January 28, 31, 1903, February 9, 1903; Brown, Shipley & Co. to AWM, February 4, 1903.

61. AWM papers: AWM divorce deposition, pp. 5–6.

62. AWM papers: AWM divorce deposition, pp. 7–8.

63. AWM papers: AWM divorce deposition, p. 8; NMM to AWM, June 7, 1903.

64. AWM papers: AWM divorce deposition, p. 9; *RSS*, p. 35.

65. AWM papers: AWM divorce deposition, pp. 9–10.

66. AWM papers: AWM divorce deposition, pp. 7, 9–10.

67. AWM papers: N. McMullen to AWM, February 2, 1904.

68. AWM papers: AWM divorce deposition, p. 14; BJH papers: A. Curphey to AWM, June 30, 1904.

69. AWM papers: AWM divorce deposition, p. 15; BJH papers: Mrs. McMullen to AWM, August 17, 1904.

70. AWM papers: AWM divorce deposition, pp. 16–17; *RSS*, p. 37.

71. AWM papers: Brown, Shipley & Co. to AWM, July 20, 29, 1904, August 3, 1904.

72. AWM papers: AWM divorce deposition, pp. 16–18.

73. AWM papers: AWM divorce deposition, p. 19; BJH papers: NMM to AWM, November 24, 1905; AWM papers: NMM to AWM, January 25, 28, 1905, February 2, 1905, May 19, 1905; M. F. S. Sanger, *Henry Clay Frick: An Intimate Portrait* (New York, 1998), pp. 294–95.

74. AWM papers: Letterbooks, 1903–1925, AWM to Messrs. M. Samuel & Co., December 1, 1905.

75. AWM papers: AWM divorce deposition, pp. 19–21.

76. P. Kelly, "At Home at Ballamoar," *Manx Life*, April 1981, pp. 9–14; P. Kelly, "Alfred Curphey—A Manx Mystery Man," *Manx Independent*, March 22, 1996, p. 10; *Isle of Man Examiner*, August 27, 1904; *Ramsay Courier and Northern Advertiser*, November 11, 1904, September 1, 1905. For the broader context, see: R. Prentice, "Social Infrastructure," in V. Robinson and D. McCarroll (eds.), *The Isle of Man: Celebrating a Sense of Place* (Liverpool, 1990), pp. 171–72; G. Davies, "Agriculture, Forestry and Fishing," in Robinson and McCarroll, *Isle of Man*, pp. 207–208; D. Kermode, "Constitutional Development and Public Policy, 1900–79," in J. Belchem (ed.), *A New History of the Isle of Man*, vol. 5, *The Modern Period, 1830–1999* (Liverpool, 2000), pp. 94–125; D. Winterbottom, "Economic History, 1830–1966," in Belchem, *Modern Period*, pp. 219–35.

77. NA: PRO: Court for Divorce and Matrimonial Causes papers: J77/833/5342: G. D. H. Curphey v. A. G. Curphey, Document no. 4; *Peel City Guardian and Chronicle*, September 22, 1906; *Ramsay Courier and Northern Advertiser*, September 14, 1906.

78. *The Times*, May 27, 1909; Y. Toussaint, *Les Barons Empain* (Paris, 1996), p. 120; F. Hassan, "The Wonderful Wizard of On," *Al-Ahram Weekly On-line*, July 9–15, 1998: http://weekly.ahram.org.eg/1998/385/feature.htm.

79. *Ramsay Courier and Northern Advertiser*, November 23, 1906.

80. Warren, *Triumphant Capitalism*, pp. 336–37; E. Morris, *Theodore Rex* (New York, 2001), pp. 61–62, 329–30.

81. L. L. Gould, *Grand Old Party: A History of the Republicans* (New York, 2003), p. 148; Morris, *Theodore Rex*, pp. 27–34, 59–65, 71–76, 87–94, 304–305, 313–16; Strouse, *Morgan*, pp. 431–34, 440–43, 460–61, 533–35.

82. R. Sylla, "American Banking and Growth in the Nineteenth Century: A Partial View of the Terrain," *Explorations in Economic History* 9 (1971–72), pp. 200–201.

83. Samber, pp. 197–99.

84. Sparkes papers: interview, W. Bierman, June 25, 1945, pp. 1–2.

85. BJH papers: interview, Mr. Gillespie, April 30, 1941, p. 1.

86. BJH papers: interview, Col. F. Drake, June 9, 1942, pp. 8–9.

87. For this section, see: Hendrick, ch. 12, pp. 1–49; Samber, pp. 201–204; S. A. Swensrud, *"Gulf Oil": The First Fifty Years* (New York, 1951), pp. 8–14.

88. AWM papers: T. Mellon & Sons Letterbooks, W. S. Mitchell to J. M. Guffey, December 29, 1900, April 1, 1901; J. M. Guffey and J. H. Galey in account with T. Mellon & Sons, April 2, 1901; AWM to A. F. Lucas, May 21, 1901.

89. J. A. Clark and M. T. Halbouty, *Spindletop* (New York, 1952), pp. 28–206; BJH papers: interview, WLM, March 17, 1941, p. 2.

90. Hendrick, ch. 12, p. 17.

91. *JMS*, pp. 255–70; AWM papers: T. Mellon & Sons Letterbooks, C. F. Farren to J. M. Guffey, November 21, 1901.

92. AWM papers: T. Mellon & Sons Letterbooks, C. F. Farren to I. Willis, October 16, 1901; AWM to A. C. Dustin, January 22, 1902; AWM to W. B. Dana & Co., June 20, 1902; T. Mellon & Sons to C. M. Schwab, June 24, 1902.

93. Hendrick, ch. 12, pp. 24–25; *JMS*, pp. 269–70; R. Chernow, *Titan: The Life of John D. Rockefeller, Sr.* (New York, 1998), p. 430; BJH papers: interview, G. S. Davison, April 29, 1941, p. 2; AWM papers: AWM Letterbooks, AWM to M. Hunsiker, November 4, 1905.

94. BJH papers: interviews, the Misses Guffey, May 3, 1941, p. 3; J. F. Grundy, March 4, 1941, p. 2; G. S. Davison, April 29, 1941, pp. 3–4.

95. Clark and Halbouty, *Spindletop*, pp. 137–42.

96. *JMS*, pp. 271–87.

97. BJH papers: interview, G. S. Davison, May 2, 1941, pp. 3–4; Chernow, *Titan*, pp. 519–22, 537–59.

98. Hendrick, ch. 12, p. 42; BJH papers: interview, Mr. Hartman, March 13, 1941, p. 2.

99. *Pittsburgh Press*, March 20, 1930; AWM papers: *17 Federal Reporter, 24 Series, Guffey v. Gulf Production Co.*, February 3, 1927, pp. 930–34; BJH papers: G. S. Davison to BJH, September 19, 1941; interview, H. A. Phillips, May 3, 1941, pp. 1–2.

100. AWM papers: T. Mellon & Sons, Statement of Financial Condition at Close of Business, February 28, 1902.

101. Hendrick, ch. 6, pp. 11–12.

102. Samber, pp. 177, 180–83, 185–89.

103. HSWP, Library and Archives Division: *Report on the Pittsburgh Transportation Problem* (Pittsburgh, 1910), pp. 1–11.

104. BJH papers: AWM Letterbooks, AWM to A. W. Thompson, June 24, 1925; D. T. Rodgers, *Atlantic Crossings: Social Politics in a Progressive Age* (Cambridge, Mass., 1998), pp. 140–59.

105. BJH papers: AWM to Miss Stephens, July 15, 1917.

106. BJH papers: interview, J. Nelson, March 8, 1941, p. 1.

107. McIntosh, "Demand and Supply," p. 165.

108. McIntosh, "Demand and Supply," p. 161; Kopper, p. 55; Knoedler papers: London Letterbook, July 17, 1906–February 16, 1907, CSC to AWM, December 28, 1906; Domestic Letterbook, December 10, 1906–March 9, 1907, R. Knoedler to AWM, January 28, 1907.

109. Knoedler papers: London Letterbook, July 17, 1906–February 16, 1907, CSC to John Singer Sargent, January 29, 1907; R. Ormond and E. Kilmurray, *John Singer Sargent: Complete Paintings*, vol. 3, *The Later Portraits* (London, 2003), pp. 87, 111, 15, 156–57, 163.

110. Knoedler papers: Domestic Letterbook, March 9, 1907–July 10, 1907, CSC to AWM, March 6, 1907; C. M. Mount, *John Singer Sargent: A Biography* (New York, 1955), pp. 262–80; T. Fairbrother, *John Singer Sargent* (New York, 1994), pp. 118–20; DEF, notes of a conversation with AWM, July 28, 30, 1929. I am most grateful to David A. Doheny for this reference.

111. Knoedler papers: Domestic Letterbook, March 9, 1907–July 10, 1907, CSC to AWM, April 10, 1907; Domestic Letterbook, December 13, 1907–March 28, 1908; Knoedler & Co. to Mellon National Bank, February 3, 6, 1908; Private Letterbook, August 9, 1907–August 19, 1908, CSC to AWM, April 2, 1908, Knoedler & Co. to Mellon National Bank, July 8, 1908; McIntosh, "Demand and Supply," pp. 162–64.

112. *JMS*, pp. 288–89; AWM papers: Letterbooks, AWM to T. Jefferson Coolidge Jr., October 27, 1906, November 3, 1906; AWM et al. to Gulf Oil Corporation, February 19, 1907; AWM et al. to Union Trust, February 19, 1907; T. Mellon & Sons to Gulf Oil Corporation, April 16, 1907, June 17, 1907.

113. Samber, pp. 190, 204.

114. Koskoff, p. 125.

115. Koskoff, p. 128; PM papers: interview no. 2, p. 8.

116. AWM papers: AWM divorce deposition, pp. 21–22; *RSS*, pp. 38–39.

6. The First Scandal: Separation and Divorce, 1907–12

1. AWM papers: NMM to AWM, October 23, 24, 27, 1907, November 17, 1907.

2. AWM papers: NMM to AWM, October 22, 23, 1907, November 17, 1907.

3. AWM papers: AWM divorce deposition, pp. 22–23; NMM to AWM, October 27, 1907 (emphasis added), December 2, 1907.

4. AWM papers: NMM to AWM, November 22, 1907, December 2, 1907.

5. AWM papers: NMM to AWM, December 6, 1907 (emphasis in original).

6. *TMT*, p. 385.

7. TM papers: TM to "My dear Sons," September 24, 1895.

8. BJH papers: WAM to BJH, June 11, 1942.

9. Judge, pp. 294–95; Carnegie papers: Container 148, AWM to A. Carnegie, February 8, 1908; TM papers: Memorial meeting of the Allegheny County Bar Association, The tenth Day of February, Nineteen Hundred Eight; Funeral Service for Thomas Mellon (Feb. 3, 1813, Feb. 3, 1908).

10. *Pittsburgh Dispatch*, January 20, 1909; TM papers: Funeral Service for Sarah Negley Mellon (Feb. 3, 1817, Jan. 19, 1909).

11. AWM papers: NMM to AWM, March 12, 17, 1908 (emphasis in original).

12. AWM papers: AWM divorce deposition, pp. 22–23; NMM to AWM, June 22, 1908.

13. *Burke's Peerage and Baronetage* (London, 1908), pp. 1740–41; J. Bateman, *The Great Landowners of Great Britain and Ireland*, 4th ed. (London, 1883, repr. New York, 1970), p. 458; *New York Times*, December 30, 1940.

14. *The Times*, December 18, 1907; *Daily Mail*, December 18, 1907.

15. AWM papers: C. E. Long, Deposition, July 31, 1911–August 2, 1911, pp. 9–13.

16. NA: PRO: Court for Divorce and Matrimonial Causes papers: J77/923/8023: *Baron Vivian v. Lady Vivian and A. Curphey*, Document no. 5; *Ramsay Courier and Northern Advertiser*, October 4, 1907, December 6, 10, 24, 1907.

17. *Ramsay Courier and Northern Advertiser*, January 10, 17, 1908.

18. *The Times*, December 18, 1907, May 27, 1909; *Ramsay Courier and Northern Advertiser*, January 28, 1908.

19. P. Kelly, "At Home at Ballamoar," *Manx Life*, April 1981, pp. 13–14; *Isle of Man Examiner*, March 28, 1908; *Ramsay Courier and Northern Advertiser*, March 24, 1908; AWM papers: C. E. Long, Deposition, July 31, 1911–August 2, 1911, pp. 163, 173–74.

20. A. McQueen, "Private Art Collections in Pittsburgh: Displays of Culture, Wealth and Connoisseurship," in G. P. Weisberg, D. E. McIntosh, and A. McQueen (eds.), *Collecting in the Gilded Age: Art Patronage in Pittsburgh, 1890–1910* (Pittsburgh, 1997), pp. 74–75, 101; D. E. McIntosh, "Demand and Supply: The Pittsburgh Art Trade and M. Knoedler & Co.," in Weisberg et al., *Collecting in the Guilded Age*, pp. 127, 129, 164; Knoedler papers: Domestic Letterbook, September 10, 1908–January 4, 1909, Knoedler & Co. to AWM, December 5, 14, 1908.

21. M. F. S. Sanger, *Henry Clay Frick: An Intimate Biography* (New York, 1998), pp. 315, 488, 490, 545.

22. BJH papers: interview, CRH and CHM, November 10, 1941, p. 2.

23. J. Holsby and P. Harris (eds.), *Dictionary of Scottish Painters, 1600 to the Present* (Edinburgh, 1998), p. 149; H. Mann, *The Technique of Portrait Painting* (Philadelphia, 1943); "Exhibition, Jacques Seligmann Galleries," *Art News*, March 18, 1933, p. 6; R. Beer, "As They Are," *Art News*, May 12, 1934, p. 11.

24. AWM papers: NMM to AWM, June 23, 1908; Knoedler papers: Domestic Letterbook, October 22, 1908–February 3, 1909, CSC to AWM [undated]; Domestic Letterbook, January 4, 1909–April 1909, Knoedler & Co. to AWM, March 17, 1909; Domestic Letterbook, November 22, 1909–February 7, 1910, CSC to AWM, January 21, 1910; PM papers: interview no. 4, pp. 12–13.

25. *Oxford Dictionary of National Biography* (Oxford, 2004), vol. 49, p. 989; B. D. Gallati, "Portraits of Aristocracy and Artifice: The Career of Sir James J. Shannon, 1862–1923" (Ph.D. diss., City University of New York, 1992), pp. 98–111; PM papers: interview no. 4, p. 14.

26. AWM papers: AWM to NMM, September 27, 1909; Knoedler papers: Domestic Letterbook, September 20, 1911–November 24, 1911, R. F. Knoedler to AWM, November 3, 1911; AWM to M. Knoedler, November 30, 1912; Domestic Letterbook, April 2, 1912–May 20, 1912, Knoedler & Co., to AWM, May 8, 1912; AWM to Knoedler & Co. [undated, but received July 11, 1913].

27. AWM papers: Divorce hearing, testimony of AWM, May 20, 1912, pp. 44–46.

28. *RSS*, pp. 44–45; AWM papers: C. E. Long, deposition, July 31, 1911–August 2, 1911, pp. 115–17; AWM divorce deposition, pp. 23–29.

29. AWM papers: C. E. Long, deposition, July 31, 1911–August 2, 1911, pp. 71, 108–10, 125; *RSS*, p. 39; PM papers: interview no. 2, p. 15.

30. AWM papers: C. E. Long, deposition, July 31, 1911–August 2, 1911, pp. 16–28; divorce hearing, testimony of AWM, May 20, 1912, pp. 34–35.

31. AWM papers: AWM divorce deposition, p. 29; R. S. Taylor, Son & Humbert to AWM, October 29, 1908.

32. AWM papers: C. E. Long, deposition, July 31, 1911–August 2, 1911, pp. 41–60.

33. AWM papers: Divorce hearing, testimony of AWM, May 20, 1912, pp. 36–37.

34. AWM papers: C. E. Long, deposition, July 31, 1911–August 2, 1911, p. 63; AWM divorce deposition, p. 30.

35. *RSS*, p. 41.

36. AWM papers: C. E. Long, deposition, July 31, 1911–August 2, 1911, pp. 76–85.

37. AWM papers: C. E. Long, deposition, July 31, 1911–August 2, 1911, pp. 88–93; AWM divorce deposition, pp. 31–33; *RSS*, p. 42.

38. AWM papers: C. E. Long, deposition, July 31, 1911–August 2, 1911, pp. 117, 168; *The Times*, April 7, 27, 28, 1909; *London Gazette*, March 12, 1909, April 27, 1909, May 10, 1910.

39. *RSS*, pp. 42–43.

40. AWM papers: AWM divorce deposition, pp. 35–37; divorce hearing, testimony of AWM, May 20, 1912, p. 55.

41. J. N. Ingham, "Steel City Aristocrats," in S. P. Hayes (ed.), *City at the Point: Essays on the Social History of Pittsburgh* (Pittsburgh, 1989), pp. 267, 285; Lorant, pp. 301–14.

42. N. M. Blake, *The Road to Reno: A History of Divorce in the United States* (New York, 1963), esp. pp. 116–88; W. L. O'Neill, *Divorce in the Progressive Era* (New Haven, Conn., 1967), esp. pp. 20, 179–80, 255; G. Riley, *Divorce: An American Tradition* (New York, 1991), pp. 85–129.

43. J. P. Lichtenberger, *Divorce: A Study in Social Causation* (New York, 1909), pp. 169–70; E. T. May, *Great Expectations: Marriage and Divorce in Post-Victorian America* (Chicago, 1980), p. 3.

44. *RSS*, p. 44; AWM papers: Divorce hearing, testimony of James Reed, May 20, 1912, pp. 5–7.

45. AWM papers: AWM divorce deposition, pp. 39–41; divorce hearing, testimony of AWM, May 20, 1912, pp. 61, 66.

46. *RSS*, p. 45.

47. AWM papers: AWM divorce deposition, pp. 42–46; divorce hearing, testimony of AWM, May 20, 1912, p. 57.

48. AWM papers: Chief of County Detectives, Allegheny County, to Superintendent of Detectives, Scotland Yard, May 10, 1909; Acting Secretary, Department of State, to Diplomatic and Consular Officials of the United States, May 14, 1909.

49. AWM papers: AWM divorce deposition, pp. 45–46; AWM and NMM, separation agreements, July 24, 1909, August 4, 1909; Hendrick, ch. 13, pp. 16–17.

50. AWM papers: AWM divorce deposition, pp. 47–48; NMM to AWM, November 30, 1909; A. McMullen to NMM, August 21, 30, 1909, July 15, 1910.

51. AWM papers: C. E. Long, deposition, July 31, 1911–August 2, 1911, pp. 95–102; AWM divorce deposition, pp. 49–50; NMM to AWM, August 26, 28, 29, 1909, September 22, 1909, October 12, 19, 1909, November 16, 28, 30, 1909; AMB to AWM, November 1, 1909, January 21, 27, 1910.

52. AWM papers: E. P. Mellon to AWM, November 3, 5, 1909, December 2, 1909, January 28, 1910, February 6, 1910.

53. AWM papers: AWM to AMB, October 10, 1909.

54. AWM papers: AWM to NMM, April 10, 17, 24, 1910, May 1, 8, 1910.

55. AWM papers: AWM diary, March 23, 26, 28, 1910, April 3, 8, 11, 17, 24, 1910; NMM to AWM, March 28, 1910, April 10, 1910; "Memma" [Miss Abernethy] to NMM, June 1910; A. J. Greenop to AWM, April 2, 1910, June 1, 1910, July 27, 1910, October 15, 1910.

56. *RSS*, pp. 48–49; AWM papers: C. E. Long, deposition, July 31, 1911–August 2, 1911, pp. 133–34, 196–97, 205–12; AWM divorce deposition, pp. 50–51.

57. *RSS*, pp. 49–50; AWM papers: AWM diary, June 12, 13, 14, 1910.

58. AWM papers: AWM divorce deposition, pp. 52–53.

59. AWM papers: AWM diary, June 28, 29, 1910.

60. *RSS*, pp. 51–52, 55; AWM papers: AWM divorce deposition, pp. 54–56; divorce hearing, testimony of AWM, May 20, 1912, pp. 89–90; letters and telegrams from Curphey to NMM in July 1910.

61. AWM papers: AWM divorce deposition, pp. 56–57; divorce reports, September 21, 1910–October 31, 1910.

62. AWM papers: AWM diary, September 14, 15, 1910; "Exemplification of Record," September 15, 1910; R. H. Demmler, *The First Century of an Institution: Reed Smith Shaw & McClay* (Pittsburgh, 1977), pp. 27–28, 46, 57–61; Koskoff, p. 131.

63. AWM papers: AWM diary, March 11, 1911, May 30, 1911, July 14, 17, 19, 1911, August 10, 19, 1911, September 11, 13, 25, 27, 1911, February 12, 1912, May 25, 1912; L. McMullen to AWM, June 18, 23, 1909, March 18, 1910, May 21, 1910, September 21, 1910, October 15, 1910.

64. AWM papers: J. A. McMullen to AWM, October 14, 1910, December 16, 1910; N. McMullen to AWM, December 17, 1910.

65. *RSS*, p. 51; *TMT*, pp. 161–68. For divorce in Pennsylvania, see: G. E. Howard, *A History of Matrimonial Institutions*, 3 vols. (Chicago, 1904), vol. 3, pp. 108–11; Blake, *Road to Reno*, pp. 56–57, 117; T. R. Meehan, " 'Not Made Out of Levity': Evolution of Divorce in Early Pennsylvania," *Pennsylvania Magazine of History and Biography* 92 (1968), pp. 441–64.

66. AWM papers: Divorce reports, September 21, 1910–October 31, 1910.

67. *RSS*, p. 52.

68. AWM papers: AWM diary, November 16, 18, 1910, December 6, 1910, February 6, 23, 1911.

69. *RSS*, pp. 52–54.

70. *Boston Herald*, October 17, 1910; J. F. Rishel, "The Founding Families of Allegheny County: An Examination of Nineteenth-Century Elite Continuity" (Ph.D. diss., University of Pittsburgh, 1975), p. 176.

71. *RSS*, p. 51.

72. AWM papers: C. E. Long, deposition, July 31, 1911–August 2, 1911, pp. 106–107; "Exemplification of Record," June 2, 1911, November 10, 1910, December 2, 9, 20, 1910.

73. AWM papers: J. G. Leishman to AWM, October 28, 1910.

74. E. N. Akin, *Flagler: Rockefeller Partner and Florida Baron* (Gainesville, Fla., 1988), pp. 149–51.

75. AWM papers: AWM diary, February 13, 16, 17, 20, 21, 1910, March 3, 7, 8, 9, 10, 12, 13, 14, 15, 20, 1910, April 1, 6, 8, 12, 17, 19, 20, 1911.

76. Hendrick, ch. 13, pp. 18–20.

77. *RSS*, p. 56.

78. *Pittsburgh Leader*, May 20, 27, 28, 1911.

79. Koskoff, p. 136; G. Seldes, *Witness to a Century* (New York, 1987), pp. 17–20; AWM papers: Divorce hearing, May 20, 1912, testimony of James Reed, p. 21;

testimony of AWM, pp. 69–70; BJH papers: AWM letterbooks, AWM to Dr. Addinsell, December 5, 1910.

80. Hendrick, ch. 13, p. 18; BJH papers: interview, J. T. McKirdy, April 30, 1941, pp. 1–4.

81. *North American*, May 7, 1911.

82. Ibid.

83. *RSS*, pp. 56–60; *North American*, May 8, 1911, June 28, 29, 1911; *Parliamentary Debates, House of Commons*, vol. 26, May 23, 1911, col. 123.

84. *North American*, June 14, 1911.

85. AWM papers: AWM diary, May 6, 8, 1911; *North American*, May 6, 8, 1911, June 13, 1911.

86. *North American*, June 10, 11, 1911.

87. *Daily Telegraph*, June 17, 1911; AWM papers: "Exemplification of Record," June 10, 14, 1911; AWM diary, June 9–15, July 8, 14.

88. AWM papers: C. E. Long, deposition, July 31, 1911–August 2, 1911, pp. 136–51.

89. *North American*, June 28, 1911, August 11, 1911.

90. AWM papers: AWM diary, February 10, 1912, April 4, 1912; "Exemplification of Record," May 25, 1911, November 24, 1911, December 2, 1911, February 10, 1912, April 4, 1912.

91. *North American*, November 15, 1911.

92. AWM papers: AWM diary, February 16, 1912, June 3, 6, 1912; PM papers: interview no. 1, p. 6, 22; no. 2, p. 7; no. 3, pp. 3–4; no. 4, p. 8.

93. AWM papers: AWM diary, April 16, 23, 1912, May 2, 21, 29, 1912, June 19, 1902.

94. AWM papers: AWM diary, May 29, 1912.

95. AWM papers: AWM diary, June 4, 1912.

96. AWM papers: AWM diary, July 3, 1912.

97. *North American*, May 26, 1912.

98. Hendrick, ch. 13, pp. 17–18; AWM papers: Decrees in the Court of Common Pleas, June 1, 1912, July 2, 1912; Court of Common Pleas of Allegheny County, Pennsylvania, AWM v. NMM, no. 229, November Term, 1910: Order, August 8, 1912; AWM diary, October 1, 1912.

99. *New York Times*, December 10, 1945; *National Cyclopaedia of American Biography*, vol. 94 (New York, 1962), pp. 262–63; AWM papers: AWM diary, April 22, 1911, May 2, 29, 1911, November 3, 1911, December 19, 20, 1911, January 3, 11, 1912, February 21, 1912.

100. BJH papers: AWM to Mr. and Mrs. Long, September 5, 1912; Mrs. Long to AWM, January 25, 1915, February 1915, May 13, 1915; AWM papers: C. Long, deposition, July 31–August 2, 1911, pp. 150–52; Greenop & Co. to AWM, October 18, 1915.

101. *The Times*, November 24, 25, 1937; Koskoff papers: K. G. Raffield to D. E. Koskoff, October 7, 1977.

102. *TMT*, pp. 441–42; AWM papers: Divorce hearing, testimony of James Reed, May 20, 1912, p. 13 (emphasis in original).

103. See L. Stone, *Road to Divorce: England, 1530–1987* (Oxford, 1990), pp. 211–28.

104. *North American*, May 26, 1912.

105. AWM papers: L. McMullen to AWM, June 23, 1909.

106. Sparkes papers: interview, H. M. Johnson, June 8, 1945, p. 5.

7. Life Goes On: Business (Almost) as Usual, 1907-14

1. *Pittsburgh Post*, January 1, 1907; Samber, p. 384.

2. N. Faires, "Immigrants and Industry: Peopling the 'Iron City,'" in S. P. Hays (ed.), *City at the Point: Essays on the Social History of Pittsburgh* (Pittsburgh, 1989), p. 10.

3. Samber, pp. 384-85; R. M. Smith, "The Politics of Pittsburgh Flood Control, 1908-1936," *Pennsylvania History* 42 (1975), pp. 5-10.

4. Samber, pp. 397-400.

5. *JMS*, p. 180; F&S, pp. 156-60.

6. L. L. Gould, *Grand Old Party: A History of the Republicans* (New York, 2003), p. 163; R. Sobel, *Panic on Wall Street* (New York, 1968), pp. 297-321; E. Morris, *Theodore Rex* (New York, 2002), pp. 495-99, 504-505; Samber, pp. 385-86; F&S, pp. 166-67.

7. Samber, pp. 165-66, 280-81; J. Strouse, *Morgan: American Financier* (New York, 1999), pp. 573-96.

8. Samber, pp. 258-59, 271, 279-80, 295, 320, 344.

9. Samber, pp. 147, 386-88; Trade Dollar Consolidated Mining Company papers: Box 2, T. B. McKaig to F. Irwin, November 5, 1907; AWM papers: J. R. Mellon to AWM, August 24, 1908.

10. Quoted in E. L. Davin, "Blue Collar Democracy: Ethnic Workers and Class Politics in Pittsburgh's Steel Valley, 1914-1948" (Ph.D. diss., University of Pittsburgh, 1999), p. 47.

11. Lorant, pp. 261-64, 274-75, 288; P. Kleppner, "Government, Parties and Voters in Pittsburgh," in Hays, *City at the Point*, pp. 168-73; R. Lubove, *Twentieth-Century Pittsburgh*, vol. 1, *Government, Business and Environmental Change* (Pittsburgh, 1995), pp. 20-25; F. G. Couvares, *The Remaking of Pittsburgh: Class and Culture in an Industrializing City, 1877-1919* (Albany, N.Y., 1984), pp. 128-29.

12. The six volumes were E. Butler, *Women and the Trades* (New York, 1909); C. Eastman, *Work-Accidents and the Law* (New York, 1910); M. Byington, *Homestead: Households of a Mill Town* (New York, 1910); J. Fitch, *The Steelworkers* (New York, 1911); P. Kellogg et al., *Pittsburgh District: Civic Frontage* (New York, 1914); and P. Kellogg et al., *Wage-Earning Pittsburgh* (New York, 1914). For the fullest discussion of the genesis, contents, reception, and (limited) impact of the Pittsburgh Survey, see M. W. Greenwald and M. Anderson (eds.), *Pittsburgh Surveyed: Social Science and Social Reform in the Early Twentieth Century* (Pittsburgh, 1996).

13. Lubove, *Twentieth-Century Pittsburgh*, vol. 1, pp. 7-19.

14. S. R. Cohen, "Reconciling Industrial Conflict and Democracy: The Pittsburgh Survey and the Growth of Social Research in the United States" (Ph.D. diss., Columbia University, 1981), pp. 52-54; E. K. Muller, "The Pittsburgh Survey and 'Greater Pittsburgh,'" in Greenwald and Anderson, *Pittsburgh Surveyed*, pp. 85-87; M. W. Greenwald, "Visualizing Pittsburgh in the 1900s: Art and

Photography in the Service of Social Reform," in Greenwald and Anderson, pp. 149–51; J. F. Bauman and M. Spratt, "Civic Leaders and Environmental Reform: The Pittsburgh Survey and Urban Planning," in Greenwald and Anderson, pp. 159–60.

15. J. A. Tarr, "Infrastructure and City Building in the Nineteenth and Twentieth Centuries," in Hays, *City at the Point*, pp. 240–44, 248; S. P. Hays, "The Politics of Reform in Municipal Government in the Progressive Era," *Pacific Northwest Quarterly* 55 (1964), pp. 157–69; Lubove, *Twentieth-Century Pittsburgh*, vol. 1, pp. 23–57; Samber, pp. 390–96, 403–409.

16. Lubove, pp. 107–108; Lubove, *Twentieth-Century Pittsburgh*, vol. 1, pp. 5, 61–63; Samber, pp. 389, 449–50.

17. G. E. McLaughlin and R. J. Watkins, "The Problem of Industrial Growth in a Mature Economy," *American Economic Review* 29 (1939), pt. 2, supplement, pp. 6–14; Samber, pp. 446–53.

18. Samber, pp. 167–70.

19. AWM papers: AWM diary, July 7, 1913.

20. AWM papers: RBM to AWM, August 5, 1913.

21. D. T. Rodgers, "In Search of Progressivism," *Reviews in American History*, 10 (1982), pp. 113–32.

22. E. E. Morison et al. (eds.), *The Letters of Theodore Roosevelt*, 8 vols. (Cambridge, Mass. 1954), vol. 5, pp. 855, 859, and vol. 6, p. 1842; J. M. Blum, *The Republican Roosevelt* (New York, 1954), pp. 115ff.; Gould, *Grand Old Party*, pp. 156–60, 165–66, 173, 179–82, 196–97.

23. R. Chernow, *Titan: The Life of John D. Rockefeller, Sr.* (New York, 1998), pp. 425–65, 519–25.

24. Hendrick, ch. 5, pp. 28–30, quoting AWM to F. W. Haskell, February 3, 1911.

25. Chernow, *Titan*, pp. 538–59.

26. Hendrick, ch. 8, pp. 34–47.

27. Smith, pp. 110–12.

28. AWM papers: AWM diary, May 16, 1912.

29. C. C. Carr, *Alcoa: An American Enterprise* (New York, 1952), pp. 75–83.

30. Smith, pp. 107–109.

31. B. J. Klebaner, *American Commercial Banking: A History* (Boston, 1990), pp. 93, 103.

32. Strouse, *Morgan*, pp. 3–14, 659–62.

33. AWM papers: AWM diary, February 17, 1914, November 4, 1914.

34. AWM papers: F. W. Haskell to AWM, March 31, 1913.

35. A. S. Link (ed.), *The Papers of Woodrow Wilson*, vol. 25 (Princeton, N.J., 1978), p. 153.

36. AWM papers: AWM diary, May 19, 1914, June 25, 1914.

37. M. A. Jones, *The Limits of Liberty: American History, 1607–1992*, 2nd ed. (New York, 1995), pp. 390–91; N. I. Painter, *Standing at Armageddon: The United States, 1877–1914* (New York, 1987), pp. 276–78.

38. F&S, pp. 189–96; Klebaner, *Commercial Banking*, pp. 101–15.

39. HCF papers: Letterbook, November 28, 1906–April 27, 1908, HCF to AWM, October 16, 1907.

40. Samber, pp. 218, 298, 341; HCF papers: Letterbook, November 28, 1906–April

27, 1908, HCF to AWM, October 16, 1907; BJH papers: interview, T. M. Galey, September 11, 1941, pp. 1–2; reminiscences, T. M. Galey [undated], pp. 3–4.

41. Samber, p. 353.
42. Lorant, pp. 242–54; BJH papers: WAM, notes for BJH biography, p. 65.
43. Samber, pp. 342–71; Sparkes papers: interview, W. H. Donner, June 25, 1945, p. 8.
44. Samber, pp. 306–42.
45. Samber, pp. 200, 298.
46. Pittsburgh Coal Company papers: Minutes of Directors' Meetings, September 24, 1911; AWM papers: Memorandum Covering Four Separate Propositions [sale of coal lands], May 16, 1911; Samber, pp. 207–21. For a broader discussion of the failure of consolidations of labor-intensive firms, see A. D. Chandler, *The Visible Hand: The Managerial Revolution in American Business* (Cambridge, Mass., 1977), ch. 10; and G. Porter, *The Rise of Big Business, 1860–1910* (Arlington Heights, Ill., 1973), pp. 79–80.
47. *JMS*, pp. 326–27.
48. Samber, p. 197; AWM papers: Standard Steel Car Company interests, June 1, 1913; *50 Years: New York Shipbuilding Corporation* (Camden, N.J., 1949), pp. 23–27; *JMS*, pp. 326–27.
49. Hendrick, ch. 12, pp. 51–53; AWM papers: [Gulf Oil] to Messrs. Kuhn Loeb & Co., December 1912; Gulf Oil Corporation, statement, December 31, 1909–December 31, 1910; Gulf Oil Corporation, plant investments, December 31, 1910; Gulf Oil, result of combined operations, 1913–1914; AWM Letterbooks, AWM to A. Hill, January 2, 1909, March 3, 1909; Hendrick, ch. 8, p. 6; Smith, pp. 77–104, 445; Samber, p. 191.
50. Mellon Bank papers: Box 604, f04-01-02-002-0001; *The Story of the Mellon Bank* (Pittsburgh, 1911), passim.
51. Union Trust papers: Box 1216, f06-01-00-011-009, Financial papers; Samber, pp. 175–77, 353.
52. Mellon Bank papers: Box 1301, Farmers' Deposit National Bank, f3, picture of bank from *Palmer's Pittsburgh* (1903); Box 1303, Farmers' Deposit National Bank: f06-02-00-007-008, list of directors; *New York Times*, July 12, 14, 15, 1913.
53. Samber, pp. 148–49; Hendrick, ch. 6, p. 7.
54. HCF papers: List of pictures, January 1910; AWM papers: AWM & RBM, 1918–1919.
55. AWM papers: AWM trial balances, 1904–1929.
56. F. C. Jaher, "The Gilded Elite: American Multimillionaires, 1865 to the Present," in W. D. Rubinstein (ed.), *Wealth and the Wealthy in the Modern World* (London, 1980), p. 222; Strouse, *Morgan*, pp. 14–15.
57. *JMS*, pp. 289, 327.
58. This is the argument famously advanced in Chandler, *The Visible Hand*. After 1920, this was the direction in which the Mellon enterprises developed, but there was little sign of it before 1914, when their structure remained "intensely personal and informal." See Smith, pp. 113–26.
59. *TMT*, p. 149.
60. AWM papers: AWM Letterbooks, AWM to WLM, July 31, 1912.

61. Smith, pp. 55–56.

62. BJH papers: interview, G. S. Davison, April 29, 1941, p. 1.

63. Sparkes papers: interview, W. H. Donner, June 25, 1945, pp. 14, 20.

64. Acheson papers: Container 24, Folder Mellon, Andrew, Mellon Bank, Mellon, R.: AWM to E. G. Acheson, May 23, 1907; AWM papers: Letterbooks, AWM to M. Hunsiker, January 21, 1910; AWM papers: AWM diary, January 3, 1911, October 21, 1912.

65. BJH papers: interview, Mr. Kerrigan, September 9, 1940, pp. 1–2; Sparkes papers: interview, H. M. Johnson, June 5, 1945, pp. 1, 4–7; AWM papers: AWM diary, January 14, 24, 1914, February 5, 1914, March 26, 1914; *JMS*, pp. 240, 251, 275, 277, 343–44.

66. HCF papers: Letterbook, March 20, 1903–March 26, 1904, HCF to AWM, October 23, 1903.

67. Sparkes papers: interview, H. M. Johnson, June 5, 1945, p. 5.

68. AWM papers: Contract between T. Mellon & Sons [i.e., AWM and RBM] and G. S. Davison, September 15, 1910.

69. J. N. Ingham, "Steel City Aristocrats," in Hays, *City at the Point*, pp. 271–73.

70. Lorant, p. 241; BJH papers: interview, H. A. Phillips, April 11, 1940, p. 4; AWM papers: H. McCullough interview, July 8, 1996, pp. 2, 6; AWM papers: AWM, speech in New York, January 12, 1925, p. 5. For AWM and RBM's attendance at the funeral of Charles Hall (Alcoa), see Huntland Downs papers: RBM diary, December 30, 31, 1914.

71. BJH papers: interview, Dr. M. A. Rosanoff, April 13, 1940 (2nd interview that day), p. 2.

72. BJH papers: interview, Dr. M. A. Rosanoff, April 15, 1940, pp. 1–2.

73. Hendrick, ch. 6, p. 35; Sparkes papers: interview, H. M. Johnson, June 5, 1945, p. 9.

74. AWM papers: F. G. Haskell to AWM, December 23, 1910.

75. AWM papers: F. G. Haskell to AWM, December [1914?].

76. Strouse, *Morgan*, pp. xiv–xv.

77. With thanks to D. Landes, *The Unbound Prometheus: Technological Change and Industrial Development in Western Europe from 1750 to the Present* (Cambridge, 1969), p. 231.

78. Huntland Downs papers: RBM diary, January 1, 1914–March 15, 1914; AWM papers: E. P. Mellon to AWM, February 28, 1914; Sparkes papers: interview, H. M. Johnson, June 8, 1945, p. 7; *JMS*, p. 383.

79. AWM papers: AWM diary, March 21–30, 1911; Sparkes papers: interview, RKM, October 18, 1944, p. 15.

80. AWM papers: AWM diary: September 1, 8, 1911, October 2, 1911, November 18, 21, 1911.

81. Hendrick, ch. 6, pp. 42–43.

82. AWM papers: AWM diary, July 8, 12, 30, 1912, August 10, 12, 13, 23, 28, 1912, November 7, 16, 19, 20, 1912, December 3–6, 17, 19, 1912, February 5, 27, 1913, April 27–30, 1913, May 1, 2, 15, 1913, September 9, 1913, December 2, 12, 1913, January 3, 12, 15, 1914, February 2, 3, 1914; Letterbooks: AWM to WLM, July 31, 1912; [Gulf Oil] to Messrs. Kuhn, Loeb & Co., December 1912;

Huntland Downs papers: RBM diary, January 31, 1914, February 4, 1914; B. E. Supple, "A Business Elite: German-Jewish Financiers in Nineteenth-Century New York," *Business History Review* 31 (1957), pp. 143–78.

83. Burnham papers: Letterbook 5, D. Burnham to HCF, September 16, 1908, February 17, 1909, December 22, 1909, December 18, 1911, January 2, 1912; HCF papers: Letterbook, February 19, 1914–October 19, 1914, HCF to AWM, March 31, 1914; AWM papers: AWM diary, April 1, 1914; J. N. Ingham, "Reaching for Respectability: The Pittsburgh Industrial Elite at the Turn of the Century," in G. P. Weisberg, D. E. McIntosh, and A. McQueen (eds.), *Collecting in the Gilded Age: Art Patronage in Pittsburgh, 1890–1910* (Pittsburgh, 1997), pp. 34–37; K. Warren, *Triumphant Capitalism: Henry Clay Frick and the Transformation of America* (Pittsburgh, 1996), pp. 338–39.

84. Hendrick, ch. 14, p. 4; J. W. Servos, "Changing Partners: The Mellon Institute, Private Industry, and the Federal Patron," *Technology & Culture* 35 (1994), pp. 226–27; M. B. W. Graham and B. H. Pruit, *R&D for Industry: A Century of Technical Innovation at Alcoa* (New York, 1990), pp. 59–97. For the broader background, see L. Galambos, "Technology, Political Economy, and Professionalization: Central Themes of the Organizational Synthesis," *Business History Review* 57 (1983), pp. 472–78.

85. B. D. Karl and S. N. Katz, "Foundations and Ruling Class Elites," *Daedalus* 116 (1987), pp. 5–27; D. J. Kelves, "Foundations, Universities, and Trends in Support for the Physical and Biological Sciences, 1900–1992," *Daedalus* 121 (1992), pp. 195–97; P. Krass, *Carnegie* (Hoboken, N.J., 2002), pp. 414–15, 463–66, 491–94, 502–503; Chernow, *Titan*, pp. 469–87, 491–500, 563–71.

86. Samber, pp. 413–20.

87. Samber, pp. 435–38, thinks these claims exaggerated, and that the number of new jobs created was nearer 2,000 than 8,000—though even this was a significant figure.

88. AWM papers: List of Contributions, 1902–1937.

89. AWM papers: AWM trial balances, 1904–1927, trial balance, January 1, 1906; BJH papers: interview, Dr. H. Kohman, August 20, 1941, pp. 1–2; Hendrick, ch. 14, pp. 23–24; Servos, "Mellon Institute," pp. 227–28.

90. Hendrick, ch. 14, pp. 4–15; R. K. Duncan, *The Chemistry of Commerce* (New York, 1907), esp. pp. 3–8, 250–51; Servos, "Mellon Institute," pp. 223–26.

91. AWM, Speech at the Dedication of the New Building of the Mellon Institute, Pittsburgh, May 6, 1937, quoted in Hendrick, ch. 14, pp. 2–3.

92. Ibid.; *JMS*, pp. 346–53.

93. Servos, "Mellon Institute," p. 226.

94. Hendrick, ch. 14, pp. 15–21.

95. Hendrick, ch. 14, pp. 25–26; AWM papers: AWM diary, December 9, 1912.

96. Hendrick, ch. 14, pp. 29–31; Lubove, *Twentieth-Century Pittsburgh*, vol. 1, p. 48; Samber, pp. 410–12.

97. R. C. Alberts, *Pitt: The Story of the University of Pittsburgh, 1787–1987* (Pittsburgh, 1986), p. 68; AWM papers: AWM diary, January 20, 23, 30, 1913, February 14, 1913, April 17, 24, 1913, May 21, 26, 1913, June 6, 1913.

98. Hendrick, ch. 14, pp. 32–33; Servos, "Mellon Institute," p. 229.

99. Servos, "Mellon Institute," p. 229; D. Noble, *America by Design: Science, Technology and the Rise of Corporate Capitalism* (Oxford, 1977), pp. 122–23.

100. BJH papers: interviews, E. O. Rhodes, August 22, 1941, pp. 1–2; Dr. R. H. Brownlee, August 22, 1941, pp. 1–2; Hendrick, ch. 14, pp. 26–27.

101. AWM papers: R. K. Duncan to AWM, March 10, 1911; BJH papers: interview, Dr. M. A. Rosanoff, April 13, 1940, p. 4; Hendrick, ch. 14, pp. 33–34.

102. BJH papers: interview, Dr. Tillotson, August 20, 1941, pp. 4–5; Huntland Downs papers: RBM diary, February 18–19, 1914; AWM papers: AWM diary, January 19, 1914, February 14, 16, 1914, April 3, 1914.

103. Hendrick, ch. 14, p. 35.

104. AWM papers: W. P. Potter to AWM, April 13, 1913; AWM diary, May 15, 1914.

105. *JMS*, pp. 370–76.

106. Hendrick, ch. 15, pp. 1–3.

107. Samber, pp. 50–54; Hendrick, ch. 15, pp. 5–7.

108. Hendrick, ch. 15, pp. 7–10.

109. *JMS*, pp. 370–77; Hendrick papers: interviews, Mr. Ulmer, August 9, 1941, p. 1; C. S. Ramsburg and Mr. X, August 27, 1941, pp. 2–3.

110. Hendrick, ch. 15, pp. 14–16; BJH papers: E. S. W. Hickes to Hendrick, January 17, 1941, p. 3.

111. BJH papers: H. B. Rust, "The Koppers Company" (Historical Notes), June 18, 1930, pp. 1–4.

112. AWM papers: AWM diary, November 4, 9, 10, 14, 17, 30, 1914, December 2, 3, 28, 1914.

113. Samber, p. 56.

114. F&S, pp. 173–74; Painter, *Standing at Armageddon*, p. 295.

115. Samber, pp. 440, 449, 452.

8. New Careers for Old: Single Parent, Aging Plutocrat, Emerging Politician, 1914–21

1. Hendrick, ch. 16, pp. 11–13; BJH papers: interviews, S. and A. Scaife, November 4, 1940, pp. 3–4; Dr. E. R. Weidlein, April 14, 1940, pp. 1–2; PM papers: interview no. 1, pp. 23–24, 26–27; interview no. 4, pp. 15–16.

2. PM papers: interview no. 1, p. 4; AWM papers: AWM diary, August 20, 1912, October 22, 1917.

3. AWM papers: AWM diary, April 12, 1910.

4. S. J. Kleinberg, *The Shadow of the Mills: Working-Class Families in Pittsburgh, 1870–1907* (Pittsburgh, 1989), pp. 166–69; R. Rosen, *The Lost Sisterhood: Prostitution in America, 1900–1918* (Baltimore, 1982), pp. 71–74, 86.

5. *Report and Recommendation of the Morals Efficiency Commission* (Pittsburgh, 1913); D. J. Pivar, *Purity Crusade, Sexual Morality and Social Control, 1868–1900* (Westport, Conn., 1973), pp. 267–77; M. T. Connelly, *The Response to Prostitution in the Progressive Era* (Chapel Hill, N.C., 1980), pp. 11–27, 48–66, 114–35; Rosen, *Lost Sisterhood*, pp. 14–37, 71–74, 94, 112–35, 183 note 2.

6. For the difference between courtesan and mistress, see K. Hickman, *Courtesans: Money, Sex and Fame in the Nineteenth Century* (London, 2003), pp. 3–4.

7. AWM papers: AWM diary, November 4, 1914; P. Gay, *The Bourgeois Experience, Victoria to Freud*, vol. 2, *The Tender Passion* (New York, 1986), pp. 355, 360, 371, 384–88.

8. AWM papers: AWM diary, April 14, 1919.

9. AWM papers: AWM diary, October 5, 1913.

10. *JMS*, p. 395; BJH papers: interview, Dr. M. A. Rosanoff, April 15, 1940, p. 4; PM papers: interview no. 4, pp. 5–7.

11. AWM papers: AWM diary, June 19, 1913 to August 20, 1913.

12. *RSS*, pp. 70–75.

13. AWM papers: AWM diary, November 8, 1915, February 17, 1919; PM papers: interview no. 4, pp. 9–13.

14. AWM papers: AWM diary, October 1, 1915; *JMS*, p. 396; *RSS*, pp. 93–94; R. J. Jucha, "The Anatomy of a Streetcar Suburb: A Development and Architectural History of Pittsburgh's Shadyside District, 1860–1920" (Ph.D. diss., George Washington University, 1980), pp. 94–95.

15. BJH papers: interview, S. and A. Scaife, November 4, 1940, pp. 1–2.

16. AWM papers: AWM diary, July 20, 27, 1912, October 30, 1912, January 11, 1913; PM papers: interview no. 1, pp. 1, 7; *RSS*, pp. 67–69.

17. AWM papers: AWM diary, August 2, 4, 1912.

18. AWM papers: AWM diary, June 3, 1912, August 8, 1912, January 25, 1913, May 24, 1913, October 23, 1913, October 5, 1914, January 6, 10, 11, 1916; PM papers: interview no. 1, p. 22.

19. AWM papers: AWM diary, March 30, 1914, January 10, 1916.

20. AWM papers: AWM diary, July 27, 1912, April 23, 1912, January 11, 1913, March 24, 1913, January 11, 1916, July 19, 1917, October 8, 1917.

21. AWM papers: AWM diary, September 20, 22, 25, 1914, December 6, 1914.

22. AWM papers: AWM diary, October 17, 1914, January 16, 1915, July 19, 1915, June 22, 1916, November 20, 1917, April 27, 1920, May 1, 1920; J. A. McMullen to AWM, September 18, 1914, January 4, 6, 1918, April 10, 1918; L. McMullen to AWM, October 17, 1915, February [1916?].

23. *JMS*, pp. 360–66; AWM papers: AWM diary, February 5, 14, 1914, July 7, 1914, November 20, 1914.

24. AWM papers: AWM diary, January 28, 1916, April 16, 1916, August 1, 1916, October 10, 1916.

25. AWM papers: AWM to AMB, November 17, 1916, December 14, 1916, January 21, 28, 1917, May 22, 1917; AMB to AWM, October 23, 31, 1916, November 16, 1916, December 7, 1916.

26. AWM papers: AWM diary, February 21, 1917, May 15, 1919; Knoedler papers: Domestic Letterbook, June 23, 1917–October 9, 1917, CHM to AWM, September 11, 1917.

27. AWM papers: AWM diary, April 15, 1917, September 23, 1917, October 8–26, 1917, November 8, 1917, September 11, 1918, January 9, 1919; AWM to Mrs. Keep, October 16, 1917 AMB to AWM, October 23, 1917; Mrs. Keep to AWM, November 1, 1917; AWM to Mrs. Keep, November 8, 1917; AWM to AMB [draft of letter, October 1917]; AMB papers: AMB to NMM, undated letters [c. 1916–17].

28. AWM papers: AWM diary, April 24, 25, 1917, July 2, 11, 1917, March 31, 1919, May 16, 1919; AMB to AWM, December 7, 1916, March 1917, May 23, 1918, December 18, 1918, February 14, 1919, May 21, 1919; PM papers: interview no. 4, p. 2.

29. AWM papers: PM to AWM, July 15, 1917; *JMS*, pp. 390–93.

30. AWM papers: AWM diary, July 2, 1918.

31. O'Connor, p. 64.

32. AWM papers: AWM diary, August 8, 1914, September 3, 1914.

33. Lorant, pp. 476–77.

34. P. A. C. Koistinen, *Mobilizing for Modern War: The Political Economy of American Warfare, 1865–1919* (Lawrence, Kans., 1997), pp. 126–36; K. Burk, *Britain, America and the Sinews of War, 1914–1918* (London, 1985), pp. 61–95; U.S. Congress, Senate, *Special Committee Investigating the Munitions Industry, Hearings*, pt. 27, *World War Financing*, pp. 8306, 8315; pt. 32, *Exhibits on Wartime and Post-War Financing*, pp. 10261, 10292, 10294, 10309, 10312; AWM papers: AWM diary, October 1, 4, 1915, June 21, 1916, July 31, 1916.

35. AWM papers: AWM diary, April 11, 1917, May 14, 28, 1917, October 23, 1917.

36. AWM papers: T. Roosevelt to AWM, November 8, 1918; AWM diary, May 25, 31, 1917; June 2, 11, 23, 1917; July 3, 1918; December 28, 1918.

37. Hendrick, ch. 15, pp. 13–20.

38. AWM papers: AWM diary, March 25, 1916; BJH papers: "The Koppers Company's Contribution to the Winning of the War" [undated typescript, no author given]; interview, C. S. Ramsburg and Mr. X, August 27, 1941, pp. 4–5.

39. AWM papers: AWM diary, October 15, 1917; BJH papers: interview, Mr. Ulmer, August 9, 1941, pp. 1–2.

40. Hendrick, ch. 15, pp. 20–22; BJH papers: "A Preliminary Survey of the General History of the Koppers Group of Companies" [typescript, April 24, 1939, no author given], p. 11.

41. Samber, p. 206.

42. AWM papers: AWM diary, May 23, 1919, July 9, 1919, August 5, 1919; T. H. Price to H. B. Rust, August 29, 1918; H. B. Rust to T. H. Price, September 7, 11, 1918; BJH papers: AWM Letterbooks, AWM to C. D. Marshall, November 28, 1921; interview, S. Brown, August 27, 1941, p. 1; Hendrick, ch. 15, p. 23.

43. AWM papers: AWM diary, June 7, 1915, March 1, 1917; Gulf Oil assets, December 31, 1917–June 30, 1920; Smith, pp. 126–31, 445; C. C. Carr, *Alcoa: An American Enterprise* (New York, 1952), pp. 147–64; Samber, pp. 191, 205, 220.

44. AWM papers: AWM diary, January 13, 1915, February 22, 1915, September 16, 1915, March 12, 1917, December 9, 1919; E. P. Mellon to AWM, February 28, 1914, August 20, 1914, February 7, 1915, June 8, 1915; Mellon Bank papers: Box 1216, f06-01-00-008-0001: *A Brief History of the Union Trust Company of Pittsburgh* (Pittsburgh, 1946); Union Trust papers: f06-01-00-011-0009, Union Trust Company financial records; Samber, pp. 149, 184.

45. AWM papers: AWM Deceased, Report and Accounts, August 26, 1937, Exhibit F, Exhibit G.

46. Hendrick, ch. 16, pp. 8–10.

47. AWM papers: diary, May 2, 8, 1915, February 12, 1917, April 16, 1917, May 9, 1917; AWM Deceased, Report and Accounts, August 26, 1937, p. 59.

48. AWM papers: AWM diary, July 9, 12, 1917.

49. F&S, pp. 231–39.

50. D. Brody, *Steelworkers in America: The Nonunion Era* (Cambridge, Mass., 1960), pp. 231–62; D. Brody, *Labor in Crisis: The Steel Strike of 1919* (Philadelphia, 1965), pp. 89–95, 148–55, 160–64.

51. Lorant, pp. 321–22, 477–78; AWM papers: AWM diary, May 12, 15, 1919, June 5–6, 1919.

52. N. I. Painter, *Standing at Armageddon: The United States, 1877–1919* (New York, 1987), p. 378.

53. Smith, pp. 136–37, 445; AWM papers: AWM diary, December 27, 1920.

54. AWM papers: AWM diary, January 18, 1916, September 6–15, 1916, December 11, 1916, April 22, 1919.

55. AWM papers: AWM diary, August 18, 1914, September 17, 1914, April 6, 1915, May 13, 1919, December 21, 23, 1919, February 3, 1920, April 14, 1920; Agreement Between AWM, RBM, T. A. Mellon Jr., E. P. Mellon, and Mary Mellon McClung, June 19, 1919.

56. AWM papers: AWM diary, December 11, 1919, February 21, 1920; Samber, pp. 446–51.

57. AWM papers: AWM diary: May 15, 1919, November 25, 1919, December 2, 5, 1919.

58. AWM papers: AWM diary, December 2–6, 1919; Frick papers: AWM to Col. Harvey, June 25, 1927; M. F. S. Sanger, *Henry Clay Frick: An Intimate Portrait* (New York, 1998), p. 409.

59. Between 1913 and 1919, AWM was mentioned once in the *New York Times* index, and the entry, for October 30, 1919, was merely the announcement that he had been appointed a director of the Crucible Steel Company.

60. AWM papers: AWM diary, November 5, 1915, March 17, 1917, May 13, 1917, July 6, 7, 1917, September 30, 1917; BJH papers: interview, S. and A. Scaife, November 4, 1940, p. 3.

61. AWM papers: AWM diary, December 26–31, 1915, January 1–6, 1917, February 19, 1919, March 12, 1919, November 19, 1919, February 21, 26, 1920, April 16, 21, 1920.

62. BJH papers: WAM, Notes for BJH biography, p. 131.

63. W. C. Kidney, *Landmark Architecture: Pittsburgh and Allegheny County* (Pittsburgh, 1985), p. 276.

64. AWM papers: AWM diary: March 5, 8, 12–14, 1916, December 23, 25, 1916.

65. AWM papers: AWM diary, September 29, 1916, February 21, 1917, March 8, 1917, October 2, 1917, November 14, 1917.

66. AWM papers: AWM diary, January 1, 1918.

67. AWM papers: AWM diary, August 11, 1913, November 19, 1914.

68. AWM papers: AWM diary, November 18, 1914, November 7, 1914, March 23, 1920; *RSS*, p. 96. In late 1918, HCF corresponded with Philander Knox about inserting into the pending revenue bill a clause which exempted collections of art and the building in which they were housed from inheritance tax, thereby saving

taxes of $10 million to $12 million on his own house and collection, which were worth between $20 million and $30 million. See Knox papers: vol. 22, HCF to P. C. Knox, September 2, 1918.

69. AWM papers: AWM diary, September 29, 1916, November 21, 1917; AWM Deceased, Report and Accounts, August 26, 1937, Exhibit D, pp. 4–7; Knoedler papers: Telegrams and Cables, March 13, 1917–March 4, 1920: CHM to Miss Sylvester, January 24, 1918; CHM to AWM, February 8, 1918; Domestic Letterbook, December 13, 1917–February 16, 1918: CHM to AWM, January 25, 1918; Domestic Letterbook, February 16, 1918–April 24, 1918: CHM to AWM, March 14, 1918; PM papers: interview no. 4, p. 15.

70. AWM papers: AMB to AWM, November 16, 1916, and also January 22, 1918, November 25, 1918, January 23, 1919.

71. AWM papers: AWM diary, February 15, 1919, March 14, 1919, November 18, 24–26, 1920, October 2, 1920; Knoedler papers: Domestic Letterbook, February 6, 1918–April 24, 1919, CHM to AWM, April 8, 1918; Domestic Letterbook, April 25, 1918–July 9, 1918, CHM to AWM, April 26, 1918; Domestic Letterbook, September 20, 1919–November 18, 1919, CHM to AWM, October 23, 1919, November 15, 1919; Domestic Letterbook, November 19, 1919–January 17, 1920, CHM to AWM, December 26, 1919; Domestic Letterbook, May 5, 1920–July 9, 1920, CHM to AWM, June 7, 1920.

72. M. Secrest, *Duveen: A Life in Art* (New York, 2004), pp. 60–63, 88–90, 100–102, 134–39, 300; PM papers: interview no. 1, p. 8.

73. Secrest, *Duveen*, pp. 300–303.

74. AWM papers: AWM diary, March 10, 26, 1915, January 9, 1919, February 19, 1919, December 17, 1919, February 20, 1920, March 23, 1920; Duveen papers: JD to AWM, February 6, 1918, September 5, 1918, November 7, 1918, December 24, 1918, January 4, 1919, March 4, 1920; AWM to JD, February 26, 1920.

75. AWM papers: AWM diary, July 3, 1918; Knoedler papers: Domestic Letterbook, January 8, 1921–February 24, 1921, CHM to AWM, February 11, 1921.

76. Knoedler papers: Domestic Letterbook, January 8, 1921–February 24, 1921, R. F. Knoedler to AWM, February 1, 1921.

77. AWM papers: AWM diary, December 17, 1919, January 28, 1920; Duveen papers: AWM to JD, February 26, 1920; JD to AWM, March 3, 1920, June 23, 1920; Secrest, *Duveen*, pp. 303–304.

78. Duveen papers: JD to AWM, September 24, 1920, January 27, 1921, AWM to JD, January 29, 1921.

79. AWM papers: AWM diary, December 21, 1918.

80. AWM papers: AWM diary, March 14, 1919, April 20, 1919.

81. AWM papers: AWM diary, March 15, 1919, September 29, 1919; PM papers: interview no. 1, p. 15; no. 4, p. 8.

82. AWM papers: AWM diary, June 6, 21, 1919, July 11, 1919; PM papers: interview no. 3, pp. 3–4; *RSS*, pp. 90, 98.

83. AWM papers: AWM diary, November 15, 17, 1919.

84. AWM papers: AWM diary, April 13, 1919, September 2, 28, 1919, October 23–24, 1919, November 21–22, 1919, December 7, 14, 16, 18, 22, 1919.

85. AWM papers: AWM diary, January 4, 1919; R. P. Keep to AWM, February 2,

1919, A. H. Sylvester to AWM, February 14, 1919; AWM to NMM, November 9, 1919.

86. AWM papers: AWM diary, June 6, 28, 1920, August 30, 1920, September 21, 1920, October 1, 1920, December 13, 1920; PM papers: interview no. 4, p. 12.

87. AWM papers: PM to AWM, October 19, 1919, March 2, 11, 17, 23, 1920, February 6, 1921; *RSS*, pp. 98–100; PM papers: interview no. 4, pp. 2–3.

88. AWM papers: AWM diary, September 26, 1919, October 15, 1919, November 2–4, 1919, May 29, 1920, August 21, 30, 1920, September 25, 1920; PM papers: interview no. 2, p. 5.

89. Frick papers: Excelsior diary, October 29, 1919.

90. BJH papers: J. W. Chalfant to AWM, October 4, 1888; AWM papers: AWM diary, December 31, 1911, October 5, 1914; Knox papers: vol. 9: AWM to P. C. Knox, November 12, 17, 1909; P. C. Knox to AWM, November 16, 1909.

91. AWM papers: AWM diary, March 20, 1912, April 10, 1912, September 14, 1914, January 7, 1916, February 3, 1916, December 19, 1917, September 23, 1920.

92. AWM papers: AWM diary, February 28, 1919; G. W. Pepper, *Philadelphia Lawyer: An Autobiography* (Philadelphia, 1944), pp. 124–29; G. Harvey, *Henry Clay Frick: The Man* (New York, 1928), pp. 325–29; R. Stone, *The Irreconcilables: The Fight Against the League of Nations* (Lexington, Ky., 1970), pp. 78–82.

93. AWM papers: AWM diary, May 14, 27, 1920, June 6–13, 1920; BJH papers: W. C. Sproul to AWM, June 17, 1920. For other expressions of support for Knox, see Knox papers: vol. 30, A. A. Davis to B. Penrose, April 30, 1920; H. K. Daugherty to P. C. Knox, May 25, 1920.

94. L. L. Gould, *Grand Old Party: A History of the Republicans* (New York, 2003), pp. 221–23.

95. AWM papers: AWM diary, April 21, 24, 1920, May 3, 1920, September 23, 1920.

96. BJH papers: J. G. Blaine Jr. to AWM, October 30, 1920; W. B. Thompson to AWM, November 30, 1920.

97. For standard accounts of AWM's appointment, see: Hendrick, ch. 17, pp. 7–24; *JMS*, pp. 394–405; J. M. Chapple, *The Life and Times of Warren G. Harding: Our After-War President* (Boston, 1924), pp. 131–39; A. Sinclair, *The Available Man: Warren Gamaliel Harding* (New York, 1965), pp. 183–89; E. P. Trani and D. L. Wilson, *The Presidency of Warren G. Harding* (Lawrence, Kans., 1977), pp. 131–39; J. W. Dean, *Warren G. Harding* (New York, 2004), pp. 84–87; Murray, pp. 4–18.

98. Knox papers: vol. 30, W. G. Harding to P. C. Knox, June 14, 24, 1920, July 28, 1920, August 10, 1920, November 5, 1920; AWM papers: AWM diary, November 3, 29, 1920, December 1, 8, 14, 1920.

99. AWM papers: AWM diary, December 14, 31, 1920; AMB to AWM [undated: late 1920, early 1921]; *New York Times*, January 1, 3, 15, 21, 24, 1921, February 4, 8, 1921; R. D. Bowden, *Boies Penrose: Symbol of an Era* (New York, 1937), pp. 200, 219, 244, 259.

100. AWM papers: AWM diary, January 1, 1921; AWM to P. C. Knox, January 1, 1921.

101. AWM papers: AWM diary, February 15, 1921.

102. AWM papers: W. G. Harding to AWM, January 2, 1921.

103. Sinclair, *Available Man*, p. 185.

104. *JMS*, pp. 400–401; BJH papers: BJH to DEF, November 13, 1941; DEF to BJH, November 21, 1941.

105. AWM papers: AWM diary, January 7–8, 1921; *Pittsburgh Gazette-Times*, January 8, 1921; *Pittsburgh Leader*, January 8, 1921; *New York Herald*, January 8, 1921.

106. BJH papers: P. C. Knox to J. T. Williams, January 23, 1921.

107. BJH papers: J. T. Williams to P. C. Knox, January 24, 1921; C. Woods to AWM, January 24, 1921; *Boston Evening Transcript*, January 24, 1921.

108. Knox papers: vol. 22, P. C. Knox to McClintic-Marshall Construction Co., April 20, 1920; J. D. Marshall to P. C. Knox, April 22, 1920.

109. AWM papers: AWM diary, January 11–15, 22, 1921.

110. AWM papers: AWM diary, January 24–27, 1921.

111. AWM papers: AWM diary, February 1–2, 1921.

112. AWM papers: AWM diary, February 6–7, 1921.

113. *New York World*, February 10, 11, 1921; *New York Times*, February 11, 14, 1921.

114. Knox papers: vol. 30, AWM to P. C. Knox, February 7, 1921; AWM papers: AWM diary, February 8–11, 1921.

115. HCF papers: Letterbook, September 13, 1918–May 26, 1919, HCF to RBM, October 24, 26, 1918, November 7, 27, 1918, December 4, 1918, January 8, 9, 21, 1919.

116. AWM papers: AWM Deceased, Report and Accounts, August 26, 1937, pp. 47–48; Hendrick, ch. 17, pp. 21–24; *New York World*, February 13, 1921; *New York Times*, February 28, 1921.

117. AWM papers: AWM diary, February 11–13, 1921.

118. AWM papers: AWM diary, February 24, 1921; BJH papers: W. G. Harding to P. C. Knox, February 20, 1921; *New York World*, February 20, 21, 1921.

119. *New York World*, February 26, 1921.

120. Knox papers: vol. 30, J. H. Reed to P. C. Knox, January 14, 1921, February 1, 1921.

121. AWM papers: AWM diary, February 28, 1921; *New York Times*, March 1, 1921.

122. AWM papers: H. C. Frick to AWM, February 16, 1921; AWM diary, February 26, 1921, March 2, 1921; Transfer agreement between AWM and RBM, March 1, 1921; *New York Times*, March 3, 1921.

123. AWM papers: PM to AWM, March 3, 1921.

124. *New York Times*, March 5, 6, 1921; *JMS*, p. 405.

9. Hard Times with Harding: Political Realities, Getting Started, Settling In, 1921–23

1. M. Klein, *Rainbow's End: The Crash of 1929* (New York, 2001), p. 6.

2. R. K. Murray, *The Harding Era: Warren G. Harding and His Administration* (Minneapolis, 1969), pp. 172, 227–64, 390–91.

3. Murray, *Harding Era*, pp. 54, 70; Murray, p. 38.

4. Hendrick, ch. 18, pp. 17–19.

5. Murray, *Harding Era*, pp. 81–86; Klein, *Rainbow's End*, pp. 25–26; *Report of the Secretary of the Treasury, 1923*, p. 2.

6. Steiner, pp. 182–213; F. Costigliola, *Awkward Dominion: American Political, Eco-*

nomic and Cultural Relations with Europe, 1919–1933 (Ithaca, N.Y., 1984), pp. 25–56.

7. CFOST: Box 254, Treasury Department—Secretary—Articles for Publication, AWM to Dr. M. Jordan, December 15, 1924.

8. M. J. Hogan, *Informal Entente: The Private Structure of Cooperation in Anglo-American Economic Diplomacy* (Columbia, Mo., 1977), pp. 78–84; W. L. Cohen, *Empire Without Tears: America's Foreign Relations, 1921–1933* (New York, 1987), pp. 18–37; E. S. Rosenberg, *Financial Missionaries to the World: The Politics and Culture of Dollar Diplomacy, 1900–1930* (Cambridge, Mass., 1999), pp. 97–107; L. V. Chandler, *Benjamin Strong, Central Banker* (Washington, D.C., 1958), pp. 247–69.

9. DEF papers (NGA): The Treasury Department: An outline of the duties of the Secretary of the Treasury, and the various offices and bureaus in the Treasury Department, prepared by the Section of Statistics, April 1924; AWM papers: AWM, Speech at the Lotos Club, New York, February 6, 1926; Kennedy, pp. 55, 57, 171, 285, 340.

10. Hendrick, ch. 18, pp. 12–13.

11. Hendrick, ch. 18, p. 31; BJH papers: AWM Letterbooks, AWM to Col. S. H. Church, January 23, 1922.

12. *JMS*, pp. 432–33; Murray, *Harding Era*, pp. 185–86.

13. Murray, *Harding Era*, pp. 108, 181, 191.

14. Murray, *Harding Era*, pp. 193–97, 211–12.

15. Murray, *Harding Era*, pp. 127–28, 315–16.

16. Murray, *Harding Era*, pp. 206–11, 318–19.

17. CFOST: Box 21, Federal Budget January–June 1921, S. Parker Gilbert to AWM, April 18, 1921, May 8, 28, 1921; AWM to W. H. King, May 20, 1921, June 7, 1921; Murray, pp. 56–58.

18. CFOST: Box 21, Federal Budget 1922, C. G. Dawes to S. Parker Gilbert, June 14, 1922; S. Parker Gilbert to AWM, November 9, 1922; Box 22, Federal Budget 1923, S. Parker Gilbert to Mr. Hand, August 15, 1923; AWM to W. G. Harding, October 24, 1923; Murray, *Harding Era*, pp. 172–78; C. G. Dawes, *The First Year of the Budget of the United States* (New York, 1923), pp. 49, 57, 63, 80–86, 104–107.

19. AWM, "What Future for the Federal Reserve?," *The 3-C Book*, vol. 8, August 1925, pp. 19–22.

20. CFOST: Box 83, Foreign Trade 1920–23, B. F. Strong to S. Parker Gilbert, May 23, 1921; S. Parker Gilbert to B. F. Strong, May 28, 1921; Box 66, Federal Reserve Banks—Discount Rates 1923–26, AWM to J. A. Check, February 14, 1920; S. Parker Gilbert to D. A. Cressinger, August 3, 1923; Klein, *Rainbow's End*, pp. 71–79; Meltzer, pp. 132–38.

21. Strong papers: 012.3, B. F. Strong to AWM, March 5, 1921; AWM to B. F. Strong, March 9, 1921; Hamlin papers: Index-Digest, March 10, 1921; AWM papers: W. G. Harding to AWM, March 7, 1921; AWM to W. G. Harding, August 11, 1922; CFOST: Box 72, Federal Reserve Board—Farmer Member on Board 1921–23, AWM to J. S. Frelinghuysen, July 15, 1921; B. F. Strong to S. Parker Gilbert, June 12, 1922; Murray, *Harding Era*, pp. 215–16, 300–301; Murray, pp. 71–73, 91–93.

22. Murray, *Harding Era*, pp. 125; Murray, pp. 47–50.

23. Murray, *Harding Era*, pp. 271–80.

24. Murray, pp. 67–70; BJH papers: AWM Letterbooks, AWM to R. P. Ernst, July 2, 1921, AWM to B. Penrose, July 26, 1921.

25. K. Middlemas and J. Barnes, *Baldwin: A Biography* (London, 1969), p. 137.

26. Hendrick, ch. 18, pp. 21–27.

27. Hendrick, ch. 18, pp. 31–35.

28. AWM papers: AWM to W. G. Harding, November 15, 1921, April 7, 1922; W. G. Harding to AWM, November 10, 28, 1921.

29. Sparkes papers: interview, E. Irey, October 10, 1945, pp. 1–5; Hendrick, ch. 18, pp. 28–31, 36–38; *JMS*, pp. 419–22.

30. AWM papers: W. G. Harding to AWM, May 4, 6, 18, 1922, August 26, 1922.

31. CFOST: Box 29, Civil Service—Miscellaneous, 1919–1932, AWM Statement, June 16, 1922; Hendrick, ch. 18, pp. 38–41.

32. Murray, pp. 44–45; Hendrick, ch. 18, p. 42; BJH papers: AWM Letterbooks, AWM to J. W. Dunbar, June 17, 1922.

33. BJH papers: AWM Letterbooks, AWM to R. H. MacMichael, August 17, 1922.

34. BJH papers: interview, A. E. Sixsmith, March 5, 1941, p. 1.

35. *JMS*, pp. 405–406, 411–16; BJH papers: interview, Col. F. Drake, June 9, 1942, pp. 1–7; Sparkes papers: interview, Col. F. Drake, June 19, 1945, pp. 1, 5–7.

36. CFOST: Box 301, Individual Correspondence, Le–Lh, AWM to B. Penrose, February 8, 1921; S. Parker Gilbert to R. C. Leffingwell, March 1, 1921.

37. CFOST: Box 160, Taxation (General), January–April 1921, S. Parker Gilbert to AWM, March 14, 1921; Box 155, Tariff (General), 1919–21, S. Parker Gilbert to AWM, March 15, 1921; Box 261, Memoranda to AWM, S. Parker Gilbert to AWM, August 29, 1921.

38. Hamlin papers: Index-Digest, March 29, 1921, April 4, 1921; F&S, p. 234; Meltzer, p. 132; Murray, pp. 71–72.

39. BJH papers: AWM Letterbooks, AWM to J. W. Fordney, May 12, 1921.

40. Hendrick, ch. 18, pp. 19–20; *JMS*, p. 410.

41. Hendrick, ch. 18, pp. 43–44.

42. Hendrick, ch. 18, p. 47.

43. AWM papers: AWM to A. J. Beveridge, December 4, 1923.

44. *JMS*, pp. 428–29; Hendrick, ch. 19, pp. 9–14, 19–21; BJH papers: AWM Letterbooks, AWM to H. S. Pritchett, January 23, 1923.

45. CFOST: Box 160, Taxation (General), August 1921, AWM Statement to Committee on Ways and Means, August 4, 1921; AWM to J. J. Fordney, August 10, 1921.

46. Murray, pp. 50–55, 59–61; Murray, *Harding Era*, pp. 182–84.

47. Murray, pp. 61–66; Murray, *Harding Era*, pp. 184–91.

48. CFOST: Box 134, Soldiers' Bonus, January–June 1921, S. Parker Gilbert to AWM, June 4, 1921.

49. BJH papers: AWM Letterbooks, AWM to C. S. Hamlin, July 14, 1921.

50. CFOST: Box 135, Soldiers' Bonus, July–December 1921, AWM to J. S. Frelinghuysen, July 2, 1921; *Wall Street Journal*, July 12, 1921.

51. CFOST: Box 135, Soldiers' Bonus, January–February 1922, S. Parker Gilbert to AWM, January 21, 1922, February 23, 1922; AWM to J. W. Fordney, February

10, 1922; AWM to W. G. Harding, February 22, 1922; Box 136, Soldiers' Bonus, April–June 1922, S. Parker Gilbert to AWM, April 7, 20, 27, 1922, May 9, 1922; Box 136, Soldiers' Bonus, July–December 1922, S. Parker Gilbert to AWM, July 8, 1922; Box 261, Treasury Department—Secretary—Memoranda to AWM, S. Parker Gilbert to AWM, June 3, 1922; *New York Times*, February 8, 1922.

52. Hendrick, ch. 18, pp. 45–47; Murray, *Harding Era*, pp. 186, 309–14; Murray, pp. 78–84.

53. Hendrick, ch. 20, pp. 1–36; Murray, pp. 93–96; Middlemas and Barnes, *Baldwin*, pp. 128–47.

54. *JMS*, pp. 445–49.

55. *JMS*, p. 449.

56. H. Clay, *Lord Norman* (London, 1957), pp. 172–79; Hendrick, ch. 20, p. 27.

57. BJH papers: interview, E. Wadsworth, February 21, 1942, pp. 2–7.

58. BJH papers: AWM Letterbooks, AWM to M. McMullen, March 18, 1923.

59. CFOST: Box 77, Financial General 1924: G. B. Winston to AWM, January 10, 1924; Murray, *Harding Era*, p. 364.

60. AWM papers: W. G. Harding to AWM, October 7, 13, 1922, December 12, 18, 28, 1922; AWM to W. G. Harding, October 7, 13, 1922, November 18, 1921, December 22, 1922.

61. Murray, *Harding Era*, p. 39; BJH papers: AWM Letterbooks, AWM to Dr. W. E. Crafts, March 29, 1921; AWM to C. C. Simmington, November 8, 1921; CFOST: Box 42, Reorganization of Departments, 1920–1932, AWM to K. Nelson, March 17, 1922; AWM to R. Smoot, January 30, 1924, May 19, 1926.

62. Murray, pp. 43–44.

63. Murray, *Harding Era*, pp. 403–407; Murray, pp. 73–74.

64. CFOST: Box 71, Federal Reserve Board 1923–31, B. F. Strong to S. Parker Gilbert, January 8, 1923.

65. Hendrick, ch. 18, p. 49; Murray, *Harding Era*, pp. 172–79; Murray, pp. 96–97.

66. CFOST: Box 188, Tax—Exemption of State and Municipal Bonds, January–March 1922, AWM to J. W. Fordney, January 16, 1922; Box 262, Treasury Department—Secretary—Memoranda to AWM 1923–31, S. Parker Gilbert to AWM, February 26, 1923; Murray, pp. 85–89; Hendrick, ch. 19, pp. 17–18; Murray, *Harding Era*, pp. 380–81, 407.

67. *JMS*, p. 411.

68. BJH papers: AWM Letterbooks, AWM to J. R. Mellon, September 13, 1921; AWM to E. P. Mellon, October 28, 1922.

69. *JMS*, pp. 407–408; Hendrick, ch. 18, p. 2; Murray, *Harding Era*, p. 181.

70. Hendrick, ch. 18, p. 6.

71. Hendrick, ch. 18, pp. 9–10.

72. BJH papers: AWM Letterbooks, AWM to C. E. Woods, January 30, 1922; February 24, 26, 1923; AWM to E. P. Mellon, July 26, 1921, May 4, 1922.

73. BJH papers: AWM Letterbooks, AWM to Mrs. E. O. Rea, July 14, 1921; AWM to C. L. Lyon, August 1, 1921; AWM to Senator B. Penrose, August 3, 1921; AWM to Senator W. W. Crow, [January 1922]; AWM to V. G. Palmer, February 7, 1922; AWM to Major Magee, April 21, 1922; AWM to Judge Buffington, June 6, 1922.

74. BJH papers: AWM Letterbooks, AWM to Col. S. H. Church, October 13, 1921, January 23, 1922; AWM to C. E. Woods, October 25, 1921, January 30, 1922; C. E. Woods to AWM, February 14, 1922.

75. S. J. Astorino, "The Decline of the Republican Dynasty in Pennsylvania, 1929–1934" (Ph.D. diss., University of Pittsburgh, 1962), pp. 9–11.

76. Astorino, "Republican Dynasty in Pennsylvania," p. 7.

77. BJH papers: interview, WLM, November 4, 1940, p. 1.

78. Astorino, "Republican Dynasty in Pennsylvania," pp. 11–18.

79. J. A. Falco, "Political Background and First Gubernatorial Administration of Gifford Pinchot, 1933–1927" (Ph.D. diss., University of Pittsburgh, 1956), pp. 114–48.

80. Murray, *Harding Era*, p. 317; BJH papers: AWM Letterbooks, AWM to C. E. Woods, February 24, 1923.

81. Hersh, p. 302; BJH papers: interview, Col. F. Drake, June 9, 1942, p. 7.

82. BJH papers: AWM Letterbooks, AWM to RBM, November 8, 1921.

83. Sparkes papers: interview, H. M. Johnson, June 8, 1945, p. 7.

84. Koskoff, p. 183; BJH papers: AWM Letterbooks, AWM to C. D. Marshall, June 20, 1921, October 5, 1921, November 28, 1921.

85. BJH papers: AWM Letterbooks, AWM to H. B. Rust, February 18, 1922; AWM to M. H. Taylor, March 6, 1922.

86. BJH papers: AWM Letterbooks, AWM to C. D. Marshall, June 22, 1921; AWM to F. J. Tone, June 6, 1922.

87. Smith, p. 139; BJH papers: AWM Letterbooks, AWM to A. B. Davis, April 2, 1921; AWM to F. J. Tone, March 6, 1922.

88. BJH papers: AWM Letterbooks, AWM to H. E. Scully, October 7, 1922; AWM to M. A. Neeland, October 26, 1921; AWM to Rev. F. E. Johnson, November 29, 1922; U.S. Congress, *Hearings Before the Committee on the Judiciary, House of Representatives, on House Resolution 92,* 72nd Congress, 1st Session, 1932, p. 10.

89. *JMS,* pp. 403, 424; Hersh, pp. 245–46.

90. Hendrick, ch. 19, p. 25; Murray, p. 282; *United States Congressional Record,* 67th Congress, 2nd Session, 1922, vol. 62, pt. 3, pp. 2605–2608.

91. Koskoff, p. 252.

92. BJH papers: AWM Letterbooks, AWM to D. L. Marsh, December 15, 1922; AWM to W. R. Nicholson Jr., December 11, 1922; AWM to J. A. Frear, October 20, 1922; AWM to B. C. Marsh, November 28, 1922.

93. Knoedler papers: Letterbook, February 24, 1921–April 18, 1921, CHM to AWM, March 4, 1921; Duveen papers: JD to AWM, March 1, 17, 1921; M. Secrest, *Duveen: A Life in Art* (New York, 2004), p. 304.

94. BJH papers: AWM Letterbooks, AWM to JD, March 21, 1921.

95. *JMS,* p. 406; BJH papers: AWM Letterbooks, AWM to J. Reed, March 22, 1921.

96. Kopper, pp. 63–68; National Trust for Historic Preservation, "1785 Massachusetts Avenue, NW" (mimeo, c. 1980); Commission of Fine Arts, *Massachusetts Avenue Architecture,* vol. 1, *North West Washington, D.C.* (Washington, D.C., 1973), pp. 60–79.

97. BJH papers: AWM Letterbooks, A. E. Sixsmith to C. L. Harrison, August 2, 1922; *JMS,* pp. 424–25.

98. BJH papers: AWM Letterbooks, AWM to JD, February 28, 1922; Duveen papers: JD to AWM, July 5, 1921, November 21, 1921, February 27, 1922, May 29, 1922.

99. Duveen papers: JD to Miss Sylvester, June 5, 1922, JD to AWM, July 26, 1922; unsigned telegrams, August 2, 9; JD to Duveen Bros., October 3, 1922.

100. Kopper, pp. 67–68; AWM papers: AWM, Deceased, Report and Accounts, August 26, 1937, Exhibit D.

101. Kopper, p. 97; Secrest, *Duveen*, p. 303.

102. Duveen papers: JD to AWM, July 25, 1922, April 7, 1923; Duveen Bros. to W. Flore (c/o AWM), March 26, 1923, May 7, 1923.

103. Secrest, *Duveen*, pp. 299–300.

104. Duveen papers: Duveen Bros. [New York] to Duveen Bros. [London], June 1, 5, 1923; Duveen Bros. [London] to Duveen Bros. [New York], June 6, 1923; JD to Duveen Bros. [New York], July 20, 1923.

105. Secrest, *Duveen*, pp. 303–304; Duveen papers: JD to AWM, June 9, 12, 1922; BJH papers: AWM Letterbooks, AWM to JD, June 10, 1922, AWM to Duveen Bros., July 6, 1922.

106. BJH papers: AWM Letterbooks, AWM to JD, June 2, 1923; Duveen papers: JD to AWM, June 5, 1923.

107. BJH papers: AWM Letterbooks, AWM to CRH, June 24, 1921; Knoedler papers: Domestic Letterbook, February 24, 1921–April 18, 1921, Knoedler & Co. to AWM [undated]; Tax Book, May 1, 1921–April 23, 1926: CRH to AWM, May 24, 1921, December 14, 1921, June 22, 1921, August 9, 1921; Domestic Letterbook, December 9, 1922–January 30, 1923, R. F. Knoedler to AWM, December 30, 1922.

108. Knoedler papers: Domestic Letterbook, February 24, 1921–April 18, 1921, CHM to AWM, March 4, 1921, April 13, 1921; Domestic Letterbook, June 8, 1921–September 17, 1921, CHM to AWM, June 23, 1921; Domestic Letterbook, February 2, 1922–April 15, 1922, CHM to AWM, March 4, 10, 1922; Domestic Letterbook, March 19, 1923–May 4, 1923, CHM to AWM, April 27, 1923.

109. Knoedler papers: Domestic Letterbook, January 9, 1922–February 21, 1922, CHM to AWM, February 7, 18, 1922; BJH papers: AWM Letterbooks, AWM to CHM, February 17, 1922.

110. Knoedler papers: Domestic Letterbook, April 15, 1922–July 8, 1922, CHM to AWM, May 8, 17, 19, 24, 1922; BJH papers: AWM Letterbooks, AWM to CHM, May 10, 1922; AWM to Knoedler & Co., May 23, 1922.

111. Knoedler papers: Domestic Letterbook, January 8, 1921–February 24, 1921, CHM to AWM, February 5, 11, 1921; Domestic Letterbook, June 8, 1921–September 17, 1921, CHM to AWM, June 23, 1921; BJH papers: AWM Letterbooks, AWM to Knoedler & Co., July 6, 1922.

112. Knoedler papers: Domestic Letterbook, December 9, 1922–January 30, 1923, CHM to AWM, December 18, 1922.

113. Knoedler papers: Domestic Letterbook, April 15, 1922–July 8, 1922, CHM to AWM, May 1, 1922.

114. BJH papers: AWM Letterbooks, AWM to J. G. Butler, November 18, 1922; AWM to T. Rousseau, August 28, 31, 1923; Duveen papers: JD to AWM, June 1, 1923, enclosing letter from S. Soudbiniere; AWM papers: AWM Deceased,

Report and Account, August 26, 1937, Exhibit D; *TMT*, pp. 408–10; Judge, pp. 332–34. This was a doubly ill-judged purchase: for not only was Harriet no relation, the painting was not by Lawrence, and on AWM's death it was valued at only $500: AWM papers: Estate of AWM, Paintings at Woodland Road, Affidavit of CHM, February 10, 1938, p. 6.

115. AWM papers: PM to AWM, March 6, 1921; BJH papers: Letterbooks, AWM to AMB, April 26, 1922; AWM to Mrs. H. G. Bowman, May 12, 1921; AWM to J. R. Mellon, December 19, 1921.

116. NMM papers: NMM to P. Ache, March 25 [1922]; Lankford, pp. 71–73.

117. BJH papers: Letterbooks, AWM to W. G. Shute, February 17, 1923.

118. AWM papers: PM report cards, May 7, 1921, May 8, 1922.

119. BJH papers: AWM Letterbooks, AWM to G. C. St. John, July 7, 1921, November 28, 1922.

120. NMM papers: AWM to NMM, July 7, 1922; NMM to AWM, August 6, 15, 1922.

121. AWM papers: NMM to AWM, November 11, 1922, February 25, 1923.

122. AWM papers: NMM to AWM, April 24, 1923.

123. AWM papers: L. McMullen to AWM, November 14, 1922, April 19, 1923 (enclosing [undated] copy of letter from NMM to AWM), July 24, 30, 1923.

124. AWM papers: N. McMullen to AWM, March 25, 1923, September 2, 1923, November 6, 1923.

125. AWM papers: P. McMullen to AWM, April 9, 1923; H. M. J[ohnson?] to AWM, June 30, 1924.

126. BJH papers: AWM Letterbooks, AWM to L. McMullen, May 30, 1921, October 5, 1922. Murray McMullen was also in debt to AWM. See BJH papers: AWM Letterbooks, AWM to M. McMullen, March 18, 1923.

127. AWM papers: NMM to AWM, November 11, 1922, February 4, 1923.

128. NMM papers: NMM to B. McCrory, June 22, [1927].

129. AWM papers: NMM to AWM, November 8, 10, 1922; NMM papers: NMM to B. McCrory, November 6, 1922.

130. NMM papers: NMM to P. Ache, March 25, 1922, October 8, 1922; AWM to NMM, February 19, 1922.

131. AWM papers: NMM to AWM, November 11, 1923, February 4, 25, 1923, April 3, 24, 1923; N. McMullen to AWM, December 31, 1922.

132. AWM papers: NMM to AWM, March 7, 1923.

133. AWM papers: NMM to AWM, March 9, 1923.

134. *RSS*, pp. 105–106.

135. AWM papers: NMM to AWM, March 9, 1923.

136. *RSS*, p. 106.

137. Hendrick, ch. 18, p. 48; Murray, *Harding Era*, pp. 382–83.

138. Klein, *Rainbow's End*, pp. 27–30, 70.

139. Hendrick, ch. 10, pp. 51–52.

140. *JMS*, p. 429; Hendrick, ch. 18, p. 50.

141. BJH papers: AWM Letterbooks, AWM to G. C. St. John, January 27, 1923; AWM to E. F. Clark, May 25, 1922.

142. BJH papers: AWM Letterbooks, AWM to S. Parker Gilbert, June 22, 1923.

143. BJH papers: AWM Letterbooks, AWM to Ambassador M. T. Herrick [France],

June 22, 1923; AWM to Ambassador A. P. Moor [Spain], June 7, 1923; AWM to Gov. W. C. Sproul, June 15, 1923.

144. AWM papers: NMM to AWM, June 23, 1923; AWM to NMM, June 28, 1923; BJH papers: AWM Letterbooks, AWM to S. Baldwin, May 22, 1923; Murray, p. 96; *JMS*, p. 452; *New York Times*, July 25, 1923.

145. AWM papers: J. A. McMullen to AWM, July 15, 1923.

146. AWM papers: N. McMullen to AWM, March 25, 1923; L. McMullen to AWM, April 19, 1923.

147. Hendrick, ch. 18, p. 2; Murray, *Harding Era*, pp. 426, 438–39, 451.

148. BJH papers: AWM Letterbooks, AWM to A. J. Greenop, September 6, 1923; AWM to C. M. Schwab, January 18, 1924; AWM to J. F. Herson, June 4, 6, 1925; AWM to C. J. Schmidlapp, August 19, 1925; AWM papers: AWM Contributions, 1902 to 1937, listed under "Public and Civic" Gifts; Murray, pp. 105–107; Murray, *Harding Era*, pp. 429, 492–93.

10. Better Years with Coolidge: Mellonizing America, Aggrandizing Himself, 1923–26

1. CFOST: Box 27, Cables 1923, S. Parker Gilbert to AWM, August 4, 1923; Murray, pp. 107–108; G. W. Pepper, *Philadelphia Lawyer: An Autobiography* (Philadelphia, 1944), p. 196; NMM papers: NMM to B. McCrory, September 4, [1923]; C. Amory, *Who Killed Society?* (New York, 1960), p. 363.

2. Murray, pp. 119–20; *New York Times*, November 1, 1924; W. A. White, *Puritan in Babylon* (New York, 1938), p. 251; BJH papers: AWM Letterbooks, AWM to W. H. Taft, April 29, 1924; L. L. Gould, *Grand Old Party: A History of the Republicans* (New York, 2003), pp. 239, 242.

3. Sparkes papers: interview, Col. F. Drake, June 19, 1945, p. 11; CFOST: Box 266, Treasury Department—Under Secretary (Garrard B. Winston), 1923–27, G. B. Winston, speech [undated].

4. Sparkes papers: interview, DEF, March 1, 1945, p. 4; D. Doheny, *David Finley: A Quiet Force for America's Arts* (Washington, D.C., 2006), pp. 7–49; Murray, pp. 104–105.

5. CFOST: Box 17, Treasury Department—Speeches and Articles by AWM, 1923–26, AWM to W. R. Green, November 10, 1923; Treasury Department—Press Releases and Speeches, 1922–31, AWM to the editor, *The Outlook*, December 22, 1923.

6. Hendrick, ch. 19, p. 40.

7. CFOST: Box 171, Taxation—Board of Tax Appeals, 1923–24, AWM to R. Smoot, May 5, 1924; Box 213, Taxation—Returns, Inspection and Publicity, 1920–24, AWM comments in *New York World*, June 14, 1924.

8. Murray, p. 118.

9. AWM papers: AWM to C. L. Gifford, December 19, 1923; AWM to W. H. Newton, January 29, 1924; AWM, Speech to Bankers' Club of Richmond, March 17, 1925; CFOST: Box 138, Soldiers' Bonus, April–May 1924, AWM to C. Coolidge, April 28, 1924; BJH papers: AWM Letterbooks, AWM to G. M. Morris, May 26, 1926; Hendrick, ch. 19, pp. 41–42; Murray, pp. 132–34.

10. CFOST: Box 204, Taxation—Mellon Tax Reduction Plan, January 1–8, 1924, Acceptances, National Citizens' Committee in Support of the Mellon Tax Reduction Proposal, January 3, 1924; BJH papers: AWM Letterbooks, AWM to L. Livingston, January 9, 1924; AWM to H. H. Patterson, January 7, 1924.

11. Sparkes papers: interview, DEF, March 1, 1945, p. 5; CFOST: Box 208, Mellon Tax Reduction Plan—Book, DEF to G. B. Winston, April 10, 26, 1924; AWM to Macmillan & Co., April 25, 1924; *New York Times*, April 29, 1924.

12. AWM, *Taxation: The People's Business* (New York, 1924), pp. 11–13, 22, 71–72; BJH papers: AWM Letterbooks, AWM to T. S. Adams, May 19, 1924; Murray, pp. 122–23.

13. CFOST: Box 109, The President (Calvin Coolidge), 1923–26, AWM to C. Coolidge, May 28, 1924; Box 195, Taxation—Inheritance, January–June 1924, AWM to C. Coolidge, June 2, 1924; BJH papers: AWM Letterbooks, AWM to A. J. Beveridge, May 31, 1924; Murray, pp. 117, 127.

14. *JMS*, pp. 440–42; Hendrick, ch. 24, pp. 1–3.

15. BJH papers: AWM Letterbooks, AWM to E. E. Brown, May 22, 1924; AWM to A. P. Moore, May 23, 1924; R. K. Murray, *The Harding Era: Warren G. Harding and His Administration* (Minneapolis, 1969), pp. 506–14; Gould, *Grand Old Party*, pp. 240–41.

16. CFOST: Box 254, Treasury Department—Secretary—Articles for Publication (AWM), January–June 1924, AWM to *New York World*, May 13, 1924; Box 112, Prohibition—National, 1924, D. H. Blair to G. D. Winston, October 16, 1924, enclosing Accomplishments in Prohibition Enforcement from June 11, 1921, to September 11, 1924; BJH papers: AWM Letterbooks, AWM to D. L. Marsh, February 5, 1924; AWM to Mrs. E. D. Harnbrook, August 26, 1925; Murray, *Harding Era*, pp. 404–405.

17. CFOST: Box 112, Prohibition—National, 1925–26, Treasury press release, June 23, 1925; *New York Times*, April 3, 1925; BJH papers: AWM Letterbooks, AWM to President Coolidge, December 1, 1925.

18. CFOST: Box 164, Taxation (General), January–June 1926, AWM to C. Coolidge, February 25, 1926; Hendrick, ch. 19, pp. 40–44.

19. BJH papers: AWM Letterbooks, AWM, Memorandum for Secretary Kellogg, October 5, 1926; Koskoff, p. 237; Hendrick, ch. 20, p. 17.

20. AWM, "What I Am Trying to Do," *World's Work*, November 1923, p. 31; Murray, p. 159.

21. Murray, pp. 176–80.

22. S. V. O. Clark, *Central Bank Cooperation, 1924–31* (New York, 1967), pp. 45–69; E. S. Rosenberg, *Financial Missionaries to the World: The Politics and Culture of Dollar Diplomacy, 1900–1930* (Cambridge, Mass., 1999), pp. 166–76; Steiner, pp. 240–50.

23. CFOST: Box 24, Treasury Department—Secretary—Articles for Publication, July–December 1924, AWM to Dr. M. Jordan, December 15, 1924, plus enclosure; Strong papers: 1000.0, B. F. Strong to AWM, September 21, 1925; K. P. Jones, "Discord and Collaboration: Choosing an Agent-General for Reparations," *Diplomatic History* 1 (1977), pp. 119–39.

24. Murray, pp. 144–45; Steiner, p. 240.

25. Hendrick, ch. 21, pp. 1–5; BJH papers: AWM Letterbooks, AWM to R. Olney, August 26, 1925.

26. BJH papers: interview, C. S. Dewey, March 3, 1942, pp. 1–2; CFOST: Box 255, Treasury Department—Secretary—Articles for Publication, 1926, AWM to *Yale Daily News*, February 10, 1926; BJH papers: AWM Letterbooks, AWM to G. B. Winston, July 7, 1925, May 1, 1926; Hendrick, ch. 21, pp. 5–38.

27. CFOST: Box 250, Treasury Department—Secretary Mellon, 1925–26, AWM to F. W. Peabody, July 18, 1926; Coolidge papers: CC 30, AWM to C. Coolidge, February 10, 1926; CC 91, AWM to C. Coolidge, February 18, 1926; AWM, *Taxation: The People's Business*, pp. 31–32; Hendrick, ch. 22, pp. 1–4.

28. Hendrick, ch. 21, pp. 38–41; BJH papers: AWM Letterbooks, AWM to W. D. Guthrie, May 17, 1926; E. Moreau, *The Golden Franc: Memoirs of a Governor of the Bank of France: The Stabilization of the Franc, 1926–1928*, trans. S. D. Stoller and T. C. Roberts (Boulder, Colo., 1991), pp. 58–59, 62–63, 76, 89, 208, 385.

29. L. V. Chandler, *Benjamin Strong, Central Banker* (Washington, D.C., 1958), pp. 291–331, 332–69, 381–415; F. Costigliola, *Awkward Dominion: American Political, Economic, and Cultural Relations with Europe, 1919–1933* (Ithaca, N.Y., 1984), pp. 111–39.

30. CFOST: Box 86, Gold (Miscellaneous), 1922–25, B. F. Strong to AWM, May 27, 1924; Box 304, Federal Reserve Bank of New York, G. L. Harrison to G. B. Winston, May 11, 1925, enclosing memorandum by B. F. Strong, January 13, 1925; Hamlin papers: Index-Digest, January 8, 1925, May 18, 1925.

31. Meltzer, pp. 170–73, 198, 203; F&S, p. 255; Chandler, *Benjamin Strong*, pp. 251–58.

32. Chandler, *Benjamin Strong*, pp. 258–71.

33. BJH papers: AWM Letterbooks, AWM to J. F. Burke, September 25, 1925.

34. BJH papers: AWM Letterbooks, AWM to A. T. Smith, March 18, 1926.

35. AWM papers: Address of James Speyer presenting portrait of AWM to the Chamber of Commerce of New York State, May 6, 1925; F. H. Ecker to AWM, April 10, 1926; AWM to F. H. Ecker, April 17, 1926; BJH papers: AWM Letterbooks, AWM to Dr. N. M. Butler, February 12, 1924; AWM to F. D. Fackenthal, May 16, 1924; AWM to J. Speyer, January 27, 1926; AWM to Dr. G. D. Olds, April 17, 1926; AWM to Dr. J. R. Angell, April 17, 1926; AWM to Dr. A. L. Lowell, April 17, 1926; AWM to G. F. Baker, September 20, 1926; AWM to Dean W. B. Donham, May 20, 1927.

36. BJH papers: interview, J. G. Bowman, January 10, 1940, p. 4; AWM Letterbooks, AWM to A. R. Holcombe, January 24, 1927; AWM to W. H. Taft, April 29, 1924.

37. BJH papers: AWM Letterbooks, AWM to Senator G. W. Pepper, June 24, 1924; AWM to C. E. Woods, October 13, 1924; AWM to W. L. Clause, February 9, 1925; AWM to A. W. Thompson, August 10, 1925.

38. BJH papers: AWM Letterbooks, AWM to C. D. Marshall and H. H. McClintic, March 6, 1925; AWM to H. V. Loss, March 9, 1924; AWM to T. H. Caraway, March 4, 1924; AWM to C. E. Hughes, September 17, 22, 1924, December 18, 1925; AWM to G. S. Davison, December 19, 1925; AWM to J. R. Sheffield, January 9, 1926; Koskoff, p. 291; Smith, pp. 141–44.

39. BJH papers: interview, A. E. Sixsmith, March 5, 1941, p. 3; interview, C. S. Dewey, March 3, 1942, pp. 3–4; Kopper, p. 68. For the broader Washington social scene in AWM's day, see Mrs J. K. van Rensselaer, *The Social Ladder* (New York, 1924), pp. 247–76; W. M. Kiplinger, *Washington Is Like That* (New York, 1942), pp. 397–418; O. E. Clapper, *Washington Tapestry* (New York, 1946), pp. 157–71; C. Hurd, *Washington Cavalcade* (New York, 1948), pp. 197–212.

40. Duveen papers: JD to AWM, October 25, 1924; note, November 19, 1924; AWM to JD, January 3, 1925; JD to AWM, January 14, 1925; AWM to Duveen Bros., March 21, 1925.

41. Duveen papers: JD to AWM, January 6, 1925; Duveen Bros. [New York] to Duveen Bros. [London], April 13, 1925; JD to AWM, September 14, 1925; Duveen Bros. [New York] to Duveen Bros. [Paris], December 9, 1925; AWM to JD, January 30, 1926; Duveen Bros. [New York] to Duveen Bros. [Paris], February 2, 1926; Duveen Bros. [New York] to AWM, February 4, 1926.

42. Duveen papers: JD to AWM, September 14, 1925; M. Secrest, *Duveen: A Life in Art* (New York, 2004), pp. 292–93.

43. Duveen papers: JD to AWM, February 15, 19, 1925.

44. Duveen papers: Duveen Bros. to AWM, April 15, 1925; AWM to JD, April 20, 1925; JD to AWM, April 21, 1925.

45. BJH papers: AWM Letterbooks, AWM to Miss H. C. Frick, May 11, 1927; *JMS*, p. 426; Secrest, *Duveen*, p. 475; Kopper, p. 68.

46. BJH papers: AWM Letterbooks, AWM to Knoedler & Co., September 6, 1923; Knoedler papers: Domestic Letterbook, May 4, 1923–August 2, 1923, CHM to AWM, May 9, 1923; Domestic Letterbook, August 2, 1923–October 31, 1923, CHM to AWM, October 22, 1923.

47. Knoedler papers: Domestic Letterbook, April 18, 1924–June 16, 1924, CHM to AWM, June 12, 1924; Domestic Letterbook, June 16, 1924–October 21, 1924, CRH to AWM, September 19, 1924, October 1, 1924; Domestic Letterbook, October 21, 1924–December 16, 1924, CHM to AWM, November 19, 1924.

48. Knoedler papers: Domestic Letterbook, February 25, 1925–April 28, 1925, CRH to AWM, April 11, 15, 1925; Domestic Letterbook, October 27, 1925–December 16, 1925, CHM to AWM, November 9, 21, 30, 1925.

49. Knoedler papers: Tax Book, May 1, 1921–April 23, 1926, R. F. Knoedler to AWM, November 28, 1923; CRH to AWM, November 30, 1923; Knoedler & Co. to AWM, January 25, 1924, February 2, 1924; Domestic Letterbook, February 27, 1924–April 17, 1924, CHM to AWM, March 27, 1924; R. F. Knoedler to AWM, April 1, 1924; CHM to RBM, March 27, 1924; Domestic Letterbook, December 17, 1924–February 25, 1925, Knoedler & Co. to AWM, January 5, 1925; CHM to AWM, February 2, 21, 1925; AWM to Sir W. Orpen, February 20, 1925; Domestic Letterbook, February 25, 1925–April 28, 1925, Knoedler & Co. to AWM, March 30, 1925; Domestic Letterbook, April 28, 1925–July 28, 1925, Knoedler & Co. to AWM, May 28, 1925, June 1, 1925; BJH papers: AWM Letterbooks, AWM to Sir W. Orpen, August 11, 13, 1925; Duveen papers: Duveen Bros. [Paris] to Duveen Bros. [New York], April 15, 1925.

50. Duveen papers: Duveen Bros. [New York] to JD, June 16, 20, 23, 1925, October

6, 1925, September 21, 1926; Knoedler papers: Domestic Letterbook, April 18, 1924–June 16, 1924, CRH to AWM, May 28, 1924.

51. AWM papers: NMM to AWM, January 31, 1924, March 2, 1924, April 19, 1924 [postmark], June 4, 1924, December 7, 1925, January 25, 1926.

52. AWM papers: NMM to AWM, February 4, 1924, June 25, 1924, September 15, 1924.

53. AWM papers: NMM to AWM, August 31, 1923, December 5, 1923; NMM papers: AWM to NMM, December 9, 1923; NMM to AWM, April 19, 1924 [postmark], March 2, 7, 1925.

54. AWM papers: NMM to AWM, February 21, 1924, June 4, 1924, October 5, 1925.

55. AWM papers: NMM to AWM, November 6, 21, 1924.

56. AWM papers: AWM to NMM, April 9, 1925; NMM to AWM, December 5, 1923, March 2, 1924, April 19, 1924 [postmark], September 9, 1924, March 7, 29, 1925, April 16, 1925.

57. AWM papers: NMM to AWM, January 31, 1924, February 4, 21, 1924, January 6, 1925, April 20, 1925, May 4, 1925, June 6, 1925.

58. AWM papers: NMM to AWM, April 19, 1924 [postmark], October 9, 1924, December 12, 18, 1924, January 6, 1925, March 29, 1925, October 5, 1925.

59. AWM papers: L. McMullen to AWM, September 4, 1924, December 24, 1924, June 18, 1926, July 9, 1926, August 15, 20, 28, 1926, February 21, 1927, April 7, 26, 1927; N. McMullen to AWM, November 6, 1923, May 9, 1924.

60. AWM papers: NMM to AWM, December 5, 1923; NMM papers: NMM to B. McCrory, January 22, [1925], February 4, [1925?], December 29, [1925], March 24, [1927]; B. McCrory to NMM, November 16, 1927.

61. NMM papers: NMM to B. McCrory, September 4, [1923], June 6, [1925], August 10, [1925], March 23, [1926], May 8, [1926]; AWM papers: NMM to AWM, April 19, 1924 [postmark], June 4, 20, 1924, September 9, 1924.

62. AMB papers: AWM to AMB, September 13, 1923, September 14, 25, 1924, April 6, 1925, May 2, 1925.

63. AWM papers: NMM to AWM, March 19, 1925; Anonymous, *Boudoir Mirrors of Washington* (Philadelphia, 1923), pp. 187–88.

64. Lankford, pp. 8–13.

65. Lankford, pp. 13–64.

66. Lankford, pp. 65–75.

67. Kopper, pp. 71–72; Lankford, p. 101.

68. BJH papers: AWM Letterbooks, AWM to J. S. Vance, January 26, 1924.

69. DEF papers (NGA): Box 1, Folder Bruce-Mellon, Order of Seating at Cathedral; Order of Procedure for Mellon-Bruce Wedding; *New York Tribune*, May 26, 1926; *Washington Times*, May 29, 1926; *Washington Post*, May 30, 1926; Doheny, *David Finley*, p. 87; Lankford, pp. 75–78.

70. AWM papers: NMM to AWM, April 28, 1925, undated [April 1926], April 28, 1926; NMM papers: NMM to B. McCrory, May 8, 1926.

71. NMM papers: NMM to B. McCrory, May 26, 1926, June 12, 1926.

72. Duveen papers: Duveen Bros. [Paris] to Duveen Bros. [New York], March 23, 1925; Duveen Bros. [London] to Duveen Bros. [Paris], March 26, 1925; AMB to

JD, March 28, 1925; O. Birley to JD, November 16, 1925; JD to AMB, May 5, 1926, and undated.

73. Duveen papers: Duveen Bros. [New York] to Duveen Bros. [London], May 28, 1926, June 1, 1926, June 24, 1926; Secrest, *Duveen*, p. 305.

74. Lankford, p. 83; Koskoff, pp. 416–17.

75. *RSS*, pp. 101–102; AWM papers: NMM to AWM, October 5, 1925.

76. AWM papers: P. T. Walden to AWM, May 28, 1926; DEF papers (NGA): Box 19, Folder Personal Correspondence—PM, 1925–1926: PM to DEF, January 1926, February 1, 8, 1926, March 23, 1926; Folder Personal Correspondence—PM, 1927–1928: PM to DEF, January 29, 1927, February 1927, March 31, 1927; BJH papers: AWM Letterbooks, C. Coolidge to AWM, June 28, 1927.

77. *RSS*, pp. 107–14.

78. PM papers: interview no. 2, p. 5.

79. DEF papers (NGA): Box 19, Folder Personal Correspondence—PM, 1927–1928, DEF to PM, March 31, 1927, June 8, 1927; *RSS*, p. 102; BJH papers: AWM Letterbooks, AWM to PM, June 11, 1925. AWM claimed his favorite poem was Gray's "Elegy": BJH papers: AWM Letterbooks, AWM to C. A. Worden, October 19, 1925.

80. BJH papers: AWM Letterbooks, AWM to W. T. Johnson, September 28, 1923; AWM to H. Heinz, October 11, 1924.

81. R. Lubove, *Twentieth-Century Pittsburgh*, vol. 1, *Government, Business and Environmental Change* (Pittsburgh, 1995), pp. 63–64; Lorant, pp. 327–29; Samber, pp. 448–51.

82. See the self-boosting essays delivered as lectures in 1927–28 and gathered in Chamber of Commerce, *Pittsburgh and the Pittsburgh Spirit* (Pittsburgh, 1929), including AWM on "Banking and Finance in Pittsburgh," pp. 257–78.

83. Union Trust papers: Box 1216, f06-01-00-011-0009, Dividends paid July 1916 to October 1942; Mellon Bank papers: Box 627, f04-05-00-002-0001, Mellon National Bank, Resources and Liabilities, June 30, 1927.

84. *MNBTC*, p. 38.

85. BJH papers: AWM Letterbooks, AWM to E. P. Mellon, May 4, 1922; interview, J. Nelson, March 14, 1941, pp. 1–2.

86. AWM papers: Anonymous, *The Union Trust Company of Pittsburgh, AD 1922* (Pittsburgh, 1923); W. C. Kidney, *Pittsburgh's Landmark Architecture: The Historic Buildings of Pittsburgh and Allegheny County* (Pittsburgh, 1997), pp. 244–45.

87. Union Trust papers: Box 1216, f06-01-00-007-0012, Announcement of Union Trust Co. removal to new offices, November 13, 1923; Invitation to a "formal inspection of the new Banking Room in the Union Trust Building . . . ," November 22, 1923; f06-01-00-007-0013: Invitation to Mr. H. C. McEldowney's dinner, November 22, 1923; *Pittsburgh Post*, November 22, 1922

88. Kidney, *Pittsburgh's Landmark Architecture*, p. 236; AWM papers: E. P. Mellon to AWM, February 7, 1915, June 8, 1915.

89. AWM papers: "Notes for an address delivered by AWM at banquet in connection with opening of new building of Mellon National Bank, March 20, 1924," p. 7.

90. BJH papers: AWM Letterbooks, AWM to G. S. St. John, November 25,

1924; AWM papers: AWM Contributions, 1902–1937, list C, Education; Speech by AWM on laying the foundation stone for the library at Choate School [undated].

91. AWM papers: H. S. Pritchett to AWM, October 16, 1920; R. C. Alberts, *Pitt: The Story of the University of Pittsburgh, 1787–1987* (Pittsburgh, 1986), pp. 79–88.

92. BJH papers: AWM Letterbooks, AWM to H. D. Williams, January 28, 1925; AWM Contributions, 1902–1937, list C, Education; Bowman papers: J. G. Bowman to AWM, February 20, 25, 1926, April 21, 1926; J. G. Bowman, *Unofficial Notes* (Pittsburgh, 1963), pp. 57–69; Alberts, *Pitt*, pp. 89–115, 122; Kidney, *Pittsburgh's Landmark Architecture*, pp. 355–56.

93. BJH papers: AWM Letterbooks, AWM to Mrs W. Flinn, February 21, 1924.

94. BJH papers: AWM Letterbooks, AWM press statement, June 18, 1927; M. Brignano and J. Tomlinson Fort, *Reed Smith: A Law Firm Celebrates 125 Years* (Pittsburgh, 2002), pp. 53–54.

95. BJH papers: AWM Letterbooks, AWM to H. Heinz, October 11, 1924.

96. Pittsburgh Coal Company papers: Minutes of Directors' Meetings, March 23, 1921, March 26, 1924.

97. Pittsburgh Coal Company papers: Minutes of Directors' Meetings, August 28, 1923, March 25, 1925, December 22, 1926; S. J. Astorino, "The Decline of the Republican Dynasty in Pennsylvania, 1929–1934" (Ph.D. diss., University of Pittsburgh, 1962), p. 96; Koskoff, p. 303.

98. For the fullest account of these episodes, see Astorino, "Republican Dynasty in Pennsylvania," pp. 20–22; L. L. Murray, "The Mellons, Their Money, and the Mythical Machine: Organizational Politics in the Republican Twenties," *Pennsylvania History* 42 (1975), pp. 221–41; Hendrick, ch. 24, pp. 10–35.

99. Pepper papers: 70/Part 1, R. B. Vale to G. W. Pepper, August 7, 13, 1925; CFOST, Box 112; Prohibition—National, 1925–26, Speech of Gifford Pinchot to the Biennial National Convention of the Anti-Saloon League of America, Chicago, November 8, 1925; G. Pinchot to AWM, November 14, 1925; AWM to G. Pinchot, November 16, 1925; Koskoff, p. 246; J. A. Falco, "Political Background and First Gubernatorial Administration of Gifford Pinchot, 1923–1927" (Ph.D. diss., University of Pittsburgh, 1956), pp. 221–24, 229–30.

100. Pepper papers: 70/Part 1, D. A. Reed to G. W. Pepper [undated, late 1925].

101. BJH papers: interview, G. W. Pepper, May 21, 1942, pp. 1–4.

102. BJH papers: AWM Letterbooks, AWM to T. Rousseau, March 6, 1926; AWM to W. W. Griest, May 8, 1926; AWM to F. B. Gernerd, May 8, 1926.

103. AWM papers: AWM, Speech in Pittsburgh, May 14, 1926; Pepper papers: 70/Part 2, G. W. Pepper to E. E. Overdorf, June 19, 1926; G. W. Pepper to J. R. Sheffield, June 19, 1928; Astorino, "Republican Dynasty in Pennsylvania," pp. 28–40.

104. BJH papers: AWM Letterbooks, AWM to WLM, July 15, 1926. For WLM's evidence, see *Sixty-ninth Congress, First Session, United States Senate, Senatorial Campaign Expenditures, Hearings Before a Special Committee* (Washington, D.C., 1926), pp. 154–98.

105. Koskoff, p. 249.

106. Murray, p. 127.

107. AWM, *Taxation: The People's Business*, pp. 10, 17; Hendrick, ch. 19, pp. 19–20; Murray, p. 126.

108. Murray, pp. 125, 129–31; G. Smiley and R. Keehn, "Federal Personal Income Tax Policy in the 1920s," *Journal of Economic History* 55 (1995), pp. 285–303.

109. Hendrick, ch. 19, pp. 23–24; Murray, pp. 128–29.

110. AWM, *Taxation: The People's Business*, pp. 9, 56–57; W. E. Brownlee, "Tax Regimes, National Crisis, and State-Building in America," in W. E. Brownlee (ed.), *Founding the Modern American State, 1941–1995: The Rise and Fall of the Era of Easy Finance* (Cambridge, 1996), pp. 67–69; R. F. King, "From Redistributive to Hegemonic Logic: The Transformation of American Tax Politics, 1894–1963," *Politics and Society* 12 (1983), pp. 1–52; R. F. King, *Money, Time and Politics: Investment Tax Subsidies and American Democracy* (New Haven, Conn., 1993), pp. 104–11.

111. Murray, *Harding Era*, pp. 479–82.

112. Koskoff, pp. 192–229; Hendrick, ch. 24, pp. 4–9.

113. CFOST: Box 143, Soldiers' Bonus—Book no. 1, J. Couzens to AWM, December 20, 1923; Hendrick, ch. 19, pp. 35–37.

114. CFOST, Box 179, Taxation—Couzens Correspondence, 1924–29, J. Couzens to AWM, January 11, 1924; Murray, pp. 136–39.

115. CFOST: Box 143, Soldiers' Bonus—Book no. 1, AWM to J. Couzens, January 15, 24, 1924; Box 179, Taxation—Couzens Correspondence, 1924–29, J. Couzens to AWM, January 18, 1924.

116. Hendrick, ch. 23, pp. 1–16.

117. Murray, pp. 138–39.

118. Coolidge papers: CC 30, AWM to President Coolidge, April 10, 1924; AWM papers: AWM, Speech to Pittsburgh Chamber of Commerce, April 12, 1924.

119. Murray, p. 139; *New York Times*, April 12, 1924.

120. Smith, pp. 139, 193–94; C. C. Carr, *Alcoa: An American Enterprise* (New York, 1952), pp. 201–208; CFOST: Box 1, Aluminum, 1921–31, Treasury press release, September 27, 1924; Department of Justice press release, February 7, 1925; FTC complaint, July 21, 1925; Alcoa response, July 21, 1925; Page papers: T. Walker Page, "Comments on Secretary Mellon's Statement" [undated, ?October 1924]; *New York Times*, September 28, 1924, October 6, 7, 8, 9, 14, 22, 30, 1924.

121. BJH papers: AWM Letterbooks, AWM to A. Brisbane, January 11, 1926; Koskoff, p. 231; Murray, *Harding Era*, pp. 379–80; G. C. Davis, "The Transformation of the Federal Trade Commission, 1914–1929," *Mississippi Valley Historical Review* 49 (1962), pp. 450–51.

122. *New York World*, April 23, 1927, May 25, 1928; *Washington Evening Star*, April 4, 1930; *New York Times*, November 27, 1930. In the spring of 1924, Alcoa was also charged, by the House Committee on Military Affairs, with wartime profiteering. Once again, the charges were denied: BJH papers: AWM Letterbooks, AWM to B. Baruch, April 7, 1924.

123. CFOST: Box 179, Taxation—Couzens Correspondence, 1924–29, D. H. Blair to J. Couzens, March 7, 1925; Treasury press release, March 9, 1925; Statement by AWM, March 9, 1925.

124. CFOST: Box 179, Taxation—Couzens Correspondence, 1924–29, *James Couzens v. Commissioner of Internal Revenue*, Memorandum re Decision of Board of Tax Appeals, May 7, 1925; Koskoff, pp. 276–77.
125. Hendrick, ch. 23, pp. 23–28.
126. Murray, pp. 124, 131–32, 282–83; F. Kent, "Andrew Mellon," *New Republic*, March 29, 1926, p. 135.
127. Hendrick, ch. 22, pp. 4, 9; BJH papers: AWM Letterbooks, AWM to F. B. Kellogg, October 5, 1926, enclosing Memorandum for Secretary Kellogg, October 5, 1926; AWM Memorandum, Government and Finance and Taxation in 1927, November 23, 1926.
128. AWM papers: T. A. Edison to AWM, June 14, 1928; AWM to T. A. Edison, October 30, 1928.
129. CFOST: Box 164, Taxation (General), July–December 1926, Treasury press release, November 8, 1926; Mellon Bank papers: Box 627, fo4-05-00-02-1 to 3, Mellon National Bank, resources and liabilities, 1926–28.
130. Koskoff, p. 238; Hendrick, ch. 19, p. 11; AWM papers: AWM, Deceased, Report and Accounts, August 26, 1937, Exhibit G, p. 59.
131. Murray, pp. 197–98.
132. CFOST: Box 18, Banks and Banking—Branch Banks 1923, H. M. Daugherty to AWM, October 3, 1923; Banks and Banking—Branch Banks, 1927–32, Memorandum to Federal Reserve Board, December 1, 1928.
133. Murray, pp. 193–94.
134. BJH papers: Letterbooks, AWM to M. T. Herrick, March 17, 1927.
135. Coolidge papers: CC 30, AWM to C. Coolidge, July 8, 1926; CFOST: Box 124, Rural Credits, January–February 1927, AWM to C. Coolidge, February 21, 1927; Hendrick, ch. 22, pp. 6–9; Koskoff, pp. 239–40.
136. Duveen papers: JD to Duveen Bros. [Paris], September 6, 1926; JD to AWM, September 9, 1926; AWM to JD, Thursday [September 1926]; JD to Duveen Bros. [New York], September 10, 1926; Duveen Bros. [New York] to Duveen Bros. [Paris], October 23, 1926; JD to Duveen Bros. [Paris], November 1, 1926; Duveen Bros. [New York] to Duveen Bros. [Paris], December 7, 1926; Price and Payment List, 1926–27; AWM to JD, March 24, 1927.
137. Duveen papers: JD, note, November 23, 1926; JD to AWM, November 24, 1926, April 21, 1927; Duveen Bros. [New York] to Duveen Bros. [London], July 5, 1927; Huntington papers: Box 185, JD to H. E. Huntington, March 29, 1927; Box 186, H. E. Huntington to JD, April 13, 1927; J. Thorpe, *Henry Edwards Huntington: A Biography* (Berkeley, Calif., 1994), pp. 499–500.
138. Kopper, p. 69; BJH papers: AWM Letterbooks, AWM to J. O'Connor, January 10, 1922.
139. Duveen papers: JD to AWM, February 2, 1925, September 14, 1925; JD to Duveen Bros. [Paris], December 28, 1925; JD to AWM, February 8, 1926; JD to A. E. Sixsmith, February 23, 1926, April 23, 1926.
140. Duveen papers: JD to Duveen Bros. [New York], September 10, 1926; Duveen Bros. [New York] to Duveen Bros. [Paris], September 11, 1926.
141. AMB papers: PM to AMB, July 28, 1926.
142. Lankford, pp. 78–82; AWM papers: AWM, Federal Estate Tax Return, February 25, 1939, sheet X-3; AMB papers: AWM to AMB, October 3, 1926; *RSS*, p. 107.

143. AWM papers: AWM, Federal Estate Tax Return, February 25, 1939, sheet X-4; AMB papers: AWM to AMB, November 21, 1926.

144. AMB papers: AWM to AMB, December 5, 1926.

145. CFOST: Box 260, Treasury Department—Secretary—Invitations to Dinner etc., 1926, AWM to C. E. Hughes, October 28, 1926; BJH papers: AWM Letterbooks, AWM to G. B. Winston, January 31, 1927; AWM to H. N. Straus, March 24, 1927.

146. CFOST: Box 262, Treasury Department—Secretary—Memoranda to AWM, 1923–1931, C. S. Dewey to AWM, April 1, 1927, May 18, 1927, January 17, 1929; BJH papers: AWM to Mr. Deuther, October 21, 1931; Hendrick, ch. 22, p. 11; Murray, pp. 198–99.

11. Carrying On with Hoover: Great Ideas to Great Crash, 1927–29

1. CFOST: Box 251, Treasury Department—Secretary Mellon 1927, AWM to J. G. Hibben, March 15, 1927; Box 165, Taxation (General), January–September 1927, E. R. Gray to O. Mills, March 26, 1927; AWM to J. C. White, April 30, 1927; Murray, pp. 163–64, 180.

2. Hendrick, ch. 27, pp. 1–2.

3. CFOST: Box 25, Budget—Business Organization of the Government 1921–29, AWM to C. Coolidge, June 5, 1928; Box 261, Treasury Department—Secretary—Invitations etc., 1927–28, AWM, Speech at the seventh annual lunch of the Women's National Republican Club, New York, January 14, 1928.

4. J. K. Galbraith, *The Great Crash, 1929* (Boston, 1997), p. 12; Hendrick, ch. 27, p. 4.

5. Hamlin papers: Container 362, f205.001, C. S. Hamlin to AWM, October 2, 1928, plus enclosure; F&S, p. 282; Meltzer, p. 223; L. V. Chandler, *Benjamin Strong, Central Banker* (Washington, D.C., 1958), p. 255.

6. Murray, pp. 201–10.

7. CFOST: Box 165, Taxation (General), January–April 1928, AWM to L. E. Pierson, April 19, 1928; L. E. Pierson to AWM, April 27, 1928.

8. Murray, pp. 181–84.

9. CFOST: Box 257, Treasury Department—Secretary—Distillery Holdings (Mellon), 1924–29, AWM to T. H. Caraway, October 2, 1928; BJH papers: AWM Letterbooks, AWM to Mrs. N. S. Scott, October 24, 1927.

10. CFOST: Box 66, Federal Reserve Banks—Discount Rates, 1927–28, O. Mills to A. Shaw, July 23, 1928; AWM papers: S. Parker Gilbert to AWM, September 14, 1927; Meltzer, pp. 228–30.

11. AWM, "Ours Are the Faults of Youth," *World's Work*, February 1928, p. 364; Murray, p. 235.

12. AWM papers: C. Coolidge to AWM, June 28, 1927; DEF papers (NGA): Folder—Subject File AWM, T. Rousseau to AWM, August 3, 1927; PM papers: interview no. 5, p. 12.

13. BJH papers: AWM Letterbooks, AWM to T. Rousseau, November 14, 1927; AWM papers: AWM diary, January 27, 1928; DEF papers (NGA): DEF, Anecdotes of AWM, Memorandum, October 9, 1935; Murray, p. 214.

14. D. Nasaw, *The Chief: The Life of William Randolph Hearst* (Boston, 2001), pp.

320–21, 377, 398; *Denver Post*, December 9, 1927; *Pittsburgh Post-Gazette*, July 30, 1927, August 6, 1927; AWM papers: P. McMullen to AWM, December 30, 1927.

15. AWM papers: AWM diary, February 16, 1928; CFOST: Box 251, Treasury Department—Secretary Mellon, 1928–32, R. W. Smith to AWM, January 30, 1928; Hendrick, ch. 25, p. 4.

16. AWM papers: AWM diary, March 20–23, 1928.

17. U.S. 70th Congress, Senate, *Hearings Before the Committee on Interstate Commerce, Conditions in the Coalfields of Pennsylvania, West Virginia and Ohio* (Washington, D.C., 1928), vol. 1, pp. 1351–67.

18. Ibid., p. 1366.

19. AWM papers: AWM diary, May 11, 13, 19, 1928; Hendrick, ch. 25, p. 5.

20. AWM papers: AWM diary, October 5, 1928; BJH papers: interview, G. B. Winston, April 7, 1942, p. 1; interview, H. M. Johnson, April 6, 1940, p. 1.

21. CFOST: Box 95, Labor Department (Miscellaneous), 1918–31, H. Hoover to AWM, February 2, 1922.

22. AWM papers: AWM diary, January 31, 1928, February 2, 1928, April 18, 1928; S. Parker Gilbert to AWM, May 7, 1928; AWM to S. Parker Gilbert, May 24, 1928; *New York Times*, January 17, 1928; Murray, pp. 211–14.

23. Hendrick, ch. 25, p. 18.

24. *New York Times*, June 11, 1928; Murray, p. 220.

25. AWM papers: AWM diary, June 11, 12, 16, 1928; H. Hoover, *The Memoirs of Herbert Hoover*, vol. 2, *The Cabinet and the Presidency* (New York, 1952), pp. 193–94; *New York Times*, June 13, 1928.

26. Murray, p. 221.

27. CFOST: Box 261, Treasury Department—Secretary—Invitations etc., AWM speech, "Republican Accomplishments," broadcast from station WRC, Washington, D.C., October 11, 1928.

28. AWM papers: AWM diary, May 5, 1928; Murray, p. 267; E. L. Davin, "Blue Collar Democracy: Ethnic Workers and Class Politics in Pittsburgh's Steel Valley, 1914–1948" (Ph.D. diss., University of Pittsburgh, 1999), p. 19.

29. AWM papers: AWM diary, December 25, 26, 1927, January 6, 15, 1928, February 6–8, 1928, April 13, 1928, June 22, 24, 1928, September 15, 1928.

30. BJH papers: AWM Letterbooks, AWM to D. A. Reed, April 18, 1929; AWM to F. Steiner, May 18, 1929.

31. Smith, p. 446; S. A. Swensrud, *"Gulf Oil": The First Fifty Years, 1901–1951* (New York, 1951), p. 15; BJH papers: "Some Comments on the History of Koppers" (typescript, August 6, 1940), pp. 12–15; W. C. Kidney, *Landmark Architecture: Pittsburgh and Allegheny County* (Pittsburgh, 1985), p. 163; V. S. Grash, "The Commercial Skyscrapers of Pittsburgh Industrialists and Financiers, 1885–1932" (Ph.D. diss., Pennsylvania State University, 1998), pp. 176–78.

32. BJH papers: interview, WLM, November 4, 1940, p. 1; interview, F. Denton, March 14, 1941, p. 2.

33. AWM papers: NMM to AWM, November 1926, February 18, 1927; NMM papers: NMM to B. McCrory, April 3, 1927.

34. AWM papers: NMM to AWM, [undated, summer 1927], September 16, 1927.

35. NMM papers: NMM to B. McCrory, March 24, 1927, June 9, 22, 1929, July 29, 1929; B. McCrory to NMM, November 16, 1927.

36. NMM papers: H. M. Johnson to NMM, September 16, 1927; AWM to NMM, Christmas 1927; AWM papers: NMM to AWM, November 28, 1927; AWM diary, December 25, 1927.

37. NMM papers: NMM to B. McCrory, March 11, 1927.

38. AWM papers: AWM diary, December 25, 1927, January 14, 1928; NMM to AWM, February 11, 1928, [?] July 1928, enclosing undated letter from N. McMullen.

39. AWM papers: NMM to AWM, August 21, 1929; NMM papers: NMM to B. McCrory, Thursday [? 1929].

40. NMM papers: H. A. Lee to B. McCrory, March 8, 1928, December 21, 1930, March 29, 1932; B. McCrory to American Red Cross, November 4, 1943; E. D. Kuppinger to W. B. McCrory, December 3, 1945.

41. AWM papers: AWM diary, March 14, 19, 1929.

42. AWM papers: AWM diary, May 11, 26, 1929.

43. NMM papers: NMM to B. McCrory, June 4, 1927; AWM papers: AWM, Federal Estate Tax Return, February 24, 1939, sheet X-6; NMM to AWM, March 23, 1929; Knoedler papers: Miscellaneous correspondence, NMM to Mr. Knoedler [undated].

44. AWM papers: AWM diary, July 22, 1928, August 20, 1928, September 26, 1928.

45. AWM papers: NMM to AWM, July 16, 1928, October 13, 1928, March 9, 1929; P. McMullen to AWM, December 30, 1927.

46. AWM papers: L. McMullen to AWM, February 21, 1927, March 3, 4, 1927, April 7, 1927, April 26, 1927, June 10, 1927, February 4, 1928.

47. NMM papers: NMM to B. McCrory, March 24, [1927]; BJH papers: AWM Letterbooks, AWM to D. K. E. Bruce, November 1, 1926; AWM to AMB, October 15, 1926, January 4, 1927; Duveen papers: AWM to JD, March 24, 1927; Duveen Bros. [New York] to Duveen Bros. [Paris], March 24, 1927.

48. Duveen papers: Duveen Bros. [New York] to Duveen Bros. [London], October 5, 1927.

49. NMM papers: NMM to B. McCrory, June 22, [1927]; AMB papers: PM to AMB, November 6, 1927; BJH papers: AWM Letterbooks, AWM to P. D. Cravath, October 12, 1927; Lankford, pp. 82–85.

50. AMB papers: PM to AMB, November 14, 1929.

51. AMB papers: AWM to AMB, January 21, 1929; AWM papers: AWM diary, April 3, 1928, May 31, 1928, July 1, 1928; AWM, Federal Estate Tax Return, February 24, 1939, sheets X-4-X-6.

52. AWM papers: AWM diary, January 16, 1928, May 30, 1928, June 10, 1928, March 5, 1929, June 28, 1929.

53. AWM papers: AWM diary, December 26, 1927, August 31, 1928, September 6, 15, 30, 1928, May 23, 27, 1929, June 28, 1929.

54. AWM papers: AWM diary, March 25, 1928.

55. AWM papers: AWM diary, January 16, 1929; Lankford, pp. 86–87.

56. DEF papers (NGA): Box 19, Personal Correspondence, PM, 1927–28, *A Banquet to Celebrate the Fiftieth Anniversary of the Yale Daily News*, March 26, 1928; *New York Times*, March 27, 1928.

57. AWM papers: AWM to PM, January 10, 1928; AWM diary, March 22, 1928; DEF papers (NGA): Box 19, Folder—Personal Correspondence PM,

1927–1928, PM to DEF, January 29, 1927; AWM to PM, March 20, 1928; Folder—Personal Correspondence undated, PM to DEF, March 14, 28, [1928], [April] 13, [1928].

58. AWM papers: AWM diary, May 6, 1928; PM to AWM, [March] 14, [1928], March 20, 1928; AWM, Federal Estate Tax Return, February 24, 1939, sheet X-6.

59. AWM papers: AWM diary, May 18, 1928; PM papers: interview no. 5, pp. 26–28; *RSS*, pp. 114–16.

60. M. F. S. Sanger, *Henry Clay Frick: An Intimate Portrait* (New York, 1998), pp. 416–19; *RSS*, p. 122; PM papers: interview no. 1, p. 12.

61. *Congressional Record, 70th Congress, 2nd Session*, vol. 70, no. 12, December 15, 1928, p. 710. For the broader background, see T. S. Hines, "The Imperial Mall: The City Beautiful Movement and the Washington Plan of 1901–02," and J. A. Peterson, "The Mall, the McMillan Plan, and the Origins of American City Planning," both in R. Longstreth (ed.), *The Mall in Washington, 1791–1991* (Washington, D.C., 1991), pp. 79–99, 100–115.

62. CFOST: Box 261, Treasury Department—Secretary—Memoranda to AWM, S. Parker Gilbert to AWM, June 10, 1921, July 13, 1921; Box 264, Treasury Department—Supervising Architect, 1918–32, AWM to C. Coolidge, January 8, 1925; CFA papers: Entry 17 150/Public Buildings Program—General, 1923–26, C. Moore to General Lord, March 16, 1924; Coolidge papers: CC 30, AWM to C. Coolidge, June 2, 1925.

63. CFA papers: PF 150/1927–34, W. C. Bruce to C. Moore, December 24, 1929; Entry 31C 7777/Contemplated Buildings—General—DC, January 1923–December 1924, R. N. Elliott to AWM, May 28, 1924, December 8, 1924; Entry 31C 7779/Contemplated Buildings—General—DC, March 1909–December 1940, J. A. Wetmore, Suggested Building Program in the District of Columbia, February 2, 1925; Coolidge papers: Reel 140, W. C. Bruce to C. Coolidge, November 9, 1925.

64. Moore papers: 21/Memoirs, chs. 24–25; C. Moore, *Washington Past and Present* (New York, 1930), pp. 3–13, 318–32; S. A. Kehler, *The Commission of Fine Arts: A Brief History* (Washington, D.C., 1966), pp. 51–52; C. M. Green, *Washington: Capital City, 1879–1950* (Princeton, N.J., 1963), pp. 268–91; J. W. Reps, *Monumental Washington: The Planning and Development of the Capital Center* (Princeton, N.J., 1967), pp. 153–54, 169, 173.

65. For the general context of these developments, see R. G. Wilson, "High Noon on the Mall: Modernism Versus Traditionalism, 1910–1970," in Longstreth, *The Mall in Washington*, pp. 143–50, and S. K. Tompkins, *A Quest for Grandeur: Charles Moore and the Federal Triangle* (Washington, D.C., 1993), pp. 37–52.

66. CFA papers: PF 150/1923–26, Memorandum for CFA, March 19, 1926; Entry 31B 780/1926–27, M. B. Medary Jr. to AWM, July 9, 1926.

67. Bennett papers: EHB diary, September 30, 1926, October 22, 1926; 63/12, C. S. Dewey to EHB, October 20, 1926; CFA papers: PF 150/1923–26, C. Moore to M. B. Medary Jr., September 22, 1926; M. B. Medary Jr. to C. Moore, September 30, 1926; Entry 31B 780/1926–27, EHB to C. S. Dewey, October 7, 1926; AWM to R. Smoot, November 3, 1926; R. Smoot to AWM, November 19, 1926.

68. CFA papers: Entry 1, Minutes of CFA meetings, December 2, 1926; J. E. Draper, *Edward H. Bennett: Architect and City Planner, 1874–1954* (Chicago, 1982), pp. 6–41.

69. CFA papers: Entry 1, Minutes of CFA meetings, April 14–15, 1927; Entry 31B 780/1926–27, C. Moore to AWM, April 5, 1927; C. S. Dewey to C. Moore, April 18, 1927; C. S. Dewey to EHB, April 27, 1927.

70. CFA papers: Entry 31B 780/1926–27, A. Garfield to AWM, December 28, 1926; PF 150/1927–34, M. B. Medary Jr. to C. Moore, March 30, 1927; AWM to W. A. Delano, May 13, 1927; W. A. Delano to C. Moore, May 14, 1927; CFOST: Box 264, Treasury Department—Supervising Architect, 1918–32, C. S. Dewey to AWM, May 12, 1927; BAC records: C. S. Dewey to L. Ayers, May 23, 1927; C. S. Dewey to EHB, May 28, 1927; EHB to C. S. Dewey, June 7, 1927; Bennett papers: EHB diary, June 2, 1927.

71. CFA papers: Entry 168, C. E. Moore to J. Russell Pope, July 17, 1928; Bennett papers: EHB diary, June 3, 1927; S. M. Bedford, *John Russell Pope: Architect of Empire* (New York, 1998), p. 143.

72. DEF papers (LOC): 67/Federal Triangle, EHB, Memorandum for use of the Secretary of the Treasury, January 6, 1928; AWM papers: AWM diary, September 13, 18, 20, 1928, October 14, 16–18, 1928; *Pittsburgh Post-Gazette*, October 19, 1928; *Pittsburgh Press*, October 18, 1928.

73. R. Rathbun, *The National Gallery of Art* (Smithsonian Institution, Washington, D.C., 1909).

74. Smithsonian archives: RU 45 Box 79 f6, C. D. Walcott to H. C. Lodge, May 1, 1920; W. H. Holmes to C. D. Walcott, June 15, 1920; Minutes of first annual meeting of National Gallery of Art Commission, December 6, 1921; W. H. Holmes, "The Story of the National Gallery of Art," *Art and Architecture* 15 (1923), pp. 251–60.

75. R. Cortissoz, "The National Gallery of Art," *American Magazine of Art* 16 (March 1925), pp. 115–22; Smithsonian archives: RU 45 Box 79 f8, JD to Mr. Farmelee, February 9, 1924.

76. Smithsonian archives: RU 45 Box 79 f8, L. Mechlin to C. D. Walcott, April 23, 1924; Box 79 f13, C. Moore to C. D. Walcott, March 3, 1924; C. D. Walcott to C. A. Platt, November 21, 1924; C. D. Walcott to AWM, November 28, 1924.

77. CFA papers: Entry 1, Minutes of CFA meetings, July 7, 1926; BAC papers: 1928, W. A. Delano to L. A. Simon, August 7, 1928.

78. Smithsonian archives: RU 311 Box 19 f11, R. P. Tolman to Dr. A. Wetmore, August 15, 1944; RU 312 Ser 1 f7, P. Buswell to W. H. Holmes, February 9, 1928; W. H. Holmes to P. Buswell, February 10, 1928; Mrs. R. V. S. Berry to W. H. Holmes, May 18, 1928; W. H. Holmes to Mrs. R. V. S. Berry, May 23, 1928.

79. BJH papers: AWM Letterbooks, AWM to G. Blair, November 14, 1927.

80. Bennett papers: EHB diaries, October 1, 1926, November 16, 18, 1926, December 14, 1926, January 1, 1927; Huntington papers: transcript of Alfonso Gomez interview, February 7, 1959, pp. 5–6; Sparkes papers: interview, DEF, March 1, 1945, p. 15.

81. PM papers: interview no. 1, p. 8; D. Doheny, *David Finley: A Quiet Force for the Arts in America* (Washington, D.C., 2006), pp. 59–60, 65; *Washington Times,*

November 9, 1927. Much of DEF's time thereafter was spent fending off owners of paintings who wished AWM to buy them: see the many letters contained in DEF papers (LOC): 16/1921–28, 16/1929, 16/1930, 16/1931, 16/1932–37.

82. AWM papers: AWM diary, February 26, 1928, September 3, 1928. Unfortunately, AWM kept no diary for 1927, or if he did, it has not survived.

83. Duveen papers: JD to AWM, May 16, 1927; Duveen Bros. [Paris] to Duveen Bros. [New York], September 6, 1927; Duveen Bros. [New York] to Duveen Bros. [Paris], September 6, 1927.

84. Duveen papers: Price list, November 1, 1927; Duveen Bros. [New York] to Duveen Bros. [Paris], November 4, 23, 1927; A. E. Sixsmith to JD, November 25, 1927; JD to A. E. Sixsmith, November 26, 1927; Secrest, *Duveen*, pp. 306, 493, 498. The famous Vermeer forgeries by van Meegeren only began after 1932, and were not discovered until after the end of the Second World War: see P. B. Coremans, *Van Meegeren's Faked Vermeers and De Hooghs: A Scientific Examination* (Amsterdam, 1949); J. Godley, *The Master Forger: The Story of Han van Meegeren* (New York, 1950); Lord Kilbracken, *Van Meegeren: Master Forger* (New York, 1967).

85. Duveen papers: Duveen Bros. [New York] to JD, January 10, 14, 27, 1927; Duveen Bros. [New York] to Duveen Bros. [Paris], November 4, 1927; Duveen Bros. [Paris] to Duveen Bros. [New York], November 5, 1927.

86. Knoedler papers: Domestic Letterbook, October 11, 1926–December 2, 1926, CRH to AWM, November 24, 1926; Domestic Letterbook, December 2, 1926–January 29, 1927, CHM to AWM, December 14, 1926, January 21, 1927; Domestic Letterbook, January 29, 1927–April 2, 1927, Knoedler & Co. to AWM, March 9, 1927; Domestic Letterbook, April 2, 1927–June 7, 1927, CHM to AWM, May 17, 1927; Knoedler & Co. to AWM, May 20, 1927.

87. Knoedler papers: Domestic Letterbook, October 3, 1927–December 3, 1927, CHM to AWM, October 24, 29, 1927, November 23, 1927, December 2, 1927; CHM, Private Letterbook, January 1, 1919–December 29, 1930, CHM to AWM, November 23, 1927; Domestic Letterbook, December 3, 1927–January 24, 1928, CHM to AWM, January 3, 1928; BJH papers: Letterbooks, AWM to CHM, December 27, 29, 1927.

88. Duveen papers: Duveen Bros. [New York] to Duveen Bros. [Paris], December 31, 1927; Duveen Bros. [Paris] to Duveen Bros. [New York], January 2, 1928; Price list, April 25, 1928; AWM statement, January 9, 1929.

89. AWM papers: AWM diary, April 25, 1928; Duveen papers: Duveen Bros. [New York] to Duveen Bros. [Paris], March 10, 20, 1928; Duveen Bros. [Paris] to Duveen Bros. [New York], March 12, 1928, April 3, 1928; JD to T. Rousseau, July 22, 1928; JD to AWM, July 26, 1928; Duveen Bros. [Paris] to JD, July 31, 1928; AWM to JD, August 18, 1928.

90. Knoedler papers: Domestic Letterbook, December 3, 1927–January 24, 1928, CSC and CRH to AWM, January 3, 1928; CHM to AWM, January 3, 14, 1928; Domestic Letterbook, March 7, 1929–May 3, 1929, CHM to AWM, April 2, 1929.

91. AWM papers: AWM diary, January 5, 1928; Knoedler papers: Domestic Letterbook, May 22, 1928–September 7, 1928, CHM to AWM, June 8, 1928.

92. Knoedler papers: Domestic Letterbook, December 3, 1927–January 24, 1928, CHM to AWM, January 14, 1928.

93. BJH papers: interview, H. M. Johnson, April 6, 1940, p. 1; AWM papers: C. Coolidge to AWM, February 27, 1929, December 23, 1929.

94. Murray, pp. 222–25.

95. W. C. Murphy, "President Hoover's Cabinet," *Current History* 30 (May 1929), p. 270.

96. Hoover, *Cabinet and the Presidency*, pp. 59–60.

97. Doheny, *David Finley*, p. 57.

98. PM papers: interview no. 1, p. 14; Sparkes papers: interview DEF, March 1, 1945, p. 4.

99. H. Barnard, *Independent Man: The Life of Senator James Couzens* (New York, 1958), p. 165; Murray, pp. 225–27.

100. Murray, pp. 228–30.

101. Murray, pp. 230–31.

102. AWM papers: J. F. Burke to AWM, November 12, 1928; AWM to H. Hoover, November 13, 1928; BJH papers: interview, H. M. Johnston, April 6, 1940, p. 2.

103. AWM papers: H. Hoover to AWM, March 5, 7, 1929.

104. Hendrick, ch. 26, pp. 23–24.

105. CFOST: Box 113, Prohibition–National, 1928–29, H. Hoover to AWM, May 31, 1929, plus enclosure; AWM to H. Hoover, May 31, 1929; Murray, p. 230.

106. *Pittsburgh Press*, May 6, 1929.

107. AWM papers: AWM diary, January 8, 1929, February 21, 1929, March 4, 6, 1929, April 18, 1929.

108. Hendrick, ch. 26, pp. 27–28.

109. Murray, p. 233.

110. AWM papers: P. McMullen to AWM, March 23, 1929.

111. AWM papers: *The City of Washington: A Meeting at the United States Chamber of Commerce Building, Washington, D.C., April 25, 1929*; CFOST: Box 43, Development of the City of Washington, 1928–32, press releases, April 15, 24, 1929; *New York Herald-Tribune*, April 26, 1929.

112. DEF papers (LOC): 68/H. Hoover, AWM to H. Hoover, March 9, 1929; 77/Henry L. Stimson, H. L. Stimson to AWM, July 1, 1929; AWM to H. L. Stimson, July 3, 1929; Doheny, *David Finley*, pp. 62–64; *Time*, May 6, 1929, pp. 9–11. This was the article that coined the phrase "Mr. Mellon's Finley."

113. AWM papers: AWM diary, September 11, 1929; CFA papers: Entry 1, Minutes of CFA meetings, May 28, 1929, September 10–11, 1929; PF 150/1927–34, W. A. Delano to C. Moore, June 21, 1929; C. Moore to W. A. Delano, June 22, 1929; A. Garfield to C. Moore, July 12, 1929; C. Moore to AWM, September 21, 1929; BAC records: 1929, Office of J. Russell Pope to Office of Supervising Architect, October 3, 1929; Bedford, *John Russell Pope*, p. 146.

114. AWM papers: AWM diary, April 18, 24, 1928, May 9, 17, 1928; DEF papers (NGA): Box 37, Folder AWM, The Pilgrims, Speech Prepared but Not Delivered: DEF, Memorandum, June 8, 1935; Doheny, *David Finley*, pp. 65–68.

115. AWM papers: AWM diary, January 5, 1929; Duveen papers: Duveen Bros. [Paris] to Duveen Bros. [New York], January 5, 1929; Duveen Bros. [London] to

Duveen Bros. [New York], January 7, 1929; D. A. Brown, *Raphael and America* (Washington, D.C., 1983), esp. pp. 29, 88–91.

116. Knoedler papers: Domestic Letterbook, January 11, 1929–March 7, 1929, CHM to AWM, January 30, 1929.

117. Duveen papers: Duveen Bros. [New York] to Duveen Bros. [Paris], March 25, 1929, May 7, 1929; Duveen Bros. [Paris] to Duveen Bros. [New York], April 12, 1929.

118. AWM papers: AWM diary, February 14, 1929; DEF papers (LOC): 16/1929, DEF to L. Venturi, February 15, 19, 1929; DEF to AWM, February 18, 1929; L. Venturi to DEF, March 1, 1929.

119. Knoedler papers: Letterbooks, 1926–1929, Hermitage Paintings, Note by DEF, February 14, 1929; Doheny, *David Finley*, pp. 64–65, 73–75, 81.

120. PM, "To Sail Beyond the Sunset," *Yale Literary Magazine* 99 (March 1929), pp. 178–80.

121. Finley papers (NGA): Box 19, Folder—Personal Correspondence—PM, 1929–1939, AWM to E. D. Woodyard, March 19, 1929.

122. AWM papers: AWM diary, May 11, 12, 1929; *RSS*, p. 117.

123. AWM papers: AWM, Federal Estate Tax Return, February 24, 1939, sheet X-6; AWM to NMM, August 8, 1929, September 12, 1929.

124. AWM papers: NMM to AWM, August 17, 1929, September 20, 1929; P. McMullen to AWM, March 23, 1929, August 19, 1929.

125. AWM papers: L. McMullen to AWM, October 22, 1929; NMM to AWM, July 2, 30, 1929, August 8, 9, 1929.

126. Knoedler papers: CHM Private Letterbook, January 1, 1919–December 29, 1930, CHM to AWM, December 31, 1929.

127. Duveen papers: JD to AWM, July 27, 1929, September 20, 1929; Duveen Bros. [New York] to Duveen Bros. [Paris], August 9, 1929.

128. Hendrick, ch. 27, p. 23.

129. Hendrick, ch. 27, pp. 8–9, 20–21.

130. AWM papers: AWM diary, March 14, 1929; *New York Times*, March 15, 1939; Murray, pp. 236–38.

131. Warburg papers: 5/65, O. Mills to P. M. Warburg, March 8, 1929; Meltzer, p. 238.

132. AWM papers: AWM diary, March 12, 1929; H. Hoover to AWM, May 3, 1929; Hendrick, ch. 27, p. 24.

133. Harrison papers: 2210.1, Confidential files, March 21, 1929, April 25, 26, 29, 1929; F&S, pp. 374, 407–19; *JMS*, pp. 469–70; Murray, pp. 238–39.

134. AWM papers: AWM diary, March 26, 1929, April 25, 1929, May 16, 23, 1929, August 8, 1929; Hamlin papers: Index-Digest, March 26, 1929, April 18, 25, 1929, May 16, 22, 1929; Meltzer, pp. 238–41; F&S, pp. 255–64.

135. BJH papers: interview, G. B. Winston, April 8, 1942, p. 1; CFOST: Box 15, Business and Banking, 1928–29, AWM to J. J. McSwain, January 11, 1929; Meltzer, p. 250; Kennedy, p. 37.

136. AWM, "What Future for the Federal Reserve?," *The 3-C Book*, vol. 7, August 1925, p. 20; H. Hoover, *The Memoirs of Herbert Hoover*, vol. 3, *The Great Depression, 1929–1941* (New York, 1952), p. 513.

137. AWM papers: AWM diary, August 8, 1929; CFOST: Box 69, Federal Reserve

Banks—Purchase and Holdings of Government Securities—Weekly Report of Open Market Operations, 1929–32, Preliminary memorandum for the O. Mills Investment Committee, September 24, 1929; Meltzer, p. 242.

138. There are many accounts of the "great crash": I have followed the most recent, M. Klein, *Rainbow's End: The Crash of 1929* (New York, 2001), pp. 194–98 and, throughout this section, chs. 9 and 10.

139. P. H. Love, *Andrew W. Mellon: The Man and His Work* (Baltimore, 1929), p. 308; Murray, pp. 244–45.

140. Love, *Mellon*, pp. 9–10, 318–19.

141. AWM papers: AWM diary, July 17, 1929; BJH papers: AWM Letterbooks, AWM to J. M. Chapple, April 3, 1929; AWM to P. S. Ache, June 7, 1929; AWM to F. H. Coggins, June 20, 1929, November 9, 1929.

142. Hendrick, ch. 26, pp. 29–30.

143. AWM papers: AWM diary, October 15, 1929, October 21, 1929.

144. AWM papers: AWM diary, October 24, 28, 1929.

145. AWM papers: AWM diary, November 13, 1929.

146. Kennedy, pp. 39–41; AWM papers: AWM diary, October 25, 1929; see also his entry for October 15, 1929.

147. AWM papers: AWM diary, October 29–31, 1929.

148. F&S, p. 304; Meltzer, pp. 285–86, 299.

149. CFOST: Box 166, Taxation (General), July–December 1929, Statement of O. Mills before Ways and Means Committee, December 4, 1929; *New York Times*, December 5, 1929.

150. AWM papers: AWM diary, November 15, 18, 19, 1929.

151. AWM papers: AWM diary, October 27, 1929; BJH papers: AWM Letterbooks, AWM to H. C. McEldowney, October 28, 1929.

152. AWM papers: AWM diary, September 23, 26, 29, 1929, October 6, 13, 18, 21, 1929, November 1, 3, 7, 17, 19, 1929, December 2, 5, 7, 1929.

153. AWM papers: AWM diary, September 4–9, 11, 24, 1929, October 2, 4, 14, 22, 24, 1929, November 29, 1929, December 3, 1929.

154. AWM papers: Contract between the Standard Steel Car Company and Pullman (1930); BJH papers: AWM Letterbooks, AWM to M. Muchnic, January 6, 1930; Sparkes papers: interview, Col. F. Drake, June 19, 1945, pp. 1–5; *Pittsburgh Post-Gazette*, December 28, 1929.

155. AWM papers: AWM diary, September 4, 6, 14, 1929, November 26, 1929, December 5, 6, 13, 1929; *JMS*, pp. 33–34.

156. AWM papers: AWM to NMM, December 1, 1929.

12. Triumphs amid Troubles: Fortune's Zenith, Russian Pictures, Pittsburgh Woes, 1929–31

1. H. Hoover, *The Memoirs of Herbert Hoover*, vol. 2, *The Cabinet and the Presidency, 1920–1933* (New York, 1952), p. 58.

2. A. M. Schlesinger Jr., *The Crisis of the Old Order, 1919–1933* (Boston, 1957), p. 164; Kennedy, p. 40; Murray, p. 255.

3. Steiner, pp. 470–89, 602–32; *New York Times*, January 1, 1930; Kennedy, pp. 72–73.

4. S. V. O. Clark, *Central Bank Co-operation, 1924–31* (New York, 1967), pp. 168–70; Steiner, pp. 638–44.

5. Murray, pp. 270–71.

6. *New York Times,* October 31, 1930.

7. CFOST: Box 113, Prohibition—National—1930–31, Statement by AWM, January 22, 1930; Murray, pp. 263–64.

8. J. H. Wilson, *Ideology and Economics: U.S. Relations with the Soviet Union, 1918–1933* (Columbia, Mo., 1974), pp. 104–105.

9. AWM papers: AWM to NMM, May 9, 1930; CFOST: Box 156, Federal Tariff 1930, AWM press release, June 21, 1930; D. Burner, *Herbert Hoover: A Public Life* (New York, 1979), p. 298; R. N. Smith, *An Uncommon Man: The Triumph of Herbert Hoover* (New York, 1984), p. 112.

10. BJH papers: AWM Letterbooks, AWM to B. E. Dart, January 29, 1930; H. Hoover, *The Memoirs of Herbert Hoover,* vol. 3, *The Great Depression, 1929–1941* (New York, 1952), p. 58; Schlesinger, *Crisis of the Old Order,* p. 231.

11. J. A. Schwartz, *The Interregnum of Despair: Hoover, Congress and the Depression* (Urbana, Ill. 1970), p. 15.

12. BAC records: 1929, BAC to AWM, November 12, 1929; C. Moore to EHB, November 20, 1929; CFA Collection: Entry 1, Minutes of CFA meetings, February 10, 1930, March 3, 20, 1930, December 4, 1930; S. K. Tompkins, *A Quest for Grandeur: Charles Moore and the Federal Triangle* (Washington, D.C., 1993), pp. 56–57.

13. DEF papers (LOC): 67/Federal Triangle, J. Russell Pope, Report to the Board of Architectural Consultants, February 10, 1930; CFA Collection: Entry 1, Minutes of CFA meetings, July 1, 1931. P. Pennoyer and A. Walker, *The Architecture of Delano and Aldrich* (New York, 2003), pp. 64–65, 158–63; S. M. Bedford, *John Russell Pope: Architect of Empire* (New York, 1998), p. 148.

14. CFA Collection: Entry 1, Minutes of CFA meetings, December 17, 1931; *New York Times,* August 4, 1935.

15. G. Gurney, *Sculpture and the Federal Triangle* (Washington, D.C., 1985), pp. 337–39.

16. BJH papers: AWM Letterbooks, AWM, "The New Washington" [undated and unpaginated].

17. AWM papers: H. Hoover to AWM, October 17, 1930; Kennedy, pp. 58–59.

18. PM papers: AWM to PM, October 23, 1930.

19. *New York Times,* October 30, 1930; Murray, pp. 259–60.

20. Kennedy, pp. 65–67; F&S, p. 357; R. Chernow, *The House of Morgan* (New York, 1990), pp. 323–24.

21. DEF papers (NGA): Box 1, AWM Biography, 1927–32, DEF to F. H. Coggins, April 10, 1931; Murray, pp. 272–73.

22. CFOST: Box 139, Soldiers' Bonus, December 1930, AWM to A. H. Vandenberg, December 4, 1930; A. H. Vandenberg to AWM, December 6, 1930; Soldiers' Bonus, January 1–20, 1931, AWM to W. C. Hawley, January 29, 1931; Soldiers' Bonus, January 29–31, 1931, AWM, Statement to Senate Finance Committee, January 28, 1931.

23. CFOST: Box 139, Soldiers' Bonus, February 13–28, 1931, E. Kammerer to AWM, February 16, 1931.

24. PM papers: AWM to PM, April 13, 1931; BJH papers: AWM Letterbooks, AWM to J. E. Ransdell, December 8, 1930; AWM to F. K. Breithut, February 26, 1931.

25. F&S, p. 313.

26. AWM papers: AWM, Speech to American Bankers' Association, May 5, 1931; *New York Times*, May 6, 1931; Murray, pp. 260–61.

27. AWM papers: AWM Deceased, Report and Accounts, August 26, 1937, Exhibit F, p. 3; Exhibit G, p. 3.

28. BJH papers: interview, H. M. Johnson, April 9, 1940, p. 1.

29. W. M. Kiplinger, *Washington Is Like That* (New York, 1942), p. 423.

30. W. C. Kidney, *Landmark Architecture: Pittsburgh and Allegheny County* (Pittsburgh, 1985), p. 163; V. S. Gash, "The Commercial Skyscrapers of Pittsburgh Industrialists and Financiers, 1885–1932" (Ph.D. diss., Pennsylvania State University, 1998), pp. 178–81.

31. BJH papers: interview, J. Nelson, March 14, 1941, p. 2.

32. AWM papers: AWM Deceased, Reports and Accounts, August 26, 1937, Exhibit K, pp. 1–4.

33. Bowman papers: RBM to J. G. Bowman, June 21, 1932; R. A. Cram, *My Life in Architecture* (Boston, 1936), pp. 253–57; Kidney, *Landmark Architecture*, p. 257.

34. DEF papers (NGA): Box 2, AWM Personal, 1928–32, AWM to H. R. Young, June 4, 1930; AWM to Mrs. B. Gosford, July 24, 1930.

35. AWM papers: AWM diary, September 26, 1929; *MNBTC*, p. 39.

36. F. Lundberg, *America's Sixty Families* (New York, 1937), pp. 212–15.

37. AWM papers: AWM diary, March 12, 1929, April 30, 1929; E. E. Freudenthal, *The Aviation Business: From Kitty Hawk to Wall Street* (New York, 1940), pp. 105–107, 167–72; O'Connor, pp. 422–23.

38. *JMS*, pp. 308–309, 510–11.

39. AWM papers: AWM diary, August 26, 1929.

40. AWM papers: Deed of Trust, December 30, 1930, Article 3.

41. PM papers: AWM to PM, October 30, 1930; AMB papers: AWM to AMB, May 23, 1931.

42. PM papers: RKM to AWM, May 17, 1932.

43. AWM papers: AWM Deceased, Report and Accounts, August 26, 1937, Exhibit F, p. 3; Exhibit H, p. 1.

44. AWM papers: K. McMullen to AWM, November 12, 1931.

45. AWM papers: L. McMullen to AWM, October 22, 29, 1929, January 24, 1930, March 4, 1930, July 10, 1930, August 5, 8, 21, 22, 1930, March 3, 1931, May 8, 1931.

46. AWM papers: NMM to AWM, August 9, 1929, June/July [?1930].

47. AWM papers: AWM, Federal Estate Tax Return, February 24, 1939, sheet X-7; AWM to NMM, December 1, 1929; NMM to AWM, December 27, 1929, January 30, 1930.

48. NMM papers: NMM to B. McCrory, June 25, 1930; AWM papers: AWM to NMM, June 11, 1930, August 12, 1930; NMM to AWM, June 9, 14, 1930, June/July [?1930], August 6, 1930.

49. AWM papers: NMM to AWM, August 21, 1929, January 30, 1930, October 27, 31, 1930, November 11, 1930.

50. AWM papers: NMM to AWM, September 25, 1930.

51. NMM papers: NMM to B. McCrory, November 3, 1929; AWM papers: NMM to AWM, August 9, 1929; AWM to NMM, September 12, 1929. For PM's own account of his time in Cambridge, see *RSS*, pp. 118–27.
52. DEF papers (NGA): Box 19, Personal Correspondence, PM, 1929–39, PM to DEF, October 17, 1929; NMM papers: NMM to B. McCrory, February 24, 1930.
53. AWM papers: NMM to AWM, January 30, 1930.
54. AWM papers: AWM to NMM, May 9, 1938.
55. DEF papers (NGA): Box 19, Personal Correspondence, PM, 1929–39, AWM to PM, February 25, 1930.
56. AWM papers: AWM to NMM, May 9, 1930.
57. DEF papers (NGA): Box 19, Personal Correspondence, PM, 1929–39, PM to DEF, February 11, 1930; A. E. Sixsmith to R. L. Scaife, July 18, 1930; A. E. Sixsmith to F. B. Robinson, July 21, 1930; A. E. Sixsmith to H. Rising, August 15, 1930; press cuttings, *New York Herald-Tribune*, July 6, 1930; *Pittsburgh Press*, July 9, 1930; *Washington Evening Star*, July 10, 1930.
58. AMB papers: PM to AMB, July 30, 1930; *RSS*, p. 122.
59. AMB papers: PM to AMB, October 19, 1930; PM papers: AWM to PM, October 24, 1930; DEF papers (NGA): Box 19, Personal Correspondence, PM, 1929–39, PM to DEF, May 29, 1930.
60. AMB papers: PM to AMB, January 27, 1931, March 22, 1931; PM papers: AWM to PM, February 22, 1931.
61. PM papers: AWM to PM, October 23, 1930, November 2, 1930, February 22, 1931.
62. PM papers: AWM to PM, October 30, 1930, February 7, 1931, April 15, 1931.
63. PM papers: AWM to PM, February 22, 1931, April 13, 1931; AWM papers: H. R. Dulany Jr. to DEF, March 4, 1931; NMM to AWM, April 21, 1931, May 1931; AWM to NMM, October 14, 31, 1930, May 14, 1931; DEF papers (NGA): Box 19, Personal Correspondence, PM, 1929–39, PM to DEF, April 10, 1931; AWM papers: AWM, Federal Estate Tax Return, February 25, 1939, sheet X-8; AWM, Deceased, Report and Accounts, August 26, 1937, Exhibit K, p. 2; *Loudoun-Fauquier Breeders' Magazine* (spring 1931), p. 9.
64. AMB papers: PM to AMB, October 19, 1930.
65. Smithsonian archives: RU 46 Box 66 f2, C. G. Abbot to AWM, March 8, 1930; AWM to C. G. Abbot, March 11, 1930; RU 312 ser. 1 7, W. A. Holmes to C. G. Abbot, May 8, 1930.
66. Smithsonian archives: RU 46 Box 140 f12, C. G. Abbot to J. H. Gest, March 16, 1934.
67. G. Retlinger, *The Economics of Taste*, vol. 1, *The Rise and Fall of Picture Prices, 1760–1960* (New York, 1982), pp. 207–209.
68. Knoedler papers: London Letterbook, August 8, 1928–May 2, 1930, CRH to O. Gutekunst, January 15, 1930; CRH to F. C. G. Menzies, April 15, 1930; Knoedler & Co. [New York] to Knoedler & Co. [London], March 28, 1930; Foreign Letterbook, June 3, 1928–August 1, 1930, CRH to G. H. Davey; Foreign Letterbook, August 4, 1930–December 14, 1934, CRH to F. Zatzenstein, October 23, 1930; CRH to O. Gutekunst, November 26, 1930; Duveen papers: J. H. Allen to E. Duveen, March 31, 1931.

69. Duveen papers: Duveen Bros. [New York] to AWM, January 6, 1930; JD to AWM, January 27, 1930.

70. Duveen papers: Duveen Bros. [New York] to AWM, April 9, 24, 1930.

71. Knoedler papers: Domestic Letterbook, February 19, 1930–April 25, 1930, CHM to AWM, March 5, 26, 1930; Telegrams and Cables, February 3, 1930–December 29, 1930, Knoedler & Co. to Colnaghi, March 27, 1930; Foreign Letterbook, June 3, 1928–August 1, 1930, CRH to G. H. Davey, April 4, 1930.

72. Knoedler papers: Telegrams and Cables, February 3, 1930–December 29, 1930, CRH to Colnaghi, March 13, 1930; London Letterbook, August 8, 1928–May 2, 1930, CRH to F. C. G. Menzies, April 15, 1930.

73. This extraordinary episode has been frequently written about. Among the fullest accounts in English are R. C. Williams, *Russian Art and American Money, 1900–1940* (Cambridge, Mass., 1980), pp. 147–90; J. Walker, *Self-Portrait with Donors: Confessions of an Art Collector* (Boston, 1974), pp. 108–22; Kopper, pp. 86–96; G. Norman, *The Hermitage: The Biography of a Great Museum* (London, 1997), pp. 179–201. See also Hendrick, ch. 31, pp. 20–33. The recent Russian accounts are: I. N. Zhukov, *Operatsiia Ermitazh* (Moscow, 1993), passim; B. B. Piotrovskii, *Stranitsy iz moei zhizni* (St. Petersburg, 1995), pp. 86–89; B. B. Piotrovskii, *Istoriia Ermitazha Kratkii ocherk. Material I dokumenty*, ed. with an introduction by M. B. Piotrovski (Moscow, 2000), pp. 85–89, 363–90, 419–76.

74. See, for example, A. Troubnikoff, "Art in Russia," *Burlington Magazine* (February 15, 1909), pp. 320–25; K. Baedeker, *Russia: A Handbook for Travelers* (Leipzig, 1914), pp. 145, 153. For the early Communist period, see M. Conway, *Art Treasures in Soviet Russia* (London, 1925), pp. 147–70.

75. BJH papers: interview, CRH and CHM, November 10, 1941, p. 5.

76. BJH papers: interview, CRH, October 24, 1942, p. 9.

77. Russian State Archive of the Economy, f5240, op. 19, d. 846, lines 198–200: Instructions of January 6, 1930, establishing a special brigade for the requisition from all museums of art objects to be sold abroad by the Antiquariat.

78. BJH papers: interview, CRH, October 24, 1942, p. 11.

79. Russian State Archive of the Economy, f5240, op. 19, d. 846, lines 21–24: C. Gulbenkian to G. L. Piatakov, July 17, 1930; J. Perdigao, *Calouste Gulbenkian, Collector* (Lisbon, 1975), pp. 116–24.

80. BJH papers: interview, CRH, October 24, 1942, p. 1.

81. T. Krakauer, *Family Portrait: History and Genealogy of the Gottschalk, Molling and Benjamin Families from Hannover, Germany* (Durham, N.C., 1995), pp. 35–37, 51–53.

82. Russian State Archive of the Economy, f5420, op. 19, d. 846, lines 88–92: G. A. Samueli to Gorskii, January 3, 1930.

83. Knoedler papers: London Letterbooks, August 8, 1928–May 2, 1920, CRH to O. Gutekunst, January 15, 1930.

84. BJH papers: CRH to BJH, March 2, 1943.

85. Wilson, *Ideology and Economics*, pp. 1–49.

86. Sparkes papers: interview, DEF, March 1, 1945, p. 20; BJH papers: interview, CRH, October 24, 1942, p. 9.

87. Knoedler papers: Hermitage Paintings Letterbook, 1930, CRH to G. H. Davey,

January 15, 1930; G. H. Davey to CRH, April 7, 15, 1930; Walker papers: Personal Papers Box 10, G. H. Davey, Notes in Leningrad.

88. BJH papers: interview, CRH, October 24, 1942, p. 2.

89. Knoedler papers: Domestic Letterbook, February 19, 1930–April 25, 1930, CHM to AWM, March 5, 1930.

90. Knoedler papers: Domestic Letterbook, February 19, 1930–April 25, 1930, CHM to AWM, April 24, 1930.

91. Knoedler papers: Hermitage Paintings Letterbook 1931, Information on Paintings, F. Zatzenstein to CRH, January 14, 1931.

92. Knoedler papers: Domestic Letterbook, February 19, 1930–April 25, 1930, CHM to AWM, April 24, 1930; Domestic Letterbook, April 26–July 21, 1930, CHM to AWM, May 23, 1930; Archive of the State Hermitage, f1, op. 17, d. 157 (160) [materials on transfer of valuables, 1930], 11. 35–41: Deeds of transfer, March 18, 1930, April 24, 26, 1930.

93. BJH papers: interview, CRH and CHM, November 10, 1941, p. 7; interview, CRH, October 24, 1942, p. 4.

94. Archive of the State Hermitage, f1 op. 17, d. 157 (160) [materials on transfer of museum valuables, 1930], lines 60–64, concerning transfer of Van Eyck *Annunciation*, June 2–3, 1930; B. B. Piotrovskii and M. B. Piotrovskii, "K istorii prodazhi 'Blagoveeshcheniia' Van Eika," in *Hermitage Readings in Memory of B. B. Piotrovsky* (St. Petersburg, 1997), pp. 5–10; M. Piotrovsky, "The Two Sales of Van Eyck's Annunciation," in *Masterpieces from Major World Museums at the Hermitage: Jan Van Eyck, The Annunciation* (St. Petersburg, 1997), pp. 11–13; Piotrovskii, *Istoriia Ermitazha*, pp. 447–50.

95. Knoedler papers: Miscellaneous Letters, Knoedler & Co. [London] to CHM, July 9, 1930.

96. BJH papers: interview, CRH, October 24, 1942, pp. 5–8; Archive of the State Hermitage, f1, op. 17, d. 147 (160) [materials on transfer of museum valuables, 1930], 11. 79–80, 117: Deeds of transfer, August 1, 11, 1930, November 11, 1930.

97. Knoedler papers: Miscellaneous Letters, Knoedler & Co. [London] to CHM, July 15, 1930.

98. PM papers: AWM to PM, November 2, 1930.

99. Duveen papers: JD to Duveen Bros. [Paris], February 25, 1930.

100. Duveen papers: JD to Duveen Bros. [New York], August 10, 1930; Duveen Bros. [New York] to JD, August 12, 1930; AWM to JD, September 4, 1930; M. Secrest, *Duveen: A Life in Art* (New York, 2004), p. 200. See also AWM papers: Alexandra Galleries to AWM, February 5, 9, 13, 1931; AWM to Alexandra Galleries, February 7, 12, 13, 1931.

101. Duveen papers: Duveen Bros. [New York] to JD, August 12, 1930; Duveen Bros. [New York] to Duveen Bros. [Paris], September 12, 16, 17, 1930; B. Boggis to JD, September 17, 1930; Duveen Bros. [Paris] to Duveen Bros. [New York], September 17, 18, 1930.

102. Duveen papers: Duveen Bros. [New York] to DEF, November 26, 1930; Duveen Bros. [New York] to Duveen Bros. [Paris], December 5, 1930; Price list, January 5, 1931.

103. Walker, *Self-Portrait*, p. 113.

104. Knoedler papers: Foreign Letterbook, August 4, 1930–December 14, 1934, CRH to F. Zatzenstein, October 23, 1930, November 25, 1930; Domestic Letterbook, October 24, 1930–December 29, 1930, CHM to AWM, December 11, 1930.

105. Knoedler papers: Hermitage Paintings Letterbook 1931, CRH to F. Zatzenstein, January 2, 1931; CRH to Matthiesen Gallery, January 9, 1931.

106. Archive of the State Hermitage, f1, op. 17, d. 205 (177) [Materials on transfer of museum valuables, 1931], line 60: Deed of transfer, January 21, 1931; Knoedler papers: Hermitage Paintings Letterbook 1931, F. Zatzenstein to CRH, January 9, 1931.

107. Archive of the State Hermitage, f1, op. 17, d. 157 (160) [materials on transfer of museum valuables, 1930], line 122: Deed of transfer, December 6, 1930; f1, op. 17, d. 205 (177) [materials on transfer of museum valuables, 1931], line 72: Deed of transfer, February 23, 1931; Knoedler papers: Hermitage Paintings Letterbook 1931, F. Zatzenstein to Knoedler & Co., January 29, 1931; CRH to F. Zatzenstein, January 29, 1931; CRH to Matthiesen Gallery, January 30, 1931; F. Zatzenstein to CRH, February 21, 1931; CRH to F. Zatzenstein, March 10, 1931. For a recent account of the sale of Raphael's *St. George and the Dragon*, see J. Pittman, *The Raphael Trail* (London, 2006), pp. 241–79.

108. PM papers: AWM to PM, February 7, 1931.

109. Archive of the State Hermitage, f1, op. 17, d. 205 (177) [materials on transfer of museum valuables, 1931], lines 78, 83: Deeds of transfer, March 23, 1931, April 23, 1931; Hendrick papers: interview, CRH, October 24, 1942, p. 8; Knoedler papers: Hermitage Paintings Letterbook 1931, CRH to Matthiesen Gallery, March 16, 1931; CRH to B. Kraevsky, March 16, 1931; N. Ilyn to Knoedler & Co., March 17, 1931; CRH to B. Kraevsky, April 2, 1931; N. Ilyn to Knoedler & Co., April 3, 1931.

110. Archive of the State Hermitage, f1, op. 17, d. 205 (177) [materials on transfer of museum valuables, 1931], line 90: Deed of transfer, April 27, 1931.

111. D. A. Brown, *Raphael and America* (Washington, D. C., 1983), pp. 88–94.

112. Knoedler papers: Hermitage Paintings Letterbook 1931, CRH to Matthiesen Gallery, May 4, 1931; PM papers: AWM to PM, April 15, 1931.

113. Walker, *Self-Portrait*, pp. 50, 119.

114. BJH papers: interview, CRH and CHM, November 10, 1941, p. 9; interview, CRH, October 24, 1942, p. 9.

115. Knoedler papers: Hermitage Painting Letterbook 1931, CHM to AWM, April 11, 1931; CRH to CHM, May 12, 1931; Walker papers: Personal Papers Box 10, Knoedler's Files, draft account of "The Greatest Picture Deal in History" [n.d., 1931].

116. Knoedler papers: Hermitage Paintings Letterbook 1931, R. Knoedler to CRH, May 19, 1931; Knoedler & Co. to CRH, May 21, 1931; G. H. Davey to CRH, May 30, 1931; BJH papers: CRH to BJH, March 2, 1943; Walker, *Self-Portrait*, p. 125; DEF, *A Standard of Excellence: Andrew W. Mellon Founds the National Gallery of Art in Washington* (Washington, D.C., 1973), pp. 21–22; Kopper, pp. 69–70.

117. Knoedler papers: Miscellaneous Letters, Knoedler & Co. [London] to CHM,

July 15, 1930; BJH papers: interview, CRH, October 24, 1942, p. 11; Duveen papers: B. Boggis to JD, September 17, 1930.

118. *New York Times*, September 28, 1930, November 1, 1930, May 11, 1931; *Art News*, October 17, 1931, pp. 1, 13; *Burlington Magazine* (December 1931), p. 323; AWM papers: AWM to C. P. Minnegerode, March 30, 1931; Knoedler papers: Hermitage Paintings Letterbook 1931, CHM to C. Powell Minnegerode, March 28, 1931; London Letterbooks, Knoedler & Co. [London] to Knoedler & Co. [New York], February 9, 1932; Duveen papers: Duveen Bros. [New York] to JD, April 25, 1931; Duveen Bros. [Paris] to Duveen Bros. [New York], November 12, 1931.

119. AWM papers: AWM, Deceased, Report and Accounts, August 26, 1937, Exhibit J, p. 1.

120. BJH papers: interview, CRH, October 24, 1942, pp. 8–9.

121. Duveen papers: B. Boggis to JD, September 17, 1930.

122. BJH papers: AWM Letterbooks, AWM to Mrs. H. C. Frick, March 25, 1930; AWM to J. R. Mellon, March 28, 1930.

123. AWM papers: AWM, Speech at Pittsburgh Golf Club, March 24, 1930.

124. Lorant, p. 482.

125. S. J. Astorino, "The Decline of the Republican Dynasty in Pennsylvania, 1929–1934" (Ph.D. diss., University of Pittsburgh, 1962), pp. 146–50; PM papers: AWM to PM, October 23, 1936.

126. Lorant, p. 482; PM papers: AWM to PM, November 23, 1930; AWM papers: AWM, Deceased, Report and Accounts, May 1, 1939, Exhibit K, p. 2.

127. PM papers: AWM to PM, April 13, 1931.

128. BJH papers: AWM Letterbook, AWM to J. M. Witherow, January 21, 1930, June 24, 1930.

129. Astorino, "Republican Dynasty in Pennsylvania," pp. 96–99.

130. The next paragraphs are much indebted to Astorino, "Republican Dynasty in Pennsylvania," pp. 99–130.

131. AWM papers: AWM diary, December 9, 1929; Hendrick, ch. 25, p. 3.

132. Stimson papers: H. L. Stimson diary, October 29, 31, 1930.

133. Astorino, "Republican Dynasty in Pennsylvania," pp. 66–73, 80, 82.

134. E. L. Davin, "Blue Collar Democracy: Ethnic Workers and Class Politics in Pittsburgh's Steel Valley, 1914–1948" (Ph.D. diss., University of Pittsburgh, 1999), p. 25.

135. R. L. Duffus, "Is Pittsburgh Civilized?" *Harper's Monthly Magazine* (October 1930), pp. 537–45; reprinted in Lubove, pp. 158–70.

136. AWM papers: S. H. Church to AWM, January 28, 1932.

137. *Pittsburgh Post-Gazette*, May 30, 1941.

13. "The Man Who Stayed Too Long":
Depression, Departure, London and Back, 1931–33

1. Steiner, pp. 646–50.

2. H. Hoover, *The Memoirs of Herbert Hoover*, vol. 3, *The Great Depression, 1929–1941* (New York, 1952), p. 61.

3. PM papers: AWM to PM, February 22, 1931; AMB papers: PM to AMB, March 22, 1931, April 22, 1931, May 7, 1931; Bank of England papers: OV 32/5, G. L. Harrison to M. Norman, June 16, 1931; *Pittsburgh Post-Gazette*, June 23, 1931; *New York Times*, June 23, 1931.

4. AWM papers: N. McMullen to AWM, June 23, 1931; A. McMullen to AWM, June 22, 1931; P. McMullen to AWM, June 22, 23, 1931.

5. AWM papers: NMM to AWM, June 3, 1931, enclosing H. Thirkill to A. P. McMullen, May 23, 1931.

6. Kennedy, pp. 72–74.

7. Hoover papers: Foreign Affairs, Box 1015, Diary of Developments of the Moratorium, June 5, 18, 1931; Koskoff papers: f12, H. L. Stimson to AWM, June 22, 1931; H. L. Stimson to American Embassy, Paris, June 22, 1931 [copies]; Murray, pp. 273–74.

8. Stimson papers: H. L. Stimson diary, June 18, 24, 25, 1931; Koskoff papers: f12, Transcript of telephone conversation between H. Hoover, O. Mills, and AWM, July 6, 1931 [copies].

9. Bank of England papers: OV 32/5, M. Norman to G. Harrison, June 18, 1931; Transcript to M. Norman and G. Harrison telephone conversations, June 23, 1931, pp. 2–3, June 27, 1931, p. 2; M. Norman diary, June 18, 19, 22, 24, 1931; Harrison papers: 3115.2, Confidential files, June 19, 23, 30, 1931.

10. Hoover papers: Foreign Affairs, Box 1015, Diary of Developments of the Moratorium, July 5–6, 1931; *New York Times*, July 18, 1931.

11. Steiner, pp. 653–58.

12. Stimson papers: H. L. Stimson diary, July 17–18, 1931; Koskoff papers: f12, Transcript of telephone conversation between H. Hoover, H. Stimson, O. Mills, and AWM, July 21, 1931 [copy]; H. L. Stimson to H. Hoover, August 11, 1931 [copy], gives a full account of the negotiations.

13. Steiner, pp. 659–66.

14. AWM papers: AWM to NMM, May 14, 1931, August 17, 1931; DEF papers (NGA): Box 19, Personal Correspondence, AWM, W. Flore to DEF, July 28, 1931.

15. CFOST: Box 15, Banks and Banking, October 1931, S. J. Block to AWM, October 3, 1931; Kennedy, pp. 77–78.

16. *New York Sun*, August 24, 1931; *New York Times*, August 25, 1931.

17. PM papers: AWM to PM, September 6, 1931; Stimson papers: H. L. Stimson diary, September 8, 1931.

18. CFOST: Box 22, Budget 1931, Press release, July 1, 1931; F&S, p. 317.

19. White, pp. 14–16, 57.

20. PM papers: AWM to PM, September 28, 1931.

21. *American Examiner*, April 22, 1933.

22. Stimson papers: H. L. Stimson diary, September 22, 1931; *American Examiner*, April 22, 1933.

23. *Pittsburgh Press*, November 29, 1931; BJH papers: interview, Mr. Richards, March 15, 1941, pp. 3–4; *Pittsburgh Press*, December 8, 1931; AWM papers: J. F. Burke to AWM, December 8, 1931; AWM to J. F. Burke, December 11, 1931; BJH papers: WAM notes on BJH biography, p. 166.

24. B. M. Stave, *The New Deal and the Last Hurrah: Pittsburgh Machine Politics* (Pittsburgh, 1970), p. 35; CFOST, 1933–56: Box 210, Tax Cases (AWM), R. H. Jackson to H. Morgenthau, February 28, 1935; R. H. Jackson to R. Magill, March 14, 1935.

25. Stimson papers: H. L. Stimson diary, October 5, 1931; DEF papers (LOC): 65/J. J. Davies, AWM to J. J. Davies, October 30, 1931; Meltzer, p. 345.

26. CFOST: Box 118, Reconstruction Finance Corporation October 1931–February 1932, AWM to F. C. Walcott, January 5, 1932; G. D. Nash, "Herbert Hoover and the Origins of the Reconstruction Finance Corporation," *Mississippi Valley Historical Review* 46 (1959), p. 463.

27. PM papers: interview no. 1, p. 13; S. E. Kennedy, *The Banking Crisis of 1933* (Lexington, Ky., 1973), p. 26.

28. BJH papers: interview, H. M. Johnson, April 6, 1940, p. 3; AWM papers: J. M. Witherow to AWM, December 16, 1931.

29. BJH papers: AWM Letterbooks, AWM to J. S. Ruedy, December 9, 1931.

30. BJH papers: AWM Letterbooks, AWM to Mrs. D. A. Reed, March 3, 1930.

31. Murray, pp. 268–70.

32. Stimson papers: H. L. Stimson diary, May 19, 1931, June 5, 1931, November 17, 1931.

33. *New York Times*, December 20, 1931; R. S. Allen and D. Pearson, *Washington Merry-Go-Round* (New York, 1931), p. 163.

34. A. J. Toynbee, *Survey of International Affairs, 1931* (London, 1932), p. 1.

35. Kennedy, pp. 85–93.

36. Stimson papers: H. L. Stimson diary, September 8, 1931; Hoover, *Great Depression*, p. 30; R. N. Smith, *An Uncommon Man: The Triumph of Herbert Hoover* (New York, 1984), pp. 118–19.

37. A. U. Romasco, *The Poverty of Abundance: Hoover, the Nation, the Depression* (New York, 1965), p. 25; Kennedy, pp. 51–52.

38. PM papers: AWM to PM, September 28, 1931; AWM papers, AWM Deceased, Report and Accounts, August 26, 1937, Exhibit G, p. 3.

39. Mellon Bank papers: f04-05-00-0002-0001, Resources/Liabilities, March 25, 1931, March 31, 1933; AWM papers: WLM to AWM, May 6, 26, 1932; S. A. Swensrud, *"Gulf Oil": The First Fifty Years, 1901–1951* (New York, 1951), pp. 17–22; Koskoff, pp. 300–305; Hersh, p. 312.

40. Duveen papers: Duveen Bros. [New York] to JD, June 2, 1931; Duveen Bros. [London] to Duveen Bros. [New York], June 17, 1931; Knoedler papers, Letterbook Carbons, October 31, 1931–December 31, 1931, CRH to H. Mansfeld, November 25, 1931; Hermitage Paintings Letterbook 1931, CRH to H. Mansfeld, December 23, 1931; BJH papers: AWM Letterbook, AWM to R. L. Douglas, June 5, 1933.

41. Knoedler papers, Letterbook Carbons, January 1, 1932–March 31, 1932, CRH to H. Mansfeld, March 8, 1932.

42. *RSS*, p. 128.

43. *RSS*, pp. 134–36.

44. G. Gurney, *Sculpture and the Federal Triangle* (Washington, D.C., 1985), pp. 124, 338–39.

45. BJH papers: AWM Letterbooks, AWM to J. M. Witherow, April 29, 1931; Murray, p. 275; Kennedy, p. 79.

46. Stimson papers: H. L. Stimson diary, May 26, 1931, September 8, 1931.

47. CFOST: Box 23, Federal Budget January–March 1932, AWM, Statement Before Ways and Means Committee, January 13, 1932.

48. For other expressions of Treasury policy, see CFOST: Box 166, Taxation (General), January–June 1931, Memorandum for O. Mills, June 4, 1931; Memorandum for AWM, June 4, 1931; Taxation (General), July–December 1931, Statement by O. Mills, December 30, 1931; Taxation (General), January–March 1932, Statement by O. Mills, March 6, 1932.

49. M. H. Leff, *The Limits of Symbolic Reform: The New Deal and Taxation, 1933–1939* (Cambridge, 1984), pp. 20–25, 30, 49–52.

50. J. A. Schwartz, *The Interregnum of Despair: Hoover, Congress and the Depression* (Urbana, Ill., 1970), pp. 125–27.

51. BJH papers: interview, M. A. Rosanoff, April 13, 1940, p. 3; Smith, *Uncommon Man*, pp. 137–40.

52. N. B. Young, *Wright Patman: Populism, Liberalism and the American Dream* (Dallas, Tex., 2000), pp. 38–41.

53. For example, Patman papers: 1511B-5, V. E. Fox, Compilation of current subsidiaries and assets of those companies listed in the Directory of Directors for the Pittsburgh district, of which AWM was director or trustee in 1919, November 13, 1931.

54. Patman papers: 1511C-10, J. B. Smith to W. Patman, February 11, 1932; see also 1511C-5, "A Pittsburgher" to W. Patman, January 6, 1932. The letters came from all over the country. For the broader background of protest against scheming financiers and debauched plutocrats, see A. Brinkley, *Voices of Protest: Huey Long, Father Coughlin and the Great Depression* (New York, 1982), pp. 143–68.

55. *Congressional Record*, 72nd Congress, 1st Session, 1932, vol. 75, pt. iii, pp. 1400–1401.

56. Young, *Wright Patman*, pp. 42–43; Murray, p. 289.

57. Murray, p. 287.

58. U.S. Congress, 72nd Congress, 1st Session, *House Committee on the Judiciary, Hearings Before the Committee on the Judiciary, Charges of the Hon. Wright Patman Against the Secretary of the Treasury*, p. 233; *New York Times*, January 16, 1932.

59. Stimson papers: H. L. Stimson diary, February 1, 3, 1932.

60. Stimson papers: H. L. Stimson diary, January 19, 24, 1932, February 1, 1932; T. G. Joslin, *Hoover Off the Record* (New York, 1934), p. 183.

61. Gurney, *Sculpture and the Federal Triangle*, p. 124.

62. Murray, p. 291.

63. *Pittsburgh Press*, March 1, 2, 1932.

64. W. Patman, *Bankerteering, Bonuseering, Melloneering* (privately printed, 1934), esp. pp. 129–69.

65. AWM papers: AWM to Bishop J. E. Freeman, February 11, 1932; S. Parker Gilbert to AWM, February 6, 1932.

66. BJH papers: AWM to H. Hoover, February 8, 1932; AWM papers: H. Hoover to AWM, February 12, 1932.

67. AWM papers: NMM to AWM, February 1, 1932.

68. Duveen papers: JD to AWM, February 4, 14, 1932.

69. Docket 76499, pp. 4375–79.

70. AWM papers: AWM, Federal Estate Tax Return, February 25, 1939, sheets X-9–X-11; AWM Deceased, Report and Accounts, August 26, 1937, Exhibit H, p. 1; Exhibit J, pp. 1–2.

71. DEF papers (NGA): Box 2, AWM Personal, 1928–1932, DEF to AWM, March 1, 18, 1932; AWM papers: AWM to H. Hoover, March 29, 1932.

72. AWM papers: J. H. Metcalf to AWM, March 1, 11, 1932; AWM to J. H. Metcalf, March 17, 1932; AWM, Remarks at a dinner given by Senator Metcalf at the New Willard Hotel, March 16, 1932.

73. *The Times*, April 9, 1932; Hendrick, ch. 30, pp. 22–23, 27; C. Black, *Franklin Delano Roosevelt: Champion of Freedom* (London, 2003), p. 439.

74. *Daily Express*, April 8, 1932; *Daily Mail*, April 8, 1932; *The Times*, April 9, 1932; *Observer*, April 10, 1932.

75. *The Times*, February 5, 1932; Lankford, p. 88.

76. BJH papers: AWM to Secretary of State, February 24, 1932; AWM papers: AWM to Mrs. W. Burns, May 3, 1932; PM papers: interview no. 5, pp. 1–2; J. Strouse, *Morgan: American Financier* (New York, 1999), p. 688.

77. Duveen papers: List of Paintings sent to Europe for Mr. Mellon, March 28, 1932.

78. Knoedler papers, London Letterbook, June 16, 1931–December 29, 1933, Knoedler & Co. [London] to Knoedler & Co. [New York], April 12, 22, 1932, May 3, 1932.

79. Hendrick, ch. 30, pp. 23–25.

80. AWM papers: Sir John Hanbury-Williams to AWM, March 7, 1932, April 8, 1932.

81. AWM papers: AWM diary, April 19, 1932, May 11, 1932; Hendrick, ch. 30, pp. 26–27.

82. D. Lloyd George, *The Truth About Reparations and War Debts* (London, 1932), pp. 116, 118–19.

83. Hendrick, ch. 30, pp. 26, 28; R. J. Cruickshank, "The Man with the Talking Eyes," *News Chronicle*, April 8, 1932; C. Price, "The Varied Job of Being an Ambassador," *New York Times Magazine*, May 15, 1932, p. 7.

84. *The Times*, April 15, 1932; AWM papers, *The Pilgrims, Dinner in Honour of AWM*, April 14, 1932.

85. AWM papers: AWM diary, April 14, 1932; CFOST: Box 298, Individuals Fh–Fz, DEF to O. Mills, April 15, 1932; *Pittsburgh Press*, May 21, 1932.

86. AWM papers: NMM to AWM, May 28, 1932.

87. AWM papers: Invitations book, lists AWM's visits to lunch, dinner, at homes, receptions and "country visits"; Lady Desborough to AWM, April 30, 1932; AWM to Lady Desborough, June 15, 1932; Mrs. R. Greville to AWM, May 10, 1932; AWM to Mrs. R. Greville, May 11, 1932; List of Guests at Lady Astor's Dinner, February 28, 1932; List of Guests at Embassy Receptions, November 28 & 30, 1932; AMB papers: D. K. E. Bruce to AMB, March 7, 1933; PM papers: interview no. 5, pp. 4, 6.

88. Hendrick, ch. 30, p. 26; AWM papers: Lord Derby to R. Atherton, May 23,

1932; AWM to Lord Derby, September 15, 1932; J. D. Lyon to AWM, May 25, 1932; AWM to J. D. Lyon, June 15, 1932; A. Flower to AWM, March 2, 1932; AWM to Lord Derby, February 9, 1932; Lord Mayor of London to AWM, April 15, 1932; BJH papers: AWM, List of honorary degrees; *The Times*, May 7, 1932, June 1, 1932, July 1, 1932; Lankford, p. 33.

89. Finley papers (NGA): Box 19, PM to DEF, March 21, 1932.

90. AWM papers: PM to AWM, November 18, 1932.

91. Knoedler papers, Miscellaneous Letters: Knoedler & Co. [London] to Knoedler & Co. [New York], March 31, 1933; Letterbook Carbons, May 1933 to June 1933, CHM to PM, June 26, 1933.

92. *RSS*, p. 141.

93. *RSS*, pp. 132–33.

94. Duveen papers: Duveen Bros. [Paris] to Duveen Bros. [New York], August 5, 1932.

95. Steiner, pp. 639, 665, 689.

96. Stimson papers: H. L. Stimson diary, January 3, 1933; State Department Records: *Papers Relating to the Foreign Relations of the United States*, 1932, vol. 1, pp. 623–25, 754–80.

97. Hendrick, ch. 30, pp. 29–36; Kennedy, pp. 103–106.

98. Kennedy, pp. 98–103.

99. CFOST: Box 298, Individuals Fh–Fz, O. Mills to DEF, September 17, 1932; *New York Times*, September 9, 1932.

100. H. L. Stimson, *The Far Eastern Crisis: Recollections and Observations* (New York, 1936); W. I. Cohen, *Empire Without Tears: Americas Foreign Relations, 1921–1933* (Philadelphia, 1987), pp. 106–18.

101. BJH papers: J. R. Nutt to AWM, July 1, 1932; AWM papers: AWM Deceased, Report and Accounts, August 26, 1937, Exhibit K, p. 1.

102. Duveen papers: [?] to Duveen Bros. [London], April 11, 1932; Duveen Bros. [London] to Duveen Bros. [New York], April 16, 1932, July 5, 1932.

103. M. Secrest, *Duveen: A Life in Art* (New York, 2004), pp. 199–200; Duveen papers: Duveen Bros. [Paris] to Duveen Bros. [New York], August 5, 1932.

104. AWM papers: CRH to AWM, May 10, 1932, June 6, 1932.

105. Knoedler papers: Letterbook Carbons, January 3, 1933–February 28, 1933, CHM to AWM, January 19, 21, 1933; CRH to H. Mansfeld, January 10, 1933; Letterbook Carbons, March 1, 1933–April 28, 1933, CRH to H. Mansfeld, March 3, 1933; London Letterbooks, June 16, 1931–December 29, 1933, Knoedler & Co. [London] to Knoedler & Co. [New York], May 3, 1932, June 20, 29, 1932.

106. Knoedler papers: London Letterbook, June 2, 1932–December 30, 1932, CRH to H. Mansfeld, June 31, 1932.

107. Knoedler papers: London Letterbook, June 16, 1931–December 1933, Knoedler & Co. [London] to Knoedler & Co. [New York], June 20, 29, 1932.

108. PM papers: interview no. 1, p. 13.

109. AWM papers: AWM Deceased, Report and Accounts, August 26, 1937, Exhibit F, p. 3; Exhibit H, p. 1; Exhibit J, p. 1.

110. PM papers: RKM to AWM, May 17, 1932; AMB papers: AWM to AMB, May 10, 1932; D. K. E. Bruce to AMB, December 7, 1934.

111. G. Hulme et al., *The National Portrait Gallery: An Architectural History* (London, 2000), pp. 149–51.

112. D. Doheny, *David Finley: A Quiet Force for America's Arts* (Washington, D.C., 2006), pp. 105–106, 324; DEF, *A Standard of Excellence: Andrew W. Mellon Founds the National Gallery of Art in Washington* (Washington, D.C., 1973), pp. 31–32.

113. For this episode, I have been much helped by F. Venn, "A Futile Paper Chase: Anglo-American Relations and Middle East Oil, 1918–1934," *Diplomacy and Statecraft* 1 (1990), pp. 165–84; F. Venn, *A Struggle for Supremacy? Great Britain, the United States and Kuwait Oil in the 1930s*, University of Essex, Department of History, Working Paper 2 (Colchester, 2000), passim. I am also grateful to Dr. Venn for showing me her unpublished work on the subject.

114. R. W. Ferrier, *The History of the British Petroleum Company*, vol. 1, *The Developing Years, 1901–1932* (Cambridge, 1982), pp. 544–75; J. H. Bamberg, *The History of the British Petroleum Company*, vol. 2, *The Anglo-Iranian Years, 1928–1954* (Cambridge, 1996), pp. 147–49.

115. AWM papers: W. T. Wallace to AWM, November 19, 1931, enclosing Memorandum on Koweit Oil Concession and British Nationality Clause; State Department Records: *Papers Relating to the Foreign Relations of the United States, 1932*, vol. 2, pp. 1–16; B. J. C. McKercher, *Transition of Power: Britain's Loss of Global Pre-eminence to the United States, 1930–1945* (Cambridge, 1999), pp. 151–54.

116. State Department Records: Box 7056, RG 59, 1930–39, decimal file 890B.6363, Gulf Oil Corporation, W. Murray to Secretary of State, March 22, 1932; W. R. Castle to R. Atherton, April 1, 1932; W. Murray to R. Atherton, April 7, 1932; W. Murray to Secretary of State, December 28, 1932.

117. FO papers: F/0371/16002, E54/10/121/91, Memorandum of conversation between the U.S. Ambassador and Sir R. Vansittart, October 17, 1932; State Department Records: Box 7056, RG 59, 1930–39, decimal file 890B.6363, Gulf Oil Corporation, AWM to Secretary of State, October 18, 1932; Sir R. Vansittart to AWM, November 23, 1932; W. Murray to R. Atherton, January 21, 1935.

118. AWM papers: AWM, Memorandum of a meeting with Sir John Cadman, March 1, 1933; Bamberg, *Anglo-Iranian Years*, pp. 146–55; A. H. T. Chisholm, *The First Kuwait Oil Concession: A Record of the Negotiations for the 1934 Agreement* (London, 1975), pp. 189–91.

119. AWM papers: PM to AWM, November 18, 1932.

120. Duveen papers: AWM to JD, January 8, 1933.

121. Duveen papers: Duveen Bros. [New York] to JD, June 13, 1933.

122. Stimson papers: H. L. Stimson diary, February 10, 1932; State Department Records: *Papers Relating to the Foreign Relations of the United States, 1932*, vol. 3, pp. 219–21, 562–63, 577, 588–89, 620–21, 635, 654–72.

123. Stimson papers: H. L. Stimson diary, January 16, 1933; State Department Records, *Papers Relating to the Foreign Relations of the United States, 1932*, vol. 4, pp. 25, 32–33, 41–42, 44, 47, 74–75, 300, 304–305, 315, 326–30; vol. 5, pp. 64, 88–90, 124–25, 135–42.

124. *The Times*, February 22, 1933; AMB papers: The Pilgrims, *Speeches at the Dinner in Honour of His Excellency AWM . . . , February 21, 1933*, pp. 8–9.

125. Kennedy, p. 163.

126. F&S, pp. 324–32.

127. *The Times*, March 2, 1933; AWM papers: WLM to AWM, February 2, 1933; NMM to AWM, March 12, 1933; Kennedy, pp. 131–33.

128. AWM papers: Dr. W. W. G. Maclachlan to AWM, May 25, 1932; BJH papers: interview, Mr. Richards, March 15, 1941, pp. 3–4; A. W. Schmidt to BJH, December 10, 1942; *MNBTC*, pp. 40–42.

129. BJH papers: interview, Mr. Richards, March 15, 1941, pp. 3–4; CFOST 1933–1956: Box 201, Tax Cases (AWM), R. H. Jackson to H. Morgenthau, February 28, 1935; R. H. Jackson to R. Magill, March 14, 1935.

130. AWM papers: Department of State to AWM, August 11, 1932.

131. AWM papers: H. Hoover to AWM, February 25, 1933.

132. AWM papers: AWM to H. Hoover, March 16, 1933.

133. AWM papers: H. Hoover to AWM, March 2, 1933; *TMT*, p. 181.

134. AWM papers: AWM to R. W. Bingham, March 14, 1933; Duveen papers: Duveen Bros. [London] to Duveen Bros. [New York], February 7, 11, 22, 1933; AWM to JD, March 17, 1933.

14. His World Turned Upside Down: An Unhappy Homecoming, 1933–34

1. Knoedler papers: London Letterbook, June 16, 1931–December 29, 1933, Knoedler & Co. [London] to Knoedler & Co. [New York], February 16, 29, 1933, March 8, 14, 1933; Duveen papers: Duveen Bros. [New York], to JD, March 24, 1933, April 19, 1933; Hendrick, ch. 30, p. 36.

2. Sparkes papers: interview, DEF, March 1, 1945, p. 19.

3. AMB papers: D. K. E. Bruce to AMB, February 26, 1933.

4. N. Painter, *Standing at Armageddon: The United States, 1877–1919* (New York, 1987), p. 214.

5. *PPAFDR*, vol. 1, pp. 742–56.

6. CFOST: Box 62, Federal Reserve Banks, 1923–24, AWM to H. P. Fulmer, April 18, 1924.

7. Kennedy, p. 134.

8. There are many accounts of FDR's first inaugural. For the most recent, see C. Black, *Franklin Delano Roosevelt: Champion of Freedom* (London, 2003), pp. 270–72.

9. *PPAFDR*, vol. 2, p. 11.

10. *PPAFDR*, vol. 2, p. 12.

11. *PPAFDR*, vol. 2, pp. 12–13.

12. Kennedy, pp. 135–37.

13. BJH MS: A. W. Schmidt to BJH, December 10, 1942.

14. Black, *Franklin Delano Roosevelt*, pp. 276–77.

15. Kennedy, pp. 153, 366.

16. T. F. McCraw, *American Business, 1920–2000: How It Worked* (Wheeling, Ill., 2000), pp. 71–72; G. J. Benston, *The Separation of Commercial and Investment Banking: The Glass-Steagall Act Revisited and Reconsidered* (London, 1990), pp. 1–4, 11–16.

17. Kennedy, pp. 140–49.

18. Kennedy, pp. 140–43, 151.

19. Steiner, pp. 692–94.

20. CFOST: Box 62, Federal Reserve Banks, 1923–24, AWM to F. G. Tracy, June 26, 1924.

21. AWM papers: O. Mills to AWM, May 16, 1934; DEF to O. Mills, June 1, 1934.

22. E. S. Rosenberg, *Financial Missionaries to the World: The Politics and Culture of Dollar Diplomacy, 1900–1930* (Cambridge, Mass., 1999), pp. 247–54.

23. W. E. Leuchtenburg, *Franklin D. Roosevelt and the New Deal, 1932–1940* (New York, 1963), pp. 19–22; R. Jenkins, *Franklin Delano Roosevelt* (New York, 2003), p. 84.

24. For this whole section, I am much indebted to S. J. Astorino, "The Decline of the Republican Dynasty in Pennsylvania, 1929–1934" (Ph.D. diss., University of Pittsburgh, 1962), pp. 155–221.

25. S. O. Shames, "David Lawrence, Mayor of Pittsburgh: Development of a Political Leader" (Ph.D. diss., University of Pittsburgh, 1958), pp. 17–18.

26. E. L. Davin, "Blue Collar Democracy: Ethnic Workers and Class Politics in Pittsburgh's Steel Valley" (Ph.D. diss., University of Pittsburgh, 1999), p. 112.

27. A. M. Schlesinger Jr., *The Politics of Upheaval* (Boston, 1960), p. 442; B. M. Stave, *The New Deal and the Last Hurrah: Pittsburgh Machine Politics* (Pittsburgh, 1970), pp. 9–10.

28. Davin, "Blue Collar Democracy," p. 200.

29. DEF papers (LOC): 74/O'Connor, H. O'Connor to AWM, February 15, 1932; DEF to H. O'Connor, February 24, 1932.

30. O'Connor, pp. 56–63, 272–300.

31. O'Connor papers: W. M. Ward to H. O'Connor, June 7, 1932; W. W. Copeland to H. Maitree, June 11, 1932; Anna R. —— to H. O'Connor, November 26, 1931, February 18, 1932; M. Schreiner to H. O'Connor, August 1, 1932; A. McDowell to H. O'Connor, July 7, 1932; Patman papers: 1511C-10, H. O'Connor to W. Patman, May 24, 1932; W. Patman to H. O'Connor, May 27, 1932; O'Connor, pp. 402–21.

32. AWM papers: J. R. Mellon to AWM, October 3, 1933; *Pittsburgh Press*, August 11, 13, 1933; *New York Times*, October 3, 1933.

33. *Time*, August 14, 1933, pp. 47–48.

34. DEF papers (LOC): 65/J. W. Davis, J. W. Davis to AWM, June 30, 1933; AWM papers: J. M. Daiger to AWM, July 30, 1933, August 2, 8, 1933.

35. AWM papers: D. E. Shepard to AWM, August 2, 1933; *New York Times*, August 11, 1933; *Pittsburgh Press*, August 11, 1933.

36. AWM papers: DEF to AWM, August 26, 1933.

37. Stave, *New Deal and the Last Hurrah*, pp. 53–84.

38. Astorino, "Decline of the Republican Dynasty in Pennsylvania," p. 200.

39. Davin, "Blue Collar Democracy," pp. 240, 243.

40. *New York Times*, November 9, 1933.

41. E. B. Bronner, "The New Deal Comes to Pennsylvania: The Gubernatorial Election of 1934," *Pennsylvania History* 27 (1960), pp. 44–69.

42. O'Connor papers: R. G. Taylor to G. Pinchot [draft], November 28, 1933; R. G. Taylor to H. Evans, January 8, 1934.

43. Davin, "Blue Collar Democracy," p. 254.

44. H. Ickes diary: August 26, 29, 1934, October 20, 1934.

45. AWM papers: AWM to H. Hoover, May 25, 1934.

46. H. F. Gosnell and W. G. Colman, "Political Trends in Industrial America: Pennsylvania an Example," *Public Opinion Quarterly* 4 (1940), p. 483.

47. *New York Times*, November 8, 1934; Stave, *New Deal and the Last Hurrah*, pp. 24, 157–61; Davin, "Blue Collar Democracy," pp. 349, 358–71.

48. D. Doheny, *David Finley: A Quiet Force for America's Arts* (Washington, D.C., 2006), p. 106; DEF, *A Standard of Excellence: Andrew W. Mellon Founds the National Gallery of Art at Washington DC* (Washington, D.C., 1973), p. 35; AWM papers: S. L. M. Grange to AWM, November 9, 26, 1933.

49. BJH papers: interview, J. G. Bowman, January 10, 1940, p. 4.

50. Duveen papers: Duveen Bros. [New York] to JD, April 19, 1933.

51. AWM papers: H. M. Johnson to AWM, March 15, 1933; A. K. Oliver to AWM, January 23, 1934; BJH papers: interview, Mr. Kerrigan, September 4, 1940, p. 5.

52. Davin, "Blue Collar Democracy," pp. 127–29.

53. AWM papers: S. L. M. Grange to AWM, November 9, 1933.

54. Kennedy, pp. 160–69; R. Lowitt and M. Beasley (eds.), *One Third of a Nation: Lorena Hickok Reports on the Great Depression* (Urbana, Ill., 1981), pp. 3–13.

55. Smith, p. 446; G. H. Love, *An Exciting Century in Coal, 1864–1964* (New York, 1955), pp. 14–15.

56. BJH papers: AWM Letterbooks, AWM to Mr. Evans, October 9, 1930.

57. CFOST: Box 261, Treasury Department—Secretary—Invitations etc., 1929–32, AWM Speech at Welfare Fund emergency mass meeting, Pittsburgh, November 8, 1933.

58. AWM papers: AWM Deceased, Report and Accounts, August 26, 1937, Exhibit K, pp. 2–3.

59. Smith, pp. 180–84.

60. R. C. Alberts, *Pitt: The Story of the University of Pittsburgh, 1787–1987* (Pittsburgh, 1986), pp. 148–56.

61. AWM papers: H. M. Johnson to AWM, March 15, 1933; A. K. Oliver to AWM, January 23, 1934, enclosing Memorial Minute on RBM for the Carnegie Institute by W. M. Moorhead; *Pittsburgh Press*, December 1, 1933; *New York Times*, December 2, 1933.

62. Koskoff, pp. 305–306.

63. F. Lundberg, *America's 60 Families* (New York, 1937), pp. 357–58; *Pittsburgh Press*, May 31, 1935.

64. Sparkes papers: interview, H. M. Johnson, June 8, 1945, p. 6; *MNBTC*, p. 42.

65. AWM papers: D. N. Seely to AWM, December 10, 1933; AWM to NMM, December 11, 1933; NMM to AWM, December 12, 1933; Koskoff, pp. 306–307.

66. *Pittsburgh Press*, March 5, 1934, March 10, 1935; *Pittsburgh Sun-Telegraph*, March 9, 1935; *Pittsburgh Post-Gazette*, March 11, 12, 1935.

67. BJH papers: interview, A. E. Sixsmith, March 6, 1941, p. 1.

68. AWM papers: AWM diary, February 13, 1929, March 7, 13, 1929; PM papers: interview, no. 2, p. 10.

69. AWM papers: M. McClung to AWM, January 18, 1914, January 10, [?1915], November 2, [?1922], April 21, 1924; AWM to M. McClung, November 10, 1922, April 30, 1924.

70. AWM papers: T. A. Mellon and Mary Mellon McClung v. AWM and the Estate of RBM, 1934: Campbell, Wick, Houck and Thomas to J. G. Frazer, July 26, 1934.

71. AWM papers: T. A. Mellon and Mary Mellon McClung v. AWM and the Estate of RBM, 1934: Statement as to the claim of T. A. Mellon and Mary Mellon McClung against AWM and the estate of RBM.

72. AWM papers: AWM Federal Estate Tax Return, February 25, 1939, sheet X-17.

73. BJH papers: D. D. Shepard to BJH, June 13, 1941.

74. AWM papers: J. M. Budd to AWM, May 10, 1932; R. Evans to AWM, June 21, 1933, March 3, 1934; A. W. Negley to AWM, August 9, 1933, April 9, 1934; G. G. Negley to AWM, undated [1933–34]; NMM to AWM, February 16, 1933; P. McMullen to AWM, January 2, 1934; L. McMullen to AWM, November 10, 1932, December 7, 1932, June 29, 1933, September 6, 1933.

75. AWM papers: NMM to AWM, December 12, 1933.

76. AWM papers: AWM to NMM, December 11, 1933, December 12, 1933.

77. AWM papers: J. R. Mellon to AMB, December 18, 1933, January 15, 1934; R. Evans to AMB, February 3, 1934; S. L. M. Grange to AWM, November 26, 1933; Mrs. Cabell Bruce to AWM, July 3, 1933; Lankford, pp. 98–99.

78. AWM papers: AWM, Federal Estate Tax Return, February 24, 1939, sheet X-10.

79. AMB papers: D. K. E. Bruce to AMB, December 7, 1934; Lankford, pp. 101–102.

80. PM papers: interview no. 5, pp. 6–7.

81. BJH papers: AWM, Notes [undated], pp. 1–3.

82. Hoover papers: H. Hoover to AWM, December 5, 1933; AWM to H. Hoover, December 13, 1933.

83. AWM papers: NMM to AWM, May 23, 1933, June 24, 1933, July 31, 1933.

84. PM papers: interview no. 5, p. 7; RSS, pp. 141–43.

85. AWM papers: T. Rousseau to AWM, May 7, 1933; Pittsburgh Coal Company papers: Minutes of Directors' Meetings, March 23, 1932, April 27, 1933.

86. RSS, pp. 136–37.

87. RSS, pp. 143–46.

88. BJH papers: interview, J. Nelson, March 14, 1941, p. 1; interview, Mr. Richards, March 15, 1941, p. 2.

89. AMB papers: PM to AMB, August 24, 1934; Duveen papers: Duveen Bros. [New York] to Duveen Bros. [London], July 26, 1934, August 1, 1934; E. Duveen to JD, August 17, 1934.

90. AMB papers: PM to AMB, September 7, 1934.

91. Duveen papers: Duveen Bros. [New York] to JD, March 24, 1933.

92. Knoedler papers: Letterbook Carbons, October 2, 1933–December 1933, CHM to AWM, November 17, 1933; Duveen papers: Duveen Bros. [New York] to Duveen Bros. [London], April 22, 1933; JD to AWM, February 20, 1934.

93. AWM papers: AWM Deceased, Report and Accounts, August 26, 1937, Exhibit F, p. 3.

94. AMB papers: D. D. Shepard to AMB, December 24, [1934].

95. AMB papers: Mrs. W. C. Bruce to AMB, August 5, 1934.

15. The Second Scandal: The "Tax Trial" and the National Gallery of Art, 1933–36

1. AWM and FDR had certainly corresponded and "conversed" before, but it is not definite that they had previously met face-to-face: AWM papers: FDR to AWM, March 4, 1930; BJH papers: AWM Letterbooks, AWM to Mr. Crumbine, December 22, 1930.

2. PM papers: interview no. 2, p. 3; Hendrick, ch. 31, p. 2; *RSS*, pp. 137–38.

3. FDR papers: FDR speech files, container 4/251, FDR Speech at Democratic State Convention, Syracuse, September 27, 1926, p. 8; Duveen papers: Duveen Bros. [New York] to Duveen Bros. [London], April 22, 1933; Smith, p. 198.

4. Lankford, pp. 90–91; AMB papers: W. C. Bruce to D. K. E. Bruce, February 24, 25, 1933; D. K. E. Bruce to AMB, February 18, 26, 1933, March 1, 7, 12, 1933.

5. AWM papers: H. M. Johnson to AWM, January 30, 1933.

6. Duveen papers: AWM to JD, March 12, 1933.

7. AWM papers: D. D. Shepard to AWM, March 9, 1933; Duveen papers: D. D. Shepard to JD, March 14, 1933; AWM to JD, March 17, 1933.

8. AWM papers: D. D. Shepard to AWM, March 6, 1933.

9. AWM papers: Memorandum of Certain Facts Pertaining to the Investigation and Determination of the Income Tax Liability of AWM for the Calendar Year 1931 [1963], pp. 2–6, quoting D. A. Olson to D. Burnett, April 14, 1933, and McFadden's speech in the House, May 5, 1933.

10. Cummings papers: 212/Speech by H. Cummings, "Crime in High Places," April 24, 1933.

11. AWM papers: Memorandum of Certain Facts . . . , pp. 8–9, quoting H. M. Johnson to W. P. Mays, September 21, 1933.

12. AWM papers: AWM, Deceased, Report and Accounts, August 26, 1937, p. 59, lists refunds and additional assessments, 1916–29.

13. FDR papers: PPF 4250 [undated, c 1933].

14. J. M. Blum, *From the Morgenthau Diaries: Years of Crisis, 1928–1938* (Boston, 1959), p. 323.

15. Hendrick, ch. 32, pp. 7–11.

16. He also made this point to JD: Duveen papers: Duveen Bros. [New York] to JD, June 13, 1933.

17. O'Connor papers: Department of Justice press release, January 18, 1934.

18. E. L. Irey [and W. J. Slocum], *The Tax Dodgers* (New York, 1948), pp. xii–xiii.

19. E. C. Gerhart, *America's Advocate: Robert H. Jackson* (Indianapolis, Ind., 1958), pp. 62–66; Blum, *From the Morgenthau Diaries*, pp. 324–25.

20. AWM papers: AWM, Statement, March 11, 1934.

21. AWM papers: Memorandum of Certain Facts . . . , p. 14.

22. Cummings papers: H. Cummings diaries, May 16, 1934; *Pittsburgh Post-Gazette*, May 9, 1934; *Philadelphia Inquirer*, May 9, 1934.

23. Hendrick, ch. 32, pp. 15–20.

24. AWM papers: W. S. Morris to WLM, May 11, 1934; Bennett papers: 63/12, EHB to AWM, May 9, 1934; AWM to EHB, May 19, 1934; Stimson papers: Reel 87, Frame Z, H. L. Stimson to AWM, [May 1934]; AWM to H. L. Stimson, May 9, 1934.

25. AWM papers: H. Hoover to AWM, May 18, 1934; AWM to H. Hoover, May 25, 1934.

26. *New York Tribune*, May 12, 1934; *Pittsburgh Post-Gazette*, May 12, 1934.

27. R. Steel, *Walter Lippmann and the American Century* (London, 1980), p. 291; Kennedy, p. 101.

28. Cummings papers: H. Cummings to Rev. A. MacColl, June 5, 1934.

29. AWM papers: AWM Deceased, Report and Accounts, August 26, 1937, p. 59, lists refunds and additional assessments, 1916–29.

30. M. H. Leff, *The Limits of Symbolic Reform: The New Deal and Taxation, 1933–1939* (Cambridge, 1984), pp. 58–59.

31. A. M. Schlesinger Jr., *The Coming of the New Deal* (Boston, 1958), p. 570.

32. Schlesinger, *Coming of the New Deal*, pp. 569–70.

33. Leff, *Limits of Symbolic Reform*, p. 59.

34. D. Burnham, *A Law unto Itself: Power, Politics and the IRS* (New York, 1989), pp. 228–31; C. Ogden, *Legacy: A Biography of Moses and Walter Annenberg* (Boston, 1999), pp. 205–27.

35. CFOST: Box 297, Individual Tax Cases, Ca–Cn, Capone; *New York Times*, April 19, 1931.

36. *New York Times*, March 14, 1934.

37. Cummings papers: H. Cummings diary, March 10, 1934; H. Ickes diary: April 9, 1934; R. H. Jackson, *That Man: An Insider's Portrait of Franklin D. Roosevelt* (Oxford, 2003), pp. 125–26.

38. Smith, pp. 194–96; C. C. Carr, *Alcoa: An American Enterprise* (New York, 1952), pp. 209–16.

39. Cummings papers: 112/George D. Haskell, 1933–1941, G. D. Haskell to H. Cummings, May 26, 1933; H. Cummings to G. D. Haskell, February 7, 1934, March 11, 1935.

40. Kennedy, pp. 367–68.

41. Leff, *Limits to Symbolic Reform*, pp. 61, 107.

42. Leff, *Limits to Symbolic Reform*, pp. 64–77.

43. C. Black, *Franklin Delano Roosevelt: Champion of Freedom* (London, 2003), pp. 334–35.

44. Kennedy, pp. 249–57.

45. Kennedy, p. 274.

46. Leff, *Limits of Symbolic Reform*, pp. 93–168.

47. *PPAFDR*, vol. 4, pp. 271–75.

48. Kennedy, pp. 275–77, 284.

49. *PPAFDR*, vol. 5, pp. 13–16.

50. Kennedy, pp. 278–79.

51. Kennedy, pp. 279–80.

52. A. M. Schlesinger Jr., *The Politics of Upheaval* (Boston, 1960), p. 392; Kennedy, p. 280.

53. DEF papers (LOC): 17/1932–37, AWM to DEF, August 31, 1935; PM papers: AWM to PM, February 2, 1936.

54. *MNBTC*, p. 40.

55. E. E. Freudenthal, *The Aviation Business* (New York, 1940), pp. 193–216; F. Lundberg, *America's 60 Families* (New York, 1937), p. 216.

56. Bennett papers: 63/12, AWM to EHB, April 17, 1934, May 19, 1934.

57. G. Gurney, *Sculpture and the Federal Triangle* (Washington, D.C., 1985), pp. 122–24, 337–43.

58. Hendrick, ch. 32, p. 23.

59. Duveen papers: JD to Duveen Bros. [New York], May 8, 1934; Duveen Bros. [New York] to Duveen, May 9, 1934.

60. CFOST, 1933–56: Box 210, Tax Cases (AWM), R. H. Jackson to H. Oliphant (undated [July–August 1934]); Duveen papers: ? [on behalf of D. E. Shepard] to JD, January 9, 1935.

61. AWM papers: Memorandum of Certain Facts . . . , pp. 16–19.

62. Hendrick, ch. 32, p. 25.

63. BJH papers: interview, F. J. Hogan, December 1, 1942, pp. 1–2; L. Cohen, *Frank Hogan Remembered* (Washington, D.C., 1985), pp. 82–88.

64. CFOST, 1933–56: Box 210, Tax Cases (AWM), R. H. Jackson to H. Morgenthau and H. Oliphant, May 26, 1934; R. H. Jackson to H. Oliphant, June 22, 1934; Jackson, *That Man*, p. 125.

65. Stimson papers: H. L. Stimson diary, May 17, 1934.

66. Cummings papers: H. Cummings diary, May 25, 1934; CFOST, 1933–56: Box 210, Tax Cases (AWM), R. H. Jackson to H. Oliphant, June 22, 1934; H. Cummings to H. Morgenthau, June 28, 1934.

67. Jackson papers: Container 67, O. Hamele to R. H. Jackson, August 8, 1934.

68. Duveen papers: Duveen Bros. [New York] to Dr. Valentiner, May 3, 1935.

69. FDR papers: PSF 79/HM, H. Morgenthau to FDR, February 25, 1935, enclosing R. H. Jackson to H. Oliphant, February 22, 1935.

70. Docket 76499: AWM testimony, pp. 4349–5246.

71. AWM papers: J. K. Evans to AWM, May 18, 1935.

72. Jackson papers: Containter 68, R. H. Jackson, Opening statement, February 18, 1935.

73. Docket 76499: AWM testimony, pp. 4375–79, 4433–38.

74. Docket 76499: Reply Brief for the Respondent, vol. i, pt. i, Fraud and Stock Loss Issues, pp. 40–43.

75. Docket 76499: H. M. Johnson testimony, pp. 957–66.

76. H. Hoover, *The Memoirs of Herbert Hoover*, vol. 2, *The Cabinet and the Presidency, 1920–1933* (New York, 1952), p. 60.

77. Hendrick, ch. 32, p. 39.

78. Docket 76499: AWM testimony, p. 4422.

79. BJH papers: interview, F. J. Hogan, December 1, 1942, p. 2.

80. AWM papers: C. F. Russell to D. E. Shepard, April 3, 1935.

81. Docket 76499: AWM testimony, pp. 5236–37, 5243–46; BJH papers: interview, F. J. Hogan, December 1, 1942, p. 5.

82. Hoover, *Cabinet and the Presidency*, p. 59.

83. *Washington Herald*, February 20, 1935; *Art News*, February 23, 1935, pp. 3–5.

84. Docket 76499: CRH testimony, pp. 7646–71; CHM testimony, pp. 7671–80.

85. CFOST, 1933–56: Box 210, Tax Cases (AWM), R. H. Jackson to H. Oliphant, February 22, 1935; Cohen, *Frank Hogan*, p. 87.

86. CFOST, 1933–56: Box 210, Tax Cases (AWM), R. H. Jackson to H. Oliphant, April 29, 1935; Docket 76499: JD testimony, pp. 7490–7636.

87. Docket 76499: JD testimony, pp. 7633–34.

88. Duveen papers: ? to JD, May 11, 1935; D. D. Shepard to J. H. Allen, May 18, 1935; J. H. Allen to D. D. Shepard, May 20, 1935.

89. BJH papers: D. D. Shepard to BJH, January 15, 1943.

90. CFOST, 1933–56: Box 210, Tax Cases (AWM), R. H. Jackson to H. Oliphant, February 24, 1935, April 11, 29, 30, 1935.

91. CFOST, 1933–56: Box 210, Tax Cases (AWM), R. H. Jackson to H. Oliphant, February 25, 1935, April 11, 1935; *Jacksonville* (Florida) *Times-Union*, March 4, 1936.

92. DEF papers (NGA): Box 38, Personal Correspondence O. and D. Mills, O. Mills to DEF, October 1, 1934.

93. CFOST, 1933–56: Box 210, Tax Cases (AWM), R. H. Jackson to H. Morgenthau and H. Oliphant, September 17, 1934.

94. Duveen papers: Duveen Bros. [New York] to Duveen Bros. [London], May 25, 29, 1935.

95. DEF papers (NGA): Box 1, Anecdotes of AWM [undated memorandum]; Mellon Bank papers: 04-05-00-002-0001 et seq., Reserves/liabilities, 1931–36.

96. AWM papers: AWM to PM, February 2, 1936.

97. AWM papers: AWM Deceased, Report and Accounts, August 26, 1937, Exhibit F, p. 3; Exhibit G, p. 3; Exhibit H, p. 2.

98. Bowman papers: J. G. Bowman to H. M. Johnson, March 31, 1936; J. G. Bowman, "Notes about AWM," pp. 23–25; R. C. Alberts, *Pitt: The Story of the University of Pittsburgh, 1787–1987* (Pittsburgh, Pa., 1986), pp. 129–30.

99. Knoedler papers: Letterbook Carbons [undated], CHM to AWM, March 6, 1935.

100. D. Doheny, *David Finley: A Quiet Force for America's Arts* (Washington, D.C., 2006), p. 114.

101. BJH papers: AWM Letterbooks, AWM to J. I. McGurk, February 17, 1931.

102. Doheny, *David Finley*, p. 324; PM papers: AWM to PM, February 2, 1936; Duveen papers: B. Boggis, note, February 1, 1936; AWM, note, February 27, 1936.

103. BJH papers: AWM Letterbooks, AWM to Helen C. Frick, January 9, 1930; AWM papers: Helen C. Frick to AWM, May 12, 1933; DEF papers (LOC): Box 1, Anecdotes of AWM [undated memo]; 17/1932–37, DEF to AWM, November 20, 1935; S. M. Bedford, *John Russell Pope: Architect of Empire* (New York, 1998), pp. 78–80, 146–55, 208–10; D. G. Wilson, *The Mausoleum of Henry and Arabella Huntington* (San Marino, Calif., 1989).

104. Bedford, *John Russell Pope*, pp. 110–12, 174–85, 186, 208.

105. E. Kehoe, "Working Hard at Giving It Away: Lord Duveen, the British Museum and the Elgin Marbles," *Historical Research* 77 (2004), pp. 503–19.

106. Duveen papers: JD to J. R. Pope, October 18, 19, 1935; J. R. Pope to JD, October 18, 1935.

107. Bedford, *John Russell Pope*, pp. 186, 192.

108. Smithsonian archives: RU 46 Box 143 f2, AWM to C. G. Abbot, January 14, 1936, enclosing summary of their conversation, January 8, 1936.

109. Duveen papers: Duveen Bros. [New York] to Duveen Bros. [London], January 21, 1936; E. Duveen to JD, January 22, 1936; K. Clark to JD, January 24, 1936.

110. For a recent study of this issue, see A. Geddes Poole, "Conspicuous Presumption: The Treasury and the Trustees of the National Gallery, 1890–1939," *Twentieth Century British History* 16 (2005), pp. 1–28.

111. Smithsonian archives: RU 46 Box 140 f13, C. G. Abbot to AWM, December 14, 1935; AWM to C. G. Abbot, January 2, 1936; C. Moore to C. G. Abbot, January 20, 1936.

112. Docket 76499: AWM testimony, pp. 4582–83.

113. PM MS: interview no. 2, p. 10.

114. AMB papers: PM to AMB, February 19, 1935, April 30, 1935, May 24, 1935.

115. Smith, p. 446; AWM papers: PM to AWM, April 2, 1935.

116. AWM papers: PM to AWM, April 2, 1935.

117. *RSS*, pp. 146–47.

118. AWM papers: A Tory [D. K. E. Bruce], *Frankie in Wonderland* (New York, 1934), p. 22.

119. Lankford, pp. 92–94, 97.

120. AMB papers: D. K. E. Bruce to AMB, August 2, 7, 1935.

121. AMB papers: PM to AMB, February 17, 1936; AWM papers: M. Mellon to AWM, March 10, 1936; Duveen papers: JD to K. Clark, January 10, 1936.

122. PM papers: AWM to PM, February 2, 1936, March 25, 1936, April 15, 26, 1936.

123. Duveen papers: DEF to JD, May 6, 16, 1936; Duveen Bros. [New York] to JD, May 25, 1936.

124. Duveen papers: DEF to JD, May 16, 1936; JD to DEF, May 18, 1936.

16. Beginnings and Endings: The Gallery Established, a Life in Its Fullness, 1936–37

1. *PPAFDR*, vol. 5, pp. 231–34; Kennedy, pp. 280–81.

2. *PPAFDR*, vol. 5, p. 568; A. M. Schlesinger Jr., *The Politics of Upheaval* (Boston, 1960), pp. 638–39; Kennedy, pp. 281–84.

3. M. H. Leff, *The Limits of Symbolic Reform: The New Deal and Taxation, 1933–1939* (Cambridge, 1984), p. 159.

4. Kennedy, pp. 285–86.

5. E. L. Davin, "Blue Collar Democracy: Ethnic Workers and Class Politics in Pittsburgh's Steel Valley, 1914–1948" (Ph.D. diss., University of Pittsburgh, 1999), pp. 114–15, 298.

6. Kennedy, pp. 303–308.

7. AMB papers: J. R. Mellon to AMB, January 15, 1934; Hendrick papers: interview, Mr. and Mrs. D. K. E. Bruce, December 1, 1942, p. 2.

8. Hendrick, ch. 32, pp. 46–47.

9. BJH papers: interview, DEF, March 27, 1940, p. 4.

10. Hendrick, ch. 32, pp. 41–42.

11. *RSS*, p. 137; Hendrick papers: interview, Mr. and Mrs. D. K. E. Bruce, December 1, 1942, p. 1.

12. BJH papers: interview, H. M. Johnson, April 6, 1940, p. 3.

13. BJH papers: D. D. Shepard to D. K. E. Bruce, January 12, 1943.

14. Duveen papers: DEF to JD, May 16, 1936; JD to Mr. Anson, May 18, 1936.

15. Duveen papers: Duveen Bros. [London] to Duveen Bros. [New York], July 22, 1936.

16. Hendrick, ch. 31, pp. 44–45; M. Secrest, *Duveen: A Life in Art* (New York, 2004), p. 354.

17. Secrest, *Duveen*, pp. 319–23, 354; D. Doheny, *David Finley: A Quiet Force for America's Arts* (Washington, D.C., 2006), p. 114.

18. Duveen papers: DEF to JD, October 13, 1936, November 3, 1936.

19. Duveen papers: DEF to JD, October 26, 1936.

20. Duveen papers: Note, November 12, 1936.

21. Duveen papers: First List of October 1936; Second List of October 1936; List of April 22, 1936; Price List, November 24, 1936.

22. DEF, *A Standard of Excellence: Andrew W. Mellon Founds the National Gallery of Art at Washington* (Washington, D.C., 1973), p. 42.

23. Secrest, *Duveen*, pp. 355–56; Doheny, *David Finley*, p. 122; Duveen papers: D. D. Shepard to Duveen Bros., December 19, 1936; Duveen Bros. to Price Waterhouse, October 22, 1937.

24. DEF papers (LOC): 17/1932–37, DEF to AWM, September 3, 1936.

25. S. M. Bedford, *John Russell Pope: Architect of Empire* (New York, 1998), p. 192; DEF, *Standard of Excellence*, p. 46.

26. *RSS*, pp. 147–48.

27. *RSS*, pp. 148–53.

28. *RSS*, pp. 155–56.

29. Duveen papers: J. H. Allen to Duveen Bros. [Paris], December 16, 1936; AMB papers: W. S. Daniels to AMB, August 27, 1937; F. G. MacMurray, "Memorial: Worth B. Daniels, 1899–1978," *Transactions of the American Clinical and Climatological Association* 90 (1979), pp. xxxiii–xxxv. I am grateful to Dr. Nomi Levy-Carrick for this reference.

30. There are two copies of this letter: AWM papers: AWM to FDR, December 22, 1936; FDR papers: PPF 4250, AWM to FDR, December 22, 1936. It is also printed in full in DEF, *Standard of Excellence*, pp. 47–48.

31. Cummings papers: H. Cummings diary, December 26, 1936.

32. AWM papers: FDR to AWM, December 26, 1936; DEF, *Standard of Excellence*, p. 49.

33. Cummings papers: H. Cummings diary, December 31, 1936; DEF, *Standard of Excellence*, pp. 49–51. See also Kopper, pp. 116–17.

34. AWM papers: AWM to FDR, December 31, 1936; FDR to AWM, January 1, 1937; FDR papers: PPF 420, AWM to FDR, January 4, 1937.

35. Hendrick, ch. 31, p. 39.

36. AWM papers: S. Early to AWM, January 2, 1937; White House press release,

January 2, 1937; AWM to FDR, January 4, 1937; Duveen papers: Duveen Bros. [London] to Duveen Bros. [New York], January 4, 5, 1937; *New York Times*, January 3, 1937; *The Times* (London), January 5, 1937.

37. R. Cortissoz in *New York Herald Tribune*, January 17, 24, 31, 1937; R. Cortissoz, *An Introduction to the Mellon Collection* (privately printed; Boston, 1937).

38. Smithsonian archives: RG 46 Box 143 f2, C. G. Abbot to AWM, January 3, 1937; AWM to C. G. Abbot, January 7, 1937.

39. Kopper, pp. 120–21.

40. Cummings papers: 135/NGA, R. H. Jackson memorandum, January 29, 1937; CFOST papers 1933–1956: Box 210, Tax Cases (AWM), FDR to H. Morgenthau [undated]; Morgenthau papers: H. Oliphant to H. Morgenthau, March 2, 1937.

41. Cummings papers: 135/NGA 1936–1937, H. S. Cummings, Memorandum for Judge Townsend, January 5, 1937; H. S. Cummings to FDR, January 15, 1937; H. Cahill to H. Hopkins, January 18, 1937; FDR papers: PPF 2259, FDR to W. van Loon, January 9, 1937; H. Ickes diary: January 3, 1937.

42. AWM papers: *Seventy-fifth Congress, First Session, House of Representatives, Document no. 139:* FDR to the Congress of the United States, February 1, 1937; *PPAFDR*, vol. 6, pp. 29–30.

43. FDR papers: OF 240, W. Patman to FDR, January 10, 1937; Patman papers: 1511-C, F. La Guardia to W. Patman, February 11, 1937; Kopper, pp. 122–23.

44. Moore papers: 7/AWM 1930–37, AWM to C. Moore, February 4, 1937.

45. Bedford, *John Russell Pope*, pp. 194–96.

46. Smithsonian archives: RU 46 Box 143 f2, AWM to C. G. Abbot, March 24, 1937, April 14, 1937; Bowman papers: J. G. Bowman to AWM, March 22, 1937; AWM to J. G. Bowman, April 2, 1937.

47. C. Duncan, *Civilizing Rituals: Inside Public Art Museums* (London, 1995), pp. 72–101.

48. Doheny, *David Finley*, pp. 131–33.

49. Duncan, *Civilizing Rituals*, p. 54; *RSS*, p. 140; D. L. Lewis, *District of Columbia: A Bicentennial History* (New York, 1976), p. 35.

50. DEF, *Standard of Excellence*, pp. 36–37.

51. Sparkes papers: interview, J. G. Bowman, August 3, 1944, p. 3; BJH papers: interview, J. G. Bowman, January 10, 1940, p. 4; Hendrick, ch. 31, p. 13.

52. *PPAFDR*, vol. 6, pp. 1–6.

53. Secrest, *Duveen*, pp. 356–57; Duveen papers: Duveen Bros. to Price Waterhouse, October 22, 1937.

54. Duveen papers: DEF to JD, March 31, 1937.

55. Duveen papers: Price list, January 6, 1937; Report, April 12, 1937; JD's conversation with DEF, April 21, 1937.

56. Duveen papers: DEF to JD, May 18, 1937; Secrest, *Duveen*, pp. 460–61.

57. Duveen papers: Duveen Bros. [New York] to Duveen Bros. [London], May 14, 1937; DEF to B. Boggis, May 27, 1937; Duveen Bros. [New York] to DEF, June 1, 1937.

58. Duveen papers: Duveen Bros. [New York] to JD, May 26, 1937; Duveen Bros. [New York] to A. Berenson, June 4, 1937; Secrest, *Duveen*, p. 445.

59. AWM papers: AWM, Deceased, Report and Accounts, August 26, 1937, Exhibit F, p. 3; Exhibit G, p. 3; Exhibit H, p. 2. Mellon's income for January–August 1937 would record another loss, of $279,785, after paying federal taxes of $243,015.

60. Kopper, pp. 190–98; Secrest, *Duveen*, pp. 178–81.

61. Doheny, *David Finley*, pp. 153–57; Duveen papers: JD to J. E. Widener, January 21, 1937; J. Widener to JD, January 29, 1937; JD to J. E. Widener, January 31, 1937; JD to DEF, April 21, 1937; JD to J. E. Widener, April 21, 1937.

62. Davin, "Blue Collar Democracy," pp. 305–18.

63. Kennedy, pp. 314, 335–36.

64. Smith, pp. 183–88.

65. Cummings papers: H. S. Cummings diary, April 23, 1937; 71/US vs Aluminum Co., In the District Court of the United States for the Southern District of New York, *United States of America v. Aluminum Company of America, et al.*, filed April 1937; Department of Justice press release, April 23, 1937.

66. C. C. Carr, *Alcoa: An American Enterprise* (New York, 1952), pp. 217–18.

67. Smith, pp. 192–93, 199.

68. *RSS*, p. 147.

69. AWM papers: H. B. Kirkpatrick to AWM, March 26, 1937.

70. *A Description of the Symbolism in Mellon Institute* (Pittsburgh, 1957); C. A. Watson, "Building a Temple of Science: Pittsburgh's Mellon Institute," *Pittsburgh History* 77 (1994–95), pp. 150–60.

71. Hendrick, ch. 29, pp. 17–18.

72. PM papers: interview no. 2, p. 12; *Pittsburgh Sun-Telegraph*, May 7, 1937.

73. R. C. Alberts, *Pitt: The Story of the University of Pittsburgh, 1787–1987* (Pittsburgh, 1986), pp. 131–32.

74. PM papers: PM to AWM, May 9, 1937.

75. Duveen papers: JD to DEF, February 15, 1937.

76. Hendrick, ch. 31, p. 41.

77. BJH papers: DEF Recollections, September 14, 1937, p. 1; Bedford, *John Russell Pope*, p. 196.

78. AWM papers: Remarks of DEF, Director of the National Gallery, March 24, 1942, p. 1.

79. Duveen papers: DEF to JD, July 1, 1937.

80. Hendrick, ch. 32, p. 47; BJH papers: interview, Mr. and Mrs. D. K. E. Bruce, December 1, 1942, p. 3; Duveen papers: Duveen Bros. [New York] to JD, May 17, 26, 1937.

81. *PPAFDR*, 6, pp. 238–50; Kennedy, pp. 336–60; Leff, *Limits of Symbolic Reform*, pp. 194–202, 209–15; F. Lundberg, *America's 60 Families* (New York, 1937), esp. pp. 15–16, 160–69, 212–15.

82. Hendrick, ch. 32, p. 48.

83. Duveen papers: Duveen Bros. [New York] to JD, July 20, 1937; B. Boggis to JD, July 21, 1937; JD to Duveen Bros. [New York], July 23, 1937; Duveen Bros. [New York] to JD, July 23, 1937; Duveen Bros. [New York] to JD, August 6, 9, 1937; Secrest, *Duveen*, p. 444.

84. Duveen papers: B. Boggis to JD, July 21, 1937; Duveen Bros. [New York] to JD, August 6, 9, 1937.

85. PM papers: interview no. 3, p. 7; BJH papers: interview, Mr. and Mrs. D. K. E. Bruce, December 1, 1942, pp. 1, 3–4.

86. BJH papers: DEF Recollections, September 14, 1937, pp. 1–2.

87. AMB papers: Mrs. H. C. McEldowney to AMB, August 27, 1937; Col. T. Roosevelt to AMB, August 27, 1937; Dr. C. G. Abbot to AMB, August 27, 1937; J. D. Rockefeller Jr. to AMB, August 28, 1937; G. Winston to AMB, August 28, 1937; S. M. Fisher to AMB, August 28, 1937; Col. F. Drake to AMB, August 31, 1937; Dr. Weidlen to AMB, September 4, 1937.

88. AMB papers: F. J. Hogan to AMB, August 27, 1937; W. B. Pryon to AMB, August 27, 1937; L. Greenway to AMB, August 31, 1937.

89. AMB papers: Helen C. Frick to AMB, August 30, 1937; JD to AMB, August 31, 1937; Duveen papers: Mr. Morgan to JD, August 28, 1937, enclosing draft letters to PM and AMB.

90. Sparkes papers: interview, Col. F. Drake, June 19, 1945, pp. 5–6.

91. AMB papers: Col. F. Drake to AMB [undated], enclosing D. H. Blair to F. Drake, August 28, 1937.

92. There are three collections of newspaper clippings reporting AWM's death and funeral: AMB papers: Folder Clippings re AWM, 1937; DEF papers (NGA): Box 1, Folder AWM Newspaper Clippings re Death, 1937; NGA Leatherbound Obituary Collection: AWM (2 vols.). To avoid unnecessary duplication, I have given references directly to the newspapers.

93. See, for example, *New York Times*, August 27, 1937; *Washington Evening Star*, August 27, 1937.

94. *Washington Star*, August 27, 1937; *Washington Herald*, August 27, 1937.

95. *Baltimore Sun, Washington Post, New York Times, Washington Star*, August 27, 1937.

96. *Washington Daily News*, August 27, 1937; *Philadelphia Record*, August 28, 1937.

97. *Pittsburgh Post-Gazette*, August 28, 1937; *Pittsburgh Sun-Telegraph*, August 28, 1937; *Pittsburgh Sunday Sun-Telegraph*, August 29, 1937; Hendrick, ch. 31, p. 13.

98. FDR papers: PPF 4250, S. Early to M. H. McIntyre, August 27, 1937; M. H. McIntyre to S. Early, August 27, 28, 1937; AMB papers: Randolph & McClements to AMB and PM, August 28, 1937; Duveen papers: JD to J. H. Allen, August 27, 1937; *Pittsburgh Sunday Sun-Telegraph*, August 29, 1937.

99. AWM papers: NMM to AWM, August 12, 1931.

100. *Pittsburgh Post-Gazette*, August 28, 1937; *Pittsburgh Sunday Sun-Telegraph*, August 29, 1937.

101. AMB papers: DEF to AMB, September 2, 1937.

Epilogue: A Fortune in History

1. AWM papers: AWM, Last Will and Testament, July 2, 1936; Hendrick, ch. 32, p. 41.

2. Docket no. 76499, Promulgated December 7, 1937, pp. 1, 72, 78–79; *New York Times*, December 8, 1937; *New York Sun*, December 8, 1937; *Chicago Daily Tribune*, December 14, 1930.

3. Docket no. 76499, Promulgated December 7, 1937, pp. 1–2; Hendrick, ch. 32, pp. 38–39, 45.

4. There were some subsequent adjustments, and the final figure, agreed upon with the Treasury, was $668,029.47: CFOST 1933–1956: Box 210, H. Oliphant to H. Morgenthau, June 8, 1938; Treasury press release, June 21, 1938; Hendrick, ch. 32, p. 41.

5. Duveen papers: JD to PM, D. K. E. Bruce, D. D. Shepard, and F. J. Hogan, December 8, 1937.

6. Duveen papers: F. J. Hogan to JD, December 10, 1937; D. D. Shepard to JD, December 14, 1937.

7. Cummings papers: H. Cummings to FDR, December 10, 1937, enclosing memorandum and printed copy of the decision.

8. Morgenthau papers: F. J. Hogan to H. Morgenthau, June 4, 1938; H. Oliphant to H. Morgenthau, June 8, 15, 1938.

9. *New York Times*, September 4, 21, 1937; *Washington Times*, August 27, 1937; *New York Post*, August 28, 1937.

10. AWM papers: AWM, Deceased, Report and Accounts, August 26, 1937, Exhibit A, p. 1; Exhibit F, p. 3; AWM papers: AWM, Federal Estate Tax Return, February 25, 1939, Sheets XVII-2-3. The figures in these two ledgers do not correspond exactly, but the overall picture is the same.

11. AWM papers: AWM, Federal Estate Tax Return, February 25, 1939, Sheets XIV, XV, XVI, XVII, XVIII, XIX.

12. AWM papers: AWM Contributions, 1902 to 1937.

13. BJH papers: interview, H. M. Johnson, April 6, 1940, p. 1.

14. R. Chernow, *Titan: The Life of John D. Rockefeller, Sr.* (New York, 1998), p. 675.

15. Duveen papers: DEF to JD, December 3, 1937.

16. DEF papers (NGA): Box 37, Folder, Letters of Sympathy to DEF on AWM's Death, J. R. Pope, D. P. Higgins, and O. R. Eggers to DEF, August 27, 1937; Duveen papers: JD to DEF, September 1, 1937.

17. Duveen papers: DEF to JD, September 15, 1937.

18. Duveen papers: Duveen Bros. [New York] to JD, September 30, 1937; PM to JD, October 16, 1937; Duveen Bros. to JD, January 28, 1938; DEF to JD, June 2, 1938; JD to DEF, June 23, 1938.

19. M. Secrest, *Duveen: A Life in Art* (New York, 2004), pp. 378–79; Duveen papers: J. H. Allen to DEF, June 3, 1939.

20. Duveen papers: J. H. Allen to Lady Duveen, June 9, 1939; B. Boggis to DEF, August 24, 1939, November 10, 1939; DEF to B. Boggis, August 31, 1939, September 7, 1939, November 8, 1939.

21. Duveen papers: Duveen Bros. [New York] to JD, March 11, 1938; PM papers: interview no. 4, p. 20; interview no. 5, p. 20; D. Doheny, *David Finley: A Quiet Force for America's Arts* (Washington, D.C., 2006), pp. 133–34.

22. DEF papers (LOC): 19/NGA Correspondence 1938–39, DEF to J. Walker, May 27, 1939; Recommendation from Acquisitions Committee to Board of Trustees re Widener and Kress Collections, May 25, 1939; FDR papers: OF 302C, Gallery of Art, 1937–45, DEF to FDR, January 11, 1940; DEF to Mrs. FDR, December 13, 1940; FDR to Mrs. FDR, January 3, 1941; Doheny, *David Finley*, pp. 134–52; S. M. Bedford, *John Russell Pope: Architect of Empire* (New York, 2004), pp. 198–200; Kopper, pp. 144–203.

23. Doheny, *David Finley*, pp. 160–61; Kopper, pp. 15–25.

24. BJH papers: interview, WLM, November 4, 1940, p. 1; FDR papers: OF 302C, Gallery of Art, 1937–45, DEF to E. M. Watson, January 6, 1941; E. M. Watson to FDR, January 14, 15, 1941; E. M. Watson to FDR and Mrs. FDR, January 23, 1941.

25. *RSS*, pp. 137–39, 300.

26. BJH papers: AWM Letterbooks, AWM to C. E. Hughes, February 15, 1930.

27. Bedford, *John Russell Pope*, p. 200; *New York Times*, August 29, 1937.

28. J. Hudnut, "The Last of the Romans: Comment on the Building of the National Gallery of Art," *Magazine of Art* 34 (April 1941), pp. 169–73.

29. Kennedy, pp. 350–52.

30. C. C. Carr, *Alcoa: An American Enterprise* (New York, 1952), pp. 218–36; Smith, p. 201.

31. Hendrick, ch. 28, pp. 27–31.

32. Smith, pp. 201–205.

33. Smith, pp. 206–13.

34. Smith, pp. 214–49.

35. G. Gurney, *Sculpture and the Federal Triangle* (Washington, D.C., 1985), pp. 408–11; J. M. Goode, *The Outdoor Sculpture of Washington, D.C.: A Comprehensive Historical Guide* (Washington, D.C., 1974), p. 144.

36. AMB papers: Program of Ceremonies Dedicating the AWM Memorial Fountain, Friday, May 9, 1952, Washington, D.C.; *Congressional Record*, Proceedings and Debates of the 82nd Congress, 2nd Session: Dedication of AWM Memorial Fountain, May 12, 1952, pp. 1–4; Washington Cathedral, Dedication of Outer Aisle Bay, Friday, May 9, 1952.

37. Patman papers: 1511C-6, W. Patman to A. Summerfield, December 17, 1955; 858C, Memorandum from J. D'Arista to W. Patman re AWM's impeachment, February 5, 1968; *MNBTC*, p. 36.

38. Mellon Bank papers, 07-02-00-001-0016: Remarks of United States Senator Edward Martin of Pennsylvania at the First Day Issue Ceremonies of the Andrew W. Mellon Commemorative Stamp in the National Gallery of Art, Washington, D.C., at 12:00 noon, Tuesday, December 20, 1955.

39. Doheny, *David Finley*, pp. 323–39; M. Pointon, "1968 and All That: The Founding of the National Portrait Gallery, Washington, D.C.," in M. Pointon (ed.), *Art Apart: Art Institutions and Ideology Across England and North America* (Manchester, 1994), pp. 50–68.

40. L. L. Gould, *Grand Old Party: A History of the Republicans* (New York, 2003), p. 384.

41. R. Evans and R. Novak, *The Reagan Revolution* (New York, 1981), pp. 91–93, 114, 237; R. Dugger, *On Reagan: The Man and His Presidency* (New York, 1983), p. 103; M. Anderson, *Revolution* (San Diego, Calif., 1988), p. 142; R. R. Keller, "Supply-Side Economic Policies During the Coolidge-Mellon Era," in R. F. Himmelberg (ed.), *Business-Government Co-operation 1917–1932: The Rise of Corporatist Policies* (New York, 1994), pp. 279–95.

42. C. A. Thomas, *The Architecture of the West Building of the National Gallery of Art* (Washington, D.C., 1992); Bedford, *John Russell Pope*, p. 200; *Wall Street Journal*, November 28, 1995.

43. DEF papers (NGA): DEF to D. K. E. Bruce, June 8, 1938.

44. *PPAFDR*, vol. 6, p. 235; C. A. R. Crosland, *The Future of Socialism* (London, 1961), pp. 224–25.

45. H. Bridges, "The Robber Baron Concept in American History," *Business History Review* 32 (1958), pp. 1–13; F. G. Couvares et al. (eds.), *Interpretations of American History: Patterns and Perspectives*, vol. 2, *From Reconstruction*, 7th ed. (New York, 2000), pp. 58–76.

46. R. J. Evans, *In Defense of History* (New York, 1999), p. 162.

47. K. Warren, *Triumphant Capitalism: Henry Clay Frick and the Industrial Transformation of America* (Pittsburgh, 1996), p. 6.

48. Doheny, *David Finley*, p. 124.

49. *RSS*, p. 321.

50. PM papers: interview no. 2, p. 6; interview no. 3, p. 5.

51. *RSS*, pp. 80–82.

52. *RSS*, pp. 22, 162.

53. PM papers: interview no. 1, p. 8; J. Walker, *Self-Portrait with Donors: Confessions of an Art Collector* (Boston, 1974), p. 198.

54. *RSS*, p. 245.

55. *RSS*, pp. 356–59; *The A. W. Mellon Educational & Charitable Trust: A Report of Its Work to December 31, 1945* (Pittsburgh, 1946), pp. 18–19.

56. Lankford, pp. 163–72.

57. AMB papers: In the Fifteenth Judicial Circuit in and for Palm Beach County, Florida, In Chancery, no. 20,226, AMB (Plaintiff) vs D. K. E. Bruce (Defendant), Special Master's Report, pp. 22–24.

58. AMB papers: D. K. E. Bruce to AMB, April 7, 1945.

59. AMB papers: D. K. E. Bruce to AMB, October 25, 1945; Lankford, pp. 173–77, 349.

60. Lankford, p. 176.

61. *RSS*, pp. 158, 167–68.

62. *RSS*, pp. 177–81.

63. *RSS*, p. 193.

64. *RSS*, pp. 220–21, 224.

65. *JMS*, pp. 556–59; *RSS*, p. 181; *MNBTC*, p. 43.

66. *RSS*, p. 354.

67. *RSS*, pp. 258–59.

68. *RSS*, pp. 266, 270–71, 282, 293–95.

69. M. Randall, *The Mansions of Long Island's Gold Coast* (New York, 2003), pp. 18–19.

70. Walker, *Self-Portrait*, pp. 195–201.

71. Walker, *Self-Portrait*, pp. 45, 202–203.

72. *French Paintings from the Collections of Mr. and Mrs. Paul Mellon and Mrs. Mellon Bruce* (Washington, D.C., 1966); *RSS*, p. 272.

73. *RSS*, pp. 297–320.

74. Koskoff, p. 535.

75. *RSS*, pp. 379–80.

76. Walker, *Self-Portrait*, pp. 196–97; Lankford, pp. 349–50.

77. *RSS*, pp. 349–54.

78. R. Lubove, *Twentieth-Century Pittsburgh*, vol. 1, *Government, Business and Envi-*

ronmental Change (Pittsburgh, 1969), pp. 106–43; L. Galambos and D. van Ee (eds.), *The Papers of Dwight D. Eisenhower*, vol. 19, *The Presidency: Keeping the Peace* (Baltimore, 2001), pp. 1119–20, 1135–36, 1382–83; *Time* magazine, October 3, 1949; *Life* magazine, May 15, 1956.

79. V. Perlo, *The Empire of High Finance* (New York, 1957), pp. 196–204.

80. *RSS*, pp. 321–40, 356–70, 423–31.

81. Walker, *Self-Portrait*, p. 184; *RSS*, pp. 114, 341–43, 391.

82. *RSS*, p. 359.

83. Andrew W. Mellon Foundation: W. G. Bowen, President's Report (provisional draft, February 2005), pp. 2–3.

84. Koskoff, p. 461.

85. *RSS*, pp. 80, 355; D. Barton, R. Newell, G. Wilson, *Dangerous Markets: Managing in Financial Crises* (New York, 2003), pp. 169–75.

86. Koskoff, pp. 486, 491, 495, 559; Smith, pp. 379–80.

87. Koskoff, pp. 495, 565; V. S. Grash, "The Commercial Skyscrapers of Pittsburgh Industrialists and Financiers, 1885–1932" (Ph.D. diss., Pennsylvania State University, 1998), pp. 178, 181.

88. R. Lubove, *Twentieth-Century Pittsburgh*, vol. 2, *The Post-Steel Era* (Pittsburgh, 1996), pp. viii, 7.

89. Lubove, *Post-Steel Era*, pp. 57–85.

90. *TMT*, p. xiii.

91. PM papers: interview no. 1, p. 21.

92. PM papers: interview no. 3, pp. 8–9.

Acknowledgments

THIS BOOK HAS BEEN RESEARCHED and written across three continents and two millenniums, during two very different American presidencies, and it has taken as many years to complete as Andrew W. Mellon served as secretary of the United States Treasury. Accordingly, I have accumulated many debts, both domestic and international—and living beyond one's means was always something of which Mellon greatly disapproved, in people and countries alike. Moreover, academic obligations, as distinct from monetary indebtedness, are almost impossible to quantify or repay. But one of the pleasures of completing a book is that they can, at least and at last, be gratefully acknowledged. My first thanks must go to the late Paul Mellon, Andrew Mellon's son and heir, who asked me to undertake the life of his father, put the staff of his Washington office at my disposal, and took great trouble to ensure my unfettered access to the relevant materials, in his possession and elsewhere. He also gave a series of interviews, recalling his father and his milieu, which brought him alive in a way that, by then, scarcely anyone else could. Since Paul Mellon's death, the executors of his estate, Beverly Carter and Ted Terry, have been scrupulous in honoring his wish that I should have complete freedom to reach my own conclusions, and they have been especially helpful in providing photographs. I have also been much assisted in this biography by Andrew Mellon's great-great-nephew, James R. Mellon II, who has encouraged this enterprise from almost the beginning, and who has been exceptionally helpful to it in its final stages.

During the twelve years that this work has been in process, it has been supported by the Andrew W. Mellon Foundation of New York, and I am deeply grateful to the trustees, and to Bill Bowen, Harriet Zuckerman, and Joseph Meisel for their constancy, encouragement, wisdom, and tolerance during what has proved to be a much longer haul than any of us initially realized. I also wish to thank Martha Rusnack (and her husband, Robert J. Rusnack) for making available the entire cache of invaluable materials compiled and collected by her grandfather, Burton J. Hendrick, when writing his earlier commissioned but unpublished biography. Mellon's was, in every sense, a big life, and no full-time academic, working on his voluminous and widely dispersed papers single-handedly, could realistically hope to get through them all this side of eternity. It is, then, a particular pleasure to acknowledge the enormous contribution to this biography made by my four research assistants: Walter Friedman, Michael Flamm, David Koistinen, and

Amy Aiseirithe. Across America, and also in Europe, our researches were greatly helped by many archivists and librarians, and although a complete list would prolong these acknowledgments inordinately, some people do deserve special thanks. In Pittsburgh: John Herbst, Steve Hussman, Walter Kidney, Lauren Kintner, C. Hax McCullough Jr., DeCourcy E. McIntosh, Nathan Pearson, Martha Frick Symington Sanger, and Sheena Wagstaff. In New York: Katherine Baetjer, Ann Freedman, Susan Grace Galassi, Elaine Koss, Melissa de Medeiros, and Anne Litle Poulet. In Washington: Faya Causey, David Doheny, Maygene Daniels, Anne Halpern, Kenneth Herr, Nelson Lankford, Earl A. Powell III, and Michele Willens. In England: John Baskett, Bob Hepple, David McMullen, James McMullen, Duncan Robinson, and Kenneth Warren. In Russia: Eka-terina Betekhtina Dunatov, Ana Konivets, Patricia Kennedy Grimstead, Mark Lapitskii, Geraldine Norman, Mikhail Piotrovski, and Mark A. Steinberg.

While working on this book, I was translated from being a professor of history at Columbia University in New York to being director of the Institute of Historical Research in London. At Columbia, the then provost, Jonathan R. Cole, imaginatively allowed me to teach some years half-time while this project was being launched, and I was efficiently supported by the Department of History, where Barbara Locurto and her staff uncomplainingly processed large quantities of often complex paperwork. At the IHR, I was able to give serious and sustained attention to this biography thanks to the efficiency and enthusiasm of my assistants: Charlotte Alston, Debra Birch, Samantha Jordan, Helen McCarthy, and Cathy Pearson. Since relinquishing the directorship, my new post has been partly funded by the generous support of the Linbury Trust. Much of the book was written while I was a visiting fellow at the Council of the Humanities at Princeton University, and I am most grateful to Anthony Grafton, Amy Gutmann, and Karin Trainer for providing me with such congenial and stimulating surroundings in which to work. It was completed while I was a visiting fellow in the Humanities Research Centre at the Australian National University in Canberra, where the kindness and support of Ian Donaldson and Iain MacCalman were both exceptional and exem-plary. And it has been revised here at the National Humanities Center in North Car-olina, where I have held the Hurford Visiting Fellowship, and where it has been a pleasure to be welcomed by Geoffrey Harpham and Kent Mullikin, and to be assisted by their legendarily efficient and devoted staff.

As an interloper in American history, I have learned much across the years from Tony Badger, Bernard Bailyn, John Morton Blum, Alan Brinkley, Hugh Brogan, Eric Foner, Kenneth T. Jackson, Edmund S. Morgan, Dan Rogers, David Reynolds, Arthur M. Schlesinger Jr., and Sean Wilentz. Among historians of banking and of business, and among biographers of bankers and businessmen, I am especially grateful to the example provided by the writings of Ron Chernow, Niall Ferguson, Harold James, David Nasaw, and Jean Strouse. Behind them stand other mentors and exemplars: the late Eric Ashby, the late Alistair Cooke, Eric Hobsbawm, David Landes, Peter Mathias, the late R. K. Merton, Nicholas Mann, Emma Rothschild, Amartya Sen, Barry Supple, and F. M. L. Thompson. Several good and long-suffering friends read this book chapter by chapter: Brian Allen, John Baskett, Elaine Koss, Nomi Levy-Carrick, Joseph Meisel, John Shakeshaft, and Duncan Robinson. Tony Badger, DeCourcy E. McIntosh, James R. Mellon II, and David Reynolds went through the whole draft as it neared completion. The comments and corrections of all these readers have greatly improved this volume, though they bear no responsibility for it. My agents, Michael Carlisle in New York and Gill Coleridge in London, have never wavered in their belief that this biography would be finished, and it is a relief finally to have justified their confidence. Linda Johns has been a superb picture researcher, Susanna Sturgis has meticulously copyedited the text, and Robin Reardon has kept the whole publishing enterprise on track and on time. Special thanks to George Andreou, my brilliant, resourceful, and companionable editor in New York, and to Simon Winder, my loyal, cheerful, and inspiring friend in London. Linda Colley has endured Andrew Mellon as a third, strange person in the midst of our marriage for well over half of its duration; having at last completed this book, I once again offer up to her my thanks and my love.

DAVID CANNADINE

National Humanities Center
Research Triangle Park
North Carolina
April 2006

Index

Revenue Act (1924), 315–16, 318, 328, 448, 518
Revenue Act (1926), 317–18, 348, 350, 354, 355, 357
Revenue Act (1928), 448
Revenue Act (1932), 448–9, 452
Revenue Act (1934), 518, 519, 529–30
Revenue Act (1935), 519
Reynolds, Joshua, xiii, 132, 159, 324, 325, 326, 379, 456, 552, 609
Richardson, H. H., 70
"Robber Barons," xiii, 114, 127–8
Robbia, Andrea della, 553
Robbins, Francis L., 227, 233
Robertson, Minnie Caldwell, 77, 80, 114, 149, 246
Robinson, Henry, 383
Rockefeller, John D., xiii, 90, 99–101, 121, 127, 132, 140, 165, 166, 174, 178–9, 216–17, 220–1, 230, 237, 349, 366, 521, 569, 581, 587, 599, 601, 602, 604
Rockefeller Center, 493
Rockefeller Foundation, 406, 618
Rogers, H. H., 118, 121, 179
Rom, Francis, 191
Romney, George, 130, 182–3, 192, 261, 326, 378, 456, 504
Roosevelt, Eleanor, 504, 581, 589
Roosevelt, Franklin Delano, 473–90; agricultural policies of, 476, 477, 478–9, 480; AM's meeting with (1933), 505–6; AM's meeting with (1936), xi–xii, 561; AM's National Gallery letter to (1936), 559–61; AM's opposition to, xi–xii, xiv, xvi, 464, 473–82, 491, 493, 495, 504–6, 522–3, 537, 541, 547, 557, 558–9, 560, 571–2, 581, 589–90, 594, 596, 598, 600, 605–6; AM's tax trial supported by, 348, 505–6, 509, 511, 512, 513–16, 524, 525, 527, 534–5, 543, 549–50, 566–7, 585, 605–6; background of, 474, 476, 514; banking policies of, 505–6, 517–18, 522, 547, 548; business interests criticized by, 473–6, 477, 480–2, 490, 504, 506, 514–21, 534, 546–7, 548,

591; capitalism preserved by, 474–5, 490, 517, 605; congressional support for, 477, 541, 560; death of, 592; Democratic National Convention speech of (1936), 546–7; Democratic support for, 477, 487–90, 522, 541, 546–7, 563, 590; economic reforms of, xi, xiv, xv, xvi, 224, 473–82, 535, 577, 591, 593, 594, 595, 597, 605; effectiveness of, 547–8, 577–8, 591; Federal Triangle project and, 452, 523; financial policies of, 476–81, 488–9, 504–6, 517–18, 547, 594, 595, 603; "fireside chats" of, 478; foreign policy of, 455, 479–80, 481; government intervention used by, 475–82, 493, 547, 577–8, 598, 605; as governor of New York, 506; "hundred days" legislation of, 476–82, 486, 505, 517–19, 521–2; inaugural address of (1933), 476–7, 505, 517, 522; industrial policies of, 476, 493–4, 516–17, 518, 522, 547; job creation by, 476, 478–9, 481, 493, 518, 522; labor policies of, 475–6, 479, 480, 493–5, 570–2; Madison Square Garden speech of (1936), 547; National Gallery of Art accepted by, 537, 541, 558–67, 589–90, 605, 607; New Deal programs of, xi–xii, xiv, xvi, 110, 441, 460, 473–95, 516–23, 547, 557, 560, 570–2, 577–8, 580, 591, 594, 595, 596, 598, 603, 605, 606, 607–8; polio contracted by, 268, 476, 514; popular support for, 487, 488, 489–90, 512, 518–19, 522–3, 547–8; presidential campaign of (1932), 460–1, 464, 466, 490, 548, 606; presidential campaign of (1936), xii, 490, 520–1, 541, 543, 546–8, 568; presidential campaign of (1940), 589–90; Prohibition repealed by, 480, 484; Republican opposition to, xv, 473–6, 476–7, 478, 480–2, 488–9, 504, 522–3, 547, 548, 591, 596; speeches of, 474, 476–7, 518, 520–1, 546–7; State of the Union address of

ILLUSTRATION CREDITS

CARNEGIE LIBRARY OF PITTSBURGH: Pittsburgh, 1859; Early-twentieth-century Pittsburgh; Charles Martin Hall; Arthur Vining Davis; Colonel James M. Guffey; James H. Reed; Christopher Magee; William Flinn; Mellon National Bank; Mellon Institute.

CENTER FOR AMERICAN HISTORY, THE UNIVERSITY OF TEXAS AT AUSTIN: John Nance Garner, Collection Brisco (Dolph) Papers (Swofford's Studio Photographer).

CORBIS CORPORATION: Sir Joseph Duveen; Andrew Mellon returning to New York, August 24, 1932, on one of two stateside visits as ambassador; FDR and Hoover ride to FDR's inauguration, March 4, 1933.

DAVID FINLEY PAPERS, NATIONAL GALLERY OF ART, WASHINGTON, D.C., GALLERY ARCHIVES: David Finley (Harris & Ewing Photographer); Andrew W. Mellon with Ogden L. Mills, his successor as secretary of the treasury, February 6, 1932 (Harris & Ewing Photographer); Andrew W. Mellon places a wreath on the statue of Alexander Hamilton in front of the Treasury Building, 1931 (Harris & Ewing Photographer); Andrew W. Mellon during tax proceeding.

THE FRICK COLLECTION: Courtesy of The Frick Collection/Frick Art Reference Library Archives, Copyright Frick Art Reference Library. Andrew Mellon with Henry Clay Frick and two other friends set off to tour Europe, June 1880; Henry Clay Frick as art collector.

GETTY IMAGES: Andrew Mellon on boat, 1920s, Hulton Archive, Photographer: E. Bacon; Federal Triangle, Getty Images News, Photographer: National Archives; The Hermitage, Hulton Archive, Photographer: Hulton Archive.

THE KNOEDLER GALLERY: Knoedler & Company partners Carman Messmore, Charles R. Henschel, Charles Carstairs, and Carrol C. Carstairs.

THE LIBRARY OF CONGRESS: Senator Boise Penrose, Philander Knox, Senator David A. Reed, S. Parker Gilbert, Senator James Couzens, Representative Wright Patman, Robert H. Jackson, Charles Moore, Frederic A. Delano.

COLLECTION OF JAMES R. MELLON II: The Judge's Building, Mellon Bank 1871; Andrew Mellon in mid-twenties; The Thomas Mellon family; Andrew and Richard Mellon with Henry C. McEldowney; E. P. Mellon and W. L. Mellon; Andrew and Paul Mellon in Cambridge, 1931; Andrew in extremis.

THE ESTATE OF PAUL MELLON: Camp Hill Cottage; Thomas Mellon ca. 1850; Mellon family home at 401 Negley; Andrew Mellon earliest extant photo; The McMullens of Hertfordshire, Christmas 1885; Nora McMullen and Andrew Mellon on the *Germanic*; Andrew and Nora Mellon's official wedding photo; Andrew and Nora Mellon's home at 5052 Forbes Street, exterior and interior photos; The Andrew Mellon family in 1907; Nora Mellon's portrait by James Jebusa Shannon; Andrew, Ailsa, and Paul Mellon; Ailsa's wedding; Ailsa and David Bruce's house at Syosset, Long Island; David K. E. Bruce, Ailsa's husband; The Harding cabinet; Andrew Mellon with Calvin Coolidge and Herbert Hoover; Andrew and granddaughter Audrey; Andrew Mellon with Joseph Duveen at tax trial.

GIFT OF PAUL MELLON, NATIONAL GALLERY OF ART, WASHINGTON, D.C., GALLERY ARCHIVES: Ambassador Andrew W. Mellon accompanying his daughter and official hostess, Ailsa Mellon Bruce, to appear at the court of King George V (Keystone View Co., Photographer); Interior of the residence of the United States Ambassador, Prince's Gate, London, displaying paintings from the Mellon Collection, 1932–33; National Gallery of Art building construction progress, September 18, 1939; Andrew W. Mellon with his daughter, Ailsa, on Long Island, 1937.

MELLON FAMILY PAPERS, NATIONAL GALLERY OF ART, WASHINGTON, D.C., GALLERY ARCHIVES: Alfred George Curphey.

THE MELLON FINANCIAL INSTITUTE: Mellon Brothers Bank, the Bismarck branch in Dakota Territory, 1882, in *One Hundred Years of Banking*.

NATIONAL GALLERY OF ART, WASHINGTON, D.C., GALLERY ARCHIVES: The first home of T. Mellon & Sons' Bank, courtesy The Mellon Bank; Andrew W. Mellon in his apartment at 1785 Massachusetts Avenue, N.W., Washington, D.C., ca. 1930; Secretary of the Treasury Andrew W. Mellon with the Federal Triangle model; Otto Eggers, rendering of the proposed National Gallery of Art and proposed landscape development of the adjacent plot, 1938; Aerial view of the construction of the National Gallery of Art, 1938; President Franklin D. Roosevelt speaking at the National Gallery of Art dedication ceremony, March 17, 1941.

THE NATIONAL GALLERY OF ART LIBRARY, WASHINGTON, D.C.: National Gallery and Trafalgar Square, London (ca. 1880), Gramstorff Archive, Department of Image Collections.

COLLECTION OF THE NEW-YORK HISTORICAL SOCIETY: John Russell Pope, architect of the National Gallery of Art, Pirie MacDonald Portrait Photograph Collection, PR 039, Box 13, Folder 306, negative number 78562d.

ST. LOUIS POST DISPATCH: Cartoon by Daniel R. Fitzpatrick ("It seems there are two Uncle Sams and two Andy Mellons").

EDWARD SOREL: Cartoon of Duveen and Andrew Mellon.

THOMAS MELLON AND HIS TIMES BY THOMAS MELLON, UNIVERSITY OF PITTSBURGH: Sarah Jane Negley.

UNITED STATES POSTAL SERVICE: The Andrew Mellon stamp, Washington D.C., December 20, 1955. Andrew Mellon stamp image © 1955 United States Postal Service. All rights reserved. Used with permission.